Lecture Notes in Computer Science 8689

Commenced Publication in 1973
Founding and Former Series Editors:
Gerhard Goos, Juris Hartmanis, and Jan van Leeuwen

Editorial Board

David Hutchison
Lancaster University, UK

Takeo Kanade
Carnegie Mellon University, Pittsburgh, PA, USA

Josef Kittler
University of Surrey, Guildford, UK

Jon M. Kleinberg
Cornell University, Ithaca, NY, USA

Alfred Kobsa
University of California, Irvine, CA, USA

Friedemann Mattern
ETH Zurich, Switzerland

John C. Mitchell
Stanford University, CA, USA

Moni Naor
Weizmann Institute of Science, Rehovot, Israel

Oscar Nierstrasz
University of Bern, Switzerland

C. Pandu Rangan
Indian Institute of Technology, Madras, India

Bernhard Steffen
TU Dortmund University, Germany

Demetri Terzopoulos
University of California, Los Angeles, CA, USA

Doug Tygar
University of California, Berkeley, CA, USA

Gerhard Weikum
Max Planck Institute for Informatics, Saarbruecken, Germany

David Fleet Tomas Pajdla Bernt Schiele
Tinne Tuytelaars (Eds.)

Computer Vision – ECCV 2014

13th European Conference
Zurich, Switzerland, September 6-12, 2014
Proceedings, Part I

Volume Editors

David Fleet
University of Toronto, Department of Computer Science
6 King's College Road, Toronto, ON M5H 3S5, Canada
E-mail: fleet@cs.toronto.edu

Tomas Pajdla
Czech Technical University in Prague, Department of Cybernetics
Technicka 2, 166 27 Prague 6, Czech Republic
E-mail: pajdla@cmp.felk.cvut.cz

Bernt Schiele
Max-Planck-Institut für Informatik
Campus E1 4, 66123 Saarbrücken, Germany
E-mail: schiele@mpi-inf.mpg.de

Tinne Tuytelaars
KU Leuven, ESAT - PSI, iMinds
Kasteelpark Arenberg 10, Bus 2441, 3001 Leuven, Belgium
E-mail: tinne.tuytelaars@esat.kuleuven.be

Videos to this book can be accessed at
http://www.springerimages.com/videos/978-3-319-10589-5

ISSN 0302-9743 e-ISSN 1611-3349
ISBN 978-3-319-10589-5 e-ISBN 978-3-319-10590-1
DOI 10.1007/978-3-319-10590-1
Springer Cham Heidelberg New York Dordrecht London

Library of Congress Control Number: 2014946360

LNCS Sublibrary: SL 6 – Image Processing, Computer Vision, Pattern Recognition, and Graphics

© Springer International Publishing Switzerland 2014
This work is subject to copyright. All rights are reserved by the Publisher, whether the whole or part of the material is concerned, specifically the rights of translation, reprinting, reuse of illustrations, recitation, broadcasting, reproduction on microfilms or in any other physical way, and transmission or information storage and retrieval, electronic adaptation, computer software, or by similar or dissimilar methodology now known or hereafter developed. Exempted from this legal reservation are brief excerpts in connection with reviews or scholarly analysis or material supplied specifically for the purpose of being entered and executed on a computer system, for exclusive use by the purchaser of the work. Duplication of this publication or parts thereof is permitted only under the provisions of the Copyright Law of the Publisher's location, in ist current version, and permission for use must always be obtained from Springer. Permissions for use may be obtained through RightsLink at the Copyright Clearance Center. Violations are liable to prosecution under the respective Copyright Law.
The use of general descriptive names, registered names, trademarks, service marks, etc. in this publication does not imply, even in the absence of a specific statement, that such names are exempt from the relevant protective laws and regulations and therefore free for general use.
While the advice and information in this book are believed to be true and accurate at the date of publication, neither the authors nor the editors nor the publisher can accept any legal responsibility for any errors or omissions that may be made. The publisher makes no warranty, express or implied, with respect to the material contained herein.

Typesetting: Camera-ready by author, data conversion by Scientific Publishing Services, Chennai, India

Printed on acid-free paper

Springer is part of Springer Science+Business Media (www.springer.com)

Foreword

The European Conference on Computer Vision is one of the top conferences in computer vision. It was first held in 1990 in Antibes (France) with subsequent conferences in Santa Margherita Ligure (Italy) in 1992, Stockholm (Sweden) in 1994, Cambridge (UK) in 1996, Freiburg (Germany) in 1998, Dublin (Ireland) in 2000, Copenhagen (Denmark) in 2002, Prague (Czech Republic) in 2004, Graz (Austria) in 2006, Marseille (France) in 2008, Heraklion (Greece) in 2010, and Florence (Italy) in 2012. Many people have worked hard to turn the 2014 edition into as great a success. We hope you will find this a mission accomplished.

The chairs decided to adhere to the classic single-track scheme. In terms of the time ordering, we decided to largely follow the Florence example (typically starting with poster sessions, followed by oral sessions), which offers a lot of flexibility to network and is more forgiving for the not-so-early-birds and hard-core gourmets.

A large conference like ECCV requires the help of many. They made sure there was a full program including the main conference, tutorials, workshops, exhibits, demos, proceedings, video streaming/archive, and Web descriptions. We want to cordially thank all those volunteers! Please have a look at the conference website to see their names (http://eccv2014.org/people/). We also thank our generous sponsors. Their support was vital for keeping prices low and enriching the program. And it is good to see such a level of industrial interest in what our community is doing!

We hope you will enjoy the proceedings ECCV 2014.

Also, willkommen in Zürich!

September 2014

Marc Pollefeys
Luc Van Gool
General Chairs

Preface

Welcome to the proceedings of the 2014 European Conference on Computer Vision (ECCV 2014) that was in Zurich, Switzerland. We are delighted to present this volume reflecting a strong and exciting program, the result of an extensive review process. In total, we received 1,444 paper submissions. Of these, 85 violated the ECCV submission guidelines and were rejected without review. Of the remainder, 363 were accepted (26,7%): 325 as posters (23,9%) and 38 as oral presentations (2,8%). This selection process was a combined effort of four program co-chairs (PCs), 53 area chairs (ACs), 803 Program Committee members and 247 additional reviewers.

As PCs we were primarily responsible for the design and execution of the review process. Beyond administrative rejections, we were not directly involved in acceptance decisions. Because the general co-chairs were permitted to submit papers, they played no role in the review process and were treated as any other author.

Acceptance decisions were made by the AC Committee. There were 53 ACs in total, selected by the PCs to provide sufficient technical expertise, geographical diversity (21 from Europe, 7 from Asia, and 25 from North America) and a mix of AC experience (7 had no previous AC experience, 18 had served as AC of a major international vision conference once since 2010, 8 had served twice, 13 had served three times, and 7 had served 4 times).

ACs were aided by 803 Program Committee members to whom papers were assigned for reviewing. There were 247 additional reviewers, each supervised by a Program Committee member. The Program Committee was based on suggestions from ACs, and committees from previous conferences. Google Scholar profiles were collected for all candidate Program Committee members and vetted by PCs. Having a large pool of Program Committee members for reviewing allowed us to match expertise while bounding reviewer loads. No more than nine papers were assigned to any one Program Committee member, with a maximum of six to graduate students.

The ECCV 2014 review process was double blind. Authors did not know the reviewers' identities, nor the ACs handling their paper(s). We did our utmost to ensure that ACs and reviewers did not know authors' identities, even though anonymity becomes difficult to maintain as more and more submissions appear concurrently on arXiv.org.

Particular attention was paid to minimizing potential conflicts of interest. Conflicts of interest between ACs, Program Committee members, and papers were based on authorship of ECCV 2014 submissions, on their home institutions, and on previous collaborations. To find institutional conflicts, all authors,

Program Committee members, and ACs were asked to list the Internet domains of their current institutions. To find collaborators, the DBLP (www.dblp.org) database was used to find any co-authored papers in the period 2010–2014.

We initially assigned approximately 100 papers to each AC, based on affinity scores from the Toronto Paper Matching System and authors' AC suggestions. ACs then bid on these, indicating their level of expertise. Based on these bids, and conflicts of interest, approximately 27 papers were assigned to each AC, for which they would act as the primary AC. The primary AC then suggested seven reviewers from the pool of Program Committee members (in rank order) for each paper, from which three were chosen per paper, taking load balancing and conflicts of interest into account.

Many papers were also assigned a secondary AC, either directly by the PCs, or as a consequence of the primary AC requesting the aid of an AC with complementary expertise. Secondary ACs could be assigned at any stage in the process, but in most cases this occurred about two weeks before the final AC meeting. Hence, in addition to their initial load of approximately 27 papers, each AC was asked to handle three to five more papers as a secondary AC; they were expected to read and write a short assessment of such papers. In addition, two of the 53 ACs were not directly assigned papers. Rather, they were available throughout the process to aid other ACs at any stage (e.g., with decisions, evaluating technical issues, additional reviews, etc.).

The initial reviewing period was three weeks long, after which reviewers provided reviews with preliminary recommendations. Three weeks is somewhat shorter than normal, but this did not seem to cause any unusual problems. With the generous help of several last-minute reviewers, each paper received three reviews.

Authors were then given the opportunity to rebut the reviews, primarily to identify any factual errors. Following this, reviewers and ACs discussed papers at length, after which reviewers finalized their reviews and gave a final recommendation to the ACs. Many ACs requested help from secondary ACs at this time.

Papers, for which rejection was clear and certain, based on the reviews and the AC's assessment, were identified by their primary ACs and vetted by a shadow AC prior to rejection. (These shadow ACs were assigned by the PCs.) All papers with any chance of acceptance were further discussed at the AC meeting. Those deemed "strong" by primary ACs (about 140 in total) were also assigned a secondary AC.

The AC meeting, with all but two of the primary ACs present, took place in Zurich. ACs were divided into 17 triplets for each morning, and a different set of triplets for each afternoon. Given the content of the three (or more) reviews along with reviewer recommendations, rebuttals, online discussions among reviewers and primary ACs, written input from and discussions with secondary ACs, the

AC triplets then worked together to resolve questions, calibrate assessments, and make acceptance decisions.

To select oral presentations, all strong papers, along with any others put forward by triplets (about 155 in total), were then discussed in four panels, each comprising four or five triplets. Each panel ranked these oral candidates, using four categories. Papers in the two top categories provided the final set of 38 oral presentations.

We want to thank everyone involved in making the ECCV 2014 Program possible. First and foremost, the success of ECCV 2014 depended on the quality of papers submitted by authors, and on the very hard work of the reviewers, the Program Committee members and the ACs. We are particularly grateful to Kyros Kutulakos for his enormous software support before and during the AC meeting, to Laurent Charlin for the use of the Toronto Paper Matching System, and Chaohui Wang for help optimizing the assignment of papers to ACs. We also owe a debt of gratitude for the great support of Zurich local organizers, especially Susanne Keller and her team.

September 2014

David Fleet
Tomas Pajdla
Bernt Schiele
Tinne Tuytelaars

Organization

General Chairs

Luc Van Gool	ETH Zurich, Switzerland
Marc Pollefeys	ETH Zurich, Switzerland

Program Chairs

Tinne Tuytelaars	KU Leuven, Belgium
Bernt Schiele	MPI Informatics, Saarbrücken, Germany
Tomas Pajdla	CTU Prague, Czech Republic
David Fleet	University of Toronto, Canada

Local Arrangements Chairs

Konrad Schindler	ETH Zurich, Switzerland
Vittorio Ferrari	University of Edinburgh, UK

Workshop Chairs

Lourdes Agapito	University College London, UK
Carsten Rother	TU Dresden, Germany
Michael Bronstein	University of Lugano, Switzerland

Tutorial Chairs

Bastian Leibe	RWTH Aachen, Germany
Paolo Favaro	University of Bern, Switzerland
Christoph Lampert	IST Austria

Poster Chair

Helmut Grabner	ETH Zurich, Switzerland

Publication Chairs

Mario Fritz	MPI Informatics, Saarbrücken, Germany
Michael Stark	MPI Informatics, Saarbrücken, Germany

Demo Chairs

Davide Scaramuzza — University of Zurich, Switzerland
Jan-Michael Frahm — University of North Carolina at Chapel Hill, USA

Exhibition Chair

Tamar Tolcachier — University of Zurich, Switzerland

Industrial Liaison Chairs

Alexander Sorkine-Hornung — Disney Research Zurich, Switzerland
Fatih Porikli — ANU, Australia

Student Grant Chair

Seon Joo Kim — Yonsei University, Korea

Air Shelters Accommodation Chair

Maros Blaha — ETH Zurich, Switzerland

Website Chairs

Lorenz Meier — ETH Zurich, Switzerland
Bastien Jacquet — ETH Zurich, Switzerland

Internet Chair

Thorsten Steenbock — ETH Zurich, Switzerland

Student Volunteer Chairs

Andrea Cohen — ETH Zurich, Switzerland
Ralf Dragon — ETH Zurich, Switzerland
Laura Leal-Taixé — ETH Zurich, Switzerland

Finance Chair

Amael Delaunoy — ETH Zurich, Switzerland

Conference Coordinator

Susanne H. Keller — ETH Zurich, Switzerland

Area Chairs

Lourdes Agapito	University College London, UK
Sameer Agarwal	Google Research, USA
Shai Avidan	Tel Aviv University, Israel
Alex Berg	UNC Chapel Hill, USA
Yuri Boykov	University of Western Ontario, Canada
Thomas Brox	University of Freiburg, Germany
Jason Corso	SUNY at Buffalo, USA
Trevor Darrell	UC Berkeley, USA
Fernando de la Torre	Carnegie Mellon University, USA
Frank Dellaert	Georgia Tech, USA
Alexei Efros	UC Berkeley, USA
Vittorio Ferrari	University of Edinburgh, UK
Andrew Fitzgibbon	Microsoft Research, Cambridge, UK
JanMichael Frahm	UNC Chapel Hill, USA
Bill Freeman	Massachusetts Institute of Technology, USA
Peter Gehler	Max Planck Institute for Intelligent Systems, Germany
Kristen Graumann	University of Texas at Austin, USA
Wolfgang Heidrich	University of British Columbia, Canada
Herve Jegou	Inria Rennes, France
Fredrik Kahl	Lund University, Sweden
Kyros Kutulakos	University of Toronto, Canada
Christoph Lampert	IST Austria
Ivan Laptev	Inria Paris, France
Kyuong Mu Lee	Seoul National University, South Korea
Bastian Leibe	RWTH Aachen, Germany
Vincent Lepetit	TU Graz, Austria
Hongdong Li	Australian National University
David Lowe	University of British Columbia, Canada
Greg Mori	Simon Fraser University, Canada
Srinivas Narasimhan	Carnegie Mellon University, PA, USA
Nassir Navab	TU Munich, Germany
Ko Nishino	Drexel University, USA
Maja Pantic	Imperial College London, UK
Patrick Perez	Technicolor Research, Rennes, France
Pietro Perona	California Institute of Technology, USA
Ian Reid	University of Adelaide, Australia
Stefan Roth	TU Darmstadt, Germany
Carsten Rother	TU Dresden, Germany
Sudeep Sarkar	University of South Florida, USA
Silvio Savarese	Stanford University, USA
Christoph Schnoerr	Heidelberg University, Germany
Jamie Shotton	Microsoft Research, Cambridge, UK

Kaleem Siddiqi	McGill, Canada
Leonid Sigal	Disney Research, Pittsburgh, PA, USA
Noah Snavely	Cornell, USA
Raquel Urtasun	University of Toronto, Canada
Andrea Vedaldi	University of Oxford, UK
Jakob Verbeek	Inria Rhone-Alpes, France
Xiaogang Wang	Chinese University of Hong Kong, SAR China
Ming-Hsuan Yang	UC Merced, CA, USA
Lihi Zelnik-Manor	Technion, Israel
Song-Chun Zhu	UCLA, USA
Todd Zickler	Harvard, USA

Program Committee

Gaurav Aggarwal
Amit Agrawal
Haizhou Ai
Ijaz Akhter
Karteek Alahari
Alexandre Alahi
Andrea Albarelli
Saad Ali
Jose M. Alvarez
Juan Andrade-Cetto
Bjoern Andres
Mykhaylo Andriluka
Elli Angelopoulou
Roland Angst
Relja Arandjelovic
Ognjen Arandjelovic
Helder Araujo
Pablo Arbelez
Vasileios Argyriou
Antonis Argyros
Kalle Astroem
Vassilis Athitsos
Yannis Avrithis
Yusuf Aytar
Xiang Bai
Luca Ballan
Yingze Bao
Richard Baraniuk
Adrian Barbu
Kobus Barnard
Connelly Barnes
Joao Barreto
Jonathan Barron
Adrien Bartoli
Arslan Basharat
Dhruv Batra
Luis Baumela
Maximilian Baust
Jean-Charles Bazin
Loris Bazzani
Chris Beall
Vasileios Belagiannis
Csaba Beleznai
Moshe Ben-ezra
Ohad Ben-Shahar
Ismail Ben Ayed
Rodrigo Benenson
Ryad Benosman
Tamara Berg
Margrit Betke
Ross Beveridge
Bir Bhanu
Horst Bischof
Arijit Biswas
Andrew Blake
Aaron Bobick
Piotr Bojanowski
Ali Borji
Terrance Boult
Lubomir Bourdev
Patrick Bouthemy
Edmond Boyer
Kristin Branson
Steven Branson
Francois Bremond
Michael Bronstein
Gabriel Brostow
Michael Brown
Matthew Brown
Marcus Brubaker
Andres Bruhn
Joan Bruna
Aurelie Bugeau
Darius Burschka
Ricardo Cabral
Jian-Feng Cai
Neill D.F. Campbell
Yong Cao
Barbara Caputo
Joao Carreira
Jan Cech
Jinxiang Chai
Ayan Chakrabarti
Tat-Jen Cham
Antoni Chan
Manmohan Chandraker
Vijay Chandrasekhar
Hong Chang
Ming-Ching Chang
Rama Chellappa
Chao-Yeh Chen
David Chen
Hwann-Tzong Chen

Tsuhan Chen
Xilin Chen
Chao Chen
Longbin Chen
Minhua Chen
Anoop Cherian
Liang-Tien Chia
Tat-Jun Chin
Sunghyun Cho
Minsu Cho
Nam Ik Cho
Wongun Choi
Mario Christoudias
Wen-Sheng Chu
Yung-Yu Chuang
Ondrej Chum
James Clark
Brian Clipp
Isaac Cohen
John Collomosse
Bob Collins
Tim Cootes
David Crandall
Antonio Criminisi
Naresh Cuntoor
Qieyun Dai
Jifeng Dai
Kristin Dana
Kostas Daniilidis
Larry Davis
Andrew Davison
Goksel Dedeoglu
Koichiro Deguchi
Alberto Del Bimbo
Alessio Del Bue
Hervé Delingette
Andrew Delong
Stefanie Demirci
David Demirdjian
Jia Deng
Joachim Denzler
Konstantinos Derpanis
Thomas Deselaers
Frederic Devernay
Michel Dhome
Anthony Dick
Ajay Divakaran
Santosh Kumar Divvala
Minh Do
Carl Doersch
Piotr Dollar
Bin Dong
Weisheng Dong
Michael Donoser
Gianfranco Doretto
Matthijs Douze
Bruce Draper
Mark Drew
Bertram Drost
Lixin Duan
Jean-Luc Dugelay
Enrique Dunn
Pinar Duygulu
Jan-Olof Eklundh
James H. Elder
Ian Endres
Olof Enqvist
Markus Enzweiler
Aykut Erdem
Anders Eriksson
Ali Eslami
Irfan Essa
Francisco Estrada
Bin Fan
Quanfu Fan
Jialue Fan
Sean Fanello
Ali Farhadi
Giovanni Farinella
Ryan Farrell
Alireza Fathi
Paolo Favaro
Michael Felsberg
Pedro Felzenszwalb
Rob Fergus
Basura Fernando
Frank Ferrie
Sanja Fidler
Boris Flach
Francois Fleuret
David Fofi
Wolfgang Foerstner
David Forsyth
Katerina Fragkiadaki
Jean-Sebastien Franco
Friedrich Fraundorfer
Mario Fritz
Yun Fu
Pascal Fua
Hironobu Fujiyoshi
Yasutaka Furukawa
Ryo Furukawa
Andrea Fusiello
Fabio Galasso
Juergen Gall
Andrew Gallagher
David Gallup
Arvind Ganesh
Dashan Gao
Shenghua Gao
James Gee
Andreas Geiger
Yakup Genc
Bogdan Georgescu
Guido Gerig
David Geronimo
Theo Gevers
Bernard Ghanem
Andrew Gilbert
Ross Girshick
Martin Godec
Guy Godin
Roland Goecke
Michael Goesele
Alvina Goh
Bastian Goldluecke
Boqing Gong
Yunchao Gong
Raghuraman Gopalan
Albert Gordo
Lena Gorelick
Paulo Gotardo
Stephen Gould
Venu Madhav Govindu
Helmut Grabner

Roger Grosse
Matthias Grundmann
Chunhui Gu
Xianfeng Gu
Jinwei Gu
Sergio Guadarrama
Matthieu Guillaumin
Jean-Yves Guillemaut
Hatice Gunes
Ruiqi Guo
Guodong Guo
Abhinav Gupta
Abner Guzman Rivera
Gregory Hager
Ghassan Hamarneh
Bohyung Han
Tony Han
Jari Hannuksela
Tatsuya Harada
Mehrtash Harandi
Bharath Hariharan
Stefan Harmeling
Tal Hassner
Daniel Hauagge
Søren Hauberg
Michal Havlena
James Hays
Kaiming He
Xuming He
Martial Hebert
Felix Heide
Jared Heinly
Hagit Hel-Or
Lionel Heng
Philipp Hennig
Carlos Hernandez
Aaron Hertzmann
Adrian Hilton
David Hogg
Derek Hoiem
Byung-Woo Hong
Anthony Hoogs
Joachim Hornegger
Timothy Hospedales
Wenze Hu
Zhe Hu
Gang Hua
Xian-Sheng Hua
Dong Huang
Gary Huang
Heng Huang
Sung Ju Hwang
Wonjun Hwang
Ivo Ihrke
Nazli Ikizler-Cinbis
Slobodan Ilic
Horace Ip
Michal Irani
Hiroshi Ishikawa
Laurent Itti
Nathan Jacobs
Max Jaderberg
Omar Javed
C.V. Jawahar
Bruno Jedynak
Hueihan Jhuang
Qiang Ji
Hui Ji
Kui Jia
Yangqing Jia
Jiaya Jia
Hao Jiang
Zhuolin Jiang
Sam Johnson
Neel Joshi
Armand Joulin
Frederic Jurie
Ioannis Kakadiaris
Zdenek Kalal
Amit Kale
Joni-Kristian Kamarainen
George Kamberov
Kenichi Kanatani
Sing Bing Kang
Vadim Kantorov
Jörg Hendrik Kappes
Leonid Karlinsky
Zoltan Kato
Hiroshi Kawasaki
Verena Kaynig
Cem Keskin
Margret Keuper
Daniel Keysers
Sameh Khamis
Fahad Khan
Saad Khan
Aditya Khosla
Martin Kiefel
Gunhee Kim
Jaechul Kim
Seon Joo Kim
Tae-Kyun Kim
Byungsoo Kim
Benjamin Kimia
Kris Kitani
Hedvig Kjellstrom
Laurent Kneip
Reinhard Koch
Kevin Koeser
Ullrich Koethe
Effrosyni Kokiopoulou
Iasonas Kokkinos
Kalin Kolev
Vladimir Kolmogorov
Vladlen Koltun
Nikos Komodakis
Piotr Koniusz
Peter Kontschieder
Ender Konukoglu
Sanjeev Koppal
Hema Koppula
Andreas Koschan
Jana Kosecka
Adriana Kovashka
Adarsh Kowdle
Josip Krapac
Dilip Krishnan
Zuzana Kukelova
Brian Kulis
Neeraj Kumar
M. Pawan Kumar
Cheng-Hao Kuo
In So Kweon
Junghyun Kwon

Junseok Kwon
Simon Lacoste-Julien
Shang-Hong Lai
Jean-François Lalonde
Tian Lan
Michael Langer
Doug Lanman
Diane Larlus
Longin Jan Latecki
Svetlana Lazebnik
Laura Leal-Taixé
Erik Learned-Miller
Honglak Lee
Yong Jae Lee
Ido Leichter
Victor Lempitsky
Frank Lenzen
Marius Leordeanu
Thomas Leung
Maxime Lhuillier
Chunming Li
Fei-Fei Li
Fuxin Li
Rui Li
Li-Jia Li
Chia-Kai Liang
Shengcai Liao
Joerg Liebelt
Jongwoo Lim
Joseph Lim
Ruei-Sung Lin
Yen-Yu Lin
Zhouchen Lin
Liang Lin
Haibin Ling
James Little
Baiyang Liu
Ce Liu
Feng Liu
Guangcan Liu
Jingen Liu
Wei Liu
Zicheng Liu
Zongyi Liu
Tyng-Luh Liu
Xiaoming Liu
Xiaobai Liu
Ming-Yu Liu
Marcus Liwicki
Stephen Lombardi
Roberto Lopez-Sastre
Manolis Lourakis
Brian Lovell
Chen Change Loy
Jiangbo Lu
Jiwen Lu
Simon Lucey
Jiebo Luo
Ping Luo
Marcus Magnor
Vijay Mahadevan
Julien Mairal
Michael Maire
Subhransu Maji
Atsuto Maki
Yasushi Makihara
Roberto Manduchi
Luca Marchesotti
Aleix Martinez
Bogdan Matei
Diana Mateus
Stefan Mathe
Yasuyuki Matsushita
Iain Matthews
Kevin Matzen
Bruce Maxwell
Stephen Maybank
Walterio Mayol-Cuevas
David McAllester
Gerard Medioni
Christopher Mei
Paulo Mendonca
Thomas Mensink
Domingo Mery
Ajmal Mian
Branislav Micusik
Ondrej Miksik
Anton Milan
Majid Mirmehdi
Anurag Mittal
Hossein Mobahi
Pranab Mohanty
Pascal Monasse
Vlad Morariu
Philippos Mordohai
Francesc Moreno-Noguer
Luce Morin
Nigel Morris
Bryan Morse
Eric Mortensen
Yasuhiro Mukaigawa
Lopamudra Mukherjee
Vittorio Murino
David Murray
Sobhan Naderi Parizi
Hajime Nagahara
Laurent Najman
Karthik Nandakumar
Fabian Nater
Jan Neumann
Lukas Neumann
Ram Nevatia
Richard Newcombe
Minh Hoai Nguyen
Bingbing Ni
Feiping Nie
Juan Carlos Niebles
Marc Niethammer
Claudia Nieuwenhuis
Mark Nixon
Mohammad Norouzi
Sebastian Nowozin
Matthew O'Toole
Peter Ochs
Jean-Marc Odobez
Francesca Odone
Eyal Ofek
Sangmin Oh
Takahiro Okabe
Takayuki Okatani
Aude Oliva
Carl Olsson
Bjorn Ommer
Magnus Oskarsson
Wanli Ouyang

Geoffrey Oxholm
Mustafa Ozuysal
Nicolas Padoy
Caroline Pantofaru
Nicolas Papadakis
George Papandreou
Nikolaos Papanikolopoulos
Nikos Paragios
Devi Parikh
Dennis Park
Vishal Patel
Ioannis Patras
Vladimir Pavlovic
Kim Pedersen
Marco Pedersoli
Shmuel Peleg
Marcello Pelillo
Tingying Peng
A.G. Amitha Perera
Alessandro Perina
Federico Pernici
Florent Perronnin
Vladimir Petrovic
Tomas Pfister
Jonathon Phillips
Justus Piater
Massimo Piccardi
Hamed Pirsiavash
Leonid Pishchulin
Robert Pless
Thomas Pock
Jean Ponce
Gerard Pons-Moll
Ronald Poppe
Andrea Prati
Victor Prisacariu
Kari Pulli
Yu Qiao
Lei Qin
Novi Quadrianto
Rahul Raguram
Varun Ramakrishna
Srikumar Ramalingam
Narayanan Ramanathan
Konstantinos Rapantzikos
Michalis Raptis
Nalini Ratha
Avinash Ravichandran
Michael Reale
Dikpal Reddy
James Rehg
Jan Reininghaus
Xiaofeng Ren
Jerome Revaud
Morteza Rezanejad
Hayko Riemenschneider
Tammy Riklin Raviv
Antonio Robles-Kelly
Erik Rodner
Emanuele Rodola
Mikel Rodriguez
Marcus Rohrbach
Javier Romero
Charles Rosenberg
Bodo Rosenhahn
Arun Ross
Samuel Rota Bul
Peter Roth
Volker Roth
Anastasios Roussos
Sebastien Roy
Michael Rubinstein
Olga Russakovsky
Bryan Russell
Michael S. Ryoo
Mohammad Amin Sadeghi
Kate Saenko
Albert Ali Salah
Imran Saleemi
Mathieu Salzmann
Conrad Sanderson
Aswin Sankaranarayanan
Benjamin Sapp
Radim Sara
Scott Satkin
Imari Sato
Yoichi Sato
Bogdan Savchynskyy
Hanno Scharr
Daniel Scharstein
Yoav Y. Schechner
Walter Scheirer
Kevin Schelten
Frank Schmidt
Uwe Schmidt
Julia Schnabel
Alexander Schwing
Nicu Sebe
Shishir Shah
Mubarak Shah
Shiguang Shan
Qi Shan
Ling Shao
Abhishek Sharma
Viktoriia Sharmanska
Eli Shechtman
Yaser Sheikh
Alexander Shekhovtsov
Chunhua Shen
Li Shen
Yonggang Shi
Qinfeng Shi
Ilan Shimshoni
Takaaki Shiratori
Abhinav Shrivastava
Behjat Siddiquie
Nathan Silberman
Karen Simonyan
Richa Singh
Vikas Singh
Sudipta Sinha
Josef Sivic
Dirk Smeets
Arnold Smeulders
William Smith
Cees Snoek
Eric Sommerlade
Alexander Sorkine-Hornung
Alvaro Soto
Richard Souvenir

Anuj Srivastava
Ioannis Stamos
Michael Stark
Chris Stauffer
Bjorn Stenger
Charles Stewart
Rainer Stiefelhagen
Juergen Sturm
Yusuke Sugano
Josephine Sullivan
Deqing Sun
Min Sun
Hari Sundar
Ganesh Sundaramoorthi
Kalyan Sunkavalli
Sabine Süsstrunk
David Suter
Tomas Svoboda
Rahul Swaminathan
Tanveer Syeda-Mahmood
Rick Szeliski
Raphael Sznitman
Yuichi Taguchi
Yu-Wing Tai
Jun Takamatsu
Hugues Talbot
Ping Tan
Robby Tan
Kevin Tang
Huixuan Tang
Danhang Tang
Marshall Tappen
Jean-Philippe Tarel
Danny Tarlow
Gabriel Taubin
Camillo Taylor
Demetri Terzopoulos
Christian Theobalt
Yuandong Tian
Joseph Tighe
Radu Timofte
Massimo Tistarelli
George Toderici
Sinisa Todorovic
Giorgos Tolias
Federico Tombari
Tatiana Tommasi
Yan Tong
Akihiko Torii
Antonio Torralba
Lorenzo Torresani
Andrea Torsello
Tali Treibitz
Rudolph Triebel
Bill Triggs
Roberto Tron
Tomasz Trzcinski
Ivor Tsang
Yanghai Tsin
Zhuowen Tu
Tony Tung
Pavan Turaga
Engin Türetken
Oncel Tuzel
Georgios Tzimiropoulos
Norimichi Ukita
Martin Urschler
Arash Vahdat
Julien Valentin
Michel Valstar
Koen van de Sande
Joost van de Weijer
Anton van den Hengel
Jan van Gemert
Daniel Vaquero
Kiran Varanasi
Mayank Vatsa
Ashok Veeraraghavan
Olga Veksler
Alexander Vezhnevets
Rene Vidal
Sudheendra Vijayanarasimhan
Jordi Vitria
Christian Vogler
Carl Vondrick
Sven Wachsmuth
Stefan Walk
Chaohui Wang
Jingdong Wang
Jue Wang
Ruiping Wang
Kai Wang
Liang Wang
Xinggang Wang
Xin-Jing Wang
Yang Wang
Heng Wang
Yu-Chiang Frank Wang
Simon Warfield
Yichen Wei
Yair Weiss
Gordon Wetzstein
Oliver Whyte
Richard Wildes
Christopher Williams
Lior Wolf
Kwan-Yee Kenneth Wong
Oliver Woodford
John Wright
Changchang Wu
Xinxiao Wu
Ying Wu
Tianfu Wu
Yang Wu
Yingnian Wu
Jonas Wulff
Yu Xiang
Tao Xiang
Jianxiong Xiao
Dong Xu
Li Xu
Yong Xu
Kota Yamaguchi
Takayoshi Yamashita
Shuicheng Yan
Jie Yang
Qingxiong Yang
Ruigang Yang
Meng Yang
Yi Yang
Chih-Yuan Yang
Jimei Yang

Bangpeng Yao
Angela Yao
Dit-Yan Yeung
Alper Yilmaz
Lijun Yin
Xianghua Ying
Kuk-Jin Yoon
Shiqi Yu
Stella Yu
Jingyi Yu
Junsong Yuan
Lu Yuan
Alan Yuille
Ramin Zabih
Christopher Zach
Stefanos Zafeiriou
Hongbin Zha
Lei Zhang
Junping Zhang
Shaoting Zhang
Xiaoqin Zhang
Guofeng Zhang
Tianzhu Zhang
Ning Zhang
Lei Zhang
Li Zhang
Bin Zhao
Guoying Zhao
Ming Zhao
Yibiao Zhao
Weishi Zheng
Bo Zheng
Changyin Zhou
Huiyu Zhou
Kevin Zhou
Bolei Zhou
Feng Zhou
Jun Zhu
Xiangxin Zhu
Henning Zimmer
Karel Zimmermann
Andrew Zisserman
Larry Zitnick
Daniel Zoran

Additional Reviewers

Austin Abrams
Hanno Ackermann
Daniel Adler
Muhammed Zeshan Afzal
Pulkit Agrawal
Edilson de Aguiar
Unaiza Ahsan
Amit Aides
Zeynep Akata
Jon Almazan
David Altamar
Marina Alterman
Mohamed Rabie Amer
Manuel Amthor
Shawn Andrews
Oisin Mac Aodha
Federica Arrigoni
Yuval Bahat
Luis Barrios
John Bastian
Florian Becker
C. Fabian Benitez-Quiroz
Vinay Bettadapura
Brian G. Booth
Lukas Bossard
Katie Bouman
Hilton Bristow
Daniel Canelhas
Olivier Canevet
Spencer Cappallo
Ivan Huerta Casado
Daniel Castro
Ishani Chakraborty
Chenyi Chen
Sheng Chen
Xinlei Chen
Wei-Chen Chiu
Hang Chu
Yang Cong
Sam Corbett-Davies
Zhen Cui
Maria A. Davila
Oliver Demetz
Meltem Demirkus
Chaitanya Desai
Pengfei Dou
Ralf Dragon
Liang Du
David Eigen
Jakob Engel
Victor Escorcia
Sandro Esquivel
Nicola Fioraio
Michael Firman
Alex Fix
Oliver Fleischmann
Marco Fornoni
David Fouhey
Vojtech Franc
Jorge Martinez G.
Silvano Galliani
Pablo Garrido
Efstratios Gavves
Timnit Gebru
Georgios Giannoulis
Clement Godard
Ankur Gupta
Saurabh Gupta
Amirhossein Habibian
David Hafner
Tom S.F. Haines
Vladimir Haltakov
Christopher Ham
Xufeng Han
Stefan Heber
Yacov Hel-Or

David Held
Benjamin Hell
Jan Heller
Anton van den Hengel
Robert Henschel
Steven Hickson
Michael Hirsch
Jan Hosang
Shell Hu
Zhiwu Huang
Daniel Huber
Ahmad Humayun
Corneliu Ilisescu
Zahra Iman
Thanapong Intharah
Phillip Isola
Hamid Izadinia
Edward Johns
Justin Johnson
Andreas Jordt
Anne Jordt
Cijo Jose
Daniel Jung
Meina Kan
Ben Kandel
Vasiliy Karasev
Andrej Karpathy
Jan Kautz
Changil Kim
Hyeongwoo Kim
Rolf Koehler
Daniel Kohlsdorf
Svetlana Kordumova
Jonathan Krause
Till Kroeger
Malte Kuhlmann
Ilja Kuzborskij
Alina Kuznetsova
Sam Kwak
Peihua Li
Michael Lam
Maksim Lapin
Gil Levi
Aviad Levis
Yan Li
Wenbin Li
Yin Li
Zhenyang Li
Pengpeng Liang
Jinna Lie
Qiguang Liu
Tianliang Liu
Alexander Loktyushin
Steven Lovegrove
Feng Lu
Jake Lussier
Xutao Lv
Luca Magri
Behrooz Mahasseni
Aravindh Mahendran
Siddharth Mahendran
Francesco Malapelle
Mateusz Malinowski
Santiago Manen
Timo von Marcard
Ricardo Martin-Brualla
Iacopo Masi
Roberto Mecca
Tomer Michaeli
Hengameh Mirzaalian
Kylia Miskell
Ishan Misra
Javier Montoya
Roozbeh Mottaghi
Panagiotis Moutafis
Oliver Mueller
Daniel Munoz
Rajitha Navarathna
James Newling
Mohamed Omran
Vicente Ordonez
Sobhan Naderi Parizi
Omkar Parkhi
Novi Patricia
Kuan-Chuan Peng
Bojan Pepikj
Federico Perazzi
Loic Peter
Alioscia Petrelli
Sebastian Polsterl
Alison Pouch
Vittal Premanchandran
James Pritts
Luis Puig
Julian Quiroga
Vignesh Ramanathan
Rene Ranftl
Mohammad Rastegari
S. Hussain Raza
Michael Reale
Malcolm Reynolds
Alimoor Reza
Christian Richardt
Marko Ristin
Beatrice Rossi
Rasmus Rothe
Nasa Rouf
Anirban Roy
Fereshteh Sadeghi
Zahra Sadeghipoor
Faraz Saedaar
Tanner Schmidt
Anna Senina
Lee Seversky
Yachna Sharma
Chen Shen
Javen Shi
Tomas Simon
Gautam Singh
Brandon M. Smith
Shuran Song
Mohamed Souiai
Srinath Sridhar
Abhilash Srikantha
Michael Stoll
Aparna Taneja
Lisa Tang
Moria Tau
J. Rafael Tena
Roberto Toldo
Manolis Tsakiris
Dimitrios Tzionas
Vladyslav Usenko
Danny Veikherman
Fabio Viola

Minh Vo
Christoph Vogel
Sebastian Volz
Jacob Walker
Li Wan
Chen Wang
Jiang Wang
Oliver Wang
Peng Wang
Jan Dirk Wegner
Stephan Wenger
Scott Workman
Chenglei Wu
Yuhang Wu
Fan Yang
Mark Yatskar
Bulent Yener
Serena Yeung
Kwang M. Yi
Gokhan Yildirim
Ryo Yonetani
Stanislav Yotov
Chong You
Quanzeng You
Fisher Yu
Pei Yu
Kaan Yucer
Clausius Zelenka
Xing Zhang
Xinhua Zhang
Yinda Zhang
Jiejie Zhu
Shengqi Zhu
Yingying Zhu
Yuke Zhu
Andrew Ziegler

Table of Contents

Tracking and Activity Recognition

Recognition

Poster Session 1

Learning and Inference

Visual Tracking by Sampling Tree-Structured Graphical Models

Seunghoon Hong and Bohyung Han

Department of Computer Science and Engineering, POSTECH, Korea
{maga33,bhhan}@postech.ac.kr

Abstract. Probabilistic tracking algorithms typically rely on graphical models based on the first-order Markov assumption. Although such linear structure models are simple and reasonable, it is not appropriate for persistent tracking since temporal failures by short-term occlusion, shot changes, and appearance changes may impair the remaining frames significantly. More general graphical models may be useful to exploit the intrinsic structure of input video and improve tracking performance. Hence, we propose a novel offline tracking algorithm by identifying a tree-structured graphical model, where we formulate a unified framework to optimize tree structure and track a target in a principled way, based on MCMC sampling. To reduce computational cost, we also introduce a technique to find the optimal tree for a small number of key frames first and employ a semi-supervised manifold alignment technique of tree construction for all frames. We evaluated our algorithm in many challenging videos and obtained outstanding results compared to the state-of-the-art techniques quantitatively and qualitatively.

Keywords: Visual tracking, tree-structured graphical model, Markov Chain Monte Carlo (MCMC), manifold alignment.

1 Introduction

Although visual tracking problem has been studied extensively for decades, the underlying graphical model of most existing probabilistic tracking algorithms is limited to linear structure, *i.e.*, first-order Markov chain. Such chain model is a reasonable choice since it is simple and typically well-suited for online tracking algorithms. However, in offline tracking algorithms (or online tracking algorithms allowing some time delay), more general graphical models are potentially helpful to overcome typical limitations of tracking algorithms relying on graphical models with linear structure. For example, when we track an object with view point changes or alternating appearances, tracking by a graphical model with multiple branches may be a better option to handle multi-modality of target and scene. Also, in chain model, inference of the target posterior at the current frame depends only on the previous frame, which may be problematic when the previous frame is not sufficiently correlated with the current one due to large motion, shot changes, occlusion, etc.

D. Fleet et al. (Eds.): ECCV 2014, Part I, LNCS 8689, pp. 1–16, 2014.
© Springer International Publishing Switzerland 2014

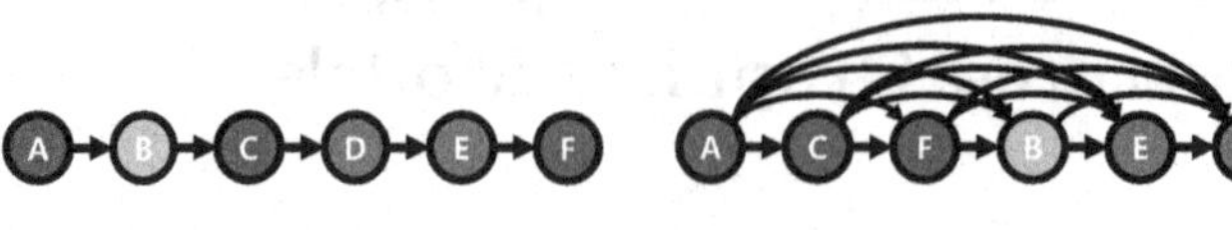

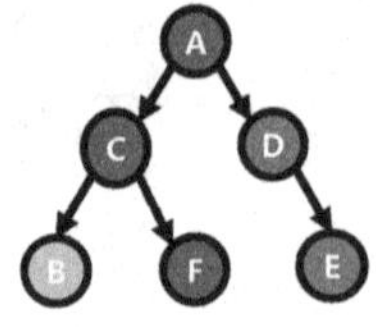

(a) Linear structure (b) Bayesian model averaging (c) Tree structure

Fig. 1. Potential graphical models for tracking. Each frame is represented by a node, where the color in each node indicates the type of target variation and the temporal order of frames is given by the alphabetical order. (a) In chain model, target is tracked by the temporal order of frames regardless of target variations. (b) Bayesian model averaging [1] infers target states in an increasing order of variations and makes a blind average of the posteriors obtained from all tracked frames. (c) In tree structure, we reorder frames based on target variations similar to (b) and estimate the posterior of a node by propagating density from a single parent, one of the frames already tracked.

Motivated by these facts, we propose a novel offline tracking algorithm based on a tree-structured representation of a video, where a node corresponds to a frame and the posterior is propagated from root to leaves sequentially along multiple branches in the tree. We claim that tracking in a tree-structured graphical model be more advantageous than chain model or Bayesian model averaging [1] due to the following reasons. First, it is natural to handle multi-modality of target and scene by identifying a reasonable tree structure and maintaining only relevant frames in each branch. Second, it is possible to achieve orderless tracking as in [1] by organizing frames based on their tracking complexity, where challenging frames are located near leaf nodes. Third, each node always has a single parent and existing sequential inference techniques can be employed directly without sophisticated posterior aggregation methods. Figure 1 illustrates the main concept of our algorithm compared to chain model and Bayesian model averaging method.

In this work, our goal is to find the optimal tree structure appropriate for tracking and improve performance by exploiting the identified tree. To achieve better tracking performance, the obtained tree structure should reflect correct dependency between frames with respect to target and scene. However, the identification of a good tree structure may require the estimation of target state in each frame. Learning the optimal tree structure and performing accurate tracking is a chicken-and-egg problem since it is practically infeasible to know which tree is optimal before tracking[1].

Therefore, we propose an iterative framework that learns tree structure and solves target tracking jointly, where a new tree structure is proposed by sampling and validated by tracking in each iteration. The proposed iterative algorithm is formulated by a Markov Chain Monte Carlo (MCMC) technique, which improves

[1] It is still difficult to determine the goodness of a tree even after tracking without evaluating results using ground-truth.

the quality of solution and provides the convergence of algorithm. For computational efficiency, the procedure is performed on a small subset of frames, and the learned tree is extended to the rest of frames in the input sequence by semi-supervised manifold alignment. Tracking in a tree-structured graphical model is similar to the standard sequential Bayesian filtering except that there exist multiple branches for density propagation. Main contributions of our study are summarized below:

- We propose an offline tracking algorithm based on a tree-structured graphical model, which is conceptually more general and reasonable compared to chain model; tree structures are well-suited to handle appearance variations, fast motion, shot changes, occlusion, temporal failures, etc.
- We formulate a unified framework of optimizing tree structure and tracking target in a principled way based on MCMC sampling.
- For efficiency, we estimate the optimal tree using a small number of key frames first, and employ a semi-supervised manifold alignment technique to construct a tree for all frames.

This paper is organized as follows. We first review related work in Section 2. The main framework of our algorithm is discussed in Section 3, and the hierarchical tree construction by semi-supervised manifold alignment is presented in Section 4. Section 5 illustrates experimental results.

2 Related Work

Visual tracking algorithm involves two main components, appearance modeling and tracker control. Recently, research on online appearance modeling is active, and various techniques have been proposed so far, *e.g.*, sparse reconstruction [2–4], online density estimation [5], incremental subspace learning [6], multi-task learning [7], multiple instance learning [8], P-N learning [9], and so on. However, the progress on tracker control issue is slow and many recent tracking algorithms still rely on sequential Bayesian filtering, tracking-by-detection or their variations, which are based on chain models with temporal smoothness assumption. Tracking algorithms based on temporally ordered chain models are inherently weak in abrupt motion, shot changes, significant appearance changes, and occlusion; [10] proposes an online tracking algorithm to tackle abrupt motion and shot changes by adopting Wang-Landau Monte Carlo sampling, but it still has the weakness of chain models and suffers from weak observation model.

Offline trackers utilize all frames in input video, and are more suitable to tackle abrupt target variations. They typically formulate tracking as a global optimization problem and solve it with standard techniques such as dynamic programming [11–14], Hidden Markov Model [15], and so on. However, even most of offline tracking algorithms employ chain models, which are not flexible enough to handle various challenges. The problem is sometimes alleviated by employing multiple key frames given beforehand [12, 15] or by user interaction [11, 14]. Recently, [1] proposes an algorithm to actively search an appropriate order of frames for tracking, where the posterior of a new frame is estimated by propagating posteriors from all tracked frames and aggregating them through Bayesian model averaging. This method seems to be better than chain models, but the blind averaging of density functions may contaminate the target posterior due to propagation of unreliable density functions.

MCMC is a useful and flexible tool to explore large solution space efficiently in many applications. Learning a graph structure by MCMC sampling is not new in computer vision community; [16] investigates image segmentation problem by constructing a tree and [17] samples graph structures of video for event summarization and rare event detection. However, to the best of our knowledge, there is no prior study about learning a graphical model for visual tracking problems through MCMC or any other methods.

3 Main Framework

Given an input video, we aim to simultaneously obtain tree structure for tracking and improve tracking based on the tree. Let $\mathbf{G} = (\mathcal{V}, \mathcal{E})$ be a tree, where $\mathcal{V} = \{v_1, \ldots, v_N\}$ denotes a set of nodes corresponding to N frames and $\mathcal{E} = \{e_1, \ldots, e_{N-1}\}$ denotes a set of directed edges defining conditional dependency between frames. Our goal is to obtain a set of target states for all frames $\mathcal{X} = \{\mathbf{x}_1, \ldots, \mathbf{x}_N\}$ and corresponding target templates $\mathcal{Y} = \{\mathbf{y}_1, \ldots, \mathbf{y}_N\}$ through tracking on $\mathbf{G}$. Since tracking is impossible without a tree and the optimal tree is difficult to obtain without tracking, we alternate the following steps in each iteration of our algorithm.

- Given a tree structure $\mathbf{G}$, perform tracking on the current tree-based probabilistic graphical model, and obtain the target states $\mathcal{X}$ and templates $\mathcal{Y}$ in all frames.
- Given tracking results $\mathcal{X}$ and $\mathcal{Y}$, propose a new tree structure $\mathbf{G}^*$ based on individual edge reliabilities in $\mathbf{G}$.

These procedures are repeated until it converges to a local optimum or reaches the predefined number of iterations. The final outputs of the algorithm are an optimal tree structure $\widehat{\mathbf{G}}$ and corresponding tracking results, $(\widehat{\mathcal{X}}, \widehat{\mathcal{Y}})$. We discuss each step of the MCMC framework in detail.

3.1 Learning Tree Structure by MCMC

There are a tremendous number of tree-structured graphical models to represent a video, and it is not straightforward to find an optimal tree for tracking efficiently. Hence, we design a good strategy to find the optimal solution in a limited number of iterations by employing MCMC sampling.

Each iteration of MCMC is composed of two steps—proposal step and acceptance step; the former draws a sample from a proposal distribution and the latter performs a probabilistic test to accept or reject the sample.

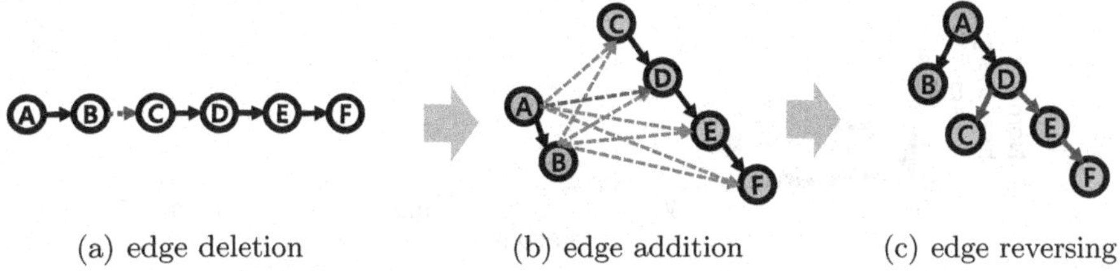

(a) edge deletion (b) edge addition (c) edge reversing

Fig. 2. Proposal of a new tree by $Q(\mathbf{G}^*|\mathbf{G})$. Given a current tree, deleting and adding edges are determined based on P_{delete} and P_{add}, respectively. Then, the directions of some edges are reversed to make all edges be directed from root to leaves.

Proposal Step. Given a current tree structure denoted by $\mathbf{G}$, a new tree sample $\mathbf{G}^*$ is proposed from proposal distribution $Q(\mathbf{G}^*|\mathbf{G})$. A new tree is sampled by replacing a subset of existing edges in $\mathbf{G}$ with new ones. For simplicity, we limit the space of $Q(\mathbf{G}^*|\mathbf{G})$ to a single edge *delete-and-add* operation as

$$Q(\mathbf{G}^*|\mathbf{G}) = P_{delete} \cdot P_{add} \tag{1}$$

where P_{delete} and P_{add} denote the probabilities to delete and add an edge, respectively.

It is practically impossible to compute the two probabilities without tracking on $\mathbf{G}$. We assume that a set of target templates $\mathcal{Y}$ is obtained by tracking on $\mathbf{G}$ in the previous MCMC iteration. Note that detailed tracking algorithm is presented in Section 3.2. The reliability of an edge is measured by the distance based on the amount of deformation between target templates in two connected frames, which is given by

$$d(i,j) \equiv \underset{m}{\text{median}} \left(||\mathbf{v}_i^m - f_{PM}(\mathbf{v}_i^m; \mathbf{y}_j)|| \right), \tag{2}$$

where $f_{PM}(\mathbf{v}_i^m; \mathbf{y}_j)$ is a patch matching function [18] from the mth patch located at $\mathbf{v}_i^m$ in $\mathbf{y}_i$ to $\mathbf{y}_j$. P_{delete} and P_{add} between two frames i and j are defined as

$$P_{delete}(i,j) = \frac{\exp(d(i,j))}{\sum_{(a,b)\in\mathcal{E}} \exp(d(a,b))} \qquad (i,j) \in \mathcal{E} \tag{3}$$

$$P_{add}(i,j) = \frac{\exp(-d(i,j))}{\sum_{(a,b)\in\overline{\mathcal{E}}} \exp(-d(a,b))} \qquad (i,j) \in \overline{\mathcal{E}} \tag{4}$$

where $\overline{\mathcal{E}}$ is the complement of $\mathcal{E}$ and does not include the edges creating loops.

By sampling from Eq. (1), deleting and adding edges are determined and a new tree $\mathbf{G}^*$ is proposed. If necessary, we change the directions of some edges and make all edges have the same direction—from root to leaves. The procedure to propose a new tree sample $\mathbf{G}^*$ from $Q(\mathbf{G}^*|\mathbf{G})$ is illustrated in Figure 2. By replacing an unreliable edge in $\mathcal{E}$ with a probable one in $\overline{\mathcal{E}}$, our algorithm learns a better tree $\mathbf{G}^*$, which does not rely on temporal order, and improves tracking performance by potentially utilizing a different path to track frames failed in the previous iterations.

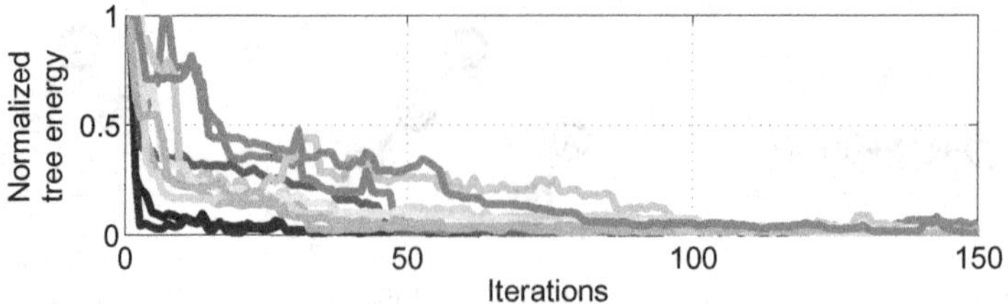

Fig. 3. Tree energy in each MCMC iteration for 10 videos used in our experiment

Acceptance Step. Once a new tree $\mathbf{G}^*$ is proposed, acceptance step decides whether the tree is accepted or not. To make the decision, we define recursively a tree energy to measure the quality of tree for tracking as

$$-\log p(\mathcal{Y}|\mathbf{G}) = \sum_{i}^{N} c_i = \sum_{i}^{N} \max(d(i, p_i), c_{p_i}) \tag{5}$$

where c_i denotes the cost to track from root to frame i, and p_i is the frame index of i's parent. Given the proposed tree structure $\mathbf{G}^*$ from Eq. (1), MCMC framework accepts or rejects the sample based on the acceptance ratio α, which is given by

$$\alpha = \min\left[1, \frac{(-\log p(\mathcal{Y}^*|\mathbf{G}^*))^{-1} Q(\mathbf{G}|\mathbf{G}^*)}{(-\log p(\mathcal{Y}|\mathbf{G}))^{-1} Q(\mathbf{G}^*|\mathbf{G})}\right]. \tag{6}$$

An important property of the tree energy function defined in Eq. (5) is that tracking error in any node is propagated to its descendants; internal nodes receive much larger penalty for tracking failures than leaf nodes. Therefore, large tracking errors in internal nodes tend to be corrected at an early iteration of MCMC and the algorithm gradually places the challenging frames to near leaf nodes, which isolates tracking failures to local areas (subtrees) and reduces error propagation. Most energy functions converge fast as illustrated in Figure 3, which may result from the reason described above.

Once MCMC iterations are completed, we take the best tree by

$$\widehat{\mathbf{G}} = \arg\min_{\mathbf{G}^l} -\log p(\mathcal{Y}^l|\mathbf{G}^l), \quad l = 1, \ldots, M \tag{7}$$

where l is the sample index and M is the number of iterations. Overall algorithm is summarized in Algorithm 1. In our algorithm, tree sampling and target tracking are tightly coupled to learn a graphical model; tracking is used to measure tree energy in MCMC iterations. We set the initial tree $\mathbf{G}^0$ to the conventional chain model in temporal order.

Due to huge search space, it is difficult to achieve the globally optimal solution after convergence. However, the tree structure obtained from MCMC sampling typically reduces tracking complexity and consequently is much better than temporally ordered chain model. In practice, tracking on the converged tree structure improves performance significantly, which will be presented in Section 5.

Algorithm 1. Tree construction by MCMC sampling

Input: Initial tree $\mathbf{G}^0$
Output: Best tree $\widehat{\mathbf{G}}$, $\widehat{\mathcal{X}} = \{\mathbf{x}_1^*, \ldots, \mathbf{x}_N^*\}, \widehat{\mathcal{Y}} = \{\mathbf{y}_1^*, \ldots, \mathbf{y}_N^*\}$
foreach $l = 0, ..., M-1$ **do**
  Propose $\mathbf{G}^*$ from $Q(\mathbf{G}^*|\mathbf{G}^l)$ by Eq. (1)
  Evaluate edge cost of $\mathbf{G}^*$ by
    1) Running tracking on $\mathbf{G}^*$ by Section 3.2
    2) Obtaining $\mathcal{Y}^*$
    3) Calculating $d(i, j)$ by Eq. (2)
  Calculate α with $-\log p(\mathcal{Y}^*|\mathbf{G}^*)$ in Eq. (5)
  $\theta \sim U[0, 1]$
  if $\alpha \geq \theta$ **then**
    $\mathbf{G}^{l+1} = \mathbf{G}^*$
  else
    $\mathbf{G}^{l+1} = \mathbf{G}^l$
  end
end

3.2 Tracking on Tree Structure

When a tree is proposed, we estimate the posterior of each frame based on the tree and decide its acceptance. This subsection describes a tracking algorithm to evaluate the proposed tree and generate the final tracking result.

Our tracking algorithm on a tree structure $\mathbf{G}$ has the following properties: 1) we set the root of tree as the initial frame for tracking, and 2) there exists a unique path from the root to any other node in the tree, which is modeled by a first-order Markov chain. Given these properties, the target posterior at frame t is estimated by a sequential Bayesian filtering as

$$P(\mathbf{x}_t|\{\mathbf{z}_i\}_{i=1,\ldots,t}, \mathbf{G}) \propto P(\mathbf{z}_t|\mathbf{x}_t) \int_{\mathbf{x}_{p_t}} P(\mathbf{x}_t|\mathbf{x}_{p_t}) P(\mathbf{x}_{p_t}|\{\mathbf{z}_i\}_{i=1,\ldots,p_t}, \mathbf{G}) d\mathbf{x}_{p_t} \quad (8)$$

where $\{\mathbf{z}_i\}_{i=1,\ldots,t}$ denotes a set of observations on the path up to node t and p_t denotes the index of t's parent. We start the density propagation from the root, which is performed independently in each branch by Eq. (8). It enables separate branches to model different types of the target variations. This property has another benefit in the next iteration of the MCMC; it makes it possible to reuse posteriors of common branches in different trees. In other words, although we track on a new tree $\mathbf{G}^*$ in each iteration, we do not need to track all frames again because the update in tree structure is minimal and the posteriors in many frames often remain unchanged. In addition, difficult frames for tracking tend to be relocated near leaf nodes, and computational cost gets smaller in later iterations since modified parts in a new tree $\mathbf{G}^*$ are mostly small.

To propagate the target posterior from parent to child, we need to define transition and likelihood model, $P(\mathbf{z}_t|\mathbf{x}_t)$ and $P(\mathbf{x}_t|\mathbf{x}_{p_t})$, respectively, in Eq. (8). Since the temporal order of frames may not be preserved in tree hierarchy, we cannot assume temporal smoothness or spatial coherency between connected frames. For this reason, we adopt patch matching and voting process as in [1] because of its robustness in this situation. For the purpose, we represent the posterior in Eq. (8) with a set of discrete samples as

$$P(\mathbf{x}_t|\{\mathbf{z}_i\}_{i=1,\ldots,t},\mathbf{G}) \approx \sum_{\mathbf{x}^j_{p_t}\in\mathbb{S}_{p_t}} P(\mathbf{z}_t|\mathbf{x}_t)P(\mathbf{x}_t|\mathbf{x}^j_{p_t}), \tag{9}$$

where $\mathbb{S}_{p_t}$ denotes a set of samples drawn from $P(\mathbf{x}_{p_t}|\{\mathbf{z}_i\}_{i=1,\ldots,p_t},\mathbf{G})$ denoting the posterior of parent. The prediction and measurement steps are modeled jointly by patch matching and voting process; for every rectangular patches in frame p_t, we apply the patch matching function f_{PM} to finding patch correspondences between frame p_t and t. Similar to the method in implicit shape model [19], every matched patch votes to the target center as

$$P(\mathbf{x}_t|\{\mathbf{z}_i\}_{i=1,\ldots,t},\mathbf{G}) \approx \sum_{\mathbf{x}^j_{p_t}\in\mathbb{S}_t}\sum_{m=1}^{K_j} \mathcal{N}(\mathbf{x}_t; f_{PM}(\mathbf{v}^m_j) - \mathbf{c}^m_j, \mathbf{\Sigma}), \tag{10}$$

where K_j is the number of patches in a sample bounding box, and $\mathbf{c}^m_j$ is the offset from $\mathbf{v}^m_j$ to $\mathbf{x}^j_{p_t}$. Each voting is smoothed by a Gaussian kernel with bandwidth $\mathbf{\Sigma}$. An efficient matching function f_{PM} is obtained from coherency sensitive hashing [18] as suggested in [1]. To further reduce voting errors, the voting map from the initial frame is used as an additional source of observation and the posterior is updated by the following equation:

$$P(\mathbf{x}_t|\{\mathbf{z}_i\}_{i=1,\ldots,t},\mathbf{G}) \approx P(\mathbf{x}_t|\mathbf{z}_1,\mathbf{z}_t)\left[\sum_{\mathbf{x}^j_{p_t}\in\mathbb{S}_t}\sum_{m=1}^{K_j} \mathcal{N}(\mathbf{x}_t; f_{PM}(\mathbf{c}^m_j) - \mathbf{a}^m_j, \mathbf{\Sigma})\right], \tag{11}$$

where $P(\mathbf{x}_t|\mathbf{z}_1,\mathbf{z}_t)$ denotes density propagation from the initial frame. Note that this term is not related to graph structure. We can estimate target posterior in every frame by propagating density based on Eq. (11). The target state in each frame is obtained by

$$\mathbf{x}^*_t = \arg\max_{\mathbf{x}_t} P(\mathbf{x}_t|\{\mathbf{z}_i\}_{i=1,\ldots,t},\mathbf{G}). \tag{12}$$

4 Hierarchical Construction of Tree Structure

The computational complexity of our tree construction algorithm is $O(MN)$, where M and N denote the numbers of iterations and frames, respectively, and tracking on a tentative tree in an MCMC iteration is time consuming. Tracking results in some frames, *e.g.*, frames with smooth or repetitive motion patterns in temporal neighborhood, are strongly correlated, and we propose a hierarchical approach to construct the tree by performing MCMC iterations only for a small subset of frames and extending the tree to the remaining frames. We perform a hierarchical tree construction based on semi-supervised manifold alignment.

4.1 Tree Construction on Key Frames

To obtain a meaningful tree structure of a video based on a small number of key frames, they should be representative and preserve crucial information about the variations in the input video. We adopt k-means clustering for key frame selection, for which we define the distance between frames. A patch-based bidirectional dissimilarity is employed as distance measure, which is given by

$$\mathbf{\Delta}_f(i,j) = \frac{1}{n_i} \sum_{\mathbf{a} \in I_i} \min_{\mathbf{b} \in I_j} \delta(\mathbf{a},\mathbf{b}) + \frac{1}{n_j} \sum_{\mathbf{b} \in I_j} \min_{\mathbf{a} \in I_i} \delta(\mathbf{b},\mathbf{a}), \tag{13}$$

where I_i and I_j denote a pair of images that contain n_i and n_j patches, respectively, and $\delta(\mathbf{a},\mathbf{b})$ denotes dissimilarity between patches $\mathbf{a} \in I_i$ and $\mathbf{b} \in I_j$. Since triangle inequality is not preserved with the measure in Eq. (13), all frames are embedded onto a metric space by Isomap [20]. Simple k-means clustering is applied on the embedded space, and the closest frame to each cluster center is selected as a key frame. This idea is similar to [21] except that k-means clustering is used instead of k-center method.

Once we select a set of key frames, MCMC iterations are performed on the key frames as described in Section 3. After convergence, we obtain the optimal tree structure $\widehat{\mathbf{G}}$ and tracking results $(\widehat{\mathcal{X}}, \widehat{\mathcal{Y}})$ for key frames.

4.2 Tree Extension by Manifold Alignment

It is a reasonable idea to construct a tree by simply running a minimum spanning tree algorithm in the metric space identified in Section 4.1. However, it is based only on scene dissimilarities and does not count target-specific information. Therefore, it would be better to find a joint embedding space that considers both scene and target distances. Suppose that we have another embedding for key frames based on target distance $\mathbf{\Delta}_o(i,j)$ similar to Eq. (13), where patches are extracted from target templates instead of whole images. Then, we construct a tree to cover all frames by extending $\widehat{\mathbf{G}}$ using the partial correspondences between two embeddings, which are given by key frames.

We adopt a semi-supervised manifold alignment algorithm [22] to establish the joint metric space. Given two dissimilarity matrices, $\mathbf{\Delta}_f$ and $\mathbf{\Delta}_o$, and the correspondences between key frames across two embeddings, our goal is to find a new metric space given by $\mathbf{h} = [\mathbf{s}^{\mathrm{T}}\ \mathbf{t}^{\mathrm{T}}]^{\mathrm{T}}$, where $\mathbf{s}$ and $\mathbf{t}$ represent the embedding coordinates extracted separately for scene and target, respectively. Key frames in the two different spaces are mapped to similar locations in the new space by optimizing the following objective function:

$$\min_{\mathbf{s},\mathbf{t}} \Phi(\mathbf{s},\mathbf{t}) \equiv \mu \sum_{i \in \mathcal{K}} |s_i - t_i|^2 + \mathbf{s}^{\mathrm{T}}\mathbf{L}^s\mathbf{s} + \mathbf{t}^{\mathrm{T}}\mathbf{L}^t\mathbf{t}, \tag{14}$$

where μ is a weighting factor, $\mathcal{K}$ is a set of key frames, and $\mathbf{L}^s$ and $\mathbf{L}^t$ are graph Laplacian matrices based on scene and target distances, respectively. The optimization of Eq. (14) is an ill-posed problem, but can be solved by minimizing Rayleigh quotient as

$$\min_{\mathbf{h}} \hat{\Phi}(\mathbf{h}) = \min_{\mathbf{h}} \frac{\mathbf{h}^{\mathrm{T}}\mathbf{L}^{c}\mathbf{h}}{\mathbf{h}^{\mathrm{T}}\mathbf{h}} \tag{15}$$

where $\mathbf{L}^c$ is the combined graph Laplacian matrix, which is given by

$$\mathbf{L}^{c} = \begin{bmatrix} \mathbf{L}^{s} + \mathbf{U}^{ss} & -\mathbf{U}^{st} \\ -\mathbf{U}^{ts} & \mathbf{L}^{t} + \mathbf{U}^{tt} \end{bmatrix}, \tag{16}$$

where $[\mathbf{U}]_{ij} = \mu$ if $i = j \in \mathcal{K}$ and 0 otherwise.

After we obtain the solution of Eq. (15), all frames are embedded to new metric space defined by $\mathbf{h}$. We first add edges between key frames by $\widehat{\mathbf{G}}$ optimized in Section 3. Then, the tree is extended to remaining frames based on a similar way to minimum spanning tree algorithm in the new metric space, and tracking is performed on the extended tree with all frames. The computational complexity of this approach is $O(kM + N - k)$, where k ($\ll N$) is the number of key frames. The complexity of a comparable algorithm OMA [1] is $O(kN)$, which shows that our algorithm is more efficient than OMA since M is typically smaller than N.

5 Experiments

We describe the details about our experiment setting, and illustrate the performance of our algorithm compared to the state-of-the-art techniques in challenging video sequences.

5.1 Datasets

For the evaluation of our tracking algorithm, we collected 10 video sequences, which are collected from [1, 23, 24] and also included new sequences. These sequences are often too difficult to be handled by traditional online tracking algorithms and appropriate to test the benefit of our offline tracking algorithm since they involve interesting challenges such as low frame rate (*tennis*), shot changes (*boxing, young, skating, dance*), occlusion (*campus, TUD*), appearance changes (*sunshade*), fast motion (*bike*), motion blur (*jumping*), etc.

5.2 Identified Tree Structure

The tree structures learned from our MCMC sampling and semi-supervised manifold alignment are reasonable and appropriate for tracking in many cases. We illustrate two examples of key frame trees. As shown in Figure 4(a), the identified tree structure of key frames for *sunshade* sequence divides two cases effectively—when human face is located in sunny side and under shadow—and enables tracker to handle them independently. On the other hand, in Figure 4(b), frames that are difficult to track due to occlusion are placed close to leaf nodes. These two

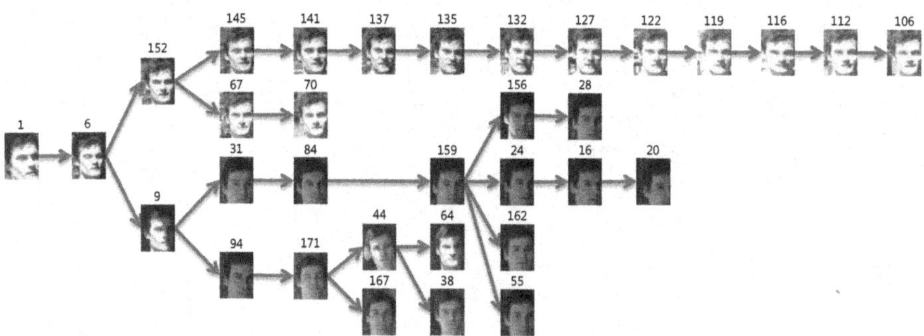

(a) Tree obtained from the key frames in *sunshade* sequence. Two main subtrees maintain bright and dark sides of face appearances.

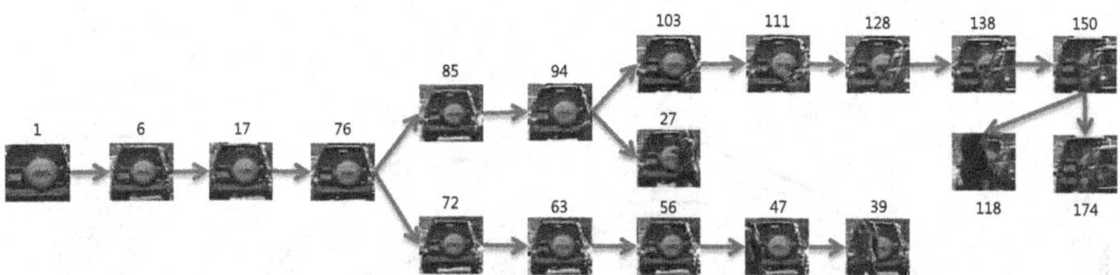

(b) Tree obtained from the key frames in *campus* sequence. Frames with occlusion are near leaf nodes, which minimizes error propagation.

Fig. 4. Examples of tree structures identified with key frames

examples present the effectiveness of our tree construction algorithm and the potential to improve tracking performance. Also, Figure 5 visualizes a tree with all frames for *skating* sequence, where we can observe a complex tree structure completely different from chain model.

5.3 Quantitative and Qualitative Performance

We compared the proposed algorithm with 18 state-of-the-art tracking methods. Most of them are online trackers, which include MIL [8], LSK [25], CSK [26], DFT [27], IVT [6], MTT [7], VTD [28], VTS [29], FRAG [30], L1APG [2], CXT [31], ASLA [32], SCM [4], Struck [33], TLD [9] and WLMC [10], while OTLE [12] and OMA [1] are offline trackers. We received source codes or binaries from authors of individual tracking algorithms. Our tracking algorithm is denoted by TST (Tracking by Sampling Tree). Among the tracking algorithms, OMA is most related to ours since it uses the same observation model and shares the temporal orderlessness property.

To evaluate performance, two most common measures—center location error and bounding box overlap ratio—are employed. For patch matching, the same parameter setting with [1] is employed; patch size is 8×8 and 900 samples are drawn in 9 scales from 0.6 to 1.4 to populate hypotheses to other frames. The

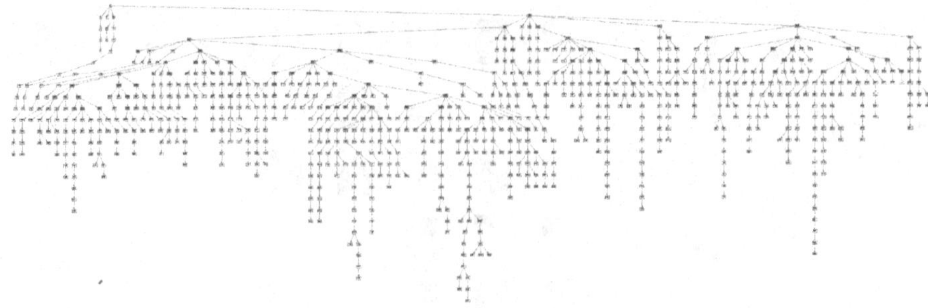

Fig. 5. An example of the entire tree structure for *skating* sequence. The solid (magenta) nodes indicate key frames. There exist multiple branches that are expected to model various aspects of target and scene.

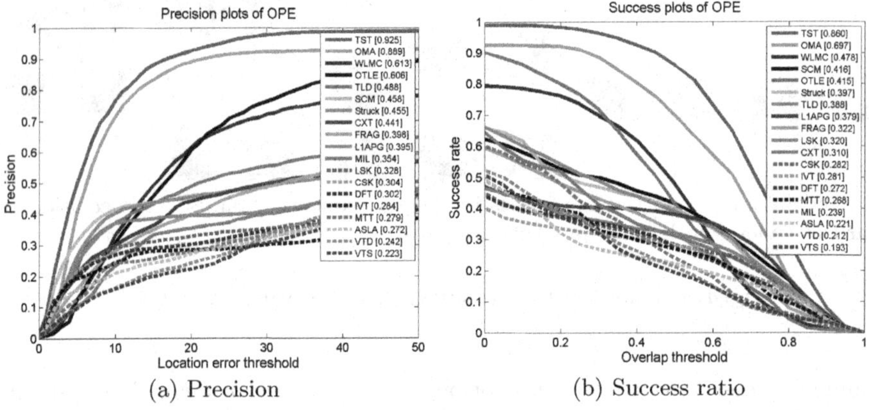

(a) Precision (b) Success ratio

Fig. 6. Precision and success ratio of all compared algorithms. Precision and success ratio are measured by center location error and bounding box overlap ratio, respectively. The ranks are determined at center location error 25 and overlap ratio 0.5.

number of key frames in each sequence is set to 10% of all frames. Note that all parameters are fixed across sequences.

Figure 6 summarizes quantitative evaluation results for all tested sequences and algorithms in terms of center location error and bounding box overlap ratio. Table 1 and 2 present more comprehensive results for the selected algorithms that perform well either in tracking benchmark [24] or Figure 6. Our algorithm generally outperforms other methods and this fact is clear in Figure 6. Performance of OMA is comparable to ours, especially in the sequences with shot changes, but its overall accuracy is lower than ours according to our experiment. OMA fails to handle strong bi-modal target appearance as in *sunshade* sequence due to its blind model-averaging property. When we construct a tree structure for all frames from the initial chain model with key frames and run our tracking algorithm, we obtain 17.8 and 0.64 for the center location error

Fig. 7. Tracking results for all sequences: from top to bottom, *bike, campus, TUD, sunshade, jumping, tennis, boxing, youngki, skating* and *dance* sequence

Table 1. Average center location error (in pixels). Red: best, blue: second best.

	FRAG	L1APG	CXT	ASLA	SCM	Struck	TLD	WLMC	OTLE	OMA	TST
bike	104.2	39.3	22.2	88.6	13.8	8.4	16.9	34.4	20.1	17.7	15.6
campus	3.3	16.1	33.4	12.2	12.2	83.1	46.7	13.5	5.8	3.2	1.4
TUD	17.3	7.4	36.4	72.6	12.2	54.4	18.9	68.2	27.3	4.4	4.1
sunshade	35.8	42.8	30.6	37.2	44.9	3.9	19.9	61.1	9.1	88.1	5.3
jumping	21.8	3.2	12.6	49.0	3.1	3.3	11.7	127.6	20.2	3.4	2.8
tennis	67.4	84.9	129.8	67.2	65.9	109.5	64.5	30.9	36.2	6.9	5.6
boxing	80.0	117.4	137.3	137.3	96.0	122.7	73.3	11.7	41.6	10.5	10.6
youngki	97.5	144.1	68.1	144.1	115.0	115.1	60.2	16.0	15.7	11.4	13.5
skating	35.4	143.9	41.5	45.2	49.4	23.8	35.3	14.7	18.3	8.0	6.1
dance	132.4	167.2	176.8	117.5	208.0	107.1	105.0	39.7	118.8	15.1	18.6
Average	59.5	76.6	68.9	77.1	62.1	63.1	45.2	45.2	31.3	16.9	8.4

Table 2. Average bounding box overlap ratio. Red: best, blue: second best.

	FRAG	L1APG	CXT	ASLA	SCM	Struck	TLD	WLMC	OTLE	OMA	TST
bike	0.08	0.18	0.39	0.16	0.46	0.54	0.45	0.39	0.27	0.40	0.56
campus	0.77	0.52	0.56	0.63	0.62	0.24	0.50	0.52	0.72	0.78	0.86
TUD	0.59	0.85	0.51	0.30	0.67	0.30	0.67	0.38	0.49	0.82	0.80
sunshade	0.33	0.32	0.49	0.43	0.45	0.78	0.57	0.24	0.60	0.29	0.70
jumping	0.31	0.77	0.40	0.20	0.76	0.75	0.56	0.07	0.26	0.74	0.79
tennis	0.11	0.29	0.08	0.12	0.11	0.28	0.10	0.43	0.33	0.63	0.74
boxing	0.22	0.13	0.01	0.03	0.13	0.04	0.21	0.65	0.38	0.70	0.71
youngki	0.19	0.02	0.38	0.12	0.13	0.09	0.24	0.62	0.54	0.62	0.66
skating	0.25	0.02	0.25	0.13	0.20	0.40	0.33	0.46	0.41	0.42	0.55
dance	0.14	0.02	0.08	0.10	0.07	0.08	0.07	0.45	0.30	0.52	0.52
Average	0.30	0.31	0.32	0.22	0.36	0.35	0.36	0.42	0.43	0.60	0.70

and the bounding box overlap ratio on average, respectively, which are better than OMA but non-trivially worse than our algorithm. These results indicate the benefit of tracking on tree structure learned from MCMC procedure. The results for qualitative evaluation are illustrated in Figure 7.

6 Conclusion

We presented a novel offline tracking algorithm based on automatic tree-structured graphical model construction. Our algorithm optimizes the structure of input video through MCMC sampling and performs tracking using the identified tree structure. Since an MCMC iteration is computationally expensive, we proposed a hierarchical tree construction algorithm by a semi-supervised manifold alignment technique. The learned tree structure tends to locate challenging frames near leaf nodes and isolate potential tracking failures in a small region. The proposed algorithm improves tracking performance substantially.

Acknowledgments. This work was supported partly by MEST Basic Science Research Program through the NRF of Korea (NRF-2012R1A1A1043658), ICT R&D program of MSIP/IITP [14-824-09-006, Novel computer vision and machine learning technology with the ability to predict and forecast; 14-824-09-014, Basic software research in human-level lifelong machine learning (Machine Learning Center)], and Samsung Electronics Co., Ltd.

References

1. Hong, S., Kwak, S., Han, B.: Orderless tracking through model-averaged posterior estimation. In: ICCV (2013)
2. Bao, C., Wu, Y., Ling, H., Ji, H.: Real time robust l1 tracker using accelerated proximal gradient approach. In: CVPR (2012)
3. Mei, X., Ling, H.: Robust visual tracking using $l1$ minimization. In: ICCV (2009)
4. Zhong, W., Lu, H., Yang, M.H.: Robust object tracking via sparsity-based collaborative model. In: CVPR (2012)
5. Han, B., Comaniciu, D., Zhu, Y., Davis, L.: Sequential kernel density approximation and its application to real-time visual tracking. TPAMI 30 (2008)
6. Ross, D.A., Lim, J., Lin, R.S., Yang, M.H.: Incremental learning for robust visual tracking. IJCV 77 (2008)
7. Zhang, T., Ghanem, B., Liu, S., Ahuja, N.: Robust visual tracking via multi-task sparse learning. In: CVPR (2012)
8. Babenko, B., Yang, M.H., Belongie, S.: Robust object tracking with online multiple instance learning. TPAMI 33 (2011)
9. Kalal, Z., Mikolajczyk, K., Matas, J.: Tracking-Learning-Detection. TPAMI (2012)
10. Kwon, J., Lee, K.M.: Tracking of abrupt motion using wang-landau monte carlo estimation. In: Forsyth, D., Torr, P., Zisserman, A. (eds.) ECCV 2008, Part I. LNCS, vol. 5302, pp. 387–400. Springer, Heidelberg (2008)
11. Buchanan, A.M., Fitzgibbon, A.W.: Interactive feature tracking using K-D trees and dynamic programming. In: CVPR (2006)
12. Gu, S., Zheng, Y., Tomasi, C.: Linear time offline tracking and lower envelope algorithms. In: ICCV (2011)
13. Uchida, S., Fujimura, I., Kawano, H., Feng, Y.: Analytical dynamic programming tracker. In: Kimmel, R., Klette, R., Sugimoto, A. (eds.) ACCV 2010, Part I. LNCS, vol. 6492, pp. 296–309. Springer, Heidelberg (2011)
14. Wei, Y., Sun, J., Tang, X., Shum, H.Y.: Interactive offline tracking for color objects. In: ICCV (2007)
15. Sun, J., Zhang, W., Tang, X., Yeung Shum, H.: Bi-directional tracking using trajectory segment analysis. In: ICCV (2005)
16. Tu, Z., Zhu, S.C.: Image segmentation by data-driven markov chain monte carlo. TPAMI 24, 657–673 (2002)
17. Kwon, J., Lee, K.M.: A unified framework for event summarization and rare event detection. In: CVPR (2012)
18. Korman, S., Avidan, S.: Coherency sensitive hashing. In: ICCV (2011)
19. Leibe, B., Leonardis, A., Schiele, B.: Combined object categorization and segmentation with an implicit shape model. In: ECCV Workshop on Statistical Learning in Computer Vision (2004)
20. Tenenbaum, J.B., de Silva, V., Langford, J.C.: A global geometric framework for nonlinear dimensionality reduction. Science 290 (2000)
21. Han, B., Hamm, J., Sim, J.: Personalized video summarization with human in the loop. In: WACV (2011)
22. Ham, J., Lee, D., Saul, L.: Semisupervised alignment of manifolds. In: 10th International Workshop on Artificial Intelligence and Statistics (2005)
23. Kwak, S., Nam, W., Han, B., Han, J.H.: Learning occlusion with likelihoods for visual tracking. In: ICCV (2011)
24. Wu, Y., Lim, J., Yang, M.H.: Online object tracking: A benchmark. In: CVPR (2013)

25. Liu, B., Huang, J., Yang, L., Kulikowski, C.A.: Robust tracking using local sparse appearance model and k-selection. In: CVPR, pp. 1313–1320 (2011)
26. Henriques, J.F., Caseiro, R., Martins, P., Batista, J.: Exploiting the circulant structure of tracking-by-detection with kernels. In: Fitzgibbon, A., Lazebnik, S., Perona, P., Sato, Y., Schmid, C. (eds.) ECCV 2012, Part IV. LNCS, vol. 7575, pp. 702–715. Springer, Heidelberg (2012)
27. Sevilla-Lara, L., Learned-Miller, E.: Distribution fields for tracking. In: CVPR (2012)
28. Kwon, J., Lee, K.M.: Visual tracking decomposition. In: CVPR (2010)
29. Kwon, J., Lee, K.M.: Tracking by sampling trackers. In: ICCV (2011)
30. Adam, A., Rivlin, E., Shimshoni, I.: Robust fragments-based tracking using the integral histogram. In: CVPR (2006)
31. Dinh, T.B., Vo, N., Medioni, G.: Context tracker: Exploring supporters and distracters in unconstrained environments. In: CVPR (2011)
32. Jia, X., Lu, H., Yang, M.H.: Visual tracking via adaptive structural local sparse appearance model. In: CVPR (2012)
33. Hare, S., Saffari, A., Torr, P.H.S.: Struck: Structured output tracking with kernels. In: ICCV (2011)

Tracking Interacting Objects Optimally Using Integer Programming*

Xinchao Wang[1,**], Engin Türetken[1,**], François Fleuret[2,1], and Pascal Fua[1]

[1] Computer Vision Laboratory, EPFL, Lausanne, Switzerland
[2] Computer Vision and Learning Group, Idiap Research Institute, Martigny, Switzerland

Abstract. In this paper, we show that tracking different kinds of interacting objects can be formulated as a network-flow Mixed Integer Program. This is made possible by tracking all objects simultaneously and expressing the fact that one object can appear or disappear at locations where another is in terms of linear flow constraints. We demonstrate the power of our approach on scenes involving cars and pedestrians, bags being carried and dropped by people, and balls being passed from one player to the next in a basketball game. In particular, we show that by estimating jointly and globally the trajectories of different types of objects, the presence of the ones which were not initially detected based solely on image evidence can be inferred from the detections of the others.

1 Introduction

Tracking people or objects over time can be achieved by first running detectors that compute probabilities of presence in individual images and then linking high probabilities of detections into complete trajectories. This can be done recursively [6,19], using dynamic programming [26,11,23], or using Linear Programming [25,15,5].

Most of these approaches focus on one kind of object, such as pedestrians or cars, and only model simple interactions, such as the fact that different instances may repel each other to avoid bumping into each other or synchronize their motions to move in groups [20,28]. In this paper, we introduce a Mixed Integer Programming framework that lets us model the more complex relationship between the presence of objects of a certain kind and the appearance or disappearance of objects of another. For example, when tracking people and cars on a parking lot, this enables us to express that people may only appear or disappear either at the edge of the field of view or as they enter or exit cars that have stopped. Similarly, when attempting to check if a bag has been abandoned in a public place where we can track the people, we can express that this can only happen at locations through which somebody has been the instant before. The same goes for the ball during a basketball match; it is usually easiest to detect when it has left the hands of one player and before it has been caught by another.

We will show that enforcing the fact that one object can only appear or disappear at locations where another is or has been can be done by imposing linear flow constraints.

* This work was funded in part by the SNSF DACH Project "Advanced Learning for Tracking and Detection in Medical Workflow Analysis".

** Authors contributed equally.

D. Fleet et al. (Eds.): ECCV 2014, Part I, LNCS 8689, pp. 17–32, 2014.
© Springer International Publishing Switzerland 2014

(a) POM [11] (b) KSP [5] (c) Ours

Fig. 1. Motivation for our approach. (a) Thresholding the detector [11] scores for cars and people produces only one strong detection in this specific frame of a complete video sequence. (b) Linking people detections across frames [5] reveals the presence of an additional person. (c) This additional person constitutes evidence for the presence of a car he will get in. This allows our algorithm to find the car as well in spite of the car detection failure. Because we treat people and cars symetrically, the situation could have been reversed: The car could have been unambiguously detected and have served as evidence for the appearance of a person stepping out of it. This would not be the case if we tracked cars first and people potentially coming out of them next.

This results in a Mixed Integer Programming problem, for which the global optimum can be found using standard optimization packages [14]. Since different object types are handled in symmetric fashion, the presence of one can be evidence for the appearance of the other and vice-versa. For example, Fig. 1 depicts a case where simply thresholding the response of the car detector we use leads to a car being missed. However, because people are properly detected disappearing at a location in the middle of the parking lot, the algorithm eventually concludes correctly that there must have been a car there which they entered. So, in this scenario, not only does the presence of a vehicle "allow" the disappearance of pedestrians but the disappearance of pedestrians is treated as evidence for the presence of a vehicle.

This is much more general than what is done in approaches such as [28], in which the appearance of people is used to infer the possible presence of a static entrance. It also goes beyond recent work on interaction between people and objects [2]. Due to the global nature of the optimization and the generality of the constraints, we can deal with objects that may be completely hidden during large portions of the interaction and do not require any training data.

Our contribution is therefore a mathematically principled and computationally feasible approach to accounting for the relationship between flows representing the motions of different object types, especially with regard to their container/containee relationship and appearance/disappearance. We will demonstrate this in the case of people entering and leaving cars, bags being carried and dropped, and balls being passed from one player to the next in a ball-game.

2 Related Work

Multiple target tracking has a long tradition, going back many years for applications such as radar tracking [7]. These early approaches to data association usually relied on gating and Kalman filtering, which have later made their way into our community [6,19]. Because of their recursive nature, they are prone to errors that are difficult to recover from by using a post processing step. Particle-based approaches such as

[13,24,8], among many others, partially address this issue by simultaneously exploring multiple hypotheses. However, they can handle only relatively small batches of temporal frames without their state space becoming unmanageably large, and often require careful parameter setting to converge.

In recent years, techniques that optimize a global objective function over many frames have emerged as powerful alternatives. They rely on Conditional Random Fields [17,27], belief Propagation [29,9], Dynamic or Linear Programming [3,10]. Among the latter, some operate on graphs whose nodes can either be all the spatial locations of potential people presence [26,11,5,1], only those where a detector has fired [25,15], or short temporal sequences of consecutive detections that are very likely to correspond to the same person [21,30,23,4].

On average, these more global techniques are more robust than the earlier ones but, especially among those that focus on tracking people, do not handle complex interactions between them and other scene objects. In papers such as [18], which looks into the behavior of sports players, their trajectories are assumed to be given. In [20,28], group behavior is considered during the tracking process by including priors that account for the fact that people tend to avoid hitting each other and sometimes walk in groups.

In [28], there is also a mechanism for guessing where entrances and exits may be by recording where tracklets start and end. However, this is very different from having objects that may move, thereby allowing objects of a different nature to appear or disappear at varying locations. In [2], person-to-person and person-to-object interactions are exploited to more reliably track all of them. This approach relies on a Bayesian Network model to enforce frame-to-frame temporal coherence, and on training data to learn object types and appearances. Furthermore, it requires the objects to be at least occasionally visible during the interaction. By contrast, we propose a global optimization framework that does not require training and can handle objects that remain invisible during extended periods of time, such as a person inside a car or a ball being carried and hidden by a player.

3 Method

In this section, we first formulate the problem of simultaneously tracking multiple instances of two kinds of objects, one of which can contain the other, as a constrained Bayesian inference problem. Here, we take "contain" to mean either fully enclosing the object, as the car does to its occupants, or simply being in possession of and partially hiding it, as a basketball player holding the ball. We then discuss these constraints in more details and show that they result in a Mixed Integer Program (MIP) on a large graph, which we solve by first pruning the graph and then using a standard optimizer.

3.1 Bayesian Inference

Given image sequences from one or more cameras with overlapping fields of view, we will refer to the set of images acquired simultaneously as a *temporal frame*. Let the number of time instants be T and the corresponding set of temporal frames $\mathbf{I} = (\mathbf{I}^1, \ldots, \mathbf{I}^T)$.

Assuming the position of target objects to be completely defined by their ground plane location, we discretize the area of interest into a grid of L square cells, which we will refer to as *spatial locations*. Within each one, we assume that a target object can be in any one of O *poses*. In this work, we define this pose space to be the set of regularly spaced object orientations on the ground plane.

For any pair k of location l and orientation o, let $\mathcal{N}(k) \subset \{1, \ldots, LO\}$ denote the neighborhood of k, that is, the locations and orientations an object located at l and oriented at o at time t can reach at time $t+1$. Let also $l(k)$ and $o(k)$ respectively denote the location and orientation of k.

Similar to [5], which treats spatial locations as graph vertices, we build a directed acyclic graph $G = (V, E)$ on the locations and orientations, where the vertices $V = \{v_k^t\}$ represent pairs of orientation angles and locations at each time instant, and the edges $E = \{e_{kj}^t\}$ represent allowable transitions between them. More specifically, an edge $e_{kj}^t \in E$ connects vertices v_k^t and v_j^{t+1} if and only if $j \in \mathcal{N}(k)$. The number of vertices and edges are therefore roughly equal to OLT and $|\mathcal{N}(.)|\, OLT$, respectively.

Recall that we are dealing with two kinds of objects, one of which can contain the other. Let $\mathbf{X} = \{X_k^t\}$ be the vector of binary random variables denoting whether location $l(k)$ is occupied at time t by a *containee* type object with orientation $o(k)$, and $\mathbf{x} = \{x_k^t\}$ a realization of it, indicating presence or absence of a *containee* object. Similarly, let $\mathbf{Y} = \{Y_k^t\}$ and $\mathbf{y} = \{y_k^t\}$ respectively be the random occupancy vector and its realization for the *container* object class.

As will be discussed in Section 4, we can estimate image-based probabilities $\rho_k^t = P(X_k^t = 1 \mid \mathbf{I}^t)$ and $\beta_k^t = P(Y_k^t = 1 \mid \mathbf{I}^t)$ that a containee or container object is present at grid location $l(k)$, with orientation $o(k)$, and at time t in such a way that their product over all k and t is a good estimate of the joint probability $P(\mathbf{X} = \mathbf{x},\ \mathbf{Y} = \mathbf{y} \mid \mathbf{I})$. Among other things, this is done by accounting for objects potentially occluding each other.

Given the graph G and the probabilities ρ_k^t and β_k^t, we look for the optimal set of paths as the solution of

$$(\mathbf{x},\mathbf{y})^* = \operatorname*{argmax}_{(\mathbf{x},\mathbf{y})\in\mathcal{F}} P(\mathbf{X} = \mathbf{x},\ \mathbf{Y} = \mathbf{y} \mid \mathbf{I}) \tag{1}$$

$$\approx \operatorname*{argmax}_{(\mathbf{x},\mathbf{y})\in\mathcal{F}} \prod_{t,k} P(X_k^t = x_k^t \mid \mathbf{I}^t) P(Y_k^t = y_k^t \mid \mathbf{I}^t) \tag{2}$$

$$= \operatorname*{argmax}_{(\mathbf{x},\mathbf{y})\in\mathcal{F}} \sum_{t,k} \log P(X_k^t = x_k^t \mid \mathbf{I}^t) + \log P(Y_k^t = y_k^t \mid \mathbf{I}^t)$$

$$= \operatorname*{argmax}_{(\mathbf{x},\mathbf{y})\in\mathcal{F}} \sum_{t,k} x_k^t \log \rho_k^t + (1 - x_k^t) \log(1 - \rho_k^t)$$
$$+ y_k^t \log \beta_k^t + (1 - y_k^t) \log(1 - \beta_k^t) \tag{3}$$

$$= \operatorname*{argmax}_{(\mathbf{x},\mathbf{y})\in\mathcal{F}} \sum_{t,k} \log\left(\frac{\rho_k^t}{1-\rho_k^t}\right) x_k^t + \log\left(\frac{\beta_k^t}{1-\beta_k^t}\right) y_k^t \tag{4}$$

where $\mathcal{F}$ stands for the set of all feasible solutions as defined in the following section. Eq. 2 comes from the above-mentioned property that the product of image-based probabilities is close to true posterior of Eq. 1, which will be discussed in more details in

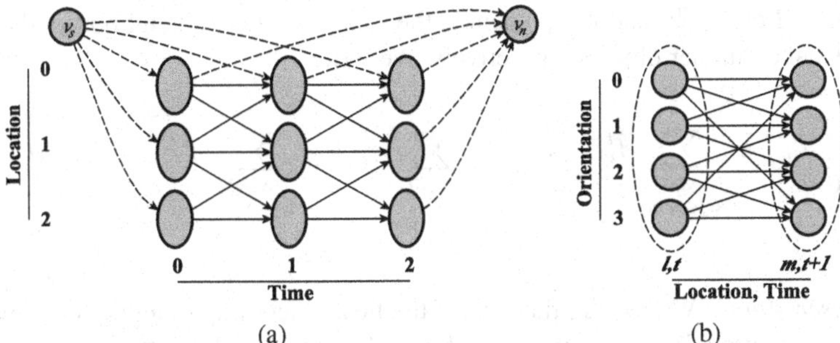

Fig. 2. A graph representing 3 spatial locations at 3 consecutive times. (a) Each ellipse corresponds to one spatial location at one time instant. Some are connected to a source and a sink node to allow entrances and exits. (b) Within each ellipse are four nodes, one for each possible orientation and the arrows represent possible transitions from one location and orientation to those in the neighboring ellipse.

§ 4, and from the assumption that all feasible transitions from time t to time $t+1$ are equally likely. Eq. 3 is true because both x_k^t and y_k^t are binary variables. Finally, Eq. 4 is obtained by dropping constant terms that do not depend on x_k^t or y_k^t. The resulting objective function is therefore a linear combination of these variables.

However, not all assignments of these variables give rise to a plausible tracking result. Therefore, the optimization of Eq. 4 must be performed subject to a set of constraints defined by $\mathcal{F}$, which we describe next.

3.2 Flow Constraints

To express all the constraints inherent to the tracking problem we introduce two additional sets of binary indicator variables that describe the flow of objects between pairs of discrete spatial locations and orientations at consecutive time instants. More specifically, we introduce the flow variables f_{kj}^t and g_{kj}^t, which stand respectively for the number of containee and container type objects moving from orientation $o(k)$ and location $l(k)$ at time t to orientation $o(j)$ and location $l(j)$ at time $t+1$.

In the following, in addition to the integrality constraints on the flow variables, we define six sets of constraints to obtain structurally plausible solutions.

Upper Bound on Flows: We set an upper-bound of one to the sum of all incoming flows to a given spatial location because it cannot be simultaneously occupied by multiple objects of the same kind.

$$\sum_{\substack{k:l=l(k),\\ i:k\in\mathcal{N}(i)}} f_{ik}^{t-1} \leq 1, \qquad \sum_{\substack{k:l=l(k),\\ i:k\in\mathcal{N}(i)}} g_{ik}^{t-1} \leq 1, \qquad \forall t,l\,. \tag{5}$$

Spatial Exclusion: As detailed in § 4.1, we model objects such as cars or people as rectangular cuboids, whose size is usually larger than that of a single grid cell. We impose spatial exclusion constraints to disallow solutions that contain overlapping cuboids in the 3D space. Let $\mathcal{N}_f(k)$ and $\mathcal{N}_g(k)$ denote the spatial exclusion neighborhoods for the containee and container objects respectively. We write

$$\sum_{i:k\in\mathcal{N}(i)} f_{ik}^{t-1} + \sum_{\substack{j\in\mathcal{N}_f(k),\\ i:j\in\mathcal{N}(i)}} f_{ij}^{t-1} \leq 1, \qquad \sum_{i:k\in\mathcal{N}(i)} g_{ik}^{t-1} + \sum_{\substack{j\in\mathcal{N}_g(k),\\ i:j\in\mathcal{N}(i)}} g_{ij}^{t-1} \leq 1, \qquad \forall t,k\,. \quad (6)$$

Flow Conservation: We require the sum of the flows incoming to a graph vertex v_k^t to be equal to the sum of the outgoing flows for each container object type.

$$y_k^t = \sum_{i:k\in\mathcal{N}(i)} g_{ik}^{t-1} = \sum_{j\in\mathcal{N}(k)} g_{kj}^t,\ \forall t,k\,. \quad (7)$$

This ensures that the container objects cannot appear or disappear at locations other than the ones that are explicitly designated as entrances or exits. Graph vertices associated to these entrance and exit points serve respectively as a source and a sink for the flows. To allow this, we introduce two additional vertices v_s and v_n into our graph G, which are linked to all the vertices representing positions through which objects can respectively enter or leave the observed area. Furthermore, we add directed edges from v_s to all the vertices of the first time instant and from all the vertices of the last time instant to v_n, as illustrated by Fig. 2.

To ensure that the total container flow is conserved in the system, we enforce the amount of flow generated at the source v_s to be equal to the amount consumed at the sink v_n.

$$\sum_{j\in\mathcal{N}(s)} g_{sj} = \sum_{i:n\in\mathcal{N}(i)} g_{in}\ . \quad (8)$$

Consistency of Interacting Flows: We allow a containee type object to appear or disappear at a location not designated as entrance or exit only when it comes into contact with or is separated from a container object. We write

$$-\sum_{\substack{m:l(k)=l(m),\\ i:m\in\mathcal{N}(i)}} g_{im}^{t-1} \leq a(t,k) \leq \sum_{\substack{m:l(k)=l(m),\\ j\in\mathcal{N}(m)}} g_{mj}^t,\ \forall t,k \quad (9)$$

$$a(t,k) = \sum_{i:k\in\mathcal{N}(i)} f_{ik}^{t-1} - \sum_{j\in\mathcal{N}(k)} f_{kj}^t \quad (10)$$

In Eq. 9, the total amount of container flow passing through the location k is denoted by the two sums on both sides of the inequality. When they are zero, these constraints impose the conservation of flow for the containee objects at location k. When they are equal to one, a containee object can appear or disappear at k. Note that, here we assume the containee objects never come to interact with the container one at exactly the same moment. For example, at one time instance only one person is allowed to enter the car.

Note that all four sums in Eqs. 9 and 10 can be equal to one. As a result, these constraints allow for a container and a containee object to coexist at the same location and at the same time instant, which can give rise to several undesirable results as shown

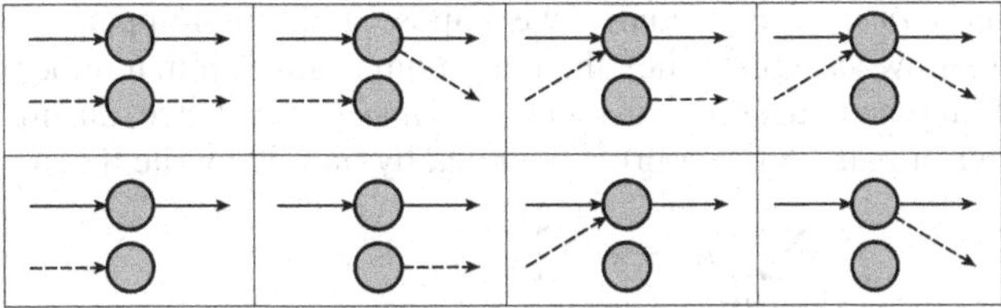

Fig. 3. Flow constraints in a two-orientation case. In each of the eight examples shown here, the two circles represent two orientation nodes at the same spatial location. The solid and the dotted arrows represent respectively non-zero flows g^t_{kj} and f^t_{kj} of the container and of the visible containee objects. **Top Row.** Forbidden configurations, which are all cases where a containee and a container coexist at the same location and at the same time instant without interacting with each other. For example, the configuration on the left could be interpreted as someone jumping in and out of the car at the same time. **Bottom Row**: Feasible configurations.

in the top row of Fig. 3. To avoid this, we bound the total amount of containee flow incoming to and outgoing from a location by one when there is a container object at that location.

$$\sum_{\substack{k:l=l(k),\\ i:k\in\mathcal{N}(i)}} f^{t-1}_{ik} + \sum_{\substack{k:l=l(k)\\ j\in\mathcal{N}(k)}} f^t_{kj} \leq 2 - \sum_{\substack{k:l=l(k)\\ j\in\mathcal{N}(k)}} g^t_{kj}, \ \forall t, l \tag{11}$$

Tracking the Invisible: We say a containee object is *invisible* when it is carried by a container. The four sets of constraints described above do not allow us to keep track of the number of invisible instances carried by a container object at a time. To facilitate their tracking even when they are invisible, we introduce additional flow variables h^t_{kj}, which stand for the number of invisible containees moving from orientation $o(k)$ and location $l(k)$ at time t to orientation $o(j)$ and location $l(j)$ at time $t+1$. These variables act as counters that are incremented or decremented when a containee object respectively disappears or appears in the vicinity of a container.

$$\sum_{\substack{k:l=l(k)\\ j\in\mathcal{N}(k)}} h^t_{kj} = \sum_{\substack{k:l=l(k),\\ i:k\in\mathcal{N}(i)}} h^{t-1}_{ik} + \sum_{\substack{k:l=l(k),\\ i:k\in\mathcal{N}(i)}} f^{t-1}_{ik} - \sum_{\substack{k:l=l(k)\\ j\in\mathcal{N}(k)}} f^t_{kj}, \ \forall t, l \tag{12}$$

$$h^t_{kj} \leq c * g^t_{kj}, \ \forall t, k, j : j \in \mathcal{N}(k) \tag{13}$$

where c is a fixed integer constant standing for the maximum number of containee instances a container can hold. For example, in the case of cars and people, this constant is set to 5. As a result, unlike the flow variables f^t_{kj} and g^t_{kj} that are binary, h^t_{kj} usually have a higher but finite upper bound. Note that, in Eq. 12, the h^t_{kj} variables are incremented or decremented always by an integer value. Therefore, during the optimization, we allow these variables to be continuous, except only those that are connected to the source, i.e., h_{sj}, which we restrict to be integers. Our experimental results show that allowing $h^t_{kj:k\neq s}$ to be continuous slightly speeds up the optimization, compared to imposing the integrality constraints on these variables.

Additional Bound Constraints: Finally, we impose additional upper or lower bound constraints on the flow variables when the maximum or minimum number of object instances of a certain type in the scene is known *a priori*. For instance, during a basketball game, the number of balls in the court is bounded by one. We write this as

$$\sum_{\substack{v_k^t \in V(t),\\ j \in \mathcal{N}(k)}} h_{kj}^t + \sum_{\substack{v_k^t \in V(t),\\ j \in \mathcal{N}(k)}} f_{kj}^t \leq 1\,, \qquad \forall t \tag{14}$$

where $V(t)$ denotes the set of graph vertices of time instant t. Together with the invisible flow constraints expressed in Eqs. 12 and 13, these constraints allow us to keep track of where the ball is and who has possession of it even when it is invisible. Another interesting case arises from the fact that a moving vehicle must have a driver inside. We express this as

$$h_{kj}^t \geq g_{kj}^t, \qquad \forall t, k, j : j \in \mathcal{N}(k), l(k) \neq l(j) \tag{15}$$

3.3 Mixed Integer Programming

The formulation defined above translates naturally into a Mixed Integer Program (MIP) with variables f_{kj}^t, g_{kj}^t, h_{kj}^t and a linear objective

$$\sum_{\substack{t \in \{1,\cdots,T\},\\ v_k^t \in V(t)}} \sum_{j \in \mathcal{N}(k)} \left(\alpha_k^t\, f_{kj}^t + \gamma_k^t\, g_{kj}^t\right), \tag{16}$$

with

$$\alpha_k^t = -\log\left(\frac{\rho_k^t}{1-\rho_k^t}\right), \text{ and } \gamma_k^t = -\log\left(\frac{\beta_k^t}{1-\beta_k^t}\right). \tag{17}$$

This objective is to be minimized subject to the constraints introduced in the previous section. Since there is a deterministic relationship between the occupancy variables (x_k^t, y_k^t) and the flow variables (f_{kj}^t, g_{kj}^t), this is equivalent to maximizing the expression of Eq. 4.

Solving the Linear Program (LP) obtained by relaxing the integrality constraints may, in some cases, result in fractional flow values as will be shown in the results section. That is why, we explicitly enforce the integrality constraints in our final results.

3.4 Graph Size Reduction

In most practical situations, the MIP of Eq. 16 has too many variables to be handled by ordinary solvers. To reduce the computational time, we eliminate spatial locations whose probability of occupancy is low.

A naive way to do this would be to simply eliminate grid locations $l(k)$ whose purely image-based probabilities ρ_k^t and β_k^t are below a threshold. However, this would be self-defeating because it would preclude the algorithm from doing what it is designed to do, such as inferring that a car that was missed by the car detector must nevertheless be present because people are seen to be coming out of it.

Instead, we implemented the following two-step algorithm. First, we designate all grid locations as potential entries and exits, and run the K-Shortest Paths Algorithm (KSP) [5] for containers and containees independently. In our experiments, we used the publicly available KSP code, which is shown to be very efficient. This produces a set of container and containee tracklets that can start and end anywhere and anytime on the grid. Second, we connect all these tracklets both to each other and to the original entrance and exit locations using the Viterbi algorithm [12]. Finally, we obtain a subgraph of G, whose nodes belong either to the tracklets or the paths connecting them.

In this way, the resulting subgraph still contains the low ρ_k^t and β_k^t locations that may correspond to missed detections while being considerably smaller than the original grid graph. For example, on a 20-frame *PETS2006* [22] image sequence that will be introduced in the results section, this procedure reduces the number of edges from around 22M to 17K. The resulting graphs are small enough to solve the MIP of Eq. 16 on batches of 500 to 1000 frames using the branch-and-cut procedure implemented in the Gurobi optimization library [14]. It minimizes the gap between a lower bound obtained from LP relaxations and an upper bound obtained from feasible integer solutions. The algorithm stops when the gap drops below the specified tolerance value. In practice, we set it to $1e^{-4}$ indicating the solution it finds is very close to the global optimum.

4 Estimating Probabilities of Occupancy

Our approach to computing the image-based probabilities of presence ρ_k^t and β_k^t that appear in Eq. 3 and Eq. 4 is an extension of the one proposed in [11].

This earlier algorithm was designed to estimate such probabilities for pedestrians given the output of background subtraction on a set of images taken at the same time. Its basic ingredient is a generative model that represents humans as cylinders that it projects into the images to create synthetic ideal images we would observe if people were at given locations. Under this model of the image given the true occupancy, the probabilities of occupancy at every location are taken to be the marginals of a product law minimizing the Kullback-Leibler divergence from the "true" conditional posterior distribution. This makes it possible to evaluate the probabilities of occupancy at every location as the fixed point of a large system of equations.

Importantly, probabilities computed in this way exhibit the property that allows us to go from Eq. 1 to Eq. 2 in our derivation of the objective function. We have therefore extended the approach to handling multiple classes of objects simultaneously as follows.

4.1 Oriented Objects

To handle objects such as cars or bags, we extend [11] by introducing simple wireframe models to represent them, as shown in Fig. 4. The only difficulty is that in the case of cylinders, orientation is irrelevant whereas the projections of our wireframe models depend on it. We solve this by allowing the generative model to model objects of any type at any one of the O regularly spaced orientations. This means that the projections of our 3D models can have arbitrary shapes and that we cannot use the integral image

(a) (b)

Fig. 4. Simultaneously detecting people and cars. (a) A person and a car is detected, as indicated by the red and green wireframes. (b) The same boxes are projected and filled as black boxes to create a synthetic image that approximates as closely as possible the background subtraction results, shown in green. Note that the white car is the same as the one that appears in Fig. 1. It remains undetected because the background subtraction algorithm fails to extract it.

trick of the publicly available software anymore [11]. We therefore use an "integral line" variant, which is comparably efficient. More specifically, we compute an integral image by taking integral of the image values only along the horizontal axis. At detection time, we then take the difference between the left-most and right-most integral pixels of a projected region and sum the resulting differences obtained from each row. This lets us detect objects of different types simultaneously and compute the probabilities of occupancy ρ_k^t and β_k^t introduced in § 3.1.

Note however, that the white car in Fig. 4 is missed because its color is similar to that of the background used for training, which is taken under direct sunlight. Arguably, we could have used a more powerful car detector but all detectors sometime fail and the point of this paper is that our technique can recover from such failures by leveraging information provided by other objects, in this case the people getting out of the car.

4.2 Objects Off the Ground Plane

In [11], objects of interest are assumed to be on the ground and the fact that they can move in the vertical direction, such as when people jump, is ignored. For people, this is usually not an issue because the distance of their feet to the ground tends to be small compared to their total height and the generative model remains roughly correct. However, in the case of an object such as a ball, which is small and can be thrown high into the air, this is not true anymore.

In theory, this could be handled by treating height over ground as a state variable, much as we do for orientation. However, in the specific case of the basketball competition we show in the result section that when the ball is in the air it also often is in front of the spectators, making the background non-constant and the results of [11] unsatisfactory. Therefore, in this specific case, we use a discriminative approach and run a ball detector based on color and roundness in each one of the frames taken at the same time, triangulate the 2D detections to obtain candidate 3D detections, and project the resulting probability estimate on the ground plane. Due to the small size of the ball compared to that of people, its presence or absence in a frame has little effect on the estimated probabilities of presence of people and we can assume conditional independence of

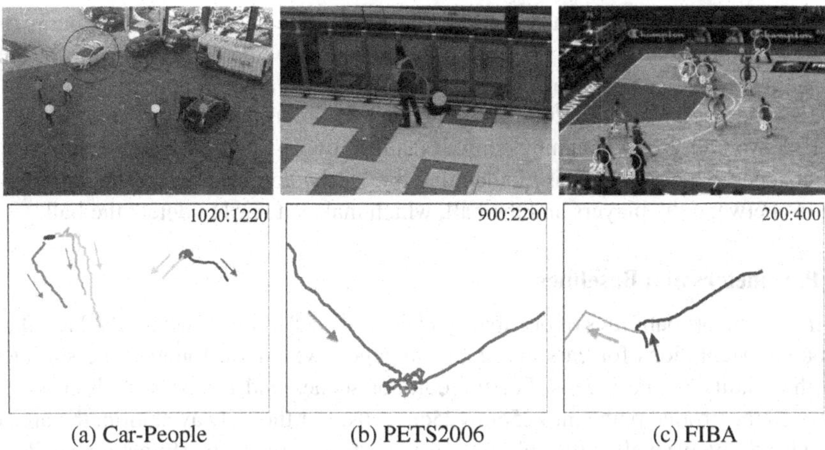

(a) Car-People (b) PETS2006 (c) FIBA

Fig. 5. Tracking results on three representative subsequences taken from our datasets. **Top row.** Sample frames with the detected container objects highlighted with circles and containee ones with dots. **Bottom Row.** Corresponding color-coded top-view trajectories for interacting objects in the scene. The arrows indicate the traversal direction. Note that, in the FIBA case, even though there are many players in the field, we plot only two trajectories: one for the ball the other for the player first holding it and then throwing it.

presence of people and ball given the images, which means we can still multiply the probabilities as required for the derivation of Eq. 2.

5 Experiments

In this section, we briefly describe the sequences we used for validation and give implementation details of our approach. We then introduce several baseline methods and finally present our comparative results. We show that our approach outperforms state-of-the-art methods on complex scenes with multiple interacting objects.

5.1 Test Sequences

We tested our approach on three datasets featuring three very different scenarios: people and vehicles on a parking lot (Car-People dataset), people and luggage in a railway station (PETS2001 dataset), and basketball players and the ball during a high-level competition (FIBA dataset). These datasets are multi-view and we processed a total of about 15K temporal frames. They all involve multiple people and objects interacting with each other. In Fig. 5, we show one image from each dataset with recovered trajectories. We summary the datasets as follows.

- **Car-People Dataset:** We captured several 300- to 5000-frame sequences from 2 cameras that feature many instances of people getting in and out of the cars. We show experimental evaluation on two sequences in the manuscript and provide further results in the supplementary material.

- **PETS2006 Dataset:** We use a 3020-frame sequence acquired by 2 cameras that shows people entering and leaving a railway station while carrying bags. Notably, one person brings a backpack into the scene, puts it on the ground, and leaves.
- **FIBA Dataset:** We use a 2600-frame sequence captured by 6 cameras at the 2010 FIBA Women World Championship. It features two 5-player-teams, 3 referees and 2 coaches. This sequence is challenging due to the complex and frequent interactions between the players and the ball, which makes it hard to detect the ball.

5.2 Parameters and Baselines

To compute the probabilities of occupancy ρ_k^t and β_k^t of Section 4, we used 12 regularly distributed orientations for cars and 2 for luggages, which we found to be sufficient given the quality of the videos. For the outdoor scenes and the basketball court, we discretized the ground plane into 25cm$\times$25cm cells. For the railway station, the area of interest is relatively small, which allowed us to perform a finer sampling with a cell size of 10cm$\times$10cm to improve the localization accuracy.

We compared our approach, denoted as **OURS-MIP**, against six baseline methods, which we summarize below.

- **POM:** We keep those orientation nodes, for which one of the occupancy probabilities ρ_k^t or β_k^t is greater than 0.5, and suppress the others. The resulting detections lack temporal consistency and may not satisfy the constraints introduced in § 3.2.
- **SSP:** The Successive Shortest Path (SSP) [23] is a algorithm for tracking multiple objects. It first builds a graph by linking pairs of object detections in consecutive temporal frames and then applies Dynamic Programing to find solutions. We run the publicly available SSP code and compared the results with ours.
- **KSP-free:** As discussed in Section 3.4, the KSP approach of [5] can be used to compute object trajectories for the container and containee objects independently using their occupancy probabilities. We designate all the grid locations as potential entries and exits prior to running the KSP algorithm. As a result, this approach allows objects to appear or disappear at any location at a certain cost value, which we take to be 40.
- **KSP-fixed:** This algorithm is similar to KSP-free, except that we use the original entrances and exits of the scene, such as the edge of the field of view. Therefore, objects can only appear or disappear at these predetermined locations.
- **KSP-sequential:** We first use the KSP-fixed algorithm to track the container objects and designate all the nodes that belong to the resulting trajectories as potential entrances and exits for the containees. We then use the same algorithm to find the containee trajectories, which may emerge from or enter the container ones. In other words, unlike in our approach, the two object classes are *not* treated symmetrically.
- **OURS-LP:** The linear programming approach (LP) solves the problem introduced in § 3.3 with the integrality constraints relaxed. The resulting flow variables are then rounded to the nearest integer to obtain the final solution.

5.3 Results

We ran all the baseline algorithms and ours on all the test sequences introduced in § 5.1. We show some qualitative results in Fig. 5. In the following, we present quantitative results on a representative subset of the sequences. We provide additional ones as well as videos overlaid with detection results in the supplementary material.

To quantify these results, we use the standard CLEAR [16] metrics, Multiple Object Detection Accuracy (MODA) and Multiple Object Tracking Accuracy (MOTA). MODA focuses on missed and false detections, while MOTA also accounts for identity switches. They are defined as a function of the amount of overlap between the detections and the ground-truth.

In Fig. 6, we plot MOTA and MODA for our approach (OURS-MIP) against those of our baselines on two sequences in the Car-People dataset, the PETS06 dataset, and the FIBA dataset. For the results of the remaining sequences in the Car-People dataset, we refer the reader to the supplementary material.

The sequence Car-People Seq.0 is the one from which we extracted the image shown in Fig. 1 and the corresponding results are shown in the first column of Fig. 6. It involves three people getting into a car stopped at the center of a parking lot. As discussed in § 4.1, the POM detector often fails to detect the car due to poor background subtraction. As a result, both KSP-fixed and KSP-sequential yield poor results because they do not create a car track, and hence are forced to explain the people in the scene by hallucinating them entering from the edges of the field of view. SSP and KSP-free do better by allowing the car to appear and disappear as needed but this does not correspond to physically plausible behavior. POM does even better because the people are in fact detected most of the time. OURS-MIP approach performs best because the evidence provided by the presence of the people along with the constraint that they can only appear or disappear in the middle of the scene, where there is a stopped car, forces the algorithm to infer that there is one at the right place.

The Car-People Seq.1 features two people getting into the first car, staying for a while, and getting out and entering the second one. Here, KSP-sequential and KSP-free do slightly better than KSP-fixed, which needs to hallucinate two false positive tracks to allow for the people emerging from the first car. The same happens in the PETS2006 sequence when the bag suddenly becomes visible in the middle of the image. Again, our approach performs best on both sequences mainly because we do not allow solutions that contain overlapping detections in the 3D space, which is enforced by the spatial exclusion constraints of § 3.2. In contrast, all the baseline methods produce overlapping spurious detections that are not physically plausible.

For the FIBA sequence, we show in Fig. 6(d) the MODA and MOTA scores for the ball only because the people detection scores for both the baselines and our approach are all very similar and the differences would not be visible in print. KSP-sequential yields a poor performance because of the weak image evidence that gives rise to several spurious ball detections. KSP-fixed eliminates some of these detections by forcing the ball to enter the scene only from the designated locations, and KSP-free does so by requiring that a cost to be paid for every appearance or disappearance of the ball. Our approach achieves the best performance by reasoning simultaneously for both players and ball, and enforcing that there can be at most one ball in the field during the game.

Note that solving the LP problem of § 3.3 and subsequently rounding the resulting fractional flow variables as in OURS-LP systematically performs either very similarly or worse than explicitly imposing the integrality constraints as we do in the OURS-MIP

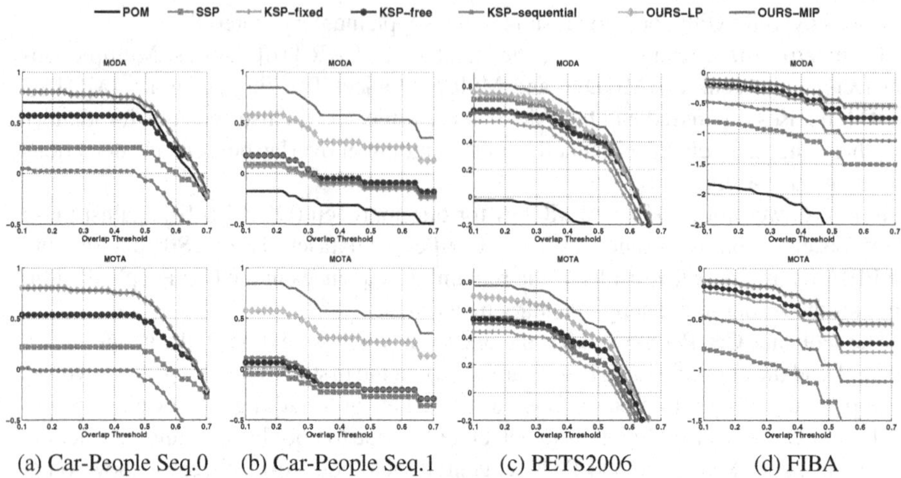

(a) Car-People Seq.0 (b) Car-People Seq.1 (c) PETS2006 (d) FIBA

Fig. 6. Comparing our proposed approach (OURS-MIP) against the baselines in terms of the MOTA and MODA scores. Our tracker yields a significant improvement on all datasets, thanks to the joint-global optimization on both container and containee objects.

approach. In Car-People Seq.1 and PETS2006, where OURS-MIP significantly outperforms OURS-LP, the ratio of fractional flows to non-zero flows using OURS-LP are 39% and 12% respectively. In the other two sequences the ratio are lower than 1%, therefore the performance of OURS-LP and OURS-MIP are very similar.

Finally, in the Car-People dataset, we observe a few failure cases where a person gets into the car but the associated counter variable is not incremented. This is because the car is parked on the boundary of the monitored area and the person is detected closer to the boundary than to the car, therefore the optimizer prefers the explanation that the person leaves the monitored area than he enters the car.

6 Conclusion

We have introduced a new approach to tracking multiple objects of different types and accounting for their complex and dynamic interactions. It relies on Mixed Integer Programming and ensures convergence to a global optimum using a standard optimizer. Furthermore, not only does it explicitly handle interactions, it also provides an estimate for the *implicit* transport of objects for which the only evidence is the presence of other objects that can contain or carry them.

We demonstrated our method on real-world sequences that feature people boarding and getting out of cars, carrying and dropping luggages, and passing the ball during a basketball match. The same approach could be applied to more complex situations and future work will aim at extending it to scenarios with more than two types of objects.

References

1. Andriyenko, A., Schindler, K., Roth, S.: Discrete-Continuous Optimization for Multi-Target Tracking. In: CVPR (2012)
2. Baumgartner, T., Mitzel, D., Leibe, B.: Tracking People and Their Objects. In: CVPR, pp. 3658–3665 (2013)
3. Bellman, R.: Dynamic programming and lagrange multipliers. Proceedings of the National Academy of Sciences 42, 767–769 (1956)
4. Ben Shitrit, H., Berclaz, J., Fleuret, F., Fua, P.: Multi-Commodity Network Flow for Tracking Multiple People. PAMI (2013)
5. Berclaz, J., Fleuret, F., Türetken, E., Fua, P.: Multiple Object Tracking Using K-Shortest Paths Optimization. PAMI 33, 1806–1819 (2011)
6. Black, J., Ellis, T., Rosin, P.: Multi-View Image Surveillance and Tracking. In: IEEE Workshop on Motion and Video Computing (2002)
7. Blackman, S.: Multiple-Target Tracking with Radar Applications. Artech House (1986)
8. Breitenstein, M., Reichlin, F., Leibe, B., Koller-Meier, E., Van Gool, L.: Online Multi-Person Tracking-By-Detection from a Single Uncalibrated Camera. PAMI (2010)
9. Choi, W., Savarese, S.: A Unified Framework for Multi-target Tracking and Collective Activity Recognition. In: Fitzgibbon, A., Lazebnik, S., Perona, P., Sato, Y., Schmid, C. (eds.) ECCV 2012, Part IV. LNCS, vol. 7575, pp. 215–230. Springer, Heidelberg (2012)
10. Dantzig, G.B.: Linear Programming and Extensions. Princeton University Press (1963)
11. Fleuret, F., Berclaz, J., Lengagne, R., Fua, P.: Multi-Camera People Tracking with a Probabilistic Occupancy Map. PAMI 30(2), 267–282 (2008)
12. Forney, G.: The Viterbi Algorithm. Proceedings of IEEE, 268–278 (March 1973)
13. Giebel, J., Gavrila, D.M., Schnörr, C.: A Bayesian Framework for Multi-Cue 3D Object Tracking. In: Pajdla, T., Matas, J. (eds.) ECCV 2004. LNCS, vol. 3024, pp. 241–252. Springer, Heidelberg (2004)
14. Gurobi: Gurobi Optimizer (2012), `http://www.gurobi.com/`
15. Jiang, H., Fels, S., Little, J.: A Linear Programming Approach for Multiple Object Tracking. In: CVPR (2007)
16. Kasturi, R., Goldgof, D., Soundararajan, P., Manohar, V., Garofolo, J., Boonstra, M., Korzhova, V., Zhang, J.: Framework for Performance Evaluation of Face, Text, and Vehicle Detection and Tracking in Video: Data, Metrics, and Protocol. PAMI 31(2), 319–336 (2009)
17. Lafferty, J., Mccallum, A., Pereira, F.: Conditional Random Fields: Probabilistic Models for Segmenting and Labeling Sequence Data. In: ICML (2001)
18. Lucey, P., Bialkowski, A., Carr, P., Morgan, S., Matthews, I., Sheikh, Y.: Representing and Discovering Adversarial Team Behaviors Using Player Roles. In: CVPR (2013)
19. Mittal, A., Davis, L.: M2Tracker: A Multi-View Approach to Segmenting and Tracking People in a Cluttered Scene. IJCV 51(3), 189–203 (2003)
20. Pellegrini, S., Ess, A., Schindler, K., Van Gool, L.: You'll Never Walk Alone: Modeling Social Behavior for Multi-Target Tracking. In: ICCV (2009)
21. Perera, A., Srinivas, C., Hoogs, A., Brooksby, G., Wensheng, H.: Multi-Object Tracking through Simultaneous Long Occlusions and Split-Merge Conditions. In: CVPR (2006)
22. PETS: Performance Evaluation of Tracking and Surveillance (2009), `http://www.cvg.rdg.ac.uk/slides/pets.html`
23. Pirsiavash, H., Ramanan, D., Fowlkes, C.: Globally-Optimal Greedy Algorithms for Tracking a Variable Number of Objects. In: CVPR (June 2011)
24. Smith, K., Gatica-Perez, D., Odobez, J.M.: Using Particles to Track Varying Numbers of Interacting People. In: CVPR (2005)

25. Storms, P., Spieksma, F.: An Lp-Based Algorithm for the Data Association Problem in Multitarget Tracking. Computers and Operations Research 30(7), 1067–1085 (2003)
26. Wolf, J., Viterbi, A., Dixon, G.: Finding the Best Set of K Paths through a Trellis with Application to Multitarget Tracking. IEEE Transactions on Aerospace and Electronic Systems 25(2), 287–296 (1989)
27. Yang, B., Nevatia, R.: An Online Learned CRF Model for Multi-Target Tracking. In: CVPR (2012)
28. Yang, B., Nevatia, R.: Multi-Target Tracking by Online Learning of Non-Linear Motion Patterns and Robust Appearance Models. In: CVPR (2012)
29. Yedidia, J.S., Freeman, W.T., Weiss, Y.: Generalized Belief Propagation. In: NIPS, pp. 689–695 (2000)
30. Zhang, L., Li, Y., Nevatia, R.: Global Data Association for Multi-Object Tracking Using Network Flows. In: CVPR (2008)

Learning Latent Constituents for Recognition of Group Activities in Video*

Borislav Antic and Björn Ommer

HCI & IWR, University of Heidelberg, Germany
borislav.antic@iwr.uni-heidelberg.de, ommer@uni-heidelberg.de

Abstract. The collective activity of a group of persons is more than a mere sum of individual person actions, since interactions and the context of the overall group behavior have crucial influence. Consequently, the current standard paradigm for group activity recognition is to model the spatiotemporal pattern of individual person bounding boxes and their interactions. Despite this trend towards increasingly global representations, activities are often defined by semi-local characteristics and their interrelation between different persons. For capturing the large visual variability with small semi-local parts, a large number of them are required, thus rendering manual annotation infeasible. To automatically learn activity constituents that are meaningful for the collective activity, we sample local parts and group related ones not merely based on visual similarity but based on the function they fulfill on a set of validation images. Then max-margin multiple instance learning is employed to jointly i) remove clutter from these groups and focus on only the relevant samples, ii) learn the activity constituents, and iii) train the multi-class activity classifier. Experiments on standard activity benchmark sets show the advantage of this joint procedure and demonstrate the benefit of functionally grouped latent activity constituents for group activity recognition.

Keywords: Group Activity Recognition, Latent Parts, Multiple-Instance Learning, Functional Grouping, Video Retrieval.

1 Introduction

Over the last years there has been an ever growing interest in recognizing activities of groups of persons in video [24,29,32]. Whereas action recognition has a focus on the actions individual persons perform, group activities involve a group of people that perform the same or a related action in the scene such as talking to another. Thus, collective activity recognition is especially challenging as it depends on interactions and group behavior and so it is more than just the sum of individual person actions. For example the activity of lining up in a queue and the activity of waiting for a green light both exhibit the same individual standing actions and thus cannot be distinguished on that level. Conversely, analyzing the behavior of a single person benefits from recognition of group activities since noise and local occlusions can be overcome given the

* Electronic supplementary material -Supplementary material is available in the online version of this chapter at http://dx.doi.org/10.1007/978-3-319-10590-3. Videos can also be accessed at http://www.springerimages.com/videos/978-3-319-10589-5

D. Fleet et al. (Eds.): ECCV 2014, Part I, LNCS 8689, pp. 33–47, 2014.
© Springer International Publishing Switzerland 2014

Fig. 1. Collective activities in videos can be recognized from semi-local characteristic parts that are grouped into a set of activity constituents by their common function on a validation set. Colors indicate different constituents and for legibility only a subset is shown.

observations from the whole group. A main goal of this field is therefore to recognize the activity of a varying number of people and localize it on the level of person bounding boxes by identifying for each person what activity they partake in.

The main theme is presently to estimate the activity of a complete person bounding box based on its visual features, motion, etc. [21,8]. Thereafter contextual interactions are incorporated by re-classifying the activity at each bounding box based on the activities at neighboring boxes. The underlying rationale is that activities depend on the *overall* visual pattern of a bounding box and the activities in its neighborhood. Our hypothesis is that activities are much better characterized not on the level of bounding boxes but based on a large number of characteristic activity constituents and their interactions within the group. For example, if a detected constituent features a hand holding a tray, this indicates a person waiting in a queue.

Obviously, there are many different characteristic activity constituents and interactions thereof conceivable. Therefore, we cannot expect users to label them beforehand as in [5] and models limited to a small number of parts such as [14,15] are not suited. Activities call for a large number of latent constituents with flexible but characteristic mutual arrangements and they need to be learned automatically without manual annotation. Training a large number of part classifiers, however, leaves only few samples per classifier. Moreover, many of these parts might be redundant (related regions coming from different persons) and recognition with too many redundant constituent classifiers is an unnecessary computational burden. Consequently, related parts need to be grouped into meaningful activity constituents before training a constituent classifier for each group. Fig. 1 shows a subset of the detected activity constituents for recognizing group activity in these two scenes. However, due to the curse of dimensionality, visual similarity becomes quickly unreliable in high-dimensional feature spaces. Consequently, the resulting groups would be cluttered and impair the subsequent learning of models for all parts within a group. As an example consider two patches on the legs of a person, one patch being larger and showing a shifted crop-out w.r.t. the other. Their feature vectors are vastly different, although both patches have the same function, i.e., they represent the gait of a walking person. Therefore, we match each patch to a set of validation images. Comparing their activations on a large number of validation samples, groups parts according to what *function* they have in these images, thus going beyond a mere visual similarity. Since the grouped parts are sampled from noisy, cluttered scenes the resulting functional groups contain outliers. We thus frame the training of the constituent classifiers for each group as a multiple instance learning problem. Discriminating the activity constituent from negatives and removing irrelevant candidate instances from its group are tackled jointly. All of these activity constituents are then combined in a multi-class activity classifier, which is optimized together with its activity constituents to model their characteristic co-activations. Learning the activity constituents, selecting meaningful part samples for this learning, and optimizing the overall activity classifier are then coupled in a single objective function to represent concerted group activities.

2 Related Work

Action recognition in video has made significant progress over the last decade [29,32]. A large body of literature on action recognition includes sparse feature representations by Dollar et al. [12], compositional models [27], action descriptions using correlations by Laptev et al. [22] or latent semantic analysis by Niebles et al. [26]. A very good summary on the action recognition techniques is provided in the survey [31].

Whereas action recognition is only concerned with actions performed by a single person or pairs of persons, recognition of group activities is about inferring the collective behavior of a group of persons that perform related actions. As the actions of individual persons are interrelated, the context of other persons in the scene is important for the overall activity. Pairwise interactions between persons in a scene are used for recognizing human activities in [28]. [3] propose a joint parsing of entire scenes for detecting abnormalities in video. Xiang and Gong [33] reason about temporal and causal correlations among scene events in a video. The recognition of group activities is very challenging because of the complex interactions between persons in a scene. Some authors proposed various contextual descriptors for representing the group activities [9,19,10]. Hierarchical models that unify individual actions, pairwise interactions and group activities were proposed in [20,8].

Recent work on collective activity recognition aims to jointly solve the problems of group activity recognition and person tracking [18,17,7]. Choi and Savarese [7] leverage target interactions for guiding target associations, and use different levels of granularity for encoding the activities. Amer and Todorovic [1] allow for arbitrarily large numbers of activity participants and localize parts of the activity using a chain model of group activity. In [2] the authors use a three-layered AND-OR graph to jointly model group activities, individual actions, and participating objects. Khamis et al. [18] combine per-track and per-frame cues for action recognition and bounding box tracking.

Human body patches with similar pose and appearance have been obtained in Poselets [23] by a very detailed manual annotation of the joints of persons. In contrast to this tedious labeling task, our method automatically discovers functionally related parts and learns the latent constituents jointly with the activity classifier using multiple-instance learning. Related work on mid-level discriminative patches [30] and intermediate compositional parts [13] learn the patches independently from the overall classifier. Consequently, mid-level patches do not directly maximize the overall classification

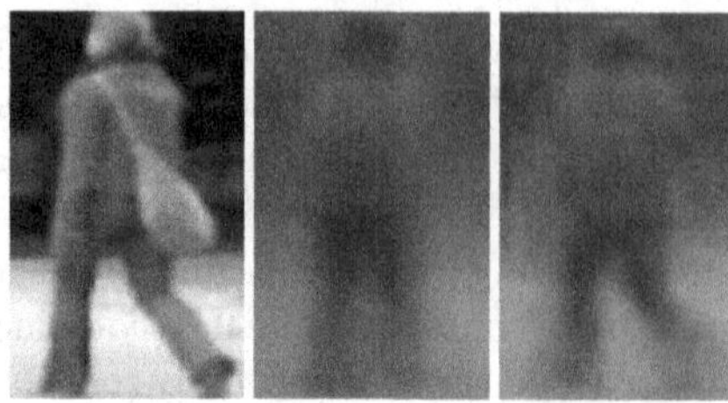

Fig. 2. Reconstructing query image (left) using groups of parts found by visual similarity based clustering (middle) and using functional grouping (right). See text for the details.

performance. In contrast, our approach jointly optimizes constituent parts and the group activity classifier. Moreover, a functional grouping based on similarity of part activation patterns on a validation set leads to more consistent initial part clusters than those based on visual part similarity.

3 Learning Functional Constituents of Group Activities

Group activity recognition requires for each person to infer which collective activity they partake in. That is, for each person bounding box we seek the activity that is consistent with other interacting persons in the scene. To capture the peculiarities of activities we have to go beyond a mere representation on the level of bounding boxes and grasp the semi-local constituents of activities. Due to the large within-class variability this requires a large number of parts, so learning a separate model for each part is neither statistically feasible (few training samples in high-dimensional feature space) nor computationally practical (high complexity).

Our approach adaptively seeks the feasible middle-ground between two extremes: (i) a single or only few complex classifiers that try to capture all characteristics of activities with all their multi-modal variabilities, and (ii) an impossibly large number of separate classifiers for each part with too few training samples for each and redundancies between them. Thus we aim at grouping related semi-local parts from different training images according to the function they take in a set of validation images, so we can train a single, more powerful classifier for each group of related activity constituents. Functional grouping yields a candidate set of part instances per activity constituent, but groups may still contain clutter and spurious part samples. That is why classifiers for activities and their latent constituents are learned jointly by employing multiple-instance learning to select only the relevant instances for each constituent from its candidate set (see Fig. 3).

3.1 Functional Grouping of Part Instances

Our goal is to learn the latent constituents that make up the group activities without having manual annotations for these components. Constituents are semi-local regions that cover characteristic parts of persons and their surroundings. Due to their number and flexible arrangement they successfully bridge the gap between local features and the group activity with its large spatial extend. To this end we need to resolve the crucial limitations of present activity recognition systems: they are limited to only a small set of predefined parts and require manually annotated training samples for each [8,17,21]. Therefore, we seek to automatically learn a large number of constituents that effectively capture the characteristics of an activity.

To learn the latent constituents of group activities, we first randomly sample a large number of parts R_i at different locations $\mathbf{x}_i \in \mathbb{R}^2$ and sizes $s_i \in \mathbb{R}_+$ within person bounding boxes so that there is a good coverage of all training instances of an activity class. To be comparable to previous work, we follow the same person detection approach as in [18,21] to obtain the person boxes.

The probability of sampling a part R_i is inversely proportional to its overlap with already previously sampled parts $R_{i_1}, R_{i_2}, \ldots, R_{i_n}$,

$$\omega_i \propto \left(\max_n \frac{|R_i \cap R_{i_n}|}{|R_i \cup R_{i_n}|} + \epsilon \right)^{-1}. \tag{1}$$

Parts that are sampled from different bounding boxes do not have any pixel in common, so their intersection is zero. Therefore, regions that have not yet been sampled will have a high likelihood of being selected, thus improving the overall coverage.

A part instance R_i that is extracted from a person bounding box is described by the feature vector $\mathbf{f}_i \in \mathcal{F}$. To compare to previous work we utilize the same feature space $\mathcal{F}$ as in [7], a bag-of-feature (BoF) [12] and histograms of oriented gradients (HoG) features.

Despite variations in their feature vectors $\mathbf{f}_i$, many of the sampled parts are related instances with the same function or meaning for the overall activity. They are instances of the same component of an activity such as different images of a knee bent at right angle represent the same aspect of the *jogging* activity. Training a separate classifier for each sampled part instance is not feasible, since this would yield a large number of mutually redundant classifiers with few training data for each. Moreover, recognition would not be practicable, because a large set of related classifiers would all need to be evaluated. Thus we need to group functionally related parts that represent the same characteristic within the overall activity.

Inferring useful groups of parts is a challenging problem. Parts with the same meaning are commonly not close in the high-dimensional feature space of their descriptors. Consequently, feature similarities are quickly becoming arbitrary given only little noise or visual variation. The problem of visual grouping can, however, be circumvented by observing the activation pattern of each part on an independent validation set. Part instances that are simultaneously active or inactive on many validation samples in similar regions are related to the same target concept. These parts have the same function in explaining the group activity and so we refer to this process as *functional grouping* in contrast to a grouping based on feature descriptor similarity.

We first divide the positive training samples into a training and validation set T and V (3/4 vs. 1/4). Then we find for each part $\{\mathbf{f}_i\}_{i \in T}$ from the training set its k best matches from the validation set $\{\mathbf{f}'_i\}_{i' \in V}$. To find these matching parts we employ an approximate nearest neighbor search [25]. Let $V_i \subseteq V$ refer to the k best matches for the i-th training part. The activation pattern of this training part is then given as a Gibbs distribution over the validation set, with support V_i,

$$\alpha_i(v) := \begin{cases} \frac{1}{Z_i} \exp\big(-\beta \Delta(\mathbf{f}_i, \mathbf{f}_v)\big), & \text{if } v \in V_i \\ 0, & \text{if } v \in V \setminus V_i \end{cases} \tag{2}$$

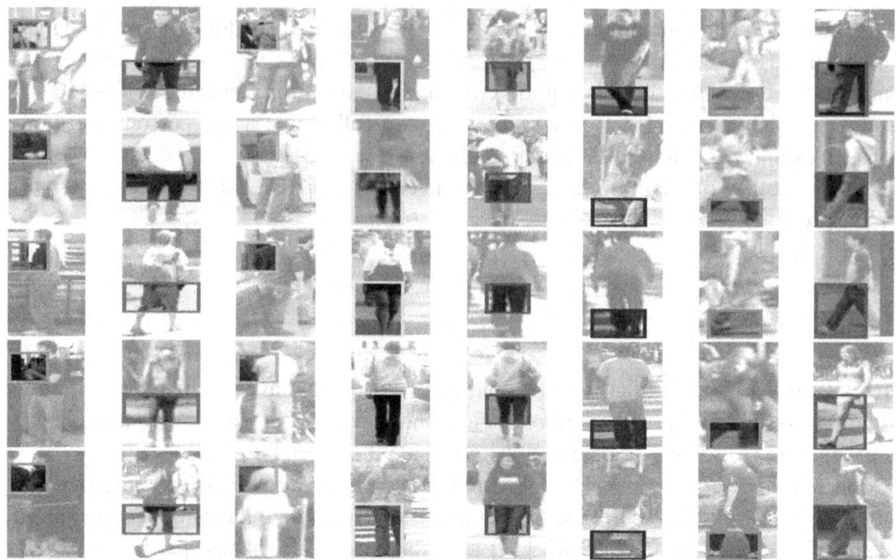

Fig. 3. Visualization of latent constituents of the group activities from the 5-class datasets. Columns show eight randomly drawn activity constituents. For each constituent five of its randomly sampled parts are shown.

where $\Delta(\cdot,\cdot)$ is a distance function between the sampled parts which combines the distance $d(\cdot,\cdot)$ in the feature space $\mathcal{F}$ with the differences in parts' location and size,

$$\Delta(\mathbf{f}_i, \mathbf{f}_v) := d(\mathbf{f}_i, \mathbf{f}_v) + \lambda_x \|\mathbf{x}_i - \mathbf{x}_v\| + \lambda_s |s_i - s_v|. \tag{3}$$

To balance individual distances, we use λ_x and λ_s as the quotients of the feature variance to the variances of parts' location and size, respectively. Z_i is the partition function of the Gibbs distribution,

$$Z_i = \sum_{v \in V_i} \exp\Big(-\beta \Delta(\mathbf{f}_i, \mathbf{f}_v)\Big). \tag{4}$$

To group related parts into a set of meaningful activity constituents, we perform agglomerative clustering (Ward's Method) based on the functional relatedness of parts $\mathbf{f}_i$ and $\mathbf{f}_{i'}$, $i, i' \in T$, estimated by calculating the distance between part activation patterns α_i and $\alpha_{i'}$. As a result of clustering, training instances of all parts $\{R_i\}_{i \in T}$ are divided into disjoint groups of related parts $\{T_1, T_2, \ldots, T_G\}$. Each group T_g contains part instances that are related to the same concept. Now we can train a discriminative classifier with weight vector $\mathbf{w}_g$ for g-th activity constituent that separates its positive training samples in T_g from a set of random negatives N_g drawn from other activities. Note that these classifiers do not distinguish between activities but only detect the presence of certain characteristic components of an activity.

Activity Reconstruction with Functional Groups: Let us now reconstruct a query image using the functional groups, Fig. 2. For each part sampled in the query image we infer the activity constituent g with maximal score from its linear classifier $\mathbf{w}_g$ on that part. Then we randomly select a training part $i \in T_g$ from its functional group. The final reconstructed image is then obtained as the weighted average (weighted with the classifier scores) of all individual sampled parts i which are then placed at locations of the original parts of the query image. As an additional experiment we cluster parts according to their mere feature similarity (also using Ward's method) and sample from the resulting groups. As illustrated in Fig. 2 the reconstruction from functional groups captures the characteristics of activities, whereas the reconstruction based on the visual similarity leads to fuzzy clusters and therefore looses important details during reconstruction.

3.2 From Constituent Classifiers to Activity Classification

Since our final goal is not only to discover group activities, but also to localize them by labeling each person with the activity it is part of, for each person the context of other persons in the group matters. A commonly used representation for action context is the descriptor from [19]. Here we extend this representation and employ it not once per person as in [21,17], but for each activity constituent g. Consequently, we are establishing context on the level of constituents rather than merely between person bounding boxes.

The action context descriptor for a constituent g divides the spatio-temporal volume around the j-th person detection that this constituent belongs to into disjoint sub-volumes $\{\mathcal{N}_{j,1}, \ldots, \mathcal{N}_{j,M}\}$ (parameters as in [19]). Then the constituent classifier $\mathbf{w}_g$ searches for other occurrences of the same constituent in each of the neighboring regions $\mathcal{N}_{j,m}$. The response for $\mathcal{N}_{j,m}$ is the maximal score of the classifier on all $\mathbf{f}_i$ within $\mathcal{N}_{j,m}$,

$$q_j(m, g) = \max_{i \in \mathcal{N}_{j,m}} \mathbf{w}_g^\top \mathbf{f}_i. \tag{5}$$

q then expresses relationships between different detections of a constituent in the neighborhood.

The joint activity representation $\mathbf{q}_j$ for person j is obtained by concatenating score function values $q_j(m, g)$ for all sub-volumes m and constituents g. The activity score of a person j for group activity $a \in \mathcal{A}$ is calculated using a linear classifier $\mathbf{w}_a^\top \mathbf{q}_j$, where $\mathcal{A}$ is the set of all group activity labels and $\mathbf{w}_a$ is a hyperplane that separates instances with activity label a from instances of other group activities, i.e., this is a multi-class classification problem which will be discussed in Sect. 3.4. Due to the max operation in Eq. 5, the group activity is more than just a mere sum of activity constituents.

3.3 Inference in Novel Query Scenes

In the recognition phase, we need to detect group activities $a \in \mathcal{A}$ and localize them on the level of bounding boxes. To get this process started, person bounding boxes are first localized as in [18,21]. Then the constituent classifiers $\mathbf{w}_g$ detect occurrences and then

Table 1. Comparing the latent constituent model with the baseline method (no constituents, parts are whole bounding boxes), and method that uses constituents learned by visual grouping. The gain of the latent constituent approach with functional grouping over the baseline are 3.7% and 5.9% on 5-class and 6-class benchmark sets, respectively. Last row shows the results of the classification if standard feature representation for the latent constituents is augmented with dense trajectories [32].

	5 Activities	6 Activities
Baseline (no latent constituents)	70.4%	83.3%
Constituents from Visual Grouping	71.7%	87.4%
Lat. Constituents + Functional Grouping	74.1%	89.2%
Lat. Constit. + Func. Grouping + Dense Traject.	75.1%	90.1%

compute the context scores $q_j(m, g)$ for each person j using Eq. 5. The group activity which a person j belongs to results from applying the overall activity classifiers,

$$a_j = \underset{a' \in \mathcal{A}}{\operatorname{argmax}} \, \mathbf{w}_{a'}^\top \mathbf{q}_j. \tag{6}$$

3.4 Joint Learning of Group Activity and Constituent Classifiers

Let us now jointly learn the weights $\mathbf{w}_g$ of all constituent classifiers and of the overall activity models $\mathbf{w}_a$ for all activity classes by adopting a max-margin rationale. The $\mathbf{w}_g$ should discriminate positive instances $\{\mathbf{f}_i\}_{i \in T_g}$ of a constituent group from negative ones $\{\mathbf{f}_i\}_{i \in N_g}$. However, since the training set T contains clutter (regions that are noisy, contain outliers, or have been sampled from uninformative areas), the decomposition of T into disjoint sets T_g by means of functional grouping in Sect. 3.1 still contains these outliers. Identifying these outliers with the constituent classifiers $\mathbf{w}_g$ and training the $\mathbf{w}_g$ with only the remaining meaningful instances are interrelated problems that need to be solved jointly. We follow a Multiple Instance Learning (MIL) approach [16,4], which selects positive instances from a positive bag that are used for training a discriminative classifier. Our approach is motivated by the AL-SVM method [16] that uses deterministic annealing to train the classifier and find the unknown instance labels with the entropy regularizer $\mathcal{H}(\cdot)$. We associate a probability $p_i \in [0, 1]$ to each part $i \in T_g$, that indicates how meaningful i is for learning the g-th constituent classifier, i.e., zero implies an outlier. The MIL objective is then to find at least $\rho|T_g|$ positive examples in a functional group g (we simply set $\rho = 0.7$ and observed only little influence when changing ρ), so that the hinge loss error $\ell(\mathbf{w}_g^\top \mathbf{f}_i) = \max(0, 1 - \mathbf{w}_g^\top \mathbf{f}_i)$ of a regularized classifier $\mathbf{w}_g$ is minimal,

$$\min_{\mathbf{w}_g, p_i} \|\mathbf{w}_g\|^2 + C_g \{ \sum_{i \in T_g} p_i \ell(\mathbf{w}_g^\top \mathbf{f}_i) + \sum_{i \in N_g} \ell(-\mathbf{w}_g^\top \mathbf{f}_i) \} - T \sum_{i \in T_g} \mathcal{H}(p_i), \tag{7}$$

$$\text{s.t.} \sum_{i \in T_g} p_i \geq \rho |T_g| \quad \wedge \quad p_i \in [0, 1], \forall i. \tag{8}$$

Activity classification with $\mathbf{w}_a$ (Eq. 6) now depends on all $\mathbf{w}_g$ and their context scores $\mathbf{q}_j$ (Eq. 5). Thus we should not only optimize the $\mathbf{w}_a$, but jointly estimate the

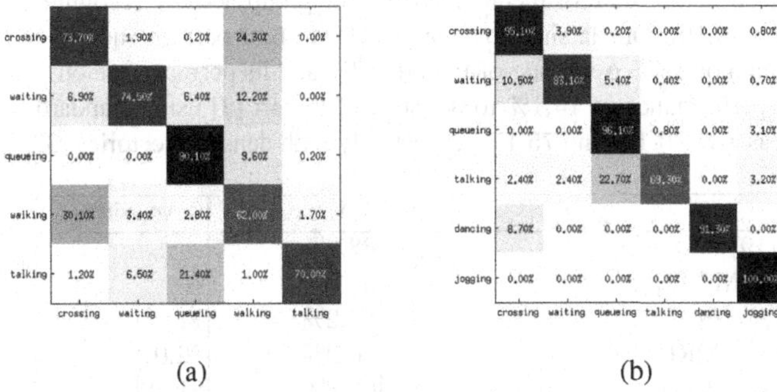

(a) (b)

Fig. 4. a) Per-class categorization results (confusion matrix) on the 5-class collective activity dataset [9]. The results are obtained by the proposed latent constituent method with functional grouping using standard features. The average classification accuracy is 74.1%. b) The confusion matrix for the 6-class benchmark set [10]. Average classification accuracy is 89.2%.

$\mathbf{w}_g$, so that they improve the discrimination between activities in Eq. 6. Following the standard training protocol of [9], training bounding boxes are provided for each person j, together with their activity labels $y_{j,a} \in \{1, -1\}$, where $y_{j,a} = 1$ if person j participates in activity a. Thus, optimizing $\mathbf{w}_g$ and finding meaningful representative parts $i \in T_g$ with MIL in Eq. 7 and max-margin training of $\mathbf{w}_a$ are coupled,

$$\min_{\mathbf{w}_a, \mathbf{w}_g, p_i} \sum_a \Big\{ \|\mathbf{w}_a\|^2 + C_a \sum_j \ell(y_{j,a} \mathbf{w}_a^\top \mathbf{q}_j) \Big\} + \sum_g \Big\{ \|\mathbf{w}_g\|^2 + C_g \big[\sum_{i \in T_g} p_i \ell(\mathbf{w}_g^\top \mathbf{f}_i) + \sum_{i \in N_g} \ell(-\mathbf{w}_g^\top \mathbf{f}_i) \big] - T \sum_{i \in T_g} \mathcal{H}(p_i) \Big\}, \tag{9}$$

$$\text{s.t.} \sum_{i \in T_g} p_i \geq \rho |T_g|, \forall g \quad \wedge \quad p_i \in [0,1], \forall i. \tag{10}$$

The joint optimization problem in Eq. 9 is non-convex, therefore we solve it using alternating optimization.

(i) To find the most meaningful samples in each group T_g we need to solve for the probabilities $p_i, i \in T_g$. Finding the optimal value of the Lagrangian,

$$\min_{\{p_i\}_{i \in T_g}} \mathcal{L}(\{p_i\}_{i \in T_g}, \lambda) = C_g \sum_{i \in T_g} p_i \ell(\mathbf{w}_g^\top \mathbf{f}_i) + T \sum_{i \in T_g} \big(p_i \log p_i + (1-p_i)\log(1-p_i)\big) - \lambda \big(\sum_{i \in T_g} p_i - \rho |T_g| \big), \text{ s.t. } \lambda \geq 0, \tag{11}$$

together with the Karush-Kuhn-Tucker conditions following from Eq. 10, the solution can be derived in analytical form

$$p_i = \sigma\Big(-\frac{C_g \ell(\mathbf{w}_g^\top \mathbf{f}_i)}{T}\Big) \cdot \max\Big(\rho |T_g| \Big\{ \sum_{i \in T_g} \sigma\Big(-\frac{C_g \ell(\mathbf{w}_g^\top \mathbf{f}_i)}{T}\Big)\Big\}^{-1}, 1\Big), \forall i \in T_g, \tag{12}$$

Table 2. Comparison of the state-of-the-art methods for group activity recognition on 5-class and 6-class datasets [9,10]. Our latent constituents achieve best performance of 89.2% on the 6-class dataset (a gain of 3.4% over state-of-the-art [17]), and its performance on 5-class dataset has a comparable performance of 74.1% to the state-of-the-art [7] using standard features and performance increases to 90.1% and 75.1% respectively with dense trajectories [32].

	5 Activities	6 Activities
AC [19]	68.2%	-
STV + MC [9]	65.9%	-
RSTV [10]	67.2%	71.2%
RSTV + MRF [10]	70.9%	82.0%
AC (Unary) [18]	68.8%	81.5%
AC + Track Cues [18]	70.9%	83.7%
AC + Frame + Track Cues [17]	72.0%	85.8%
Unified Track. + Recognit. [7]	74.4%	-
Latent Constituents	74.1%	89.2%
Latent Constituents + Dense Traject.	**75.1%**	**90.1%**

where $\sigma(x) = \big(1+\exp(-x)\big)^{-1}$ is the sigmoid function.

(ii) Now we can discuss the training of constituent classifiers $\mathbf{w}_g$. Note from Eq. 5 that the score function related to person j can be written in linear form $q_j(m,g) = \mathbf{w}_g^\top \mathbf{f}_{i_g^*}$, where $i_g^* = \text{argmax}_{i \in \mathcal{N}_{j,m}} \mathbf{w}_g^\top \mathbf{f}_i$. By concatenating the features $\mathbf{f}_{i_g^*}$ over all neighbors m into a matrix $\mathbf{F}_j$ the score vector becomes $\mathbf{q}_j = \mathbf{F}_j^\top \mathbf{w}_g$. The constituent classifier is solved as a convex optimization problem using ILOG CPLEX solver for the problem

$$\min_{\mathbf{w}_g} \|\mathbf{w}_g\|^2 + C_g\big[\sum_{i\in T_g} p_i \ell(\mathbf{w}_g^\top \mathbf{f}_i) + \sum_{i\in N_g} \ell(-\mathbf{w}_g^\top \mathbf{f}_i)\big] + C_a \sum_j \ell\big(y_{j,a} \mathbf{w}_g^\top (\mathbf{F}_j \mathbf{w}_a)\big). \tag{13}$$

(iii) Based on p_i and $\mathbf{w}_g$, optimizing $\mathbf{w}_a$ becomes a multi-class linear SVM problem of the same formulation as [6], which is solved using LIBLINEAR,

$$\min_{\mathbf{w}_a} \sum_a \|\mathbf{w}_a\|^2 + C_a \sum_j \ell(y_{j,a} \mathbf{w}_a^\top \mathbf{q}_j). \tag{14}$$

We alternate between these three steps until convergence that is typically achieved within on the order of ten iterations. Visualization of the learned latent constituents for a benchmark set that we use in our experiments is given in Fig. 3.

4 Experimental Results

4.1 Experimental Protocol

We evaluate our approach on two standard benchmark sets for group activity recognition that were recently proposed in [9,10]. Both datasets are recorded with a hand-held camera in realistic indoor and outdoor environments. Popular action recognition

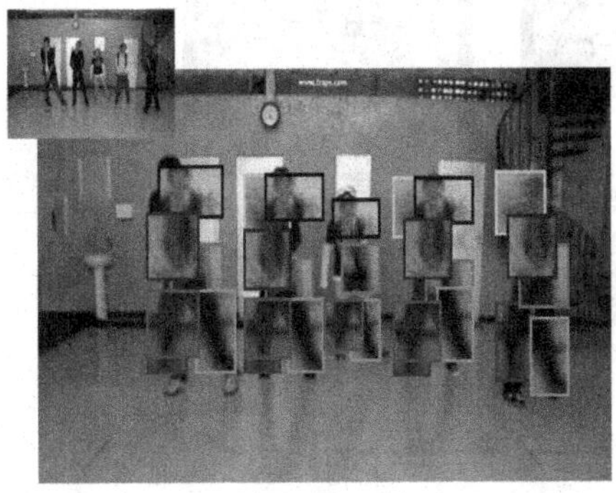

Fig. 5. Visualization of detected latent constituents of two example group activities. Detected parts that correspond to the same latent constituent are framed in the same color. Each part is then visualized by averaging over the training patches that define the latent constituent.

datasets such as KTH, Weizmann, Hollywood or UCF Sports are not appropriate for evaluation, since they contain only isolated human actions, but not any group activity.

The first benchmark set [9] consists of 44 videos showing 5 group activities (*crossing*, *standing*, *queueing*, *walking*, and *talking*). The length of videos ranges from less than 100 frames to more than 2000 frames. The second benchmark set [10] contains 72 videos and involves 6 group activity classes. This dataset is created by augmenting the first dataset, adding *dancing* and *jogging* and removing *walking* categories. We follow the common experimental protocol [21,17,18,7] that provides bounding boxes for persons in the training set with corresponding group activity labels and uses a leave-one-out framework for testing. To assess localized group activity recognition performance, we follow the standard protocol and evaluate on a per-bounding-box level.

Following recent practice in the group activity recognition literature [7,8], we use the combination of HOG [11] and bag-of-feature (BoF) [12] features to represent the constituents of group activities, c.f. Sect. 3.1. We also adhere to a common practice in group activity recognition [7,17] that associates object detections from different frames of a video by object tracking. Learning begins by randomly sampling (Eq. 1) 10000 parts from training person bounding boxes. The functional grouping of Sect. 3.1 then creates $G = 100$ constituents. Max-margin MIL training learns the importance $\mathbf{w}_a$ of each constituent for group activity recognition. Constituents with small value in the activity classifier $\mathbf{w}_a$ can be skipped during inference. The number of constituents that is used for testing is chosen so that 80% of the classifier's energy $\|\mathbf{w}_a\|^2$ is retained. Typically around 50 constituents are retained after such selection process, which is why we observed only little influence when changing G.

4.2 Group Activity Recognition

Fig. 5 shows latent constituents for two example group activities (*dancing* and *jogging*). Different colors represent different latent constituents. Moreover, each constituent is visualized by averaging the training patches that defined it during learning.

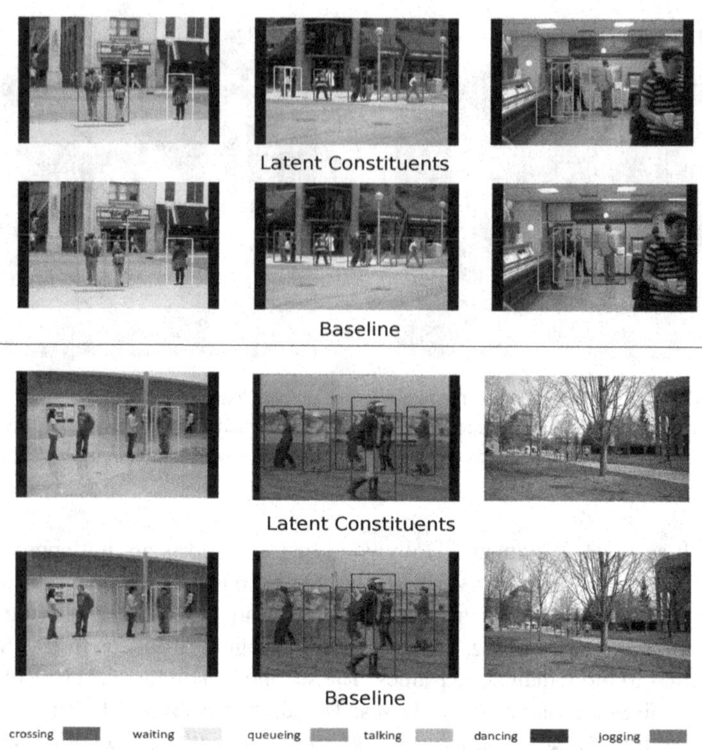

Fig. 6. Visualization of the classification results on test videos comparing our latent constituent model and the baseline approach that uses bounding boxes as is common but no further constituents. Frames are taken from the test videos.

Table 1 presents the results of group activity recognition on the benchmark sets. We compare our latent constituent approach to the baseline method that does not use any latent constituents, but is merely based on the whole bounding box of a person as in other activity approaches such as [18,19]. Our method achieves a gain of 3.7% over the baseline for the 5-class dataset, and 5.9% for the 6-class dataset. We also compare our latent constituents found by functional grouping and MIL with the baseline approach of performing visual clustering, i.e., directly clustering the part feature vectors. Our method achieves an improvement of 2.4% over the visual grouping method for the 5-class dataset, and 1.8% on the 6-class dataset. We also conduct an experiment in which we update the standard feature representation used for the latent constituents with recent dense trajectory features [32]. We obtain an increase in the performance and achieve 75.1% for the 5-class dataset and 90.1% for the 6-class dataset.

Per-category classification results of our latent constituent method based on standard features on the two benchmark sets are given in confusion matrices of Fig. 4a and 4b. We notice that the greatest confusion is between *walking* and *crossing* activities, because they have many constituents in common. *Talking* activity is also often missclassified as *queueing* because of their similarity.

  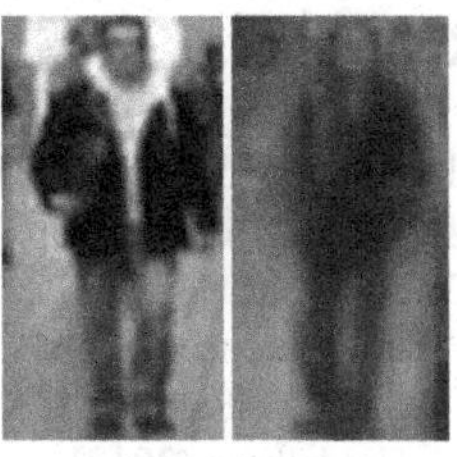

Fig. 7. Sampling parts and reconstructing (explaining) them from the training parts that belong to the same constituents as the original part. Samples are taken from *waiting*, *crossing* and *walking* activities.

We next compare our performance with other state-of-the-art results in Table 2. Our method achieves an average accuracy of 74.1% on the 5-class dataset, that is almost the same as the best performing method [7] that uses additional manual labels. Our method achieves 89.2% on the 6-class dataset, which is 3.4% better than the state-of-the-art. The visual results of our group activity classification and of the baseline method are shown in Fig. 6.

Activity Reconstruction with Latent Constituents: Fig. 2 shows reconstructions provided by groups of parts obtained by functional grouping with those coming from groups of parts obtained by clustering with visual similarity, i.e., clustering the part appearance features. Fig. 7 presents additional reconstructions for person bounding boxes in several activity classes: *crossing*, *waiting* and *walking*. Each image part is replaced by a randomly sampled part from the training set that belongs to the same constituent as the original image part. The final reconstructed image is obtained by averaging. Again one can see that key characteristics of an activity class are captured by latent constituents.

5 Conclusion

This paper has demonstrated that activity recognition significantly benefits from modeling human behavior using a large number of semi-local parts and their interaction between persons. Learning the underlying classifier becomes feasible by grouping functionally related parts into activity constituents and removing clutter with multiple instance learning while training constituent classifiers and the multi-class activity model. The approach has shown a significant performance gain on standard activity benchmarks.

Acknowledgements. This work has been partially supported by the Ministry for Science, Baden-Wuerttemberg and German Research Foundation (DFG) within the program Spatio-/Temporal Graphical Models and Applications in Image Analysis, grant GRK 1653. The authors would also like to thank Timo Milbich for additional support and Till Kroeger for helpful discussions.

References

1. Amer, M.R., Todorovic, S.: A chains model for localizing participants of group activities in videos. In: ICCV, pp. 786–793 (2011)
2. Amer, M.R., Xie, D., Zhao, M., Todorovic, S., Zhu, S.-C.: Cost-sensitive top-down/bottom-up inference for multiscale activity recognition. In: Fitzgibbon, A., Lazebnik, S., Perona, P., Sato, Y., Schmid, C. (eds.) ECCV 2012, Part IV. LNCS, vol. 7575, pp. 187–200. Springer, Heidelberg (2012)
3. Antic, B., Ommer, B.: Video parsing for abnormality detection. In: ICCV, pp. 2415–2422 (2011)
4. Antić, B., Ommer, B.: Robust multiple-instance learning with superbags. In: Lee, K.M., Matsushita, Y., Rehg, J.M., Hu, Z. (eds.) ACCV 2012, Part II. LNCS, vol. 7725, pp. 242–255. Springer, Heidelberg (2013)
5. Bourdev, L., Maji, S., Brox, T., Malik, J.: Detecting people using mutually consistent poselet activations. In: Daniilidis, K., Maragos, P., Paragios, N. (eds.) ECCV 2010, Part VI. LNCS, vol. 6316, pp. 168–181. Springer, Heidelberg (2010)
6. Chapelle, O., Keerthi, S.S.: Multi-class feature selection with support vector machines. In: Proc. of the American Statistical Assoc. (2008)
7. Choi, W., Savarese, S.: A unified framework for multi-target tracking and collective activity recognition. In: Fitzgibbon, A., Lazebnik, S., Perona, P., Sato, Y., Schmid, C. (eds.) ECCV 2012, Part IV. LNCS, vol. 7575, pp. 215–230. Springer, Heidelberg (2012)
8. Choi, W., Savarese, S.: Understanding collective activities of people from videos. Pattern Analysis and Machine Intelligence (99), 1 (2013)
9. Choi, W., Shahid, K., Savarese, S.: What are they doing?: Collective activity classification using spatio-temporal relationship among people. In: Proc. of 9th International Workshop on Visual Surveillance (VSWS 2009) in Conjuction with ICCV (2009)
10. Choi, W., Shahid, K., Savarese, S.: Learning context for collective activity recognition. In: Proceedings of the IEEE International Conference on Computer Vision and Pattern Recognition (2011)
11. Dalal, N., Triggs, B.: Histograms of oriented gradients for human detection. In: Schmid, C., Soatto, S., Tomasi, C. (eds.)International Conference on Computer Vision & Pattern Recognition, vol. 2, pp. 886–893 (2005)
12. Dollár, P., Rabaud, V., Cottrell, G., Belongie, S.: Behavior recognition via sparse spatio-temporal features. In: 2nd Joint IEEE International Workshop on Visual Surveillance and Performance Evaluation of Tracking and Surveillance, pp. 65–72. IEEE (2005)
13. Eigenstetter, A., Takami, M., Ommer, B.: Randomized Max-Margin Compositions for Visual Recognition. In: CVPR - International Conference on Computer Vision and Pattern Recognition, Columbus, USA (2014)
14. Felzenszwalb, P.F., Girshick, R.B., McAllester, D.A., Ramanan, D.: Object detection with discriminatively trained part-based models. IEEE Trans. Pattern Anal. Mach. Intell. 32(9), 1627–1645 (2010)
15. Fergus, R., Perona, P., Zisserman, A.: Object class recognition by unsupervised scale-invariant learning. In: Proceedings of the IEEE Conference on Computer Vision and Pattern Recognition, vol. 2, pp. 264–271 (2003)
16. Gehler, P.V., Chapelle, O.: Deterministic annealing for multiple-instance learning. In: International Conference on Artificial Intelligence and Statistics, pp. 123–130 (2007)
17. Khamis, S., Morariu, V.I., Davis, L.S.: Combining per-frame and per-track cues for multi-person action recognition. In: Fitzgibbon, A., Lazebnik, S., Perona, P., Sato, Y., Schmid, C. (eds.) ECCV 2012, Part I. LNCS, vol. 7572, pp. 116–129. Springer, Heidelberg (2012)

18. Khamis, S., Morariu, V.I., Davis, L.S.: A flow model for joint action recognition and identity maintenance. In: IEEE Conference on Computer Vision and Pattern Recognition (2012)
19. Lan, T., Wang, Y., Mori, G., Robinovitch, S.: Retrieving actions in group contexts. In: International Workshop on Sign Gesture Activity (2010)
20. Lan, T., Wang, Y., Yang, W., Mori, G.: Beyond actions: Discriminative models for contextual group activities. In: Advances in Neural Information Processing Systems, NIPS (2010)
21. Lan, T., Wang, Y., Yang, W., Robinovitch, S., Mori, G.: Discriminative latent models for recognizing contextual group activities. IEEE Transactions on Pattern Analysis and Machine Intelligence (2012)
22. Laptev, I., Marszałek, M., Schmid, C., Rozenfeld, B.: Learning realistic human actions from movies. In: Conference on Computer Vision & Pattern Recognition (2008)
23. Maji, S., Bourdev, L., Malik, J.: Action recognition from a distributed representation of pose and appearance. In: IEEE International Conference on Computer Vision and Pattern Recognition, CVPR (2011)
24. Marszałek, M., Laptev, I., Schmid, C.: Actions in context. In: Conference on Computer Vision & Pattern Recognition (2009)
25. Muja, M., Lowe, D.G.: Fast approximate nearest neighbors with automatic algorithm configuration. In: International Conference on Computer Vision Theory and Application (VISSAPP 2009), pp. 331–340. INSTICC Press (2009)
26. Niebles, J.C., Wang, H., Fei-Fei, L.: Unsupervised learning of human action categories using spatial-temporal words. Int. J. Comput. Vision 79(3), 299–318 (2008)
27. Ommer, B., Mader, T., Buhmann, J.M.: Seeing the objects behind the dots: Recognition in videos from a moving camera. International Journal of Computer Vision 83(1), 57–71 (2009)
28. Ryoo, M.S., Aggarwal, J.K.: Stochastic representation and recognition of high-level group activities. International Journal of Computer Vision 93(2), 183–200 (2011)
29. Schüldt, C., Laptev, I., Caputo, B.: Recognizing human actions: A local svm approach. In: ICPR (3), pp. 32–36 (2004)
30. Singh, S., Gupta, A., Efros, A.A.: Unsupervised discovery of mid-level discriminative patches. In: Fitzgibbon, A., Lazebnik, S., Perona, P., Sato, Y., Schmid, C. (eds.) ECCV 2012, Part II. LNCS, vol. 7573, pp. 73–86. Springer, Heidelberg (2012)
31. Turaga, P.K., Chellappa, R., Subrahmanian, V.S., Udrea, O.: Machine recognition of human activities: A survey. IEEE Trans. Circuits Syst. Video Techn. 18(11), 1473–1488 (2008)
32. Wang, H., Kläser, A., Schmid, C., Liu, C.L.: Action Recognition by Dense Trajectories. In: IEEE Conference on Computer Vision & Pattern Recognition, Colorado Springs, United States, pp. 3169–3176 (2011)
33. Xiang, T., Gong, S.: Beyond tracking: Modelling activity and understanding behaviour. International Journal of Computer Vision 67(1), 21–51 (2006)

Large-Scale Object Classification Using Label Relation Graphs

Jia Deng[1,2], Nan Ding[2], Yangqing Jia[2], Andrea Frome[2], Kevin Murphy[2], Samy Bengio[2], Yuan Li[2], Hartmut Neven[2], and Hartwig Adam[2]

[1] University of Michigan, USA
[2] Google Inc., USA

Abstract. In this paper we study how to perform object classification in a principled way that exploits the rich structure of real world labels. We develop a new model that allows encoding of flexible relations between labels. We introduce Hierarchy and Exclusion (HEX) graphs, a new formalism that captures semantic relations between any two labels applied to the same object: mutual exclusion, overlap and subsumption. We then provide rigorous theoretical analysis that illustrates properties of HEX graphs such as consistency, equivalence, and computational implications of the graph structure. Next, we propose a probabilistic classification model based on HEX graphs and show that it enjoys a number of desirable properties. Finally, we evaluate our method using a large-scale benchmark. Empirical results demonstrate that our model can significantly improve object classification by exploiting the label relations.

Keywords: Object Recognition, Categorization.

1 Introduction

Object classification, assigning semantic labels to an object, is a fundamental problem in computer vision. It can be used as a building block for many other tasks such as localization, detection, and scene parsing. Current approaches typically adopt one of the two classification models: multiclass classification, which predicts one label out of a set of mutually exclusive labels(e.g. entries in ILSVRC [9]), or binary classifications, which make binary decisions for each label independently(e.g. entries in PASCAL VOC classification competitions [13]).

Both models, however, do not capture the complexity of semantic labels in the real world. Multiclass classification tasks typically assume a set of mutually exclusive labels. Although efforts have been made to artificially constrain the label set in benchmarks (e.g. the ImageNet Challenges [9] select a subset of mutually exclusive labels from WordNet), this assumption becomes increasingly impractical as we consider larger, more realistic label sets. This is because the same object can often be described by multiple labels. An object classified as "husky" is automatically a "dog"; meanwhile it may or may not be a "puppy". Making "husky", "dog", and "puppy" mutually exclusive labels clearly violates real world semantics.

D. Fleet et al. (Eds.): ECCV 2014, Part I, LNCS 8689, pp. 48–64, 2014.
© Springer International Publishing Switzerland 2014

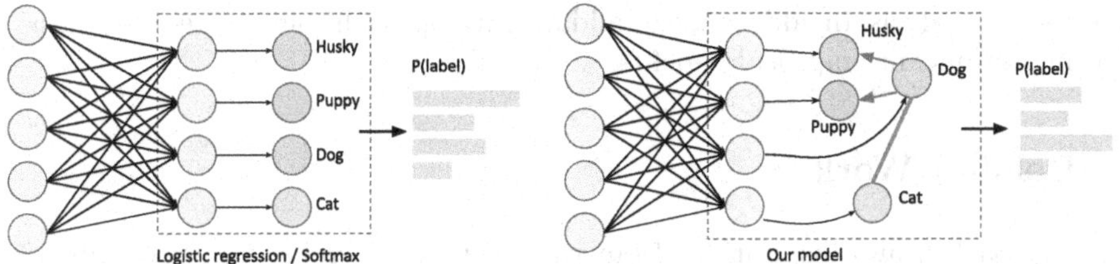

Fig. 1. Our model replaces traditional classifiers such as softmax or independent logistic regressions. It takes as input image features (e.g. from an underlying deep neural network) and outputs probabilities consistent with pre-specified label relations.

Independent binary classifiers, on the other hand, ignore the constraints between labels and can thus handle overlapping labels. But this can lead to inconsistent predictions such as an object being both a dog and a cat, or a husky but not a dog. In addition, discarding the label relations misses the opportunity to transfer knowledge during learning. For example, in practical settings training images are not always annotated to the most specific labels — many Internet images are simply labeled as "dog" instead of "husky" or "German Shepherd". Intuitively, learning a good model for "dog" should benefit learning breeds of dogs (and vice versa) but training independent binary classifiers will not be able to capitalize on this potential knowledge transfer.

In this paper we study how to perform classification in a principled way that exploits the rich structure of real world labels. Our goal is to develop a new classification model that allows flexible encoding of relations based on prior knowledge, thus overcoming the limitations of the overly restrictive multiclass model and the overly relaxed independent binary classifiers (Fig. 1).

We first introduce Hierarchy and Exclusion (HEX) graphs, a new formalism allowing flexible specification of relations between labels applied to the same object: (1) mutual exclusion (e.g. an object cannot be dog and cat), (2) overlapping (e.g. a husky may or may not be a puppy and vice versa), and (3) subsumption (e.g. all huskies are dogs). We provide theoretical analysis on properties of HEX graphs such as consistency, equivalence, and computational implications.

Next, we propose a probabilistic classification model leveraging HEX graphs. In particular, it is a special type of Conditional Random Field (CRF) that encodes the label relations as pairwise potentials. We show that this model enjoys a number of desirable properties, including flexible encoding of label relations, predictions consistent with label relations, efficient exact inference for typical graphs, learning labels with varying specificity, knowledge transfer, and unification of existing models.

Finally, we evaluate our approach using the ILSVRC2012 [9], a large-scale benchmark for object classification. We also perform experiments on zero-shot recognition. Empirical results demonstrate that our model can significantly improve object classification by exploiting the label relations.

Our main contribution is *theoretical*, i.e. we propose a new formalism (HEX graphs), a new classification model, and a new inference algorithm, all grounded on rigorous analysis. In addition, we validate our approach using large-scale data, showing significant empirical benefits.

2 Related Work

Our approach draws inspirations from various themes explored in prior literature, including hierarchies, multilabel annotation, large-scale classification, and knowledge transfer. The main novelty of our work is unifying them into a single probabilistic framework with a rigorous theoretical foundation.

Exploiting hierarchical structure of object categories has a long history [34]. In particular, label hierarchies have been used to share representations [15,2,8,17] and combine models [18,38,27].

Correlations between labels have been explored in multilabel annotation (e.g. [20]), but most prior work addresses contextual relations between co-occurring objects (e.g. [10]), as opposed to our setting of multiple labels on the same object. Lampert et al. and Bi and Kwok studied hierarchical annotations as structured predictions [24,4,3]. Chen et al. considered exclusive relations between labels [6]. To our knowledge we are the first to *jointly* model hierarchical *and* exclusive relations. By treating unobserved labels as latent variables, our approach also connects to prior work on learning from partial or incomplete labels [19,7,5].

Our model is a generalized multiclass classifier. It is designed to run efficiently and can thus be adapted to work with techniques developed for large-scale classification involving many labels and large datasets [32,29].

Finally, by modeling the label relations and ensuring consistency between visual predictions and semantic relations, our approach relates to work in transfer learning [31,30], zero-shot learning [28,12,25], and attribute-based recognition [1,36,33,14], especially those that use semantic knowledge to improve recognition [16,30] and those that propagate or borrow annotations between categories [26,22].

3 Approach

3.1 Hierarchy and Exclusion (HEX) Graphs

We start by introducing the formalism of Hierarchy and Exclusion (HEX) graphs, which allow us to express prior knowledge about the labels. Due to space limit, all proofs and some lemmas are provided in the supplemental material.

Definition 1. *A HEX graph $G = (V, E_h, E_e)$ is a graph consisting of a set of nodes $V = \{v_1, \ldots, v_n\}$, directed edges $E_h \subseteq V \times V$, and undirected edges $E_e \subseteq V \times V$, such that the subgraph $G_h = (V, E_h)$ is a directed acyclic graph (DAG) and the subgraph $G_e = (V, E_e)$ has no self loop.*

Each node $v \in V$ represents a distinct label. An edge $(v_i, v_j) \in E_h$ is a hierarchy edge, indicating that label i subsumes label j, e.g. "dog" is a parent,

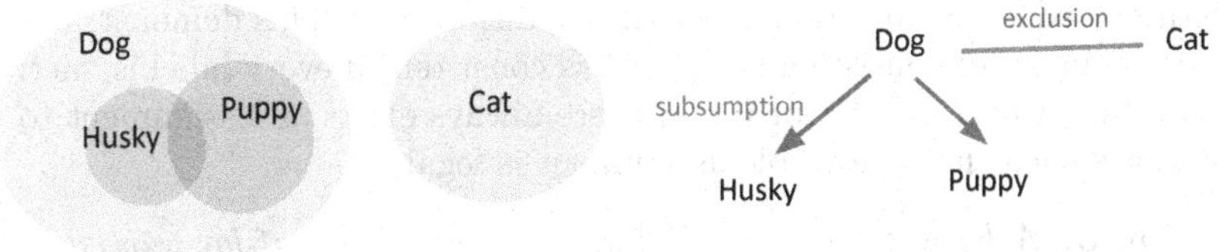

Fig. 2. HEX graphs capture relations between labels applied to the same object

or superclass of "husky". The subgraph with only those edges form a semantic hierarchy. An edge $(v_i, v_j) \in E_e$ is called an exclusion edge, indicating that label v_i and v_j are mutually exclusive, e.g. an object cannot be dog and cat. If two labels share no edge, it means that they overlap, i.e. each label can turn on or off without constraining the other.

Alternatively one can think of each label as representing a set of object instances and the relations between labels as relations between (distinct) sets (Fig. 2). A hierarchy edge corresponds to one set containing the other. An exclusion edge corresponds to two disjoint sets. No edge corresponds to overlapping sets—the only remaining case.

It is worth nothing that while it is convenient to assume mutually exclusive children in a hierarchy, this is not the case for real world hierarchies, e.g. "child", "male", "female" are all children of "person" in WordNet. Thus we need a HEX graph to express those complexities.

Each label takes binary values, i.e. $v_i \in \{0,1\}$. Each edge then defines a constraint on values the two labels can take. A hierarchy edge $(v_i, v_j) \in E_h$ means that an assignment of $(v_i, v_j) = (0,1)$ (e.g. a husky but not a dog) is illegal. An exclusion edge $(v_i, v_j) \in E_e$ means that $(v_i, v_j) = (1,1)$ (both cat and dog) is illegal. These local constraints of individual edges can thus define legal global assignments of labels.

Definition 2. *An assignment (state) $y \in \{0,1\}^n$ of labels V in a HEX graph $G = (V, E_h, E_e)$ is legal if for any $(y_i, y_j) = (1,1)$, $(v_i, v_j) \notin E_e$ and for any $(y_i, y_j) = (0,1)$, $(v_i, v_j) \notin E_h$. The state space $S_G \subseteq \{0,1\}^n$ of graph G is the set of all legal assignments of G.*

We now introduce some notations for further development. Let $\alpha(v_i)$ the set of all ancestors of $v_i \in V$ and $\bar{\alpha}(v_i) = \alpha(v_i) \cup \{v_i\}$ (ancestors and the node itself). Let $\sigma(v_i)$ be the set of all descendants of $v_i \in V$ and $\bar{\sigma}(v_i) = \sigma(v_i) \cup \{v_i\}$. Let $\epsilon(v_i)$ be the set of exclusive nodes, those sharing an exclusion edge with v_i. Let $o(v_i)$ be the set of overlapping nodes, those sharing no edges with v_i.

Consistency. So far our definition of the HEX graph allows arbitrary placement of exclusion edges. This, however, can result in non-sensible graphs. For example, it allows label v_i and v_j to have both hierarchy and exclusion edges, i.e. v_i subsumes v_j and v_i and v_j are exclusive. This makes label v_j "dead", meaning that it is always 0 and thus cannot be applied to any object instance without causing a contradiction: if it takes 1, then it's parent v_i must take value 1 per the hierarchy edge and also take 0 per the exclusion edge. This demonstrates the need for a concept of consistency: a graph is consistent if every label is "active", i.e. it can take value either 1 or 0 and there always exists an assignment to the rest of labels such that the whole assignment is legal.

Definition 3. *A HEX graph* $G = (V, E_h, E_e)$ *is consistent if for any label* $v_i \in V$*, there exists two legal assignments* $y, y' \in \{0,1\}^n$ *such that* $y_i = 1$ *and* $y_i' = 0$.

Consistency is in fact solely determined by the graph structure—it is equivalent to the condition that for any label, there is no exclusion edge between its ancestors or between itself and its ancestors:

Theorem 1. *A HEX graph* $G = (V, E_h, E_e)$ *is consistent if and only if for any label* $v_i \in V$, $E_e \cap (\bar{\alpha}(v_i) \times \bar{\alpha}(v_i)) = \emptyset$.

We thus have an algorithm to check consistency without listing the state space. As will become clear, consistency is very important algorithmically.

3.2 Classification Model

A HEX graph encodes our prior knowledge about label relations. We can thus define a probabilistic classification model based on a HEX graph $G = (V, E_h, E_e)$. Let $x \in \mathcal{X}$ be an input and $f(x; w) : \mathcal{X} \rightarrow \mathcal{R}^n$ be a function with parameters w that maps an input image (or bounding box) to a set of scores, one for each label. The form of f is not essential (e.g. it can be a linear model $w_i^T x$ or a deep neural network) so we leave it unspecified. We define a joint distribution of an assignment of all labels $y \in \{0,1\}^n$ as a Conditional Random Field (CRF) [23]:

$$\tilde{P}(y|x) = \prod_i e^{f_i(x;w)[y_i=1]} \prod_{(v_i,v_j)\in E_h} [(y_i, y_j) \neq (0,1)] \prod_{(v_i,v_j)\in E_e} [(y_i, y_j) \neq (1,1)], \quad (1)$$

where $\tilde{P}$ is the unnormalized probability. The probability is then $\Pr(y|x) = \tilde{P}(y|x)/Z(x)$, where $Z(x) = \sum_{\hat{y}} \tilde{P}(\hat{y}|x)$ is the partition function. To compute the probability of a label, we marginalize all other labels. The scores $f_i(x; w)$ can be thought of as raw classification scores (local evidence) for each label and our model can convert them into marginal probabilities.

It is easy to verify a few facts about the model: (1) the probability of any illegal assignment is zero; (2) to compute the probability of a legal assignment, we take all labels with value 1, sum their scores, exponentiate, and then normalize; (3) the marginal label probabilities are always consistent with the label relations: probability of "dog" is always bigger than that of "husky" and probabilities of "dog" and "cat" cannot add to more than 1; (4) the model assumes an open world to gracefully handle unknown categories. For each node on the hierarchy, it is legal to assign itself a value 1 and all its descendants value 0. e.g. an object is a "dog" but none of the known dog subcategories. If the model sees novel dog subcategory, it can produce a large marginal for dog but will not be compelled to assign a large probability to a known subcategory.

Special Cases. A nice property is that it unifies standard existing models. If we use a HEX graph with pairwise exclusion edges and no hierarchy edges, i.e. all nodes are mutually exclusive, it is easy to verify that we arrive at the popular softmax (or multinomial regression)[1]: $\Pr(y_i = 1|x) = e^{f_i}/(1 + \sum_j e^{f_j})$. Another special case is when the HEX graph has no edges at all, i.e. all labels are independent. Eqn. 1 thus fully decomposes: $\Pr(y|x) = \prod_i e^{f_i[y_i=1]}/(1 + e^{f_i})$, i.e. independent logistic regressions for each label.

Joint Hierarchical Modeling. We highlight another property: our model allows flexible joint modeling of hierarchical categories, thus enabling potential knowledge transfer. It is easy to verify that for all graphs the marginal probability of a label depends the sum of its ancestors' scores, i.e. $\Pr(y_i = 1|x)$ has the term $\exp(f_i + \sum_{v_j \in \alpha(v_i)} f_j)$, because all its ancestors must be 1 if the label takes value 1. Thus the model allows the score for "dog" to influence decisions about "husky". If the score function $f_i(x; w)$ is a linear model $w_i^T x$, then $\Pr(y_i = 1|x) \propto \exp(\tilde{w}_i^T x)$, where $\tilde{w}_i = w_i + \sum_{v_j \in \alpha(v_i)} w_j$, i.e the weights decompose along the hierarchy—the weights for "husky" are a combination of weights for "husky-ness", "dog-ness", and "animal-ness". This enables a form of sharing similar to prior work [8]. Note that depending on the applications, sharing can also be disabled by using constant scores (e.g. zeros).

Conversely, the probability of an internal node of the hierarchy also depends on the probabilities of its descendants because we need to marginalize over all possible states of the descendants. For example, if we have a tree hierarchy with mutually exclusive siblings, it can be shown that the unnormalized probability $\tilde{P}$ of an internal node is a simple recursive form involving its own score, its ancestors' scores, and the sum of unnormalized probabilities of its direct children $c(v_i)$, i.e. $\tilde{P}(y_i = 1|x) = \exp\left(f_i + \sum_{v_k \in \alpha(v_i)} f_k\right) + \sum_{v_j \in c(v_i)} \tilde{P}(y_j = 1|x)$. Again we can use constant scores for internal nodes, in which case the model is a collection of "local leaf models" and we simply sum the probabilities of leaves.

Learning. In learning we maximize the (marginal) likelihood of the observed ground truth labels using stochastic gradient descent (SGD). Given training examples $\mathcal{D} = \{(x^{(l)}, y^{(l)}, g^{(l)})\}, l = 1, \dots, m$, where $y^{(l)} \in \{0,1\}^n$ is the complete ground truth label vector and $g^{(l)} \subseteq \{1, \dots, n\}$ is the indices of the observed labels, the loss function is :

$$\mathcal{L}(\mathcal{D}, w) = -\sum_l \log \Pr(y^{(l)}_{g^{(l)}} | x^{(l)}; w) = -\sum_l \log \sum_{y: y_{g^{(l)}} = y^{(l)}_{g^{(l)}}} \Pr(y|x^{(l)}; w) \quad (2)$$

In training we often have incomplete ground truth. Labels can be at any level of the hierarchy. We may only know the object is a "dog" but uncertain about the specific breed. Incomplete ground truth also occurs with labels that are not hierarchical but can still overlap ("husky" and "puppy"). Our model can

[1] There is an additional constant 1 in the denominator because for n labels there are $n + 1$ states. The extra one is "none of the above", i.e. all labels zero. This makes no practical difference. See supplemental material for further discussions.

naturally handle this by treating the unobserved labels as latent variables and marginalizing them in computing the likelihood.

3.3 Efficient Inference

Inference—computing the partition function and marginalizing unobserved labels—is exponential in the number of labels if performed with brute force. Treated as a generic CRF, our model can easily be densely connected and full of loops, especially when there are many mutual exclusions, as is typical for object labels. Thus at first glance exact inference is intractable.

However, in this section we show that exact inference is tractable for a large family of HEX graphs with dense connections, especially in realistic settings. The main intuition is that when the graph is densely connected, the state space can be small due to the special form of our binary potentials—all illegal states have probability zero and they can simply be eliminated from consideration. One example is the standard multiclass setting where all labels are mutually exclusive, in which case the size of the state space is $O(n)$. On the other hand, when a graph is sparse, i.e. has small treewidth, then standard algorithms such as junction trees apply. Our algorithm will try to take the best of both worlds by transforming a graph in two directions: (1) to an equivalent sparse version with potentially small treewidth; (2) to an equivalent dense version such that we can afford to exhaustively list the state space for any subset of nodes. The final algorithm is a modified junction tree algorithm that can be proven to run efficiently for many realistic graphs.

Equivalence. Two HEX graphs are *equivalent* if they have the same state space:

Definition 4. *HEX graphs G and G' are equivalent if* $S_G = S_{G'}$.

Intuitively equivalent graphs can arise in two cases. One is due to the transitivity of the subsumption relation—if "animal" subsumes "dog" and "dog" subsumes "husky" then "animal" should be implied to subsume "husky". Thus a hierarchy edge from "animal" to "husky" is redundant. The other case is that mutual exclusion can be implied for children by parents. For example, if "cat" and "dog" are exclusive, then all subclasses of "dog" should be implied to be exclusive with "cat". Thus an exclusion edge between "husky" and "cat" is redundant. Formally redundant edges are those that can be removed or added without changing the state space:

Definition 5. *Given a graph $G = (V, E_h, E_e)$, a directed edge $e \in V \times V$ (not necessarily in E_h) is redundant if $G' = (V, E_h \setminus \{e\}, E_e)$ and $G'' = (V, E_h \cup \{e\}, E_e)$ are both equivalent to G. An undirected edge $e \in V \times V$ (not necessarily in E_e) is redundant if $G' = (V, E_h, E_e \setminus \{e\})$ and $G'' = (V, E_h, E_e \cup \{e\})$ are both equivalent to G.*

For consistent graphs, redundant edges can be found by searching for certain graph patterns: for a directed hierarchy edge (v_i, v_j), it is redundant if and only if there is an alternative path from v_i to v_j. For an undirected exclusion edge

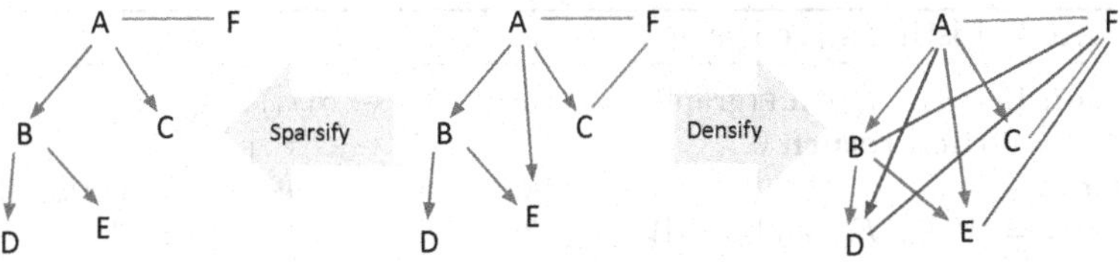

Fig. 3. Equivalent HEX graphs

(v_i, v_j), it is redundant if and only if there is an another exclusion edge that connects their ancestors (or connects one node's ancestor to the other node).

Lemma 1. *Let $G = (V, E_h, E_e)$ be a consistent graph. A directed edge $e \in V \times V$ is redundant if and only if in the subgraph $G = (V, E_h)$ there exists a directed path from v_i to v_j and the path doesn't contain e. An undirected edge $e = (v_i, v_j) \in V \times V$ is redundant if and only if there exists an exclusion edge $e' = (v_k, v_l) \in E_e$ such that $v_k \in \bar{\alpha}(v_i)$, $v_l \in \bar{\alpha}(v_j)$ and $e \neq e'$.*

Lemma 1 in fact gives an algorithm to "sparsify" or "densify" a graph. We can remove one redundant edge a time until we obtain a *minimally sparse* graph. We can also add edges to obtain a *maximally dense* equivalent. (Fig. 3).

Definition 6. *A graph G is* minimally sparse *if it has no redundant edges. A graph G is* maximally dense *if every redundant edge is in G.*

In fact for a consistent graph, its minimally sparse or maximally dense equivalent graph is unique, i.e. we always arrive at the same graph regardless of the order we remove or add redundant edges:

Theorem 2. *For any consistent graphs G and G′ that are both minimally sparse (or maximally dense), if $S_G = S_{G'}$, then $G = G'$.*

Thus given any consistent graph, we can "canonicalize" it by sparsifying or densifying it[2]. This can help us reason about the size of the state space.

Size of State Space. If a graph has very dense connections, its state space tends to be tractable, such as the case of pairwise mutually exclusive labels. Intuitively, for labels applied to real world objects, there should be many mutual exclusions. For example, if we randomly pick two labels from the English dictionary, most likely they will have a relation of exclusion or subsumption when applied to the same object. In other words, for the same object, there shouldn't be too many overlapping labels. Otherwise the state space can grow exponentially with the amount of overlap. We can formalize this intuition by first introducing the quantity *maximum overlap*.

Definition 7. *The maximum overlap of a consistent graph $G = (V, E_h, E_e)$ is $\Omega_G = \max_{v \in V} |o_{\bar{G}}(v)|$, where $o_{\bar{G}}(v) = \{u \in V : (u, v) \notin \bar{E}_h \wedge (v, u) \notin \bar{E}_h \wedge (u, v) \notin \bar{E}_e\}$ and $\bar{G} = (V, \bar{E}_h, \bar{E}_e)$ is the maximally dense equivalent of G.*

[2] Note that Lemma 1 and Theorem 2 do not apply to inconsistent graphs because of "dead" nodes. See supplemental materials for more details.

Algorithm 1. Listing state space

```
function ListStateSpace(graph G)
    if G = ∅ then return ∅
    end if
    Let G = (V, E_h, E_e) and n = |V|.
    Pick an arbitrary v_i ∈ V.
    V^0 ← α(v_i) ∪ ϵ(v_i) ∪ o(v_i).
    G^0 ← G[V^0]
    S_{G^0} ← ListStateSpace(G^0)
    S_G^0 ← {y ∈ {0,1}^n : y_i = 0 ∧ y_{σ(v_i)} = 0 ∧ y_{V^0} ∈ S_{G^0}}.
    V^1 ← σ(v_i) ∪ o(v_i).
    G^1 ← G[V^1]
    S_{G^1} ← ListStateSpace(G^1)
    S_G^1 = {y ∈ {0,1}^n : y_i = 1 ∧ y_{α(v_i)} = 1 ∧ ϵ(v_i) = 0 ∧ y_{V^1} ∈ S_{G^1}}
    return S_G^0 ∪ S_G^1.
end function
```

That is, we first convert a graph to its maximally dense equivalent and then take the max of the per-node overlap—the number of non-neighbours of a node. In other words, the overlap of a label is the number of other non-superset and non-subset labels you can additionally apply to the same object. We can now use the maximum overlap of a graph to bound the size of its state space:

Theorem 3. *For a consistent graph* $G = (V, E_h, E_e)$, $|S_G| \leq (|V| - \Omega_G + 1)2^{\Omega_G}$.

As an interesting fact, if a HEX graph consists of a tree hierarchy and exclusion edges between all siblings, then it's easy to verify that its maximum overlap is zero and its state space size is exactly $|V| + 1$, a tight bound in this case.

Listing State Space. A tractable size of the state space is useful for inference only if the legal states can also be enumerated efficiently. Fortunately this is always the case for HEX graphs. To list all legal assignments for an input, we can first pick an arbitrary node as a "pivot" and fix its value to 1. Also we fix all its parents to 1 and exclusive neighbours to 0 because otherwise we would violate the constraints. We then recursively apply the same procedure to the subgraph induced by the rest of the nodes (children and non-neighbours). For each returned assignment of the subgraph, we generate a new assignment to the full graph by concatenating it with the fixed nodes. Similarly, we fix the pivot node to 0 and fix its children to 0, and then recurse on the subgraph induced by the rest of the nodes. See Alg. 1 for pseudo-code. We can formally prove that if the graph is consistent and maximally dense, this greedy procedure returns all legal assignments and runs in time linear in the size of the state space:

Lemma 2. *If graph* $G = (V, E_h, E_e)$ *is consistent and maximally dense, Alg. 1 runs in* $O\left((|V| + |E_h| + |E_e|)|S_G|\right)$ *time and returns the state space* S_G.

Full Inference Algorithm. We now describe the full inference algorithm (Alg. 2). Given a graph, we first generate the minimally sparse and maximally dense equivalents. We treat the minimally sparse graph as a generic CRF and generate a junction tree. For each clique of the junction tree, we list its state

Algorithm 2. Exact Inference

Input: Graph $G = (V, E_h, E_e)$.
Input: Scores $f \in \mathcal{R}^{|V|}$.
Output: Marginals, e.g. $\Pr(v_i = 1)$.
1: $G^* \leftarrow$ SPARSIFY(G)
2: $\bar{G} \leftarrow$ DENSIFY(G)
3: $T \leftarrow$BUILDJUNCTIONTREE(G^*).
4: For each clique $c \in T$, $S_c \leftarrow$LISTSTATESPACE($\bar{G}[c]$).
5: Perform (two passes) message passing on T using only states S_c for each clique c.

space using the subgraph induced by the clique on the maximally dense graph. To do inference we run two passes of sum-product message passing on the junction tree, performing computation only on the legal states of each clique.

This algorithm thus automatically exploits dynamic programming for sparse regions of the graph and small state spaces for dense regions of the graph. For example, it is easy to verify that for pairwise mutually exclusive labels, the inference cost is $O(n)$, the same as hand-coded softmax, due to the small state space. For fully independent labels (no edges), the inference cost is also $O(n)$, the same as n hand-coded logistic regressions, because the junction tree is n disconnected cliques, each containing a single label. We can formally bound the complexity of the inference algorithm:

Theorem 4. *The complexity of the exact inference (Line 5 in Alg. 2) for graph* $G = (V, E_h, E_e)$ *is* $O\left(\min\{|V|2^w, |V|^2 2^{\Omega_G}\}\right)$, *where* w *is the width of the junction tree* T *(Line 3).*

Note that this is a worst case bound. For example, a graph can have two disconnected components. One has a large treewidth but small overlap (e.g. many mutual exclusions between object labels). The other has a small treewidth but large overlap (e.g. attribute labels). The bound in Theorem 4 for the whole graph will assume the worst, but Alg. 2 can perform inference for this graph efficiently by automatically treating the two components differently.

4 Experiments

4.1 Implementation

We implement our model as a standalone layer in a deep neural network framework. It can be put on top of any feed-forward architecture. The layer takes as input a set of scores $f(x; w) \in \mathbb{R}^n$ and outputs (marginal) probability of a given set of observed labels. During learning, we use stochastic gradient descent and compute the derivative $\frac{\partial \mathcal{L}}{\partial f}$, where $\mathcal{L}$ is the loss as defined in Eqn. 2 but treated here as a function of the label scores f instead of the raw input x. This derivative is then back propagated to the previous layers represented by $f(x; w)$.

For exact inference as described in Alg. 2, Step 1 to Step 4 (processing the graph, building the junctions trees, listing state space etc.) only depend on the graph structure and are performed offline. Only the message passing on the junction tree (Step 5) needs to be performed for each example online. Given a junction tree and the legal assignments for each clique, we perform a "dry run" of message passing and record the sequence of sum-product operations. Then the online inference for each example simply follows this pre-determined sum-product sequence and thus has negligible extra overhead compared to hand-coded implementations of softmax or independent logistic regressions.

4.2 Object Classification on ImageNet

Dataset. We evaluate our model using the ILSVRC2012 dataset [9]. It consists of 1.2M training images from 1000 object classes[3]. These 1000 classes are mutually exclusive leaf nodes of a semantic hierarchy based on WordNet that has 820 internal nodes. All images are labeled to the leaf nodes.

WordNet provides hierarchical relations but no exclusive relations. We thus adopt the assumption of "exclusive whenever possible", i.e. putting an exclusive edge between two nodes unless it results in an inconsistent graph. This means that any two labels are mutually exclusive unless they share a descendant. Note that the WordNet hierarchy is a DAG instead of a tree. For example, "dog" appear under both "domestic animal" and "canine".

Setup. In this experiment we test the hypothesis that our method can improve object classification by exploiting label relations, in particular by enabling joint modeling of hierarchical categories. To this end, we evaluate the recognition performance in the typical test setting—multiclass classification at the leaf level—but allow the training examples to be labeled at different semantic levels. This setting is of practical importance because when one collects training examples from the Internet, the distribution of labels follow a power law with many more images labeled at basic levels ("dog","car") than at fine-grained levels ("husky", "Honda Civic"). While it is obvious that with a semantic hierarchy, one can aggregate all training examples from leaf nodes to learn a classifier for internal nodes, the other direction—how to use higher level classes with many training examples to help train fine-grained classes with fewer examples—is not as clear.

Since ILSVRC2012 has no training examples at internal nodes, we create training examples for internal nodes by "relabelling" the leaf examples to their immediate parent(s) (Fig. 4), i.e. some huskies are now labeled as "dog". Note that each image still has just one label; an image labeled as "husky" is not additionally labeled as "dog".

We put our model on top of the convolutional neural network (CNN) developed by Krizhevsky et al. [21,37]. Specifically, we replace the softmax classifier layer (fully connected units with a sigmoid activation function followed by normalization to produce the label probabilities) with our layer — fully connected units followed by our inference to produce marginals for each label (see Fig. 1 for an illustration). We only use fully connected units for the leaf nodes and fix input

[3] Since ground truth for test set is not released and our experiments involve non-standard settings and error measures, we use the validation set as our test images and tune all parameters using cross-validation on the training set.

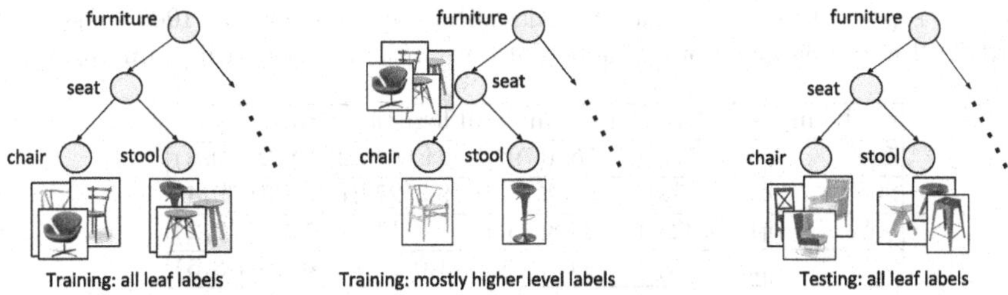

Fig. 4. Instead of training with data all labeled at leaf nodes, we train with examples leveled at different levels but still evaluate classification at leaf nodes during test

scores (f_i in Eqn. 1) of internal nodes to zero because we found that otherwise it takes longer to train but offer no significant benefits on ILSVRC2012.

We compare our model with three baselines, all on top of the same CNN architecture and all trained with full back propagation from scratch: (1) softmax on leaf nodes only i.e. ignoring examples labeled to internal nodes; (2) softmax on all labels, i.e. treating all labels as mutually exclusive even though "dog" subsumes "husky"; (3) independent logistic regressions for each label[4]. For the logistic regression baseline, we need to specify positive and negative examples individually for each class—we add to positives by aggregating all examples from descendants and use as negatives all other examples except those from the ancestors. During test, for each method we use its output probabilities for the 1000 leaf nodes (ignoring others) to make predictions.

Results. Table 1 reports the classification accuracy on the leaf nodes with different amounts of relabelling (50%, 90%, 95%, 99%). As a reference, our implementation of softmax with all examples labeled at leaf nodes (0% relabeling) gives a hit rate (accuracy) of 62.6% at top 1 and 84.3% at top 5[5].

Our approach outperforms all baselines in all settings except that in the extreme case of 99% relabelling, our approach is comparable with the best baseline. Even with 90% of labels at leaf nodes "weakened" into internal nodes, we can still achieve 55.3% top 1 accuracy, not too big a drop from 62.6% by using all leaf training data. Also independent logistic regressions perform very abysmally, likely because of the lack of calibration among independent logistic regressions and varying proportions of positive examples for different classes.

Interestingly the baseline of softmax on all labels, which seems non-sensible as it trains "dog" against "husky", is very competitive. We hypothesize that this is because softmax treats examples in internal nodes as negatives. It is in fact a mostly correct assumption: the "dog" examples contain some huskies but are mostly other types of dogs. Softmax thus utilizes those negative examples effectively. On the other hand, our model treats labels in internal nodes as weak positive examples because the marginal of an internal node depends on the scores

[4] They are trained jointly but, unlike softmax, without normalization of probabilities.

[5] Our model gives the same result—with scores for internal nodes fixed to zero it is equivalent to softmax up to an additional constant in the partition function.

Table 1. Top 1 (top 5 in brackets) classification accuracy on 1000 classes of ILSVRC2012 with relabeling of leaf node data to internal nodes during training

relabeling	softmax-leaf	softmax-all	logistic	**ours**
50%	50.5(74.7)	56.4(79.6)	21.0(45.2)	**58.2(80.8)**
90%	26.2(47.3)	52.9(77.2)	9.3(27.2)	**55.3(79.4)**
95%	16.0(32.2)	50.8(76.0)	5.6(17.2)	**52.4(77.2)**
99%	2.5 (7.2)	**41.5**(68.1)	1.0(3.8)	**41.5(68.5)**

of its descendants. This is semantically correct, but makes no assumption about the proportion of real positive examples. This suggests a future direction of including stronger assumptions during learning to further improve our model.

In the case of 99% relabelling, softmax-all is comparable to our model (41.5% versus 41.5% top 1 accuracy). This is likely because there are too few images labeled at the leaf nodes (around 10 images per class). During learning, our model "softly" assigns the images labeled at internal nodes to leaves (by inferring the distribution of unobserved labels), which improves the leaf models (weights for generating leaf input scores). However, with too few training examples labeled at leaf nodes, the leaf models can "drift away" with noisy assignment.

4.3 Zero-Shot Recognition on Animals with Attributes

In this experiment we evaluate whether our HEX graph based model can be used to model relations between objects and attributes, although not by design. We use the Animal with Attributes (AWA) dataset [25] that includes images from 50 animal classes. For each animal class, it provides binary predicates for 85 attributes, e.g. for zebra, "stripes" is yes and "eats fish" is no. We evaluate the zero-shot setting where training is performed using only examples from 40 classes and testing is on classifying the 10 unseen classes. The binary predicates and the names of the unseen classes are both known a priori.

Here we show that our model can be easily adapted to perform zero-shot recognition exploiting object-attribute relations. First we build a HEX graph for all animals and attributes by assuming mutual exclusion between the animal classes and then adding the object-attribute relations: "zebra has stripes" establish a subsumption edge from "stripes" to "zebra"; "zebra doesn't eat fish" means an exclusion edge between them.

We use the same published, pre-computed features x from [25] and use a linear model to map the features to score $f_i(x) = w_i^T \phi(x)$ for label i, where $\phi(x)$ is computed by the Nystrom method [35] with rank 8000 to approximate the Chi-squared kernel used in [25]. In training, we observe the class labels for examples from the first 40 classes. The system is trained to maximize the likelihood of the class labels, but indirectly it learns to also predict the (latent) attributes given the image features. At test time, the class labels are not observed (and are drawn from a distinct set of 10 new labels); however, the model can predict the attributes given the image, and since the mapping from attributes to classes is known (for all 50 classes), the model can also (indirectly) predict the novel class

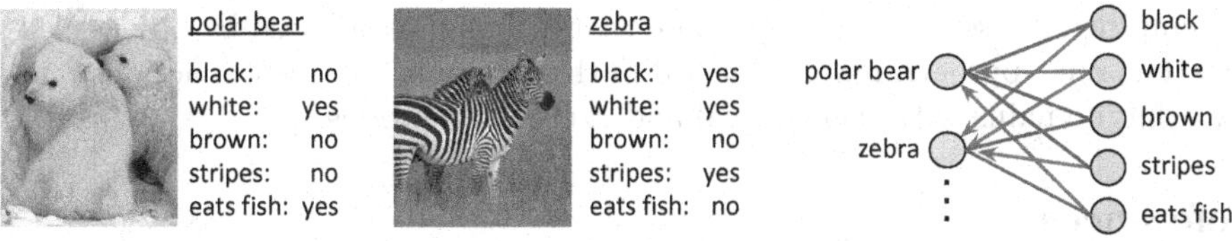

Fig. 5. We can build a HEX graph using relations between objects and attributes

label. This can be done by performing inference in the model and reading out the marginals for the 10 unknown classes. We achieve a 38.5% mean accuracy (and 44.2% using the recently released DECAF features [11]) as compared to 40.5% in [25]. Given that our model is not explicitly designed for this task and the kernel approximation involved, this is a very encouraging result.

4.4 Efficiency of Inference

We evaluate the empirical efficiency of inference by counting the number of basic operations (summations and multiplications) needed to compute the marginals for all labels from the scores (not including computation for generating the scores). For the HEX graph used with ILSVRC2012, i.e. a DAG hierarchy and dense mutual exclusions, the inference cost is 6 relative to softmax for the same number of labels. For AWA, the cost is 294 relative to softmax. In both cases, the overhead is *negligible* because while softmax costs $O(n)$, simply computing the scores from d-dimensional inputs costs $O(nd)$ using a linear model ($d = 4096$ for ILSVRC2012 and $d = 8000$ for AWA), let alone multilayer neural networks.

Moreover, it is worth noting that the HEX graph for AWA (Fig. 5) has 85 overlapping attributes with no constraints between them. Thus it has at least 2^{85} legal states. Also it has a large treewidth—the 50 animal classes are fully connected with exclusion edges, a complexity of 2^{50} for a naive junction tree algorithm. But our inference algorithm runs with negligible cost. This again underscores the effectiveness of our new inference algorithm in exploiting both dynamic programming and small state space.

5 Discussions and Conclusions

We now briefly mention a couple of possible future directions. Efficient exact inference depends on the relations being "absolute" such that many states have probability zero. But it does not allow non-absolute relations ("taxi is mostly yellow"). Thus it remains an open question how to use non-absolute relations in conjunction with absolute ones. Another direction is to integrate this model developed for single objects into a larger framework that considers spatial interactions between objects.

To conclude, we have provided a unified classification framework that generalizes existing models. We have shown that it is flexible, theoretically principled, and empirically useful. Finally, we note that although motivated by object classification, our approach is very general in that it applies to scenes, actions, and any other domains with hierarchical and exclusive relations.

References

1. Akata, Z., Perronnin, F., Harchaoui, Z., Schmid, C.: Label-embedding for attribute-based classification. In: 2013 IEEE Conference on Computer Vision and Pattern Recognition (CVPR), pp. 819–826. IEEE (2013)
2. Amit, Y., Fink, M., Srebro, N., Ullman, S.: Uncovering shared structures in multiclass classification. In: Proceedings of the 24th International Conference on Machine Learning, pp. 17–24. ACM (2007)
3. Bi, W., Kwok, J.T.: Multi-label classification on tree-and dag-structured hierarchies. In: Proceedings of the 28th International Conference on Machine Learning (ICML 2011), pp. 17–24 (2011)
4. Bi, W., Kwok, J.T.: Mandatory leaf node prediction in hierarchical multilabel classification. In: NIPS, pp. 153–161 (2012)
5. Bucak, S.S., Jin, R., Jain, A.K.: Multi-label learning with incomplete class assignments. In: 2011 IEEE Conference on Computer Vision and Pattern Recognition (CVPR), pp. 2801–2808. IEEE (2011)
6. Chen, X., Yuan, X.T., Chen, Q., Yan, S., Chua, T.S.: Multi-label visual classification with label exclusive context. In: 2011 IEEE International Conference on Computer Vision (ICCV), pp. 834–841. IEEE (2011)
7. Cour, T., Sapp, B., Taskar, B.: Learning from partial labels. The Journal of Machine Learning Research 12, 1501–1536 (2011)
8. Dekel, O., Keshet, J., Singer, Y.: Large margin hierarchical classification. In: Proceedings of the Twenty-first International Conference on Machine Learning, p. 27. ACM (2004)
9. Deng, J., Berg, A., Satheesh, S., Su, H., Khosla, A., Fei-Fei, L.: Imagenet large scale visual recognition challenge 2012 (2012), `http://www.image-net.org/challenges/LSVRC/2012`
10. Desai, C., Ramanan, D., Fowlkes, C.C.: Discriminative models for multi-class object layout. International Journal of Computer Vision 95(1), 1–12 (2011)
11. Donahue, J., Jia, Y., Vinyals, O., Hoffman, J., Zhang, N., Tzeng, E., Darrell, T.: Decaf: A deep convolutional activation feature for generic visual recognition. arXiv preprint arXiv:1310.1531 (2013)
12. Elhoseiny, M., Saleh, B., Elgammal, A.: Write a classifier: Zero-shot learning using purely textual descriptions. In: ICCV (2013)
13. Everingham, M., Van Gool, L., Williams, C.K., Winn, J., Zisserman, A.: The pascal visual object classes (voc) challenge. International Journal of Computer Vision 88(2), 303–338 (2010)
14. Farhadi, A., Endres, I., Hoiem, D.: Attribute-centric recognition for cross-category generalization. In: 2010 IEEE Conference on Computer Vision and Pattern Recognition (CVPR), pp. 2352–2359. IEEE (2010)
15. Fergus, R., Bernal, H., Weiss, Y., Torralba, A.: Semantic label sharing for learning with many categories. In: Daniilidis, K., Maragos, P., Paragios, N. (eds.) ECCV 2010, Part I. LNCS, vol. 6311, pp. 762–775. Springer, Heidelberg (2010)
16. Frome, A., Corrado, G.S., Shlens, J., Bengio, S., Dean, J., Mikolov, T.: Devise: A deep visual-semantic embedding model. In: Advances in Neural Information Processing Systems, pp. 2121–2129 (2013)

17. Hwang, S.J., Sha, F., Grauman, K.: Sharing features between objects and their attributes. In: 2011 IEEE Conference on Computer Vision and Pattern Recognition (CVPR), pp. 1761–1768. IEEE (2011)
18. Jia, Y., Abbott, J.T., Austerweil, J., Griffiths, T., Darrell, T.: Visual concept learning: Combining machine vision and bayesian generalization on concept hierarchies. In: Advances in Neural Information Processing Systems, pp. 1842–1850 (2013)
19. Jin, R., Ghahramani, Z.: Learning with multiple labels. In: Advances in Neural Information Processing Systems, pp. 897–904 (2002)
20. Kang, F., Jin, R., Sukthankar, R.: Correlated label propagation with application to multi-label learning. In: 2006 IEEE Computer Society Conference on Computer Vision and Pattern Recognition, vol. 2, pp. 1719–1726. IEEE (2006)
21. Krizhevsky, A., Sutskever, I., Hinton, G.E.: Imagenet classification with deep convolutional neural networks. In: NIPS, vol. 1, p. 4 (2012)
22. Kuettel, D., Guillaumin, M., Ferrari, V.: Segmentation propagation in imageNet. In: Fitzgibbon, A., Lazebnik, S., Perona, P., Sato, Y., Schmid, C. (eds.) ECCV 2012, Part VII. LNCS, vol. 7578, pp. 459–473. Springer, Heidelberg (2012)
23. Lafferty, J.D., McCallum, A., Pereira, F.C.N.: Conditional random fields: Probabilistic models for segmenting and labeling sequence data. In: Proceedings of the Eighteenth International Conference on Machine Learning, ICML 2001, pp. 282–289. Morgan Kaufmann Publishers Inc., San Francisco (2001), `http://dl.acm.org/citation.cfm?id=645530.655813`
24. Lampert, C.H.: Maximum margin multi-label structured prediction. In: NIPS, vol. 11, pp. 289–297 (2011)
25. Lampert, C.H., Nickisch, H., Harmeling, S.: Learning to detect unseen object classes by between-class attribute transfer. In: IEEE Conference on Computer Vision and Pattern Recognition, CVPR 2009, pp. 951–958. IEEE (2009)
26. Lim, J.J., Salakhutdinov, R., Torralba, A.: Transfer learning by borrowing examples for multiclass object detection. In: Neural Information Processing Systems, NIPS (2011)
27. Marszalek, M., Schmid, C.: Semantic hierarchies for visual object recognition. In: IEEE Conference on Computer Vision and Pattern Recognition, CVPR 2007, pp. 1–7. IEEE (2007)
28. Palatucci, M., Pomerleau, D., Hinton, G.E., Mitchell, T.M.: Zero-shot learning with semantic output codes. In: NIPS, vol. 3, pp. 5–2 (2009)
29. Perronnin, F., Akata, Z., Harchaoui, Z., Schmid, C.: Towards good practice in large-scale learning for image classification. In: 2012 IEEE Conference on Computer Vision and Pattern Recognition (CVPR), pp. 3482–3489. IEEE (2012)
30. Rohrbach, M., Stark, M., Schiele, B.: Evaluating knowledge transfer and zero-shot learning in a large-scale setting. In: 2011 IEEE Conference on Computer Vision and Pattern Recognition (CVPR), pp. 1641–1648. IEEE (2011)
31. Rohrbach, M., Stark, M., Szarvas, G., Gurevych, I., Schiele, B.: What helps where–and why? semantic relatedness for knowledge transfer. In: 2010 IEEE Conference on Computer Vision and Pattern Recognition (CVPR), pp. 910–917. IEEE (2010)
32. Sánchez, J., Perronnin, F., Mensink, T., Verbeek, J.: Image classification with the fisher vector: Theory and practice. International Journal of Computer Vision 105(3), 222–245 (2013)
33. Sharmanska, V., Quadrianto, N., Lampert, C.H.: Augmented attribute representations. In: Fitzgibbon, A., Lazebnik, S., Perona, P., Sato, Y., Schmid, C. (eds.) ECCV 2012, Part V. LNCS, vol. 7576, pp. 242–255. Springer, Heidelberg (2012)

34. Tousch, A.M., Herbin, S., Audibert, J.Y.: Semantic hierarchies for image annotation: A survey. Pattern Recognition 45(1), 333–345 (2012)
35. Williams, C., Seeger, M.: Using the nyström method to speed up kernel machines. In: Advances in Neural Information Processing Systems 13. Citeseer (2001)
36. Yu, F.X., Cao, L., Feris, R.S., Smith, J.R., Chang, S.F.: Designing category-level attributes for discriminative visual recognition. In: 2013 IEEE Conference on Computer Vision and Pattern Recognition (CVPR), pp. 771–778. IEEE (2013)
37. Zeiler, M.D., Fergus, R.: Visualizing and understanding convolutional neural networks. arXiv preprint arXiv:1311.2901 (2013)
38. Zweig, A., Weinshall, D.: Exploiting object hierarchy: Combining models from different category levels. In: IEEE 11th International Conference on Computer Vision, ICCV 2007, pp. 1–8. IEEE (2007)

30Hz Object Detection with DPM V5

Mohammad Amin Sadeghi and David Forsyth

Computer Science Department, University of Illinois at Urbana, Champaign, USA
{msadegh2,daf}@illinois.edu

Abstract. We describe an implementation of the Deformable Parts Model [1] that operates in a user-defined time-frame. Our implementation uses a variety of mechanism to trade-off speed against accuracy. Our implementation can detect all 20 PASCAL 2007 objects simultaneously at 30Hz with an mAP of 0.26. At 15Hz, its mAP is 0.30; and at 100Hz, its mAP is 0.16. By comparison the reference implementation of [1] runs at 0.07Hz and mAP of 0.33 and a fast GPU implementation runs at 1Hz. Our technique is over an order of magnitude faster than the previous fastest DPM implementation. Our implementation exploits a series of important speedup mechanisms. We use the cascade framework of [3] and the vector quantization technique of [2]. To speed up feature computation, we compute HOG features at few scales, and apply many interpolated templates. A hierarchical vector quantization method is used to compress HOG features for fast template evaluation. An object proposal step uses hash-table methods to identify locations where evaluating templates would be most useful; these locations are inserted into a priority queue, and processed in a detection phase. Both proposal and detection phases have an any-time property. Our method applies to legacy templates, and no retraining is required.

Keywords: Fast Object Detection, Real-time Object Detection, Fast Deformable Parts Model.

1 Introduction

A major burden in using object detectors in practice is speed. Except for certain objects including face, pedestrians and certain rigid objects, detectors do not currently run at video rate. We employ a series of techniques to detect several objects together at video rate. The architecture we present in this paper can detect the 20 PASCAL VOC categories simultaneously at 30Hz.

We focus on speeding up DPM [1] because it is a mature and stable technology. While other detection methods are more accurate, the full potential of these technologies has not yet been explored, and they will not take their final form for some time. We believe that our speed-up techniques exploit fundamental properties of templates and will apply to deep leaning methods.

We build up our detector based on Deformable Parts Model [1] and compare to its latest implementation [21]. The latest implementation detects 20 PASCAL VOC object categories in about 13 seconds per image from the PASCAL

D. Fleet et al. (Eds.): ECCV 2014, Part I, LNCS 8689, pp. 65–79, 2014.
© Springer International Publishing Switzerland 2014

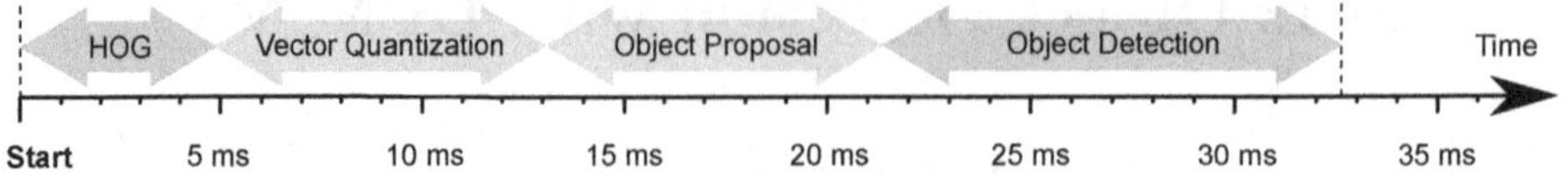

Fig. 1. Our fast implementation of Deformable Parts Model can jointly detect 20 PASCAL categories at 30fps or faster. The pipeline consists of four steps that together run at video rate speed. To achieve this speed we used optimized techniques for each step. Optimizations for HOG feature computation are discussed in Section 2; Fast Vector Quantization is discussed in Section 3; The object proposal technique is discussed in Section 4; and object scoring is discussed in Section 5. For details about the exact computation time of our implementation please refer to Section 6. Allocation of time between the proposal and the detection phase can be balanced according to the processor architecture, dataset properties and application requirements; time allocation is discussed in Section 7.

dataset. Several techniques have been developed to speed up DPMs [3][11][2]. These techniques can speed up computation time to about 0.5 seconds (2Hz) with almost no loss of accuracy. Our techniques obtains a further speed-up to 30Hz with a minor loss of accuracy. Furthermore, our technique allow an explicit trade-off of accuracy for speed.

Furthermore, our technique can maintain a fixed frame rate at 30.0Hz that is essential in practical applications. Most speed-up techniques optimize average speed and cannot guarantee a fixed time per frame.

Our technique consists of four major steps that are illustrated in Figure 1. Given a query image, we first extract a lightweight version of HOG features from the image (details in Section 2). We then vector quantize HOG features according to Section 3. We use a data-structure to obtain object proposal to identify the promising locations (Section 4). We finally score the proposals by evaluating the corresponding templates (Section 5).

We employ separate optimization techniques to speed up each of the four main stages. We implemented a highly optimized code to extract HOG features very quickly. Our implementation utilize various low-level optimizations including vector operations, multiple cores and CPU cache management. We also use a lightweight version of the HOG pyramid that further speeds up the process. After the HOG features are computed we use a hierarchical clustering process to vector quantize the HOG features (Section 3).

We use a data-structure to provide cheap object-dependent proposals in Section 4. Our proposal stage uses a hashing scheme that allows us to process only a small fraction of templates at each location. Our object scoring stage (Section 5) can also operate in a user-defined time-frame. It processes as many locations as it can within the specified time-frame.

Our implementation is fast and light-weight. The code is implemented in C++ but can be called from MATLAB. Our implementation will be available online for public use upon paper acceptance. Our algorithm not only can process an image to detect 20 pascal categories simultaneously at 30fps, it can further trade off accuracy for time to achieve a detection rate of 100Hz.

1.1 Prior Work

There is a rich literature of fast object detection built up on the original Deformable Parts Model [1] algorithm. Several successful speed-up techniques have been introduced in the last few years.

Cascades speed up evaluation by using rough tests to identify promising locations to further process using fine tests. For example, Felzenszwalb et al. [3] evaluate root models, and then evaluate the part scores only in promising locations. At each iteration their method evaluate the corresponding template only if the current score of the object is higher than a certain threshold. Sadeghi et al. [2] follow a similar approach but they use a fast vector quantization technique that is compatible with cascades to further boost the speed. Pedersoli et al. [12] estimate the score of a location using a lower resolution version of root templates and use higher resolution templates in high-scoring locations. Dollár et al. [10] enable neighbouring locations to communicate when a template is being evaluated. Cascade approach to object detection has been shown to be very successful for speed-ups.

Transform Methods evaluate templates at all locations simultaneously by exploiting properties of the Fast Fourier Transform. The advantage of these methods, pioneered by Dubout et al. [11] is that the computation is fast and exact at the same time. In comparison, most other techniques involve approximation. The disadvantage of this approach is that it is not *random-access*; a large chunk of the locations are processed in one pass making the algorithm incompatible with cascade techniques.

Hash Tables exploit locality sensitive hashing [15] to get a system that can detect many thousands of object categories in a matter of seconds [14]. This strategy appears effective and achieves a good speed-up with very large numbers of categories. Dean et al. [14] use a hash table at the core of their technique that allows them to spend computation for only the high-scoring locations. The advantage of this technique compared to cascades is that they don't require any computation for low chance locations whereas cascade algorithms examine every location at least once.

Vector Quantization is well-studied for data compression [18]. In the past few years several algorithms have used vector quantization to speed up computation. These techniques operate in situations where arithmetic accuracy is not crucial. Jégou et al. [17] successfully apply vector quantization to approximate nearest neighbour search. Kokkinos [13], Vedaldi et al. [16] and Sadeghi et al. [2] apply different variations of this approach to object detection and demonstrate significant speed-ups.

Hierarchical Classification techniques run detectors in a tree structure with a depth of $\Theta(\log C)$ to be able to cover C categories. Nistér et al. [8] clusters categories using hierarchical k-means. Bengio et al. [24] use detectors that are suitable to discriminate between groups of categories. Both techniques are scalable in terms of C.

Object Proposals are used in object detection techniques that need to avoid a dense sliding window search. Some object proposal algorithms produce category-independent proposals (e.g. Endres et al. [6] and Cheng et al. [7]) while others [14] provide category-dependent proposals. The main source of speed-up in these techniques is that they significantly limit the number of locations to evaluate detectors. Category-dependent proposals are preferred in speed-up applications as they need to be evaluated by fewer detectors.

GPU Implementation can be used to speed up object detectors as well. Vanilla DPM [22] is a version of DPM that can harness the power of GPU to speed-up object detectors.

These techniques have improved the object detection speed so much that the feature computation stage has became a major bottleneck. Dollár et al. [4] present elegant techniques to speed-up features computation. We use a version of [4] to speed up our feature computation (Section 2).

2 Pyramid of Features vs. Pyramid of Templates

Conventional object detectors operate at various scales to be able to detect objects with variable sizes. Template based object detectors extract local features at various scales (e.g. HOG pyramid [5] and histogram of sparse codes [19]) and evaluate a given template at all scales. In practice ten scales per octave is typical.

Feature computation is a major bottleneck for pedestrian detection. Dollár et al. [4] present an elegant technique to process features for certain key scales (one or two per octave) and interpolate for the rest of scales. Their experiments with pedestrian detection show that this leads to a significant speed-up for feature computation. Benenson et al. [25] interpolate templates for integral channel features. Our approach is similar to Dollár et al. [4]; however, instead of rescaling features we rescale templates (Figure 2). We rescale each template to several scales in order to make a *Pyramid of Templates*. Our experiments show that this works as accurate as rescaling features while being faster in practice. The pyramid of templates has two major advantages over the regular pyramid of features:

1. Because HOG templates are several times smaller in size than HOG features (2K cells per object category vs. 100K cells per image) processing and storing HOG features takes much more time than templates. Furthermore, categories are often fixed for several images while every new image comes with a new feature. As a result, reducing the number of feature levels per octave directly limits the space required to store features. In our experiments HOG features are compressed from 8MB to 1.6MB per image. The benefits include more efficient caching and more efficient mobile application.
2. Several speed-up techniques are based on having a large number of templates (e.g. Pirsiavash et al. [9] and Dean et al. [14]). The computational complexity of [14] is claimed to be independent of C the number of templates. Their computational complexity depends only on L the number of locations to

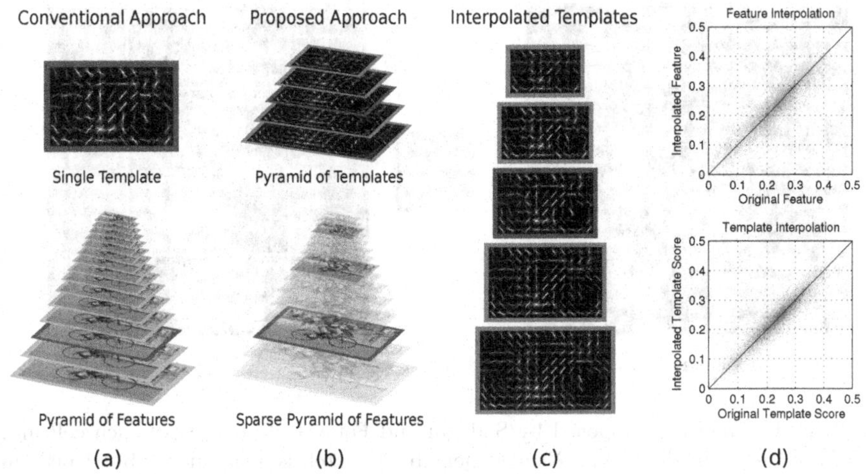

Fig. 2. **a**: Conventional object detectors run templates on a pyramid of features to capture a range of scales (ten scales per octave is typical). Dollár et al. [4] compute two scales per octave then interpolate the rest of the scales to considerably speed up feature computation at the cost of about 2% loss of average precision. **b**: Instead of interpolating features we interpolate templates. We show that interpolating templates is faster and leads to further speed-up techniques. **c**: We generate new templates by interpolating templates to different scales. **d**: This process introduces some error. The two scatter plots illustrate original template score versus the score produced by interpolated features/templates. **d**: **Top**: Features are interpolated according to [4]. **Bottom**: Templates are interpolated instead of features. Although interpolating templates is faster than interpolating feature pyramids, the errors are in the same range.

evaluate templates (whereas most algorithms have at least a $\Theta(CL)$ term in their complexity). Our technique uses $5C$ templates and $\frac{1}{5}L$ locations; therefore, it can directly benefit from speed-up techniques presented by Pirsiavash et al. [9] and Dean et al. [14].

A few technical issues arise when resizing templates for object detection. All part templates need to be resized as well as deformation costs and part locations. The interpolation method can affect the quality of the new template. In order to resize a HOG template we interpolate every layer separately. We compared bilinear and bicubic interpolations and bicubic interpolation appears to be the best. The interpolated weights are adjusted by a factor to maintain the mean and the standard deviation of the scores. Our experiments show that this optimization leads to an mAP loss of about 0.02, compatible to that of [4].

3 Hierarchical Vector Quantization

Several optimization techniques have been employed to speed up Deformable Parts Model object detectors. The fastest was proposed by Sadeghi and Forsyth

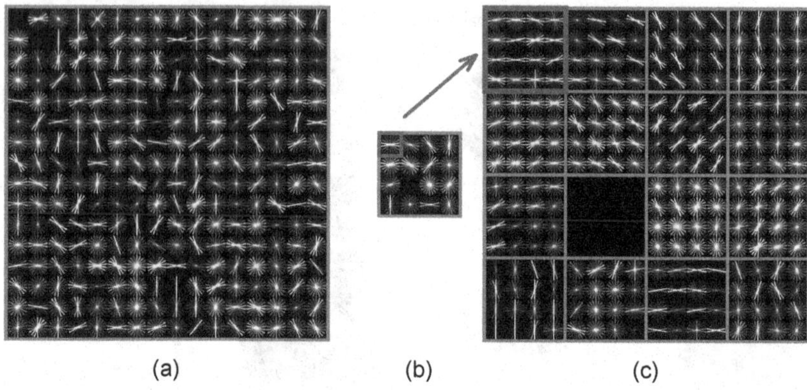

Fig. 3. a: The method proposed by Sadeghi and Forsyth [2] quantizes each cell into one of 256 pre-defined clusters. Nearest neighbour search is a significant bottleneck in their technique. In this paper we use hierarchical clustering instead of flat clustering. **b**: each cell is first quantized into one of the 16 clusters. **c**: Depending on the first level, the cell is clustered into one of 16 clusters in the respective group in c. Note that hierarchical clustering reduces the number of comparisons from 256 per cell to two stages of 16 comparisons per cell.

[2]. This is nearly two orders of magnitude faster than the original implementation of [21]. The key to their success is a vector quantization technique that decreases the computation demand by a large factor. They vector quantize HOG features and compute template scores by indexing certain look-up tables and adding their scores.

We use vector quantization for the same purpose but with a slightly different approach. The main computation bottleneck in [2] is vector quantization. They need 70ms per image to quantize HOG features for one image. The high computational demand is due to the fact that each HOG cell needs to be compared against every one of 256 cluster centers. (Figure 3, a). We use a hierarchical clustering technique to speed up this process. We first cluster each cell into 16 clusters (Figure 3, b). Then according to the nearest cluster in the first step we compare against 16 other clusters to find the nearest cluster (Figure 3, c). We pre-compute clusters using k-means algorithm.

Our experiments show that the proposed hierarchical clustering technique leads to a negligible loss of 0.001 in mAP. In contrast, the speed-up gain is about 8-fold.

4 Object Proposal Using Hash Table

We cannot evaluate all templates at all locations fast enough. Instead, we use a hashing technique to identify promising locations and insert them into priority queues (Figure 4). Proposals will then be processed in the object scoring stage

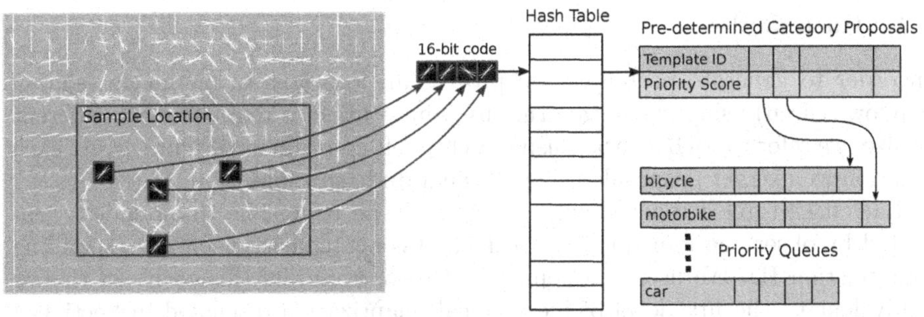

Fig. 4. Our proposal generation data-structure. We use a few look-up tables that are filled with pre-determined proposals. For each location we make a hash code by observing four pre-specified cells. We index the code into a hash table and obtain a list of pre-determined category proposals for each location. We store the proposals in category specific priority lists and later use them to evaluate the score of each location for each proposed category.

(Section 5). This architecture means that both the proposal process and the template evaluation process can be terminated at any time allowing our method to operate at fixed frame rate and trade-off accuracy for speed.

The cascade framework applied to Deformable Parts Model first evaluates a rough version of a given root template and then evaluates the corresponding part scores and finally re-estimate the scores by using fine templates (e.g. Felzenszwalb et al. [3] and Sadeghi et al. [2]). Although cascade methods prune the majority of locations, they need to at least evaluate all root templates at all locations (they can prune part templates but not root templates). To process the 20 PASCAL categories this step takes about 400ms in [3] and about 90ms in [2]. The two techniques are both too slow for video rate speed.

Several algorithms are introduced to generate object proposals for object detection (e.g. Endres et al. [6] and Cheng et al. [7]). We use a proposal generation data-structure to limit template evaluation to a sparse set of proposals rather than dense sliding window search. Our data-structure uses a hash table similar to Dean et al. [14]. Our hash table is distinguished from [14] in three aspects:

1. Instead of Winner Takes All (WTA) hash we use a hashing scheme compatible to our hierarchical vector quantization (Figure 4).
2. The data-structure used by Dean et al. [14] proposes template ID's without proposed scores. Our data-structure provides a *priority score* with each template ID. The priorities help us later choose which templates to process further.
3. The data-structure used by Dean et al. [14] uses hundreds or thousands of hash tables. We instead use 10 hash tables. The fact that we need fewer hash tables is partly due to our pre-stored priority scores.

4.1 Hash Codes

In order to generate proposals, we process all locations in an image (sliding window search) using our data-structure. Since different templates are different in size, we refer to each location using its top left co-ordinate (Figure 4). At each location we extract proposals using 10 separate hash tables.

Each hash table is indexed with a distinct 16-bit code. The 16-bit code is generated by observing four quantized cells and concatenating their corresponding quantization ID. We use a dictionary of 16 words (4-bits) for each cell that is equivalent to the first level of hierarchical quantization discussed in Section 3 (Figure 3). Reference cells are randomly determined for each hash table while initializing the data-structure.

Each cell of the hash tables is linked to a list of proposed templates and their corresponding priorities. A template can be determined by its category, root index and scale. For the PASCAL dataset and Deformable Parts Model version 5, there are 20 categories, 6 root templates per category and 5 scales (Figure 2): a total of 1200 root templates. We store 20 templates for each cell of the hash table. However, most of the proposals are not used in most cases.

4.2 Priority Lists

For each root template we store a separate priority list (Figure 4). Each list stores several proposal locations with their corresponding priority scores. The priority scores are used to determine the priorities between locations given a root template. Each root template has a limited budget of locations to examine that are chosen according to priority scores.

We use a simple array to store each priority list. After the lists are populated with proposals we keep a number of proposals that are expected to complete within the specified time-frame. We then evaluate root templates on remaining locations and update their priority score with the actual responses from the root templates.

The reason we store a separate priority list per template – as opposed to one joint priority list – is that the scores of different root templates are not directly comparable. Also the user may need to specify more process time on a certain template depending on the application. In our experiments we process equal number of locations per root template. Process allocation could be adjusted depending on the architecture of processor and the application. We discuss time allocation in more detail in Section 7.

4.3 Hash Table Initialization

We use 10 parallel hash tables each indexed with a separate 16-bit code. A hash code is generated by concatenating the quantization ID's of four cells. We randomly choose the cells in a 12×12 window and build the look up tables accordingly. For each possible hash code we compute a rough approximation score using the look-up tables used by Sadeghi and Forsyth [2]. We choose the

20 top categories according to the approximation scores. We perform a score adjustment process to make sure all templates are equally likely to be proposed.

We process the 10 hash tables in a sequence to balance proposals among all locations in case of early termination. If not enough time is available to go through all hash tables, the tables used will cover image locations fairly.

5 Object Scoring

Our proposal generation process provides a separate priority queue for each template. Because the number of proposals is often more than what we afford to process, many proposals cannot be evaluated.

We use a version of Round-Robin algorithm to process priority queues corresponding to different templates. We process one location from each queue in a circular order, handling all queues with equal priority. As soon as one proposal from one queue is done we process an example from the next queue. We continue this process until time is out. Our algorithm is parallelized with OpenMP to harness the power of all processor cores. Each thread in our process is responsible for an equal number of templates. All threads stop when time is up and return their detections. The time required for Non-max suppression (NMS) is also negligible.

We follow the technique presented by Felzenszwalb et al. [3] to process each location. Given a proposal, we first approximate the score of the root template using FTVQ [2]. We then add the approximated score of the first part together with its deformation cost. We continue adding the score of all other parts in a sequence. After we evaluate a part score we may stop and reject the proposal according to a pre-trained threshold.

After computing the approximated scores using FTVQ, we replace the approximated score of the root template and the part templates with their exact score in the same order. Again we may stop the process in each step according to a threshold. If the proposal is able to pass all steps we may report it according to NMS results.

Felzenszwalb et al. [1] and Sadeghi et al. [2] cache part template scores in their implementation to avoid re-computation. Because we operate in a sparse set of locations, the chances that a part template score is re-used at a certain location is small. Therefore we don't cache any scores. We observed that not caching scores could improve speed in our implementation as we need to allocate lower memory so we can utilize hardware cache more effectively.

6 Experimental Results

To evaluate our algorithm we compare it to a set of algorithms that are all based on Deformable Parts Model [1]. We evaluate our algorithm with three frequency settings: 15fps, 30fps and 100fps. We compare the techniques on PASCAL VOC 2007 that is established as a standard baseline.

Table 1. Comparison of different frame rates of our method with two major implementations of Deformable Parts Model: Fast Template evaluation using Vector Quantization (FTVQ) [2] and Deformable Parts Model (DPM) Version 5 [21]. We report per category AP that is computed as the average of precisions at 11 recall rates. Frequency is computed as $\frac{1}{t}$ where t is the time to detect all the 20 PASCAL VOC categories in one image. This time includes features computation time but excludes the time to load the image. We compare the algorithms on PASCAL VOC 2007 challenge that is a standard for benchmarking detection performance. Precision-Recall curves are illustrated in Figure 5.

Method	Ours	Ours	Ours	FTVQ [2]	DPM V5 [21]
Frequency	**100Hz**	**30Hz**	**15Hz**	**2Hz**	**0.07Hz**
aeroplane	0.1630	0.2695	0.3029	0.3320	0.3318
bicycle	0.3563	0.5735	0.5946	0.5933	0.5878
bird	0.0021	0.0909	0.0909	0.1027	0.1019
boat	0.0303	0.0303	0.1141	0.1568	0.1801
bottle	0.0909	0.1938	0.2425	0.2664	0.2535
bus	0.2989	0.4130	0.4720	0.5129	0.5056
car	0.2505	0.4240	0.4996	0.5373	0.5271
cat	0.1368	0.1725	0.1931	0.2251	0.1904
chair	0.0909	0.0909	0.1053	0.2010	0.2046
cow	0.0909	0.1062	0.1994	0.2432	0.2444
diningtable	0.1743	0.2500	0.2510	0.2685	0.2750
dog	0.0507	0.1159	0.1159	0.1260	0.1238
horse	0.2724	0.4735	0.5539	0.5651	0.5709
motorbike	0.2019	0.3850	0.4399	0.4849	0.4838
person	0.1962	0.3736	0.3971	0.4322	0.4327
pottedplant	0.0909	0.1179	0.1129	0.1345	0.1366
sheep	0.0000	0.0909	0.1702	0.2085	0.2154
sofa	0.1208	0.2860	0.3497	0.3568	0.3633
train	0.2801	0.3962	0.4198	0.4520	0.4651
tvmonitor	0.3075	0.3703	0.3840	0.4216	0.3943
mean AP	0.1603	0.2612	0.3004	0.3310	0.3294

We evaluated our algorithm by looking at the detection time and average precision (AP) score with respect to our baseline. We use DPM V5 [21] as our Average Precision baseline that is the most recent and most accurate implementation of DPM. To evaluate the time we compare to [2] that runs nearly two orders of magnitude faster than [21] and is the fastest algorithm before this publication. Our algorithm run on a system with an Intel Xeon E5-1650 processor and 32GB of RAM. Both our proposed algorithm and the baseline utilize all the 6 cores of the CPU at full load.

Our algorithm runs legacy models from DPM V5 [21] that are trained to have 6 root templates per category and 8 parts per root template. Our algorithm doesn't need to train a new model, we build up our model by processing the pre-trained detectors of DPM V5 [21].

We use a separate optimization techniques to speed up each of the stages of [2]. We implemented a highly optimized function to extract HOG features very

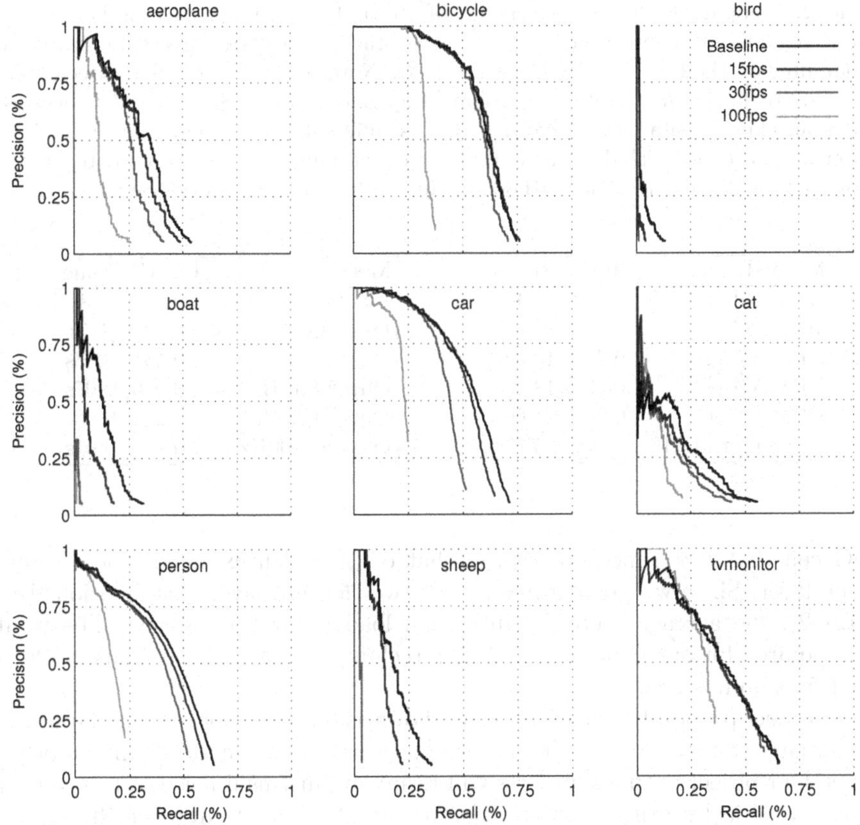

Fig. 5. Precision-Recall curves for 9 objects in PASCAL dataset comparing to the baseline. The black curve (above) corresponds to the accuracy of deformable parts model at regular speed (Table 1). In the blue curve all 20 PASCAL categories are detected at once in a time frame of 67ms (15fps). In the red curve all 20 PASCAL categories are detected at once in a time frame of 33ms (30fps). In the green curve all 20 PASCAL categories are detected at once in a time frame of 10ms (100fps). For all precision recall curves a threshold is chosen so each PR curve would cover precision > 0.05. In practical applications often one working point is chosen in the high precision area. Note that the gap between the curves in the high precision are tiny within the red, the blue and the black curves. This means in applications where a high precision working point is set, the loss is less noticeable. Note that the green curve fails to produce any detections for bird, boat and sheep categories. More information about APs can be found in Table 1.

quickly. Our implementation uses AVX vector operations and multiple cores. It is also optimized to utilizes CPU cache carefully. We also limit the number of layers to extract HOG features by a factor of 5. These optimizations together speed up HOG feature computation from 40ms in [2] to an average of 4ms.

We use a hierarchical clustering process to vector quantize HOG features (Section 3). Our hierarchical algorithm examines two sets of 16 clusters per

Table 2. Comparison of various versions of DPM [1]. The reported time here is the time to complete the detection of 20 categories starting from raw image. Performance is computed on the PASCAL VOC 2007 dataset. Note that our method is three orders of magnitude faster than that of the original implementation. HSC [19] is slow because it uses an experimental set of features that is different than HOG. The method by Yan et al. [23] is not included in the table as its running time (0.22s per category) is reported on a single core. The methods in this table run 20 categories on six cores.

Method	mAP	time
HSC [19]	0.343	180s
WTA [14]	0.240	26s
DPM V5 [21]	0.330	13.3s
DPM V4 [20]	0.301	13.2s
DPM V3 [1]	0.268	11.6s
Vedaldi et al. [16]	0.277	7s

Method	mAP	time
FFLD [11]	0.323	1.8s
DPM Cascade [3]	0.331	1.7s
FTVQ [2]	0.331	0.53s
Ours at 15Hz	0.300	0.07s
Ours at 30Hz	0.261	0.03s
Ours at 100Hz	0.160	0.01s

HOG cell that is 8 times lower than that of [2] which examines 256 clusters in one layer. Since we process five times fewer feature layers (as mentioned in Section2), the average vector quantization load is further reduced. The total time required for our vector quantization technique is down from 70ms in [2] to about 5ms on average.

Our object proposal stage (Section 4) allows us to process only a small fraction of templates at each location. It can terminate early to acomodate time for other stages. Our object proposal process will terminate in 7ms if it is not terminated early. Our object scoring stage (Section 5) can also operate in a specified time-frame. On average it takes about 1.2μs to process one location for one category (including root and part scores). This algorithm processes as many locations as it affords in the specified time-frame. In the fastest case it can run at 100Hz. In this speed our algorithm affords to process only one location per root template (For PASCAL 2007 we have 1200 root templates that is 20 categories $\times 6$ components $\times 5$ scales).

Our implementation is very fast and light-weight. The code is implemented in C++ but can be called from MATLAB. Our algorithm can process an image to detect 20 pascal categories simultaneously at 30fps or faster. It can further trade off accuracy for time; it can run at 100Hz while detecting 20 PASCAL categories in a time frame of 10ms. It also requires less than 10MB of memory at its peak demand to process an image for 20 categories (PASCAL Images are mostly 350×500 pixels large). This is three orders of magnitude faster than the original DPM V5 [21] implementation that itself is highly optimized.

Table 1 compares our algorithm with two established baselines. Our algorithm achieves 30Hz with an mAP of 0.26. At 15Hz, its mAP is 0.30; and at 100 Hz, its mAP is 0.16. Frequency is computed as $\frac{1}{t}$ where t is the time to detect all the 20 PASCAL VOC categories together in one image. This time includes features computation time but excludes the time to load image. We exclude the time to load the image because the time highly depends on the media.

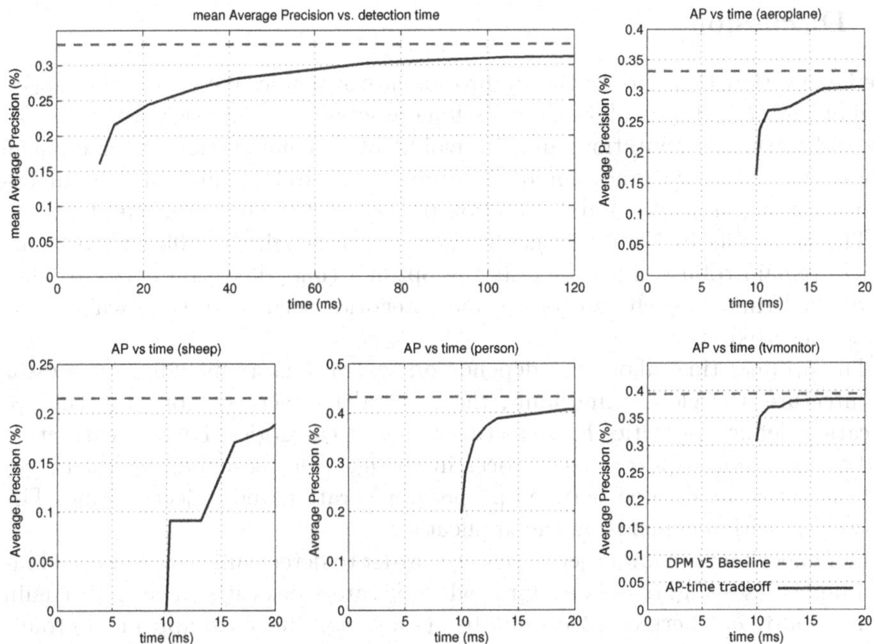

Fig. 6. Our method operates within a time limit specified by the user. It can jointly detect the entire set of PASCAL VOC challenge categories in about 10ms, that is about 0.5ms per category. The top-left plot shows the trade-off between operation time-frame and mean Average Precision (mAP) of the 20 PASCAL categories. In this setting all 20 objects are detected jointly within the time-frame. The rest of the plots show that this trade-off for detecting a single category. In this setting only one category is detected within the time-frame. Note that different categories respond differently to the time-limit. The Sheep detector fails at 100fps while the tvmonitor detector remains robust. The red dashed line shows DPM V5 [21] baseline while the solid blue curve shows Average Precision vs. time trade-off.

Precision-Recall curves for our experiments are illustrated in Figure 5. Note that the gap between the curves in the high precision area in tiny between the red, the blue and the black curves. This is very important in practical applications as they often consider false positives costly and work in high precision regimes.

Table 2 compares our algorithm to several variations of DPM in terms of speed and accuracy. We report running time to detect all 20 PASCAL categories from raw image. We also compare our mean Average Precision to other techniques. In this table we compared to only algorithms that run on CPU. The fastest algorithm on GPU is Vanilla DPM [22] that runs at about 1Hz to detect the 20 PASCAL categories in a 640×480 image. It cannot sacrifice accuracy for speed.

Our algorithm can trade off accuracy for speed. Figure 6 illustrates the trade-off for both detecting all objects jointly and also detecting only a single object. This figure shows some detectors fail at 100fps while some others remain robust.

7 Discussion

We believe that there are further improvements available. We expect that speed could be improved by exploring our hashing process to: (a) interleave image loading and feature computation; and (b) avoid feature computation at some image blocks. We expect accuracy could be improved by careful tuning of time allocation (a) between proposal and detection process and (b) between templates.

The trade-offs in Figure 6 shows some detectors fail at 100fps while some others remain robust. This suggests the optimal time allocation is not to allocate equal time to each category; some categories need more time while some categories need less.

The optimal time allocation depends on several factors including: processor architecture, the global time limit, the demand by each category and the application defined priorities for detecting different categories. Feature extraction and quantization require a fixed processing budget. Our design allows the rest of the budget to be divided between proposal generation and object scoring. The optimal partition depends on the application.

Our experiments show objects that are harder to detect suffer more with a limited budget (see Figure 5, boat, bird) whereas categories with higher AP remain more robust. Furthermore, Certain objects are more likely to appear in groups (e.g. sheep, person) so they are more sensitive to limiting the number of locations to process. The study of optimal process allocation in different situations requires an extensive study that doesn't fit into the context of this paper.

Our trade-off allows for any speed improvement technique to directly result in accuracy improvement. The choice of working point in speed-accuracy trade-off allows for further data such as video or depth to be used for speed or accuracy.

References

1. Felzenszwalb, P.F., Girshick, R.B., McAllester, D., Ramanan, D.: Object Detection with Discriminatively Trained Part Based Models. IEEE Transactions on Pattern Analysis and Machine Intelligence (2010)
2. Sadeghi, M.A., Forsyth, D.: Fast Template Evaluation with Vector Quantization. In: Advances in Neural Information Processing Systems, NIPS (2013)
3. Felzenszwalb, P.F., Girshick, R.B., McAllester, D.: Cascade Object Detection with Deformable Part Models. In: IEEE Conference on Computer Vision and Pattern Recognition (2010)
4. Dollár, P., Appel, R., Belongie, S., Perona, P.: Fast Feature Pyramids for Object Detection In. IEEE Transactions on Pattern Analysis and Machine Intelligence (2014)
5. Dalal, N., Triggs, B.: Histograms of oriented gradients for human detection. In: IEEE Conference on Computer Vision and Pattern Recognition (2005)
6. Endres, I., Hoiem, D.: Category Independent Object Proposals. In: Daniilidis, K., Maragos, P., Paragios, N. (eds.) ECCV 2010, Part V. LNCS, vol. 6315, pp. 575–588. Springer, Heidelberg (2010)
7. Cheng, M., Zhang, Z., Lin, W., Torr, P.: Bing: Binarized Normed Gradients for Objectness Estimation at 300fps. In: IEEE Conference on Computer Vision and Pattern Recognition (2014)

8. Nister, D., Stewenius, H.: Scalable Recognition with a Vocabulary Tree. In: IEEE Conference on Computer Vision and Pattern Recognition (2006)
9. Pirsiavash, H., Ramanan, D.: Steerable part models. In: IEEE Conference on Computer Vision and Pattern Recognition (2012)
10. Dollár, P., Appel, R., Kienzle, W.: Crosstalk Cascades for Frame-Rate Pedestrian Detection. In: Fitzgibbon, A., Lazebnik, S., Perona, P., Sato, Y., Schmid, C. (eds.) ECCV 2012, Part II. LNCS, vol. 7573, pp. 645–659. Springer, Heidelberg (2012)
11. Dubout, C., Fleuret, F.: Exact Acceleration of Linear Object Detectors. In: Fitzgibbon, A., Lazebnik, S., Perona, P., Sato, Y., Schmid, C. (eds.) ECCV 2012, Part III. LNCS, vol. 7574, pp. 301–311. Springer, Heidelberg (2012)
12. Pedersoli, M., Gonzàlez, J., Bagdanov, A.D., Villanueva, J.J.: Recursive Coarse-to-Fine Localization for Fast Object Detection. In: Daniilidis, K., Maragos, P., Paragios, N. (eds.) ECCV 2010, Part VI. LNCS, vol. 6316, pp. 280–293. Springer, Heidelberg (2010)
13. Kokkinos, I.: Bounding Part Scores for Rapid Detection with Deformable Part Models. In: Fusiello, A., Murino, V., Cucchiara, R. (eds.) ECCV 2012 Ws/Demos, Part III. LNCS, vol. 7585, pp. 41–50. Springer, Heidelberg (2012)
14. Dean, T., Ruzon, M., Segal, M., Shlens, J., Vijayanarasimhan, S., Yagnik, J.: Fast, Accurate Detection of 100,000 Object Classes on a Single Machine. In: IEEE Conference on Computer Vision and Pattern Recognition (2013)
15. Indyk, P., Motwani, R.: Approximate nearest neighbours: Towards removing the curse of dimensionality. In: ACM Symposium on Theory of Computing (1998)
16. Vedaldi, A., Zisserman, A.: Sparse Kernel Approximations for Efficient Classification and Detection. In: IEEE Conference on Computer Vision and Pattern Recognition (2012)
17. Jgou, H., Douze, M., Schmid, C.: Product quantization for nearest neighbour search. IEEE Transactions on Pattern Analysis and Machine Intelligence (2010)
18. Gray, R.M., Neuhoff, D.L.: Quantization. IEEE Transactions on Information Theory (1998)
19. Ren, X., Ramanan, D.: Histograms of Sparse Codes for Object Detection. In: IEEE Conference on Computer Vision and Pattern Recognition (2013)
20. Felzenszwalb, P., Girshick, R., McAllester, D.: Discriminatively Trained Deformable Part Models, Release 4, `http://people.cs.uchicago.edu/pff/latent-release4/`
21. Girshick, R., Felzenszwalb, P., McAllester, D.: Discriminatively Trained Deformable Part Models, Release 5, `http://people.cs.uchicago.edu/rbg/latent-release5/`
22. Song, H.O., Zickler, S., Althoff, T., Girshick, R., Fritz, M., Geyer, C., Felzenszwalb, P., Darrell, T.: Sparselet Models for Efficient Multiclass Object Detection. In: Fitzgibbon, A., Lazebnik, S., Perona, P., Sato, Y., Schmid, C. (eds.) ECCV 2012, Part II. LNCS, vol. 7573, pp. 802–815. Springer, Heidelberg (2012)
23. Yan, J., Lei, Z., Wen, L., Li, S.Z.: The Fastest Deformable Part Model for Object Detection. In: IEEE Conference on Computer Vision and Pattern Recognition (2014)
24. Bengio, S., Weston, J., Grangier, D.: Label embedding trees for large multi-class tasks. In: Advances in Neural Information Processing Systems (2010)
25. Benenson, R., Mathias, M., Timofte, R., Van Gool, L.: Pedestrian detection at 100 frames per second. In: IEEE Conference on Computer Vision and Pattern Recognition (2012)

Knowing a Good HOG Filter When You See It: Efficient Selection of Filters for Detection

Ejaz Ahmed[1,*], Gregory Shakhnarovich[2], and Subhransu Maji[3]

[1] University of Maryland, College Park, USA
ejaz@umd.edu
[2] Toyota Technological Institute at Chicago, USA
greg@ttic.edu
[3] University of Massachusetts, Amherst, USA
smaji@cs.umass.edu

Abstract. Collections of filters based on histograms of oriented gradients (HOG) are common for several detection methods, notably, poselets and exemplar SVMs. The main bottleneck in training such systems is the selection of a subset of good filters from a large number of possible choices. We show that one can learn a universal model of part "goodness" based on properties that can be computed from the filter itself. The intuition is that good filters across categories exhibit common traits such as, low clutter and gradients that are spatially correlated. This allows us to quickly discard filters that are not promising thereby speeding up the training procedure. Applied to training the poselet model, our automated selection procedure allows us to improve its detection performance on the PASCAL VOC data sets, while speeding up training by an *order of magnitude*. Similar results are reported for exemplar SVMs.

1 Introduction

A common approach to modeling a visual category is to represent it as a mixture of appearance models. These mixtures could be part-based, such as those in poselets [1,2], and deformable part-based models [3], or defined globally, such as those in exemplar SVMs [4]. Histograms of oriented gradient (HOG) [5] features are often used to model the appearance of a single component of these mixtures. Details on how these mixture components are defined, and discovered, vary across methods; in this paper our focus is on a common architecture where a pool of candidate HOG filters is generated from instances of the category, and perhaps some negative examples, followed by a selection stage in which filters are, often in a greedy fashion, selected based on their incremental contribution to the detection performance.

The candidate generation step is, typically, at most moderately expensive. The selection stage, however, requires an expensive process of evaluating each candidate on a large set of positive and negative examples. There are two sources of inefficiency in this: (i) **Redundancy**, as many of the candidates are highly similar to each other, since

* This author was partially supported by a MURI from the Office of Naval Research under Grant N00014-10-1-0934.

D. Fleet et al. (Eds.): ECCV 2014, Part I, LNCS 8689, pp. 80–94, 2014.
© Springer International Publishing Switzerland 2014

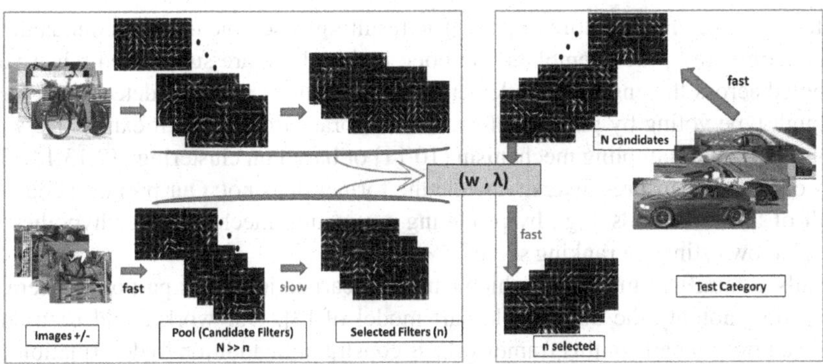

Fig. 1. Outline of our approach: Left block shows the training pipeline which is used to obtain a linear ranker (**w**) and diversity tradeoff parameter λ (described in Sect. 3) on a set of categories. Our system improves the bottleneck of the selection procedure by learning to predict the utility of filters for a new category.

the generation process is driven by frequency of keypoint configurations for poselets, of examples for exemplar SVMs; (ii) **Noise**, as many of the candidates are not discriminative, not localizable (e.g., due to aperture effect) or not repeatable.

In this paper we address both of these inefficiencies, and propose a method that automatically selects from a large pool of filters generated for a category, a small subset that is likely to contain non-redundant discriminative ones. We do this by learning to predict relative discriminative value (quality rank) of a filter from its intrinsic properties, and by combining the ranking scores with a diversity-inducing penalty on inter-filter similarity. Fig. 1 shows an overview of our approach.

The components of this automatic selection mechanism, once learned on a set of categories, can be applied to a novel target category. In that sense, it is a category-independent method for part selection. Of course, some information about the target category enters the process in the form of candidate parts, and our method can not "hallucinate" them from scratch; but it can rank them, as we show in our experiments, as accurately as a direct evaluation on thousands of examples for the category.

As its main contribution, this paper offers a practical way to speed up training detection architectures based on poselets, and exemplar SVMs, by an order of magnitude, with no loss, and in fact sometimes a moderate gain, in detection performance. This eliminates a significant computational bottleneck, as computer vision advances towards the goal of detecting thousands of categories [6]. As an additional contribution, our ranking-with-diversity approach may provide insight into what makes a good filter for object detection, with implications for design of part-based models and in descriptors and interest operators.

1.1 Related Work

The most relevant body of work that uses part generation and selection for building detectors is the poselet model [1,2,7] which forms the basis for our work and which we review in detail in the next section. Alternative methods for generating part libraries/ensembles include exemplar SVMs [4], where every positive example leads to a detector (typically for an entire object). The resulting ensemble is very redundant, and may contain many poor exemplars; the hope is that these are suppressed when votes are pooled across the ensemble at detection time. In many methods detection is based on Hough-type voting by part detectors, with a library of parts built exhaustively [8], randomly [9], by a sampling mechanism [10,11] or based on clustering [12,13,14]. The latter construction ensures diversity, while the former does not. Our proposal could affect all of these methods, e.g., by providing a rejection mechanism for hypothesized parts with low estimated ranking score.

Finally, a family of models in which parts are learned jointly as part of a generative model, most notably the deformable part model of [3]. Our work could be used to provide a prior on parts in this framework, as constraint in addition to deformation cost already in the model.

There has been relatively little work on predictive measures for part or filter quality. Most notably, in [15] and [16] a structured prior for HOG filters is intended to capture spatial structure typical of discriminative image regions. [15] is the work closest to ours in spirit, and we evaluate it in our experiments. Our results show that while this "structured norm" approach is helpful, additional features that we introduce further improve our ability to distinguish good filters from bad ones.

2 Background

We are interested in a sliding window approach to detection [5,2] in which an object template is specified by a filter $\mathbf{f}$. An image subwindow is represented by its feature vector $\mathbf{x}$ and is scored by the inner product $\mathbf{f}^T\mathbf{x}$. Feature vector $\mathbf{x}$ is computed by spatially dividing the subwindow to $m \times n$ cells and computing a histogram of oriented gradients for each cell. Feature vector consists of cell-level features, $\mathbf{x} = [\mathbf{x_1}; \mathbf{x_2}; \ldots; \mathbf{x_{mn}}] \in \mathbb{R}^{mnd}$, where $\forall c \in \{1, \ldots, mn\}, \mathbf{x}_c \in \mathbb{R}^d$ and d is the dimension of the cell-level features. In the same way model parameter can be broken down into $\mathbf{f} = [f_1; f_2; \ldots; f_{mn}] \in \mathbb{R}^{mnd}$. The template $\mathbf{f}$ is learned from labeled training set $\mathcal{X}, \mathcal{Y} = \{(x^{(i)}, y^{(i)})\}_{i=1}^N$ by training a linear classifier, for instance by an SVM (we refer to such filters as SVM filters) or by a linear discriminant analysis (LDA filters).

We consider the category-level transfer settings: having learned filters for (training) categories $g = 1, \ldots, G$ we want to predict filter quality for a new (test) category $G+1$. Our pipeline is outlined in Fig. 1. For each training category g, we start by constructing a pool of N candidate filters $\{\mathbf{f}_{g,i}\}$. Then we train a model which includes only $n \ll N$ parts. Once the models are fully trained, we can in hindsight look at the initial set of N parts and the selected set of n for each category. We train a ranking function with the objective to reproduce the order of filter quality. Furthermore, we tune a weight which controls tradeoff between estimated rank of a filter and the diversity it adds; we want to discourage adding a part similar to the ones already selected, even if this part is highly ranked. The objective in tuning the diversity tradeoff is to as closely as possible reproduce the selection of n out of N filters done by the expensive full process.

For the test category, we construct the pool of N candidate filters $\{\mathbf{f}_{g+1,i}\}$ in the same process as for training categories. This stage is typically inexpensive, especially using the LDA method (Sect. 3.4). Then, we apply the learned ranker function to order

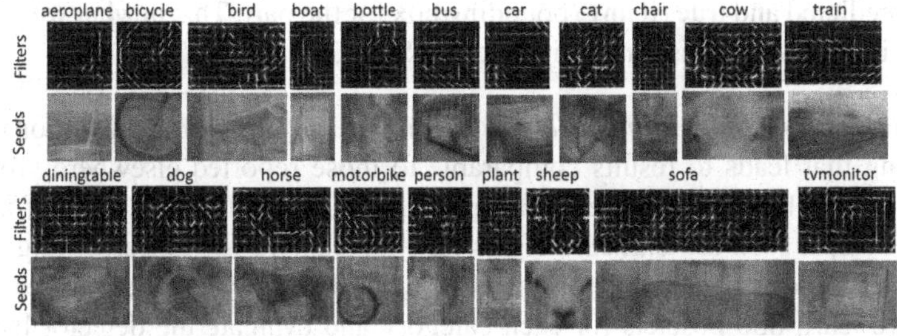

Fig. 2. Poselet filters and the average of 10 nearest examples to its seed for various categories

the candidate parts according to their estimated relative quality. Finally, we combine suitably normalized relative scores with a diversity term tuned on training categories, and select a set of n estimated high quality candidates by a greedy procedure. This small set is used to train the full model. Thus, the expensive stage only includes n parts, instead of N. In our experiments these steps are done as part of training a poselet model [2,1], or exemplar SVMs [4]. We briefly describe the two models below.

2.1 An Overview of Poselets for Object Detection

Poselets [1,2] are semantically aligned discriminative patterns that capture parts of objects at a fixed pose and viewpoint. For person these include frontal faces, upper bodies, or side facing pedestrians; for bicycles these include side views of front wheels, etc. These patterns are *discovered* from the data using a combination of supervision in the form of landmark annotations, discriminative filter training, and a selection procedure that selects a subset of these patterns.

In more detail, each poselet is trained to detect a stable and repeatable configuration of a subset of landmarks ("part") using HOG features and linear SVMs. This step is identical to pipelines typically used for training object detectors such as [5]. Technically, a poselet filter is obtained by randomly sampling a *seed* window covering a subset of landmarks in a positive example, then a list of matching windows, sorted by the alignment error of the landmarks (up to a similarity transform to the landmarks within the seed) is obtained. Top examples on the list (3% in our implementation) along with some negative examples are used to retrain the HOG filter, which is retained as a poselet detector. Fig. 2 shows examples of HOG filters, along with visualization of the average of the top 10 matching examples used to train them.

Some of the resulting poselet detectors may not be discriminative. For instance, limb detectors are often confused by parallel lines. Some others, e.g., detectors of faces and upper bodies, are more discriminative. In order to identify the set of discriminative poselets, they are evaluated as *part detectors* on the entire training set, and a subset is selected using a 'greedy coverage algorithm' that iteratively picks poselets that offer highest increase in detection accuracy at a fixed false positive rate. We can compute the detection average precision (AP) of each poselet independently, by looking at overlap between predicted and true (if any) bounding box for the part. This is what we will learn to predict in our using a discriminative ranker (Sect. 3).

Our poselet training and testing baseline. We use an in-house implementation of poselets training that leads to results comparable to those reported elsewhere. To isolate the effect of poselet selection, we use a simplified model that avoids some of the post-processing steps, such as, learned weights for poselets (we use uniform weights), and higher-order Q-poselet models (we use q-poselets, i.e., raw detection score). During training we learn 800 poselets for each category and evaluate the detector by selecting 100 poselets. Our models achieve a mean AP (MAP) of 29.0% across 20 categories of the PASCAL VOC 2007 *test* set. This is consistent with the full-blown model that achieves 32.5% MAP. The combination of Q-poselets, and learned weights per poselet, typically lead to a gain of 3% across categories. Our baseline implementation is quite competitive to existing models that use HOG features and linear SVMs, such as, the Dalal & Triggs detector (9.7%), exemplar SVMs (22.7%) [4] and DPM (33.7%). These scores are without inter-object context re-scoring, or any other post-processing.

Breakdown of the training time. Our implementation takes 20 hours to train a single model on a 6-core modern machine. About 24% of the time is spent in the initial poselet training, i.e., linear classifiers for each detector. The rest 76% of the time is spent on poselet selection, an overwhelming majority of which is spent on evaluating the 800 poselets on the training data. The actual selection, calibration and construction of the models takes less than 0.05% of the time.

2.2 An Overview of Exemplar SVMs for Object Detection

Exemplar SVMs [4] is a method for category representation where each positive example of a category is used to learn a HOG filter that discriminates the positive example from background instances. Thus, the number of exemplar SVMs for a given category is equal to the number of positive examples in the category, similar in the spirit to a nearest neighbor classifier. At test time each of these SVMs are run as detectors, i.e., using a multi-scale scanning window method, and the activations are collected. Overall detections are obtained by pooling spatially consistent set of activations from multiple exemplars within an image.

By design, the exemplars are likely to be highly redundant since several examples within a category are likely to be very similar to one another. Hence, a good model may be obtained by considering only a subset of the exemplars. Experimentally, we found that using only 100 best exemplars (based on the learned weights of the full model), a small fraction of the total, we obtain a performance of MAP $= 21.89\%$, compared to MAP $= 22.65\%$. We use publicly available models [1] for our experiments, and report results using **E-SVM + Co-occ** method reported in [4].

The training time scales linearly with the number of exemplars in the model. Hence, we would save significantly in training time we could quickly select a small set of relevant exemplars. We describe the details of the experimental setup in Sect. 5.

[1] `https://github.com/quantombone/exemplarsvm`

3 Ranking and Diversity

One could attempt to predict the AP value of a filter, or some other direct measure of filter's quality, directly in a regression settings. However this is unlikely to work[2] due to a number of factors: noisy estimates of AP on training filters/categories, systemic differences across categories (some are harder than others, and thus have consistently lower performing parts), etc.

3.1 Learning to Rank Parts

Our approach instead is to train a scoring function. Given a feature representation of a part, this function produces a value (score) taken to represent the quality of the filter. Ordering a set of filters by their scores determines the predicted ranking of their quality; note that the scores themselves are not important, only their relative values are.

Let $\phi(\mathbf{f})$ be a representation of a filter $\mathbf{f}$ in terms of its *intrinsic features*; we describe the choice of ϕ in Sect. 3.3. We model the ranking score of f by a linear function $\langle \mathbf{w}, \phi(\mathbf{f}) \rangle$. The training data consists of a set of filters $\{\mathbf{f}_{g,i}\}$ for $g = 1, \ldots, G$ (training categories) and $i = 1, \ldots, N$, where N is the number of filters per category (assumed for simplicity of notation to be the same for all categories). For each $\mathbf{f}_{g,i}$ we have the estimated quality $y_{g,i}$ measured by the explicit (expensive) procedure on the training data of the respective categories. Let $\mathbf{f}_{g,i}$ be ordered by descending values of $y_{g,i}$. For $i > j$, we denote $\Delta_{g,i,j} \doteq y_{g,i} - y_{g,j}$; this measures how much better $\mathbf{f}_{g,i}$ is than $\mathbf{f}_{g,j}$.

We train the ranking parameters $\mathbf{w}$ to minimize the large margin ranking objective

$$\min_{\mathbf{w}} \frac{1}{2}\|\mathbf{w}\|^2 + C \sum_{g=1}^{G} \sum_{i=1}^{N-1} \sum_{j=i+1}^{N} \left[1 - \langle \mathbf{w}, \delta\phi_{g,i,j} \rangle\right]_+ \Delta_{g,i,j} \tag{1}$$

where $\delta\phi_{g,i,j} \doteq \phi(\mathbf{f}_{g,i}) - \phi(\mathbf{f}_{g,j})$. and $[\cdot]_+$ is the hinge at 0. The value C determines the tradeoff between regularization penalty on $\mathbf{w}$ and the empirical ranking hinge loss. Additionally, per-example scaling by $\Delta_{g,i,j}$ is applied only to pairs on which the ranking makes mistakes; this is known as slack rescaled[3] hinge loss [17]. We minimize (1) in the primal, using conjugate gradient descent [19].

3.2 Selecting a Diverse Set of Parts

A set of parts that are good for detection should be individually good and complementary. We can cast this as a maximization problem. Let $x_i \in \{0, 1\}$, $i \in \{1, \ldots, N\}$, denote the indicator variable that part i is selected. Let $\widehat{y}_i$ denote the (estimated) score of part i, and A_{ij} denote the similarity between parts i, j; we defer the details of evaluating A_{ij} until later. Then the problem of selecting n parts can be cast as:

$$\max_{\mathbf{x} \in \{0,1\}^N, \sum_i x_i = n} \sum_i \widehat{y}_i x_i - \lambda \sum_i \max_{j \neq i} A_{ij} x_i x_j. \tag{2}$$

[2] And indeed did poorly in our early experiments.

[3] In our experiments slack rescaling performed better than margin rescaling, consistent with results reported elsewhere [17,18].

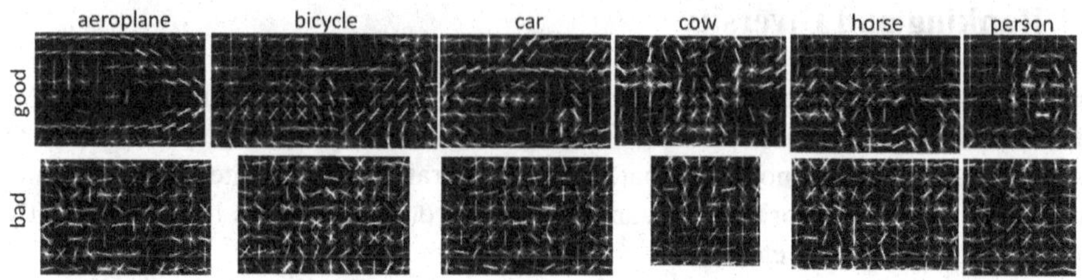

Fig. 3. Examples of good and bad filters from the poselets model. Good filters exhibit less clutter, and stronger correlations among nearby spatial locations, than bad ones.

This is a submodular function, which can be made monotone by additive shift in the values of $\widehat{y}$. For such functions, although exact maximization of this function subject to cardinaty constraint $\sum x_i = n$ is intractable, the simple greedy agorithm described below is known [20] to provide near-optimal solution, and to work well in practice.

First part selected is $\operatorname{argmax}_i \widehat{y}_i$. Now, suppose we have selected t parts, without loss of generality let those be $1, \ldots, t$. Then, we select the next part as

$$\underset{i}{\operatorname{argmax}} \left\{ \widehat{y}_i - \lambda \max_{j=1,\ldots,t} A_{i,j} \right\}.$$

We can further relax the diversity term, by replacing the max with the k-th order value of similarity between candidate part and those already selected. For instance, if $k = 10$, we select the first ten parts based on scores $\widehat{y}$ only, and then start penalizing candidates by the tenth highest value of similarity to selected parts. Suppose this value is σ; this means that ten parts already selected are similar to the candidate by *at least* σ. This makes it less likely that we will reject a good part because a single other part we selected is somewhat similar to it.

3.3 Features for Part Ranking

Recall that filter $\mathbf{f}$ is considered to be good if during prediction it does not confuse between a negative sub-window and a sub-window belonging to the object class. Or in other words it results in high average precision for that object/part/poselet. Fig. 3 shows some examples of good and bad filters. We propose to capture the properties of a good filter by considering various low level features that can be computed from the filter itself which are described below.

- *Norm:* The first feature we consider is the ℓ_2-norm of the filter $\sqrt{\mathbf{f}^T\mathbf{f}}$. Intuitively, high norm of filter weights is consistent with high degree of alignment of positive windows similar to the seed that initiated the part, and may indicate a good part.
- *Normalized norm:* The norm is not invariant to the filter dimension $(m \times n)$, which may vary across filters. Therefore we introduce *normalized norm* $\sqrt{\mathbf{f}^T\mathbf{f}}/(mn)$.
- *Cell covariance:* For good filters, the activations of different gradient orientation bins within a cell are highly structured. Neighboring gradient orientation bins are active simultaneously and majority of them are entirely suppressed. This is because the template has to account for small variations in local gradient directions in order to be robust, and if a certain gradient orientation is encouraged, its orthogonal

counterpart is often penalized. For each filter $\mathbf{f} \in \mathbb{R}^{mnd}$, a $d \times d$ feature vector is obtained which captures average covariance of the filter weights within a cell.

- *Cell cross-covariance:* Similarly, there is also a strong correlation between filter weights in nearby spatial locations. Dominant orientations of neighboring cells tend to coincide to form lines, curves, corners, and parallel structures. This could be attributed to the fact that the template has to be robust to small spatial variations in alignment of training samples, and that contours of objects often exhibit such traits. We model 4 types of features: cross-covariance between pairs of cells that are (a) horizontal (b) vertical, (c) diagonal 1 ($+45°$), and (d) diagonal 2 ($-45°$). This leads to a $4d \times d$ dimensional feature vector.

Our covariance features are inspired by [15] who used them in a generative model of filters that served as a prior for learning filters from few examples. In contrast, we use these features in a discriminative framework for selecting good filters. Our experiments suggests that the discriminative ranker outperforms the generative model (Sect. 4).

3.4 The LDA Acceleration

Instead of ranking SVM filters, one can also learn to rank the filters that are obtained using linear discriminant analysis (LDA) instead [21]. The key advantage is that this can be computed efficiently in closed form as $\mathbf{\Sigma}^{-1}(\boldsymbol{\mu}_+ - \boldsymbol{\mu}_-)$, where $\mathbf{\Sigma}$ is a covariance matrix of HOG features computed on a large set of images, and $\boldsymbol{\mu}_+$ and $\boldsymbol{\mu}_-$ are the mean positive and negative features respectively. The parameters $\mathbf{\Sigma}$ and $\boldsymbol{\mu}_-$ need to be estimated once for all classes. *In our experiments the LDA filter by itself did not perform very well.* The LDA based detector with poselets was 10% worse in AP on bicycles, but we found that the performance of the LDA filters and that of the SVM filters are highly correlated. If the selection is effective using the LDA filters we can train the expensive SVM filters only for the selected poselets, providing a further acceleration in training time. We consider additional baseline where the ranker is trained on the LDA filters instead of the SVM filters in our experiments.

4 Experiments with Poselets

We perform our poselet selection on the models described in Sect. 2.1. For each category we have a set of 800 poselets, each with learned HOG filter trained with a SVM classifier, and its detection AP computed on the training set. We evaluate our selection in a *leave-one-out* manner – for a given category the goal is to select a subset (say of size 100) out of all the poselets by training a ranker on the remaining categories. The code can be downloaded from our project page[4].

We compare the various selection algorithms in two different settings. The first is **ranking task** where algorithms are evaluated by comparing the *predicted ranking* of poselets to the *true ranking* according to their AP. We report overlaps at different depths of the lists to measure the quality. In addition, we also evaluate the selected poselets in the **detection task**, by constructing a detector out of the selected poselets and evaluating it on the PASCAL VOC 2007 *test* set. All the poselets are trained on the PASCAL VOC

[4] `http://www.umiacs.umd.edu/~ejaz/goodParts/`

2010 *trainval* set for which the keypoint annotations are publicly available, and the images in our training set are disjoint from the test set.

4.1 Training the Ranking Algorithm

As described in Sect. 3.1 for each category we train a ranking algorithm that learns to order the poselets from the remaining 19 categories according to their detection AP. We normalize the APs of each class by dividing by maximum for that category to make them comparable across categories. Note that this does not change the relative ordering of poselets within a class.

The learning is done according to 1. From the pool of all the poselet filters (19×800) we generate ordering constraints for pairs of poselets i, j for which $\Delta_{c,i,j} > 0.05$; this significantly reduces computation with negligible effect on the objective.[5] The cost of reversing the constraint is set proportional to the difference of the APs of the pair under consideration. The constant of proportionality C in Eqn. 1 is set using cross-validation. We consider values ranging from 10^{-13} to 10^{3}. As a criteria for cross-validation we check for ranking on the held-out set. We consider the ranked list at depth one fourth of the number of samples in the held-out set. The cross-validation score is computed as follows, $\frac{list_{predicted} \cap list_{actual}}{list_{predicted} \cup list_{actual}}$, and set using 3 fold cross validation. Note, that at any stage of the learning, the filters for the target class are not used.

4.2 Training the Diversity Model

The actual set of filters selected by the poselet model is not simply the top performing poselets, instead they are selected greedily based on highest incremental gain in detection AP. We can model this effect by encouraging diversity among the selected poselets as described in Sect 3.2. To do so, we first need a model of similarity between poselets. In our experiments we use a simple notion of similarity that is based on the overlap of their training examples. Note that poselets use keypoint annotations to find similar examples and provide an ordering of the training instances. For two different poselets i, j we compute the overlap of the top $r = 3\%$ (which is used for training the filters) of the ordered list of training examples Top_i and Top_j to compute the similarity, i.e., $A_{ij} = \frac{Top_i \cap Top_j}{Top_i \cup Top_j}$. We ignore the actual filter location and simply consider the overlap between indices of training examples used. More sophisticated, but slower, versions of similarity may include computing the responses of a filter on the training examples of another.

The only parameter that remains is the term λ (Eqn. 3.2) controlling the tradeoff between diversity and estimated AP rank. We tune it by cross-validation. Note that unlike the previous setting for ranking where we learn to match the AP scores, here we train the diversity parameter λ to match the set of "poselets" that were *actually picked* by the poselet training algorithm. This process closely approximates the true diversity based selection algorithm. For each category, we pick a λ that matches the predicted list of other categories best on average. In practice, we found λ to be very similar across categories.

4.3 Selection Methods Considered

Below are the methods we consider for various ranking and detection tasks in the poselets framework:

[5] The results are not sensitive to the choice of threshold on Δ.

- `Oracle` - poselets ordered using the poselet selection algorithm (Sect 2.1).
- `10%` - only 10% of the training images are used for poselet selection.
- `Random` - select a random subset of poselets.
- `Norm(svm)` - poselets ordered in descending order of ℓ_2-norm of their SVM filter.
- Σ-`Norm(svm)` - poselets ordered in descending order on SVM filters, according to $\mathbf{f}^T(\mathbf{I} - \lambda_\mathbf{s}\mathbf{\Sigma}_s)\mathbf{f}$, where λ_s is set such that the largest eigenvalue of $\lambda_s\mathbf{\Sigma}_s = 0.9$ as defined in [15]. We construct $\mathbf{\Sigma}_s$ from top 30 filters (according to AP) from each category to create a model of a good filter. While constructing $\mathbf{\Sigma}_s$ for one category we consider all the other category's filters.
- `Rank(svm)` - poselets ordered according to the score of the ranker trained on the SVM filters (Sect. 4.1).
- `Rank(lda)` - poselets ordered according to the score of the ranker trained on LDA filters (Sect 3.4).

In addition we consider variants with diversity term added (Sect. 4.2), which is shown as $+$ `Div` appended to the end of the method name.

4.4 Ranking Results

Tab. 1 displays the performance of various ranking methods on the ranking task. Ranked list was looked at various depths (top 50, 100 etc.) and its overlap was found with top 100 poselets in the groundtruth ranking (i.e. ranking according to actual AP, Sec. 2). Table shows number of poselets in top 100 groundtruth by considering various depths in the ranked list, averaged across categories. Note that `Rank(svm)` performs best at all the depths considered, and is closely matched by ranking using the LDA filter `Rank(lda)`. It is worth noting that the ranking task is a proxy for the real task (detection). In the next section we examine how the differences (some of them minor) between methods in Table 1 translate to difference in detection accuracy.

4.5 PASCAL VOC Detection Results

Tab. 2 summarizes the accuracy of the detectors, reported as the mean average precision (`MAP`) across the 20 categories using the model constructed from the top 100 poselets using various algorithms. We also report the speedups and relative `MAP` (δ`MAP` $=$ `MAP` $-$ $\texttt{MAP}_{\texttt{oracle}}$), that various methods can provide over the actual implementation for training model consisting of 100 poselets from a pool of 800 poselets.

Table 1. The number of common filters in the ranked list for various methods and the ground truth list based on the poselet detection AP for different lengths of the list

Methods	50	100	150	200
`Norm(svm)`	30.25	52.80	68.60	80.00
Σ-`Norm(svm)`	29.30	52.20	67.85	79.70
`Rank(lda)`	31.50	54.30	70.20	80.20
`Rank(svm)`	**31.55**	**55.35**	**71.20**	**81.10**

Ranking with SVM filters. The Random baseline performs poorly with δMAP $= -2.37\%$. Norm based ordering does well – the ℓ_2-norm based ordering already comes close with a δMAP $= -1.65\%$, while the structured norm, Σ-Norm(svm) is slightly better with a δMAP $= -1.50\%$. Our learned ranker outperforms the norm based methods (not surprising since the features include norm and the co-variance structure of the HOG cells). The ranker trained on the SVM filters achieves a δMAP $= -1.22\%$.

Adding diversity term leads to improvements across the board. Notably, the performance of the Rank(svm) + Div is indistinguishable from the original model δMAP $= +0.01\%$. Examination of the sets of 100 filters obtained with and without diversity with Rank(svm) reveals that on average (across categories) 40% of the filters are different.

All these methods provide a speedup of $8\times$ in the poselet selection step relative to Oracle, and an overall speed up of $3\times$, since the initial training of expensive SVM filters still has to be done which consumes 24% of the overall training time as described in Sect. 2.1 (except for Random which provides a speedup of $8\times$, but at significant loss of accuracy). Finally, an alternative way to achieve such speedup is to evaluate the AP of the filters directly, but on only the fraction of the data; this 10% method does significantly worse than our proposed methods, and provides a smaller speedup of $2.4\times$ since all the filters need to be evaluated on 10% of the data. One likely reason for the low performance: most poselets, including useful ones, are rare (hence the pretty low APs even for the top performing parts), and subsampling the training set might remove almost all true positive examples for many parts, skewing the estimated APs. Larger subsets, e.g., 25% would lead to even smaller speedups, $1.9\times$ in this case.

Ranking with LDA filters. Next we consider LDA filters, and we find the the performance of the selection of poselets based on the LDA filters is slightly worse. The diversity based ranker trained on the LDA filters, Rank(lda) + Div, achieves a δMAP $= -0.84\%$. The key advantage of ranking using the LDA filters is that it speeds up the initial poselet training time as well, since only 100 poselets are further trained using SVM bootstrapping and data-mining. Thus the overall speed up provided by this procedure is $8\times$, almost an order of magnitude. On a six-core machines it takes about 2.5 hours to train a single model, compared to 20 hours for the original model. Note that we only use the LDA filter for ranking as we found that the LDA filters themselves are rather poor for detection on a number of categories. Notably, the bicycle detector was 10% worse – the LDA based wheel detector has many false positives on wheels of cars, which the hard-negative mining stage of SVM training learns to discriminate.

The $2\times$ poselets experiment. We can select twice as many seeds and select an even better set of 100 poselets using the diversity based ranker based on the LDA filters. This has a negligible effect on the training time as the seed generation and LDA filter computation takes a small amount of additional time ($< 1\%$). However, this improves the performance which is better than the original model with δMAP $=$ **0.43**%, while still being an *order of magnitude* faster than the original algorithm.

PASCAL VOC 2010 results. We evaluated the oracle and the best performing method (Rank(lda) + Div (2x seeds)), on the PASCAL VOC 2010 detection test set and achieved a δMAP $=$ **0.56**%.

Table 2. Performance of poselet selection algorithms on PASCAL VOC 2007 detection

Method	VOC 2007 test		Training speedup		
	MAP	δMAP	Initial	Selection	Overall
Oracle	29.03				
Random	26.66	−2.37	8×	8×	8×
10%	27.78	−1.25	1×	4.4×	2.4×
Norm(svm)	27.38	−1.65	1×	8×	3×
Norm(svm) + Div	28.34	−0.69	1×	8×	3×
Σ-Norm(svm)	27.53	−1.50	1×	8×	3×
Σ-Norm(svm) + Div	28.51	−0.52	1×	8×	3×
Rank(svm)	27.81	−1.22	1×	8×	3×
Rank(svm) + Div	29.04	+0.01	1×	8×	3×
Rank(lda) + Div	28.19	−0.84	8×	8×	8×
Rank(lda) + Div (2× seeds)	**29.46**	**+0.43**	8×	8×	8×

5 Experiments with Exemplar SVMs

Here we report experiments on training exemplar SVMs. As described in Sect. 2.2, exemplar SVMs' training time scales linearly with the number of positive examples in the category. On the PASCAL VOC 2007 dataset, each category has on average 630 exemplars. Our goal is to select a set of 100 exemplars such that they reproduce the performance of the optimal set of 100 exemplars. This is obtained as follows: we use the model trained using all the exemplars and use the weights learned per exemplar in the final scoring model as an indicator of its importance. The oracle method picks the 100 most important exemplars, and obtains a performance of $\text{MAP} = 21.89\%$.

Unlike poselet filters, some of these exemplars are likely to be rare. Thus even though the filter looks good, it may not be useful for detection since it is likely to detect only a small number of positive examples. Hence, we need to consider the *frequency* of the filter, in addition to its quality as a measure of importance. We use a simple method for frequency estimation. Each exemplar filter is evaluated on the every other positive instance, and the highest response is computed among all locations that have overlap > 50%. Let, s_{ij}, denote the normalized score of exemplar i on instance j, i.e, $s_{ii} = 1$. Then, the frequency of the ith filter is the number of detections with score $> \theta$, where θ is set to be the 95 percentile of the entries in s. The overall quality of the filter **f** is the sum of score obtained from the ranker and is frequency, $\text{Rank}(\mathbf{f}) + \text{Freq}(\mathbf{f})$.

The same metric can be used for diversity. In our experiments we say that $\tau = 5\%$ of the nearest exemplars are considered similar. For each category the ranker itself was trained on the poselets of the other 19 categories, i.e., we use Rank(lda) model described in Sect. 4.3. The diversity tradeoff parameter λ is estimated again by cross-validation within the 19 categories.

To summarize, our overall procedure for exemplar selection is, (a) we train an LDA filter for each exemplar, (b) using the ranker (trained on poselet model for the training categories) select a set of 100 filters and associated exemplars, (c) train the full model with SVM filters for these 100 exemplars. Steps (a) and (b) are relatively inexpensive, hence the training time is dominated by step (c). Compared to the oracle model with 100 exemplars, our fast selection procedure offers a $6.3\times$ speedup.

5.1 PASCAL VOC Detection Results

Here we compare several selection strategies listed below:

- `Oracle` - top 100 filters picked according to learned weights (as described earlier)
- `Random` - a random set of 100 filters.
- `Freq` - the set of 100 most frequent filters.
- `Rank(lda)` - the set of 100 highest ranked filters according to the LDA ranker.
- `Rank(lda)` + `Freq` - the set of 100 filters according to the rank and frequency.
- `Rank(lda)` + `Freq` + `Div` - previous step with diversity term added.

Tab. 3 shows the performance of various methods on the PASCAL VOC 2007 dataset reported as the mean average precision (MAP) across 20 categories. The `Oracle` obtains 21.89%, while `Random` does poorly at 18.53%. Frequency alone is insufficient, and does even worse at 16.23%. Similarly rank alone is insufficient with performance of 17.93%. Our ranker combined with frequency obtains 18.75%, while adding the diversity term improves the performance to 19.62%. Note that we obtain this result using the model trained on the poselet filters and using LDA for training the exemplars. Replacing this with SVM filters may close the gap even further as we observed in the poselet based experiments.

Table 3. Performance of selection algorithms for detection on the PASCAL VOC 2007 dataset. All these methods provide a speed up of 6.3× relative to the `Oracle` as there are on average 630 exemplars per category.

Method	MAP on VOC 2007 test
`Oracle`	21.89
`Random`	18.53
`Freq`	16.23
`Rank(lda)`	17.93
`Rank(lda)` + `Freq`	18.75
`Rank(lda)` + `Freq` + `Div`	19.62

5.2 An Analysis of Bicycle HOG Filters

Finally, we look at the bicycle category to get some insight into the ranker. We take the filters obtained from the poselets model, as well as exemplar SVMs. To decouple the effect of frequency we only consider side-facing bicycle exemplars. The assumption here is that all side-facing exemplars have the same frequency.

Fig. 4 (top) shows a scatterplot of the score obtained by the ranker (higher is better) and the true ranks of the filters (lower is better) for poselets and exemplar SVMs. For poselets there is a strong (anti) correlation between the predicted score and quality (*correlation coefficient* = *-0.64*). For exemplar SVMs, the prediction is weaker, but it does exhibit high (anti) correlation (*correlation coefficient* = *-0.42*). Fig. 4 (bottom) shows the 10 least and highest ranked side-facing exemplars. The ranker picks the exemplars that have high figure-ground contrast revealing the relevant shape information and little background clutter.

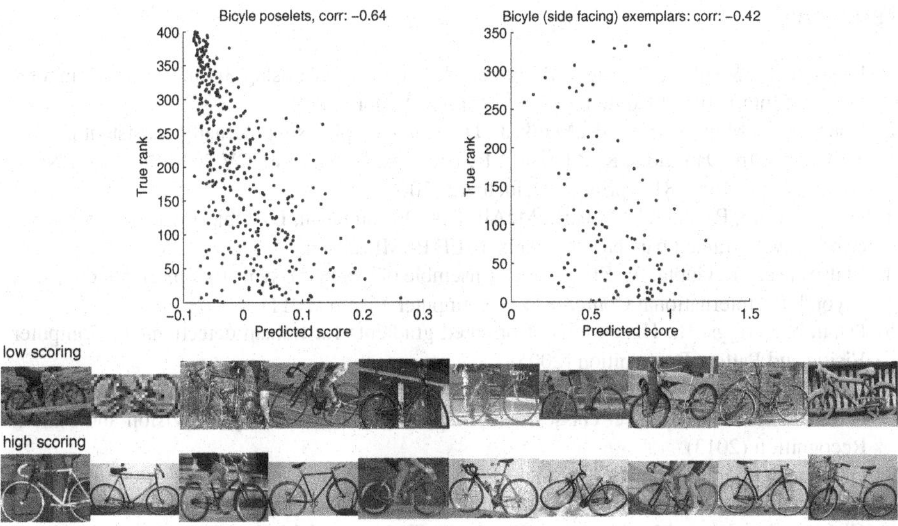

Fig. 4. An analysis of bicycle filters. (Top-left) Scatter plot of true ranks and the ranker score of the bicycle poselets. (Top-right) the same for all the exemplars of side-facing bicycles. The high scoring side-facing exemplars (Bottom row) exhibit high contrast and less clutter than the low scoring exemplars (Middle row).

6 Conclusion

We described an automatic mechanism for selecting a diverse set of discriminative parts. As an alternative to the expensive explicit evaluation that is often the bottleneck in many methods, such as poselets, this has the potential to dramatically alter the tradeoff between accuracy of a part based model and the cost of training. In our experiments, we show that combined with LDA-HOG, an efficient alternative to SVM, for training the part candidates, we can reduce the training time of a poselet model by an order of magnitude, while actually improving its detection accuracy. Moreover, we show that our approach to prediction of filter quality transcends specific detection architecture: rankers trained for poselets allow efficient filter/exemplar ranking for exemplar SVMs as well. This also reduced the training time for exemplar SVMs by an order of magnitude while suffering a small loss in performance.

The impact of such a reduction would be particularly important when one wants to experiment with many variants of the algorithm – situation all too familiar to practitioners of computer vision. Our work suggests that it is possible to evaluate the discriminative quality of a set of filters based purely on their intrinsic properties. Beyond direct savings in training time for part-based models, this evaluation may lead to speeding up part-based detection methods at *test time*, when used as an attention mechanism to reduce number of convolutions and/or hashing lookups.

Our plans for future work include investigation of the role of class affinity in generalization of part quality; e.g., one might benefit from using part ranking from vehicle classes when the test class is also a vehicle.

References

1. Bourdev, L., Malik, J.: Poselets: Body part detectors trained using 3D human pose annotations. In: International Conference on Computer Vision (2009)
2. Bourdev, L., Maji, S., Brox, T., Malik, J.: Detecting people using mutually consistent poselet activations. In: Daniilidis, K., Maragos, P., Paragios, N. (eds.) ECCV 2010, Part VI. LNCS, vol. 6316, pp. 168–181. Springer, Heidelberg (2010)
3. Felzenszwalb, P.F., Girshick, R.B., McAllester, D., Ramanan, D.: Object detection with discriminatively trained part-based models. IEEE PAMI (2010)
4. Malisiewicz, T., Gupta, A., Efros, A.A.: Ensemble of exemplar-svms for object detection and beyond. In: International Conference on Computer Vision (2011)
5. Dalal, N., Triggs, B.: Histograms of oriented gradients for human detection. In: Computer Vision and Pattern Recognition (2005)
6. Dean, T., Ruzon, M.A., Segal, M., Shlens, J., Vijayanarasimhan, S., Yagnik, J.: Fast, accurate detection of 100,000 object classes on a single machine. In: Computer Vision and Pattern Recognition (2013)
7. Gkioxari, G., Hariharan, B., Girshick, R., Malik, J.: Using k-poselets for detecting people and localizing their keypoints. In: Computer Vision and Pattern Recognition, CVPR (2014)
8. Glasner, D., Galun, M., Alpert, S., Basri, R., Shakhnarovich, G.: Viewpoint-aware object detection and pose estimation. In: International Conference on Computer Vision (2011)
9. Gall, J., Lempitsky, V.: Class-specific hough forests for object detection. In: Computer Vision and Pattern Recognition (2009)
10. Singh, S., Gupta, A., Efros, A.A.: Unsupervised discovery of mid-level discriminative patches. In: Fitzgibbon, A., Lazebnik, S., Perona, P., Sato, Y., Schmid, C. (eds.) ECCV 2012, Part II. LNCS, vol. 7573, pp. 73–86. Springer, Heidelberg (2012)
11. Aytar, Y., Zisserman, A.: Immediate, scalable object category detection. In: IEEE Conference on Computer Vision and Pattern Recognition (2014)
12. Leibe, B., Leonardis, A., Schiele, B.: Combined object categorization and segmentation with an implicit shape model. In: Workshop on Statistical Learning in Computer Vision, ECCV (2004)
13. Maji, S., Malik, J.: Object detection using a max-margin hough transform. In: Computer Vision and Pattern Recognition (2009)
14. Maji, S., Shakhnarovich, G.: Part discovery from partial correspondence. In: Computer Vision and Pattern Recognition (2013)
15. Gao, T., Stark, M., Koller, D.: What makes a good detector? – structured priors for learning from few examples. In: Fitzgibbon, A., Lazebnik, S., Perona, P., Sato, Y., Schmid, C. (eds.) ECCV 2012, Part V. LNCS, vol. 7576, pp. 354–367. Springer, Heidelberg (2012)
16. Aubry, M., Russell, B., Sivic, J.: Painting-to-3D model alignment via discriminative visual elements. ACM Transactions on Graphics 33(2) (2014)
17. Tsochantaridis, I., Joachims, T., Hofmann, T., Altun, Y.: Large margin methods for structured and interdependent output variables. Journal of Machine Learning Research (2005)
18. Sarawagi, S., Gupta, R.: Accurate max-margin training for structured output spaces. In: ICML (2008)
19. Chapelle, O.: Training a support vector machine in the primal. Neural Computation 19(5) (2007)
20. Nemhauser, G.L., Wolsey, L.A., Fisher, M.L.: An analysis of approximations for maximizing submodular set functions. Mathematical Programming 14(1) (1978)
21. Hariharan, B., Malik, J., Ramanan, D.: Discriminative decorrelation for clustering and classification. In: Fitzgibbon, A., Lazebnik, S., Perona, P., Sato, Y., Schmid, C. (eds.) ECCV 2012, Part IV. LNCS, vol. 7575, pp. 459–472. Springer, Heidelberg (2012)

Linking People in Videos with "Their" Names Using Coreference Resolution

Vignesh Ramanathan[1], Armand Joulin[2], Percy Liang[2], and Li Fei-Fei[2]

[1] Department of Electrical Engineering, Stanford University, USA
[2] Computer Science Department, Stanford University, USA
{vigneshr,ajoulin,pliang,feifeili}@cs.stanford.edu

Abstract. Natural language descriptions of videos provide a potentially rich and vast source of supervision. However, the highly-varied nature of language presents a major barrier to its effective use. What is needed are models that can reason over uncertainty over both videos and text. In this paper, we tackle the core task of person naming: assigning names of people in the cast to human tracks in TV videos. Screenplay scripts accompanying the video provide some crude supervision about who's in the video. However, even the basic problem of knowing who is *mentioned* in the script is often difficult, since language often refers to people using pronouns (e.g., "he") and nominals (e.g., "man") rather than actual names (e.g., "Susan"). Resolving the identity of these mentions is the task of *coreference resolution*, which is an active area of research in natural language processing. We develop a joint model for person naming and coreference resolution, and in the process, infer a latent alignment between tracks and mentions. We evaluate our model on both vision and NLP tasks on a new dataset of 19 TV episodes. On both tasks, we significantly outperform the independent baselines.

Keywords: Person naming, coreference resolution, text-video alignment.

1 Introduction

It is predicted that video will account for more than 85% of Internet traffic by 2016 [1]. To search and organize this data effectively, we must develop tools that can understand the people, objects, and actions in these videos. One promising source of supervision for building such tools is the large amount of natural language text that typically accompanies videos. For example, videos of TV episodes have associated screenplay scripts, which contain natural language descriptions of the videos (Fig. 1).

In this paper, we tackle the task of *person naming*: identifying the name (from a fixed list) of each person appearing in a TV video. Since the script accompanying a video also mentions these people, we could use the names in the text as labels for person naming. But as seen in Fig. 1, the text does not always use proper names (e.g., "Leonard") to refer to people. Nominal expressions (e.g., 'engineer") and pronouns (e.g., "he") are also employed, accounting for 32% of

D. Fleet et al. (Eds.): ECCV 2014, Part I, LNCS 8689, pp. 95–110, 2014.
© Springer International Publishing Switzerland 2014

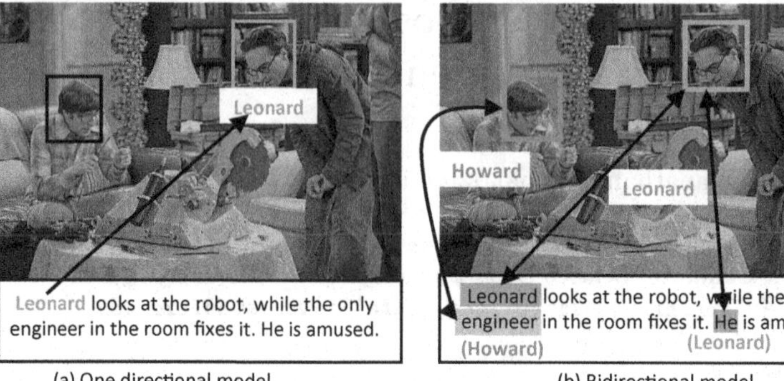

Fig. 1. Name assignment to people in a video can be improved by leveraging richer information from the text. (a) A traditional unidirectional approach only transfers unambiguous mentions of people ("Leonard") from the text to the video. (b) Our proposed bidirectional approach reasons about both proper mentions and ambiguous nominal and pronominal mentions ("engineer", "he").

the human mentions in our dataset. A human reading the text can understand these mentions using context, but this problem of *coreference resolution* remains a difficult challenge and an active area of research in natural language processing [17, 25].

Pioneering works such as [11, 37, 7, 38, 4, 6] sidestep this challenge by only using proper names in scripts, ignoring pronouns and nominals. However, in doing so, they fail to fully exploit the information that language can offer. At the same time, we found that off-the-shelf coreference resolution methods that operate on language alone are not accurate enough. Hence, what is needed is a model that tackles person naming and coreference resolution jointly, allowing information to flow bidirectionality between text and video.

The main contribution of this paper is a new bidirectional model for person naming and coreference resolution. To the best of our knowledge, this is the first attempt that jointly addresses both these tasks. Our model assigns names to tracks and mentions, and constructs an explicit alignment between tracks and mentions. Additionally, we use temporal constraints on the order in which tracks and mentions appear to efficiently infer this alignment.

We created a new dataset of 19 TV episodes along with their complete scripts, collected from 10 different TV shows. On the vision side, our model outperforms unidirectional models [6, 7] in name assignment to human tracks. On the language side, our model outperforms state-of-the-art coreference resolution systems [27, 17] for name assignment to mentions in text.

2 Related Work

Track naming using screenplay scripts. In the context of movies or TV shows, scripts have been used to provide weak labels for person naming [11, 37,

7, 38, 4, 6], and action recognition [26, 28, 9, 6]. All these works use the names from scripts as weak labels in a multiple instance learning (MIL) setting [40]. A similar line of work [32] links person names with faces based on image captions. These methods offer only a unidirectional flow of information from language to vision, and assume very little ambiguity in the text. In contrast, our model propagates information both from text to video (for person naming) and from video to text (for coreference resolution).

Joint vision and language models. Many works have combined NLP and computer vision models; we mention the ones most relevant to our setting. Some focus on creating textual descriptions for images or videos [8, 24, 30, 31, 41, 12, 35]. Others propagate image captions to uncaptioned images using visual similarities [41, 3, 14, 33]. Another line of work focuses on learning classifiers from images with text [5, 15, 21]. Rohrbach et al. [34] introduced semantic relatedness between visual attributes and image classes. Recently, Fidler et al. [13] used image descriptions to improve object detection and segmentation. These methods assume relatively clean text and focus only on propagating information from text to either videos or images. We work in a more realistic setting where text is ambiguous, and we show that vision can help resolve these ambiguities.

Grounding words in image/videos. This is the task of aligning objects or segments in an image/video with corresponding words or phrases in the accompanying text. This problem has been handled in different scenarios, depending on the entity to be grounded: Tellex et al. [39] addressed this challenge in a robotics setting, while others have worked on grounding visual attributes in images [36, 29]. Gupta et al. grounded storylines based on annotated videos [16].

Coreference resolution. Coreference resolution is a core task in the NLP community, and we refer the reader to Kummerfeld et al. [25] for a thorough set of references. Hobbs et al. [19] tried to extend the idea of coreference resolution for entities and events occurring in video transcripts. Hodosh et al. [20] and more recently, Kong et al. [23] have reported improvement in coreference resolution of objects mentioned in a text describing a static scene, when provided with the image of the scene. Unlike these works, we focus on the coreference resolution of humans mentioned in a TV script, where people reappear at multiple time points in the video. In our work, we build a discourse-based coreference resolution model similar to that of Haghighi and Klein [17]. We also take advantage of properties of TV scripts, such as the fixed set of cast names and constraints on the gender of the mentions.

3 Problem Setup

We are given a set of video-script pairs representing one TV episode. Let $\mathcal{P}$ be the set of P names appearing in the cast list, which we assume to be known. We also include a special "NULL" person in $\mathcal{P}$ to represent any person appearing in the episode, but not mentioned in the cast list.

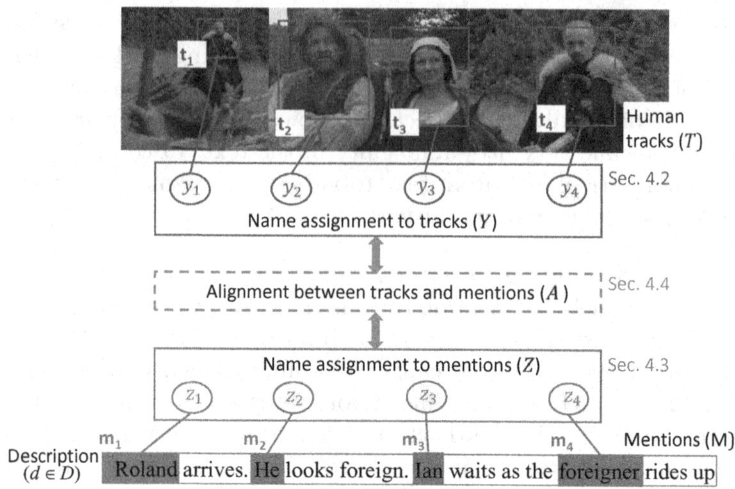

Fig. 2. The problem setup is illustrated for a sample scene. Our task is to assign a person $p \in \mathcal{P}$ to each human track t (red bounding box in the figure) and to each mention m (highlighted in green) from the text.

On the vision side, let $\mathcal{T}$ be a set of T human tracks extracted from the video (see Sec. 6 for details). For each track $t \in \mathcal{T}$, let $y_t \in \mathcal{P}$ denote the person name assigned to track t. We also define a matrix $Y \in \{0,1\}^{T \times P}$, where $Y_{tp} = 1$ iff $y_t = p$.

On the language side, each script is a sequence of *scenes*, and each scene is a sequence of *dialogues* $\mathcal{D}$ and *descriptions* $\mathcal{E}$. From the descriptions, we extract a set $\mathcal{M}$ of M *mentions* corresponding to people (see Sec. 6 for details). A mention is either a proper noun (e.g., "Roland"), pronoun (e.g., "he") or nominal (e.g., "foreigner"). For each mention $m \in \mathcal{M}$, let $z_m \in \mathcal{P}$ denote the person assigned to mention m. Define a matrix $Z \in \{0,1\}^{M \times P}$, where $Z_{mp} = 1$ iff $z_m = p$.

Each dialogue and description is also crudely aligned to a temporal window in the video, using the subtitle-based method from [11]. Our goal is to infer the person assignment matrices Y and Z given the crude alignment, as well as features of the tracks and mentions (see Fig. 2).

4 Our Model

In this section, we describe our model as illustrated in Fig. 2. First, let us describe the variables:

- Name assignment matrix for tracks $Y \in \{0,1\}^{T \times P}$.
- Name assignment matrix for mentions $Z \in \{0,1\}^{M \times P}$.
- Antecedent matrix $R \in \{0,1\}^{M \times M}$ where $R_{mm'}$ indicates whether the mention m (e.g., "he") refers to m' (e.g., "Roland") based on the text (and hence refer to the same person). In this case, m' is called the antecedent of m.

– Alignment matrix $A \in \{0,1\}^{T \times M}$ between tracks and mentions, where A_{tm} indicates whether track t is aligned to mention m.

The first two (Y and Z) are the output variables introduced in the previous section; the other variables help mediate the relationship between Y and Z.

We define a cost function over these variables which decomposes as follows:

$$C(Y,Z,R,A) \stackrel{\text{def}}{=} \gamma_t \cdot C_{\text{track}}(Y) + \gamma_m \cdot C_{\text{mention}}(Z,R) + C_{\text{align}}(A,Y,Z), \quad (1)$$

where γ_t and γ_m are hyperparameters governing the relative importance of each term. The three terms are as follows:

– $C_{\text{track}}(Y)$ is only based on video (face recognition) features (Sec. 4.2).
– $C_{\text{mention}}(Z,R)$ is only based on text features, using coreference features to influence R, and thus the name assignment Z (Sec. 4.3).
– $C_{\text{align}}(A,Y,Z)$ is based on a latent alignment A of the video and which imposes a soft constraint on the relationship between Y and Z (Sec. 4.4).

We minimize a relaxation of the cost function $C(Y,Z,R,A)$; see Sec. 5. Note that we are working in the transductive setting, where there is not a separate test phase.

4.1 Regression-Based Clustering

One of the building blocks of our model is a regression-based clustering method [2]. Given n points $x_1,\ldots,x_n \in \mathbb{R}^d$, the task is to assign, for each point x_i, a binary label vector $y_i \in \{0,1\}^p$ so that nearby points tend to receive the same label. Define the matrix $X = (x_1,\ldots,x_n)^\top \in \mathbb{R}^{n\times d}$ of points and $Y \in \{0,1\}^{n\times p}$ the labels. The regression-based clustering cost function is as follows:

$$\begin{aligned} C_{\text{cluster}}(Y;X,\lambda) &= \arg\min_{\mathbf{W}\in\mathbb{R}^{d\times p}} \sum_{t\in\mathcal{T}} \|Y - X\mathbf{W}\|_F^2 + \lambda\|\mathbf{W}\|_F^2 \\ &= \operatorname{tr}(Y^\top \underbrace{(I - X(X^\top X + \lambda I)^{-1}X^\top)}_{\stackrel{\text{def}}{=} B(X,\lambda)} Y), \end{aligned} \quad (2)$$

where the second line follows by analytically solving for the optimal weights. (see Bach and Harchaoui [2]). Note that if we relax $Y \in \{0,1\}^{n\times p}$ to $Y \in [0,1]^{n\times p}$, then $C_{\text{cluster}}(Y;X,\lambda)$ becomes a convex quadratic function of Y, and can be minimized efficiently. We will use this building block in the next two sections.

4.2 Name Assignment to Tracks

In this section, we describe $C_{\text{track}}(Y)$, which is responsible for the name assignment to tracks based on visual features. Many different models [7, 6, 26, 28] have been proposed to assign names to tracks based on face features. In this work, we adopt the recent model from Bojanowski et al. [6], which was shown to achieve state-of-the-art performance for this task. Specifically, let $\Phi^{\text{track}} \in \mathbb{R}^{T \times d}$ be a matrix of face features (rows are tracks $t \in \mathcal{T}$ and columns are features). We set $C_{\text{track}}(Y)$ in our cost function (Eq. 1) to be the clustering cost:

$$C_{\text{cluster}}(Y; \Phi^{\text{track}}, \lambda^{\text{track}}) \quad \text{(face features)} \tag{3}$$

We also enforce that each track is be associated with exactly one name: $Y\mathbf{1}_P = \mathbf{1}_T$. This hard constraint (and all subsequent constraints) is included in $C_{\text{track}}(Y)$ by adding a term equal to 0 if the constraint is satisfied and ∞ otherwise.

Additionally, as with standard approaches [7, 6, 26, 28], we include hard constraints based on the crude alignment of the script with the video:

Dialogue alignment constraint. Each dialogue $d \in \mathcal{D}$ is associated with a subset $\mathcal{P}_d$ of speakers, and a subset $\mathcal{T}_d$ of tracks which overlaps with the dialogue. This overlap is obtained from the crude alignment between tracks and dialogues [11]. Similar to [6], we add a *dialogue alignment* constraint enforcing that each speaker in $\mathcal{P}_d$ should align to at least one track in $\mathcal{T}_d$.

$$\forall\, d \in \mathcal{D},\ \forall\, p \in \mathcal{P}_d : \sum_{t \in \mathcal{T}_d} Y_{tp} \geq 1 \quad \text{(dialogue alignment)} \tag{4}$$

Scene alignment constraint. Each scene $s \in \mathcal{S}$ is associated with a subset of names $\mathcal{P}_s$ mentioned in the scene, and a subset of tracks $\mathcal{T}_s$ which overlaps with the scene (also from crude alignment [11]). We observe in practice that *only* names in $\mathcal{P}_s$ appear in the scene, so we add a *scene alignment* constraint enforcing that a name *not mentioned* in scene s should not be aligned to a track in $\mathcal{T}_s$:

$$\forall s \in \mathcal{S},\ p \notin \mathcal{P}_s : \sum_{t \in \mathcal{T}_s} Y_{tp} = 0 \quad \text{(scene alignment)} \tag{5}$$

Note that this constraint was absent from [6].

4.3 Name Assignment to Mentions and Coreference Resolution

In this section, we describe $C_{\text{mention}}(Z, R)$, which performs name assignment to mentions. The nature of name assignment to mentions is notably different from that of tracks. Proper mentions such as "Roland" are trivial to map to the fixed set of cast names based on string match, but nominal (e.g., "foreigner") and pronominal (e.g., "he") mentions are virtually impossible to assign based on the mention alone. Rather, these mentions reference previous *antecedent* mentions (e.g., "Roland" in Fig. 3). The task of determining antecedent links is called coreference resolution in NLP [25].[1]

To perform coreference resolution, we adapt the discourse model of [17], retaining their features, but using our clustering framework (Sec. 4.1).

[1] Our setting differs slightly from classic coreference resolution in that we must resolve each mention to a fixed set of names, which is the problem of *entity linking* [18].

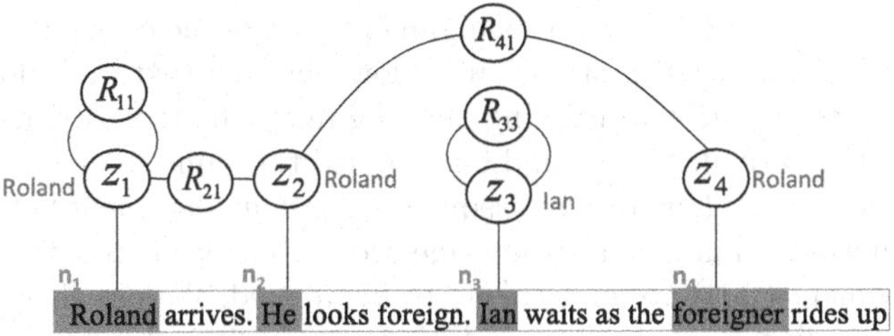

Fig. 3. An example illustrating the mention naming model from Sec. 4.3. The mentions in the sentence are highlighted in green. The antecedent variable R and name assignment matrix Z are shown for the correct coreference links. The final names assigned to the mentions are shown in red.

Coreference resolution. Each pair of mentions (m, m') is represented by a d-dimensional feature vector, and let $\Phi^{\text{mention}} \in \mathbb{R}^{M^2 \times d}$ be the corresponding feature matrix.[2] We apply the clustering framework (Sec. 4.1) to predict the antecedent matrix, or more precisely, its vectorized form $\text{vec}(R) \in \mathbb{R}^{M^2}$. We first include in $C_{\text{mention}}(R, Z)$ (Eq. 1) the clustering cost:

$$C_{\text{cluster}}(\text{vec}(R); \Phi^{\text{mention}}, \lambda^{\text{mention}}) \quad \text{(coreference features)} \tag{6}$$

We also impose hard constraints, adding them to $C_{\text{mention}}(R, Z)$. First, each mention has at most one antecedent:

$$\forall\, m \leq M: \sum_{m' \leq m} R_{mm'} = 1 \quad \text{(one antecedent)} \tag{7}$$

In addition, we include linguistic constraints to ensure gender consistency and to avoid self-association of pronouns (see supplementary material for the details).

Connection constraint. When m has an antecedent m' ($R_{mm'} = 1$), they should be assigned the same name ($Z_m = Z_{m'}$). Note that the converse is not necessarily true: two mentions not related via the antecedent relation ($R_{mm'} = 0$) can still have the same name. For example, in Fig. 3, the mentions "Roland" and "foreigner" are not linked, but still refer to the same person. This relation between Z and R can be enforced through the following constraint:

$$\forall\, m' \leq m, \forall\, p \in \mathcal{P}: \; |Z_{mp} - Z_{m'p}| \leq 1 - R_{mm'} \quad (R \text{ constrains } Z) \tag{8}$$

Finally, each mention is assigned exactly one name: $Z\mathbf{1}_P = \mathbf{1}_M$.

4.4 Alignment between Tracks and Mentions

So far, we have defined the cost functions for the name assignment matrices for tracks Y and mentions Z, which use video and text information separately.

[2] The features are described in [17]. They capture agreement between different attributes of a pair of mentions, such as the gender, cardinality, animacy, and position in the parse tree.

Now, we introduce $C_{\text{align}}(A, Y, Z)$, the alignment part of the cost function, which connects Y and Z, allowing information to flow between text and video.

There are three intuitions involving the alignment matrix A: First, a track and a mention that are aligned should be assigned the same person. Second, the tracks $\mathcal{T}$ and mentions $\mathcal{M}$ are ordered sequences, and an alignment between them should be monotonic. Third, tracks and mentions that occur together based on the crude alignment ([11]) are more likely to be aligned. We use these intuitions to formulate the alignment cost $C_{\text{align}}(A, Y, A)$, as explained below:

Monotonicity constraint. The tracks $\mathcal{T}$ are ordered by occurrence time in the video, and the mentions $\mathcal{M}$ are ordered by position in the script. We enforce that no alignment edges cross (this assumption is generally but not always true): if $t_2 > t_1$ and $A_{t_1 m} = 1$, then $A_{t_2 m'} = 0$ for all $m' < m$.

Mention mapping constraint. Let $\mathcal{M}_e$ be the set of mentions in a description $e \in \mathcal{E}$ and $\mathcal{T}_e$ be the set of tracks in the crudely-aligned time window. We enforce each mention from $\mathcal{M}_e$ to be mapped to exactly one track from $\mathcal{T}_e$: for each $e \in \mathcal{E}$ and $m \in \mathcal{M}_e$, $\sum_{t \in \mathcal{T}_e} A_{tm} = 1$. Conversely, we allow a track to align to multiple mentions. For example, in "John sits on the chair, while he is drinking his coffee", a single track might align to both "John" and "he".

$$\forall\, e \in \mathcal{E},\ m \in \mathcal{M}_e,\ \sum_{t \in \mathcal{T}_e} A_{tm} = 1 \quad \text{(mention mapping)}. \tag{9}$$

Connection penalty. If a track t is assigned to person p ($Y_{tp} = 1$), and track t is aligned to mention m ($A_{tm} = 1$), then mention m should be assigned to person p as well ($Z_{mp} = 1$). To enforce this constraint in a soft way, we add the following penalty:

$$\|A^\top Y - Z\|_F^2 = -2\text{tr}(A^\top Y Z) + \text{constant}, \tag{10}$$

where the equality leverages the fact that Y and Z are discrete with rows that sum to 1 (see supplementary material for details). Note that $C_{\text{align}}(A, Y, Z)$ is thus a linear function of A with monotonicity constraints. This special form will be important for optimization in Sec. 5.

5 Optimization

Now we turn to optimizing our cost function (Eq. 1). First, the variables Z, Y, R and A are matrices with values in $\{0, 1\}$. We relax the domains of all variables except A from $\{0, 1\}$ to $[0, 1]$. Additionally, to account for noise in the tracks and mentions, we add a slack to all inequalities involving Y and Z.

We solve the relaxed optimization problem using block coordinate descent, where we cycle between minimizing Y, (Z, R), and A. Each block is convex given the other blocks. For the smaller matrices Z, Y and R (which have on the order of 10^4 elements), we use interior-point methods [6], whose complexity is cubic in the number of variables. The alignment matrix A has on the order of 10^6 elements, but fortunately, due to the special form of $C_{\text{align}}(A, Y, Z)$, we can use an efficient dynamic program similar to dynamic time warping [10] to optimize A (see supplementary material for details).

Initialization. Since our cost function is not jointly convex in all the variables, initialization is important. We initialize our method with the solution to simplified optimization problem that excludes any terms involving more than one block of variables.

Rounding. The variables Y and Z are finally rounded to integer matrices, with elements in $\{0, 1\}$. The rounding is carried out similar to [6], by projecting the matrices on the corresponding set of integer matrices. This amounts to taking the maximum value along the rows of Y and Z.

6 Experiments

We evaluated our model on the two tasks: (i) name assignment to tracks in videos and (ii) name assignment to mentions in the corresponding scripts.

Dataset. We created a new dataset of TV episode videos along with their scripts.[3] Previous datasets [6, 7, 38] come with heavily preprocessed scripts, where no ambiguities in the text are retained. In contrast, we use the original scripts. We randomly chose 19 episodes from 10 different TV shows. The complete list of the episodes is shown in the supplementary material. Sample video clips from the dataset with descriptions are shown in Fig. 4. The dataset is split into a development set of 14 episodes and a test set of 5 episodes. Note that there is no training set, as we are working in the transductive setting. The number of names in the cast lists varies between $9 - 21$.

To evaluate the name assignment task in videos, we manually annotated the names of human tracks from 3 episodes of the development set, and all 5 episodes of the test set. There are a total of 3329 tracks with ground truth annotations in the development set, and 4757 tracks in the test set. To evaluate the name assignment to mentions, we annotated the person names of the pronouns and nominal mentions in all episodes. To ensure that a mention always refers to a person physically in the scene, we retain only the mentions which are the subject of a verb. This resulted in a total of 811 mentions in the development set and 300 mentions in the test set.

Implementation details. The tracks were obtained by running an off-the-shelf face detector followed by tracking [22]. We retain all tracks extracted by this scheme, unlike previous works which only use a subset of clean tracks with

[3] The scripts were collected from `https://sites.google.com/site/tvwriting/`.

Fig. 4. Sample video clips from the dataset are shown along with their corresponding script segments. The mentions extracted from the script are underlined. The ones corresponding to nominal subjects are shown in green. These are the mentions used in our full model for person name assignment. The face tracks from the video are shown by red bounding boxes.

visible facial features. We further extracted a set of features between pairs of mentions using the Stanford CoreNLP toolbox [27] (see supplementary material). We tuned the hyperparameters on the development set, yielding $\lambda^{\text{mention}} = 0.0001$, $\lambda^{\text{track}} = 0.01$, $\gamma_t = 0.2$ and $\gamma_m = 20$.

Table 1. The Average Precision (AP) scores for person name assignment in videos is shown for episodes with face annotations in the development and test set. We also show the mean AP (MAP) value for the development and test sets. The description of the different methods are provided in the text.

Set	Development				Test					
Episode ID	E1	E2	E3	*MAP*	E15	E16	E17	E18	E19	*MAP*
RANDOM	0.266	0.254	0.251	0.257	0.177	0.217	0.294	0.214	0.247	0.229
COUR [7]	0.380	0.333	0.393	0.369	0.330	0.327	0.342	0.306	0.337	0.328
BOJ [6]	0.353	0.434	0.426	0.404	0.285	0.429	0.378	0.383	**0.454**	0.385
OURUNIDIR	0.512	0.560	0.521	0.531	0.340	0.474	0.503	0.399	0.384	0.420
OURUNICOR	0.497	0.572	0.501	0.523	**0.388**	0.470	0.512	0.424	0.401	0.431
OURUNIF	0.497	0.552	0.561	0.537	0.345	0.488	0.516	0.410	0.388	0.429
OURBIDIR	**0.567**	**0.665**	**0.573**	**0.602**	0.358	**0.518**	**0.587**	**0.454**	0.376	**0.459**

6.1 Name Assignment to Tracks in Video

We use the Average Precision (AP) metric previously used in [6, 7] to evaluate the performance of person naming in videos. We compare our model (denoted by OURBIDIR) to state-of-the-art methods and various baselines:

1. RANDOM: Randomly picks a name from the set of possible names consistent with the crude alignment.
2. BOJ [6]: Similar to the model described in Sec. 4.2 but without the scene constraints. We use the publicly available code from the authors.

3. COUR [7]: Weakly-supervised method for name assignment using a discriminative classifier. We use the publicly available code from the authors.
4. OURUNIDIR: Unidirectional model which does not use any coreference resolution, but unlike BOJ, it includes the "scene alignment" constraint.
5. OURUNICOR: We first obtain the person names corresponding to the mentions in the script by running our coreference model from Sec. 4.3. These are then used to specify additional constraints similar to the "dialogue alignment" constraint.
6. OURUNIF: All the tracks appearing in the temporal window corresponding to the mention are given equal values in the matrix A.
7. OURBIDIR: Our full model which jointly optimizes name assignment to mentions and tracks.

Tab. 1 shows the results. First, note that even our unidirectional model (OURUNIDIR) performs better than the state-of-the-art methods from [6, 7]. As noted in [6], the ridge regression model from Bach et al [2] might be more robust to noise. This could explain the performance gain over [7]. The improvement of our unidirectional model over [6] is due to our addition of scene based constraints, which reduces the ambiguity in the names that can be assigned to a track.

The improved performance of our bidirectional model compared to OURUNIDIR and OURUNICOR, shows the importance of the alignment variable in our formulation. On the other hand, when A is fixed through uniform assignment (OURUNIF), the model performs worse than our bidirectional model. This shows the benefit of inferring the alignment variable in our method.

In Fig. 5, we show examples where our model makes correct name assignments. Here, our model performs well even when tracks are aligned with pronouns and nominals.

Finally, we conducted an oracle experiment where we fix the alignment between tracks and mentions (A) and mention name assignment (Z) to manually-annotated ground truth values. The resulting OURBIDIR obtained a much improved MAP of 0.565 on the test set. We conclude that person naming could be improved by inferring a better alignment variable.

6.2 Name Assignment to Mentions

Now we focus on the language side. Here, our evaluation metric is accuracy, the fraction of mentions that are assigned the correct person name. We compare the performance of our full bidirectional model (OURBIDIR) with standard coreference resolution systems and several baselines:

1. CORENLP: This is the coreference resolution model used in the Standord CoreNLP toolbox [27].
2. HAGHIGHI ([17] modified): We modify the method from [17] to account for the fixed set of cast names in our setting (see supplementary material for more details).

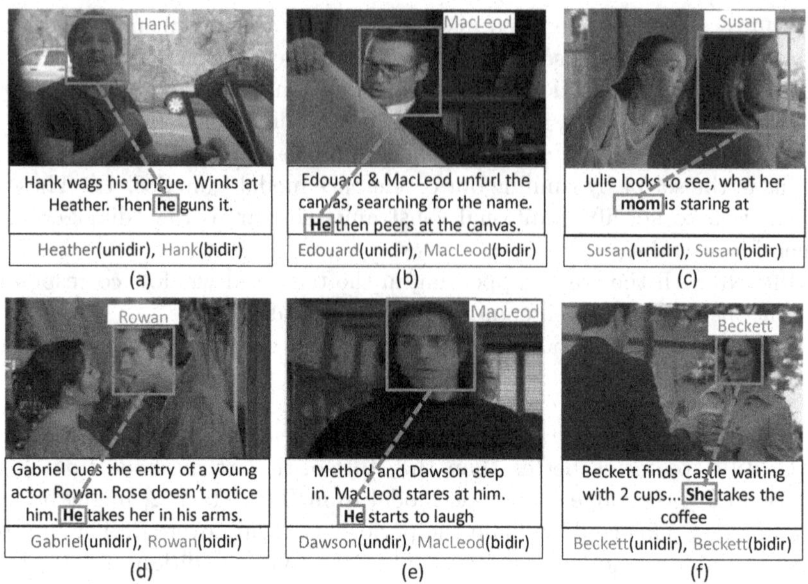

Fig. 5. Examples where the person name assignment by our bidirectional model is correct, both in the video and the text. The alignment is denoted by the blue dotted line. The name assignment to the tracks are shown near the bounding box. The name assignment to mentions by our unidirectional and bidirectional models are shown in the box below the videos. The correct assignment is shown in green, and the wrong one in red.

3. OurUnidir: This is the unidirectional model from Sec. 4.3.
4. OurUnif: Same as OurUnif for name assignment to tracks.
5. OurBidir: Same as OurBidir for name assignment to tracks.

The Stanford CoreNLP coreference system uses a fixed set of rules to iteratively group mentions with similar properties. These rules were designed for use with well structured news articles which have a higher proportion of nominals compared to pronouns. Also, our model performs explicit entity linking by associating every mention to a name from the cast list, unlike standard coreference resolution methods. While comparing to CoreNLP, we performed entity linking by assigning each mention in a coreference chain to the head mention of the chain, which is usually a proper noun corresponding to one of the cast names. These factors contribute to the gain of OurUnidir, which uses constraints specific to the TV episode setting. The modified version of Haghighi and Klein's model [17] is a probabilistic variant of OurUnidir. Note that our formulation is convex whereas theirs is not.

We also a gain from our bidirectional model over the unidirectional model, due to additional visual cues. This is especially true when there text is truly ambiguous. In Fig. 5(d), "Rowan" is not the subject of the sentence preceding the pronoun "He". This causes a simple unidirectional model to associate the

Table 2. The percentage accuracy of mentions associated to the correct person name across all episodes in the development and test set is shown. The description of the different methods in the table are provided in the text.

Set	Dev.	Test
CoreNLP [27]	54.99 %	41.00 %
Haghighi [17] modified	53.02 %	38.67 %
OurUnidir	58.20 %	49.00 %
OurUnif	59.56 %	48.33 %
OurBidir	**60.42 %**	**56.00 %**

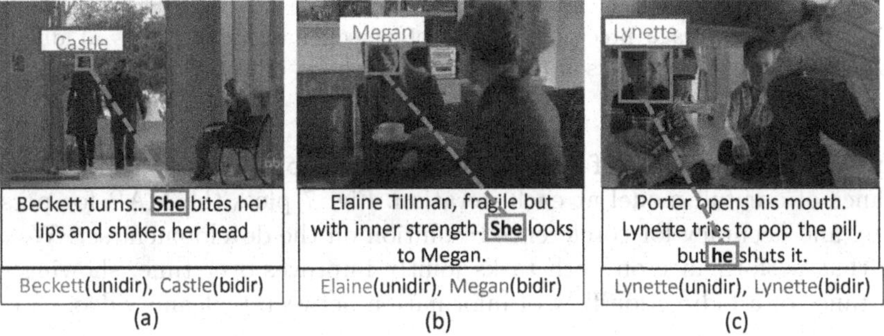
Castle
Beckett turns... She bites her lips and shakes her head
Beckett(unidir), Castle(bidir)
(a)
Megan
Elaine Tillman, fragile but with inner strength. She looks to Megan.
Elaine(unidir), Megan(bidir)
(b)
Lynette
Porter opens his mouth. Lynette tries to pop the pill, but he shuts it.
Lynette(unidir), Lynette(bidir)
(c)

Fig. 6. Examples of videos are shown, where our full model fails to predict the correct names The alignment is shown by the blue dotted line. The name assignment to tracks are shown over the bounding box. The wrong name assignments are shown in red. The name assignment to mentions by our bidirectional and unidirectional models are shown in the box below the videos. The correct name assignment is shown in green, and the wrong one in red.

pronoun with a wrong antecedent mention. Our bidirectional model avoids these errors by using the name of the tracks mapped to the mentions.

Finally, we explore the full potential of improving mention name assignment from visual cues by fixing the matrices A and Y to their ground truth values. This yields an oracle accuracy of 68.98% on the test data, compared to 52.15% for OurBidir. Interestingly, the oracle improvement here on the language side is significantly higher than on the vision side.

Error analysis. We show sample video clips in Fig. 6, where our bidirectional model (OurBidir) fails to predict the correct name for mentions. As seen in Fig. 6(a), one typical reason for failure is incorrect name assignments to low-resolution faces; the error then propagates to the mentions. In the second example, the face detector fails to capture the face of the person mentioned in the script. Hence, our model maps the pronoun to the only face available in the description, which is incorrect.

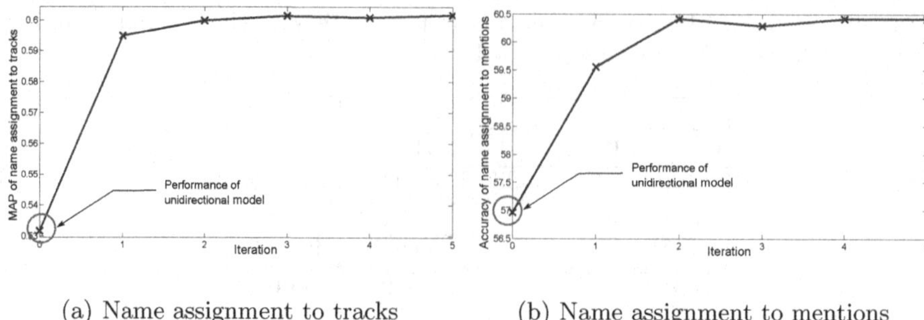

(a) Name assignment to tracks

(b) Name assignment to mentions

Fig. 7. (a) Mean average precision (MAP) of person naming of tracks at different iterations. (b) Accuracy of person naming of mentions at different iterations.

Empirical justification of our joint optimization. We also show the performance of our full model at each iteration. Fig. 7 plots the MAP for person naming and accuracy for coreference resolution on the development set. We observe that performance on both tasks jointly improves over time, showing the importance of a bidirection flow of information between text and video.

7 Conclusion

In this work, we tackled the problem of name assignment to people in videos based on their scripts. Compared to previous work, we leverage richer information from the script by including ambiguous mentions of people such as pronouns and nominals. We presented a bidirectional model to jointly assign names to the tracks in the video and the mentions in the text; a latent alignment linked the two tasks. We evaluated our method on a new dataset of 19 TV episodes. Our full model provides a significant gain for both vision and language tasks compared to models that handle the tasks independently. We plan to extend our bidirectional model to not only share information about the identity of the tracks and mentions, but also to link the actions in video with relations in text.

Acknowledgements. We thank A. Fathi, O. Russakovsky and S. Yeung for helpful comments and feedback. This research is partially supported by Intel, the NFS grant IIS-1115493 and DARPA-Mind's Eye grant.

References

1. Cisco visual networking index: Global mobile data traffic forecast update. Tech. rep., Cisco (February 2014)
2. Bach, F., Harchaoui, Z.: Diffrac: A discriminative and flexible framework for clustering. In: NIPS (2007)

3. Barnard, K., Duygulu, P., Forsyth, D., de Freitas, N., Blei, D.M., Jordan, M.I.: Matching words and pictures. Journal of Machine Learning Research 3, 1107–1135 (2003)
4. Bäuml, M., Tapaswi, M., Stiefelhagen, R.: Semi-supervised Learning with Constraints for Person Identification in Multimedia Data. In: IEEE Conference on Computer Vision and Pattern Recognition, CVPR (June 2013)
5. Berg, T.L., Berg, A.C., Edwards, J., Maire, M., White, R., Teh, Y.W., Learned-Miller, E.G., Forsyth, D.A.: Names and faces in the news. In: IEEE Conference on Computer Vision and Pattern Recognition (CVPR), vol. 2, pp. 848–854 (2004)
6. Bojanowski, P., Bach, F., Laptev, I., Ponce, J., Schmid, C., Sivic, J.: Finding actors and actions in movies. In: ICCV (2013)
7. Cour, T., Sapp, B., Jordan, C., Taskar, B.: Learning from ambiguously labeled images. In: CVPR (2009)
8. Das, P., Xu, C., Doell, R.F., Corso, J.J.: A thousand frames in just a few words: Lingual description of videos through latent topics and sparse object stitching. In: CVPR (2013)
9. Duchenne, O., Laptev, I., Sivic, J., Bach, F., Ponce, J.: Automatic annotation of human actions in video. In: ICCV (2009)
10. Duda, R.O., Hart, P.E., Stork, D.G.: Pattern classification. John Wiley & Sons (2012)
11. Everingham, M., Sivic, J., Zisserman, A.: Hello! my name is... buffy automatic naming of characters in tv video. In: BMVC (2006)
12. Farhadi, A., Hejrati, M., Sadeghi, M., Young, P., Rashtchian, C., Hockenmaier, J., Forsyth, D.: Every picture tells a story: Generating sentences from images. In: Daniilidis, K., Maragos, P., Paragios, N. (eds.) ECCV 2010, Part IV. LNCS, vol. 6314, pp. 15–29. Springer, Heidelberg (2010)
13. Fidler, S., Sharma, A., Urtasun, R.: A sentence is worth a thousand pixels. In: CVPR. IEEE (2013)
14. Guillaumin, M., Mensink, T., Verbeek, J., Schmid, C.: Tagprop: Discriminative metric learning in nearest neighbor models for image auto-annotation. In: CVPR (2009)
15. Gupta, A., Davis, L.S.: Beyond nouns: Exploiting prepositions and comparative adjectives for learning visual classifiers. In: Forsyth, D., Torr, P., Zisserman, A. (eds.) ECCV 2008, Part I. LNCS, vol. 5302, pp. 16–29. Springer, Heidelberg (2008)
16. Gupta, A., Srinivasan, P., Shi, J., Davis, L.S.: Understanding videos, constructing plots learning a visually grounded storyline model from annotated videos. In: IEEE Conference on Computer Vision and Pattern Recognition, CVPR 2009, pp. 2012–2019. IEEE (2009)
17. Haghighi, A., Klein, D.: Coreference resolution in a modular, entity-centered model. In: HLT-NAACL (2010)
18. Han, X., Sun, L., Zhao, J.: Collective entity linking in web text: a graph-based method. In: ACM SIGIR Conference on Research and Development in Information Retrieval, pp. 765–774 (2011)
19. Hobbs, J.R., Mulkar-Mehta, R.: Using abduction for video-text coreference. In: Proceedings of BOEMIE 2008 Workshop on Ontology Evolution and Multimedia Information Extraction (2008)
20. Hodosh, M., Young, P., Rashtchian, C., Hockenmaier, J.: Cross-caption coreference resolution for automatic image understanding. In: Conference on Computational Natural Language Learning (2010)
21. Jie, L., Caputo, B., Ferrari, V.: Who's doing what: Joint modeling of names and verbs for simultaneous face and pose annotation. In: NIPS (2009)

22. Kalal, Z., Mikolajczyk, K., Matas, J.: Tracking-learning-detection. IEEE Transactions on Pattern Analysis and Machine Intelligence 34(7), 1409–1422 (2012)
23. Kong, C., Lin, D., Bansal, M., Urtasun, R., Fidler, S.: What are you talking about? text-to-image coreference. In: CVPR (2014)
24. Kulkarni, G., Premraj, V., Dhar, S., Li, S., Choi, Y., Berg, A.C., Berg, T.L.: Baby talk: Understanding and generating simple image descriptions. In: CVPR (2011)
25. Kummerfeld, J.K., Klein, D.: Error-driven analysis of challenges in coreference resolution. In: Proceedings of EMNLP (2013)
26. Laptev, I., Marszałek, M., Schmid, C., Rozenfeld, B.: Learning realistic human actions from movies. In: CVPR (2008)
27. Lee, H., Peirsman, Y., Chang, A., Chambers, N., Surdeanu, M., Jurafsky, D.: Stanford's mulit-pass sieve coreference resolution system at the conll-2011 shared task. In: CoNLL 2011 Shared Task (2011)
28. Marszałek, M., Laptev, I., Schmid, C.: Actions in context. In: CVPR (2009)
29. Matuszek, C., FitzGerald, N., Zettlemoyer, L., Bo, L., Fox, D.: A joint model of language and perception for grounded attribute learning. In: ICML (2012)
30. Motwani, T.S., Mooney, R.J.: Improving video activity recognition using object recognition and text mining. In: ECAI (2012)
31. Ordonez, V., Kulkarni, G., Berg, T.L.: Im2text: Describing images using 1 million captioned photographs. In: NIPS (2011)
32. Pham, P., Moens, M.F., Tuytelaars, T.: Linking names and faces: Seeing the problem in different ways. In: Proceedings of the 10th European Conference on Computer Vision: Workshop Faces in 'Real-life' Images: Detection, Alignment, and Recognition, pp. 68–81 (2008)
33. Ramanathan, V., Liang, P., Fei-Fei, L.: Video event understanding using natural language descriptions. In: ICCV (2013)
34. Rohrbach, M., Stark, M., Szarvas, G., Schiele, B.: What helps where – and why? semantic relatedness for knowledge transfer. In: CVPR (2010)
35. Rohrbach, M., Wei, Q., Titov, I., Thater, S., Pinkal, M., Schiele, B.: Translating video content to natural language descriptions. In: ICCV (2013)
36. Silberer, C., Ferrari, V., Lapata, M.: Models of semantic representation with visual attributes. In: ACL (2013)
37. Sivic, J., Everingham, M., Zisserman, A.: "Who are you?" - learning person specific classifiers from video. In: CVPR (2009)
38. Tapaswi, M., Bäuml, M., Stiefelhagen, R.: "Knock! Knock! Who is it?" Probabilistic Person Identification in TV Series. In: IEEE Conference on Computer Vision and Pattern Recognition, CVPR (June 2012)
39. Tellex, S., Kollar, T., Dickerson, S., Walter, M.R., Banerjee, A.G., Teller, S., Roy, N.: Understanding natural language commands for robotic navigation and mobile manipulation. AAAI (2011)
40. Vijayanarasimhan, S., Grauman, K.: Keywords to visual categories: Multiple-instance learning for weakly supervised object categorization. In: IEEE Conference on Computer Vision and Pattern Recognition, CVPR 2008, pp. 1–8. IEEE (2008)
41. Wang, Y., Mori, G.: A discriminative latent model of image region and object tag correspondence. In: NIPS (2010)

Optimal Essential Matrix Estimation via Inlier-Set Maximization

Jiaolong Yang[1,2], Hongdong Li[2], and Yunde Jia[1]

[1] Beijing Laboratory of Intelligent Information Technology, Beijing Institute of Technology, China
[2] Australian National University and NICTA, Australia
{yangjiaolong,jiayunde}@bit.edu.cn, hongdong.li@anu.edu.au

Abstract. In this paper, we extend the globally optimal "rotation space search" method [11] to essential matrix estimation in the presence of feature mismatches or outliers. The problem is formulated as inlier-set cardinality maximization, and solved via branch-and-bound global optimization which searches the entire essential manifold formed by all essential matrices. Our main contributions include an explicit, geometrically meaningful essential manifold parametrization using a 5D direct product space of a solid 2D disk and a solid 3D ball, as well as efficient closed-form bounding functions. Experiments on both synthetic data and real images have confirmed the efficacy of our method. The method is mostly suitable for applications where robustness and accuracy are paramount. It can also be used as a benchmark for method evaluation.

Keywords: Essential matrix, robust estimation, global optimization, branch-and-bound.

1 Introduction

Essential matrix estimation is a basic building block for Structure from Motion (SfM). Given two views of a rigid scene from a calibrated perspective camera, the task is to estimate the relative pose or motion between the two views. Essential matrix can be estimated with image point correspondences using epipolar geometry. In reality, correspondence outliers are ubiquitous. For instance, natural or man-made scenes often contain similar structures, flat (and ambiguous) regions, repetitive patterns *etc.*, making flawless feature matching nearly impossible.

To deal with outliers in the context of multiple-view geometry, RANSAC [7] and its variants have played a major role. These methods, which are based on random sampling, cannot provide an optimality guarantee, and the inlier sets they find often vary from time to time. Moreover, in most RANSAC algorithms (*e.g.* [8,26]), to ensure efficiency an algebraic solver (*e.g.* the 5-point method [24,20]) and the 8-point method [21,10]) is often adopted to compute tentative estimation, followed by a thresholding stage using geometric reprojection error or Sampson error. The apparent inconsistency here, *i.e.* algebraic solver versus geometric threshold, can lead to inferior estimate.

D. Fleet et al. (Eds.): ECCV 2014, Part I, LNCS 8689, pp. 111–126, 2014.
© Springer International Publishing Switzerland 2014

In contrast, this work seeks a consistent, and globally optimal solution to essential matrix estimation, based on meaningful geometric error. By optimal, we adopt the consensus set maximization idea of RANSAC, *i.e.* to find the maximal-sized inlier set that is compatible with the input image measurements. To distinguish inliers from outliers, we use angular reprojection error. With a calibrated camera, it is natural to use angular reprojection error, because a calibrated camera behaves just like an angle measurement device, and every image point (represented by a unit vector) gives the actual viewing angle.

To achieve globally maximal inlier-set, a naive way would be exhaustively enumerating all possible combinations of inliers/outliers. However, this soon becomes intractable as combinations grow exponentially with point number. No efficient solver to this combinational problem exists to our knowledge. Our idea in this paper is: rather than searching over all *discrete* combinations of inliers, we search the entire *continuous* parameter space of essential matrix. To this end, it is necessary to find a suitable domain representation (parametrization) of the space, with which the bounds can be easily derived and efficiently evaluated.

The proposed method is based on systematically searching two (reduced) rotation spaces using branch-and-bound (BnB). It is inspired by the rotation search technique proposed in [11], which has been used in several vision problems [13,1,31]. To minimize the L_∞-norm of angular errors, [11] uses BnB to recursively search SO(3) with elegant bounding. However, L_∞-optimization is known to be extremely vulnerable to outliers, and [11] assumes outlier-free correspondences. Contrastly, our method works in the presence of outliers.

1.1 Related Work

Our method is closely related to [11], and extends [11] to optimal inlier-set maximization which is non-trivial. A key insight for [11] to applying rotation search to essential matrix estimation is that, given rotation, the translation can be optimally solved with convex optimization (SOCP/LP). Contrasty, optimally solving the translation maximizing inlier-set cardinality is not trivial. The optimal essential matrix problem considered in this paper is more challenging. Method of [1] achieves inlier-set maximization with rotation search, however translation is assumed to be known. In this paper, we optimally solve the problem by searching the essential manifold with BnB, based on a novel parametrization scheme.

There have been some research efforts devoted to optimal essential matrix estimation with inlier-set maximization criterion [5,6]. Most closely related to our method is [5] in which a brute-force search method is proposed using triangulation feasibility test. The solution is exhaustively searched over the discretized parameter space formed by two unit spheres, and GPU implementation is used to speed up the computation. In [6], double pairs of correspondences are used, from which camera pose is found by searching the two epipoles via BnB. An approximation is made to solve an otherwise NP-hard problem (minimum vertex cover), which compromises the global optimality guarantee. The closed-form bounding functions we use in this paper are inspired by [5] (with necessary extension);

we however introduce other innovations in both parametrization scheme and optimization technique. By our method, an exact optimality can be achieved.

Some approaches use branch-and-bound methods for finding globally optimal fundamental matrix [19,32]. In particular, inlier-set is optimally maximized in [19] with algebraic error. Geometrically meaningful error is investigated in [32], but the goal is optimal error minimization assuming no outlier. These works discuss uncalibrated cases only, where the underlying Euclidean constraints of essential matrix are not exploited.

Another line of related work is outlier removal using convex optimization [28,16,18,25]. These methods are able to detect potential outliers with respect to a given threshold. However, the goal is not inlier-set maximization and outliers may be removed at the expense of losing some true inliers. Moreover, in SfM they assume known rotation to formulate the problem to be (quasi-)convex. Our work is also related to the study of SfM without pre-built correspondences [4,23], in a sense that we all compute the motion yielding most agreeable correspondences.

2 Essential Manifold Parametrization

A rigid motion comprises rotation and translation. As such, an essential matrix E relates to a 3D rotation $\hat{\mathrm{R}} \in \mathrm{SO}(3)$ and a 3D translation $\hat{\mathbf{t}} \in \mathbb{R}^3$ from the first camera to the second one by $\mathrm{E} = [\hat{\mathbf{t}}]_\times \hat{\mathrm{R}}$ where $[\cdot]_\times$ denotes the skew-symmetric matrix representation. Essential matrix can only be determined up to an unknown scale. To resolve this scale indeterminacy one can set the length of $\hat{\mathbf{t}}$, *i.e.* $\|\hat{\mathbf{t}}\|$ to be fixed (*e.g.* to be 1). Therefore, we have $\hat{\mathbf{t}} \in \mathbb{S}^2$, *i.e.* a 2-sphere embedded in $\mathbb{R}^3$. In this way the essential manifold can be parameterized with 5 degrees of freedom (dofs) in $\mathrm{SO}(3) \times \mathbb{S}^2$. In this paper we advocate different coordinate system and parametrization scheme to facilitate our BnB algorithm.

In solving the relative pose problem, one has the freedom to arbitrarily choose a coordinate system as the world frame. Different from a common practice which sets the first camera matrix to be $[\mathbf{I} \mid \mathbf{0}]$, we fix the first camera's center at the origin, *i.e.* $\mathbf{C} \equiv \mathbf{0}$, and fix the second camera's center at $\mathbf{C}' \equiv [0, 0, 1]^\mathrm{T}$ on the Z-axis.[1] We use R to denote the *absolute orientation* of the first camera (relative to the world frame), and R' for the second camera. Then, it is easy to see that, under this configuration the essential matrix can be written as

$$\mathrm{E} = [-\mathrm{R}'\mathbf{C}']_\times \mathrm{R}'\mathrm{R}^\mathrm{T} = \mathrm{R}'[-\mathbf{C}']_\times \mathrm{R}^\mathrm{T} = \mathrm{R}' \begin{bmatrix} 0 & 1 & 0 \\ -1 & 0 & 0 \\ 0 & 0 & 0 \end{bmatrix} \mathrm{R}^\mathrm{T}. \tag{1}$$

Using two absolute rotations $(\mathrm{R}, \mathrm{R}') \in \mathrm{SO}(3) \times \mathrm{SO}(3)$ to represent essential matrix is clearly an over-parametrization, because the essential manifold has only five dofs. The excess one dof can further be removed, as we will show next.

[1] Note that, the second camera's center can be set on either X-, Y-, or Z-axis; the resultant parametrization using X- or Y-axis can be similarly derived. We opt for Z-axis for the convenience of closed-form bounding function evaluation (*cf.* Sec. 4.3).

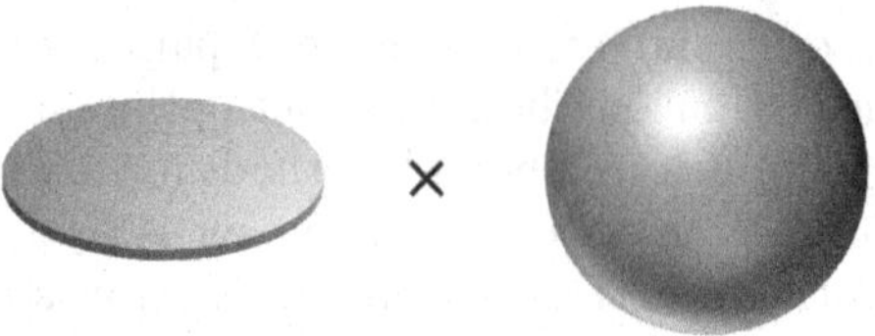

Fig. 1. The essential manifold is parameterized as the product space of a solid 2D disk $\mathbb{D}^2_\pi$ and a solid 3D ball $\mathbb{B}^3_\pi$, corresponding to rotations of the first and second camera respectively. (Note that the disk is thickened to aid in visualization).

Observe that, under our special camera setup, any rotation about Z-axis (*i.e.* the axis joining the two camera centers) applied to both cameras will leave the essential matrix invariant. In other words, they form an *equivalence class* which is a member of the 2D rotation group SO(2). In order to "factor out" these Z-axis rotations, we apply *group quotient operator* to one of the two SO(3) groups as SO(3)/SO(2). In this way we can represent the essential space as $\mathrm{SO}(3) \times \big(\mathrm{SO}(3)/\mathrm{SO}(2)\big)$, i.e. the product space of SO(3) – rotation space for one camera, and SO(3)/SO(2) for the other camera. Note that there are still equivalence classes remaining, and each of them corresponds to four relative pose configurations [12,30]. It is necessary to leave these equivalence classes there, as only one (unknown) configuration out of the four depicts the true relative pose.

We adopt the angle-axis representation for 3D rotations, with which any rotation is representable as a point in a solid radius-π ball in 3-space, *i.e.* $\mathbb{B}^3_\pi$. Thus SO(3) can be parameterized as $\mathbb{B}^3_\pi$. The remaining problem is how to parameterize SO(3)/SO(2). It is known in topology [17] that SO(3)/SO(2) is homeomorphic to $\mathbb{S}^2$. Instead of this, we directly parameterize SO(3)/SO(2) using angle-axis representation of camera rotation, as detailed in the following.

With angle-axis representation, it is easy to verify that, in our setup the X-Y plane of $\mathbb{B}^3_\pi$ effectively encodes all "Z-axis-free" rotations we need. This is because the X-Y plane of $\mathbb{B}^3_\pi$ contains all rotations whose Z-axis components are zero, while X-axis and Z-axis components are arbitrary. Concretely, let $\mathbf{v}$ be the angle-axis vector of R, *i.e.* $\mathrm{R} = \exp([\,\mathbf{v}\,]_\times)$, we avoid the freedom of Z-axis rotation by setting v^3, the 3rd element of vector $\mathbf{v}$, to be 0. Thus our search space for the first rotation $\mathrm{R} = \exp([v^1, v^2, 0]_\times)$ is reduced to the 2D disk $\mathbb{D}^2_\pi$ on the equator plane of the π-ball. Now, we have "squeezed" a 3D radius-π ball to a flat 2D radius-π disk in the X-Y plane.

Without loss of generality, we assume the first camera's rotation R is of 2-dof and "Z axis free"; we denote this as $\mathbf{v} \in \mathbb{D}^2_\pi$. Let $\mathrm{R}' = \exp([\,\mathbf{v}'\,]_\times)$, then the essential manifold is parameterized by 5D vectors $(\mathbf{v}, \mathbf{v}') \in \mathbb{D}^2_\pi \times \mathbb{B}^3_\pi$. To recover a 3×3 essential matrix E from $(\mathbf{v}, \mathbf{v}')$, one simply needs to recover rotations matrices $(\mathrm{R}, \mathrm{R}')$ from $(\mathbf{v}, \mathbf{v}')$, then compute E with Eq. (1).

Comparison to previous work. Some previous works such as [14,29] base their parametrization on Singular Value Decomposition (SVD) of essential matrix. Although these representations also originate from $\mathrm{SO}(3) \times \mathrm{SO}(3)$, they do not provide the geometric interpretation of their parameters, and are not suitable for our BnB search. Very recently, an independent work [30] chooses the same coordinate system as ours and uses the essential matrix formulation in Eq. (1). One difference between [30] and our work is that, [30] computes geodesic distance between two equivalence classes of two 6D $SO(3) \times SO(3)$ elements, while we propose an explicit parametrization of the 5D manifold $SO(3) \times (SO(3)/SO(2))$.

3 Optimization Criteria

With the parametrization described above, we are ready to formally define the optimality, and formulate the problem we will solve.

Let $(\mathbf{x}, \mathbf{x}')$ be a putative feature correspondence pair represented as unit 3D vectors, both corresponding to an unknown 3D scene point $\mathbf{X} \in \mathbb{R}^3$. Note $(\mathbf{x}, \mathbf{x}')$ may be subject to outliers and measurement noise. We represent the two cameras by their absolute orientations R and R′, which jointly encode the essential matrix $\mathrm{E} = \mathrm{E}(\mathrm{R}, \mathrm{R}')$. The epipolar equation $\mathbf{x}'^{\mathrm{T}}\mathrm{E}\mathbf{x} = 0$ gives an algebraic error metric for measuring the optimality of an essential matrix. In this work, we will use the geometrically meaningful angular reprojection error, which is defined as

$$\begin{aligned} \measuredangle(\mathrm{R}^{\mathrm{T}}\mathbf{x}, \mathrm{R}'^{\mathrm{T}}\mathbf{x}') &\doteq \min_{\mathbf{X}} \max \left(\angle(\mathrm{R}^{\mathrm{T}}\mathbf{x}, \mathbf{X}), \angle(\mathrm{R}'^{\mathrm{T}}\mathbf{x}', \mathbf{X} - \mathbf{C}') \right) \\ &= \min_{\mathbf{X}} \max \left(\angle(\mathbf{x}, \mathrm{R}\mathbf{X}), \angle(\mathbf{x}', \mathrm{R}'(\mathbf{X} - \mathbf{C}')) \right) \end{aligned} \tag{2}$$

where $\angle(\cdot\,,\,\cdot)$ denotes the angle between two vectors, and $\mathbf{C}' \equiv [0, 0, 1]^{\mathrm{T}}$. We use the symbol $\measuredangle(\cdot\,,\,\cdot)$ to denote the angular reprojection error, which is the maximum of the two angular residuals.

With this angular error definition, there are two options to define the optimality of essential matrix $\mathrm{E}(\mathrm{R}, \mathrm{R}')$, corresponding to the following two problems.

Problem 1 (Inlier-set cardinality maximization). Given feature correspondences $(\mathbf{x}_i, \mathbf{x}'_i)$ and a prescribed angular error tolerance ϵ, the optimal essential matrix $\mathrm{E}(\mathrm{R}, \mathrm{R}')$ maximizes the cardinality of the inlier set (or consensus set) as

$$\max_{\mathrm{R},\mathrm{R}'} |\mathcal{I}|, \quad s.t. \;\; \forall i \in \mathcal{I}, \;\; \measuredangle(\mathrm{R}^{\mathrm{T}}\mathbf{x}_i, \mathrm{R}'^{\mathrm{T}}\mathbf{x}'_i) \leq \epsilon \tag{3}$$

where $\mathcal{I}$ denotes the inlier set and $|\cdot|$ represents cardinality. A pair of correspondences $(\mathbf{x}_i, \mathbf{x}'_i)$ is considered to be an inlier *w.r.t.* ϵ if $\measuredangle(\mathrm{R}^{\mathrm{T}}\mathbf{x}_i, \mathrm{R}'^{\mathrm{T}}\mathbf{x}'_i) \leq \epsilon$.

Problem 2 (Angular reprojection error minimization). Given feature correspondences $(\mathbf{x}_i, \mathbf{x}'_i)$, the optimal essential matrix $\mathrm{E}(\mathrm{R}, \mathrm{R}')$ is found by

$$\min_{\mathrm{R},\mathrm{R}'} \|\mathbf{e}\|, \quad s.t. \;\; e_i = \measuredangle(\mathrm{R}^{\mathrm{T}}\mathbf{x}_i, \mathrm{R}'^{\mathrm{T}}\mathbf{x}'_i) \tag{4}$$

where $\|\cdot\|$ is a certain norm.

Solving Problem 2 gives rise to an exact essential matrix minimizing angular error; however the result is sensitive to outliers. The goal of this paper is to optimally solve Problem 1 with an exact inlier-set cardinality, thus it is intrinsically robust. Note that the solution to Problem 1 may not be unique. To solve essential matrix both robustly and exactly, one can solve Problem 2 with existing methods (*e.g.* [11]) after obtaining the true inliers with the proposed method.

Although global optimization for Problem 2 is studied in [11], solving the cardinality maximization problem globally optimally is still extremely difficult due to its obvious combinatorial and discrete nature. In this paper, we approach the problem as a continuous optimization, and solve it by BnB search over the continuous parameter domain – the 5D product space $\mathbb{D}_\pi^2 \times \mathbb{B}_\pi^3$.

4 Branch and Bound over $\mathbb{D}_\pi^2 \times \mathbb{B}_\pi^3$

Recall that the goal is to globally maximize the inlier-cardinality as shown in Eq. (3). We treat this problem as continuous optimization, and solve it via 5D space BnB. A high level description of our method is given below. For the ease of manipulation, we use a 5D cube $\mathbb{C}_\pi^5$ with half side-length π to enclose the space of $\mathbb{D}_\pi^2 \times \mathbb{B}_\pi^3$. The initial cube $\mathbb{C}_\pi^5$ can be divided into smaller cubes. For each such cube, we compute the lower-bound (LB) as well as the upper-bound (UB) of the inlier-set cardinality for all rotations within it. LB and UB will be compared with the best value found so far, then this cube will be discarded or sub-divided. In the following we will denote a cube by $C_\sigma(\bar{\mathrm{R}}, \bar{\mathrm{R}}')$, where σ is its half side-length, and $\bar{\mathrm{R}}, \bar{\mathrm{R}}'$ are the center rotations of the corresponding 2D square and 3D cube respectively.

As is true for any BnB algorithm, the key to success is to find effective and efficient bounds. Below we will explain how we achieve this.

4.1 Lower-Bound Computation

Finding a lower-bound for the cardinality maximization problem is relatively easy. It can be done simply by evaluating the cardinality function at a single point within the cubical domain. Obviously, the cardinality obtained in this way is necessarily a lower-bound, as it must not be greater than the true maximal cardinality with rotation in that cube.

The following algorithm computes a lower-bound for a cube $C_\sigma(\bar{\mathrm{R}}, \bar{\mathrm{R}}')$ *w.r.t.* a prescribed angular error tolerance ϵ.

1. Check all candidate correspondences $(\mathbf{x}_i, \mathbf{x}_i')$, with center rotations $\bar{\mathrm{R}}, \bar{\mathrm{R}}'$.
2. Count how many *feasibility inequalities* $\angle(\mathrm{R}^\mathrm{T}\mathbf{x}_i, \mathbf{X}_i) \le \epsilon$ and $\angle(\mathrm{R}'^\mathrm{T}\mathbf{x}_i', \mathbf{X}_i - \mathbf{C}') \le \epsilon$ can be satisfied with some $\mathbf{X}_i$.
3. Report the above count as a lower-bound for this cube.

Step 2 of the algorithm is done by solving a series of *feasibility test problems.* How to perform such tests will be explained in Sec. 4.3.

4.2 Upper-Bound Computation via Relaxation

In solving maximization (as opposed to minimization) with BnB, it is in general more difficult to find a proper upper-bound (than to find a lower-bound).

The following algorithm gives our solution to finding suitable upper-bound of the cardinality function for a given cube $C_\sigma(\bar{\mathrm{R}}, \bar{\mathrm{R}}')$ and tolerance ϵ.

1. Check all correspondences $(\mathbf{x}_i, \mathbf{x}_i')$ with center rotations $\bar{\mathrm{R}}, \bar{\mathrm{R}}'$.
2. Count how many *relaxed feasibility inequalities* $\angle(\bar{\mathrm{R}}^{\mathrm{T}}\mathbf{x}_i, \mathbf{X}_i) \leq \epsilon + \sqrt{2}\sigma$ and $\angle(\bar{\mathrm{R}}'^{\mathrm{T}}\mathbf{x}_i', \mathbf{X}_i - \mathbf{C}') \leq \epsilon + \sqrt{3}\sigma$ can be satisfied with some $\mathbf{X}_i$.
3. Report the above count as an upper-bound for this cube.

Note in Step 2 of this algorithm, we solve a *relaxed* feasibility test problem, as the thresholds in the right side of the inequalities have been enlarged (relaxed), leading to more correspondences to be claimed as inliers, hence increasing the inlier cardinality.

To show that the upper-bound is valid (*i.e.* no solution in the cube yields larger inlier-set cardinality), a lemma and its proof are given below.

Lemma 1. *For a 5D cubic domain $C_\sigma(\bar{\mathrm{R}}, \bar{\mathrm{R}}')$, solving the above relaxed feasibility problem gives a valid upper-bound of the inlier-set cardinality.*

Proof. Our proof follows from two lemmas of paper [11], which show that, for any vector $\mathbf{x} \in \mathbb{R}^3$, given two arbitrary rotations $\mathrm{R}, \bar{\mathrm{R}}$ (with $\mathbf{v}$ and $\bar{\mathbf{v}}$ as their angle-axis representations), one must have $\angle(\mathrm{R}\mathbf{x}, \bar{\mathrm{R}}\mathbf{x}) \leq \angle(\mathrm{R}, \bar{\mathrm{R}}) \leq \|\mathbf{v} - \bar{\mathbf{v}}\|$.

Let's first fix R', and consider a 2D square domain of R centered at $\bar{\mathrm{R}}$ with half side-length σ. Suppose R^* is the optimal rotation, among all rotations within this domain, such that the corresponding inlier-set $\mathcal{I}$ is maximized. Therefore R^* must be feasible for inlier points, *i.e.* $\forall i \in \mathcal{I}$ one has $\angle(\mathrm{R}^{*\mathrm{T}}\mathbf{x}_i, \mathrm{R}'^{\mathrm{T}}\mathbf{x}_i') \leq \epsilon \Rightarrow \angle(\mathrm{R}^{*\mathrm{T}}\mathbf{x}_i, \mathbf{X}_i) \leq \epsilon$ with some $\mathbf{X}_i$. Then for the center rotation $\bar{\mathrm{R}}$ we have

$$\begin{aligned}\angle(\bar{\mathrm{R}}^{\mathrm{T}}\mathbf{x}_i, \mathbf{X}_i) &\leq \angle(\mathrm{R}^{*\mathrm{T}}\mathbf{x}_i, \mathbf{X}_i) + \angle(\bar{\mathrm{R}}^{\mathrm{T}}\mathbf{x}_i, \mathrm{R}^{*\mathrm{T}}\mathbf{x}_i)\\ &\leq \epsilon + \angle(\bar{\mathrm{R}}, \mathrm{R}^*)\\ &\leq \epsilon + \|\bar{\mathbf{v}} - \mathbf{v}^*\|\\ &\leq \epsilon + \sqrt{2}\sigma.\end{aligned} \tag{5}$$

This result implies that, if we relax the right side of the feasibility inequality from ϵ to $\epsilon + \sqrt{2}\sigma$ and evaluate inlier cardinality with respect to the center rotation, then the obtained cardinality will be no less than the optimal cardinality obtained within this cube, *i.e.* the one corresponding to R^*.

For the other rotation R' (which is a 3-dof rotation) and vector $\mathbf{x}'$, a similar result can be obtained, except that in this case one has $\sqrt{3}\sigma$ for a 3D cubic domain instead of $\sqrt{2}\sigma$. Combining both rotations we have: for each point i in the optimal inlier-set with rotations in $C_\sigma(\bar{\mathrm{R}}, \bar{\mathrm{R}}')$, both $\angle(\bar{\mathrm{R}}^{\mathrm{T}}\mathbf{x}_i, \mathbf{X}_i) \leq \epsilon + \sqrt{2}\sigma$ and $\angle(\bar{\mathrm{R}}'^{\mathrm{T}}\mathbf{x}_i', \mathbf{X}_i - \mathbf{C}') \leq \epsilon + \sqrt{3}\sigma$ must be satisfied with some $\mathbf{X}_i$. This completes the proof and the upper-bound is valid.

4.3 Efficient Bounding with Closed-Form Feasibility Test

Solving upper-bound and lower-bound necessitates the feasibility test task. This task is: given a pair of camera rotations R, R' (along with $\mathbf{C} \equiv \mathbf{0}, \mathbf{C}' \equiv [0, 0, 1]^{\mathrm{T}}$), test whether or not a correspondences pair $(\mathbf{x}, \mathbf{x}')$ is an inlier *w.r.t.* the given angular reprojection error threshold ϵ. It can be formally formulated as

Problem 3 (Feasibility test for determining inliers).

$$\begin{array}{ll} \textit{Given} & \mathbf{x}, \mathbf{x}', \mathrm{R}, \mathrm{R}', \mathbf{C}, \mathbf{C}', \varepsilon, \varepsilon' \\ \textit{does there exist} & \mathbf{X} \\ \textit{such that} & \angle(\mathrm{R}^{\mathrm{T}}\mathbf{x}, \mathbf{X} - \mathbf{C}) \leq \varepsilon \\ \textit{and} & \angle(\mathrm{R}'^{\mathrm{T}}\mathbf{x}', \mathbf{X} - \mathbf{C}') \leq \varepsilon' \end{array}$$

where $\varepsilon = \varepsilon' = \epsilon$ for the feasibility test in lower-bound computation, and $\varepsilon = \epsilon + \sqrt{2}\sigma$, $\varepsilon' = \epsilon + \sqrt{3}\sigma$ for the relaxed one in upper-bound computation.

One way to do such a test is by *two-view triangulation*. It has been shown in [16,15] that this problem can be solved by Second Order Cone Programming (SOCP). We have tested this method experimentally using a commercial SOCP solver (MOSEK). It worked successfully on very small numbers of feature points but with high computational demand, preventing us from doing larger experiment. We were therefore motivated to seek a faster solution.

In this paper, built upon previous work [5], our bounds are derived with efficient feasibility test in closed-form. The intuition is: to verify whether or not $(\mathbf{x}, \mathbf{x}')$ is compatible with a tentatively given essential matrix, one does not have to recover the corresponding 3D point $\mathbf{X}$. Instead, it is sufficient to check whether or not the epipolar relationship of the two points is satisfied. A similar idea was proposed in [11], where a Linear Programming solver is used for feasibility tests.

Our method avoids using convex programming. It is a direct application of the following theorem which is a simple extension of that in [5]. Recall that, the first camera is centered the origin and the second one is on Z-axis. If we represent the unit vectors $\mathrm{R}^{\mathrm{T}}\mathbf{x}$ and $\mathrm{R}'^{\mathrm{T}}\mathbf{x}'$ in spherical coordinates, they become

$$\mathrm{R}^{\mathrm{T}}\mathbf{x} = \begin{bmatrix} \sin\theta\cos\varphi \\ \sin\theta\sin\varphi \\ \cos\theta \end{bmatrix}, \quad \mathrm{R}'^{\mathrm{T}}\mathbf{x}' = \begin{bmatrix} \sin\theta'\cos\varphi' \\ \sin\theta'\sin\varphi' \\ \cos\theta' \end{bmatrix}. \tag{6}$$

Theorem 1. *Given a pair of correspondences* $\mathbf{x}, \mathbf{x}'$, *rotation matrices* R, R' *and camera centers* $\mathbf{C} \equiv \mathbf{0}, \mathbf{C}' \equiv [0,0,1]^{\mathrm{T}}$, *representing* $\mathrm{R}^{\mathrm{T}}\mathbf{x}$ *and* $\mathrm{R}'^{\mathrm{T}}\mathbf{x}'$ *in spherical coordinates as* (θ, φ) *and* (θ', φ'), *we have: Problem 3 is feasible if and only if* $\begin{cases} \theta \leq \theta' + \varepsilon + \varepsilon' \\ |\varphi - \varphi'| \leq \omega \end{cases}$, *where* ω *is given below:*

$$\omega = \begin{cases} \arcsin(\frac{\sin\varepsilon}{\sin\theta}) + \arcsin(\frac{\sin\varepsilon'}{\sin\theta'}), & \textit{if } \theta < \theta' \\ \arccos(\frac{\cos(\varepsilon+\varepsilon') - \cos\theta\cos\theta'}{\sin\theta\sin\theta'}), & \textit{if } \theta \in [\theta', \theta'+\varepsilon+\varepsilon'] \\ \pi, \ \textit{if any of the above is undefined} \end{cases} \cdot \tag{7}$$

Proof of this theorem can be found in [5]. The geometric intuition behind Theorem 1 is easy to discern. Consider the limit case when $\varepsilon \to 0$ and $\varepsilon' \to 0$ (thus $\omega \to 0$), then $|\varphi - \varphi'| \leq \omega \Rightarrow \varphi = \varphi'$ says that the two viewing rays of the two points lie in the same *half-plane* containing the baseline, and $\theta < \theta' + \varepsilon + \varepsilon' \Rightarrow \theta < \theta'$ entails that the two viewing rays intersect in this half-plane.

Based on this theorem, both lower-bound and upper-bound for a cube can be made in closed-form. The evaluation is efficient with elementary computation (and counting), using basic trigonometric functions.

Algorithm 1. BnB search in $\mathbb{D}_\pi^2 \times \mathbb{B}_\pi^3$ for optimal essential matrix maximizing the inlier set

---

Input: Images point pairs $(\mathbf{x}_i, \mathbf{x}_i')$, $i = 1, \ldots, M$; angular error threshold ϵ.
Output: Optimal essential matrix E^* and corresponding inlier set $\mathcal{I}^*$ of size N^*.

Divide $[-\pi, \pi]^5$ into small sub-cubes and push them into Q.
Set $N^* = 4$. %*we need to find at least* $N^* = 5$ *points*
begin
  Read out a cube with the highest upper-bound UB from Q.
  Quit the loop if $UB = N^*$.
  Divide it into $2^5 = 32$ sub-cubes with equal side length.
  foreach sub-cube $C_\sigma(\bar{\mathrm{R}}, \bar{\mathrm{R}}')$ **do**
    Set its lower-bound LB and upper-bound UB to be 0.
    foreach correspondence pair $(\mathbf{x}_i, \mathbf{x}_i')$ **do**
      $LB{+}{+}$, if Problem 3 is feasible with $\bar{\mathrm{R}}, \bar{\mathrm{R}}', \epsilon, \epsilon$.
      $UB{+}{+}$, if Problem 3 is feasible with $\bar{\mathrm{R}}, \bar{\mathrm{R}}', \epsilon{+}\sqrt{2}\sigma, \epsilon{+}\sqrt{3}\sigma$.
    end
    if $LB > N^*$ **then**
      Update $N^* = LB$, $\mathrm{E}^* = \mathrm{E}(\bar{\mathrm{R}}, \bar{\mathrm{R}}')$ and also $\mathcal{I}^*$.
    end
    Discard this cube if $UB \leqslant N^*$; otherwise put it into Q.
  end
end

Degeneracy. Note that when a feature point (θ, φ) either falls on Z-axis or is sufficiently close to it ($\theta < \epsilon$ or $\theta < \epsilon'$), the above functions for ω are not defined. In such cases the feasibility test always returns true.

4.4 The Main Algorithm

Armed with the above developments of domain parametrization, lower and upper bounds, and closed-form feasibility test, we are now ready to present our main algorithm. Although it appears to be a bit technically heavy, the central idea and the implementation are rather simple: for each parameter domain, *i.e.* a 5D cube, count the number of feature correspondences that pass the feasibility test (or, relaxed feasibility test) as the lower-bound (or, upper-bound) of the cardinality, and try to update the solution and discard this cube accordingly. Algorithm 1 summarizes the algorithm in pseudo-code form.

Initial cubes. Before the BnB loop we divide the initial cube $[-\pi, \pi]^5$ into smaller cubes as it is less likely that a large cube can be discarded. In our implementation we use $6^5 = 7776$ inital cubes with equal side length.

Search strategy. The BnB algorithm uses the *best-first-search* strategy. Concretely, it maintains a priority queue of the active cubes, whose priorities are set to be their upper-bounds. In this way, the BnB algorithm always explores the most promising cube first.

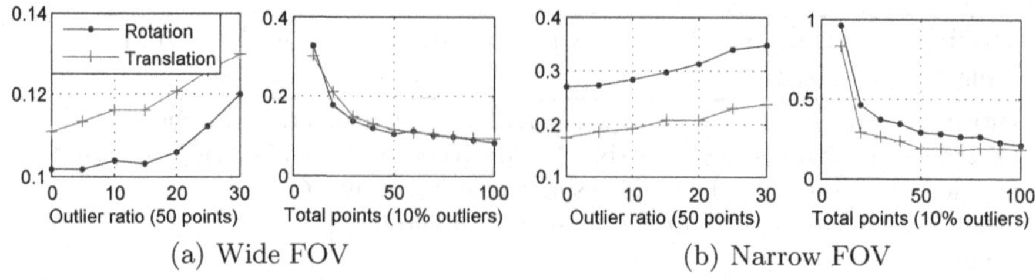

(a) Wide FOV (b) Narrow FOV

Fig. 2. Average rotation and translation error (both in degrees) for 50 runs of our method in synthetic wide-FOV (*left*) and narrow-FOV (*right*) tests *w.r.t* different outlier ratios and total points

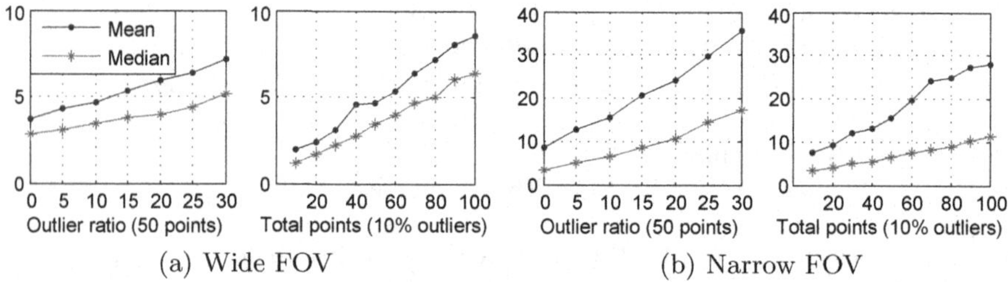

(a) Wide FOV (b) Narrow FOV

Fig. 3. Running time (in seconds) for 50 runs of our method in synthetic wide-FOV (*left*) and narrow-FOV (*right*) tests *w.r.t* different outlier ratios and total points

Proof of convergence. The convergence of the algorithm is easy to see, as when the side-lengths of all cubes asymptotically diminish to zero, the gap between the upper-bound and lower-bound will be zero too.

5 Experiment Results

In this section, we report the experimental results on synthetic scenes and real imageries. Our method is implemented in C++, and tested on a standard PC with Intel i7 3.4GHz 4-core CPU and 8GB memory.

5.1 Synthetic Scene Test: Normal Cases

The main goal of experiments on synthetic data is to verify the correctness of the proposed method, including the essential manifold parametrization and the BnB algorithm. In these experiments we set the angular error threshold to be 0.002 radians (about 0.115 degrees). Inlier number is the main index for essential matrix evaluation as our goal is to optimally maximize it. Nevertheless, we will also report the estimation error of essential matrix. For better comprehension, we use classic parametrization $\mathrm{E} = [\hat{\mathbf{t}}]_\times \hat{\mathrm{R}}$, and evaluate error of $\hat{\mathrm{R}}$ and $\hat{\mathbf{t}}$. Rotation error is the angle between $\hat{\mathrm{R}}$ and ground truth rotation. As $\hat{\mathbf{t}}$ is obtained up to a scale, we define translation error as the angle between $\hat{\mathbf{t}}$ and ground

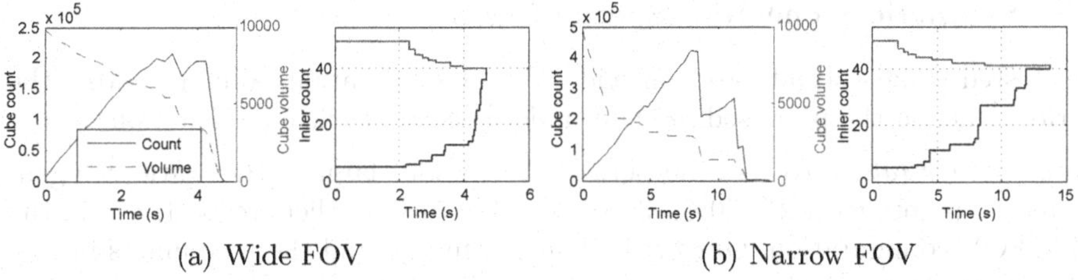

Fig. 4. Typical cube and bound evolutions of BnB in synthetic wide-FOV (*left*) and narrow-FOV (*right*) tests using 50 points with 20% (*i.e.* 10) outliers

truth translation. Note that, as discussed in Sec. 3, these results can be further improved by minimizing the reprojection error of obtained inliers (which is not used here).

Wide Field-Of-View (Omnidirectional Camera). In this test synthetic data with random points and two omnidirectional cameras which have 360° field of view were used. We synthesized 50 configurations of different points and camera poses. The points were generated in a cube centered at origin with side length 4, and camera centers were generated from Gaussian distribution centered at origin with $\sigma = 0.5$. Gaussian noise with $\sigma = 0.001$ was added to all the projected image points. To generate outliers, we randomly perturbed the image points in the first camera by over 10 degrees. We tested our method first on different numbers of outliers with fixed total points (50), and then on different numbers of points with fixed outlier ratio (10%). As expected, *our method succeeded in all the tests in terms of finding out all the true inliers.* Average rotation and translation errors of the 50 configurations are shown in Fig. 2. Clearly, the error increases with outlier ratio, and decreases with total point number. Average running time is shown in Fig. 3. In general, it took the method longer time to converge when higher levels of outliers were present. To visualize the behavior of BnB, we present typical evolution curves of active cubes and global bounds as a function of time in Fig. 4.

Narrow Field-Of-View. We then tested our method with narrow field of view. We synthesized the situation where the points are confined in approximately 60° FOV of two regular pinhole cameras. The points were generated in a cube centered at origin with side length 4, and cameras were randomly placed at a distance of about 4 facing the origin. Other settings were the same with that in wide-FOV tests. Again, our method successfully found out all the true inliers. The estimation error, running time, and typical BnB evolution are also shown in Fig. 2, Fig. 3 and Fig. 4 respectively. It is clear that solving the problem with narrow-FOV is generally more difficult than that with wide-FOV, as evidenced by the larger rotation and translation errors as well as the longer running time of our method.

5.2 Synthetic Scene Test: Special Cases

We tested some special cases on wide FOV configuration, aiming to test the performance of the proposed method under special or extreme situations.

Large outlier ratio. To test the performance under large outlier ratio, we generated 50 points with 25 (50%), 30 (60%), 35 (70%) outliers respectively in the wide FOV configuration. Our method successfully found the true inliers in 11s, 26s and 81s respectively.

Pure translational motion. In this experiment, two cameras with pure (and random) translation as the ground-truth transformation and 50 points were synthesized. We ran our method on these points, and the angle between the two estimated rotations R and R′ is about 0.11 degrees, which indicates that our method successfully identified the equal rotation case.

All scene points on a plane. We synthesized a planar case where all 50 points lie on a plane. This is a well-known degenerate case for fundamental matrix estimation, however it should not affect essential matrix estimation, as explained in [24]. Our experiment on this case obtained positive result and we successfully recovered the correct essential matrices with and without outliers. The rotation and translation errors are all below 0.15 degrees.

5.3 Real Image Test

Images from both narrow-FOV and wide-FOV cameras were then used to evaluate the real-life performance of our method. We also tested RANSAC and LO-RANSAC [2] (with Option 4 of local optimization described in [2]) methods. In both RANSAC implementations, the 8-point method[2] was used and angular error threshold is adopted to distinguish outliers; the outlier ratio and probability parameter η were set to be 30% and 0.99 respectively. Note that, the goal of this paper is not to replace the popular RANSAC and its variants in essential matrix estimation, but to provide a complementary (yet important) optimal method.

Narrow Field-Of-View. We tested our method on two image pairs from the Corridor and Valbonne data sets[3]. 94 and 106 SIFT matches [22] were generated respectively for the two pairs as shown in Fig. 5. The angular error threshold was set to 0.0015 radians. We parallelized the BnB search with 8 threads, and our method converged in 221s and 453s respectively. Apparently, it takes quite more time than on synthetic data of the same size. However, this is reasonable as will be analyzed as follows. On a 600×600 image from a 60°-FOV camera, a small pixel difference, say 3 pixels, yields about 0.3-degree angle difference. To tell outliers from inliers at this accuracy of both camera orientations, the 5D cube would have to be divided into $(\frac{180}{0.3/\sqrt{2}})^2 \times (\frac{180}{0.3/\sqrt{3}})^3 \approx 8 \times 10^{14}$ blocks for a complete search method, and this is also a very difficult task for our BnB. The number

[2] The 5-point method (with [9]'s solver) was also tested. It performed comparably with or slightly worse than the 8-point method; the latter one is thus presented.

[3] http://www.robots.ox.ac.uk/~vgg/data/data-mview.html

Table 1. Inlier-set maximization performance of different methods. The first column lists the images and correspondence numbers. The second and third columns show the maximal and mean inlier number detected by RANSAC and LO-RANSAC in their 1,000 runs. The last column shows the inlier number from our method and the running time (with 8 threads).

Images (#points)	RANSAC max/mean #inliers	LO-RANSAC max/mean #inliers	Our method #inliers (time)
Corridor (94)	63 / 32.5	65 / 50.0	66 (221s)
Church (106)	82 / 32.8	87 / 35.5	89 (453s)
Building (202)	160 / 146.9	161 / 151.7	163 (52s)
Office (151)	124 / 91.4	126 / 104.2	126 (43s)

(a) Corridor (b) Church

Fig. 5. Results on narrow-FOV images. Green and red dots are respectively inlier and outlier correspondences found by our method. For outliers we labeled their angular reprojection errors in radius. (Best viewed on screen and with zoom-in)

of detected inliers is 66 for Corridor image and 89 for Church image, indicating 29.8% and 16% outlier ratios respectively. The detected inliers and outliers are shown in Fig. 5. For some outliers we show their angular errors (optimally solved via bi-section and SOCP [15]) with the obtained essential matrix.

We then repeated both RANSAC and LO-RANSAC 1,000 times with the same angular error threshold; the resulting inlier numbers are shown in the first two columns of Tab. 1. The heuristic and stochastic nature of random sampling scheme can be clearly seen, as the mean performances of the 1,000 runs are not satisfactory. Moreover, both the two methods failed to detect the same inlier number as ours. This can be explained by the fact that algebraic solution of essential matrix is not consistent with the meaningful geometric error metric. In future we plan to compare our method with RANSAC methods in high-noise situation where algebraic solutions can be severely biased.

Wide Field-Of-View (Fisheye Camera). In order to test our method in real-life wide-FOV case, a camera with a fisheye lens was used to capture images of the scene with up to 190° FOV. The camera was calibrated with the method of [27].

Fig. 6 shows two typical pairs referred as Building and Office. The angular threshold was set to be 0.003 radians for these images. Our method converged

(a) Building (b) Office

Fig. 6. Results on wide-FOV images taken with a fisheye camera. See caption of Fig. 5.

in 52s and 43s for the two image pairs respectively as shown in Tab. 1, and the results indicate 19.3% and 16.6% outlier ratios. In general, the angular errors of outliers are larger than that in the narrow-FOV case (see Fig. 6), and our method ran faster on wide-FOV images. This result is in consistent with our synthetic experiments and similar discoveries reported in previous works [3,11,6,13].

6 Conclusion and Future Work

A branch-and-bound global optimization method is proposed for essential matrix estimation via inlier-set cardinality maximization under geometric (angular) error. An explicit and geometrically meaningful parametrization of the 5D essential manifold, *i.e.* $\mathbb{D}_\pi^2 \times \mathbb{B}_\pi^3$, is used to perform the BnB search. Based on previous works [11] and [5], closed-form bounding functions of inlier-set cardinality are derived, leading to efficient bound evaluation in the 5D space BnB.

Currently the proposed method is slow especially for cameras with small field of view. Nevertheless, due to its optimality the method can be used as a benchmark for method evaluation, or be applied in situations where robustness or accuracy is highly desired while speed is not crucial.

To make the method faster and more practical, there are some strategies we would like to investigate in future. For example, a possible one is to get an initial essential matrix estimate using RANSAC, then search the parameter space with the proposed BnB in a small region around this estimate. Taking advantage of prior knowledge on motion to confine the parameter space is a metric of continues optimization in contrast to discrete combinatorial optimization. Since our BnB algorithm can be easily parallelized, another idea would be porting it onto modern GPU where a significant speedup can be expected.

Acknowledgements. This work was funded in part by the Natural Science Foundation of China (NSFC) under Grant No 61375044, and ARC Discovery grants: DP120103896, DP130104567, and CE140100016. The first author is funded by the Chinese Scholarship Council to be a joint PhD student from BIT to ANU. We would like to thank the anonymous reviewers for their valuable comments.

References

1. Bazin, J.-C., Seo, Y., Pollefeys, M.: Globally optimal consensus set maximization through rotation search. In: Lee, K.M., Matsushita, Y., Rehg, J.M., Hu, Z. (eds.) ACCV 2012, Part II. LNCS, vol. 7725, pp. 539–551. Springer, Heidelberg (2013)
2. Chum, O., Matas, J., Kittler, J.: Locally optimized RANSAC. Pattern Recognition (2003)
3. Daniilidisl, K., Spetsakisz, M.E.: Understanding noise sensitivity in structure from motion. In: Visual Navigation: from Biological Systems to Unmanned Ground Vehicles. Psychology Press (1997)
4. Dellaert, F., Seitz, S.M., Thorpe, C.E., Thrun, S.: Structure from motion without correspondence. In: CVPR (2000)
5. Enqvist, O., Jiang, F., Kahl, F.: A brute-force algorithm for reconstructing a scene from two projections. In: CVPR (2011)
6. Enqvist, O., Kahl, F.: Two view geometry estimation with outliers. In: BMVC (2009)
7. Fischler, M.A., Bolles, R.C.: Random sample consensus: a paradigm for model fitting with applications to image analysis and automated cartography. Comm. ACM (1981)
8. Goshen, L., Shimshoni, I.: Balanced exploration and exploitation model search for efficient epipolar geometry estimation. T-PAMI (2008)
9. Hartley, R., Li, H.: An efficient hidden variable approach to minimal-case camera motion estimation. T-PAMI (2012)
10. Hartley, R.I.: In: defense of the eight-point algorithm. T-PAMI (1997)
11. Hartley, R.I., Kahl, F.: Global optimization through searching rotation space and optimal estimation of the essential matrix. In: ICCV (2007)
12. Hartley, R.I., Zisserman, A.: Multiple View Geometry in Computer Vision, 2nd edn. Cambridge University Press (2004)
13. Heller, J., Havlena, M., Pajdla, T.: A branch-and-bound algorithm for globally optimal hand-eye calibration. In: CVPR (2012)
14. Helmke, U., Hüper, K., Lee, P.Y., Moore, J.: Essential matrix estimation using gauss-newton iterations on a manifold. IJCV (2007)
15. Kahl, F., Hartley, R.: Multiple-view geometry under the l_∞-norm. T-PAMI (2008)
16. Ke, Q., Kanade, T.: Quasiconvex optimization for robust geometric reconstruction. In: ICCV (2005)
17. Lee, J.: Introduction to topological manifolds. Springer (2010)
18. Li, H.: A practical algorithm for l_∞ triangulation with outliers. In: CVPR (2007)
19. Li, H.: Consensus set maximization with guaranteed global optimality for robust geometry estimation. In: ICCV (2009)
20. Li, H., Hartley, R.: Five-point motion estimation made easy. In: ICPR (2006)
21. Longuet-Higgins, H.C.: A computer algorithm for reconstructing a scene from two projections. Nature (1981)
22. Lowe, D.G.: Distinctive image features from scale-invariant keypoints. IJCV (2004)
23. Makadia, A., Geyer, C., Daniilidis, K.: Correspondence-free structure from motion. IJCV (2007)
24. Nistér, D.: An efficient solution to the five-point relative pose problem. T-PAMI (2004)
25. Olsson, C., Eriksson, A., Hartley, R.: Outlier removal using duality. In: CVPR (2010)

26. Raguram, R., Chum, O., Pollefeys, M., Matas, J., Frahm, J.: USAC: A universal framework for random sample consensus. T-PAMI (2013)
27. Scaramuzza, D., Martinelli, A., Siegwart, R.: A toolbox for easily calibrating omnidirectional cameras. In: IROS (2006)
28. Sim, K., Hartley, R.: Removing outliers using the l_∞ norm. In: CVPR (2006)
29. Subbarao, R., Genc, Y., Meer, P.: Robust unambiguous parametrization of the essential manifold. In: CVPR (2008)
30. Tron, R., Daniilidis, K.: On the quotient representation for the essential manifold. In: CVPR (2014)
31. Yang, J., Li, H., Jia, Y.: Go-ICP: Solving 3D registration efficiently and globally optimally. In: ICCV (2013)
32. Zheng, Y., Sugimoto, S., Okutomi, M.: A branch and contract algorithm for globally optimal fundamental matrix estimation. In: CVPR (2011)

UPnP: An Optimal $O(n)$ Solution to the Absolute Pose Problem with Universal Applicability

Laurent Kneip[1], Hongdong Li[1], and Yongduek Seo[2]

[1] Research School of Engineering, Australian National University, Australia
[2] Department of Media Technology, Sogang University, Korea

Abstract. A large number of absolute pose algorithms have been presented in the literature. Common performance criteria are computational complexity, geometric optimality, global optimality, structural degeneracies, and the number of solutions. The ability to handle minimal sets of correspondences, resulting solution multiplicity, and generalized cameras are further desirable properties. This paper presents the first PnP solution that unifies all the above desirable properties within a single algorithm. We compare our result to state-of-the-art minimal, non-minimal, central, and non-central PnP algorithms, and demonstrate universal applicability, competitive noise resilience, and superior computational efficiency. Our algorithm is called *Unified PnP* (UPnP).

Keywords: PnP, Non-perspective PnP, Generalized absolute pose, linear complexity, global optimality, geometric optimality, DLS.

1 Introduction

The Perspective-n-Point (PnP) algorithm is a fundamental problem in geometric computer vision. Given a certain number of correspondences between 3D world points and 2D image measurements, the problem consists of fitting the absolute position and orientation of the camera to the measurement data. Our contribution is a PnP solution that unifies most desirable properties within one and the same algorithm. We call our method *Unified PnP* (UPnP), and the benefits are summarized as follows:

- *Universal applicability*: UPnP is applicable to both central and non-central camera systems (i.e. generalized cameras). In contrast, existing methods are often designed exclusively for the central case (e.g. [6], [17]).
- *Optimality*: Similarly to [16], we employ the object space error. However, we do not rely on convex relaxation techniques, which is why our solution is theoretically guaranteed to return a geometrical optimum. Likewise, UPnP is guaranteed to find the global optimum.
- *Linear complexity*: Similarly to many recent works (e.g. [11]), our algorithm solves the PnP problem with $O(n)$ (linear) complexity in the number of points. From a practical point of view, the $O(n)$-complexity argument is

D. Fleet et al. (Eds.): ECCV 2014, Part I, LNCS 8689, pp. 127–142, 2014.
© Springer International Publishing Switzerland 2014

stronger than simple algebraic linearity of the solution. Despite of returning comparable results to [16] in terms of noise resilience, our method does not employ any iterative parts and therefore turns out to be **faster by about two orders of magnitude**.
- *Completeness*: The proposed solution is complete in the sense of returning multiple solutions. It therefore supports the minimal case, as well as other possible ambiguous-pose situations [15]. Moreover—in contrast to recent works such as [6] and [17]—our algorithm still does not return any spurious solutions. The returned number of solutions is precisely equal to the maximum number of solutions in the minimal case. Similarly to [17], we furthermore exploit 2-fold symmetry in the space of quaternions in order to avoid solution duplicates.
- *Homogeneity*: We parametrize rotations in terms of unit-quaternions—a non-minimal parametrization of rotations that is free of singularities and leads to homogeneous accuracy.

UPnP unifies all listed properties. It is inspired by several recent works, and—using first-order optimality conditions—solves the problem by a closed-form computation of all stationary points of the sum of squared object space errors. The conceptual innovations lie in the avoidance of a Lagrangian formulation, a geometrically consistent application of the Gröbner basis methodology, and a general technique to circumvent 2-fold symmetry in quaternion-based parametrizations.

The paper is structured as follows: The related work is presented in the following subsection. Section 2 then outlines the core theoretical contributions behind our approach. Section 3 finally contains a detailed comparison to existing algorithms, show-casing state-of-the-art noise resilience at superior computational efficiency.

1.1 Related Work

While an exhaustive review of the vast literature on the PnP problem goes beyond the extend of this introduction, we nonetheless note that—after more than 170 years of related research—still new solutions with interesting properties keep being discovered. The most recent advancement in the minimal case—the P3P problem—was presented in 2011 [9]. The P3P problem uses 3 correspondences and returns at most 4 solutions. One of the major recent achievements in the PnP case then consists of proving that the problem can be solved accurately in linear time with respect to the number of correspondences. The first solution to provide accurate results under linear complexity is EPnP [11] (2009). This algorithm is computationally efficient, however depends on a special variant with only 3 control points in the planar case, minimizes only an algebraic error, and fails in situations of solution multiplicity (i.e., in situations of pose-ambiguity such as for instance the minimal case). The first $O(n)$-successor that succeeds in all these criteria was presented in 2011 and is called DLS [6]. It performs measurement data compression in linear time and then computes all stationary points of the sum of squared object-space errors in closed-form, using polynomial resultant techniques. It achieves a least-squares geometric error in linear time,

Table 1. Comparison of properties of various $O(n)$ PnP algorithms. Note, however, that [16] contains an iterative convex relaxation part, which means that the effective computational complexity of SOS is in fact unbounded (hence the brackets).

	EPnP	DLS	OPnP	SOS	GPnP	UPnP
reference	[11]	[6]	[17]	[16]	[8]	this
year	2009	2011	2013	2008	2013	2014
central cameras	✓	✓	✓	✓		✓
non-central cameras				✓	✓	✓
geometric optimality		✓		✓		✓
linear complexity	✓	✓	✓	(✓)	✓	✓
multiple solutions		✓	✓			✓
singularity-free rotation param.	✓		✓	✓	✓	✓

however employs a singularity-affected rotation matrix parametrization [2]. The most recent contribution in $O(n)$-complexity PnP solvers is then given by the OPnP algorithm [17] (2013), which essentially replaces the Cayley parametrization by the singularity-free non-unit quaternion parametrization, thus leading to improved accuracy. They also exploit 2-fold symmetry in the solver, thus avoiding the duality of quaternion solutions. Although they achieve very good accuracy, we still note that—from a theoretical point of view—their algorithm again falls back to an algebraic error.

An interesting fact is that—while searching for all stationary points—the DLS and OPnP algorithms find 27 and 40 solutions, respectively. In other words, despite of using more than the minimum amount of information, those algorithms return far more solutions than a minimal solver. It is true that many of the stationary points can be neglected because they are either complex or local maxima/saddle points, but still the computation at least intermediately reaches a seemingly too high level of complexity.

More recently, people have also started to consider the generalized PnP problem, which consists of estimating the position of a non-central or generalized camera given correspondences between arbitrary non-central rays in the camera frame and points in the world frame. [3], [14], and [8] present minimal solvers for the generalized PnP problem, proving that 3 correspondences are still enough and that the maximum number of possible solutions corresponds to 8. Regarding the generalized PnP problem, there has been less progress to date. [5] presents the first linear complexity solution, however minimizes only an algebraic error. It fails in situations of multiple solutions (e.g. the minimal case), and depends on a special variant for the planar case. The linear complexity solution presented in [16] (SOS) minimizes a geometric error, however again fails in the mentioned special cases, and depends on a computationally intensive, iterative convex relaxation technique. Yet another algebraic $O(n)$ solution to the generalized PnP problem has been discovered in 2013 [8] (GPnP), and essentially consists of a generalization of the EPnP algorithm to the non-central case. It thus comes with similar drawbacks.

Table 1 shows a summary of all relevant algorithms and their properties, including the proposed UPnP algorithm.

2 Theory

We now proceed to the theoretical part of our method. We start by recalling the geometry of the absolute pose problem in the generalized case, which covers the classical perspective situation as well. We then derive a cost-function in the space of quaternions reflecting the geometrical error as a function of absolute orientation. All local minima are found by a closed-form computation of all stationary points. This is achieved by computing a Gröbner basis over the first-order optimality conditions and the quaternion unit-norm constraint. We also present an alternative unit-norm constraint allowing us to exploit 2-fold symmetry in quaternion-space, thus reducing the number of solutions by a factor of two. We finally obtain an ideal number of solutions, and also introduce an easy way to verify second-order optimality and polish the final result.

2.1 Geometry of the Absolute Pose Problem

Let $\mathbf{p}_i \in \mathbb{R}^3$ describe a point in the world frame, $\mathbf{R} \in SO^3$ the rotation from the world frame to the camera frame, and $\mathbf{t} \in \mathbb{R}^3$ the position of the world origin seen from the camera frame. The measurements of $\mathbf{p}_i$ in the camera frame are given by non-central rays expressed by $\alpha_i \mathbf{f}_i + \mathbf{v}_i$, where $\mathbf{v}_i \in \mathbb{R}^3$ represents a point on the ray, $\mathbf{f}_i \in \mathbb{R}^3$ the normalized direction vector of the ray, and α_i the depth. The situation is explained in Figure 1. The non-central projection equation results to

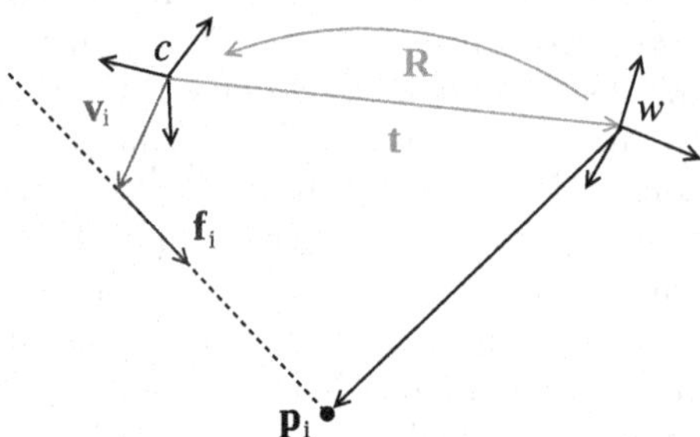

Fig. 1. Point measurements of a generalized camera

$$\alpha_i \mathbf{f}_i + \mathbf{v}_i = \mathbf{R}\mathbf{p}_i + \mathbf{t}, i = 1, \ldots, n. \tag{1}$$

$\mathbf{R}$, $\mathbf{t}$, and α_i are the parameters to be computed from the inputs $\mathbf{f}_i$, $\mathbf{v}_i$, and $\mathbf{p}_i$. In case the generalized camera is given by a multi-camera system, the $\mathbf{v}_i$'s are simply the positions of the respective camera centers inside the main common frame. In this case, some $\mathbf{f}_i$'s may obviously have the same $\mathbf{v}$ for reflecting the non-centrality of their measurement. For a central camera, $\mathbf{v}_i = \mathbf{0},\ i = 1, \ldots n$.

Let $\mathbf{I}$ be the 3×3 identity matrix. We can stack all constraints into

$$\begin{bmatrix} \mathbf{f}_1 & & & -\mathbf{I} \\ & \cdots & & \vdots \\ & & \mathbf{f}_n & -\mathbf{I} \end{bmatrix} \begin{bmatrix} \alpha_1 \\ \vdots \\ \alpha_n \\ \mathbf{t} \end{bmatrix} = \begin{bmatrix} \mathbf{R} & & \\ & \cdots & \\ & & \mathbf{R} \end{bmatrix} \begin{bmatrix} \mathbf{p}_1 \\ \vdots \\ \mathbf{p}_n \end{bmatrix} - \begin{bmatrix} \mathbf{v}_1 \\ \vdots \\ \mathbf{v}_m \end{bmatrix} \Leftrightarrow \mathbf{A}\mathbf{x} = \mathbf{W}\mathbf{b} - \mathbf{w}. \tag{2}$$

2.2 Derivation of the Objective Function

The derivation of the objective function is based on the work of [6]:

- We start by applying block-wise matrix inversion to eliminate the unknown translation and point depths from the projection equations. *(Result 1)*
- The obtained expressions are then transformed into a residual that notably corresponds to the object-space error. *(Definition 1)*
- Factorization of the rotation matrix in the sum of squared object space errors then results in a fourth-order energy function of the quaternion variables. The measurement data inside this expression is compressed in form of linear-complexity summation terms. *(Results 2 & 3)*

We now proceed to the details of this derivation.

Result 1: $\mathbf{x}$ appears linearly in (2) and can be eliminated by

$$\mathbf{x} = (\mathbf{A}^T\mathbf{A})^{-1}\mathbf{A}^T(\mathbf{W}\mathbf{b} - \mathbf{w}) = \begin{bmatrix}\mathbf{U}\\ \mathbf{V}\end{bmatrix}(\mathbf{W}\mathbf{b} - \mathbf{w}). \tag{3}$$

The pseudo-inverse of $\mathbf{A}$ is hence partitioned such that the depth parameters are a function of $\mathbf{U} = \left[\mathbf{u}_1^T \ldots \mathbf{u}_n^T\right]^T$, and the translation is a function of $\mathbf{V}$. Back-substitution results in the rotation-only projection equation

$$\left[\mathbf{u}_i^T(\mathbf{W}\mathbf{b} - \mathbf{w})\right]\mathbf{f}_i + \mathbf{v}_i = \mathbf{R}\mathbf{p}_i + \mathbf{V}(\mathbf{W}\mathbf{b} - \mathbf{w}). \tag{4}$$

Proof: The symbolic solution of $\mathbf{x}$ is mainly based on [6]. The derivation of the symbolic form of $\mathbf{U}$ and $\mathbf{V}$ is based on a) $\|\mathbf{f}_i\| = 1$, b) the Schur-complement, and c) block-wise matrix inversion. It results in

$$\begin{aligned}
\mathbf{V}_{3\times 3n} &= [\mathbf{V}_1, ..., \mathbf{V}_n], \text{ with} \\
\mathbf{V}_i &= \mathbf{H}[\mathbf{f}_i\mathbf{f}_i^T - \mathbf{I}] \in \mathbb{R}^{3\times 3} \quad i = 1, ..., n, \text{ and} \qquad (5)\\
\mathbf{H}_{3\times 3} &= \left(n\mathbf{I} - \sum_{i=1}^{n}\mathbf{f}_i\mathbf{f}_i^T\right)^{-1} \qquad (6)\\
\mathbf{U}_{n\times 3n} &= \begin{bmatrix}\mathbf{f}_1^T & & \\ & \cdots & \\ & & \mathbf{f}_n^T\end{bmatrix} + \begin{bmatrix}\mathbf{f}_1^T\\ \vdots \\ \mathbf{f}_n^T\end{bmatrix}\mathbf{V} = \begin{bmatrix}\mathbf{u}_1^T\\ \vdots \\ \mathbf{u}_n^T\end{bmatrix}, \text{ with} \\
\mathbf{u}_i^T &= [\mathbf{u}_{i1}^T, \ldots, \mathbf{u}_{in}^T]_{1\times 3n}, \quad i = 1, ..., n, \text{ and} \\
\mathbf{u}_{ij}^T &= \mathbf{f}_i^T\delta(i,j) + \mathbf{f}_i^T\mathbf{V}_j \in \mathbb{R}^{1\times 3}, \quad i, j = 1, ..., n. \qquad (7)
\end{aligned}$$

$\mathbf{u}_i^T$ represents row i of $\mathbf{U}$, and $\mathbf{u}_{ij}^T$ represents the 1×3 element of $\mathbf{U}$ in row i and column $3j$. We obtain $\alpha_i = \mathbf{u}_i^T(\mathbf{W}\mathbf{b} - \mathbf{w})$ and $\mathbf{t} = \mathbf{V}(\mathbf{W}\mathbf{b} - \mathbf{w})$, and back-substitution in (1) yields the rotation-only constraint (4).[1] ■

[1] It is worth noting here that the DLS mechanism is the only one to solve for the linear elements (i.e. depth and translation) in a homogeneous way. While this might be irrelevant for the central case, where we can assume that the z-coordinate in the camera frame is bigger than 1, there is no guarantee on any coordinate in the generalized camera situation. In the non-central case, the presented resolution therefore has better accuracy than the ones in [11] and [17].

Definition 1: The residual of an estimate for $\mathbf{R}$ is the *object space error*

$$\begin{aligned}\eta_i &= \left[\mathbf{u}_i^T(\mathbf{Wb}-\mathbf{w})\right]\mathbf{f}_i + \mathbf{v}_i - \mathbf{R}\mathbf{p}_i - \mathbf{V}(\mathbf{Wb}-\mathbf{w}) \\ &= \sum_{j=1}^{n}\mathbf{u}_{ij}^T\mathbf{R}\mathbf{p}_j\mathbf{f}_i - \sum_{j=1}^{n}\mathbf{V}_j\mathbf{R}\mathbf{p}_j - \mathbf{R}\mathbf{p}_i - \sum_{j=1}^{n}\mathbf{u}_{ij}^T\mathbf{v}_j\mathbf{f}_i + \sum_{j=1}^{n}\mathbf{V}_j\mathbf{v}_j + \mathbf{v}_i. \qquad (8)\end{aligned}$$

Result 2: The residual vector of a correspondence can be expressed as $\eta_i = \mathcal{A}_i\mathbf{s} + \beta_i$, where the elements of $\mathbf{s}$ are quadratic functions of the quaternion variables, and $\mathcal{A}_i$ and β_i depend on the measurements only, and can be computed with linear complexity in the number of correspondences.

Proof: By substituting (7) in (8) and resolving the summations over terms including $\delta(i,j)$, we arrive at

$$\eta_i = \mathbf{f}_i^T\mathbf{R}\mathbf{p}_i\mathbf{f}_i - \mathbf{R}\mathbf{p}_i + \mathbf{f}_i^T\left[\sum_{j=1}^{n}\mathbf{V}_j\mathbf{R}\mathbf{p}_j\right]\mathbf{f}_i - \sum_{j=1}^{n}\mathbf{V}_j\mathbf{R}\mathbf{p}_j - \mathbf{f}_i^T\mathbf{v}_i\mathbf{f}_i + \mathbf{v}_i - \mathbf{f}_i^T\mathcal{J}\mathbf{f}_i + \mathcal{J}, \qquad (9)$$

where $\mathcal{J} = \sum_{j=1}^{n}\mathbf{V}_j\mathbf{v}_j$ does not depend on any unknowns or i anymore, so it can be computed ahead with linear complexity (just like $\mathbf{H}$). All elements that do not depend on $\mathbf{R}$ can be summarized in

$$\beta_i = -(\mathbf{f}_i^T\mathbf{v}_i\mathbf{f}_i - \mathbf{v}_i + \mathbf{f}_i^T\mathcal{J}\mathbf{f}_i - \mathcal{J}) = -(\mathbf{f}_i\mathbf{f}_i^T - \mathbf{I})(\mathbf{v}_i + \mathcal{J}) \in \mathbb{R}^3. \qquad (10)$$

We then adopt the singularity-free unit-quaternion parametrization $\mathbf{q} = [q_0, q_1, q_2, q_3]^T$ such that $q_0^2 + q_1^2 + q_1^2 + q_3^2 = 1$. $\mathbf{R}$ in function of $\mathbf{q}$ is given by

$$\mathbf{R} = \begin{pmatrix} q_0^2 + q_1^2 - q_2^2 - q_3^2 & 2q_1q_2 - 2q_0q_3 & 2q_1q_3 + 2q_0q_2 \\ 2q_1q_2 + 2q_0q_3 & q_0^2 - q_1^2 + q_2^2 - q_3^2 & 2q_2q_3 - 2q_0q_1 \\ 2q_1q_3 - 2q_0q_2 & 2q_2q_3 + 2q_0q_1 & q_0^2 - q_1^2 - q_2^2 + q_3^2 \end{pmatrix}. \qquad (11)$$

$\mathbf{R}\mathbf{p}_i$ is a 3-vector of polynomials, each one having quadratic monomials in the quaternion parameters. Grouping those monomials in

$$\mathbf{s} = [q_0^2, q_1^2, q_2^2, q_3^2, q_0q_1, q_0q_2, q_0q_3, q_1q_2, q_1q_3, q_2q_3]^T \in \mathbb{R}^{10}, \qquad (12)$$

we obtain $\mathbf{R}\mathbf{p}_i = \Phi(\mathbf{p}_i)_{3\times 10}\mathbf{s}$, where Φ is given by

$$\Phi(\mathbf{p}_i) = \begin{pmatrix} p_{ix} & p_{ix} & -p_{ix} & -p_{ix} & 0 & 2p_{iz} & -2p_{iy} & 2p_{iy} & 2p_{iz} & 0 \\ p_{iy} & -p_{iy} & p_{iy} & -p_{iy} & -2p_{iz} & 0 & 2p_{ix} & 2p_{ix} & 0 & 2p_{iz} \\ p_{iz} & -p_{iz} & -p_{iz} & p_{iz} & 2p_{iy} & -2p_{ix} & 0 & 0 & 2p_{ix} & 2p_{iy} \end{pmatrix}. \qquad (13)$$

Using (13) and (10) in (9) results in

$$\eta_i = \mathbf{f}_i^T\Phi(\mathbf{p}_i)\mathbf{s}\mathbf{f}_i - \Phi(\mathbf{p}_i)\mathbf{s} + \mathbf{f}_i^T\left[\sum_{j=1}^{n}\mathbf{V}_j\Phi(\mathbf{p}_j)\right]\mathbf{s}\mathbf{f}_i - \left[\sum_{j=1}^{n}\mathbf{V}_j\Phi(\mathbf{p}_j)\right]\mathbf{s} + \beta_i, \qquad (14)$$

and defining $\mathcal{G} = \sum_{j=1}^{n}\mathbf{V}_j\Phi(\mathbf{p}_j)$—another linear complexity term that can be computed ahead—we finally obtain

$$\begin{aligned}\eta_i &= \mathbf{f}_i^T \Phi(\mathbf{p}_i)\mathbf{s}\mathbf{f}_i - \Phi(\mathbf{p}_i)\mathbf{s} + \mathbf{f}_i^T \mathcal{G}\mathbf{s}\mathbf{f}_i - \mathcal{G}\mathbf{s} + \beta_i \\ &= \left[(\mathbf{f}_i\mathbf{f}_i^T - \mathbf{I})(\Phi(\mathbf{p}_i) + \mathcal{G})\right]\mathbf{s} + \beta_i = \mathcal{A}_i\mathbf{s} + \beta_i. \quad \blacksquare \end{aligned} \tag{15}$$

Result 3: The squared scalar residual for the i-th measurement is given by

$$\epsilon_i = \eta_i^T \eta_i = \tilde{\mathbf{s}}^T \begin{bmatrix} \mathcal{A}_i^T \mathcal{A}_i & \mathcal{A}_i^T \beta_i \\ \beta_i^T \mathcal{A}_i & \beta_i^T \beta_i \end{bmatrix} \tilde{\mathbf{s}}, \tag{16}$$

where $\tilde{\mathbf{s}} = \left[\mathbf{s}^T 1\right]^T$. This notably corresponds to the squared object-space error (i.e. the squared spatial orthogonal distance between point and ray)[2]. The total error over all measurements finally results in

$$E = \sum_i \epsilon_i = \tilde{\mathbf{s}}^T \left\{ \sum_i \begin{bmatrix} \mathcal{A}_i^T \mathcal{A}_i & \mathcal{A}_i^T \beta_i \\ \beta_i^T \mathcal{A}_i & \beta_i^T \beta_i \end{bmatrix} \right\} \tilde{\mathbf{s}} = \tilde{\mathbf{s}}^T \mathbf{M} \tilde{\mathbf{s}}. \tag{17}$$

Since each $\mathcal{A}_i$ and β_i can be computed in $O(1)$ (assuming that $\mathbf{H}$, $\mathcal{J}$, and $\mathcal{G}$ are computed ahead), $\mathbf{M}$ is computed in $O(n)$. We call this error the compressed generalized object space error.
Proof: By induction. ■

2.3 Universal, Closed-Form Least-Squares Solution

The energy E is always positive, and its minimization corresponds to solving the generalized PnP problem with minimal geometric error. Following the concept presented in [6], the first-order optimality conditions constitute a system of polynomial equations that allows us to compute all stationary points in closed-form and constant time. They are given by the 4 equations

$$\frac{\partial E}{\partial q_j} = 2\tilde{\mathbf{s}}^T \mathbf{M} \cdot \frac{\partial \tilde{\mathbf{s}}}{\partial q_j} = 0, \ j = 0, \ldots, 3. \tag{18}$$

It is easy to recognize that (17) reduces to the central formulation presented in [6] in case $\mathbf{v}_i = \mathbf{0} \ \forall i \in \{1, \ldots, n\}$. Moreover, since all elements of $\mathbf{s}$ are quadratic in q_i, any $k \cdot \mathbf{q}_0, k \in \mathbb{R}$ represents a valid solution to the problem if $\mathbf{q}_0$ is also a solution. We avoid this infinity of solutions in the central case by adding the unit-norm constraint $\mathbf{q}^T\mathbf{q} - 1 = 0$. The solutions are finally computed using the Gröbner basis approach.

Our solver leads to 16 solutions only, which is substantially less than the 81 solutions reported in [17] (without considering 2-fold symmetry for the moment), and less than the 27 solutions reported in [6] despite of using a quaternion parametrization. The reason lies in the way we search for the Gröbner basis. Readers familiar with the procedure might recall that the Gröbner basis method

[2] The object-space error corresponds to the moment distance and has proven to perform very well for pose estimation. Good alternatives are given by angular (geodesic) distance, and the reprojection error. The latter one, however, does not make sense in the generalized camera situation, which does not bare a planar projective subspace.

requires to first solve the problem in a finite prime field, where exact zero cancellations are taking place[3]. $\mathbb{Z}_p$—the field of integers modulo a large prime number p—is a popular choice. The typical way consists of drawing random values in $\mathbb{Z}_p$ for the coefficients of all polynomials, and then proceeding to the Gröbner basis derivation. This might work in any situation where the polynomial coefficients are independent. In the present problem, however, this is not the case, and we can reduce the size of the Gröbner basis by chosing coefficients that inherently reflect the geometry of the problem. This requires to setup the entire random problem in $\mathbb{Z}_p$, which is done as follows:

- Chose random values in $\mathbb{Z}_p$ for $\mathbf{q}$, $\mathbf{t}$, $\mathbf{v}_i$, and $\mathbf{p}_i$.
- Derive the rotation matrix $\mathbf{R}$ and the measurement vectors $\mathbf{f}_i$.
- Derive the coefficients of the polynomials by applying Section 2.2 in $\mathbb{Z}_p$.

Beware that—by chosing random values in $\mathbb{Z}_p$—neither $\mathbf{q} \in \mathbb{Z}_p^4$ nor $\mathbf{f}_i \in \mathbb{Z}_p^3$ fulfill the unit-norm constraint unless we apply the square root in $\mathbb{Z}_p$. As an alternative, we simply derive $\mathbf{R}$ from $\mathbf{q}$ using the non-unit quaternion parametrization, and apply a modified version of the symbolic block-wise inversion of $(\mathbf{A}^T\mathbf{A})$ that accepts non-unit-norm $\mathbf{f}_i$ (presented in the supplemental material). Note that these changes only concern the derivation of the random coefficients before computing the Gröbner basis, we constantly use the unit-quaternion parametrization in the objective system of equations.

The norm constraint on the quaternion is not needed in the non-central case. A wrong quaternion-scale only scales the point cloud, and it seems intuitive that non-central measurements are no longer invariant with respect to such changes. Interestingly, including the same set of equations than in the central case (i.e. including the norm constraint) still in combination with properly posed problems in $\mathbb{Z}_p$ again reduces the number of solutions from 81 to 16. As can be observed, the reduction from 81 to 16 solutions is caused by different modifications in the central and the non-central case. While this might be just a coincidence given by analogies in the corresponding algebraic varieties, it requires a deeper investigation going beyond the scope of this paper.

In conclusion, we generate a solver from a properly-posed generalized P3P problem in $\mathbb{Z}_p$ as outlined above. We use first-order optimality conditions and the unit-norm constraint, and the obtained compact generalized P3P solver works for all scenarios, including P3P, PnP, and generalized PnP. We use our own Gröbner basis solver generator, which follows the idea presented in [10].

2.4 Comparison to a Lagrangian Formulation

The reader might ask why we did not chose a Lagrangian formulation with unit-norm constraint. We verified by experimentation that, in both the central and the non-central case, the number of solutions falls back to 80—even if chosing geometrically consistent coefficients. This is natural, since the Lagrangian formulation eventually computes the projections orthogonal to the level lines of all 80 stationary points onto the unit sphere in the space of quaternions.

[3] For details about the Gröbner basis method, the reader is referred to [4] and [10].

Our formulation is better than the Lagrangian one. In the unconstrained central case, the infinitly many solutions of $\frac{\partial E}{\partial q_j} = 0$ lie on one-dimensional varieties that correspond to radial lines intersecting with the origin. Constrained solutions are obtained by intersecting those varieties with the unit-norm sphere. It is intuitively clear that the gradient of the norm constraint and the gradient of (17) are orthogonal in the intersection points, which means that the Lagrangian multipliers have to be zero for any correct solution. In the non-central case, we again exploit the speciality of our optimization problem that the constraints appear to be fulfilled exactly by 16 of our 81 stationary points. This is clear from the fact that the number of solutions reduces from 81 to 16 if adding the unit-norm constraint. With $\frac{\partial E}{\partial q_j} = 0$, the partial derivatives of the Lagrangian by the quaternion variables therefore result in $\lambda q_j = 0$, where λ represents the Lagrangian multiplier. Since all quaternion variables can never be simultaneously zero, this implies that $\lambda = 0$.

We proved that λ ideally has to be zero, and thus that the Lagrangian formulation implicitly transitions to ours. Instead of computing the projection of a large variety (i.e. all stationary points), we provide a closed-form solution for a smaller variety (i.e. those 16 stationary points that idealy fulfill the norm constraint exactly). Moreover, our formulation leads to a substantially easier elimination template as well as a 5 times smaller action matrix (note that the theoretical complexity of an Eigen decomposition is $O(n^3)$, which means that in our case the action matrix decomposition is up to 125 times faster).

2.5 Elimination of Two-Fold Symmetry

Similar to [17], we employ the technique outlined in [1] to eliminate double roots in our polynomial equation system. The general idea consists of using only monomials with even total degree in order to create new equations in the Macaulay matrix. The pre-condition however consists of having monomials with either only even or only uneven total degrees in the initial equations. We do not yet fulfill this condition because the first-order optimality conditions only contain uneven total degrees, while the norm constraint contains only even ones. The condition is met by applying a small trick. We consider the squared unit-norm constraint $(\mathbf{q}^T\mathbf{q} - 1)^2 = 0$ depicted for 2D in Figure 2 instead of the standard unit-norm constraint. It can be observed that this function is stationary at $\mathbf{q} = \mathbf{0}$ and when the norm constraint is fulfilled. Adding all first-order derivatives of the squared norm constraint therefore results in the following system of 8 third-order equations which contains only uneven total degrees in the monomials

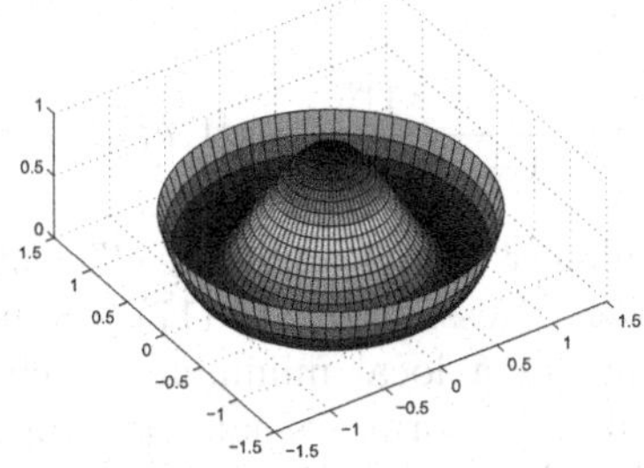

Fig. 2. The squared norm constraint in 2D

$$\begin{cases} \tilde{\mathbf{s}}^T \mathbf{M} \cdot \frac{\partial \tilde{\mathbf{s}}}{\partial q_j} & = 0, \; j = 0, \ldots, 3 \\ (\mathbf{q}^T \mathbf{q} - 1) q_j & = 0, \; j = 0, \ldots, 3 \end{cases}. \tag{19}$$

Since there is one additional solution now ($\mathbf{q} = \mathbf{0}$), the size of the action matrix for this system becomes 17×17. Applying the technique for eliminating 2-fold symmetry however reduces the number of solutions to 8. The size of our final elimination template shrinks to 141×149, which is substantially smaller than all elimination templates mentioned in [17]. The action matrix has a size of 8×8 only, leading to very efficient Eigenvector decomposition. The result is a drastic reduction in execution time of geometric error minimizers. Moreover, we note that the number of solutions now elegantly agrees with the maximum number of solutions for the generalized P3P problem.

2.6 Second-Order Optimality and Root Polishing

The above method only computes complex stationary points of (17). Disambiguation is done by checking the energy $\mathbf{E}$. Besides, one can easily solve the chirality ambiguity by checking the sign of the resulting depth parameters. However, there exist further sanity checks that do not depend on the number of correspondences. For instance, the magnitude of the imaginary part of each Eigenvalue from the Action matrix decomposition should be very small. In order to also verify second-order optimality, we apply another small trick. Let $\mathbf{R}_0(\mathbf{q}_0)$ be a solution of (17). We can easily compensate for this rotation by replacing all $\mathbf{p}_i$ by $\mathbf{R}_0\mathbf{p}_i$, and recomputing $\mathbf{M}$. The stationary point now lies at identity rotation. The well-conditioned 3D subspace of rotations around $\mathbf{q}_0 = [1\;0\;0\;0]^T$ is now entered by simply switching to the Cayley rotation parametrization $\mathbf{c} = [c_1\;c_2\;c_3]^T$. $\mathbf{s}$ as a function of the Cayley parameters is given by

$$\mathbf{s} = \frac{1}{1 + c_1^2 + c_2^2 + c_3^2} [1, c_1^2, c_2^2, c_3^2, c_1, c_2, c_3, c_1c_2, c_1c_3, c_2c_3]^T \in \mathbb{R}^{10}. \tag{20}$$

It is almost trivial and very efficient to compute the 3×1 Jacobian J_E and the 3×3 Hessian H_E of (17) around $\mathbf{c} = \mathbf{0}$. This allows to easily verify the presence of a local minimum by checking for positive-definitness of $H_E|_{\mathbf{c}=\mathbf{0}}$, as well as perform a single Newton step for root pollishing which is given by $\delta_{\mathbf{c}} = -(H_E|_{\mathbf{c}=\mathbf{0}})^{-1} \cdot J_E|_{\mathbf{c}=\mathbf{0}}$. More information is provided in the supplemental material.

3 Experimental Evaluation

In this section, we compare UPnP to both central and non-central state-of-the-art PnP solvers using simulation experiments. We reuse the experimental evaluation toolbox from [17], and only extend it by an additional algorithm for the non-central case, plus the proposed UPnP algorithm. We start by looking at the central case, and include experiments on regular, planar, near-singular, and minimal situations. Near-singular configurations are defined as world point distributions with low variance. We then show a comparative study for the non-central case, again including both the n-point and the minimal situation. We conclude the section by evaluating the computational efficiency. Due to space limitations, we constrain our results to the rotation errors only. However, the conclusions wouldn't change if we would instead evaluate the translational error. The absolute rotation error between the ground truth rotation $\mathbf{R}_{\text{true}}$ and the estimated rotation $\mathbf{R}$ is given by $\epsilon_{\text{rot}} = max_{k\in\{1,2,3\}} \cos^{-1}(\mathbf{r}_{k,\text{true}}^T \mathbf{r}_k)$, where $\mathbf{r}_{k,\text{true}}$ and $\mathbf{r}_k$ are the k-th column of $\mathbf{R}_{\text{true}}$ and $\mathbf{R}$, respectively. This error metric might not be standard, but we use it in order to remain consistent with [17].

3.1 The Central Case

In the central case, we create random experiments by assuming a virtual perspective camera with focal length 800, and add different levels of Gaussian noise to the measurements in the image plane. Up to 20 random world points are then generated with varying distribution depending on the type of experiment. In the normal case, the points are distributed such that they lie in the range $[-2,2]\times[-2,2]\times[4,8]$ in the camera frame, and then transformed into the world frame by assuming a random transformation. In the planar case, they are picked in the range $[-2,2]\times[-2,2]$ in the plane $z=0$ in the world frame, and then transformed into the camera frame using a random transformation. In the quasi-singular case, they are again defined in the camera frame with a distribution of $[1,2]\times[1,2]\times[4,8]$.

The comparison algorithms in the central case are the exact same algorithms than the ones used in [17]. They are given by EPnP+GN (or EPnP in the planar case) [11], RPnP [12], DLS [6] (plus its non-degenerate version DLS+++), SDP [16], LHM [13] (plus the planar variant SP+LHM), and OPnP itself [17]. We name the SDP algorithm here in agreement with [17], but note however that the original, more accurate name of this method is SOS. As indicated in Figures 3 and 4, our algorithm leads to state-of-the-art noise resilience in all situations. Figure 4 also shows a comparison to [9], proving that the minimal case is still accurately solved.

The careful reader might notice that we plot only the median error in the minimal, planar, and quasi-singular cases. The reason is that the universal applicability and the superior computational efficiency naturally lead to reduced robustness in special situations. As clearly underlined by the low median errors, the solver is however able to generally find a good solution in any special situation too. Failures are easily pruned when all sanity checks are enabled. For the present experiments, however, we configured UPnP to always return at least one solution.

3.2 The Non-central Case

In the non-central case, we assume a multi-camera system with 4 virtual spherical cameras with focal length 800, and add noise in the tangential plane of each

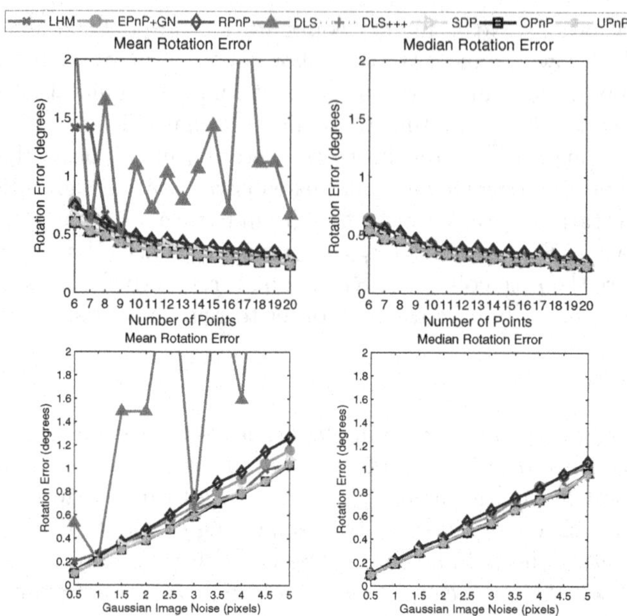

Fig. 3. Comparison of various central state-of-the-art PnP solvers w.r.t. varying point numbers (1st row, noise level=2 pixels) and varying noise levels (2nd row, n=10) in case of normal 3D points

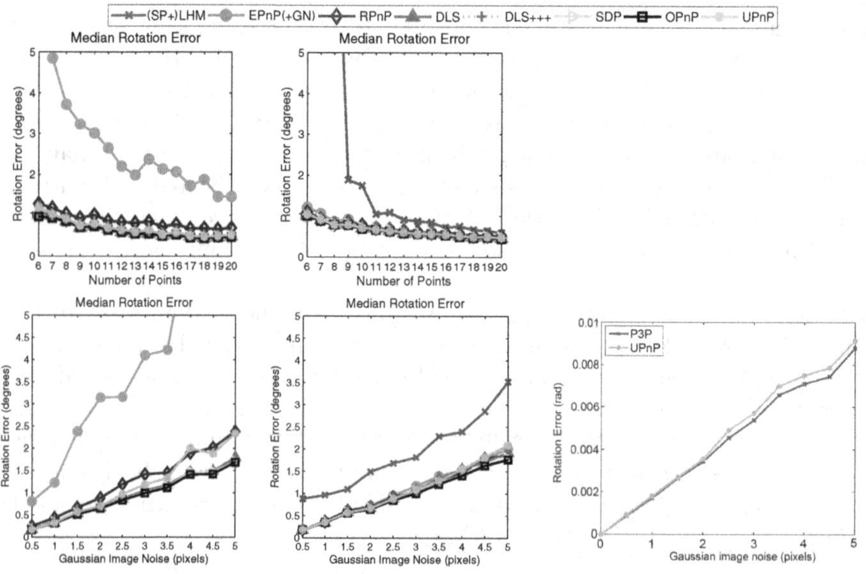

Fig. 4. Comparison of various central state-of-the-art PnP solvers w.r.t. varying point numbers (1st row, noise level=2 pixels) and varying noise levels (2nd row, n=10) in the case of planar (1st column) and near singular (2nd column) point configurations. The last figure indicates a comparison to the state-of-the-art minimal solver.

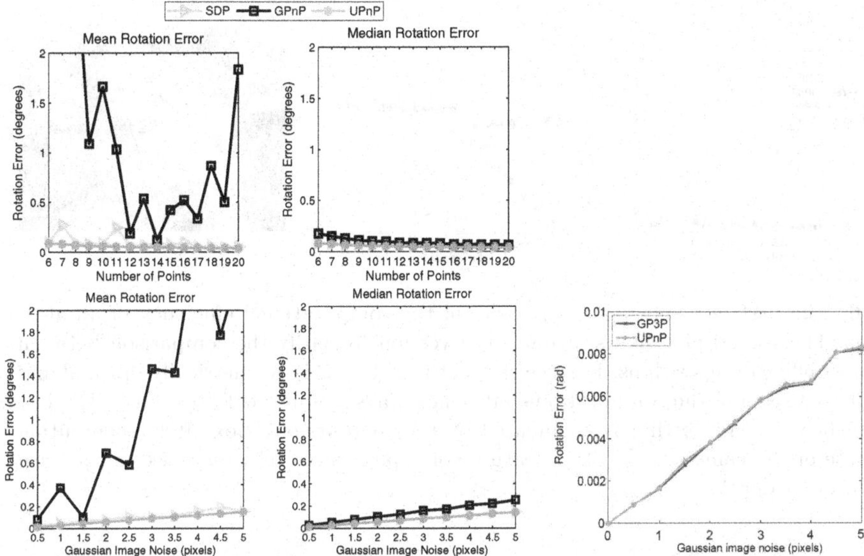

Fig. 5. Comparison of various noncentral state-of-the-art PnP solvers w.r.t. varying point numbers (1st row, noise level=2 pixels) and varying noise levels (2nd row, n=10) in case of normal 3D points. The last figure indicates a comparison to a minimal solver

measurement. The points are now always defined in the world frame, and the camera to world transformation is picked such that the distance between the camera and the world origin does not exceed 2. The world points are picked such that they have an average distance between 4 and 8 from the world frame origin, and are evenly distributed in all directions.

We compare our algorithm against SDP [16] and GPnP [8]. SDP (i.e. SOS) is the only alternative algorithm that is also applicable to both the central and the non-central case. As indicated in Figure 5, UPnP maintains state-of-the-art noise resilience in the non-central case too, slightly outperforming SDP. The figure also shows a comparison to the minimal solver of [8], proving that the minimal case is still accurately solved.

3.3 Computational Efficiency

Figure 6 illustrates the computational efficiency, highlighting the clear advantage of our method. For 100 points, our method outperforms OPnP by a factor of 10, and SDP—the only general alternative that can handle both the central and the non-central case—by a factor of 150. We have to emphasize that the core part of our algorithm is implemented in a mex-file. Some algorithms, such as EPnP, have a more efficient pendant in C++ too, but we sticked here to a baseline implementation. All experiments have been executed on an Intel Core 2 Duo with 2.8 GHz.

Note: Our algorithm is publically available within the open-source library OpenGV[7], and all results can easily be reproduced.

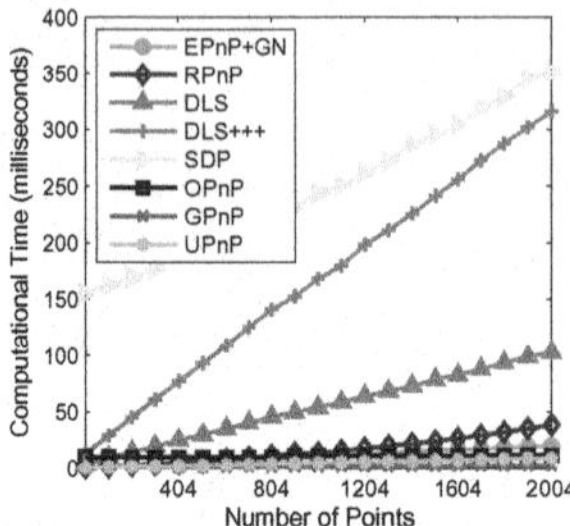

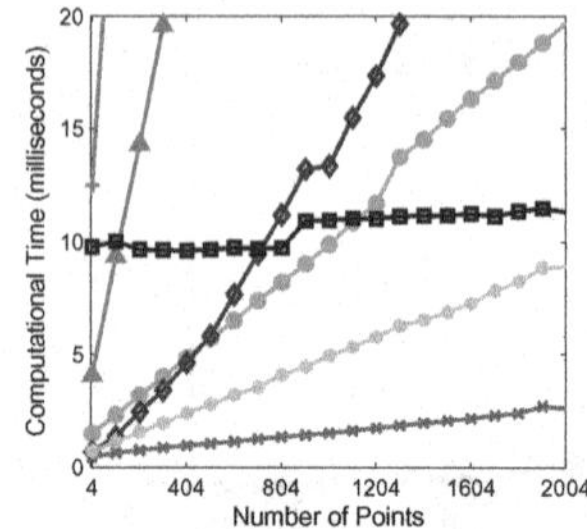

Fig. 6. The first plot shows a comparison of the computational efficiency of all algorithms. The second plot shows a zoomed-in version to clarify the comparison between the most efficient algorithms. Despite the fact that UPnP is geometrically optimal and completely general, the computational efficiency stays among the fastest ones. The last figure shows an image that is augmented by the contours of a box after recomputing the pose of the camera from SIFT feature correspondences to a reference image with known point depths.

3.4 Results on Real Data

We again repeat the experiments from [17], and recompute the pose of the camera in front of a box from matched SIFT feature correspondences. An augmented image with the contours of the box is indicated in Figure 6, showing the similarly visually pleasing results.

4 Conclusion

The scientific relevance of the presented material is given by the fact that we provide for the first time a completely general and highly computationally efficient solution to one of the most fundamental problems in geometric vision. We present a non-iterative minimization of a geometric error in linear time, and are able to handle the minimal, non-minimal, central, and non-central cases, as well as any special situations in which multiple solutions can appear. With an execution time of only a couple of ms for hundreds of points, we outperform the state-of-the art generalized geometric error minimizer by about two orders of magnitude, while having improved noise resilience. Besides our generalized formulation, the conceptual cornerstones of our method that lead to a reduced number of solutions are a geometrically consistent application of the Gröbner basis method, as well as the avoidance of Lagrangian multipliers in the special case of optimization problems that are known to fulfill the constraints exactly in the noise-free case. We furthermore provide an alternative to L2-norm constraints with only uneven terms, which potentially eases the general exploitation of p-fold symmetries in polynomial solvers.

Acknowledgment. The research leading to these results has received funding from ARC grants DP120103896 and DP130104567. We furthermore want to thank Stergios Roumeliotis, Joel Hesch, and Erik Ask for their supportive feedback.

References

1. Ask, E., Yubin, K., Astrom, K.: Exploiting p-fold symmetries for faster polynomial equation solving. In: Proceedings of the International Conference on Pattern Recognition (ICPR), Tsukuba, Japan (2012)
2. Cayley, A.: About the algebraic structure of the orthogonal group and the other classical groups in a field of characteristic zero or a prime characteristic. Reine Angewandte Mathematik 32 (1846)
3. Chen, C.S., Chang, W.Y.: On pose recovery for generalized visual sensors. IEEE Transactions on Pattern Analysis and Machine Intelligence (PAMI) 26(7), 848–861 (2004)
4. Cox, D.A., Little, J., O'Shea, D.: Ideals, Varieties, and Algorithms: An Introduction to Computational Algebraic Geometry and Commutative Algebra, 3rd edn. Undergraduate Texts in Mathematics. Springer-Verlag New York, Inc., Secaucus (2007)
5. Ess, A., Neubeck, A., Van Gool, L.: Generalised linear pose estimation. In: Proceedings of the British Machine Vision Conference (BMVC), pp. 22.1–22.10. Warwick, UK (2007)
6. Hesch, J.A., Roumeliotis, S.I.: A Direct Least-Squares (DLS) Method for PnP. In: Proceedings of the International Conference on Computer Vision (ICCV), Barcelona, Spain (2011)
7. Kneip, L., Furgale, P.: OpenGV: A Unified and Generalized Approach to Real-Time Calibrated Geometric Vision. In: Proceedings of the IEEE International Conference on Robotics and Automation (ICRA), Hongkong (2014)
8. Kneip, L., Furgale, P., Siegwart, R.: Using Multi-Camera Systems in Robotics: Efficient Solutions to the NPnP Problem. In: Proceedings of the IEEE International Conference on Robotics and Automation (ICRA), Karlsruhe, Germany (2013)
9. Kneip, L., Scaramuzza, D., Siegwart, R.: A novel parametrization of the perspective-three-point problem for a direct computation of absolute camera position and orientation. In: Proceedings of the IEEE Conference on Computer Vision and Pattern Recognition (CVPR), Colorado Springs, USA (2011)
10. Kukelova, Z., Bujnak, M., Pajdla, T.: Automatic generator of minimal problem solvers. In: Forsyth, D., Torr, P., Zisserman, A. (eds.) ECCV 2008, Part III. LNCS, vol. 5304, pp. 302–315. Springer, Heidelberg (2008)
11. Lepetit, V., Moreno-Noguer, F., Fua, P.: EPnP: An accurate O(n) solution to the PnP problem. International Journal of Computer Vision (IJCV) 81(2), 578–589 (2009)
12. Li, S., Xu, C., Xie, M.: A robust O(n) solution to the perspective-n-point problem. IEEE Transactions on Pattern Analysis and Machine Intelligence (PAMI) 34(7), 1444–1450 (2012)
13. Lu, C., Hager, G., Mjolsness, E.: Fast and globally convergent pose estimation from video images. IEEE Transactions on Pattern Analysis and Machine Intelligence (PAMI) 22(6), 610–622 (2000)
14. Nistér, D., Stewénius, H.: A minimal solution to the generalized 3-point pose problem. Journal of Mathematical Imaging and Vision (JMIV) 27(1), 67–79 (2006)

15. Schweighofer, G., Pinz, A.: Robust pose estimation from a planar target. IEEE Transactions on Pattern Analysis and Machine Intelligence (PAMI) 28(12), 2024–2030 (2006)
16. Schweighofer, G., Pinz, A.: Globally optimal O(n) solution to the PnP problem for general camera models. In: Proceedings of the British Machine Vision Conference (BMVC), Leeds, UK (2008)
17. Zheng, Y., Kuang, Y., Sugimoto, S., Astrom, K., Okutomi, M.: Revisiting the PnP problem: A fast, general and optimal solution. In: Proceedings of the International Conference on Computer Vision (ICCV), Sydney, Australia (2013)

3D Reconstruction of Dynamic Textures in Crowd Sourced Data

Dinghuang Ji, Enrique Dunn, and Jan-Michael Frahm

The University of North Carolina at Chapel Hill, USA
{jdh,dunn,jmf}@cs.unc.edu

Abstract. We propose a framework to automatically build 3D models for scenes containing structures not amenable for photo-consistency based reconstruction due to having dynamic appearance. We analyze the dynamic appearance elements of a given scene by leveraging the imagery contained in Internet image photo-collections and online video sharing websites. Our approach combines large scale crowd sourced SfM techniques with image content segmentation and shape from silhouette techniques to build an iterative framework for 3D shape estimation. The developed system not only enables more complete and robust 3D modeling, but it also enables more realistic visualizations through the identification of dynamic scene elements amenable to dynamic texture mapping. Experiments on crowd sourced image and video datasets illustrate the effectiveness of our automated data-driven approach.

1 Introduction

State of the art crowd sourced 3D reconstruction systems deploy structure from motion (SfM) techniques leveraging large scale imaging redundancy in order to generate photo-realistic models of scenes of interest. The estimated 3D models reliably depict both the shape and appearance of the captured environment under the joint assumptions of shape constancy and appearance congruency, commonly associated with static structures. Accordingly, the attained 3D models are unable to robustly capture dynamic scene elements not in compliance with the aforementioned assumptions. In this work, we strive to estimate more complete and realistic 3D scene representations by addressing the 3D modeling of dynamic scene elements within the context of crowd sourced input imagery.

In our crowd sourced 3D modeling framework, dynamic scene content can only be determined through the observation of visual motion. Nelson and Polana [16] categorized visual motion into three classes: activities, motion events and dynamic (temporal) texture. *Activities*, such as walking or swimming, are defined as motion patterns that are periodic in time; *motion events*, like opening a door, lack temporal or spatial periodicity; *dynamic textures*, i.e. fire, smoke and flowing water, exhibit statistical regularity but have uncertain spatial and temporal extent. Dynamic scenes may contain visual motions in any combination of these three categories. Our work focuses on modeling the 3D shape of scene elements belonging to the dynamic texture category, working under the assumption of a

D. Fleet et al. (Eds.): ECCV 2014, Part I, LNCS 8689, pp. 143–158, 2014.
© Springer International Publishing Switzerland 2014

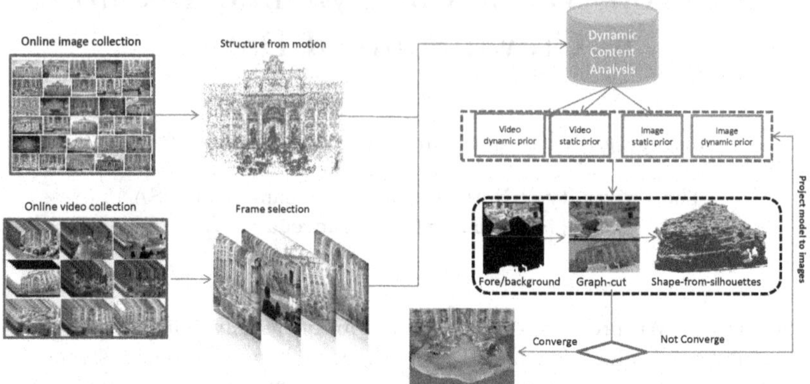

Fig. 1. Workflow overview of the proposed framework

rigid supporting surface. Moreover, while our framework assumes the geometry of scene elements having time-varying appearance (i.e. such as active billboards or bodies of water) to be approximated by a single surface, our solution is completely data-driven and does not impose geometric or shape priors to perform our estimation.

We briefly summarize the functionality of our processing pipeline. The input data to our framework encompasses both online image and video collections capturing a common scene. We initially leverage photo-collection data to perform sparse reconstruction of the rigid scene elements. Then, video collection data is analyzed to reap video segments amenable for 1) registration to our existing rigid model and 2) coarse identification of dynamic scene elements. We use these coarse estimates, along with the knowledge of our sparse rigid 3D structure, to pose the segmentation of dynamic elements within an image as a global two-label optimization problem. The attained dynamic region masks are subsequently fused through shape-from-silhouette techniques in order to generate an initial 3D shape estimate from the input videos. The preliminary 3D shape is then back projected to the original photo-collection imagery, all image labelings recomputed and then fused to generate an updated 3D shape. This process is iterated until convergence of the output photo-collection imagery segmentation process. Figure 1 depicts an overview of the proposed pipeline.

Our developed system improves upon existing 3D modeling system by increasing the coverage of the generated modeling, mitigating spurious geometry caused by dynamic scene elements and enabling more photo-realistic visualizations through the explicit identification and animation of model surfaces having time varying appearance. The remainder of this document describes the design choices and implementation details of different modules comprising our dynamic scene content modeling pipeline.

2 Related Work

Dense 3D reconstruction of dynamic scenes in uncontrolled environments is a challenging problem for computer vision research. Several systems have been developed for building multiview dynamic outdoor scenes. Jiang et al. [11] and Taneja et. al. [21] propose a probabilistic framework to model outdoor scenes with handheld cameras. Kim et al. [12] design a synchronized portable multiple camera system. These systems rely on a set of pre-calibrated or synchronized cameras, while our method just uses Internet downloaded imagery, which may extensively vary in environment and camera parameters.

Foreground segmentation, which generates the 2D shape of foreground objects, is a critical problem of multiview 3D reconstruction. Many dynamic scene modeling methods only consider controlled environments, where the background is known or can be accurately estimated. Hasler et al. [9] address outdoor scenarios using scene priors, while Ballan et al.[1] limit the reconstruction quality at the billboard level. Taneja et al.[21] propose a method to estimate scene dynamics without making any assumptions on the shape or the motion of elements to be reconstructed. They use the precomputed geometry of the static parts of the scene to transfer the current background appearance across multiply views. Kim et al.[12] propose a multiple view trimap (with foreground, background and unknown labels) propagation algorithm, which allows trimaps to be propagated across multiple views given a small number of manually specified key-frame trimaps. Jiang et al.[11] propose a novel dense depth estimation method, which simultaneously solves bilayer segmentation and depth estimation in a unified energy minimization framework.

Shape from silhouettes is one popular class of methods to estimate shape of scenes from multiple views. Most of these techniques compute the visual hull, which is the maximal volume consistent with a given set of silhouettes. It was first introduced by Baumgart[2], and extensively reviewed by Laurentini[15]. Visual hull is usually in the format of 3D volume, which is a subdivision of space into elementary regions, typically as voxels. Many 3D volume-based visual hull methods, including [6][19][3], are widely used. However, due to camera calibration errors and foreground self-occlusion, traditional shape from silhouette is not robust to noisy input data. Franco et al. [5] propose a sensor fusion method to modify this process and generate more accurate models. In order to address occlusion inference and multi objects modeling, Guan et al.[8] further propose a Bayesian fusion framework.

Scenes with uncontrolled imaging conditions cause many false matches, leading to noisy sparse 3D reconstructions. Tetrahedra-carving-based methods [13] [14][23] mitigate this problem by: (1)transforming a dense point cloud into a visibility consistent mesh (2) refine the mesh by geometric and photometric consistency. Jancosek et al.[10] further use visual hull to construct weakly supported surfaces (i.e. road, transparent layers) which are not densely sampled. However, their method does not explore scenarios where dynamic appearance changes are the cause of the reduced support of a given surface.

3 Initial Model Generation

3.1 Static Reconstruction from Photo Collections

The first step in our pipeline is to build a preliminary 3D model of the environment using photo-collection imagery. To this end we perform keyword and location based queries to photo sharing websites such as Flickr & Panoramio. We perform GIST based K-means clustering to attain a reduced set images on which to perform exhaustive geometric verification. We take the largest connected component in the resulting camera graph, consisting of pairwise registered cluster centers, as our initial sparse model and perform intra-cluster geometric verification to densify the camera graph. The final set of registered images is fed to the publicly available VisualSfM module to attain a final sparse reconstruction. The motivation for using VisualSfM is the availability for direct comparison against two input compatible surface reconstruction modules: PMVS2[7] by Furukawa & Ponce and CMPMVS[10] by Jancosek & Pajdla. Once a static sparse model is attained the focus shifts to identifying additional video imagery enabling the identification and modeling of dynamic scene content.

3.2 Coarse Dynamic Textures Priors from Video

Video collections are the natural media to identify and analyze dynamic content. To this end we download videos from YouTube using tag queries of the scenes of interest. Our goal is to identify and extract informative video fragments within our downloaded set of videos. We consider as informative, those video subsequences where the dynamic texture content can be distinguished and reliably correlated with our existing sparse model of the scene's static structure.

Video Frame Registration. We temporally sample each video at a $1/50$ ratio to obtain a reduced set of video frames for analysis. For illustration, a set of 500 videos generated little over 80K frame samples. We introduce into the video frame set a random subset of 30% of the registered cameras from the rigid scene modeling. We again perform GIST based clustering on the augmented image set and re-run intra cluster geometric verification to identify registered video frames.

Video Sub-sequence Selection. Given a reduced set of registered video frames we want to select compact frame sub-sequences having reduced camera motion in order to simplify the detection of dynamic scene content. Namely, we compute the HOG descriptor of the frames immediately preceding and following a reg0istered video frame in the original sequence. We count the number of neighboring frames having an NCC value in the range $(0.9, 1)$ w.r.t. the registered frame and keep those sequences having cardinality above a given threshold τ_{seq_len}. We favor such image content based approach instead of pairwise camera motion estimation due to the difficulty in defining suitable capture dependent thresholds (i.e. camera motion, lighting changes, varying zoom, etc.). Discarding fully correlated (i.e. NNC=1) pairwise measurements enables the elimination of duplicates. Moreover, we found measuring the NCC over the HOG descriptors

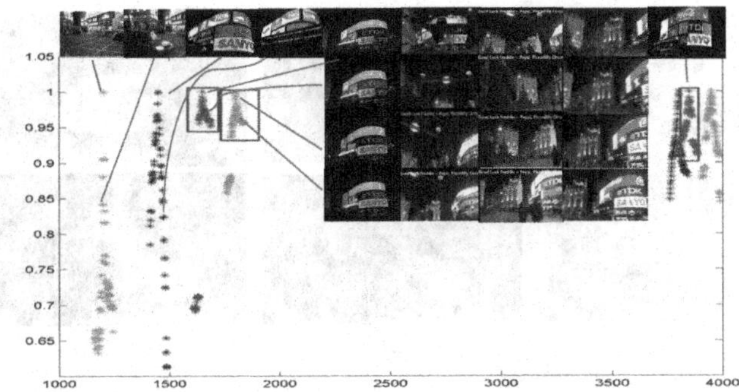

Fig. 2. Keyframe selection for an input video. The plot shows the frame number count vs the NCC similarity of each frame's HOG descriptor. Red boxes indicate selected video fragments centered on sampled frames. Sequences that are not been selected usually have large viewpoint change or severe occlusions(i.e. cars, pedestrians etc.).

to be robust against abrupt dynamic texture variation as long such changes were restricted to reduced image regions. Figure 2 describes the selection thresholds utilized for subsequence detection.

Barebones Dynamic Texture Estimation. In order to analyze and synthesize dynamic texture from static backgrounds on the selected short video sequences, Soatto et al.[20] and Fitzgibbon [4] propose to model dynamic texture as parametrized auto-regressive model, and compute it with autoregressive moving average process, their works can generate "videotextures" that play forever without repetition. Vidal et al. [22] further work on modeling a scene containing dynamic textures undergoing rigid-body motions, and propose a method to compute both dynamic texture and motion flow of the scene. Since we only want to find the region containing dynamic textures, we deploy basic frame differencing by accumulating the inter-frame pixel intensity differences. We compensate for (the reduced) camera motion by performing RANSAC based homography warping of all sub-sequence frames to the anchor (i.e. registered) video frame. The accumulated difference image is then binarized using non-parametric Otsu thresholding [17]. The attained mask is then modified by a sequence of erosion-dilation-erosion morphological operations with respective window sizes of 2×2 (remove noise), 11×11 (fill holes) and 9×9 (reduce over-grow) for an input image of VGA resolutions. We sort the connected component of the binary output image w.r.t. their area and eliminate all individual components ranked at the bottom 10% of total image area (shown in Figure 3).

3.3 Coarse Static Background Priors from Video Frames

We leverage the dense temporal sampling within a single video sub-sequence in order to estimate a mask for static texture observed on all selected reference video frames. Instead of naively using the complement of the precomputed

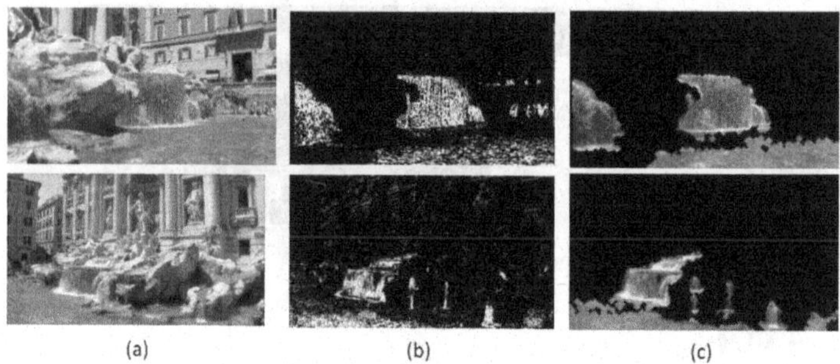

Fig. 3. Dynamic content priors from video fragments. Left to right: (a) Reference frame (b) Accumulated frame differencing (c) Result after post processing.

dynamic texture mask for a given video frame, we strive to deploy a more data-driven approach. To this end we analyze the sparse feature similarity among the reference frame and one of its immediate neighbors. We retrieve the set putative SIFT matches previously used for homography based stabilization of the video sequence and perform RANSAC based epipolar geometry estimation. We consider the attained set of inlier image features in the reference videoframe as a sparse sample of the observed static structure. To mitigate spurious dynamic features being registered due to low frequency appearance variations, we exclude from this set any features contained within the regions described by dynamic texture mask. From the final image feature set we compute the concave hull and use the attained 2D polygon as an area-based prior for static scene content (shown in Figure 4).

Fig. 4. Static content prior from video fragments. First and third columns depict SIFT features matches among neighboring frames as red dots. Second and fourth columns depict the concave hull defined by detected features not overlapping with the existing dynamic content prior.

3.4 Graph-Cut Based Dynamic Texture Refinement

Once a preliminary set of segmentation masks for static and dynamic object regions are attained, they are refined trough a two label (e.g. foreground/ background) graph-cut labeling optimization framework. We will denote static structure as background and dynamic content as foreground. The optimization problem is Graphcut defined as:

$$\min E(f) = \sum_{u \in \mathcal{U}} D_{\mathcal{U}}(f_u) + \sum_{u,v \in \mathcal{N}} V_{u,v}(f_u, f_v) \tag{1}$$

where $f_u, f_v \in \{0, 1\}$ are the labels for pixels u and v, $\mathcal{N}$ is the set of neighboring pixels for u and $\mathcal{U}$ denotes the set of all the pixels with unknown labels. Similarly to the work of Rother et. al. [18], we use a Gaussian mixture model to compute the foreground/background membership probabilities of a pixel. Hence, the smoothness term is defined to be:

$$V_{u,v}(f_u, f_v) = |f_u - f_v| \exp(-\beta(I_u - I_v)^2), \tag{2}$$

where I_u, I_v denote the RGB values of pixels u and v, while $\beta = (2 \left\langle (I_u - I_v)^2 \right\rangle)^{-1}$, for $\langle \cdot \rangle$ denoting the expectation over an image sample. Conversely, the data term is defined as:

$$D_u(f_u) = \log \left(\frac{p(f_u = 1)}{p(f_u = 0)} \right), \tag{3}$$

$$\begin{aligned} p(f_u = 1) &= p(I_u|\lambda_1) = \textstyle\sum_{i=1}^{M} \omega_{i1} g(I_u|\mu_{i1}, \Sigma_{i1}) \\ p(f_u = 0) &= p(I_u|\lambda_0) = \textstyle\sum_{i=1}^{M} \omega_{i0} g(I_u|\mu_{i0}, \Sigma_{i0}) \\ \lambda_{1|0} &= \{\omega_{i1|0}, \mu_{i1|0}, \Sigma_{i1|0}\}, i \in \{1, 2, ..., M\} \end{aligned}$$

and $g(I_u|\mu_i, \Sigma_i)$ belongs to a mixture-of-gaussian model using $M = 3$, and we assume the labels for fore/background are 1/0. Figure 5 exemplifies the result of our graph-cut segmentation.

3.5 Shape from Silhouettes

We leverage the output of our graph-cut segmentation module to estimate the 3D visual hull of the dynamic texture through space carving methods. Namely, we utilize the refined dynamic content mask as an object silhouette, along with the corresponding camera poses and calibration estimates, to deploy a 3D fusion method estimating a volumetric shape representation in accordance to the steps described in Algorithm 1.

We first use dynamic appearance silhouettes to determine a visual hull through weighted volume intersection. We observed that segmentation errors occasionally caused overextension of the 3D volume. Our second pass enforces free-space constraints associated with the static background by carving away from 3D volume the silhouettes of the static background. There are two dataset specific thresholds used for space carving: θ_1 and θ_2. θ_1 was empirically set to values from 70% to 90% of total cameras, θ_2 was set from 5% to 15%, roughly (1-θ_1)/2. Higher values of θ_1 slow down convergence by contracting the dynamic texture volume of each iteration, while lower values increase the risk of model over extension. Space carving weight ω_i is set to be 1 in Algorithm 1, in subsection 4.4 we show this value should be adjusted according to camera distribution.

Fig. 5. Graph-cut label refinement. First and third rows depict (alternatively from left to right) single image dynamic and static content priors. Second and fourth rows depict the outputs of the label optimization, where green regions are dynamic textures.

4 Closed Loop 3D Shape Refinement

The preceding section described a video-based approximation of the observed shape of dynamic texture within the scene. The motivation for exclusively using video keyframes until now has been the lack of a mechanism to estimate dynamic texture priors for static images. In this section, we describe an iterative mechanism to effectively transfer the labelings attained from video sequences to the available photo-collection imagery. Such label transferring will enable us to leverage and augmented imagery dataset offering 1) increased robustness through additional redundancy and viewpoint diversity, as well as 2) increased level of detail afforded by larger available imaging resolutions.

4.1 Geometry Based Video to Image Label Transfer

In order to transfer dynamic content masks from videos into static images we leverage the estimated preliminary 3D volume. The process is as follows:

1. Generate static background priors for each image.
2. Project the preliminary 3D shape model to all registered images and use its silhouette as a dynamic foreground prior for each image.
3. Execute graph-cut based label optimization for each image.
4. Generate an updated 3D model using the shape from silhouettes module.

Steps 2 to 4 in the above method will iterate until convergence of the dynamic foreground prior mask. Note that in such a framework the static background priors are kept constant while the dynamic texture content is a function of an evolving 3D shape. In general, the preliminary model attained from videos sequences may suffer from variability in viewpoint coverage or be sensitive to errors in our video based dynamic texture segmentation estimates. While the

Algorithm 1. SHAPE FROM SILHOUETTES FUSION

Input: Sets of camera poses $\{\mathbb{C}_i\}$ and corresponding foreground silhouettes $\{\mathbb{M}_i\}$ and background silhouettes $\{\mathbb{M}'_i\}$, camera weight w_i where $i \in [1, \cdots, N]$, 3D occupancy grid O, threshold θ_1, θ_2

Output: Labeled 3D occupancy grid V

Set all $O(x, y, z) = 0, w_i = 1$
for $i \in [1, N]$ **do**
  for *pixel* $\mathbf{M}_{ij} \in \{\mathbb{M}_i\}$ **do**
    Find all voxels $O_{x,y,z}, \{x, y, z\} \in O_1 \subset O$,$Proj^i(O_1) = M_{ij}$
    $O_1 \leftarrow O_1 + w_i$
$V = Find(\{x, y, z\}|O_{x,y,z} > \theta_1), \{x, y, z\} \in V \subset O$
Set all $V(x, y, z) = 0$
for $i \in [1, N]$ **do**
  for *pixel* $\mathbf{M}'_{ij} \in \{\mathbb{M}'_i\}$ **do**
    Find all voxels $V_{x,y,z}, \{x, y, z\} \in V_1 \subset V$,$Proj^i(V_1) = M'_{ij}$
    $V_1 \leftarrow V_1 + w_i$
$V = Find(\{x, y, z\}|V_{x,y,z} < \theta_2), \{x, y, z\} \in V$
Label voxels in V as occupied.

former may either under-constrain or bias the attained 3D shape, the latter may arbitrarily corrupt the estimate. Both of these challenges are addressed through the additional sampling redundancy afforded by image photo-collections. The remaining challenges consist then in robustly defining static content priors for single images and adapting the shape estimation framework to adequately handle the heterogeneous additional imaging data.

4.2 Mitigating Dynamic Texture in SfM Estimates

The variability in the temporal behavior and extent of dynamic textures may enable its spurious inclusion within SfM estimates. Namely, it is possible for changes in appearance to manifest themselves at time scales larger than those encompassed through short video subsequences or to present periodic behavior that would enable feature correspondence across multiple unsynchronized image. We evaluate the appearance variability of sparse reconstructed features across the imaging dataset to classify them having either persistent or sporadic color.

In principle, static 3D structure with constant appearance should provide consistent color throughout all images observing said structure. Conversely, features with sporadic color are mainly observed from dynamic structures, for example: rocks under the flowing water, flashing letters on a billboard etc. The existence of reconstructed features within a dynamic texture obeys mainly to the transient nature of their appearance. That is, while such appearance is observable at multiple different times, the same structure element may alternatively display appearance independent of the one used for matching.

Moreover, according to Lambert's cosine law, if the colors of a static structure remains constant, the observed pixels are linearly correlated to the intensity of the incoming light, as described by

$$I_D = \mathbf{L} \cdot \mathbf{N} C I_L = C I_L \cos\alpha, \tag{4}$$

where **L** and **N** are the normalized incoming light direction and the normalized normal for 3D object, C and I_L the color of the model and the intensity of incoming light respectively, making the reflection color I_D a linear function of I_L (with slope $\cos\alpha$). Given that robust features (e.g. SIFT, SURF) enable the robust detection even in the presence of such lighting variation, we can generally expect the color variability of a static feature to comply with such linear behavior. Based on this assumption, we propose a simple method for consistency detection. First we re-project each reconstructed feature to all cameras observing the same structure and record the observed RGB pixel color. Note we re-project to all cameras where the feature falls within the viewing frustum, not just those cameras where the feature was detected. We perform RANSAC based line fitting on the set of measured RGB values to determine the inlier ratio ϵ for a pre-specified distance $d_1 = 0.08$ in the RGB unit color cube. We consider any feature with an estimated inlier ratio below 0.6 to have sporadic color. Figure 6 shows the results running our method on a billboard dataset. Moreover, the set of features classified as having sporadic color will be subsequently used to filter sparse SfM estimates corresponding to static structure.

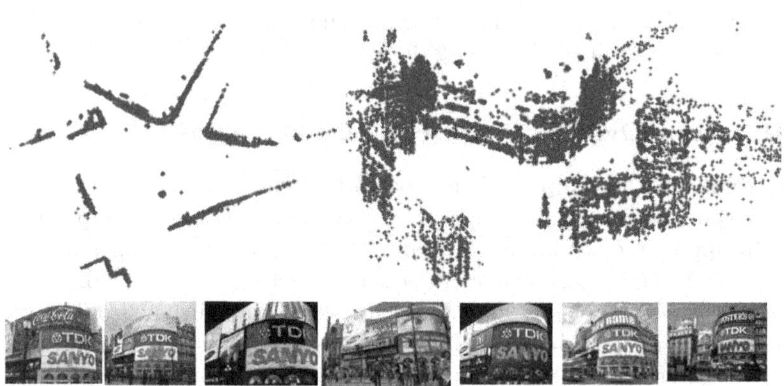

Fig. 6. Identification of dynamic textures within existing SfM estimates. Top Row: birds-eye and fontal view of estimated sparse structure for Piccadilly Circus. Blue dots are 3D features with persitent color across the dataset. Red dots are 3D features determined to have sporadic color. The bottom row shows sample images in the dataset. We associate color persistance with predominantly linear variation in the RGB space.

4.3 Building a Static Background Prior for Single Images

We leverage the dense spatial sampling within image photo-collections in order to estimate a mask for the static structure observed on all images registered by SfM. In order to achieve as dense as possible sampling of static structure within the image, we retrieve the set of inlier feature matches previously attained by pairwise geometric verification to its closest registered neighbor in GIST-space. We then exclude from this set any features in close proximity to features having sporadic color across the entire dataset. There is a coverage to accuracy trade-off in selecting the pairwise inlier feature set instead of the final reconstructed feature set for each image. In order to mitigate the effect of spurious dynamic texture features, we define a sparse background prior, where each feature location is dilated to define a background mask comprising multiple (possibly overlapping) blob structures. We note the contrast with the area based static prior masks estimated from video (i.e. determined by the concave hull of features). Our rationale is that while the dense spatial sampling of video sequences affords strong spatial correlations, the viewpoint and temporal variability of sparse SfM features provides tightly localized correlations. Moreover, the elimination of features having sporadic color from the static prior enables more robust segmentation by the subsequent graph-cut label refinement.

4.4 Mitigating of Non-uniform Spatial Sampling

In order to generate accurate 3D shape models of dynamic scene elements through space carving methods, wide spatial coverage of cameras is a requisite. In fact, this is the motivation for using photo-collection images. However, the availability of abundant images also presents challenges when said imagery is not uniformly distributed within the scene. Namely, we require a large number of viewing rays tangent to the shape's surface in order for the estimated visual hull to accurately approximate the observed surface. Moreover, our basic shape from silhouettes method will favor the identification of commonly observed image regions. Figure 7 shows the reconstruction of Piccadilly circus using 5800 iconic images (from more than 60,000 images). We can see the camera distribution is not uniform providing scarce coverage of the tangent views of the billboard. In order to compensate for the uncontrolled viewpoint distribution, we deploy a weighting mechanism (Algorithm 2) within our image base shape from silhouettes framework. The procedure reduces the contribution/weight of the cameras having common viewpoint configurations and reduced fields of view. Camera distribution is represented as a histogram of angle values between a reference vector and each of the vectors connecting each camera to the centroid of the 3D initial model.

5 Experiments

We downloaded 4 online datasets from the Internet, with videos attained from Youtube and images from Flickr. The statistics of our systems data associations are presented in Table 1. For all datasets, the set of registered images was

Algorithm 2. camera weighting strategy

Input: A initial model M_0, camera centers $C_i, i \in [1, \cdots, N]$, cameras field-of-view angles $f_i, i \in [1, \cdots, N]$

Output: Space carving weight w_i for each camera

for $i \in [1, \cdots, N]$ **do**
- Direction vector of each camera center $v_i \leftarrow C_i - centroid(M_0)$
- Direction angle of each camera center $a_i \leftarrow \arccos \frac{v_i * v_{N/2}}{norm(v_i) norm(v_{N/2})}$
- $w_i = 1$

Discretize the direction angles into 5 bins histogram centered at $B_j, j \in [1, \cdots, 5]$, with frequency $H_j, j \in [1, \cdots, 5]$

for $i \in [1, \cdots, N]$ **do**
- $idx = find(j | B_j \le a_i < B_{j+1})$
- $w_i \leftarrow w_i * min(H)/H_{idx}$
- $w_i \leftarrow w_i * min(f)/f_i$

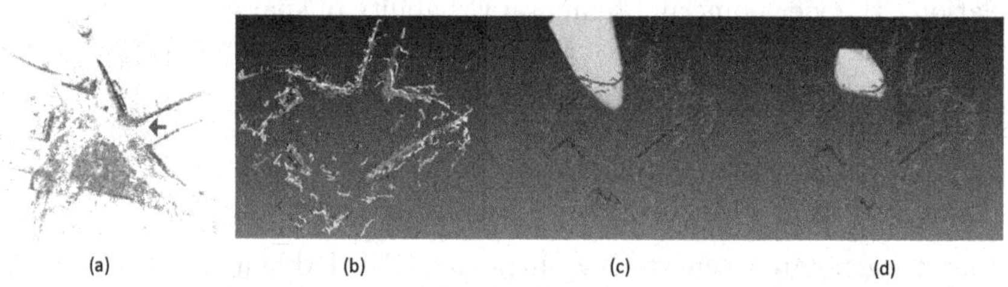

Fig. 7. Mitigation of non uniform spatial sampling. Left to right: (a) Cameras in the red arrow direction are scarse in the SfM model (b) Quasi-dense output from PMVS (c) Dynamic Shape estimation with uniformly weighted carving. The reconstructed 3D volume will be extended towards the camera centroid (d) Shape estimate with weighted carving.

attained using our own SfM implementations, while the final sparse SfM was generated using visualSfM. Figure shows our results combining PMVS quasi-dense model and our dynamic texture shape estimate.

To illustrate the iterative space carving method, we show the segmented estimated visual hull result in each iteration using the Trevi Fountain dataset (Fig. 8). For the the first iteration we use an interaction count ratio (θ_1) of 0.90 and decrease this value by 0.03 each iteration. To ensure convergence of the iteration, we choose a random subset of wide field-of-view images and test their segmentation change in each iteration.

The efficacy of our weighted space carving method for photo collection imagery is illustrated for the Piccadilly Circus Billboard dataset in Figure 7. We can see in the absence of camera contribution weighting, the model will outstretch in the direction of greater camera density. The effect is effectively mitigated by our weighting approach. However, we can still observe slight protrusions w.r.t. the expected surface facade. These are mitigated by a post-processing refinement

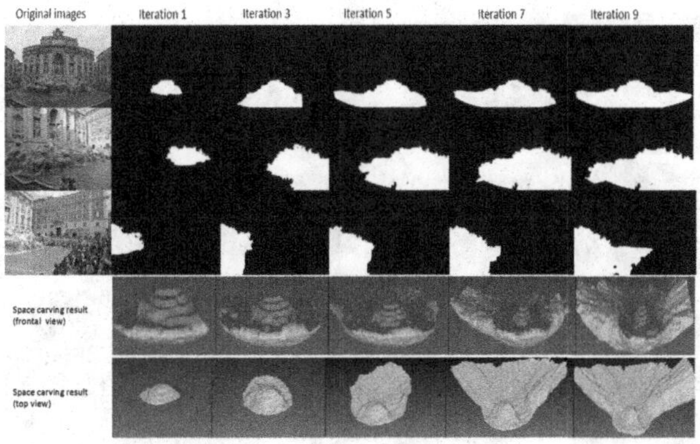

Fig. 8. Evolution of estimated 3D dynamic content in Trevi Fountain model. The video-based model only identified the water motion in the central part of the fountain. Iterative refinement extends the shape to the brim of the fountain. Top rows depict the evolving segmentation mask. Bottom rows depict the evolving 3D shape.

step leveraging the 3D locations of the features determined to have sporadic color (i.e. dynamic texture features reconstructed by SfM) and perform non rigid registration of the final attained dynamic texture shape. We also generate the textured 3D model and compare the results generated by the state-of-the-art method CMPMVS [10] (Fig. 9). For all the experiments, we use the same input dataset for comparison. Each dataset takes approximately 24 hours of processing using both methods.

To illustrate the generality of the proposed framework, we also considered a controlled capture scenario of an indoor scene containing a flat surface with varying illumination. Adapting our method to work with a single input video, instead of crowd sourced data, we were able to generate a 3D approximation of the screen surface of an electronic tablet displaying dynamic texture (shown in Fig. 10). In practice, the inability to attain observations of the dynamic texture of a flat surface from completely oblique views yielded a pice-wise planar 3D surface with a slight outside of plane protrusions. Nevertheless, our attained 3D model was amenable for video texture mapping yielding a realistic animation of the captured video.

Table 1. Composition of our downloaded crowd sourced datasets

Dataset	Videos Downloaded	Keyframes Extracted	Images Downloaded	Images Registered
Trevi Fountain	481	68629	6000	810
Navagio Beach	300	45823	1000	520
Piccadilly Circus Billboard	460	75983	5000	496
Mooney Falls	200	17850	1000	723

Fig. 9. Top two rows: sample dataset imagery, respective outputs for PMVS, CMPMVS and our proposal. Bottom two rows: sample dataset imagery, respective outputs for PMVS and our proposal; CMPMVS failed to generate on the same input data.

Fig. 10. From left to right: sample dataset imagery, respective outputs of PMVS, CMPMVS and our proposed method

6 Conclusion

We proposed a crowd sourced 3D modeling framework encompassing scene elements having dynamic appearance but constant shape. By leveraging both online video and photo-collections we enable the analysis of scene appearance variability across different time scales and spatial layout. Building upon standard SfM, scene labeling and silhouette fusion modules our system can provide, in a fully automated way, more complete representations of captured landmarks containing dynamic elements, such as bodies of water surfaces and active billboards. Moreover, the segregation of the scene content into static and dynamic elements enables compelling visualizations that incorporate the texture dynamics and effectively "bring 3D models to life".

Acknowledgement. This material is based upon work supported by the National Science Foundation under Grant No. IIS-1252921 and No. IIS-1349074. We gratefully acknowledge the support of NVIDIA Corporation with the donation of the Titan GPU used for this research.

References

1. Ballan, L., Brostow, G., Puwein, J., Pollefeys, M.: Unstructured video-based rendering: Interactive exploration of casually captured videos. ACM Transactions on Graphics (2010)
2. Baumgart, B.: Geometric modeling for computer vision. Ph. D. Thesis (Tech. Report AIM-249), Stanford University (1974)
3. Bonet, J.S.D., Viola, P.A.: Roxels: Responsibility weighted 3D volume reconstruction. In: Proceedings of ICCV, vol. 1, p. 418 (1999)
4. Fitzgibbon, A.W.: Stochastic rigidity: Image registration for nowhere-static scenes. In: Proceedings of ICCV, p. 662 (2001)
5. Franco, J.-S., Boyer, E.: Fusion of multi-view silhouette cues using a space occupancy grid. In: Proceedings of ICCV, vol. 2, p. 1747 (2005)
6. Furukawa, Y., Ponce, J.: Carved visual hulls for image-based modeling. In: Leonardis, A., Bischof, H., Pinz, A. (eds.) ECCV 2006, Part I. LNCS, vol. 3951, pp. 564–577. Springer, Heidelberg (2006)
7. Furukawa, Y., Ponce, J.: Towards internet-scale multi-view stereo. In: Proceedings of CVPR, p. 1434 (2010)
8. Guan, L., Franco, J.S., Pollefey, M.: Multi-object shape estimation and tracking from silhouette cues. In: Proceedings of CVPR (2008)
9. Hasler, N., Rosenhahn, B., Thormahlen, T., Wand, M., Gall, J., Seidel, H.: Markerless motion capture with unsynchronized moving cameras. In: Proceedings of CVPR, p. 224 (2009)
10. Jancosek, M., Pajdla, T.: Multi-view reconstruction preserving weakly-supported surfaces. In: Proceedings of CVPR, p. 3121 (2011)
11. Jiang, H., Liu, H., Tan, P., Zhang, G., Bao, H.: 3D reconstruction of dynamic scenes with multiple handheld cameras. In: Fitzgibbon, A., Lazebnik, S., Perona, P., Sato, Y., Schmid, C. (eds.) ECCV 2012, Part II. LNCS, vol. 7573, pp. 601–615. Springer, Heidelberg (2012)
12. Kim, H., Sarim, M., Takai, T., Guillemaut, J., Hilton, A.: Dynamic 3D scene reconstruction in outdoor environments. In: Proceedings of 3DPVT (2010)
13. Labatut, P., Pons, J., Keriven, R.: Efficient multi-view reconstruction of large-scale scenes using interest points, delaunay triangulation and graph cuts. In: Proceedings of ICCV, p. 1 (2007)
14. Labatut, P., Pons, J., Keriven, R.: Robust and efficient surface reconstruction from range data. Computer Graphics Forum 28, 2275 (2009)
15. Laurentini, A.: The visual hull concept for silhouette-based image understanding. IEEE Trans. on Pattern Analysis and Machine Intelligence 16(2), 150 (1994)
16. Nelson, R., Polana, R.: Qualitative recognition of motion using temporal texture. CVGIP: Image Understanding 56, 78 (1992)
17. Otsu, N.: A threshold selection method from gray-level histograms. IEEE Trans. Sys., Man., Cyber. 9(1), 62 (1979)
18. Rother, C., Kolmogorov, V., Blake, A.: Grabcut – interactive foreground extraction using iterated graph cuts. ACM Transactions on Graphics 23(3), 309 (2004)

19. Sinha, S.N., Pollefeys, M.: Multi-view reconstruction using photo-consistency and exact silhouette constraints: A maximum-flow formulation. In: Proceedings of ICCV (2005)
20. Soatto, S., Doretto, G., Wu, Y.N.: Dynamic textures. In: Proceedings of ICCV, p. 439 (2001)
21. Taneja, A., Ballan, L., Pollefeys, M.: Modeling dynamic scenes recorded with freely moving cameras. In: Kimmel, R., Klette, R., Sugimoto, A. (eds.) ACCV 2010, Part III. LNCS, vol. 6494, pp. 613–626. Springer, Heidelberg (2011)
22. Vidal, R., Ravich, A.: Optical flow estimation and segmentation of multiple moving dynamic textures. In: Proceedings of CVPR, p. 516 (2005)
23. Vu, H., Keriven, R., Labatut, P., Pons, J.P.: Towards highresolution large-scale multi-view stereo. In: Proceedings of CVPR, p. 1430 (2009)

3D Interest Point Detection via Discriminative Learning

Leizer Teran[1] and Philippos Mordohai[2]

[1] Drexel University, USA
[2] Stevens Institute of Technology, USA

Abstract. The task of detecting the interest points in 3D meshes has typically been handled by geometric methods. These methods, while designed according to human preference, can be ill-equipped for handling the variety and subjectivity in human responses. Different tasks have different requirements for interest point detection; some tasks may necessitate high precision while other tasks may require high recall. Sometimes points with high curvature may be desirable, while in other cases high curvature may be an indication of noise. Geometric methods lack the required flexibility to adapt to such changes. As a consequence, interest point detection seems to be well suited for machine learning methods that can be trained to match the criteria applied on the annotated training data. In this paper, we formulate interest point detection as a supervised binary classification problem using a random forest as our classifier. We validate the accuracy of our method and compare our results to those of five state of the art methods on a new, standard benchmark.

Keywords: 3D computer vision.

1 Introduction

The identification of important points in images has been a long standing problem in computer vision. Once detected, these important, or interest, points are encoded in one of many invariant representations, such as SIFT [19], and are used within a multitude of applications such as image registration, retrieval, object tracking and structure from motion. Note that Lowe [19] presents techniques for detecting and describing interest points, but one can use a different detector and then apply the SIFT descriptor. A similar two-stage approach can be applied to 3D data. However, due to concerns about the reliability of interest point detectors in 3D, in many cases descriptors are computed at uniformly sampled locations of the 3D model [15,9,24]. The reliability of 3D interest point detectors was recently studied by Dutagaci et al. [7] who created a benchmark (Fig. 1) and evaluated several state of the art methods. In this paper, we go beyond pure geometry for 3D interest point detection by learning to detect such points from a corpus of annotated data. Note that descriptor computation is out of scope here.

D. Fleet et al. (Eds.): ECCV 2014, Part I, LNCS 8689, pp. 159–173, 2014.
© Springer International Publishing Switzerland 2014

Fig. 1. David and glasses with marked ground truth points

One of the main difficulties in predicting interest points lies in the discrepancy between quantifiable importance and perceived importance. Many methods assume that quantitatively important points, usually found by optimization of a function, correspond to perceptually important points. This assumption works well for vertices that are co-located with sharp changes in the model, e.g. corners. For smoother regions and perceptually ambiguous points, the previous assumption along with a multi-scale approach have been met with varying success. Another layer of difficulty arises when semantic ambiguity is considered. This is due to varying, task-specific requirements and, in the case of our data, due to subjectivity of the annotators.

A successful algorithm should be invariant to rotation, translation and scaling, capture points that are appealing to a large consensus of people and have enough flexibility to deal with ambiguity and subjectivity. One approach to capturing subjectivity, which has not been fully explored in the 3D shape analysis literature, is discriminative learning that attempts to identify patterns associated with the annotators' preferences.

In this paper, we formulate 3D interest point detection as a binary classification problem. We use several geometric detectors to produce attributes which are the inputs to a learning algorithm that gives competitive performance against five state of the art methods on the benchmark of Dutagaci et al. [7]. The peculiarity of this benchmark is that the ground truth interest points were selected by non-expert users who were asked to click on the models. As a result, points with widely varying geometric properties are selected in each case. For example, as seen in Fig. 1, the high curvature of David's hair does not attract the attention of the annotators. In fact in many cases, such as the teddy bear in Fig. 2, the interest points lie on smooth hemi-spheres. Subjectivity and semantics play a large role in feature selection in this data set posing significant challenges to geometric methods. In some sense, our approach aims at encoding the potential subjective criteria of the annotators and then transferring them to unseen meshes in order to detect interest points according to these criteria. The results in Section 4.5 show that our approach is able to cope with this variability to a very satisfactory degree. Furthermore, consistent performance across widely varying 3D models is an indication of our algorithm's generalizability.

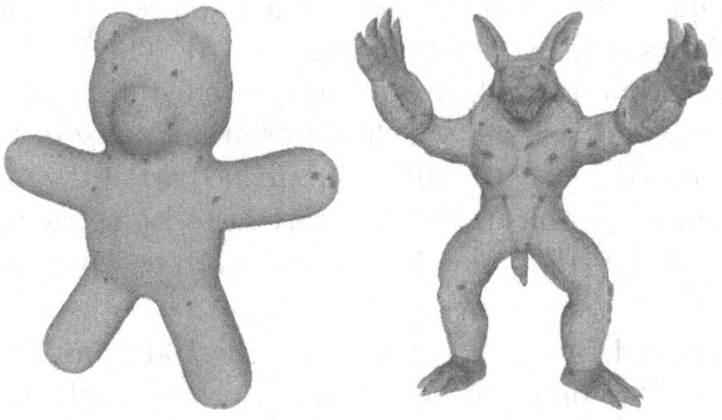

Fig. 2. Teddy bear and armadillo with marked ground truth points

2 Related Work

In a recent survey, Dutagaci et al [7] introduced a benchmark and an evaluation methodology for algorithms designed to predict interest points in 3D. The benchmark comprises 43 triangular meshes and the associated paper evaluated the performance of six algorithms [17,22,2,28,27,12] in interest point detection. Since we also use this benchmark, we focus our attention to these six methods in this section. Other methods for interest point detection on meshes include those based on distinctiveness compared with other local regions [11,10,26], as well as others based on thresholding geometric features [20] or detection in scale-space [16]. We refer readers to recent surveys [21,25,7,18,31] for more details.

Mesh Saliency. Lee et al. [17] address interest point detection through the use of local curvature estimates coupled with a center surround scheme at multiple scales. The total saliency of a vertex is defined as the sum of Difference of Gaussian (DoG) operators over all scales. Interest points are selected after non-max suppression on total saliency.

Scale Dependent Corners. Novatnack and Nishino [22] measure the geometric scale variability of a 3D mesh on a 2D representation of the surface geometry given by its normal and distortion maps, which can be obtained by unwrapping the surface of the model onto a 2D plane. A geometric scale-space which encodes the evolution of the surface normals on the 3D model while it is gradually smoothed is constructed and interest points are extracted as points with high curvature at multiple scales. The appropriate scale is automatically selected for each point.

Salient Points. Castellani et al. [2] also adopt a multi-scale approach. DoG filters are applied to vertex coordinates to compute a displacement vector of each vertex at every scale. The displacement vectors are then projected onto the normals of the vertices producing a "scale map" for each scale. Interest points are extracted among the local maxima of the scale maps after an inhibition process.

Heat Kernel Signature. Sun et al. [28] apply the Laplace-Beltrami operator over the mesh to obtain its Heat Kernel Signature (HKS). The HKS captures neighborhood structure properties which are manifested during the heat diffusion process on the surface model and which are invariant to isometric transformations. The time required for heat to diffuse from one part of the model to another can be used to form a signature which is invariant to isometric transformations. The local maxima of the HKS are selected as the interest points of the model.

3D Harris. Sipiran and Bustos [27] generalize the Harris and Stephens corner detector [13] to 3D. The computation is now performed on the rings of a vertex, which play the role of neighboring pixels. A quadratic surface is fitted to the points around each vertex. This enables the use of a filter similar to the Harris operator, the maximal responses of which are selected as interest points.

3D SIFT. Godil and Wagan [12] initially convert the mesh model into a voxel representation. Then, 3D Gaussian filters are applied to the voxel model at various scales as in the standard SIFT algorithm. DoG filters are used to compute the difference between the original model and the model at a particular scale and their extrema are taken as candidate interest points. The final set of interest points are those that also lie on the surface of the 3D object.

Related to our work is the approach of Holzer et al. [14] that detects interest points in range images using a regression forest. The key differences with our approach are that it operates on sequences of RGB-D images instead of meshes, it is designed for real-time processing and thus uses a simpler set of features, and it considers only objective, geometric criteria. Donner et al. [6] propose an approach for detecting class-specific landmarks, such as the finger tips of a human hand, in volumetric data. A similar problem of detecting facial features in meshes is addressed by Creusot et al. [4]. The two latter approaches [6,4] differ from ours in that they aim at detecting different instances of the same feature, while we aim at transferring the knowledge gained from human annotation from a set of meshes to a completely different mesh.

3 Attributes and Learning

In this section, we focus on the geometric attributes that are used as inputs to our classifier. The attributes capture characteristics that intuitively should help discriminate between interest and regular points, such as curvature, saliency compared to neighboring vertices, etc. Since interest points may become salient at different scales, we capture information at multiple scales by applying Difference of Gaussian (DoG) filters on the attributes [17,2]. The DoG filters are an implementation of the center-surround principle for detecting salient regions based on their differences with the surrounding context. All attributes are invariant to rotation, translation and scale. The latter is achieved by normalizing the lengths in each mesh by its diameter.

First, we present the attributes that serve as the basic building blocks for all the others. The motivation behind this basic set is to create descriptors that capture the local geometric properties and context of a given vertex. We attempt to quantify the basic properties of every vertex, v, through the following 10 attributes, the first 7 of which use the 100 nearest Euclidean neighbors, denoted as $\nu(v)$.

3.1 Basic Attributes

The first 5 attributes involve the scatter matrix about a vertex v:

$$S(v) = \sum_{x \in \nu(v)} \exp^{-\frac{||\mathbf{x}-\mathbf{v}||^2}{\tau^2/2}} \frac{(\mathbf{x}-\mathbf{v})(\mathbf{x}-\mathbf{v})^T}{||\mathbf{x}-\mathbf{v}||^2}, \tag{1}$$

with $\mathbf{x}$ being the coordinates of vertex x and $\mathbf{v}$ being the coordinates of vertex v. The parameter τ, was taken to be the radius of $\nu(v)$. The contribution of each neighbor is weighted according to its proximity with v to limit the influence of neighboring points that may be located across discontinuities.

Attributes 1 to 3 are ratios of eigenvalues of $S(v)$:

$$F_1(v) = \lambda_{1,v}/\lambda_{2,v} \tag{2}$$
$$F_2(v) = \lambda_{1,v}/\lambda_{3,v} \tag{3}$$
$$F_3(v) = \lambda_{2,v}/\lambda_{3,v}, \tag{4}$$

where $\lambda_{i,v}$ is the i-th largest eigenvalue of $S(v)$. These capture properties of the surface, such as planarity in which case $S(v)$ is almost rank deficient, or corners that have three eigenvalues of similar magnitude.

We look at the differences between the eigenvalues for the next two attributes, as follows:

$$F_4(v) = \lambda_{2,v} - \lambda_{1,v} \tag{5}$$
$$F_5(v) = \lambda_{3,v} - \lambda_{2,v}. \tag{6}$$

Attribute 6 is the vertex density about the point, whereas attribute 7 is the average inner product of vertex v's normal with the normals of its 100 nearest neighbors:

$$F_6(v) = \frac{100}{\text{Vol}(\nu(v))} \tag{7}$$
$$F_7(v) = \frac{\sum_{x \in \nu(v)} \mathbf{n}(v) \cdot \mathbf{n}(x)}{100} \tag{8}$$

Where $\mathbf{n}(x)$ is the vertex normal of vertex x.

Attributes 8 and 9 are the principal curvatures at vertex v and the 10th attribute is its Gaussian curvature.

$$F_8(v) = \kappa_1(v) \tag{9}$$
$$F_9(v) = \kappa_2(v) \tag{10}$$
$$F_{10}(v) = \kappa_1(v)\kappa_2(v) \tag{11}$$

To compute the principal curvatures, we look at the one-ring of the current vertex. Then, directional curvatures along the edges are approximated and used to compute the tensor of curvature [30].

3.2 DoG Attributes

The basic attributes described above are generally not sufficient to detect all interest points, since they may become salient at different scales. Inspired by the success of the multi-scale approach adopted by other algorithms [17,2], we compute a set of DoG attributes that are functions of the basic attributes.

The DoG attribute computations were performed within Euclidean neighborhoods of radius r centered at vertex v, which will be referred to as $N(v, r)$. We compute the Gaussian weighted average within the $\delta, 2\delta, 4\delta$ and 6δ neighborhoods of vertex v, for each basic attribute. We use 0.3% of the model diameter as δ. In addition, we compute the Gaussian weighted neighborhood averages of the mean curvature for vertex v, which was not included in the set of basic attributes because it is a linear combination of the principal curvatures.

Attributes 11 through 20 are the DoGs between the δ and 2δ neighborhoods at each vertex for each basic attribute.

$$G_{\delta,j}(v) = \frac{\sum_{x \in N(v,\delta)} F_j(x) \exp^{-||x-v||^2/(2\delta^2)}}{\sum_{x \in N(v,\delta)} \exp^{-||x-v||^2/(2\delta^2)}} \tag{12}$$

$$F_{j+10}(v) = |G_{2\delta,j}(v) - G_{\delta,j}(v)| \; , j \in \{1...10\}. \tag{13}$$

Attribute 21 is the DoG of the mean curvature for the δ and 2δ neighborhoods:

$$\mu_\delta(v) = \frac{\sum_{x \in N(v,\delta)} C(x) \exp^{-||x-v||^2/(2\delta^2)}}{\sum_{x \in N(v,\delta)} \exp^{-||x-v||^2/(2\delta^2)}} \tag{14}$$

$$F_{21}(v) = |\mu_{2\delta} - \mu_\delta| \tag{15}$$

with $C(x)$ being the mean curvature at vertex x.

Attributes 22 through 31 are DoGs for the basic attributes but use the 2δ and 4δ neighborhoods instead. The 32nd attribute is the mean curvature DoG for the 2δ and 4δ neighborhoods. Finally, we look at the DoGs for the 4δ and 6δ neighborhoods to define the 33rd through 43rd attributes in the same way.

To summarize, each vertex has a total of 43 attributes, denoted by $F_i(v)$ with $i \in 1, ..., 43$. The attribute set for each vertex can be broken down into a set of basic attributes $\{F_1(v)...F_{10}(v)\}$ and a set of DoG attributes $\{F_{11}(v)...F_{43}(v)\}$ that are functions of the basic attributes at varying scales. Having defined the inputs to our classifier, we now shift our attention to the random forest.

3.3 Random Forest

Random forest classifiers are ensembles of classification and regression trees that have gained popularity due to their high accuracy and ability to generalize [1,5].

The key idea during training is to generate decisions trees that partition the attribute space in a way that separates the training data according to their labels, interest and non-interest points in our case. In the training stage, a new training set is created for each tree by sampling with replacement (bootstrapping) from the original training set. Each node performs randomly generated tests on random subsets of the full attribute set. The attribute and threshold value that optimize a function of the input samples is selected and the data are divided to the node's children. The Gini gain and the information gain are standard functions used for the selection. We use the former in our analysis.

Once the forest has been trained, the test set vertices are fed to each trained tree in the forest. The current vertex is run down each tree and decisions are made at every node based on the optimal splits computed during training. This process continues until the terminal node is reached and a decision is made about the current vertex's class label. The class label that is output by the majority of the trees in the forest is assigned to the vertex. We use Scikit-Learn [23] to implement the random forests.

The performance of the forest is controlled by its parameters: the depth of each tree, the number of attributes at each node and the the number of trees in the forest. Following Breiman's recommendation [1], we do not prune the trees and allow them to grow until each leaf contains one example. In general, the full attribute set is not used while sampling at each node. This is done to keep the trees in the forest as uncorrelated as possible. Following common practice, we use $\sqrt{p}$ attributes, where p is the total number of attributes, as a guideline to search for the optimal number of attributes used at each node. As discussed in Section 4, we use cross-validation to determine the number of trees.

3.4 Imbalanced Classes

Imbalanced classes present a challenge for most classifiers. Poor predictive performance arises because the standard implementation aims to reduce the overall error rate. As a consequence, the random forest can afford to misclassify almost all the minority class examples and still achieve a very low error rate. To make matters worse, the minority class may not even be selected during bootstrapping and therefore may be missing almost entirely during the training process. For our problem, the ratio of interest to non interest points can range anywhere from 1:100 to even 1:240 within our training data set.

There are a few strategies to deal with the misrepresentation of classes. We chose a technique proposed by Chen et al [3] where the dominant class is down-sampled, while the minority class is over-sampled. For a set of labelled vertices, we randomly select n interest points, where n is one half of the total interest points. During training each tree is given a balanced set of vertices that have a ratio of k non interest vertices to n interest vertices, where $k \geq n$. The parameter k and the bootstrap ratio will be discussed in Section 4.

4 Ground Truth and Experiments

In this section we describe the data we used, the experimental setup and our results.

4.1 Ground Truth

Dutagaci et al. [7] used a web-based application to collect user clicks on 43 mesh models. These models were organized in two overlapping data sets, Data Set A and Data Set B, consisting of 24 and 43 triangular mesh models respectively. Through the web-based application, a user was shown the models from a data set one at a time and was allowed to freely click on them. Data Set A was annotated by 23 human subjects while Data Set B was annotated by 16 human subjects. The positions of the individual user clicks showed some variability as well as some consensus. The variability may be due to imprecise clicking or the subjective nature of interest points.

In order to determine user consensus and remove outliers, the authors considered two criteria while constructing each set's ground truth. The first is the radius, σd_M, of an interest region and the second is the number of users n that clicked within the region. The radius of the interest region is model-specific with d_M denoting the diameter of the model and σ is a parameter in [0.01, 0.02, 0.03, ... , 0.1]. Individual user clicks are clustered together if their geodesic distances are less than $2\sigma d_M$. If the number of clicks in a cluster is less than n that cluster is ignored. If not, the point that minimizes the sum of geodesic distances to the other points is chosen as the representative of the cluster and included in the ground truth. In case the distance between cluster representatives is less than $2\sigma d_M$, the clusters are merged and the representative with the highest number of cluster points is chosen as the final representative.

The parameters, σ and n, affect the number of ground truth points. For a fixed σ, fewer ground truth points are observed as n increases since a higher consensus among users is needed. With small σ and large n, there tends to be better localization around the points and typically fewer ground truth points are observed. As can be seen in Fig. 3, as σ increases, more ground truth points are observed. This trend continues until the clusters are large and close enough to be merged with adjacent clusters, consequently decreasing the overall number of ground truth points for large σ.

4.2 Experiments

We use the human generated ground truth to compare the random forest with the five following methods: Mesh Saliency [17], Salient Points [2], Heat Kernel Signature [28], 3D Harris [27] and Scale Dependent Corners [22], across Data Sets A and B. There are a few models within these data sets that are not watertight and therefore do not allow volumetric representations. As a consequence, the output of 3D SIFT for these models was not provided at the benchmark website.

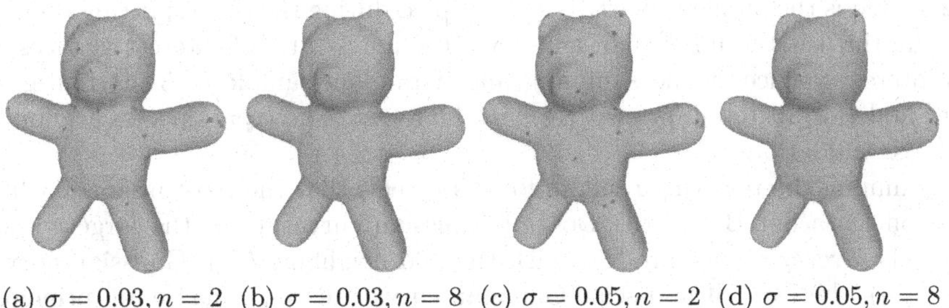

(a) $\sigma = 0.03, n = 2$ (b) $\sigma = 0.03, n = 8$ (c) $\sigma = 0.05, n = 2$ (d) $\sigma = 0.05, n = 8$

Fig. 3. Ground truth points for the teddy bear for four σ/n combinations

This led to its exclusion from our analysis, but partial results can be seen in [7]. (3D SIFT is not among the top performing methods on the benchmark.)

Data Sets A and B are treated as distinct experiments where we measure the effects of user consensus, n, and ground truth localization, σ, on algorithmic performance. Adhering to the evaluation protocol [7], we adopt the following σ/n combinations for Data Set A: 0.03/2, 0.03/11, 0.05/2 and 0.05/11. For Data Set B we use the following combinations: 0.03/2, 0.03/8, 0.05/2 and 0.05/8. In other words, for a given mesh model M, we assess how well the algorithms perform in detecting ground truth points agreed upon by at least two subjects or by at most one half of the subjects labeling each set.

4.3 Training and Predicting

For all experiments, we apply three-fold cross validation for both Data Sets A and B. Specifically, Data Set B was partitioned into three disjoint sets consisting of 14 models each (igea was removed since igea and bust2 are duplicates). Data Set A was split into three disjoint sets consisting of eight models each. Once the splits are established for a given set, we train the random forest, using the attributes from Section 3 as the classifier input, on the first two folds and predict the interest points of the last fold (test set), then the folds are rotated between the test and training sets. The test data are never seen by the classifiers and are not used for parameter selection.

Every vertex of every model in the training set of a given fold has a set of labels. Because the ground truth points vary by σ and n, we have to make a compromise between the number of ground truth points available and high consensus among the annotators. For Data Set B, the representative of clusters σ/n, $n \in [11...22]$, are placed in the positive class for all values of σ provided. All other vertices are placed in the negative class. Likewise, for Data Set A we place the representative of clusters σ/n, $n \in [8...15]$, in the positive class for every available value of σ. The remaining vertices are considered members of the negative class.

Our classifier has three main parameters. The first is the bootstrap ratio of interest vertices to non-interest vertices that is used to balance the training set.

The second is the number of attributes sampled during the node splitting process and the third is the number of trees. We use a 1:1 ratio of interest vertices to non-interest vertices while sampling and a random sample of 5 attributes at every node for all 100 unpruned trees in the forest. These parameters are found via cross validation.

Examining the resulting random forests reveals that the most important features on Data Set B are: the DoG of Gaussian curvature at the largest scale (f_{42}), the average inner product with the 100 neighbors (f_7), Gaussian curvature (f_{10}), the DoG of mid-scale Gaussian curvature (f_{31}), maximum principal curvature (f_9) and two of the eigenvalue ratios (f_1 and f_2). Most feature types, at some scale, contribute to the classifier.

In general, the random forest returns a large number of interest points, as nearby vertices that have similar attributes form clusters. To address this, non-max suppression is performed on the test set vertices that are chosen by the forest. The suppression is done within the $c\psi$ Euclidean neighborhood of the chosen vertices, where c is found to be 5 for Data Set A and 2 for Data Set B via cross validation. ψ is the average minimum geodesic distance between ground truth vertices of the training set.

Note, that the competing methods cannot be trained. Adjusting some threshold is their only means for adaptation. Their outputs were downloaded from the website provided by the authors of [7] and compared with our method's output on each test set. A detailed explanation of the test set scoring is given in the following section.

4.4 Evaluation Criteria

Dutagaci et al. [7] evaluated the performance of the algorithms based on the following definitions and criteria. Let A_M be the set of vertices selected by the algorithm for a given mesh model, M, with diameter d_M. A ground truth point, $g \in G$, is correctly identified if there exists $a \in A_M$ such that the geodesic distance between them is less than some error tolerance, ϵ, and that no other point in G is closer to a. Or in other words, g_0 is correctly identified by the algorithm if: $g_0 = \text{argmin}_{g \in G}(d(a,g) \leq \epsilon)$ for some $a \in A_M$. The following error tolerances are used: $\epsilon = rd_M$ with $r \in [0, 0.1, 0.2...0.12]$.

This definition allows each correctly detected point in the ground truth set to be in correspondence with a unique $a \in A$. The number of false positives (FP) is then $N_A - N_C$ and the false negatives (FN) are $N_G - N_C$ where N_A, N_C and N_G are the number of algorithm selected points, correctly identified points and number of ground truth points respectively. The geodesic distances were computed using publicly available software [29].

In addition to the evaluation criteria proposed by the authors of the benchmark, we also adopt the Intersection Over Union (IOU) criterion, which has been used to evaluate object detection in images [8]. We choose the IOU as our main metric because FN and FP rates can be misleading in isolation. For a mesh model, M, and algorithm, A, we use FP, FN and TP (true positives) as defined above to compute the IOU of an algorithm over a mesh model as:

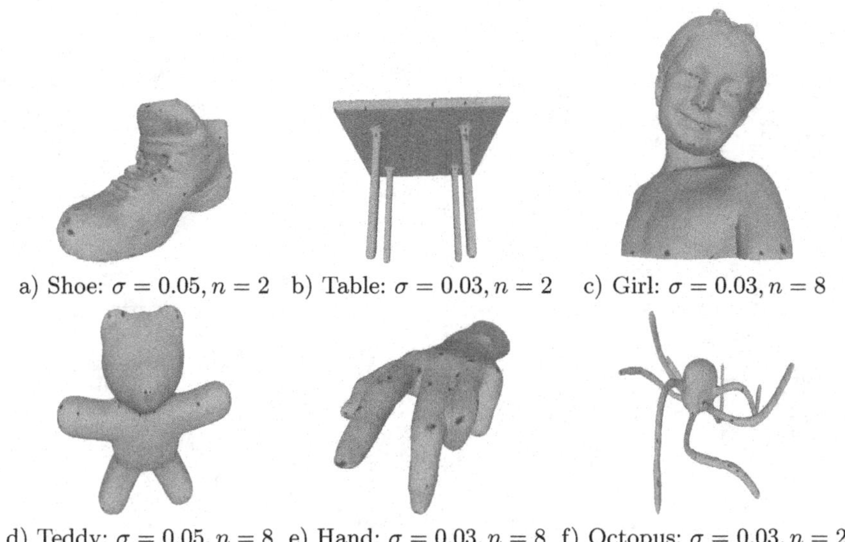

Fig. 4. Random Forest predictions for six Set B models. Ground truth points for various σ/n pairs in red. Random forest predictions in blue. Purple points are ground truth vertices that are predicted exactly.

$$\mathrm{IOU}_{A,M} = \frac{\mathrm{TP}}{\mathrm{FP} + \mathrm{TP} + \mathrm{FN}} \tag{16}$$

The definition for the IOU given above is for a mesh model. To find the IOU score of an algorithm over a set of models, as is done in the experiments, a running total of the false positives, false negatives and true positives were kept over all vertices in the test set and then used to compute a set-wise IOU. We compute the set-wise IOU score for the σ/n combinations in the experiments section. For a given σ/n combination the IOU scores are found for values of $r \in [0, 0.1, 0.2...0.12]$.

4.5 Results

In this section, we present the results of the algorithm evaluations for Data Set A and Data Set B under the IOU metric. Figure 4 contains some visualizations of the results, while Fig. 5 shows the set-wise IOU scores averaged over the three folds as the radius r varies. The legends show the Area Under the Curve (AUC) for the different values of r. In addition, we compare the methods at $\sigma = 0.03/n = 2$ and $\sigma = 0.05/n = 2$ using the evaluation criteria proposed by [7] in the last column of Fig. 5. Here, FNE and FPE are defined as $1 - N_C/N_G$ and FP/N_A respectively. It is important to note that the points detected by the methods are constant when σ and n change.

Figure 5 shows that the random forest is either first or second across Data Set B's σ/n settings. It performs especially well when the localization is relaxed, as

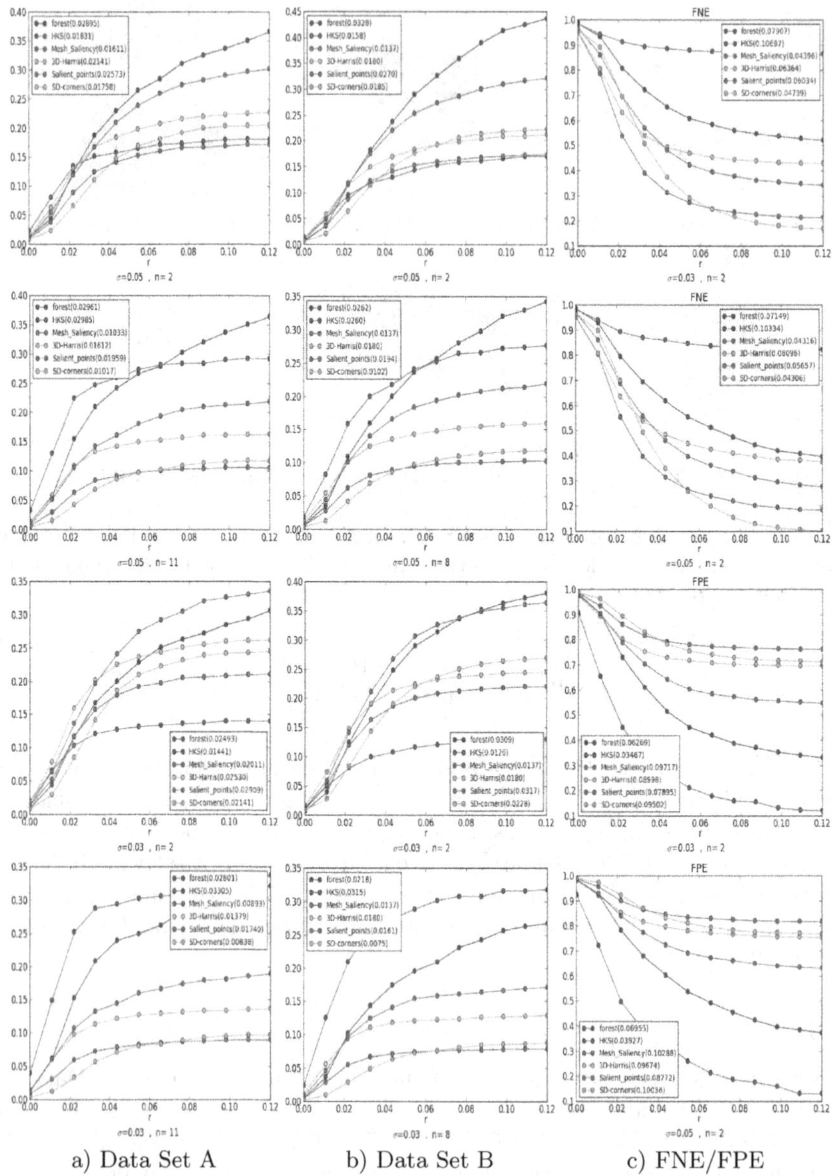

Fig. 5. Column 1 shows the IOU curves for Data Set A at various σ/n pairs. Column 2 contains the IOU curves for Data Set B and Column 3 has the FNE and FPE rates for Data Set B with $\sigma = 0.03, n = 2$ and $\sigma = 0.05, n = 2$. The parameter r is mentioned in Section 4.4. The AUC for each method is provided in the legend.

can be seen when $\sigma = 0.05$. One possible cause for this is that new ground truth points emerge when σ increases for $n = 8$. This is indicative of an ambiguous region within the model, as seen in the teddy bear's neck in Fig. 4. The random forest captures these regions more effectively than the other methods.

Small values of n result in large numbers of ground truth interest points, favoring aggressive methods, such as Salient Points. On the other hand, when n is large, conservative methods are able to identify the truly salient points without producing too many false positives. In this sense, the HKS algorithm is an outlier compared to the rest of the algorithms, including ours. HKS can reliably detect a very small number of very salient points but is unable to detect even slightly more ambiguous points. The last column of Fig. 5 contains FPE and FNE curves for Data Set B with $n = 2$. These curves reveal how aggressive or conservative the algorithms are. The random forest performs well according to all criteria over the parameter range.

Data Set A is expected to be more challenging for a learning-based method, since the training set is smaller. Nevertheless, our algorithm is the top performing one according to IOU. To reach an overall ranking, we average the IOU AUCs over all settings. The results are summarized in Table 1.

Table 1. Average IOU AUCs for all methods on both data sets

Method	Data Set A	Data Set B
Random Forest	0.0279	0.0279
HKS	0.0239	0.0215
Salient Points	0.0230	0.0236
3D Harris	0.0192	0.0180
SD Corners	0.0144	0.0148
Mesh Saliency	0.0139	0.0137

5 Conclusions

In this paper, we have presented a discriminative learning approach to 3D interest point detection that gives competitive performance over state of the art methods. Experiments on a new, publicly available benchmark demonstrate that our method handles variability in the ground truth, or the desirable output, more steadily than other methods. A closer look at Figs. 1, 2 and 4 reveals the diversity of the data, which combined with the relatively small number of models on which our classifier is trained, serves as evidence of generalizability. This translates to an increased ability to cope with human subjectivity in these experiments, and it is equivalent to the ability to adapt to different task-specific requirements imposed on the algorithm. This is they key difference between our work and other approaches that rely on purely geometric criteria for detecting interest points.

References

1. Breiman, L.: Random forests. Machine Learning 45(1), 5–32 (2001)
2. Castellani, U., Cristani, M., Fantoni, S., Murino, V.: Sparse points matching by combining 3D mesh saliency with statistical descriptors. Computer Graphics Forum 27(2), 643–652 (2008)
3. Chen, C., Liaw, A., Breiman, L.: Using random forest to learn imbalanced data. Tech. rep., University of California, Berkeley (2004)
4. Creusot, C., Pears, N., Austin, J.: A machine-learning approach to keypoint detection and landmarking on 3D meshes. IJCV 102(1-3), 146–179 (2013)
5. Criminisi, A., Shotton, J., Konukoglu, E.: Decision forests: A unified framework for classification, regression, density estimation, manifold learning and semi-supervised learning. Found. Trends. Comput. Graph. Vis. 7(2-3), 81–227 (2012)
6. Donner, R., Birngruber, E., Steiner, H., Bischof, H., Langs, G.: Localization of 3D anatomical structures using random forests and discrete optimization. In: Menze, B., Langs, G., Tu, Z., Criminisi, A. (eds.) MICCAI 2010. LNCS, vol. 6533, pp. 86–95. Springer, Heidelberg (2011)
7. Dutagaci, H., Cheung, C., Godil, A.: Evaluation of 3D interest point detection techniques via human-generated ground truth. The Visual Computer 28, 901–917 (2012)
8. Everingham, M., Van Gool, L., Williams, C.K.I., Winn, J., Zisserman, A.: The pascal visual object classes (VOC) challenge. IJCV 88(2), 303–338 (2010)
9. Frome, A., Huber, D., Kolluri, R., Bülow, T., Malik, J.: Recognizing objects in range data using regional point descriptors. In: Pajdla, T., Matas, J. (eds.) ECCV 2004, part III. LNCS, vol. 3023, pp. 224–237. Springer, Heidelberg (2004)
10. Gal, R., Cohen-Or, D.: Salient geometric features for partial shape matching and similarity. ACM Transactions on Graphics 25(1), 130–150 (2006)
11. Gelfand, N., Mitra, N.J., Guibas, L.J., Pottmann, H.: Robust global registration. In: Proceedings of the Third Eurographics Symposium on Geometry Processing (2005)
12. Godil, A., Wagan, A.I.: Salient local 3D features for 3D shape retrieval. arXiv 1105.2796[cs.CV] (2011)
13. Harris, C., Stephens, M.: A combined corner and edge detector. In: Proceedings of the 4th Alvey Vision Conference, pp. 147–151 (1988)
14. Holzer, S., Shotton, J., Kohli, P.: Learning to efficiently detect repeatable interest points in depth data. In: Fitzgibbon, A., Lazebnik, S., Perona, P., Sato, Y., Schmid, C. (eds.) ECCV 2012, Part I. LNCS, vol. 7572, pp. 200–213. Springer, Heidelberg (2012)
15. Johnson, A., Hebert, M.: Using spin images for efficient object recognition in cluttered 3D scenes. PAMI 21(5), 433–449 (1999)
16. Knopp, J., Prasad, M., Willems, G., Timofte, R., Van Gool, L.: Hough transform and 3D SURF for robust three dimensional classification. In: Daniilidis, K., Maragos, P., Paragios, N. (eds.) ECCV 2010, Part VI. LNCS, vol. 6316, pp. 589–602. Springer, Heidelberg (2010)
17. Lee, C.H., Varshney, A., Jacobs, D.: Mesh saliency. ACM Transactions on Graphics 24(3), 659–666 (2005)
18. Lian, Z., Godil, A., Bustos, B., Daoudi, M., Hermans, J., Kawamura, S., Kurita, Y., Lavoué, G., Van Nguyen, H., Ohbuchi, R., et al.: A comparison of methods for non-rigid 3D shape retrieval. Pattern Recognition 46(1), 449–461 (2013)

19. Lowe, D.: Distinctive image features from scale-invariant keypoints. IJCV 60(2), 91–110 (2004)
20. Matei, B., Shan, Y., Sawhney, H.S., Tan, Y., Kumar, R., Huber, D., Hebert, M.: Rapid object indexing using locality sensitive hashing and joint 3D-signature space estimation. PAMI 28(7), 1111–1126 (2006)
21. Mian, A.S., Bennamoun, M., Owens, R.A.: On the repeatability and quality of keypoints for local feature-based 3D object retrieval from cluttered scenes. IJCV 89(2-3), 348–361 (2010)
22. Novatnack, J., Nishino, K.: Scale-dependent 3D geometric features. In: ICCV (2007)
23. Pedregosa, F., Varoquaux, G., Gramfort, A., Michel, V., Thirion, B., Grisel, O., Blondel, M., Prettenhofer, P., Weiss, R., Dubourg, V., Vanderplas, J., Passos, A., Cournapeau, D., Brucher, M., Perrot, M., Duchesnay, E.: Scikit-learn: Machine learning in Python. Journal of Machine Learning Research 12, 2825–2830 (2011)
24. Rusu, R., Blodow, N., Beetz, M.: Fast point feature histograms (FPFH) for 3D registration. In: ICRA, pp. 3212–3217 (2009)
25. Salti, S., Tombari, F., Di Stefano, L.: A performance evaluation of 3D keypoint detectors. In: 3DIMPVT, pp. 236–243 (2011)
26. Shilane, P., Funkhouser, T.: Distinctive regions of 3D surfaces. ACM Transactions on Graphics 26(2) (2007)
27. Sipiran, I., Bustos, B.: Harris 3d: a robust extension of the harris operator for interest point detection on 3D meshes. Visual Computer 27(11), 963–976 (2011)
28. Sun, J., Ovsjanikov, M., Guibas, L.: A concise and provably informative multi-scale signature based on heat diffusion. In: Proceedings of the Symposium on Geometry Processing, pp. 1383–1392 (2009)
29. Surazhsky, V., Surazhsky, T., Kirsanov, D., Gortler, S.J., Hoppe, H.: Fast exact and approximate geodesics on meshes. ACM Transactions on Graphics 24(3), 553–560 (2005)
30. Taubin, G.: Estimating the tensor of curvature of a surface from a polyhedral approximation. In: ICCV, pp. 902–907 (1995)
31. Yu, T.H., Woodford, O.J., Cipolla, R.: A performance evaluation of volumetric 3D interest point detectors. IJCV 102(1-3), 180–197 (2013)

Pose Locality Constrained Representation for 3D Human Pose Reconstruction

Xiaochuan Fan, Kang Zheng, Youjie Zhou, and Song Wang

Department of Computer Science & Engineering, University of South Carolina, USA
{fan23,zheng37,zhou42}@email.sc.edu, songwang@cec.sc.edu

Abstract. Reconstructing 3D human poses from a single 2D image is an ill-posed problem without considering the human body model. Explicitly enforcing physiological constraints is known to be non-convex and usually leads to difficulty in finding an optimal solution. An attractive alternative is to learn a prior model of the human body from a set of human pose data. In this paper, we develop a new approach, namely pose locality constrained representation (PLCR), to model the 3D human body and use it to improve 3D human pose reconstruction. In this approach, the human pose space is first hierarchically divided into lower-dimensional pose subspaces by subspace clustering. After that, a block-structural pose dictionary is constructed by concatenating the basis poses from all the pose subspaces. Finally, PLCR utilizes the block-structural pose dictionary to explicitly encourage pose locality in human-body modeling – nonzero coefficients are only assigned to the basis poses from a small number of pose subspaces that are close to each other in the pose-subspace hierarchy. We combine PLCR into the matching-pursuit based 3D human-pose reconstruction algorithm and show that the proposed PLCR-based algorithm outperforms the state-of-the-art algorithm that uses the standard sparse representation and physiological regularity in reconstructing a variety of human poses from both synthetic data and real images.

Keywords: 3D human pose reconstruction, subspace clustering, hierarchical pose tree.

1 Introduction

3D human pose reconstruction plays an important role in many vision applications, such as image retrieval, video surveillance and human-computer interaction. In this paper, we focus on the problem of reconstructing 3D human poses from the 2D locations of human joints that are annotated in a monocular image. Without considering any prior knowledge on human body, this is obviously an ill-posed problem. Previous works have explicitly utilized physiological knowledge of the human body, such as the body-segment length [6,11], the joint-angle limits [1] and the skeletal size [9], to regularize the 3D pose reconstruction. However, due to the large diversity of human poses, it is usually intractable to find an optimal solution under non-convex physiological constraints [13].

D. Fleet et al. (Eds.): ECCV 2014, Part I, LNCS 8689, pp. 174–188, 2014.
© Springer International Publishing Switzerland 2014

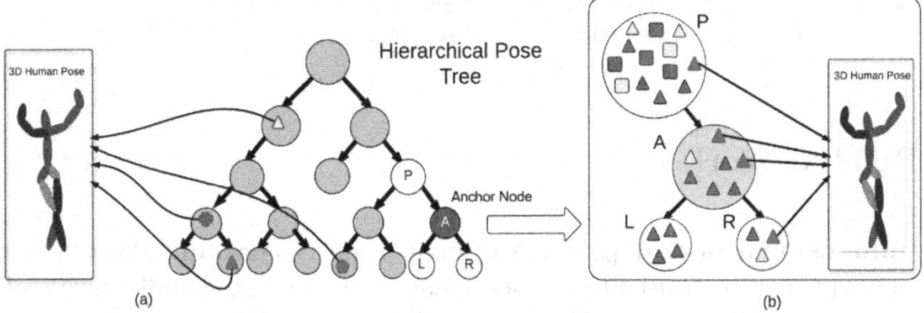

Fig. 1. An illustration of the proposed method. (a) The standard sparse representation allows the non-zero coefficients to be assigned to blocks (nodes) that are distant from each other. (b) The proposed PLCR-based algorithm assigns the non-zero coefficients only to a small set of blocks (nodes) that are close to each other. Basis poses are shown in different-shape elements (e.g., triangles, squares). The selected basis poses for 3D pose reconstruction are linked to the final reconstruction with arrows.

Recently, many efforts have been made in inferring the semantic concepts of the pose or action presented in the 2D image and then using these semantic concepts to help the 3D pose reconstruction. Ramakrishna et al [11] categorize human poses by the human actions, like walking and jumping, and construct sparse representations of human poses. Recently, supervised action classification [23,22,10] was also introduced to automate the action categorization for 3D pose reconstruction. While human actions are semantically well defined, one action may still consist of a variety of human poses and the action-based categorization may not provide sufficiently specific knowledge for 3D pose reconstruction. To address this problem, in this paper we propose a pose locality constrained representation (PLCR) approach for improving the 3D pose reconstruction. In this approach, we construct a hierarchical pose tree, as shown in Figure 1 to model the human poses by subspace clustering [8], where each tree node represents a lower-dimensional pose subspace and nodes with a larger depth in the tree represents more specific pose subspaces. In addition, nodes that are closer to each other in this tree indicate pose subspaces with higher similarity and/or overlap.

In using PLCR for 3D pose reconstruction, we build a block-structural dictionary by concatenating the basis poses from all the nodes of the tree and basis poses from each node constitute a block. With the dictionary, we apply the projected matching pursuit (PMP) algorithm to estimate the most likely 3D human pose. The proposed method explicitly encourages pose locality – nonzero coefficients are only assigned to the basis poses from a small number of blocks (tree nodes) that are close to each other. A comparison between the proposed PLCR representation and the standard sparse representation is shown in Figure 1, where the standard sparse representation may assign nonzero coefficients to distant blocks. Wang et al [19] have shown that locality is more important than sparsity in the image classification. In this paper, we show that, this observation also holds true for the ill-posed problem of 3D human pose reconstruction

– the proposed method can achieve better performance than the state-of-the-art method that uses the standard sparse representation.

2 Related Work

Low-dimensional action priors for pose reconstruction. Many human motion analysis systems used low-dimensional action priors to handle their problems such as human motion optimization [12], human action classification [21], and 3D human body pose tracking [5]. Recently, action priors were also used to assist 3D human pose reconstruction. Yao et al [22] used 2D action recognition as a prior for 3D pose reconstruction, where action specific regression models were trained separately based on low-level appearance features. More recently, Yu et al [23] used action detection on video snippets to derive strong spatiotemporal action priors, which was combined with part-based 2D pose estimation for 3D pose reconstruction. While providing a prior for reconstructing the 3D pose, action labels are still not sufficiently specific since poses from one action class may still show a large diversity.

3D pose reconstruction with physiological regularity. An example of early works on reconstructing 3D poses using physiological regularity is [4] in which physical and motion constraints were applied to prune a binary interpretation tree that records all possible body configurations. Liebowitz and Carlsson [6] assumed known body segment lengths and reconstructed 3D poses from uncalibrated multiple views by using articulated structural constraints. Taylor et al [16] recovered the poses from a single view by assuming known skeletal sizes and resolving the depth ambiguity manually. In [1], the maximum a posterior 3D trajectory was estimated based on a 3D kinematic model including joint angle limits, dynamic smoothing, and 3D key frames. [9] assumed known skeletal size and dealt with a perspective uncalibrated camera. Wei and Chai [20] reconstructed 3D human poses using the bone symmetric constraint from biomechanical data. Valmadre and Lucey [17] extended Wei and Chai [20]'s work by using a deterministic structure-from-motion method. As discussed above, due to the large diversity of human poses, it is usually intractable to find an optimal solution under non-convex physiological constraints [13].

Sparse representation for 3D pose reconstruction. Recently, Ramakrishna et al [11] presented an activity-independent pose-reconstruction method in which the 3D pose is sparsely represented by an overcomplete dictionary learned from a large motion capture dataset. A projected matching pursuit (PMP) algorithm was proposed to infer the underlying 3D poses and the camera settings by minimizing the reprojection error greedily. In this paper, we further introduce pose locality into 3D pose reconstruction – the sparse set of basis poses selected for reconstruction are always from a small number of specific subspaces with high similarity. Through experiments, we will show that the introduction of pose locality can further improve the accuracy of 3D pose reconstruction.

3 Proposed Method

In this section, we first give a formal definition of 3D human pose reconstruction from a 2D projection in Section 3.1. Then, in Section 3.2, we describe an unsupervised pose subspace clustering method for constructing hierarchical pose tree. Based on this tree, we detail the idea of the PLCR and the algorithm that use PLCR for 3D human pose reconstruction in Section 3.3. Finally, we summarize the entire PLCR-based algorithm for 3D pose reconstruction in Section 3.4.

3.1 Problem Description

A 3D human pose can be represented by a set of human joints $\mathbf{J} = \{\mathbf{j}_i\}_{i=1}^{L} \in \mathbb{R}^{3L\times1}$, where $\mathbf{j}_i$ denotes the 3D coordinates of joint i and L is the number of human joints. In this paper, we are interested in estimating 3D joint locations $\mathbf{J}$ from their 2D projections $\mathbf{p} \in \mathbb{R}^{2L\times1}$, with unknown camera parameters.

Under the weak perspective camera projection model, the projected 2D coordinates can be represented as

$$\mathbf{p} = (\mathbf{I}_L \otimes \mathbf{M})\,\mathbf{J} + \mathbf{1}_{L\times1} \otimes \mathbf{T} \tag{1}$$

where $\otimes$ is the Kronecker product, $\mathbf{T} \in \mathbb{R}^{2\times1}$ is the translation vector, and $\mathbf{M} \in \mathbb{R}^{2\times3}$ contains both rotation and scaling parameters. Assuming that the camera intrinsic parameters are known, the degree of freedom of the camera parameters is 7. Therefore, in total there are $3L + 7$ unknowns while only $2L$ equations are available. Obviously, this is an under-determined problem, and we need to apply dimensionality reduction to make it determined.

However, due to the large diversity of human poses, a direct application of linear dimensionality reduction on the entire pose space is difficult and usually results in large reconstruction errors. This problem can be solved by restricting the pose reconstruction on a more specific pose subspace. To achieve this goal, two problems need to be addressed: 1) effectively dividing the entire pose space into subspaces, 2) finding the subspace in which the underlying 3D pose belongs to, based only on its 2D projection. For the first problem, we construct a hierarchical pose tree, where each node represents a pose subspace and the node with a larger depth in the tree represents a more specific pose subspace. For the second problem, given a 2D pose projection we find an anchor node in the tree by minimizing the reprojection error. In practice, the underlying 3D pose may not exactly belong to the subspace defined by the anchor node because of the information loss in 2D projection. To address this issue, we additionally include nodes close to the anchor node in the tree and use all their basis poses for 3D pose reconstruction.

3.2 Hierarchical Pose Tree

We construct pose subspaces with different levels of specificity by using subspace clustering. In particular, given a large set of 3D pose training data, we cluster them into different groups in a hierarchical way, such that each group of pose data represents a subspace.

Unsupervised Human Pose Subspace Clustering. Considering the code efficiency and availability, in this paper we use the low-rank representation algorithm [8,7] for 3D human pose subspace clustering. Other subspace clustering algorithms, such as the K-subspaces algorithm [18] and the sparse subspace clustering (SSC) algorithm [2,15], can also be used here.

Specifically, given a set of 3D human poses $\mathcal{J} = \{\mathbf{J}_i\}_{i=1}^N \in \mathbb{R}^{3L\times N}$, we first construct the lowest-rank representation $\mathbf{Z} \in \mathbb{R}^{N\times N}$ that satisfies $\mathcal{J} = \mathcal{J}\mathbf{Z}$. Let the skinny SVD of $\mathbf{Z}$ be $U\Sigma V^T$. We define the affinity matrix $\mathbf{W}$ as

$$w_{ij} = \left(\left[\widetilde{U}\widetilde{U}^T\right]_{ij}\right)^2,$$

where $\widetilde{U}$ is formed by $U\Sigma^{\frac{1}{2}}$ with normalized rows. Each element $w_{ij} \in \mathbf{W}$ measures the likelihood that two poses $\mathbf{J}_i$ and $\mathbf{J}_j$ are located in the same subspace. Finally, we apply the spectral clustering [14] on the affinity matrix $\mathbf{W}$.

Pose Data Normalization. The goal of subspace clustering is to group similar poses, even performed by different subjects, into a same subspace. However, in practice, we found that the physiological difference between subjects may dominate the pose clustering, e.g., different poses from similar-size subjects may be clustered together. To address this problem, we propose to normalize all the 3D pose data before applying the above subspace clustering. In this paper, we normalize the length of each segment between adjacent joints in the human skeleton.

A segment that connects two joints $\mathbf{j}_a$ and $\mathbf{j}_b$ in the human skeleton can be written as $\mathbf{j}_a - \mathbf{j}_b$. We then convert it to the spherical coordinates as

$$\mathbf{j}_a - \mathbf{j}_b = (\theta_{ab}, \phi_{ab}, r_{ab}),$$

where, θ_{ab} is the zenith angle from the z axis, ϕ_{ab} is the azimuth angle from the x axis in the xy plane, and r_{ab} is the radius or the length of the segment. Obviously, r_{ab} is a constant for all the poses performed by a same subject, but different for the poses performed by different subjects. We normalize r_{ab} to the average length of this segment over all the training pose data. For the rigid parts of the human body, such as clavicles and hips, we also normalize the zenith and azimuth angles to be constants, by averaging over all the training pose data. After normalizing in the spherical coordinates, we convert the pose data back to the Cartesian coordinates. In this step, to ensure the segments are connected at the corresponding joints, we take advantage of the tree structure of the human skeleton – starting from the root (e.g., human head), normalized segments are assembled layer by layer to determine the coordinates of each joint. Figure 2 shows the sample subspace clusters with and without the normalization step. We can see that, with the data normalization, similar poses from different subjects can be clustered together.

Hierarchical Pose Tree. To construct subspaces with various levels of specificity, we recursively perform subspace clustering to construct a hierarchical pose

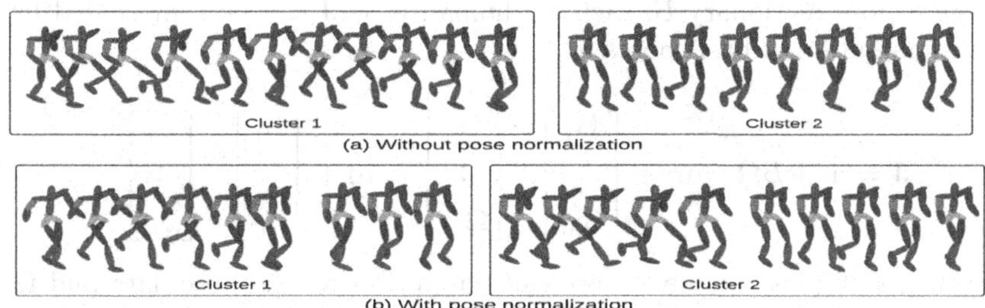

Fig. 2. Sample subspace clustering results (a) without and (b) with the pose data normalization. With the normalization, the data that describe similar poses from different subjects are successfully clustered together, e.g., cluster 1 for the pose of moving right foot ahead and cluster 2 for the pose of moving left foot ahead.

tree – a cluster of pose data may be further clustered into smaller groups, where each group represents a more specific pose subspace. In this paper, we use two parameters, the branch factor K and a subspace complexity k, to control the number of clusters and the height of the resulting pose tree. A branch factor K indicates that each node in the pose tree, except for the leaves, has K children – each subspace is partitioned into K more specific subspaces in the recursive clustering. The subspace complexity k can be estimated using the method proposed in [7] – a subspace will not be further divided if $k < K$ and this subspace becomes a leaf node in the pose tree. This way, nodes with a larger depth in the constructed pose tree represent more specific pose subspaces and the pose similarity between different subspaces can be measured by the shortest-path distance between the corresponding nodes in the pose tree.

3.3 Pose Locality for Reconstruction

In this section, we first build a block-structural pose dictionary based on all the subspaces (nodes) in the constructed pose tree, taking the basis poses at each node as a block. We then describe a new pose locality constrained representation (PLCR) for reconstructing the 3D pose.

Block-Structural Pose Dictionary. As described in Section 3.2, each node in the constructed pose tree represents a pose subspace, which is described by a cluster of training pose data. At each node i, we can draw all pose data in the corresponding cluster and apply PCA to construct D_i basis poses, denoted as a block $\mathbf{B}_i$. The pose dictionary $\mathcal{B} = \{\mathbf{B}_i\}_{i=1}^{M}$ is constructed by concatenating the basis poses over all the M nodes. The total number of basis poses in the dictionary is $D = \sum_{i=1}^{M} D_i$. Thus, the pose dictionary can also be written as $\mathcal{B} = \{\mathbf{b}_j\}_{j=1}^{D}$, where each $\mathbf{b}_j$ denotes one basis pose.

Given a pose dictionary $\mathcal{B}$, each 3D human pose $\mathbf{J}$ can be represented by a linear combination of basis poses in $\mathcal{B}$, i.e.,

$$\mathbf{J} = \mathbf{m} + \mathcal{B}\boldsymbol{\Omega} = \mathbf{m} + \begin{bmatrix} \mathbf{B}_1 \\ \vdots \\ \mathbf{B}_M \end{bmatrix}^T \begin{bmatrix} \boldsymbol{\Omega}_1 \\ \vdots \\ \boldsymbol{\Omega}_M \end{bmatrix} = \mathbf{m} + \begin{bmatrix} \mathbf{b}_1 \\ \vdots \\ \mathbf{b}_D \end{bmatrix}^T \begin{bmatrix} \omega_1 \\ \vdots \\ \omega_D \end{bmatrix} \tag{2}$$

where $\mathbf{m} \in \mathbb{R}^{3L\times 1}$ is the mean pose calculated over all the pose data and $\boldsymbol{\Omega} \in \mathbb{R}^{D\times 1}$ are the coefficients. We also denote $E = \|\boldsymbol{\Omega}\|_0$ to be the sparsity of $\boldsymbol{\Omega}$, with which the number of unknowns in Eq. (1) can be reduced to $E + 7$.

Pose Reconstruction with PLCR. For reconstructing the 3D pose from a 2D projection, we need to select E basis poses from the dictionary. Previous method [11] uses sparse representation to sequentially select E basis poses that minimize the reprojection error

$$\mathbf{R}(\mathcal{B}, \boldsymbol{\Omega}, \mathbf{M}, \mathbf{T}) = \mathbf{p} - (\mathbf{I}_L \otimes \mathbf{M}) \left(\mathbf{m} + \sum_{i=1}^{M} \mathbf{B}_i \boldsymbol{\Omega}_i \right) - \mathbf{1}_{L\times 1} \otimes \mathbf{T},$$

where the weak-projective camera parameters $\mathbf{M}$ and $\mathbf{T}$ can be refined iteratively with an initialization.

However, standard sparse representation does not enforce pose locality – the selected basis poses can be drawn from subspaces (nodes) that are far from each other in the pose tree. In this section, our main goal is to ensure that the E selected basis poses are drawn from a small number of subspaces (nodes) that are close to each other. To achieve this goal, we calculate the initial reprojection error $\mathbf{r}_i$ for each block $\mathbf{B}_i$ based on the initial camera parameters, i.e.

$$\mathbf{r}_i = \mathbf{R}\left(\mathbf{B}_i, \boldsymbol{\Omega}_i^*, \mathbf{M}, \mathbf{T}\right),$$

where the coefficients $\boldsymbol{\Omega}_i^*$ can be calculated by

$$\boldsymbol{\Omega}_i^* = \arg\min_{\boldsymbol{\Omega}_i} \|\mathbf{R}\left(\mathbf{B}_i, \boldsymbol{\Omega}_i, \mathbf{M}, \mathbf{T}\right)\|_2. \tag{3}$$

Given the 2D projection $\mathbf{p}$ of the pose and initial camera parameters, we define the *anchor node* $A(\mathbf{p})$ to be the node in the pose tree that leads to the smallest reprojection error, by using the basis poses at this node (subspace), i.e.,

$$A(\mathbf{p}) = \arg\min_i \|\mathbf{r}_i\|_2. \tag{4}$$

To make the search process of anchor node more efficient, we use the following top-down search algorithm.

1. Examine the root of the tree and calculate the reprojection error.
2. Examine all the K child nodes of the root and pick the one with the smallest reprojection error.

3. For the picked node, we further examine its K children and pick the one with the smallest reprojection error and repeat this process until we reach a leaf node.
4. All the picked nodes constitute a path from the root to a leaf and each node along this path has an associated reprojection error. We then pick the node along this path with the smallest reprojection error as the anchor node.

Given the information loss in the 2D projection, the anchor node may not provide a subspace that well describes the underlying 3D pose. We select E basis poses not only from the subspace described by the anchor node, but also from the nodes nearby. Specifically, we use the projected matching pursuit (PMP) to select the basis poses and in each iteration, a new pose basis $\mathbf{b}_{j*}$ is chosen from $\mathcal{B}$ by

$$j^* = \arg\min_j \left(|\theta_j| + \lambda d_j\right), \tag{5}$$

where θ_j is the angle between $(\mathbf{I} \otimes \mathbf{M})\,\mathbf{b}_j$ and the reprojection error $\mathbf{r}$ in the current iteration, λ is the locality weight. The locality adaptor

$$d_j = \begin{cases} e^{\frac{d(N(j),A(\mathbf{p}))}{\sigma}}, & \text{if } d\left(N\left(j\right), A\left(\mathbf{p}\right)\right) \le d_M, \\ +\infty, & \text{otherwise,} \end{cases}$$

controls the pose locality – only the nodes (subspaces) that are close to the anchor node in the pose tree are included for basis-pose selection. $N\left(j\right)$ denotes the node (subspace) that $\mathbf{b}_j$ belongs to and $d\left(N\left(j\right), A\left(\mathbf{p}\right)\right)$ is the distance or the length of the shortest path between two nodes $N\left(j\right)$ and $A\left(\mathbf{p}\right)$ in the pose tree. d_M is a pre-set threshold and the nodes with a distance to the anchor that is larger than this threshold will not be included for basis-pose selection. Following [19], σ controls the weight decay speed for the locality adaptor. Using this technique to select basis poses, we can iteratively refine the reconstruction of the 3D pose and camera parameters using the PMP algorithm [11]. Note that, the proposed algorithm only selects one more basis pose $\mathbf{b}_j^*$ in each iteration and this is different from the group sparsity technique [3], where all the basis poses at the node $N(j^*)$ are selected in an iteration.

3.4 Algorithm Summary

The complete PLCR-based algorithm for 3D pose reconstruction is summarized in Algorithm 1. As described above, we first construct a hierarchical pose tree, build a block-structural pose dictionary and search for an anchor node. We then iteratively pick the new basis poses that not only reduce the reprojection error, but also satisfy the pose locality constraint. In each iteration, we re-estimate the camera parameters based on the updated pose representations. Specifically, we use the PMP algorithm in [11] for camera parameter estimation. This iterative process is terminated when the 2D reprojection error is lower than a tolerance value, or a pre-set sparsity E has been reached. Using this iterative algorithm, a 3D human pose can be reconstructed using a linear combination of a small number of basis poses.

Algorithm 1. PLCR-based 3D pose reconstruction

Input: $\mathbf{p}$: 2D projection of a human pose
$\mathcal{J}$: a set of 3D human poses
E: pre-set sparsity
τ: tolerance value for the 2D reprojection error

```
Construct a hierarchical pose tree using method proposed in Sec. 3.2 and
  build the pose dictionary B.
Estimate initial camera parameters ⟨M = M_1, T = T_1⟩[11].
Search for an anchor node A(p) using the method proposed in Sec. 3.3
  and initialize S = ∅.
FOR l from 1 to E
  j* = arg min_j (|θ_j| + λ d_j)
  S = S ∪ b_{j*}
  Update the coefficients Ω and camera parameters ⟨M, T⟩ according to
  the updated S.
  Calculate the reprojection error r = R(S, Ω, M, T).
  IF ||r||_2 > τ
    BREAK
Calculate the 3D pose J by Eq.(2) and return.
```

Output: 3D pose $\mathbf{J}$ and camera parameters $\mathbf{M}$ and $\mathbf{T}$

4 Experiments

We use the CMU Motion Capture dataset for quantitative evaluations. This dataset contains more than three million 3D human poses collected on 144 subjects performing 30 different actions, and it has been widely used for evaluating 3D human pose reconstruction [11,17,20]. We also qualitatively evaluate the proposed method on real images collected from the Internet. As in previous works [11,17,20], we randomly selected a subset of 29,336 3D human poses from 5 different action categories: 'walking', 'jumping', 'running', 'boxing' and 'climbing' for quantitative performance evaluation. Details on the selected data is shown in Table 1. We can see that, for each action category except for 'climbing', the collected data are preformed by a number of different subjects. We use the 18-joint pose representation for our experiments [20].

Table 1. Detailed information on the 29,336 3D poses that are used for quantitative performance evaluation

	Walking	Jumping	Running	Boxing	Climbing
# of Pose	5752	5808	5352	8072	4352
# of Subjects	8	3	8	3	1

To study the generalizability of the proposed method, we use the "leave-one-subject-out" strategy for performance evaluation – the test data and the training data are from different subjects. Furthermore, we exclude the data from the 'climbing' action from training and only use them for testing to examine the generalizability of the proposed 3D pose reconstruction method across different action categories. As shown in Table 1, we in total conducted 23 rounds of experiments. Out of them, we have 22 rounds of experiments that use the pose data from the first four categories, excluding the data from 'climbing' category. In each of these 22 rounds of experiments, we leave out pose data from one subject in one action category for testing, while using the remaining data for training. We then conduct one additional round of experiment which uses pose data from 'climbing' category for testing and all the pose data from the other four categories for training.

When using a pose for testing, we first project it (i.e., the 18 joints) into 2D using a randomly generated camera parameters – both the camera location and orientation conform to a Gaussian distribution. We then reconstruct the 3D pose from this 2D projection (assuming camera parameters are unknown) and measure the reconstruction error at each joint as Euclidean distance between the ground-truth location of this joint and the reconstructed location of this joint. We then take the **maximum** reconstruction error over all the 18 joints and normalize it over the distance between the chest and waist as the *(normalized) reconstruction error* of this pose. Another performance metric used in this paper is the pose *reconstruction rate*, defined as the percentage of the tested poses that result in a low (normalized) reconstruction error, defined by a given threshold, which we use 0.3 for all the experiments.

The parameters that need to be tuned for our algorithms are: the branch factor K, the sparsity E, and the locality-adaptor related ones (λ, σ and d_M). In our experiments, we set $K = 2$, $E = 10$, $\sigma = 1$ and $d_M = 2$. We vary the parameter λ in the experiment to examine its effect to the performance. The choice of the parameters E and d_M will be further discussed at the end of this section.

4.1 Quantitative Results

Table 2 shows the reconstruction error (*rec_error*) and the reconstruction rates (*rec_rate*), averaged over all the subjects for each action category, with varying parameter λ. For comparison, we also report in Table 2 the performance of a state-of-the-art algorithm developed by Ramakrishna et al [11] on the same training and testing data. This comparison method [11] uses standard sparse representation and physiological regularity for 3D pose reconstruction. Note that, to examine the effectiveness of the proposed pose-locality constraints, we do not include any physiological regularity in the proposed method. We can see that, the proposed PLCR-based 3D pose reconstruction method outperforms the Ramakrishna's algorithm for all the action categories.

The 2D joint locations annotated in monocular images are often noisy. To examine the performance of 3D pose reconstruction under the 2D annotation noise, we add Gaussian white noise with different standard deviation *std* to the projected 2D joint locations, and then perform the 3D reconstruction, and the average performance over all the action categories is reported in Table 3, where

Table 2. The 3D reconstruction errors and reconstruction rates for different action categories

Action Category	Performance Metrics	Proposed method				Ramakrishna et al [11]
		$\lambda = 0$	$\lambda = 0.1$	$\lambda = 0.2$	$\lambda = 0.3$	
Walking	*rec_error*	0.360	0.300	**0.260**	0.272	0.446
	rec_rate	53.4%	71.2%	**73.9%**	70.4%	29.6%
Running	*rec_error*	0.417	0.390	**0.385**	0.432	0.453
	rec_rate	29.8%	35.1%	**38.2%**	34.0%	23.0%
Jumping	*rec_error*	0.343	0.322	**0.316**	0.321	0.374
	rec_rate	34.12%	39.5%	**41.6%**	40.2%	31.6%
Boxing	*rec_error*	0.579	**0.530**	0.535	0.534	0.584
	rec_rate	13.3%	**17.0%**	16.4%	16.8%	10.7%
Climbing	*rec_error*	0.560	0.528	**0.522**	0.526	0.533
	rec_rate	21.7%	27.9%	27.0%	**28.1%**	20.1%

Table 3. The average 3D reconstruction errors and reconstruction accuracy rates when different levels of noise are added to the 2D projections

std		0.0	0.1	0.2	0.3	0.4
Proposed method	*rec_error*	0.414	0.449	0.485	0.561	0.630
	rec_rate	32.6%	28.7%	24.4%	18.1%	13.1%
Ramakrishna et al [11]	*rec_error*	0.466	0.497	0.558	0.634	0.704
	rec_rate	23.9%	20.5%	13.8%	9.3%	4.8%

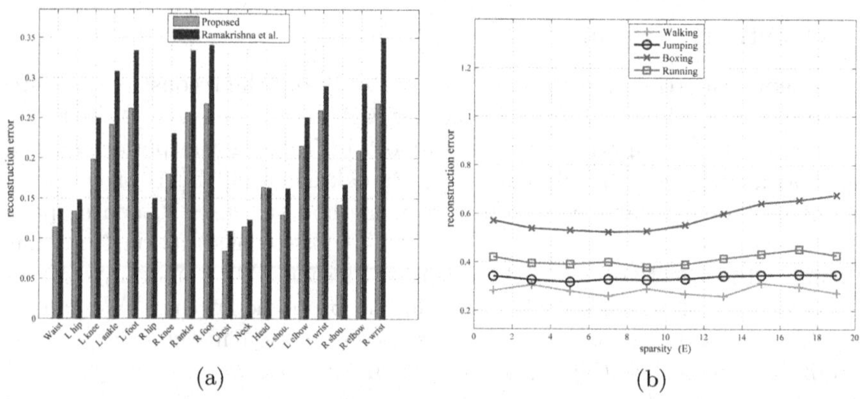

Fig. 3. (a) Reconstruction errors at each of the 18 joints – a comparison between the proposed method and the Ramakrishna et al's algorithm. (b) Average reconstruction errors for four actions by varying the value of E.

the performance under $std = 0.0$ is the one without adding any noise. The values of the std are normalized by the width of the bounding box around the 2D projected pose. We can see that, the stronger the added noise, the larger the 3D reconstruction error and the lower the reconstruction rate. However, with the same level of noise, the proposed method still outperforms the comparison method.

Figure 3(a) shows the reconstruction error at each of the 18 joints, averaged over all rounds of experiments and all action categories. We can see that the proposed method achieves lower reconstruction error at all 18 joints than the Ramakrishna et al's algorithm. We can also see that, the reconstruction errors at feet, wrists, and ankles are larger than those at other joints, because of the larger movements of the hands and feet. Similar phenomena has been reported in [23].

4.2 Qualitative Evaluation

3D pose reconstruction results on four pose samples drawn from CMU Motion Capture dataset are shown in Figure 4. For each sample, we show (from left to right) the ground-truth 3D pose, its 2D projection, the 3D reconstruction using the proposed method, and the 3D reconstruction using the Ramakrishna's algorithm [11], respectively. For all these four cases, we can see that the proposed method generates more accurate and physiologically correct reconstructions, which are particularly clear at the locations indicated by the thick blue arrows on the results from the Ramakrishna et al's algorithm [11].

We also evaluate the proposed method on several images downloaded from the Internet, by manually annotating the 2D locations of the 18 joints on each image. The pose reconstruction results are shown in Figure 5. The reconstructed 3D human poses are shown from two different view angles. We can see that, the proposed method produces reasonable human pose reconstruction results on these real images.

4.3 The Selection of Parameters d_M and E

The parameter d_M defines a range around the anchor node that is allowed to be used for drawing the basis poses for 3D pose reconstruction. Intuitively, this parameter should be the distance between the real node (subspace) a pose belongs to and the anchor node searched by the proposed method. In our case, a pose belongs to one node (subspace) at each level of the tree and all these real nodes from all levels constitute a path from the root to a leaf. We can examine the shortest distance between the anchor node and this path, called *node-path distance,* to select an appropriate value for d_M. Table 4 shows the distribution of this node-path distance for all the collected pose data. We can see that most poses (86%) show such a distance to be no more than 2 (edges). Therefore, in our experiments, we set $d_M = 2$.

The parameter E indicates the sparsity, i.e., the number of basis poses used for 3D pose reconstruction. Figure 3(b) shows the average reconstruction error curves by varying the value of E, one curve for each action category. We can see

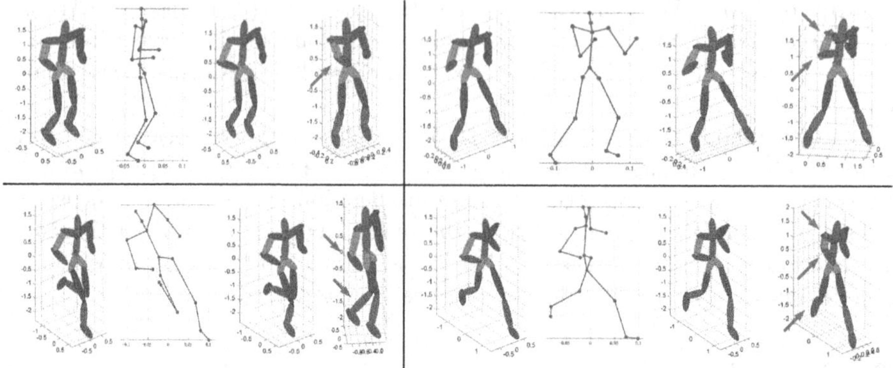

Fig. 4. Qualitative comparison between the proposed method and the Ramakrishna et al's algorithm [11] on the CMU Motion Capture dataset. For each pose, from left to right are the ground-truth 3D pose, its 2D projection, the 3D reconstruction using the proposed method, and the 3D reconstruction using the Ramakrishna et al's algorithm [11], respectively. Indicated by the blue arrows (on the 3D reconstruction produced by the Ramakrishna et al's algorithm) are the locations where the proposed method produces much better 3D reconstruction than the Ramakrishna et al's algorithm.

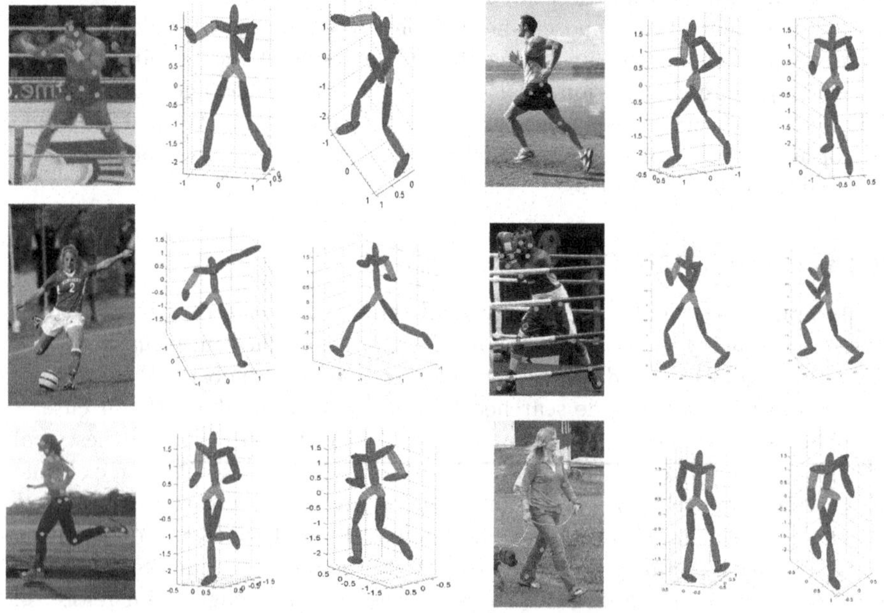

Fig. 5. 3D pose reconstruction from six images collected from Internet

Table 4. Distribution of the distance between the anchor node and the true path in the pose tree

Node-path distance	0	1	2	3	4	5	6	7
% Poses	60.3	14.0	11.8	7.8	3.4	1.0	1.2	0.0

that, varying the value of E from 1 to 19 does not lead to substantial performance difference for the 3D pose reconstruction. In our experiments, we simply select $E = 10$.

4.4 Distribution of Anchor-Node Depth

The depth of the searched anchor nodes in the pose tree reflects the specificity of the subspace used for 3D pose reconstruction – the deeper the anchor node, the more specific the corresponding subspace and the stronger the regularization for the ill-posed 3D reconstruction. Table 5 shows the distribution of anchor-node depth for all the tested pose data. We can see that for more than 80% of the poses, the searched anchor nodes have a depth larger than or equal to 2.

Table 5. Distribution of the anchor-node depth in the pose tree

Depth	0	1	2	3	4	5	6	7
% Poses	4.0	12.1	21.7	12.9	19.3	19.7	7.2	3.1

5 Conclusions

In this paper, we developed a new pose locality constrained representation (PLCR) of 3D human poses and used it to improve the 3D pose reconstruction from a single 2D image. We first used subspace clustering to construct a hierarchical pose tree, where each node represents a pose subspace and the nodes with larger depth in the tree represent more specific pose subspaces. To reconstruct a 3D pose, an anchor node is searched from the pose tree based on the input 2D projection. We then use the projected matching pursuit algorithm to search for a sparse set of basis poses from the anchor node (subspace) and its nearby nodes, which enforces the pose locality. We tested on $29,336$ pose data randomly selected from five action categories of the CMU Motion Capture dataset and found that the proposed PLCR-based algorithm outperforms a state-of-the-art algorithm using only sparse representation without considering pose locality. Reasonable qualitative results were also shown on real images collected from the Internet.

Acknowledgement. This work was supported in part by AFOSR FA9550-11-1-0327 and NSF IIS-1017199.

References

1. Di Franco, D.E., Cham, T.J., Rehg, J.M.: Reconstruction of 3D figure motion from 2D correspondences. In: CVPR (2001)
2. Elhamifar, E., Vidal, R.: Sparse subspace clustering. In: CVPR (2009)
3. Jenatton, R., Mairal, J., Obozinski, G., Bach, F.: Proximal methods for hierarchical sparse coding. The Journal of Machine Learning Research 12, 2297–2334 (2011)
4. Lee, H.J., Chen, Z.: Determination of 3D human body postures from a single view. Computer Vision, Graphics, and Image Processing 30(2), 148–168 (1985)
5. Li, R., Tian, T.P., Sclaroff, S., Yang, M.H.: 3D human motion tracking with a coordinated mixture of factor analyzers. IJCV 87(1-2), 170–190 (2010)
6. Liebowitz, D., Carlsson, S.: Uncalibrated motion capture exploiting articulated structure constraints. IJCV 51(3), 171–187 (2003)
7. Liu, G., Lin, Z., Yan, S., Sun, J., Yu, Y., Ma, Y.: Robust recovery of subspace structures by low-rank representation. TPAMI 35(1), 171–184 (2013)
8. Liu, G., Lin, Z., Yu, Y.: Robust subspace segmentation by low-rank representation. In: ICML (2010)
9. Parameswaran, V., Chellappa, R.: View independent human body pose estimation from a single perspective image. In: CVPR (2004)
10. Raja, K., Laptev, I., Pérez, P., Oisel, L.: Joint pose estimation and action recognition in image graphs. In: ICIP (2011)
11. Ramakrishna, V., Kanade, T., Sheikh, Y.: Reconstructing 3D human pose from 2D image landmarks. In: Fitzgibbon, A., Lazebnik, S., Perona, P., Sato, Y., Schmid, C. (eds.) ECCV 2012, Part IV. LNCS, vol. 7575, pp. 573–586. Springer, Heidelberg (2012)
12. Safonova, A., Hodgins, J.K., Pollard, N.S.: Synthesizing physically realistic human motion in low-dimensional, behavior-specific spaces. TOG 23(3), 514–521 (2004)
13. Salzmann, M., Urtasun, R.: Implicitly constrained gaussian process regression for monocular non-rigid pose estimation. In: NIPS (2010)
14. Shi, J., Malik, J.: Normalized cuts and image segmentation. TPAMI, 888–905 (2000)
15. Soltanolkotabi, M., Elhamifar, E., Candes, E.: Robust subspace clustering. arXiv preprint arXiv:1301.2603 (2013)
16. Taylor, C.J.: Reconstruction of articulated objects from point correspondences in a single uncalibrated image. In: CVPR (2000)
17. Valmadre, J., Lucey, S.: Deterministic 3D human pose estimation using rigid structure. In: Daniilidis, K., Maragos, P., Paragios, N. (eds.) ECCV 2010, Part III. LNCS, vol. 6313, pp. 467–480. Springer, Heidelberg (2010)
18. Vidal, R.: Subspace clustering. Signal Processing Magazine 28(2), 52–68 (2011)
19. Wang, J., Yang, J., Yu, K., Lv, F., Huang, T., Gong, Y.: Locality-constrained linear coding for image classification. In: CVPR, pp. 3360–3367 (2010)
20. Wei, X.K., Chai, J.: Modeling 3D human poses from uncalibrated monocular images. In: ICCV (2009)
21. Yang, A.Y., Iyengar, S., Sastry, S., Bajcsy, R., Kuryloski, P., Jafari, R.: Distributed segmentation and classification of human actions using a wearable motion sensor network. In: CVPRW (2008)
22. Yao, A., Gall, J., Van Gool, L.: Coupled action recognition and pose estimation from multiple views. IJCV (2012)
23. Yu, T.H., Kim, T.K., Cipolla, R.: Unconstrained monocular 3D human pose estimation by action detection and cross-modality regression forest. In: CVPR (2013)

Synchronization of Two Independently Moving Cameras without Feature Correspondences

Tiago Gaspar[1], Paulo Oliveira[1], and Paolo Favaro[2]

[1] Instituto Superior Técnico, Universidade de Lisboa, Lisbon, Portugal
[2] University of Bern, Bern, Switzerland

Abstract. In this work, a method that synchronizes two video sequences is proposed. Unlike previous methods, which require the existence of correspondences between features tracked in the two sequences, and/or that the cameras are static or jointly moving, the proposed approach does not impose any of these constraints. It works when the cameras move independently, even if different features are tracked in the two sequences. The assumptions underlying the proposed strategy are that the intrinsic parameters of the cameras are known and that two rigid objects, with independent motions on the scene, are visible in both sequences. The relative motion between these objects is used as clue for the synchronization. The extrinsic parameters of the cameras are assumed to be unknown. A new synchronization algorithm for static or jointly moving cameras that see (possibly) different parts of a common rigidly moving object is also proposed. Proof-of-concept experiments that illustrate the performance of these methods are presented, as well as a comparison with a state-of-the-art approach.

1 Introduction

In the last few years, the proliferation of digital cameras transformed the acquisition and manipulation of videos into common tasks. Having several videos of a given event, recorded by different people from different viewpoints, is thus more and more common. Synchronizing these videos is essential to merge all the available information, which can then be used in a wide range of areas, such as 3D reconstruction, human action recognition, calibration of multiple cameras, or dynamic depth estimation, see examples in [22], [24], [16], and [26], respectively.

In professional applications, it is possible to synchronize two cameras using proper hardware. However, such hardware is expensive and is usually not available to the common user. Moreover, in many situations, synchronizing the videos turns out to be important only after their acquisition. Therefore, since accurate manual synchronization is both tedious and difficult, the problem of synchronizing two videos, usually acquired by cameras with unknown relative inter-camera extrinsic parameters, has received a lot of attention in the last decade.

1.1 Previous Work

The video synchronization problem that has received more attention from the scientific community considers that the cameras are static and that there exist

D. Fleet et al. (Eds.): ECCV 2014, Part I, LNCS 8689, pp. 189–204, 2014.
© Springer International Publishing Switzerland 2014

correspondences between the features observed in the two videos. Two of the directions of work that have been pursued to solve this problem are presented by Tresadern and Reid in [20] and by Caspi and Irani in [2], in what they called the "feature-based sequence alignment" approach. In the first case, the time offset is found by searching for the minimum of the relative magnitude of the fourth singular value of the "measurement matrix" introduced by Tomasi and Kanade in [19]. The second strategy aligns video sequences, in time and space, when the two sequences are related by a homography or by the projective epipolar geometry. To overcome the requirement that the cameras are static or jointly moving, i.e., that the relative inter-camera extrinsic parameters do not change, and that correspondences between the features observed in the two videos exist, some research has been done on algorithms that drop one of these assumptions.

In [2], Caspi and Irani present a second method, the "direct intensity-based sequence alignment", which exploits spatio-temporal brightness variations within each sequence. This approach can handle complex scenes and drops the need for having feature correspondences across the two sequences, but still requires that the cameras are static or jointly moving and that they see the same scene. In [22], Wolf and Zomet propose a strategy that builds on the idea that every 3D point tracked in one sequence results from a linear combination of the 3D points tracked in the other sequence. This approach copes with articulated objects, but still requires that the cameras are static or moving jointly.

There are also some works that can deal with independently moving cameras, but at the cost of requiring the existence of correspondences between features tracked in the two video sequences. Tuytelaars and Van Gool were the first to address the problem of automatic video synchronization for independently moving cameras and general 3D scenes, see [21]. This is done by reformulating the video synchronization problem in terms of checking the rigidity of at least 5 non-rigidly moving points, matched and tracked throughout the two sequences. Another example is the work by Meyer et al. [11], which consists of a two-step algorithm that leads to subframe-accurate synchronization results. First, an algorithm that estimates a frame-accurate offset by analysing the motion trajectories observed in the images and by matching their characteristic time patterns is used. After this step, subframe-accurate results are obtained by estimating a fundamental matrix between the two cameras, using a correspondence of 9 non-rigidly moving points in the scene. Both the motion of the cameras and the motion of the tracked object are assumed to be linear between consecutive time instants.

Video synchronization has been addressed from different perspectives. However, to the best of our knowledge, the most general and complex case, which arises when the cameras move independently and the parts of the moving object in the field of view of each camera do not intersect, is yet to be solved. None of the previous strategies would work in this situation, as there is no correspondence between the features observed in the two cameras. In [23], Yan and Pollefeys suggest a novel algorithm that uses the correlation between the distributions of space-time interest points, which represent special events in the videos, to synchronize them. This method does not explicitly require feature correspondences and static or jointly moving cameras, but their fields of view must intersect and its performance degrades as the baseline between the cameras gets wider.

1.2 Contributions

The main contribution of our work is a method that synchronizes two video sequences acquired by independently moving cameras that see (possibly) different parts of a common rigidly moving object, see Fig. 1. The scene recorded by the cameras must also include a second common object (typically a static background), whose motion must be independent of the one of the first object. From now on, this second object is referred to as the background. The fields of view of the two cameras may not intersect and no knowledge about the correspondence between the two video sequences, in terms of which trajectories belong to which objects, is required. This is one of the most common video synchronization problems, as it occurs every time two people use handheld cameras to record a rigid object moving on a static background (e.g., a car moving on the street). The relative inter-camera extrinsic parameters are unknown and the intrinsic parameters of the cameras (which can be calibrated *a priori* using the typical approaches, see [25] and [1]) are assumed to be known. The idea is to track two sets of features in each video sequence: one on the moving object and other on the background. These sets are used to retrieve the motion of the two objects with respect to each camera, using state-of-the-art structure and motion methods, see [8] and [18]. These results can be used to obtain information about the motion of one object with respect to the other, which is used as clue for the synchronization process. When the correspondences between the features and the two trajectories are not known, subspace clustering algorithms, such as the ones presented in [4] and [9], can be used to segment the two motions.

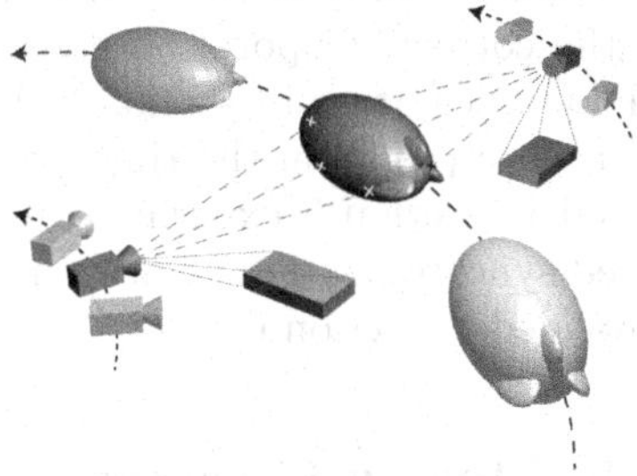

Fig. 1. Example of setup for the synchronization problem with independently moving cameras. The blimp and the parallelepipeds represent, respectively, a moving object and a static background.

In addition to the previous contribution, a new method that synchronizes two video sequences acquired by static or jointly moving cameras that see (possibly) different parts of a common rigidly moving object is also presented. This method is closely related to the one mentioned in the previous paragraph, and is introduced first in the paper as it serves as a starting point for the more general case of independently moving cameras. The assumptions about the intrinsic parameters, extrinsic parameters, and fields of view of the cameras are the same as before. In this case, the motion of the object with respect to each camera can be used directly as clue for the synchronization, due to the constraints imposed on the motion of the cameras. A study of the uniqueness of the solutions obtained with this method is also presented.

The two video sequences, which are the only available data, are assumed to be acquired by cameras with the same frame rate, thus a single temporal offset between them is considered. This is without loss of generality since the multirate problem can be tackled by interpolating the measurements of the features in the video acquired with the lowest frame rate (note that typical object motions are smooth). The strategies proposed in this paper can be used after this resampling.

1.3 Notation and Paper Organization

In this document, the identity matrix with dimensions $k \times k$ is denoted I_k, and $0_{k \times n}$ is used to represent a matrix of zeros with k lines and n columns. The notation $||v||$ denotes the Euclidean norm of the vector v and $[v]_\times$ is used to represent the skew-symmetric matrix obtained from a given vector $v \in \mathbb{R}^3$. This matrix is such that $[v]_\times s = v \times s$, for any vector $s \in \mathbb{R}^3$, where $\times$ represents the cross-product. For a generic rotation matrix $R \in SO(3)$, the corresponding unit quaternion is given by $q = [\sin(\theta/2)v^T \; \cos(\theta/2)]^T$, where θ and v denote, respectively, the associated non-negative angle of rotation and the unit Euler axis. These quantities are such that $R = e^{[v]_\times \theta}$.

The remaining of this paper is organized as follows. A new algorithm that synchronizes video sequences acquired by static or jointly moving cameras is presented in section 2, as well as a study of the object trajectories that lead to a unique identification of the correct temporal offset. This algorithm is generalized for independently moving cameras in section 3. In section 4, a strategy that recovers the motion of an object from the time evolution of the images of its features is described, and in section 5 experimental results illustrating the performance of the proposed synchronization algorithms are presented. Finally, concluding remarks are provided in section 6.

2 Static and Jointly Moving Cameras

In this section, the synchronization of static or jointly moving cameras, when no correspondences between the features tracked in the two videos exist, is addressed. Instead of explicitly using the features to solve the synchronization problem, the rigid body transformations that explain their motion in the reference frame of each one of the cameras are used.

Let $X_i(k) \in \mathbb{R}^3$, for $k \in [k_0, k_0 + F]$, where k_0 and $k_0 + F$ correspond to the times of acquisition of the first and final frames of the videos, denote the

3D coordinates of an object feature expressed in the reference frame of camera i, $i = 1, 2$, at the time of the acquisition of the k-th frame. These coordinates can be obtained from the coordinates of the same feature at k_0 as $X_i(k) = R_i(k)X_i(k_0) + T_i(k)$, $i = 1, 2$, for all $k \in [k_0, k_0 + F]$, where $R_i(k) \in SO(3)$ and $T_i(k) \in \mathbb{R}^3$ denote, respectively, rotation matrices and translation vectors that describe the evolution in time of the coordinates of object features expressed in the reference frame of camera i.

Since the cameras are static or jointly moving, the relative inter-camera extrinsic parameters are constant, i.e., there exist a constant rotation matrix and a constant translation vector that transform coordinates expressed in the reference frame of camera 1 into the one of camera 2, similarly to what happens in the hand-eye calibration problem, see [7]. If these rotation and translation are denoted $R \in SO(3)$ and $T \in \mathbb{R}^3$, respectively, then it is possible to show that $X_2(k) = RR_1(k)R^T X_2(k_0) + RT_1(k) + (I_3 - R_2(k))T$, and consequently

$$R_2(k) = RR_1(k)R^T \quad \text{and} \quad T_2(k) = RT_1(k) + (I_3 - R_2(k))T, \tag{1}$$

for all $k \in [k_0, k_0 + F]$, when the two videos are synchronized. These expressions are not valid for unsynchronized videos, except in the cases detailed in section 2.2.

2.1 Video Synchronization

There are several methods that can be used to track a set of features belonging to an object moving on a video, being one of the most used the KLT feature tracker [15]. By combining such strategies with algorithms that recover structure and motion from image sequences, see [8] and [18], it is possible to retrieve the motion of the object, apart from a non-negative scaling factor in the magnitude of its translational component. More details about this procedure are provided in section 4. By applying this strategy to the two video sequences, the quantities $R_1(k)$, $\alpha_1 T_1(k)$, $R_2(k)$, and $\alpha_2 T_2(k)$, are obtained for all $k \in [k_0, k_0 + F]$. The constants α_1 and α_2 are non-negative scalars that account for the scaling ambiguity in the magnitude of the translation of the moving object.

According to the discussion above, for unsynchronized videos the expressions in (1) have the form

$$R_2(k') = RR_1(k)R^T \tag{2}$$

$$\alpha_2 T_2(k') = RT_1(k) + (I_3 - R_2(k'))T, \tag{3}$$

for all $k \in [k_0, k_0 + F]$, with $k' = k + \delta$, where δ denotes the temporal offset between the two sequences. This offset is considered to belong to a given interval, $\delta \in [-\Delta, \Delta]$, with $\Delta \leq F$ positive and known. Even though the two videos are unsynchronized, they are assumed to have at least $F + 1$ frames acquired at the same time instants. In the expressions, α_1 is considered to be the unit. This is without loss of generality, as there is an overall ambiguity in the magnitude of the two terms of equation (3).

If quaternions are used to parameterize the attitude associated with the rotation matrices in (2), this expression takes the form $q_2(k').q = q.q_1(k)$, where

"$\cdot$" denotes quaternion multiplication, and $q_2(k')$, $q_1(k)$, and q, are the unit quaternions (quaternions with unit norm) associated with $R_2(k')$, $R_1(k)$, and R, respectively (see [12] for details about the use of quaternions to represent rotations and section 1.3 for details about the notation used to represent quaternions). This expression can be written as

$$M(q_1(k), q_2(k'))q = 0_{4\times 1}, \tag{4}$$

with $M(q_1(k), q_2(k')) = \begin{bmatrix}\Psi(q_2(k')) - \Xi(q_1(k)) & q_2(k') - q1(k)\end{bmatrix}$. For a given quaternion $g = [w^T\ g_4]^T$, the matrices $\Xi(g)$ and $\Psi(g)$ have the form

$$\Xi(g) = \begin{bmatrix} g_4 I_3 + [w]_\times \\ -w^T \end{bmatrix} \quad \text{and} \quad \Psi(g) = \begin{bmatrix} g_4 I_3 - [w]_\times \\ -w^T \end{bmatrix}, \tag{5}$$

where $w \in \mathbb{R}^3$ is a vector and $g_4 \in \mathbb{R}$ a scalar, see [3].

If (3) is also written as a function of the unit quaternion q, we have that

$$\alpha_2 T_2(k') = \Xi^T(q)\Psi(q)T_1(k) + (I_3 - R_2(k'))T, \tag{6}$$

as $R = \Xi^T(q)\Psi(q)$, see [3]. The use of quaternions in this paper allows avoiding singularities in the representation of rotations, see [12].

By combining (4) and (6), the synchronization problem for static or jointly moving cameras can be cast into the form of the minimization problem

$$\hat{\delta} = \arg\min_{\delta}\ E_s(\delta), \tag{7}$$

where $\hat{\delta}$ denotes the estimated temporal offset and $E_s(\delta)$ is the error function

$$E_s(\delta) = \min_{(q,T,\beta_2)} \mu_R E_R(\delta, q) + \mu_T E_T(\delta, q, T, \beta_2) + \mu_q (q^T q - 1)^2, \tag{8}$$

with μ_R, μ_T, and μ_q, positive weighting coefficients. The last term in the expression forces $||q||$ to be the unit and the other two are obtained from

$$E_R(\delta, q) = \sum_{k=k_0+\Delta}^{k_0+F-\Delta} ||M(q_1(k), q_2(k+\delta))q||^2 \quad \text{and}$$

$$E_T(\delta, q, T, \beta_2) = \sum_{k=k_0+\Delta}^{k_0+F-\Delta} ||\beta_2^2 T_2(k+\delta) - \Xi^T(q)\Psi(q)T_1(k) - (I_3 - R_2(k+\delta))T||^2.$$

The scalar β_2 is used to guarantee that α_2, with $\alpha_2 = \beta_2^2$, is not negative.

The optimization problem in (8) is a nonlinear least-squares problem due to the nonlinear dependence of $E_T(\delta, q, T, \beta_2)$ on q and β_2, thus it can be solved using the Levenberg-Marquardt method [10]. This problem transforms into a linear least-squares problem if α_2 is used and if R, in (3), is considered to be a generic constant matrix $P \in \mathbb{R}^{3\times 3}$. Linear constraints on the trace of P and on the l_1 and l_∞ norms of its line and column vectors are imposed to guarantee that P is close to a rotation matrix, see [5] for details about these norms. If this relaxation is used and if the estimate found for P, by solving the linear version of the problem, is approximated by a rotation matrix, an initial guess for q, T, and β_2, is easily found. This approximation can be obtained using the algorithm proposed in [14], which can be used to approximate a given matrix by the closest rotation matrix in the least-squares sense.

The temporal offset between the two videos is the one that solves (7), and is found by evaluating the error function in (8) for all the offsets in a given range.

2.2 Uniqueness of Solution

There are situations in which the motion of the object does not have enough information for the synchronization process (imagine for instance that the object is stopped or moves with constant velocity). In these cases, the solution of the minimization problem introduced in the previous section is not unique, i.e., there are several temporal offsets that minimize the error function in (8).

According to (2) and (3), it is possible to conclude that the solution of the optimization problem in (7) is unique in terms of the temporal offset δ (meaning that $E_s(\delta)$ is null only for the correct offset), if and only if there not exist a non-negative constant scaling factor α, a constant rotation matrix R, and a constant translation vector T, that verify such equations for some temporal offset, different from the real δ. The trajectories of the objects that violate this condition are summarized in Lemma 1, where $\theta_i(k) \in \mathbb{R}$ and $v_i(k) \in \mathbb{R}^3$ are used to denote, respectively, the non-negative rotation angle and the corresponding Euler axis associated with $R_i(k)$, for all $k \in [k_0 - \Delta, k_0 + F + \Delta]$. The conditions presented on the lemma depend on T_i and R_i, but they do not need to be tested for both $i = 1$ and $i = 2$. It is enough to choose one of the cameras, for instance camera 1, and test if T_1 and R_1 verify any of such conditions.

Lemma 1. *The solution of the optimization problem presented in* (7) *is unique if and only if none of the following three conditions are met for some non-null $\overline{\delta}$ verifying $|\overline{\delta}| \leq \Delta$:*

1. *$\theta_i(k) = 0$ for all $k \in [k_0 + \overline{\delta}_1, k_0 + F + \overline{\delta}_2]$ and there exist a non-negative constant scalar $\overline{\alpha}$ and a constant rotation matrix $\overline{R}$ such that $\overline{\alpha}\, T_i(k + \overline{\delta}) = \overline{R}\, T_i(k)$, for all $k \in [k_0, k_0 + F]$.*
2. *$\theta_i(k)$ is periodic with period $|\overline{\delta}|$ for $k \in [k_0 + \overline{\delta}_1, k_0 + F + \overline{\delta}_2]$, the direction of $\theta_i(k)v_i(k)$ is constant in the same interval, and there exist a non-negative constant scalar $\overline{\alpha}$ and a constant rotation matrix $\overline{R}$ such that $\theta_i(k+\overline{\delta})v_i(k+\overline{\delta}) = \overline{R}\,\theta_i(k)v_i(k)$, for all $k \in [k_0, k_0 + F]$, and $\overline{\alpha}\,[T_i(k + 2\overline{\delta}) - T_i(k + \overline{\delta})] = \overline{R}\,[T_i(k + \overline{\delta}) - T_i(k)]$, for all $k \in [k_0 - \overline{\delta}_1, k_0 + F - \overline{\delta}_2]$.*
3. *$\theta_i(k)$ is periodic with period $|\overline{\delta}|$ for $k \in [k_0 + \overline{\delta}_1, k_0 + F + \overline{\delta}_2]$, the direction of $\theta_i(k)v_i(k)$ is not constant in the same interval, and there exist a non-negative constant scalar $\overline{\alpha}$, a constant vector $\overline{T}$, and a constant rotation matrix $\overline{R}$ such that*

$$
\begin{aligned}
\theta_i(k + \overline{\delta})v_i(k + \overline{\delta}) &= \overline{R}\,\theta_i(k)v_i(k) \\
\overline{\alpha}\, T_i(k + \overline{\delta}) &= \overline{R}\, T_i(k) + (I_3 - R_i(k + \overline{\delta}))\overline{T}\ , \text{ for all } k \in [k_0, k_0 + F].
\end{aligned}
$$

In the previous expressions, $\overline{\delta}_1 = \min\left[\overline{\delta}, 0\right]$ *and* $\overline{\delta}_2 = \max\left[0, \overline{\delta}\right]$.

The conditions presented on the lemma can be easily tested for a given trajectory of the moving object. The procedure used to test them and the proof of the lemma are omitted here due to space constraints.

3 Independently Moving Cameras

When videos are acquired with independently moving cameras, tracking features on a single rigidly moving object is not enough for the synchronization. This is because the projection of such 3D features into acquired images results both from the motion of the object, which includes information for the synchronization, and from the motion of the camera, which does not. In this situation, features on a second rigidly moving object, for instance a static background, must be used. If the motion of this object is independent from the one of the first object, the relative motion between the two objects has information for the synchronization.

Let ${}^{c_0}M_i^j(k) \in \mathbb{R}^4$, for $k \in [k_0, k_0 + F]$, denote the homogeneous coordinates of a point of the j-th object, $j = 1, 2$, at the time of acquisition of the k-th frame. The superscript c_0 and the subscript i indicate that these coordinates are expressed in the reference frame $\{c_0\}$ of camera i, $i = 1, 2$, at the time of acquisition of the first frame k_0 of the video sequence. The evolution in time of the coordinates of this point is given by ${}^{c_0}M_i^j(k) = g_i^j(k)\,{}^{c_0}M_i^j(k_0)$, where $g_i^j(k)$ denotes a homogeneous transformation. Moreover, let ${}^{c_k}_{c_0}g_i(k)$ denote another homogeneous transformation, which converts coordinates of points expressed in $\{c_0\}$, into the coordinates of the same points expressed in $\{c_k\}$. Here, $\{c_k\}$ is used to identify the reference frame of camera i at the time of acquisition of frame k. This transformation represents the motion of camera i. If these two transformations are combined, a new transformation $g_{T_i^j}(k)$ that includes both the motion of the j-th object and the motion of the i-th camera, results

$$ {}^{c_k}M_i^j(k) = \underbrace{{}^{c_k}_{c_0}g_i(k)\; g_i^j(k)}_{g_{T_i^j}(k)}\; {}^{c_0}M_i^j(k_0). $$

This transformation relates ${}^{c_0}M_i^j(k_0)$, the homogeneous coordinates in the initial time instant of points of object j expressed in $\{c_0\}$, with ${}^{c_k}M_i^j(k) \in \mathbb{R}^4$, their homogeneous coordinates at the time of acquisition of frame k expressed in $\{c_k\}$.

From the three aforementioned transformations, only $g_{T_i^j}(k)$ can be obtained from the available features (apart from a non-negative scaling factor, as discussed in section 3.1), for all $k \in [k_0, k_0 + F]$. Thus, any relation used for the synchronization process has to be based on such transformation. Consider, for instance, the homogeneous transformation $g_{T_i^1}(k) = {}^{c_k}_{c_0}g_i(k)\; g_i^1(k)$, associated with the motion of object 1 with respect to camera i, which can be written as $g_{T_i^1}(k) = {}^{c_k}_{c_0}g_i(k)\; g_i^2(k)\; [g_i^2(k)]^{-1}\, g_i^1(k)$, since $g_i^2(k)[g_i^2(k)]^{-1} = I_4$. If $[g_i^2(k)]^{-1}\, g_i^1(k)$, which does not depend on the motion of the cameras, is denoted by $g_i(k)$, the previous expression can be rearranged in the form

$$ g_i(k) = [g_{T_i^2}(k)]^{-1}\; g_{T_i^1}(k). \tag{9} $$

If the homogeneous transformation from the reference frame of camera 1, at the initial instant, to the reference frame of camera 2, at the same instant, is denoted g, it is easy to show that $g_2^j(k) = g\, g_1^j(k)\, g^{-1}$, $j = 1, 2$, and consequently

$$g_2(k) = g\, g_1(k)\, g^{-1}, \tag{10}$$

as $g_i(k) = [g_i^2(k)]^{-1}\, g_i^1(k)$. When the two video sequences are synchronized, this expression is valid for all $k \in [k_0, k_0 + F]$.

If the rotations and translations associated with g and $g_i(k)$, $i = 1, 2$, are denoted by $R \in SO(3)$ and $T \in \mathbb{R}^3$, and by $R_i(k) \in SO(3)$ and $T_i(k) \in \mathbb{R}^3$, respectively, then (10) can be cast into the form of (1). The difference is that in section 2, $T_i(k)$ was determined using structure and motion strategies, which is not possible in this case. Here, the translational components of $g_{T_i^j}(k)$ can also be determined using structure and motion strategies, thus they are known up to a scaling factor, but $T_i(k)$ cannot. For independently moving cameras, $T_i(k)$ is obtained using (9). This procedure induces some structure on $T_i(k)$, which cannot be modelled with a single scaling factor. This is why the strategy proposed in section 2.1 cannot be used for independently moving cameras.

3.1 Video Synchronization

By using the strategy described in the beginning of section 2.1, it is possible to retrieve the values of $R_{T_i^j}(k)$ and $\alpha_i^j T_{T_i^j}(k)$, with $i = 1, 2$, and $j = 1, 2$, for all $k \in [k_0, k_0 + F]$. The rotation $R_{T_i^j}(k)$ and translation $T_{T_i^j}(k)$ are the ones associated with the homogeneous transformation $g_{T_i^j}(k)$, and α_i^j is a non-negative constant that accounts for the ambiguity in the magnitude of the translation of the j-th object, when it is estimated using the features observed in camera i.

According to the discussion above and to (9), we have that

$$\begin{aligned} R_i(k) &= [R_{T_i^2}(k)]^T R_{T_i^1}(k) \\ T_i(k) &= \alpha_i^1 \underbrace{[R_{T_i^2}(k)]^T T_{T_i^1}(k)}_{h_i^1(k)} - \alpha_i^2 \underbrace{[R_{T_i^2}(k)]^T T_{T_i^2}(k)}_{h_i^2(k)}, \end{aligned}$$

for all $k \in [k_0, k_0 + F]$ and for $i = 1, 2$. Note that the use of a single scaling factor is not enough to model the structure of the ambiguity in the determination of $T_i(k)$. The vectors $h_i^1(k) \in \mathbb{R}^3$ and $h_i^2(k) \in \mathbb{R}^3$, introduced in the expression, are used in this section with the single purpose of becoming the notation clearer.

If the expression in (10) is separated into its rotational and translational parts, it takes the following form for unsynchronized video sequences

$$R_2(k') = R R_1(k) R^T \tag{11}$$

$$\alpha_2^1 h_2^1(k') - \alpha_2^2 h_2^2(k') = R\left[h_1^1(k) - \alpha_1^2 h_1^2(k)\right] + (I_3 - R_2(k'))T, \tag{12}$$

for all $k \in [k_0, k_0 + F]$, and with $k' = k + \delta$, where δ is as defined in section 2.1. Note that α_1^1 was omitted from (12) as it is assumed to be the unit. This is without loss of generality since there is an overall ambiguity in the magnitude of the two terms of equation (12).

If quaternions are used, the equation in (11) reduces to the form of (4), see details in section 2.1, where $q_1(k)$, $q_2(k')$, and q, are the unit quaternions associated, respectively, with the rotation matrices $R_1(k)$, $R_2(k')$, and R, redefined in this section for the case of independently moving cameras.

The expression in (12) can also be written as a function of the quaternion q, associated with the rotation R that relates the reference frames of the two cameras in the initial time instant. In this case, this expression takes the form $\alpha_2^1 h_2^1(k') - \alpha_2^2 h_2^2(k') = \Xi^T(q)\Psi(q)\left[h_1^1(k) - \alpha_1^2 h_1^2(k)\right] + (I_3 - R_2(k'))T$, where the matrices $\Xi(q)$ and $\Psi(q)$ are as defined in (5).

By combining the previous expression with the one relating the rotations perceived from both sequences, the synchronization problem for independently moving cameras can be cast into the form of the minimization problem

$$\hat{\delta} = \arg\min_{\delta} \; E_m(\delta), \tag{13}$$

where $\hat{\delta}$ denotes the estimated temporal offset and $E_m(\delta)$ is the error function

$$E_m(\delta) = \min_{(q,T,\beta_2^1,\beta_2^2,\beta_1^2)} \mu_R E_R(\delta,q) + \mu_T E_T(\delta,q,T,\beta_2^1,\beta_2^2,\beta_1^2) + \mu_q(q^T q - 1)^2, \tag{14}$$

with μ_R, μ_T, and μ_q, positive weighting coefficients and

$$E_R(\delta,q) = \sum_{k=k_0+\Delta}^{k_0+F-\Delta} ||M(q_1(k), q_2(k+\delta))q||^2$$

$$E_T(\delta,q,T,\beta_2^1,\beta_2^2,\beta_1^2) = \sum_{k=k_0+\Delta}^{k_0+F-\Delta} ||(\beta_2^1)^2 h_2^1(k+\delta) - (\beta_2^2)^2 h_2^2(k+\delta) - $$
$$-\Xi^T(q)\Psi(q)\left[h_1^1(k) - (\beta_1^2)^2 h_1^2(k)\right] - (I_3 - R_2(k+\delta))T||^2.$$

The scalars β_2^1, β_2^2, and β_1^2 are used in these expressions to guarantee that α_2^1, α_2^2, and α_1^2 (with $\alpha_2^1 = (\beta_2^1)^2$, $\alpha_2^2 = (\beta_2^2)^2$, and $\alpha_1^2 = (\beta_1^2)^2$) are not negative.

The optimization problem in (14) is a nonlinear least-squares problem due to the nonlinear dependence of $E_T(\delta,q,T,\beta_2^1,\beta_2^2,\beta_1^2)$ on q, β_2^1, β_2^2, and β_1^2, thus it can be solved using the Levenberg-Marquardt method [10]. An initial guess for the unknowns q, T, β_2^1, β_2^2, and β_1^2, can be obtained by relaxing the problem, similarly to what was done in the end of section 2.1.

The temporal offset between the two videos is the one that solves (13), and is found by evaluating the error function in (14) for all the offsets in a given range. Moreover, note that with the proposed strategy it is possible to estimate the relative scales between the two objects. This is only possible because two cameras are used. In the monocular multi-body structure-from-motion problem, for instance, each reconstructed object has a different unknown scale, thus objects are distorted with respect to each other, see [13].

In this work, the correspondence between the two video sequences, in terms of which trajectories belong to which objects, is assumed to be unknown. A set of features in one camera may correspond to any of the two sets in the other camera, thus two possible combinations between the sets are possible (once an association is assumed, the other is implicitly defined). The correct combination can be found by solving the previous optimization problem for the two cases, and choosing the one that leads to the minimum value for $E_m(\delta)$.

4 Object Motion Recovery

There are several methods to retrieve structure and motion from a sequence of images, see [8]. In this work, a strategy based on the concept of epipolar geometry is used to estimate the rotation matrices and translation vectors that define the motion of a set of 3D rigidly moving features, see [6].

Given the projection of a set of 3D features into two images, the essential matrix (the intrinsic parameters of the cameras are known) that relates the two views can be obtained using different strategies, depending on the number of available features, see examples in [6] and [17]. By using such methods, the essential matrices that relate the coordinates of features at a given time instant with their coordinates in the initial instant result. Moreover, if the standard algorithms described in [6] are used, these matrices can be converted into rotations and normalized translations of the object with respect to that instant. These rigid body transformations do not enforce a globally consistent geometry, as only the directions of the translations are retrieved, rather than the full 3D translation vectors. Strategies that enforce such global consistency are described in [8] and [18]. In this work, a modified version of such approaches, not described here in detail due to space constraints, is used. It is based on the alignment of 3D point clouds, and leads to translation vectors that are defined up to an overall ambiguity (in this case, a non-negative scaling factor) in their magnitude. This ambiguity cannot be removed unless some metric information about the scene is considered to be available, which is not the case.

5 Experimental Results

In this section, experimental results illustrating the performance of the proposed methods are presented, as well as a comparison with a state-of-the-art approach.

The videos were acquired with cameras of regular mobile phones, at 29 fps, and images with the spatial resolution 960×540 pixel were used. The intrinsic parameters of the cameras were calibrated using the toolbox in [1].

The features used in the synchronization were selected manually in the first frame of each sequence, and then tracked along the videos with the KLT feature tracker [15]. No strategy to deal with occlusions or outliers was implemented, as this is not the focus of this work, thus good features must be selected to guarantee that the motion recovery algorithm performs properly.

For the proof-of-concept experiments presented in this section, in which the video sequences are small, $\Delta = 10$ frames was considered. Larger values for Δ

can be used, specially for long sequences. The ground truth information was obtained using a photo-flash to mark some of the frames, as suggested in [21].

Two experiments are presented. In the first, two cameras were mounted on the same rigid platform, in such a way that their fields of view do not intersect (they were facing opposite directions). The inter-camera extrinsic parameters between the two remain constant over time, and features on the static background are used. This problem is the same as the more common situation where the cameras record an object that is moving between the two. In the second experiment, a tram was recorded with independently moving cameras, and the static background is used as a second object. The strategies proposed in this work were implemented using $\mu_T = 1$, $\mu_R = 10$, and $\mu_q = F$.

The results obtained with our algorithms are compared to the ones obtained with the method proposed in [22]. This method was developed to synchronize videos acquired with static or jointly moving cameras, when no correspondence between the features tracked in both videos exists. It consists in using an heuristic to examine the effective rank of a matrix constructed from the measurements. The heuristic proposed in the paper and the suggested threshold were used in the implementation of this algorithm. The comparisons with [22] serve two purposes: i) understand how our algorithm for static or jointly moving cameras compares to a state-of-the-art approach, and ii) confirm that such approach cannot be used to synchronize videos acquired with cameras that move independently.

The videos used in the first experiment have 121 frames and were obtained with two cameras moving jointly in the center of a public square. The first and final frames of the two sequences are depicted in Fig. 2, with the motion of the

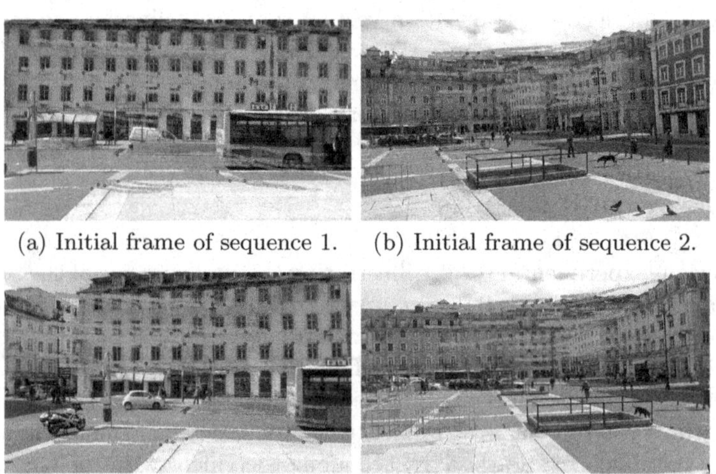

(a) Initial frame of sequence 1. (b) Initial frame of sequence 2.

(c) Final frame of sequence 1. (d) Final frame of sequence 2.

Fig. 2. Initial and final frames of the two videos in the experiment with jointly moving cameras. Green dots represent the evolution over time of features on the background, and black dots identify their position at the time of acquisition of the presented frames.

features used in the synchronization (that results from the motion of the platform in which the cameras were installed) superimposed on them. No correspondence between the features tracked in the two sequences exists, as the fields of view of the cameras do not intersect at any point.

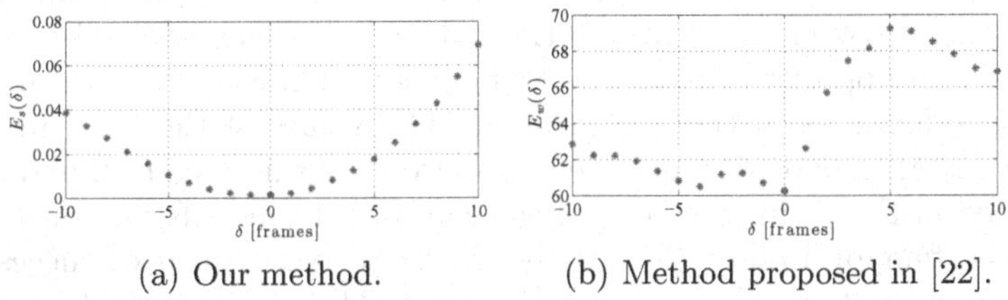

(a) Our method. (b) Method proposed in [22].

Fig. 3. Error functions for the experiment with jointly moving cameras (videos previously synchronized using the ground truth obtained by marking some of the frames with a photo-flash). The dots in red identify the minima of the functions.

A comparison between the approach presented in section 2 and the one presented in [22] can be found in Fig. 3. In particular, the values of the error functions $E_s(\delta)$ and $E_w(\delta)$, proposed respectively in section 2.1 of this document and in [22], are presented for each one of the considered temporal offsets. Both methods correctly identify the temporal offset between the two video sequences ($\delta = 0$ as the videos were previously synchronized using the ground truth).

(a) Initial frame of sequence 1. (b) Initial frame of sequence 2.

(c) Final frame of sequence 1. (d) Final frame of sequence 2.

Fig. 4. Initial and final frames of the two sequences in the experiment with independently moving cameras. The evolution along time of features in the tram and features in the background are represented in green and blue, respectively. The black dots identify the position of the features at the time of acquisition of the presented frames.

The sequences used in the experiment with independently moving cameras have 96 frames. As before, there is no time offset between the two as they were previously synchronized using the ground truth. The first and final frames of the two videos are depicted in Fig. 4, with the time evolution of the features used in the synchronization superimposed on them. The motion of the features in blue result from the motion of the users that were holding the cameras. No correspondence between the features tracked in both sequences exists, as the cameras were in opposite sides of the tram (note for instance the open/closed door or the differences in the background). The values of the error functions $E_m(\delta)$ and $E_w(\delta)$, proposed respectively in section 3 of this document and in [22], are presented in Fig. 5, for each one of the considered time offsets. Our method identifies the temporal offset ($\delta = 0$) between the two sequences successfully, whereas the methods proposed in [22] does not. This was expected, since this algorithm was proposed for the case of static or jointly moving cameras.

The two curves in Fig. 5(a) correspond to the two combinations between the sets of features acquired by the cameras. The combination associated with the green curve is the correct, as it minimizes the minimum of the error function.

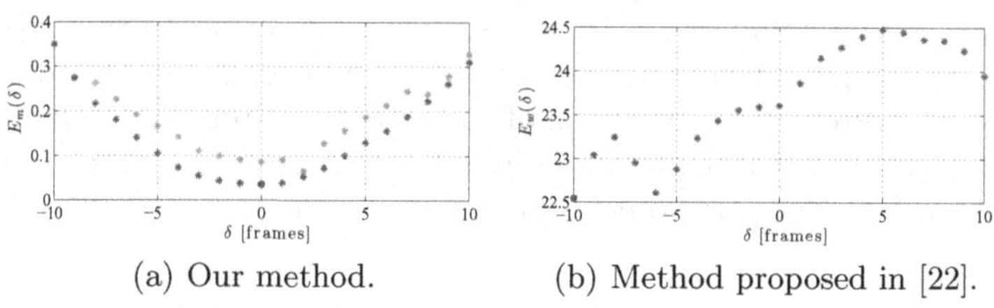

(a) Our method. (b) Method proposed in [22].

Fig. 5. Error functions for the experiment with independently moving cameras (videos previously synchronized using the ground truth obtained by marking some of the frames with a photo-flash). The dots in red identify the minima of the functions. The two curves in (a) result from evaluating $E_m(\delta)$ for the two possible combinations between the set of features associated with the moving object and with the static background.

6 Conclusions

In this paper, the video synchronization problem for cameras with fields of view that may not intersect was addressed. Our approach differs from previous methods as it can deal with independently moving cameras. Features on two rigidly moving objects with independent motions are tracked in both sequences, and used to retrieve the relative motion between the objects, which is used as clue for the synchronization. A similar approach is used to solve this problem for the particular case of static or jointly moving cameras. Both methods were tested and validated with real data, and the strategy proposed for static or jointly moving cameras was shown to perform similarly to a state-of-the-art approach.

References

1. Bouguet, J.: Camera Calibration Toolbox for Matlab, `http://www.vision.caltech.edu/bouguetj/calib_doc/`
2. Caspi, Y., Irani, M.: Spatio-temporal alignment of sequences. IEEE Transactions on Pattern Analysis and Machine Intelligence 24(11), 1409–1424 (2002)
3. Crassidis, J., Markley, F., Cheng, Y.: Survey of nonlinear attitude estimation methods. Journal of Guidance, Control, and Dynamics 30(1), 12–28 (2007)
4. Elhamifar, E., Vidal, R.: Sparse subspace clustering. In: IEEE Conference on Computer Vision and Pattern Recognition, pp. 2790–2797 (2009)
5. Golub, G.H., Loan, C.F.V.: Matrix Computations, 3rd edn., vol. 1. JHU Press (1996)
6. Hartley, R., Zisserman, A.: Multiple View Geometry in Computer Vision, 2nd edn. Cambridge University Press (2004)
7. Horaud, R., Dornaika, F.: Hand-eye calibration. The International Journal of Robotics Research 14(3), 195–210 (1995)
8. Kanade, T., Morris, D.: Factorization methods for structure from motion. Philosophical Transactions of the Royal Society of London. Series A: Mathematical, Physical and Engineering Sciences 356, 1153–1173 (1998)
9. Liu, G., Lin, Z., Yan, S., Sun, J., Yu, Y., Ma, Y.: Robust recovery of subspace structures by low-rank representation. IEEE Transactions on Pattern Analysis and Machine Intelligence 35(1), 171–184 (2013)
10. Marquardt, D.: An algorithm for least-squares estimation of nonlinear parameters. Journal of the Society for Industrial & Applied Mathematics 11(2), 431–441 (1963)
11. Meyer, B., Stich, T., Magnor, M., Pollefeys, M.: Subframe temporal alignment of non-stationary cameras. In: British Machine Vision Conference (2008)
12. Murray, R., Li, Z., Sastry, S.: A Mathematical Introduction to Robotic Manipulation, 1st edn. CRC Press, Inc. (1994)
13. Ozden, K.E., Schindler, K., Van Gool, L.: Multibody structure-from-motion in practice. IEEE Transactions on Pattern Analysis and Machine Intelligence 32(6), 1134–1141 (2010)
14. Schönemann, P.: A generalized solution of the orthogonal procrustes problem. Psychometrika 31(1), 1–10 (1966)
15. Shi, J., Tomasi, C.: Good features to track. In: IEEE Conference on Computer Vision and Pattern Recognition, pp. 593–600 (June 1994)
16. Sinha, S.N., Pollefeys, M.: Synchronization and calibration of camera networks from silhouettes. In: International Conference on Pattern Recognition, vol. 1, pp. 116–119 (August 2004)
17. Stewénius, H., Engels, C., Nistér, D.: Recent developments on direct relative orientation. Journal of Photogrammetry and Remote Sensing 60(4), 284–294 (2006)
18. Sturm, P., Triggs, B.: A factorization based algorithm for multi-image projective structure and motion. In: Buxton, B., Cipolla, R. (eds.) ECCV 1996. LNCS, vol. 1065, pp. 709–720. Springer, Heidelberg (1996)
19. Tomasi, C.: Shape and motion from image streams under orthography: a factorization method. International Journal of Computer Vision 9, 137–154 (1992)
20. Tresadern, P., Reid, I.: Synchronizing image sequences of non-rigid objects. In: British Machine Vision Conference, pp. 629–638 (2003)
21. Tuytelaars, T., Van Gool, L.: Synchronizing video sequences. In: IEEE Conference on Computer Vision and Pattern Recognition, vol. 1, pp. 762–768 (June 2004)

22. Wolf, L., Zomet, A.: Correspondence-free synchronization and reconstruction in a non-rigid scene. In: Workshop on Vision and Modelling of Dynamic Scenes (2002)
23. Yan, J., Pollefeys, M.: Video synchronization via space-time interest point distribution. Advanced Concepts for Intelligent Vision Systems (2004)
24. Yilma, A., Shah, M.: Recognizing human actions in videos acquired by uncalibrated moving cameras. In: IEEE International Conference on Computer Vision, vol. 1, pp. 150–157 (October 2005)
25. Zhang, Z.: A flexible new technique for camera calibration. IEEE Transactions on Pattern Analysis and Machine Intelligence 22(11), 1330–1334 (2000)
26. Zhou, C., Tao, H.: Dynamic depth recovery from unsynchronized video streams. In: IEEE Conference on Computer Vision and Pattern Recognition, vol. 2, pp. 351–358 (June 2003)

Multi Focus Structured Light for Recovering Scene Shape and Global Illumination

Supreeth Achar and Srinivasa G. Narasimhan

Robotics Institute, Carnegie Mellon University, USA

Abstract. Illumination defocus and global illumination effects are major challenges for active illumination scene recovery algorithms. Illumination defocus limits the working volume of projector-camera systems and global illumination can induce large errors in shape estimates. In this paper, we develop an algorithm for scene recovery in the presence of both defocus and global light transport effects such as interreflections and sub-surface scattering. Our method extends the working volume by using structured light patterns at multiple projector focus settings. A careful characterization of projector blur allows us to decode even partially out-of-focus patterns. This enables our algorithm to recover scene shape and the direct and global illumination components over a large depth of field while still using a relatively small number of images (typically 25-30). We demonstrate the effectiveness of our approach by recovering high quality depth maps of scenes containing objects made of optically challenging materials such as wax, marble, soap, colored glass and translucent plastic.

Keywords: Structured Light, Depth from Focus/Defocus, Global Light Transport.

1 Introduction

Active illumination techniques that use projectors as programmable light sources have been applied to many problems in computer vision including depth recovery [15], surface normal estimation [9], BRDF estimation [4], separating direct and global components of illumination [12] and probing light transport [14,13]. Because projectors have large apertures, most active illumination algorithms are limited to a shallow working volume in which the projector is in focus. This limits their applicability to scenarios where the scene relief is small and laboratory or industrial settings where the relative geometry between the scene and the projector-camera system can be carefully controlled. Additionally, global light transport effects like inter-reflections and sub-surface scattering are often ignored, but they can induce large, systematic errors in active shape recovery techniques like structured light and photometric stereo. Since global illumination effects are present in virtually all scenes to some extent, it is important to be able to account for their effects during shape recovery.

Pattern coding strategies like gray codes [10] degrade gracefully when illumination is defocused. In [6] patterns are designed such that they are all attenuated

D. Fleet et al. (Eds.): ECCV 2014, Part I, LNCS 8689, pp. 205–219, 2014.
© Springer International Publishing Switzerland 2014

to roughly the same extent by projector blur and [8] uses a sliding projector as the light source. These methods have some robustness to illumination blur but they do not explicitly model illumination blur and use a single projector focus setting. When depth variation in a scene is very large, the structured light patterns in some areas will be blurred too severely for shape recovery to be possible.

Global illumination can be handled in structured light depth recovery by using suitably designed illumination patterns. When the spatial frequency of the pattern is high compared to the frequency of the scene's global illumination, the contribution of the global illumination to the observed radiance at each scene point becomes almost independent of the pattern [12]. Thus, using high frequency patterns can ameliorate problems caused by global light transport during shape recovery but it makes designing and decoding patterns more difficult as projector-pixel correspondences become ambiguous. Previous solutions to this ambiguity include using a very large number of patterns like in [3] or using techniques like phase unwrapping as was done in [6].

In this paper, we present a structured light algorithm that extends the working volume of the projector-camera system and is capable of producing high resolution depth maps over large working volumes. Our algorithm models both illumination defocus and global illumination effects like scattering and interreflection. In addition to a depth map of the scene, our algorithm recovers the direct and global components of illumination. It can be used to scan optically challenging materials like wax, marble and translucent plastic.

A naïve approach to expanding the depth of field would be to project a complete set of structured light patterns at each focus setting and then combine the resulting depth maps, but such an approach would require an inordinately large number of images. Our algorithm uses multiple focus settings but projects only a small number of patterns at each setting, keeping the overall number of images required small. The key insight of our method is that even an illumination pattern that is not in focus at a scene point can aid in pattern decoding, provided the projector blur kernel has been carefully characterized. We do this characterization by calibrating the projector to find the blur kernel as a function of scene point depth for each focus setting.

Previous work in structured light associates a fixed, depth independent code word with each projector pixel. In contrast, in our approach a projector pixel's code has a defocus induced dependency on the depth of the point it is illuminating. To test a candidate projector-camera pixel correspondence hypothesis, we first compute the scene point depth implied by the hypothesis. This depth value can be used to predict the defocused illumination received by the scene point from the projector. If the candidate correspondence is correct, this projector output prediction should match well with the intensity values observed at the camera pixel. By using a range of focus settings, we ensure that at least some segment of a projector code is always in sharp focus at a point in the scene. Our algorithm seamlessly combines two complementary depth cues - triangulation based cues which provide high depth resolution but require sharp illumination focus (and thus suffer from narrow working ranges) and defocus based cues which work over a large range of depths but provide coarse depth estimates. Our shape recovery algorithm is purely temporal and does not use spatial windows for decoding projector patterns which allows it to recover high quality depth maps with few artefacts at scene discontinuities. Once the shape has been predicted, we automatically have an estimate of the illumination received by each point of the scene in each image. We use this information to recover the direct and global components of illumination.

1.1 Related Work

The idea of exploiting projector defocus as a cue to recover shape was proposed in [19]. The approach involved estimating a measure of the projector pattern blur occurring at each illuminated scene point and mapping this measure to a depth value using a calibration function. They could recover accurate depth maps, but the fixed blur-to-depth mapping could not handle global light transport effects like sub-surface scattering. Gupta et al. [7] proposed a method to simultaneously model both projector defocus and global illumination. Their technique allows for depth recovery in the presence of global illumination and is based on the observation that unlike defocus blur, the blur induced by global light transport effects is almost independent of projector focus. Both [19] and [7] use colocated projector-camera systems and recover depth solely from focus/defocus cues.

In contrast, our approach does not use a colocated configuration but performs stereo triangulation between the camera and projector to measure depth. It has been shown that in principle, depth from defocus is similar to stereo triangulation [16] but focus/defocus cues have a baseline equal to the size of the aperture. Since triangulation cues are computed over the wider projector-camera baseline, our method is capable of producing more fine grained depth estimates. Although we do not use defocus cues explicitly (by using an illumination sharpness measure for instance), they are used implicitly as our projector codes are modeled as being depth dependent due to defocus. Previous work that combines camera defocus and stereo cues includes [18] and [17].

In structured light literature, some methods have been proposed to prevent errors due to global light transport. In [3] a large number of high frequency random bandpass illumination patterns were used to mitigate pattern decoding errors caused by inter reflections. In [5], global illumination effects are handled by designing a set of light pattern codes that work well with long range effects like inter reflections and a second set of patterns that work well with short range effects like sub-surface scattering. For scenes with both types of effects, ensembles of codes are generated and a voting scheme is used to estimate depth. Unlike [5], we do not seek to assign a binary code to each pixel and instead attempt to fit a model to the observed projector and camera values at a pixel, so we can use a single set of patterns to handle both types of global illumination effects.

Modulated phase shifting [2] modulates the sinusoids used in phase shifting by high frequency signals so both shape and global illumination of a scene can be recovered, but it does not consider the effects of illumination defocus.

Micro phase shifting [6] is a phase shifting variant that uses a narrow band set of high frequency sinusoids as the projected patterns. All the patterns are high frequency so the effects of global illumination are avoided. Because the patterns all have similar frequency they are attenuated similarly by projector defocus which lends some robustness to projector blurring. However, it should be noted that while this has some robustness to blur, it does not model defocus or use multiple focus settings so it can not handle large variations in scene depth.

In [11] illumination defocus is exploited towards a different end. Sinusoidal patterns are generated by projecting binary patterns with a defocused projector. DLP projectors can project binary patterns at very high frame rates which allows the phase shift algorithm to run in real time and recover dynamic scenes.

2 Modeling Image Formation and Illumination

Let $S^t(x)$ be the value of the projected structured light pattern at time t at a scene point imaged by camera pixel x. The brightness $I^t(x)$ observed by a camera pixel is a weighted sum of the direct illumination $I_d(x)$ and the global illumination $I_g(x)$ of the scene point. When the pattern $S^t(x)$ has a high spatial frequency and a 50% duty cycle, it can be shown that the contribution of the global illumination to the observed brightness is approximately pattern independent and equal to $\frac{1}{2}I_g(x)$ [12]. The pattern modulates the direct component so its contribution to the observed brightness is $S^t(x)I_d(x)$. Thus we have

$$I^t(x) = \tfrac{1}{2}I_g(x) + S^t(x)I_d(x) \tag{1}$$

We use π to denote the correspondence between projector pixels and camera pixels that illuminate/image the same scene point, $p = \pi(x)$. The projector value seen at time t at a scene point at depth z illuminated by projector pixel p, is a defocused version of the projector pattern value at that pixel $L^t(p)$. It has been shown that unlike camera defocus blur, the defocus blur kernel for a projector is scene independent in the sense that the kernel at a scene point depends only on the depth of the point, not on the geometry of the neighborhood surrounding the point [19]. Thus, without resorting to assumptions like local fronto-planarity, the effects of projector defocus blur can be modeled by convolving the projector pattern $L^t(p)$ with a spatially varying blur kernel $G(p, z, f)$.

$$S^t(x) = \tilde{L}^t(\pi(x)) = \left(L^t * G(\pi(x), z, f)\right)(\pi(x)) \tag{2}$$

The blur kernel G depends on the scene point depth z and the projector focus setting f. Additionally, we allow the function G to vary spatially with projector pixel coordinate as this helps better model the projector's optical aberrations.

Although the original high frequency illumination pattern $L^t(p)$ is blurred due to defocus, Equation 1 still holds. The defocus blur reduces the amplitude

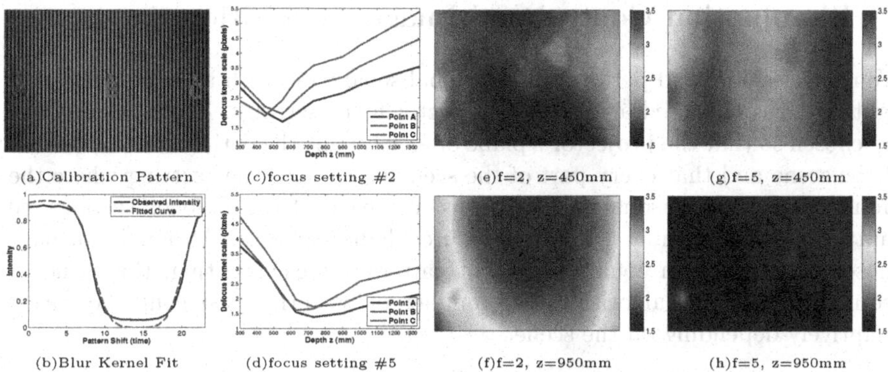

(a)Calibration Pattern (c)focus setting #2 (e)f=2, z=450mm (g)f=5, z=450mm

(b)Blur Kernel Fit (d)focus setting #5 (f)f=2, z=950mm (h)f=5, z=950mm

Fig. 1. Characterizing Projector Defocus: (a) - image of one of the square wave patterns for estimating projector blur. (b) is the temporal intensity profile at point B and the Gaussian smoothed square wave fit. (c) and (d) - the blur kernel scale σ for the projector pixels A,B and C for two different focus settings as the scene depth is varied. (e) to (h) - maps of blur scale σ across the projector image for different combinations of focus setting and scene point depth. The value of σ clearly varies across the image, especially when the projector is out of focus.

of the high frequency components of the pattern but does introduce any low frequency content into the signal. We use a small aperture on the camera ($f/10$ in our experiments) and model it as a pinhole camera that does not introduce any additional blurring due to camera defocus.

Characterizing Projector Defocus. We model the projector blur using a spatially varying, isotropic Gaussian kernel. The scale of the blur kernel $\sigma(p, z, f)$ is a function of projector pixel location p, the depth z of the scene point being illuminated and the current focus setting of the projector f. A more general class of kernels may allow for a more accurate characterization and allow more complex types of aberrations to be modeled, but we found that isotropic Gaussians were sufficient for our purpose.

For a given focus setting f and target depth z we estimate the defocus blur by projecting a sequence of patterns onto a planar target at depth z. The patterns are horizontal square waves with a period of 24 pixels (fig. 1a). We capture 24 images as the pattern translates one pixel at a time. The temporal profile of intensity values observed at a pixel is modeled as a square wave convolved by the blur kernel (fig. 1b). A similar scheme was used in [19] to estimate a mapping between illumination defocus and scene point depth. We find the blur kernel scale $\sigma(p, z, f)$ that best fits the observed temporal profile for each projector pixel. This characterizes the defocus blur at one depth and focus setting (example σ maps are figs. 1e-1h). We repeat the process at a set of depths for each focus setting ($f = 1, 2, ...|F|$). We sample $G(p, z, f)$ at every projector pixel p and focus setting f, but only sparsely in depth z. When queried for the blur kernel at a given focus setting and depth, we return the kernel at that focus for the nearest calibrated depth. Projector characterization is a one time, off line process.

3 Illumination Control and Image Acquisition

We recover shape and perform direct-global separation with a set of structured light patterns captured at different projector focus settings. The focus settings are chosen so that the projector's plane of focus spans the entire working volume of the scene and that every part of the scene has at least one setting where the illumination is in reasonably good focus. For each of the F focus settings we capture a small number (N) of structured light patterns. Although we have chosen to capture an equal number of patterns at each setting, this is not a requirement for the algorithm, the number of patterns used could be varied adaptively depending on the scene.

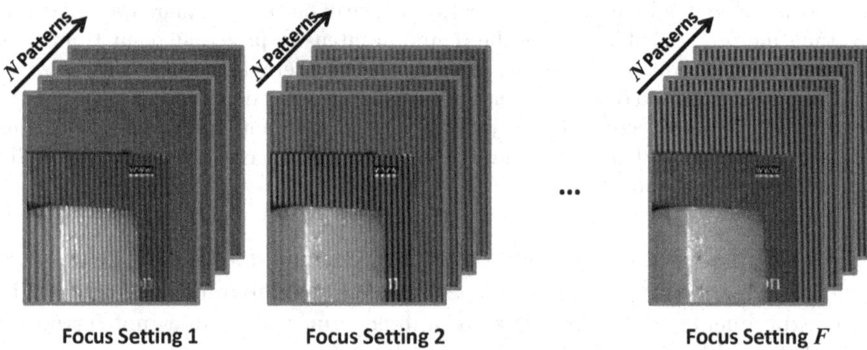

Fig. 2. Input to our Algorithm: We use binary stripe patterns of varying width. Unlike most other structured light algorithms that use a fixed focus setting on the projector, we change the focus setting to move the plane of focus backwards during the image capture process (the camera focus however remains fixed). We capture a total of $T = F \times N$ images. In our experiments, T typically ranged between 20 and 30. As the figure illustrates, near by objects receive focused illumination in the earlier parts of the sequence and distant objects come into focus later on.

The structured light patterns we use are vertical binary stripes with randomly varying widths. Higher frequencies are less susceptible to global illumination errors, but very high frequency patterns are not displayed well by projectors. We let the period of the stripes in a pattern fluctuate between 10 and 14 pixels. This frequency range is high enough to prevent global illumination errors in most situations while still being in the band where contemporary projectors works effectively. We select patterns that do not correlate with each other to ensure that there is little redundancy between patterns.

4 Recovering Shape with Defocused Light Patterns

Temporal structured light algorithms project a series of patterns onto the scene, the time sequence of values emitted by a projector pixel form a code for that pixel. Camera-projector correspondence is established by finding the projector code that best matches the time sequence of intensity values observed at each camera pixel. The code can be binary (eg. gray codes) or continuous (eg. phase shifting), but it assumed that the code for each projector pixel is independent of the scene geometry.

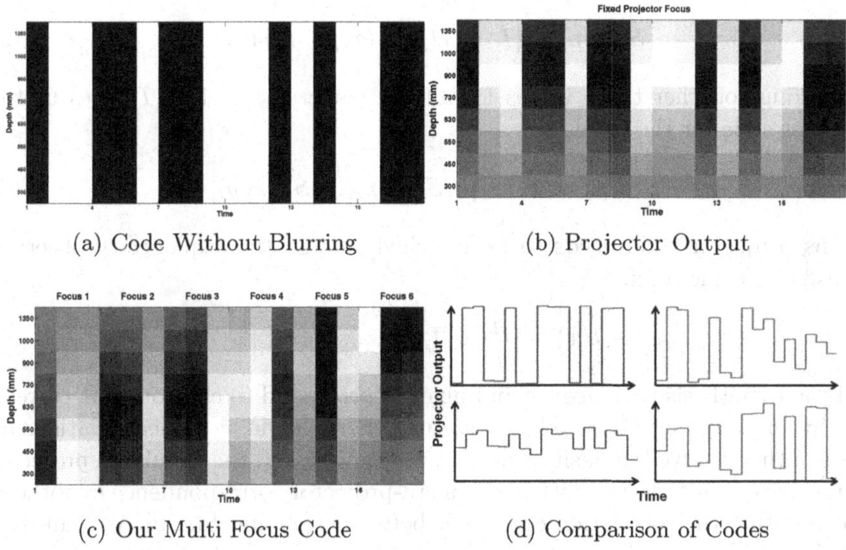

(a) Code Without Blurring (b) Projector Output

(c) Our Multi Focus Code (d) Comparison of Codes

Fig. 3. Effect of Defocus on Codes: When illumination defocus is not modeled, the temporal code associated with a projector pixel (a horizontal cross section of (a)) is independent of depth. However, as (b) shows, outside a narrow working range, the actual appearance of the code is depth dependent. In (c), we use 6 focus settings and 3 patterns per focus. Using multiple focus settings allows us to expand the systems working volume. Also, we model illumination defocus so blurred codes do not cause errors. When regular codes are in focus, they work well (upper blue graph in (d)), however for scene points that are out of focus, contrast is very poor (lower blue graph in (d)). On the other hand, our multiple focus codes always have parts that are well focused and thus have high contrast (red graphs in (d)).

In contrast, our multi-focal structured light algorithm explicitly models illumination defocus effects, so a projector pixel's code becomes a function of the depth of the scene point it is illuminating. This idea is illustrated in figure 3. It is clear, that when the depth variation in a scene is large, defocus can strongly affect how a projector code manifests in a scene. As seen in figure 3b, when a pattern is out of focus, different values become difficult to distinguish. Decoding such a blurred pattern reliably with a defocus-blind algorithm would necessitate very high illumination power and high dynamic range on the imaging sensor. As figure 3c shows, even in large working volumes, some part of our code is always in sharp focus. This allows our method to work at lower illumination power levels over extended depths.

If we hypothesize that projector pixel p corresponds to camera pixel x, we can perform triangulation to find the scene point depth $\tau_z(x,p)$ implied by the hypothesis. Using our defocus model (equation 2), we can then simulate the projector value $\tilde{S}^t(x,p)$ that would be observed at this scene point by convolving the projector illumination pattern L^t with the defocus kernel,

$$\tilde{S}^t(x,p) = \left(L^t * G\left(p, \tau_z\left(x,p\right), f\right)\right)(p) \tag{3}$$

Stacking together these values for all the patterns $t = 1, ..., T$ gives us the projector code for the pixel.

$$\tilde{S}(x,p) = [\tilde{S}^1(x,p), \tilde{S}^2(x,p), ..., \tilde{S}^T(x,p)] \tag{4}$$

This projector code needs to be matched against the sequence of observed intensity at camera pixel $I(x)$

$$I(x) = [I^1(x), I^2(x), ..., I^T(x)] \tag{5}$$

If the hypothesis that pixel x and pixel p correspond to each other is correct, then by our illumination model (equation 1), there should be a linear relationship between the observed intensity values at the camera and the simulated projector values. We quantify the quality of a camera-projector correspondence hypothesis by computing the correlation coefficient between $I(x)$ and $\tilde{S}(x,p)$. We can then find the projector pixel $p = \pi(x)$ corresponding to camera pixel x by maximizing this correlation.

$$\pi(x) = \underset{p}{\operatorname{argmax}}\ \rho\left(I\left(x\right), \tilde{S}\left(x,p\right)\right) \tag{6}$$

We use a calibrated projector-camera system so with the epipolar constraint we limit the search in equation 6 to a $1D$ search along the epipolar line. We compute $\rho(I(x), \tilde{S}(x,p))$ for every p along the epipolar line corresponding to a positive depth (Figure 4). To compute disparity to sub-pixel accuracy, we interpolate ρ scores between projector pixels when searching for maximae.

5 Recovering Direct and Global Illumination Components

Once the camera-projector correspondence map π has been estimated, we can compute $S^t(x)$, the projector pattern value at each camera pixel taking defocus blur into account using equation 2. Under the image formation model (equation 1), there is a linear relationship between the projected pattern value at a point $S^t(x)$ and the brightness observed by the camera $I^t(x)$. Fitting a line to this model at each pixel yields estimates of the global and direct illumination. However, it is possible that even over the entire sequence of projected light patterns, some camera pixels would have seen seen only a small range of projector intensity values. There will be significant ambiguity while fitting a line to data at

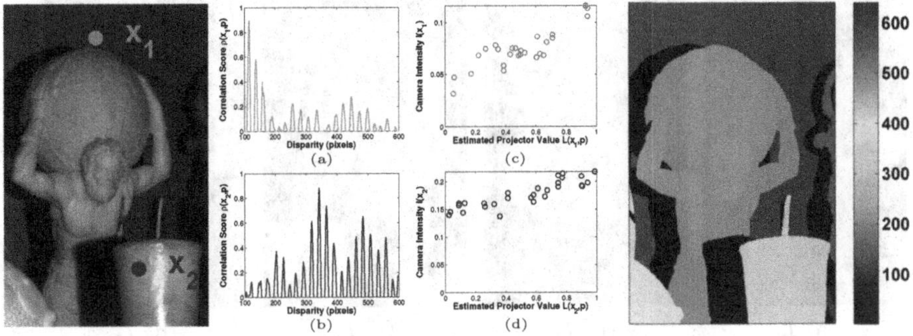

Fig. 4. Part of a scene (left) and the computed disparity map (right). Graph (a) shows the correlation score for point x_1 as a function of disparity to the projector. The disparity that leads to the best match is 115. There are many peaks in the correlation score graph, but modeling of illumination blur causes the peaks to decay as we move away from the correct disparity value. Graph (c) shows the intensity observed by the camera against the simulated projector illumination value for the best disparity. Graph (b) and (d) are the same trends for point x_2. Because of strong sub-surface scattering at x_2, the global illumination component is large and the direct component is relatively small. This can be seen in (d).

these pixels and hence there will be numerous plausible solutions to the direct-global separation. We resolve these ambiguities using a smoothness prior as was done in [1] by finding the direct image I_d and global image I_g that solve

$$\underset{I_d, I_g}{\operatorname{argmin}} \sum_{t \in T} \|I^t - \tfrac{1}{2} I_g - S \circ^t I_d\|_2^2 + \lambda_d TV(I_d) + \lambda_g TV(I_g) \tag{7}$$

λ_d and λ_g are scalar parameters that weight the smoothness terms for the direct and global components respectively. $A \circ B$ is the Hadamard (element-wise) product between A and B. $TV(F)$ is the isotropic total variation of the function $F(x, y)$

$$TV(F) = \sum_{Domain(F)} \sqrt{\left(\frac{\partial F}{\partial x}\right)^2 + \left(\frac{\partial F}{\partial y}\right)^2} \tag{8}$$

Parts of the scene far away from the projector receive less light that regions close to the projector. As a result, there is a pronounced falloff in the recovered direct and global illumination images. Because we have recovered scene geometry, we can roughly correct for this falloff by assuming it follows an inverse square relationship with depth. We can compute depth dependent correction factor $K(x)$ at each pixel

$$K(x) = \frac{\alpha}{\tau_z^2(x, \pi(x))} \tag{9}$$

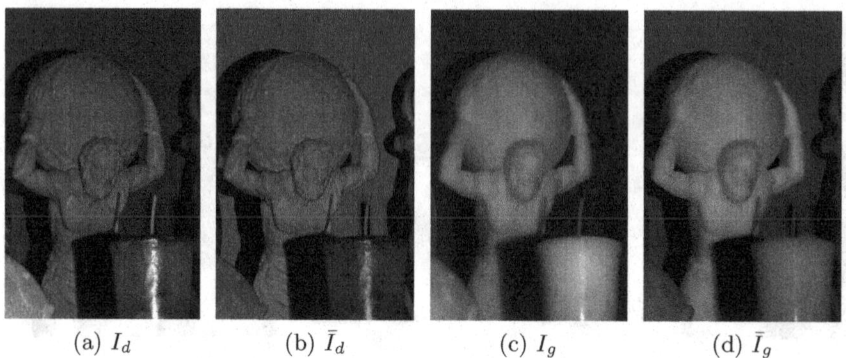

(a) I_d (b) $\bar{I}_d$ (c) I_g (d) $\bar{I}_g$

Fig. 5. The direct (a) and global (c) components of illumination estimated by our algorithm. Since we have recovered a depth map of the scene, we can also correct for projector fall off. This is particularly useful in scenes with large depth variations where objects in the background appear much darker than those in the foreground because they are further away from the light source. After accounting for the fall off, we get corrected estimates for the direct and global component illumination (images (b) and (d) respectively).

where α is an (arbitrary) positive scale factor. We can then solve for the corrected direct and global illumination components ($\bar{I}_d$ and $\bar{I}_g$) by modifying equation 7:

$$\underset{\bar{I}_d,\bar{I}_g}{\operatorname{argmin}} \sum_{t \in T} \|I^t - \tfrac{1}{2} K \circ \bar{I}_g - K \circ S \circ^t \bar{I}_d\|_2^2 + \lambda_d TV(\bar{I}_d) + \lambda_g TV(\bar{I}_g) \tag{10}$$

6 Results

Experimental Setup. Our experimental setup consists of a projector and a camera mounted in a stereo configuration. We use a 500 lumen DLP projector with a resolution of 1280×800 (InFocus IN1144). The camera is a 2448×2048 color CCD (Point Gray Research GRAS-50S5-C). The camera is calibrated geometrically and radiometrically. The projector is calibrated geometrically at each focus setting and its blur kernel has been characterized (as described in Section 2). Our method uses only binary stripe patterns but we calibrated the projector radiometrically so that we could compare our method to micro phase shifting [6]. The projector-camera baseline is fixed and known. Since the projector intrinsics change with focus setting, we correct for this by warping images before projecting them so that geometrically they all appear to be projected by a projector with fixed intrinsic parameters.

In our experiments the focus ring position was changed by hand and we used 4 positions ($F = 4$). Between the shortest and longest focus settings, the working range of the system covers depths from $350mm$ to $1600mm$. For all experiments the camera lens aperture was set to $f/10$, the exposure time was $133ms$ and the camera was configured to capture 8 bit images.

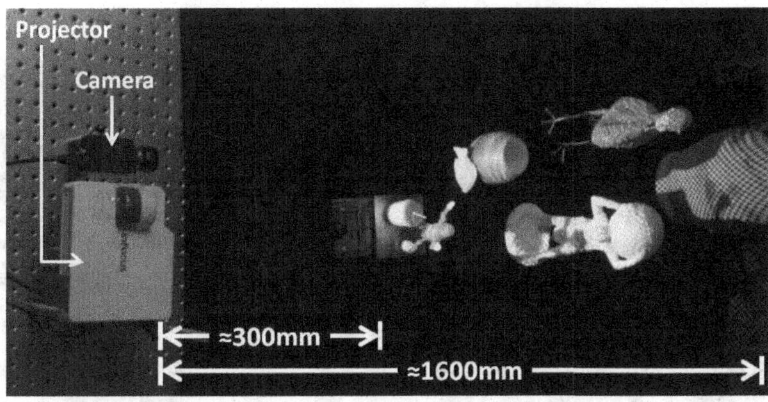

Fig. 6. Experimental Setup: With a small, 500 lumen DLP projector and a small number of images, we are able to scan scenes over a large working volume to recover accurate depth maps and perform illumination separation.

6.1 Depth Recovery

We present results from our depth map recovery algorithm on two challenging scenes (top row in fig 7). Depth maps from our algorithm (second row in fig 7) were generated using 7 structured light patterns at each of 4 focal lengths, a total of 28 images. Our algorithm is able to recover accurate depth maps of both scenes with very few errors. We compare against a simple depth from illumination focus algorithm (bottom row) and micro phase shifting (third row).

The illumination defocus algorithm we compared against projects a shifted sequence of square waves (14 images) at each of 8 projector focus settings and then finds the focus setting at which each camera pixel's illumination contrast was maximized. Each focus setting can be mapped to the depth of its corresponding plane of focus to find the depth map. Since the baseline for this method is limited to the aperture of the projector, the resulting depth estimates are coarse along z and tend to be inaccurate at large distances.

For the micro phase shifting experiments, we chose the high frequency (16 pixels per cycle) pattern set with 15 frequencies [6]. Micro phase shifting uses a fixed projector focus so we set the projector to be in focus in the middle of the scenes. The total number of patterns used is 17. Using more patterns at this frequency is difficult because micro phase shifting requires all projected pattern frequencies to be in a narrow band.

Micro phase shift has some robustness to illumination blur but since it does not actually model defocus, it breaks down when the depth variation in a scene is too large. This is evident in scene 1 where the shape of green plastic robot in the foreground is not recovered by micro phase shifting. In comparison, our method is able to recover the robot. Our algorithm also works better on low albedo or poorly lit regions like the red funnel in scene 2. Since we change focus settings, there are always some images where the contrast of our projected illumination is high, so low signal to noise ratios are less of a problem for our algorithm.

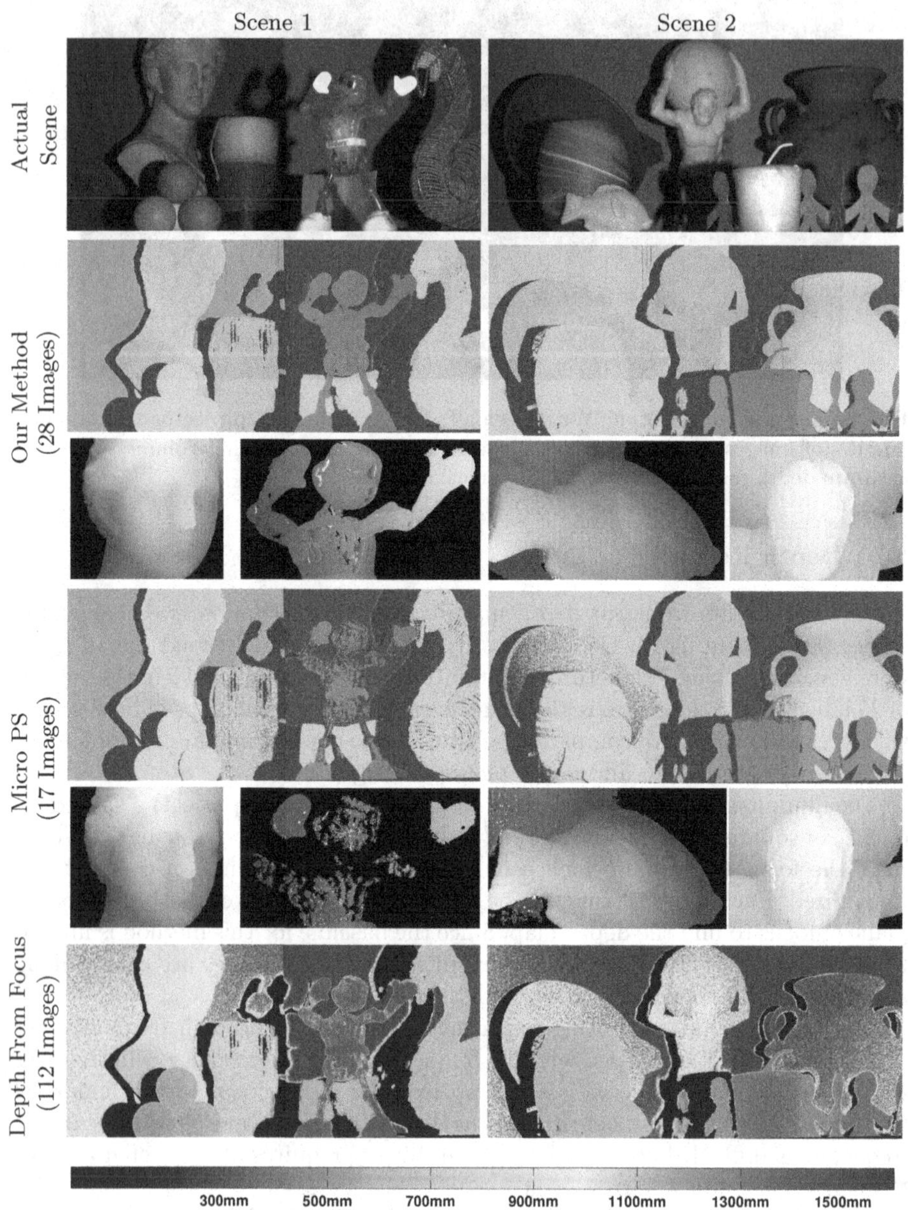

Fig. 7. Recovering Depth: Our structured light algorithm is able to recover depth maps for scenes containing challenging objects over an extended working volume with relatively few images. The insets for our method and micro phase shifting show (rescaled) depth maps for small parts of the scene. Many fine details on objects like the scales on the soap fish are successfully resolved.

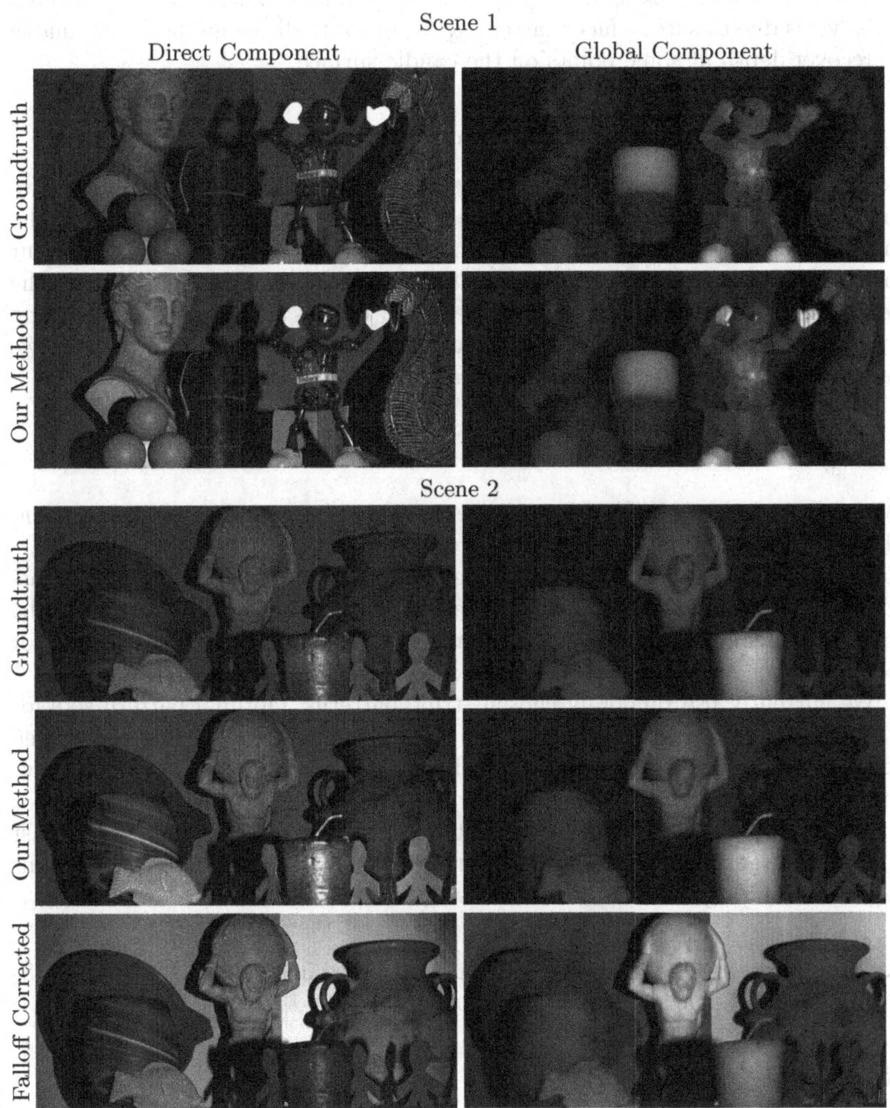

Fig. 8. Direct-Global Separation. Groundtruth was computed using 112 images and our method used 28. In scene 1, the white hands on the robot toy appear much brighter in the global image computed by our method than the ground truth. This is because our algorithm tried to fit a linear trend to saturated (completely white) camera pixels. In scene 2, the shading on the soap fish and the white statue becomes is very clear in the direct illumination image.

The candle in scene 1 is very difficult to reconstruct as from some directions, it reflects almost no light directly back to the camera, almost all the observed radiance is due to sub-surface scattering. As a result, all the methods are unable to recover depth at some points on the candle surface.

6.2 Recovering Direct and Global Illumination

To obtain ground truth direct and global illumination images for our scenes, we projected 14 shifted stripe patterns at 8 projector focus settings and used the multiple focus separation technique proposed in [7]. The results presented for our method are computed using the same 28 images that were used to estimate the depth maps. Although our technique uses fewer images and involves a smoothing term, it generates output that is similar to the ground truth. Additionally, we can correct for the effects of projector fall off as demonstrated in Figure 8.

7 Discussion

We presented an algorithm that can reconstruct shape and recover direct and global illumination in a large working volume with a small number of images.

Our algorithm's robustness to global illumination effects relies on the assumption used in [12]- the global illumination must vary slowly compared to the spatial frequency of the projected patterns. If this assumption does not hold, for example when specular interreflections occur, our method fails.

We currently use randomly chosen stripe patterns. Optimal pattern sets for structured light are usually derived by trying to maximize the distance between codes to minimize the chance of a decoding error. In our setting, we would have to consider the fact that defocus causes our codes to vary with depth. Also, for the direct-global component separation to work well, each pixel's code word must contain a large range of projector intensity values. Carefully designed patterns may allow our algorithm to work well with fewer images.

Acknowledgements. This research was supported in parts by NSF grants IIS-1317749 and IIS-0964562 and ONR grant N00014-11-1-0295.

References

1. Achar, S., Nuske, S.T., Narasimhan, S.G.: Compensating for Motion During Direct-Global Separation. In: International Conference on Computer Vision (2013)
2. Chen, T., Seidel, H.P., Lensch, H.P.: Modulated phase-shifting for 3D scanning. In: IEEE Conference on Computer Vision and Pattern Recognition, pp. 1–8 (June 2008)
3. Couture, V., Martin, N., Roy, S.: Unstructured light scanning to overcome interreflections. In: International Conference on Computer Vision (2011)
4. Goldman, D.B., Curless, B., Hertzmann, A., Seitz, S.M.: Shape and spatially-varying BRDFs from photometric stereo. IEEE Transactions on Pattern Analysis and Machine Intelligence 32(6), 1060–1071 (2010)

5. Gupta, M., Agrawal, A., Veeraraghavan, A., Narasimhan, S.G.: Structured light 3D scanning in the presence of global illumination. In: IEEE Conference on Computer Vision and Pattern Recognition, pp. 713–720 (June 2011)
6. Gupta, M., Nayar, S.K.: Micro Phase Shifting. In: IEEE Conference on Computer Vision and Pattern Recognition (2012)
7. Gupta, M., Tian, Y., Narasimhan, S.G., Zhang, L.: A Combined Theory of Defocused Illumination and Global Light Transport. International Journal of Computer Vision 98(2), 146–167 (2011)
8. Hermans, C., Francken, Y., Cuypers, T., Bekaert, P.: Depth from sliding projections. In: IEEE Conference on Computer Vision and Pattern Recognition (2009)
9. Hern, C., Gabriel, V., Bjorn, J.B., Roberto, S.: Non-rigid Photometric Stereo with Colored Lights. In: International Conference on Computer Vision (October 2007)
10. Inokuchi, S., Sato, K., Matsuda, F.: Range imaging system for 3-d object recognition. In: International Conference on Pattern Recognition (1984)
11. Lei, S., Zhang, S.: Digital sinusoidal fringe pattern generation: Defocusing binary patterns VS focusing sinusoidal patterns. Optics and Lasers in Engineering 48(5), 561–569 (2010)
12. Nayar, S.K., Krishnan, G., Grossberg, M.D., Raskar, R.: Fast separation of direct and global components of a scene using high frequency illumination. ACM Transactions on Graphics 25(3), 935 (2006)
13. O'Toole, M., Raskar, R., Kutulakos, K.N.: Primal-dual coding to probe light transport. ACM Transactions on Graphics 31(4), 1–11 (2012)
14. Reddy, D., Ramamoorthi, R., Curless, B.: Frequency-Space Decomposition and Acquisition of Light Transport under Spatially Varying Illumination. In: Fitzgibbon, A., Lazebnik, S., Perona, P., Sato, Y., Schmid, C. (eds.) ECCV 2012, Part VI. LNCS, vol. 7577, pp. 596–610. Springer, Heidelberg (2012)
15. Scharstein, D., Szeliski, R.: High-accuracy stereo depth maps using structured light. In: IEEE Conference on Computer Vision and Pattern Recognition (2003)
16. Schechner, Y., Kiryati, N.: Depth from defocus vs. stereo: How different really are they? International Journal of Computer Vision 39(2), 141–162 (2000)
17. Tao, M., Hadap, S., Malik, J., Ramamoorthi, R.: Depth from Combining Defocus and Correspondence Using Light-Field Cameras. In: International Conference on Computer Vision (2013)
18. Yuan, T., Subbarao, M.: Integration of Multiple-Baseline Color Stereo Vision with Focus and Defocus Analysis for 3-D. In: Proceedings of SPIE, No. i, pp. 44–51 (November 1998)
19. Zhang, L., Nayar, S.: Projection defocus analysis for scene capture and image display. ACM Transactions on Graphics (2006)

Coplanar Common Points in Non-centric Cameras

Wei Yang[1], Yu Ji[1], Jinwei Ye[2], S. Susan Young[2], and Jingyi Yu[1]

[1] University of Delaware, Newark, DE 19716, USA
[2] US Army Research Laboratory, Adelphi, MD 20783, USA

Abstract. Discovering and extracting new image features pertaining to scene geometry is important to 3D reconstruction and scene understanding. Examples include the classical vanishing points observed in a centric camera and the recent coplanar common points (CCPs) in a crossed-slit camera [21,17]. A CCP is a point in the image plane corresponding to the intersection of the projections of all lines lying on a common 3D plane. In this paper, we address the problem of determining CCP existence in general non-centric cameras. We first conduct a ray-space analysis to show that finding the CCP of a 3D plane is equivalent to solving an array of ray constraint equations. We then derive the necessary and sufficient conditions for CCP to exist in an arbitrary non-centric camera such as non-centric catadioptric mirrors. Finally, we present robust algorithms for extracting the CCPs from a single image and validate our theories and algorithms through experiments.

1 Introduction

An important task in computer vision is to identify and then extract image features pertaining to scene geometry for reliable 3D reconstruction. A classical example is the vanishing point (VP) in centric (perspective) cameras: a VP in the image plane Π corresponds to the intersection of a set of parallel lines in space. The VP and the direction of the lines form one-to-one correspondence and tremendous efforts [6,5,3,2] have been focused on scene reconstruction using the VP. Recent studies [20] have shown that VPs generally exist in non-centric cameras such as the crossed-slit [21,10], linear oblique [9], etc.

The VP, in essence, is the characteristics of line directions. In contrast, the recently proposed coplanar common point or CCP is the characteristics of positions: for a set of (oblique) lines lying on a 3D plane, will their images still intersect at a common pixel in the image plane? The answer is generally no for centric cameras as these lines will map to 2D lines with different directions and origins in the image plane, with a singular case when the plane also pass through the camera's Center-of-Projection (CoP). Surprisingly, CCP generally exists for some special non-centric cameras such as the crossed-slit (XSlit) camera [21]. Although 3D lines map to curves (e.g., hyperbolas) as shown in Fig. 1, these curves intersect at the CCP as far as they lie on the same plane. In fact, the CCP and the 3D plane forms one-to-one mapping, a highly useful property for 3D scene reconstruction and understanding.

In this paper, we address the problem of determining CCP existence in general non-centric cameras[13]. On the theory front, we conduct a comprehensive analysis in ray-space and show that finding the CCP of a 3D plane is equivalent to solving an array

D. Fleet et al. (Eds.): ECCV 2014, Part I, LNCS 8689, pp. 220–233, 2014.
© Springer International Publishing Switzerland 2014

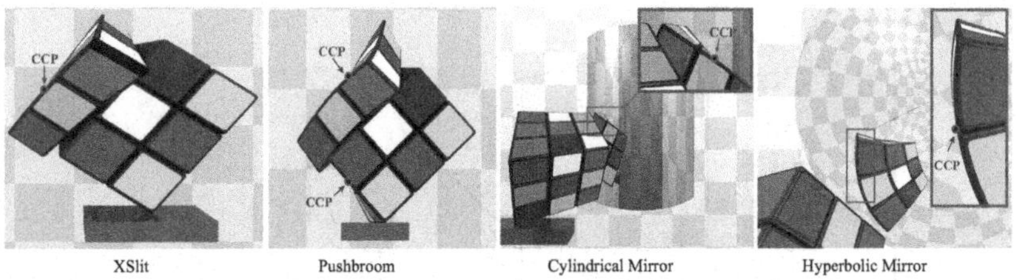

Fig. 1. CCPs in several non-centric cameras

of ray constraint equations. We then derive the necessary and sufficient conditions for CCP to exist in general non-centric cameras such as catadioptric mirrors. Our analysis further reveals the relationship between the CCP and the caustic (focal) surfaces of rays. Despite being largely theoretical, our framework finds its uses in 3D plane localization and reconstruction. Specifically, we develop robust algorithms for fitting curved images of 3D lines, locating the CCPs, and mapping them back to 3D planes. We validate our theory and algorithms on both synthetic data and real non-centric cameras, and we show that the CCP analysis provides useful insights on scene composition and configuration.

2 Ray Space Analysis

To characterize CCPs in an arbitrary non-centric camera, we conduct a ray space analysis. We describe a camera, centric or non-centric, as 2D manifold of rays, where each pixel on the sensor maps to a unique ray. Given a set of lines lying on a 3D plane Π, if their images in the camera pass through a CCP, then the CCP (which is a pixel) should map to a ray that lie on plane Π. We therefore can reformulate the problem of finding the CCP into finding the ray that satisfies a specific set of constraints.

Before proceeding, we explain our notations. To represent the ray space, we adopt the two-plane parametrization (2PP) model [7]. In 2PP, each ray is parameterized by its intersections with two parallel planes where $[s, t]$ is the intersection with the first plane Π_{st} and $[u, v]$ the second Π_{uv}. To simply our analysis, we choose the $z = 0$ plane to be Π_{uv}, and $z = 1$ plane to be Π_{st}. Further, we use $\sigma = s - u$ and $\tau = t - v$ to parameterize the ray direction as $[\sigma, \tau, 1]$. All rays are parameterized as the 4-tuple $[u, v, \sigma, \tau]$.

Given a 3D plane with normal $[n_x, n_y, n_z]$ can be parameterized as $\Pi : n_x x + n_y y + n_z z + d = 0$, any ray $r[u, v, \sigma, \tau]$ lying on Π should satisfy two constraints: 1) r's origin must lie on the plane and 2) r's direction is orthogonal to Π's normal. Therefore, we can derive the *ray-on-plane constraints* as:

$$\begin{cases} n_x u + n_y v + d = 0 \\ n_x \sigma + n_y \tau + n_z = 0 \end{cases} \tag{1}$$

To find whether CCP exists in a general non-centric camera, we set out to combine the *ray-on-plane constraints* with the camera's ray constraints and determine if there exists a solution that satisfies all constraints.

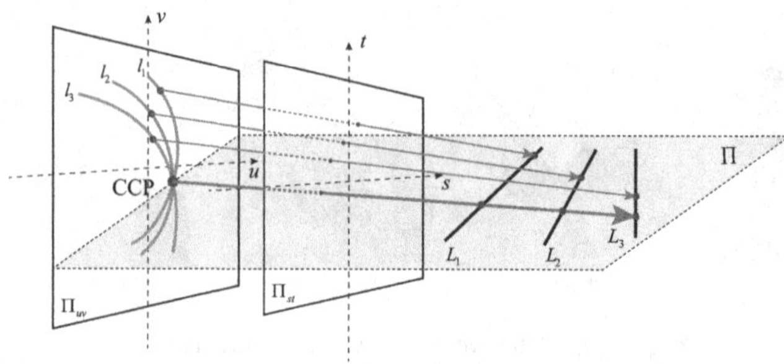

Fig. 2. CCP in 4D ray space. CCP is a pixel on the image plane corresponding to the intersection of the projections of all lines lying on a common 3D plane.

2.1 CCPs in General Linear Cameras

Yu and McMillan [19] introduced a class of primitive non-centric cameras called the general linear cameras or GLC. They correspond to 2D affine subspaces embedded in the 4D light field space [20] and they can be used to describe a broad range of commonly used non-centric cameras including pushbroom [4], XSlit, and linear oblique cameras.

A GLC is constructed by three generator rays r_1, r_2, r_3 so that all rays that collected by GLC are affine combinations of these three rays:

$$GLC = \{r : r = \alpha r_1 + \beta r_2 + (1 - \alpha - \beta) r_3, \forall \alpha, \beta\} \tag{2}$$

where α, β are affine coefficients.

Without loss of generality, we can pick three special generator rays originating from $[1, 0]$, $[0, 1]$ and $[0, 0]$ on Π_{uv} and rewrite the GLC equation as two linear constraints:

$$\begin{cases} \sigma = u\sigma_1 + v\sigma_2 + (1 - u - v)\sigma_3 \\ \tau = u\tau_1 + v\tau_2 + (1 - u - v)\tau_3 \end{cases} \tag{3}$$

where $[\sigma_i, \tau_i]$, $i = 1, 2, 3$ are the directions of the three ray generators.

Now that given a 3D plane Π, to determine if it has a CCP in the GLC, we can simply set out to find if there exists a ray that simultaneously satisfy the *ray-on-plane constraints* (Eqn. 1 and the GLC constraints (Eqn. 3). Notice that combining the two sets of equations result in a 4×4 linear system in $[u, v, \sigma, \tau]$:

$$\begin{bmatrix} -n_x & -n_y & 0 & 0 \\ 0 & 0 & -n_x & -n_y \\ \sigma_3 - \sigma_1 & \sigma_3 - \sigma_2 & 1 & 0 \\ \tau_3 - \tau_1 & \tau_3 - \tau_2 & 0 & 1 \end{bmatrix} \begin{bmatrix} u \\ v \\ \sigma \\ \tau \end{bmatrix} = \begin{bmatrix} d \\ n_z \\ \sigma_3 \\ \tau_3 \end{bmatrix} \tag{4}$$

Whether the linear system has a solution depends on the determinant J:

$$J = n_x^2(\sigma_2 - \sigma_3) + n_x n_y(\tau_2 - \tau_3 - \sigma_1 + \sigma_3) - n_y^2(\tau_1 - \tau_3)$$

By solving the linear system (Eqn. 4), the CCP coordinate on the image plane can be computed as:

$$\begin{cases} u = \dfrac{1}{J}[n_y(n_x\sigma_3 + n_y\tau_3 + n_z) - d \cdot m_2] \\ v = \dfrac{1}{J}[d \cdot m_1 - n_x(n_x\sigma_3 + n_y\tau_3 + n_z)] \end{cases} \quad (5)$$

Where $m_1 = n_x(\sigma_1 - \sigma_3) + n_y(\tau_1 - \tau_3)$, $m_2 = n_x(\sigma_2 - \sigma_3) + n_y(\tau_2 - \tau_3)$. Now that let us look at specific types of GLCs. To simplify our analysis, we assume that we translate the uv plane so that the third generator ray passes both the origins of the st and uv plane, i.e., $r_3 = [0, 0, 0, 0]$.

Pinhole: Assume the camera's CoP is at $[0, 0, f]$, by using the similitude relationship, we have $\sigma_2 = \sigma_3 = 0$, $\tau_1 = \tau_3 = 0$, $\sigma_1 - \sigma_3 = \tau_2 - \tau_3 = -1/f$. Therefore, we have $J = 0$ for any plane Π. Hence, CCPs do not exist in a pinhole camera.

Pushbroom: A pushbroom camera collects rays that pass through a common slit and parallel to a plane. We assume that the slit is parallel to Π_{uv} at distance Z. It is easy to see that we have $\sigma_2 = \sigma_3 = 0$, $\tau_1 = \tau_3 = 0$, $\sigma_1 - \sigma_3 = 0$, $\tau_2 - \tau_3 = -1/Z$. Therefore, $J \neq 0$ for a general 3D plane and CCPs exist in a pushbroom camera.

XSlit: A XSlit camera collects rays that pass through two slits. We assume the two slits are orthogonal and both parallel to Π_{uv}. The horizontal and vertical slits are at depth Z_1 and Z_2 respectively. We have $\sigma_2 = \sigma_3 = 0$, $\tau_1 = \tau_3 = 0$, $\sigma_1 - \sigma_3 = -1/Z_2$, $\tau_1 - \tau_3 = -1/Z_1$. Therefore, $J \neq 0$ for a general 3D plane and CCPs exist in XSlit cameras.

Pencil and Bilinear: If we assume that the slit is parallel to Π_{uv} at depth Z, we have $\sigma_2 = 1/Z$, $\sigma_3 = 0$, $\tau_1 = \tau_3 = 0$, $\sigma_1 - \sigma_3 = -1/Z$, $\tau_2 - \tau_3 = -1/Z$. Therefore, $J \neq 0$ for a general 3D plane and therefore CCPs exist. A similar conclusion holds for the bilinear (linear oblique) [9] cameras. The complete results are showed in Table. 1.

Table 1. CCP existence in popular GLCs

	Pinhole	XSlit	Pushbroom	Pencil	Bilinear
CCP Existence	×	√	√	√	√

Our analysis reveals that the pinhole camera is one of the very few singular cases where a 3D general does not exhibit a CCP. Notice that many of the GLC models have real world implementations. For example, pushbroom and XSlit and pencil images can be captured by a rolling shutter camera [8] or synthesized by stitching specific rows or columns from a row of pinhole images, as shown in Section 4.2. Therefore, CCPs can be potentially benefit scene reconstruction using these cameras.

2.2 Concentric Mosaics

There are other widely used non-centric cameras, for example, concentric mosaics [16,12] or circular XSlit [22]. These camera models are generally synthesized from

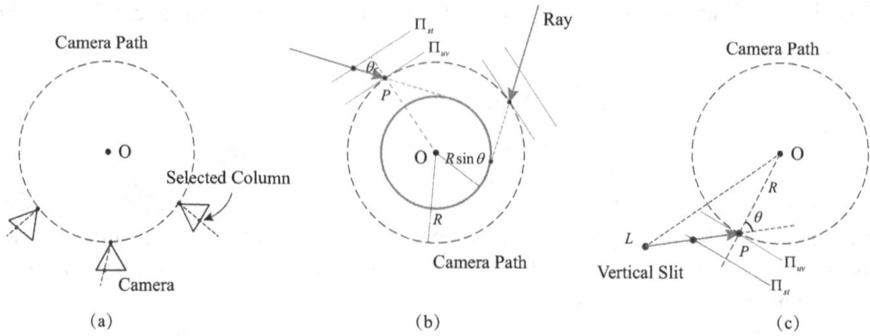

Fig. 3. (a) Concentric mosaics are synthesized from a sequence of images captured by a perspective camera moving along a circular path. (b) We define 2PP tangent to the camera path and rotating with the camera. (c) Circular XSlit panorama.

rotational panoramas. To acquire a concentric mosaics, it is common practice to rotate a camera off-axis on a circle. For each camera position, a column is sampled according to its angle from the optical axis. Then all selected columns are stitched together to form a panorama, as showed in Fig. 3(a).

To investigate the existence of CCP, we set the origin of the coordinate system as the rotation axis. Assume the xy plane is the the camera path plane and we can also adopt 2PP model for ray parametrization. However instead of using two fixed planes, we use two parallel planes that rotate along with the camera. We set Π_{uv} tangent to the camera path at P and vertical to the xy plane. Π_{st} is parallel to Π_{uv} with distance 1. At each position, the column with angle θ is sampled. The set of all collected ray intersect Π_{st} at $[x + (x - y\tan\theta)/R, y + (y + x\tan\theta)/R]$. This allows us to map rays collected by the camera as a 2D manifold defined by x, y and θ:

$$[u, v, \sigma, \tau] = [x, y, (x - y\tan\theta)/R, (y + x\tan\theta)/R] \tag{6}$$

Notice the z value of the intersection on Π_{st} is not necessarily 1 as in the conventional 2PP case. Assume $z = \lambda$, we can rewrite the *ray-on-plane constraints* as:

$$\begin{cases} n_x x + n_y y + d = 0 \\ \sin\theta(\sin\theta x + \cos\theta y) \cdot n_x + \sin\theta(\sin\theta y - \cos\theta x) \cdot n_y + \lambda n_z + d = 0 \end{cases} \tag{7}$$

Notice though that the solution to Eqn. 7 is actually the intersection of Π and a cylinder centered at origin and with radius $R\sin\theta$. Therefore Eqn. 7 essentially indicates that the plane should have intersections both with the camera path circle and the cylinder, as showed in Fig. 3(b). This analysis is consistent with the geometric interpretation: the cylinder is the inner viewing surface and all rays the collected by the camera should be tangent to the cylinder. This type of concentric mosaics resembles the pushbroom camera where the central columns are stitched together.

A different way to construct concentric mosaic is proposed in [22], analogous to stitching an XSlit panorama from a translational array of images. Using the same acquisition setup, we select, at each camera position, the column with the ray that passes a predefined vertical slit, as showed in Fig 3(c). The result is a circular XSlit model with one vertical slit and one circular slit where the circular slit is the trajectory of the camera. In this set up, θ is a nonlinear function of x and y. The intersections of the rays collected by P and Π_{st} is along PL. Hence $\sigma = \widetilde{\lambda}(s_x - x), \tau = \widetilde{\lambda}(s_y - y)$, s_x, s_y are x and y coordinates of the vertical slit. Eqn. 7 now becomes: $n_x\widetilde{\lambda}(s_x - x) + n_y\widetilde{\lambda}(s_y - y) + \lambda n_z = 0$. Since λ, $\widetilde{\lambda}$ are both scalers, we can eliminate $\widetilde{\lambda}$ as:

$$\begin{cases} n_x x + n_y y + d = 0 \\ n_z s_x + n_z s_y + \lambda n_z + d = 0 \end{cases} \tag{8}$$

This indicates that for a plane Π to have a CCP, it should intersect with both the vertical slit and the camera path.

3 CCPs in Catadioptric Mirrors

A commonly used class of real non-centric cameras are catadioptric mirrors [1,15] in which a regular pinhole camera is positioned in front of a curved mirror for acquiring images with much wider field-of-view (FoV).

3.1 Ray Space vs. Caustics

Recall that our goal is to determine if we can find an incident ray collected by the camera that lies on Π. Notice that each point $P(x, y, z)$ on the mirror surface corresponds to a reflection ray. Hence we can also potentially map the CCP problem into the ray space similar to the GLC and concentric mosaic case: assume the mirror surface is in form $z(x, y)$, the incident ray $\mathbf{v}_i = [i^x, i^y, 1]$ can be computed as:

$$\mathbf{v}_i = \mathbf{v}_r - 2\frac{\mathbf{n}_s \cdot \mathbf{v}_r}{\parallel \mathbf{n}_s \parallel^2}\mathbf{n}_s \tag{9}$$

$\mathbf{n}_s$ is the surface normal and $\mathbf{v}_r$ is the reflection ray. Intersect this ray with Π_{uv} and Π_{st}, we can get the 4D representation:

$$[u, v, \sigma, \tau] = [x - z \cdot i^x, y - z \cdot i^y, i^x, i^y] \tag{10}$$

u, v, σ, τ are functions in x and y. The set of rays collected by the mirror surface form a ray-space parametric manifold in x and y.

$$\Sigma(x, y) = [u(x, y), v(x, y), \sigma(x, y), \tau(x, y)] \tag{11}$$

We have the *ray-on-plane constraints*:

$$\begin{cases} u(x, y)n_x + v(x, y)n_y + d = 0 \\ \sigma(x, y)n_x + \tau(x, y)n_y + n_z = 0 \end{cases} \tag{12}$$

For a given plane Π, we have two equations, two unknowns. In theory, we can determine if Π has a CCP by testing if Eqn. 12 has a solution. In reality, $\Sigma(x, y)$ can become highly complex and searching for the solution is a challenging algebraic problem.

A different and more intuitive solution is to view the problem from the caustic perspective. Caustic is a curve or surface where the light rays concentrate[14]. The caustic surface can be computed using Jacobian method which results in a quadratic equation. A quadratic equation generally produces two solutions, hence the caustic surfaces always appear in pairs and locally they can be interpreted as XSlit[18]. If a plane has CCP, then the plane has to intersect with the two caustic surfaces, a necessary condition for CCP to exist. However, the condition is insufficient: the resulting intersections are two curves on the caustic surfaces. Since the caustic surfaces need to appear in pairs, the two curves do not necessarily form valid correspondences. Therefore, we would need to check for, every ray originating from the first curve, whether it will pass through the second curve. If there exists such a ray, then CCP exists. Otherwise, it does not. The procedure above provides a simple but effective recipe for determining CCP existence. In the following sections, we analyze several commonly used catadioptric mirrors.

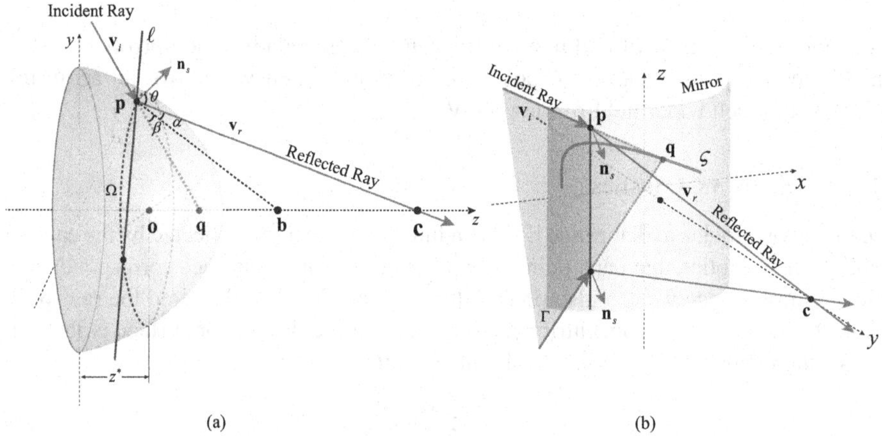

Fig. 4. (a) CCP condition in a rotationally symmetric mirror: the plane has to intersect with z-axis at a point $\mathbf{q}$ and have intersections with the Ω that determined by $\mathbf{q}$. (b) CCP condition in a cylinder mirror: the plane has to intersect with the caustic ζ and not perpendicular to the xy plane.

3.2 Rotationally Symmetric Mirrors

A rotationally symmetric mirror is formed by rotating a quadric curve about its symmetric axis. Assume the symmetric axis is aligned with the z-axis, the mirror surface can be parameterized as

$$r^2 + Az^2 + 2Bz - C = 0, x^2 + y^2 = r^2 \tag{13}$$

A, B and C are the curve parameters that determine the mirror shape. In particular, $A = 1, B = 0, C > 0$, the mirror is a sphere; $A > 0, C > 0$, elliptical mirror; and $A < 0, C > 0$, hyperbolic mirror. We assume that the pinhole viewing camera is on the symmetric axis of the mirror. The only singular case is when the pinhole coincides with curve's foci that emulates a virtual pinhole, in which the CCP does not exist. Therefore, in order to observe the CCP, we need to place the viewing camera off the foci.

By the symmetry, all reflection rays that collected by the view camera should intersect the symmetric axis. Hence the the symmetric axis is one of the two caustic surfaces.

CCP Condition 1: *The 3D plane must have an intersection with the symmetric axis.*

The projection under a rotationally symmetric mirror is shown in Fig. 4(a). Given an incident ray $\mathbf{v}_i$ from the scene towards the mirror surface, to produce image in the viewing camera, its reflection ray $\mathbf{v}_r$ must pass through the CoP $\mathbf{c} = [0, 0, c]$, lying on the z-axis. Since $\mathbf{v}_i$ and $\mathbf{v}_r$ are coplanar, $\mathbf{v}_i$ also have an intersection with the z-axis. Therefore, a valid CCP projection must intersects with the z-axis, and hence the plane.

As mentioned above, the plane that intersects with the symmetric axis does not necessarily have a CCP. Assume $\mathbf{q} = [0, 0, d'], d' = -d/n_z$ is the intersection point between the common plane and symmetric axis. We now only need to check the set of rays determined by $\mathbf{q}$. Assume the incident ray is reflected at $\mathbf{p}$ on the mirror surface and we have $\mathbf{v}_i = \mathbf{p} - \mathbf{q}$. It is important to note that ruled by the law of reflection, there only exists one circle of $\mathbf{p}$ on the mirror whose resulting reflection ray can enter $\mathbf{c}$. Assume the circle is $\Omega : x^2 + y^2 = r^{*2}$ for $\mathbf{p}$, we can obtain the set of rays as a cone that connects $\mathbf{q}$ and Ω.

To compute Ω, we orthogonally project $\mathbf{p}$ onto the z-axis and obtain $\mathbf{o} = [0, 0, z^*]$. By Eqn. 13, the surface normal at $\mathbf{p}$ can be computed as $[x^*, y^*, Az^* + B]$. Thus the tangent plane at $\mathbf{p}$ is $x^*x + y^*y + (Az^* + B)z + (Bz^* - C) = 0$. Hence we can compute the intersection point $\mathbf{b}$ of the tangent plane and z-axis. Since $\forall p \in \Omega$, the corresponding reflection rays pass through $\mathbf{c}$, the tangent plane bisect the angle formed by $\mathbf{v}_i$ and $\mathbf{v}_r$, i.e, $\alpha = \beta = 90° - \theta$, by the law of reflection, as shown in Fig. 4. Consider the triangle formed by $\mathbf{q}$,$\mathbf{p}$ and $\mathbf{c}$, we can formulate the following equation by applying the angle bisector theorem to solve for z^*

$$\frac{\sqrt{r^{*2} + (d' - z^*)^2}}{\sqrt{r^{*2} + (c - z^*)^2}} = \frac{C - Bd' - (B + d'A)z^*}{(cA + B)z^* + cB - C} \tag{14}$$

The solution to Eqn. 14 corresponds to valid reflection points on the mirror surface.

CCP Condition 2: *The 3D plane must have intersection with Ω.*

Recall that not all the planes contain $\mathbf{q}$ will intersect with the circle Ω. To test the plane-circle intersection, we compute the distance from the plane to the z-axis at $z = z^*$ as:

$$D = \frac{|n_z(z^* - d')|}{\sqrt{n_x^2 + n_y^2}} \tag{15}$$

If $D > r^*$, the plane will have no intersection with the circle and thus has no CCP. If $D = r^*$, the plane has one intersection with the circle and thus has a single CCP; When $D < r^*$, the plane has two intersections with the circle and will have two CCPs.

Plane Reconstruction from CCPs. In rotationally symmetric mirrors, a plane can be directly located from its CCPs. Recall that a plane may have one or two CCPs. We consider the two cases separately.

Case I: One CCP. If there is only one CCP, the plane must be the tangent plane of the circle Ω. Therefore, we can first find the tangent line l at $z = z^*$ of Ω. The plane can be reconstructed through the l and the CCP's corresponding $\mathbf{q}$.
Case II: Two CCPs. If two CCPs exist, we can instantly recover the plane by three points on it, i.e, the two CCPs and their corresponding $\mathbf{q}$.

3.3 Cylinder Mirrors

Another commonly used class of catadioptric mirrors is cylinder mirrors. Given a quadratic curve on the xy-plane, instead of rotating it about its symmetric axis, we extrude the curve along the z-axis to form a cylinder. By aligning the y-axis with symmetric axis, a cylinder mirror can be parameterized as

$$x^2 + Ay^2 + 2By - C = 0, z = t \tag{16}$$

Same as the rotational symmetric mirror, A, B and C are the quadratic curve parameters. When $A = 1, B = 0, C > 0$, we have a cylindrical mirror; $A > 0, C > 0$, elliptical cylinder mirror; and $A < 0, C > 0$, hyperbolic cylinder mirror. We place the camera on the y-axis such that the CoP can be written as $\mathbf{c} = [0, c, 0]$.

Whether the cylinder mirrors have one dimensional caustic is not as clear as the rotationally symmetric mirrors. We start with considering the forward projection problem, i.e, finding the incident ray constraints whose corresponding reflection ray will pass through the CoP, as shown in Fig. 4(b). Assume $\mathbf{p} = [x, y, z]$ is a point on the mirror surface where reflection occurs. First, we can determine the direction of the reflection ray $\mathbf{v}_r$ by connecting $\mathbf{p}$ and $\mathbf{c}$. Thus we have $\mathbf{v}_r = [-x, -y, c - t]$. The surface normal at $\mathbf{p}$ can be computed as $\mathbf{n}_s = [x, Ay + B, 0]$. By specular reflection, we can compute the incident ray from Eqn. 9 as:

$$\mathbf{v}_i = [\frac{2g - f}{f}x, \frac{2Ag - f}{f}y + (\frac{2g}{f}B + c), -t] \tag{17}$$

Where $f(x) = (1 - A)x^2 + (B^2 - AC), g(y) = -(B + Ac)y + (Bc - C)$. The incident ray can be parameterized in the point-direction form as $\mathbf{p} + \lambda\mathbf{v}_i$. Let $\lambda = 1$, we have the intersection point of the incident ray and the xy-plane ($z = 0$) as $\mathbf{q} = [2gx/f, 2g(Ay + B)/f + c, 0]$. Notice that $\mathbf{q}$ is independent of the z component of $\mathbf{p}$. This indicates that for all $\mathbf{p}$ on a vertical line (parallel to z-axis) on the mirrors surface, the corresponding effective incident ray will pass through the same point $\mathbf{q}$ on xy-plane. From the geometric perspective, $\mathbf{q}$ is actually the reflection point of the CoP w.r.tthe tangent plane of the mirror surface at $\mathbf{p}$ and hence it is equivalent to a virtual CoP. Since all points on a vertical line share the same tangent plane, the CoP reflection $\mathbf{q}$ remains the same. Further, by sliding the vertical line on the mirror surface, we obtain a set of $\mathbf{q}$ that form a curve ζ. ζ is the one dimensional caustic of cylinder mirrors and can be derived in $\mathbf{q}$ as:

$$\zeta(x, y) = \Sigma\{[\frac{2gx}{f}, 2\frac{g}{f}(Ay + B) + c, 0]\} \tag{18}$$

For all x, y on the cylinder mirror surface.

CCP Condition: *the 3D plane must intersect with* ζ.

As mentioned before, each point on ζ determines a set of rays on a vertical plane Γ, as show in Fig. 4(b). If only the common plane does not perpendicular to the x-y plane, i.e $n_z \neq 0$, there will be one valid CCP projection ray which is the intersection line of the common plane and Γ. Similar to the rotationally symmetric mirror example, the number of intersections between the common plane and ζ determines the number of CCPs.

4 Experiments

To validate our theory and analysis, we experiment on both synthetic and real data.

4.1 Synthetic Experiment

We render catadioptric mirror images using the POV-Ray ray tracer (www.povray.org). Our first experiment is performed on a cylindrical mirror $x^2 + (y - 10)^2 = 16, z = t$ where the viewing camera is place at the origin $(0, 0, 0)$ facing towards the cylindrical mirror. Our scene consists with two planes: $\Pi_1 : 2.7475y + z - 12 = 0$ and $\Pi_2 : 3.9153y + z - 8.9378 = 0$. Each plane consists of five lines, among which three are parallel. The camera and scene setups are shown in Fig. 5(a). As shown in Fig. 5(b), Π_1 has one intersection with ζ while Plane Π_2 has two. Fig. 5(c) shows the captured catadioptric images of Π_1 and Π_2 and we can observe that Π_1 has one CCP and Π_2 has two. Our results are hence consistent with the theoretical prediction.

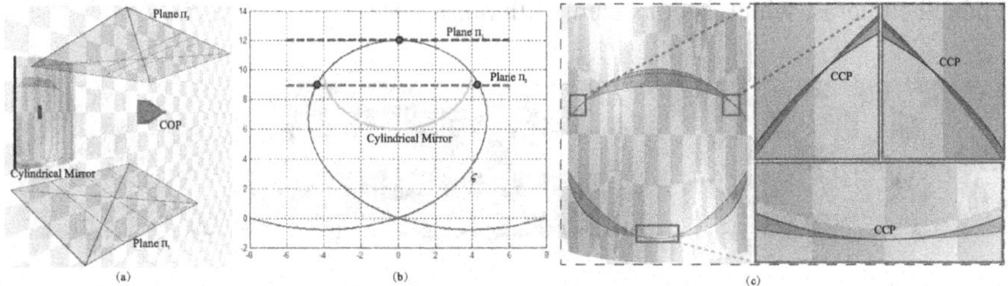

Fig. 5. Experiments on a cylindrical mirror. (a) Experimental setup; (b) Intersections between each plane and ζ; (c) Rendered catadioptric image with close-up view at each CCP.

Next, we test on a hyperbolic mirror $z^2/16 - r^2/9 = 1$ with the viewing camera the origin. The scene consists of two planes: $\Pi_3 : 0.6608y - z + 5.1530 = 0$ and $\Pi_4 : 0.7908y + z - 5.4184 = 0$. Same as our first experiment, we place five lines on each plane. The experimental setup is shown in Fig. 6(a). Fig. 6(b) shows the captured catadioptric image of the two planes and the numbers and position of CCP are consistent with the intersection points between the plane and Ω as predicted by our theory. We can further map the CCPs back to 3D space, showed in Fig. 6(c). The recovery of the 3D planes are highly accurate.

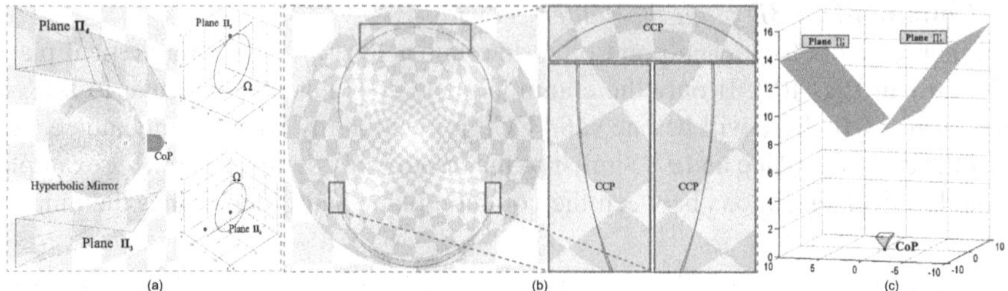

Fig. 6. Experiments on a hyperbolic rotationally symmetric mirror. (a) Experimental setup; (b) Rendered catadioptric image with close-up view at each CCP; (c) The recovered planes.

4.2 Real Experiment

Next, we conduct experiments on real non-centric cameras.

General Linear Cameras. We synthesize several popular GLC images by stitching specific rows/columns from a row of pinhole images. We mount a Cannon 60D SLR with 50mm F1.8 lens on translation track. Two planes are placed in front of the camera and the planes intersect with the camera path. We record a video while the camera is moving at a constant velocity. The resolution of the captured video is 1280×720. From each frame, we choose a specific column or row and stitch them together to form a new image. For pushbroom, we choose column 480 in all frames, as showed in Fig. 7(b). We linearly increase the column index in terms of frame number and stitch these columns to form an XSlit image, as showed in Fig. 7(c). Finally, we linear increase the row index in terms of the frame number and stitch these rows to form a pencil camera, as showed in Fig. 7(d). The highlighted rectangles illustrate where CCPs occur in pushbroom, XSlit and pencil cameras, which is consistent with our theory.

Fig. 7. Synthesized GLC images through stitching pinhole images. (a) The perspective view of the scene. (b) Pushbroom Image. (c) XSlit Image. (d) Pencil Image. Notice lines on a common 3D plane coverage t CCP in Pushbroom, XSlit and Pencil images.

Concentric Mosaics. To construct a concentric mosaic, we mount a Cannon 60D SLR with 50mm F1.8 lens on a rotation table. We align the optical axis to pass through the rotation axis. Two planes are placed in front of the camera and the planes intersect the camera path. We record a video as the camera rotates. The system setup is showed in Fig. 8(a). From the recorded view, we select specific columns from different frames and stitch them to form a concentric mosaic image. Fig. 8(b) shows the images formed by stitching column 560 from all frames. Fig. 8(c) shows the result by stitching column 840. The highlighted regions show where the CCPs occur.

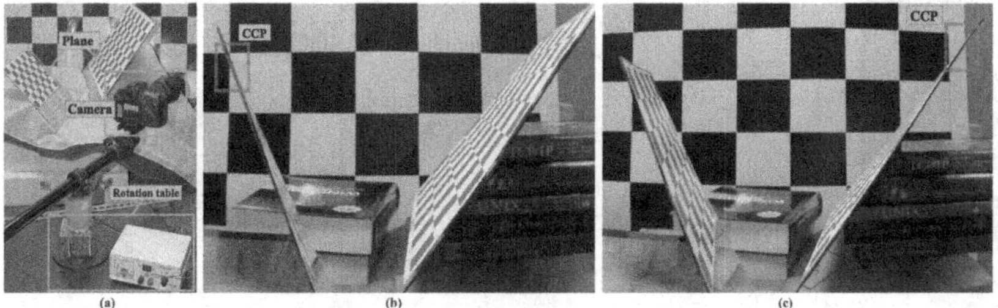

Fig. 8. Captured CCP in concentric mosaics

Cylindrical Mirror. We place a PointGrey FL2-08S2C camera in front of a cylindrical mirror and align the optical axis with the cylindrical axis, as showed in Fig. 9(a). The resolution of the captured images is 1024×768. We place a plane in front of the mirror and the catadioptric images of the plane is shown in Fig. 9(b) and (c). Notice that the plane exhibits the CCP. To understand why this is the case, recall that our analysis shows that as far as the plane has an intersection with the caustic circle, the plane generally has a CCP. In our case, we position the plane near the center of the mirror and tilt it so that it is guaranteed to intersect with the circle and hence has a CCP.

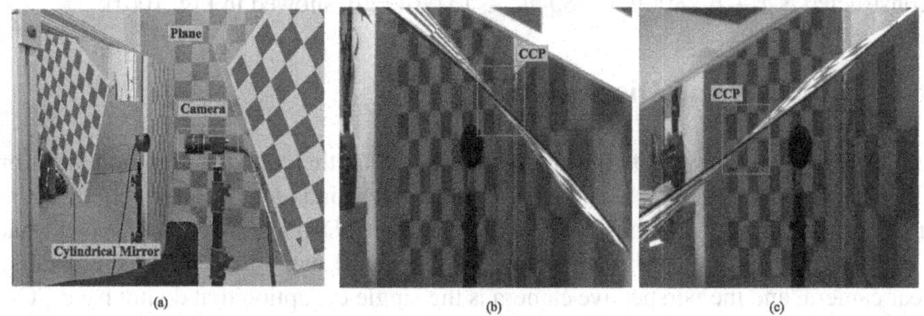

Fig. 9. Captured CCP in cylinder mirror

Spherical Mirror. Our analysis shows that catadioptric systems based on rotationally symmetric mirrors generally cannot capture the CCP of a plane. In fact, even the CCP does exist, it can lie outside the image plane. We have developed a curve-fitting algorithm to handle this case and details can be found in the supplementary materials. In our experiment, we first mount a spherical mirror on a vertical reference plane. The radius of the mirror is 51.64mm. We place the PointGrey FL2-08S2C camera with focal length 7.85mm in front of the spherical mirror. The camera is pre-calibrated. Next, we align the optical axis to pass through the center of sphere using the reference plane, as showed in Fig. 10(b). We set the center of the spherical mirror to be the origin of the coordinate system and connect it with the camera's CoP as the z axis. As a result, the CoP is at $[0, 0, 182.37]$ in our coordinate system.

We attach three parallel white stripes on to a black plane and place it in front of the mirror. The captured image is showed in Fig. 10(a). We then apply our curve fitting algorithm of the white stripes and the fitted results are showed in Fig. 10(c). Our results reveal that the images of these stripes (lines) intersect at two CCPs in

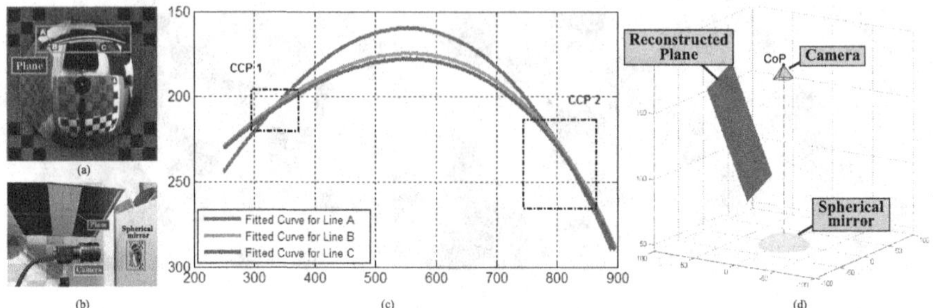

Fig. 10. Line projection in a symmetric catadioptric mirror. Left: We show the line image and the mirror profile; Middle: Located CCPs by curve fitting; Right: Reconstructed plane by using CCPs.

addition to the vanishing points. The 3 fitted curves, however do not exactly intersect at the same CCPs due to errors in curve fitting. We therefore average the estimation as the final detected CCPs. In this example, the two CCPs have pixel coordinate as $[332.5, 207.1]$ and $[809.45, 232.5]$. We map them back to their reflection points on the mirror at $z^* = 33.675$ and finally locate the plane from the two CCPs and z^*. The plane reconstructed is $x + 6.2806y - 3.8944z + 131.14 = 0$, showed in Fig. 10(d).

5 Conclusions and Discussions

We have explored a new type of image features called the coplanar common point or CCP in general non-centric cameras. A CCP corresponds to the intersection of the curved projections of all lines lying on a common 3D plane. We have shown that CCPs generally exist in a broad range of non-centric cameras such as the general linear camera, and the perspective camera is the single exception that do not have CCP. We have further derived the necessary and sufficient conditions for a plane to have CCP in an arbitrary non-centric camera such as non-centric catadioptric mirrors. Our experiments have validated our theories and the detected CCPs can facilitate 3D plane localization tasks, which is crucial to 3D scene reconstruction.

There are several future directions we plan to explore. First, the accuracy of CCP largely depends on curve fitting. Since the curves in catadioptric mirrors are of a high-order, our current solution is to search for the optimal solution from a set of basis functions using a look-up table. In particular, we do not consider the mirror geometry when fitting curves and as a result, it can be sensitive to discretization errors. In the future, we plan to develop tailored curve fitting algorithm by imposing mirror geometry as constraints. In addition, although our caustic-based analysis is applicable to arbitrary catadioptric mirrors, we have by far only studied in depth the cylindrical and rotationally symmetric mirrors. In the future, we will explore efficient testing schemes for general catadioptric mirrors. Finally, we intend to integrate the VP and CCP analysis under a unified geometric framework. Conceptually VPs present directions and CCPs represent positions. A unified representation under projective geometry [11] may sufficiently address both problems via a more elegant model.

Acknowledgements. This project was partially supported by the National Science Foundation under grants IIS-CAREER-0845268 and IIS-1218156.

References

1. Baker, S., Nayar, S.K.: A theory of single-viewpoint catadioptric image formation. IJCV 35(2) (1999)
2. Caglioti, V., Gasparini, S.: "How many planar viewing surfaces are there in noncentral catadioptric cameras?" towards singe-image localization of space lines. In: 2006 IEEE Computer Society Conference on Computer Vision and Pattern Recognition, vol. 1, pp. 1266–1273 (June 2006)
3. Delage, E., Lee, H., Ng, A.Y.: Automatic single-image 3D reconstructions of indoor manhattan world scenes. In: ISRR (2005)
4. Gupta, R., Hartley, R.I.: Linear pushbroom cameras. IEEE TPAMI, 963–975 (1997)
5. Hoiem, D., Efros, A.A., Hebert, M.: Geometric context from a single image. In: ICCV (2005)
6. Hoiem, D., Efros, A.A., Hebert, M.: Automatic photo pop-up. In: ACM SIGGRAPH (2005)
7. Levoy, M., Hanrahan, P.: Light field rendering. In: ACM SIGGRAPH, pp. 31–42 (1996)
8. Meingast, M., Geyer, C., Sastry, S.: Geometric models of rolling-shutter cameras. CoRR (2005)
9. Pajdla, T.: Stereo with oblique cameras. In: IEEE Workshop on Stereo and Multi-Baseline Vision, pp. 85–91 (2001)
10. Pajdla, T.: Geometry of two-slit camera. Rapport Technique CTU-CMP-2002-02, Center for Machine Perception, Czech Technical University, Prague (2002)
11. Ponce, J.: What is a camera? In: The IEEE Conference on Computer Vision and Pattern Recognition (2009)
12. Shum, H.Y., He, L.W.: Rendering with concentric mosaics. In: Proceedings of the 26th Annual Conference on Computer Graphics and Interactive Techniques, pp. 299–306. ACM Press/Addison-Wesley Publishing Co. (1999)
13. Sturm, P., Ramalingam, S., Tardif, J.P., Gasparini, S., Barreto, J.: Camera models and fundamental concepts used in geometric computer vision. Foundations and Trends in Computer Graphics and Vision 6(1-2), 1–183 (2011)
14. Swaminathan, R., Grossberg, M., Nayar, S.: Caustics of Catadioptric Cameras. In: IEEE International Conference on Computer Vision (ICCV), vol. 2, pp. 2–9 (July 2001)
15. Swaminathan, R., Grossberg, M.D., Nayar, S.K.: Non-single viewpoint catadioptric cameras: Geometry and analysis. Int. J. Comput. Vision 66(3), 211–229 (2006)
16. Tom, H.B.: Rendering novel views from a set of omnidirectional mosaic images. In: Proceedings of Omnivis 2003: Workshop on Omnidirectional Vision and Camera Networks. IEEE Press (2003)
17. Ye, J., Ji, Y., Yu, J.: Manhattan scene understanding via xslit imaging. In: CVPR (June 2013)
18. Yu, J., McMillan, L.: Modelling reflections via multiperspective imaging. In: IEEE Computer Society Conference on Computer Vision and Pattern Recognition, CVPR 2005, vol. 1, pp. 117–124 (June 2005)
19. Yu, J., McMillan, L.: General linear cameras. In: Pajdla, T., Matas, J. (eds.) ECCV 2004. LNCS, vol. 3022, pp. 14–27. Springer, Heidelberg (2004)
20. Yu, J., McMillan, L., Sturm, P.: Multiperspective modeling, rendering, and imaging. In: ACM SIGGRAPH ASIA 2008 Courses, pp. 14:1–14:36 (2008)
21. Zomet, A., Feldman, D., Peleg, S., Weinshall, D.: Mosaicing new views: the crossed-slits projection. IEEE TPAMI 25(6), 741–754 (2003)
22. Zomet, A., Feldman, D., Peleg, S., Weinshall, D.: Non-perspective imaging and rendering with the crossed-slits projection. Tech. rep., Leibnitz Center, Hebrew University of Jerusalem (2002)

SRA: Fast Removal of General Multipath for ToF Sensors

Daniel Freedman[1], Yoni Smolin[1], Eyal Krupka[1], Ido Leichter[1], and Mirko Schmidt[2]

[1] Microsoft Research, Haifa, Israel
[2] Microsoft Corporation, Mountain View, CA, USA
{danifree,t-yonis,eyalk,idol,mirko.schmidt}@microsoft.com

Abstract. A major issue with Time of Flight sensors is the presence of multipath interference. We present Sparse Reflections Analysis (SRA), an algorithm for removing this interference which has two main advantages. First, it allows for very general forms of multipath, including interference with three or more paths, diffuse multipath resulting from Lambertian surfaces, and combinations thereof. SRA removes this general multipath with robust techniques based on L_1 optimization. Second, due to a novel dimension reduction, we are able to produce a very fast version of SRA, which is able to run at frame rate. Experimental results on both synthetic data with ground truth, as well as real images of challenging scenes, validate the approach.

1 Introduction

The field of depth sensing has attracted much attention over the last few years. By providing direct access to three-dimensional information, depth sensors make many computer vision tasks considerably easier. Examples include object tracking and recognition, human activity analysis, hand gesture analysis, and indoor 3D mapping; see the comprehensive review in [11].

Amongst depth sensing technologies, Time of Flight (ToF) imaging has recently shown a lot of promise. A phase modulated ToF sensor works by computing the time – measured as a phase-shift – it takes a ray of light to bounce off a surface and return to the sensor. ToF sensors are generally able to achieve very high accuracy, and – since they use light in the infrared spectrum – to operate in low illumination settings.

The main issue with ToF sensors is that they suffer from *multipath interference* (henceforth simply "multipath"). Since rays of light are being sent out for each pixel, and since light can reflect off surfaces in myriad ways, a particular pixel may receive photons originally sent out for other pixels as well. An illustration is given in Figure 2. Significant multipath is observed, for example, in scenes with shiny or specular-like floors.

The key problem is that multipath results in corrupted sensor measurements. These corruptions do not look like ordinary noise, and can be quite large, resulting in highly inaccurate depth estimates; see Figure 1. Removing the effect of multipath is therefore a crucial component for ToF systems.

D. Fleet et al. (Eds.): ECCV 2014, Part I, LNCS 8689, pp. 234–249, 2014.
© Springer International Publishing Switzerland 2014

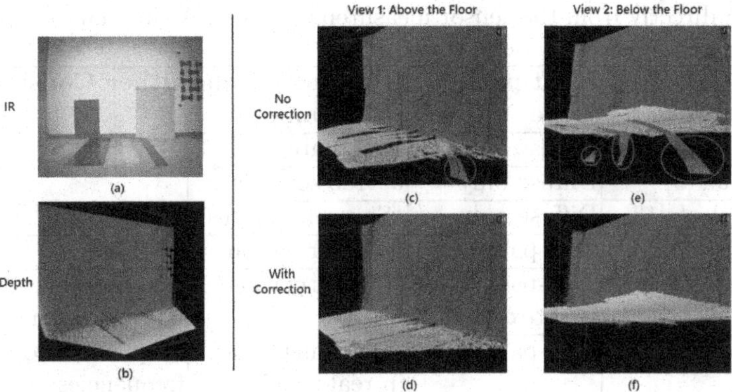

Fig. 1. Effect of Multipath and its Removal. Multipath is caused by specular floor materials. (a) IR image. (b) Depth reconstruction using our proposed SRA algorithm, rendered from a side-on viewpoint; the floor is shown in green, the wall in blue. (c, e) Results of not correcting for multipath, shown from two viewpoints – above and below the floor; gross errors are circled in red. (d, f) Output of our proposed SRA algorithm.

1.1 Contributions

Our work addresses two areas in which we improve on the state-of-the-art:

1. More General Multipath. As we will discuss more explicitly in Section 2, prior work mostly falls into two categories. The first class of algorithms focuses on the case with diffuse multipath, arising from Lambertian surfaces. The second class of algorithms focuses on the case of "two-path" multipath, which arises from specular surfaces.[1] But multipath can often be more general than this: specular multipath with more than two paths is possible, as are combinations of diffuse and specular multipath.

We formalize the problem of general multipath estimation as an L_1 optimization problem; this is the basis for our Sparse Reflections Analysis (SRA) approach. SRA is posed in such a way as to admit the computation of a global optimum, which is crucial for the robust cancellation of general multipath even in the presence of considerable measurement noise.

2. Speed. Prior work targeting diffuse multipath is very slow, typically requiring a few minutes per frame. By contrast, SRA is able to run at frame-rate, i.e. 30 fps. This speed would not be possible with a pure L_1-based approach; we accelerate SRA through the use of a novel dimension reduction which allows for a look-up table based approach. This gives extremely fast performance in practice.

2 Prior Work

Earlier work proposed removing multipath by using additional sensors based on structured light [7,6], while more recent work has attempted to remove the

[1] An exception is the contemporaneous work [1], see Section 2.

multipath directly from the sensor measurement itself. A summary of this more recent work is given in the following table.

Paper	**Multipath Type**	**Running Time Per Frame**	**Other Constraints**
Fuchs [8]	Diffuse only	10 minutes	
Fuchs *et al.* [9]	Diffuse only	60-150 seconds	
Jiménez *et al.* [13]	Diffuse only	"Several minutes"	
Dorrington *et al.* [5]	Two-path only	No information	
Godbaz *et al.* [10]	Two-path only* (see text)	No information	Requires 3 or 4 modulation frequencies
Kirmani *et al.* [15]	Two-path only	"Implementable in real-time"	Requires 5 modulation frequencies

The works of Fuchs [8], Fuchs *et al.* [9], and Jiménez *et al.* [13] all model only diffuse multipath (arising from Lambertian surfaces). [8] estimates the scene by a point cloud and updates the multipath from all pixels to all pixels by ray tracing. A single pass approximation is performed, whose complexity is quadratic in the number of pixels. [9] is a generalization of [8] to a spatially varying, unknown reflection coefficient. It requires an iterative solution consisting of multiple passes. [13] performs a somewhat different iterative optimization of a global function involving scene reconstruction and ray tracing. As is noted in the table, none of these methods are close to real-time, requiring anywhere between 1-10 minutes of processing per frame.

The works of Dorrington *et al.* [5], Godbaz *et al.* [10], and Kirmani *et al.* [15] all model two-path multipath, arising from specular surfaces. All of these methods work on a per pixel basis, using either closed form solutions [10,15] or optimizations [5]. Thus, while they do not report on their running times explicitly, it is reasonable to expect that they may be close to real-time. [15] requires 5 modulation frequencies; one of the two methods presented in [10], which is based on a Cauchy distribution approximation to the backscattering of a single return, requires 4. Several commercial ToF sensors, including the variant of Microsoft's Kinect for Windows beta sensor (henceforth "K4W") on which we perform our experiments, use only 3 modulation frequencies; thus, these methods are rendered impracticable for such sensors. By contrast, the second method presented in [10], which uses a more standard delta-function approximation to a single return, only requires 3 modulation frequencies. Given the additional fact that this method runs in or near real-time, it is therefore our nearest competitor.

We also note the extremely recent work of Bhandari *et al.* [1], whose publication was simultaneous with our submission to ECCV, and which we became aware of after submission. The formulation of the problem in [1] is quite similar to the formulation proposed in this paper; however, the solution is different. This is due to a crucial difference in the setups: while we assume 3 modulation frequencies, [1] assumes an extremely large number of modulation frequencies – 77, in fact. Such a massively large number of frequencies is infeasible in many scenarios of interest: for example, in dynamic scenes with fast movement, especially if there is high pixel resolution. [1] reports an integration time of 47 ms for an image with 19,200 pixels; this means that purely based on integration time – i.e., even if the depth computation is instantaneous – the frame-rate would top out at 20 fps, and this on a very small image. By contrast, in our case the K4W integration time is 10 ms for 217,088 pixels – that is, the integration time is nearly 5 times smaller for 11 times as many pixels. This is possible because only 3 modulation frequencies are used. (We note that all of the competing methods except for [1] use between 2 and 5 modulation frequencies, for related reasons.)

Given the use of 77 modulation frequencies, [1] successfully solves for a sparse solution through a greedy approach, Orthogonal Matching Pursuit (OMP). When restricting to a small number of modulation frequencies – 3, rather than 77 – we found that a greedy optimization approach based on OMP is not effective. Instead, our method is based on an L_1-style global optimization, which works considerably better in practice. The drawback of L_1 is that it tends to be slow, which is why our novel LUT-based approach is crucial; it allows us to both gain from the accuracy of L_1, while not suffering from its speed disadvantage.

Finally, we note [14] and [12], which use related signal representations.

3 Sparse Reflections Analysis

3.1 The Multipath Representation

The ToF Measurement. We begin by describing the vector which is measured by a ToF sensor. For a given pixel, the sensor emits infra-red (IR) light modulated by several frequencies. The light bounces off a surface in the scene, and some of the light (depending on the reflectivity and orientation of the surface) is returned to the detector. For each of m modulation frequencies, this light is then integrated against sinusoids with the same frequency, such that the phase of the measurement v is based on the distance to the surface:

$$v \in \mathbb{C}^m, \text{ with } v_k = xe^{2\pi id/\lambda_k}, \quad k = 1, \ldots, m \tag{1}$$

where d is the distance to the surface, $\lambda_k = c/2f_k$ is half of the wavelength corresponding to the kth modulation frequency f_k, and x is a real scalar corresponding to the strength of the signal received. A typical choice for the number of frequencies is $m = 3$; this is generally sufficient to prevent aliasing effects.

Multipath. Equation (1) assumes that there is no multipath in the scene. If there is single extra path (the "two-path" scenario), as shown in Figure 2(a), then the above equation is modified to

$$v_k = x_1 e^{2\pi id_1/\lambda_k} + x_2 e^{2\pi id_2/\lambda_k} \tag{2}$$

where d_1 and d_2 are the distances of the two paths, and x_1 and x_2 give the strengths of the two paths. If $d_1 < d_2$, then d_1 is the true distance and d_2 is the multipath component; and the ratio x_2/x_1 gives the strength of the multipath.

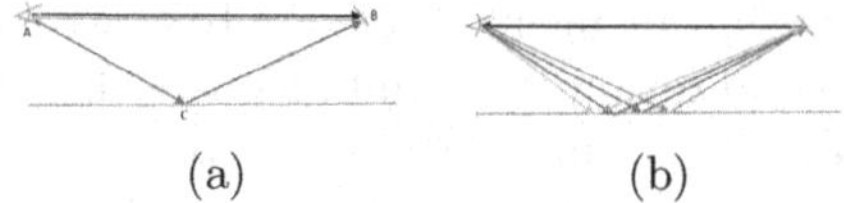

(a) (b)

Fig. 2. Illustration of Multipath. (a) Two-Path Multipath. The camera (A) and surface (B) are shown in blue, and light rays in other colours. The correct path is A-B-A; the second, incorrect path is A-C-B-A. (b) Diffuse Multipath. This results from small reflections from many nearby points, shown illustratively as four colored paths.

Of course, one can have more general multipath, including: three or more paths; diffuse plus two-path; and so on. Equation (2) generalizes naturally as

$$v_k = \sum_{j=1}^{n} x_j e^{2\pi i d_j/\lambda_k} \tag{3}$$

where d_j is over the relevant interval. In typical examples, we take the range of object distances to be 20 cm to 450 cm, with increments of 1 cm. Thus, in this case $n = 431$. The vector x is referred to as the **backscattering**.

Equation (3) includes the case of diffuse multipath. An ideal Lambertian surface receives light from a given direction, and reflects infinitesimal amounts in all directions. In fact, an infinite number of nearby points on the surface reflect infinitesimal amounts, and the result is finite. This is shown in Figure 2(b). Diffuse multipath typically has the form $v_k = x_\ell e^{2\pi i d_\ell/\lambda_k} + \sum_{j=\ell+\Delta}^{n} x_L(d_{j-\Delta}) e^{2\pi i d_j/\lambda_k}$ for some $\Delta \geq 0$. The shape of $x_L(\cdot)$ can be determined by looking at simulations of diffuse multipath, and turns out to be well approximated by $x_L(d) \approx A d^\alpha e^{-\beta d}$, where α and β depend on the geometry of the underlying scene.

We can rewrite Equation (3) in vector-matrix form as $v = \Phi x$, where $\Phi \in \mathbb{C}^{m \times n}$ and $x \in \mathbb{R}^n$. We further turn complex measurements into real ones, by stacking the real part on top of the imaginary part, and abuse notation by denoting the $2m$-dimensional result also as v. We do the same with Φ, yielding

$$\Phi \in \mathbb{R}^{2n \times m}, \quad \text{with} \quad \Phi_{kj} = \begin{cases} \cos(2\pi d_j/\lambda_k) & \text{if } k = 1, \ldots, m \\ \sin(2\pi d_j/\lambda_{k-m}) & \text{if } k = m+1, \ldots, 2m \end{cases}$$

Then we may still write

$$v = \Phi x \tag{4}$$

but now all quantities are real.

A Characterization of the Backscattering. Let us now characterize the class of backscatterings x which capture the multipath phenomenon.

Property 1: Non-Negativity The first property is that x is non-negative: $x \geq 0$. That is, there can only be positive or zero returns for any given distance.

Property 2: Compressibility The second property is more interesting. We saw that the two-path scenario involved an x which was zero at all indices except for two (corresponding to d_1 and d_2 in Equation (2)). Such an x is sparse.

On the other hand, the diffuse multipath, which has the form $x_L(d) \approx Ad^{\alpha}e^{-\beta d}$, is not sparse. Rather, its discretized version has the following property: when the x coefficients are sorted from greatest to smallest, the resulting vector falls off quickly to 0. This property is referred to as compressibility.

Formally, given a vector $x = (x_1, \ldots, x_n)$, let $(x_{I(1)}, \ldots, x_{I(n)})$ denote the vector sorted in descending order. Then x is compressible if $x_{I(i)} \leq Ri^{-1/r}$ with $r \leq 1$. That is, the sorted entries of x fall off as a power law.

3.2 The SRA Algorithm

We have represented multipath via the backscattering x, and have further characterized the important properties of the backscattering – non-negativity and compressibility. We now go on to show how to use this information to cancel the effects of multipath, and hence find a robust and accurate depth estimate from the raw ToF measured vector.

Multiplicity of Solutions. We are given v, and we know that a backscattering x has generated v; i.e. following Equation (4), we have $v = \Phi x$. Given that $x \in \mathbb{R}^n$ and $v \in \mathbb{R}^{2m}$ where $n \gg 2m$, there are many possible x's which can generate v. But our characterization of the backscattering says that x is non-negative and compressible, which leads to a much more restrictive set of possible backscatterings.

In fact, due to sensor noise we will not have $v = \Phi x$ exactly. Rather, we may expect that $v = \Phi x + \eta$, where η is generally taken to be Gaussian noise, with zero mean and known covariance matrix C.[2]

L_0 Minimization. Let us suppose, for the moment, that x is *sparse* rather than compressible – that is, x has a small number of non-zero entries. The number of non-zero entries of x is often denoted as it's 0-norm, i.e. $\|x\|_0$. In this case, one would like to solve the following problem:

$$\min_{x \geq 0} \|x\|_0 \quad \text{subject to} \quad (\Phi x - v)^T C^{-1} (\Phi x - v) \leq \epsilon^2 \|v\|^2 \tag{5}$$

for some parameter ϵ, which we fix to be 0.05 in our experiments. (Note that we have indicated the non-negativity of x under the min itself.) That is, we want the sparsest backscattering x which yields the measurement vector v, up to some noise tolerance. Unfortunately, the above problem, which is combinatorial in nature, is NP-hard to solve.

L_1 Minimization. However, it turns out that subject to certain conditions on the matrix Φ, solving the problem

$$\min_{x \geq 0} \|x\|_1 \quad \text{subject to} \quad (\Phi x - v)^T C^{-1} (\Phi x - v) \leq \epsilon^2 \|v\|^2 \tag{6}$$

will yield a similar solution [3,2,4] to the optimization in (5). Note that the only difference between the two optimizations is that we have replaced the 0-norm

---

[2] Due to the physics of the sensor, there is often a shot noise component involved. We will ignore this consideration, though our method can be adapted to handle it.

with the 1-norm. The key implication is that the optimization in (6) is *convex*, and hence may be solved in polynomial time.

In fact, the conditions mentioned in [3,2,4], such as the Restricted Isometry Property, are generally not satisfied by our matrix Φ. This is due to the redundancy present in nearby columns of Φ, i.e. nearby columns tend to have high inner products with each other. Nevertheless, we can use the optimization in (6), with the understanding that certain theoretical guarantees given in [3,2,4] do not hold. Note that this is in the same vein as other computer vision work, such as the celebrated paper by Wright *et al.* on robust face recognition [16], which used L_1 optimization under conditions which differed from those specified in [3,2,4].

Until now we have been assuming that x is sparse, rather than compressible. It turns out, however, that even if x is compressible and not sparse, then solving the L_1 optimization in (6) still yields the correct solution [3,2,4].

L_1 with L_1 Constraints. Although the optimization (6) is convex, it is a second-order cone program which can be slow to solve in practice. We therefore make the following modification. Note that the L_2 constraint above may be written $\|C^{-1/2}(\Phi x - v)\|_2 \leq \epsilon \|v\|_2$. We may consider approximating these constraints by their equivalent L_1 constraints, i.e. $\|C^{-1/2}(\Phi x - v)\|_1 \leq \epsilon \|v\|_1$. In this case, the resulting optimization becomes

$$\min_{x \geq 0} \|x\|_1 \quad \text{subject to} \quad \|C^{-1/2}(\Phi x - v)\|_1 \leq \epsilon \|v\|_1 \tag{7}$$

The advantage of this formulation over (6) is that it can be recast as a linear program. As such, it can be solved considerably faster. To perform the conversion, first notice that since $x \geq 0$, $\|x\|_1 = \sum_{i=1}^{n} x_i = \mathbf{1}^T x$. Second, note that the constraint $\|z\|_1 \leq \gamma$ for $z \in \mathbb{R}^\ell$ can be converted into the set of linear constraints $Q_\ell z \leq \gamma \mathbf{1}$, where Q_ℓ is a $2^\ell \times \ell$ matrix, whose rows consist of all elements of the set $\{-1, +1\}^\ell$. While this might be prohibitive for ℓ large, in our case $\ell = 2m$, and we generally have $m = 3$; this leads to 64 extra constraints, much fewer than the number of non-negativity constraints. This yields the linear program

$$\min_{x \geq 0} \mathbf{1}^T x \quad \text{subject to} \quad Ax \leq b$$

where $A = Q_{2m} C^{-1/2} \Phi$ and $b = Q_{2m} C^{-1/2} v + \epsilon \|v\|_1 \mathbf{1}$.

Computing Depth from Backscattering. The various optimization problems we have just described yield the backscattering x. Of course, in the end our goal is an estimate of the depth; we now explain how to extract the depth from x.

The main path must have the shortest distance; this results from the geometry of the imaging process. Thus, we have simply that the depth corresponds to the first non-zero index of x, i.e. the index $i_1(x) \equiv \arg\min_i \{i : x_i > 0\}$. Then the depth is just $\delta = d_{i_1(x)}$. In practice, due to numerical issues there will be many small non-zero elements of x. Thus, we take $i_1(x) \equiv \arg\min_i \{i : x_i > c \max_{i'} x_{i'}\}$ for some small c; typically, we use $c = 0.01$.

If we have a reasonably accurate noise model, we can be more sophisticated. For each peak of the backscattering x, we can compute the probability that the peak is generated by noise rather than signal. Then the probability that the first peak is the true return is just one minus the probability that it is generated by noise; the probability that the second peak is the true return is the probability that the first peak is generated by noise times one minus the probability that the second peak is generated by noise; and so on. If no return has probability greater than a threshold (e.g. 0.9), we can "invalidate" the pixel – that is, declare that we do not know the true depth. We will make use of this kind of invalidation in Section 5.

4 Fast Computation

SRA allows us to compute the backscattering x from a sensor measurement v; from the backscattering, one can compute the depth. The issue that now arises is related to the speed of the computation. Solving the optimization in (7) typically requires about 50 milliseconds per instance on a standard CPU. Given that a ToF image may consist of several hundred thousand pixels, this yields on the order at least an hour per frame. To achieve a frame rate of 30 Hz, therefore, a radically different approach is needed. The method we now describe allows for SRA to run at frame rate on ordinary hardware, for images of size 424×512.

Dimension Reduction: Motivation. Real-time computation is often aided by performing pre-computation in the form of a look-up table (LUT). If we construct a LUT directly on the measurement vector v, then the table will be $2m$-dimensional, as this is the dimensionality of v. It is easy to see that multiplying v by a scalar does not change the results of any of the SRA optimizations, except to scale x by the same scalar. Thus, one can easily normalize v so that its L_2 norm (or L_1 norm) is equal to 1, yielding a reduction of a single dimension. The resulting table will then be $(2m-1)$-dimensional.

Our goal is a further reduction of a single dimension, to $(2m-2)$ dimensions. Recall that the size of an LUT is *exponential* in its dimension; thus, the reduction of two dimensions reduces the total memory for the LUT by a factor of L^2, where each dimension has been discretized into L cells. This reduction makes the LUT approach feasible in practice.

A Useful Transformation. Let us return to the complex formulation of the problem; this will make the ensuing discussion easier, though it is not strictly necessary. Let us define the $m \times m$ complex matrix $F_{s,\Delta}$ by

$$F_{s,\Delta} = s \cdot \text{diag}(e^{-2\pi i \Delta/\lambda_1}, \ldots, e^{-2\pi i \Delta/\lambda_m})$$

where $\Delta \in \mathbb{R}$; $s > 0$ is any real positive scalar; and diag() denotes the diagonal matrix with the specified elements on the diagonal. Then we have the following theorem, from which we can derive our dimension reduction.

Theorem 1. *Let x^* be the solution to the optimization (6), and let $x^*_{s,\Delta}$ be the solution to (6) with $F_{s,\Delta}v$ replacing v and $F_{s,\Delta}\Phi$ replacing Φ. Suppose that the covariance C is diagonal, and satisfies $C_{jj} = C_{j+m,j+m}$. Then $x^*_{s,\Delta} = x^*$.*

The proof is included in the supplementary material. The implication of Theorem 1 is that multiplying both the measurement v and the matrix Φ by the matrix $F_{s,\Delta}$ does not change the backscattering (assuming the theorem's conditions on the covariance matrix hold, which is a reasonable model of sensor noise). Of course, the corresponding range of distances has been shifted by by $-\Delta$, so in extracting the depth from $x^*_{s,\Delta}$, one must add on Δ afterwards.

Before going on, we note that Theorem 1 applies to optimization (6) rather than (7), which we use in practice. However, as (7) is a reasonable approximation to (6), we proceed to use Theorem 1 to construct our dimension reduction.

The Canonical Transformation. The Canonical Transformation is derived from $F_{s,\Delta}$ by a particular choice of s and Δ. Let $k \in \{1, \ldots, m\}$ be a specific frequency index; then Canonical Transformation of v, $\rho^{(k)}(v)$, is given by

$$\rho^{(k)}(v) \equiv F_{s,\Delta} v \quad \text{with} \quad s = \|v\|^{-1}, \ \Delta = \lambda_k (\angle v_k / 2\pi)$$

where $\angle v_k$ denotes the phase of v_k, taken to lie in $[0, 2\pi)$. It is easy to see that $\rho^{(k)}$ has the following property. The kth element of $\rho^{(k)}(v)$ is real, i.e. has 0 phase. Furthermore, the kth element of $\rho^{(k)}(v)$ may be found from the other elements of $\rho^{(k)}(v)$ by $\rho^{(k)}_k(v) = \left(1 - \sum_{k' \neq k} |\rho^{(k)}_{k'}(v)|^2\right)^{1/2}$.

In other words, in the Canonical Transformation, one of the elements is *redundant*, in that it is completely determined by the other elements. Hence, this element can be removed without losing information. Of course, the component is complex, meaning that we have removed two real dimensions, hence enabling the promised dimension reduction from $2m$ to $2m - 2$. A LUT can be built on the remaining $2m - 2$ dimensions, simply by discretizing over these dimensions.

Note that having transformed v by $F_{s,\Delta}$ (with s and Δ given by the Canonical Transformation), we must also apply $F_{s,\Delta}$ to Φ in order to use Theorem 1. In fact, this is straightforward: this transformation simply "shifts" the columns of Φ. So if before they represented distances in the range $[D_{min}, D_{max}]$, they now represent distances in the range $[D_{min} - \Delta, D_{max} - \Delta]$. Rather than actually do the shifting, we simply enlarge this range. Note that the minimal value that Δ can take on is 0, while the maximal value is λ_k; thus, after the Canonical Transformation the potential distances can now fall between $D_{min} - \lambda_k$ and D_{max}. Thus, the matrix Φ is now enlarged to have columns corresponding to distances in the range $[D_{min} - \lambda_k, D_{max}]$. A natural method for choosing k is to keep the above range as small as possible, and hence to choose the k corresponding to the smallest half-wavelength λ_k.

5 Experiments

5.1 Running Time

As one of the main claims of this paper is a fast algorithm, we begin by presenting the speed of the algorithm. We have benchmarked SRA on images of size 424 × 512, which are the standard for Microsoft's Kinect for Windows beta sensor ("K4W"). The code is run on an Intel Core i7 processor, with 4 cores, 8 logical processors, and a clockspeed of 2.4 GHz. The code runs in 31.2 milliseconds per

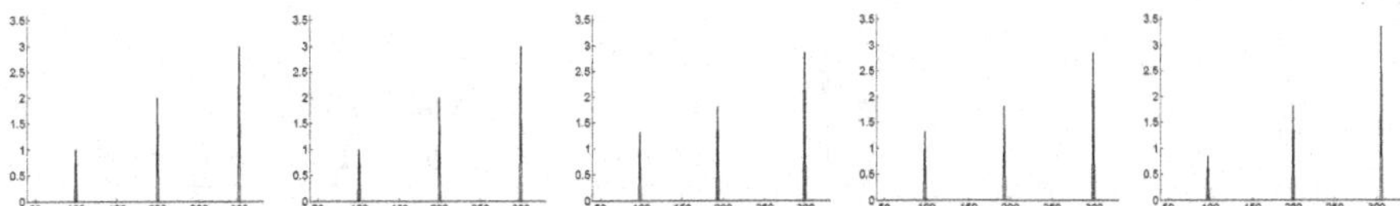

Fig. 3. Three-Path Simulation. Left: true backscattering. Following 4 plots: SRA reconstruction of the backscattering, for SNR= $\infty, 20, 10, 5$. See discussion in the text.

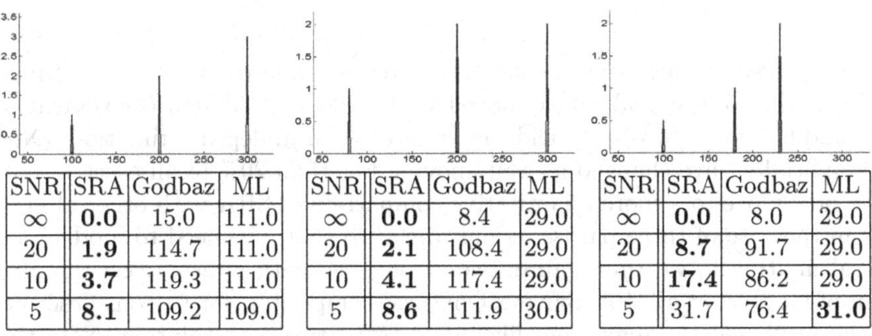

SNR	SRA	Godbaz	ML
∞	**0.0**	15.0	111.0
20	**1.9**	114.7	111.0
10	**3.7**	119.3	111.0
5	**8.1**	109.2	109.0

SNR	SRA	Godbaz	ML
∞	**0.0**	8.4	29.0
20	**2.1**	108.4	29.0
10	**4.1**	117.4	29.0
5	**8.6**	111.9	30.0

SNR	SRA	Godbaz	ML
∞	**0.0**	8.0	29.0
20	**8.7**	91.7	29.0
10	**17.4**	86.2	29.0
5	31.7	76.4	**31.0**

Fig. 4. Three-Path Simulation. Each column shows the true backscattering (top), and the median absolute error in cm of three algorithms under various noise levels (bottom). The best algorithm is indicated in bold. See discussion in the text.

frame, which is real-time given a frame-rate of 30 fps. Note that our code is largely unoptimized Matlab (the only optimization we make is to use the CPU's 8 logical processors for parallelization); the speed comes from the LUT-based approach. It is to be expected that optimized C code would be even faster.

5.2 General Multipath: Examples

Specular Three Path. We begin by motivating the relevance of general multipath. Specular multipath with three or more paths results naturally from simple scene geometries. Suppose that we have the geometry shown in Figure 2(a), where the object (B) lies on a Lambertian surface and the scene element (C) is taken to be purely specular. Then it can be shown that by varying the position and normal of the scene element, we can generate any relative amplitudes we wish between the direct (A-B-A) and interfering (A-C-B-A) paths, as well as any pair of path distances; please see the supplementary material for more details. Generating three (or more) paths then becomes straightforward, by adding an extra (or multiple extra) specular surfaces to the scene.

Figure 3 shows an example of three path specular interference. The leftmost plot shows the true backscattering, corresponding to object distances of 100, 200, and 300 cm, with amplitudes in the ratio 1:2:3. That is, the multipath is $2 + 3 = 5$ times stronger than the initial return. Moving from left to right, the following four plots show the backscattering computed by the SRA algorithm under different levels of noise: SNR= $\infty, 20, 10, 5$. Note that the backscattering extracted is exactly correct for the case of SNR= ∞, and remains fairly close to

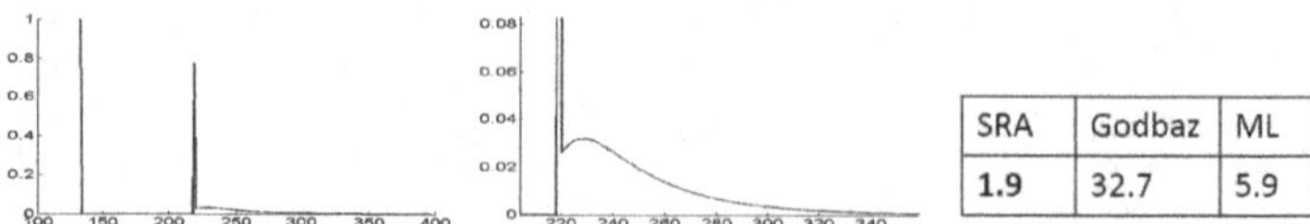

SRA	Godbaz	ML
1.9	32.7	5.9

Fig. 5. Combined Diffuse and Specular Multipath. Left: true backscattering. Middle: detail of the backscattering, showing the diffuse part. Right: Absolute error in cm.

the true backscattering as the noise level increases. Indeed, for the highest noise level of SNR= 5, the peaks have moved to 97, 200, and 306 cm (movements of -3, 0, and 6 cm resp.), which yields an error of 3 cm in depth estimation. (Note the amplitudes have changed as well, moving less than 20% in all cases.)

We now move to a more quantitative comparison of SRA with other alternatives in the case of three paths. As our aim is to show the need to model more general multipath, we run against two strong two-path alternatives: the algorithm of Godbaz *et al.* [10] (our most natural competitor, for reasons described in Section 2) and the maximum likelihood (ML) two-path solution. Note that the ML solution is not a practical algorithm, as it requires a slow, exhaustive examination of all pairs of paths; but we include it as it represents the best possible two path solution. Figure 4 shows three separate configurations; the top row shows the true backscatterings, while the tables below show the performance of SRA vs. the two alternatives. The performance is given by the median absolute error of the depth; as we are adding noise, we average over 1,000 samples.

We note that SRA outperforms the two alternatives, and does so by a wide margin once even a small amount of noise is added. In the first example, the accuracies of SRA are very high, staying under 4 cm for SNR levels up to 10; the second example is similar. The third case has been chosen to be more difficult for SRA: the multipath is 6 times stronger than the original path, and the second and third returns are fairly closely spaced. SRA's errors here are higher, though still considerably lower than the alternatives (except in the case of SNR = 5, where performance is similar to ML). In all three cases, Godbaz gives reasonable results in the noiseless case, but fails once even a small amount of noise (SNR = 20) is added. ML is much more resistant to noise, but does not give very high accuracy in any of the examples, regardless of noise level.

Combined Diffuse and Specular Multipath. We now show an example which leads to a combination of diffuse and specular multipath. The geometry is again simple, and consists of an object and a single plane; both object and plane have both specular and diffuse reflectivity. The backscattering, which we generate by use of our own light-transport simulator, is shown in Figure 5; note the fact that the backscattering is no longer sparse (but is still compressible).

The depth estimate errors are shown in Figure 5. The method of Godbaz generates fairly large errors. ML is considerably better: it turns out that there is a reasonably good two path approximation to the measurement v produced by this backscattering. SRA produces the lowest error: not surprisingly, allowing for a more complex backscattering – as SRA does – leads to the best result.

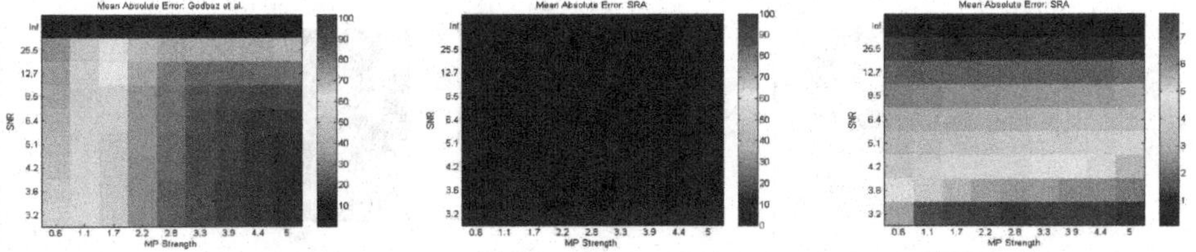

Fig. 6. Two-Path Simulation: Mean Absolute Error (cm). Left: Godbaz. Middle: SRA, with the same scale as Godbaz, i.e. [0, 100] . Right: SRA, with errors rescaled to [0,8].

5.3 Comprehensive Two-Path Evaluation

Setup. We have shown the ability of SRA to deal with general multipath. However, standard two-path interference is a very important case, and we would like to show SRA's capabilities in this regime. We challenge SRA in two ways: by simulating high multipath, up to a factor of 5 times as high as the direct return; and by simulating high noise regimes. We again compare against Godbaz *et al.* [10], our most natural competitor (for reasons described in Section 2).

In particular, we simulate returns of the form $v_k = x_1 e^{2\pi i d_1/\lambda_k} + x_2 e^{2\pi i d_2/\lambda_k} + \eta_k$; the noise η_k has independent real and imaginary components, and is taken to be Gaussian with variance σ^2 for each component. There are two critical parameters: (1) Multipath Strength is defined as x_2/x_1, and takes on values in the set $\{0.6, 1.1, 1.7, 2.2, 2.8, 3.3, 3.9. 4.4, 5.0\}$. (2) SNR is defined as $x_1/\sqrt{6}\sigma$, since there are 6 independent noise components to the measurement. It takes on values in the set $\{\infty, 25.5, 12.7, 8.5, 6.4, 5.1, 4.2, 3.6, 3.2\}$.

We also allow d_1 to vary over values between 20 cm and 380 cm, and the return separation $d_2 - d_1$ to vary between 40 cm and 250 cm; and each instance is generated with many noise vectors. In total, we generate 261,000 examples.

We visualize the results in Figure 6, in which we show the mean absolute error (MAE) of the depth estimates as a function of multipath strength and SNR. Each square corresponds to a (multipath strength, SNR) pair; we average over all examples falling into the square to compute the MAE.

Discussion. In general, SRA's behavior is as we would imagine: as multipath strength increases, MAE increases; likewise, as SNR decreases, MAE increases.

There are two notable facts about the results. First, the MAE is quite small for "realistic" values of multipath strength and SNR. Focus on the upper left rectangle of Figure 6 consisting of SNRs from ∞ to 8.5 and multipath strengths from 0.6 to 2.2; note that these are still quite challenging values. In this regime, the MAE is low: it is less than 2.6 cm in all squares, with an average of 1.4 cm.

Second, SRA's performance degrades in a graceful way: the MAE increases gradually in both dimensions. In fact, even when the multipath is 5 times stronger than the true return and the SNR has a low value of 3.2, the MAE is 7.9 cm, which is a very reasonable error in such circumstances.

It is interesting to compare SRA's MAE with that of Godbaz *et al.* [10], recalling that Godbaz's algorithm was designed with two-path multipath in mind.

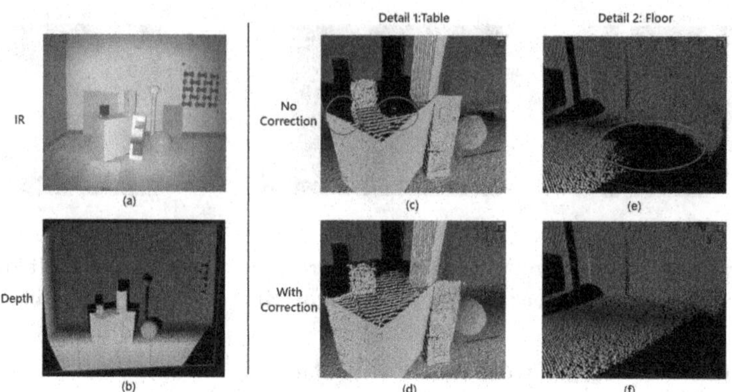

Fig. 7. "Geometric". (a) IR image. (b) SRA depth estimate. (c,e) Optimal depth estimates without multipath correction; errors are circled in red. (d,f) SRA depth.

Godbaz gives good results when there is no noise: the MAE is nearly 0. Once even a small amount of noise is added in, however, Godbaz's performance drops significantly. For example, with SNR = 25.5, the errors range from 30.8 cm (MP Strength = 0.6) to 69.7 cm (MP Strength = 5). Performance worsens significantly as SNR decreases.

5.4 Real Images

We now discuss the results of running SRA on three different challenging images. The images are collected using a variant of the K4W sensor, which has $m = 3$ modulation frequencies – 15, 80, and 120 MHz – and a resolution of 424×512. The images have been placed in the publicly available repository `http://research.microsoft.com/sparsereflections/`; researchers should also be able to acquire similar images on their own, using the K4W sensor.

Unfortunately, we are not able to compare with any of the real-time competing methods due to their incompatibility with the K4W imaging setup. Specifically, Godbaz *et al.* [10] and Dorrington *et al.* [5] require a very particular relation between the modulation frequencies, which is not satisfied by K4W's modulation frequencies. Kirmani *et al.* [15] requires 5 modulation frequencies, while a second method described in [10] requires 4; K4W uses only 3 modulation frequencies. Thus, for comparison purposes in this section, we run SRA against a variant of SRA which looks for the optimal single path which best describes the sensor measurement, which we call "Opt-Single".

"Strips" Image. See Figure 1. This image is a simple scene – a floor and a wall; however, the floor is composed of strips of different materials, each of which has different reflectance properties. This can be seen clearly in the IR image in Figure 1.

The more specular materials tend to lead to very high multipath: a path which bounces off the wall, and from there to the floor, will generally have strength higher than the direct return from the floor. This is due to the fact that the direct path is nearly parallel to the floor, leading to a weak direct return.

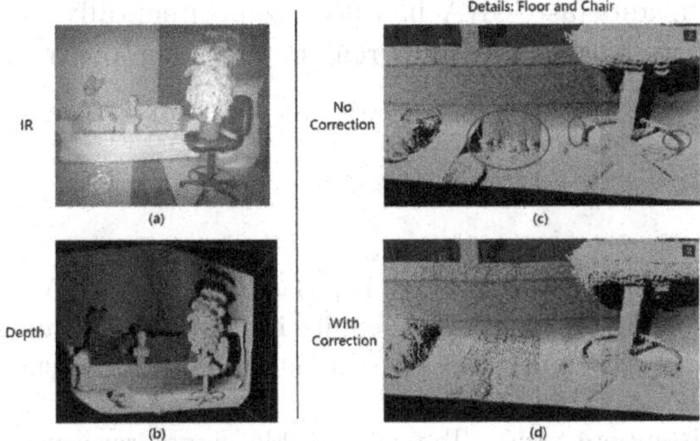

Fig. 8. "Living Room". (a) IR image. (b) SRA depth estimate. (c) Optimal depth estimate without multipath correction; errors are circled in red. (d) SRA depth estimate.

Results of the depth reconstruction are shown in Figure 1. To see the effect of multipath removal, we compare SRA's depth estimate to Opt-Single. In Figure 1, one can see details of the scene which show the effect of "specular floor" multipath: the wall is effectively reflected into the floor, leading to grossly inaccurate estimates for the floor. By contrast, SRA reconstructs a very clean floor, which is seen to be almost completely flat, the exceptions being a few small depressions of less than 4 cm.

Note in Figure 1 that SRA invalidates a number of pixels at the top right part of the image, corresponding to a patterned wall-hanging; this is due to the low reflectivity of this part of the scene, leading to very noisy measurements.

"Geometric" Image. See Figure 7. This image consists of a similar set-up to "Strips", but with various geometric objects inserted. These objects include many sharp angles, as well as several thin structures. SRA reconstructs the scene quite well, see Figure 7. Again, note the scene details in Figure 7, which show the performance of SRA vs. Opt-Single. Much of the surface of the rectangular table is lost without accounting for multipath, whereas SRA is able to reconstruct it. And the corner where the wall joins the floor is lost – actually reflected into the floor – without accounting for multipath, whereas SRA recovers it.

"Living Room" Image. See Figure 8. This image consists of a couch as well as a number of objects inserted. As in "Strips", there is a strip of reflective material on the floor; Opt-Single has trouble accounting for this strip, as can be seen in Figure 8. Perhaps more interestingly, the thin structure which is the wheel at the base of the swivel chair is largely reconstructed by SRA, whereas large portions of it, on both the right and left sides, are lost by Opt-Single.

6 Conclusions

We have presented the SRA algorithm for removing multipath interference from ToF images. We have seen that the method is both general, dealing with many types of multipath, and fast. SRA has been experimentally validated on both synthetic data as well as challenging real images, demonstrating its superior performance.

References

1. Bhandari, A., Kadambi, A., Whyte, R., Barsi, C., Feigin, M., Dorrington, A., Raskar, R.: Resolving multipath interference in time-of-flight imaging via modulation frequency diversity and sparse regularization. Optics Letters 39(6), 1705–1708 (2014)
2. Candes, E.J., Romberg, J.K., Tao, T.: Stable signal recovery from incomplete and inaccurate measurements. Communications on Pure and Applied Mathematics 59(8), 1207–1223 (2006)
3. Candes, E.J., Tao, T.: Decoding by linear programming. IEEE Transactions on Information Theory 51(12), 4203–4215 (2005)
4. Donoho, D.L.: Compressed sensing. IEEE Transactions on Information Theory 52(4), 1289–1306 (2006)
5. Dorrington, A.A., Godbaz, J.P., Cree, M.J., Payne, A.D., Streeter, L.V.: Separating true range measurements from multi-path and scattering interference in commercial range cameras. In: IS&T/SPIE Electronic Imaging, pp. 786404. International Society for Optics and Photonics (2011)
6. Falie, D., Buzuloiu, V.: Further investigations on ToF cameras distance errors and their corrections. In: European Conference on Circuits and Systems for Communications (ECCSC), pp. 197–200 (2008)
7. Falie, D., Buzuloiu, V.: Distance errors correction for the time of flight (ToF) cameras. In: IEEE International Workshop on Imaging Systems and Techniques, IST 2008, pp. 123–126. IEEE (2008)
8. Fuchs, S.: Multipath interference compensation in time-of-flight camera images. In: International Conference on Pattern Recognition (ICPR), pp. 3583–3586 (2010)
9. Fuchs, S., Suppa, M., Hellwich, O.: Compensation for multipath in ToF camera measurements supported by photometric calibration and environment integration. In: Chen, M., Leibe, B., Neumann, B. (eds.) ICVS 2013. LNCS, vol. 7963, pp. 31–41. Springer, Heidelberg (2013)
10. Godbaz, J.P., Cree, M.J., Dorrington, A.A.: Closed-form inverses for the mixed pixel/multipath interference problem in amcw lidar. In: IS&T/SPIE Electronic Imaging, pp. 829618. International Society for Optics and Photonics (2012)
11. Han, J., Shao, L., Xu, D., Shotton, J.: Enhanced computer vision with Microsoft Kinect sensor: A review. IEEE Transactions on Cybernetics 43(5), 1318–1334 (2013)
12. Heide, F., Hullin, M.B., Gregson, J., Heidrich, W.: Low-budget transient imaging using photonic mixer devices. ACM Transactions on Graphics (TOG) 32(4), 45 (2013)
13. Jiménez, D., Pizarro, D., Mazo, M., Palazuelos, S.: Modelling and correction of multipath interference in time of flight cameras. In: IEEE Conference on Computer Vision and Pattern Recognition (CVPR), pp. 893–900 (2012)

14. Kadambi, A., Whyte, R., Bhandari, A., Streeter, L., Barsi, C., Dorrington, A., Raskar, R.: Coded time of flight cameras: sparse deconvolution to address multipath interference and recover time profiles. ACM Transactions on Graphics (TOG) 32(6), 167 (2013)
15. Kirmani, A., Benedetti, A., Chou, P.A.: Spumic: Simultaneous phase unwrapping and multipath interference cancellation in time-of-flight cameras using spectral methods. In: IEEE International Conference on Multimedia and Expo (ICME), pp. 1–6 (2013)
16. Wright, J., Yang, A.Y., Ganesh, A., Sastry, S.S., Ma, Y.: Robust face recognition via sparse representation. IEEE Transactions on Pattern Analysis and Machine Intelligence 31(2), 210–227 (2009)

Sub-pixel Layout for Super-Resolution with Images in the Octic Group

Boxin Shi[1,2], Hang Zhao[1], Moshe Ben-Ezra[1], Sai-Kit Yeung[2], Christy Fernandez-Cull[3], R. Hamilton Shepard[3], Christopher Barsi[1], and Ramesh Raskar[1]

[1] MIT Media Lab, Cambridge, MA, USA
[2] Singapore University of Technology and Design, Singapore
[3] MIT Lincoln Lab, Lexington, MA, USA

Abstract. This paper presents a novel super-resolution framework by exploring the properties of non-conventional pixel layouts and shapes. We show that recording multiple images, transformed in the octic group, with a sensor of asymmetric sub-pixel layout increases the spatial sampling compared to a conventional sensor with a rectilinear grid of pixels and hence increases the image resolution. We further prove a theoretical bound for achieving well-posed super-resolution with a designated magnification factor w.r.t. the number and distribution of sub-pixels. We also propose strategies for selecting good sub-pixel layouts and effective super-resolution algorithms for our setup. The experimental results validate the proposed theory and solution, which have the potential to guide the future CCD layout design with super-resolution functionality.

Keywords: Super-resolution, CCD sensor, Sub-pixel layout, Octic group.

1 Introduction

High-resolution imaging is a goal commonly desired for many applications in computer vision. To overcome the upper limit of spatial frequency, determined by the interval between sampling points of the sensor, super-resolution (SR) can be performed by taking multiple frames with sub-pixel displacements of the same scene. However, even with a large number of images under sufficiently small-step displacements, the performance of SR algorithms can hardly extend beyond small magnification factors of 2 to 4 [1,12], partially due to the challenges associated with proper alignment of local patches with finer translations [19].

We note here that the geometry of the pixels usually has been assumed to lie on a rectangular grid. This geometric restriction limits the information captured for each sub-pixel shift, because repeating the observations at integer pixel intervals are redundant. An aperiodic pixel layout [2] or a random disturbance to pixel shapes [17] could break the theoretical bottleneck of conventional SR by effectively avoiding the redundancy due to translational symmetry. These structures provide greater variation with sub-pixel displacements to result in more independent equations for recovering high-frequency spatial information.

D. Fleet et al. (Eds.): ECCV 2014, Part I, LNCS 8689, pp. 250–264, 2014.
© Springer International Publishing Switzerland 2014

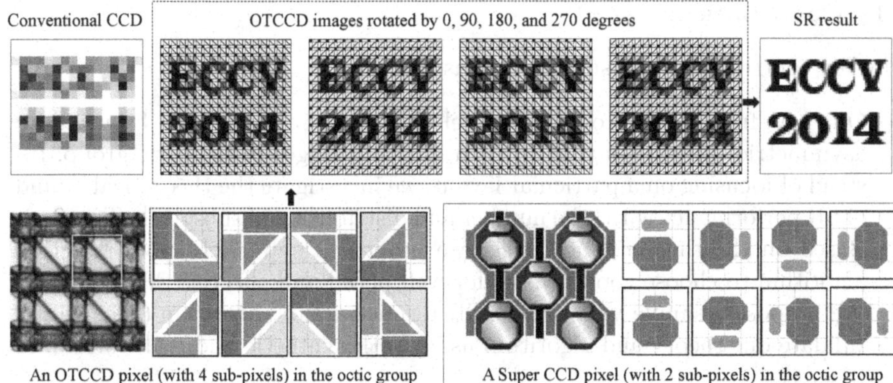

Fig. 1. Existing CCD sensors with non-conventional sub-pixel layouts (bottom row). By transforming the image plane, their images in the octic group show different sub-pixel layouts, which can be combined for significant resolution enhancement (top row). The OTCCD images under 4 rotations can perform 4× SR. Comparing the OTCCD with the super CCD, it can be seen that sub-pixels with an asymmetric layout produce more variation in their images in the octic group.

This paper explores the properties of non-conventional pixel layouts and shapes. Some existing CCDs contain sub-pixels of different shapes and spatial locations within one pixel. We show two examples in the bottom row of Fig. 1. The Orthogonal-Transfer Charge-Coupled Device (OTCCD) sensor [4] has four sub-pixels[1], and the super CCD [10] has two[2]. These sub-pixels naturally increase the spatial sampling rate. Instead of relying on sub-pixel displacements, however, we focus on forming multiple images via transformations in the octic group, *i.e.*, all symmetries of a square. We assume the pixel shape is square, so that each element in the octic group corresponds to one pose of a pixel. The sub-pixel layout varies with different poses of a pixel, and depends on the layout's symmetry. For example, the OTCCD can form 8 different sub-pixel layouts (through four 90° rotations and their reflections), but the super CCD has left-right symmetry and therefore shows only 4 different layouts. By combining multiple images recorded with different poses, a super-resolved image with higher resolution can be obtained. The intuition here is that more sub-pixels with asymmetric layouts can construct a higher resolution image. We discuss here the exact relationship between sub-pixel layout (including the number and distribution of sub-pixels) in the octic group and the magnification factor.

[1] The OTCCD actually consists four phases in one pixel. Photon charge can integrate separately in each phase and shift between the phases. Here we interpret the four "phases" as four "sub-pixels".

[2] If we treat the gap among sub-pixels as another sub-pixel that does not record photon charges, the number of sub-pixels could be five for the OTCCD and three for the super CCD.

1.1 Contributions

Our key contributions are summarized as below:

- Our new framework provides a novel view to the SR problem by using an asymmetric sub-pixel layout to form multiple mages in the octic group. Instead of focusing on a particular layout, we investigate the theoretical bound of SR performance w.r.t. the number and distribution of sub-pixels (Sec. 2.2).
- Based on the theoretical analysis, we propose a sub-pixel layout selection algorithm to choose good layouts for well-posed and effective SR (Sec. 2.3).
- We propose a simple yet effective SR reconstruction algorithm (Sec. 3) and validate our theory and algorithm using both synthetic and real-world data (Sec. 4).

1.2 Related Work

Our approach belongs to the category of reconstruction-based SR with multiple images. SR algorithms using single images such as learning-based methods (*e.g.*, [9]) are beyond the scope of this paper. We refer the readers to survey papers (*e.g.*, [16]) for a discussion of various categories of SR algorithms.

For regular pixel layouts and shapes, there are various SR reconstruction methods for images with sub-pixel displacements. Popular approaches include iterative back projection (IBP) [11], maximum a posteriori and regularized maximum likelihood [6] and sparse representation [18]. These reconstruction techniques focus on solving the ill-posed inverse problem with a conventional sensor and setup.

In contrast, this paper studies asymmetric sub-pixel layouts and is therefore similar to previous techniques using non-conventional pixel layouts [2] and pixel shapes [17]. The former work used a Penrose pixel layout, which never repeats itself, on an infinite plane. The latter work implemented random pixel shapes by spraying fine-grained black powder on the CCD. Both methods focus on one type of layout or shape and use multiple images with sub-pixel displacements. Our work is different from them in two ways: 1) We transform the image plane to form multiple images in the octic group; 2) We propose a general theory and categorize good sub-pixel layouts for deeper understanding of SR performance with non-conventional pixels.

2 Good Sub-pixel Layout for Super-Resolution

2.1 Single Image Case

Similar to Penrose tiling [2], we ignore optical deblurring and assume that it can be applied after sub-pixel sampling. Thus, in the discrete domain, reconstruction-based SR can be represented as a linear system as

$$\mathbf{L} = \mathbf{P}\mathbf{H} + \mathbf{E}, \tag{1}$$

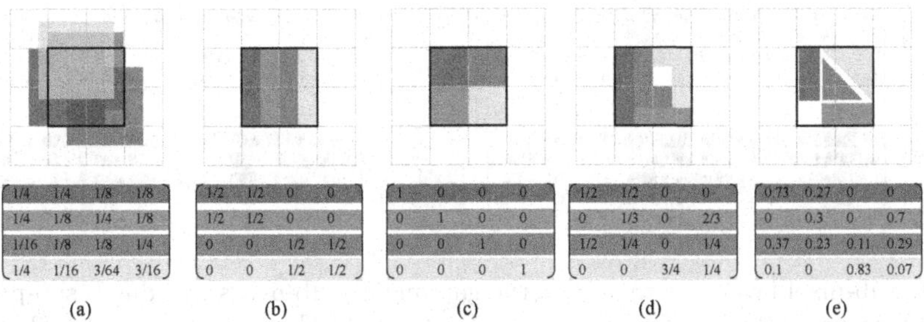

Fig. 2. Different sub-pixel layouts and their HR-to-LR mapping matrices **P**, with magnification factor $\mathcal{M} = 2$. (a) Conventional SR: LR pixels with double the size as HR pixels undergo a sub-pixel displacement; (b)-(e): examples of different sub-pixel layouts. Different color-shaded areas (RGBYW here) represent different sub-pixels, and the white area within one pixel is to simulate a gap that does not record photon charges.

where **H** includes all pixels of a high resolution (HR) image in a column vector, **L** concatenates column vectors formed by all low resolution (LR) images, **P** is the matrix that maps HR to LR images, and **E** is the per-pixel noise.

In the ideal case when noise can be ignored, to double the resolution (2× SR), we need at least 4 LR images with exactly half-pixel shifts to produce a full reconstruction (the inverse problem is well-posed). In general, the displacements of LR images can be arbitrary, and they determine the values in **P**. An example of **P** is shown in Fig. 2(a). The HR grid is drawn with dashed lines, and the shaded squares with different colors represent LR pixels from different images. In this example, **P** is evaluated for the 2×2 area indicated by the bold black square (values out of this area are not shown). Each row of **P** corresponds to one displaced-LR pixel (shaded area with the same color), and the element in each row is calculated for all HR pixels (bold black square in Fig. 2) as the area ratio of overlapping regions to the LR pixel size. The analysis of **P** plays a key role in understanding the performance of SR.

Similar to sub-pixel displacement with multiples images, the increase in spatial sampling can also be implemented by splitting one LR pixel into smaller sub-pixels with a single image. The most straightforward example for the 2× SR is splitting one LR pixel into 4 square regions, as shown in Fig. 2(c). In such a case, **P** is an identity matrix. By treating each sub-pixel as a displaced LR pixel, we can build **P** for sub-pixel layouts in Fig. 2(b), (d), and (e) in a similar way as Fig. 2(a). Note the layout in (b) has $\text{rank}(\mathbf{P}) = 2$, so it cannot produce 2× SR. The layouts in (d) and (e) have $\text{rank}(\mathbf{P}) = 4$, so they can achieve 2× SR. For easy analysis, we assume the sub-pixels completely cover one LR pixel, so the layouts in Fig. 2(d) and (e) actually have 5 sub-pixels. We treat the gap among sub-pixels as a dumb sub-pixel that does not record photon charges; therefore, strictly speaking, **P** for layouts (d) and (e) should have an all-zero row, which is omitted in the figure.

In general, the size of **P** equals to $r \times \mathcal{M}^2$, where r is the number of sub-pixels, and $\mathcal{M}$ as the magnification factor. It is easy to infer that for a single pixel with

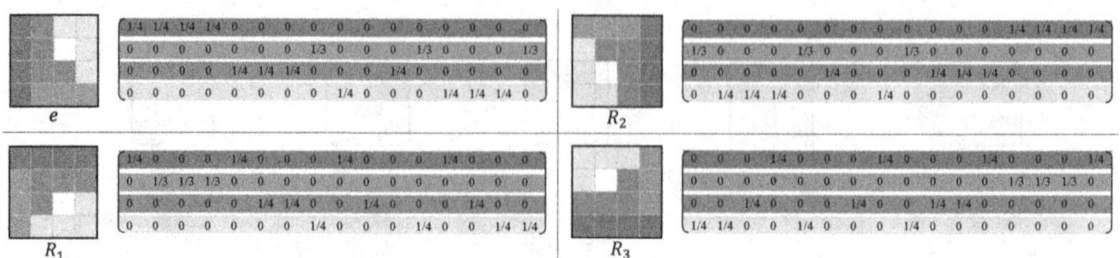

Fig. 3. Sub-pixel layouts with $r = 5$ (the gap among sub-pixels is a dumb sub-pixel) in a sub-group of the octic group $\hat{\mathcal{G}} = \{e, R_1, R_2, R_3\}$. These layouts could build a $\mathbf{P}$ with rank($\mathbf{P}$) = 16. Four images captured with such sub-pixel layouts can be used to perform 4× SR.

r sub-pixels, to achieve $\mathcal{M}\times$ SR, the sufficient condition for full reconstruction is when $r \geq \mathcal{M}^2$. Because the full reconstruction is achieved when rank($\mathbf{P}$) $= \mathcal{M}^2$ and $\mathbf{P}$ has the size of $r \times \mathcal{M}^2$, rank($\mathbf{P}$) $< \mathcal{M}^2$ holds if $r < \mathcal{M}^2$.

2.2 Multiple Images in the Octic Group

Enhancing the resolution by only using sub-pixels in one image has limited performance (requires $r \geq \mathcal{M}^2$). Further, in practice, increasing the sub-pixel number cannot continue indefinitely, due to manufacturing limitations and the proportionality between pixel size and light collection efficiency (*i.e.*, signal-to-noise ratio (SNR) decreases with pixel size). Combining different sub-pixel layouts for one pixel can further enhance the resolution, but physically modifying the layout in a fabricated sensor is cost prohibitive. Instead, we observe that simple operations on the image plane can serve to change the sub-pixel layouts, if we make multiple images to form the octic group.

Octic Group. In group theory, a square belongs to the octic group, which is the 4-th order dihedral group. This group contains 8 components that keep all symmetric properties of a square, denoted as

$$\mathcal{G} = \{e, R_1, R_2, R_3, S_e, S_{R_1}, S_{R_2}, S_{R_3}\}, \tag{2}$$

where e represents the original pose; R_1, R_2 and R_3 represent 90°, 180° and 270° rotations of the original pose; and S_e, S_{R_1}, S_{R_2}, and S_{R_3} represent the reflections (horizontal or vertical mirror flipping) to the first 4 elements, respectively. These 8 poses can transform into each other according to the multiplication table of the octic group.

An Intuitive Example. We show an intuitive example in Fig. 3. Given a rotation-asymmetric sub-pixel layout with $r = 5$ (4 effective sub-pixels and 1 dumb sub-pixel), the maximum $\mathcal{M}$ allowed for such a structure is 2 (see Fig. 2(c)-(e)) for a single image. We denote $\hat{\mathcal{G}} = \{e, R_1, R_2, R_3\}$ as the sub-group of $\mathcal{G}$ with the first 4 elements. By rotating the image plane three times with a step of 90°, we obtain 4 images in group $\hat{\mathcal{G}}$. Similar to Fig. 2, we reconstruct $r-1$ (exclude the gap) rows of $\mathbf{P}$ for each pose in $\hat{\mathcal{G}}$, and by stacking the layouts with all 4 poses we obtain $\mathbf{P}$. Here $\text{rank}(\mathbf{P}) = 16$, so it is well-posed for full reconstruction of 4× SR.

We assume the image plane is square and all pixels are congruent squares, then all images in the octic group will have their pixel contours exactly overlapped with different sub-pixel layouts inside. This makes the following analysis and SR reconstruction independent of pixel locations.

Full Reconstruction Conditions. The full reconstruction of SR is determined by $\text{rank}(\mathbf{P})$. The structure of $\mathbf{P}$ is determined by various factors: the size and distribution of sub-pixels, denoted as Γ; the number of sub-pixels r; the number of elements in $\mathcal{G}$ or its subgroup, denoted as t (it is equal to the number of different images used for SR); and the magnification factor $\mathcal{M}$. We denote P as the function constructing $\mathbf{P}$: $\mathbf{P} = P(\Gamma, r, t, \mathcal{M})$. Assuming we have found a Γ that satisfies $\text{rank}(\mathbf{P}^\Gamma) = \text{argmax}_\Gamma \, \text{rank}(P(\Gamma, r, t, \mathcal{M}))$ given a fixed combination of $(r, t, \mathcal{M})$, the exact value of $\text{rank}(\mathbf{P}^\Gamma)$ depends on $(r, t, \mathcal{M})$. According to Fig. 2 and Fig. 3, the intuition is that Γ should be a rotation/reflection-asymmetric sub-pixel layout. In this paper, we restrict the discussion to two different t values: $t = 4$ means 4 images in the group $\hat{\mathcal{G}}$ (only rotations), and $t = 8$ means 8 images that form the group $\mathcal{G}$ (rotations and reflections). With these constraints on Γ and t, we explore the relationship between r and $\mathcal{M}$.

1) For small $\mathcal{M}$: If $\mathcal{M}^2 << rt$, the upper bound U_1 of $\text{rank}(\mathbf{P}^\Gamma)$ is determined by $\mathcal{M}$ as $U_1 = \mathcal{M}^2$. This is understood by noting that $\mathbf{P}^\Gamma$ has a size of $rt \times \mathcal{M}^2$. But, this case is not very meaningful for practical applications, since people expect larger $\mathcal{M}$ with smaller r and t.

2) For large $\mathcal{M}$: If $\mathcal{M}^2 >> rt$, the upper bound U_2 of $\text{rank}(\mathbf{P}^\Gamma)$ is determined by the values of rt. Unfortunately, $\text{rank}(\mathbf{P}^\Gamma)$ might not reach the maximum number of rows of $\mathbf{P}^\Gamma$, which is rt, because of some linear dependence across the rows of $\mathbf{P}^\Gamma$. For example, the layout in Fig. 3 has $r = 5$ and $t = 4$, and Lemma 1 below explains that it is impossible to produce $\text{rank}(\mathbf{P}^\Gamma) = 16$ with only $r = 4$.

Lemma 1. *Given a group of pixels with t poses in $\mathcal{G}$, with each pixel containing r sub-pixels, for a sufficiently large $\mathcal{M}$, the upper bound of* $\text{rank}(\mathbf{P}^\Gamma)$*, denoted as U_2, is $U_2 = t(r-1) + 1$.*

Proof. A sufficiently large $\mathcal{M}$ means the HR pixel is quite small comparing to the LR pixel. So we can assume that each sub-pixel covers several integer HR pixels (*e.g.*, the example in Fig. 3). Set the image plane as its original pose, and assume the i-th ($1 \le i \le r$) sub-pixel has an area of a_i by covering a_i unit-area HR pixels. Then, the i-th row of $\mathbf{P}^\Gamma$ denoted as $\mathbf{P}^\Gamma_{i*}$ contains a_i elements with value of $\frac{1}{a_i}$ and all other elements of 0. Given $r-1$ such rows, and a $1 \times \mathcal{M}^2$ row vector $\mathbf{I}$ with all values as 1, we can represent the r-th row as:

$$\mathbf{P}^\Gamma_{r*} = \frac{1}{\mathcal{M}^2 - \sum_{i=1}^{r-1} a_i} \left(\mathbf{I} - \sum_{i=1}^{r-1} a_i \mathbf{P}^\Gamma_{i*} \right). \tag{3}$$

According to the composition of $\mathbf{P}^\Gamma$, each sub-matrix of r rows corresponds to one image with a pose from $\mathcal{G}$. Therefore, the i-th row and the $(i+kr)$-th row $(1 \leq k \leq t-1, k \in \mathbb{Z})$ have the same values permutated to different columns (compare all rows with the same color in Fig. 3). Then, the r-th row in each sub-matrix can also be calculated by using $\mathbf{I}$ and Eq. (3).

Finally, $\mathbf{P}^\Gamma$ is concatenated by t sub-matrices of $r-1$ rows, plus another row vector $\mathbf{I}$. Thus, its maximum rank is equal to its number of rows $t(r-1)+1$. □

Combining the inequality relationships above, we naturally come up with the following proposition about the upper bound of $\text{rank}(\mathbf{P}^\Gamma)$.

Proposition 1. *Given a group of pixels with t poses in $\mathcal{G}$ with each pixel containing r sub-pixels, for a designated magnification factor $\mathcal{M}$, the value of* $\text{rank}(\mathbf{P}^\Gamma)$ *is bounded as*

$$\text{rank}(\mathbf{P}^\Gamma) \leq \min(U_1, U_2) = \min(\mathcal{M}^2, t(r-1)+1). \tag{4}$$

Validation. If $\mathcal{M}^2 \approx rt$, $\text{rank}(\mathbf{P}^\Gamma)$ might have a value below the upper bound of Proposition 1, but the exact value is very difficult to write as a closed-form solution, because rank maximization is a highly nonlinear problem. We use numerical simulation to plot these exact values and verify Proposition 1.

We randomly select r positions within one pixel area as centers and expand these centers in all 8 discrete directions. The expanding process is stopped when the whole pixel is filled. The pixel is transformed to different poses and forms a group $\mathcal{G}$. Then $\mathbf{P}$ is built and evaluated. This process is repeated 100 times to avoid symmetric sub-pixel layouts. We empirically observe that the possibility of generating a rank-deficient (partially or completely symmetric) layout is usually less than 1%, and almost all layouts have constant $\text{rank}(\mathbf{P}^\Gamma)$.

The $\text{rank}(\mathbf{P}^\Gamma)$ value distribution with varying r and $\mathcal{M}$ is shown in Fig. 4. The top row corresponds to $\hat{\mathcal{G}}$ $(t=4)$ and the bottom row shows the case for $\mathcal{G}$ $(t=8)$. The exact value distribution is illustrated in the first column, and the upper bound calculated from Proposition 1 is shown in the second column. The third column is the 2D planar view of the first column. It is interesting to note that the left side of the distribution shows a parabolic shape corresponding to U_1, while the right side of the distribution shows a planar shape corresponding to U_2. For $t=4$, the exact values perfectly match the upper bound. As the number of images in the group increases, the possibility that $\mathbf{P}^\Gamma$ has more linearly dependent rows increases, so when $t=8$ some values around $\mathcal{M} \approx rt$ cannot reach the upper bound. From the similarity of (d) to (e) and their small offsets indicated by numbers in (f), it can be seen that the upper bound is quite tight.

With the analysis above, it is easy to evaluate the SR performance for a specific sensor. For the two real sensors in Fig. 1, the OTCCD has an asymmetric layout with $r=5$, it could perform 4× SR with $t=4$ images in $\hat{\mathcal{G}}$ and 5× SR with $t=8$ images in $\mathcal{G}$; while the super CCD has $r=3$ sub-pixels with left-right symmetric, it only performs 2× SR ($\text{rank}(\mathbf{P})=8$) with both $\hat{\mathcal{G}}$ and $\mathcal{G}$.

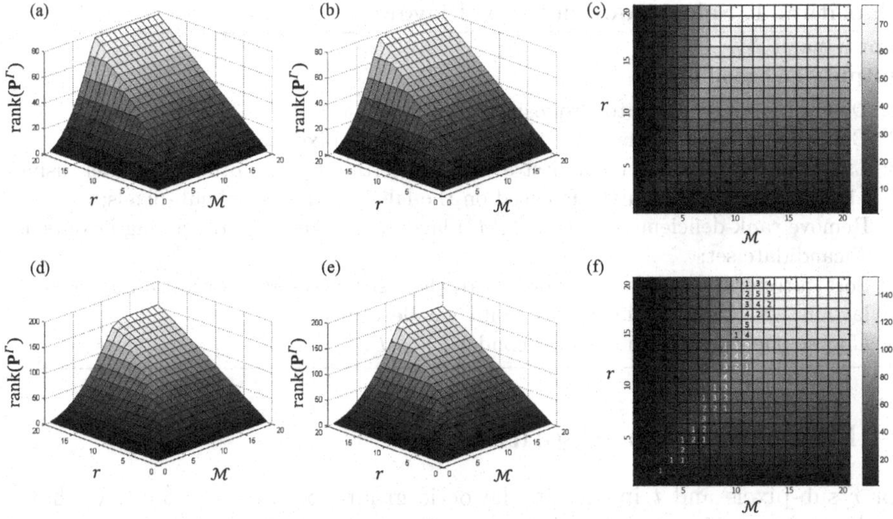

Fig. 4. Values of rank($\mathbf{P}^{\Gamma}$) varying with different r, t, and $\mathcal{M}$. Top row: $t = 4$; bottom row: $t = 8$. (a) and (d) are exact values from simulation; (b) and (e) are upper bound from Proposition 1; (c) and (f) are 2D planar views of (a) and (d). The numbers overlaid on the matrix area of (f) indicate difference from (d) to (e) (cells without numbers mean the upper bound is reached).

2.3 Good Sub-pixel Layout

The theoretical analysis in Sec. 2.2 explains the relationship of $(r, t, \mathcal{M})$ by assuming a good layout Γ has been found. We propose four merits to select good sub-pixel layout Γ, from randomly generated candidates. The first and most important one is to ensure the full SR reconstruction as Proposition 1: 1) With t images in a group, the pixel should contain at least r sub-pixels to ensure rank($\mathbf{P}^{\Gamma}$) $= \mathcal{M}^2$, which we call full-rank layouts (note that there can be infinite many solutions for full-rank layouts Γ).

Three additional constraints benefiting the sensor layout design and SR performance should be considered among candidates with full-rank layouts: 2) We set the sub-pixel with smallest area as a dumb sub-pixel (or gap), so we actually use only $r - 1$ effective sub-pixels to achieve the same performance of r sub-pixels. We do not use larger sub-pixels as the dumb one to maximize the size of effective sub-pixels for capturing more light. 3) The layouts with smaller sub-pixel area variance are preferred. Because our goal is to increase the spatial sampling rather than the dynamic range, sub-pixels with approximately equal areas will perform similarly in receiving light, thus too bright or too dark sub-pixels are easily avoidable. 4) We prefer $\mathbf{P}^{\Gamma}$ with smaller condition number, denoted as cond($\mathbf{P}^{\Gamma}$), which makes the inverse problem better-conditioned under noise. Considering the above four merits, we propose the good sub-pixel layout selection method in Algorithm 1.

Algorithm 1. Select good sub-pixel layout.

Input: t and $\mathcal{M}$.

Output: The good layout Γ.

1: Determine r according to Proposition 1 and Fig. 4;
2: Generate sufficiently many (> 10000) random sub-pixel layouts;
3: Label the sub-pixel with smallest area using 0 (dumb), and other sub-pixels using $\{1, 2, \cdots, r-1\}$; Calculate $\mathbf{P}$ based on the labels and areas of sub-pixels;
4: Remove rank-deficient ($\text{rank}(\mathbf{P}) < \mathcal{M}^2$) layouts and keep the remaining layouts as Γ candidate set;
5: Sort current Γ candidates according to their sub-pixel area variance and remove layouts with larger variance (keep only smallest 10%);
6: Choose the layout with smallest $\text{cond}(\mathbf{P}^{\Gamma})$ as Γ.

3 Reconstruction Algorithm

For r sub-pixels and t images in the octic group (or its sub-group), we have rt observations for each pixel location[3]. By concatenating these observations, we obtain the LR observations $\mathbf{L}$. $\mathbf{P}$ is determined by the sub-pixel layout and image poses in the octic group as described in Sec. 2. For good layouts Γ with proper r and t, $\text{rank}(\mathbf{P})$ is equal to $\mathcal{M}^2$. Therefore, the HR image $\mathbf{H}$ can be easily recovered by solving the linear system in Eq. (1).

The reconstruction is performed independently for each pixel by solving the linear least squares (ℓ^2) with a Tikhonov regularization term, denoted as

$$\underset{\mathbf{H}}{\text{argmin}} \, \|\mathbf{PH} - \mathbf{L}\|_2^2 + \lambda \|\mathbf{H}\|_2^2, \tag{5}$$

where λ is the weight of regularization term. This problem can be solved by using the LSQR method in [15].

When the noise is stronger, the problem can also be solved by minimizing the total variation (TV) with quadratic constraints as

$$\underset{\mathbf{H}}{\text{argmin}} \, \text{TV}(\mathbf{H}) \quad \text{subject to} \quad \|\mathbf{PH} - \mathbf{L}\|_2^2 < \epsilon, \tag{6}$$

where ϵ is the constraint relaxation parameter. We solve the above problem using "ℓ^1-Magic" [5]. This approach needs more computation, but can better suppress the noise. We empirically find that under moderate noise, the ℓ^2-based solution is accurate with far less computation. We will verify this in Sec. 4.

The modified IBP algorithm in [2] dealing with non-conventional pixel layouts and shapes can also be naturally applied to solve our problem. Similar to [2], we can apply IBP in the HR domain. The average of all LR images is used as an initial HR image. Then the iterations are performed to update the residual between LR images upsampled to the HR domain and the images resampled using our sub-pixel layouts in the octic group. Please refer to [2] for details. We will also evaluate and compare this approach in Sec. 4.

[3] If there is one dumb sub-pixel, the effective size of $\mathbf{P}$ could be $(r-1)t$ by removing rows with all elements as 0.

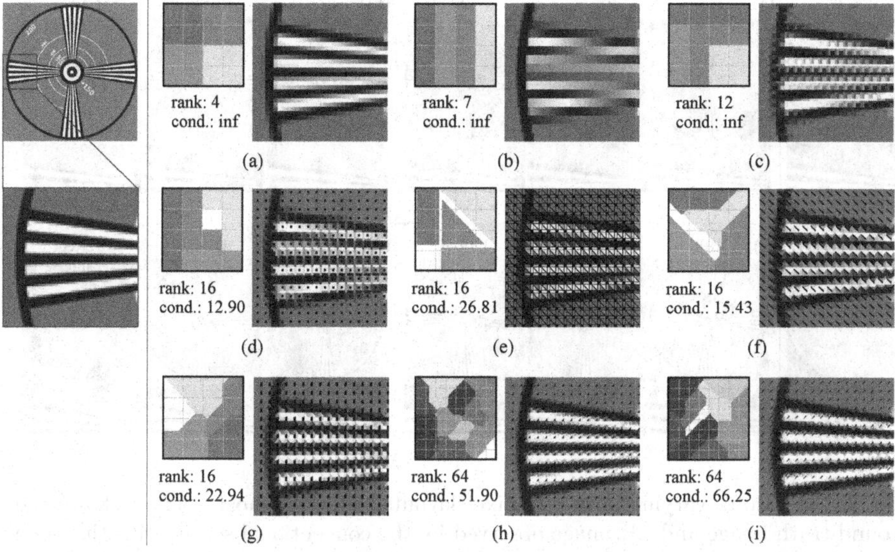

Fig. 5. Simulated images under various sub-pixel layouts for 4× SR. The rank and condition number of their corresponding **P** are indicated below the sub-pixel layout. (a)-(c): $r = 4$; (d)-(g): $r = 5$; (h), (i): $r = 11$. For each layout, white means the dumb sub-pixel, and other colors indicate other effective sub-pixels.

4 Performance Evaluation

4.1 Synthetic Test

Sub-pixel Layouts. We show image appearances under sensors with different sub-pixel layouts in Fig. 5. We model spatial integration of photon charges by using a box function by overlaying the sensor plane on the HR grid and taking average values within each sub-pixel region. The layouts in the first row have $r = 4$. They cannot reach full rank for $t = 4$, because for $r = 4$ the maximum rank is only 13 according to Lemma 1. Fig. 5(d)-(g) show some full-rank layouts with $r = 5$ and $t = 4$, and they could produce 4× SR; (d) is a manually designed layout; (e) is from the real structure of an OTCCD sensor (Fig. 1); (f) and (g) are generated from Algorithm 1; (h) and (i) with $r = 11$ are also generated by Algorithm 1, they could produce 8× SR with $t = 8$.

SR Results with Different Layouts. We then evaluate the SR performance by using the sub-pixel layouts in Fig. 5. In addition to the three reconstruction methods introduced in Sec. 3, we also compare SR using sub-pixel shift with our sub-pixel layouts, denoted as "IBP-shift" [2]. All test images contain 8-bit quantization noise. With only quantization noise, we found solving Eq. (5), denoted as "L2Reg", and Eq. (6) (TV) give almost the same results, so we omit the results from TV-based method here. For the IBP-based method, we run the

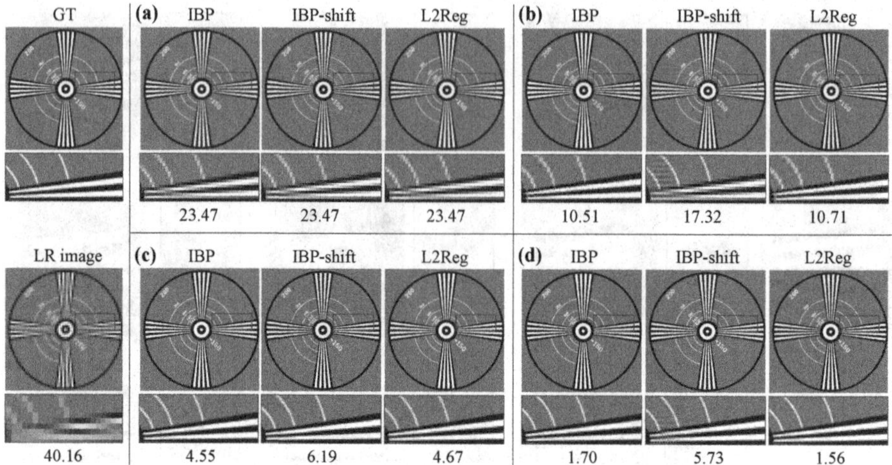

Fig. 6. SR results varying with sub-pixel layouts. The left most column shows the ground truth image and LR image observed by the conventional sensor with the same pixel size as our pixel. (a)-(d) here show 4× SR results under various sub-pixel layouts from Fig. 5(a)-(d). The number below each image is the RMSE value w.r.t. ground truth.

algorithm for 1000 iterations, and for L2Reg, we use $\lambda = 0.01$. These parameters are consistent for all of the following experiments, unless otherwise specified.

From the results in Fig. 6, we can tell that the conventional grid structure shows the worst accuracy, which actually performs 2× SR, because it keeps the layout unchanged for all images in the octic group. The layouts in (b) and (c) also show (partial) symmetric properties for different images, thus have limited enhancement in resolution. Generally, higher rank($\mathbf{P}$) produces higher resolution.

For the full-rank layouts, we show the reconstructed images using Fig. 5(d) as an example. All full-rank layouts are equivalently optimal in terms of full SR reconstruction. When there is no noise, all of them produce perfect reconstruction with RMSE = 0. Even if there is noise, these layouts produce SR images with similar appearances. There are some slight differences in RMSEs depending on the condition number of $\mathbf{P}$, *e.g.*, the SR result from layout in Fig. 5(e) has RMSE of 2.42, while Fig. 5(f) has 2.18. Fig. 5(d) has the smallest condition number, whose RMSE is also the smallest (1.56). However, this manually designed layout is not well-balanced in sub-pixel sizes.

For different reconstruction methods, L2Reg provides results similar to those of IBP. With full-rank layouts, L2Reg shows even higher accuracy. The asymmetric pixel structure also benefits the SR using sub-pixel shift (IBP-shift), but its accuracy is not as good as using images in the octic group (IBP). For a fair comparison, we evaluate only half-pixel displacement compared to our $t = 4$ rotations here. Using finer steps in shifting and more images further increases the resolution [2], but it is equivalent to using more sub-pixels with smaller sizes.

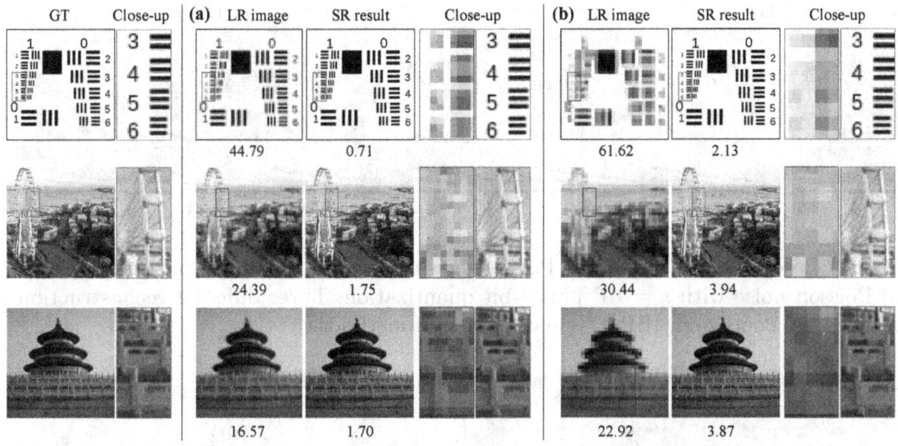

Fig. 7. (a) 4× SR results and (b) 8× SR results with full-rank sub-pixel layouts from Fig. 5(d) and Fig. 5(h). The left most column shows the ground truth image. The LR image refers to the results from a conventional sensor. Close-up views are shown in the rightmost of each column.

We show more SR results with full-rank layouts in Fig. 7 solved by L2Reg. Column (a) shows 4× SR with the layout in Fig. 5(d) and $t = 4$; column (b) shows the 8× SR results with the layout in Fig. 5(h) and $t = 8$.

Results Varying with Noise. We show the influence of noise on the results in Fig. 8. 4× SR with full-rank layouts are evaluated by using three different reconstruction methods. We use a Matlab built-in function "imnoise" to add signal-dependent Poisson noise, which more closely models shot noise than does zero-mean Gaussian noise. We use a scaling factor η to adjust the strength of the noise[4] before quantizing the data to 8 bits.

In the presence of Poisson noise, IBP does not show good convergence, and the errors accumulate after a local minimum has been reached. To show the best results that IBP can obtain, we manually stop the iterations at 150 and 50 for the test in Fig. 8(a) and (b) (larger noise makes IBP worse in convergence), respectively. Even with manual interference, IBP still shows worse performance than ℓ^2- and TV-based methods. TV could produce reconstructions with smaller errors with noisy images. We use $\epsilon = 2$ in Eq. (6) for this experiment.

4.2 Real Data Test

We use a Canon EOS Rebel T3i camera to capture images with real noise. For each $\mathcal{M} \times \mathcal{M}$ area of the captured image, we create one pixel according to a

[4] For double-precision data, "imnoise" interprets pixel values as means of Poisson distributions scaled up by 10^{12}. To adjust the noise level, we scale the data by $\frac{1}{\eta}$ before applying "imnoise," and then scale it back by η.

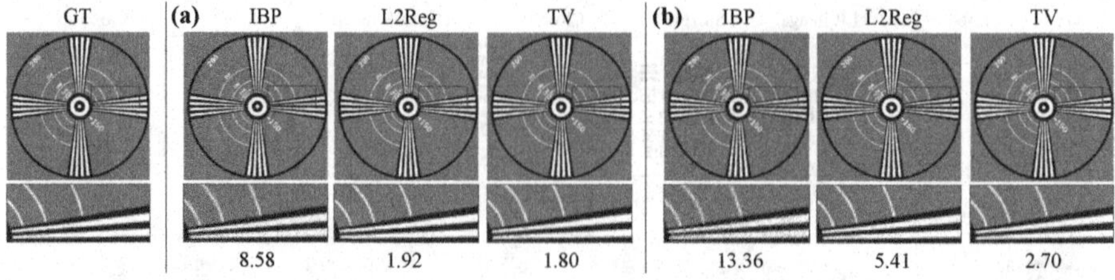

Fig. 8. SR results with noise. (a) Poisson noise with $\eta = 10^7$ plus 8-bit quantization; (b) Poisson noise with $\eta = 10^8$ plus 8-bit quantization. Three different reconstruction methods are compared: IBP, ℓ^2-, and TV-based methods.

Fig. 9. SR results using real data. (a) 4× SR with OTCCD sub-pixel layout in Fig. 1, (b) 8× SR with our good sub-pixel layout in Fig. 5(h). From left to right: images using conventional sensor, image views from an sensor with sub-pixel layouts, and SR result.

sub-pixel layout. Here we evaluate the OTCCD layout in Fig. 1 for 4× SR and the layout in Fig. 5(h) for 8× SR. We manually rotate and flip the image plane in a controlled manner to obtain images in the octic group. The captured images are further registered using the method in [7].

Various noise are included in the captured images, such as the registration error, image blur, sensor noise, and JPEG compression noise, so we apply the TV-based method with $\epsilon = 30$ to reconstruct the HR images. We show the results in Fig. 9. Note that the images from sensors with several sub-pixels already have some resolution enhancement, but with multiple images in the octic group the resolution could be further increased. Even with various types of real noise, our SR results could clearly recover delicate details in the original scene.

5 Discussion

A Potential Hardware Implementation. We suggest a potential implementation for building a prototype camera to realize our SR framework. As shown in Fig. 1, there are existing CCD sensors with asymmetric sub-pixel layouts. The image rotation can be implemented by placing a Dove prism in front of the main lens, similarly as done in rotational-shearing interferometry [14,13]. The Dove prism has the property of rotating the image plane 2θ for its own rotation of θ. It can be controlled with great precision using a rotary engine (such as a stepper motor or an ultrasound motor used to focus lenses), which is mechanically simpler and more accurate than XY translation stages used in previous SR work [3]. This will be sufficient for realizing the $t = 4$ group. Note that all the images after a single Dove prism will be mirror-flipped, so another, cascaded Dove prism would be required to obtain all images in the octic group.

Other Considerations in SR System Design. As compared to conventional SR that involves inter-pixel overlapping, the proposed method based on octic groups can work independently and equivalently on each pixel, which has advantages in supporting parallel computation and saving memory in encoding $\mathbf{P}$ (do not need to consider neighboring pixels) for real-time functionality.

We do not directly compare our approach with SR algorithms that use conventional sensors, because the goal of this paper is to show the condition for full reconstruction rather than developing an advanced method for solving the inverse problem. As validated in the experiments, even with simple solutions in Sec. 4 the accuracy could be very high. We believe that by using more complicated regularization terms (*e.g.*, [8]) and modern robust methods (*e.g.*, [18]), the reconstruction accuracy could be further improved under severe noise.

6 Conclusion

The key observation of this paper is that when one pixel is split into several asymmetrically distributed sub-pixels, the images in the octic group could further increase the spatial sampling. This group of images can be combined to perform super-resolution. We analyzed the theoretical bound for this setup. With proper sub-pixel layouts, SR with desired magnification factor could be accurately achieved with simple computation. We verify our theory and algorithm with both synthetic and real-world data.

Acknowledgement. The Lincoln Laboratory portion of this work is sponsored by the Assistant Secretary of Defense for Research & Engineering under Air Force Contract #FA8721-05-C-0002. Opinions, interpretations, conclusions and recommendations are those of the author and are not necessarily endorsed by the United States Government. Boxin Shi is supported by SUTD-MIT joint postdoctoral programme. Sai-Kit Yeung is supported by SUTD StartUp Grant ISTD 2011 016 and Singapore MOE Academic Research Fund MOE2013-T2-1-159.

References

1. Baker, S., Kanade, T.: Limits on super-resolution and how to break them. IEEE Transactions on Pattern Analysis and Machine Intelligence 24(9), 1167–1183 (2002)
2. Ben-Ezra, M., Lin, Z., Wilburn, B., Zhang, W.: Penrose pixels for super-resolution. IEEE Transactions on Pattern Analysis and Machine Intelligence 33(7), 1370–1383 (2011)

3. Ben-Ezra, M., Zomet, A., Nayar, S.K.: Video super-resolution using controlled subpixel detector shifts. IEEE Transactions on Pattern Analysis and Machine Intelligence 27(6), 977–987 (2005)
4. Burke, B.E., Tonry, J., Cooper, M., Luppino, G., Jacoby, G., Bredthauer, R., Boggs, K., Lesser, M., Onaka, P., Young, D., Doherty, P., Craig, D.: The orthogonal-transfer array: A new CCD architecture for astronomy. In: Proceedings of the SPIE, Optical and Infrared Detectors for Astronomy, vol. 5499, pp. 185–192 (2004)
5. Candes, E., Romberg, J.: ℓ^1-magic: Recovery of sparse signals via convex programming (2005), `http://users.ece.gatech.edu/~justin/l1magic/`
6. Elad, M., Feuer, A.: Restoration of single super-resolution image from several blurred, noisy and down-sampled measured images. IEEE Transactions on Image Processing 6(12), 1646–1658 (1997)
7. Evangelidis, G.D., Psarakis, E.Z.: Parametric image alignment using enhanced correlation coefficient maximization. IEEE Transactions on Pattern Analysis and Machine Intelligence 30(10), 1858–1865 (2008)
8. Farsiu, S., Elad, M., Milanfar, P.: Multiframe demosaicing and super-resolution of color images. IEEE Transactions on Image Processing 15(1), 141–159 (2006)
9. Freeman, W.T., Pasztor, E.C.: Learning low-level vision. In: Proc. of International Conference on Computer Vision (ICCV), pp. 1182–1189 (1999)
10. Fuji film Super CCD (2003), `http://www.dcviews.com/press/fuji_superccd_4.htm`
11. Irani, M., Peleg, S.: Improving resolution by image restoration. Computer Vision, Graphics, and Image Processing 53, 231–239 (1991)
12. Lin, Z., Shum, H.Y.: Fundamental limits of reconstruction-based superresolution algorithms under local translation. IEEE Transactions on Pattern Analysis and Machine Intelligence 26(1), 83–97 (2004)
13. Moreno, I., Paez, G., Strojnik, M.: Dove prism with increased throughput for implementation in a rotational-shearing interferometer. Applied Optics 42(22), 4514–4521 (2003)
14. Murty, M.V.R.K., Hagerott, E.C.: Rotational shearing interferometry. Applied Optics 5(4), 615–619 (1966)
15. Paige, C.C., Saunders, M.A.: LSQR: An algorithm for sparse linear equations and sparse least squares. ACM Transactions on Mathematical Software 8(1), 43–71 (1982)
16. Park, S.C., Park, M.K., Kang, M.G.: Super-resolution image reconstruction: A technical overview. IEEE Signal Processing Magazine 20(3), 21–36 (2003)
17. Sasao, T., Hiura, S., Sato, K.: Super-resolution with randomly shaped pixels and sparse regularization. In: Proc. of International Conference on Computational Photography (ICCP), pp. 1–11 (2013)
18. Yang, J., Wright, J., Huang, T.S., Ma, Y.: Image super-resolution via sparse representation. IEEE Transactions on Image Processing 19(11), 2861–2873 (2008)
19. Zhao, W.Y., Sawhney, H.S.: Is super-resolution with optical flow feasible? In: Heyden, A., Sparr, G., Nielsen, M., Johansen, P. (eds.) ECCV 2002, Part I. LNCS, vol. 2350, pp. 599–613. Springer, Heidelberg (2002)

Simultaneous Feature and Dictionary Learning for Image Set Based Face Recognition

Jiwen Lu[1], Gang Wang[1,2], Weihong Deng[3], and Pierre Moulin[1,4]

[1] Advanced Digital Sciences Center, Singapore
[2] Nanyang Technological University, Singapore
[3] Beijing University of Posts and Telecommunications, Beijing, China
[4] University of Illinois at Urbana-Champaign, IL USA

Abstract. In this paper, we propose a simultaneous feature and dictionary learning (SFDL) method for image set based face recognition, where each training and testing example contains a face image set captured from different poses, illuminations, expressions and resolutions. While several feature learning and dictionary learning methods have been proposed for image set based face recognition in recent years, most of them learn the features and dictionaries separately, which may not be powerful enough because some discriminative information for dictionary learning may be compromised in the feature learning stage if they are applied sequentially, and vice versa. To address this, we propose a SFDL method to learn discriminative features and dictionaries simultaneously from raw face images so that discriminative information can be jointly exploited. Extensive experimental results on four widely used face datasets show that our method achieves better performance than state-of-the-art image set based face recognition methods.

Keywords: Face recognition, image set, feature learning, dictionary learning, simultaneous learning.

1 Introduction

Image set based face recognition has attracted increasing interest in computer vision in recent years [41,33,27,12,15,2,11,7,23,38,3,17,37,4,6,5,30,19,29]. Different from conventional image based face recognition systems where each training and testing example is a single face image, for image set based face recognition, each training and testing example contains a face image set captured from different poses, illuminations, expressions and resolutions. While more information can be provided to describe the person with image sets, image set based face recognition is still challenging because there are usually large intra-class variations within a set, especially when they are captured in unconstrained environments.

There has been a number of work on image set based face recognition over the past decade [41,33,27,12,15,2,11,7,23,38,3,17,37,4,6,5,30,19], and dictionary-based methods have achieved state-of-the-art performance [4,6,5] because the pose, illumination and expression information in face image sets can be implicitly

D. Fleet et al. (Eds.): ECCV 2014, Part I, LNCS 8689, pp. 265–280, 2014.
© Springer International Publishing Switzerland 2014

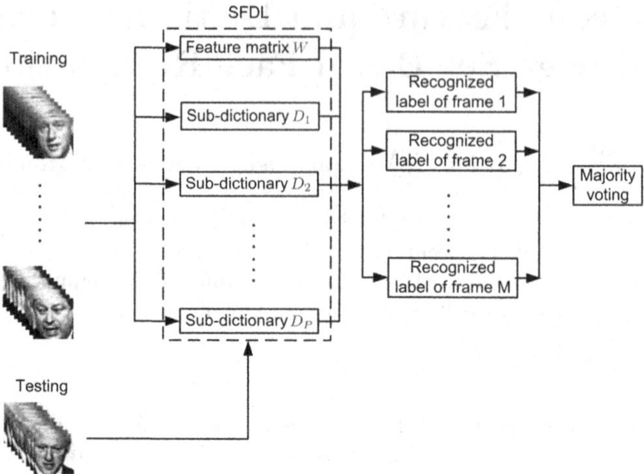

Fig. 1. The basic idea of our image set based face recognition approach, where discriminative features and dictionaries are learned simultaneously to encode the pose, illumination and expression information in face image sets, so that it is more robust to noise. In the training stage, we learn a feature projection matrix W and a structured dictionary $D = [D_1, D_2, \cdots, D_P]$ (one sub-dictionary per class) by using the proposed SFDL method, where P is the number of subjects in the training set. Given a testing face image set containing M image frames, we first apply the learned feature projection matrix W to project each sample into a feature and recognize its label by using the smallest reconstruction error corresponding to the associated sub-dictionary. Lastly, the majority voting strategy is used to classify the whole testing face image set.

encoded into the learned dictionaries. However, most existing dictionary-based image set based face recognition methods are unsupervised [4,6,5], which are not discriminative enough to classify face sets. Moreover, these methods learn dictionaries using the original raw pixels, which may contain some noisy components that are irrelevant to dictionary learning. Since face images usually lie on a low-dimensional manifold, it is desirable to seek the most discriminative features in a low-dimensional subspace and suppress the useless information to promote learning dictionaries for image sets.

In this paper, we propose a new simultaneous feature and dictionary learning (SFDL) method for image set based face recognition, where the basic idea is illustrated in Fig. 1. The goal of our method is to jointly learn a feature projection matrix and a structured dictionary, where each frame within a set is projected into a low-dimensional subspace and encoded with a discriminative coding coefficient, and face image sets from each person are represented by a sub-dictionary so that person-specific dictionaries can be learned to extract more discriminative information, simultaneously. Extensive experimental results on four widely used face datasets show that our method achieves better performance than state-of-the-art image set based face recognition methods.

2 Related Work

Image Set Based Face Recognition: Over the past recent years, we have witnessed a considerable interest in developing new methods for image set based face recognition [33,27,12,15,2,11,23,38,36,3,17,8,4,6,5,30]. These methods can be mainly categorized into two classes: parametric and non-parametric. Parametric methods first model each face image set as a distribution function and then compute the divergence between two distributions as the similarity of two face image sets. The key shortcoming of these methods is that if there are not strong correlations between two face image sets, the estimated model cannot well characterize the sets and may fail to measure their similarity. Non-parametric methods usually represent each face image set as a single or mixture of linear subspaces, and then use the subspace distance to measure the similarity of face image sets. Representative subspace distance methods include principal angle [16], affine/convext hull similarity [3], and nearest points distance [17,18,44]. However, these methods are generally sensitive to outliers and occlusions. To address this, Chen *et al.* [4,6,5] presented a dictionary-based approach for image set based face recognition by building one dictionary for each face image set and using these dictionaries to measure the similarity of face image sets. While reasonably good recognition rates can be obtained, their approach is generative and the dictionaries are learned from the original raw pixels, which may contain some noisy and irrelevant components.

Dictionary Learning: There have been extensive work on dictionary learning in the literature [1,32,45,20,34,42,31,24,14,28,39,46,9,10]. Dictionary learning aims to seek a collection of atoms for sparse representation of the input samples, where each data is linearly represented by a small number of atoms. Existing dictionary learning methods can be mainly classified into two categories: unsupervised [1] and supervised [42,24]. In recent years, dictionary learning has been extensively used in face recognition and also shown good performance [42,24]. However, most existing dictionary learning methods have been developed for image based face recognition and little progress has been made for image set based face recognition. More recently, Chen *et al.* [4] presented a discretionary learning method for video-based face recognition, where each face video is first clustered into several clusters and then the dictionary is learned for each cluster. However, their method is unsupervised, which may not be discriminative enough for classification.

3 Proposed Approach

Fig. 1 shows the basic idea of our proposed approach, and the following subsections present the details of the proposed approach.

3.1 SFDL

Generally, there are two key components in an image set based face recognition approach [36,37,30]: image set representation and image set matching. Previous work [36] has shown that feature learning is an effective tool for image set representation because it can extract discriminative information from face image sets. Recent study [4] has also shown that dictionary learning is a promising solution to image set matching because face images with varying poses, illuminations and expressions within a set can be encoded as dictionaries so that the noise can be effectively alleviated and better matching performance can be obtained. However, most previous image set based face recognition methods learned features and dictionaries separately, which may not be powerful enough because some discriminative information for dictionary learning may be compromised in the feature learning stage, and vice versa. That is because the objective of feature learning is usually inconsistent to that of dictionary learning because feature learning is essentially a feature selection problem while dictionary learning is intrinsically a clustering problem. Hence, it is suboptimal to apply feature learning and dictionary learning for image set based face recognition. To address this shortcoming, we propose a SFDL method to learn discriminative features and dictionaries simultaneously in the following.

Let $X = [X_1, X_2, \cdots, X_P]$ be the training set of face image sets from P different subjects. Assume there are N images in total in the training set by concatenating all the frames from image sets, we rewrite X as $X = [x_1, x_2, \cdots x_N] \in R^{d\times N}$, where x_i is a d-dimensional vector of the cropped face image. To extract more discriminative and robust information from the training set, SFDL aims to simultaneously learn a feature projection matrix and a discriminative structured dictionary to project each image frame in all image sets into a low-dimensional subspace, under which each image frame is encoded by a discriminative coding coefficient. To achieve this, we formulate the following optimization problem:

$$\begin{aligned}\min_{W,D,A} J &= J_1 + \lambda_1 J_2 + \lambda_2 J_3 \\ &= \sum_{i=1}^{N} (\|Wx_i - D\alpha_i\|_2^2 + \eta_1 \|\alpha_i\|_1) + \sum_{p=1}^{P}\sum_{i=1}^{N_p} \|Wx_{ip} - D_p \alpha_{ip}^p\|_2^2 \\ &+ \lambda_1 \sum_{i=1}^{N} (\|W^T W x_i - x_i\|_2^2 + \eta_2 \sum_{j=1}^{k} h(W_j x_i)) \\ &+ \lambda_2 \sum_{i=1}^{N}\sum_{j=1}^{N} \|\alpha_i - \alpha_j\|_2^2 S_{ij} \end{aligned} \quad (1)$$

where W is the feature projection matrix, $D = [D_1, D_2, \cdots, D_P]$ is the structured dictionary, D_p is the sub-dictionary for the pth class in D, x_{ip} is the ith raw pixel sample from the pth class, N_p is the number of samples in the pth class, $A = [\alpha_1, \alpha_2, \cdots, \alpha_N]$ is the sparse representation of the training samples in X, α_i is the coefficient vector of x_i, α_{ip}^p is the representation coefficient vector of α_i from the pth class, h is a nonlinear convex function which is defined as a smooth l_1 penalty: $h(\cdot) = \log(\cosh(\cdot))$ [25], λ_1, λ_2, η_1 and η_2 are four parameters to balance the importance of different terms, S is an affinity matrix to measure the similarity of the sparse codes α_i and α_j according to their label and appearance information, which is defined as follows:

$$S_{ij} = \begin{cases} 1, & \text{if } x_i \in N_{k_1}(x_j) \text{ or } x_j \in N_{k_1}(x_i) \\ & \text{and } l(x_i) = l(x_j) \\ -1, & \text{if } x_i \in N_{k_2}(x_j) \text{ or } x_j \in N_{k_2}(x_i) \\ & \text{and } l(x_i) \neq l(x_j) \\ 0, & \text{otherwise} \end{cases} \tag{2}$$

where $N_k(x_i)$ and $l(x_i)$ denote the k-nearest neighbors and the label of x_i, respectively.

The first term J_1 in Eq. (1) is to ensure that for each face sample x_i from the pth class in the low-dimensional feature subspace, it is not only well reconstructed by the whole dictionary D, but also the sub-dictionary D_p of the pth class. The second term J_2 in Eq. (1) is to ensure that the feature projection matrix W can preserve the energy of each x_i as much as possible and each column in W is to be as sparse as possible. The third term J_3 in Eq. (1) is to ensure that the difference of the sparse codes of two face images is minimized if they are from the same class and look similar, and the difference of the sparse codes of two face images is maximized if they are from different classes and also look similar, such that discriminative information can be discovered when learning sparse representation coefficients.

We rewrite A as $A = [A_1, A_2, \cdots, A_P]$, where A_p denotes the sub-matrix from the pth class containing the coding coefficients of X_p over D. Let A_p^p be the coding coefficient of X_p over the sub-dictionary D_p. Then, J_1 in Eq. (1) can be re-written as follows:

$$\begin{aligned} J_1 &= \sum_{p=1}^{P} (\|WX_p - DA_p\|_F^2 + \|WX_p - D_p A_p^p\|_F^2) + \eta_1 \|A\|_1 \\ &= \sum_{p=1}^{P} G_p(W, X_p, D, A_p) + \eta_1 \|A\|_1 \end{aligned} \tag{3}$$

where

$$G_p(W, X_p, D, A_p) \triangleq \|WX_p - DA_p\|_F^2 + \|WX_p - D_p A_p^p\|_F^2 \tag{4}$$

We can also simplify J_2 and J_3 in Eq. (1) as follows:

$$J_2 = \|W^T WX - X\|_2^2 + \eta_2 H(WX) \tag{5}$$

$$J_3 = tr(A^T CA) - tr(A^T SA) = tr(A^T LA) \tag{6}$$

where $H(Z)$ is the sums of the outputs of the nonlinear convex function h which is applied on all elements in the matrix Z, $C = diag\{c_1, c_2, \cdots, c_N\}$ is a diagonal matrix whose diagonal elements are the sums of the row elements of S, and $L = C - S$.

Combining Eqs. (4)-(6) into Eq. (1), we have the following SFDL model:

$$\min_{W,D,A} J = \sum_{p=1}^{P} G_p(W, X_p, D, A_p) + \eta_1 \|A\|_1 + \lambda_1(\|W^T W X - X\|_2^2 + \eta_2 H(WX)) + \lambda_2 tr(A^T L A) \tag{7}$$

While the objective function in Eq. (7) is not convex for W, D and A simultaneously, it is convex to one of them when the other two are fixed. Following the work in [20], [42], [14], [24], we iteratively optimize W, D and A by using the following three-stage method.

Step 1: Learn W with fixed D and A: when D and A are fixed, Eq. (7) can be rewritten as

$$\min_{W} J = \sum_{p=1}^{P} (\|WX_p - DA_p\|_F^2 + \|WX_p - D_p A_p^p\|_F^2) + \lambda_1(\|W^T W X - X\|_2^2 + \eta_2 H(WX)) \tag{8}$$

Eq. (8) is an unconstrained optimization problem and many existing fast unconstrained optimizers can be applied to solve this problem. In our implementations, we use the conjugate gradient decent method in [25] to get W.

Step 2: Learn A with fixed W and D: when W and D are fixed, Eq. (7) can be rewritten as

$$\min_{A} J = \sum_{p=1}^{P} (\|Y_p - DA_p\|_F^2 + \|Y_p - D_p A_p^p\|_F^2) + \eta_1 \|A\|_1 + \lambda_2 tr(A^T L A) \tag{9}$$

where $Y_p = WX_p$ is the projection of X_p in the feature space. We compute A_p sequentially by fixing the other coefficient matrices A_q ($q \neq p$, and $1 \leq q \leq P$). Then, Eq. (9) can be simplified as

$$\min_{A_p} J = \|Y_p - DA_p\|_F^2 + \|Y_p - D_p A_p^p\|_F^2 + \eta_1 \|A_p\|_1 + \lambda_2 tr(A_p^T L A_p) \tag{10}$$

Following the work in [26], we optimize each α_{ip} in A_p alternatively. To obtain each α_{ip}, we fix the encoding coefficients α_{jp} ($j \neq i$) for other samples, and rewrite Eq. (10) as

$$\min_{\alpha_{ip}} J = \|Y_p - D\alpha_{ip}\|_F^2 + \|Y_p - D_p \alpha_{ip}^p\|_F^2 + \eta_1 \|\alpha_{ip}\|_1 + \lambda_2 F(\alpha_{ip}) \tag{11}$$

where

$$F(\alpha_{ip}) = \lambda_2(\alpha_{ip}^T (A_p L_i) + (A_p L_i)^T \alpha_{ip} - \alpha_{ip}^T L_{ii} \alpha_{ip}) \tag{12}$$

L_i is the ith column of L, and L_{ii} is the entry in the ith row and ith column of L. We apply the feature sign search algorithm [26] to solve α_{ip}.

Input: Training set $X = [X_1, X_2, \cdots, X_P]$, affinity matrix S, parameters λ_1, λ_2, η_1 and η_2, iteration number T, convergence error ϵ.
Output: Feature weighting matrix W, dictionary D, and coding coefficient matrix A.
Step 1 (Initialization):
1.1: Initialize each column d_p^i in D_p as a random vector with unit l2-norm.
1.2: Initialize each column in A as a random vector.
Step 2 (Local optimization):
For $t = 1, 2, \cdots, T$, repeat
2.1. Solve W^t with fixed D^{t-1} and A^{t-1} via Eq. (8).
2.2. Solve A^t with fixed W^t and D^{t-1} via Eq. (11).
2.3. Solve D^t with fixed W^t and A^t via Eq. (14).
2.3. If $|D^t - D^{t-1}| < \epsilon$ or $|W^t - W^{t-1}| < \epsilon$ and $t > 2$, go to Step 3.
Step 3 (Output):
Output $W = W^t$, $D = D^t$, and $A = A^t$.

Algorithm 1. SFDL

Step 3: Learn D with fixed W and A: when W and A are fixed, Eq. (7) can be rewritten as

$$\min_D J = \sum_{p=1}^{P} (\|Y_p - DA_p\|_F^2 + \|Y_p - D_p A_p^p\|_F^2) \tag{13}$$

We update D_p sequentially by fixing the other sub-dictionaries D_q ($q \neq p$, and $1 \leq q \leq P$). Then, Eq. (13) can be reduced as

$$\min_{D_p} J = \|Y_p - D_p A_p\|_F^2 + \|Y_p - D_p A_p^p\|_F^2 \tag{14}$$

We restrict that each column d_p^i in D_p is a unit vector, where $1 \leq i \leq K_p$, K_p is the number of atoms in D_p. Eq. (14) is a quadratic programming problem and can be solved by using the algorithm in [43], which updates D_p atom by atom.

We repeat the above three steps until the algorithm is convergent. The proposed SFDL algorithm is summarized in **Algorithm 1**.

3.2 Identification

Given a testing face video $X^q = [x_1^q, x_2^q, \cdots, x_M^q]$, where x_j^q is the jth ($1 \leq j \leq M$) frame of this video and M is the number of image frames in this video, we first apply the learned feature projection matrix W to project each frame x_j^q in this video into a feature and recognize its label by using the smallest reconstruction error corresponding to each sub-dictionary D_p ($q \leq p \leq P$), which is computed as follows:

$$p' = \arg\min_p \|Wx_j^q - D_p D_p^\dagger x_j^q\|_2 \tag{15}$$

where $D_p^\dagger = (D_p^T D_p)^{-1} D_p^T$ is the pseudoinverse of D_p.

Then, we adopt the majority voting strategy to classify the whole testing face video:

$$p^* = \arg\max_p Z_p \tag{16}$$

where Z_p is the total number of votes from the pth class.

3.3 Verification

Different from face identification, the goal of video face verification is to determine whether a pair of given face videos belongs to the same person or not. Assume $X^a = [x_1^a, x_2^a, \cdots, x_{M_1}^a]$ and $X^b = [x_1^b, x_2^b, \cdots, x_{M_2}^b]$ be the given testing face video pair, x_i^a and x_j^b are the ith and jth frames of these two videos, M_1 and M_2 are the number of image frames in these two videos, $1 \leq i \leq M_1$, $1 \leq j \leq M_2$, we first apply the learned feature projection matrix W to project each x_i^a and x_j^b in these two videos into a low-dimensional feature and recognize their labels by using the smallest reconstruction error corresponding to each sub-dictionary D_p $(1 \leq p \leq P)$ as defined in Eq. (15). Then, we compute the number of votes from each class for these two videos by counting the labels of all frames in each video and get two voting vectors $H^a = [h_1^a, h_2^a, \cdots, h_P^a]$ and $H^b = [h_1^b, h_2^b, \cdots, h_P^b]$, where h_p^a and h_p^b denote the total voting number of votes from the pth class of X^a and X^b, respectively. Lastly, the intersection metric is applied to measure the similarity of the normalized H^a and H^b as follows:

$$s(H^a, H^b) = \sum_{p=1}^{P} \min(\bar{h_p^a}, \bar{h_p^b}) \tag{17}$$

where $\bar{h_p^a} = \frac{1}{M_1} h_p^a$ and $\bar{h_p^a} = \frac{1}{M_2} h_p^b$.

4 Experimental Results

We evaluate our proposed approach on four publicly available video face databases including the Honda [27], Mobo [13], YouTube Celebrities (YTC) [22] and YouTube Face (YTF) [40] datasets. The Honda, MoBo, and YTC datasets are used to show the effectiveness of our approach for face classification with image sets, and the YTF dataset is selected to show the effectiveness of our approach to face verification with image sets.

4.1 Datasets

The Honda dataset [27] contains 59 face videos of 20 subjects, where there are large pose and expression variations and the average length of these videos are approximately 400 frames.

There are 96 videos from 24 subjects in the MoBo dataset [13]. For each subject, four videos corresponding to different walking patterns on a treadmill such as slow, fast, inclined and carrying a ball were captured and each video corresponds to one walking pattern. For each video, there are around 300 frames covering pose and expression variations.

The YTC dataset [22] contains 1910 video sequences of 47 celebrities (actors, actresses and politicians) which are collected from YouTube. Most videos are low resolution which leads to noisy and low-quality image frames. The number of frames for these videos varied from 8 to 400.

The YTF dataset [40] contains 3425 videos of 1596 subjects which are also downloaded from YouTube. The average length of each video clip is about 180 frames. There are large variations in pose, illumination, and expression, and resolution in these videos.

For face videos in the Honda, Mobo and YTC datasets, each image frame is first automatically detected by applying the face detector method proposed in [35] and then resized to a 30×30 intensity image. For the YTF dataset, each image frame was cropped into 30×30 according to the provided eye coordinates. Hence, each video is represented as an image set. For each image frame in all these four datasets, we only perform histogram equalization to remove the illumination effect.

4.2 Experimental Settings

To make a fair comparison with state-of-the-art image set based face recognition methods, we follow the same protocol used in [38], [36], [3], [17], [37], [40]. On the Honda, MoBo, and YTC datasets, we conduct experiments 10 times by randomly selecting training and testing sets, compute and compare the average identification rate. For both the Honda and MoBo datasets, we randomly select one face video per person to construct the training set and the remaining videos as the testing set. For the YTC dataset, we equally divide the whole dataset into five folds (with minimal overlapping), and each fold contains 9 videos for each person. For each fold, we randomly select 3 face videos for each person for training and use the remain 6 for testing. For the YTF dataset, we follow the standard evaluation protocol and evaluate our approach by using 5000 video pairs which were randomly selected in [40], where half of them are from the same person and the remaining half are from different persons. These pairs are equally divided into 10 folds and each fold contains 250 intra-personal pairs and 250 inter-personal pairs. We also use the 10-fold cross validation strategy in our experiments [40]. Specifically, we use 6 folds from the 9 folds in the training set to train the SFDL model and the rest 3 to learn a discriminative distance metric by using the method in [21].

In our implementations, the feature dimension of W and the parameters λ_1, λ_2, η_1 and η_2 of our SFDL method were empirically specified as 200, 1, 1, 0.05, and 0.2, respectively, and the number of atoms per person (K_p) for different datasets are summarized in Table 1.

Table 1. Summary of number of atoms per person (K_p) for different face datasets in our experiments

Dataset	Honda	MoBo	YTC	YTF
K_p	20	25	35	40

4.3 Results and Analysis

Comparison with Existing State-of-the-Art Image Set Based Face Recognition Methods: We compare our approach with ten state-of-the-art image set based face recognition methods, including Mutual Subspace Method (MSM) [41], Discriminant Canonical Correlation analysis (DCC) [23], Manifold-to-Manifold Distance (MMD) [38], Manifold Discriminant Analysis (MDA) [36], Affine Hull based Image Set Distance (AHISD) [3], Convex Hull based Image Set Distance (CHISD) [3], Sparse Approximated Nearest Point (SANP) [17], Covariance Discriminative Learning (CDL) [37], Dictionary-based Face Recognition from Video (DFRV) [4], and Local Multi-Kernel Metric Learning (LMKML) [30].

The standard implementations of all the other compared methods were provided by the original authors except the CDL and DFRV methods because their codes have not been publicly available. We carefully implemented their methods by following their settings in [37] and [4]. We tuned the parameters of different methods as follows: For MSM and DCC, we performed PCA to learn a linear subspace for each face image set where each subspace dimension was set as 10 to preserve 90% of the energy to compute the similarity of two image sets. For MMD and MDA, the parameters were configured according to [38] and [36], respectively. Specifically, the maximum canonical correlation was used to compute MMD, and the number of connected nearest neighbors for computing geodesic distance in both MMD and MDA was fixed as 12. No parameter is required in AHISD. For CHISD and SANP, we follow the same parameter settings as those in [3] and [17]. For CDL, the KLDA was employed for discriminative learning and the regularization parameter was set the same as that in [37]. For DFRV, we followed the parameter settings in [4]. For the DCC, CDL and LMKML methods, if there is a single video from each class in the Honda, MoBo and YTF datasets, we randomly and equally divided each video clip into two image sets to model the within-class variation.

Table 2 tabulates the average recognition rates of different image set based face recognition methods on these four datasets. We see that our approach performs better than the other ten compared image set based face recognition methods on the Honda, MoBo, and YTF datasets, and achieves comparable results on the YTC dataset. Compared with the existing unsupervised image set based face recognition methods such as MSM, DCC, MMD, AHISD, CHISD, SANP, and DFRV, our SFDL can exploit more discriminative information in the learned feature projection matrix and dictionary. Compared with the existing supervised image set based face recognition methods such as MDA, CDL, and LMKML, our SFDL can project each image frame into a discriminative feature subspace

Table 2. Average recognition rates (%) of different image set based face recognition methods on different video face datasets

Method	Honda	MoBo	YTC	YTF	Year
MSM [41]	92.5	85.5	61.5	62.5	1998
DCC [23]	94.9	88.1	64.8	70.8	2007
MMD [38]	94.9	91.7	66.7	65.0	2008
MDA [36]	97.4	94.4	68.1	72.5	2009
AHISD [3]	89.5	94.1	66.5	66.5	2010
CHISD [3]	92.5	95.8	67.4	66.3	2010
SANP [17]	93.6	96.1	68.3	63.7	2011
CDL [37]	97.4	87.5	69.7	74.5	2012
DFRV [4]	97.4	94.4	74.5	78.6	2012
LMKML [30]	98.5	96.3	78.2	77.8	2013
SFDL	**100.0**	**96.7**	**76.7**	**80.2**	

Table 3. Average recognition rates (%) of different feature and dictionary learning strategies on different face datasets

Method	Honda	MoBo	YTC	YTF
Structured IFDL	98.3	94.1	74.3	78.5
Structured SFDL	**100.0**	**96.7**	**76.7**	**80.2**

and encode it with a class-specific dictionary, so that more person-specific information can be extracted.

Simultaneous vs. Individual Feature and Dictionary Learning: The feature learning and dictionary learning can also be learned in an individual manner. To show the effect of SFDL, we compare our SFDL method with the individual feature and dictionary learning (IFDL) method. IFDL means the feature projection matrix and the structured dictionaries are learned from the training set separately. Table 3 tabulates the average recognition rates of these two methods. We can observe that our simultaneous method can achieve higher recognition rate than the individual method, which shows that jointly learning the feature subspace and dictionary is better because some useful information for dictionary learning may be lost in the feature learning phase in the individual method.

Structured vs. Shared SFDL: To demonstrate the advantage of the structured dictionary in our SFDL, we also compare it with a shared SFDL method which learns a common dictionary in SFDL rather than a structured dictionary. Table 4 tabulates the average recognition rates of these two types of SFDL methods. We can observe that the structured SFDL achieves higher recognition rate than the shared SFDL method. This is because the structured SFDL can characterize more class-specific information than the shared SFDL.

Parameter Analysis: We first evaluate the effect of the feature dimension of the learned feature projection matrix of our SFDL on the recognition performance. Fig. 2 shows the recognition accuracy of our SFDL versus different

Table 4. Average recognition rates (%) of the structured and shared dictionary learning methods on different face datasets

Method	Honda	MoBo	YTC	YTF
Shared SFDL	98.3	95.3	74.7	78.9
Structured SFDL	**100.0**	**96.7**	**76.7**	**80.2**

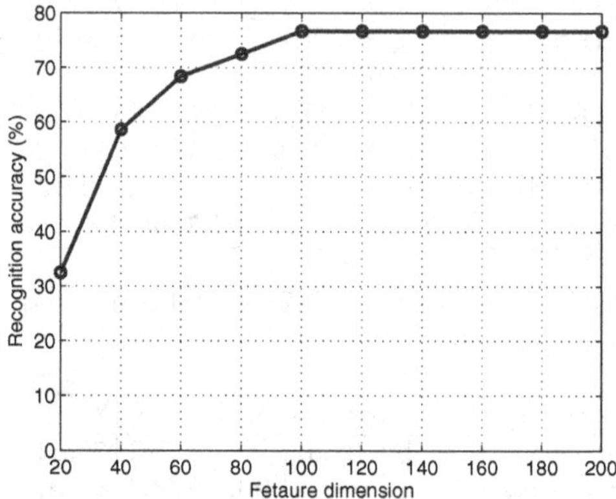

Fig. 2. Average recognition rate (%) of our SFDL versus different feature dimension of the learned feature projection matrix on the YTC dataset

feature dimensions on the YTC dataset. We can see that our proposed SFDL can achieve stable performance when the feature dimension reaches 100.

We also investigate the performance of our SFDL versus different number of iterations. Fig. 3 shows the recognition accuracy of our SFDL over different number of iterations on the YTC dataset. We see that our proposed SFDL can achieve stable performance in several iterations.

Robustness Analysis: We first test the robustness of our proposed approach versus different amount of noisy data in face videos. We follow the settings in [3], [37], [30] and conducted three experiments where the training and/or testing face image sets were corrupted by adding one image from each of the other classes. The original data and three noisy scenarios are called as "original", "NTR" (only training videos have noisy data), "NTE" (only testing videos have noisy data), and "NTT" (both training and testing videos have noisy data), respectively. Table 5 records the recognition accuracy of different image set based face recognition methods with different amounts of noisy data on the YTC dataset.

We also evaluate the performance of our approach when face videos contain varying number of image frames. We randomly selected N frames from each face image set (both training and testing) and used them for recognition. If there are less than N image frames for one face image set, all image frames within this image set were used for recognition. Fig. 4 shows the performance of different methods on the YTC dataset with varying image frames. From Table 5 and

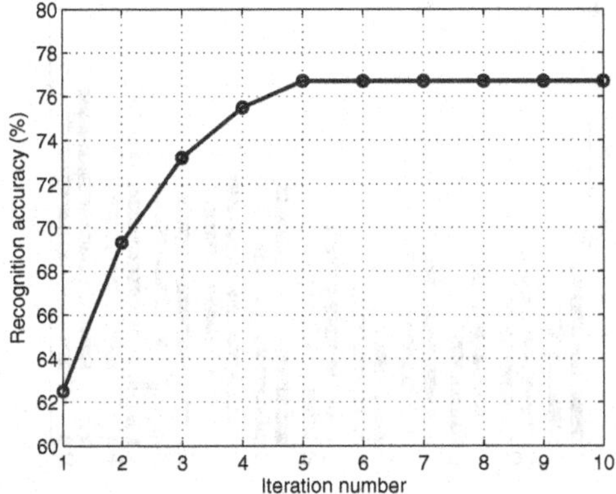

Fig. 3. Average recognition rate (%) of our approach versus different number of iterations on the YTC dataset

Table 5. Average recognition rates (%) of different image set based face recognition methods with different amounts of noisy data on the YTC dataset

Method	Original	NTR	NTE	NTT
MSM [41]	62.8	59.7	45.3	52.2
DCC [23]	64.8	58.7	49.9	54.2
MMD [38]	66.7	62.5	46.4	55.4
MDA [36]	68.1	65.8	52.5	53.4
AHISD [3]	66.5	62.5	44.5	35.6
CHISD [3]	67.4	66.8	42.5	38.5
SANP [17]	68.3	67.2	47.5	39.4
CDL [37]	69.7	68.4	54.5	58.4
DFRV [4]	74.5	71.1	60.8	62.1
LMKML [30]	78.2	76.1	64.5	66.1
SFDL	**76.7**	**76.3**	**64.8**	**67.2**

Fig. 4, we observe that our approach demonstrates strong robustness with some slight performance drop than the other compared methods. That is because we use dictionaries to represent each face image set and such dictionary-based methods are robust to noise and the number of samples in face image set. Hence, the effects of the noisy samples and varying data size can be alleviated in our proposed approach.

Computational Time: Lastly, we report the computational time of different methods using the YTC dataset. Our hardware configuration is a 2.8-GHz CPU and a 24GB RAM. Table 6 shows the computational time for different methods under the Matlab paltform. It is to be noted that training time is only required for some discriminative learning and dictionary learning methods such as DCC, MDA, CDL, DFRV, LMKML and our SFDL. We see that the computational

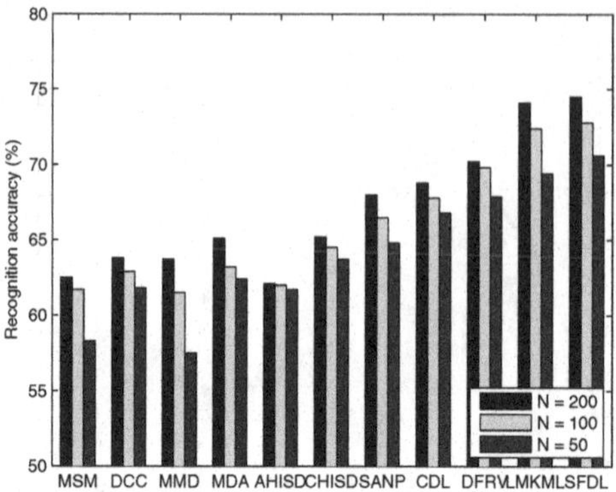

Fig. 4. Average recognition rates (%) of different image set based face recognition methods with different number of image frames on the YTC dataset

Table 6. Computation time (seconds) of different image set based face recognition methods on the YTC dataset for the training and testing phases per face video

Method	MSM	DCC	MMD	MDA	AHISD	CHISD	SANP	CDL	DFRV	LMKML	SFDL
Training	N.A.	98.6	N.A.	185.3	N.A.	N.A.	N.A.	68.5	8656.5	4232.8	7532.5
Testing	2.7	2.5	3.5	3.2	8.7	6.7	48.6	12.8	5.4	210.6	6.5

time of our SFDL is generally larger than many other compared methods for training and is comparable to them for testing.

5 Conclusion and Future Work

In this paper, we propose a new simultaneous feature and dictionary learning (SFDL) method for image set based face recognition. By jointly learning the feature projection matrix and the structured dictionary, our approach extracts more discriminative information for image set based face representation. Experimental results on four widely used face datasets have shown the superiority of our approach over the state-of-the-art image set based face recognition methods in terms of accuracy and robustness. How to design more efficient optimization methods to improve the speed of our SFDL method appears to be an interesting future work.

Acknowledgement. This work is supported by the research grant for the Human Cyber Security Systems (HCSS) Program at the Advanced Digital Sciences Center from the Agency for Science, Technology and Research of Singapore, and the research grant of MOE Tier 1 RG84/12, MOE Tier 2 ARC28/14 and SERC 1321202099.

References

1. Aharon, M., Elad, M., Bruckstein, A.: Ksvd: An algorithm for designing overcomplete dictionaries for sparse representation. TSP 54(11), 4311–4322 (2006)
2. Arandjelovic, O., Shakhnarovich, G., Fisher, J., Cipolla, R., Darrell, T.: Face recognition with image sets using manifold density divergence. In: CVPR, pp. 581–588 (2005)
3. Cevikalp, H., Triggs, B.: Face recognition based on image sets. In: CVPR, pp. 2567–2573 (2010)
4. Chen, Y.-C., Patel, V.M., Phillips, P.J., Chellappa, R.: Dictionary-based face recognition from video. In: Fitzgibbon, A., Lazebnik, S., Perona, P., Sato, Y., Schmid, C. (eds.) ECCV 2012, Part VI. LNCS, vol. 7577, pp. 766–779. Springer, Heidelberg (2012)
5. Chen, Y.C., Patel, V.M., Phillips, P.J., Chellappa, R.: Dictionary-based face recognition from video. Tech. rep., University of Maryland (2013)
6. Chen, Y.C., Patel, V.M., Shekhar, S., Chellappa, R., Phillips, P.J.: Video-based face recognition via joint sparse representation. In: FG, pp. 1–8 (2013)
7. Chin, T.J., Schindler, K., Suter, D.: Incremental kernel svd for face recognition with image sets. In: FG, pp. 461–466 (2006)
8. Cui, Z., Shan, S., Zhang, H., Lao, S., Chen, X.: Image sets alignment for video-based face recognition. In: CVPR, pp. 2626–2633 (2012)
9. Deng, W., Hu, J., Guo, J.: Extended src: Undersampled face recognition via intraclass variant dictionary. PAMI 34(9), 1864–1870 (2012)
10. Deng, W., Hu, J., Lu, J., Guo, J.: Transform-invariant pca: A unified approach to fully automatic face alignment, representation, and recognition. PAMI 36(6), 1275–1284 (2014)
11. Fan, W., Yeung, D.: Locally linear models on face appearance manifolds with application to dual-subspace based classification. In: CVPR, pp. 1384–1390 (2006)
12. Fitzgibbon, A., Zisserman, A.: Joint manifold distance: a new approach to appearance based clustering. In: CVPR, pp. 26–33 (2003)
13. Gross, R., Shi, J.: The cmu motion of body (mobo) database. Tech. rep., Carnegie Mellon University (2001)
14. Guo, H., Jiang, Z., Davis, L.S.: Discriminative dictionary learning with pairwise constraints. In: Lee, K.M., Matsushita, Y., Rehg, J.M., Hu, Z. (eds.) ACCV 2012, Part I. LNCS, vol. 7724, pp. 328–342. Springer, Heidelberg (2013)
15. Hadid, A., Pietikainen, M.: From still image to video-based face recognition: an experimental analysis. In: FG, pp. 813–818 (2004)
16. Hotelling, H.: Relations between two sets of variates. Biometrika 28(3/4), 321–377 (1936)
17. Hu, Y., Mian, A., Owens, R.: Sparse approximated nearest points for image set classification. In: CVPR, pp. 121–128 (2011)
18. Hu, Y., Mian, A.S., Owens, R.: Face recognition using sparse approximated nearest points between image sets. PAMI 34(10), 1992–2004 (2012)
19. Huang, L., Lu, J., Tan, Y.P.: Co-learned multi-view spectral clustering for face recognition based on image sets. IEEE Signal Processing Letters 21(7), 875–879 (2014)
20. Jiang, Z., Lin, Z., Davis, L.S.: Learning a discriminative dictionary for sparse coding via label consistent k-svd. In: CVPR, pp. 1697–1704 (2011)
21. Kan, M., Shan, S., Xu, D., Chen, X.: Side-information based linear discriminant analysis for face recognition. In: BMVC, pp. 1–12 (2011)
22. Kim, M., Kumar, S., Pavlovic, V., Rowley, H.: Face tracking and recognition with visual constraints in real-world videos. In: CVPR, pp. 1–8 (2008)

23. Kim, T., Kittler, J., Cipolla, R.: Discriminative learning and recognition of image set classes using canonical correlations. PAMI 29(6), 1005–1018 (2007)
24. Kong, S., Wang, D.: A dictionary learning approach for classification: Separating the particularity and the commonality. In: Fitzgibbon, A., Lazebnik, S., Perona, P., Sato, Y., Schmid, C. (eds.) ECCV 2012, Part I. LNCS, vol. 7572, pp. 186–199. Springer, Heidelberg (2012)
25. Le, Q.V., Karpenko, A., Ngiam, J., Ng, A.: Ica with reconstruction cost for efficient overcomplete feature learning. In: NIPS, pp. 1017–1025 (2011)
26. Lee, H., Battle, A., Raina, R., Ng, A.: Efficient sparse coding algorithms. In: NIPS, pp. 801–808 (2006)
27. Lee, K., Ho, J., Yang, M., Kriegman, D.: Video-based face recognition using probabilistic appearance manifolds. In: CVPR, pp. 313–320 (2003)
28. Lin, T., Liu, S., Zha, H.: Incoherent dictionary learning for sparse representation. In: ICPR, pp. 1237–1240 (2012)
29. Lu, J., Tan, Y.P., Wang, G., Yang, G.: Image-to-set face recognition using locality repulsion projections and sparse reconstruction-based similarity measure. TCSVT 23(6), 1070–1080 (2013)
30. Lu, J., Wang, G., Moulin, P.: Image set classification using multiple order statistics features and localized multi-kernel metric learning. In: ICCV, pp. 1–8 (2013)
31. Ma, L., Wang, C., Xiao, B., Zhou, W.: Sparse representation for face recognition based on discriminative low-rank dictionary learning. In: CVPR, pp. 2586–2593 (2012)
32. Mairal, J., Bach, F., Ponce, J., Sapiro, G., Zisserman, A.: Discriminative learned dictionaries for local image analysis. In: CVPR, pp. 1–8 (2008)
33. Shakhnarovich, G., Fisher III, J.W., Darrell, T.: Face recognition from long-term observations. In: Heyden, A., Sparr, G., Nielsen, M., Johansen, P. (eds.) ECCV 2002, Part III. LNCS, vol. 2352, pp. 851–865. Springer, Heidelberg (2002)
34. Tosic, I., Frossard, P.: Dictionary learning. IEEE Signal Processing Magazine 28(2), 27–38 (2011)
35. Viola, P., Jones, M.: Robust real-time face detection. IJCV 57(2), 137–154 (2004)
36. Wang, R., Chen, X.: Manifold Discriminant Analysis. In: CVPR, pp. 1–8 (2009)
37. Wang, R., Guo, H., Davis, L., Dai, Q.: Covariance discriminative learning: A natural and efficient approach to image set classification. In: CVPR, pp. 2496–2503 (2012)
38. Wang, R., Shan, S., Chen, X., Gao, W.: Manifold-manifold distance with application to face recognition based on image set. In: CVPR, pp. 1–8 (2008)
39. Wang, X., Wang, B., Bai, X., Liu, W., Tu, Z.: Max-margin multiple-instance dictionary learning. In: ICML, pp. 846–854 (2013)
40. Wolf, L., Hassner, T., Maoz, I.: Face recognition in unconstrained videos with matched background similarity. In: CVPR, pp. 529–534 (2011)
41. Yamaguchi, O., Fukui, K., Maeda, K.: Face recognition using temporal image sequence. In: FG, pp. 318–323 (1998)
42. Yang, M., Zhang, L., Feng, X., Zhang, D.: Fisher discrimination dictionary learning for sparse representation. In: ICCV, pp. 543–550 (2011)
43. Yang, M., Zhang, L., Yang, J., Zhang, D.: Metaface learning for sparse representation based face recognition. In: ICIP, pp. 1601–1604 (2010)
44. Yang, M., Zhu, P., Van Gool, L., Zhang, L.: Face recognition based on regularized nearest points between image sets. In: FG, pp. 1–7 (2013)
45. Zhang, Q., Li, B.: Discriminative k-svd for dictionary learning in face recognition. In: CVPR, pp. 2691–2698 (2010)
46. Zuo, Z., Wang, G.: Learning discriminative hierarchical features for object recognition. IEEE Signal Processing Letters 21(9), 1159–1163 (2014)

Read My Lips: Continuous Signer Independent Weakly Supervised Viseme Recognition

Oscar Koller[1,2], Hermann Ney[1], and Richard Bowden[2]

[1] Human Language Technology and Pattern Recognition, RWTH Aachen, Germany
[2] Centre for Vision Speech and Signal Processing, University of Surrey, UK
{koller,ney}@cs.rwth-aachen.de, r.bowden@surrey.ac.uk

Abstract. This work presents a framework to recognise signer independent mouthings in continuous sign language, with no manual annotations needed. Mouthings represent lip-movements that correspond to pronunciations of words or parts of them during signing. Research on sign language recognition has focused extensively on the hands as features. But sign language is multi-modal and a full understanding particularly with respect to its lexical variety, language idioms and grammatical structures is not possible without further exploring the remaining information channels. To our knowledge no previous work has explored dedicated viseme recognition in the context of sign language recognition. The approach is trained on over 180.000 unlabelled frames and reaches 47.1% precision on the frame level. Generalisation across individuals and the influence of context-dependent visemes are analysed.

Keywords: Sign Language Recognition, Viseme Recognition, Mouthing, Lip Reading.

1 Introduction

Sign Languages, the natural languages of the Deaf, are known to be as grammatically complete and rich as their spoken language counterparts. However, their grammar is different to spoken language. They are not international and convey meaning by more than just the movements of hands. Sign languages make use of both 'manual features' (hand shape, position, orientation and movement) and linguistically termed 'non-manual features' consisting of the face (eye gaze, mouthing/mouth gestures and facial expression) and of the upper body posture (head nods/shakes and shoulder orientation). All of these parameters are used in parallel to complement each other, but depending on the context a specific component may or may not be required to interpret the sign, sometimes playing an integral role within the sign, sometimes modifying the meaning and sometimes providing context. Furthermore, the different information channels don't share a fixed temporal alignment, but are rather loosely tied together. For example, the mouthing 'ALPS' may span over the two manual signs 'MOUNTAIN' and 'REGION'. Historically, research on automatic recognition of sign language has

D. Fleet et al. (Eds.): ECCV 2014, Part I, LNCS 8689, pp. 281–296, 2014.
© Springer International Publishing Switzerland 2014

focused extensively on the manual components [1–3]. These manual parameters are widely considered to cover an important part of the information conveyed by sign language. However, it is clear that a full understanding of sign language, particularly with respect to its lexical variety, language idioms and grammatical structures is not possible without further exploring the remaining information channels [4]. Computer vision methods exist to extract features for these non-manual channels. However, sign language constitutes an extremely challenging test bed as it incorporates huge variations inherent to natural languages. Further, ambiguity is inherent to sign languages, as each movement, each change in eye gaze or each appearance of the tongue may or may not have a grammatical or semantic function depending on the context. Thus, learning features and training classifiers that can be applied to sign language recognition must cope with a natural variation seldom present in other tasks.

The unsolved challenges in sign language recognition are to increase the number of signs to distinguish, recognise signs in a continuous fashion and generalise across different signers. Annotating the parallel information streams is cumbersome and time consuming, also due to the fact that sign languages don't have a standardised annotation system. Thus, possible annotation sources are noisy. This paper explores automatic identification and classification of mouthings in German Sign Language (DGS), as such it directly addresses each of these key challenges and our results are shown to generalise well across signers. They also scale well with increasing vocabulary (due to viseme sub-units) and the approach requires only weak supervision and no manual annotation. To our knowledge no previous work has modelled mouthings explicitly by sequences of visemes in the context of sign language recognition.

In Section 2 we specify the term 'mouthings' in the context of sign language and discuss difficulties when used for recognition. In Section 3 related work in viseme and facial recognition is shown. Further, the employed data sets and features are presented in Sections 4 and 5, respectively. In Section 6 the overall approach is explained. Results are given in Section 7 and finally the paper closes with a conclusion and future work in Section 8.

2 Mouthings in Sign Language, Challenging?

During signing the mouth of a signer performs notable and valuable actions. In sign language, two different types of actions are distinguished: mouth gestures and mouthings. Mouthings originate from speech contact [5] and represent at least part of a pronounced word, while mouth gestures are patterns that are unrelated to spoken language. Some signs are often accompanied by mouthings, others by mouth gestures and sometimes no mouth movement is present at all. Mouthing can be observed in many European sign languages, where it occurs more with nouns than with verbs. The latter are often accompanied by mouth gestures [6]. Nevertheless, the exact linguistic function of mouthings is still debated [7], but signing people state that it is evident they help to discriminate signs which are identical with respect to the manual components of the sign.

In audio-visual speech, recognising visemes, referring to visual patterns of the mouth while speaking, has been shown to be very challenging (even to humans) with error rates usually around 50% [8]. In sign language, and for this paper, additional challenges need to be tackled: 1. Mouthings may or may not occur with specific signs; 2. they can be stretched across several manual signs;

3. viseme sequences of a specific sign are not consistent (sign 'ALPS' sometimes is accompanied by the full mouthing 'A L P', but sometimes only an 'A' or an 'L' suffices); 3. phonemes and visemes don't share a one-to-one correspondence, rather a many-to-many [9]; 4. no standard viseme inventory for sign language exists; 5. huge variability in practises are observed, depending on context (see Fig. 1) and individuals; 6. sign language and spoken language sentence structure differs; 7. the video often has a low spatial resolution (mouth is small in videos); 8. there is an inherent lack of annotation, annotation is difficult; and time consuming especially due to ambiguity; 9. speech recognition cannot be used to bootstrap a viseme mapping. Our approach faces all these problems and suggests ways to solve them.

3 State of the Art

In 1968 Fisher [10] was the first to mention differences between spoken phonemes and corresponding visemes in the mouth area. Nowadays lipreading and viseme recognition is a well established, yet challenging research field in the context of audio-visual speech recognition. The first system was reported in 1984 by Petajan [11] who distinguished letters from the alphabet and numbers from zero to nine and achieved 80% accuracy on that task. Since then the field has advanced in terms of recognition vocabulary, features and modelling approaches. In 2011 Zhou et al. [12] achieve a Frame Recognition Accuracy (FRA) of 56% on the speaker independent OuluVS database [13] proposing a method to project visual mouthing features to a low dimensional graph representation. Lan et al. [8] achieve an accuracy of 45% on their challenging 12 speakers audio-visual corpus. A good overview of the field is given in [14] and [15]. Neti et al. [16] present audio-visual but also visual only recognition results. In their report they briefly evaluate phonetic decision trees and context-dependent modelling of visemes. Not much work has been done training viseme models in an unsupervised or weakly supervised fashion. Most deals with the problem of clustering visemes in order to find an optimal phoneme to viseme mapping [17].

In facial expression recognition mouth features and classifiers can also be found [18], e.g. [19] recognizes action units (and models the mouth with only three different states: open, closed, very closed).

With respect to sign language, several works exist that exploit weak supervision to learn hand-based sign models [20–24]. Facial features have also been used before. Michael et al. [25] employs spatial pyramids of Histogram of Oriented Graphs (HOG) and SIFT features together with 3D head pose and its first order derivative to distinguish three grammatical functions trained on isolated American Sign Language (ASL) data of three signers. Vogler and Goldstein [26] present a facial tracker specifically for ASL.

Pfister et al. [27] employ mouth openness as feature to distinguish signing from silence. This is used to reduce the candidate sequences in multiple instance learning (which besides manual features employs a sift descriptor of the mouth region). However, to our knowledge no previous work has explicitly modelled dedicated visemes in the context of sign language recognition.

4 Corpora

The proposed approach uses the publicly available RWTH-PHOENIX-Weather corpus, which contains 7 hearing interpreter's performing continuous signing in DGS. The corpus consists of a total of 190 TV broadcasts of weather forecast recorded on German public TV. It provides a total of 2137 manual sentence segmentations and 14717 gloss annotations, totalling to 189.363 frames. Glosses constitute a less labour intense way of annotating sign language corpora. They can be seen as an approximate semantic description of a sign, usually annotated w.r.t. the manual components (i.e. the hand shape, orientation, movement and position), neglecting many details. For instance, the same gloss 'MOUNTAIN' denotes the sign alps but also any other mountain, as they share the same hand configuration and differ only in mouthing. Moreover, the RWTH-PHOENIX-Weather corpus contains 22604 automatically transcribed and manually corrected German speech word transcriptions. The boundaries of the signing sentences are matched to the speech sentences. It is worth noting that the sentence structures for spoken German and DGS do not correlate. This is a translation rather than a transcript.

For the purpose of evaluating this work, we annotated 5 sentences per signer on the frame level with viseme labels totalling 3687 labelled frames. The annotation was performed three times by a learning non-native signer with profound knowledge of sign language. While annotating, the annotator had access to the video sequence of signing interpreters showing their whole body (not just the mouth), the gloss annotations and the German speech transcriptions. In each of the three annotation iterations the frame labels varied slightly due to the complexity and ambiguity of labelling visemes (see [8] for a human evaluation of viseme annotations). We consider each annotation to be valid, yielding more than a single label per frame for parts of the data. Refer to Tab. 1 for details.

5 Mouthing Features

The features extracted from the mouth region consist of ten continuous distance measurements around the signers mouth and the average colour intensity of three areas inside the mouth (to capture tongue and teeth presence), as shown in Fig. 2. First and second order derivatives and an additional temporal window of 1 frame are added to the feature vector. In a later stage of the proposed algorithm Linear Discriminant Analysis (LDA) is used to reduce the dimensionality to 15.

The mouth-distance measurements are based on lower-level facial features, which are defined as a set of consistent, salient point locations on the interpreter's

Fig. 1. Illustration of context-dependency of visemes in the annotated data. All frames share the same annotation, but occur in different context. They stem from the phoneme /s/ which is mapped to 'T'. The first two frames originate from the pronounced sequence 'Island' (engl: Iceland), while the second two occurred within 'Küste' (engl: coast).

face. Since the structure of the human face as described by a set of such point features exhibits a lot of variability due to changes in pose and expression, we chose to base our tracking strategy on the deformable model registration method known as Active-Appearance-Models (AAMs).

In this work, we chose to use the efficient version of the simultaneous inverse-compositional AAM (SICAAM) proposed in [28]. The implementation is more robust to large variations in shape and appearance, which typically occur when dealing with facial expressions in the context of sign language. Moreover, it copes well with large out-of-plane head rotations, also commonly present in sign language, which can lead a 2D AAM to fail. We also use the refinement proposed in [29]. Following the work in [30] a 3D Point Density Model (PDM) is estimated using a non-rigid structure-from-motion algorithm on the training shapes, and is then involved in the optimisation process which incorporates a regularisation term encouraging the 2D shape controlled by the 2D PDM to be a valid projection of the 3D PDM. To estimate the high-level mouth distances

Table 1. Frame annotation statistics for 11 visemes on the RWTH-PHOENIX-Weather corpus. The penultimate line shows relative annotation per viseme in [%]. 'gb' denotes frames labelled as non-mouthings/garbage. 'ratio' refers to the average labels per frame (last row) or per viseme (last line), which reflects the uncertainty of the annotator.

	frames	A	E	F	I	L	O	Q	P	S	U	T	gb	ratio
Signer 1	489	45	34	42	48	12	73	55	62	19	36	112	240	1.6
Signer 2	484	66	46	38	30	28	47	59	36	31	44	94	298	1.7
Signer 3	556	69	27	26	57	20	65	105	65	21	29	127	326	1.7
Signer 4	517	92	62	47	42	21	58	70	40	26	45	116	161	1.5
Signer 5	596	62	62	64	97	44	53	57	50	36	54	121	268	1.6
Signer 6	522	76	42	68	29	13	73	77	36	16	42	136	241	1.6
Signer 7	523	46	29	40	87	23	71	57	57	9	36	127	256	1.6
$\sum$	3687	12.4	8.2	8.8	10.6	4.4	11.9	13.0	9.4	4.3	7.8	22.6	48.6	1.6
ratio	1.6	1.8	1.9	1.9	2.0	2.0	1.8	2.2	1.8	1.9	1.9	2.0	1.9	

we project the registered shape and remove its global translation and rotation by means of the 3D PDM. Then, for each point features subset given in Fig. 3, we estimate the corresponding local area-based measurements and normalise it between 0 and 1 according to the minimum and maximum values obtained during training. To capture the mouth cavity, we extract the pixels in the quadrilateral defined by its four mouth corners and project it to a fixed-sized square. The pixel intensities are averaged over three regions: patch top, centre and bottom, yielding 3 features.

6 Weakly Supervised Mouthing Recognition

6.1 Overview

The approach exploits the fact that mouthings are related to the corresponding spoken words, for which automatic spoken language transcripts are part of the RWTH-PHOENIX-Weather corpus. However, there is a loose relation between speech and mouthings, which holds for some signs only. An overview of the scheme is given in Fig. 4

Visual features of the mouth region are extracted and clustered using Gaussian clustering and Expectation Maximization (EM) while constraining the sequence of features to the sequence of automatically transcribed German words in a Hidden-Markov-Model (HMM) framework. For increased accuracy, the word sequence can be optionally reordered by using manual gloss annotations and techniques commonly used in statistical machine translation to align source and target language. Furthermore, a lexicon is built that includes a finite set of possible pronunciations for each German word. This lexicon consists of different phoneme sequences for each word and an entry for 'no-mouthing'. Finally, to account for the difference in articulatory phonemes and visual visemes, we need to map phonemes to visemes. Two different ways are explored to achieve this: either apply the mapping directly to the lexicon or to include it later in the pipeline in the estimation of context-dependent visemes. During the EM-iterations, the pronunciation probabilities in the lexicon are constantly updated based on the pronunciation counts in the current cluster. In the last step, context-dependent

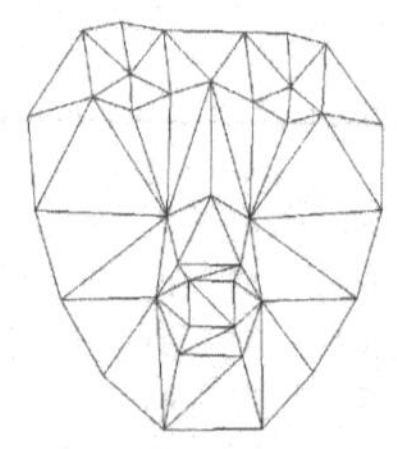

Fig. 2. Feature extraction, left: fitted AAM grid and inner mouth cavity patch, centre: rotated and normalised AAM grid, right: high-level feature values over time

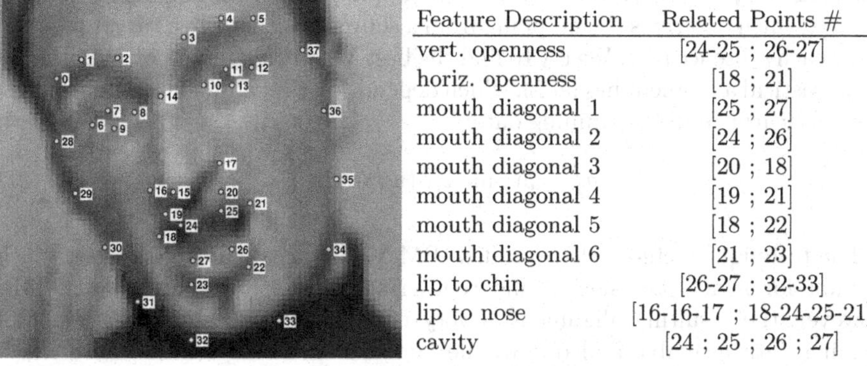

Feature Description	Related Points #
vert. openness	[24-25 ; 26-27]
horiz. openness	[18 ; 21]
mouth diagonal 1	[25 ; 27]
mouth diagonal 2	[24 ; 26]
mouth diagonal 3	[20 ; 18]
mouth diagonal 4	[19 ; 21]
mouth diagonal 5	[18 ; 22]
mouth diagonal 6	[21 ; 23]
lip to chin	[26-27 ; 32-33]
lip to nose	[16-16-17 ; 18-24-25-21]
cavity	[24 ; 25 ; 26 ; 27]

Fig. 3. Visualisation of distance measures employed as features

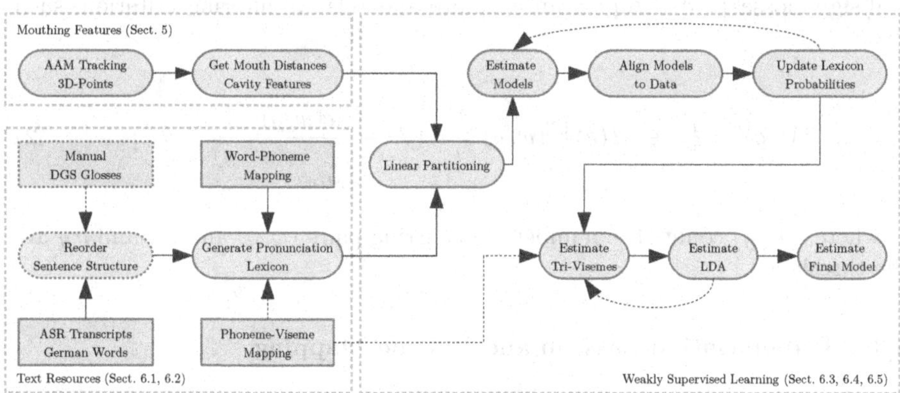

Fig. 4. Overview of the proposed approach. Dotted lines represent optional usage for better results. Round boxes represent procedures, while squared boxes are resources.

tri-visemes are estimated. In order to cope with limited data, a visemic Classification And Regression Tree (CART) is used to cluster those tri-visemes that share similar characteristics. The fine-grained tri-viseme alignments are used to perform a LDA on the input features, while adding more temporal context to the features.

6.2 Reordering Sentence Structure

Sign languages and their spoken counterparts do not share the same word order, nor does one word always translate to exactly one sign. Spoken German typically follows the 'subject (S), verb (V), object (O)' structure, while DGS prefers 'SOV'. Inspired by statistic machine translation, we employ a technique presented in [31], which maximises the alignment likelihood on a training corpus of sentence pairs each with a pair of sequences of German words $\mathbf{w} = w_1^J := w_1, \ldots, w_J$ and DGS glosses $\mathbf{g} = g_1^I := g_1, \ldots, g_I$ $(\mathbf{w}, \mathbf{g})$. The approach uses an alignment variable $\mathbf{a} = a_1^J$, which describes the mapping from a source position j to a target position a_j for each sentence pair. We try to find the best Viterbi alignment by maximising the statistical alignment model p_θ, which depends on a set of unknown parameters θ that is learnt from the training data:

$$\hat{a}_1^J = \arg\max_{a_1^J} p_\theta(w_1^J, a_1^J | g_1^I) \tag{1}$$

The technique includes the so called IBM Models as alignment models, which account for lexical translation and reordering. For more details refer to [31]. However, the resulting alignment is very noisy, due to the limited amount of training data available and due to the fact that not every source word has a single target. We thus apply filtering to the generated (w, g) pairs constituting a mapping $M : \mathcal{G} \rightarrow \mathcal{P}(\mathcal{W})$, where $w \in \mathcal{W} = \{\text{all spoken words}\}$ and $g \in \mathcal{G} = \{\text{all sign glosses}\}$. We employ an absolute and relative filtering criterion, such that

$$M(g)' = \left\{ w \in M(g) \,\middle|\, c(w,g) > \vartheta_A \wedge \frac{c(w,g)}{\sum\limits_{w' \in M(g)} c(w',g)} > \vartheta_R \right\}, \tag{2}$$

where $c(w, g)$ counts the number of occurring pairs (w, g) and ϑ_A and ϑ_R are the thresholds.

6.3 Pronunciation Lexicon and Viseme Mapping

Based on German words, we can build a pronunciation lexicon, which defines the finite set of possible pronunciations that occur with a sign. We first need a phoneme representation of the German words. For this purpose we use a word-phoneme mapping which has been generated with the publicly available Sequitur Grapheme-to-Phoneme converter [32].

However, mouthings produced by signers often do not constitute fully pronounced words, but rather discriminating bits of words. Thus, for each full pronunciation we add multiple shortened versions to our lexicon ψ by truncating the word w which consists of a sequence of phonemes $s_1^N = s_1, \ldots, s_N$, such that

$$\psi = \left\{ w' : s_1^{N-\phi} | \phi \in \{0, \ldots, \phi_{trunc}\} \wedge N - \phi \geq \phi_{min} \right\} \tag{3}$$

Moreover a 'no-mouthing' is added to the lexicon for each word. We are aware of the fact that visemes have a different inventory than phonemes. In the literature there is some specific work on viseme sets for Deaf people. Elliott [33] suggests a phoneme to viseme mapping resulting in 11 visemes (A, E, F, I, L, O, P, Q, S, T, U).

We choose two different ways to include this viseme knowledge into our pipeline: 1. We map our phoneme pronunciations to viseme sequences. 2. We use phoneme classes as models and include the viseme mapping in a visemic clustering of tri-visemes, as described later in this paper (Section 6.5).

6.4 Training Viseme Models

We use EM with Gaussian clustering in an HMM-framework to train viseme models from our data. Thus, we consider the weakly supervised viseme training to be a search problem of finding the sequence of visemes $v_1^Z := v_1, \ldots, v_Z$ belonging to a sequence of mouthings (pronounced words) $m_1^N := m_1, \ldots, m_N$, where the sequence of features $x_1^T := x_1, \ldots, x_T$ best matches the viseme models. We maximise the posterior probability $p(v_1^N | x_1^T)$ over all possible viseme sequences for the given sequence of glosses.

$$x_1^T \to \hat{v}_1^Z(x_1^T) = \arg\max_{v_1^Z} \{p(m_1^N) p(x_1^T | v_1^Z)\}, \tag{4}$$

where $p(m_1^N)$ denotes the pronunciation probability for a chosen mouthing. In a first step we model each viseme by a 3 state HMM and a no-mouthing model having a single state. The emission probability of an HMM state is represented by a single Gaussian density with a diagonal covariance matrix. The HMM states have a strict left to right structure. Global transition probabilities are used for the visemes. The no-mouthing model has independent transition probabilities. We initialise the viseme models by linearly partitioning the data. We then use the EM algorithm to iteratively 1. estimate the best alignment based on the current models and 2. to accumulate updated viseme models and 3. update pronunciation probabilities based on the alignments. To prevent abrupt changes in the pronunciation probabilities due to limited data, we average the probabilities over the last three alignments.

6.5 Context-Dependent Visemes with a Visemic Classification and Regression Tree

Visemes are known to be context dependent, e.g. the viseme /s/ in the words 'sue' and 'sea' is likely to have very different properties. Refer to Fig. 1 for a visual example. Co-articulation effects stem from the constraints enforced by the human muscular system, which does not allow immediate, ad-hoc execution or stops of motions, but rather blends one movement into another [34, 35].

We model the viseme context using both the previous and subsequent viseme (so-called tri-visemes). However, due to data limitations, not all tri-visemes can be observed during training. It is necessary to tie states of less frequent tri-visemes together and pool their model parameters. We follow the approach of phonetic decision trees presented in [36] for Automatic Speech Recognition (ASR). We cluster the tri-visemes with respect to visual properties of the visemes. The method uses a decision tree whose internal nodes are tagged with questions on these properties, as listed in Tab. 2. The leafs of the tree represent the actual tri-visemes. The

Table 2. Common visemic properties of the mouthings, used for decision tree based clustering

Common Property	Visemes
Consonant	F, P, T
Vowel	A, E, I, O, U, Q
Alveolar	T, Q
Labial	F, P
Round	U, O ,S
Not-round	I, E
Open	A, Q ,L
Semi-open	U, Q, L, E, T

observations within each node are modelled by a single Gaussian density with diagonal covariance. Starting at the root, the leafs of the tree are consecutively split by the questions regarding the visemic properties, where the order of questions is based on the maximum local gain in likelihood. Splitting is stopped, when there are less than 200 observations in a leaf or when the likelihood gain falls below a threshold. The tree can also be used to incorporate further linguistic knowledge such as the mapping from phonemes to visemes.

6.6 Linear Discriminant Analysis

LDA helps to find a linear transformation of our feature vectors to a lower dimensional space, while maximising class separability. Inspired from a quasi-standard in ASR [37], we apply LDA to the estimated tri-visemes. At this stage we also take into account the temporal context by concatenating the preceding $n = 3$ frames to the feature vector x_t^T, which yields a context feature vector X_t^T consisting of context frames plus the current frame. Finally, a reduced feature representation y_t is achieved by projecting X_t into a subspace of reduced dimensionality 15 with $y_t = V^T X_t$. The transformation matrix V^T is constructed by LDA such that it maximises interclass, while minimising intra-class variance.

7 Results

In this section, we present results that allow assessment of all training steps proposed in this framework. We evaluate four different setups in terms of their alignment performance during weakly supervised training and in classification performance on the frame level ground truth annotation (see Tab. 3). Due to the weakly supervised nature, the latter can be understood as a recognition constrained by the accompanying manual signs. If not otherwise stated, all results have been trained in a signer independent fashion, i.e. leaving one signer's data out of the training and averaging over all signers. Furthermore, we show how the visemes generalise across different signers comparing a multi-signer setup (no unseen signer in test) with a signer independent setup (see Tab. 4) and how the systems behave with a variation of precision and recall based on classifier confidence thresholding (see Fig. 5). Finally, we also analyse the classification errors on the viseme level (see Fig. 6)

We perform classification based on the highest pooled posterior probability per frame $\hat{p}(v|x)$ of the viseme v given the feature vector x,

$$\hat{p}(v|x) = \max_{v \in \mathcal{V}} p(v|x) = \max_{v \in \mathcal{V}} \sum_{v_c \in \mathcal{C}_v} p(v_c|x), \tag{5}$$

where $\mathcal{C}_v = \{v_{c1}, \ldots, v_{cN}\}$ contains all context-dependent tri-visemes of v. The classification does not rely on any priors, such as a grammar. The standard classification task distinguishes 11 visemes and a 'no-mouthing' class, whereas in a second task ('excl. Garbage') we exclude all frames that have been manually labelled with 'garbage' and evaluate only the 11 viseme classes.

As evaluation criterion we chose precision $= \frac{\text{tp}}{\text{tp+fp}}$ and recall $= \frac{\text{tp}}{\text{tp+fn}}$, where a classification is counted as true positive (tp) if it corresponds to any of the annotated ground truth labels (1.6 labels/frame, see Section 4). The reference labels count a false negative (fn) if no classified label matches them. If the chosen label was other than 'garbage' it counts additionally as false positive (fp).

In Tab. 3 we see four different experiments. The first experiment does not compensate for different word order (see Section 6.2) and applies the viseme mapping at an early stage straight to the lexicon (see Section 6.3), while experiment (3) and (4) incorporate the phoneme-viseme mapping into the clustering of tri-visemes (see Section 6.5). Precision and recall are given for each training step of all experiments: after the initial linear bootstrapping of the models, after 25/50 iterations of the EM-algorithm (see Section 6.4) and after successive tri-viseme clustering and incorporation of temporal context with a LDA (see Section 6.6). The results in Tab. 3 show the strength of our weakly supervised learning approach in detail. Furthermore, Fig. 6 shows the confusions on the viseme level achieved by the best system, split up by each signer, allowing to asses the quality of the approach in general and also qualify its signer independent capabilities. Following statements can be drawn from the results:

1. **Reordering is important.** The alignment precision during training improves in all cases (see right columns in Tab. 3, 34.1 → 41.3% and 34.3 → 41.3%). Reordering has in all cases a positive impact on the final classification performance (43.4 → 44.1% and 40.8 → 47.1%). Earlier EM-iteration steps in some cases show a slight degradation, which may be due to introduced noise by the reordering technique. In Fig. 5 we also see that systems (2) and (4) outperform the others.
2. **Integration of a viseme mapping through a visemic decision tree is advisable when reordering is applied.** The late integration outperforms the early viseme mapping with 44.1 → 47.1%.
3. **Visemes have signer independent properties.** Tab. 4 shows that the recognition precision only degrades by 3.2% (32.1% → 29.0%) on average from the multisigner to the unseen signer (signer independent) case. Signer specific models have a slightly better performance, but their data is very

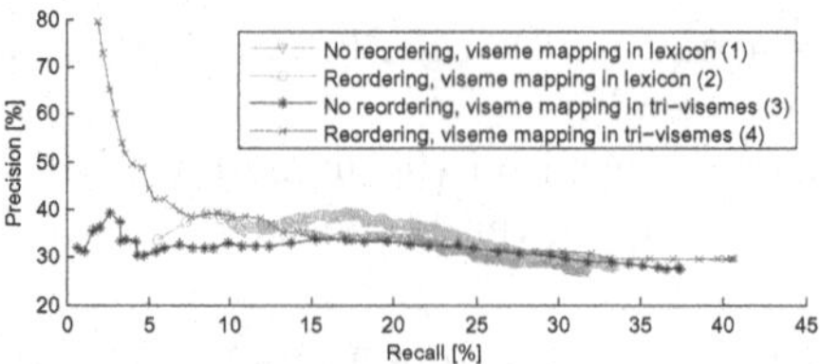

Fig. 5. Performance curves of the four competing systems. Precision and recall varied by applying a confidence threshold to the joint classifier

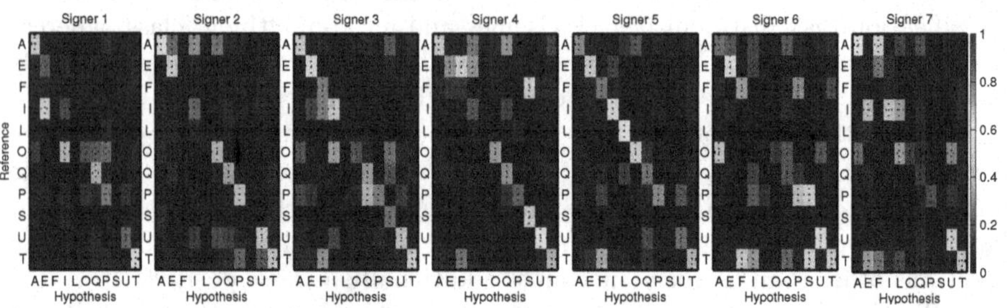

Fig. 6. Confusion matrices per signer of the best system (4) ('Reordering & viseme mapping in tri-visemes') excluding frames manually labelled as garbage on a signer independent task. Colours on the diagonal correspond to the precision of a certain viseme. This setup achieves 47.1% precision averaged over all signers.

limited. However, Fig. 6 shows that not all visemes are equally well recognized across all signers. Thus, improved adaptation methods are still required.

4. **Context-dependent modelling is very important.** Context-dependent outperform context-independent visemes heavily (e.g. 27.0 → 44.9%)
5. **Frames ground-truthed as 'garbage' are problematic.** Results excluding 'garbage' are constantly better than including it.
6. **LDA with added temporal context seems to require more and cleaner training alignments.** In cases without applied reordering , the LDA does not improve results. This may be due to low recall and limited precision achieved by the weakly supervised training (see 'Alignment during Training' in Tab. 3: 35.8 → 36.9% and 35.9 → 38.5%).
7. **Normalization of features w.r.t. the signer and to the out of plane rotation is important.** Comparative experiments have been done replacing the AAM distance features by a sift descriptor (128 dim., placed in the centre of the mouth, resized to match the mouth opening). This only yields 26.4% prec. and 26.0% recall in the 'no garbage' task and compares to 44.9% and 41.7% with the original features.

In terms of computational complexity, the algorithm requires around 50 minutes to train using all 189.363 frames on a single core of a AMD Opteron

Table 3. Precision and recall in [%] measured on the frame-level of continuous viseme recognition without any grammar constraints in a signer independent task averaged over all seven signers

	Testing				Alignment during Training			
	Standard		no Garb.		Standard		no Garb.	
	prec.	recall	prec.	recall	prec.	recall	prec.	recall
No Reordering & viseme mapping in lexicon (1)								
Partition linearly	11.9	10.6	17.9	11.8	23.7	23.5	33.8	25.8
25 EM-iterations	11.4	12.4	18.1	13.9	33.9	32.8	49.1	35.7
50 EM-iterations	11.5	12.5	18.3	14.1	34.0	32.9	49.2	35.8
1st Tri-visemes	29.3	34.6	43.5	38.3	34.1	33.0	49.4	35.9
LDA	29.0	38.0	43.4	42.3	"	"	"	"
Reordering & viseme mapping in lexicon (2)								
Partition linearly	10.2	9.6	16.0	10.7	30.0	26.4	40.3	28.3
25 EM-iterations	11.9	13.4	19.1	15.1	40.9	36.0	55.9	38.3
50 EM-iterations	11.9	13.4	19.1	15.1	41.2	36.2	56.2	38.4
1st Tri-visemes	29.0	35.5	43.5	39.6	41.3	36.3	56.3	38.5
LDA	29.5	39.0	44.1	43.7	"	"	"	"
No Reordering & viseme mapping in tri-visemes (3)								
Partition linearly	16.8	17.7	25.1	19.8	24.1	24.2	33.9	26.4
25 EM-iterations	16.7	20.9	26.1	23.9	33.9	32.9	47.7	35.5
50 EM-iterations	17.0	21.3	26.6	24.4	34.5	33.4	48.4	36.0
1st Tri-visemes	27.3	34.0	41.7	38.1	34.3	33.2	48.0	35.8
LDA	26.6	36.9	40.8	41.6	"	"	"	"
Reordering & viseme mapping in tri-visemes (4)								
Partition linearly	17.0	23.2	26.4	26.4	31.4	28.2	42.1	30.2
25 EM-iterations	17.4	22.3	27.2	25.5	41.0	34.6	54.5	36.4
50 EM-iterations	17.2	22.1	27.0	25.3	41.4	35.1	55.1	36.9
1st Tri-visemes	29.7	37.2	44.9	41.7	41.3	35.1	55.1	36.9
LDA	**31.3**	**43.2**	**47.1**	**48.2**	41.3	35.1	55.1	36.9
Chance	13.3	-	13.9	-	-	-	-	-

Table 4. Precision and recall in [%] on the frame-level of continuous viseme recognition without grammar constraints. Results are given for signer specific models (Single Signer), all signers trained jointly (Multi Signer) and for all signers trained jointly with exclusion of any data of the tested signer (Signer Independent).

	Single Signer		Multi Signer		Signer Indep.	
	prec.	recall	prec.	recall	prec.	recall
Average	33.5	36.1	32.1	38.1	29.0	35.5
Signer 1	41.9	45.1	31.5	38.2	24.1	28.8
Signer 2	29.9	37.2	22.3	33.3	25.0	37.4
Signer 3	27.7	30.4	22.9	28.7	17.9	23.7
Signer 4	39.5	34.8	49.6	41.2	38.1	37.2
Signer 5	34.3	42.0	37.9	46.9	36.4	45.2
Signer 6	30.8	31.7	31.5	37.4	30.2	36.4
Signer 7	29.8	30.2	31.4	37.5	30.4	37.2

Processor 6176 with 2300 Mhz. Each of the 25 EM iterations takes approximately 20 minutes. Frame recognition runs at around 9000 frames per second (fps), whereas feature extraction (matlab implementation) runs at only 0.07 fps.

8 Conclusions

This paper has proposed a framework to build a mouthing recogniser for continuous sign language. To our knowledge no previous work has achieved to apply a dedicated viseme recognition to the particularities of sign language recognition. We use no hand labelled training data, but just a pool of 189.363 frames. Our approach reaches 47.1% precision on the frame level on a challenging signer independent task, facing low quality 'real-life' data recorded from TV, with low spatial resolution. The approach requires only weak supervision and does not rely on any grammar priors.

The approach uses AAM-based distance features around the mouth to model 11 visemes and a 'no-mouthing class. The visemes are modelled as context-dependent tri-visemes which are clustered using a visemic decision tree. An extensive quantitative analysis in four different experimental settings allows to deduce new knowledge about recognition of mouthings in sign language.

We find that the modelling of visemes drastically improves with context dependent tri-visemes. Furthermore, accounting for differences in sentence structure between spoken and sign language improves the visual models. We further show that the visemes generalise well to unseen signers with a drop of only 3.2% precision.

Besides adding adaptation methods to enhance generalisation across signers, we identify the task of distinguishing between mouthings and mouth gestures in sign language as important future research. Moreover, work is needed to integrate the viseme recognition into a multimodal recognition pipeline. Finally, finding the actual number and properties of visemes best suited for sign language recognition also remains an open question.

Acknowledgements. The work presented has been supported by the EPSRC project "Learning to Recognise Dynamic Visual Content from Broadcast Footage" (EP/I011811/1). Special thanks to Thomas Hoyoux (University of Innsbruck) for continuous support related to the AAMs.

References

1. Starner, T., Weaver, J., Pentland, A.: Real-time American sign language recognition using desk and wearable computer based video. IEEE Pattern Analysis and Machine Intelligence 20(12), 1371–1375 (1998)
2. Vogler, C., Metaxas, D.: Handshapes and movements: Multiple-channel American sign language recognition. In: Camurri, A., Volpe, G. (eds.) GW 2003. LNCS (LNAI), vol. 2915, pp. 247–258. Springer, Heidelberg (2004)

3. Zaki, M.M., Shaheen, S.I.: Sign language recognition using a combination of new vision based features. Pattern Recognition Letters 32(4), 572–577 (2011)
4. Ong, S.C., Ranganath, S.: Automatic sign language analysis: A survey and the future beyond lexical meaning. IEEE Pattern Analysis and Machine Intelligence 27(6), 873–891 (2005)
5. Lucas, C., Bayley, R., Valli, C.: What's your sign for pizza?: an introduction to variation in American Sign Language. Gallaudet University Press, Washington, D.C (2003)
6. Emmorey, K.: Language, Cognition, and the Brain: Insights From Sign Language Research. Psychology Press (November 2001)
7. Sandler, W.: Sign Language and Linguistic Universals. Cambridge University Press (February 2006)
8. Lan, Y., Harvey, R., Theobald, B.-J.: Insights into machine lip reading. In: 2012 IEEE International Conference on Acoustics, Speech and Signal Processing (ICASSP), pp. 4825–4828 (March 2012)
9. Hilder, S., Theobald, B.J., Harvey, R.: In pursuit of visemes. In: Proceedings of the International Conference on Auditory-Visual Speech Processing, pp. 154–159 (2010)
10. Fisher, C.G.: Confusions among visually perceived consonants. Journal of Speech, Language and Hearing Research 11(4), 796 (1968)
11. Petajan, E.D.: Automatic Lipreading to Enhance Speech Recognition (Speech Reading). PhD thesis, University of Illinois at Urbana-Champaign, Champaign, IL, USA (1984)
12. Zhou, Z., Zhao, G., Pietikainen, M.: Towards a practical lipreading system. In: Computer Vision and Pattern Recognition, pp. 137–144 (2011)
13. Zhao, G., Barnard, M., Pietikainen, M.: Lipreading with local spatiotemporal descriptors. IEEE Transactions on Multimedia 11(7), 1254–1265 (2009)
14. Potamianos, G., Neti, C., Gravier, G., Garg, A., Senior, A.: Recent advances in the automatic recognition of audiovisual speech. Proceedings of the IEEE 91(9), 1306–1326 (2003)
15. Chiţu, A., Rothkrantz, L.J.M.: Automatic visual speech recognition. In: Ramakrishnan, S. (ed.) Speech Enhancement, Modeling and Recognition- Algorithms and Applications. InTech (March 2012)
16. Neti, C., Potamianos, G., Luettin, J., Matthews, I., Glotin, H., Vergyri, D., Sison, J., Mashari, A., Zhou, J.: Audio-visual speech recognition. In: Final Workshop 2000 Report, vol. 764 (2000)
17. Aghaahmadi, M., Dehshibi, M.M., Bastanfard, A., Fazlali, M.: Clustering persian viseme using phoneme subspace for developing visual speech application. Multimedia Tools and Applications, 1–21 (2013)
18. Shan, C., Gong, S., McOwan, P.W.: Facial expression recognition based on local binary patterns: A comprehensive study. Image and Vision Computing 27(6), 803–816 (2009)
19. Tian, Y.L., Kanade, T., Cohn, J.: Recognizing action units for facial expression analysis. IEEE Transactions on Pattern Analysis and Machine Intelligence 23(2), 97–115 (2001)
20. Buehler, P., Everingham, M., Zisserman, A.: Employing signed TV broadcasts for automated learning of British sign language. In: Proceedings of 4th Workshop on the Representation and Processing of Sign Languages: Corpora and Sign Language Technologies, pp. 22–23 (2010)
21. Cooper, H., Ong, E.J., Pugeault, N., Bowden, R.: Sign language recognition using sub-units. The Journal of Machine Learning Research 13(1), 2205–2231 (2012)

22. Kelly, D., McDonald, J., Markham, C.: Weakly supervised training of a sign language recognition system using multiple instance learning density matrices. IEEE Transactions on Systems, Man, and Cybernetics, Part B: Cybernetics 41(2), 526–541 (2011)
23. Cooper, H., Holt, B., Bowden, R.: Sign language recognition. In: Moeslund, T.B., Hilton, A., Krüger, V., Sigal, L. (eds.) Visual Analysis of Humans, pp. 539–562. Springer, London (2011)
24. Koller, O., Ney, H., Bowden, R.: May the force be with you: Force-aligned SignWriting for automatic subunit annotation of corpora. In: IEEE International Conference on Automatic Face and Gesture Recognition, Shanghai, PRC (April 2013)
25. Michael, N., Neidle, C., Metaxas, D.: Computer-based recognition of facial expressions in ASL: from face tracking to linguistic interpretation. In: Proceedings of the 4th Workshop on the Representation and Processing of Sign Languages: Corpora and Sign Language Technologies, LREC, Malta (2010)
26. Vogler, C., Goldenstein, S.: Facial movement analysis in ASL. Universal Access in the Information Society 6(4), 363–374 (2008)
27. Pfister, T., Charles, J., Zisserman, A.: Large-scale learning of sign language by watching TV (using co-occurrences). In: Proceedings of the British Machine Vision Conference, U. K. Leeds (2013)
28. Gross, R., Matthews, I., Baker, S.: Generic vs. person specific active appearance models. Image and Vision Computing 23(12), 1080–1093 (2005)
29. Xiao, J., Baker, S., Matthews, I., Kanade, T.: Real-time combined 2D+ 3D active appearance models. In: CVPR (2), pp. 535–542 (2004)
30. Schmidt, C., Koller, O., Ney, H., Hoyoux, T., Piater, J.: Enhancing gloss-based corpora with facial features using active appearance models. In: International Symposium on Sign Language Translation and Avatar Technology, Chicago, IL, USA, vol. 2 (2013)
31. Och, F.J., Ney, H.: A systematic comparison of various statistical alignment models. Comput. Linguist. 29(1), 19–51 (2003)
32. Bisani, M., Ney, H.: Joint-sequence models for grapheme-to-phoneme conversion. Speech Communication 50(5), 434–451 (2008)
33. Elliott, E.A.: Phonological Functions of Facial Movements: Evidence from deaf users of German Sign Language. Thesis, Freie Universität, Berlin, Germany (2013)
34. Jiang, J., Alwan, A., Bernstein, L.E., Auer, E.T., Keating, P.A.: Similarity structure in perceptual and physical measures for visual consonants across talkers. In: 2002 IEEE International Conference on Acoustics, Speech, and Signal Processing (ICASSP), vol. 1, pp. I–441–I–444 (May 2002)
35. Turkmani, A.: Visual Analysis of Viseme Dynamics. Ph.d., University of Surrey (2008)
36. Beulen, K.: Phonetische Entscheidungsbäume für die automatische Spracherkennung mit großem Vokabular. Mainz (1999)
37. Haeb-Umbach, R., Ney, H.: Linear discriminant analysis for improved large vocabulary continuous speech recognition. In: IEEE International Conference on Acoustics, Speech, and Signal Processing (ICASSP), vol. 1, pp. 13–16 (1992)

Multilinear Wavelets: A Statistical Shape Space for Human Faces*,**

Alan Brunton[1], Timo Bolkart[2,3], and Stefanie Wuhrer[2]

[1] Fraunhofer Institute for Computer Graphics Research IGD, Germany
[2] Cluster of Excellence MMCI, Saarland University, Germany
[3] Saarbrücken Graduate School of Computer Science, Germany

Abstract. We present a statistical model for 3D human faces in varying expression, which decomposes the surface of the face using a wavelet transform, and learns many localized, decorrelated multilinear models on the resulting coefficients. Using this model we are able to reconstruct faces from noisy and occluded 3D face scans, and facial motion sequences. Accurate reconstruction of face shape is important for applications such as tele-presence and gaming. The localized and multi-scale nature of our model allows for recovery of fine-scale detail while retaining robustness to severe noise and occlusion, and is computationally efficient and scalable. We validate these properties experimentally on challenging data in the form of static scans and motion sequences. We show that in comparison to a global multilinear model, our model better preserves fine detail and is computationally faster, while in comparison to a localized PCA model, our model better handles variation in expression, is faster, and allows us to fix identity parameters for a given subject.

Keywords: Statistical shape models, human faces, multilinear model, wavelets.

1 Introduction

Acquisition of 3D surface data is continually becoming more commonplace and affordable, through a variety of modalities ranging from laser scanners to structured light to binocular and multi-view stereo systems. However, these data are often incomplete and noisy, and robust regularization is needed. When we are interested in a particular class of objects, such as human faces, we can use prior knowledge about the shape to constrain the reconstruction. This alleviates not only the problems of noise and incomplete data, but also occlusion. Such priors can be learned by computing statistics on databases of registered 3D face shapes.

Accurate 3D face capture is important for many applications, from performance capture to tele-presence to gaming to recognition tasks to ergonomics,

* Electronic supplementary material -Supplementary material is available in the online version of this chapter at `http://dx.doi.org/10.1007/978-3-319-10590-20`. Videos can also be accessed at `http://www.springerimages.com/videos/978-3-319-10589-5`

** This work has partially been funded by the German Research Foundation (DFG).

D. Fleet et al. (Eds.): ECCV 2014, Part I, LNCS 8689, pp. 297–312, 2014.
© Springer International Publishing Switzerland 2014

and considerable resources of data are available from which to learn a statistical prior on the shape of the human face (e.g. [5,33,32,24]).

In this paper, we propose a novel statistical model for the shape of human faces, and use it to fit to input 3D surfaces from different sources, exhibiting high variation in expression and identity, and severe levels of data corruption in the forms of noise, missing data and occlusions. We make the following specific technical contributions:

- A novel statistical shape space based on a wavelet decomposition of 3D face geometry and multilinear analysis of the individual wavelet coefficients.
- Based on this model, we develop an efficient algorithm for learning a statistical shape model of the human face in varying expressions.
- We develop an efficient algorithm for fitting our model to static and dynamic point cloud data, that is robust with respect to highly corrupted scans.
- We publish our statistical model and code to fit it to point cloud data [6].

Our model has the following advantages. First, it results in algorithms for training and fitting that are highly efficient and scalable. By using a wavelet transform, we decompose a high-dimensional global shape space into many localized, decorrelated low-dimensional shape spaces. This dimensionality is the dominant factor in the complexity of the numerical routines used in both training and fitting. Training on thousands of faces takes a few minutes, and fitting to an input scan takes a few seconds, both using a single-threaded implementation on a standard PC.

Second, it allows to capture fine-scale details due to its local nature, as shown in Figure 5, while retaining robustness against corruption of the input data. The wavelet transform decomposes highly correlated vertex coordinates into decorrelated coefficients, upon which multilinear models can be learned independently. Learning many low-dimensional statistical models, rather than a single high-dimensional model, as used in [5,30,7], greatly reduces the risk of over-fitting to the training data; it avoids the curse of dimensionality. Thus, a much higher proportion of the variability in the training data can be retained in the model. During fitting, tight statistical bounds can be placed on the model parameters for robustness, yet the model can still fit closely to valid data points.

Third, it is readily generalizable and extendable. Our model requires *no explicit segmentation* of the face into parts; the wavelet transform decomposes the surface hierarchically into overlapping patches, and the inverse transform recombines them. Unlike manually decomposed part-based models, eg. [14,13,26], it requires no sophisticated optimization of blending weights and the decomposition is not class-specific. Further, it can be easily extended to include additional information such as texture.

2 Related Work

This work is concerned with learning 3D statistical shape models that can be used in surface fitting tasks. To learn a statistical shape model, a database of shapes with known correspondence information is required. Computing correspondences between a set of shapes is a challenging problem in general [28].

However, for models of human faces, correspondences can be computed in a fully automatic way using template deformation methods (e.g. [20,23]).

The most related works to our work are part-based multilinear models that were recently proposed to model 3D human body shapes [9]. To define the part-based model, a segmentation of the training shapes into meaningful parts is required. This is done manually by segmenting the human models into body parts, such as limbs. Lecron et al. [17] use a similar statistical model on human spines, that are manually segmented into its vertebrae. In contrast, our method computes a suitable hierarchical decomposition automatically, thereby eliminating the need to manually generate a meaningful segmentation.

Many statistical models have been used to analyze human faces. The first statistical model for the analysis of 3D faces was proposed by Blanz and Vetter [5]. This model is called the morphable model, and uses Principal Component Analysis (PCA) to analyze shape and texture of registered faces, mainly in neutral expression. It is applied to reconstruct 3D facial shapes from images [5] and 3D face scans [4,22]. Amberg et al. [1] extend the morphable model to consider expressions, by combining it with a PCA model for expression offsets with respect to the neutral expression geometry. An alternative way to incorporate expression changes is to use use a multilinear model, which separates identity and expression variations. This model has been used to modify expressions in videos [30,11,31], or to register and analyze 3D motion sequences [7]. Multilinear models are mathematically equivalent to TensorFaces [29] applied to 3D data rather than images, and provide an effective way to capture both identity and expression variations, and thus in Section 6 we compare to a global multilinear model and show that our model better captures local geometric detail.

Blanz and Vetter [5] manually segmented the face into four regions and learned a morphable model on each segment. The regions are fitted to the data independently and merged in a post-processing step. This part-based model was shown to lead to a higher data accuracy than the global morphable model. As part-based models are suitable to obtain good fitting results in localized regions, they have been used in multiple follow-up works, eg. [14,13,26]. While the model of Kakadiaris et al. [14] shares some similarities with our model, they use a fixed annotated face model, and wavelet transforms to compare facial geometry images. In contrast, we learn multilinear models on subdivision wavelet coefficients.

All of the methods discussed so far model shape changes using global or part-based statistical models. In contrast, by applying a wavelet transform to the data first, statistical models can be constructed that capture shape variation in both a local and multi-scale way. Such wavelet-domain techniques have been used extensively for medical imaging [12,21,18], and Brunton et al. [8] proposed a method to analyze local shape differences of 3D faces in neutral expression in a hierarchical way. This method decomposes each face hierarchically using a wavelet transform and learns a PCA model for each wavelet coefficient independently. This approach has been shown to capture more facial details than global statistical shape spaces. Hence, in Section 6 we compare to a wavelet-domain approach and show that our model better captures expression variation.

We propose a method that combines this localized shape space with a multilinear model, thereby allowing to capture localized shape differences of databases of 3D faces of different subjects in different expressions.

3 Multilinear Wavelet Model

Our statistical shape space for human faces consists of a multilinear model for each wavelet coefficient resulting from a spherical subdivision wavelet decomposition of a template face mesh. The wavelet transform takes a set of highly correlated vertex positions and produces a set of decorrelated wavelet coefficients. This decorrelation means that we can treat the coefficient separately and learn a distinct multilinear model for each coefficient. These multilinear models capture the variation of each wavelet coefficient over changes in identity and expression. In the following, we review the two components of our model.

3.1 Second Generation Spherical Wavelets

Spherical wavelets typically operate on subdivision surfaces [25] following a standard subdivision hierarchy, giving a multi-scale decomposition of the surface. This allows coarse-scale shape properties to be represented by just a few coefficients, while localized fine-scale details are represented by additional coefficients. Second generation wavelets can be accelerated using the lifting scheme [27], factoring the convolution of the basis functions into a hierarchy of local lifting operations, which are weighted averages of neighboring vertices. When combined with subsampling, the transform can be computed in time linear in the number of vertices. The particular wavelet decomposition we use [3] follows Catmull-Clark subdivision, and has been used previously for localized statistical models in multiple application domains [18,8]. The wavelet transform is a linear operator, denoted D. For a 3D face surface $\mathcal{X}$, the wavelet coefficients are $\mathbf{s} = D\mathcal{X}$.

3.2 Multilinear Models

To statistically analyze a population of shapes, which vary in multiple ways, such as identity and expression for faces, one can use a multilinear model. In general, one constructs a multilinear model by organizing the training data into an N-mode tensor, where the first mode is the vector representation of each training sample, and the remaining modes contain training samples varied in distinct ways.

We organize our set of parametrized training shapes into a 3-mode tensor $\mathcal{A} \in \mathbb{R}^{d_1 \times d_2 \times d_3}$, where d_1 is the dimension of each shape, and d_2 and d_3 are the number of training samples in each mode of variation; in our case, identity and expression. It would be straightforward to extend this model to allow for more modes, such as varying textures due to illumination changes, if the data were available. We use a higher-order Singular Value Decomposition (HOSVD) [16] to decompose $\mathcal{A}$ into

$$\mathcal{A} = \mathcal{M} \times_2 \mathbf{U}_2 \times_3 \mathbf{U}_3, \tag{1}$$

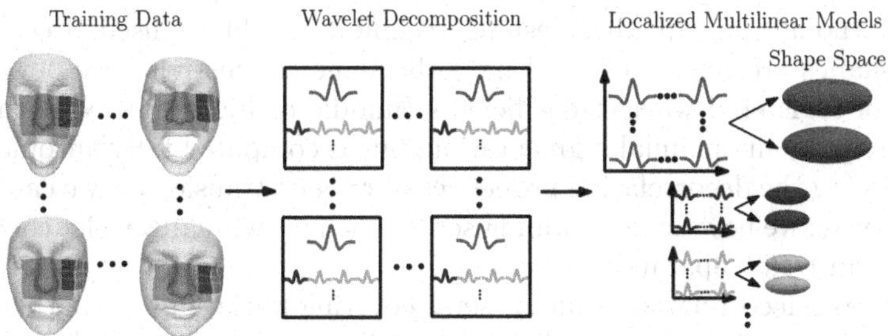

Fig. 1. Overview of the training. Left: Training data with highlighted impact of the basis function. Middle: Wavelet decomposition of each face of the training data. Right: Corresponding wavelet coefficients and learned multilinear model shape spaces.

where $\mathcal{M} \in \mathbb{R}^{d_1 \times m_2 \times m_3}$ is a tensor called a multilinear model, and $\mathbf{U}_2 \in \mathbb{R}^{d_2 \times m_2}$ and $\mathbf{U}_3 \in \mathbb{R}^{d_3 \times m_3}$ are orthogonal matrices. The i-th mode product $\mathcal{M} \times_i \mathbf{U}_i$ replaces each vector $\mathbf{m} \in \mathbb{R}^{m_i}$ of $\mathcal{M}$ in the direction of i-th mode by $\mathbf{U}_i\mathbf{m} \in \mathbb{R}^{d_i}$. To compute the orthogonal matrix U_2, $\mathcal{A}$ is unfolded in the direction of 2-nd mode to the matrix $\mathbf{A}_{(2)} \in \mathbb{R}^{d_2 \times d_1 d_3}$, where the columns of $\mathbf{A}_{(2)}$ are the vectors of $\mathcal{A}$ in direction of 2-nd mode.

The decomposition in (1) is exact, if $m_i = \text{rank}(\mathbf{U}_{(i)})$ for all i. If $m_i < \text{rank}(\mathbf{U}_{(i)})$ for at least one i, the decomposition approximates the data. This technique is called truncated HOSVD, and we use this to reduce the dimensionality of the training data.

The multilinear model represents a shape $\mathbf{s} \in \mathbb{R}^{d_1}$ by

$$\mathbf{s} \approx \bar{\mathbf{f}} + \mathcal{M} \times_2 \mathbf{w}_2^T \times_3 \mathbf{w}_3^T, \tag{2}$$

where $\bar{\mathbf{f}}$ is the mean of the training data (over all identities and expressions), and $\mathbf{w}_2 \in \mathbb{R}^{m_2}$ and $\mathbf{w}_3 \in \mathbb{R}^{m_3}$ are identity and expression coefficients. Varying only $\mathbf{w}_2$ changes identity while keeping the expression fixed, whereas varying only $\mathbf{w}_3$ changes the expression of a single identity.

4 Training

In this section, we describe the process of learning the multilinear wavelet model from a database of registered 3D faces in a fixed number of expressions. Using the notation from Section 3.2, the database contains d_2 identities, each in d_3 expressions. We discuss in Section 6 how to obtain such a registered database. The training process is depicted graphically in Figure 1.

The first stage in our training pipeline is to apply a wavelet transform to every shape in our training database. The left-most part of Figure 1 shows the influence region of two wavelet coefficients on four face shapes (two identities in two expressions). To obtain a template with the proper subdivision connectivity, we use a registration-preserving stereographic resampling onto a regular grid [8], although any quad-remeshing technique could be used. Because the training shapes are registered, and have the same connectivity, we now have a database of registered wavelet coefficients (middle of Figure 1). Note that this does *not* require any manual segmentation, but is computed fully automatically. By considering the decorrelating properties of wavelet transforms, we can look at it another way: we now have a training set for each individual wavelet coefficient, which we can treat separately.

From these decorrelated training sets, covering variations in both identity and expression, we can learn a distinct multilinear model for each coefficient, resulting in many localized shape spaces as shown in the right part of Figure 1. This allows a tremendous amount of flexibility in the model.

Training our model has the following complexity. Each wavelet transform has complexity $O(n)$, for n vertices, and we perform $d_2 d_3$ of them. The complexity of the HOSVD is $O(d_1^2(d_2 d_3^2 + d_3 d_2^2))$ [16], and we compute n of them. Because every multilinear model is computed for only a single wavelet coefficient over the training set, $d_1 = 3$ so the complexity is $O(d_2 d_3^2 + d_3 d_2^2)$ per wavelet coefficient and $O(n(d_2 d_3^2 + d_3 d_2^2))$ overall. Thus, our model allows highly efficient and scalable training, as detailed in Section 6.

Training many low-dimensional models has statistical benefits too. We retain a large amount of the variation present in the training data by truncating modes 2 and 3 at $m_2 = 3$ and $m_3 = 3$. We chose $m_2 = m_3 = 3$ because $d_1 = 3$ is the smallest mode-dimension in our tensor.

Our model generates a 3D face surface $\mathcal{X}$ as follows. The vertex positions $\mathbf{x} \in \mathcal{X}$ are generated from the wavelet coefficients via the inverse wavelet transform, denoted by D^{-1}. The wavelet coefficients are generated from their individual multilinear weights for identity and expression. Thus, following (2), wavelet coefficients are generated by

$$\mathbf{s}_k = \bar{\mathbf{s}}_k + \mathcal{M}_k \times_2 \mathbf{w}_{k,2}^T \times_3 \mathbf{w}_{k,3}^T \tag{3}$$

where k is the index of the wavelet coefficient, and the surface is generated by $\mathcal{X} = D^{-1}\mathbf{s}$ where $\mathbf{s} = [\mathbf{s}_1 \ \dots \ \mathbf{s}_n]^T$.

5 Fitting

In this section, we discuss the process of fitting our learned model to an input oriented point cloud or mesh $\mathcal{P}$, which may be corrupted by noise, missing data or occlusions. The process is depicted graphically in Figure 2. We fit our model by minimizing a fitting energy that captures the distance between $\mathcal{X}$ and $\mathcal{P}$, subject to the constraints learned in our training phase. We minimize the energy in a coarse-to-fine manner, starting with the multilinear weights of the coarse-scale wavelet coefficients, and refining the result by optimizing finer-scale multilinear weights.

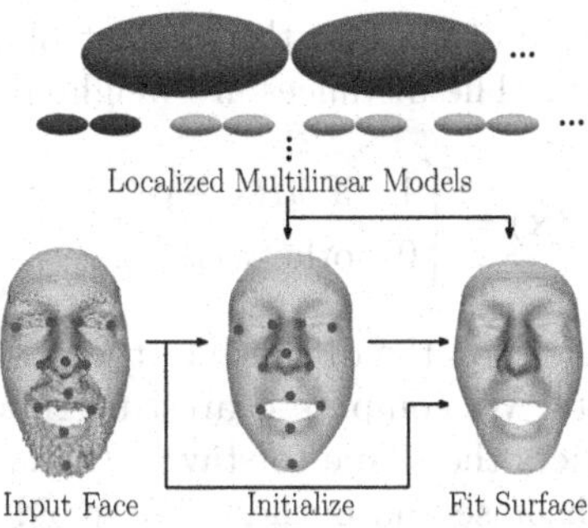

Fig. 2. Overview of the fitting. Top: Localized multilinear models. Bottom, left to right: input face scan, result after initialization, result of full surface fitting.

5.1 Fitting Energy

We optimize our model parameters to minimize an energy measuring the distance between $\mathcal{X}$ and $\mathcal{P}$. Our model parameters consist of the per-wavelet coefficient multilinear weights, $\mathbf{w}_{k,2}$, $\mathbf{w}_{k,3}$ for $k = 1, \ldots, n$, and a similarity transform (rigid plus and uniform scaling) R mapping the coordinate frame of $\mathcal{X}$ to the coordinate frame of $\mathcal{P}$.

Our fitting energy consists of four parts: a landmark term, a surface fitting term, a surface smoothing term, and a prior term. That is,

$$E_{\text{fit}} = E_{\mathcal{L}} + E_{\mathcal{X}} + E_S + E_P \tag{4}$$

where $E_{\mathcal{L}}$, $E_{\mathcal{X}}$, E_S and E_P are the landmark energy, surface fitting energy, surface smoothing energy and prior energy, respectively. We now describe each of these energies in turn.

The landmark energy measures the Euclidean distance between corresponding landmark sets $\mathcal{L}^{(m)} \subset \mathcal{X}$ and $\mathcal{L}^{(d)} \subset \mathcal{P}$ located on the model surface and input data, respectively. These landmarks may be obtained in a variety of ways, including automatically [10,23], and do not restrict our method. In Section 6, we demonstrate how our method performs using landmarks from multiple sources. The landmarks are in correspondence such that $|\mathcal{L}^{(m)}| = |\mathcal{L}^{(d)}|$ and $\ell_i^{(m)}$ and $\ell_i^{(d)}$ represent the equivalent points on $\mathcal{X}$ and $\mathcal{P}$ respectively. With this, we define our landmark energy as,

$$E_{\mathcal{L}} = \rho_{\mathcal{L}} \frac{|\mathcal{X}|}{|\mathcal{L}^{(m)}|} \sum_{i=1}^{|\mathcal{L}^{(m)}|} \left\| R\ell_i^{(m)} - \ell_i^{(d)} \right\|_2^2 \tag{5}$$

where $\rho_{\mathcal{L}} = 1$ is a constant balancing the relative influence of landmarks against that of the rest of the surface.

The surface fitting energy measures the point-to-plane distance between vertices in $\mathcal{X}$ and their nearest neighbors in $\mathcal{P}$. That is,

$$E_{\mathcal{X}} = \sum_{\mathbf{x} \in \mathcal{X} \setminus \mathcal{L}^{(m)}} \rho(\mathbf{x}) \left\| R\mathbf{x} - \mathbf{y}(\mathbf{x}) \right\|_2^2 \tag{6}$$

where $\mathbf{y}(\mathbf{x})$ is the projection of $R\mathbf{x}$ into the tangent plane of $\mathbf{p}$, where $\mathbf{p} \in \mathcal{P}$ is the nearest neighbor of $R\mathbf{x}$. The distances are weighted by

$$\rho(\mathbf{x}) = \begin{cases} 1 & \text{if } \|R\mathbf{x} - \mathbf{p}\|_2 \leq \tau \\ 0 & \text{otherwise} \end{cases} \tag{7}$$

where $\tau = 1\text{cm}$ is a threshold on the distance to the nearest neighbor, providing robustness to missing data. We compute nearest neighbors using ANN [2].

The prior energy restricts the shape to stay in the learned shape space, providing robustness to both noise and outliers. We avoid introducing undue bias to the mean shape via a hyper-box prior [7],

$$E_P = \sum_{k=1}^{n} \left(\sum_{j=1}^{m_2} f_{k,2,j}(w_{k,2,j}) + \sum_{j=1}^{m_3} f_{k,3,j}(w_{k,3,j}) \right) \tag{8}$$

where

$$f_{k,2,j}(w) = \begin{cases} 0 & \text{if } \bar{w}_{k,2,j} - \lambda \leq w \leq \bar{w}_{k,2,j} + \lambda \\ \infty & \text{otherwise} \end{cases} \tag{9}$$

restricts each component of $\mathbf{w}_{k,2}$ to be within a constant amount λ of the same component of the mode-mean $\bar{\mathbf{w}}_{k,2}$, and similarly for each component of $\mathbf{w}_{k,3}$.

The smoothing energy is the bi-Laplacian energy, which penalizes changes in curvature between neighboring vertices. It is needed due to the energy minimization algorithm, described in Section 5.2, which optimizes each multilinear wavelet independently. Without a smoothing energy, this can result in visible patch boundaries in the fitted surface, as can be seen in Figure 4.

Formally, we write

$$E_S = \rho_S \sum_{\mathbf{x} \in \mathcal{X}} \left\| U^2(\mathbf{x}) \right\|_2^2 \tag{10}$$

where $U^2(\mathbf{x})$ is the double-umbrella discrete approximation of the bi-Laplacian operator [15], and ρ_S is a constant weight.

The smoothing energy poses a trade-off: visually pleasing smooth surfaces versus fitting accuracy and speed. Leaving out E_S allows the energy minimization to get closer to the data (as expected), and leads to faster fitting due to the energy being more localized. Hence, we retain the option of not evaluating this energy in case the scenario would favor close fitting and fast performance over visually smooth results. We use either $\rho_S = 100$ or $\rho_S = 0$ in all our experiments. Section 6 discusses this trade-off in more concrete terms.

5.2 Energy Minimization

We minimize (4) in a two-step procedure. In the first step, we iteratively minimize $E_{\mathcal{L}} + E_P + E_S$ with respect to R and the multilinear weights of each wavelet coefficient. This rigidly aligns the model and the data, and coarsely deforms the surface to fit the landmarks, giving a good initialization for subsequent surface fitting. We solve for R that minimizes $E_{\mathcal{L}}$, given the landmark positions $\mathcal{L}^{(m)}$ and $\mathcal{L}^{(d)}$. This involves solving a small over-determined linear system. Then, we optimize $\mathbf{w}_{k,2}$ and $\mathbf{w}_{k,3}$ for $k = 1, \ldots, n$ to minimize $E_{\mathcal{L}} + E_{\mathcal{P}}$. Figure 2 (bottom, middle) shows the result of landmark fitting for a given input data.

In the second step, we fix R and minimize (4) with respect to only the multilinear weights. This deforms the surface so that it closely fits the input data $\mathcal{P}$. Figure 2 (bottom, right) shows the final fitting result.

The energies $E_{\mathcal{L}}$, $E_{\mathcal{X}}$ and $E_{\mathcal{S}}$ are nonlinear with respect to the multilinear weights, and we minimize them using the L-BFGS-B [19] quasi-Newton method. This bounded optimization allows the prior (8) to be enforced simply as bounds on the multilinear weights. The hierarchical and decorrelating nature of the wavelet transform allows us to minimize the energies separately for each multilinear model in a coarse-to-fine manner. During initialization, we recompute R and optimize the multilinear weights iteratively at each level of wavelet coefficients. During surface fitting, nearest neighbors are recomputed and the multilinear weights optimized iteratively at each level. During initialization, we allow greater variation in the model, $\lambda = 1$, because we assume the landmarks are not located on occlusions. During surface fitting, we restict the shape space further, $\lambda = 0.5$, unless the particular weight component is already outside this range from the initialization.

Fitting many low-dimensional local multilinear models is more efficient than fitting a single high-dimensional global multilinear model, because the dimensionality of the variables to be optimized is the dominant factor in the complexity of the quasi-Newton optimization, which achieves super-linear convergence by updating an estimate of the Hessian matrix in each iteration. For a problem size $d = m_2 + m_3$ the Hessian contains $\Omega(d^2)$ unique entries, which favors solving many small problems even if the total number of variables optimized is greater. This is confirmed experimentally in Section 6. Further, each multilinear model has compact support on $\mathcal{X}$, which reduces the number of distances that must be computed in each evaluation of (6) and its gradient.

5.3 Tracking

As an application of our shape space, we show how a simple extension of our fitting algorithm can be used to track a facial motion sequence. To the first frame, we fit both identity and expression weights. Subsequently, we fix identity weights and only fit expression weights. This ensures that shape changes over the sequence are only due to expression, not identity. A more elaborate scheme, which averages the identity weights, would also be feasible.

To avoid jitter, we introduce a temporal smoothing term on the vertex positions. Approaches based on global multilinear models often place a temporal smoothing term on the expression weights themselves [31,7] since these are usually much lower dimension than the surface $\mathcal{X}$. In our case, the combined dimensionality of all expression weights is equal to that of the vertex positions, so no efficiency is to be gained by operating on the weights rather than the vertex positions. Further, placing a restriction on the vertex positions fits easily into our energy minimization. We use a simple penalty on the movement of the vertices $\mathbf{x} \in \mathcal{X}$ between frames. This is easily incorporated into our fitting algorithm by simply adding a Euclidean distance penalty to our energy function (4) during surface fitting:

$$E_T = \sum_{\mathbf{x}_t \in \mathcal{X}_t} \rho_T \left\| \mathbf{x}_t - \mathbf{x}_{t-1} \right\|_2^2 \tag{11}$$

where $\rho_T = 1$ is a constant balancing allowing the surface to move versus reducing jitter.

6 Evaluation

6.1 Experimental Setup

Training Data: For a training database, we use the BU3DFE database [33] registered using an automatic template-fitting approach [23] with ground truth landmarks. This database contains 100 subjects in 25 expressions levels each. We successfully registered 99 subjects in all expressions and used this for training in our experiments.

Test Data: To test our fitting accuracy we use 200 scans from the Bosphorus database [24] including variation in identity, expression and types of occlusions. We specifically do *not* test on scans from the same database we use for training to avoid bias. Further, the Bosphorus scans typically have higher noise levels than those in BU3DFE, and contain occlusions. This database contains landmarks on each scan; we use the subset of those shown in Figure 2 present on a given surface (not blocked by an occlusion). In Section 6.4, we show the performance of our method when tracking facial motion sequences from the BU4DFE database [32] with landmarks automatically predicted using an approach based on local descriptors and a Markov network [23].

Comparison: We compare our fitting results to the localized PCA model [8] and the global multilinear model [7]. All three models are trained with the same data, with the exception that because the local PCA model does not model expression variation, we train it separately for each expression and give it the correct expression during fitting. The other two are given landmarks for fitting.

Performance: We implemented our model, both training and fitting, in C++ using standard libraries. We ran all tests on a workstation running windows with an Intel Xeon E31245 at 3.3GHz. Training our model on 2475 face shapes each with 24987 vertices takes $<$ 5min using a single-threaded implementation. In practice we found our training algorithm to scale approximately linearly in the number of training shapes. Fitting takes 5.37s on average with $\rho_S = 0$, and 14.76s with $\rho_S = 100$, for a surface with approximately 35000 vertices (Sections 6.2 and 6.3). For the motion sequences with approximately 35000 vertices per frame (Section 6.4), fitting takes 4.35s per frame on average without smoothing and 11.14s with smoothing. The global multilinear model takes $\approx$ 2 min for fitting to a static scan. A single-threaded implementation of the local PCA model takes 5 min due to the sampling-based optimization, which avoids local minima.

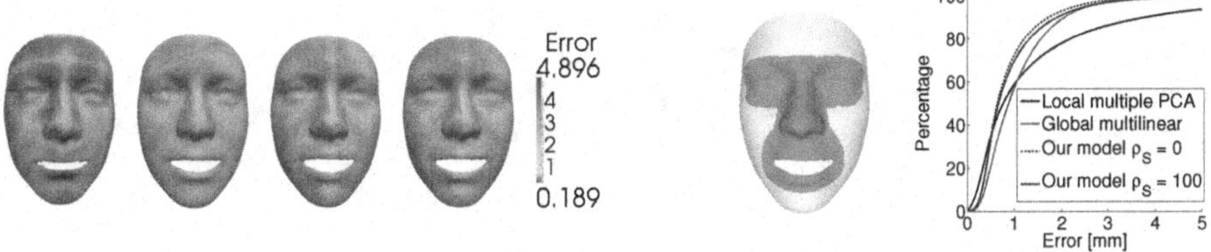

Fig. 3. Left block: Median reconstruction error for noisy data using multiple localized PCA models, a global multilinear model, our model ($\rho_S = 0$), and our model ($\rho_S = 100$). Right block: mask showing the characteristic detail regions of the face, and cumulative error plot for varying identity and expression. Errors in millimeters.

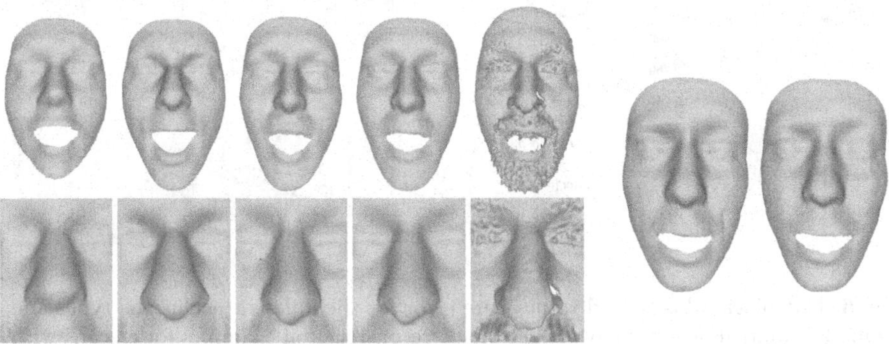

Fig. 4. Effect of smoothing energy E_S on an example noisy scan. Left block: fitting results for a scan in surprise expression, with a close-up of the nose region in the bottom row. Left to right: local multiple PCA, global multilinear model, our model ($\rho_S = 0$), our model ($\rho_S = 100$), and input data. Right block: our reconstructions for a fear expression for $\rho_S = 0$ (left) and $\rho_S = 100$. Note the faint grid-artifacts that appear without smoothing, eg. in the cheek region and around the mouth. The input data can be seen in Figure 5 (left block).

6.2 Reconstruction of Noisy Data

In this section, we demonstrate our model's ability to capture fine-scale detail in the presence of identity and expression variation, and high noise levels. We fit it to 120 models (20 identities in up to 7 expressions) from the Bosphorus database [24]. We measure the fitting error as distance-to-data, and the per-vertex median errors are shown for all three models in Figure 3 (left). Our model has a greater proportion of sub-millimeter errors than either of the other models. Specifically, the local PCA and the global multilinear have 63.2% and 62.0%, respectively, of vertices with error < 1mm, whereas our model has 71.6% with $\rho_S = 100$ and 72.4% with $\rho_S = 0$. Figure 3 (right) shows cumulative error plots for all three methods for vertices in the characteristic detail region of the face, which is shown next to the plot. This region contains prominent facial features with the most geometric detail. We see that our model is more

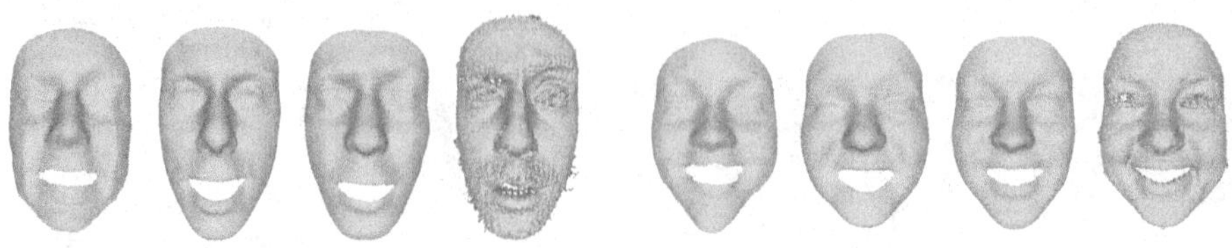

Fig. 5. Reconstruction examples for noisy scans in different expressions. Left block: fear expression. Right block: happy expression. Each block, from left to right: local multiple PCA [8], global multilinear [7], proposed ($\rho_S = 100$), input data.

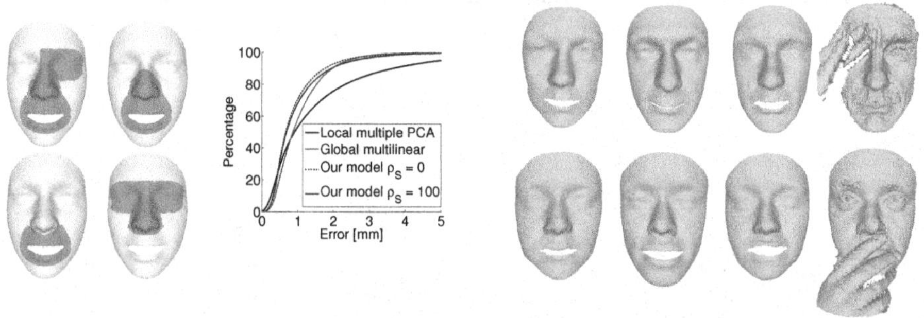

Fig. 6. Left block: Masks used to measure error for the different occlusions types and combined cumulative error plot. Right block: reconstruction examples for a scans with occlusions. Top: eye occlusion. Bottom: mouth occlusion. Each row: local multiple PCA model, global multilinear model, our reconstruction with $\rho_S = 100$, input data.

accurate than previous models in this region and has many more sub-millimeter errors; the local PCA and global multilinear have 60.4% and 58.0% of errors < 1mm, respectively, whereas our model has 70.2% with $\rho_S = 100$ and 72.7% with $\rho_S = 0$. This shows that our model has improved accuracy for fine-scale detail compared to existing models, in particular in areas with prominent features and high geometric detail.

Figures 4 and 5 show examples of fitting to noisy scans of different subjects in different expressions. These scans contain acquisition noise, missing data and facial hair. Figure 4 (left) shows a surprise expression and close-ups of the nose region; our reconstruction both $\rho_S = 100$ and $\rho_S = 0$ capture significantly more fine-scale detail than previous models. The right part of the figure demonstrates the effect of the smoothing energy in preventing faint grid artifacts appearing in the reconstruction due to the independent optimization scheme. Figure 5 shows two subjects in fear and happy expressions. We again see the increased accuracy of our model in terms of fine-scale detail on facial features compared to previous models. Note the accuracy of the nose and mouth shapes in all examples compared to the other models, and the accurate fitting of the underlying face shape in the presence of facial hair. Further note how our model captures the asymmetry in the eyebrow region for the fear expression.

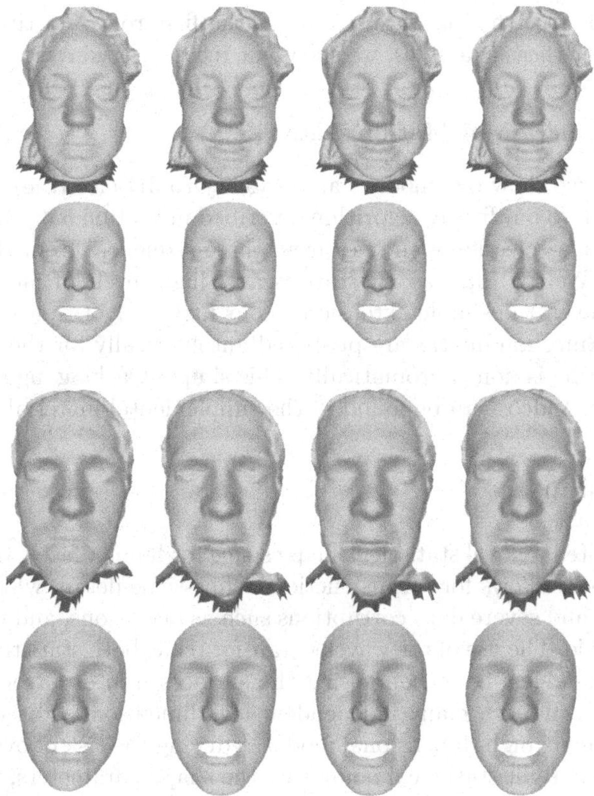

Fig. 7. Tracking results for the application of our fitting algorithm given in Section 5.3. Each block shows frames 0, 20, 40 and 60 of a sequence of a subject performing an expression. Top: happy expression. Bottom: fear expression.

6.3 Reconstruction of Occluded Data

In this section, we demonstrate our model's robustness to severe data corruptions in the form of occlusions. We fit all three models to 80 scans (20 subjects, 4 types of occlusions) from the Bosphorus database [24]. Figure 6 (left) shows the cumulative error for all three models. Since distance-to-data is not a valid error measure in occluded areas, we apply different masks, shown next to the error plot, depending on the type of occlusion so that only unoccluded vertices are measured. Clockwise from top-left: the mask used for eye, glasses, mouth and hair occlusions. From the cumulative error curves, we see that our model retains greater accuracy in unoccluded parts of the face than previous models.

Figure 6 (right) shows example reconstructions in the presence of severe occlusions. All models show robustness to occlusions and reconstruct plausible face shapes, but our model provides better detail in unoccluded parts of the face than previous models (see the mouth and chin in the first row, and the nose in the second row). For these examples, we show our reconstruction with $\rho_S = 100$.

6.4 Reconstruction of Motion Data

In this section, we show our model's applicability to 3D face tracking using the simple extension to our fitting algorithm described in Section 5.3. Figure 7 shows some results for a selection of frames from three sequences from the BU4DFE database [32]. We see that, as for static scans, high levels of facial detail are obtained, and even the simple extension of our fitting algorithm tracks the expression well. Since landmarks are predicted automatically for these sequences, the entire tracking is done automatically. This simple tracking algorithm is surprisingly stable. Videos can be found in the supplemental material.

7 Conclusion

We have presented a novel statistical shape space for human faces. Our multilinear wavelet model allows for reconstruction of fine-scale detail, while remaining robust to noise and severe data corruptions such as occlusions, and is highly efficient and scalable. The use of the wavelet transform has both statistical and computational advantages. By decomposing the surfaces into decorrelated wavelet coefficients, we can learn many independent low-dimensional statistical models rather than a single high-dimensional model, reducing the risk of overfitting and allowing us to set tight statistical bounds on the shape parameters, thereby providing robustness to data corruptions while capturing fine-scale detail. Model dimensionality is the dominant factor in the numerical routines used for fitting the model to noisy input data, and fitting many low-dimensional models is much faster than a single high-dimensional model even when the total number of parameters is much greater. We have confirmed these properties experimentally with a thorough evaluation on noisy data with varying expression, occlusions and missing data. We have further shown how our fitting procedure can be easily and simply extended to stable tracking of 3D facial motion sequences. Future work includes making our model applicable for real-time tracking. Virtually all aspects of our fitting algorithm are directly parallelizable, and an optimized GPU implementation could likely achieve real-time fitting rates. Such high-detail real-time tracking could have tremendous impact in tele-presence and gaming applications. We have made our statistical model and code to fit it to point cloud data available for research purposes [6].

References

1. Amberg, B., Knothe, R., Vetter, T.: Expression invariant 3D face recognition with a morphable model. In: FG, pp. 1–6 (2008)
2. Arya, A., Mount, D.: Approximate nearest neighbor queries in fixed dimensions. In: SODA, pp. 271–280 (1993), `http://www.cs.umd.edu/~mount/ANN/`

3. Bertram, M., Duchaineau, M., Hamann, B., Joy, K.I.: Generalized B-Spline subdivision-surface wavelets for geometry compression. TVCG 10(3), 326–338 (2004)
4. Blanz, V., Scherbaum, K., Seidel, H.P.: Fitting a morphable model to 3D scans of faces. In: ICCV, pp. 1–8 (2007)
5. Blanz, V., Vetter, T.: A morphable model for the synthesis of 3D faces. In: SIGGRAPH, pp. 187–194 (1999)
6. Bolkart, T., Brunton, A., Salazar, A., Wuhrer, S.: Statistical 3D shape models of human faces (2013), `http://statistical-face-models.mmci.uni-saarland.de/`
7. Bolkart, T., Wuhrer, S.: Statistical analysis of 3D faces in motion. In: 3DV, pp. 103–110 (2013)
8. Brunton, A., Shu, C., Lang, J., Dubois, E.: Wavelet model-based stereo for fast, robust face reconstruction. In: CRV, pp. 347–354 (2011)
9. Chen, Y., Liu, Z., Zhang, Z.: Tensor-based human body modeling. In: CVPR, pp. 105–112 (2013)
10. Creusot, C., Pears, N., Austin, J.: A machine-learning approach to keypoint detection and landmarking on 3D meshes. IJCV 102(1-3), 146–179 (2013)
11. Dale, K., Sunkavalli, K., Johnson, M.K., Vlasic, D., Matusik, W., Pfister, H.: Video face replacement. TOG 30(6), 130:1–130:10 (2011)
12. Davatzikos, C., Tao, X., Shen, D.: Hierarchical active shape models, using the wavelet transform. TMI 22(3), 414–423 (2003)
13. ter Haar, F.B., Veltkamp, R.C.: 3D face model fitting for recognition. In: Forsyth, D., Torr, P., Zisserman, A. (eds.) ECCV 2008, Part IV. LNCS, vol. 5305, pp. 652–664. Springer, Heidelberg (2008)
14. Kakadiaris, I., Passalis, G., Toderici, G., Murtuza, M., Lu, Y., Karamelpatzis, N., Theoharis, T.: Three-dimensional face recognition in the presence of facial expressions: An annotated deformable model approach. TPAMI 29(4), 640–649 (2007)
15. Kobbelt, L., Campagna, S., Vorsatz, J., Seidel, H.P.: Interactive multi-resolution modeling on arbitrary meshes. In: SIGGRAPH 1998, pp. 105–114 (1998)
16. Lathauwer, L.D.: Signal processing based on multilinear algebra. Ph.D. thesis, K.U. Leuven, Belgium (1997)
17. Lecron, F., Boisvert, J., Mahmoudi, S., Labelle, H., Benjelloun, M.: Fast 3D spine reconstruction of postoperative patients using a multilevel statistical model. In: Ayache, N., Delingette, H., Golland, P., Mori, K. (eds.) MICCAI 2012, Part II. LNCS, vol. 7511, pp. 446–453. Springer, Heidelberg (2012)
18. Li, Y., Tan, T.S., Volkau, I., Nowinski, W.: Model-guided segmentation of 3D neuroradiological image using statistical surface wavelet model. In: CVPR, pp. 1–7 (2007)
19. Liu, D., Nocedal, J.: On the limited memory method for large scale optimization. Math. Prog.: Ser. A, B 45(3), 503–528 (1989)
20. Mpiperis, I., Malassiotis, S., Strintzis, M.G.: Bilinear models for 3-D face and facial expression recognition. TIFS 3, 498–511 (2008)
21. Nain, D., Haker, S., Bobick, A., Tannenbaum, A.R.: Multiscale 3D shape analysis using spherical wavelets. In: Duncan, J.S., Gerig, G. (eds.) MICCAI 2005. LNCS, vol. 3750, pp. 459–467. Springer, Heidelberg (2005)
22. Patel, A., Smith, W.: 3D morphable face models revisited. In: CVPR, pp. 1327–1334 (2009)
23. Salazar, A., Wuhrer, S., Shu, C., Prieto, F.: Fully automatic expression-invariant face correspondence. MVAP 25(4), 859–879 (2014)

24. Savran, A., Alyüz, N., Dibeklioğlu, H., Çeliktutan, O., Gökberk, B., Sankur, B., Akarun, L.: Bosphorus database for 3D face analysis. In: Schouten, B., Juul, N.C., Drygajlo, A., Tistarelli, M. (eds.) BIOID 2008. LNCS, vol. 5372, pp. 47–56. Springer, Heidelberg (2008)
25. Schröder, P., Sweldens, W.: Spherical wavelets: Efficiently representing functions on the sphere. In: SIGGRAPH, pp. 161–172 (1995)
26. De Smet, M., Van Gool, L.: Optimal regions for linear model-based 3D face reconstruction. In: Kimmel, R., Klette, R., Sugimoto, A. (eds.) ACCV 2010, Part III. LNCS, vol. 6494, pp. 276–289. Springer, Heidelberg (2011)
27. Sweldens, W.: The lifting scheme: A custom-design construction of biorthogonal wavelets. Appl. Comp. Harm. Anal. 3(2), 186–200 (1996)
28. Tam, G., Cheng, Z.Q., Lai, Y.K., Langbein, F., Liu, Y., Marshall, D., Martin, R., Sun, X.F., Rosin, P.: Registration of 3D point clouds and meshes: A survey from rigid to nonrigid. TVCG 19(7), 1199–1217 (2013)
29. Vasilescu, M.A.O., Terzopoulos, D.: Multilinear analysis of image ensembles: TensorFaces. In: Heyden, A., Sparr, G., Nielsen, M., Johansen, P. (eds.) ECCV 2002, Part I. LNCS, vol. 2350, pp. 447–460. Springer, Heidelberg (2002)
30. Vlasic, D., Brand, M., Pfister, H., Popović, J.: Face transfer with multilinear models. TOG 24(3), 426–433 (2005)
31. Yang, F., Bourdev, L., Wang, J., Shechtman, E., Metaxas, D.: Facial expression editing in video using a temporally-smooth factorization. In: CVPR, pp. 861–868 (2012)
32. Yin, L., Chen, X., Sun, Y., Worm, T., Reale, M.: A high-resolution 3D dynamic facial expression database. In: FG, pp. 1–6 (2008)
33. Yin, L., Wei, X., Sun, Y., Wang, J., Rosato, M.J.: A 3D facial expression database for facial behavior research. In: FG, pp. 211–216 (2006)

Distance Estimation of an Unknown Person from a Portrait

Xavier P. Burgos-Artizzu[1,2], Matteo Ruggero Ronchi[2], and Pietro Perona[2]

[1] Technicolor - Cesson Sévigné, France
[2] California Institute of Technology, Pasadena, CA, USA
xavier.burgos@technicolor.com, {mronchi,perona}@caltech.edu

Abstract. We propose the first automated method for estimating distance from frontal pictures of unknown faces. Camera calibration is not necessary, nor is the reconstruction of a 3D representation of the shape of the head. Our method is based on estimating automatically the position of face and head landmarks in the image, and then using a regressor to estimate distance from such measurements. We collected and annotated a dataset of frontal portraits of 53 individuals spanning a number of attributes (sex, age, race, hair), each photographed from seven distances. We find that our proposed method outperforms humans performing the same task. We observe that different physiognomies will bias systematically the estimate of distance, i.e. some people look closer than others. We expire which landmarks are more important for this task.

Keywords: Camera-subject distance, Perspective distortion, Pose estimation, Face recognition.

1 Introduction

Consider a standard portrait of a person – either painted or photographed. Can one estimate the distance between the camera (or the eye of the painter) and the face of the sitter? Can one do so accurately even when the camera and the sitter are unknown? These questions are not just academic – we have four applications in mind. First, faces are present in most consumer pictures; if faces could provide a cue to distance, this would be useful for scene analysis. Second, psychologists have pointed out that the distance from which a portrait is captured affects its emotional valence [1]; therefore, estimating this distance from a given picture would provide a cue to automate the assessment of its emotional valence. Third, estimating the distance from which master paintings were produced will provide art historians with useful information on art practices throughout the ages [2]. The fourth potential application is forensics: inconsistency in the distance from which faces were photographed may help reveal photographic forgeries [3].

The most informative visual cues for distance are stereoscopic disparity [4], motion parallax [5],[6] and structured lighting [7, 8]. However, we are interested in the case of a static monocular brightness picture, such as a painting hanging in a museum or a photograph in a newspaper, where none of these cues is available.

D. Fleet et al. (Eds.): ECCV 2014, Part I, LNCS 8689, pp. 313–327, 2014.
© Springer International Publishing Switzerland 2014

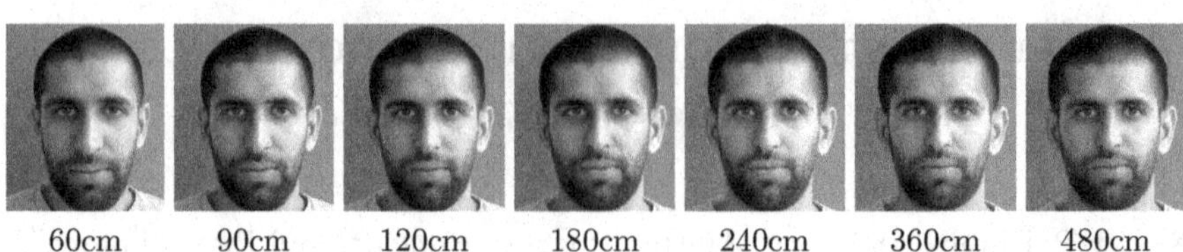

Fig. 1. Portrait pictures of a subject taken from 7 different distances ranging between 60 cm (left-most image) and 480 cm (right-most image). The effect of perspective, improperly called 'perspective distortion', is clearly noticeable. In portraits taken from a closer distance (left) the nose and mouth appear bigger, the ears are partially occluded by the cheeks and the face appears longer. This systematic deformation in the image plane is related to distance. We explore whether, and how accurately, the distance from which the portrait was taken may be estimated from the image when both the person and the camera are unknown.

The most reliable remaining cue is object familiarity [9]; however, there are several obstacles to a straightforward use of this cue. First, if the camera is unknown one does not have calibration parameters, which rules out straightforward use of the distance of known points, such as the distance between the pupils. Second, when the sitter is unknown only statistical, rather than exact, knowledge of the 3D shape of the object is available. However, it is known that one image of a constellation of at least five 3D points whose mutual position is known is sufficient both for camera calibration and pose computation [10], and therefore one would expect that some useful signal is available, see Fig. 1.

In this paper we study the feasibility and accuracy of automatically estimating the distance of a person from a camera, using a single 2D frontal portrait image without requiring any prior knowledge on the camera used or the person being photographed. Our approach is to first detect automatically facial features and then estimate distance from their mutual positions in the image. Our main contributions are:

1. A novel approach for estimating the camera-head distance from a single 2D portrait photograph when both the camera and the sitter are unknown. Our method yields useful signal and outperforms humans by 16%, see Fig. 6.
2. The introduction of a new dataset of portraits, *Caltech Multi-Distance Portraits* (**CMDP**), composed of 53 subjects belonging to both sexes, a variety of ages, ethnic backgrounds and physiognomies. Each subject was photographed from seven different distances and each portrait manually labeled with 55 keypoints over the head and face. The dataset is available online.
3. In-depth analysis and discussion of the feasibility of the proposed approach. We study two different variants of the task and analyze what are the most important input visual cues. We compare our method's performance using machine estimated landmarks vs. ground-truth landmarks. Finally, we also compare with the performance of human observers. Interestingly, we found that the main source of error for both humans and our method is the variability of physiognomies.

2 Related Work

Estimating the pose of a human head from an image was explored in [11, 12]. The literature focuses on the estimation of the three degrees of freedom (DOF) - yaw, pitch and roll - under the assumption that the human head can be modeled as a disembodied rigid object. Knowledge of the intrinsic camera parameters or depth information is required.

Psychophysics experiments [13, 14] show that human face recognition performance can be impaired by perspective transformation. As one might expect, the severity of this deficit depends on the difference between the amount of 'perspective distortion' at the learning and testing phases. They also established that both global perspective information and local image similarity features such as ears, eyes, mouth or nose play a fundamental role in this task. Their conclusion is that perspective distortion impairs face recognition, similarly to other visual cues such as lighting and head orientation. This poses the question of whether perspective distortion or, equivalently, distance may be estimated.

Psychologists [1] observed that portrait photographs taken from within personal space elicit lower investments in an economic trust game and lower ratings of social traits such as strength, attractiveness or trustworthiness. These findings could not be explained by width-to-height ratio, explicit knowledge of the camera distance or typicality of the presented faces, thus suggesting the existence of a facial cue influencing social judgments as a function of interpersonal distance. They suggest that there is an "optimal distance" at which portraits should be taken. This idea of choosing the optimal viewpoint and distance to subject is also known to be of great importance in traditional portraiture [2].

To our knowledge, Flores et al. [15] are the first to propose a method that recovers camera distance from a single image of a previously unseen subject. Their work is based on the Efficient Perspective n-Point algorithm (EPnP) [16], a non-iterative solution to the perspective n-point problem for pose estimation of a calibrated camera given n 3D-to-2D point correspondences. The main difference with our work is that this approach is based on explicit computation of 3D information; therefore it requires 3D models of heads. We argue this is an unnecessary complication. Moreover, Flores et al.'s method is not fully automated and requires hand-annotated landmarks on the test image.

In contrast with all prior work, we propose to train and test in image space without the need for 3D head features or pose information. Furthermore, no calibration or knowledge of camera parameters is needed. Finally, thanks to the recent improvement of automatic facial landmark estimation [17–21], our method is fully automated; it uses automatically estimated landmarks instead of manual annotations.

3 Caltech Multi-Distance Portraits Dataset

We collected a novel dataset, the *Caltech Multi-Distance Portraits* (**CMDP**). This collection is made of high quality frontal portraits of 53 individuals against a blue background imaged from seven distances spanning the typical range of distances between photographer and subject: 60, 90, 120, 180, 240, 360, 480 cm, see Fig 1. For distances exceeding 5m, perspective projection approaches a parallel projection (the depth of a face is about 10cm), therefore no samples beyond 480cm were needed. Participants were selected among both genders, different ages and a variety of ethnicities, physiognomies, hair and facial hair styles, to make the dataset as heterogeneous and representative as possible.

Table 1. Diversity in the *Anonymous Portrait Faces* dataset. Individuals may belong to multiple categories.

Category	Number of Subjects	Percentage
African-American	4	7.5%
Asian	5	9.4%
Caucasian	36	68.2%
Latino	8	15%
Female	7	13.2%
Male	46	86.8%
With Facial Hair	13	24.5%
With Occlusions	11	20.7%

Pictures were collected with a Canon Rebel Xti DSLR camera mounting a 28-300mm L-series Canon zoom lens. Participants standing in front of a blue background were instructed to remain still and maintain a neutral expression. The photographer used a monopod to support the camera-lens assembly. The monopod was adjusted so that the height of the center of the lens would correspond to the bridge of the nose, between the eyes. Markings on the ground indicated seven distances. After taking each picture, the photographer moved the foot of the monopod to the next marking, adjusted the zoom to fill the frame of the picture with the face, and took the next picture. This procedure resulted in seven pictures (one per distance) being taken within 15-20 seconds. Images were then cropped and resampled to a common format. The lens was calibrated at different zoom settings to verify the amount of barrel distortion, which was found to be very small at all settings, and thus left uncorrected. Lens calibration was then discarded and not used further in our experiments.

As the camera approaches the subject the relationship of the size of the picture of the main parts of the face changes (Fig. 1). It is important to clarify that this 'perspective distortion' is not a lens error (this was verified, as explained in the previous paragraph): it arises from the projection of the three dimensional world into a two dimensional image and is easily observable with our own eyes. We could have used any other lens, including one with fixed focal length, or a pinhole camera, and there would have been no difference in the amount of 'perspective distortion' measured at a given distance (that is, assuming that the lens has no internal flaws or distortion). Using a lens with a shorter focal length and wider field of view will result in a coarser pixel sampling of the face, but the perspective geometry and proportions would only depend on distance, or, equivalently, on the visual angle subtended by the face. Regardless of the lens used, crops of two images taken from the same distance would be identical, apart from sampling resolution. We used a zoom lens to obtain maximum pixel resolution at all distances.

3.1 Annotating CMDP

All images in the dataset were manually annotated with 55 facial landmarks distributed over and along the face and head contour, see Fig. 2(a). The location of our landmarks is very different from landmark positions typically used in the literature, more focused towards the center and bottom of the face, as for example Multi-pie [22] format, Fig. 2(b). We purposely wanted to have landmarks around the head contour (in green) and all around the face (in red), to sample a larger area of the face.

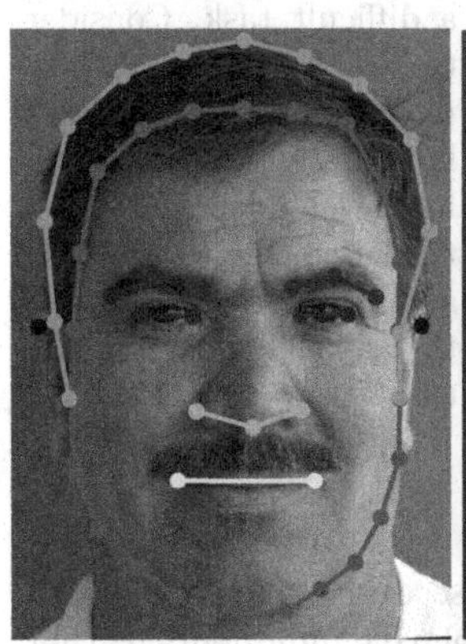

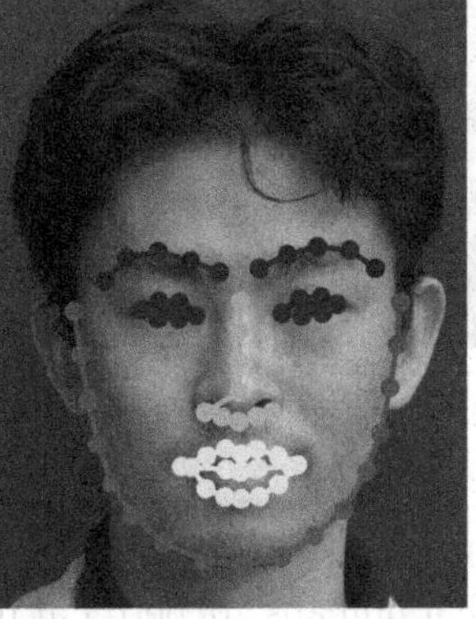

Fig. 2. Our 55 face landmarks (left) compared to the 68 facial keypoints in Multi-pie format [22] (right). With landmarks around the hair line and top of the forehead our landmarks allow to test whether these regions provide useful signal, despite their intrinsic variability.

The dataset was annotated by three different human annotators. Portraits from the same subject were always annotated by the same annotator in sequence, minimizing the variance in the location of landmarks between pictures at different distances. To check consistency of annotations, we doubly annotated several images from different subjects. Annotators are very consistent, showing an average disagreement between them less than 3% of the interocular distance, and not varying much across distances, see Fig 4.

4 Problem Formulation

The goal is to estimate the camera-head distance from a single 2D portrait photograph when both the camera and the sitter are unknown. From this initial problem formulation, we derive two different tasks:

1. Sorting the seven images belonging to a single previously unseen subject according to their distance.
2. Estimating the distance from which a single image of a previously unseen subject was taken.

While the difference between the two might seem subtle, it affects the entire procedure. Firstly, from a machine learning point of view, the former is a classification task, while the latter is a pure regression problem, meaning that feature normalization schemes and error metrics will be different in each case.

Secondly, pure regression is a much harder task. Since the person has never been seen before, it is difficult to account for his/her physiognomy. For example, a person with a round face or a big nose will often appear closer than a squared face with a small nose, see Fig. 3.

Fig. 3. Estimating the relative distance of previously unseen subjects is a difficult task. Consider these portraits. Their physiognomy confuses human annotators, which have a tendency to pick the left image (d=240cm) as the closest one, while the right hand side one (d=180cm) was closer.

In fact, while humans are able to perform the first task rather accurately, see Fig. 6, they are completely unable to perform the second task. Part of the reason is the well known fact that humans are better at relative judgments, rather than estimating absolute values. Another reason may be that having access to several pictures of the same subject allows to ignore physiognomy and focus on the important signal. For real-life applications the regression task is far more relevant; we use the ordering task exclusively to benchmark our method against human performance and guide our thoughts.

Error Metrics: In the re-ordering problem, we measure for each portrait the probability of being correctly classified into its distance category (from 1 to 7). In the regression task we measure both the Pearson correlation coefficient (Corr) and the coefficient of determination (R^2) between prediction and ground truth distance on all 7 images of the test subject:

$$Corr(sbj) = \frac{COV(gt(sbj), pred(sbj))}{std(gt(sbj)) * std(pred(sbj))}, R^2(sbj) = 1 - \frac{(gt(sbj) - pred(sbj))^2}{(gt(sbj) - \overline{gt})^2}$$

Where the terms *gt(sbj)* and *pred(sbj)* are respectively the ground-truth and predicted distances of each picture belonging to the subject being evaluated and $\overline{gt}$ is the average of all ground truth distances.

5 Method

We use the position of the face's landmarks to capture the 2D shape of the face and therefore measure how much it changes with distance. Input landmarks can be both the result of manual annotations or the output of a landmark estimation algorithm. After computing the facial landmarks, we apply a supervised learning approach, see Sec 5.2. A subset of the subjects in the dataset are used to train a regressor capable of mapping the shape of their face at different distances to the ground truth distances. Then, the performance of the learned regressor is evaluated on the remaining subjects in the dataset according to each of the tasks defined in the previous Section.

5.1 Facial Landmarks

Encouraged by the recent success of facial landmark estimation approaches, we decided to benchmark its feasibility for this task. We use *Random Cascaded Pose Regression (RCPR)* [20], due to its performance, speed and availability of code.

We trained RCPR on 70% of the individuals in our CMDP dataset (259 images in total), with the same parameters as in the original publication. When applied to the remaining 30% of our dataset, RCPR yields an average landmark error of 6.9% and a 16% failure rate, see Fig 4(a). Errors are measured as the average landmark distance to ground-truth, normalized as a percentage with respect to interocular distance. A failure is an average error above 10%, as in [20].

We also trained RCPR on the more exhaustive 300-Faces-in-the wild dataset [21] which contains more than 2K faces taken from previously existing datasets and re-annotated following Multi-Pie 68 landmarks [22] convention, see Fig 2(b). To compare its result on our test images, we only evaluate it on the 22 set of landmarks our convention shares with Multi-Pie format. This version of RCPR, applied to the same 30% subset of subjects achieves an average error of 7.8%, but with a much lower failure rate (4%), see Fig 4(a).

Both RCPR versions are still far from human performance, struggling slightly more with faces from both distance extremes, less common in face recognition datasets, see Fig 4(b). The distribution of errors by landmarks reveals that RCPR trained on CMDP struggles particularly with the head contour and the ears due to their inherent variability, while RCPR trained on 300F struggles with the nose and eyebrows. However, both versions still have a low number of failure cases and therefore these issues affect only slightly the final performance of distance estimation when compared with using ground-truth landmarks, as shown in next Section.

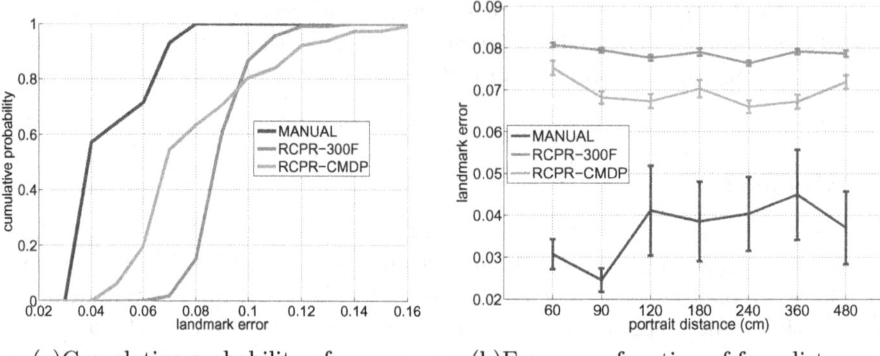

(a)Cumulative probability of errors (b)Error as a function of face distance

Fig. 4. Landmark estimation error. Human annotators are very consistent, showing a low disagreement (3% average), and not varying much across distances. Training RCPR using images from CMDP achieves good average performance except for its high number of failures (16%), struggling in close-range images. RCPR trained on 300-Faces yields slightly worse average performance while with a lower number of failures (4%). A failure is an average error above 10%, as in [20].

5.2 Proposed Approach

After collecting the facial landmarks, we use them as input to learn a regressor that maps face shapes to their ground-truth distances. More specifically, shape $\mathcal{S}$ is represented as a series of P landmark locations $\mathcal{S} = [(x_p, y_p)|p \in 1..P \wedge x, y \in \mathbb{R}]$. For each subject $i \in 1..N$ we dispose of seven different shape vectors associated to each one of the $d \in 1..7$ different distance images, $\mathcal{S}^i_d$. The goal is to learn a robust mapping from each one of the seven shapes to their respective distance: $f : \mathcal{S}^i_d \mapsto \mathbb{R}$.

Shape Vector Normalization: Due to the heterogeneity of face physiognomies contained in our dataset, a prior normalization step of the face shapes is crucial to learn a robust mapping. First, we standardize all portraits using the individual shape vectors $\mathcal{S}^i_d$ cropping the image around the face and removing scale and rotation variations. Then, we propose two different normalization schemes for each one of the tasks defined previously.

In the re-ordering task, we can compute the average subject face shape across all seven distances ($\overline{\mathcal{S}}^i = \frac{1}{7}\sum_{d=1}^{7} \mathcal{S}^i_d$) and use it to normalize each shape, subtracting the mean from the landmark's position (${\mathcal{S}'}^i_d = \mathcal{S}^i_d - \overline{\mathcal{S}}^i$). This filters out the variations in the shape of the face due to the physiognomy of the individual, leaving only the changes due to perspective distortion.

In the case of the regression task, at test time we only have access to one shape $\mathcal{S}^i_d$ at a time. During training, however, we can compute the average shape for each distance ($\overline{\mathcal{S}}_d = \frac{1}{N}\sum_{i=1}^{N} \mathcal{S}^i_d$). These average shapes can then be used to codify the current shape as the concatenation of the differences between $\mathcal{S}^i_d$ and each one of the d average faces $\overline{\mathcal{S}}_d$: (${\mathcal{S}'}^i_d = \langle \mathcal{S}^i_d - \overline{\mathcal{S}}_{d=1}, .., \mathcal{S}^i_d - \overline{\mathcal{S}}_{d=7} \rangle$).

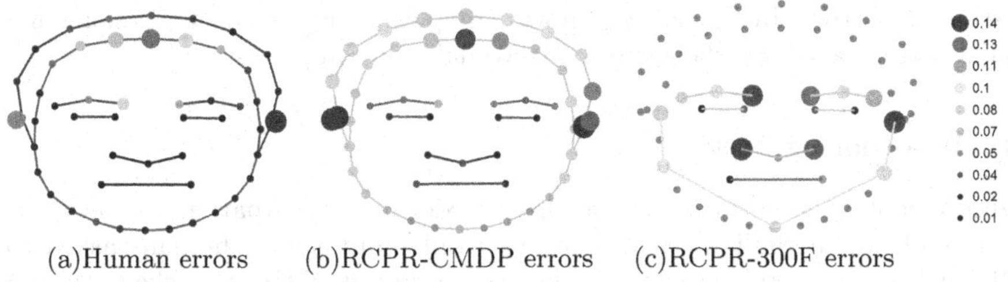

(a)Human errors (b)RCPR-CMDP errors (c)RCPR-300F errors

Fig. 5. Individual landmark errors (blue=low average error, red=high average error). (a) Humans concentrate their disagreement on the forehead (telling where it ends is somewhat subjective) and ears (which can be occluded by hair and excessive distortion). (b) RCPR trained on our faces struggles with hair and face contours. (c) RCPR trained on 300W-Faces struggles the most with the eyebrows and chin. Gray points signify non-existence of the fiducial due to use of Multi-Pie convention.

The effect of each one of these normalization schemes on performance is presented in Fig 9(b), compared also to no normalization at all. Each step improves performance significantly. It is evident that being able to average out with respect to the subject's shape makes a big difference, even compared to our distance normalization scheme.

Inverse distance: In practice, inverse distance is preferred to avoid the saturation of the signal after a certain value of distance (i.e. the difference in the measured distortion becomes negligible with respect to the change in distance).

Learning algorithm: We train a multivariate linear regressor to learn the mapping from the normalized shapes ${\mathcal{S}'}^i_d$ onto the inverse distance of a face as a weighted linear combination of the P landmark locations: $(\sum_{p=1}^{P} \mathbf{w_p}{\mathcal{S}'}^i_d(x_p, y_p))$. We tried several other regression/classification methods but none improved results w.r. to simple linear regression. This may be due to the the relatively small number of training examples, see Supp. Material for more info.

Regression vs. classification: For the classification task, we sort the values the regressor outputs for each of the 7 images belonging to the same subject and compare it against ground-truth distance ordering.

6 Results

We now discuss the results of our method on the re-ordering and pure regression tasks. We benchmark three variants of our method depending on the nature of the input landmarks: using 1) Ground-truth landmarks (MANUAL), 2) Landmarks from RCPR trained on our CMDP images (RCPR-CMDP) and 3) Landmarks from RCPR trained on 300-Faces in the wild (RCPR-300F).

All reported results are obtained using 70% of the subjects for training and the remaining 30% for testing (the same train/test set as that used to train RCPR-CMDP), except in Fig 9 where cross-validation runs are used. Variance is shown as standard errors. In Sec 6.3 we show examples of how subject physiognomy affects performance. Further analysis is available in Supp. Material.

6.1 Re-ordering Task

Figure 6 shows the performance on the re-ordering task. Apart from the three variants of our method, we also plot the result obtained by humans asked to perform the exact same task. We developed a specific GUI and asked a group of 5 people of different levels of computer vision expertise to sort a random permutation of all 7 pictures of a subject based on their conveyed distance. Each person annotated at least 10 different subjects (70 images in total).

The ground-truth landmarks based variant (MANUAL) outperforms human performance by 16%, while the automatic based ones (RCPR-CMDP and RCPR-300F) are slightly behind by 3% and 25% respectively. Closer faces appear to be much easier to classify than distant ones because of their unusual and disproportioned geometry. This has been confirmed by the human subjects of the study, stating their difficulty in telling apart images in the middle distance-range.

We find these results very encouraging. Our best variant outperforms human capabilities in the classification task, correctly reordering an average of 81% of the faces when random chance is merely 15%. The same method using machine estimated landmarks still classifies correctly 62% of the images, and could very likely be improved just by increasing the availability of training examples.

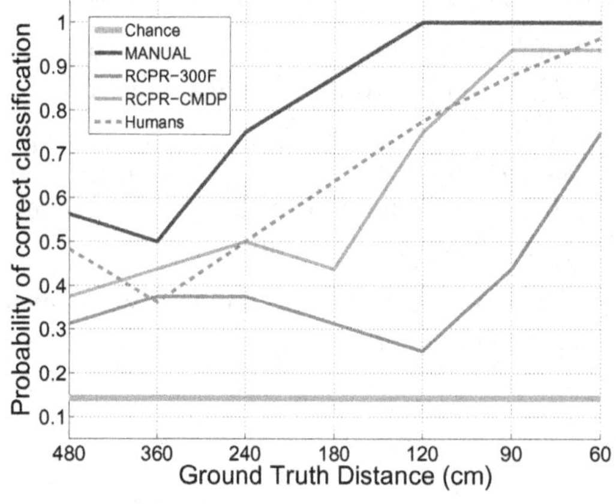

Fig. 6. Main results of our approach on the re-ordering task, measured as the probability of correctly ordering portraits of a subject according to their distance. Our methods using manual landmarks outperforms humans by 16%, while using RCPR-CMDP performance is virtually identical (lower by 3%).

Figure 7 shows which landmarks are most discriminative for the re-ordering task using both MANUAL and RCPR-CMDP input. We measure how well each landmark group (head contour, face contour, eyes, nose, mouth) compares to best performance when only that particular group is used. For both MANUAL and RCPR-CMDP, best results are achieved using the head contour and the nose, while the eyes seem to be the least useful.

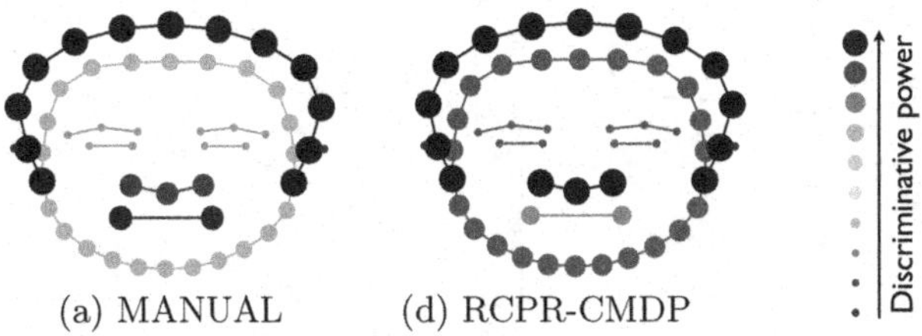

Fig. 7. Input landmarks discriminative power on the re-ordering task, measured as how well the method performs when incorporating those input landmarks into the learning, ranging from most discriminative (big blue dot) to least discriminative (small red dot). For both MANUAL and RCPR-CMDP, the most useful landmarks are the facial/head contours and the nose.

6.2 Regression Task

Figure 8 shows the results on the regression task. There is a strong correlation between ground-truth distances and predictions of our method. MANUAL achieves 75% correlation with a coefficient of determination of $R^2 = .5$, while RCPR-CMDP and RCPR-300F achieve 65% and 45% correlation and $R^2 = .48$ and .46 respectively. All variants seem to struggle more with the larger distances, as noticeable from the higher variance and greater distance to ground truth. This is an expected result considering the lower effect of perspective differences between two images taken from afar.

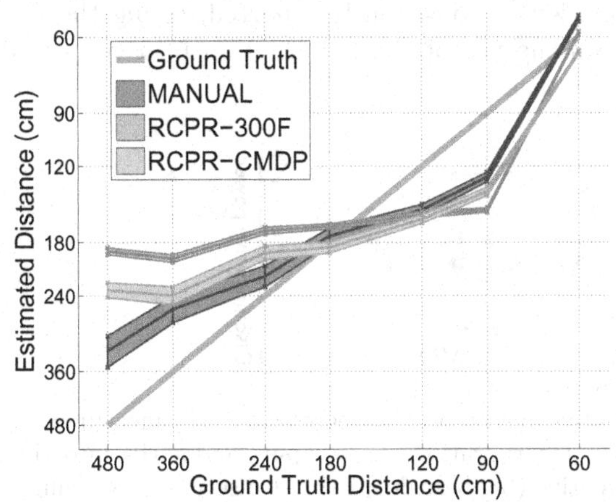

Fig. 8. Main results of our approach on the regression task, measured as the distance with ground truth distance. Using MANUAL landmarks achieves 75% correlation with a coefficient of determination of $R^2 = .5$, while RCPR-CMDP and RCPR-300F achieve 65% and 45% correlation and $R^2 = .48$ and .46 respectively.

As expected, directly estimating the distance of an unknown face proved to be a harder task. Nonetheless, a correlation of 75% with ground-truth indicates that the method is learning well. Furthermore, increasing the amount of training data results in a peek of correlation up to 85%, see Figure 9(a), with no apparent saturation of performance, suggesting that with more data performance could be close to that desired for real-life applications. Overall, our experiments suggest that the distance of a face may be estimated from an uncalibrated 2D portrait.

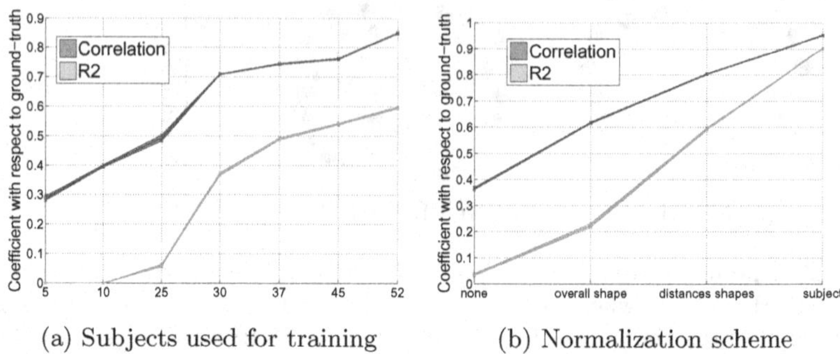

(a) Subjects used for training (b) Normalization scheme

Fig. 9. Parameters evaluation. Results computed using cross-validation runs for robustness. (a) Result of increasing the number of training subjects on the regression task using MANUAL landmarks. With each added subject, the performance continues to grow with no saturation. (b) Result of the different normalization approaches presented in Sec. 5.2 using 52 training subjects in a leave-one-out cross validation scheme. Normalizing the shape of a subject's face using his own average shape across all distances achieves best performance.

Figure 10 shows which landmarks are most discriminative for the regression task using both MANUAL and RCPR-CMDP input. We measure how well each landmark group (head contour, face contour, eyes, nose, mouth) compares to best performance when only that particular group is used. For both MANUAL and RCPR-CMDP, most discriminative group is once again the nose. This finding agrees with human annotators, which consistently reported during the reordering psychophysics experiments the use of the deformation in a subject's nose as their main visual cue for the task.

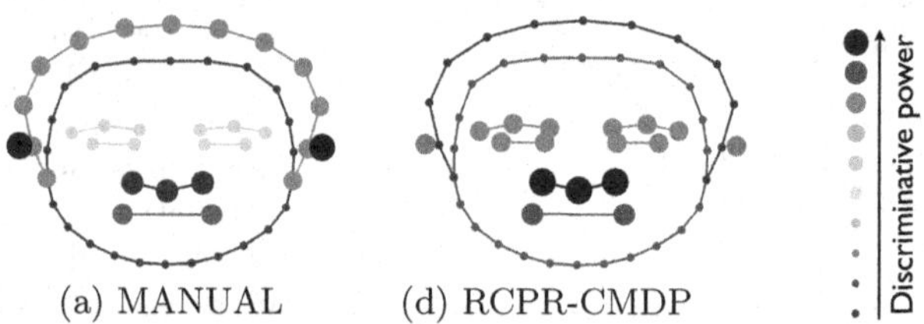

(a) MANUAL (d) RCPR-CMDP

Fig. 10. Input landmarks discriminative power on the regression task, measured as how well the method performs when incorporating those input landmarks into the learning, ranging from most discriminative (big blue dot) to least discriminative (small red dot). For both MANUAL and RCPR-CMDP, the most useful group of landmarks is the nose. For MANUAL, the head contour is once again very discriminative.

Looking at Figures 7 and 10 together is very informative. They show that as we suspected, head and facial contours are extremely important for this task, which explains why RCPR using our landmark convention works far better that RCPR using Multi-Pie convention, which does not have landmarks around head contour. The differences between both figures tells us what parts of the face vary the most across individuals, defining most important cues for physiognomy. Take the facial contour for instance: it switches from most useful in re-ordering task to least useful in regression. This is natural; if one knows the shape of a subject's face (re-ordering) it can be very useful to watch how it gets deformed by perspective. However, not being able to tell physiognomy apart from perspective (regression) makes those landmarks become useless.

6.3 Physiognomy

A final interesting observation regards physiognomy. Throughout all of the experiments we observed that physiognomy of people turned out to be one of the key factors for performance, both for human observers and for our algorithm. In fact, some people appear to be systematically closer than others exclusively due to the shape of their face, Figure 3. Therefore we discussed in Section 5 normalization schemes discarding physiognomy and preserving the signal from perspective distortion.

Accordingly, we have found that the accuracy of the method increases when we normalize using the subject's own average shape across the pictures at all distances, see Fig 9(b). However this subject-specific normalization is only applicable in the re-ordering task, where we can legitimately assume the availability of information on the subject. This has no practical bearing in the regression task where the person being portrayed is unknown.

We asked whether we could derive information on subject's physiognomy by observing the results of our method and if this could shed light on what specific attributes of a human face are most likely to bias distance estimates. We measured for all the faces in the dataset their average bias in the estimated distance over several runs with different training-test set combinations and show our findings in Figure 11. Besides a subjective feeling of roundness for the over estimated faces (judged closer by the algorithm) no evident pattern was found so far, see Supplementary Materials. Estimating physiognomy from a single picture is, thus, an open question.

Figure 12 shows an example output of our algorithm for a subject whose predicted distances are close to ground truth.

Fig. 11. Example of how physiognomy biases distance estimation. (TOP) Ten most under-estimated subjects. (BOTTOM) Ten most over-estimated subjects.

Fig. 12. Example output of the algorithm on the ordered images of a subject (ground-truth from left to right = 60, 90, 120, 180, 240, 360, 480 cm)

7 Conclusions

We proposed the first method for estimating automatically the distance from which a face was photographed. We assume that we have a single frontal photograph, where both the person and the camera are unknown. The method is based on two steps: first, estimating the position of a number of facial landmarks; second, estimating from their relative position the inverse distance by regression.

We find that the method is reasonably accurate. When using manually annotated landmarks as input, it outperforms relative depth judgments obtained from human observers. Furthermore, we find that performance does not suffer much when the method is fully automated with machine-based face landmark estimation. The fully automated method can estimate absolute distance, which human observers are unable to do. As expected, distance estimates beyond 3m, where perspective projection approaches parallel projection, are much noisier than distance estimates in the 0.5-2m range.

An interesting finding is that the main source of error is the variability of physiognomies. Some people appear to be systematically closer than others because their face is shaped differently. Once one normalizes for physiognomy the accuracy of the method increases about 30%; this has no practical bearing when the person being portrayed is unknown, and therefore it is impossible to normalize for physiognomy.

Recovering the distance of a face has a number of applications: as an additional cue to depth in scene analysis, as an indicator of the possible emotional valence of the picture [1], as a tool to study portraiture in classical paintings, and as a tool for forensic analysis of images [3]. Our experiments are encouraging, and are sufficient as a proof of principle to demonstrate feasibility. However, they indicate that accuracy would be significantly better if a much larger training set was available. It is intuitive that such a dataset should include a representative range of facial expressions, as well as a range of viewpoints.

Acknowledgments. This work is funded by ONR MURI Grant N00014-10-1-0933 and NASA Stennis NAS7.03001.

References

1. Bryan, R., Perona, P., Adolphs, R.: Perspective distortion from interpersonal distance is an implicit visual cue for social judgments of faces. PloS One 7(9), e45301 (2012)

2. Perona, P.: A new perspective on portraiture. Journal of Vision 7(9), 992 (2007)
3. Farid, H.: Image forgery detection. IEEE Signal Processing Magazine 26(2), 16–25 (2009)
4. Wheatstone, C.: Contributions to the physiology of vision. Part the first. On some remarkable, and hitherto unobserved, phenomena of binocular vision. Philosophical Transactions of the Royal Society of London 128, 371–394 (1838)
5. Gibson, E.J., Gibson, J.J., Smith, O.W., Flock, H.: Motion parallax as a determinant of perceived depth. Journal of Experimental Psychology 58(1), 40 (1959)
6. Rogers, B., Graham, M., et al.: Motion parallax as an independent cue for depth perception. Perception 8(2), 125–134 (1979)
7. Scharstein, D., Szeliski, R.: High-accuracy stereo depth maps using structured light. In: CVPR (2003)
8. Microsoft: Corp redmond wa. Kinect for xbox 360
9. Gogel, W.C.: The effect of object familiarity on the perception of size and distance. The Quarterly Journal of Experimental Psychology 21(3), 239–247 (1969)
10. Triggs, B.: Camera pose and calibration from 4 or 5 known 3D points. In: The Proceedings of the Seventh IEEE International Conference on Computer Vision, vol. 1, pp. 278–284. IEEE (1999)
11. Murphy-Chutorian, E., Trivedi, M.M.: Head pose estimation in computer vision: A survey. IEEE Transactions on Pattern Analysis and Machine Intelligence 31(4), 607–626 (2009)
12. Fanelli, G., Dantone, M., Gall, J., Fossati, A., Van Gool, L.: Random forests for real time 3D face analysis. Int. J. Comput. Vision 101(3), 437–458 (2013)
13. Liu, C.H., Chaudhuri, A.: Face recognition with perspective transformation. Vision Research 43(23), 2393–2402 (2003)
14. Liu, C.H., Ward, J.: Face recognition in pictures is affected by perspective transformation but not by the centre of projection. Perception 35(12), 1637 (2006)
15. Flores, A., Christiansen, E., Kriegman, D., Belongie, S.: Camera distance from face images. In: Bebis, G., et al. (eds.) ISVC 2013, Part II. LNCS, vol. 8034, pp. 513–522. Springer, Heidelberg (2013)
16. Lepetit, V., Moreno-Noguer, F., Fua, P.: Epnp: An accurate o(n) solution to the pnp problem. International Journal of Computer Vision 81(2), 155–166 (2009)
17. Saragih, J., Lucey, S., Cohn, J.F.: Deformable model fitting by regularized landmark mean-shift. IJCV 2(91), 200–215 (2011)
18. Zhu, X., Ramanan, D.: Face detection, pose estimation, and landmark localiz. in the wild. In: CVPR (2012)
19. Cao, X., Wei, Y., Wen, F., Sun, J.: Face alignment by explicit shape regression. In: CVPR (2012)
20. Burgos-Artizzu, X.P., Perona, P., Dollár, P.: Robust face landmark estimation under occlusion. In: ICCV (2013)
21. Sagonas, C., Tzimiropoulos, G., Zafeiriou, S., Pantic, M.: 300 faces in-the-wild challenge: The first facial landmark localization challenge. In: ICCV-Workshop (2013)
22. Gross, R., Matthews, I., Cohn, J., Kanade, T., Baker, S.: Multi-pie. In: FG (2008)

Probabilistic Temporal Head Pose Estimation Using a Hierarchical Graphical Model

Meltem Demirkus, Doina Precup, James J. Clark, and Tal Arbel

Centre for Intelligent Machines, McGill University, Montreal, Canada

Abstract. We present a hierarchical graphical model to probabilistically estimate head pose angles from real-world videos, that leverages the temporal pose information over video frames. The proposed model employs a number of complementary facial features, and performs feature level, probabilistic classifier level and temporal level fusion. Extensive experiments are performed to analyze the pose estimation performance for different combination of features, different levels of the proposed hierarchical model and for different face databases. Experiments show that the proposed head pose model improves on the current state-of-the-art for the unconstrained McGillFaces [10] and the constrained CMU Multi-PIE [14] databases, increasing the pose classification accuracy compared to the current top performing method by 19.38% and 19.89%, respectively.

Keywords: Face, hierarchical, probabilistic, video, graphical, temporal, head pose.

1 Introduction

Video cameras are ubiquitous in today's world, from street and area surveillance to intelligent digital signs and kiosks. The imagery provided by these cameras is unconstrained and capture video streams of people in many different poses and under a wide variety of lighting conditions. Robustly estimating head pose from such video is an increasingly important and necessary task. In the context of real-world scenarios, face recognition/verification, facial attribute classification and human computer interaction all generally benefit from using head pose estimates as prior information in order to boost their performance [7, 12, 16, 19, 22, 23, 41].

There is a wide literature on head pose estimation, [2–4, 6, 11, 13, 17, 18, 20, 25, 27, 28, 30, 32, 34, 35, 39, 42, 43]. The general categories of methods described in this literature include [26]: *Appearance template methods* use image-based comparison techniques to match a test image to a set of training images with corresponding pose labels. *Manifold, subspace embedding methods* project an image onto the head pose manifold using linear and nonlinear subspace techniques. When such techniques are used for video frames, they implicitly model a given video sequence temporally by mapping similar frames onto nearby locations in the manifold. *Geometric methods* use the location of facial landmarks to determine the head pose from their relative configuration. Lastly, *tracking methods* aim to estimate the global movement of a head by using the relative movement

D. Fleet et al. (Eds.): ECCV 2014, Part I, LNCS 8689, pp. 328–344, 2014.
© Springer International Publishing Switzerland 2014

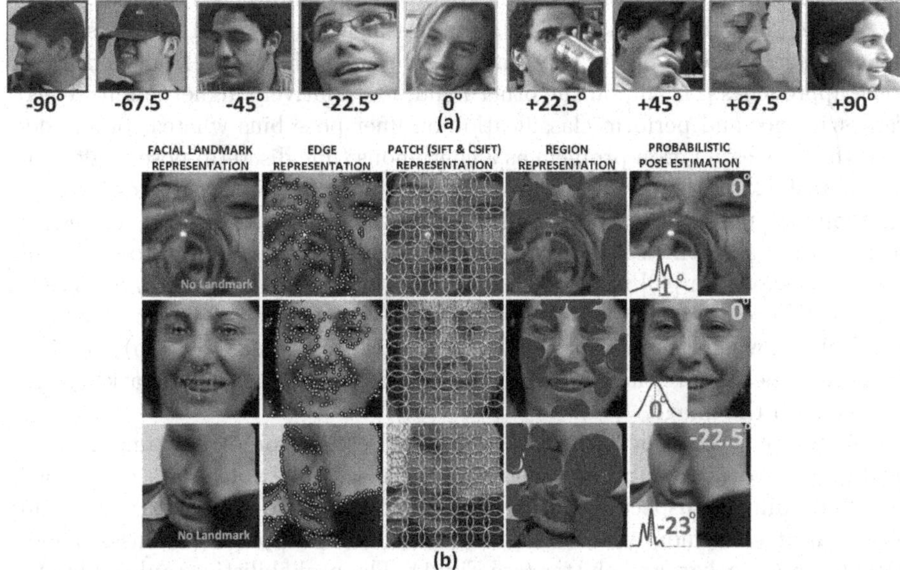

Fig. 1. Examples of tracked faces from the McGillFaces Database [10] depicting the head pose ground truth angles, extracted features and estimated pose information: (a) Head pose (yaw angle) ground truth labels of example faces, (b) Different facial representations, namely facial landmark [40], facial region (BPLR), patch (SIFT and CSIFT) and edge (GB), employed by the proposed model and the estimated pose information. The pose ground truth label obtained via [10] is shown on the top right. The yaw distribution calculated by our approach is shown on the top bottom and the corresponding MAP estimate is shown in red on the pose distribution.

between consecutive video frames. The highest accuracies published in the head pose literature are presented by the manifold learning methods, e.g.[4]. Most of these methods, however, are not designed to operate in unconstrained environments. A common assumption is that the entire set of facial features typical for frontal poses is always visible. Facial features are often manually labeled in the testing data, rather than extracted automatically. Furthermore, most approaches are trained and tested on images which do not exhibit wide variation in appearance. The testing databases mostly contain images with solid or constant background, limited facial expression, no random illumination, and limited or no facial occlusion (e.g. Multi-PIE [14]). Finally, current face tracking methods require a known initial head pose, and usually must be reinitialized whenever the tracking fails. All of these issues contribute to poor performance when applied to real-world videos.

Estimation of head pose from uncontrolled environments has recently been receiving more attention [2, 11, 12, 28, 35, 40, 43]. Orozco et al. [28] and Tosato et al. [35] address the problem of head pose estimation in single, low resolution video frames of crowded scenes under poor and/or limited, e.g. indoor, lighting, where they treat the problem as a classification problem. That is, they assign a face image to one of the coarse discrete pose bins, e.g. front and back. Some approaches [11, 43], on the other hand, use relatively higher quality video frames/images and perform classification on finer pose bins whereas others defined the pose estimation problem as a continuous (fine discrete) pose angle estimation task [2, 12, 40]. In short, most of these approaches either do not leverage the temporal pose information available between consecutive video frames, or focus on only a specific set of features (e.g. facial landmark points) to represent faces. It is shown in [40] that facial landmarks can be used successfully to estimate head pose when they are reliably located. However, it is difficult to extract such features when a significant facial occlusion is present (see Fig. 1(b)) or when the pose angle is more than 45°, leading to occlusion of facial landmark regions (e.g. eyes) in the image.

This paper is concerned with the automated estimation of very fine discrete head pose (yaw angle only) in unconstrained videos. The video data is assumed to include difficult aspects such as a wide range in face scales, extreme head poses, variable and non-uniform illumination conditions, partial occlusions, motion blur, and background clutter (see Fig. 1). The probabilistic graphical model proposed in this paper (Fig. 2 and 3) is based on a hierarchy of complementary robust local invariant facial features, which leverages the dependencies between consecutive video frames in order to substantially improve head pose estimation in real world scenarios. These features have a high degree of invariance to various transformations, such as changes in scale, viewpoint, rotation and translation. They include: (i) facial landmarks, (ii) densely sampled patch-based features, (iii) regions, mainly associated with anatomical structures such as the eyes, forehead, and cheeks, and (vi) edge points, mainly arising from the eyebrows, mouth, eyes and nose (see Fig. 1(b)). These features are complementary in that when one feature type is not reliably detected from a face image, the other feature(s) can compensate for it, in order to robustly estimate head pose. In each video frame, the system assesses the probability density function over the pose angle, ranging from -90° to $+90^o$ (Fig. 1(b)). Spatial codebook representations are inferred from the various local features. For each feature type, we calculate the codebook statistics to infer the corresponding pose distribution. These are used in the graphical model to estimate the single video frame pose probability distribution. These head pose probabilities over the given video sequence, later, are temporally modelled. Finally, the non-parametric density estimation is employed to obtain fine discrete head pose probabilities. The results show that that the proposed framework outperforms competing methods [2, 4, 12, 40, 43] when evaluated on a challenging, unconstrained, public available video database, i.e. the McGillFaces Database [10] (see Fig. 1). The proposed model is also evaluated on the CMU Multi-PIE [14] database, which is collected in a controlled environment. It is observed that compared to the next closest competitor, our method achieves a much higher pose classication accuracy.

2 Methodology

In Level 1 (Fig. 3), the framework models the relationship between the statistics learned from different local invariant features on the detected face, and their corresponding face pose distributions. In Level 2, the single frame pose distribution is inferred based on the different feature-based face pose estimates inferred at Level 1. Finally, Level 3 (Fig. 2) estimates the most likely face pose configuration Θ by leveraging the temporal information. To achieve, this we employ Belief Propagation (BP).

Assume that a video contains T video frames, each of which contains a successfully located and tracked face image via the algorithm in [10], $\boldsymbol{X^t_{int}}$, $t \in \{1, 2, \cdots, T\}$. Our goal is to estimate the set of head pose PDFs throughout the video, $\Theta = \{\theta_1, \theta_2, \cdots, \theta_t, \cdots, \theta_T\}$ given $\boldsymbol{Y} = \{Y_1, Y_2, \cdots, Y_t, \cdots, Y_T\}$, where $\theta_t = \{\phi_1, \phi_2, \cdots, \phi_M\}$ is the set of head pose angles for each video frame, and $Y_t = \{y^t_{patch}, y^t_{edge}, y^t_{region}, y^t_{landmark}\}$, which are the patch, edge, region based and facial landmark based pose distributions. The posterior distribution is $p(\Theta|\boldsymbol{Y}) = \frac{p(\Theta,\boldsymbol{Y})}{p(\boldsymbol{Y})}$, where $p(\boldsymbol{Y})$ is a normalization term, which is constant with respect to Θ. To model the head pose over a video sequence Θ, the graphical model shown in Fig. 2 is employed. This allows us to express the posterior distribution with pairwise interactions: $p(\Theta|\boldsymbol{Y}) = \frac{1}{p(\boldsymbol{Y})}\left(\prod_{t=1}^{T} \vartheta(\theta^t, Y^t)\right)\left(\prod_{t=1}^{T-1} \varphi(\theta^t, \theta^{t+1})\right)$. In this equation, the unary compatibility function accounting for local evidence (likelihood) for θ^t is represented by $\vartheta(\theta^t, Y^t)$, whereas the pairwise compatibility function between θ^t and θ^{t+1} is represented by $\varphi(\theta^t, \theta^{t+1})$.

The unary compatibility function for each node i, $\vartheta(\theta^t, Y^t)$, is defined as the joint distribution $p(\theta^t, Y^t)$ given by: $p(\theta^t, y^t_{patch}, y^t_{edge}, y^t_{region}, y^t_{landmark}) = p(\theta^t|y^t_{patch}, y^t_{edge}, y^t_{region}, y^t_{landmark})p(y^t_{patch}, y^t_{edge}, y^t_{region}, y^t_{landmark})$, where $p(\theta^t|y^t_{patch}, y^t_{edge}, y^t_{region}, y^t_{landmark})$ and $p(y^t_{patch}, y^t_{edge}, y^t_{region}, y^t_{landmark})$ are computed by a hierarchical graphical model, whose parametrization and learning are explained in the following subsections. A Gaussian distribution, $N(\mu, \Delta)$, assumption is made to model the pairwise compatibility function $\varphi(\theta^t, \theta^{t+1})$.

Belief Propagation (BP) [29] is used to calculate the MAP estimate as the most likely head pose configuration, $\Theta^* = \text{argmax}_{\Theta} p(\Theta|\boldsymbol{Y})$. In our experiments,

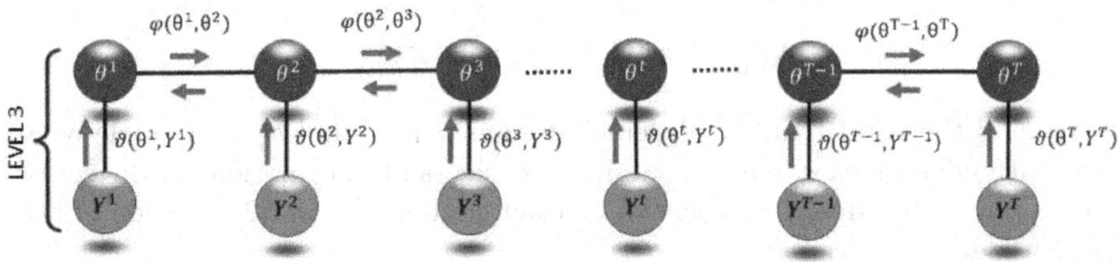

Fig. 2. Level 3 (the highest level) of the proposed framework: Belief Propagation defined over the proposed graphical model and local message passing for head pose estimation from a video sequence

we adapt the sum-product BP algorithm, which is efficient and provides the exact solution since the highest level of our model is a chain.

2.1 Hierarchical Temporal Graphical Model

$\boldsymbol{X}^t_{\boldsymbol{int}}$ is the set of intensity values in RGB space at time t for the pixels in the image of the tracked face: $\boldsymbol{X}^t_{\boldsymbol{int}} = \{x^t_{i,j} \mid \forall i \in \{1, \cdots, I\}, \forall j \in \{1, \cdots, I\}\}$, where the image has the size of $I \times I$ and $x^t_{i,j}$ is the intensity value of an individual pixel at location (i, j).

Given the challenges presented by real-world environments, local invariant features are inferred due to their high degree of robustness to various transformations, such as changes in scale, viewpoint, rotation and translation. Extensive analysis of a number of different local invariant features (e.g. [36, 37]) shows that using both densely and sparsely detected features, and representing these features with complementary descriptors is beneficial for classification/detection tasks.

The collection of the different feature representations (see Fig. 1(b)) inferred from the tracked face $\boldsymbol{X}^t_{\boldsymbol{int}}$ is denoted by $\boldsymbol{X}^t = \left\{\boldsymbol{X}^t_{\boldsymbol{patch}}, \boldsymbol{X}^t_{\boldsymbol{edge}}, \boldsymbol{X}^t_{\boldsymbol{region}}, \boldsymbol{X}^t_{\boldsymbol{landmark}}\right\}$, where $\boldsymbol{X}^t_{\boldsymbol{patch}}$ is the densely sampled patch representation, $\boldsymbol{X}^t_{\boldsymbol{edge}}$ is the sparsely sampled edge representation, $\boldsymbol{X}^t_{\boldsymbol{region}}$ is the dense region, and $\boldsymbol{X}^t_{\boldsymbol{landmark}}$ is the facial landmark representation.

Here, $\boldsymbol{X}^t_{\boldsymbol{patch}}$ is the collection of image patches extracted from $\boldsymbol{X}^t_{\boldsymbol{int}}$:

$$\boldsymbol{X}^t_{\boldsymbol{patch}} = \{x^t_p \mid \forall p \in \{1, \cdots P\}\}, \tag{1}$$

where P is the total number of patches and x^t_p denotes a single patch with index p, which contains two pieces of information: 1) the set of pixels in the patch, $\{x^t_{i,j}\}_p$, and 2) the location of the patch center, (r_p, c_p):

$$x^t_p = \left\{(\{x^t_{i,j}\}_p, r_p, c_p) \mid \{x^t_{i,j}\}_p \subset \boldsymbol{X}^t_{\boldsymbol{int}},\ r_p \in \{1, \cdots, I\}, c_p \in \{1, \cdots, I\}\right\}. \tag{2}$$

$\boldsymbol{X}^t_{\boldsymbol{edge}}$ denotes the collection of distinct points lying on the edge map inferred from X^t_{int}:

$$\boldsymbol{X}^t_{\boldsymbol{edge}} = \{x^t_e \mid \forall e \in \{1, \cdots E\}\}, \tag{3}$$

where E is the total number of detected edge points, and x^t_e is a single edge point with edge index e, which contains two pieces of information: 1) the set of pixels $\{x^t_{i,j}\}_e$ that describes the e-th distinct edge point, and 2) location of the distinct edge point (r_e, c_e):

$$x^t_e = \left\{(\{x^t_{i,j}\}_e, r_e, c_e) \mid \{x^t_{i,j}\}_e \subset \boldsymbol{X}^t_{\boldsymbol{int}},\ r_e \in \{1, \cdots, I\}, c_e \in \{1, \cdots, I\}\right\}. \tag{4}$$

$\boldsymbol{X^t_{region}}$ denotes the collection of facial regions extracted from X^t_{int}:

$$\boldsymbol{X^t_{region}} = \left\{x^t_r \mid \forall r \in \{1, \cdots R\}\right\}, \tag{5}$$

where R is the total number of facial regions extracted from $\boldsymbol{X^t_{int}}$, and x^t_r is the rth single face region, which includes three pieces of information: 1) its set of pixels $\left\{x^t_{i,j}\right\}_r$, 2) the location of the region center (r_r, c_r), and 3) the region scale (size) s_r:

$$x^t_r = \Big\{(\left\{x^t_{i,j}\right\}_r, r_r, c_r, s_r) \mid \left\{x^t_{i,j}\right\}_r \subset \boldsymbol{X^t_{int}}, \\ r_r \in \{1, \cdots, I\}, c_r \in \{1, \cdots, I\}, s_r \in Z^+\Big\}. \tag{6}$$

$\boldsymbol{X^t_{landmark}}$ denotes the collection of facial landmarks extracted from X^t_{int}:

$$\boldsymbol{X^t_{landmark}} = \left\{x^t_{fl} \mid \forall l \in \{1, \cdots L\}\right\}, \tag{7}$$

where L is the total number of facial landmarks extracted from $\boldsymbol{X^t_{int}}$, and x^t_{fl} is the flth single facial landmark, which contains the facial landmark location (r_{fl}, c_{fl}).

To model each of these representations, one can use different features. Here, the features chosen are: (i) densely sampled "SIFT" [24] and "Color SIFT (CSIFT)" [9] features for modeling the face image patches, (ii) sparsely sampled "Geometric Blur (GB)" [5] features for modeling the distinct facial edge points, (iii) "Boundary Preserving Local Region (BPLR)" [21], and (iv) facial landmark [40] features for modeling the facial anatomical regions.

For the landmark features, we use the location information directly. For the remaining features, rather than using the pixel intensities directly for each feature type, the corresponding descriptor d is extracted from each feature point's intensity representation, such as $\left\{x^t_{i,j}\right\}_p$, $\left\{x^t_{i,j}\right\}_e$ or $\left\{x^t_{i,j}\right\}_r$. For the patch representation, SIFT and CSIFT descriptors are used, $d^t_{sift,p=k}$ and $d^t_{csift,p=k}$. In the case of edge features, the GB descriptor $d^t_{GB,e=l}$ is chosen. Pyramids of Histograms of Oriented Gradients are used as the region descriptor, i.e. $d^t_{PHOG,r=m}$. A visual vocabulary (codebook) is learned for each feature type, using the corresponding feature descriptors and an appropriate mapping function which takes the extracted feature's location information into account. That is, in the encoding step, hierarchical K-means clustering is performed on this information. Learning the optimal number of codewords is achieved via cross validation on training set. In the pooling step, vector quantization is used. Next, each extracted feature is represented by a visual word (codeword), from which codeword statistics will be learned. Occurrence statistics, for example, model how likely it is to observe a codeword for a pose value of interest. These statistics will be later used in the potential functions. Note that in the rest of the formulation, instead of the pixel intensity values, the corresponding descriptors d are used in $x^t_{p=k}$, $x^t_{e=l}$ and $x^t_{r=m}$.

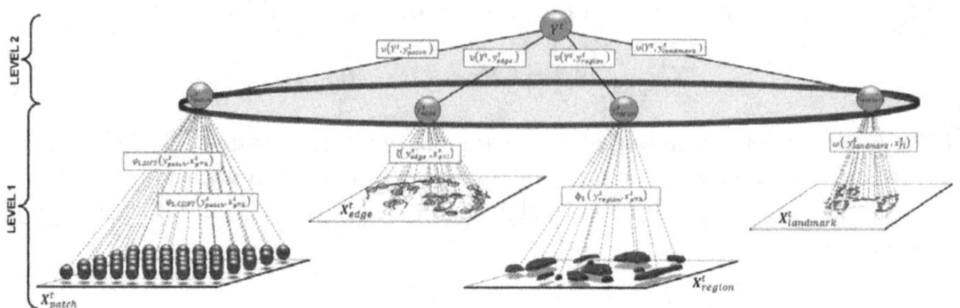

Fig. 3. An overview of Level 1 and Level 2 of the hierarchical graphical model for the t-th frame in a video sequence. The red nodes are the patch, edge, region and landmark based visual words. The yellow nodes of y^t_{patch}, y^t_{edge}, y^t_{region} and $y^t_{landmark}$ represent pose distributions for the patch, edge, region and landmark representations, respectively. The green node Y^t is the pose distribution at the t-th frame. The boxes show the potential functions used to model the relationship between the corresponding two nodes.

We now define each of the facial feature types used in the proposed model: ***The Patch-based Representation:*** A dense sampling of the given facial image is achieved by the patch representation. SIFT and CSIFT vocabularies are used to model each image patch. This choice is motivated by the observed performance increase when CSIFT is combined with SIFT, as in [31]. To map the k-th image patch $x^t_{p=k}$ to a visual word $f^t_{sift,p=k}$ learned using the SIFT and CSIFT descriptors, a mapping function g is used such that $g : x^t_{p=k} \rightarrow f^t_{sift,p=k}$ and $g : x^t_{p=k} \rightarrow f^t_{csift,p=k}$ (that is $\boldsymbol{X^t_{patch}} \rightarrow \boldsymbol{F^t_{patch}}$). To leverage the spatial information, the patch location (r_p, c_p) is used in the coding and pooling phases, similar to the IG-BOW method in [10]. By adding two more dimensions to the descriptor space, this permits modeling the spatial inter-patch relationship. Because faces are aligned in the preprocessing step, this mapping provides better modeling for the face vocabulary. ***The Edge-based Representation:*** The Geometric Blur (GB) framework ([1, 5]) is used for detecting the key facial edge points and calculating the corresponding descriptor around each edge point. Geometric blur is shown to be effective when applied to sparse edge points. Thus, first the oriented edge filter responses are extracted from face images. Then, the rejection sampling over the edge map is used to obtain sparse interest points along edges. Once these interest points are detected, GB descriptors are calculated around each point [5]. GB descriptors, unlike uniform Gaussian blur-based descriptors, models the blur as small near the corresponding points, and larger far from them. Here the motivation is that the distortion due the affine transformations should be modeled properly: the amount of blur varies linearly with distance from corresponding points. To map the l-th distinct edge point $x^t_{e=l}$ to a visual word $f^t_{GB,e=l}$ learned using GB descriptors, we use the mapping function $g : x^t_{e=l} \rightarrow f^t_{GB,e=l}$ (that is $\boldsymbol{X^t_{edge}} \rightarrow \boldsymbol{F^t_{edge}}$). Similar to the facial patch occurrence model, the location information (r_e, c_e) is used in the coding and pooling steps. ***The Region-based Representation:*** To learn the pose information inherent in the facial anatomical regions, e.g the mouth, the eyes, the ears and the eyebrows, we use the boundary-preserving local regions (BPLRs) [21], i.e. $x^t_{r=m}$. Facial BPLRs are densely sampled local regions which preserve the shape of the facial structure on which they are detected. The BPLR detection is achieved based on the following steps [21]; The algorithm first obtains multiple overlapping segmentations from a given face image, for which the corresponding distance transform maps are computed. Then, it divides each segment into regular grid cells, and samples an element feature in each cell. The cell position and scale information is determined by the maximal distance transform value in the cell. Then, it links all elements using a minimum spanning tree, which extends connections and integrates multiple segmentations. Finally, it outputs a set of overlapping regions which contains a group of linked elements within the tree, namely BPLRs. Once the BPLRs are extracted, the Pyramids of Histograms of Oriented Gradients (PHOG) descriptors are computed over the gPb (globalized probability of boundary)-edge map for each detected BPLR. The mapping function $g : x^t_{r=m} \rightarrow f^t_{PHOG,r=m}$ not only uses the spatial information in the coding and pooling steps, but also the scale (size) information for each extracted BPLR. ***The Facial Landmark-based Representation:*** As facial landmarks [40] are shown to successfully estimate head pose when they are reliably detected, we also incorporate these features to our framework. The facial landmarks locations are used in the graphical model. Robust landmark extraction is achieved via the algorithm by Xiong and De la Torre [40].

2.2 Estimation of Level 2 Probabilities

The goal of this level is to estimate the posterior distribution $p(\theta^t|y^t_{patch}, y^t_{edge}, y^t_{region}, y^t_{landmark})$ for the face image in t-th video frame, by learning different combinations of patch, edge, region and landmark classifier pose distributions. To infer the posterior probability $p(\theta^t|y^t_{patch}, y^t_{edge}, y^t_{region}, y^t_{landmark})$, given the hierarchical model in Fig. 3, the following expression is proposed:

$$p(\theta^t|y^t_{patch}, y^t_{edge}, y^t_{region}, y^t_{landmark}) = \frac{1}{\mathcal{Z}(y^t_{patch}, y^t_{edge}, y^t_{region}, y^t_{landmark})} exp\{-U\}, \quad (8)$$

where as before, the normalization function is denoted by $\mathcal{Z}$ and U is the energy function defined as:

$$U = \beta_1 \nu(\theta^t, y^t_{patch}) + \beta_2 \nu(\theta^t, y^t_{edge}) + \beta_3 \nu(\theta^t, y^t_{region}) + \beta_4 \nu(\theta^t, y^t_{landmark}) + \\ \beta_5 \nu(\theta^t, y^t_{patch}, y^t_{edge}) + \beta_6 \nu(\theta^t, y^t_{patch}, y^t_{region}) + \beta_7 \nu(\theta^t, y^t_{edge}, y^t_{region}) + ... \\ \beta_{11} \nu(\theta^t, y^t_{patch}, y^t_{edge}, y^t_{region}) + ... + \beta_{15} \nu(\theta^t, y^t_{patch}, y^t_{edge}, y^t_{region}, y^t_{landmark}). \tag{9}$$

$\{\beta_1, \cdots, \beta_{15}\}$ are the weights for each possible clique and potential function combinations, which are learned using the optimization strategy in [15], namely the de-randomized evolution strategy with covariance matrix adaptation (CMA-ES). CMA-ES is chosen since it does not require any prior information, such as the distribution shape, which is a difficult task considering the dimensionality of the β space. The potential function ν models the *unary, pairwise, triplet* and *fourth order* cliques of t-th frame pose distribution. Note that since we cannot show all 15 potential functions here, we show only a subset. The probability distribution functions are used to define corresponding ν :

$$\nu(\theta^t, y^t_{patch}) = -\log \left\{ p(\theta^t | y^t_{patch}) p(y^t_{patch}) \right\} \tag{10}$$

$$\nu(\theta^t, y^t_{patch}, y^t_{edge}) = -\log \left\{ p(\theta^t | y^t_{patch}, y^t_{edge}) p(y^t_{patch}, y^t_{edge}) \right\} \tag{11}$$

$$\nu(\theta^t, y^t_{patch}, y^t_{edge}, y^t_{region}) \\ = -\log \left\{ p(\theta^t | y^t_{patch}, y^t_{edge}, y^t_{region}) p(y^t_{patch}, y^t_{edge}, y^t_{region}) \right\} \tag{12}$$

$$\nu(\theta^t, y^t_{patch}, y^t_{edge}, y^t_{region}, y^t_{landmark}) \\ = -\log \left\{ p(\theta^t | y^t_{patch}, y^t_{edge}, y^t_{region}, y^t_{landmark}) p(y^t_{patch}, y^t_{edge}, y^t_{region}, y^t_{landmark}) \right\}. \tag{13}$$

$\left\{ y^t_{patch}, y^t_{edge}, y^t_{region}, y^t_{landmark} \right\}$ are the pose distributions, which are inferred through Section 2.3. The estimation of the joint probability $p(\theta^t, y^t_{patch})$ is achieved using the training database: $p(\theta^t, y^t_{patch}) \propto k(\theta^t, y^t_{patch}) + d_t$. The count of the joint occurrence event (θ^t, y^t_{patch}) is represented by $k(\theta^t, y^t_{patch})$, and the Dirichlet regularization parameter d_t is used to compensate for the sparsity. Because a uniform prior is assumed, d_t is constant for all t. Note that probabilities in other cliques are calculated in a similar fashion. The RFs [8], on the other hand, are used to calculate the posterior probabilities, such as $p(\theta^t | y^t_{patch})$, $p(\theta^t | y^t_{patch}, y^t_{edge})$, $p(\theta^t | y^t_{patch}, y^t_{edge}, y^t_{region})$ and $p(\theta^t | y^t_{patch}, y^t_{edge}, y^t_{region}, y^t_{landmark})$. Next, Gaussian kernel-based model fitting is employed to estimate the pose density in the range $[-90^o, +90^o]$ with 1-degree intervals. The motivation behind using such a kernel-based method is that the initial pose densities do not follow any specific parametric distribution. Note that it is possible to get even much finer pose intervals, if needed.

2.3 Estimation of Level 1 Probabilities

To infer $\left\{y^t_{patch}, y^t_{edge}, y^t_{region}, y^t_{landmark}\right\}$, we need to model the posterior distributions $p(y^t_{patch} \mid \boldsymbol{X^t_{patch}})$, $p(y^t_{edge} \mid \boldsymbol{X^t_{edge}})$, $p(y^t_{region} \mid \boldsymbol{X^t_{region}})$ and $p(y^t_{landmark} \mid \boldsymbol{X^t_{landmark}})$. The posterior distribution for the patch-based features is given by:

$$p(y^t_{patch} \mid \boldsymbol{X^t_{patch}}) = \frac{1}{\mathcal{Z}(\boldsymbol{X^t_{patch}})} exp\left\{-U_{patch}\right\}, \tag{14}$$

where $\mathcal{Z}$ is the normalization function and, given the proposed graphical model, the energy function U is defined as:

$$U_{patch} = \lambda_1 \varphi_{1,sift}(y^t_{patch}, \boldsymbol{X^t_{patch}}) + \lambda_2 \sum_{k=1}^{P} \varphi_{1,csift}(y^t_{patch}, \boldsymbol{X^t_{patch}}), \tag{15}$$

where the *unary* potential φ_1 models the relationship between patch features (e.g., SIFT or CSIFT) and the t-th frame patch-based pose distribution. The weights $\{\lambda_1, \lambda_2\}$ are learned from the training data using 2-fold cross validation.

For edge-based features, the posterior distribution is defined as:

$$p(y^t_{edge} \mid \boldsymbol{X^t_{edge}}) = \frac{1}{\mathcal{Z}(\boldsymbol{X^t_{edge}})} exp\left\{-U_{edge}\right\}, \tag{16}$$

where $\mathcal{Z}$ is the normalization function and the energy function U_{edge} is defined as: $U_{edge} = \zeta(y^t_{edge}, \boldsymbol{X^t_{edge}})$, where ζ is the edge related *unary* potential function, which models the relationship between edge features and the t-th frame edge-based pose distribution

The region and landmark posterior distributions, i.e. $p(y^t_{region} \mid \boldsymbol{X^t_{region}})$ and $p(y^t_{landmark} \mid \boldsymbol{X^t_{landmark}})$, are modeled via the *unary* potential functions of $\Phi_1(Y^t_{region}, \boldsymbol{X^t_{region}})$ and $\omega(Y^t_{landmark}, \boldsymbol{X^t_{landmark}})$, in a similar fashion to the edge-based features.

Facial Patch Potentials: The following expressions are used to model the occurrence potential function for SIFT and CSIFT based vocabulary (recall that using the codebook mapping $g : \boldsymbol{X^t_{patch}} \rightarrow \boldsymbol{F^t_{patch}}$ for SIFT and CSIFT separately):

$$\varphi_{1,sift}(y^t_{patch}, \boldsymbol{X^t_{patch}}) = -log\left\{p(y^t_{patch} \mid \boldsymbol{F^t_{patch}}) p(\boldsymbol{F^t_{patch}})\right\}, \tag{17}$$

where $\varphi_{1,csift}(y^t_{patch}, \boldsymbol{X^t_{patch}})$ is calculated similarly and uniform priors are assumed . Any classifier can be user to model the posterior probabilities $p(y^t_{patch} \mid \boldsymbol{F^t_{patch}})$ for SIFT and CSIFT. In this work, we choose to use a Random Forest (RF) [8] to perform inference. A RF is a discriminative classier that consists of an ensemble of decision tree classifiers, where the final classification is determined by summing the votes cast by each individual tree. Due to random selection of subset of training data and features, contrary to traditional decision trees, RF is less prone to overfitting,. Also The RF classifier is computationally efficient and also provides probabilistic outputs.

Table 1. The mean and standard deviation statistics of pose classification accuracy and RMSE for the different pose classification approaches, which are averaged over all folds

Method	Accuracy (%)	RMSE
Aghajanian and Prince [2]	20.68 ± 3.55	> 40
BenAbdelkader [4]	54.04 ± 8.77	> 40
Demirkus et al. [12]	55.04 ± 6.53	> 40
Xiong and De la Torre [40]	58.41 ± 9.61	29.81 ± 7.73
Zhu and Ramanan [43]	59.64 ± 7.66	35.70 ± 7.48
Our Method	**79.02± 3.79**	**12.41± 1.60**

Facial Edge Potential: The following expressions model the facial edge potential function using the mapping defined earlier, i.e. $g : \boldsymbol{X^t_{edge}} \rightarrow \boldsymbol{F^t_{edge}}$:

$$\zeta\left(y^t_{edge}, \boldsymbol{X^t_{edge}}\right) = -\log\left\{p\left(y^t_{edge} \mid \boldsymbol{F^t_{edge}}\right) p\left(\boldsymbol{F^t_{edge}}\right)\right\}, \tag{18}$$

where $p(\boldsymbol{F^t_{edge}})$ is assumed to be uniform, and the posterior probability $p(y^t_{edge} \mid \boldsymbol{F^t_{edge}})$ is also estimated using a Random Forest classifier.

Facial Region and Landmark Potentials: Modeling the potential functions $\Phi_1\left(y^t_{region}, \boldsymbol{X^t_{region}}\right)$ and $\omega\left(y^t_{landmark}, \boldsymbol{X^t_{landmark}}\right)$ is achieved by using a similar method to estimate the edge-based potential functions. To estimate the posterior probabilities $p(y^t_{region} \mid \boldsymbol{F^t_{region}})$ and $p(y^t_{landmark} \mid \boldsymbol{F^t_{landmark}})$, a Random Forest classifier is used.

2.4 Experimental Results

We begin by testing the proposed method on a fully unconstrained video dataset, and compare it to the top performing methods. To this end, we chose to test it on the McGillFaces Database [10]. This freely-accessible public database consists of 18,000 real-world video frames captured from 60 different subjects. The videos exhibit wide variability in captured head poses, with 45% of the frames showing non-frontal head poses, with more than half of these having poses beyond 45° (see Fig. 1(a)). Each frame in the database has a labeled head pose. This ground-truth pose label is obtained using the robust 2-stage labeling strategy introduced in [10]. This labeling strategy provides *pose distributions*, in the range $[-90^o, +90^o]$, which can be interpreted as a measure of the labelers' belief of the pose angle. This labeling scheme provides 9 different discrete pose labels computed using the MAP estimates of the pose distributions (see Fig. 1(a)). The competing approaches provide only discrete pose estimates rather than complete pose distributions. Hence the discrete labels are used as the ground truth when testing the alternative approaches. In all cases, the tracking algorithm described in [10] is used to locate and track the faces in each video.

The proposed graphical model is compared to: (i) Aghajanian and Princes probabilistic patch-based within-object classification framework [2], (ii) BenAbdelkaders supervised manifold-based approach which uses raw pixel intensity

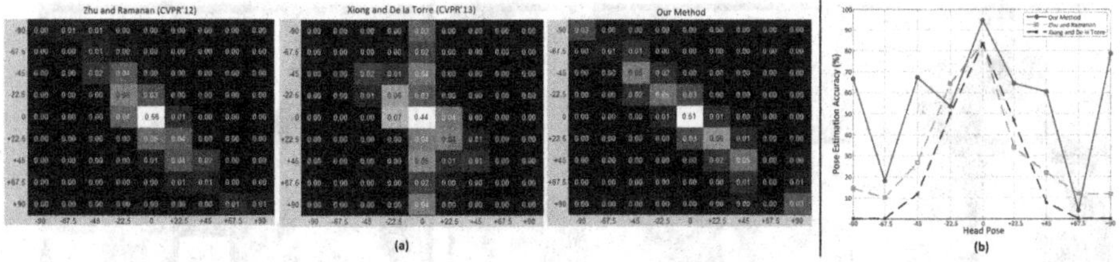

Fig. 4. Comparison of the proposed and the leading alternative methods: (a) the confusion matrices, and (b) the plot showing the pose estimation performance for each head pose label

values [4], (iii) Demirkus et al.'s Bayesian framework which uses OCI [33] features to model the pose in real-world environments [12], (iv) Zhu and Ramanan's unified model for face detection, pose estimation and landmark localization using a mixture of trees with a shared pool of parts [43], and (v) Xiong and De la Torre's Supervised Descent Method which solves a non-linear least squares problem in the context of facial feature detection and tracking (IntraFace) [40]. Ten-fold cross validation is used to evaluate the performance of each method, applied to videos taken from the McGillFaces Database.

In Table 1, quantitative comparison of the these approaches over all folds is provided. The validation metrics consist of: (1) head pose classification accuracy (results in terms of mean±std), and (2) the mean root mean square error (RMSE) based on angle error. In both categories, the proposed framework significantly (i.e., p-value of 4.9051×10^{-5} for the pose classification experiment compared to [43]) out-performs the alternative approaches. Our method provides the best accuracy and that the next closest competitors have over 19% lower accuracy. [43] and [40] are the bests among comparative approaches. [43] and [40] overall provide similar pose label estimation performance, whereas IntraFace [40] has a much lower RMSE. Note that the original implementation provided by the authors of [2, 40, 43] are optimized and used in our experiments. To accomplish a more comprehensive analysis, the confusion matrices (see Fig. 4(a)) and the plots showing the pose estimation performance for each head pose label (see Fig. 4(b)) are provided for the proposed model, [43] and [40]. The confusion matrix for [43] reveals that the approach is good at head pose estimation for face images depicting maximum of 45° head pose angle. [43] does not provide reliable pose estimation for very off frontal, i.e. more than 67.5^o, face pose images. The confusion matrix for [40] shows that [40] is better at detecting faces in the wild however it has tendency to label face images with mostly frontal (in the range of $[-45^o,+45^o]$) pose label, leading to a dominant vertical flow in the confusion matrix. The confusion matrix for the proposed approach, on the other hand, shows a more diagonal trend with small variance. It is observed in Fig. 4(b) that all the methods, including the proposed method, perform poorly for pose angles of -67.5^o and $+67.5^o$. This is due to the fact that humans showed poor ability to perform ground truth labelling for these angles when shown images that are very unconstrained (see some failure cases in Fig. 5). The proposed

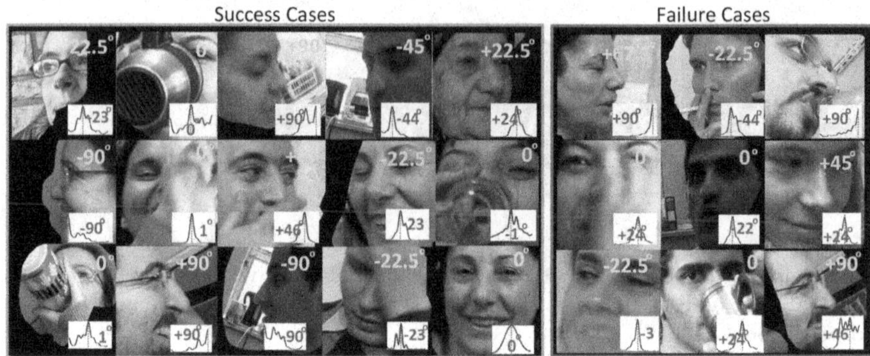

Fig. 5. Success and failure cases with the corresponding pose ground truth labels (in yellow), estimated pose distributions (in blue) and the MAP estimates (in red)

approach tends to estimate the label as being either -45° or $+90^o$, for each of these angles respectively. As such, this reduced the overall reported accuracy in terms of bin classification. However, the RMSE errors for these angles helped this problem by reflecting the angle errors. Furthermore,the proposed approach is the only method to perform accurate pose estimation even for images acquired at full profile (90°) poses. Furthermore, in Fig. 4(b), it is observed that all the three approaches do the best for the frontal images, which is expected. For [43] and [40], the performance decreases dramatically as the head pose is more off-frontal. The proposed approach, on the other hand, has a good pose estimation performance even for the images with full profile (90°) poses.

The pose estimation performance for different combination of features is also analyzed. It is observed that the patch only, edge only, region only and landmark only achieves the pose estimation accuracy of 71.75%, 71.77%, 74.6%, 60.90%, respectively. That is, the region representation achieves the best performance among single features. When the region and patch features are combined, the performance increases to 76%. Combining the top three representations, i.e. region, patch and edge, leads to an accuracy of 77.13% whereas using all types of representations provides an accuracy of 79.02%. We also do a comparison of the MAP based accuracies for each pose label before and after the temporal stage. The maximum accuracy gain of 12.2% is achieved with a pose of -67.5^o, whereas the average accuracy gain over all pose bins is 9.17%. Over all folds, the mean histogram distance between the ground truth PDF and the estimated PDF decreases by 9.37% when Earth Mover's Distance is employed.

Fig. 5 shows examples of cases in which the proposed method does well, and where it fails. For each of these cases the estimated pose distributions are shown along with the MAP estimate of the head pose as well as the ground truth labels. One can also see that the method can be successful even in challenging conditions such as the presence of occlusion, facial hair and glasses, blur and various facial expressions. On the other hand, as depicted by some examples, the method can fail in the presence of motion blur, occlusions, due to the lack of reliable features.

Finally, we wish to examine the method under more controlled conditions. To this end, we test the proposed model on CMU Multi-PIE database [14], which is collected in a controlled environment. We perform a comparison on 5200 images which include all 13 different pose (equally distributed), along with lighting and facial expression variations. Our method achieves a pose classification accuracy of 94.46% whereas [43] provides an accuracy of 74.57%. Note that the pose classification is performed over 13 head pose bins and this dataset is larger than the one reported in [43].

3 Conclusions and Future Work

In this paper, we propose a hierarchical temporal graphical model to robustly estimate fine discrete head pose angle from real-world videos, i.e. with arbitrary facial expressions, arbitrary partial occlusions, arbitrary and non-uniform illumination conditions, motion blur and arbitrary background clutter. The proposed methodology provides a probability density function (pdf) over the range $[-90^o, +90^o]$ of head poses for each video frame rather than just provide a single decision. Experiments performed on the real-world video database (McGillFaces) and the controlled CMU Multi-PIE database show that the proposed approach significantly outperforms the alternative approaches. The proposed framework is a general approach which can be directly applied to any temporal trait and can use any type of feature. Our model does not rely on any subjective notion of what features are more useful for the task of interest. Rather, it learns how to optimally combine a set of features both spatially and temporally. It infers which set of features are more useful. Furthermore, the framework outputs the entire pose distribution for a given video frame, which permits robust temporal, probabilistic fusion of pose information over the entire video sequence. This also allows probabilistically embedding the head pose information for other tasks. We are currently collecting the probabilistic head pose ground truth for the YouTube Faces DB [38] to further evaluate our framework (the probabilistic labels will be publicly available). In future work, we plan to further analyze how temporal relationships can be used to improve other inference tasks (e.g. gender and facial hair classification).

References

1. Berg, A.C., Berg, T.L., Malik, J.: Shape matching and object recognition using low distortion correspondences. In: Proc. International Conference on Computer Vision and Pattern Recognition, CVPR (2005)
2. Aghajanian, J., Prince, S.: Face pose estimation in uncontrolled environments. In: Cavallaro, A., Prince, S., Alexander, D.C. (eds.) BMVC, pp. 1–11. British Machine Vision Association (2009)

3. Balasubramanian, V.N., Ye, J., Panchanathan, S.: Biased manifold embedding: A framework for person-independent head pose estimation. In: CVPR. IEEE Computer Society (2007)
4. BenAbdelkader, C.: Robust head pose estimation using supervised manifold learning. In: Daniilidis, K., Maragos, P., Paragios, N. (eds.) ECCV 2010, Part VI. LNCS, vol. 6316, pp. 518–531. Springer, Heidelberg (2010)
5. Berg, A.C., Malik, J.: Geometric blur for template matching. In: Proceedings of the 2001 IEEE Computer Society Conf. on Computer Vision and Pattern Recognition, CVPR 2001, vol. 1, pp. 607–614 (2001)
6. Beymer, D.: Face recognition under varying pose. In: Proceedings of the 1994 IEEE Computer Society Conference on Computer Vision and Pattern Recognition CVPR 1994, pp. 756–761 (June 1994)
7. Blanz, V., Grother, P., Phillips, P., Vetter, T.: Face recognition based on frontal views generated from non-frontal images. In: IEEE Computer Society Conference on Computer Vision and Pattern Recognition, CVPR 2005, vol. 2, pp. 454–461 (June 2005)
8. Breiman, L.: Random forests. Machine Learning 45(1), 5–32 (2001)
9. Burghouts, G., Geusebroek, J.: Performance evaluation of local color invariants. Computer Vision and Image Understanding (CVIU) 113, 48–62 (2009)
10. Demirkus, M., Clark, J.J., Arbel, T.: Robust semi-automatic head pose labeling for real-world face video sequences. Multimedia Tools and Applications, 1–29 (2013)
11. Demirkus, M., Oreshkin, B.N., Clark, J.J., Arbel, T.: Spatial and probabilistic codebook template based head pose estimation from unconstrained environments. In: Macq, B., Schelkens, P. (eds.) ICIP, pp. 573–576. IEEE (2011)
12. Demirkus, M., Precup, D., Clark, J.J., Arbel, T.: Soft biometric trait classification from real-world face videos conditioned on head pose estimation. In: CVPR Workshops, pp. 130–137. IEEE (2012)
13. Demirkus, M., Precup, D., Clark, J.J., Arbel, T.: Multi-layer temporal graphical model for head pose estimation in real-world videos. In: ICIP. IEEE (2014)
14. Gross, R., Matthews, I., Cohn, J., Kanade, T., Baker, S.: Multi-pie. Image Vision Comput. 28(5), 807–813 (2010)
15. Hansen, N., Müller, S.D., Koumoutsakos, P.: Reducing the time complexity of the derandomized evolution strategy with covariance matrix adaptation (cma-es). Evol. Comput. 11(1), 1–18 (2003)
16. Hassner, T.: Viewing real-world faces in 3D. In: The IEEE International Conference on Computer Vision, ICCV (December 2013)
17. Hu, C., Xiao, J., Matthews, I., Baker, S., Cohn, J.F., Kanade, T.: Fitting a single active appearance model simultaneously to multiple images. In: Hoppe, A., Barman, S., Ellis, T. (eds.) BMVC, pp. 1–10. BMVA Press (2004)
18. Hu, N., Huang, W., Ranganath, S.: Head pose estimation by non-linear embedding and mapping. In: ICIP (2), pp. 342–345. IEEE (2005)
19. Hua, G., Yang, M., Learned-Miller, E., Ma, Y., Turk, M., Kriegman, D., Huang, T.: Special section on real-world face recognition. IEEE Trans. Pattern Anal. Mach. Intell. 33(10), 1921–1924 (2011)
20. Huang, D., Storer, M., De la Torre, F., Bischof, H.: Supervised local subspace learning for continuous head pose estimation. In: IEEE Conference on Computer Vision and Pattern Recognition (CVPR), pp. 2921–2928 (2011)

21. Kim, J., Grauman, K.: Boundary preserving dense local regions. In: Proc. International Conference on Computer Vision and Pattern Recognition, CVPR (2011)
22. Kumar, N., Berg, A., Belhumeur, P., Nayar, S.: Describable visual attributes for face verification and image search. IEEE Transactions on Pattern Analysis and Machine Intelligence (PAMI) 33(10), 1962–1977 (2011)
23. Li, H., Hua, G., Lin, Z., Brandt, J., Yang, J.: Probabilistic elastic matching for pose variant face verification. In: CVPR, pp. 3499–3506 (2013)
24. Lowe, D.G.: Distinctive image features from scale-invariant keypoints. International Journal of Computer Vision (IJCV) 60(2), 91–110 (2004)
25. Morency, L., Rahimi, A., Checka, N., Darrell, T.: Fast stereo-based head tracking for interactive environments. In: Proceedings of the Fifth IEEE International Conference on Automatic Face and Gesture Recognition, pp. 390–395 (May 2002)
26. Murphy-Chutorian, E., Trivedi, M.M.: Head pose estimation in computer vision: A survey. IEEE Trans. Pattern Anal. Mach. Intell. 31(4), 607–626 (2009)
27. Oka, K., Sato, Y., Nakanishi, Y., Koike, H.: Head pose estimation system based on particle filtering with adaptive diffusion control. In: MVA, pp. 586–589 (2005)
28. Orozco, J., Gong, S., Xiang, T.: Head pose classification in crowded scenes. In: BMVC. British Machine Vision Association (2009)
29. Pearl, J.: Probabilistic reasoning in intelligent systems: networks of plausible inference. Morgan Kaufmann (1988)
30. Raytchev, B., Yoda, I., Sakaue, K.: Head pose estimation by nonlinear manifold learning. In: Proceedings of the 17th International Conference on Pattern Recognition, ICPR 2004, vol. 4, pp. 462–466 (August 2004)
31. Van de Sande, K.E.A., Gevers, T.: Evaluating color descriptors for object and scene recognition. IEEE PAMI 32(9), 1582–1596 (2010)
32. Sherrah, J., Gong, S.: Fusion of perceptual cues for robust tracking of head pose and position. Pattern Recognition 34(8), 1565–1572 (2001)
33. Toews, M., Arbel, T.: Detection, localization, and sex classification of faces from arbitrary viewpoints and under occlusion. IEEE Transactions on Pattern Analysis and Machine Intelligence 31(9), 1567–1581 (2009)
34. Torki, M., Elgammal, A.: Regression from local features for viewpoint and pose estimation. In: 2011 IEEE International Conference on Computer Vision (ICCV), pp. 2603–2610 (November 2011)
35. Tosato, D., Farenzena, M., Spera, M., Murino, V., Cristani, M.: Multi-class classification on riemannian manifolds for video surveillance. In: Daniilidis, K., Maragos, P., Paragios, N. (eds.) ECCV 2010, Part II. LNCS, vol. 6312, pp. 378–391. Springer, Heidelberg (2010)
36. Tuytelaars, T.: Mikolajczyk, K.: Local invariant feature detectors: a survey. Foundations and Trends in Computer Graphics and Vision 3(3), pp. 177–280 (2008)
37. Tuytelaars, T., Mikolajczyk, K.: A survey on local invariant features. Tutorial at ECCV (2006)
38. Wolf, L., Hassner, T., Maoz, I.: Face recognition in unconstrained videos with matched background similarity. In: Proc. IEEE Conf. Comput. Vision Pattern Recognition (2011)
39. Wu, J., Trivedi, M.M.: A two-stage head pose estimation framework and evaluation. Pattern Recogn. 41(3), 1138–1158 (2008)

40. Xiong, X., De la Torre, F.: Supervised descent method and its application to face alignment. In: Proc. International Conference on Computer Vision and Pattern Recognition, CVPR (2013)
41. Yi, D., Lei, Z., Li, S.Z.: Towards pose robust face recognition. In: CVPR, pp. 3539–3545 (2013)
42. Zhao, G., Chen, L., Song, J., Chen, G.: Large head movement tracking using sift-based registration. In: Lienhart, R., Prasad, A.R., Hanjalic, A., Choi, S., Bailey, B.P., Sebe, N. (eds.) ACM Multimedia, pp. 807–810. ACM (2007)
43. Zhu, X., Ramanan, D.: Face detection, pose estimation, and landmark localization in the wild. In: 2012 IEEE Conference on Computer Vision and Pattern Recognition (CVPR), pp. 2879–2886 (June 2012)

Description-Discrimination Collaborative Tracking

Dapeng Chen[1], Zejian Yuan[1], Gang Hua[2], Yang Wu[3], and Nanning Zheng[1]

[1] Institute of Artificial Intelligence and Robotics, Xi'an Jiaotong University, China
[2] Department of Computer Science, Stevens Institute of Technology, USA
[3] Academic Center for Computing and Media Studies, Kyoto University, Japan

Abstract. Appearance model is one of the most important components for online visual tracking. An effective appearance model needs to strike the right balance between being adaptive, to account for appearance change, and being conservative, to re-track the object after it loses tracking (*e.g.*, due to occlusion). Most conventional appearance models focus on one aspect out of the two, and hence are not able to achieve the right balance. In this paper, we approach this problem by a max-margin learning framework collaborating a descriptive component and a discriminative component. Particularly, the two components are for different purposes and with different lifespans. One forms a robust object model, and the other tries to distinguish the object from the current background. Taking advantages of their complementary roles, the components improve each other and collaboratively contribute to a shared score function. Besides, for realtime implementation, we also propose a series of optimization and sample-management strategies. Experiments over 30 challenging videos demonstrate the effectiveness and robustness of the proposed tracker. Our method generally outperforms the existing state-of-the-art methods.

Keywords: Descriptive model, discriminative model, collaborative tracking, SVDD, structural prediction, long-term and short-term memory.

1 Introduction

Visual tracking is a fundamental research problem in computer vision and is important for a large variety of applications. Although significant progress has been made, challenges still remain due to numerous factors such as partial occlusion, illumination change, pose variation, and background clutter, etc. To handle the challenges, it is important to adopt an appropriate appearance model.

An appearance model can be built descriptively, to form a robust object model; or be built discriminatively, to separate the object from surrounding background. Both have their strengths and weaknesses in visual tracking. The former directly models the object appearance [13,17,11,20], but easily drifts to similar distractors, the latter one distinguishes the target from the background [2,10,14], but is not robust enough as the background may change dramatically.

D. Fleet et al. (Eds.): ECCV 2014, Part I, LNCS 8689, pp. 345–360, 2014.
© Springer International Publishing Switzerland 2014

Although several collaborative models have been proposed to take the best of both [26,30], they usually learn the two kinds of appearance models separately, which hinders them seeking the right level of balance between these two types of models.

Another factor needs to be considered for appearance model is adaption. In order to capture the dynamically changing appearance, it is also required that the appearance model should be adaptively updated. Some models adjust an ad-hoc learning rate to update the appearance model with most recent observations [2,11,6], which makes the tracker be prone to drift in case of erroneous updates. Some other models learn from a subset of historically observed samples [10,12], which is not sufficiently adaptive to handle fast appearance change. To cope with the well known "stability-plasticity" dilemma, Santner et. al [21] combine complementary models operated at different timescales, Xing et al[28] collect samples at different time for online dictionary learning. Their success suggest that utilizing different lifespan information is important for adaption, but how to balance this these information remains to be an open problem.

We propose a novel way to collaborate the descriptive component with the discriminative component in a unified max-margin framework for appearance modeling. The two components are with different lifespans to better exploit their complementary modeling power, leading to a more data-dependent adaption of appearance model. The main contributions of the paper lies in three aspects:

Components: We employ a descriptive component and a discriminative component to composite the appearance model. The descriptive component is based on Support Vector Data Description (SVDD) [23]. It describes the global properties of the target from all the tracked frames, using representative samples to capture their essential characteristics. Meanwhile, the discriminative component is based on Structured Output SVM (SSVM) [24]. It differentiates the targets from its surrounding background in recent frames, focusing on the most violated background samples to guide the accurate localization.

Collaboration: We cast the two relevant but distinctive components in a unified max-margin learning framework, where they are combined in a mutually beneficial way. The descriptive component uses discriminative information to modify its descriptive boundary, and the discriminative component recalls relevant descriptive samples to increase its discriminative ability. More meaningfully, as the two components have different lifespans. The adaption of the appearance model is influenced by current discriminative samples, but at the same time seeks for a consistence with previous descriptive samples.

Computation: To reduce the computational burden, two kinds of strategies are taken. The first is the learning strategy. We optimize the collaborative model in its dual form to make use of optimized solution from previous time instance, and only select the most informative samples for fast approaching the optimum. The second is the implementation strategy. As the training data increase linearly during tracking, there is a need to control the size of sample set. We adopt a series of set management operations, which boost the tracking speed without impacting much of the tracking accuracy.

2 Related Work

We compare our description-discrimination collaborative tracker with the previous methods based on generative, discriminative and collaborative models.

Generative models estimate the distribution of object appearance directly, they usually form a robust object representation in a particular feature space, including superpixel [25], and feature histograms [1,11,6], etc. Recently, subspace based generative models attract a lot of attention [20,15], and the trackers making use of sparse representation become quite popular [17,13,30]. Different from generative models, the descriptive component in our method is based on the idea of SVDD [23], which estimates the support of the target distribution rather than the full density. As shown in [7], the decision function of SVDD can well capture the density and modality of the feature distribution by using kernel techniques [7,16], which is effective to capture the changing appearance of the target.

Discriminative models aim to distinguish the target from the background. They usually train a dynamic target classifier with the most prevalent algorithms, such as boosting [9,2], random forest [21,14] and SVM [12,10]. The discriminative component in our model is inspired by a state-of-the-art discriminative tracker [27], termed "Struck" [10]. Struck predicts the change in object location using structured output SVM(SSVM) [24], which alleviates the "label jitter" and turns out to be more suitable than binary classifier for prediction. Compared with Struck, our discriminative component regards the temporal inequality between target and background. Specifically, we only utilize recent background samples, which is more suitable for tracking in the dynamic environment.

Collaborative models have already attracted a lot of attention. They collaborate different models to explore their complementary strength to enhance the tracking robustness. For example, Wen et. al [26] and Zhong et. al [30] employ the different models in parallel, and predict the targets by fusing their separate results. Meanwhile, Kalal et. al [14] integrate different models in a cascade, successively selects the best sample from the candidates. Both kinds of collaboration do not build mutual beneficial connections between different models, therefore lack a unified and consistent treatment to explore the complementary strength.

3 Description-Discrimination Collaboration

An object is represented by a bounding box. Let $\mathcal{Y}$ stand for the set of possible bounding boxes, whose element $\mathbf{y} = \{x, y, s\}$ is a three dimensional vector describing position and scale. The features extracted from image $\mathbf{x}_t$ that correspond to the area inside the bounding box $\mathbf{y}$ are denoted as $\phi(\mathbf{x}_t, \mathbf{y})$. In this paper, $\phi(\mathbf{x}_t, \mathbf{y})$ is a high dimensional normalized vector, whose L_2 norm is required to be a constant.

Instead of training a binary classifier over $\phi(\mathbf{x}_t, \mathbf{y})$, we learn a score function $F : \mathcal{X} \times \mathcal{Y} \rightarrow \mathbb{R}$ that measures the compatibility between $(\mathbf{x}_t, \mathbf{y})$ pairs. Considering its efficiency at predictive stage, F is assumed to be linear that can yield higher scores to those more similar to the target. The optimal state $\hat{\mathbf{y}}_t$ is predicted by:

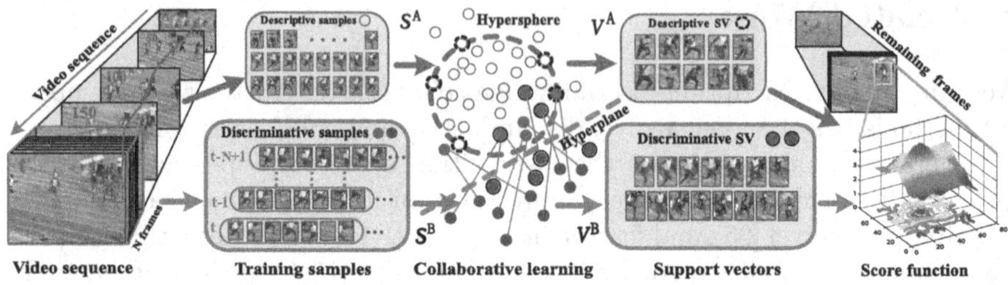

Fig. 1. Overview of our Description-Discrimination Collaborative Tracking algorithm. We crop the long-term target samples and short-term target-background samples into $\mathcal{S}^A$ and $\mathcal{S}^B$(red dot is the target while blue dot is the background). In order to keep both robustness and adaptiveness, the score the target samples are highlighted by different samples from different views. We put the learned support vectors (dots with loops) into $\mathcal{V}^A$ and $\mathcal{V}^B$. They together contribute to the score function.

$$\hat{\mathbf{y}}_t = \arg\max_{\mathbf{y}} F(\mathbf{x}_t, \mathbf{y}) = \langle \mathbf{w}, \phi(\mathbf{x}_t, \mathbf{y}) \rangle. \tag{1}$$

Parameters $\mathbf{w}$ encode the object's appearance, which is collaboratively learned from two components through a single objective function:

$$\min_{\mathbf{w}} \quad \mathcal{R}(\mathbf{w}) + C^{des} \cdot \mathcal{L}^{des}(\mathbf{w}) + C^{dis} \cdot \mathcal{L}^{dis}(\mathbf{w}), \tag{2}$$

where $\mathcal{L}^{des}$, $\mathcal{L}^{dis}$ represent the loss terms on the descriptive component and discriminative component. C^{des} and C^{dis} are scalar parameters to trade-off the impact between the two components. $\mathcal{R}(\mathbf{w}) = \|\mathbf{w}\|_2^2$ is the regularization term.

3.1 Descriptive Component

As the object appearance continuously changes in the feature space, neither offline trained detector nor the appearance template from the first frame is able to capture its variations. To built an effective prior for tracking, we focus on describing the dynamical target set $\mathcal{S}^A$, which ideally contains the features of all tracked targets until the current time instance, *i.e.* $\mathcal{S}^A = \{\phi(\mathbf{x}_i, \hat{\mathbf{y}}_i) | i = 1...t\}$.

We describe the set $\mathcal{S}^A$ using SVDD. The basic idea of SVDD is to employ a hypersphere to enclose the target set and minimize the sphere's volume to exclude outliers. Given the hypersphere's center $\mathbf{c}$, the descriptive loss term is :

$$\mathcal{L}^{des}(\mathbf{c}) = \min_{R} R^2 + \bar{C} \sum_i H(\|\phi(\mathbf{x}_i, \hat{\mathbf{y}}_i) - \mathbf{c}\|^2 - R^2), \tag{3}$$

where R is the radius of the hypersphere, and $H(z) = max(0, z)$ is the hinge loss. As mentioned above, all the features are constrained to have a constant norm a, *i.e.*, $\|\phi(\mathbf{x}_t, \mathbf{y})\|_2 = a$. Let $\mathbf{w} = 2\mathbf{c}$ and $\rho = \frac{1}{4}\|\mathbf{w}\|_2^2 + a^2 - R^2$, $\mathcal{L}^{des}(\mathbf{c})$ can be transformed to $\mathcal{L}^{des}(\mathbf{w})$:

$$\mathcal{L}^{des}(\mathbf{w}) = \min_{\rho} \frac{1}{4}\|\mathbf{w}\|_2^2 - \rho + \bar{C} \sum_i H(\rho - \mathbf{w} \cdot \phi(\mathbf{x}_i, \hat{\mathbf{y}}_i)) + const. \tag{4}$$

where $\mathcal{L}^{des}(\mathbf{w})$ is in the form of 1-class svm [22], which is convenient to be optimized and is good at handling high dimensional data. The proposed descriptive component have two advantages for object tracking. It captures the global support of the samples in $\mathcal{S}^A$, hence is robust to outlier target samples. In addition, the learning of descriptive component needs less prior knowledge but depends more on the tracked samples, enabling the tracker to adapt to the complex changes of the object.

3.2 Discriminative Component

However, if the tracker merely relies on the descriptive component, it tends to fail when the object's appearance changes rapidly. This is because the descriptive component attempts to describe the whole distribution of target samples and may not well capture the current object appearance. Opposite to the target object, the background contains important contextual cues and is effective for accurate localization. To achieve tracking adaptivity, we only focus on the most recent N frames, where the both target and background samples are cropped into a set $\mathcal{S}^B$, *i.e.* $\mathcal{S}^B = \{\phi(\mathbf{x}_j, \mathbf{y}) | \mathbf{y} \in \mathcal{Y}, j = t-N+1, ..., t\}$.

Inspired by the Struck tracker [10], we discriminate the target and the background samples in $\mathcal{S}^B$ using SSVM [24]. The basic idea of SSVM is that the scores of the target should be larger than those of the background samples in the same frame at least by a margin $\Delta(\hat{\mathbf{y}}_j, \mathbf{y})$. Therefore, $\mathcal{L}^{dis}(\mathbf{w})$ is

$$\mathcal{L}^{dis}(\mathbf{w}) = \sum_{j, \mathbf{y} \neq \hat{\mathbf{y}}_j} H(\Delta(\hat{\mathbf{y}}_j, \mathbf{y}) - \mathbf{w} \cdot \delta\phi_j(\mathbf{x}_j, \mathbf{y})), \quad (5)$$

where $\delta\phi_j(\mathbf{x}_j, \mathbf{y}) = \phi(\mathbf{x}_j, \hat{\mathbf{y}}_j) - \phi(\mathbf{x}_j, \mathbf{y})$, and $\Delta(\hat{\mathbf{y}}_i, \mathbf{y})$ is the structural loss that rescales the margin of each sample differently based on the bounding box overlap ratio, defined as $\Delta(\hat{\mathbf{y}}_i, \mathbf{y}) = 1 - \frac{\text{Area}(\hat{\mathbf{y}}_i \bigcap \mathbf{y})}{\text{Area}(\hat{\mathbf{y}}_i \bigcup \mathbf{y})}$. Different from binary classifiers, SSVM explores the structural relationship among samples that each target sample is associated with the background samples in the same frame. In this way, the contextual information contained in background samples is well oriented to the specific target instance and can be updated along with the target instance as well.

3.3 Collaborative Model

We take Eq. 4 and Eg. 5 into Eq. 2. After arranging the coefficients, the original objective function is rewritten as:

$$\min_{\mathbf{w}, \rho} \frac{1}{2} \|\mathbf{w}\|_2^2 - C_1 \rho + C_2 \sum_i H(\rho - \mathbf{w} \cdot \phi(\mathbf{x}_i, \hat{\mathbf{y}}_i)) + C_3 \sum_{j, \mathbf{y} \neq \hat{\mathbf{y}}_j} H(\Delta(\hat{\mathbf{y}}_i, \mathbf{y}) - \mathbf{w} \cdot \delta\phi_j(\mathbf{x}_j, \mathbf{y})), \quad (6)$$

Using standard Lagrangian duality and reparametrizing techniques [4], we introduce multipliers $\alpha_i, \beta_j^{\mathbf{y}}$ for each feature $\phi(\mathbf{x}_i, \hat{\mathbf{y}}_i)$ in $\mathcal{S}^A$ and $\phi(\mathbf{x}_j, \mathbf{y})$ in $\mathcal{S}^B$. Then the dual form of Eq. 6 is[1]:

[1] We leave the derivation in the supplementary materials.

$$\max_{\boldsymbol{\alpha},\boldsymbol{\beta}} \quad -\frac{1}{2}\boldsymbol{\alpha}^\top K^A \boldsymbol{\alpha} - \boldsymbol{\alpha}^\top K^{AB}\boldsymbol{\beta} - \frac{1}{2}\boldsymbol{\beta}^\top K^B \boldsymbol{\beta} - \boldsymbol{\beta}^\top \Delta,$$
$$\text{s.t.} \quad \forall i \quad \sum_i \alpha_i = C_1, 0 \le \alpha_i \le C_2; \quad \forall j, \mathbf{y} \quad \sum_{\mathbf{y}} \beta_j^{\mathbf{y}} = 0, \beta_j^{\mathbf{y}} \le C_3 \delta(\mathbf{y}, \hat{\mathbf{y}}), \tag{7}$$

where $\boldsymbol{\alpha}$, $\boldsymbol{\beta}$ and Δ are column vectors that concatenate the α_i, $\beta_j^{\mathbf{y}}$ and $\Delta(\hat{\mathbf{y}}_j; \mathbf{y})$; K^A and K^B are the kernel matrices for $\mathcal{S}^A$ and $\mathcal{S}^B$; and K^{AB} measures the inter affinities between the two sets. The entries of the three matrices are all calculated based on a linear kernel function: $k(\mathbf{x}, \mathbf{y}, \bar{\mathbf{x}}, \bar{\mathbf{y}}) = \langle \phi(\mathbf{x}, \mathbf{y}), \phi(\bar{\mathbf{x}}, \bar{\mathbf{y}}) \rangle$. With the multipliers α and $\beta_j^{\mathbf{y}}$, the parameters $\mathbf{w}$ in Eq.7 is represented as: $\mathbf{w} = \boldsymbol{\alpha}^\top \Phi_A + \boldsymbol{\beta}^\top \Phi_B$, where Φ_A and Φ_B are feature matrices that concatenate the features in $\mathcal{S}^A$ and $\mathcal{S}^B$ along the column. $\boldsymbol{\alpha}^\top \Phi_A$ corresponds to the descriptive component, which is a nonnegative linear combination of features in $\mathcal{S}^A$, while $\boldsymbol{\beta}^\top \Phi_B$ corresponds to the discriminative component, which is a linear combination of features in $\mathcal{S}^B$ highlighting the difference between target and background samples. All the features with non-zero multipliers are called *Support Vectors.*

Discussion. The proposed collaborative model intends to better exploit the different properties of the target samples and background samples to build more robust appearance model for visual tracking. Generally, there are a small number of target samples, while background samples surround the target are abundant. Furthermore, the appearances of target samples from different frames are relatively similar, while the appearances of background samples vary a lot especially in dynamic scenes. The collaborative model is well oriented to the two properties.

Firstly, the discriminative component takes advantage of SSVM [24] like Struck. SSVM makes use of structured samples, it does not need to sample around the target to obtain positive samples that may cause "label jitter", but only stresses that the score of target sample should be larger than the scores of background samples in the same frame. Secondly, the descriptive component utilizes SVDD [23]. SVDD explicitly puts a prior on the target samples to capture the major characteristic of the object. It is robust to outlier and alleviates the learning burden of SSVM by avoiding using obsolete background samples.

The collaborative strategy is superior to Struck - the tracker using SSVM, which, along with its variants has been regarded as the state-of-the-art during recent evaluations and challenges [18,27]. Under the framework of SSVM, in order to retrieve historical target samples for learning the appearance model, Struck has to use the obsolete background samples in the same frame with the target sample. However, for tracking in dynamic scenes, the obsolete background samples can hardly help the current tracking, instead it would actually contaminate the appearance model and increase the computational cost. Our collaborative model gets rid of this limitation. The descriptive component summarizes the previous target samples to be robust, while the discriminative component adopts most effective background samples to be accurate. The two components build natural connections between each other, and the samples in $\mathcal{S}^A$ and $\mathcal{S}^B$ together decide the learning of each component.

More interesting, as the two components have different lifespans, their collaboration corresponds to the theory of the long-term and short-term memory in human brain, where the long-term memory (descriptive component)recalls more about the object itself rather than the background, while the short-term memory (discriminative component) utilize the contextual information to influence the forming of the long-term memory.

4 Online Optimization

Eq.7 is a typical quadratic optimization problem for both $\boldsymbol{\alpha}$ and $\boldsymbol{\beta}$. Considering the tracking efficiency, we decompose the original problem into a sequence of subproblems inspired by the SMO algorithm [19]. Each subproblem first selects coefficient pairs (α_+, α_-) and $(\beta_j^{\mathbf{y}+}, \beta_j^{\mathbf{y}-})$, then optimizes the coefficients using an *elementary step*. In this section, we first discuss the elementary step, then explain the online selection.

4.1 Elementary Step

As constrained by $\sum_i \alpha_i = C_1$ and $\sum_{\mathbf{y}} \beta_j^{\mathbf{y}} = 0$, the elementary step modifies the coefficient pairs by opposite amounts:

$$\begin{cases} \alpha_+ \leftarrow \alpha_+ + \lambda^\alpha \\ \alpha_- \leftarrow \alpha_- - \lambda^\alpha \end{cases} \qquad \begin{cases} \beta_j^{\mathbf{y}+} \leftarrow \beta_j^{\mathbf{y}+} + \lambda^\beta \\ \beta_j^{\mathbf{y}-} \leftarrow \beta_j^{\mathbf{y}-} - \lambda^\beta \end{cases}, \tag{8}$$

where $\lambda^\alpha, \lambda^\beta \geq 0$, leading to an one-step maximization subject to the constraints in Eq. 7. In order to obtain $\lambda^\alpha, \lambda^\beta$, we first introduce $g(\alpha_i)$ and $g(\beta_j^{\mathbf{y}})$, which are the gradients of Eq.7 w.r.t. the multipliers α_i and $\beta_j^{\mathbf{y}}$, respectively:

$$g(\alpha_i) = -\langle \mathbf{w}, \phi(\mathbf{x}_i, \hat{\mathbf{y}}_i) \rangle; \qquad g(\beta_j^{\mathbf{y}}) = -\langle \mathbf{w}, \phi(\mathbf{x}_j, \mathbf{y}) \rangle - \Delta(\hat{\mathbf{y}}_j, \mathbf{y}). \tag{9}$$

We first calculate the unconstrained $\tilde{\lambda}^\alpha$ and $\tilde{\lambda}^\beta$ as:

$$\begin{aligned} \tilde{\lambda}^\alpha &= \frac{g(\alpha_+) - g(\alpha_-)}{Z_{\alpha_+\alpha_-}}, & \tilde{\lambda}^\beta &= \frac{g(\beta_j^{\mathbf{y}+}) - g(\beta_j^{\mathbf{y}-})}{Z_{\beta_j^{\mathbf{y}+}\beta_j^{\mathbf{y}-}}} \\ Z_{\alpha_+\alpha_-} &= k_{\alpha_+\alpha_+} + k_{\alpha_-\alpha_-} - 2k_{\alpha_+\alpha_-}, & Z_{\beta_j^{\mathbf{y}+}\beta_j^{\mathbf{y}-}} &= k_{\beta_j^{\mathbf{y}+}\beta_j^{\mathbf{y}+}} + k_{\beta_j^{\mathbf{y}-}\beta_j^{\mathbf{y}-}} - 2k_{\beta_j^{\mathbf{y}+}\beta_j^{\mathbf{y}-}} \end{aligned} \tag{10}$$

where $k_{\alpha_+\alpha_+}, k_{\beta_j^{\mathbf{y}+}\beta_j^{\mathbf{y}+}}, \ldots$ are kernel values for the corresponding feature pairs. We enforce the constraints in Eq.7 to get the exact adjustment of λ^α and λ^β, *i.e.*:

$$\lambda^\alpha = \max(\min(\tilde{\lambda}^\alpha, \alpha_-, C_2 - \alpha_+), 0), \quad \lambda^\beta = \max(\min(\tilde{\lambda}^\beta, C_3\delta(\mathbf{y}, \hat{\mathbf{y}}_j) - \beta_j^{\mathbf{y}+}), 0). \tag{11}$$

Finally, the parameter $\mathbf{w}$ is updated according to

$$\mathbf{w} \leftarrow \mathbf{w} + \lambda^\beta(\phi(\mathbf{x}_j, \mathbf{y}+) - \phi(\mathbf{x}_j, \mathbf{y}-)) + \lambda^\alpha(\phi(\mathbf{x}_+, \hat{\mathbf{y}}_+) - \phi(\mathbf{x}_-, \hat{\mathbf{y}}_-)). \tag{12}$$

The entire elementary step is summarized in Alg. 1.

Algorithm 1. Elementary step

Compute the gradients $g(\alpha_+), g(\alpha_-), g(\beta_j^{\mathbf{y}+}), g(\beta_j^{\mathbf{y}-})$	Eq. 9
Compute the unconstrained $\tilde{\lambda}^\alpha, \tilde{\lambda}^\beta$	Eq. 10
Enforce the constrains to obtain $\lambda^\alpha, \lambda^\beta$	Eq. 11
Update the coefficients $\alpha_+, \alpha_-, \beta_j^{\mathbf{y}+}, \beta_j^{\mathbf{y}-}$	Eq. 8
Update the parameter $\mathbf{w}$	Eq. 12

4.2 Online Selection

Online selection hinges on how to choose proper coefficient pairs that should be optimized by the elementary step. Intuitively, the pair of coefficients should define the feasible search direction with highest gradient. Even by doing so, searching such coefficients from all the samples still need large storage and expensive computation, which hinders online tracking. As it has been observed that support vectors are not updated frequently [3], it is indeed effective to select coefficients focusing on support vectors. Inspired by OLaRank [5], we design three blocks for selection, which can *update*, *retrieve*, and *adjust* the support vectors respectively:

- **UPDATE** selects the coefficients from newly incoming frame $\mathbf{x}_t$ to improve the model with new information.
- **RETRIEVE** selects the coefficients from past frames to retrieve past data to assure the model's generalization ability.
- **ADJUST** selects the coefficients of the current support vectors , and adjust them to better adapt the model.

For convenience, we define $\mathcal{V}^A$ and $\mathcal{V}^B$ as the support vectors in $\mathcal{S}^A$ and $\mathcal{S}^B$, and we also define $\mathcal{C}^{SA}$, $\mathcal{C}^{SB}$, $\mathcal{C}^{VA}$, $\mathcal{C}^{VB}$ as the coefficient sets for $\mathcal{S}^A$, $\mathcal{S}^B$, $\mathcal{V}^A$, $\mathcal{V}^B$, respectively. Each block simultaneously selects the coefficients from $\boldsymbol{\alpha}$ and $\boldsymbol{\beta}$, and the process is summarized in Tab.1. All the coefficients associated with a new frame are initialized to be zeros except α_1. We initialized $\alpha_1 = C_1$ to satisfy the constraint $\sum_i \alpha_i = C_1$, and α_1 will gradually decrease to be within $[0, C_2]$ as the online optimization proceeds. As a result, the appearance model stresses more on the first frame at the primary stage of tracking, which is reasonable before forming a stable appearance model. We schedule the three blocks as suggested by Bordes et al. [5], which is a simple scheme that considers both the computation time and the progress of the objective function.

5 Implementation

We now explain some important implementation details of our algorithm.

Features. We use intensity histograms and gradient orientation histograms to represent $\phi(\mathbf{x}, \mathbf{y})$. The bounding box region is divided into 5×5 cells, and then the intensity value and gradient orientation in a cell are quantized into 8 bins. Therefore, each cell is represented by a 16 dimensional vector. Besides, for every

Table 1. The three basic blocks for selecting the coefficient pairs to be optimized. Specifically, for $\boldsymbol{\beta}$, we first determine frame j , then select the coefficient pair from the frame.

	UPDATE	RETRIEVE	ADJUST
α_+	α_t	$\arg\max_{\alpha\in\mathcal{C}^{SA}} g(\alpha)$	$\arg\max_{\alpha\in\mathcal{C}^{VA}} g(\alpha)$
α_-	$\arg\min_{\alpha\in\mathcal{C}^{SA}} g(\alpha)$	$\arg\min_{\alpha\in\mathcal{C}^{SA}} g(\alpha)$	$\arg\min_{\alpha\in\mathcal{C}^{VA}} g(\alpha)$
frame j	t	a random k in $\mathcal{S}^B$	a random k in $\mathcal{V}^B$
$\beta_j^{\mathbf{y}+}$	$\beta_t^{\hat{\mathbf{y}}_t}$	$\arg\max_{\beta_k^{\mathbf{y}}\in\mathcal{C}^{SB}} g(\beta_k^{\mathbf{y}})$	$\arg\max_{\beta_k^{\mathbf{y}}\in\mathcal{C}^{VB}} g(\beta_k^{\mathbf{y}})$
$\beta_j^{\mathbf{y}-}$	$\arg\min_{\beta_t^{\mathbf{y}}\in\mathcal{C}^{SB}} g(\beta_t^{\mathbf{y}})$	$\arg\min_{\beta_k^{\mathbf{y}}\in\mathcal{C}^{SB}} g(\beta_k^{\mathbf{y}})$	$\arg\min_{\beta_k^{\mathbf{y}}\in\mathcal{C}^{VB}} g(\beta_k^{\mathbf{y}})$

neighbouring 2×2 cells, we calculate the histogram sum to represent the appearance of a larger region; for a set of randomly selected 30 cell pairs, we calculate the histogram difference of each pair to capture the inter-cell dependency. All these 16 dim histograms are L_2-normalized within their separate channels, and then they are concatenated together to form a 1136 dim vector. Note that the norm of the feature is made to be a constant. By using integral histogram [1], the features can be computed efficiently.

Searching Strategy. Based on the histogram features, the distribution of score values is usually smooth in the state space $\mathcal{Y}$. Hence, we employ a coarse-to-fine search strategy similar to that presented in [6]. This method iteratively samples the candidates based on SMC [8], which gradually approches the high score region without the need of hand-tuning the motion parameters for different video sequences.

Set Management. As tracking proceeds, the sizes of all the sets $\mathcal{V}^A, \mathcal{V}^B, \mathcal{S}^A, \mathcal{S}^B$ will increase incrementally, making the optimization more and more expensive. Considering efficiency, we keep these sets with fixed size $N_{VA}, N_{VB}, N_{SA}, N_{SB}$, and therefore an appropriate set management is necessary.

1. For $\mathcal{S}^A$, each time we add the feature of the optimal state. When the number of its elements exceed N_{SA}, we condense the set by sampling its elements. Specifically, we reserve the existing support vectors, then uniformly sample half of the rest features, finally combine them to form the new S^A.
2. For $\mathcal{S}^B$, each time we add the features of both target and background samples. We only consider the samples in the neighborhood of the target, hence we produce these samples by sampling around the target state on a polar grid centered on the target, which gives 81 different locations. These samples are produced with same scale as the current target state. Only the features from the last N frames are kept in $\mathcal{S}^B$.
3. We maintain the features with coefficient $\alpha > 0$ in $\mathcal{V}^A$. When $|\mathcal{V}^A| > N_{VA}$, we delete the support vector with smallest α, and transit its coefficient to the one with second smallest α.
4. We maintain features with coefficient $\beta \neq 0$ in $\mathcal{V}^B$. When $\mathcal{V}^B > N_{VB}$, we delete all the support vectors from the oldest frames.

The entire algorithm of our proposed Description-Discrimination Collaborative Tracker (DDCT) is summarized in Alg. 2.

Algorithm 2. Description-Discrimination Collaboration Tracker

Input: $\hat{\mathbf{y}}_{t-1}, \mathbf{w}, \mathcal{S}^A, \mathcal{S}^B, \mathcal{V}^A, \mathcal{V}^B$

$\hat{\mathbf{y}}_t = \arg\max_{\mathbf{y}} \langle \mathbf{w}, \phi(\mathbf{x}_t, \mathbf{y}) \rangle$ — according to Searching strategy
manage $\mathcal{S}^A$, $\mathcal{S}^B$ — according to Set management
UPDATE $\longrightarrow$ elementary step
manage $\mathcal{V}^A$, $\mathcal{V}^B$ — according to Set management
for $j = 1$ to n_R **do**
  RETRIEVE $\longrightarrow$ elementary step
  manage $\mathcal{V}^A$, $\mathcal{V}^B$ — according to Set management
  for $k = 1$ to n_A **do**
    ADJUST $\longrightarrow$ elementary step
  end for
end for

Output: $\hat{\mathbf{y}}_t, \mathbf{w}, \mathcal{S}^A, \mathcal{S}^B, \mathcal{V}^A, \mathcal{V}^B$

6 Experiments

Datasets and Metric. Experiments are conducted over 30 publicly available video sequences, which include the full MIL dataset [2] (*tiger1*, *tiger2*, *coke*, *cliffbar*, *david*, *dollar*, *face1*, *face2*, *girl*, *surfer*, *sylv*, *twinnings*), the full PROST dataset [21] (*lemming*, *board*, *box*, *liquor*), the full VTD dataset [15] (*animal*, *basketball*, *football*, *skating1*, *skating2*, *singer1*, *singer2*, *soccer*, *shaking*) and other 5 frequently used sequences (*woman*, *bolt*, *car4*, *trellis*, *jump*). The challenges of the data are summarized in Tab. 2. We use two widely accepted evaluation metrics during our experiments: the center location error (CLE) [29] and the Pascal VOC overlap ratio (VOR) [30]. Based on CLE and VOR, we employ the precision plot and success plot to demonstrate the trackers' performance. The definition of the two plots can be found in [27].

Experiment Settings. The proposed Description Discrimination Collaborative Tracker (DDCT) is implemented in MATLAB/C and runs about 12 FPS with a 3.07GHZ CPU. We empirically set the parameters as $C_1 = 8, C_2 = 0.75, C_3 = 0.75$, where C_1 is the sum for coefficients of descriptive support vectors, and C_2, C_3 restrict the influence of a single support vector in the descriptive and the discriminative component, respectively. We fix the set sizes as $N_{VA} = 20, N_{VB} = 50, N_{SA} = 50, N_{SB} = 20 \times 81$. N_{VA}, N_{VB} define the maximum number of support vectors in each component, and N_{SA}, N_{SB} are the sizes of $\mathcal{S}^A$ and $\mathcal{S}^B$. For $\mathcal{S}^B$, we only keep the last $N = 20$ frames and extract features for 81 samples in each frame. The iteration times in Alg. 2 are: $n_A = 12$ and $n_R = 10$. **All the parameters of DDCT are fixed in the experiments.**

6.1 Analysis of the Proposed Method

Component analysis. In order to investigate the properties of the descriptive component and the discriminative component, we construct two trackers using

Table 2. The challenges of experimental sequences

Main Challenges	Sequences
Distractor	*dollar, basketball, liquor, football, bolt*
Rotation	*cliffbar, face2, girl, surfer, board, shaking*
Illumination	*tiger1, tiger2, coke, david, trellis, basketball,sylv, car4 , singer1, singer2, skating1, shaking*
Occlusion	*box, football, coke, face1, face2, girl, skating2, tiger1, tiger2, basketball, lemming, liquor, woman*
Scaling	*cliffbar, david, girl, singer1, singer2, car4, lemming, board, liquor, skating1, skating2, trellis*

Fig. 2. Qualitative analysis of components. From left to right are *tiger2*, *woman*, *box* and *basketball*.

either the descriptive or the discriminative component, named as DET and DIT, respectively. For DET, we set $C_3 = 0$ excluding the influence from discriminative support vectors. For DIT, we set $C_1 = 3, C_2 = 0$ to preserve the initial object to collaborate with discriminative support vectors. Together with DDCT, we run the three trackers over all sequences. We analyze their average VORs over different datasets and challenges in Fig. 3(a). The overall performance and the detailed quantitative results are provided in Fig. 5 and Tab. 3, respectively.

DDCT significantly outperforms the other two on the overall performance, as shown in Fig. 3, 5 and Tab. 3. The results confirm the effectiveness of Description-Discrimination collaboration, which enables the two components to benefit from each other. DDCT performs most stably over different challenges, although the overall performance fluctuates a bit over different datasets. This demonstrates the robustness of our tracker, and at the same time verifies the degree of difficulty for each individual dataset.

DET performs better than DIT on sequences in the MIL dataset and the additional video sequences as shown in Fig. 3. In these Datasets, the change of the object's appearance is relatively small and mild, so that the major characteristic of objects can be well captured by the descriptive component. Typical examples are sequences *tiger2* and *woman* (Fig. 2). In *tiger2*, the target moves across the leaves, DET tolerates the interruption caused by occlusion, while DIT updates its appearance to the leaves. In *woman*, the pedestrian goes out of the occlusion by the car, and both DET and DIT fail on the abrupt appearance change, but when the target recovers its usual appearance, DET can re-track the object.

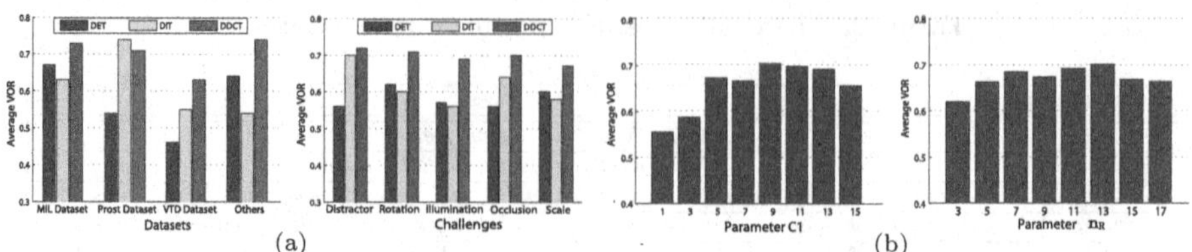

Fig. 3. Quantitative analysis of (a) different components, (b) different parameters over 15 sequences

DIT performs better than DET on the sequences in PROST dataset and VTD dataset as shown in Fig. 3. The object's appearance changes drastically in VTD dataset, and there exists similar objects in PROST dataset. The superiorities of DIT are demonstrated in sequences *box* and *basketball* (Fig. 2). In *box*, DIT can distinguish the target from a similar black box. In *basketball*, the pose of the player frequently changes, and DIT can adapt to the changing appearance rather than drift to a distracter that is similar to its previous appearance.

Parameter analysis. We study the effect of two important trade-off parameters including the parameter C_1 and the iteration number n_R. The evaluations are implemented on randomly selected 15 sequences.

Parameter C_1 reflects the descriptive ability of descriptive support vectors. Fixing other parameters, we observe how C_1 influences the tracking performance as shown in Fig. 3(b). It can be seen that C_1 should be neither too small nor too large. If C_1 is too small, C_2 in Eq.7 can not effectively constrain the coefficients $\boldsymbol{\alpha}$. Therefore the descriptive support vectors tend to overfit the samples at the initial stage, and are reluctant to adapt to newly coming samples (Fig. 4, in black dash). On the contrary, if C_1 is too large, it will drive more samples to become support vectors, and the descriptive support vectors become redundant and increase the risk of incorporating outliers (Fig. 4, in blue dash). We set a moderate C_1 to balance between the two situations, which is flexible to capture distinctive poses without redundancy.

Parameter n_R is related to appearance model updating. It balances the two blocks UPDATE and RETRIEVE as described in Alg. 2. Different from the conventional learning rates that significantly influence the tracking performance, n_R is relative mild. However, we can still observe trade-off phenomena in Fig. 3 (b), a smaller n_R leads to an adaptive tracker where small error accumulate quickly and cause the track to drift, while a larger n_R generates a conservative tracker which may not be able to respond to the changes in the appearance.

Discussion. Through the above analysis, we find that the tracking performance of DDCT is not very sensitive to the parameters C_1, C_2 and C_3. Among them, C_1 easily achieves stable performance in its range (in Fig. 3(b)). C_2 and C_3 balance influence of the two components, even independent trackers DET and DIT perform reasonably well(Fig. 3(a)). The robustness to the parameters lies in the online optimization stage, where the updating the of model is more dependent

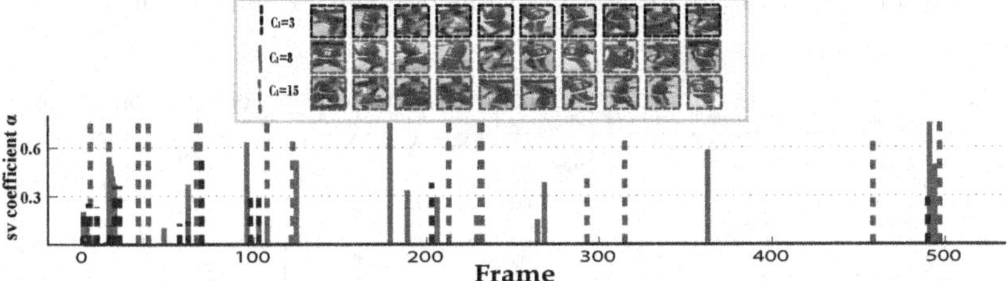

Fig. 4. The comparison of different C_1 configurations on sequence *basketball.* **Top:** The descriptive support vectors selected by different C_1, ranked in descending order of sv coefficients $\boldsymbol{\alpha}$. **Bottom:** The distribution of support vectors over time with different C_1. We display these support vectors when the tracker arrives at # 510.

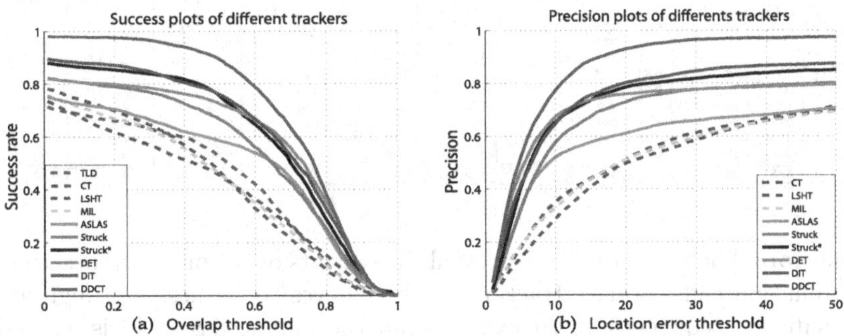

Fig. 5. The success plots and the precision plots for the comparison of different algorithms. We don't include the precision plot for TLD in (b), because some results of it are not available.

on the data – the gradients (in Eq.9). Meanwhile, parameters C_1, C_2 and C_3 play a gentle role in updating the appearance model. Specifically, C_1 controls the global updating property, and C_2 and C_3 prevent over-fitting (in Eq.11).

6.2 Empirical Comparison with Other Trackers

We compare DDCT with six competing trackers, named MIL [2], TLD [14], CT [29], ASLSA [13], LSHT [11] and Struck [10]. The tracking results are obtained by running their publicly available codes with default parameters. For a more intensive comparison with Struck, we equip the original version with the same feature as ours, named Struck*. Together with independent components DET and DIT, we quantitatively compare the 10 trackers on all the 30 sequences. Tab. 3 reports the average VOR and average CLE of each sequence respectively. Fig. 5 demonstrates their success plots and precision plots on all the frames to compare the overall performance. More quantitative and qualitative results are in the supplementary materials.

Table 3. Results in terms of CLE and VOR, the best three results are in red, orange and green

	CT		LSHT		MIL		TLD		ASLSA		Struck		Struck*		DET		DIT		DDCT	
	VOR	CLE	VOR	CLE	VOR.	CLE	VOR	CLE	VOR	CLE	VOR	CLE	VOR	CLE	VOR	CLE	VOR	CLE	VOR	CLE.
tiger1	0.46	21.7	0.09	79.4	0.46	24.3	0.50	- -	0.23	36.4	0.63	7.2	0.74	4.3	0.72	4.9	0.65	7.4	0.74	4.2
tiger2	0.55	10.1	0.14	43.3	0.58	10.2	0.31	- -	0.30	31.6	0.65	6.5	0.72	4.1	0.72	4.5	0.24	31.5	0.72	4.2
coke	0.40	15.5	0.56	7.2	0.39	14.0	0.53	7.8	0.69	4.9	0.60	5.5	0.77	3.0	0.74	3.8	0.50	9.3	0.75	3.4
ciff.	0.43	18.1	0.11	66.3	0.51	12.3	0.35	- -	0.17	49.8	0.42	14.8	0.60	6.7	0.49	19.2	0.53	13.0	0.52	12.2
david	0.57	6.1	0.56	8.5	0.43	20.7	0.57	17.2	0.50	15.9	0.55	11.3	0.58	4.6	0.83	2.8	0.51	18.6	0.73	4.2
dollar	0.62	18.1	0.87	2.4	0.68	14.7	0.05	157.3	0.86	2.4	0.65	17.4	0.86	2.6	0.38	63.0	0.77	5.4	0.84	3.7
face1	0.64	25.4	0.66	28.7	0.63	24.6	0.53	27.5	0.61	43.6	0.87	5.8	0.88	4.9	0.83	8.0	0.85	5.3	0.78	8.5
face2	0.61	17.4	0.68	9.8	0.64	13.8	0.55	11.7	0.74	8.6	0.72	8.0	0.73	7.3	0.64	10.9	0.63	11.1	0.70	9.9
girl	0.54	19.4	0.26	74.5	0.49	26.1	0.51	- -	0.30	48.9	0.64	5.9	0.60	13.4	0.74	8.7	0.29	79.5	0.76	7.1
surf	0.15	28.4	0.19	28.9	0.49	9.8	0.66	3.6	0.41	23.6	0.58	6.5	0.59	5.9	0.40	40.6	0.65	5.0	0.67	4.1
sylv	0.57	12.7	0.63	15.1	0.55	15.7	0.64	12.4	0.71	7.7	0.72	6.9	0.79	4.3	0.77	5.1	0.71	8.3	0.80	4.2
twin.	0.53	12.8	0.46	20.8	0.58	9.7	0.33	- -	0.58	10.8	0.64	7.3	0.59	9.8	0.61	7.5	0.56	13.1	0.57	9.2
lem.	0.43	53.4	0.42	80.6	0.49	56.7	0.11	- -	0.14	200.7	0.52	75.4	0.79	8.1	0.59	30.3	0.66	13.2	0.72	7.6
board.	0.48	48.2	0.70	16.7	0.53	41.6	0.35	- -	0.75	19.0	0.71	18.9	0.71	18.0	0.78	12.6	0.73	19.0	0.78	10.8
box	0.47	33.1	0.31	109.4	0.15	111.3	0.56	- -	0.40	71.0	0.32	142.9	0.05	176.9	0.06	202.0	0.73	9.6	0.72	9.5
liquor	0.20	183.4	0.23	107.5	0.16	167.9	0.59	- -	0.21	238.5	0.61	51.4	0.62	56.4	0.72	31.4	0.82	4.4	0.71	30.9
animal	0.03	250.5	0.05	100.1	0.38	36.8	0.54	- -	0.62	19.7	0.85	3.1	0.79	6.4	0.85	3.2	0.84	3.6	0.84	3.4
basket.	0.19	136.1	0.56	22.1	0.22	97.0	0.06	- -	0.24	103.6	0.03	198.3	0.53	23.3	0.43	82.5	0.63	18.3	0.69	9.8
football	0.63	12.5	0.69	8.4	0.59	13.8	0.60	12.5	0.59	10.1	0.61	12.4	0.83	3.2	0.79	2.6	0.80	2.4	0.80	3.8
skate1	0.37	50.7	0.18	119.1	0.11	153.6	0.36	- -	0.50	49.3	0.29	83.9	0.38	64.6	0.43	60.8	0.27	61.0	0.46	59.5
skate2	0.06	120.8	0.49	31.9	0.11	109.1	0.04	- -	0.21	55.1	0.08	152.8	0.20	129.2	0.29	53.7	0.58	17.4	0.55	18.9
singer1	0.34	14.7	0.34	16.5	0.33	17.8	0.40	- -	0.77	3.8	0.34	15.2	0.34	25.2	0.76	6.8	0.79	5.8	0.78	6.5
singer2	0.09	124.9	0.72	11.4	0.39	33.2	0.02	- -	0.03	180.5	0.02	180.8	0.69	13.3	0.40	49.2	0.32	82.4	0.57	16.9
soccer	0.35	52.6	0.31	40.6	0.14	98.1	0.07	- -	0.12	131.2	0.18	111.4	0.19	113.0	0.17	164.6	0.21	120.2	0.42	23.3
shak.	0.65	8.2	0.53	17.7	0.58	14.5	0.51	- -	0.70	10.2	0.23	49.6	0.64	7.7	0.81	4.6	0.77	6.5	0.79	6.3
woman	0.13	112.7	0.14	123.8	0.14	120.0	0.62	- -	0.68	10.5	0.73	3.5	0.75	4.5	0.68	14.6	0.16	142.0	0.75	4.0
bolt	0.52	10.0	0.38	36.6	0.58	8.5	0.14	- -	0.70	4.7	0.17	80.7	0.51	8.2	0.05	250.7	0.06	126.0	0.60	8.3
car4	0.17	93.1	0.26	56.7	0.24	58.0	0.03	- -	0.86	3.3	0.55	6.3	0.25	80.8	0.57	16.6	0.37	77.6	0.74	3.3
trellis	0.32	38.5	0.37	52.5	0.23	56.9	0.33	- -	0.68	8.7	0.55	9.6	0.57	7.9	0.34	39.3	0.46	20.3	0.72	8.7
jump	0.77	3.5	0.23	30.8	0.78	2.8	0.80	- -	0.80	3.5	0.80	2.2	0.79	3	0.86	2.1	0.86	2.2	0.84	1.8
average	0.41	51.8	0.40	45.6	0.42	46.5	0.39	- -	0.50	46.9	0.51	43.4	0.60	27.4	0.58	40.1	0.57	31.3	0.70	10.3

Discussion. The results generally reveal the benefits of the proposed description discrimination collaborative tracker, which achieves robustness and high accuracy on diverse sequences. In the experiments, the enhanced Struck* is the major competitor (in Tab.3, Fig.5). During the 60 tests, Struck* achieved 14 bests, 9 seconds and 7 thirds, and DDCT achieved 19 bests, 22 seconds and 11 thirds. Struck* performs well on the sequences with rigid objects and static scenes such as *tiger1*, *tiger2*, *coke* and *face1*, etc. However, the use of obsolete background samples makes Struck* fail in dynamic scenes such as *skate1*, *skate2*, *singer1*, and *trellis*, etc. Compared with Struck*, the proposed DDCT uses historical target samples to be robust to outliers and uses current background samples to be distinctive to distractors, performing well in both static and dynamic scenes. Besides, the different performance between Struck* and Struck also suggests the superiority of employing a high-dimensional histogram feature, where the "high dimension" can better characterize an object and the "histogram" is less sensitive to the spatial alignment. In addition, from Tab. 3, we also observe the complementary property between DET and DIT, which again confirms the rationality of their collaboration.

7 Conclusion

In this paper, we have proposed a novel visual tracking method based on description discrimination collaboration. We integrate descriptive component and discriminative component in a unified max-margin learning framework, and take advantage of their complementary modeling power in both representation and lifespans. The collaborative model is not vulnerable to outliers like occlusion, and it can track the target with high accuracy.

Furthermore, the adaptation of the model is more data-dependent, which strikes for a balance between past and current appearances. To solve the whole optimization problem, we devise a set of efficient and effective online selection rules, which significantly accelerate the tracking process. Experiments on 30 sequences verified our hypothesis that the collaboration between the descriptive and discriminative components would lead to better tracking performance. It is shown that our proposed tracker generally outperforms existing methods.

Acknowledgement. This work was supported by the National Basic Research Program of China under Grant No. 2012CB316402 and the National Natural Science Foundation of China under Grant No. 91120006.

References

1. Adam, A., Rivlin, E., Shimshoni, I.: Robust fragments-based tracking using the integral histogram. In: CVPR (2006)
2. Babenko, B., Yang, M.H., Belongie, S.: Visual Tracking with Online Multiple Instance Learning. In: CVPR (2009)
3. Bordes, A., Bottou, L.: The huller: A simple and efficient online SVM. In: Gama, J., Camacho, R., Brazdil, P.B., Jorge, A.M., Torgo, L. (eds.) ECML 2005. LNCS (LNAI), vol. 3720, pp. 505–512. Springer, Heidelberg (2005)
4. Bordes, A., Bottou, L., Gallinari, P., Weston, J.: Solving multiclass support vector machines with larank. In: ICML (2007)
5. Bordes, A., Usunier, N., Bottou, L.: Sequence labelling SVMs trained in one pass. In: Daelemans, W., Goethals, B., Morik, K. (eds.) ECML PKDD 2008, Part I. LNCS (LNAI), vol. 5211, pp. 146–161. Springer, Heidelberg (2008)
6. Chen, D., Yuan, Z., Wu, Y., Zhang, G., Zheng, N.: Constructing adaptive complex cells for robust visual tracking. In: ICCV (2013)
7. Chen, Y., Zhou, X., Huang, T.S.: One-class svm for learning in image retrieval. In: ICIP, pp. 34–37 (2001)
8. Doucet, A., Johansen, A.M.: A tutorial on particle filtering and smoothing: fifteen years later (2011)
9. Grabner, H., Leistner, C., Bischof, H.: Semi-supervised on-line boosting for robust tracking. In: Forsyth, D., Torr, P., Zisserman, A. (eds.) ECCV 2008, Part I. LNCS, vol. 5302, pp. 234–247. Springer, Heidelberg (2008)
10. Hare, S., Saffari, A., Torr, P.H.S.: Struck: Structured output tracking with kernels. In: ICCV (2011)
11. He, S., Yang, Q., Lau, R.W., Wang, J., Yang, M.H.: Visual tracking via locality sensitive histograms. In: CVPR (2013)
12. JamesSteven, S., Ramanan, D.: Self-paced learning for long term tracking. In: CVPR (2013)
13. Jia, X., Lu, H., Yang, M.H.: Visual tracking via adaptive structural local sparse appearance model. In: CVPR (2012)
14. Kalal, Z., Mikolajczyk, K., Matas, J.: Tracking-learning-detection. IEEE TPAMI 34(7), 1409–1422 (2012)

15. Kwon, J., Lee, K.M.: Visual tracking decomposition. In: CVPR (2010)
16. Lampert, C.H., Blaschko, M.B.: Structured prediction by joint kernel support estimation. Machine Learning (2009)
17. Mei, X., Ling, H.: Robust visual tracking using l1 minimization. In: ICCV (2009)
18. Pang, Y., Ling, H.: Finding the best from the second bests - inhibiting subjective bias in evaluation of visual tracking algorithms. In: ICCV (2013)
19. Platt, J.C.: Sequential minimal optimization: A fast algorithm for training support vector machines. Tech. rep., Advances in Kernel Methods - Support Vector Learning (1998)
20. Ross, D.A., Lim, J., Lin, R.S., Yang, M.H.: Incremental learning for robust visual tracking. Int. J. Comput. Vision 77(1-3), 125–141 (2008), `http://dx.doi.org/10.1007/s11263-007-0075-7`
21. Santner, J., Leistner, C., Saffari, A., Pock, T., Bischof, H.: PROST Parallel Robust Online Simple Tracking. In: CVPR (2010)
22. Scholkopf, B., Williamson, R.C., Smola, A., Shawe-Taylor, J.: Sv estimation of a distribution's support. In: NIPS (1999)
23. Tax, D.M.J., Duin, R.P.W.: Support vector data description. Mach. Learn. (2004)
24. Tsochantaridis, I., Joachims, T., Hofmann, T., Altun, Y.: Large margin methods for structured and interdependent output variables. J. Mach. Learn. Res. (2005)
25. Wang, S., Lu, H., Yang, F., Yang, M.H.: Superpixel tracking. In: ICCV (2011)
26. Wen, L., Cai, Z., Lei, Z., Yi, D., Li, S.Z.: Online spatio-temporal structural context learning for visual tracking. In: Fitzgibbon, A., Lazebnik, S., Perona, P., Sato, Y., Schmid, C. (eds.) ECCV 2012, Part IV. LNCS, vol. 7575, pp. 716–729. Springer, Heidelberg (2012)
27. Wu, Y., Lim, J., Yang, M.H.: Online object tracking: A benchmark. In: CVPR (2013)
28. Xing, J., Gao, J., Li, B., Hu, W., Yan, S.: Robust object tracking with online multi-lifespan dictionary learning. In: ICCV (2013)
29. Zhang, K., Zhang, L., Yang, M.-H.: Real-time compressive tracking. In: Fitzgibbon, A., Lazebnik, S., Perona, P., Sato, Y., Schmid, C. (eds.) ECCV 2012, Part III. LNCS, vol. 7574, pp. 864–877. Springer, Heidelberg (2012)
30. Zhong, W., Lu, H., Yang, M.H.: Robust object tracking via sparsity-based collaborative model. In: CVPR (2012)

Online, Real-Time Tracking Using a Category-to-Individual Detector*

David Hall and Pietro Perona

California Institute of Technology, USA
{dhall,perona}@vision.caltech.edu

Abstract. A method for online, real-time tracking of objects is presented. Tracking is treated as a repeated detection problem where potential target objects are identified with a pre-trained category detector and object identity across frames is established by individual-specific detectors. The individual detectors are (re-)trained online from a single positive example whenever there is a coincident category detection. This ensures that the tracker is robust to drift. Real-time operation is possible since an individual-object detector is obtained through elementary manipulations of the thresholds of the category detector and therefore only minimal additional computations are required. Our tracking algorithm is benchmarked against nine state-of-the-art trackers on two large, publicly available and challenging video datasets. We find that our algorithm is 10% more accurate and nearly as fast as the fastest of the competing algorithms, and it is as accurate but 20 times faster than the most accurate of the competing algorithms.

1 Introduction

The objective of tracking is to determine the size and location of a target object in a sequence of video frames, given the initial state of the target. It is important for a variety of applications, including the tracking of pedestrians in railway stations and airports; vehicles on the road for traffic monitoring and faces for interfacing people with computers. It is a well studied problem and although many offline tracking methods exist [2,8,9,30,33,34,36,37], the focus of this work will be on online trackers.

We present a novel method for real-time, online, appearance-based tracking. Tracking is treated as a detection problem where an individual-object detector is trained online to distinguish the target-to-be-tracked from background. Objects to track are first identified with a pre-trained category detector (a face, pedestrian or vehicle detector for example); each of the detections made by the category detector are now identified as individual targets to be tracked; for each of these targets an individual detector is learnt on-the-fly using IDBoost, a category-to-individual learning algorithm [27]. During tracking, the individual detector is updated using the currently detected sample of the target but only if

* Project Website: http://vision.caltech.edu/~dhall/projects/CIT/

D. Fleet et al. (Eds.): ECCV 2014, Part I, LNCS 8689, pp. 361–376, 2014.
© Springer International Publishing Switzerland 2014

Fig. 1. Tracking individuals across a video sequence using our proposed tracking algorithm. (Top) a face from the Buffy dataset and (bottom) pedestrians from Caltech Pedestrians. The appearance of the face changes over time with a full frontal face example at initialisation (far left) to a quasi-frontal face in the final frame (far right). Despite the change in appearance, our tracker is able to track the target since the model for the target is updated over time (see Sec. 3). Pedestrians are also tracked successfully even when they are subject to occlusion. The magenta target is initialised in the first frame; is occluded by the light pole in the second and is successfully reacquired in the third. Individual tracker outputs are colour-coded. Each image is 30 frames apart (model update is still occurring every frame).

there is a coincident category detection. This ensures that the tracker is robust to drift. Crucially, the algorithm runs in real-time since the individual-object detector is obtained through elementary manipulations of the thresholds of the category detector. We then benchmark our tracking algorithm against 9 other, publicly available, state-of-the-art trackers on two challenging video datasets. We make two main contributions:

1. A fast, accurate, tracking algorithm that is robust to drift.
2. A careful and reliable benchmark of state-of-the-art trackers.

2 Related Work

Appearance-based tracking algorithms typically contain the following elements: 1) an appearance model for the target object to be tracked; 2) a search strategy to find potential candidates in subsequent frames that match the target; and 3) a mechanism to dynamically update the appearance model of the target so that changes in pose and illumination over time can be modelled.

A pitfall of dynamically updating the appearance model is that when trackers make mistakes this incorrect information is then incorporated into the model. The result is that the tracker no longer tracks the original target. This is known as drift. Designing algorithms that are robust to noisy updates is thus essential for good tracking performance.

Many trackers use generative appearance models. One of the representations used for target objects within this class of trackers are subspaces. Black and Jepson [11] learn offline an eigenbasis to model the target object along with particle filtering as a search mechanism. The IVT method of Ross et al. [38] proposes an online update of the target subspace over time using incremental PCA. Wu's ORIA [45] tracker also includes online updates but updates only occur if the new target is significantly different from the existing basis set.

Kernel based methods are also used to represent target objects. The influential work of Comaniciu et al. with their Kernel-Based Object Tracker (KMS) [13] represent the target object with a histogram in some feature space; a metric based on the Bhattacharyya coefficient is used to match the target to potential candidates; while the mean-shift algorithm [23] is used to efficiently search for these candidates. In traditional histogram-based algorithms information about the spatial distribution of features is lost; the FRAG [1] tracker of Adam et al. represents the target using multiple histograms obtained from many different patches in the target thus preserving some of the spatial information. Neither of these methods update the model online.

Alternative representations include probability distribution fields (DFT) [39]; sparse linear combinations of target and trivial templates (L1AP) [5] and the superpixels of (LOT) [35].

Discriminative appearance models are also widely used. Avidan's ensemble tracker [3] constructs a feature vector for every pixel. A classifier to separate pixels belonging to the target from those in the background is then trained by using an adaptive ensemble of weak classifiers. The compressive tracking (CT) algorithm of Zhang et al. [46] generates multi-scale features for the positive and negative samples and applies a sparse sampling matrix to reduce dimensionality. A naive Bayes classifier with online update is then used to classify windows as target or background. Grabner et al.'s online boosting method (OAB) [24] adaptively selects features to discriminate the object from the background.

To avoid drift, Grabner et al. [25] propose a semi-supervised, online boosting algorithm (SBT) where only the initial samples of the target are labelled while all of the self-learnt samples are unlabelled. The MIL tracker of Babenko et al. [4] uses multiple instance learning where a bag of positive samples are used to update the model. Kalal's [31] TLD tracker also approaches tracking as a semi-supervised learning problem with positive and negative examples being selected by an online classifier that has structural constraints. The BSBT tracker of Stalder et al. [41] combine the supervised and semi-supervised approaches into a single implementation.

For all of the approaches mentioned so far a sparse sampling strategy is used. This means that in each frame, positive samples are collected close to the predicted target while the negative samples are further from the target's centre. The CSK algorithm of Henriques et al. [28] proposes a different approach where a classifier is trained using all possible samples in a dense sampling strategy. The circulant structure of the problem is exploited allowing for not only efficient training but fast detection since all responses can be computed simultaneously rather than using a sliding-window scheme.

There are many benchmark datasets available for a number of vision problems. For pedestrians there is INRIA [14] and Caltech Pedestrians [17]; for unconstrained face recognition there is LFW [29]; and for person reidentification there is VIPeR [26]. Tracking, however, still lacks a decent benchmarking dataset although progress has been made recently to fill this gap. Wu et al. [44] have collected a benchmark that contains 50 sequences commonly used in the literature to evaluate tracking algorithms. While most algorithms have been evaluated on a subset of these sequences by their original authors, Wu et al. provide a far more comprehensive analysis by evaluating 29 tracking algorithms on all 50 sequences given the initial bounding box of the target object.

While the progress that has been made by Wu et al. is appreciable, we feel that the dataset is lacking for the following reasons: 1) The size of the dataset is too small; 2) The difficulty of most sequences is low with a focus on tracking only single objects; 3) About half of the sequences are unrealistic; they are in controlled environments and 4) trackers are perfectly initialised by a ground truth bounding box. This gives little insight into how robust trackers are to poor initialisation. Wu et al. address this by jittering the ground truth bounding box.

3 Approach

In this section we present the details of our tracking algorithm. We treat the tracking problem as a detection task and train an individual-object detector, online, to distinguish the target from background. We break down the algorithm into 5 major components: 1) identify target objects to track; 2) initialise the tracker; 3) evaluate the tracker on a new frame; 4) update the tracker; 5) stop the tracker. There is no assumption made about the number of objects being tracked and our algorithm is able to handle tracking multiple objects that enter and exit a scene. An outline of our approach is depicted in Figure 2.

3.1 Identify Target Objects to Track

Identifying new targets to track is a problem that most of the tracking literature avoids. It is usually assumed that an initial tracking window has already been provided either manually or by a 'perfect' category detector [38]. In this work, instead of providing initial locations by hand, a category detector is used. This is a more realistic setting under which trackers would operate since for most online applications, having a human operator identify potential targets would not be feasible; particularly if there are many targets to identify. This setting also allows us to evaluate how robust tracking algorithms are to poor initialisation.

A new target is identified if the category detector makes a detection and there is no coincident individual detection as shown in Figure 2.

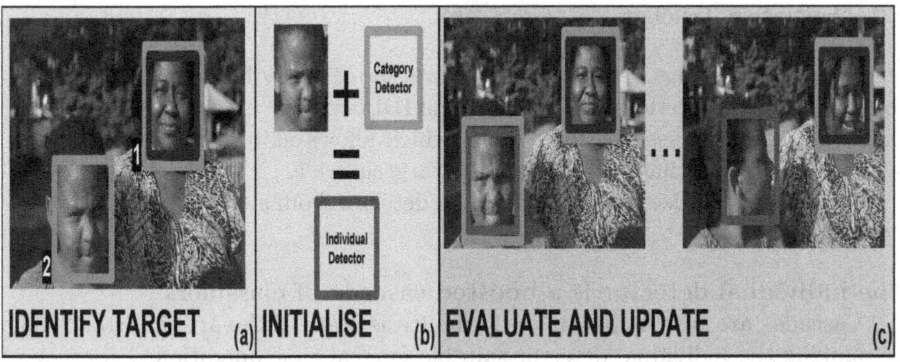

Fig. 2. Tracking Algorithm Outline. (a) A new target (2) is identified by a non-coincident category detection (green). There is also a category detection that coincides with an individual detection (blue) which indicates that this target (1) is already being tracked. (b) An individual detector (red) for target 2 is initialised using the category-to-individual learning algorithm in [27]. The only two pieces of information required to initialise the individual detector is a single positive example of the target and the category detector itself. (c) The individual detector is then evaluated on subsequent frames using a sliding window scheme. The location with the maximal score is identified as the new location of the target object. If a detection made by the individual detector is coincident with a detection made by the category detector then the individual detector is re-initialised with the current example of the target. If there is no coincident category detection the individual detector is not updated. If this occurs for more than a fixed number of frames tracking of that target stops.

Category detectors are trained offline using AdaBoost [22]. A boosted classifier takes feature vector $\mathbf{x} \in \mathbb{R}^D$ as input and outputs a binary decision:

$$H(\mathbf{x}) = \text{sign}\left(\sum_{m=1}^{M} \alpha_m h_m(\mathbf{x}) - \tau\right) \tag{1}$$

where $h_m(\mathbf{x})$ is a weak classifier; α_m its weight and the threshold τ is chosen to produce the desired trade-off between false reject rate and false alarm rate.

The family of weak classifiers used are stumps. This means that given an input $\mathbf{x} \in \mathbb{R}^D$, the decision only depends on the j-th dimension of $\mathbf{x}$, a threshold $\theta \in \mathbb{R}$ and a polarity $p \in \{\pm 1\}$

$$h_m(\mathbf{x}) = \begin{cases} 1, & p_m x_{j_m} > p_m \theta_m \\ -1, & \text{otherwise} \end{cases} \tag{2}$$

Note that any boosting method and decision trees of any depth could be used to train the category detector; our proposed method is agnostic to these choices.

3.2 Initialise Tracker

Once a new target has been identified; a tracker can now be initialised to track the object. In this section we briefly outline IDBoost, the category-to-individual learning algorithm (see [27] for details) which allows us to efficiently train the individual detector that only detects the target object.

The approach for learning an individual detector from a category detector has four elements:

The individual detector is a boosted cascade of classifiers
Cascades are fast and their performance is state-of-the-art [7,16,18,42,43], making the individual detector suitable for real-time operation.

The individual detector is learnt from a single sample
The object identified by the category detector, which we will denote by $\mathbf{u}^0 \in \mathbb{R}^D$, is used as the single positive training example to train the individual detector. Costly computations are avoided by using a single positive sample and by not mining negative samples.

The individual detector uses the same M features that were selected by AdaBoost for the category detector
We will denote this set of features by $\mathbf{J} = (j_1, \ldots, j_M)$ where $j_m \in \{1, \ldots, D\}$ and the importance of each feature through the weights $\boldsymbol{\alpha} = (\alpha_1, \ldots, \alpha_M)$. Computational cost is reduced since there is no need to compute extra features (this has already been done for the category detector). There is also no cost for selecting which features to use since they are fixed.

Only the thresholds for a single weak classifier in the boosted cascade of the individual detector are modified
Selecting the thresholds for a single weak classifier $h'(x')$, which depends on a single feature $x' \in \mathbb{R}$, can be achieved at almost zero computational cost.

Consider the target that has been detected by the category detector and call u' the value of feature x'. An interval, centred at u', can now be defined. The width of this interval is determined offline, from a small validation set that contains tracks of a few individuals. The standard deviation of feature x' for a single individual across its track is calculated; the median standard deviation or spread σ' is then computed across the set of individuals. The spread σ' gives an estimate of the width of the interval.

Formally, the interval is $(u' - \beta\sigma', u' + \beta\sigma')$ where β is a free parameter that can be tuned experimentally. If the appearance of the individual is changing slowly over time, which is a reasonable assumption to make for video (since the difference from frame-to-frame is small), this interval represents the most likely values that the feature x' will take for that individual.

The weak classifier $h'(x')$ can thus be obtained from one training example and by only setting two thresholds (making the computational cost near zero):

$$h'(x'; u', \sigma') = \begin{cases} 1 & u' - \beta\sigma' < x' < u' + \beta\sigma' \\ -1 & \text{otherwise.} \end{cases} \quad (3)$$

This weak classifier provides evidence for an individual being present (absent) if the feature x' lies inside (outside) the interval $(u' - \beta\sigma', u' + \beta\sigma')$.

An individual detector in the form of a cascaded boosted classifier can now be constructed. Given the set of features $\mathbf{J}$ and weights $\boldsymbol{\alpha}$ that were selected for the category detector, the single positive example $\mathbf{u}^0$ of the target, and an estimate of the spread $\boldsymbol{\sigma} = (\sigma_1, \ldots, \sigma_M)$ of the features $\mathbf{J}$, a classifier $F(\mathbf{x})$ for the target can be defined by:

$$F(\mathbf{x}; \mathbf{u}^0, \boldsymbol{\sigma}) = \sum_{m=1}^{M} \alpha_m h'(x_{j_m}; u_{j_m}, \sigma_m) \quad (4)$$

3.3 Evaluate Tracker

Given the next frame in the video the individual detector $F(\mathbf{x}; \mathbf{u}^0, \boldsymbol{\sigma})$ is evaluated using a sliding-window scheme. The location with the maximal classification score is identified as the new location of the target object. Since the individual detector is a cascade of boosted classifiers, sliding window detection is very efficient. It would also be possible to use a motion model to reduce the number of sub-windows evaluated (we have not done this).

3.4 Update Tracker

If at the new location of the target object (the one identified by the individual detector) there is also a coincident detection made by the category detector, then the individual detector is updated with the new sample, $\mathbf{u}^1$, of the target. The update procedure is then as simple as reinitialising the individual detector with the new sample which results in $F(\mathbf{x}; \mathbf{u}^1, \boldsymbol{\sigma})$. The updated individual detector is then applied to the next frame and so on. If there fails to be a coincident category detection then the individual detector is not updated at all and is simply applied to the next frame. Figure 2 outlines this update procedure. Drift is avoided by only updating the model when the individual detector and category detector are coincident. This strategy ensures that only "good" positive samples are used to update the model. A category detection and individual detection are coincident if their overlap is greater than 50%.

3.5 Stop Tracker

There are two conditions, either of which can be met, for tracking of the target object to cease. The first is that there are no detections made by the individual detector for T_1 consecutive frames. This condition is usually met when the target object leaves the frame. The second is that the detections made by the individual detector fail to coincide with those made by the category detector for

T_2 consecutive frames. This condition is usually met when a tracker is initialised by a false detection made by the category detector. In this work we set both of these quantities to five frames.

4 Datasets

To benchmark the performance of our tracking algorithm we use two publicly available video datasets.

The first dataset is the Caltech Pedestrians [17,19] dataset. It contains 250,000 frames of video, at a resolution of 640x480, taken from a vehicle driving through regular traffic in an urban environment. The dataset is labelled with a total of 350,000 bounding boxes and around 1900 unique individual pedestrians. Around 30% of the frames have two or more pedestrians. Pedestrians are visible for 150 frames on average. The dataset is divided into 11 sets; 6 are used for training (S0-S5) and 5 are used for testing (S6-S10). This division is provided by the authors. The training set contains 192,000 bounding boxes and the test set contains 155,000. The authors also refer to experiments conducted on pedestrians over 50 pixels tall, with no or partial occlusion as the *reasonable evaluation setting*. There are 73,256 labelled bounding boxes and 769 unique individuals that meet these requirements in the test set. All of our experiments are conducted using the reasonable evaluation setting.

The second dataset used is the Buffy dataset [40]. It has been regularly used for the automatic labelling of faces of TV characters using subtitle and script text [40,21]. In this work we use the publicly available, ground truth labels of [6]. The dataset contains episodes 1–6 from season 5 of Buffy the Vampire Slayer with around 64,000 frames per episode. The faces are labelled using an automatic algorithm rather than by a human operator. This means that the ground truth labels are noisy. In total there are 317,831 labelled bounding boxes and 5513 unique face tracks across the six episodes. There is also a wide variety in the appearance of individuals in this dataset with many shots set outdoors and at night time; there are also a number of close-up shots.

Examples of the different individuals and how their appearance changes over time for both datasets are displayed in Figure 3.

The reason we benchmark tracking performance on these datasets is 1) because of their size and 2) because of their complexity. The benchmarking procedure of Wu et al. [44] only evaluates tracking performance on 50 different individuals. In this work we make this evaluation on around 6000 individuals; a 120-fold increase. The datasets here are also more complex. Having to track multiple objects of a similar appearance is a far more difficult task than the tracking of a single object, particularly when the target objects interact with each other, which may lead to trackers swapping identities. These datasets are also less biased since they were collected independently of the authors of any the trackers mentioned in section 1. They are also more realistic in the sense that the sequences haven't been generated in a lab as around half of the sequences in [44] are.

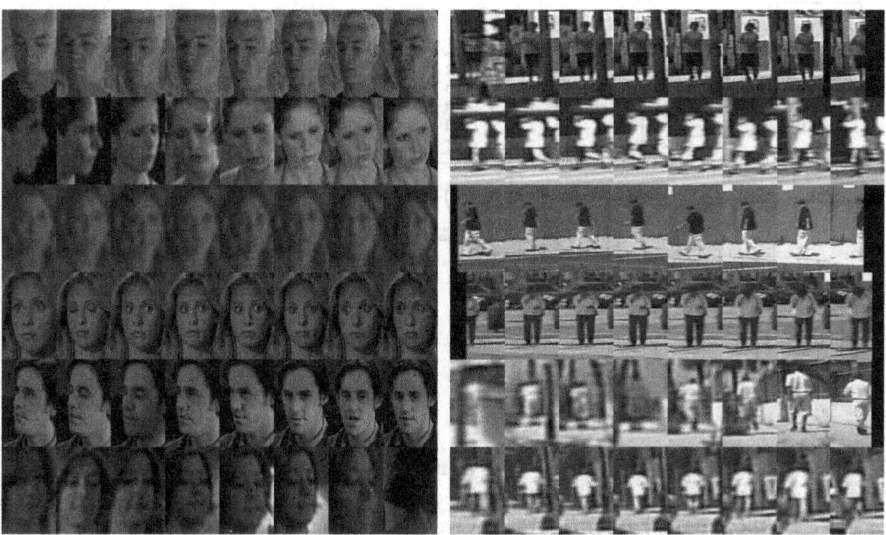

Fig. 3. Dataset Examples. (Left) Face tracks from the Buffy dataset. (Right) pedestrian tracks from Caltech Pedestrians. The ground-truth trajectories were sampled randomly from a video in each of the datasets. There are frontal and profile faces; the lighting can change considerably across a face track; facial expressions are varied. The pedestrians are low resolution; they change scale as the car mounted camera approaches and there is occlusion. The datasets are large with a combined total of 7500 individual tracks and 800,000 bounding boxes. They are also difficult due to the variety in pose, lighting, background and scale across a track as well as having multiple objects present at any one time. To the best of our knowledge this is one of the largest datasets that appearance-based tracking algorithms have been evaluated on.

5 Performance Metrics

There are a variety of methods [44,32,10] to measure the performance of a tracking algorithm. In this work we use three simple and intuitive measures to capture tracking performance (refer to Figure 4).

In a multiple-object tracking scenario, given a single frame, there are a number of options for determining whether a tracked target and ground-truth location match. The centre location error which is the Euclidean distance between the centre's of the two locations is one option [4,44,10]. This measure is not very robust to labelling error and relies heavily on the fact that the ground-truth is perfect. A more robust method to use is the bounding box overlap. Using the PASCAL criteria [20] a tracked object matches a ground-truth object if the area of overlap between their respective bounding boxes exceeds 50%.

In addition to bounding box overlap we also include another criterion for matching to occur. A tracked object matches a ground-truth object if the tracker was initialised by a target that has the same identity as the ground-truth object.

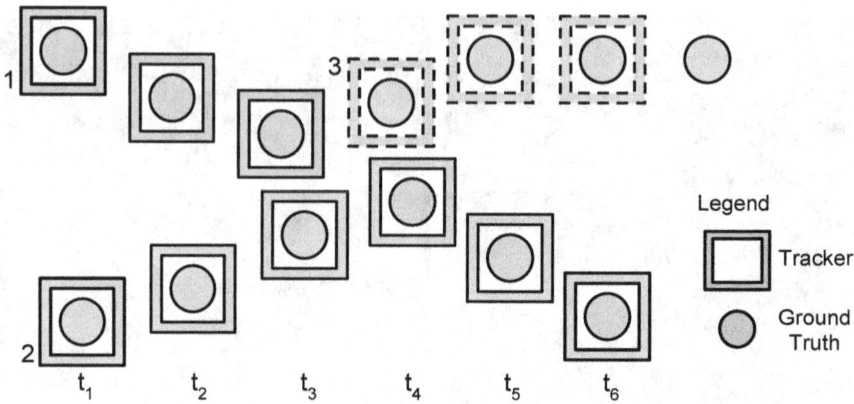

Fig. 4. A graphical example of the performance measures. The performance measures used are precision, recall and continuity/fragmentation of a trajectory. Tracker 1 (pink squares) is initialised to track the ground-truth target A (pink circles). Tracker 1 has 3 matches since it is only ever matched with target A and has a track length of 3. Tracker 2 (solid blue squares) only has 3 matches with a length of 6. This is because it is initialised to track the ground-truth target B (blue circles), however, it's last three detections coincide with ground-truth target A which is incorrect. Tracker 3 (dotted blue squares) is also initialised to track ground-truth target B and has 3 matches with a length of 3. The precision is then 9/12. Ground-truth target A has 3 matches with a length of 6. The last three ground-truth targets are unmatched due to tracker 2 being initialised to track target B. Ground-truth target B has 6 matches and a length of 7 since all of the corresponding trackers were initialised to track target B. The recall is 9/13. Target A is only covered by tracker 1 (tracker 2 is not included since it has not been initialised to track A) while target B is covered by trackers 2 and 3. The fragmentation is thus 3/2 and so the continuity is 2/3.

This is a reasonable condition to enforce since a tracker initialised by target A should not be tracking target B.

Now that single frame matching has been defined, performance across trajectories can be measured. If there are a total of N tracking trajectories and M ground truth trajectories then three quantities can be defined: precision, recall and continuity.

If $l^n_{tracker}$ is the length of tracking trajectory n and $d^n_{tracker}$ is the number of matches in trajectory n then the precision P across all tracking trajectories is defined as:

$$P = \frac{\sum_{n=1}^{N} d^n_{tracker}}{\sum_{n=1}^{N} l^n_{tracker}} \tag{5}$$

This measure is similar to the MOTP metric proposed by Bernardin and Stiefelhagen [10]. Precision gives a measure of how well a tracker initialised on target A tracks target A. If the tracker drifts or there is an identity swap precision will be low.

If l_{gt}^m is the length of ground truth trajectory m and d_{gt}^m is the number of matches in ground truth trajectory m then the recall R across all ground-truth trajectories is defined as:

$$R = \frac{\sum_{m=1}^{M} d_{gt}^m}{\sum_{m=1}^{M} l_{gt}^m} \tag{6}$$

Let f^m be the number of trackers that are required to cover ground truth trajectory m. The continuity C is then defined as:

$$C = \frac{\sum_{m=1}^{M} \mathbb{1}(f^m > 0)}{\sum_{m=1}^{M} f^m} \tag{7}$$

where $\mathbb{1}$ is the indicator function. Continuity is the inverse of the mean number of trackers needed to cover a ground truth trajectory. This is described as fragmentation in [32]. Trajectories that have no trackers covering them are not included in this calculation. The reason continuity is used instead of fragmentation is that continuity is easier to compare to precision and recall since a value of 1 for all three of these measures indicates perfect performance.

Recall and continuity give a measure of how well targets are tracked. If the tracker does not adapt to the appearance of the target, continuity will be low.

The overall performance of a tracking algorithm is given as the mean of the precision, recall and continuity. We feel that this is a reasonable metric to compare algorithms on since all three quantities are equally as important.

6 Experiments

For the remainder of this paper we will refer to our proposed tracking algorithm as the Category-to-Individual Tracker (CIT). To assess the performance of CIT we conduct experiments using the Buffy and Caltech Pedestrian datasets (refer to Sec 4). To the best of our knowledge, this is one of the largest performance evaluations for appearance-based tracking. The most important findings are reported here in this manuscript; the remainder is included as supplementary material.

The results of CIT are compared to 9 other, publicly available, appearance-based tracking algorithms. The source code for each of the algorithms was downloaded from the original author's website. Minor modifications were then made so that each tracker would operate in our multi-target, automatic initialisation framework (as opposed to single target; human initialised frameworks that these algorithms were originally tested on). If an algorithm had parameters to set then those that were recommended by the original authors were used.

For all of the experiments we use the multi-scale ACF detector of Dollar et al. [18,15] for the category detector. The code was downloaded from the website[1].

The category detector used for the Buffy dataset was trained using 882 faces from a separate dataset [12] which was also downloaded from the web. Due to

[1] `http://vision.ucsd.edu/~pdollar/toolbox/doc/`

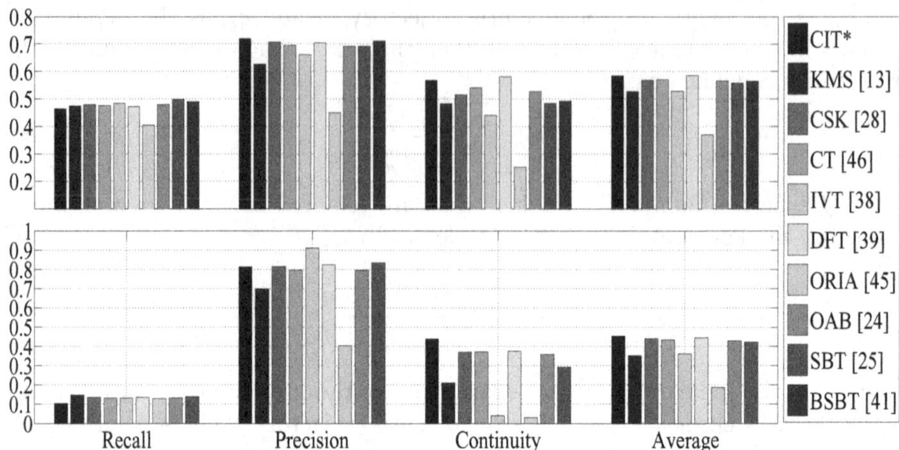

Fig. 5. Tracking Performance on Buffy (top) and Caltech Pedestrians (bottom) for a category detector operating at a recall of 0.5. Refer to Section 5 for definitions of recall, precision and continuity. The average performance is the mean of the precision, recall and continuity. The precision calculation ignores trajectories that have been initialised by false category detections. A tracker with perfect performance would have a value of 1 for each of the measurements. The results indicate that our method CIT is one of the best performers, however, most of the methods have similar performance results. The relative performance of the trackers is roughly equivalent across the two very different, very distinct datasets. The BSBT algorithm ran too slowly and so its performance on Caltech Pedestrians is omitted.

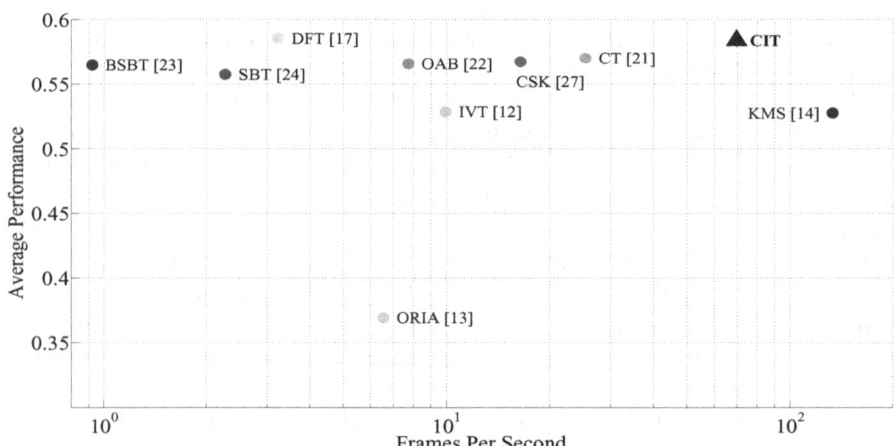

Fig. 6. The average performance and frame rate for each tracking algorithm using the Buffy dataset. The average performance is the same as the value in the top plot of Fig 5. The results indicate that our method, CIT is 10% more accurate and nearly as fast as the fastest of the competing algorithms. It is also as accurate but 20x faster than the most accurate of the competing algorithms.

the ground-truth for Buffy being noisy, an external dataset was used to train the face detector to ensure detection results were reasonable. The category detector used for the Caltech Pedestrians dataset was trained using the recommended training sets S0-S4 (refer to Sec.4).

Each category detector was then calibrated to operate at a specific recall by using a validation set. Episode 1 was used for Buffy and set S5 for Caltech Pedestrians. By operating the category detectors at different recall rates different targets are identified thus having an impact on the initialisation and update stages of tracking. We only include the results for a category detector recall of 0.5. Refer to the supplementary material for other values.

The validation sets were also used to calibrate each of the tracking methods. Each of the tracking methods have a confidence score associated with their predictions; in our regime, individuals enter and exit the scene so it is important to stop tracking a target when the confidence of the tracker is below a certain threshold otherwise the trackers will update their target model with background. To choose this threshold we evaluated each algorithm on the validation set for each dataset and selected the threshold that gave the best average performance. For the CIT tracker we selected the value of β (refer to Eqn. 3) during validation rather than the confidence threshold which was set to zero.

Each tracking algorithm was then evaluated on the test set for Buffy (episodes 2-5) and for Caltech Pedestrians (sets S6-S10) with trackers being initialised by non-coincident category detections (refer to Fig. 2). The resulting trajectories were used to compute precision, recall and continuity for each algorithm. The results for both datasets are in Figure 5 which includes the average performance which is the mean of the precision, recall and continuity. The precision calculation ignores trajectories that have been initialised by false category detections.

The speed at which each of these algorithms operate at is also important. To compute the average frame rate of a tracking algorithm we need to decouple the computation time due to the tracker and the computation time due to the category detector. The time it takes for the category detector to run without tracking is subtracted from the time it takes a tracker to run. The results are in Figure 6. We only include the results for Buffy since the results on Caltech Pedestrians (in the supplementary material) are similar. The average frame rates were computed using the first 10,000 frames of episode 3 of Buffy on an Intel i5, 3.20 GHz machine.

Qualitative examples of how our tracking method works on both Buffy and Caltech Pedestrians can be found in Figure 1. The sequences give an indication of how tracking of a target is successful despite occlusion and changes in pose.

7 Discussion and Conclusions

We have presented a novel tracking method which is designed to track objects belonging to a specific category. The method makes use of a category detector to identify target objects to track and of an individual-specific detector to track the target in subsequent video frames. The individual-specific detector is trained on-the-fly at almost no extra cost, making it possible for the tracker to operate in real-time. The well-known problem of drift is addressed by updating the individual-specific detector only when there are coincident category detections.

We compare the performance of our scheme to 9 state-of-the-art trackers and find that it is as accurate as the most accurate competitor, but 20x faster. It is only slightly slower than the fastest competitor, but 10% more accurate.

In order to carry out our benchmark comparison we developed a methodology based on considering four metrics: precision, recall, fragmentation and computational cost. Our experiments were carried out on two large (hundreds of thousands of detections), challenging and heterogeneous datasets of faces and pedestrians; we observe identical rankings of the various algorithms on the two datasets, which gives us the confidence that our findings are general and may be expected to carry over to a variety of datasets and tasks. We believe that our benchmark surpasses, both in method and set size, any such comparative evaluation in the literature.

Acknowledgements. This work is funded by the ARO-JPL NASA Stennis NAS7.03001 grant and the MURI ONR N00014-10-1-0933 grant.

References

1. Adam, A., Rivlin, E., Shimshoni, I.: Robust Fragments-Based Tracking Using the Integral Histogram. In: CVPR (2006)
2. Andriyenko, A., Schindler, K.: Globally Optimal Multi-target Tracking on a Hexagonal Lattice. In: Daniilidis, K., Maragos, P., Paragios, N. (eds.) ECCV 2010, Part I. LNCS, vol. 6311, pp. 466–479. Springer, Heidelberg (2010)
3. Avidan, S.: Ensemble Tracking. PAMI 29(2), 431–435 (2007)
4. Babenko, B., Belongie, S., Yang, M.H.: Visual Tracking with Online Multiple Instance Learning. In: CVPR (2009)
5. Bao, C., Wu, Y., Ling, H., Ji, H.: Real Time Robust L1 Tracker using Accelerated Proximal Gradient Approach. In: CVPR (2012)
6. Bauml, M., Tapaswi, M., Stiefelhagen, R.: Semi-Supervised Learning with Constraints for Person Identification in Multimedia Data. In: CVPR (2013)
7. Benenson, R., Mathias, M., Timofte, R., Van Gool, L.: Pedestrian Detection at 100 Frames per Second. In: CVPR (2013)
8. Berclaz, J., Fleuret, F., Fua, P.: Multiple Object Tracking using Flow Linear Programming. In: PETS (2009)
9. Berclaz, J., Türetken, E., Fleuret, F., Fua, P.: Multiple Object Tracking using K-Shortest Paths Optimization. PAMI 33(9), 1806–1819 (2011)
10. Bernardin, K., Stiefelhagen, R.: Evaluating Multiple Object Tracking Performance: The CLEAR MOT Metrics. EURASIP JIVP (1), 1–10 (2008)
11. Black, M.J., Jepson, A.D.: EigenTracking: Robust Matching and Tracking of Articulated Objects Using a View-Based Representation. IJCV 26(1), 63–84 (1996)
12. Burgos-Artizzu, X., Hall, D., Perona, P., Dollár, P.: Merging Pose Estimates across Space and Time. In: BMVC (2013)
13. Comaniciu, D., Ramesh, V., Meer, P.: Kernel-Based Object Tracking. PAMI 25(5), 564–577 (2003)

14. Dalal, N., Triggs, B.: Histograms of Oriented Gradients for Human Detection. In: CVPR (2005)
15. Dollár, P., Appel, R., Belongie, S., Perona, P.: Fast Feature Pyramids for Object Detection. PAMI (2014)
16. Dollár, P., Tu, Z., Perona, P., Belongie, S.: Integral Channel Features. In: BMVC (2009)
17. Dollár, P., Wojek, C., Schiele, B., Perona, P.: Pedestrian Detection: A Benchmark. In: CVPR
18. Dollár, P., Belongie, S., Perona, P.: The Fastest Pedestrian Detector in the West. In: BMVC (2010)
19. Dollár, P., Wojek, C., Schiele, B., Perona, P.: Pedestrian Detection: an Evaluation of the State of the Art. PAMI 34(4), 743–761 (2012)
20. Everingham, M., Van Gool, L., Williams, C.K.I., Winn, J., Zisserman, A.: The PASCAL Visual Object Classes Challenge 2009 (VOC) Results (2009)
21. Everingham, M.R., Sivic, J., Zisserman, A.: Hello! My Name is.... Buffy – Automatic Naming of Characters in TV Video. In: BMVC (2006)
22. Freund, Y., Schapire, R.E.: A Decision-Theoretic Generalization of On-Line Learning and an Application to Boosting. Journal of Computer and System Sciences 55(1), 119–139 (1997)
23. Fukunaga, K., Hostetler, L.: The Estimation of the Gradient of a Density Function, with Applications in Pattern Recognition. IEEE Transactions on Information Theory 21 (1975)
24. Grabner, H., Grabner, M., Bischof, H.: Real-Time Tracking Via On-line Boosting. In: BMVC (2006)
25. Grabner, H., Leistner, C., Bischof, H.: Semi-supervised On-Line Boosting for Robust Tracking. In: Forsyth, D., Torr, P., Zisserman, A. (eds.) ECCV 2008, Part I. LNCS, vol. 5302, pp. 234–247. Springer, Heidelberg (2008)
26. Gray, D., Tao, H.: Viewpoint Invariant Pedestrian Recognition with an Ensemble of Localized Features. In: Forsyth, D., Torr, P., Zisserman, A. (eds.) ECCV 2008, Part I. LNCS, vol. 5302, pp. 262–275. Springer, Heidelberg (2008)
27. Hall, D., Perona, P.: From Categories to Individuals in Real Time - A Unified Boosting Approach. In: CVPR (2014)
28. Henriques, J.F., Caseiro, R., Martins, P., Batista, J.: Exploiting the Circulant Structure of Tracking-by-Detection with Kernels. In: Fitzgibbon, A., Lazebnik, S., Perona, P., Sato, Y., Schmid, C. (eds.) ECCV 2012, Part IV. LNCS, vol. 7575, pp. 702–715. Springer, Heidelberg (2012)
29. Huang, G.B., Ramesh, M., Berg, T., Learned-Miller, E.: Labeled Faces in the Wild: A Database for Studying Face Recognition in Unconstrained Environments. Tech. Rep. 07-49, University of Massachusetts, Amherst (October 2007)
30. Jiang, H., Fels, S., Little, J.J.: A Linear Programming Approach for Multiple Object Tracking. In: CVPR (2007)
31. Kalal, Z., Mikolajczyk, K., Matas, J.: Tracking-Learning-Detection. PAMI 6(1), 1–14 (2011)
32. Li, Y., Huang, C., Nevatia, R.: Learning to Associate: HybridBoosted Multi-Target Tracker for Crowded Scene. In: CVPR (2009)
33. Ma, Y., Yu, Q., Cohen, I.: Target Tracking with Incomplete Detection. Computer Vision and Image Understanding 113(4), 580–587 (2009)
34. Nevatia, R.: Global Data Association for Multi-Object Tracking using Network Flows. In: CVPR (2008)
35. Oron, S., Bar-Hillel, A., Levi, D., Avidan, S.: Locally Orderless Tracking. In: CVPR (2012)

36. Pellegrini, S., Ess, A., Van Gool, L.: Improving Data Association by Joint Modeling of Pedestrian Trajectories and Groupings. In: Daniilidis, K., Maragos, P., Paragios, N. (eds.) ECCV 2010, Part I. LNCS, vol. 6311, pp. 452–465. Springer, Heidelberg (2010)
37. Pirsiavash, H., Ramanan, D., Fowlkes, C.C.: Globally-Optimal Greedy Algorithms for Tracking a Variable Number of Objects. In: CVPR (2011)
38. Ross, D.A., Lim, J., Lin, R.S., Yang, M.H.: Incremental Learning for Robust Visual Tracking. IJCV 77, 125–141 (2007)
39. Sevilla-Lara, L., Learned-Miller, E.: Distribution Fields for Tracking. In: CVPR (2012)
40. Sivic, J., Everingham, M., Zisserman, A.: Who are You? - Learning Person Specific Classifiers from Video. In: CVPR (2009)
41. Stalder, S., Grabner, H., Van Gool, L.: Beyond Semi-Supervised Tracking: Tracking Should be as Simple as Detection, but not Simpler than Recognition. In: ICCV Workshops (2009)
42. Viola, P., Jones, M.: Rapid Object Detection Using a Boosted Cascade of Simple Features. In: CVPR (2001)
43. Viola, P., Jones, M.J.: Robust Real-Time Face Detection. IJCV 57(2), 137–154 (2004)
44. Wu, Y., Lim, J., Yang, M.H.: Online Object Tracking: A Benchmark. In: CVPR (2013)
45. Wu, Y., Shen, B.: Online Robust Image Alignment Via Iterative Convex Optimization. In: CVPR (2012)
46. Zhang, K., Zhang, L., Yang, M.-H.: Real-Time Compressive Tracking. In: Fitzgibbon, A., Lazebnik, S., Perona, P., Sato, Y., Schmid, C. (eds.) ECCV 2012, Part III. LNCS, vol. 7574, pp. 864–877. Springer, Heidelberg (2012)

Robust Visual Tracking with Double Bounding Box Model

Junseok Kwon[1], Junha Roh[2], Kyoung Mu Lee[3], and Luc Van Gool[1]

[1] Computer Vision Laboratory, ETH Zurich, Switzerland
[2] Imaging Media Research Center, KIST, Korea
[3] Department of ECE, ASRI, Seoul National University, Korea
{kwonj,vangool}@vision.ee.ethz.ch, junha.roh@imrc.kist.re.kr, kyoungmu@snu.ac.kr

Abstract. A novel tracking algorithm that can track a highly non-rigid target robustly is proposed using a new bounding box representation called the Double Bounding Box (DBB). In the DBB, a target is described by the combination of the Inner Bounding Box (IBB) and the Outer Bounding Box (OBB). Then our objective of visual tracking is changed to find the IBB and OBB instead of a single bounding box, where the IBB and OBB can be easily obtained by the Dempster-Shafer (DS) theory. If the target is highly non-rigid, any single bounding box cannot include all foreground regions while excluding all background regions. Using the DBB, our method does not directly handle the ambiguous regions, which include both the foreground and background regions. Hence, it can solve the inherent ambiguity of the single bounding box representation and thus can track highly non-rigid targets robustly. Our method finally finds the best state of the target using a new Constrained Markov Chain Monte Carlo (CMCMC)-based sampling method with the constraint that the OBB should include the IBB. Experimental results show that our method tracks non-rigid targets accurately and robustly, and outperforms state-of-the-art methods.

1 Introduction

Visual tracking has been used in many artificial intelligence applications, including surveillance, augmented reality, medical imaging, and other intelligent vision systems [5,8,16,32,34]. In practical applications, the purpose of visual tracking is to find the best configuration of a target with a given observation [38]. As many conventional tracking methods describe the target with a single bounding box, the configuration at time t is typically represented by a three-dimensional vector $\mathbf{X}_t = (X_t^x, X_t^y, X_t^s)$, where (X_t^x, X_t^y), and X_t^s are the center coordinate and the scale of the target, respectively. This single bounding box representation is widely used because it allows the easy inference of the best configuration using a low-dimensional vector [1,4,13,17,20,24]. In addition, with the representation, tracking methods that use the tracking by detection approach [3,7,14,18,31,35] easily train a classifier using the rectangular patches described by the bounding box.

D. Fleet et al. (Eds.): ECCV 2014, Part I, LNCS 8689, pp. 377–392, 2014.
© Springer International Publishing Switzerland 2014

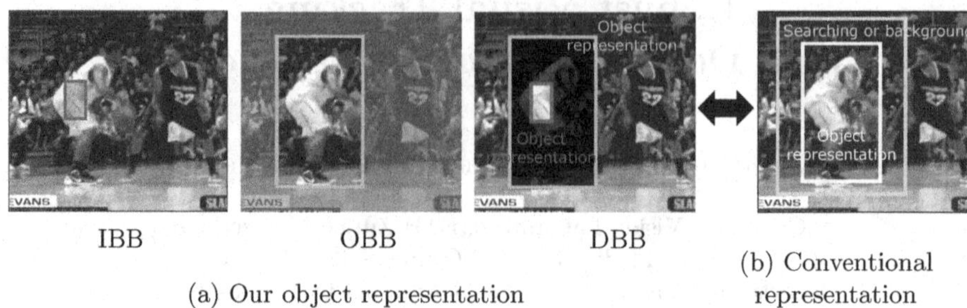

(a) Our object representation

(b) Conventional representation

Fig. 1. Example of the different bounding box representations. (a) The IBB is the bounding box that only includes the target region, but excludes some parts of it. The OBB is the bounding box that includes whole target region but also includes some background regions. In our DBB, the bounding box of the target is represented by the combination of the IBB (red) and OBB (blue). (b) The discriminative tracking approaches in [2][36] also use two BBs for visual tracking. However only one BB is used for representing the target configuration. The other BB is required only to get the background information [2] or to make a search range [36], which is quite different from our OBB. All of two BBs in our method are designed to represent the non-rigid target configuration.

However, the single bounding box representation has inherent ambiguity if a target is highly non-rigid. No single bounding box can cover the whole region of the target while excluding all the background regions, as shown in Fig.1(a). In this case, the tracking methods may choose the Inner Bounding Box (IBB), the Outer Bounding Box (OBB), or between them. The IBB is the largest bounding box that contains pure object region only. The OBB is the smallest bounding box that contains the whole object region, where the outside of the OBB is pure background. However, although the IBB in Fig.1(a) can deliver the pure target region, the IBB and bounding boxes that are smaller than the IBB lose lots of useful information about the target by excluding large parts of it. While the OBB in Fig.1(a) includes the whole target region, the OBB and bounding boxes that are larger than the OBB inevitably contain unwanted background regions. The bounding boxes between the IBB and OBB include both the target region and the background region. Now, the natural question is *which box representation can best describe a general and non-rigid target.* The present paper aims to resolve this ambiguity in the bounding box representation, and to track a non-rigid target robustly using a new bounding box representation.

In this paper, the bounding box of a target is represented by the combination of the IBB and OBB. We call this representation the DBB. By describing the bounding box with this combination, our method solves the inherent ambiguity in the single bounding box representation. In addition, this representation improves tracking performance because it does not consider the ambiguous regions (the black region between the IBB and OBB in Fig.1(a)) in determining the probable configuration of the target, which contains mixed target and background regions. Instead, our method only considers the *maximal pure foreground region*, inside of the IBB (the red region in Fig.1(a)) and the *pure background region*, outside of the OBB (the blue region in Fig.1(a)) in determining the probable configuration of the target. Our method finds the IBB and OBB using the DS theory [9,11] in Section 3.2. Following the DS theory, the IBB is obtained by maximizing the similarity between the red region and the target model, and the OBB is obtained by maximizing the dissimilarity between the green region and the target model. With the IBB and OBB, the method searches the best state of the target using the proposed Constrained Maximum a Posteriori (CMAP) estimate in Section 4.1. The best state maximizes the posterior probability while it satisfies the constraint that the OBB has to include the IBB. The best state can be achieved by the proposed CMCMC-based sampling method in Section 4.2.

The first contribution of our work is to propose a new bounding box representation. A highly non-rigid object cannot be adequately described by any single bounding box. To solve the ambiguity in the conventional bounding box representation, the target is represented by the combination of two bounding boxes, which is called the DBB. The second contribution is to apply the the DS theory to the bounding box representation problem and to provide a theoretical basis for determining the IBB and OBB. The last contribution is to present an efficient tracking system using the DBB and a new CMCMC-based sampling method. The DBB explores the complementary connection between the IBB and OBB to track highly non-rigid targets accurately. In practice, the IBB is robust to the deformation of the target but sensitive to noise because of its small size. The OBB is resistant to noise but imprecise on the deformation of the target because of its large size. Hence, these two representations complement each other, resulting in a representation that is insensitive to both deformation and noise. The CMCMC-based sampling method efficiently determines the best states of the target while maintaining the constraint in which the OBB must include the IBB.

2 Related Work

In tracking methods for non-rigid targets, the BHT tracker [26] described the target using multiple rectangular blocks, whose positions within the tracking window are adaptively determined. The BHMC tracker [22] represented the target using multiple local patches, in which the topology among local patches continuously evolves. Using multiple rectangular blocks and multiple local patches, these methods efficiently track non-rigid objects undergoing large variations in appearance and shape. Our method and aforementioned part models are similar in the sense of using multiple bounding boxes. However, the main advantages of our method over these methods are in how it determines the sizes of the IBB and OBB and how to calculate their likelihoods efficiently using the DS theory [9,11]. Therefore, our method can improve even the conventional part models by applying the aforementioned two contributions to them. In addition, compared with the part models [29], our method describes the target as a low-dimensional vector using only the IBB and OBB. Hence, the best state of the target is easily determined with a much smaller computational cost.

In sampling-based tracking methods, the particle filter [15] determines the best state by considering the non-Gaussian and the multi-modality of the target distribution in the tracking problem. Markov Chain Monte Carlo (MCMC) methods [19,33] efficiently determines the best state in high-dimensional state spaces. Compared with these methods, the CMCMC-based sampling method finds the best state while satisfying some constraints. It is a more difficult problem than the conventional sampling problems.

In tracking methods using the the DS theory [9,11], the method in [10] presented a face tracking system using a pixel fusion process from three color sources within the framework of the DS theory. The methods in [23,25] resolved the visual tracking problem by combining evidences from multiple sources using the DS theory. Unlike these methods that used the DS theory only for the observation fusion, our method employs the theory for the bounding box representation.

3 Design of the Double Bounding Box

3.1 Bounding Box Representation Using DS Theory

In the tracking method, a state $\mathbf{X}_t$ represents a bounding box of a rectangular region at t-th frame. Let us denote $\mathbb{R}(\mathbf{X}_t)$ as the region enclosed by $\mathbf{X}_t$. According to the Shafer's framework [9], we can define a mass function $m(\mathbb{R}(\mathbf{X}_t))$ for the region of a bounding box $\mathbb{R}(\mathbf{X}_t)$, which is bounded by two values, i.e., belief and plausibility:

$$bel(\mathbb{R}(\mathbf{X}_t)) \leq m(\mathbb{R}(\mathbf{X}_t)) \leq pl(\mathbb{R}(\mathbf{X}_t)), \tag{1}$$

where $bel(\mathbb{R}(\mathbf{X}_t))$ and $pl(\mathbb{R}(\mathbf{X}_t))$ denote the belief and the plausibility of $\mathbb{R}(\mathbf{X}_t)$, respectively. In this work, the mass function $m(\mathbb{R}(\mathbf{X}_t))$ is designed by the likelihood of the region of the bounding box:

$$m(\mathbb{R}(\mathbf{X}_t)) \equiv p(\mathbf{Y}_t|R = \mathbb{R}(\mathbf{X}_t)) = \frac{1}{c}e^{-dist\left(M_t, \mathbf{Y}_t(\mathbb{R}(\mathbf{X}_t))\right)}, \tag{2}$$

where $\mathbf{Y}_t(\mathbb{R}(\mathbf{X}_t))$ denotes the observation inside of the region $\mathbb{R}(\mathbf{X}_t)$ and $dist(\cdot)$ returns the distance between the observation $\mathbf{Y}_t(\mathbb{R}(\mathbf{X}_t))$ and the target model M_t. For the observation and the distance measure, we utilize the HSV color histogram and the Bhattacharyya similarity coefficient in [28]. c in (2) is a normalization constant.

Now, given an IBB $\mathbf{X}_t^i$ and an OBB $\mathbf{X}_t^o$, as shown in Fig.2, the whole region of interest can be divided by three regions $\mathbf{R}_t^1$, $\mathbf{R}_t^2$, and $\mathbf{R}_t^3$, making the frame of discernment to be $\mathbf{U}_t = \{\mathbf{R}_t^1, \mathbf{R}_t^2, \mathbf{R}_t^3\}$, where the regions are mutually exclusive $\bigcap_{i=1}^3 \mathbf{R}_t^i = \phi$ and the union of the regions compose a whole region $\bigcup_{i=1}^3 \mathbf{R}_t^i = \mathbf{U}_t$. Note that the IBB $\mathbf{X}_t^i$ represents the region $\mathbf{R}_t^1$, and the OBB $\mathbf{X}_t^o$ covers the region $\{\mathbf{R}_t^1, \mathbf{R}_t^2\}$, where $\{\mathbf{R}_t^1, \mathbf{R}_t^2\}$ denotes a union of regions $\mathbf{R}_t^1$ and $\mathbf{R}_t^2$. The power set of the universal set, $2^{\mathbf{U}_t}$, is $\{\phi$, $\mathbf{R}_t^1$, $\mathbf{R}_t^2$, $\mathbf{R}_t^3$, $\{\mathbf{R}_t^1, \mathbf{R}_t^2\}$, $\{\mathbf{R}_t^1, \mathbf{R}_t^3\}$, $\{\mathbf{R}_t^2, \mathbf{R}_t^3\}$, $\mathbf{U}_t\}$. According to the DS theory [9,11], the mass function in (2) is then normalized, such that the masses of the elements of the power set $2^{\mathbf{U}_t}$ add up to a total of 1. In this paper, the mass corresponds to the likelihood score

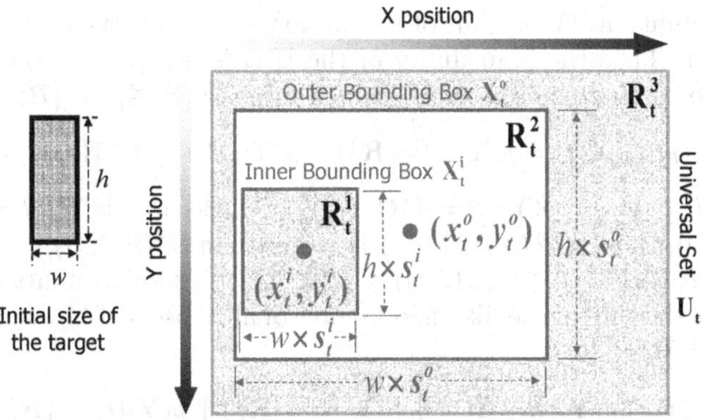

Fig. 2. Notation of the DBB. $\mathbf{R}_t^1$ indicates the region inside of the IBB $\mathbf{X}_t^i$. $\mathbf{R}_t^3$ indicates the region outside of the OBB $\mathbf{X}_t^o$. $\mathbf{R}_t^2$ indicates the region between the IBB and OBB.

$p(\mathbf{Y}_t|R)$ and, thus, we make the sum of the likelihood scores of all elements of $2^{\mathbf{U}_t}$ to be 1:

$$\begin{aligned}\sum_{r|r\in 2^{\mathbf{U}_t}} p(\mathbf{Y}_t|R=r) &= p(\mathbf{Y}_t|R=\mathbf{R}_t^1)+p(\mathbf{Y}_t|R=\mathbf{R}_t^2)+p(\mathbf{Y}_t|R=\mathbf{R}_t^3) \\ &\quad + p(\mathbf{Y}_t|R=\{\mathbf{R}_t^1,\mathbf{R}_t^2\})+p(\mathbf{Y}_t|R=\{\mathbf{R}_t^2,\mathbf{R}_t^3\})=1.\end{aligned} \tag{3}$$

In (3), $p(\mathbf{Y}_t|R=\phi)$, $p(\mathbf{Y}_t|R=\mathbf{U}_t)$, and $p(\mathbf{Y}_t|R=\{\mathbf{R}_t^1,\mathbf{R}_t^3\})$ are designed as zero because ϕ, $\mathbf{U}_t$, and $\{\mathbf{R}_t^1,\mathbf{R}_t^3\}$ make meaningless regions, which are empty region, entire region, and two separate regions, respectively.

3.2 Inner and Outer Bounding Boxes

According to the DS theory [9,11], the belief in (1) is defined as the sum of all the masses of subsets of the set of interest. In our problem, the mass corresponds to the likelihood score $p(\mathbf{Y}_t|R)$, whereas the set of interest is the IBB, $\mathbb{R}(\mathbf{X}_t^i)=\{\mathbf{R}_t^1\}$, or OBB, $\mathbb{R}(\mathbf{X}_t^o)=\{\mathbf{R}_t^1,\mathbf{R}_t^2\}$. The belief of the IBB is then modeled by the sum of the likelihood scores of all subsets of $\{\mathbf{R}_t^1\}$, as follows:

$$bel(\mathbb{R}(\mathbf{X}_t^i))=p(\mathbf{Y}_t|R=\mathbf{R}_t^1). \tag{4}$$

The belief of the OBB is modeled by the sum of the likelihood scores of all subsets of $\{\mathbf{R}_t^1,\mathbf{R}_t^2\}$, as follows:

$$bel(\mathbb{R}(\mathbf{X}_t^o))=p(\mathbf{Y}_t|R=\mathbf{R}_t^1)+p(\mathbf{Y}_t|R=\mathbf{R}_t^2)+p(\mathbf{Y}_t|R=\{\mathbf{R}_t^1,\mathbf{R}_t^2\}). \tag{5}$$

Notably, the belief is the amount of belief that directly supports the bounding box at least in part, forming a lower bound [9].

The plausibility in (1) is sum of all the masses of subsets that intersect the set of interest. Thus the plausibility of the IBB is designed as the sum of the likelihood scores of all subsets of $\mathbf{U}_t$, which intersect $\mathbb{R}(\mathbf{X}_t^i) = \{\mathbf{R}_t^1\}$.

$$pl(\mathbb{R}(\mathbf{X}_t^i)) = p(\mathbf{Y}_t|R = \mathbf{R}_t^1) + p(\mathbf{Y}_t|R = \{\mathbf{R}_t^1, \mathbf{R}_t^2\}), \tag{6}$$

where $p(\mathbf{Y}_t|R = \mathbf{U}_t) = p(\mathbf{Y}_t|R = \{\mathbf{R}_t^1, \mathbf{R}_t^3\}) = 0$. Because $p(\mathbf{Y}_t|R = \{\mathbf{R}_t^1, \mathbf{R}_t^2\})$ is positive and, thus, $pl(\mathbb{R}(\mathbf{X}_t^i))$ in (6) is larger than $bel(\mathbb{R}(\mathbf{X}_t^i))$ in (4), the IBB satisfies (1): $bel(\mathbb{R}(\mathbf{X}_t^i)) \leq m(\mathbb{R}(\mathbf{X}_t^i)) \leq pl(\mathbb{R}(\mathbf{X}_t^i))$. The plausibility of the OBB is designed as the sum of the likelihood scores of all subsets of $\mathbf{U}_t$, which intersect $\mathbb{R}(\mathbf{X}_t^o) = \{\mathbf{R}_t^1, \mathbf{R}_t^2\}$.

$$\begin{aligned} pl(\mathbb{R}(\mathbf{X}_t^o)) &= p(\mathbf{Y}_t|R = \mathbf{R}_t^1) + p(\mathbf{Y}_t|R = \mathbf{R}_t^2) + p(\mathbf{Y}_t|R = \{\mathbf{R}_t^1, \mathbf{R}_t^2\}) \\ &\quad + p(\mathbf{Y}_t|R = \{\mathbf{R}_t^2, \mathbf{R}_t^3\}) = 1 - p(\mathbf{Y}_t|R = \mathbf{R}_t^3), \end{aligned} \tag{7}$$

where the last equality holds because of (3). Because $p(\mathbf{Y}_t|R = \{\mathbf{R}_t^2, \mathbf{R}_t^3\})$ is positive and, thus, $pl(\mathbb{R}(\mathbf{X}_t^o))$ in (7) is larger than $bel(\mathbb{R}(\mathbf{X}_t^o))$ in (5), the OBB satisfies (1): $bel(\mathbb{R}(\mathbf{X}_t^o)) \leq m(\mathbb{R}(\mathbf{X}_t^o)) \leq pl(\mathbb{R}(\mathbf{X}_t^o))$. Note that the plausibility forms an upper bound because there is only so much evidence which contradicts that bounding box [9].

Then, with (4),(6),(5), and (7), we obtain

$$\begin{aligned} bel(\mathbb{R}(\mathbf{X}_t^i)) \leq pl(\mathbb{R}(\mathbf{X}_t^i)) \leq bel(\mathbb{R}(\mathbf{X}_t^o)) \leq pl(\mathbb{R}(\mathbf{X}_t^o)), \\ bel(\mathbb{R}(\mathbf{X}_t^i)) \leq m(\mathbb{R}(\mathbf{X}_t^i)), m(\mathbb{R}(\mathbf{X}_t^o)) \leq pl(\mathbb{R}(\mathbf{X}_t^o)). \end{aligned} \tag{8}$$

In terms of the DS theory, the best bounding box has the largest belief and plausibility values. Thus, (8) is maximized to obtain the best IBB and OBB: $\max bel(\mathbb{R}(\mathbf{X}_t^i)) \leq \max m(\mathbb{R}(\mathbf{X}_t^i)), \max m(\mathbb{R}(\mathbf{X}_t^o)) \leq \max pl(\mathbb{R}(\mathbf{X}_t^o))$. Thereafter, the best IBB $\hat{\mathbf{X}}_t^i$ is obtained using (4):

$$\hat{\mathbf{X}}_t^i = \arg\max_{\mathbf{X}_t^i} bel(\mathbb{R}(\mathbf{X}_t^i)) = \arg\max_{\mathbf{X}_t^i} p(\mathbf{Y}_t|R = \mathbf{R}_t^1), \tag{9}$$

where the best IBB $\hat{\mathbf{X}}_t^i$ is determined by maximizing the similarity between the whole region inside the IBB, $\mathbf{R}_t^1$, and the target model M_t. Similarly, the best OBB $\hat{\mathbf{X}}_t^o$ is obtained using (7):

$$\hat{\mathbf{X}}_t^o = \arg\max_{\mathbf{X}_t^o} pl(\mathbb{R}(\mathbf{X}_t^o)) = \arg\max_{\mathbf{X}_t^o} \left[1 - p(\mathbf{Y}_t|R = \mathbf{R}_t^3)\right], \tag{10}$$

where the OBB $\hat{\mathbf{X}}_t^o$ is determined by maximizing the dissimilarity between the region outside of the OBB, $\mathbf{R}_t^3$, and the target model M_t.

4 Visual Tracker Using the Double Bounding Box

4.1 Constrained Maximum a Posteriori

As illustrated in Fig.2, our state $\mathbf{X}_t^{DBB} = (\mathbf{X}_t^i, \mathbf{X}_t^o)$ is represented as the combination of the sub-states of the IBB and OBB. $\mathbf{X}_t^i$ and $\mathbf{X}_t^o$ consist of a three-dimensional vector including the center coordinate and the scale of the IBB and

OBB, respectively. Thus, the cardinality of the final state $\mathbf{X}_t^{DBB}$ is 6. Then, the objective of our tracking problem is to find the best state $\hat{\mathbf{X}}_t^{DBB} = (\hat{\mathbf{X}}_t^i, \hat{\mathbf{X}}_t^o)$ that maximizes the posterior $p(\mathbf{X}_t^{DBB}|\mathbf{Y}_{1:t})$:

$$\hat{\mathbf{X}}_t^{DBB} = \arg\max_{\mathbf{X}_t^i, \mathbf{X}_t^o} p(\mathbf{X}_t^i, \mathbf{X}_t^o|\mathbf{Y}_{1:t}) \textit{ subject to } \mathbb{R}(\mathbf{X}_t^i) \subset \alpha\mathbb{R}(\mathbf{X}_t^o) \subset \beta\mathbb{R}(\mathbf{X}_t^i), \tag{11}$$

where $\alpha\mathbb{R}(\mathbf{X}_t^o)$ means that the width and height of the region $\mathbb{R}(\mathbf{X}_t^o)$ are multiplied by α. $\alpha > 1$ practically makes (11) to be easily solved by relaxing the strong constraint, $\alpha = 1$, although we get the approximated solution. Because $\alpha > 1$, a small part of the IBB can be located outside of the OBB in the experimental results. In (11), $p(\mathbf{X}_t^i, \mathbf{X}_t^o|\mathbf{Y}_{1:t})$ is reformulated by

$$\begin{aligned} p(\mathbf{X}_t^i, \mathbf{X}_t^o|\mathbf{Y}_{1:t}) \propto\, & p(\mathbf{Y}_t|\mathbf{X}_t^i)p(\mathbf{Y}_t|\mathbf{X}_t^o)\times \\ & \int p(\mathbf{X}_t^i, \mathbf{X}_t^o|\mathbf{X}_{t-1}^i, \mathbf{X}_{t-1}^o)p(\mathbf{X}_{t-1}^i, \mathbf{X}_{t-1}^o|\mathbf{Y}_{1:t-1})d\mathbf{X}_{t-1}, \end{aligned} \tag{12}$$

where $p(\mathbf{Y}_t|\mathbf{X}_t^i)$ is the likelihood of the IBB and $p(\mathbf{Y}_t|\mathbf{X}_t^o)$ is the likelihood of the OBB.

In (12), we design $p(\mathbf{Y}_t|\mathbf{X}_t^i)$ to measure the similarity between the region inside of the IBB, $\mathbf{R}_t^1$, and the target model, M_t, based on (2) and (9) derived from the DS theory:

$$p(\mathbf{Y}_t|\mathbf{X}_t^i) \equiv p(\mathbf{Y}_t|R = \mathbf{R}_t^1) = \frac{1}{c}e^{-dist\left(M_t, \mathbf{Y}_t(\mathbf{R}_t^1)\right)}, \tag{13}$$

where c is a normalization constant. We design $p(\mathbf{Y}_t|\mathbf{X}_t^o)$ to measure the dissimilarity between the region outside of the OBB, $\mathbf{R}_t^3$, and the target model, M_t, based on (2) and (10) derived from the DS theory:

$$p(\mathbf{Y}_t|\mathbf{X}_t^o) \equiv 1 - p(\mathbf{Y}_t|R = \mathbf{R}_t^3) = 1 - \frac{1}{c}e^{-dist\left(M_t, \mathbf{Y}_t(\mathbf{R}_t^3)\right)}. \tag{14}$$

Note that the target model, M_t, is updated over time by averaging the initial model with the most recent model.

In (12), the dynamical part, $p(\mathbf{X}_t^i, \mathbf{X}_t^o|\mathbf{X}_{t-1}^i, \mathbf{X}_{t-1}^o)$, is realized by proposal and constraint steps of the CMCMC, explained in the next section, where a new IBB(OBB) is proposed based on the previous OBB(IBB) and a new IBB is included by a new OBB.

The first constraint in (11) makes the region described by the OBB, $\mathbb{R}(\mathbf{X}_t^o)$, to include the region described by the IBB, $\mathbb{R}(\mathbf{X}_t^i)$, while the second constraint prevents the OBB from becoming infinitely large. Compared with MAP, our CMAP in (11) is more difficult because it should satisfy the aforementioned constraints. To obtain the best state, searching all states within the state space is impractical. Thus, our method adopts the MCMC sampling method [19], which produces N number of sampled states. Among the sampled states, the sampling method easily chooses the best one that maximizes the posterior probability in (11). We modify the MCMC sampling method to satisfy the aforementioned constraint and present a new CMCMC-based sampling method, which will be explained in the next section.

(a) Modification of the IBB (b) Modification of the OBB

Fig. 3. Example of the DBB constraint

4.2 Constrained Markov Chain Monte Carlo

The CMCMC-based sampling method defines a single Markov Chain and obtains samples over the chain. As we define two sub-states, $\mathbf{X}_t^i$ and $\mathbf{X}_t^o$, we get samples of the sub-states, alternately. For example, we get samples like $\mathbf{X}_t^{i(n-1)}$, $\mathbf{X}_t^{o(n)}$, $\mathbf{X}_t^{i(n+1)}$,..., where $\mathbf{X}_t^{o(n)}$ and $\mathbf{X}_t^{i(n+1)}$ are the n-th sample for the OBB and the *(n+1)*-th sample for the IBB, respectively.

• **Proposal Step of the IBB** First, the method obtains a sample of the IBB $\mathbf{X}_t^i$ by three main steps: the proposal, constraint, and acceptance steps. The proposal step suggests a new sample of the IBB as follows: a new center of the IBB, $c(\mathbf{X}_t^{i(n+1)})$, is proposed through the Gaussian function G (mean: current center of the OBB, $c(\mathbf{X}_t^{o(n)})$, variance: 0.5). A new scale of the IBB, $s(\mathbf{X}_t^{i(n+1)})$, is proposed through G (mean: current scale of the IBB, $s(\mathbf{X}_t^{i(n-1)})$, variance: 0.01).

• **Constraint Step of the IBB** To satisfy the constraint in (11), the bounding box of the proposed sample $\mathbf{X}_t^{i(n+1)}$ shifts to the bounding box of the sample $\mathbf{X}_t^{i(n+1)^*}$, where the shifted bounding box is included by the region $\alpha\mathbb{R}(\mathbf{X}_t^{o(n)})$, as shown in Fig.3(a): $\mathbb{R}(\mathbf{X}_t^{i(n+1)^*}) \subset \alpha\mathbb{R}(\mathbf{X}_t^{o(n)}) = \mathbb{R}(\mathbf{U}_t^{(n+1)})$, where $\mathbf{U}_t^{(n+1)}$ is the *(n+1)*-th universal set. The region $\alpha\mathbb{R}(\mathbf{X}_t^{o(n)})$ has the same center as $\mathbf{X}_t^{o(n)}$ and is α times the scale of $\mathbf{X}_t^{o(n)}$, where α is empirically set to 1.2.

• **Acceptance Step of the IBB** After the proposed step, the acceptance step determines whether the proposed sample $\mathbf{X}_t^{i(n+1)^*}$ is accepted or not with the probability, $\min\left[1, \frac{p(\mathbf{Y}_t|\mathbf{X}_t^{i(n+1)^*})}{p(\mathbf{Y}_t|\mathbf{X}_t^{i(n-1)})}\right]$, where $p(\mathbf{Y}_t|\mathbf{X}_t^{i(n+1)^*})$ and $p(\mathbf{Y}_t|\mathbf{X}_t^{i(n-1)})$ are the likelihoods of the proposed and current IBB, respectively. The likelihood of the IBB is defined in (13).

• **Proposal Step of the OBB** Our method then proposes a sample of the OBB $\mathbf{X}_t^o$ as follows: a new center of the OBB, $c(\mathbf{X}_t^{o(n+2)})$, is proposed through G (mean: current center of the IBB, $c(\mathbf{X}_t^{i(n+1)})$, variance: 0.5). A new scale of the OBB, $s(\mathbf{X}_t^{o(n+2)})$, is proposed through G (mean: current scale of the OBB, $s(\mathbf{X}_t^{o(n)})$, variance: 0.01).

• **Constraint Step of the OBB** To satisfy the constraint in (11), the bounding box of the proposed sample $\mathbf{X}_t^{o(n+2)}$ shifts to the bounding box of the sample $\mathbf{X}_t^{o(n+2)^*}$, where the shifted bounding box is included by the region $\beta\mathbb{R}(\mathbf{X}_t^{i(n+1)})$,

(a) IBB only (b) DBB (c) OBB only (d) DBB

Fig. 4. Performance of the DBB in *basketball* seq. which has abrupt motions and pose variations. The red and blue rectangles are the IBB and OBB, respectively.

as shown in Fig.3(b): $\mathbb{R}(\mathbf{X}_t^{o(n+2)^*}) \subset \beta\mathbb{R}(\mathbf{X}_t^{i(n+1)}) = \mathbb{R}(\mathbf{U}_t^{(n+2)})$, where $\mathbf{U}_t^{(n+2)}$ is the *(n+2)*-th universal set. The region $\beta\mathbb{R}(\mathbf{X}_t^{i(n+1)})$ has the same center as $\mathbf{X}_t^{i(n+1)}$ and is β times the scale of $\mathbf{X}_t^{i(n+1)}$, where β is empirically set to 5.0.

• **Acceptance Step of the OBB** After the proposal step, the method accepts the proposed sample $\mathbf{X}_t^{o(n+2)^*}$ with the probability, $\min\left[1, \frac{p(\mathbf{Y}_t|\mathbf{X}_t^{o(n+2)^*})}{p(\mathbf{Y}_t|\mathbf{X}_t^{o(n)})}\right]$, where $p(\mathbf{Y}_t|\mathbf{X}_t^{o(n+2)^*})$ and $p(\mathbf{Y}_t|\mathbf{X}_t^{o(n)})$ are the likelihoods of the proposed and current OBB, respectively. The likelihood of the OBB is defined in (14). These steps iteratively continue until the number of iterations reaches the predefined value.

5 Experimental Results

To initialize the proposed method (DBB), we manually draw the IBB and OBB at the first frame. The IBB and OBB could have different width/height proportion initially. However, the proportion is fixed for each bounding box during the tracking process. The number of samples was fixed to 1000 for all sampling-based methods, including our method. For all experiments, we used the fixed parameters. Our method approximately takes 0.1 sec per frame.

5.1 Analysis of the Proposed Method

Analysis of the DBB: The performance difference between the single bounding box representation and the DBB representation were examined. The experiments were performed under the same conditions, differing only in the types of bounding box representation. As shown in Fig.4, either the IBB alone or the OBB alone is prone to drift away from the target. Fig.4(a) shows that the IBB began to drift and to track the background region around the target, as the appearance of the target became severely deformed. Our method kept tracking the target because of the constraint provided by the OBB. Thus, the OBB serves as a weak constraint that gives an estimate of the position of the target to the IBB, as it began sampling from the position of the IBB of the previous frame. If the IBB includes some parts of the background, then it will have a tendency

Table 1. Comparison of tracking results using IMCMC and CMCMC. The numbers indicate the average center location errors in pixels. These numbers were obtained by running each algorithm five times and averaging the results.

	basketball	*lazysong*	*fx*	*diving*	*gymnastics*	*faceocc*	*twinings*	*singer1*	*skating2*	**Average**
IMCMC	209	42	44	56	109	21	18	84	56	**71.0**
CMCMC	36	17	25	16	16	6	6	12	28	**18.0**

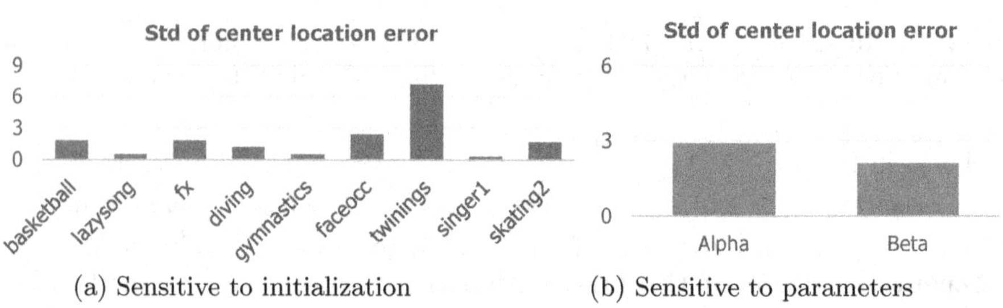

(a) Sensitive to initialization (b) Sensitive to parameters

Fig. 5. Stability of our method

to drift because it recognizes the background part as the target. However, in the DBB, the IBB is sampled at the estimated position from the OBB, pulling the IBB to the center of the target and reducing the possibility of drifting. The OBB can estimate the target position better than the IBB, owing to its large region, which makes the OBB robust to noise. Similarly, the IBB also helps the OBB. In Fig.4(c), the OBB drifted, despite being insensitive to noise. As in the previous case, the IBB complemented the OBB, as shown in Fig.4(d). The IBB usually has a higher probability of only including the target than the OBB. Thus, it also serves as a weak constraint, pulling the OBB to the target region.

Analysis of the CMCMC: The performances of the Interacting Markov Chain Monte Carlo (IMCMC) in [20] and CMCMC were also compared to demonstrate the superiority of the proposed CMCMC. The fundamental problem of IMCMC is that IMCMC has no mechanism to satisfy the constraint. Hence, we can't use IMCMC for our problem. Although we forcibly make IMCMC to satisfy the constraint, IMCMC is experimentally worse than CMCMC. For this experiment, IMCMC was applied to incorporate purposely the same capability of pulling one box to another, similar to CMCMC. IMCMC initially verifies the constraint in which the IBB must be inside the OBB. If this is verified, it separately samples each Markov Chain for each bounding box; otherwise, it provides an offset to one of the bounding boxes and probabilistically determines which one has to be adjusted. However, it cannot prevent itself from drifting away even if the two bounding boxes do satisfy the constraint. When the IBB begins to drift, it forces the OBB to drift as well because of the constraint, rendering the IBB even worse. As shown in Table 1, IMCMC cannot outperform CMCMC, because the probability that the IBB will pull the OBB toward it and the vulnerability of the IBB to noise are high.

Table 2. Quantitative comparison of tracking results with other methods. In this experiment, other tracking methods utilize the **IBB representation**. The numbers indicate the average center location errors in pixels and the amount of successfully tracked frames (score > 0.5), where the score is defined by the overlap ratio between the predicted bounding box B_p and the ground truth bounding box B_{gt}: $\frac{area(B_p \bigcap B_{gt})}{area(B_p \bigcup B_{gt})}$. The best result is shown in red and the second-best in blue. N/W means that a method does not work at the corresponding dataset. For our method, the mean of center positions and bounding boxes of the IBB and OBB are reported as the final tracking result.

	ABCShift	BHMC	BHT	MIL	IVT	VTD	VTS	MC	HT	LGT	TLD	DBB
basketball	80/33	80/34	63/40	133/22	50/49	58/42	**38**/65	110/26	197/18	160/20	178/18	36/65
lazysong	71/40	55/50	142/39	38/55	38/55	17/70	26/67	30/62	56/50	42/55	20/68	17/**69**
fx	59/49	73/39	69/41	56/49	46/54	33/65	**29/69**	144/19	70/41	126/21	30/65	25/70
diving	23/35	41/39	N/W	76/26	68/31	23/34	**16/46**	20/34	76/26	15/51	N/W	**16/46**
gymnastics	45/45	29/59	N/W	42/47	62/41	22/62	18/66	17/66	108/23	99/31	13/72	**16/68**
faceocc	29/70	50/50	N/W	36/69	61/44	21/75	20/**79**	20/78	34/70	**19**/78	25/72	6/88
twinings	18/76	5/91	34/67	15/80	17/77	9/87	8/87	14/81	31/68	22/75	15/80	**6/89**
tiger1	85/30	33/30	30/45	17/59	80/30	16/61	15/62	30/42	30/42	15/62	9/70	**13/65**
david	50/21	40/31	17/50	29/47	13/58	13/58	10/60	42/30	10/60	6/71	8/62	6/64
shaking	50/55	47/60	22/72	27/70	107/22	8/88	7/89	99/21	15/76	15/76	5/90	**6**/90
soccer	199/8	178/9	76/17	51/24	85/16	**22/33**	18/38	60/21	50/25	50/25	33/30	25/29
animal	44/34	42/35	25/75	29/60	19/80	**11/90**	17/80	28/75	20/77	30/55	20/79	8/92
skating1	99/29	98/29	57/60	80/52	150/13	**9/90**	12/88	133/22	129/22	99/24	19/75	6/93
singer1	51/54	24/71	51/54	17/80	13/83	8/90	13/83	22/72	5/95	5/95	14/83	12/83
skating2	56/46	57/45	N/W	93/19	80/22	**42/51**	43/50	68/39	97/19	74/26	99/18	28/67
Average	63/41	56/44	53/50	49/50	59/45	20/66	**19/68**	55/45	61/47	51/51	34/63	15/71

Analysis of the Parameters: Our method is less sensitive to the initialization of the IBB and OBB, as demonstrated in Fig.5(a). To get the standard deviation, we changed the initial center positions of the IBB and OBB by adding random noises, to a maximum of 5 pixels. Then, we obtained 10 center location errors from 10 different initialization settings.

We also tested the parameter sensitivity of α and β in (11). For this experiment, we obtained the standard deviation of center location errors of 10 tests. To make 10 tests, we added α and β with 10% noise. As shown in Fig.5(b), our method is not much sensitive to the parameter settings.

5.2 Comparison with Other Methods

The proposed method (DBB) was compared with 11 different state-of-the-art tracking methods [27,37]: ABCShift [36], MC [19], IVT [30], MIL [3], BHMC [22], BHT [26], HT [12], LGT [6], VTD [20], VTS [21], and TLD [18], where VTD and VTS are state-of-the-art trackers that use *color* information and BHMC, BHT, HT, and LGT are trackers that are designed especially for highly *non-rigid* targets. We tested 15 sequences[1].

[1] 12 sequences are publicly available. Only 3 sequences (*basketball*, *lazysong*, and *fx*) were made by us.

Table 3. Quantitative comparison of tracking results with other methods. In this experiment, other tracking methods utilize the **OBB representation**.

	ABCShift	BHMC	BHT	MIL	IVT	VTD	VTS	MC	HT	LGT	TLD	DBB
basketball	99/28	63/**40**	157/20	101/29	237/11	177/15	**62/40**	133/22	169/21	170/16	116/26	36/65
lazysong	60/45	74/43	115/27	48/53	43/55	**24/65**	29/61	94/31	137/22	71/45	34/57	17/69
fx	63/42	29/65	N/W	75/36	**27/69**	39/59	28/68	37/61	70/41	70/41	39/59	25/70
diving	26/31	**18/45**	74/25	88/19	91/16	70/27	98/14	29/39	83/20	29/49	84/20	16/46
gymnastics	20/64	7/87	N/W	22/60	27/51	**10/80**	92/35	76/40	102/25	98/31	74/41	16/68
faceocc	29/70	30/69	29/71	25/75	27/74	7/88	6/89	31/69	13/81	19/78	19/78	6/**88**
twinings	20/74	29/69	43/52	10/85	32/64	**7**/91	**7**/90	27/70	36/60	24/73	17/79	6/**89**
tiger1	85/30	34/39	21/58	16/60	90/29	17/59	15/60	32/41	40/39	16/60	10/69	**13/65**
david	38/37	30/34	15/50	29/47	13/58	11/60	10/60	39/33	9/62	5/72	7/64	**6/64**
shaking	38/79	50/60	20/85	37/77	130/20	7/87	**6/93**	100/21	12/79	12/79	5/94	**6**/90
soccer	71/13	150/11	43/24	43/24	104/16	**22/33**	17/39	49/26	55/22	49/26	33/30	25/29
animal	30/40	59/30	29/47	29/47	22/51	**13/88**	15/86	30/46	25/49	35/49	17/81	8/92
skating1	130/20	129/20	77/54	80/52	150/13	**11/88**	12/**88**	172/19	126/21	99/22	22/70	6/93
singer1	22/78	55/52	48/61	24/77	3/99	5/96	5/96	84/39	51/54	**4/98**	53/52	12/83
skating2	80/31	52/45	49/47	95/29	157/19	30/64	**29/66**	36/59	174/12	160/18	85/31	28/67
Average	54/45	53/47	55/47	48/51	76/43	30/**66**	**28**/65	64/41	73/40	57/50	41/56	15/71

For sufficient comparison, we used 2 different settings of the bounding box like Tables 2 and 3. Tables 2 and 3 show the quantitative evaluation of the tracking results. Our method always used the DBB representation whereas other methods used the inner and outer bounding box representations to produce results in Tables 2 and 3, respectively. These tracking results indicate that our method is robust to track deformable target objects, as the drifting problem is effectively resolved using the DBB representation. In terms of the center location error, our method outperformed the recent state-of-the-art tracking methods especially for highly non-rigid objects, which are BHMC, BHT, HT, and LGT. Our method was also better than the other tracking methods in terms of the sucess rate, because our method successfully tracked the targets to the last frame although it produces slightly inaccurate OBB. On the other hand, other tracking methods fail to track the target and drift into the background, which make the low success rate. The tracking results demonstrate that a single bounding box representation is not adequate to represent highly non-rigid objects. In addition, our method produced better results than color-based tracking methods (BHMC, VTD, VTS, and MC) because our method did not consider the ambiguous regions while calculating color histograms. Our method only calculates color histograms for the region inside the IBB and the region outside of the OBB. Notably, conventional tracking methods using a single bounding box yielded very different tracking results depending on the representation type of a single bounding box (i.e., IBB representation in Table 2 and OBB representation in Table 3). Conversely, our method does not depend on the representation type of a single bounding box because it uses both the IBB and OBB.

Fig.7(e) shows the tracking results in the *gymnastics* seq. In the sequence, VTD showed the best result, but its distance from the target became wider when the gymnast turned and changed her pose fast. Fig.6 shows the results

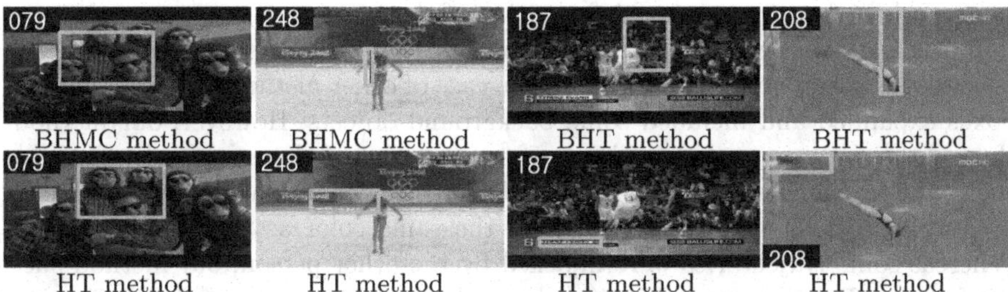

Fig. 6. Tracking results of the methods especially for highly non-rigid objects

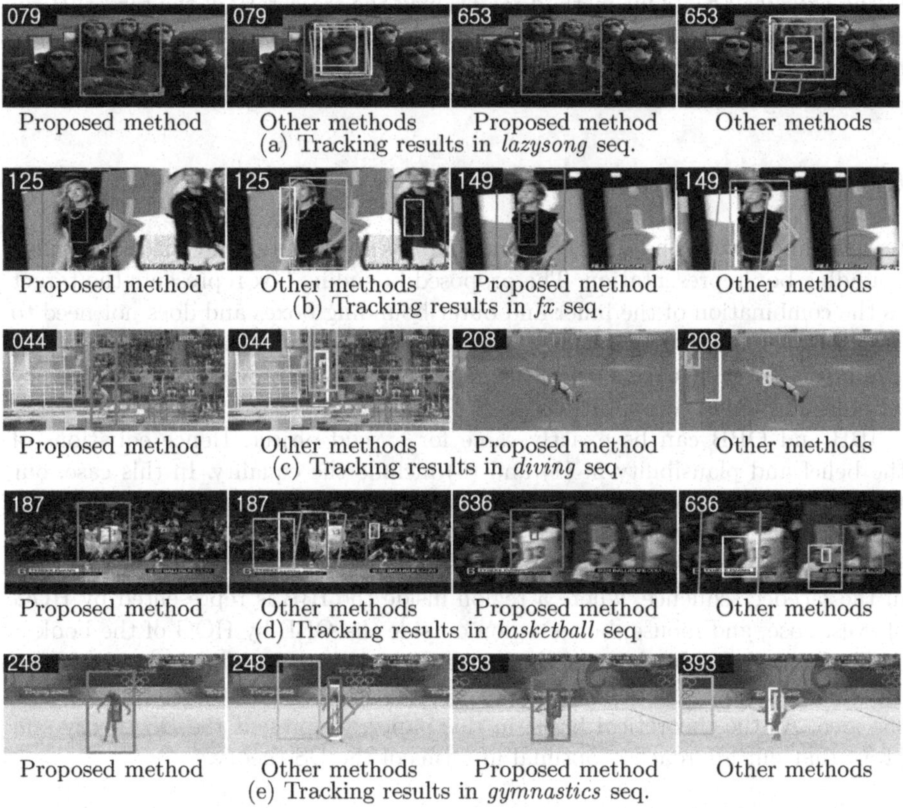

Proposed method | Other methods | Proposed method | Other methods

(a) Tracking results in *lazysong* seq.

Proposed method | Other methods | Proposed method | Other methods

(b) Tracking results in *fx* seq.

Proposed method | Other methods | Proposed method | Other methods

(c) Tracking results in *diving* seq.

Proposed method | Other methods | Proposed method | Other methods

(d) Tracking results in *basketball* seq.

Proposed method | Other methods | Proposed method | Other methods

(e) Tracking results in *gymnastics* seq.

Fig. 7. Qualitative comparison of the tracking results with other state-of-the-art tracking methods. The red and blue boxes give the results of the proposed method (Combination of the IBB and OBB). The yellow, white, orange, green, and pink boxes give the results of MCMC method using the IBB representation, VTD, VTS, IVT, and MIL using the OBB representation, respectively.

of BHMC, BHT, and HT, which are designed especially for highly non-rigid objects, and demonstrates that these methods also frequently failed to track the targets when there was severe deformation of the targets.

In Fig.7(a), the *lazysong* seq., which includes some objects similar in appearance to the target object, is tested. In the case of other methods, their bounding boxes expanded and included some background objects. However, our method showed the most accurate tracking performance among these methods. Fig.7(b) shows the tracking results of the *fx* seq. The target person was severely occluded by another person who wore clothes of the same color as that of the target. Whereas some trajectories were hijacked by the other person, our method successfully tracked the target. Fig.7(c) shows the tracking results of the *diving* seq. When the woman started spinning, our method continued to track the woman while the other methods failed to track it. Fig.7(d) shows the tracking results in the *basketball* seq. Our method maintained the trajectory of the target. However, the other methods experienced drifting problems, as they had a larger background part than the target part in their bounding boxes in frame #187 and frame #636.

6 Conclusion and Discussion

In this paper, we propose a new bounding box representation called the double bounding box representation. The proposed bounding box represents the target as the combination of the inner and outer bounding boxes and does not need to deal with the ambiguous regions, which include both the target and the background, at the same time. Hence, the method greatly improves tracking accuracy without additional computational cost.

IBB and OBB can be exactly same for a rigid object. Hence equations of the belief and plausibility in (1) and (8) include the equality. In this case, our tracking performance is similar to the single BB based tracking methods.

Although the color feature is applied to our method, other features can be also used in the method. For example, histogram of gradient (HOG) can be used in the faceocc sequence, where a region inside the IBB is represented by HOG of eyes, nose, and mouse, but a region outside the OBB by HOG of the book.

The basic idea behind our method is intuitive and can be implemented without any theories. However, there are few works that try to find a theoretical basis of the idea. As the theoretical basis, in this paper, we present the DS theory and prove that our approach is optimal in terms of the DS theory.

Acknowledgements. This work was partly supported by the ICT R&D program of MSIP/IITP, Korea [14-824-09-006, Novel Computer Vision and Machine Learning Technology with the Ability to Predict and Forecast] and the European Research Council (ERC) under the project VarCity (#273940). The authors gratefully acknowledge support by Toyota.

References

1. Adam, A., Rivlin, E., Shimshoni, I.: Robust fragments-based tracking using the integral histogram. In: CVPR (2006)
2. Avidan, S.: Ensemble tracking. PAMI 29(2), 261–271 (2007)
3. Babenko, B., Yang, M., Belongie, S.: Visual tracking with online multiple instance learning. In: CVPR (2009)
4. Bao, C., Wu, Y., Ling, H., Ji, H.: Real time robust l1 tracker using accelerated proximal gradient approach. In: CVPR (2012)
5. Birchfield, S.: Elliptical head tracking using intensity gradients and color histograms. In: CVPR (1998)
6. Cehovin, L., Kristan, M., Leonardis, A.: An adaptive coupled-layer visual model for robust visual tracking. In: ICCV (2011)
7. Collins, R.T., Liu, Y., Leordeanu, M.: Online selection of discriminative tracking features. PAMI 27(10), 1631–1643 (2005)
8. Comaniciu, D., Ramesh, V., Meer, P.: Real-time tracking of non-rigid objects using mean shift. In: CVPR (2000)
9. Dempster, A.P.: Upper and lower probabilities induced by a multivalued mapping. Ann. Math. Statist. 38(2), 325–339 (1967)
10. Faux, F., Luthon, F.: Robust face tracking using colour dempster-shafer fusion and particle filter. In: FUSION (2006)
11. Glenn, S.: A mathematical theory of evidence. Princeton University Press (1976)
12. Godec, M., Roth, P.M., Bischof, H.: Hough-based tracking of non-rigid objects. In: ICCV (2011)
13. Han, B., Davis, L.: On-line density-based appearance modeling for object tracking. In: ICCV (2005)
14. Hare, S., Saffari, A., Torr, P.H.S.: Struck: Structured output tracking with kernels. In: ICCV (2011)
15. Isard, M., Blake, A.: ICONDENSATION: Unifying low-level and high-level tracking in a stochastic framework. In: Burkhardt, H.-J., Neumann, B. (eds.) ECCV 1998. LNCS, vol. 1406, pp. 893–908. Springer, Heidelberg (1998)
16. Jepson, A.D., Fleet, D.J., Maraghi, T.F.E.: Robust online appearance models for visual tracking. PAMI 25(10), 1296–1311 (2003)
17. Jia, X., Lu, H., Yang, M.H.: Visual tracking via adaptive structural local sparse appearance model. In: CVPR (2012)
18. Kalal, Z., Mikolajczyk, K., Matas, J.: Tracking-learning-detection. PAMI 34(7), 1409–1422 (2012)
19. Khan, Z., Balch, T., Dellaert, F.: MCMC-based particle filtering for tracking a variable number of interacting targets. PAMI 27(11), 1805–1918 (2005)
20. Kwon, J., Lee, K.M.: Visual tracking decomposition. In: CVPR (2010)
21. Kwon, J., Lee, K.M.: Tracking by sampling trackers. In: ICCV (2011)
22. Kwon, J., Lee, K.M.: Tracking of a non-rigid object via patch-based dynamic appearance modeling and adaptive basin hopping monte carlo sampling. In: CVPR (2009)
23. Li, X., Dick, A., Shen, C., Zhang, Z., van den Hengel, A., Wang, H.: Visual tracking with spatio-temporal dempstershafer information fusion. TIP (2013)
24. Mei, X., Ling, H.: Robust visual tracking using l1 minimization. In: ICCV (2009)
25. Munoz-Salinas, R., Medina-Carnicer, R., Madrid-Cuevas, F., Carmona-Poyato, A.: Multi-camera people tracking using evidential filters. Ann. Math. Statist. 50, 732–749 (2009)

26. Nejhum, S.M.S., Ho, J., Yang, M.H.: Visual tracking with histograms and articulating blocks. In: CVPR (2008)
27. Pang, Y., Ling, H.: Finding the best from the second bests- inhibiting subjective bias in evaluation of visual tracking algorithms. In: ICCV (2013)
28. Pérez, P., Hue, C., Vermaak, J., Gangnet, M.: Color-based probabilistic tracking. In: Heyden, A., Sparr, G., Nielsen, M., Johansen, P. (eds.) ECCV 2002, Part I. LNCS, vol. 2350, pp. 661–675. Springer, Heidelberg (2002)
29. Ramanan, D., Forsyth, D., Zisserman, A.: Tracking people by learning their appearance. PAMI 29(1), 65–81 (2007)
30. Ross, D.A., Lim, J., Lin, R., Yang, M.: Incremental learning for robust visual tracking. IJCV 77(1), 125–141 (2008)
31. Santner, J., Leistner, C., Saffari, A., Pock, T., Bischof, H.: Prost: Parallel robust online simple tracking. In: CVPR (2010)
32. Sevilla-Lara, L., Learned-Miller, E.: Distribution fields for tracking. In: CVPR (2012)
33. Smith, K., Gatica-Perez, D., Odobez, J.M.: Using particles to track varying numbers of interacting people. In: CVPR (2005)
34. Stalder, S., Grabner, H., Van Gool, L.: Cascaded confidence filtering for improved tracking-by-detection. In: Daniilidis, K., Maragos, P., Paragios, N. (eds.) ECCV 2010, Part I. LNCS, vol. 6311, pp. 369–382. Springer, Heidelberg (2010)
35. Stenger, B., Woodley, T., Cipolla, R.: Learning to track with multiple observers. In: CVPR (2009)
36. Stolkin, R., Florescu, I., Baron, M., Harrier, C., Kocherov, B.: Efficient visual servoing with the abcshift tracking algorithm. In: ICRA (2008)
37. Wu, Y., Lim, J., Yang, M.H.: Online object tracking: A benchmark. In: CVPR (2013)
38. Yilmaz, A., Javed, O., Shah, M.: Object tracking: A survey. ACM Comput. Surv. 38(4) (2006)

Tractable and Reliable Registration of 2D Point Sets

Erik Ask[1], Olof Enqvist[2], Linus Svärm[1], Fredrik Kahl[1,2], and Giuseppe Lippolis[3]

[1] Centre for Mathematical Sciences, Lund University, Lund, Sweden
[2] Department of Signals and Systems, Chalmers University of Technology, Gothenburg, Sweden
[3] Department of Clinical Sciences, Division of Urological Cancers, Skåne University Hospital, Lund University, Malmö, Sweden

Abstract. This paper introduces two new methods of registering 2D point sets over rigid transformations when the registration error is based on a robust loss function. In contrast to previous work, our methods are guaranteed to compute the optimal transformation, and at the same time, the worst-case running times are bounded by a low-degree polynomial in the number of correspondences. In practical terms, this means that there is no need to resort to ad-hoc procedures such as random sampling or local descent methods that cannot guarantee the quality of their solutions.

We have tested the methods in several different settings, in particular, a thorough evaluation on two benchmarks of microscopic images used for histologic analysis of prostate cancer has been performed. Compared to the state-of-the-art, our results show that the methods are both tractable and reliable despite the presence of a significant amount of outliers.

1 Introduction

Image registration is a classical problem in computer vision and it appears as a subroutine for many imaging tasks. For example, it is a prerequisite for shape analysis and modeling [6] and for automated analysis of multi-modal microscopy images [17]. It is also an important component in image guided surgery where often fiducial markers are used for estimating the transformation [14,7]. In this paper, we are interested in estimating rigid image transformations under less controlled situations where there may be a substantial number of mismatches and where it is important to obtain reliable results. For example, the method should not be dependent on a good initialization.

Naturally, the registration problem has been studied in depth. When choosing the method of preference, one is often faced with the following dilemma. Using a simplified, mathematical model of the problem enables efficient computations, but sacrifices realism. While using a more realistic model incurs the computational cost of hard inference. As an example, consider the case of feature-based registration under the assumption that measurement noise in the target image can be modeled by independently distributed Gaussian noise. This is in fact the standard Procrustes problem which can be solved in closed form. However, the model is not so realistic as there are typically erroneous measurements - *outliers* - among the feature correspondences. This makes the registration estimates very unreliable. On the other hand, modeling outliers leads

D. Fleet et al. (Eds.): ECCV 2014, Part I, LNCS 8689, pp. 393–406, 2014.
© Springer International Publishing Switzerland 2014

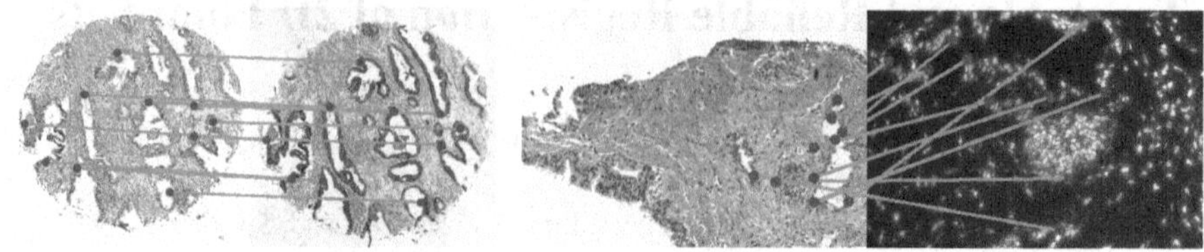

Fig. 1. Examples from our two benchmarks with 10 manually marked correspondences. *Left:* Prostate tissue stained with H&E and p63/AMACR. *Right:* Prostate tissue stained H&E and TRF (fluorescent). The goal is to find a rigid transformation that aligns the two images using features from an automated method such as SIFT.

to a much more complicated optimization problem and solving this problem exactly is sometimes dismissed as infeasible. Heuristic methods based on random sampling and expectation maximization dominate the field. We show that one can achieve a method which is both efficient (in terms of speed) and reliable (with respect to outliers).

Our own interests stem from the study of automated methods in medical imaging. In particular, we seek to develop robust registration procedures for combining information from different sources and modalities. The images may be degraded and have limited/varying fields of view. We present experimental results from two different applications. In our first setting, the objective is to perform histologic analysis of biopsies. Prostate cancer is the second most common cancer in men worldwide [16] and whose gold standard of diagnosis and prognosis is based on histologic assessment of tumours in images stained with Hematoxylin and Eosin (H&E). Several automatic pattern recognition prototypes exist [20,8]. In order to improve the accuracy in clinical practice, considerable research efforts have been directed to complement the analysis with additional types of stainings and imaging modalities [17]. One example is given in the left of Fig. 1 where two adjacent tissue sections have been stained with H&E and antibodies directed against p63/AMACR, respectively. Another example is given in the right of Fig. 1 with one H&E staining and one Time Resolved Fluorescence (TRF) image measuring the Androgen Receptor (AR) obtained from the same section. This type of images is quite challenging for any automated approach because reliable feature correspondences are hard to obtain and there are image degradations due to imperfect acquisition.

In our second setting, we are dealing with images of the human brain and the goal is to study the perfusion of blood flow through small vessels, so-called capillaries in the white and gray matter regions of the brain. This is important for patients with hydrocephalus which are treated by placing a drainage tube (shunt) between the brain ventricles and the abdominal cavity to eliminate the high intracranial pressure, see `wikipedia/hydrocephalus` [24]. To capture the anatomy of the region of interest, MR-Flair images have been obtained. The perfusion data is obtained via contrast-enhanced CT images taken at one second apart during a two-minute session. To acquire good temporal resolution, only a couple of slices can be captured at each time instant. The challenge here is to register single slices from the CT image to the full 3D volume of the MR image. As the head of the patient is in an upright position, the mapping from one CT slice to the corresponding (but unknown) slice in the MR-Flair volume is well described by a rigid 2D transformation after having adjusted for known scale differences.

In this paper, we develop two new robust methods for feature-based image registration based on the L_1-norm of the residual functions. As we shall see, from a statistical point of view, this model is well-suited for dealing with outliers. The methods are compared and extensively evaluated on two benchmarks of prostate tissue samples. The focus of our evaluation is on two important desiderata that a satisfactory solution should possess, namely *tractability* and *reliability*. The first term refers to the computational complexity. We investigate both the performance in practice and derive theoretical complexity bounds as a function of the number of feature correspondences. The second one concerns the reliability of the estimate. We are interested in methods that produce provably optimal estimates under a robust loss function. If the registration fails, then it can either due to lack of good correspondences or the algorithm's inability to find a good solution. In our approach, the latter source of error is removed from the process.

Our main contributions can be summarized as follows.

- Two new registration methods based on the L_1-norm and the truncated L_1-norm with worst-case complexity $\mathcal{O}(n^3)$ and $\mathcal{O}(n^3 \log(n))$, respectively, where n is the number of correspondences[1].
- An extensive experimental evaluation and comparison with other registration methods on benchmarks with 88 and 103 image pairs, respectively.

Note that the set of algorithms we propose is restricted to rigid point set registration in the plane, and other settings are not considered in this paper.

2 Related Work

Closed form solutions to the standard Procrustes alignment problem have been known for a long time [15] and used in various settings, for instance, in surface alignment [3]. However, as the estimate is based on least-squares (minimum of L_2-errors), outliers will have a large influence and that makes the approach unreliable. Already in [21], it is emphasized that robustness is a key issue and a multi-scale approach is proposed that integrates local measures to obtain an estimate of a rigid transformation. The method is applied to the problem of registering serial histological sections. In [19], a probabilistic method is developed that explicitly models outliers and which regards the registration problem as an inference problem. Inference is performed via expectation-maximization. The method in [13] proposes to use the Huber kernel as a residual function to make the registration less sensitive to outliers. Levenberg-Marquardt iterations are performed in order to minimize the loss function. In [22] deterministic annealing is proposed in order to optimize a robust loss function for the registration of autoradiograph slices. Yet another example is [9], where meta-heuristics is applied for the optimization step of the registration of angiograms. See also the registration survey [2]. All of these local optimization techniques are dependent on a good initial estimate and they are susceptible to local optima. Hence, they cannot guarantee the quality of their solutions.

Another popular approach for dealing with outliers is RANSAC [12]. It works by hypothesize-and-test: Pick a random minimal subset of correspondences, compute a

[1] The algorithms will be made publicly available to promote further research.

hypothetical transformation and check how many of the other correspondences are consistent with this transformation. The method is by nature random (which can be remedied by exhaustively examining all possible subsets). Still, the estimator has no guarantee of finding the optimal solution which makes the method unreliable. This will be empirically demonstrated in our evaluation.

Several works have focused on optimal estimators based on branch-and-bound. One of the first algorithms was developed in [5] and it finds the rigid transformation that maximizes the number of inliers. In [11], a robust estimator based on a vertex cover formulation is proposed and in [18], a formulation based on integer programming is given. The methods are independent of initialization and converge to a global optimum. However, as they are based on branch-and-bound, the computational complexity of the algorithm is exponential. The most closely related work to ours is [10,1], where a truncated L_2-norm algorithm is derived with complexity $\mathcal{O}(n^4)$. However, the runtime tends to be prohibitive (see experimental section), making it a less tractable alternative.

3 Choice of Loss Function

It is a common and reasonable assumption that there exist *correct* but noisy point correspondences as well as complete mismatches or outliers. The errors in the positioning of correct correspondences follow approximately a normal distribution, whereas the outliers are uniformly spread over the image. In [4] it is shown that in order to find a maximum likelihood estimate, a sum of loss functions of the following type

$$\ell(r) = -\log\left(c_1 + \exp\left(-r^2/c_2\right)\right) \tag{1}$$

should be minimized, where r is the residual error for one correspondence and the constants depend on the amount of inlier noise as well as on the rate of outliers; see Fig. 2. An approximation which is commonly used is obtained by truncating the squared error. However, the quality of this approximation depends heavily on the rate of outliers in data. At higher rates the loss function levels out much more slowly. In this case a truncated L_1-loss can be a more appropriate choice.

All these loss functions lead to a non-convex problem with many local minima. One may even wrongly conclude that the problem is intractable to solve optimally, that is, that no polynomial-time algorithm exists.

4 Fast Optimization of the Truncated L_1-Norm

Given corresponding point coordinates in two images, $\mathbf{x}_i = (x_i, y_i)^T$ and $\mathbf{x}'_i = (x'_i, y'_i)^T$, $i = 1, \ldots, n$, consider the following problem

$$\min_{R,\mathbf{t}} \sum_{i=1}^{n} \ell(||R\mathbf{x}_i + \mathbf{t} - \mathbf{x}'_i||_1) \tag{2}$$

where R is a 2×2 rotation matrix and $\mathbf{t}$ a translation vector, parameterized as

$$R(\alpha) = \begin{bmatrix} \cos\alpha & -\sin\alpha \\ \sin\alpha & \cos\alpha \end{bmatrix} \text{ and } \mathbf{t} = \begin{bmatrix} t_1 \\ t_2 \end{bmatrix},$$

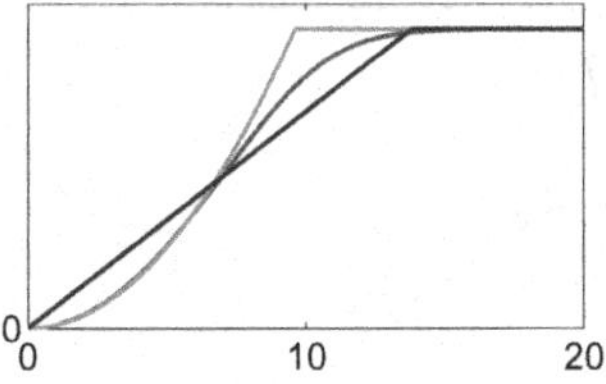

Fig. 2. The robust loss function (red) suggested in [4], the truncated L_2-error (green) and the truncated L_1-error (blue) that can be optimized using the proposed framework

respectively and where ℓ is the loss function $\ell(r) = \min\{r, \epsilon\}$ for some given threshold ϵ, that is, the truncated L_1-norm.

The following observation allows us to simplify the problem.

Lemma 1. *For any fixed rotation R, consider the minimization of (2) over* $\mathbf{t}$

$$\min_{\mathbf{t}} \sum_{i=1}^{n} l\left(|x_i \cos\alpha - y_i \sin\alpha + t_1 - x_i'| + |x_i \sin\alpha + y_i \cos\alpha + t_2 - y_i'|\right). \quad (3)$$

Then there exist two indices j and k in $\{1, \ldots, n\}$ such that

$$t_1^* = x_j' - x_j \cos\alpha + y_j \sin\alpha \text{ and } t_2^* = y_k' - x_k \sin\alpha - y_k \cos\alpha \quad (4)$$

is an optimal choice of $\mathbf{t}$.

In order to get a geometric intuition why the above lemma is true, consider the graph of the loss function in (3). Note that it is piecewise linear in $\mathbf{t}$ and a global minimum can be found by examining all break points, that is, points which are non-differentiable in all directions. There are two different causes for non-differentiability in our objective function. One is due to truncation and one is due to taking absolute values. Our proof shows that break points that are also local minima are given by (4). This means that break points caused by truncation need not be examined since all local minima are due to taking absolute values.

Proof. The optimal $\mathbf{t}^*$ to the truncated L_1-loss, denoted $L(\mathbf{t}^*)$, is also a global minimizer to the L_1-loss on the set of optimal inlier correspondences (those that have residuals less than ϵ). To see this, let $L_{inliers}(\mathbf{t}^*)$ be the optimal loss on the inliers and $L_{outliers}(\mathbf{t}^*)$ the loss on the outliers. Assume that there exists a different solution $\mathbf{t}$ with $L_{inliers}(\mathbf{t}) < L_{inliers}(\mathbf{t}^*)$. Clearly, $L_{outliers}(\mathbf{t}) \leq L_{outliers}(\mathbf{t}^*)$ as this is already maximal. Hence $L(\mathbf{t}) = L_{inliers}(\mathbf{t}) + L_{outliers}(\mathbf{t}) < L_{inliers}(\mathbf{t}^*) + L_{outliers}(\mathbf{t}^*) = L(\mathbf{t}^*)$ which is a contradiction.

This shows that an optimal $\mathbf{t}^*$ is a local optimum to the L_1-loss. The formula for the L_1-loss is given by

$$\sum_{i=1}^{n} |x_i \cos\alpha - y_i \sin\alpha + t_1 - x_i'| + |x_i \sin\alpha + y_i \cos\alpha + t_2 - y_i'|.$$

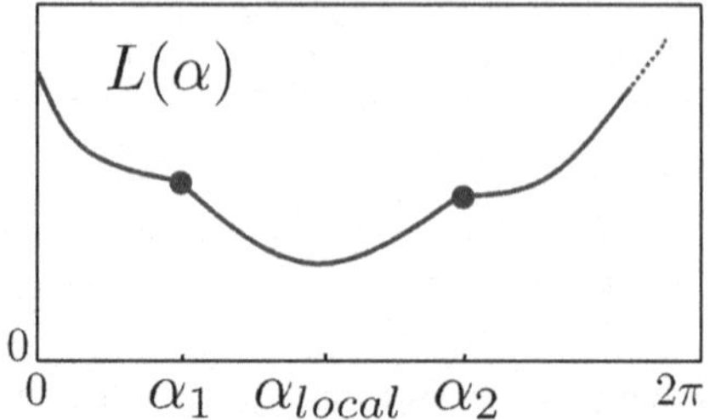

Fig. 3. Sketch of the objective function in (5), denoted $L(\alpha)$, which is piecewise smooth

As no absolute value contains both t_1 and t_2 we can write this as a function of t_1 plus a function of t_2 and the minimization with respect to t_1 and t_2 can be analyzed separately. Consider the t_1-part. We have a piecewise linear function that tends to infinity as $|t_1|$ tends to infinity and thus a minimizer of this function is at a break point. The break points are due to the absolute values - there is a break point whenever one of the absolute values is exactly zero. Hence a minimizer exists for which at least one absolute value is zero, so $t_1^* = x'_j - x_j \cos\alpha + y_j \sin\alpha$ for some j as stated in the lemma. The same argument for t_2 proves the lemma. □

The lemma shows that if the two indices j and k are given (for example, by exhaustively trying all possibilities), we can reduce the problem via substitution of $\mathbf{t}^*$ in (4) to a one-dimensional search over rotation angle α,

$$\min_{\alpha} \sum_{i=1}^{n} \ell(|\delta x_{ij} \cos\alpha - \delta y_{ij} \sin\alpha - \delta x'_{ij}| + |\delta x_{ik} \sin\alpha + \delta y_{ik} \cos\alpha - \delta y'_{ik}|), \quad (5)$$

where $\delta x_{ij} = x_i - x_j$, $\delta y_{ij} = y_i - y_j$, etc. Let us denote the resulting, piecewise smooth objective function in (5) by $L(\alpha)$, see Fig. 3 for an illustration. It has optimum either at a break point or at a stationary point. The break points are places where the derivative $L'(\alpha)$ is discontinuous and occur when an absolute value is exactly zero or the number in an input to ℓ is exactly ϵ. Hence the number of break points grows linearly with n. Given the break points $\alpha_1, \alpha_2, \ldots, \alpha_M$, consider an interval $[\alpha_i, \alpha_{i+1}]$ of $L(\alpha)$. It can be described by

$$L(\alpha) = w_1 \cos\alpha + w_2 \sin\alpha + w_3, \quad (6)$$

for some constants w_1, w_2 and w_3. By examining all intervals, we can compute the optimal rotation angle α^* using Algorithm 1.

4.1 Complexity

There are two important things to note here. First, that each time we compute w_1, w_2 and w_3 for $[\alpha_i, \alpha_{i+1}]$ in (6), we can take advantage of the constants from the previous interval $[\alpha_{i-1}, \alpha_i]$. Only the coordinates $\mathbf{x}_i$ and $\mathbf{x}'_i$ that gave rise to α_i are required for computing the update. Second, that there is only one local minimum to

$$w_1 \cos\alpha + w_2 \sin\alpha + w_3,$$

Algorithm 1. Finding the rotation angle

Set $L^* := \infty$.
Compute all break points of $L(\alpha)$ for $\alpha \in [0, 2\pi)$.
Sort the break points $\alpha_1, \alpha_2, \ldots, \alpha_M$.
for $i = 1, \ldots, M$
    Compute $L(\alpha_i)$ and compare with L^*.
    Compute w_1, w_2 and w_3 of (6) for $[\alpha_i, \alpha_{i+1}]$.
    Compute local minimum α_{local} of (6).
    if $\alpha_{local} \in [\alpha_i, \alpha_{i+1}]$,
        compute $L(\alpha_{local})$
        compare with L^*.

being

$$(\cos\alpha, \sin\alpha) = \pm(w_1, w_2)/\sqrt{w_1^2 + w_2^2}, \tag{7}$$

given by the minus sign. Hence each step in the for-loop of Algorithm 1 is $\mathcal{O}(1)$ so the computationally heaviest step is the sorting. Given the indices j and k, we can find an optimal α^* in $\mathcal{O}(n \log n)$. If we consider all possible index pairs j and k exhaustively, the total complexity is $\mathcal{O}(n^3 \log n)$. Note that the most complex arithmetic operations in the algorithm consists of computing square roots.

4.2 Fast Outlier Rejection

To increase the speed even more we propose a fast outlier rejection step as preprocessing, inspired by the work in [1]. For this we need a variant of Algorithm 1 that works with the zero-one loss (denoted by L_0), that is, counting the number of outliers rather than truncated L_1-norm. First note that the zero-one loss has the same break points as truncated L_1 and that the loss function only changes values at these break points. There, it either increases with one or decreases with one. Algorithm 2 lists the details.

Algorithm 2. Upper bound on inliers

Initialize best loss, $L_0^* = \infty$.
Compute all break points of $L_0(\alpha)$ for $\alpha \in [0, 2\pi)$.
Sort the break points $\alpha_1, \alpha_2, \ldots, \alpha_M$.
Compute $L_0(\alpha_1)$ and update L_0^*.
for $i = 2, \ldots, M$
    Depending on the type of α_i
    Set $L(\alpha_i) = L(\alpha_{i-1}) \pm 1$ and update L_0^*.

We will use this algorithm together with the following observation.

- Assume that for the optimal transformation $(R^*, \mathbf{t}^*)$, correspondence k is an inlier and there are N outliers, i.e. residuals larger than ϵ. If we change the translation to t so that $r_k(R^*, \mathbf{t}) = 0$, then, since $||\mathbf{t} - \mathbf{t}^*|| \leq \epsilon$, the error on inliers has increased with at most ϵ so there are at most N residuals larger than 2ϵ.

This means that we can use Algorithm 2 with threshold 2ϵ to produce a bound of the following kind: *If correspondence k is an inlier, then there are at least N outliers.* This also yields a bound on the truncated L_1 loss, as if N residuals are $> \epsilon$, then the truncated L_1 loss is at least $N\epsilon$. If this is a higher loss than one we have already found, we can discard correspondence k from further consideration.

Algorithm 3. Fast Outlier Rejection

Given an upper bound L_c on the optimal loss.
for $i = 1, \ldots, n$
  Set $\mathbf{t} = \mathbf{x}'_i - \mathbf{x}_i$
  Use Algorithm 2 with threshold 2ϵ to compute L_0^*
  (The output L_0^* is a bound on the number of outliers)
  if $L_0^*\epsilon > L_c$,
    discard correspondence i

A value for L_c can be found by running Algorithm 3 using ϵ in place of 2ϵ and simply storing the best loss function value rather than discarding points. As the dominating cost inside the loop is the sorting in Algorithm 2 running this scheme to remove outliers costs only $\mathcal{O}(n^2 \log n)$ and can be used as a preprocessing step while keeping guaranteed optimality.

5 Fast Optimization of the L_1-Norm

Optimizing the L_1-norm is a simpler problem compared to the truncated case. In fact, one can set $\epsilon := \infty$ and use the same algorithm, but we can do better. Lemma 1 still applies, so we can eliminate the translation and only consider the rotation problem, which simplifies to

$$\min_{\alpha} \sum_{i=1}^{n} |\delta x_{ij} \cos\alpha - \delta y_{ij} \sin\alpha - \delta x'_{ij}| + |\delta x_{ik} \sin\alpha + \delta y_{ik} \cos\alpha - \delta y'_{ik}|. \quad (8)$$

An important difference here is that we can compute the break points for the first term and the second term *independently*. This means that we can precompute and sort all the break points for $j, k = 1, \ldots, n$ in $\mathcal{O}(n^2 \log(n))$ and then use the for-loop of Algorithm 1 to find the optimal α^*. Now, the heaviest part is no longer the sorting. The total time complexity is $\mathcal{O}(n^3)$ since the for-loop is $\mathcal{O}(n)$ and exhaustively trying all combinations of j and k is $\mathcal{O}(n^2)$.

6 Experiments

The proposed methods have been evaluated on two challenging registration tasks.

6.1 Registering Histology Sections

The first set of experiments is concerned with the registration of histology sections of prostate tissue, and also serves as a quantitative evaluation. We used one dataset with 88 image pairs of adjacent slides of prostate tissue, stained using H&E and p63/AMACR, respectively. Another dataset consists of 103 images of H&E stained slides, in which sub-parts are also analyzed with TRF. Examples can be seen in Fig. 1. The size of the stained images are on the order of 1100x1100, while the TRF images are 368x546.

We used SIFT features as the basis of our point-to-point correspondences. Matching was restricted to the same scale octave and we used Lowe's ratio criterion with a threshold at 0.9 to discard poor matches. This yielded 800-1500 matches for the first dataset, and, due to TRF images being smaller, 40-500 matches in the second dataset. The inlier rate varies from 1% to 40% with a 10% average for the H&E-p63/AMACR set and from 4% to 54% for the H&E-TRF set with a 28% average.

The proposed algorithms were compared to the algorithm for truncated L_2-norm from [1] as well as standard L_2-minimization and RANSAC followed by L_2-minimization on the inlier set. For each problem instance, 10 correspondences were manually picked by an expert and used to compute an optimal transformation under the L_2-loss. Reported results are compared to the rotation and the translation of this estimate. We have also selected two failure criteria based on these comparisons. The first being that the rotation error is larger than 5°, the second that the translation error is larger than 25 pixels. The percentage of results that fail according to these criteria are presented.

Table 1. The results for the H&E - p63/AMACR benchmark. In the left column, the inlier threshold ϵ is varied. Then, for each of the methods (RANSAC with varying number of iterations, and the truncated L_1- and L_2-norms), three numbers are reported: average rotation error (degrees), average translation error (pixels) and failure rate. A failure case is one with error in rotation larger than 5° or in translation larger than 25 pixels. When $\epsilon = \infty$, no truncation takes place.

ϵ	RANSAC 100 iter.			RANSAC 500 iter.			RANSAC 1000 iter.			Truncated norms L_1			Truncated norms L_2		
1p	10.7°	204p	48%	8.38°	221p	27%	8.14°	105p	28%	2.72°	61p	11%	2.47°	58p	8%
5p	14.4°	280p	42%	2.85°	53p	9%	1.94°	28p	5%	1.21°	7p	3%	0.43°	6.4p	2%
10p	7.80°	158p	28%	1.23°	42p	6%	2.24°	43p	6%	0.29°	4.8p	1%	0.28°	4.6p	1%
20p	3.96°	78p	18%	2.43°	34p	8%	0.91°	23p	3%	0.27°	4.0p	0%	0.26°	3.9p	0%
∞		-			-			-		2.43°	6.5p	5%	6.54°	94p	69%

The experimental results on H&E-p63/AMACR are shown in Table 1. The most accurate results are obtained by the truncated L_2-method. Truncated L_1-norm performs poorly on the lowest threshold, but at more reasonable levels for this task performance is similar to truncated L_2. None of the methods based on RANSAC succeeds on all examples, although the accuracy is good at higher thresholds with 1000 iterations. We also note that regular L_1-norm (marked ∞) succeeds much more frequently than L_2-norm and with better accuracy than a majority of the RANSAC variants—on a dataset with only 10% inliers on average. For the highest threshold level (20p), we have also performed a test exhaustively trying all possible hypotheses ransac migth get. The accuracy is slightly worse but comparable to the L_1- and L_2- truncated methods. However, as the time complexity is $\mathcal{O}(n^3)$, close to the complexity of truncated L_1 with more expensive operations and no fast rejection method, it is in practice as slow or slower as the L_1- method while having no theoretical guarantees.

Table 2. The results for the H&E - TRF benchmark. See Table 1 for explanation.

ϵ	RANSAC 100 iter.			RANSAC 500 iter.			RANSAC 1000 iter.			Truncated norms L_1			Truncated norms L_2		
1p	2.53°	30.6p	6%	0.40°	6.2p	1%	0.31°	2.7p	0%	0.34°	2.9p	0%	0.31°	2.6p	0%
2p	2.27°	31.2p	5%	0.29°	2.6p	0%	0.27°	2.7p	1%	0.29°	2.6p	0%	0.28°	2.6p	0%
3p	1.75°	23.4p	4%	0.29°	2.7p	0%	0.29°	2.7p	0%	0.28°	2.6p	0%	0.28°	2.6p	0%
4p	0.66°	8.5p	3%	0.28°	2.6p	0%	0.28°	2.6p	0%	0.28°	2.6p	0%	0.27°	2.6p	0%
5p	1.14°	7.4p	2%	0.26°	2.5p	0%	0.26°	2.5p	0%	0.27°	2.5p	0%	0.26°	2.6p	0%
10p	0.76°	7.8p	1%	0.27°	2.4p	0%	0.27°	2.4p	0%	0.26°	2.5p	0%	0.26°	2.4p	0%
∞		-			-			-		15.6°	173p	57%	33.6°	341p	100%

Results from the benchmark experiment on H&E-TRF registration are shown in Table 2. This dataset has significantly fewer matches per image pair and higher inlier ratios, making it more suitable for RANSAC. With 1000 iterations, RANSAC performs on par with truncated L_1-norm and truncated L_2-norm, but with fewer iterations there are still some failures. The poor results for regular L_1-norm and L_2-norm show that for this task, aligning a sub-image to a larger image, using truncated norms is essential.

We also tested the intensity-based Image Regsitration Toolkit [23], using normalized mutual information. For the first dataset, the toolkit failed to produce a correct registration (less than 5° rotation and 25 pixels translation error) in 86% of the experiments. For the second dataset it failed to produce any corrrect results. The poor results are not surprising as these methods often are sensitive to initialization and to outlier structures in the images.

6.2 Registering CT to MR-Flair

This experiment is a demonstration of the applicability of the method. For more quantitative results, see Sections 6.1 and 6.3. The dataset consists of 44 image slices captured using the MR-Flair methodology and 4 image slices from a CT-scan of one single subject. To correlate the information provided by the different modalities, one would like to register each of the CT slices to the MR-Flair volume. As the CT slices are roughly aligned with the slices of the MR-Flair volume, we try to register each of the CT slices to each of the MR-Flair slices and then try to find the sequence of four MR-Flair slices that best match the four CT slices. We use standard 2D SIFT to obtain correspondences. To improve the matching performance, all descriptors were extracted at a fixed scale instead of using the estimated scale from the difference of Gaussians detector. The motivation is that in very noisy images the scale estimation tends to be uncertain.

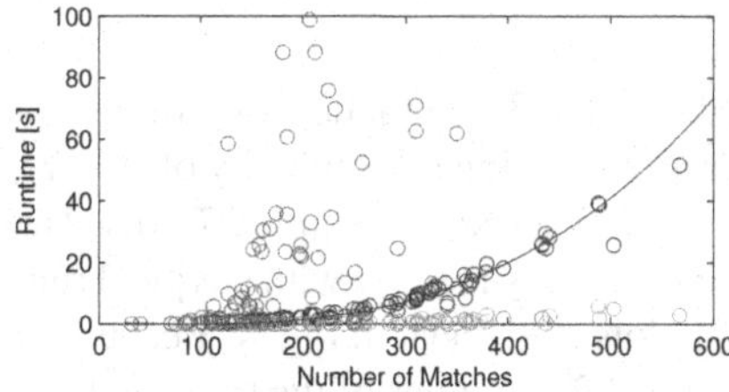

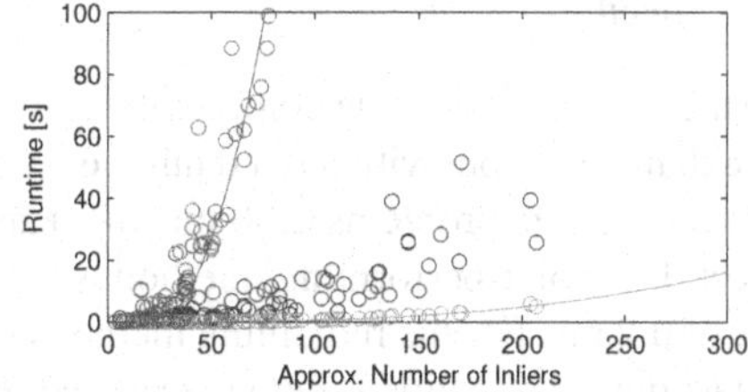

Fig. 4. *Left:* Runtime as a function of number of matches is graphed for truncated L_1-norm (green), truncated L_2-norm (red) and regular L_1-norm. The L_1-method follows closely a $\mathcal{O}(n^3)$-curve (blue). *Right:* Runtime as a function of number of inlier matches is graphed. The truncated methods are more correlated to the number of inliers, see the $\mathcal{O}(n^4)$-curve (red) and the $\mathcal{O}(n^3 \log(n))$-curve (green), respectively. ($\epsilon = 10$ pixels.)

Due to the small dataset we only present qualitative results for our truncated L_1-approach. Different slice-matches have different number of potential inliers, making the truncated L_1-cost skewed. However this is easily rectified by using a modified cost c_i defined as $c_i = N_i\epsilon - l_i^*$ where N_i is the combined number of correspondences for subsequence i, $epsilon$ the truncation level, and l_i^* the combined optimal truncated L_1-solution. Using this criterion and $\epsilon = 10$ the best subsequence evaluated at $c_{19} = 397$, with closest runners up $c_{18} = 362$, $c_{17} = 367$. All other sequence-matchings had significantly lower score. We show the found matchings for the best matching in Fig. 5.

The frequently used intensity-based method called NIFTYREG [21] using mutual information was also tested, but without any reasonable registration results at all. Note that this method was also developed to cope with outlier structures by using robust estimation techniques.

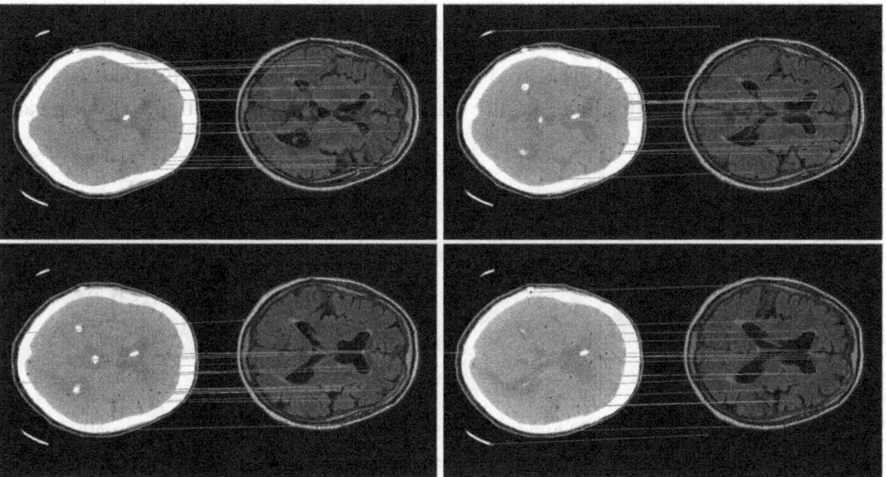

Fig. 5. The found inliers for the best subsequence obtained using our truncated L_1 algorithm

6.3 Speed

The theoretical worst time complexities are stated in Table 3. In practice RANSAC is not run exhaustively but with a fixed number of k iterations, giving a complexity of $\mathcal{O}(nk)$. For average-size problems (280 matches) and $k = 1000$, RANSAC required 73 ms. The fastest (but worst-performing) method is the closed-form L_2-method with a typical runtime of 0.2 ms. For the remaining methods timing plots are shown in Fig. 4. Because of the fast outlier rejection scheme discussed in Section 4.2, runtimes of the truncated L_1-norm and L_2-norm depend mainly on the size of the inlier sets. The full L_1-method has no such advantage. These numbers clearly show the advantage in runtime for the truncated L_1-method over both the regular L_1-norm and the truncated L_2-norm. However, on datasets consisting of a majority of inliers, the lower complexity of the L_1-norm would give faster runtimes as all operations are identical apart from the sorting strategies. The timing statistics is from experiments on H&E-TRF, though the same analysis holds for H&E-p63/AMACR.

Table 3. Characteristics of the algorithms presented or discussed in the paper. Note that the stated complexity for RANSAC is for exhaustive selection of all minimal subsets which can be thought of as a worst time complexity bound.

Algorithm	*complexity*	*tractability*	*reliability*	*reference*
RANSAC	$\mathcal{O}(n^3)$	high	medium	[12]
Truncated L_1-norm	$\mathcal{O}(n^3 \log(n))$	high	high	this paper
L_1-norm	$\mathcal{O}(n^3)$	high	medium	this paper
Truncated L_2-norm	$\mathcal{O}(n^4)$	medium	high	[1]
L_2-norm	$\mathcal{O}(n)$	high	low	[15]

7 Discussion

So what is the right way to attack feature-based image registration in presence of outliers? The literature provides us with a vast amount of choices, but many of these are based on local optimization and require a reasonable starting solution, which means

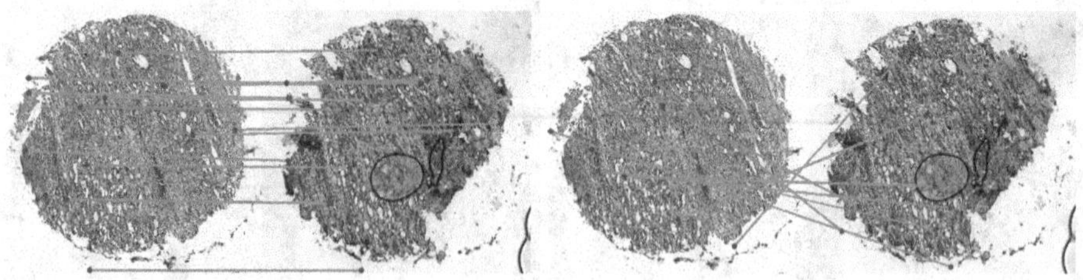

Fig. 6. *Left:* 13 inliers among 1179 hypothetical SIFT matches of the truncated L_1-method (*success*). *Right:* 8 inliers of RANSAC with 1000 iterations (*failure*). This was the hardest case to register among all pairs. ($\epsilon = 20$ pixels.)

that the outlier problem is already more-or-less solved. To handle really difficult outlier problems, RANSAC-type algorithms are the standard against which others are measured. However, as our experiments show, they are sub optimal both in terms of accuracy and with respect to the risk of failure. Some of the failures could be avoided by increasing the number of iterations - even up to exhaustively searching all the minimal subsets. But, that will increase the complexity to $\mathcal{O}(n^3)$, being practically the same as the algorithms proposed here (Table 3). More importantly, even then there is no guarantee as to the solution quality (Fig. 6). Hence, we would only recommend RANSAC when the amount of outliers is known to be low and the available runtime is very limited.

This contrasts sharply to the typical setting for medical image registration where the process is performed offline. With different image modalities, the rates of outliers are usually high. In these cases the increased reliability of optimizing a truncated norm is valuable and the L_1-based methods, although slower than RANSAC, should be efficient enough for most applications. Our experiments indicate only a small gain in accuracy for the truncated L_2-norm, so using the truncated L_1-norm would be the general recommendation.

In many applications, the actual improvement in terms of accuracy and failure rates of these methods might not be huge. This is compensated by the value of removing a possible error source and not having to tune the parameters of the algorithm. We believe that the choice between a tractable, reliable algorithm with guaranteed high-quality solutions and a fast algorithm with no guarantees whatsoever should be an easy one.

References

1. Ask, E., Enqvist, O., Kahl, F.: Optimal geometric fitting under the truncated L_2-norm. In: Conf. Computer Vision and Pattern Recognition, Portland, USA (2013)
2. Audette, M.A., Ferrie, F.P., Peters, T.M.: An algorithmic overview of surface registration techniques for medical imaging. Med. Image Anal. 4(3), 201–217 (2000)
3. Besl, P.J., McKay, N.D.: A method for registration of 3-D shapes. IEEE Trans. Pattern Analysis and Machine Intelligence 14(2), 239–256 (1992)
4. Blake, A., Zisserman, A.: Visual Reconstruction. MIT Press (1987)
5. Breuel, T.M.: Implementation techniques for geometric branch-and-bound matching methods. Computer Vision and Image Understanding 90(3), 258–294 (2003)
6. Cootes, T.F., Edwards, G.J., Taylor, C.J.: Active appearance models. IEEE Trans. Pattern Analysis and Machine Intelligence 23(6), 681–685 (2001)
7. Datteri, R.D., Dawant, B.M.: Estimation and reduction of target registration error. In: Ayache, N., Delingette, H., Golland, P., Mori, K. (eds.) MICCAI 2012, Part III. LNCS, vol. 7512, pp. 139–146. Springer, Heidelberg (2012)
8. Doyle, S., Madabhushi, A., Feldman, M., Tomaszeweski, J.: A boosting cascade for automated detection of prostate cancer from digitized histology. In: Larsen, R., Nielsen, M., Sporring, J. (eds.) MICCAI 2006. LNCS, vol. 4191, pp. 504–511. Springer, Heidelberg (2006)
9. Dreo, J., Nunes, J.C., Siarry, P.: Robust rigid registration of retinal angiograms through optimization. Comput. Med. Imaging Graph. 30(8), 453–463 (2006)
10. Enqvist, O., Ask, E., Kahl, F., Åström, K.: Robust fitting for multiple view geometry. In: Fitzgibbon, A., Lazebnik, S., Perona, P., Sato, Y., Schmid, C. (eds.) ECCV 2012, Part I. LNCS, vol. 7572, pp. 738–751. Springer, Heidelberg (2012)

11. Enqvist, O., Josephson, K., Kahl, F.: Optimal correspondences from pairwise constraints. In: Int. Conf. Computer Vision, Kyoto, Japan (2009)
12. Fischler, M.A., Bolles, R.C.: Random sample consensus: a paradigm for model fitting. Commun. Assoc. Comp. Mach. 24, 381–395 (1981)
13. Fitzgibbon, A.W.: Robust registration of 2D and 3D point sets. Image Vision Comput. 21, 1145–1153 (2003)
14. Fitzpatrick, J.M., West, J.B., Maurer, C.R.: Predicting error in rigid-body point-based registration. IEEE Trans. Medical Imaging 17(5), 694–702 (1998)
15. Horn, B.K.P.: Closed-form solution of absolute orientation using unit quaternion. Journal of the Optical Society of America A 4(4) (1987)
16. Jemal, A., Bray, F., Center, M.M., Ferlay, J., Ward, E., Forman, D.: Global cancer statistics. CA Cancer J. Clin. 61(2), 69–90 (2011)
17. Kwak, J.T., Hewitt, S.M., Sinha, S., Bhargava, R.: Multimodal microscopy for automated histologic analysis of prostate cancer. BMC Cancer 11(62) (2011)
18. Li, H.: Consensus set maximization with guaranteed global optimality for robust geometry estimation. In: Int. Conf. Computer Vision, Kyoto, Japan (2009)
19. Myronenko, A., Song, X.: Point-set registration: Coherent point drift. IEEE Trans. Pattern Analysis and Machine Intelligence 32(12), 2262–2275 (2010)
20. Nguyen, K., Sabata, B., Jain, A.K.: Prostate cancer grading: Gland segmentation and structural features. Pattern Recognition Letters 33(7), 951–961 (2012)
21. Ourselin, S., Roche, A., Subsol, G., Pennec, X., Ayache, N.: Reconstructing a 3D structure from serial histological sections. Image Vision Comput. 19, 25–31 (2001)
22. Rangarajan, A., Chui, H., Mjolsness, E., Pappu, S., Davachi, L., Goldman-Rakic, P., Duncan, J.: A robust point-matching algorithm for autoradiograph alignment. Med. Image Anal. 1(4), 379–398 (1997)
23. Studholme, C., Hill, D.L.G., Hawkes, D.J.: An overlap invariant entropy measure of 3D medical image alignment. Pattern Recognition 32(1), 71–86 (1999)
24. Wikipedia, `http://www.wikipedia.org`

Graduated Consistency-Regularized Optimization for Multi-graph Matching

Junchi Yan[1,2], Yin Li[3], Wei Liu[4],
Hongyuan Zha[3,5], Xiaokang Yang[1], and Stephen Mingyu Chu[2]

[1] Shanghai Jiao Tong University, 200240 Shanghai, China
yanjunchi@sjtu.edu.cn
[2] IBM Research - China, 201203 Shanghai China
[3] Georgia Institute of Technology, 30032 Atlanta, USA
[4] IBM T.J. Watson Research Center, 10598 New York, USA
[5] East China Normal University, 200062 Shanghai, China

Abstract. Graph matching has a wide spectrum of computer vision applications such as finding feature point correspondences across images. The problem of graph matching is generally NP-hard, so most existing work pursues suboptimal solutions between two graphs. This paper investigates a more general problem of matching N attributed graphs to each other, i.e. labeling their common node correspondences such that a certain compatibility/affinity objective is optimized. This multi-graph matching problem involves two key ingredients affecting the overall accuracy: a) the pairwise affinity matching score between two local graphs, and b) global matching consistency that measures the uniqueness and consistency of the pairwise matching results by different sequential matching orders. Previous work typically either enforces the matching consistency constraints in the beginning of iterative optimization, which may propagate matching error both over iterations and across different graph pairs; or separates score optimizing and consistency synchronization in two steps. This paper is motivated by the observation that affinity score and consistency are mutually affected and shall be tackled jointly to capture their correlation behavior. As such, we propose a novel multi-graph matching algorithm to incorporate the two aspects by iteratively approximating the global-optimal affinity score, meanwhile gradually infusing the consistency as a regularizer, which improves the performance of the initial solutions obtained by existing pairwise graph matching solvers. The proposed algorithm with a theoretically proven convergence shows notable efficacy on both synthetic and public image datasets.

1 Introduction

Due to the powerful characteristics of abstraction, Graph Matching (GM) plays a central role in tremendous computer vision applications such as image registration [39], object categorization [30], action recognition [5], shape matching [29], stereo [20,46], and so forth. The problem of graph matching is to establish a compatible node-to-node mapping among two or more graphs. In computer vision, GM has primarily been used to find correspondences among two or more sets

D. Fleet et al. (Eds.): ECCV 2014, Part I, LNCS 8689, pp. 407–422, 2014.
© Springer International Publishing Switzerland 2014

of local features extracted from images. Different from conventional matching methods such as RANSAC [15] and Iterative Closest Point (ICP) [4], GM goes beyond the first-order node-wise feature as well as the focus of location information [51], which incorporates more distinctive pairwise [43,47] or higher-order [50,13,28,33] node interactions for matching structural objects. Consequently, GM has attracted considerable research attention [12,17,22,34,16] for decades, yet remains computationally challenging due to its combinatorial nature.

Current graph matching methods mostly focused on the two-graph scenario such as [21,38,9,41,52,43,10,8,47]. In particular, there are several research groups focusing on graph matching and related problems over the past years, such as Professor Horst Bunke's group in Bern [3], Professor Edwin R. Hancock's group in York [2], and Professor Francesc Serratosa's group in Tarragona [1], to name a few. Readers are referred to the recent comparison review paper [22] for more details therein. However, on one hand, many practical computer vision tasks need matching multiple images or point sets, which is a building block for various applications that involve multi-view registration or matching. On the other hand, it is generally recognized [47,44,40,36] that simultaneously exploring all pairwise affinity information across the whole pool of graphs $\mathbb{G} = \{G_1, \cdots, G_N\}$ may improve the matching accuracy. Such an improvement is accomplished through avoiding trapping to local optima, or a false optima away from the semantic true correspondence due to the large deformation, appearing in the pairwise case since only affinity between two local graphs is explored. Therefore, it is appealing to design effective and efficient multi-graph matching algorithms beyond conventional pairwise matching solvers.

The multi-graph matching problem has been basically solved in a sequential manner [37], where each step executes a pairwise matching of two graphs. Ideally, the pairwise matching sequence can be designed by different orders that cover all graphs in a path, *e.g.*, $G_1 \rightarrow G_2 \rightarrow \ldots \rightarrow G_N$. However, whatever path order is chosen, a single error in the corresponding sequence will typically create a large number of erroneous pairwise matches. To fully explore the information across the whole graph pool $\mathbb{G}$, it is perhaps more robust to compute all or part of pairwise matching results independently, and then leave the calculation of the final solution to several post-steps [36,24]. Compared with computing a pairwise matching chain like $G_1 \rightarrow G_2 \rightarrow \ldots \rightarrow G_N$, such an exhaustive matching strategy would cause the problem of *redundancy*, or in another word, *inconsistency*, as the node mapping between two graphs cannot be uniquely determined by different pairwise matching paths. Formally, we use the term "cycle-consistency" as introduced and described in [48,26,24], i.e., that composition of correspondences between two graphs should be independent of the connecting path chosen.

2 Problem Statement

2.1 Graph Matching Formulations

For self-completeness, first we briefly introduce the widely used objective function of graph matching in the context of two graphs. Concretely, given two graphs $G_1(V_1, E_1, A_1)$ and $G_2(V_2, E_2, A_2)$, where V denotes nodes, E, edges and A, attributes, there is an affinity matrix $\mathbf{K} \in \mathbb{R}^{n_1 \times n_2}$, whereby its elements $K_{ia;jb}$ measure the affinity with the edge pair candidate $\{v_1(i), v_1(j)\}$ vs. $\{v_2(a), v_2(b)\}$. The diagonal elements $K_{ia;ia}$ represent the unary affinity of a node pair candidate $\{v_1(i), v_2(a)\}$. By introducing a permutation[1] matrix $\mathbf{P} \in \{0,1\}^{n_1 \times n_2}$ whereby P_{ia}=1 if node $v_1(i)$ matches node $v_2(a)$ (P_{ia}=0 otherwise). It can be concisely formulated as a constrained quadratic assignment problem (QAP [35]). It goes beyond the linear assignment problem that can be efficiently solved by the Hungarian method [27]. In general, the QAP is known to be NP-hard [18].

$$\mathbf{P}^* = \arg\max_{\mathbf{P}} \text{vec}(\mathbf{P})^T \mathbf{K} \text{vec}(\mathbf{P}) \quad s.t. \quad \mathbf{I}_{n_1}^T \mathbf{P} = \mathbf{1}_{n_2}^T, \mathbf{P}\mathbf{I}_{n_2} = \mathbf{1}_{n_1}, \mathbf{P} \in \{0,1\}^{n_1 \times n_2}.$$

Here vec($\mathbf{P}$) is the vectorized permutation matrix of $\mathbf{P}$, and vec($\mathbf{P})^T$ is the transpose version. The constraints refer to the one-to-one node bijection.

One step further, now we consider the formulation for the multi-graph matching. Given N graphs and the pairwise affinity matrix $\mathbf{K}_{ij}(i, j = 1, 2, \ldots, N; i>j)$, a natural extension for multi-graph matching as used in [47] is:

$$\{\mathbf{P}_{ij}\}^* = \arg\max_{\{\mathbf{P}_{ij}\}} \sum_{i,j=1,2,\ldots,N;i>j} \text{vec}(\mathbf{P}_{ij})^T \mathbf{K}_{ij} \text{vec}(\mathbf{P}_{ij}) \quad (1)$$

$$s.t. \quad \mathbf{I}_{n_1}^T \mathbf{P}_{ij} = \mathbf{1}_{n_2}^T \quad \mathbf{P}_{ij}\mathbf{I}_{n_2} = \mathbf{1}_{n_1} \quad \mathbf{P}_{ij} \in \{0,1\}^{n_i \times n_j} \quad \forall i, j = 1, 2, \ldots, N; \quad i > j$$

where $\{\mathbf{P}_{ij}\}$ is the set of pairwise permutation matrix over N graphs. Note that for notational simplicity, without loss of generality, here we omit the weight λ_{ij} for each quadratic term in the objective function as used in [47].

2.2 Notations and Preliminaries

We first give several notations and definitions which will be used throughout this paper. Without loss of generality, given a set of N graphs $\mathbb{G} = \{G_k, \sum_{k=1}^N\}$, let the assignment matrix $\mathbf{P}_{ij} \in \mathbb{R}^{n_i \times n_j}$ denote the node-to-node mapping between G_i and G_j. We also define the pairwise affinity matching score J_{ij} that measures the similarity between two aligned graphs as $J_{ij} = \text{vec}(\mathbf{P}_{ij}^T)\mathbf{K}_{ij}\text{vec}(\mathbf{P}_{ij})$. This score definition is widely used in graph matching related work, such as [9,52,43,10,8,47]. By stacking all $\mathbf{P}_{ij}$ into one whole matrix, we define the resulting *matching configuration matrix*[2] as: $\mathbf{W} = \begin{pmatrix} \mathbf{P}_{11} & \cdots & \mathbf{P}_{1N} \\ \vdots & \ddots & \vdots \\ \mathbf{P}_{N1} & \cdots & \mathbf{P}_{NN} \end{pmatrix} \in \mathbb{R}^{nN \times nN}$.

[1] We use "assignment matrix"/"permutation matrix" interchangeably in the paper.

[2] For multi-graph matching tackled in this paper, we seek the common inlier node set (via the one-to-one node matching) shared among all graphs, and admit outliers appearing in graphs i.e. $n_i = n_i^{in} + n_i^{out}$ for each graph G_i. In general, in the case of $n_i \neq n_j$, the variable $\mathbf{P}_{ij}$ in Eq. (1) is a partial assignment matrix. Similar to [52,21,40], we transform the partial assignment matrix $\mathbf{P}$ to a full square assignment matrix by augmenting proper dummy nodes (adding slack variables into $\mathbf{P}_{ij}$ accordingly), so that the one-to-one two-way constraints can always be satisfied. This is a conventional strategy used in solving linear programming, and also is previously adopted by graph matching work such as [45,14,40]. Thus throughout the paper from now on, we assume $n_i = n_j = n$ for all graphs.

Now we introduce several definitions that will facilitate the presentation of the paper: Definition (1) and (2) are used to quantify the consistency metric related to the proposed Alg.2 as we will show later. Definition (3) is regarding with using Maximum Span Tree for multi-graph matching and related to the concept of matching path in Definition (4), which is related to Alg.1 and Alg.2.

Definition 1. *Given a set of graphs* $\mathbb{G}=\{G_k, \sum_{k=1}^{N}\}$*, the consistency of graph* G_k *is defined as* $C(G_k)=1-\frac{\sum_{i=1}^{N-1}\sum_{j=i+1}^{N}(\|\mathbf{P}_{ij}-\mathbf{P}_{ik}\mathbf{P}_{kj}\|_F/2}{n(N-2)(N+1)/2}$ *where* $\mathbf{P}_{ij}$ *is the pairwise assignment matrix over the graph set* $\mathbb{G}$*.*

Definition 2. *Given a set of graphs* $\mathbb{G}=\{G_k, \sum_{k=1}^{N}\}$ *and its pairwise assignment matrix set* $\{\mathbf{P}_{ij}\}$*, we call the graph set* $\mathbb{G}$ *is fully consistent w.r.t. its pairwise matching configuration* $\mathbf{W}$ *if* $\forall i, j, k \leq N$*:* $\mathbf{P}_{ij}=\mathbf{P}_{ik}\mathbf{P}_{kj}$*. Specifically, the consistency measure of* $\mathbb{G}$ *is defined as* $C(\mathbb{G})=\frac{\sum_{k=1}^{N}C(G_k)}{N}$*. Thus* $C(\mathbb{G})=1$ *if and only if* $\mathbb{G}$ *is fully consistent.*

Definition 3. *Given a set of graphs* $\{G_k, \sum_{k=1}^{N}\}$ *and* $\mathbf{P}_{ij}$*, the super graph* $\mathcal{G}$ *is defined as an undirected weighted graph such that each node* k *denotes* G_k*, and its edge* e_{ij} *is weighted by the* $J_{ij} = vec(\mathbf{P}_{ij})^T\mathbf{K}_{ij}vec(\mathbf{P}_{ij})$*.*

Definition 4. *The matching path* $T_{ij}(k_1, k_2, \ldots, k_s)$ *from graph* G_i *to* G_j *is defined as a loop-free chain of graphs* $G_i \rightarrow G_{k_1} \rightarrow \cdots \rightarrow G_{k_s} \rightarrow G_j$ *which induces the multiplication of the pairwise matching solutions:* $\mathbf{H}_{ij}(k_1, k_2, \ldots, k_s) \triangleq \mathbf{P}_{ik_1}\mathbf{P}_{k_1k_2}\ldots\mathbf{P}_{k_sj}$*. Its order* s *is further defined as the number of the intermediate graphs between the two ending graphs* G_i, G_j*. The score* $J_{ij}(k_1, k_2, \ldots, k_s)$ *of the path is induced by the chaining matching solution* $\mathbf{H}_{ij}(k_1, k_2, \ldots, k_s)$ *as* $J_{ij}(k_1, k_2, \ldots, k_s) = vec(\mathbf{H}_{ij})^T\mathbf{K}_{ij}vec(\mathbf{H}_{ij})$*.*

Comments. By assuming full consistency of Definition (2), solving the multi-matching problem reduces to finding $N-1$ different assignment matrix, rather than $O(N^2)$ that cover all pairwise cases. The consistency measurement regarding a single graphs as defined in Definition (1) reflects its consistency contribution. The super graph is considered as a fully connected graph when each pair of graphs is matched by some means ($e_{ij} > 0$) or set to zero if the pairwise matching is unknown. In general, given a connected super graph (not necessarily fully connected), a *maximum spanning tree* (MST) [19] can be found with more or equal to the weight of every other spanning tree on the super graph.

3 Related Work

As a general problem for matching structural data, graph matching has been extensively studied for decades not only in computer vision, but also in computer science and mathematics [12]. Here we view the problem from several key aspects that account for the main threads of the related work.

Machine Learning for GM: Conventional graph matching methods first compute an affinity matrix and keep the graph unchanged during the entire matching process. Recent work leverage various leaning algorithms for estimating the optimal affinity matrix [6,32,33,23,8], and the methods can fall into either supervised [6] or unsupervised [32] or semi-supervised [33] learning paradigms.

Higher-Order Affinity Modeling: Combing the unary and pairwise edge information has been heavily investigated since such types of matching schemes play a good tradeoff between computational complexity and representation capability [9,21,29,31,42]. More recently, the higher-order (most are third order) information has been encoded to achieve more robust matching paradigms. Several representative hypergraph matching methods have been developed for computer vision applications [7,13,28,33,50] that encode higher-order information to enhance the structural distinctiveness for matching.

Optimization Methods: Most approaches first formulate an objective function, and then employ certain optimization methods to derive optimal solutions [21,29,42], which vary among a wide spectrum of optimization strategies [11]. Some recent work first relax the objective function to convex-concave formulation [52,49]. Then the optimal solutions are achieved using the so-called path following strategy and a modified version of the Frank-Wolfe algorithm [49]. Probabilistic matching paradigms are also developed, which have shown unique power in interpreting and addressing hypergraph matching problems [9,28,50].

Surprisingly, little work in computer vision community has been done for *simultaneously* addressing both matching consistency and matching affinity. The most recent methods still concentrate on one single aspect of the problem - either aiming at maximizing/minimizing the matching affinity score/cost by using a *reference graph* to ensure the matching consistency, like [47,40], or addressing the problem from a spectral smoothing perspective to enhance consistency like [36] while ignoring the affinity score between two local graphs. More specifically, Sole-Ribalta and Serratosa [40] extend the classical Graduated Assignment Graph Matching (GAGM) algorithm [21,43] from pairwise to the multi-graph case, which inherits the robustness of the original method, yet meanwhile, being less efficient as it repeatedly applies the GAGM method across graph pairs iteratively. Yan et. al. [47] propose an iterative optimization method that imposes the rigid matching consistency constraint via a closed form in each iteration. The recent work [36] employs spectral analysis and approximation to eigenvector decomposition on the matching configuration matrix comprised of all initial pairwise matching solutions, and recover the consistent matching solutions. In this paper, we formulate the multi-graph matching problem as a novel graduated regularized optimization procedure, and solve it using an iterative first-order approximating algorithm regarding with the affinity score.

The *main contribution* of this paper lies in the study of the correlation score between affinity score and matching accuracy decays as the score value increases, while consistency becomes a more informative regularizer. Based on this observation, a novel graduated consistency-regularization method is proposed to effectively improve the accuracy from the initial pairwise matching solutions.

4 Graduated Consistency-Regularized Approximating

4.1 Maximizing Matching Score under Consistency Constraints

Note that the formulation (1) does not automatically account for the matching consistency. By introducing the consistency measure associated with the configuration matrix $\mathbf{W}$ for graph set $\mathbb{G}$ as defined in Definition (2), we present the consistency-constrained version of the objective function:

$$\{\mathbf{P}_{ij}\}^* = \arg\max_{\{\mathbf{P}_{ij}\}} \sum_{i,j=1,2,\ldots,N;i>j} \text{vec}(\mathbf{P}_{ij})^T \mathbf{K}_{ij} \text{vec}(\mathbf{P}_{ij}) \tag{2}$$

$$\mathbf{I}_{n_1}^T \mathbf{P}_{ij} = \mathbf{1}_{n_2}^T \quad \mathbf{P}_{ij}\mathbf{I}_{n_2} = \mathbf{1}_{n_1} \quad \mathbf{P}_{ij} = \mathbf{P}_{ik}\mathbf{P}_{kj} \in \{0,1\}^{n_i \times n_j} \quad \forall k = 1,2,\ldots,N; k \neq i,j$$

We first transform the above objective to a "Lagrange-multiplier" form, which is more suitable for the problem as we will show later:

$$\{\mathbf{P}_{ij}\}^* = \arg\max_{\{\mathbf{P}_{ij}\}} \sum_{i,j=1,2,\ldots,N;i>j} \text{vec}(\mathbf{P}_{ij})^T \mathbf{K}_{ij} \text{vec}(\mathbf{P}_{ij}) + \lambda \sum_{k=1}^{N} \|\mathbf{P}_{ij} - \mathbf{P}_{ik}\mathbf{P}_{kj}\|_F \tag{3}$$

$$\mathbf{I}_{n_1}^T \mathbf{P}_{ij} = \mathbf{1}_{n_2}^T \quad \mathbf{P}_{ij}\mathbf{I}_{n_2} = \mathbf{1}_{n_1} \quad \mathbf{P}_{ij} = \mathbf{P}_{ik}\mathbf{P}_{kj} \in \{0,1\}^{n_i \times n_j} \quad \forall k = 1,2,\ldots,N; k \neq i,j$$

Note that we do not move the one-to-one bijection constraint to the "Lagrange-multiplier" term, this is due to existing pairwise graph matching solvers are able to handle this constraint, such as relaxing to the permutation matrix's convex hull - a doubly stochastic matrix e.g. [9].

The above objective function is challenging due to NP-hard, and even harder as more consistency constraints need being satisfied here. Thus we are more interested in devising efficient approximating algorithms, which is based on two rationales to the specific matching problem as we will show in the following.

4.2 Maximizing Pairwise Score via Approximating Path Selection

Our first key rationale is that the highest-score matching between two graphs may be found along a higher-order path (refer to Definition 4) instead of the direct (zero-order) pairwise matching. We formalize this idea as follows:

For graph G_i, G_j, all possible (loop-free) matching pathes can form the following (loop-free) path set $\mathbb{T}_{ij} = \{T_{ij}(k_1, \ldots, k_s), s = 1, 2, \ldots, N-2\}$. Its cardinality $|\mathbb{T}_{ij}| = \sum_{s=1}^{N-2} s!$. Thus exhaustively searching for the best solution T_{ij}^* is intimidating as the complexity is exponential in terms of N.

One alternative approach is to approximate T_{ij}^* by a set of consecutive first-order iterations, which involves concatenating the first-order short pathes that are chosen in each iteration, into a higher-order path. This idea is formally described in Alg.1: in each iteration s, the pairwise matching solution $\mathbf{P}_{ij}$ is updated by the highest-score one among the confined *subset* of $\mathbb{T}_{ij}$ with path order $s = 1$ (See line 8-10 in the algorithm chart). This algorithm bears solid convergence property due to the score-ascending procedure will always converge to a fixed value because the score is bounded in the discrete permutation matrix space. In general, such a greedy algorithm cannot ensure the global optimality

Algorithm 1. Iterative Approximating Pairwise Affinity Maximization

Input

One set of N graphs with n nodes: $\mathbf{V}_i = \{v_1, v_2, \dots, v_n\}, (i = 1, 2, \dots, N)$;
Pairwise affinity matrix $\mathbf{K}_{ij} (i = 1, 2, \dots, N; j = i + 1, \dots, N)$;
Maximum iteration count: S_{max}, initial iteration count: $s = 0$;

Output

Consistent matching configuration matrix $\mathbf{W} \in \mathbb{R}^{Nn \times Nn}$;

Procedure

Perform pairwise graph matching to obtain the putative assignment matrix $\mathbf{P}_{ij}^{(0)} \in \mathbb{R}^{n \times n}$ and the matching configuration matrix $\mathbf{W}^{(0)} \in \mathbb{R}^{Nn \times Nn}$;
Calculate the initial total score $J^{(0)}$ by $J^{(0)} = \sum_{i=1,j=i+1}^{N,N} \text{vec}(\mathbf{P}_{ij}^{(0)})^T \mathbf{K}_{ij} \text{vec}(\mathbf{P}_{ij}^{(0)})$;
while $s \leq S_{max}$ **do**
  for all $i = 1, 2, \dots, N; j = i + 1, \dots, N$ **do**
    Update $\mathbf{P}_{ij}^{(s)} = \mathbf{P}_{ik}^{(s-1)} \mathbf{P}_{kj}^{(s-1)}$ for k to maximize $\text{vec}(\mathbf{P}_{ij}^{(s)})^T \mathbf{K}_{ij} \text{vec}(\mathbf{P}_{ij}^{(s)})$
  end for
  Calculate the total score $J^{(s)} = \sum_{i=1,j=i+1}^{N,N} \text{vec}(\mathbf{P}_{ij}^{(s)})^T \mathbf{K}_{ij} \text{vec}(\mathbf{P}_{ij}^{(s)})$;
  If $J_s = J_{s-1}$, **break**;
  $s{+}{+}$;
end while
Update $\mathbf{W}^{(s)}$ by updating all $\mathbf{P}_{ij}^{(s)}$;
Impose full consistency by spectral smoothing method [36] when $N > n$, or via building a maximum span tree on the super graph [25] when $N <= n$.

for affinity score. The following proposition shows under certain conditions, Alg.1 can guarantee the global optimality. Proving its correctness is trivial.

Proposition 1. *For any G_i, G_j out of a fully connected super graph, denote the "highest-score" path as T_{ij}^*. If for any sub-segment $\widetilde{T}_{kl}^*$ of T_{ij}^*, it is also the "highest-score" path for the two ending graph G_k, G_l, i.e. $\widetilde{T}_{kl}^* = T_{kl}^*$, then Alg.1 is ensured to find the global optimum for the initial configuration* $\mathbf{W}$.

To satisfy the full consistency as defined in Definition (2), after iteration, a synchronization post-step [36] is performed (See the last step in Alg.1). This step can also involve other smoothing methods especially when a small number of graphs are used for matching ($n > N$). A simple alternative is finding maximum spanning tree on the super graph induced by $\mathbf{W}^{(s)}$ and populate other edges (assignment matrix) by multiplication through the maximum span tree.

The above discussion is concretized into an iterative algorithm as described in Alg.1: **Iterative Approximating Pairwise Affinity Maximization (IA-PAM)**. In each iteration, it approximates the best path w.r.t. pairwise matching score between two graphs by the best solution out of the first-order path. This algorithm is ensured to converge when the score stops increasing. Then the post-step of global consistency synchronization is performed by either a spectral smoothing method [36] or maximum span tree as discussed above. The efficacy of such a score-ascending strategy can be exemplified by a concrete analysis:

Algorithm 2. Graduated Consistency-Regularized Affinity Maximization

Input

One set of N graphs with n nodes: $\mathbf{V}_i = \{v_1, v_2, \ldots, v_n\}, (i = 1, 2, \ldots, N)$;
Pairwise affinity matrix $\mathbf{K}_{ij}(i = 1, 2, \ldots, N; j = i+1, \ldots, N)$;
Maximum iteration count: S_{max}, initial iteration count: $s = 0$;
Consistency weight initialization $\lambda = \lambda_0$ and the weight increasing rate $\rho > 1$;

Output

Consistent matching configuration matrix $\mathbf{W} \in \mathbb{R}^{Nn \times Nn}$;

Procedure

Perform pairwise graph matching to obtain the putative assignment matrix $\mathbf{P}_{ij}^{(0)} \in \mathbb{R}^{n \times n}$ and the matching configuration matrix $\mathbf{W}^{(0)} \in \mathbb{R}^{Nn \times Nn}$;
Set the constant score scale reference $J_{max}^{(0)} = \max_{\mathbf{P}_{ij}^{(0)} \in \mathbf{W}^{(0)}} \text{vec}(\mathbf{P}_{ij}^{(0)})^T \mathbf{K}_{ij} \text{vec}(\mathbf{P}_{ij}^{(0)})$;
while $s \leq S_{max}$ **do**
  for all $i = 1, 2, \ldots, N; j = i+1, \ldots, N$ **do**
    Set $\mathbf{P}_{ij}^{(s)} = \mathbf{P}_{ik}^{(s-1)} \mathbf{P}_{kj}^{(s-1)}$ for k to maximize the regularized objective: $C(G_k) + (1-\lambda)\text{vec}(\mathbf{P}_{ij}^{(s)})^T \mathbf{K}_{ij} \text{vec}(\mathbf{P}_{ij}^{(s)})/J_{max}^{(0)}$
  end for
  Increase λ by $\lambda^{(s+1)} = \rho \lambda^{(s)}$;
  Calculate the total score $J^{(s)} = \sum_{i=1,j=i+1}^{N,N} \text{vec}(\mathbf{P}_{ij}^{(s)})^T \mathbf{K}_{ij} \text{vec}(\mathbf{P}_{ij}^{(s)})/J_{max}^{(0)}$;
  s++;
end while
Update $\mathbf{W}^{(s)}$ by updating all $\mathbf{P}_{ij}^{(s)}$;
Impose full consistency by spectral smoothing method [36] when $N > n$, or via building a maximum span tree on the super graph [25] when $N <= n$.

when matching graph G_i and G_j is ambiguous due to both are deformed, it is still possible to recover the correct matching by an intermediate high quality graph that is able to find perfect matches respectively.

4.3 Graduated Consistency-Regularized Optimization Algorithm

Our second key rationale is viewing the consistency constraint as a *regularizer* for affinity score maximization. Note that maximizing pairwise matching score among all pairs cannot ensure the consistency constraint. Moreover, due to outliers and local deformation and the difficulty in setting up the affinity matrix in a parametric manner[3], there can be a case that for some pairs of graphs, the ground truth matching may not produce the highest score. Thus purely maximizing the overall matching score is biased to accuracy.

As a baseline method, Alg.1 separates score maximization and consistency synchronization into two separate steps. It is yet appealing to tackle the two aspects jointly. We make the following statements, for devising a novel algorithm that gradually introduces consistency during the score-ascending procedure:

[3] Currently the affinity function is mostly modeled by parametric functions, the fixed parameters by whatever manual setting [43], or automatically learned from training samples [6,8] etc. may still be unable to best fit the score with accuracy.

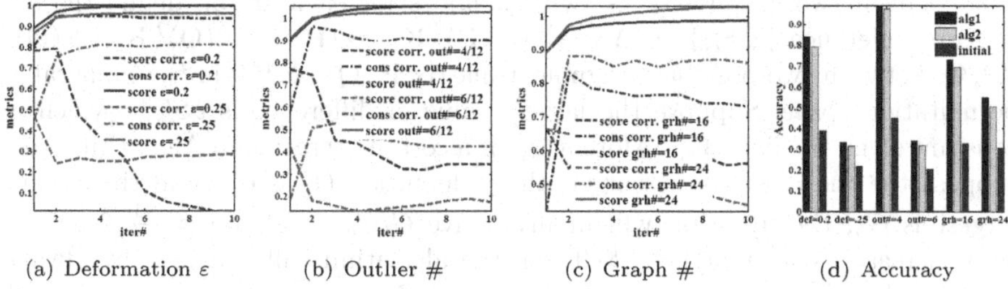

(a) Deformation ε (b) Outlier # (c) Graph # (d) Accuracy

Fig. 1. Correlation coefficient value as a function of number of iterations of Alg.1 under different synthetic settings on a set of N=24 graphs with n_{in}=8 inliers: a) varying deformation level $\varepsilon = 0.2$ and $\varepsilon = 0.25$; b) varying number of outliers for n_{out}=4 and n_{out}=6; c) varying number of graphs for N=16 and N=24. For outlier test and graph set size test, ε is set to 0.05 and 0.2 respectively. Dot dashed curve is for the correlation coefficient between consistency and accuracy; dashed curve is for score and accuracy. The solid curve is for the normalized score.

- For the initial assignment matrix $\mathbf{W}^{(0)}$ obtained by the pairwise graph matching solver, its scores are more correlated with the true accuracy.
- After rounds of iterations of score-ascending, score becomes less discriminative for accuracy and consistency becomes a more indicative measurement.

The assertions are verified on synthetic tests using Alg.1 as illustrated in Fig.1: As we continue to iterate, the overall normalized matching score (solid curve) increases, and the correlation coefficient between score and accuracy (dashed curve) drops quickly, while the correlation coefficient for consistency and accuracy (dot dashed curve) still remain at a certain level (above 0.4). This observation is consistent across deformation and outlier tests as show in Fig.1(a) and Fig.1(b) respectively. Moreover, Fig.1(c) shows a relatively larger size of graph set will further improve the correlation between consistency and accuracy. In summary, as affinity score increases along iterating, consistency *gradually* becomes more important as a *regularizer* that help dismiss the biased matching resulting from an unfitted affinity function or due to arbitrary local ambiguities.

Thus we infuse the matching consistency in each iteration by a weighted term that accounts for consistency. In line with the observation from Fig.1, its weight λ gradually increases until the procedure exceeds a certain iteration threshold or converges to a fully consistent configuration. To enhance the overall consistency, the similar post-processing can also be conducted which will stop the score growing immediately. This idea is detailed in Alg.2: **Graduated Consistency-Regularized Pairwise Affinity Maximization (GCRPAM)**. We will evaluate the two proposed algorithms in our experiments. Now we present the convergence property of Alg.2 by Proposition (2) as follows.

Proposition 2. *The iteration procedure of Alg.2 is ensured to converge to a fixed matching configuration* $\mathbf{W}^*$ *after a finite number of iterations.*

Intuitively, the matching configuration becomes more consistent as the weight λ dominates over iterations. A rigorous proof is given in below.

Proof. Given two graphs G_i, G_j with n nodes for each graph, define the set of score difference $\{\Delta S_{ij}\}$ as $\Delta S_{ij} = \text{vec}(\mathbf{P})^T\mathbf{K}_{ij}\text{vec}(\mathbf{P}) - \text{vec}(\mathbf{Q})^T\mathbf{K}_{ij}\text{vec}(\mathbf{Q})$, $\forall\mathbf{P},\mathbf{Q}$, between two possible assignment matrix $\mathbf{P}$, $\mathbf{Q} \in \mathbb{R}^{n\times n}$ in the numerable permutation space. Suppose the largest value of difference is δS_{ij}^{max} which is constant given the fixed $\mathbf{K}_{ij}$. Moreover, for a certain iteration in Alg.2 (Line 10), suppose the the most consistent graph by definition (1) is G_a, and the second largest is G_b, the iteration will finally arrive $C(G_a) - C(G_b) > \frac{(1-\lambda)}{\lambda}\delta S_{ij}^{max}$ as λ increase close enough to 1. Then, the algorithm will converge by always choosing the most consistent graph G_a for updating, as its consistency score will be further improved in next iteration. Thus we finish the proof.

Finally we discuss the computational complexity of the algorithms. In each iteration of Alg.1 and Alg.2, we re-calculate the pairwise score by $\text{vec}(\mathbf{P})^T\mathbf{K}\text{vec}(\mathbf{P})$ to update each graph pair's correspondence by using each of other graphs as the anchor graph. This complexity is $O(N^3)O(J_1)$ where $O(J_1)$ is the overhead for pairwise score computing. In addition, the Alg.2 requires the calculation of consistency for each graph by using it as the anchor graph to compare the new chaining solution with the original direct matching for all graph pairs. Its complexity is $O(N^3)O(J_2)$ where $O(J_2)$ is the overhead for the multiplication of two permutation matrix for calculating a single graph's consistency as defined in 1. Typically the affinity matrix $\mathbf{K}$ is very sparse as Delaunay triangulation is performed to sparsify the edge density. Thus it is usually significantly faster than the worst case $O(n^3)$ - note the assignment matrix is also sparse. In addition, Step 9 in Alg.1 and Step 10 in Alg.2 can also be speeded up: one can first compute all possible $\mathbf{P}_{ij}$ by choosing different intermediate graph G_k. There is a possible case that for $k_1 \neq k_2$, one has $\mathbf{P}_{ik_1}\mathbf{P}_{k_1j} = \mathbf{P}_{ik_2}\mathbf{P}_{k_2j}$. Thus we only need to compute the affinity score once given two equal derived $\mathbf{P}$. This also enables possible local search and hashing mechanism which we leave for future work.

5 Experiments

The experiments involve synthetic simulation and two public real image datasets which follow a standard protocol widely employed by related work such as [9,43] and so forth. We conduct the experiments on a laptop PC with dual cores at 3.02GHz for each. The pairwise graph matching solver is implemented in C++ and the iterative optimization procedure is implemented in Matlab. The comparing methods are [47,36][4] since we focus on the multiple-graph matching problem thus the pairwise matching solvers are in parallel with our work.

5.1 Protocol Description

Graph affinity setting. Following the widely used protocol of [52,47] etc, we use Delaunay method to triangulate the landmarks that are annotated/detected

[4] For space limitation, we did not present the results of [40]. In our test it is slightly better than the pairwise matching in accuracy while being significantly slower.

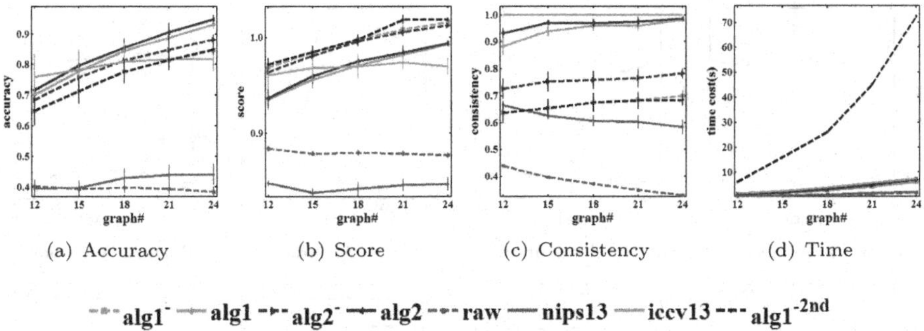

(a) Accuracy (b) Score (c) Consistency (d) Time

Fig. 2. Synthetic data evaluation via 10 random tests. alg1$^-$ (alg2$^-$) denotes Alg.1 (Alg.2) without post-synchronization, alg1^{-2nd} denotes replacing 1st-order approximation in Alg.1 with 2nd-order path selection. Deformation $\varepsilon = 0.15$, $n_{in} = 10$, $n_{out} = 2$ and edge density $\rho = 1$ (fully connected attributed graphs).

in each image. This setting can also speed up the score calculation in our algorithms as it sparsifies the affinity matrix. The edge length affinity matrix between two graphs is calculated by $K^{edge}_{ij,ab} = e^{-\frac{|q_{ij}-q_{ab}|}{0.15}}$, where q_{ij} (q_{ab}) are the Euclidean distance between two points i, j (a, b) that is further normalized to [0,1] by dividing the largest edge value. For real image test, we further add the edge angle affinity matrix in a similar way such that: $\mathbf{K} = \frac{4}{5}\mathbf{K}^{edge} + \frac{1}{5}\mathbf{K}^{angle}$.

Evaluation Setting. The comparing multi-graph matching methods [47,36] and ours all apply pairwise matching solvers as an out-of-box building block. For space limitation, we focus on Reweighted Random Walks Matching (RRWM) as it has been proven [9] in general more cost-effective[5]. Our methods are set to stop when it converges or exceeds 10 iterations and set the consistency inflating parameter in Alg.2 $\rho = 1.05$ for all tests. There are three main performance metrics: i) accuracy: the number of correctly matched inliers divided by the total number of inliers; ii) average matching affinity score over the whole graph set; iii) consistency as defined in Definition (2). In addition, we testify the comparing methods under two conditions: i) large number of graphs $N > n$; and ii) small number of graphs $N <= n$. Note that for the spectral smooth method [36], it requires the number of graphs shall be larger than the number of nodes, thus for the second case, we build a maximum span tree on the super-graph.

5.2 Dataset Description

Synthetic Dataset. The synthetic test is performed with the aim of testing the robustness against deformation and outlier in a quantitative manner. Specifically, a reference graph with n_{in} nodes is created by assigning random attribute to

[5] We have also tested three widely used pairwise matching solvers including Graduated Assignment (GAGM) [21], Reweighted Random Walks Matching (RRWM) [9] and Integer Projected Fixed Point (IPFP) [31] respectively. It is found that the overall performances are insensitive to the selection of pairwise solver.

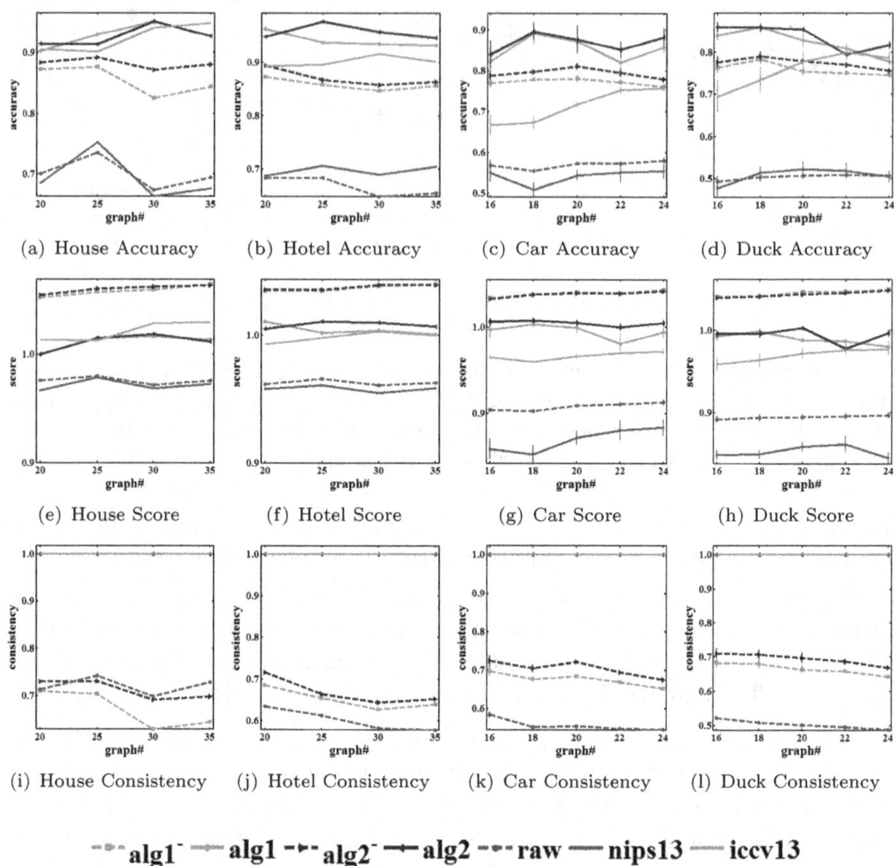

Fig. 3. Evaluation on large sized graph set ($N > n$) by 10 tests of random sampling on two object categories from CMU dataset, and two categories from WILLOW-ObjectClass. $N = 16, 18, 20, 22, 24$; $n_{in} = 10$ and $n_{out} = 3$.

each of its edge, which is uniformly sampled from the interval [0,1]. Based on the created reference graph, the "perturbed" graph set is created by adding a Gaussian noise ε, which is sampled from $N(0, \sigma^2)$, to the edge attribute d_a^{ij} by $d_b^{ij} = d_a^{ij} + \varepsilon$. Each "perturbed" graph is further added n_{out} outliers. This protocol is the same with [9,43,47] etc. Furthermore, we set n_{in} and n_{out} equal across all graphs to make $\mathbf{P}$ a square permutation matrix. This setting is adopted in comparing methods [47,36,40] and so forth.

CMU House/Hotel Dataset. The CMU house/hotel image sequence[6] was commonly used to test the performance of graph matching algorithms [9,6,52,43,47,8] etc. The hotel sequence contains 101 frames and the house sequence consists of 111 frames. Thirty landmarks are annotated in each image for both sequences.

[6] `http://vasc.ri.cmu.edu/idb/html/motion/`

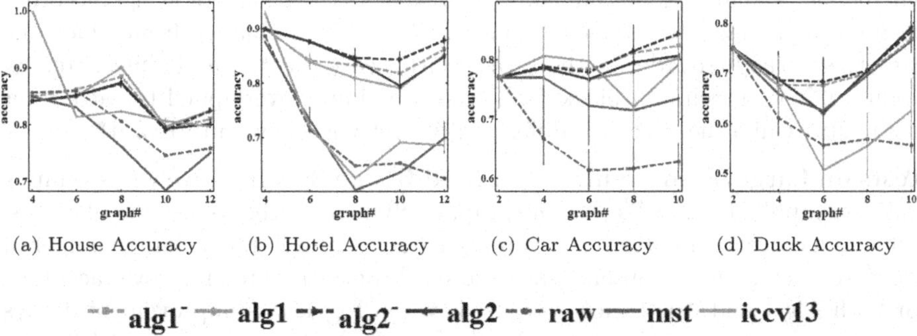

(a) House Accuracy (b) Hotel Accuracy (c) Car Accuracy (d) Duck Accuracy

Fig. 4. Evaluation on small sized graph set ($N > n$) by 10 tests of random sampling on two object categories from CMU dataset, and two categories from WILLOW-ObjectClass. $N = 4, 6, 8, 12$; $n_{in} = 10$ and $n_{out} = 3$.

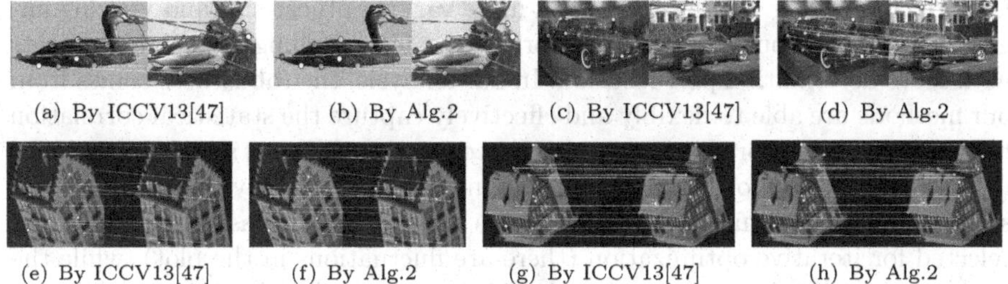

(a) By ICCV13[47] (b) By Alg.2 (c) By ICCV13[47] (d) By Alg.2

(e) By ICCV13[47] (f) By Alg.2 (g) By ICCV13[47] (h) By Alg.2

Fig. 5. Matching illustration by Alg.2 and ICCV13 [47] on Duck and Car of WILLOW-ObjectClass, and the hotel and house of CMU dataset. More yellow and less red denote more accurate matching. White circles denote outliers.

For more details of the dataset, readers are referred to [9,52]. To model the challenges in real world, we use $n_{in} = 10$ markers as the inliers, and randomly chose $n_{out} = 3$ from the rest of the markers as outliers.

WILLOW-ObjectClass dataset. The object class dataset[7] is recently created and used by Cho et al. [8]. Here we perform our tests on two categories of this dataset: Duck (50 images) and Car (40 images) which is constructed with images from Caltech-256 and PASCAL VOC2007 respectively. For each image, $n_{in} = 10$ landmarks were manually labeled on the target object. Moreover, we also add $n_{out} = 3$ outliers of detected points from the background by the SIFT detector.

5.3 Results and Discussion

Tests on Synthetic Dataset. The results on synthetic dataset is shown in Fig.2, which suggest the proposed two methods outperform other methods as the number of graphs grows, under fixed deformation and outlier configuration. The regularized maximization method (Alg.2) further improves the baseline (Alg.1)

[7] `http://www.di.ens.fr/willow/research/graphlearning/`

wherein no regularization is added. Fig.2 also plots the results of using 2nd-order path score maximization policy (termed as Alg.1^{-2nd} in black), from which one can observe the first order method (in green) is cost-effective and almost equally accurate. Note green and black dash lines are almost overlapped to each other in Fig.2(a) while the overhead differs significantly as shown in Fig.2(d).

Tests on Large/Samll Number of Real Image Set. Intuitively (also empirically exemplified in Fig.1(c)), more graphs will increase the robustness of consistency as a correlated indicator towards accuracy. From Fig.3 for large number of image sets test, one can observe the post-synchronization step improves accuracy for both Alg.1 and Alg.2. However, as shown in Fig.4, this improvement decays for small number of graph tests and the role of graduated regularization becomes more important. On the other hand, as shown in Fig.3, the effectiveness of our methods is highlighted on the Willow-Object dataset (Duck and Car) compared with the CMU dataset (House and Hotel). Fig.5 shows some comparing examples from these datasets, from which one can observe the Willow-Object dataset is more challenging for matching with more varying object size and viewing angle. This suggests our methods are more robust for matching less related objects with more deformation perturbation. In our analysis, the robustness comes from our methods are able to flexibly and effectively capture the statistical correlation behavior between score/consistency and accuracy at different score ranges (refer to Fig.1). In the opposite, the comparing method [47] strictly imposes full consistency in the beginning of iteration and is sensitive to the basis reference graph selected for iterative optimization (there are fluctuations in the plot), while the other method [36] imposes synchronization in an one-shot fashion.

6 Conclusion and Future Work

We proposed novel algorithms towards robust multi-graph matching by incorporating both matching scores and matching consistency in an iterative approximating optimization procedure. Their efficacy is demonstrated through convincing experiments conducted on both synthetic and public real image datasets. The underlying rationale is that the two aspects are statistically coupled and can thus be tackled jointly. Our future work include i) study the concept of "partial consistency" that involves part of the nodes; ii) connect unsupervised or semi-supervised machine learning methodologies with multi-graph matching, as the consistency itself can guide the matching and learning.

Acknowledgment. The work was supported in part by NSF IIS-1116886, NSF DMS-1317424, NSFC 61129001,61025005/F010403. The authors would also like to thank reviewers' valuable comments during the whole review process.

References

1. `http://deim.urv.cat/~francesc.serratosa/`
2. `http://www-users.cs.york.ac.uk/~erh/`
3. `http://www.iam.unibe.ch/fki/staff/prof.-dr.-horst-bunke`
4. Besl, P., McKay, N.: A method for registration of 3-d shapes. PAMI (1992)

5. Brendel, W., Todorovic, S.: Learning spatiotemporal graphs of human activities. In: ICCV (2011)
6. Caetano, T., McAuley, J., Cheng, L., Le, Q., Smola, A.J.: Learning graph matching. IEEE Transaction on PAMI 31(6), 1048–1058 (2009)
7. Chertok, M., Keller, Y.: Efficient high order matching. PAMI (2010)
8. Cho, M., Alahari, K., Ponce, J.: Learning graphs to match. In: ICCV (2013)
9. Cho, M., Lee, J., Lee, K.M.: Reweighted random walks for graph matching. In: Daniilidis, K., Maragos, P., Paragios, N. (eds.) ECCV 2010, Part V. LNCS, vol. 6315, pp. 492–505. Springer, Heidelberg (2010)
10. Cho, M., Lee, K.M.: Progressive graph matching: Making a move of graphs via probabilistic voting. In: CVPR (2012)
11. Cho, M., Sun, J., Duchenne, O., Ponce, J.: Finding matches in a haystack: A max-pooling strategy for graph matching in the presence of outliers. In: CVPR (2014)
12. Conte, D., Foggia, P., Sansone, C., Vento, M.: Thirty years of graph matching in pattern recognition. IJPRAI (2004)
13. Duchenne, O., Bach, F., Kweon, I., Ponce, J.: A tensor-based algorithm for high-order graph matching. In: CVPR (2009)
14. Eshera, M.A., Fu, K.S.: An image understanding system using attributed symbolic representation and inexact graph-matching. PAMI (1986)
15. Fischler, M., Bolles, R.: Random sample consensus: A paradigm for model fitting with applications to image analysis and automated cartography. Comm. of the ACM, 381–395 (1981)
16. Foggia, P., Percannella, G., Vento, M.: Graph matching and learning in pattern recognition in the last 10 years. IJPRAI (2014)
17. Gallagher, B.: Matching structure and semantics: A survey on graph-based pattern matching. In: AAAI, pp. 45–53 (2006)
18. Garey, M.R., Johnson, D.S.: Computers and Intractability; A Guide to the Theory of NP-Completeness. W. H. Freeman and Co., New York (1990)
19. Gavril, F.: Generating the maximum spanning trees of a weighted graph. Journal of Algorithms, 592–597 (1987)
20. Goesele, M., Snavely, N., Curless, B., Hoppe, H., Seitz, S.: Multi-view stereo for community photo collections. In: ICCV (2007)
21. Gold, S., Rangarajan, A.: A graduated assignment algorithm for graph matching. IEEE Transaction on PAMI (1996)
22. Hancock, E.R., Wilson, R.C.: Pattern analysis with graphs: Parallel work at bern and york. Pattern Recognition Letters, 833–841 (2012)
23. Hu, N., Rustamov, R.M., Guibas, L.: Graph mmatching with anchor nodes: a learning approach. In: CVPR (2013)
24. Huang, Q., Zhang, G., Gao, L., Hu, S., Butscher, A., Guibas, L.: An optimization approach for extracting and encoding consistent maps in a shape collection. ACM Transactions on Graphics, TOG (2012)
25. Huang, Q.X., Flory, S., Gelfand, N., Hofer, M., Pottmann, H.: Reassembling fractured objects by geometric matching. ACM Trans. Graph., 569–578 (2006)
26. Kim, V.G., Li, W., Mitra, N.J., DiVerdi, S., Funkhouser, T.: Exploring collections of 3D models using fuzzy correspondences. In: SIGGRAPH (2012)
27. Kuhn, H.W.: The hungarian method for the assignment problem. Export. Naval Research Logistics Quarterly, 83–97 (1955)
28. Lee, J., Cho, M., Lee, K.M.: Hyper-graph matching via reweighted random walks. In: CVPR (2011)
29. Leordeanu, M., Hebert, M.: A spectral technique for correspondence problems using pairwise constraints. In: ICCV (2005)

30. Leordeanu, M., Hebert, M., Sukthankar, R.: Beyond local appearance: Category recognition from pairwise interactions of simple features. In: CVPR (2007)
31. Leordeanu, M., Herbert, M.: An integer projected fixed point method for graph matching and map inference. In: NIPS (2009)
32. Leordeanu, M., Sukthankar, R., Hebert, M.: Unsupervised learning for graph matching. Int. J. Comput. Vis., 28–45 (2012)
33. Leordeanu, M., Zanfir, A., Sminchisescu, C.: Semi-supervised learning and optimization for hypergraph matching. In: ICCV (2011)
34. Livi, L., Rizzi, A.: The graph matching problem. Pattern Anal. Applic., 253–283 (2013)
35. Loiola, E.M., de Abreu, N.M., Boaventura-Netto, P.O., Hahn, P., Querido, T.: A survey for the quadratic assignment problem. EJOR, 657–690 (2007)
36. Pachauri, D., Kondor, R., Vikas, S.: Solving the multi-way matching problem by permutation synchronization. In: NIPS (2013)
37. Pevzner, P.A.: Multiple alignment, communication cost, and graph matching. SIAM JAM (1992)
38. Qiu, H., Hancock, E.R.: Spectral simplification of graphs. In: Pajdla, T., Matas, J. (eds.) ECCV 2004. LNCS, vol. 3024, pp. 114–126. Springer, Heidelberg (2004)
39. Shen, D., Hammer, C.D.: Hierarchical attribute matching mechanism for elastic registration. TMI (2002)
40. Sole-Ribalta, A., Serratosa, F.: Graduated assignment algorithm for multiple graph matching based on a common labeling. IJPRAI (2013)
41. Suh, Y., Cho, M., Lee, K.M.: Graph matching via sequential monte carlo. In: Fitzgibbon, A., Lazebnik, S., Perona, P., Sato, Y., Schmid, C. (eds.) ECCV 2012, Part III. LNCS, vol. 7574, pp. 624–637. Springer, Heidelberg (2012)
42. Cour, T., Srinivasan, P., Shi, J.: Balanced graph matching. In: NIPS (2006)
43. Tian, Y., Yan, J., Zhang, H., Zhang, Y., Yang, X., Zha, H.: On the convergence of graph matching: Graduated assignment revisited. In: Fitzgibbon, A., Lazebnik, S., Perona, P., Sato, Y., Schmid, C. (eds.) ECCV 2012, Part III. LNCS, vol. 7574, pp. 821–835. Springer, Heidelberg (2012)
44. Williams, M.L., Wilson, R.C., Hancock, E.: Multiple graph matching with bayesian inference. Pattern Recognition Letters, 1275–1281 (1997)
45. Wong, A., You, M.: Entropy and distance of random graphs with application to structural pattern recognition. IEEE Transactions on PAMI (1985)
46. Yan, J., Li, Y., Zheng, E., Liu, Y.: An accelerated human motion tracking system based on voxel reconstruction under complex environments. In: Zha, H., Taniguchi, R.-I., Maybank, S. (eds.) ACCV 2009, Part II. LNCS, vol. 5995, pp. 313–324. Springer, Heidelberg (2010)
47. Yan, J., Tian, Y., Zha, H., Yang, X., Zhang, Y.: Joint optimization for consistent multiple graph matching. In: ICCV (2013)
48. Zach, C., Klopschitz, M., Pollefeys, M.: Disambiguating visual relations using loop constraints, pp. 1246–1433 (2010)
49. Zaslavskiy, M., Bach, F.R., Vert, J.P.: A path following algorithm for the graph matching problem. PAMI (2009)
50. Zass, R., Shashua, A.: Probabilistic graph and hypergraph matching. In: CVPR (2008)
51. Zeng, Z., Chan, T.-H., Jia, K., Xu, D.: Finding correspondence from multiple images via sparse and low-rank decomposition. In: Fitzgibbon, A., Lazebnik, S., Perona, P., Sato, Y., Schmid, C. (eds.) ECCV 2012, Part V. LNCS, vol. 7576, pp. 325–339. Springer, Heidelberg (2012)
52. Zhou, F., Torre, F.D.: Factorized graph matching. In: CVPR (2012)

Optical Flow Estimation with Channel Constancy

Laura Sevilla-Lara[1], Deqing Sun[2], Erik G. Learned-Miller[1], and Michael J. Black[3]

[1] School of Computer Science, University of Massachusetts Amherst, MA, USA
{lsevilla,elm}@cs.umass.edu
[2] School of Engineering and Applied Sciences, Harvard University, Cambridge, MA, USA
dqsun@seas.harvard.edu
[3] Max Planck Institute for Intelligent Systems, Tübingen, Germany
black@tuebingen.mpg.de

Abstract. Large motions remain a challenge for current optical flow algorithms. Traditionally, large motions are addressed using multi-resolution representations like Gaussian pyramids. To deal with large displacements, many pyramid levels are needed and, if an object is small, it may be invisible at the highest levels. To address this we decompose images using a *channel representation* (CR) and replace the standard brightness constancy assumption with a descriptor constancy assumption. CRs can be seen as an over-segmentation of the scene into layers based on some image feature. If the appearance of a foreground object differs from the background then its descriptor will be different and they will be represented in different layers. We create a pyramid by smoothing these layers, without mixing foreground and background or losing small objects. Our method estimates more accurate flow than the baseline on the MPI-Sintel benchmark, especially for fast motions and near motion boundaries.

Keywords: Optical flow, channel representation, pyramids, large motions.

1 Introduction

Small, fast moving objects are easy for humans to see and track. Their motion is important for biological tasks such as obstacle avoidance, catching, and predator detection. Figure 1(a) shows an example in which a small animated character is viewed from above, running through a bamboo forest [7]. In contrast to biological vision, current optical flow algorithms perform badly in such cases (Fig. 1(e)). We find that this is particularly true for small or thin regions.

The issue stems from the basic assumptions of most current flow methods. Most techniques estimate dense optical flow using two constraints: brightness constancy and spatial smoothness of the flow field [28]. Brightness constancy assumes that the intensity value of a small region remains constant despite its change in location. The brightness term is a non-linear function of the flow and, in gradient-based formulations, is typically linearized for optimization. This linearization is valid only in the case that the displacement is small. In order to capture longer range motion, a coarse-to-fine method is employed [3,5], typically using a Gaussian pyramid [6]. The pyramid is built by successively smoothing and downsampling the images. The problem with this approach is that, for scenes with multiple moving objects, this blurs the pixel values across object

D. Fleet et al. (Eds.): ECCV 2014, Part I, LNCS 8689, pp. 423–438, 2014.
© Springer International Publishing Switzerland 2014

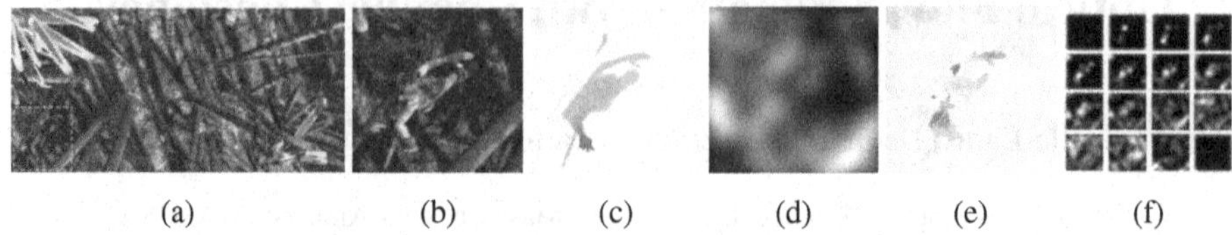

(a) (b) (c) (d) (e) (f)

Fig. 1. Problems with Gaussian pyramids: (a) Image from [7] (b) Detail of a small, fast object (c) Ground truth (d) Blurred image patch from high pyramid level (e) Flow using a Gaussian pyramid [27] (f) CR of the same patch blurred with same kernel size (g) Flow using a CR pyramid and our method

boundaries. For small or thin objects this means that at coarse (high) levels of the pyramid, the object may completely disappear; see Fig. 1(d-e) for an example of a blurred image region and the flow of the Classic+NL algorithm, which uses a pyramid [27].

Instead, if one could segment the scene into objects, then the objects could be matched across large displacements. But since object segmentation is itself an unsolved problem, we need an alternative. In this work we replace the brightness constancy assumption with a descriptor constancy assumption. For this we represent an image using a channel representation (CR). This representation contains a descriptor at each pixel location. This descriptor is a locally weighted histogram.

The advantage of this representation is that performing blurring in CR space does not introduce mixing of the brightness values of the pixels. Instead, the image is decomposed into several different channels, according to the pixel intensities (or other image property). Each of these channels is then blurred separately (Fig. 1(f)). This process allows spreading the information about the pixel values spatially. This smooths the optimization landscape, but prevents the averaging of pixel values that one sees in a Gaussian pyramid. An example of the effect of blurring using CRs in the optimization landscape is shown in Fig. 2. This descriptor constancy assumption is also linearized, to fit in the traditional approach of flow estimation. We then apply the standard coarse-to-fine framework, creating a CR-pyramid by blurring each CR and downsampling it. This prevents losing some small objects at the coarse levels and oversmoothing motion boundaries.

In this paper we start with the original Classic+NL technique, and simply replace the brightness-constancy data term by our descriptor-constancy data term, leaving the rest of the system, including the parameter values, untouched. We call this data term Channel constancy or descriptor constancy. The only parameter that we change is the weight of the smoothness term, since the statistics of the values of an image and a CR are slightly different. We compare the performance of both systems in a synthetic setting as well as on the standard benchmark for large displacements, which is the *MPI-Sintel* dataset [7]. We find that this simple change improves results overall, especially in long range motions and at motion boundaries. This suggests that replacing brightness constancy with channel constancy may also improve other optical flow algorithms.

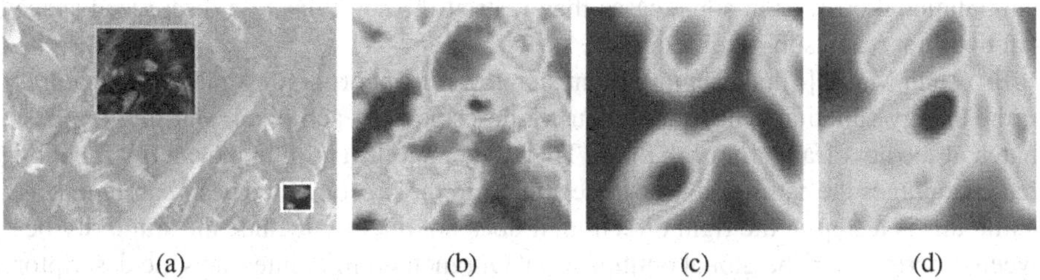

(a) (b) (c) (d)

Fig. 2. Pyramid versus CR pyramid. Computing the sum of squared difference between the hand in the white region in (a) and pixels in the yellow region gives the error surface in (b) with many local minima. The global optimum is near the center. Using a Gaussian pyramid oversmooths the energy (c) and the minimum is less clear. Decomposing the image into a CR and blurring each channel using the same kernel as in (c) yields the energy in (d), which smooths the surface but maintains the global optimum. The error increases from cold (blue) to warm (red) color.

2 Previous Work

The problem of recovering long range motion has previously been addressed [4,25,31], but results on the *MPI-Sintel* dataset [7] show that current methods still fail to capture really large motions, especially of small objects.

Many of the top performing algorithms on the standard datasets are based on the traditional approach of Horn and Schunck [14]. This method minimizes an energy function that is the sum of two terms: the smoothness term that encourages neighboring flow vectors to be similar, and the data term that encourages corresponding pixels to have the same brightness. These classical methods often use a coarse-to-fine approach [6] for computing optical flow. These methods smooth the images and, as a consequence, the optimization landscape, so that motions larger than 1 pixel can be estimated. However, smoothing the images enough to capture large motions makes it nearly impossible to recover the motion of small objects with large displacements.

In principle, this approach fails because each pixel is not discriminative enough. If we consider estimating optical flow as finding correspondences between image pixels, we would like each pixel to be uniquely identifiable so that the correspondence can be found easily. In the traditional approach, these correspondences cannot be found because the blurring makes pixels indistinguishable from each other. One way of avoiding this is adding additional features at each pixel. Estimating the flow becomes finding correspondences where not only the pixel value matches, but also other pixel features like linear filter responses, edges and information about the neighboring pixels [18,25,26,30,31]. This is typically done by including additional feature matching terms in the original energy function.

However, including these terms in the classical approach is not trivial, because it makes the optimization of the energy function difficult. For these terms to be integrated in the framework, they need to be differentiable and increase away from the global optimum, which is often not the case. Therefore, this family of methods that try to incorporate additional features are difficult to optimize, and suffer from increased computational cost, or in some cases they restrict the solutions to a discretized space that does not reach sub-pixel accuracy.

Brox and Malik [4] take an important step towards incorporating additional features in the energy function. They precompute a descriptor at each pixel, and find the best match at the next frame for each pixel. Then they include a term in the energy function that encourages the estimated flow to be similar to the precomputed best feature match. While this is a step in the right direction, it does not directly include the similarity between descriptors in the global optimization. Our method fully integrates the descriptor matching in the global optimization of the energy function.

The descriptor used in this work and its variants have been successfully applied to a variety of problems in the vision literature [2,17,20,21,24,29]. Representing an image using this descriptor at each pixel has received several names, but here we use the most common: channel representation. The descriptor has been extensively used for image denoising [9,10,11,12,16] and pose estimation [15]. It has also been used for affine image alignment [19]. In object tracking, Sevilla-Lara and Learned-Miller [23] use a distribution over grayscale values at each pixel to create an object template that can be smoothed, to reach long displacements. The success with tracking suggests that the descriptor may also be useful for optical flow. No previous work has considered this and we show that the channel representation helps recover the motion of small, fast moving objects.

3 Methods

In this section we first explain the proposed energy function and its relationship to the traditional approach. We then describe how to compute the image descriptor used in this energy function.

3.1 Energy Function

Most optical flow formulations make assumptions about brightness constancy and spatial smoothness, in one form or another. In this formulation, we minimize the following energy function

$$E(u, v) = E_{\text{brightness}}(u, v) + \lambda E_{\text{smooth}}(u, v), \tag{1}$$

where u and v represent the horizontal and vertical flow fields from the first image I_1 to the second image I_2 respectively.

The first (brightness) term assumes that the brightness of a pixel persists over time and is typically formulated as

$$E_{\text{brightness}}(u, v) = \sum_{x,y} \rho\left(I_1(x, y) - I_2(x + u_{(x,y)}, y + v_{(x,y)})\right). \tag{2}$$

where $u_{(x,y)}$ and $v_{(x,y)}$ represent the flow at a pixel (x, y) and where $\rho(\cdot)$ is a robust penalty function that downweights the influence of outliers (i.e. violations of the brightness constancy assumption) [3].

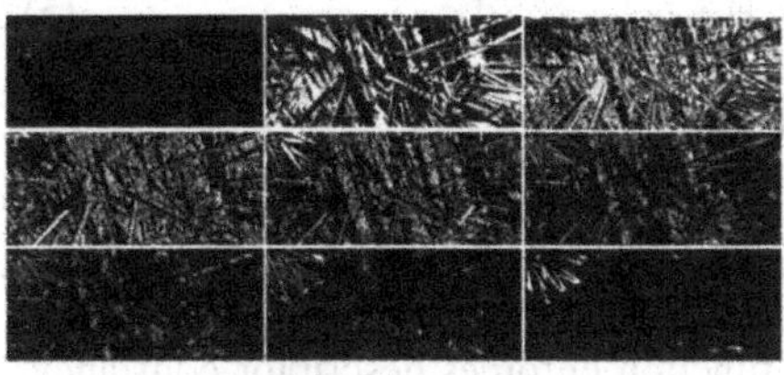
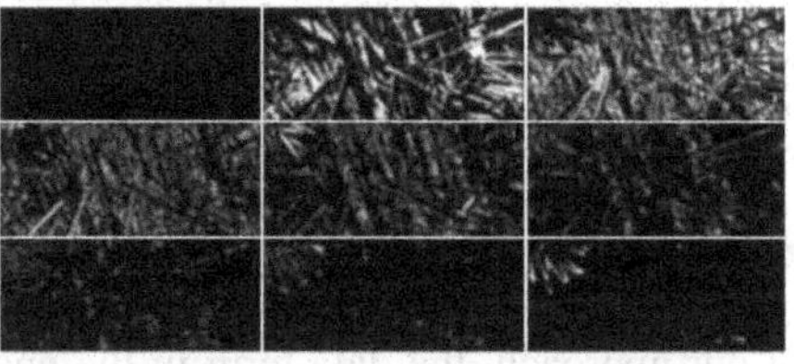

Fig. 3. Left: CR after exploding one of the images from *MPI-Sintel* (see Fig. 1). The number of brightness levels (or layers) has been quantized to 9. **Right**: The same CR after smoothing the layers spatially.

The brightness constancy term is a non-linear function of the unknown flow fields. The traditional approach linearizes the brightness constancy term for optimization and requires the smoothing of the optimization landscape. This is typically implemented by blurring the image as part of a coarse-to-fine strategy. Depending on the size of certain objects in the scene and the amount of blur, some details may be lost. To preserve the details, we need to robustly smooth the object boundaries without mixing pixel values. Next we describe the channel representation designed for this purpose.

3.2 Channel Representation

The channel representation (CR) allows robust smoothing over object boundaries. It contains a probability distribution over the feature space at each pixel location. For example, if the image is in grayscale, the probability distribution will be over values from 0 to 255. A CR is built by "exploding" an image, which places a Kronecker delta function at each pixel, according to Eq 3. At each pixel, this yields a distribution that is 0 for every value, except for the pixel's intensity:

$$d(i,j,k) = \begin{cases} 1 \ \text{if} \ \lfloor \frac{I(i,j)}{\triangle} \rfloor = k, \\ 0 \ \text{otherwise}, \end{cases} \tag{3}$$

where $\triangle$ is the quantization bin size, variable k ranges from $1 \leq k \leq K$, K is the number of bins used for quantizing the feature space, and $\lfloor \cdot \rfloor$ denotes the floor operation.

We can blur a CR to smooth the optimization landscape, by blurring each of the k channels separately as

$$d_s(k) = d(k) * h_{\sigma_s}, \tag{4}$$

where h is a 2D Gaussian kernel of standard deviation σ_s, in each dimension and $*$ is the convolution operator.

Figure 3 shows a visualization of the result of exploding an image and blurring its resulting CR. Because the layers are blurred separately, pixel values are not mixed across object boundaries. Hence we can preserve the fine image details, which is the main advantage of using CRs. Smoothing maintains the property that there is a distribution at each pixel location.

Pixel intensities may change a little over time, for example due to subpixel motion or changes in illumination. Such situations can be represented by uncertainty in the feature space. We achieve such uncertainty by smoothing in the k direction at each pixel

$$d_{ss}(i,j) = d_s(i,j) * h_{\sigma_f}, \tag{5}$$

where h_{σ_f} is a 1D Gaussian kernel of standard deviation σ_f.

3.3 Channel Constancy Assumption

In our approach, the data term in the energy function enforces descriptor constancy, which matches the descriptor at each pixel instead of the pixel intensity. The energy function becomes

$$E(u,v) = E_{CR}(u,v) + \lambda E_{\text{smooth}}(u,v), \tag{6}$$

where the descriptor constancy term enforces that each of the components in the descriptors should match. Let the descriptor at each pixel have K components, and $d_1(x,y,k)$ be the kth component (level) of the descriptor at pixel (x,y) in image I_1. Then the data term becomes

$$E_{\text{CR}}(u,v) = \sum_{x,y}\sum_{k=1}^{K} \rho\left(d_1(x,y,k) - d_2(x+u_{(x,y)}, y+v_{(x,y)}, k)\right). \tag{7}$$

Two CRs can be compared by comparing each of their corresponding components, as in Eq. 7. In this work we use two different metrics: the $L2$ distance ($\rho(x) = x^2$) and the generalized Charbonnier ($\rho(x) = (x^2+\epsilon^2)^\alpha$) [8]. These choices were made based on previous studies [27] that illustrate their advantages. Note that we apply the function to each component of the CRs, not to the pixel values.

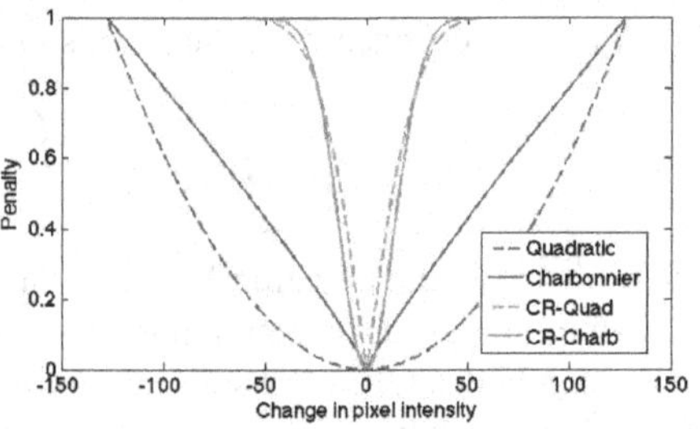

Fig. 4. Shape of the different penalty functions: The generalized Charbonnier and quadratic distance functions change shape when applied to a pair of distributions instead of to a pair of pixels. This new shape is more robust to outliers but it is still convex in CR space like the quadratic function.

To understand what it means to compute the distance between two CRs, we can consider a simple case in which each input image has one non-zero pixel. We then consider the distance as a function of the difference in pixel values. The CRs blur the pixel value across several levels and the error is computed by summing the robust error across all K levels in Eq. 7. In Fig. 4 we plot this error as a function of pixel-value difference and compare the CR case with the standard intensity case for both the quadratic and Charbonnier penalty functions. The effective shape of the error function is quite different in the case of the CR error. In fact, the error function has an interesting property of saturating like a robust error function. This saturation happens even when the penalty function is quadratic.

The intuition here is simple. If there is no blurring across layers, then the difference between two CRs will be zero only when the input pixels have the same value and will be constant for any difference in pixel values; that is, like an inverted delta function. Blur across layers allows different pixel values to be compared and the more smoothing there is the wider the convex region around zero.

4 Optimization

Our goal is to isolate and evaluate the effect of channel constancy versus brightness constancy. To that end we use the existing Classic+NL framework for flow estimation and simply replace the data term while keeping all other elements of the method the same.

4.1 Integration in Traditional Approach

Optimization in Classic+NL involves linearizing the brightness term as part of an incremental warping strategy that gradually warps the second image towards the first image.

By replacing the images with the CR, each incremental warping step linearizes the descriptor constancy term of the energy function (Eq. 7) around the current flow estimate (u_0, v_0), differentiates Eq. 6 w.r.t. the flow increment (du, dv), and sets the derivatives to be zero. The resultant linear equation system to solve for the flow increment are

$$\begin{bmatrix} \sum_k \tilde{\rho}(d) d_x(k)^2 + \lambda L & \sum_k \tilde{\rho}(d) d_x(k) d_y(k) \\ \sum_k \tilde{\rho}(d) d_x(k) d_y(k) & \sum_k \tilde{\rho}(d) d_y(k)^2 + \lambda L \end{bmatrix} \begin{bmatrix} du \\ dv \end{bmatrix} = - \begin{bmatrix} \sum_k d_x(k) d_t(k) + \lambda L u_0 \\ \sum_k d_y(k) d_t(k) + \lambda L v_0 \end{bmatrix},$$

where the weighting function $\tilde{\rho}(x) = 2(x^2 + \epsilon^2)^{a-1}$ for the generalized Charbonnier penalty $\rho(x) = (x^2 + \epsilon^2)^a$, L is the Laplacian operator, d_x and d_y are derivatives of the CR w.r.t. x and y and d_t is the derivative of the CR w.r.t. t. We compute the derivatives by taking the derivative of each layer of the CR, as if they were images.

4.2 Optical Flow Estimation

We use a coarse-to-fine warping-based approach to optimize the proposed energy function. Instead of using the traditional image pyramid [5], we use a pyramid of CRs, as shown in Fig. 5. The first level is computed by exploding the image according to Eq. 3. Each successive level is computed from the previous one by smoothing it as in Eq. 4 and downsampling. We downsample each layer of a CR as if the layer were an image and interpolate using bicubic interpolation.

We compute the flow at the coarsest level of the two pyramids and use the flow to warp the second CR toward the first CR. Each layer of a CR is warped separately. At the next level, the computation of the flow starts from the position of the previous level, interpolating for the points where there is no estimation yet. We use a 3-stage graduated non-convexity (GNC) scheme for the optimization [28]. The first one uses a quadratic penalty, the last one uses a generalized Charbonnier penalty and the middle one uses a linear combination of the two (as in [27]). In practice, since the CRs need to be differentiated, the bottom level of the pyramid is also smoothed with a small Gaussian filter. We call the resulting algorithm *Channel Flow (CFlow)*.

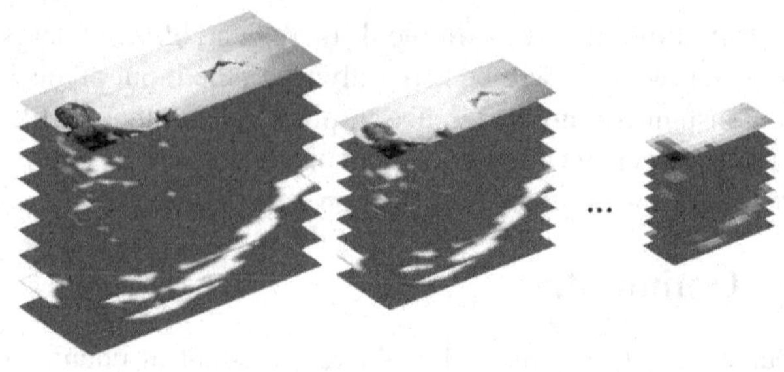

Fig. 5. Channel representation pyramid. Each level of the pyramid is a CR, created by smoothing and downsampling the previous level. The original image is also shown here but is not part of the CR.

4.3 Modeling the Change in Illumination

If there were no smoothing across layers in the k (vertical) direction, the CR would be sensitive to slight changes in image intensity. Despite smoothing across layers, we find that the descriptor constancy is still sensitive to brightness variations. Classic+NL does not actually use brightness constancy but rather uses a texture decomposition for the data term, which reduces the effects of illumination change. In the case of the CR, we take a different approach and explicitly model illumination change.

Previous work [13,32] has shown the advantage of using a model of the change in illumination for techniques that assume brightness constancy. The physics of the natural world make the changes in illumination in a scene multiplicative. However, many images have gamma-correction applied to them, which makes the changes in illumination have an additive effect on the image. Therefore, a plausible model for changes in illumination is: $I(x + u_{(x,y)}, y + v_{(x,y)}, t + 1) = I(x, y, t) + b(x, y)$.

What we need, however, is the effect of brightness changes on the CR. If a pixel changes brightness, this changes the *level* at which the pixel appears in the CR. Thus, to compensate for the brightness change we want to *warp* the CR in the direction that undoes this change. This warping is analogous to the warping we do in space using the optical flow except it happens in the vertical direction of the CR.

To better understand how brightness varies, we used the Sintel training sequences. We warped adjacent frames together using the ground truth flow and computed the brightness difference b at every pixel. We found that the distribution of b values is tightly peaked at zero with heavy tails.

This leads us to a simple method to compute the brightness change. Given the current flow estimate, we warp the input images and compute their difference. We then apply a median filter of 21×21 to obtain a robust estimate of b at every pixel. We can use the flow fields and the brightness change to apply a 3D warp (in space and level) to the CRs as follows:

1. Compute d_1 and d_2 from input images I_1 and I_2
2. Compute optical flow (u, v) using d_1 and d_2 as described in Sec. 4.2
3. Compute I_2^w by warping I_2 according to the flow (u, v)
4. Compute the change in illumination b at each pixel as: $b = I_1 - I_2^w$
5. Filter this field b with a median filter
6. Warp d_2 according to the field of 3D vectors: (u, v, b) .

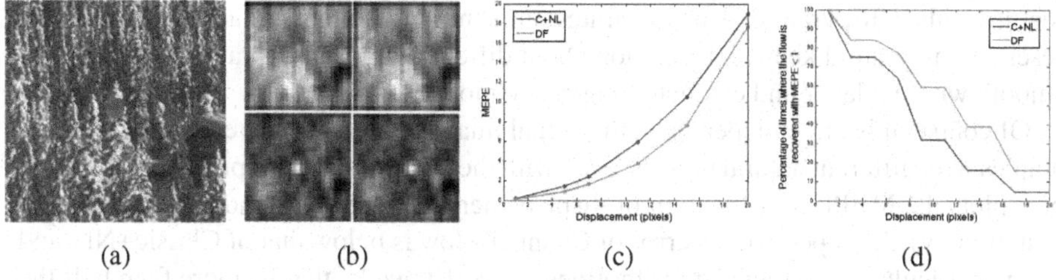

Fig. 6. Image pyramid versus CR-pyramid. The foreground object in (a) is lost at the third level of the image pyramid (b, top), while still distinguishable at the third level of the CR-pyramid (b, bottom). This results in more accurate flow estimation for longer displacements (c). The histogram in (d) shows that in our set of images, the 20-pixel foreground object can be recovered.

We also experimented with including the variable b in the main energy function and optimizing it as we optimize u and v. While this should be the optimal choice in principle, in practice we find that it is computationally considerably more expensive while presenting similar results to our approximation.

5 Experiments

We have built Channel-Flow by replacing the brightness term in Classic+NL with the intent of isolating the contribution of this new formulation. Consequently, here we provide a detailed comparison with Classic+NL. We focus our analysis on the *MPI-Sintel* dataset (both training and testing) because it contains many fast motions of small or thin objects. Below we use mean endpoint error (MEPE) as a measure of accuracy [1].

5.1 Synthetic Experiment

First we evaluate experimentally the core contribution of our technique, which is recovering large motions of small objects. Since it is difficult to create a real dataset of small objects moving fast with ground truth optical flow, we chose to create a synthetic dataset with the properties we want to test. To that end, we take natural images and create a sequence with a small (20 pixels) circular-shaped region in the foreground (Fig. 6(a)). Then for a range of foreground displacements (0-20 pixels), we compute the optical flow and we measure the error. We repeat this for several images.

We compute the optical flow with 4 levels of the pyramid, using Classic+NL and also using our method. Figure 6(b) shows the third level of the Gaussian pyramids for two consecutive frames (top). Note that the foreground object is hard to be distinguished from the background. Even though the texture of the foreground and background were originally different, the blurring of the pyramid has eliminated much of this difference. In the bottom half of Fig. 6(b) we show one of the channels of the CR-pyramid where the foreground was represented, also at the third level. Note that the object is visible as a bright spot near the center of the image in both frames. Clearly this is a trackable feature in the CR pyramid. This illustrates our central hypothesis, that the channel representation pyramid keeps information about different objects separate, allowing us to smooth within a layer and estimate long-range motions.

Of course, this effect depends on the actual image values. We generated 44 such examples with different natural images, each with the same range of displacements. Figure 6(c) plots the MEPE as a function of displacement of the foreground (the background is stationary). As expected, the error of Channel-Flow is below that of Classic+NL, and this is particularly pronounced for motions above 10 pixels; that is, more than half the diameter of the foreground region.

When the methods fail, the errors are large, and these obscure what is going on. Consequently in Fig. 6(d) we report the percentage of times that the flow is accurately estimated (with an MEPE < 1 pixel). When the object moves a distance half its size (10 pixels), we recover the true flow twice as many times as does Classic+NL.

5.2 Constant Albedo Sequences

Experiment description: In this experiment we take the traditional Classic+NL algorithm and simply substitute the traditional brightness constancy by our descriptor constancy term. The **hypothesis** is that using a CR pyramid preserves more information at high levels of the pyramid, thus making the recovery of large motions and motion boundaries more accurate. In other words, we wish to test whether the basin of attraction around the true flow is wider using the CR data term than using the brightness constancy term. **Dataset:** We want to isolate this question, that concerns the optimization landscape, from that of which data term is more accurate or robust to certain phenomena. For this reason we use the albedo sequence of the *MPI-Sintel* training dataset, where pixel values do not change from one frame to the next[1]. Here we did not use the full training set but, rather, sampled a subset at random.

Quantitative results: Numerical results are shown in Table 1. In addition to the traditional mean end point error (MEPE), we report other statistics for further analysis, following the *MPI-Sintel* standard. Categories *matched* and *unmatched* group pixels according to whether they exist in both frames or not, the s- and d- categories group pixels based on their speed and distance to a motion boundary respectively. Further details can be found in the original dataset publication [7]. The table shows that that Channel-Flow produces overall better results than Classic+NL. The two columns where Channel-Flow outperforms Classic+NL by wider margins are: closer to the boundaries ($d10$) and in the large motions ($s40$). These are areas near motion boundaries and fast moving regions. This provides some confirmation, on complex sequences, of our original hypothesis that the CR should be better for these cases.

Qualitative results: Figure 7 shows some examples of the performance of the two methods. Channel-Flow is able to recover certain details or fast motions where Classic+NL fails. On the other hand, Classic+NL produces very nice and smooth flow fields, while Channel-Flow has a stronger tendency towards piece-wise constant fields, presumably due to the data term being very robust to outliers (see Fig. 4).

[1] Here we must use the training set because the test set does not include constant albedo sequences.

Fig. 7. Details of results on the albedo training sequences. Top row: Ground truth. **Middle row:** Flow estimation with the traditional approach often fails to capture large motions, especially of smaller objects. **Bottom row:** Using CR's to represent the image improves the accuracy of the flow in such difficult regions. Some examples are (from left to right): Sintel's hair, the arm and knife, the bat's wing, Sintel's limbs, Sintel's body, Sintel's foot.

Table 1. Results on 398 non-consecutive, randomly chosen, image pairs of the albedo sequence of *MPI-Sintel*. Bold letters show the best results in the category.

Method	**MEPE all**	MEPE matched	MEPE unmatched	d0-10	d10-60	d60-140	s10	s10-40	s40
Classic+NL	4.5297	2.6450	**28.857**	5.7011	3.2381	2.0382	0.7703	3.1173	18.7098
Channel-Flow	**4.2178**	**2.1472**	30.923	**4.7790**	**2.5294**	**1.6181**	**0.6936**	**2.2110**	**15.4031**

5.3 Experiments on "Final" Pass of the Sintel Training Set

Experiment description: In this section we test our method in the same set of frames used in the previous section, but this time the frames contain complex phenomena such as changes in illumination, motion blur, fog, etc. The purpose of this experiment is to test the new data term under these additional phenomena. Then, for each of the problems that we identify we propose a solution. The main disadvantage of the CR formulation is that the penalty function is similar for pixel differences that differ by a little or a lot. This problem can be seen in Fig. 4, where the penalty is similar for a change in intensity of 50 and 100. This lack of gradient makes optimization unlikely to converge to the correct solution when there are brightness changes in the scene. To address this we use the illumination model described in Sec. 4.3.

We call the method with the illumination model C-Flow+I in Table 2. In addition, in order to have valid derivatives, the finest level of the CR pyramid needs to be spatially smoothed. Therefore, the two frames are never compared without spatial blur. To refine the output, we use a 1-level pyramid of Classic+NL, and we call this method C-Flow+I+C in Table 2.

Results: Qualitative results are shown in Table 2. We observe that both the illumination model and the 1-level pyramid steps improve results in all categories. Visualizations of the recovered change in illumination at each pixel are shown in Fig. 9. We

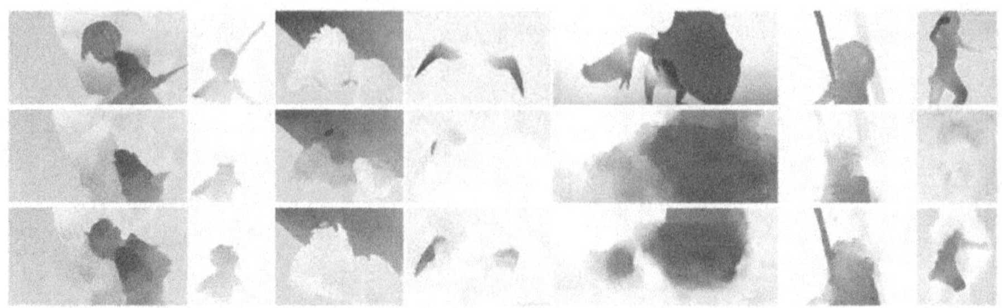

Fig. 8. Results on the "final" training sequences. Top row: Ground truth. **Middle row:** Results with Classic+NL. **Bottom row:** Results with Channel-Flow and the two additions (C-Flow+I+C).

observe that our technique often recovers successfully the low frequency changes in illumination produced by fog, specular reflections, etc. Higher frequency changes are not recovered due to the wide median filter used. Qualitatively, in Fig. 8 we see roughly the same behavior as in the albedo case.

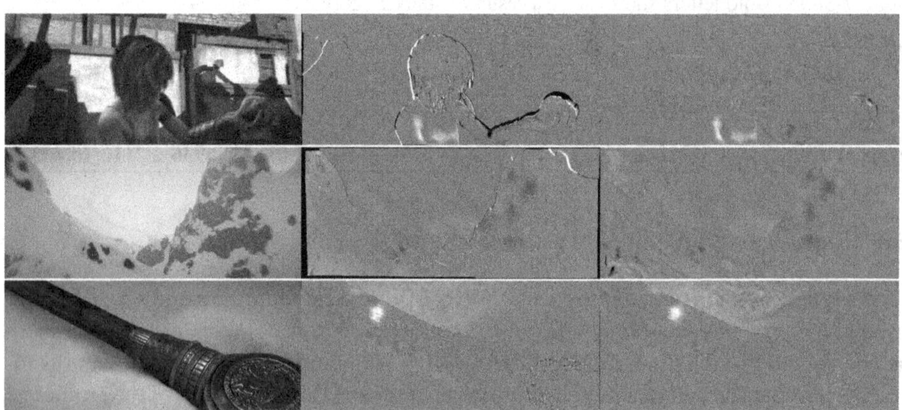

Fig. 9. Visualization of recovered change in illumination. Left: Average of the pair of input frames. **Middle:** Ground truth change in illumination. **Right:** Estimated illumination change. The ground truth change in illumination is estimated by warping the second frame according to the ground truth flow field, and subtracting this from the first frame. If brightness constancy held, the result would be a constant image of zeros. However, changes in illumination and other complex phenomena (motion blur, smoke, fog, etc) violate this.

The runtime of the Matlab code for a 1024×436 *MPI-Sintel* image pair is about 5 hours on a standard Linux desktop. Half of the computational time is spent on solving the linear equation system using the Matlab built-in backslash function. The parameter values used are: $\sigma_{sp} = 1$ and $\sigma_f = 1.2$, $\lambda = 100$, number of bins = 32, $\alpha = 0.45$, $\epsilon = 0.001$.

Table 2. Results on the same 398 non-consecutive, randomly chosen, image pairs of the final sequence of *MPI-Sintel*. C-Flow+I is Channel-Flow with illumination model. C-Flow+I+C is the same, followed by a refinement with a 1-level pyramid Classic+NL.

Method	**MEPE all**	MEPE matched	MEPE unmatched	d0-10	d10-60	d60-140	s10	s10-40	s40
Channel-Flow	8.0147	6.1496	34.418	9.4287	7.0531	5.4954	1.5578	7.3484	42.2794
C-Flow+I	7.6456	5.8759	30.823	9.3090	6.7750	5.2896	1.4564	6.8913	40.9962
C-Flow+I+C	**7.3330**	**5.5448**	**30.736**	**8.9132**	**6.3343**	**4.9935**	**1.3041**	**6.1424**	**40.1855**

5.4 Experiments on the Sintel Test Set

We evaluate our method on the test set of *MPI-Sintel* and the results are shown in Tables 3 and 4; numbers in parentheses indicate the ranking on the Sintel site at the time of submission. We show only a few methods here; see the MPI-Sintel website for the full comparison and images of our results. Consistent with the experiments above, we see a consistent improvement over the baseline Classic+NL, both in the clean and final sets. In addition we compare with LDOF [4], a popular method for dealing with large displacements. We see that a classical formulation with the CR data term largely outperforms LDOF for large displacements without the use of an external matching process. Since our method is based on Classic+NL, it does not benefit from the latest ideas in optical flow. Other methods like DeepFlow [31] are significantly more accurate, even for large motions. Our results suggest, however, that switching from classical brightness constancy to some sort of descriptor constancy may be valuable and we hypothese that this idea will apply to other methods as well.

Table 3. Select results on the *MPI-Sintel* test set for the clean pass. The simple change in data term improves results over the Classic+NL baseline. See the Sintel website for the full table.

Method	**MEPE all**	MEPE matched	MEPE unmatched	d0-10	d10-60	d60-140	s10	s10-40	s40
DeepFlow (6)	5.377	1.771	34.751	4.519	1.534	0.837	0.960	2.730	33.701
Channel-Flow (13)	7.023	3.086	39.084	5.411	3.236	1.918	0.624	2.791	49.021
LDOF (15)	7.563	3.432	41.170	5.353	3.284	2.454	0.936	2.908	51.696
Classic+NL (16)	7.961	3.770	42.079	6.191	3.911	2.509	0.573	2.694	57.374

5.5 Experiments on the Middlebury Dataset

In order to provide a more complete comparison with existing methods, we also test our method in the training set of the *Middlebury* dataset. As we do in the previous experiments, we use the parameter configuration reported by Classic+NL. The MEPE of CR-Flow is 0.287 and the MEPE of Classic+NL is 0.257. We test the statistical significance of these two results and we find them not to be significant. Note that Middlebury motions are small and the value of the CR term for dealing with large motions is not evident here.

Table 4. Select results on the *MPI-Sintel* test set for the final pass. Channel-Flow again improves over the baseline. See the Sintel website for the full table.

Method	**MEPE all**	MEPE matched	MEPE unmatched	d0-10	d10-60	d60-140	s10	s10-40	s40
DeepFlow (5)	7.212	3.336	38.781	5.650	3.144	2.208	1.284	4.107	44.118
Channel-Flow (13)	8.835	4.754	42.064	6.757	4.566	3.657	1.292	5.349	54.648
LDOF (15)	9.116	5.037	42.344	6.849	4.928	4.003	1.485	4.839	57.296
Classic+NL (16)	9.153	4.814	44.509	7.215	4.822	3.427	1.113	4.496	60.291

6 Conclusion

One of the dilemmas of optical flow is that there is a trade-off between the size of the objects and the magnitude of motions that can be estimated. The large motions and complexity of the *MPI-Sintel* optical flow database demand that such trade-offs be addressed. We have shown how to at least partially address this issue by introducing a channel representation to replace the images used in standard methods. This representation maintains more of the image information under significant blurs.

Our paradigm works with the Classic+NL framework and changes only the data term. This allows us to isolate the effects of this term from other properties of a flow method. We have demonstrated quantitative improvement over the baseline method for a controlled experiment of small regions moving quickly. We have also demonstrated improvement over baseline for the *MPI-Sintel* albedo sequences where brightness constancy holds (except at occlusion boundaries). Given that many of the top-performing methods are based on the variational approach, the channel representation may be potentially very useful for many other flow algorithms as well.

Finally we introduced a simple method to deal with changing brightness, which extends the Channel-Flow method to more complex sequences. This simple method could also be used for other flow algorithms. On the difficult *MPI-Sintel* final test set we show improvement over the baseline, especially in areas near motion boundaries and in fast moving regions.

Acknowledgement. DS has been partially supported by NSF grant OIA 1125087.

References

1. Baker, S., Scharstein, D., Lewis, J.P., Roth, S., Black, M.J., Szeliski, R.: A database and evaluation methodology for optical flow. IJCV 92(1) (March 2011), `http://dx.doi.org/10.1007/s11263-010-0390-2`
2. Berg, A.C., Malik, J.: Geometric blur for template matching. In: Proceedings of the 2001 IEEE Computer Society Conference on Computer Vision and Pattern Recognition, CVPR 2001, vol. 1. IEEE, pp. I–607 (2001)
3. Black, M.J., Anandan, P.: The robust estimation of multiple motions: Parametric and piecewise-smooth flow fields. Computer Vision and Image Understanding 63(1), 75–104 (1996)

4. Brox, T., Malik, J.: Large displacement optical flow: Descriptor matching in variational motion estimation. PAMI 33(3) (2011), http://lmb.informatik.uni-freiburg.de//Publications/2011/Bro11a
5. Bruhn, A., Weickert, J., Schnörr, C.: Lucas/Kanade meets Horn/Schunck: Combining local and global optic flow methods. IJCV 61(3), 211–231 (2005)
6. Burt, P.J., Adelson, E.H.: The Laplacian pyramid as a compact image code. IEEE Transactions on Communications 31(4), 532–540 (1983)
7. Butler, D.J., Wulff, J., Stanley, G.B., Black, M.J.: A naturalistic open source movie for optical flow evaluation. In: Fitzgibbon, A., Lazebnik, S., Perona, P., Sato, Y., Schmid, C. (eds.) ECCV 2012, Part VI. LNCS, vol. 7577, pp. 611–625. Springer, Heidelberg (2012)
8. Charbonnier, P., Blanc-Feraud, L., Aubert, G., Barlaud, M.: Two deterministic half-quadratic regularization algorithms for computed imaging. In: IEEE Int. Conf. Image Proc. (ICIP), vol. 2, pp. 168–172 (1994)
9. Felsberg, M.: Spatio-featural scale-space. In: Tai, X.-C., Mørken, K., Lysaker, M., Lie, K.-A. (eds.) SSVM 2009. LNCS, vol. 5567, pp. 808–819. Springer, Heidelberg (2009)
10. Felsberg, M.: Adaptive filtering using channel representations. In: Mathematical Methods for Signal and Image Analysis and Representation, pp. 31–48. Springer (2012)
11. Felsberg, M., Forssén, P.E., Scharr, H.: Channel smoothing: Efficient robust smoothing of low-level signal features. PAMI 28(2), 209–222 (2006)
12. Granlund, G.H.: An associative perception-action structure using a localized space variant information representation. In: Sommer, G., Zeevi, Y.Y. (eds.) AFPAC 2000. LNCS, vol. 1888, pp. 48–68. Springer, Heidelberg (2000)
13. Haussecker, H.W., Fleet, D.J.: Computing optical flow with physical models of brightness variation. IEEE Trans. Pattern Anal. Mach. Intell. 23(6), 661–673 (2001), http://dx.doi.org/10.1109/34.927465
14. Horn, B.K., Schunck, B.G.: Determining optical flow. Tech. rep., Massachusetts Institute of Technology, Cambridge, MA, USA (1980)
15. Jonsson, E., Felsberg, M.: Accurate interpolation in appearance-based pose estimation. In: Ersbøll, B.K., Pedersen, K.S. (eds.) SCIA 2007. LNCS, vol. 4522, pp. 1–10. Springer, Heidelberg (2007), http://dx.doi.org/10.1007/978-3-540-73040-8_1
16. Jonsson, E., Felsberg, M.: Efficient computation of channel-coded feature maps through piecewise polynomials. Image and Vision Computing 27(11) (2009)
17. Koenderink, J.J., Van Doorn, A.J.: The structure of locally orderless images. International Journal of Computer Vision 31(2-3), 159–168 (1999)
18. Liu, C., Yuen, J., Torralba, A., Sivic, J., Freeman, W.T.: SIFT flow: Dense correspondence across different scenes. In: Forsyth, D., Torr, P., Zisserman, A. (eds.) ECCV 2008, Part III. LNCS, vol. 5304, pp. 28–42. Springer, Heidelberg (2008), http://dx.doi.org/10.1007/978-3-540-88690-7_3
19. Mears, B., Sevilla-Lara, L., Learned-Miller, E.: Distribution fields with adaptive kernels for large displacement image alignment. In: BMVC. IEEE (2013)
20. Nordberg, K., Granlund, G., Knutsson, H.: Representation and Learning of Invariance. Report LiTH-ISY-I-1552, Computer Vision Laboratory, SE-581 83 Linköping, Sweden (1994)
21. Oron, S., Bar-Hillel, A., Levi, D., Avidan, S.: Locally orderless tracking. In: 2012 IEEE Conference on Computer Vision and Pattern Recognition (CVPR), pp. 1940–1947. IEEE (2012)
22. Sevilla-Lara, L., Learned-Miller, E.: Distribution fields. Tech. rep., UMass Amherst (2011)
23. Sevilla-Lara, L., Learned-Miller, E.: Distribution fields for tracking. In: CVPR (2012)
24. Snippe, H.P., Koenderink, J.J.: Discrimination thresholds for channel-coded systems. Biological Cybernetics 66(6), 543–551 (1992)
25. Steinbrucker, F., Pock, T., Cremers, D.: Large displacement optical flow computation without warping. In: ICCV (2009)

26. Steinbruecker, F., Pock, T., Cremers, D.: Advanced data terms for variational optic flow estimation. In: Proceedings Vision, Modeling and Visualization (2009)
27. Sun, D., Roth, S., Black, M.J.: A quantitative analysis of current practices in optical flow estimation and the principles behind them. International Journal of Computer Vision (IJCV) 106(2), 115–137 (2014)
28. Sun, D., Roth, S., Lewis, J.P., Black, M.J.: Learning optical flow. In: Forsyth, D., Torr, P., Zisserman, A. (eds.) ECCV 2008, Part III. LNCS, vol. 5304, pp. 83–97. Springer, Heidelberg (2008)
29. van Ginneken, B., ter Haar Romeny, B.M.: Applications of locally orderless images. In: Nielsen, M., Johansen, P., Fogh Olsen, O., Weickert, J. (eds.) Scale-Space 1999. LNCS, vol. 1682, pp. 10–21. Springer, Heidelberg (1999)
30. Weber, J., Malik, J., Devadas, S., Michel, P.: Robust computation of optical flow in a multiscale differential framework. IJCV 14 (1994)
31. Weinzaepfel, P., Revaud, J., Harchaoui, Z., Schmid, C.: Deepflow: Large displacement optical flow with deep matching. In: ICCV, pp. 1385–1392 (2013)
32. Werlberger, M.: Convex Approaches for High Performance Video Processing. Ph.D. thesis, Institute for Computer Graphics and Vision, Graz University of Technology, Graz, Austria (June 2012), `http://gpu4vision.icg.tugraz.at/papers/2012/werlberger_phd.pdf`

Non-local Total Generalized Variation for Optical Flow Estimation*

René Ranftl[1], Kristian Bredies[2], and Thomas Pock[1,3]

[1] Institute for Computer Graphics and Vision,
Graz University of Technology, Austria
[2] Institute for Mathematics and Scientific Computing,
University of Graz, Austria
[3] Safety & Security Department,
AIT Austrian Institute of Technology, Austria

Abstract. In this paper we introduce a novel higher-order regularization term. The proposed regularizer is a non-local extension of the popular second-order Total Generalized variation, which favors piecewise affine solutions and allows to incorporate soft-segmentation cues into the regularization term. These properties make this regularizer especially appealing for optical flow estimation, where it offers accurately localized motion boundaries and allows to resolve ambiguities in the matching term. We additionally propose a novel matching term which is robust to illumination and scale changes, two major sources of errors in optical flow estimation algorithms. We extensively evaluate the proposed regularizer and data term on two challenging benchmarks, where we are able to obtain state of the art results. Our method is currently ranked first among classical two-frame optical flow methods on the KITTI optical flow benchmark.

1 Introduction

Higher-order regularization has become increasingly popular for tackling correspondence problems like stereo or optical flow in recent years. This is not surprising since correspondences in real-world imagery can be modeled very well with the assumption of piecewise planar structures in the case of stereo estimation and piecewise affine motion in the case of optical flow.

Total Generalized Variation (TGV) [4], especially its second-order variant, has shown promising results as a robust regularization term. Consider for example the challenging KITTI Benchmark [9], where TGV-based optical flow models are currently among the top performing optical flow methods [3,23]. The merits of this regularization term are given by the fact that it is robust and allows for piecewise affine solutions. Moreover the regularization term is convex and

* René Ranftl and Thomas Pock acknowledge support from the Austrian Science Fund (FWF) under the projects No. I1148 and Y729. Kristian Bredies acknowledges support by the Austrian Science Fund special research grant SFB F32 "Mathematical Optimization and Applications in Biomedical Sciences".

D. Fleet et al. (Eds.): ECCV 2014, Part I, LNCS 8689, pp. 439–454, 2014.
© Springer International Publishing Switzerland 2014

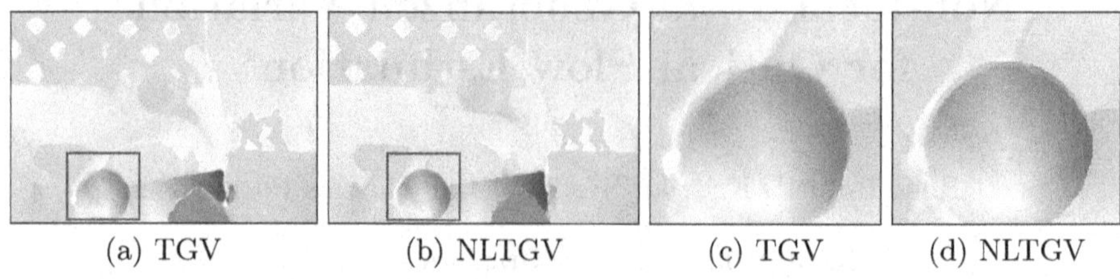

(a) TGV (b) NLTGV (c) TGV (d) NLTGV

Fig. 1. Sample optical flow result from the Middlebury benchmark [1] using the proposed NLTGV regularizer compared to TGV. The regularizer is able to provide sharp and accurate motion boundaries and piecewise affine solutions.

a direct extension of the classical Total Variation semi-norm, which allows for easy integration into existing warping-based models. Note, however, that TGV suffers from the major drawback that it is local in its nature, *i.e.* only directly neighboring pixels influence the value of the regularization term, which may result in bad performance in areas where the data term is ambiguous. Moreover, purely TGV-based models are not able to accurately locate motion and depth discontinuities.

We propose a non-trivial non-local extension to the TGV regularization term, which is designed to remedy these problems. By incorporating larger neighborhoods into the regularizer and providing additional soft-segmentation cues, we are able to show increased performance in optical flow models. Our non-local regularizer remains convex and reduces to an anisotropic variant of the classical TGV regularizer for appropriately chosen neighborhoods, thus it is easy to integrate into existing frameworks. Figure 1 compares the proposed non-local Total Generalized Variation (NLTGV) to classical TGV. It can be seen that in both cases piecewise affine optical flow fields are obtained, but NLTGV results in significantly better localized motion boundaries.

A second important development, which is mainly driven by the recent availability of benchmarks featuring realistic data, is a strong interest in robust data terms. It is evident that in realistic scenarios, good optical flow estimates can only be obtained by a combination of a good regularization term as well as robust data terms. Rashwan *et al.* [20] incorporate dense HOG descriptors directly into the classical energy minimization framework in order to gain robustness against illumination changes, whereas [8] propose a simpler patch-based correlation measure, which is invariant to illumination and morphological changes. We again refer to the KITTI Benchmark, where many of the top-performing methods rely on variants of the Census transform for matching correspondences. The Census transform has shown to be robust to illumination changes both theoretically and in practice [11], which is especially important in realistic scenarios. Note, however, that an often overlooked additional source of errors are scale changes between images, which occur when motion along the optical axis is present in the scene. Classical patch-based data terms, such as the Census transform, fail in such scenarios, since the local appearance strongly changes in this case. To this end we introduce a novel dataterm, which is motivated by the Census transform, in order to gain robustness to scale changes, while still providing robustness to challenging illumination conditions. Our experiments show that using the proposed data term, we are able to obtain increased robustness in image sequences which feature scaling motions.

Related Work. Starting from the seminal work by Horn & Schunk [13], innumerable optical flow models have been proposed. An important development was the introduction of robust regularizers, specifically in the form of Total Variation regularization, and robust data terms [29]. Much research has been devoted to different aspects of this model, like edge-preserving regularization terms [26], or the robustness to large-displacement motions [28].

A non-local variant of Total Variation has been first introduced by Gilboa and Osher [10] for image and texture restoration problems. Werlberger *et al.* successfully showed that a smoothed variant of this regularizer can be used to incorporate soft-segmentation cues into motion estimation algorithms [25]. Sun *et al.* [21] arrived at a similar non-local model by formalizing a median filtering heuristic that is present in many successful optical flow models. Both models are computationally demanding if they are defined for large support window sizes, thus they are often constrained to small support windows. Krähenbühl *et al.* [15] showed how to approximately optimize optical flow models that incorporate non-local Total Variation in the presence of large support windows.

Models which incorporate TGV regularization have seen increasing success recently. Ranftl *et al.* [19] introduced a edge-aware TGV-based model with a Census data term for the task of stereo estimation. Similar to the popular LDOF [5] framework, Braux *et al.* [3] incorporate sparse feature matches into a TGV-based model in order to handle large displacements. Vogel *et al.* [23] also use a TGV-based model and investigate the influence of different robust data terms. These models currently define the state of the art on the KITTI optical flow benchmark.

All of these models use variants of the Census transform as data term in order to be robust against illumination changes, but surprisingly none of them explicitly consider scale changes. In the context of dense descriptor matching it was shown that it is possible to derive a "scaleless" version of the popular SIFT descriptor [12], which were integrated into the discrete SIFT-Flow framework [17]. Xu *et al.* incorporate scale estimation as an additional latent variable into a classical continuous optical flow model [27]. Since they model scale selection as a labeling problem, this model is computationally demanding. Finally, Kim *et al.* propose a locally adaptive fusion of different data costs [14], which in theory could also be used to remedy the negative influence of scale changes.

2 Preliminaries

We denote the optical flow field as $v = (v^1, v^2)^T : \Omega \to \mathbb{R}^2$ and the input images as $I_1, I_2 : \Omega \to \mathbb{R}$. A generic form of an optical flow energy takes the form

$$\min_v J(v^1) + J(v^2) + \lambda \int_\Omega \rho(x, v(x), I_1, I_2)\mathrm{d}x, \tag{1}$$

where $J(.)$ are the regularizers of the individual flow components, $\rho(x, v(x), I_1, I_2)$ is a matching term that gives the cost for warping I_1 to I_2 using the flow v and λ is a scalar regularization parameter.

In order to cope with the non-convexity of the matching term which arises from the warping operation and potentially from the function ρ, we follow the strategy of approximating the data term $\rho(x, v(x), I_1, I_2)$ using a second-order Taylor expansion [25] around some initial flow $v_0(x)$:

$$\rho(x, v(x)) \approx \rho(x, v_0(x)) + (v(x) - v_0(x))^T \nabla \rho(x, v_0(x)) \\ + \tfrac{1}{2}(v(x) - v_0(x))^T (\nabla^2 \rho(x, v_0(x)))(v(x) - v_0(x)) = \hat{\rho}(x, v(x)), \quad (2)$$

where we dropped the explicit dependence on I_1 and I_2 for notational simplicity. In contrast to the approach of linearizing the matching image [29], which leads to the classical optical flow constraint, this strategy allows to incorporate complex data terms into the model. As suggested in [25] we use a diagonal positive semi-definite approximation of the Hessian matrix $\nabla^2 \rho(x, v_0(x))$ in order to keep the approximation convex. The specific form of the regularization term and the matching term will be the subject of the next sections.

3 Non-local Total Generalized Variation

For clarity we focus on second-order regularization, since such regularizers have empirically shown to provide a good tradeoff between computational complexity and accuracy in correspondence problems.

Let $\Omega \subset \mathbb{R}^2$ denote the image domain and $u : \Omega \to \mathbb{R}$ be a function defined on this domain (*e.g.* one component of a flow field). The second-order Total Generalized Variation [4] of the function u is given by

$$\mathrm{TGV}^2(u) = \min_w \alpha_1 \int_\Omega |Du - w| + \alpha_0 \int_\Omega |Dw|, \quad (3)$$

where $w : \Omega \to \mathbb{R}^2$ is an auxiliary vector field, $\alpha_0, \alpha_1 \in \mathbb{R}^+$ are weighting parameters and the operator D denotes the distributional derivative, which is well-defined for discontinuous functions. An important property of this regularizer is that $\mathrm{TGV}^2(u) = 0$ if and only if u is a polynomial of order less than two [4], *i.e.* if u is affine. This explains the tendency of models, which incorporate this regularization term, to produce piecewise affine solutions. Note that the parameter α_1 is related to the penalization of jumps in u, whereas the parameter α_0 is related to the penalization of kinks, *i.e.* second-order discontinuities.

Non-local Total Variation [10] on the other hand can be defined as:

$$\mathrm{NLTV}(u) = \int_\Omega \int_\Omega \alpha(x, y)|u(x) - u(y)| dy dx. \quad (4)$$

Here, the support weights $\alpha(x,y)$ allow to incorporate additional prior information into the regularization term, *i.e.* $\alpha(x,y)$ can be used to strengthen the regularization in large areas, which is especially useful in the presence of ambiguous data terms. Variants of this regularizer have been successfully applied to the task of optical flow estimation [25,15,21].

Motivated by non-local Total Variation (4), Definition 1 introduces a non-local extension of the TGV^2 regularizer:

Definition 1. *Let $u : \Omega \to \mathbb{R}$, $w : \Omega \to \mathbb{R}^2$ and $\alpha_0, \alpha_1 : \Omega \times \Omega \to \mathbb{R}^+$ be support weights. We define the non-local second-order Total Generalized Variation regularizer $J(u)$ as*

$$J(u) = \min_w \int_\Omega \int_\Omega \alpha_1(x,y) |u(x) - u(y) - \langle w(x), x-y \rangle| \mathrm{d}y \mathrm{d}x + \sum_{i=1}^{2} \int_\Omega \int_\Omega \alpha_0(x,y) |w^i(x) - w^i(y)| \mathrm{d}y \mathrm{d}x, \tag{5}$$

where vector components are denoted by super-scripts, i.e. $w(x) = (w^1(x), w^2(x))^T$.

The reasoning behind this definition is as follows: Considering a point $x \in \Omega$, the expression $u(x) - \langle w(x), x-y \rangle$ defines a plane through the point $(x, u(x))$, with normal vector $(w(x), -1)^T$. Consequently the inner integral of the first expression,

$$\int_\Omega \alpha_1(x,y) |u(x) - u(y) - \langle w(x), x-y \rangle| \mathrm{d}y, \tag{6}$$

measures the total deviation of u from the plane at the point x, weighted by the support function α_1. The outer integral evaluates this deviation at every point in the image. This term can be understood as a linearization of u around a point x. Note that the linearization is not constant, *i.e.* as we are interested in a field w which minimizes the total deviations from the (in the continuous setting infinitely many) local planes, the normal vector $w(x)$ can vary, although not arbitrarily as the term

$$\sum_{i=1}^{2} \int_\Omega \int_\Omega \alpha_0(x,y) |w^i(x) - w^i(y)| \mathrm{d}y \mathrm{d}x \tag{7}$$

forces the field w to have low (non-local) total variation itself. Intuitively (5) assigns low values to functions u which can be well approximated by affine functions.

We now derive primal-dual and dual representations of (5), which will later serve as the basis for the optimization of functionals that incorporate this regularizer.

Proposition 1. *The dual of* (5) *is given by*

$$J(u) = \sup_{\substack{|p(x,y)| \leq \alpha_1(x,y) \\ |q^i(x,y)| \leq \alpha_0(x,y)}} \int_\Omega \left(\int_\Omega \{p(x,y) - p(y,x)\} \, \mathrm{d}y \right) u(x) \mathrm{d}x$$

$$s.t. \quad \int_\Omega q^i(x,y) - q^i(y,x) \mathrm{d}y = \int_\Omega p(x,y)(x^i - y^i) \mathrm{d}y \quad \forall i \in \{1,2\} \quad (8)$$

Proof. Dualizing the absolute values in (5) yields

$$J(u) = \min_w \sup_{|p(x,y)| \leq \alpha_1(x,y)} \int_\Omega \int_\Omega (u(x) - u(y) - \langle w(x), x - y \rangle) \cdot p(x,y) \mathrm{d}x \mathrm{d}y$$

$$+ \sum_{i=1}^{2} \sup_{|q^i(x,y)| \leq \alpha_0(x,y)} \int_\Omega \int_\Omega (w^i(x) - w^i(y)) \cdot q^i(x,y) \mathrm{d}x \mathrm{d}y$$

$$= \min_w \sup_{\substack{|p(x,y)| \leq \alpha_1(x,y) \\ |q^i(x,y)| \leq \alpha_0(x,y)}} \int_\Omega \left(\int_\Omega \{p(x,y) - p(y,x)\} \, \mathrm{d}y \right) u(x) \mathrm{d}x$$

$$+ \sum_{i=1}^{2} \int_\Omega \left(\int_\Omega \{q^i(x,y) - q^i(y,x) + p(x,y)(y^i - x^i)\} \, \mathrm{d}y \right) w^i(x) \mathrm{d}x. \quad (9)$$

By taking the minimum with respect to w we arrive at the dual form. □

We will now show two basic properties of non-local Total Generalized Variation:

Proposition 2. *The following statements hold:*

1. *$J(u)$ is a semi-norm.*
2. *$J(u) = 0$ if and only if u is affine.*

Proof. To show the first statement, consider that the supremum in (8) is taken over linear functions with additional linear constraints on p and q. It is well-known that the supremum over linear functions is convex [2] . Since the constraints on p and q form a linear and thus convex set, $J(u)$ is convex. Moreover it is easy to see from (8) that $J(u)$ is positive one-homogeneous. As a consequence the triangle inequality holds, which establishes the semi-norm property.

In order to show the second statement, assume that u is affine, *i.e.* $u(x) = \langle a, x \rangle + b, \quad a \in \mathbb{R}^2$. By plugging into (5) it is easy to see that the minimum is attained at $w(x) = a$. As a consequence we have $J(u) = 0$. Conversely assume that $J(u) = 0$. In any case this requires that

$$\sum_{i=1}^{2} \int_\Omega \int_\Omega \alpha_0(x,y) |w^i(x) - w^i(y)| \mathrm{d}y \mathrm{d}x = 0, \quad (10)$$

which implies that $w(x) = c \in \mathbb{R}^2$, $\forall x \in \Omega$. Consequently

$$\min_{c} \int_{\Omega} \int_{\Omega} \alpha_1(x,y) |u(x) - u(y) - \langle c, x - y \rangle | \mathrm{d}y \mathrm{d}x = 0, \tag{11}$$

if and only if $u(x)$ is of the form $u(x) = \langle a, x \rangle + b$ and hence affine. □

Since the properties in Proposition 2 are shared by TGV and the non-local TGV regularizer (NLTGV), it can be expected that both behave qualitatively similar when used in an energy minimization framework. The main advantage of NLTGV is the larger support size and the possibility to enforce additional prior knowledge using the support weights α_1 and α_0. This is especially advantageous for optical flow estimation, where support weights can be readily computed from a reference image, in order to allow better localization of motion boundaries and resolve ambiguities. Akin to [25] the support weights α_1 and α_0 can be used to incorporate soft-segmentation cues into the regularizer, *e.g.* in the case of optical flow estimation it is possible to locally define regions which are forced to have similar motion based on the reference image.

Figure 2 shows a synthetic experiment which demonstrates the qualitative behavior of NLTGV. We denoise a piecewise linear function using a quadratic data term with TGV and NLTGV, respectively. We assume prior knowledge of jumps in order to compute the support weights and set $\alpha_1(x, y) = 1$ if there is no discontinuity between x and y and $\alpha_1(x, y) = 0.1$ otherwise. Support weights outside of a 5×5 window were set to zero. While prior knowledge of jumps is not

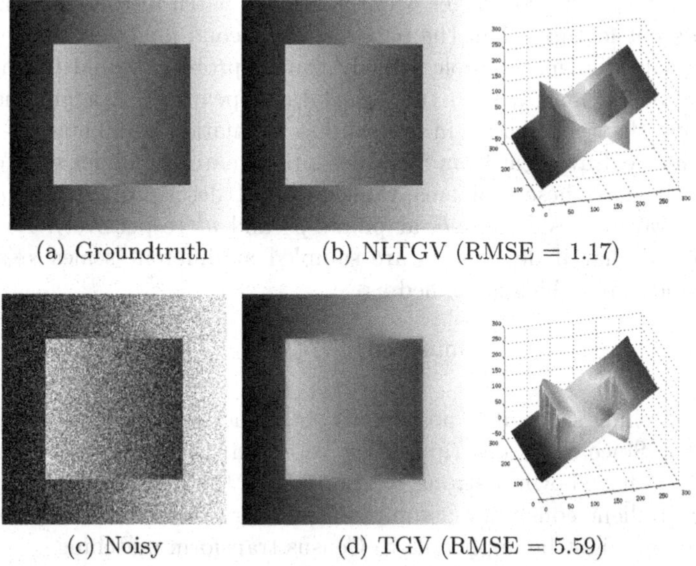

(a) Groundtruth (b) NLTGV (RMSE = 1.17)

(c) Noisy (d) TGV (RMSE = 5.59)

Fig. 2. Comparison of NLTGV and TGV for denoising a synthetic image. NLTGV is able to perfectly reconstruct the groundtruth image. TGV tends to oversmooth jumps.

available in real denoising problems, similar support weights can be easily derived in optical flow estimation from the input images. It can be seen that NLTGV nearly perfectly reconstructs the original image, while TGV has problems with accurate localization of the discontinuities.

4 Scale-Robust Census Matching

The Census transform is a popular approach to gain robustness against illumination changes in optical flow. The principal idea is to generate a binary or ternary representation, called Census signature, of an image patch and measures patch similarity using the Hamming distance between Census signatures.

Let us define the per-pixel Census assignment function for an image $I : \Omega \to \mathbb{R}$:

$$C_\varepsilon(I, x, y) = \text{sgn}(I(x) - I(y))\mathbb{1}_{|I(x)-I(y)|>\varepsilon}, \tag{12}$$

which assigns to the pixel at location y one of the values $\{-1, 0, 1\}$ based on the value of the pixel x. Given two images I_1, I_2 and a flow field $v : \Omega \to \mathbb{R}^2$, the Census matching cost of the flow v is defined via the Hamming distance of the two strings as

$$\rho_C(x, v(x), I_1, I_2) = \int_\Omega \mathbb{1}_{C_\varepsilon(I_1,x,y) \neq C_\varepsilon(I_2,x+v(x),y+v(x))} \mathcal{B}(x - y)\mathrm{d}y, \tag{13}$$

where $\mathcal{B}$ denotes a box filter, which defines the size of the matching window.

Note that classical patch-based matching approaches are problematic when scale changes between two images occur, since the patch in the first image will capture different features than the patch in the second image. If one knew the amount of scale change, a simple remedy to this problem would be to appropriately rescale the patch, such that the local appearance is again the same. Unfortunately the scale change in optical flow estimation is unknown a-priori.

To this end we draw ideas from SIFT descriptor matching under scale changes in order to alleviate these problems: Consider SIFT descriptors h^1 and h^2 computed from two images I_1 and I_2 at points p^1 and p^2 respectively. Hassner *et al.* [12] showed that if descriptors are sampled at different scales s_i and the "min-dist" measure, which is defined as

$$\min_{i,j} dist(h^1_{s_i}, h^2_{s_j}), \tag{14}$$

is used as matching score, it is possible to obtain accurate matches even under scale changes. Since SIFT descriptors are based on distributions of image gradients and [11] has shown a strong relationship of the Census transform to an anisotropic gradient constancy assumptions, it is reasonable to assume that a similar strategy might be applicable to Census transform matching.

We define a variant of the Census transform, which is easily amenable for multi-scale resampling, by using radial sampling instead of a window-based sampling strategy. An example of this sampling strategy is shown in Figure 3. We

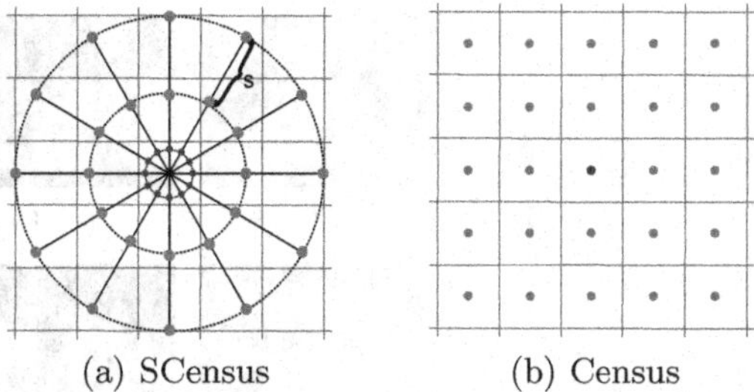

(a) SCensus (b) Census

Fig. 3. Example of the proposed sampling strategy analogous to a 5x5 census transform. The center value is computed by averaging the sampling positions on the inner most ring (red). A ternary string of length 24 is generated from the sampling positions on the outer rings (green). (Best viewed in color).

sample radially around the center point. Samples from the inner ring are averaged and serve as the basis value for generating the Census string, *i.e.* the average takes the role of the center pixel when compared to the standard Census transform. In order to generate the Census string, the gray values of samples on the outer ring are compared to the average value. All samples are extracted using bilinear interpolation, whenever a sampling point is not in the center of a pixel. This strategy allows simple rescaling of the descriptor, which is important for an efficient implementation. Note that this radial sampling shares similarities to Local Binary Patterns [18]. Formally, we fix some radial discretization step $\theta = \frac{2\pi}{K}$ and a radius r and introduce scale depended coordinates $\hat{x} = (\hat{x}^1, \hat{x}^2)^T$

$$\hat{x}^1(k,s,r) = x^1 + rs\cos(k\theta), \qquad \hat{x}^2(k,s,r) = x^2 + rs\sin(k\theta) \tag{15}$$

We define the difference between the average value of the inner ring $r_i = \frac{s}{4}$ and the l-th sample from an outer ring r as

$$f(I,x,l,s,r) = \tfrac{1}{K}\sum_{k=1}^{K}(G_s * I)(\hat{x}(k,s,\tfrac{s}{4})) - (G_s * I)(\hat{x}(l,s,r)), \tag{16}$$

where G_s denotes a Gaussian kernel with variance s. Analogous to the Census assignment function (12) we define the scale-dependent Census assignment function as

$$C_\varepsilon^s(I,x,l,r) = \operatorname{sgn}(f(I,x,l,s,r))\mathbb{1}_{|f(I,x,l,s,r)|>\varepsilon}, \tag{17}$$

This definition allows to compare descriptors at different scales s_1 and s_2 using the Hamming distance:

$$\rho_{s_2}^{s_1}(x,v(x),I_1,I_2) = \sum_{l=1}^{L}\sum_{r=1}^{R}\mathbb{1}_{C_\varepsilon^{s_1}(I_1,x,l,r)\neq C_\varepsilon^{s_2}(I_2,x+v(x),l,r)}. \tag{18}$$

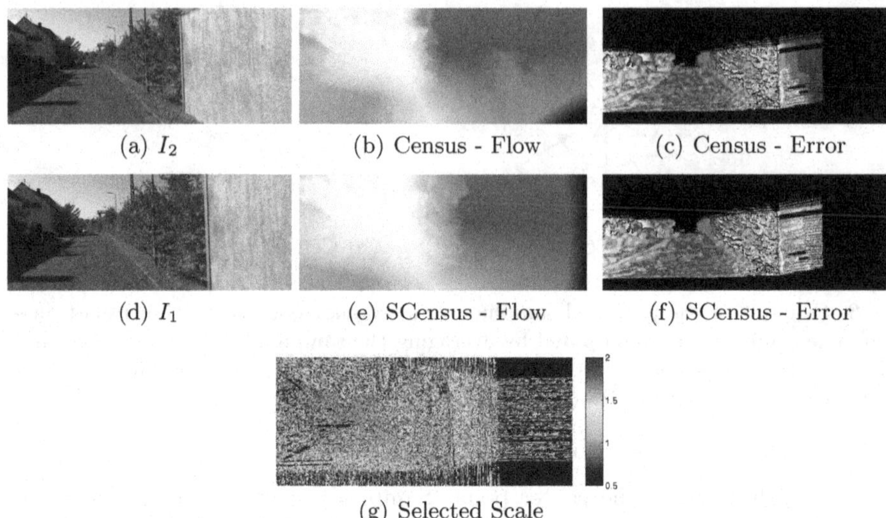

Fig. 4. Example behaviour of the Census dataterm and the scale-robust Census dataterm. The wall to the right undergoes a strong scale change. (b)-(c): Census fails in these areas. (e)-(f): Using scale-robust Census we are able to find a correct flow field. (g) shows the scale that was locally selected by the data term. (Best viewed in color).

By introducing the "min-dist" measure we finally arrive at the scale-robust Census data term:

$$\rho(x, v(x), I_1, I_2) = \min_{s_1, s_2} \rho_{s_2}^{s_1}(x, v(x), I_1, I_2). \tag{19}$$

While this data term is highly non-linear and non-convex, it can still be easily integrated into our continuous model using the convex quadratic approximation (2).

In practice we fix the scale in the first first image to the original scale and compute $\rho_{s_2}^1$ for a number of scales s_2. Note that this definition is slightly biased toward forward motion, but is also able to handle moderate scale changes in the other direction.

Figure 4 shows the qualitative behavior of the proposed data term in areas that undergo a strong scale change. It can be seen that the proposed data term is able to successfully choose the correct scale on many points, which allows the global model to achieve accurate results.

5 Discretization and Minimization

For minimization we use the preconditioned primal-dual scheme [7]. We discretize (1) on the regular rectangular pixel grid of size $M \times N$ and use the index $1 \leq i \leq MN$ to refer to individual pixels in this grid. Let $v^i \in \mathbb{R}^2$ denote the flow at the i-th pixel, which is at the location $l_i = (x^1(i), x^2(i))^T$. In order to allow for a simpler notation, we introduce a signed distance matrix

$$D_{ij} = \begin{pmatrix} d_{ij}^1 & d_{ij}^2 & 0 & 0 \\ 0 & 0 & d_{ij}^1 & d_{ij}^2 \end{pmatrix} \in \mathbb{R}^{2\times 4},$$

with $d_{ij} = (d_{ij}^1, d_{ij}^2)^T = l_j - l_i$. Let $p^{ij} \in \mathbb{R}^2$ and $q^{ij} \in \mathbb{R}^4$ be the dual variable associated to the connection of pixels i and j. The discretized model can be written in its primal-dual formulation as

$$\min_{v,w} \max_{\substack{\|p^{ij}\|_\infty \le \alpha_1^{ij} \\ \|q^{ij}\|_\infty \le \alpha_0^{ij}}} \sum_i \sum_{j>i} \left[(v^i - v^j + D_{ij} w^i) \cdot p^{ij} + (w^i - w^j) \cdot q^{ij} \right] + \lambda \sum_i \hat{\rho}(i, v^i). \tag{20}$$

Remark 1. In order to prevent double counting of edges we set the support weights in (20) to zero for all $y^1(i) \le x^1(i)$ or $(y^2(i) \le x^2(i)) \wedge (y^1(i) \le x^1(i))$.

Using (9) we can derive the optimization scheme:

$$\begin{cases} p_{n+1}^{ij} &= \max(-\alpha_1^{ij}, \min(\alpha_1^{ij}, p_n^{ij} + \sigma_p(\bar{v}_n^i - \bar{v}_n^j + D_{ij}\bar{w}_n^i)) \\ q_{n+1}^{ij} &= \max(-\alpha_0^{ij}, \min(\alpha_0^{ij}, q_n^{ij} + \sigma_q(\bar{w}_n^i - \bar{w}_n^j))) \\ v_{n+1}^i &= \mathrm{prox}_{\tau_v \lambda \hat{\rho}}(v_n^i - \tau_v \sum_{j>i}(p_{n+1}^{ij} - p_{n+1}^{ji})) \\ w_{n+1}^i &= w_n^i - \tau_w \sum_{j>i}(q_{n+1}^{ij} - q_{n+1}^{ji} + D_{ij}^T p_{n+1}^{ij}) \\ \bar{v}_{n+1}^i &= 2v_{n+1}^i - v_n^i \\ \bar{w}_{n+1}^i &= 2w_{n+1}^i - w_n^i \end{cases}$$

where minima and maxima are taken componentwise. The proximal operator $\mathrm{prox}_{t\hat{\rho}}(\hat{u})$ with respect to the quadratic approximation of the data term is given by

$$\mathrm{prox}_{t\hat{\rho}}(\hat{v}^i) = (\nabla^2 \rho(v_0^i) + \tfrac{1}{t} I)^{-1} (\tfrac{1}{t}\hat{v}^i - \nabla \rho(v_0^i) + \nabla^2 \rho(v_0^i) v_0). \tag{21}$$

We compute support weights based on color similarities and spatial proximity:

$$\alpha_1^{ij} = \frac{1}{Z^i} \exp(-\tfrac{\|I_1^i - I_1^j\|}{w_c}) \exp(-\tfrac{\|l_j - l_i\|}{w_p}), \quad \alpha_0^{ij} = c\alpha_1^{ij}, \tag{22}$$

where w_c and w_p are user-chosen parameters that allow to weight the influence of the individual terms and Z^i ensures that the support weights sum to one. Note that in practice we constrain the influence of the non-locality in a window of size $2w_p + 1$ in order to keep optimization tractable (e.g. weights outside the window are set to zero, which allows to drop corresponding dual variables from the optimization problem). Figure 5 shows the influence of the parameters w_p and and w_c on the average endpoint error (EPE), evaluated on the Middlebury training set [1]. It can be seen that larger spatial influence results in lower EPE, whereas a too large color similarity parameter results in oversmoothing and consequently yields higher EPE.

As is common, the optimization is embedded into a coarse-to-fine warping framework in order to cope with large motions.

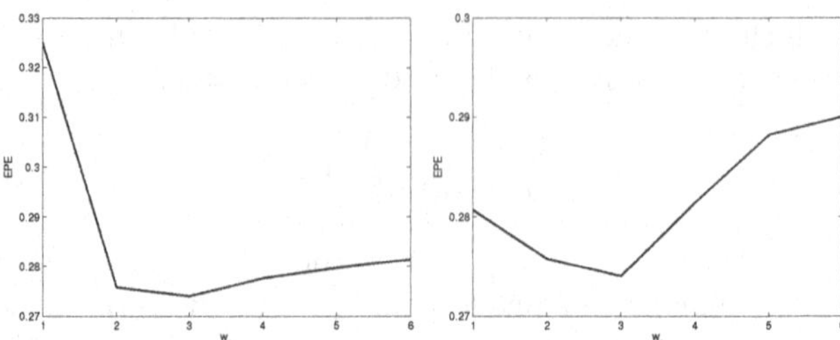

Fig. 5. Influence of the spatial proximity parameter w_p an the color proximity parameter w_c on EPE evaluated on the Middlebury training set

6 Experiments

In this section we evaluate the performance of the proposed model on two challenging data sets. The model was implemented using CUDA; all experiments were conducted on a Geforce 780Ti GPU. We use a scale factor of 0.8 for the coarse-to-fine pyramid and 15 warps per pyramid level. For the scale-robust data term we evenly sample 7 scales between 0.5 and 2 in both image. We fix $w_p = 2$, which gives a good trade-off between accuracy and computational complexity. The remaining parameters were adapted for each benchmark individually.

KITTI Benchmark. The KITTI Benchmark [9] is composed of real-world images taken from an automotive platform. The data set is split into a training set and a test set of 194 images each. We use the training set, where groundtruth optical flow is available, to show the influence of non-local TGV as well as the scale-robust data term. As a baseline model we use standard TGV with the Census term (TGV-C), as it has been shown that this combination already works well on this dataset. We compare different combinations of regularizers and data terms: Standard TGV, non-local TV, as defined in (4), and NLTGV. The suffixes -C and -SC denote Census and scale-robust Census, respectively.

We use a small subset of the training set (20% of the images) to find optimal parameters for each method using grid-search. The Census and NLTGV window sizes were set to 5×5. Since the groundtruth flow fields in this data set are not

Table 1. Average error in % for different models and different error thresholds on the KITTI NOC-training set

	TGV-C	NLTV-C	NLTGV-C	TGV-SC	NLTV-SC	NLTGV-SC
$2px$	12.86	12.38	7.58	11.73	11.29	**7.35**
$3px$	10.38	9.59	5.74	9.19	8.57	**5.50**
$4px$	8.99	8.27	4.90	7.87	7.30	**4.59**
$5px$	8.03	7.48	4.34	6.97	6.53	**4.00**

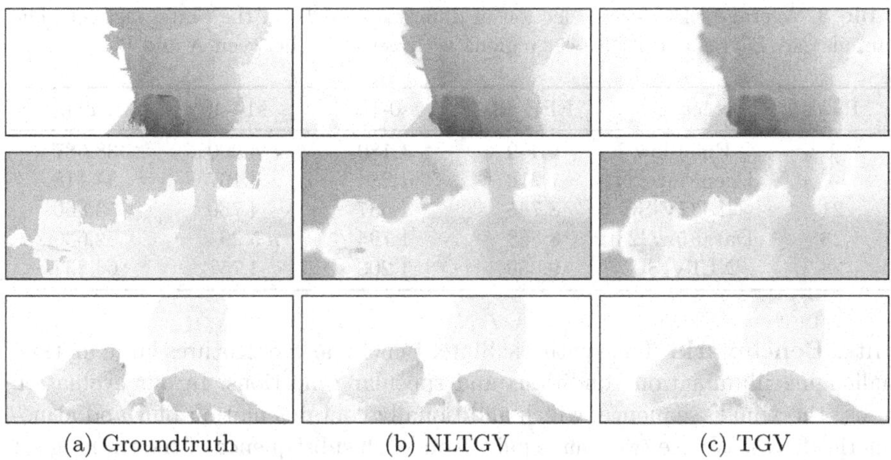

(a) Groundtruth (b) NLTGV (c) TGV

Fig. 6. Comparison between NLTGV and TGV on the Sintel Benchmark

pixel-accurate, we follow the officially suggested methodology of evaluating the percentage of pixels, which have endpoint error above some threshold [9].

Table 1 shows a comparison of TGV and NLTV to NLTGV, as well as the influence of the scale-robust Census data term. TGV and NLTV perform similar, which is in accordance to the results of similar NLTV-based models on this dataset (*cf.* [22]). NLTGV gives a significantly lower error with both data terms. This can be attributed to more accurate motion boundaries and a better behaviour in occluded and ambiguous areas. Using the scale-robust Census data term additionally lowers the error for both models, with NLTGV-SC giving the lowest overall error. Table 2 shows results on the test set of this benchmark, where our method is currently ranked first among two-frame optical flow methods.

Table 2. Average error on the KITTI test set for error thresholds $3px$ and $2px$. Suffixes "Noc" and "All" refer to errors evaluated in non-occluded and all regions, respectively. Methods "DDR-DF" and "EpicFlow" were unpublished at the time of writing. We show the six best-performing two-frame optical flow methods.

	Out-Noc [%]		Out-All [%]		Avg-Noc [px]	Avg-All [px]	Runtime [s]
	3px	2px	3px	2px			
NLTGV-SC	**5.93**	**7.64**	**11.96**	**14.55**	1.6	3.8	16
DDR-DF	6.03	8.23	13.08	16.01	1.6	**2.7**	60
TGV2ADCS [3]	6.20	8.04	15.15	17.87	1.5	4.5	12
DataFlow [23]	7.11	9.16	14.57	17.41	1.9	5.5	180
EpicFlow	7.19	9.53	16.15	19.47	**1.4**	3.7	15
DeepFlow [24]	7.22	9.31	17.79	20.44	1.5	5.8	17

Table 3. Average EPE for a selection of different models on the Sintel test set. The columns "sA-B" refer to EPE over regions with velocities between A and B.

Rank	Method	EPE all	s0-10	s10-40	s40+
1	EpicFlow	6.469	1.180	4.000	38.687
4	DeepFlow [24]	7.212	1.284	4.107	44.118
21	NLTGV-SC	8.746	1.587	4.780	53.860
23	DataFlow [23]	8.868	1.794	5.294	52.636
28	NLTV-SC	9.855	1.202	4.757	64.834

Sintel Benchmark. The synthetic Sintel Benchmark [6] features large motion, challenging illumination conditions and specular reflections. In our evaluation we use the "final" sequence, which additionally contains motion blur and atmospheric effects. We use two image pairs from each subsequence of the training set to set the parameters and report the average endpoint error as error measure.

Table 3 show results on the Sintel test set. We see an improvement over the TGV-based model [23] and an NLTV-based model (NLTV-SC). The most critical regions for the overall error are high-velocity regions, which are problematic in purely coarse-to-fine-based methods. Hence, it is not surprising that methods which integrate some form of sparse prior matching [24,16] fair better than classical coarse-to-fine-based approaches on this dataset. Note that a-priori matches could be easily integrated into our model [3]. We leave such an extension for future work. Finally, Figure 6 shows a qualitative comparison between TGV and NLTGV on this benchmark.

7 Conclusion

In this paper we have introduced a novel higher-order regularization term for variational models, called non-local Total Generalized Variation. The principal idea of this regularizer is to measure deviations of a function from local linear approximations, where an additional spatial smoothness assumption is imposed onto the linear approximations. The proposed regularization term allows for piecewise affine solutions and is able to incorporate soft-segmentation cues, which is especially appealing for tasks like optical flow estimation and stereo. Additionally, we introduced a novel data term for optical flow estimation, which is robust to scale and illumination changes, as they frequently occur in optical flow imagery. Our experiments show that an optical flow model composed of non-local Total Generalized Variation together with the proposed scale robust data term is able to significantly improve optical flow accuracy.

References

1. Baker, S., Scharstein, D., Lewis, J.P., Roth, S., Black, M.J., Szeliski, R.: A database and evaluation methodology for optical flow. International Journal of Computer Vision 92(1), 1–31 (2011)

2. Boyd, S., Vandenberghe, L.: Convex Optimization. Cambridge University Press, New York (2004)
3. Braux-Zin, J., Dupont, R., Bartoli, A.: A general dense image matching framework combining direct and feature-based costs. In: International Conference on Computer Vision, ICCV (2013)
4. Bredies, K., Kunisch, K., Pock, T.: Total generalized variation. SIAM Journal on Imaging Sciences 3(3), 492–526 (2010)
5. Brox, T., Malik, J.: Large displacement optical flow: descriptor matching in variational motion estimation. IEEE Transactions on Pattern Analysis and Machine Intelligence 33(3), 500–513 (2011)
6. Butler, D.J., Wulff, J., Stanley, G.B., Black, M.J.: A naturalistic open source movie for optical flow evaluation. In: Fitzgibbon, A., Lazebnik, S., Perona, P., Sato, Y., Schmid, C. (eds.) ECCV 2012, Part VI. LNCS, vol. 7577, pp. 611–625. Springer, Heidelberg (2012)
7. Chambolle, A., Pock, T.: A first-order primal-dual algorithm or convex problems with applications to imaging. Journal of Mathematical Imaging and Vision 40(1), 120–145 (2011)
8. Demetz, O., Hafner, D., Weickert, J.: The complete rank transform: A tool for accurate and morphologically invariant matching of structures. In: British Machine Vision Conference, BMVC (2013)
9. Geiger, A., Lenz, P., Urtasun, R.: Are we ready for autonomous driving? the kitti vision benchmark suite. In: Conference on Computer Vision and Pattern Recognition, CVPR (2012)
10. Gilboa, G., Osher, S.: Nonlocal operators with applications to image processing. Multiscale Modeling & Simulation 7(3), 1005–1028 (2008)
11. Hafner, D., Demetz, O., Weickert, J.: Why is the census transform good for robust optic flow computation? In: Kuijper, A., Bredies, K., Pock, T., Bischof, H. (eds.) SSVM 2013. LNCS, vol. 7893, pp. 210–221. Springer, Heidelberg (2013)
12. Hassner, T., Mayzels, V., Zelnik-Manor, L.: On sifts and their scales. In: Conference on Computer Vision and Pattern Recognition, CVPR (2012)
13. Horn, B.K.P., Schunck, B.G.: Determining optical flow. Artifical Intelligence 17, 185–203 (1981)
14. Kim, T.H., Lee, H.S., Lee, K.M.: Optical flow via locally adaptive fusion of complementary data costs. In: International Conference on Computer Vision, ICCV (2013)
15. Krähenbühl, P., Koltun, V.: Efficient nonlocal regularization for optical flow. In: Fitzgibbon, A., Lazebnik, S., Perona, P., Sato, Y., Schmid, C. (eds.) ECCV 2012, Part I. LNCS, vol. 7572, pp. 356–369. Springer, Heidelberg (2012)
16. Leordeanu, M., Zanfir, A., Sminchisescu, C.: Locally affine sparse-to-dense matching for motion and occlusion estimation. In: International Conference on Computer Vision, ICCV (2013)
17. Liu, C., Yuen, J., Torralba, A.: Sift flow: Dense correspondence across scenes and its applications. IEEE Transactions on Pattern Analysis and Machine Intelligence 33(5), 978–994 (2011)
18. Ojala, T., Pietikäinen, M., Harwood, D.: A comparative study of texture measures with classification based on featured distributions. Pattern Recognition 29(1), 51–59 (1996)
19. Ranftl, R., Gehrig, S., Pock, T., Bischof, H.: Pushing the Limits of Stereo Using Variational Stereo Estimation. In: Intelligent Vehicles Symposium (2012)

20. Rashwan, H.A., Mohamed, M.A., García, M.A., Mertsching, B., Puig, D.: Illumination robust optical flow model based on histogram of oriented gradients. In: Weickert, J., Hein, M., Schiele, B. (eds.) GCPR 2013. LNCS, vol. 8142, pp. 354–363. Springer, Heidelberg (2013)
21. Sun, D., Roth, S., Black, M.J.: Secrets of optical flow estimation and their principles. In: Conference on Computer Vision and Pattern Recognition (CVPR), pp. 2432–2439 (2010)
22. Sun, D., Roth, S., Black, M.: A quantitative analysis of current practices in optical flow estimation and the principles behind them. International Journal of Computer Vision 106(2), 115–137 (2014)
23. Vogel, C., Roth, S., Schindler, K.: An evaluation of data costs for optical flow. In: Weickert, J., Hein, M., Schiele, B. (eds.) GCPR 2013. LNCS, vol. 8142, pp. 343–353. Springer, Heidelberg (2013)
24. Weinzaepfel, P., Revaud, J., Harchaoui, Z., Schmid, C.: DeepFlow: Large displacement optical flow with deep matching. In: International Conference on Computer Vision, ICCV (2013)
25. Werlberger, M., Pock, T., Bischof, H.: Motion estimation with non-local total variation regularization. In: Conference on Computer Vision and Pattern Recognition, CVPR (2010)
26. Werlberger, M., Trobin, W., Pock, T., Wedel, A., Cremers, D., Bischof, H.: Anisotropic huber-l1 optical flow. In: British Machine Vision Conference, BMVC (2009)
27. Xu, L., Dai, Z., Jia, J.: Scale invariant optical flow. In: Fitzgibbon, A., Lazebnik, S., Perona, P., Sato, Y., Schmid, C. (eds.) ECCV 2012, Part II. LNCS, vol. 7573, pp. 385–399. Springer, Heidelberg (2012)
28. Xu, L., Jia, J., Matsushita, Y.: Motion detail preserving optical flow estimation. IEEE Transactions on Pattern Analysis and Machine Intelligence 34(9), 1744–1757 (2012)
29. Zach, C., Pock, T., Bischof, H.: A duality based approach for realtime tv-l1 optical flow. In: Hamprecht, F.A., Schnörr, C., Jähne, B. (eds.) DAGM 2007. LNCS, vol. 4713, pp. 214–223. Springer, Heidelberg (2007)

Learning Brightness Transfer Functions for the Joint Recovery of Illumination Changes and Optical Flow

Oliver Demetz[1,⋆], Michael Stoll[2,⋆], Sebastian Volz[2], Joachim Weickert[1], and Andrés Bruhn[2]

[1] Mathematical Analysis Group, Saarland University, Saarbrücken, Germany
{demetz,weickert}@mia.uni-saarland.de

[2] Institute for Visualization and Interactive Systems, University of Stuttgart, Germany
{stoll,volz,bruhn}@vis.uni-stuttgart.de

Abstract. The increasing importance of outdoor applications such as driver assistance systems or video surveillance tasks has recently triggered the development of optical flow methods that aim at performing robustly under uncontrolled illumination. Most of these methods are based on patch-based features such as the normalized cross correlation, the census transform or the rank transform. They achieve their robustness by locally discarding both absolute brightness and contrast. In this paper, we follow an alternative strategy: Instead of discarding potentially important image information, we propose a novel variational model that jointly estimates *both* illumination changes *and* optical flow. The key idea is to parametrize the illumination changes in terms of basis functions that are learned from training data. While such basis functions allow for a meaningful representation of illumination effects, they also help to distinguish real illumination changes from motion-induced brightness variations if supplemented by additional smoothness constraints. Experiments on the KITTI benchmark show the clear benefits of our approach. They do not only demonstrate that it is possible to obtain meaningful basis functions, they also show state-of-the-art results for robust optical flow estimation.

1 Introduction

Three decades after the seminal work of Horn and Schunck [22], dense variational optical flow methods have found their way into numerous real-world applications such as driver assistance systems [33], markerless motion capture [13], long-term trajectory analysis [32] as well as motion-aware video editing [37]. Based on the minimization of a global energy functional that combines constancy assumptions (data term) with regularity constraints (smoothness term), variational methods allow both a transparent modeling and an accurate estimation of the results. Since many real-world applications require to process outdoor sequences, it is not surprising that the robustness of optical flow methods under uncontrolled illumination has become a major challenge. This is also reflected in the design of recent real-world benchmarks such as the KITTI Vision Benchmark Suite [14]. It provides challenging data from automotive scenarios that contains typical illumination changes due to automatic camera re-adjustments, changeable weather conditions or physical effects such as shadows and highlights.

⋆ Authors have equally contributed to this work.

D. Fleet et al. (Eds.): ECCV 2014, Part I, LNCS 8689, pp. 455–471, 2014.
© Springer International Publishing Switzerland 2014

Basic Optical Flow Approaches. In order to tackle the problem of illumination changes, most approaches from the literature make use of constancy assumptions based on *illumination-invariant* image features. Such features achieve their robustness by locally discarding illumination-sensitive information such as absolute brightness or contrast [24,27,34,36,50]. In the extreme case almost all information is discarded and only a relative local ordering is stored [5,11,35]. Methods based on such illumination-invariant features use constancy assumptions on higher order derivatives such as the gradient or the Hessian [23,34,38,43,51], photometric invariants [27,45,54] as well as mutual information [21]. Moreover, recently, patch-based techniques have become very popular such as the normalized cross correlation (NCC) [50], the rank transform [11,53] and the census transform [5,35,39]. Some of the approaches also use illumination-robust descriptors from sparse feature matching such as SIFT [24,25] and HOG [8,36]. A comparison of some of these methods can be found in [40] and [46]. Similar in spirit are methods that discard illumination-relevant information via preprocessing. Typically, they employ the structure-texture-decomposition [48] or derivative-type filters [41].

What all those aforementioned methods have in common is that they discard potentially valuable image information. However, if illumination changes are only moderate or not even present, discarding brightness and contrast information may significantly deteriorate the results. Moreover, some of the transformations are highly non-linear and even lack differentiability which results in a more complex optimization. Finally, most invariants are not defined at all locations, since illumination-invariant information cannot be extracted everywhere (e.g. in homogeneous regions). Summarizing: Instead of discarding potentially valuable information that may harm the estimation, it would be desirable to keep and exploit all available information when estimating the flow.

Advanced Optical Flow Approaches. In fact, there are a few methods in the literature that follow the above mentioned idea by *jointly* estimating both illumination changes and the optical flow. On the one hand, there are approaches that seek to estimate a single *global* brightness transfer function to identify problematic image regions [10]. On the other hand, there are techniques that embed the classical brightness constancy assumption into a parametrized *local* illumination model for which the coefficients are jointly estimated. Such local models include simple additive terms [7,28], affine illumination models [15,18,30] as well as complex brightness models derived from physics [20]. Recently, also local and global ideas were combined [18]: While a local affine model allows to estimate the correspondences in a PatchMatch-like approach [1], the information is eventually condensed to a single global transfer function.

Preserving potentially valuable image information, however, is not the only advantage of approaches based on parametrized illumination models. If appropriate models are employed, imposing smoothness on the resulting parameter field allows to separate real illumination changes from motion-induced brightness variations. However, so far in the literature, the considered illumination models were either chosen ad-hoc [7,15], or specifically tailored towards a certain physical process [20]. There have been no efforts so far to determine the most suitable model for a specific type of data. Moreover, it has not yet been investigated how the smoothness term of the coefficient field should be modeled such that it allows for a good separation of motion and illumination effects. Finally, since all existing variational methods with parametrized illumination models are based on simple concepts for data and smoothness terms, it remains unclear how a more sophisticated joint method would perform on a suitable optical flow benchmark.

Our Contribution. In this paper, we address all these questions. Firstly, we use a principal components analysis (PCA)-based approach with a clustering step to learn a suitable basis for the local brightness transfer functions from training data. Secondly, we propose a joint complementary regularizer for the basis coefficients that is based on a weighting scheme derived from the eigenvalues of the PCA. Thirdly, we embed the basis functions and the regularizer into a variational model that combines brightness and gradient constancy with a second-order smoothness term. Experiments demonstrate that our approach works very well in practice. We obtain meaningful basis functions, intuitive coefficient fields as well as state-of-the art results on the KITTI benchmark.

Related Work on Basis Learning. Apart from the aforementioned techniques that jointly estimate illumination changes and optical flow, a few more related works are worth mentioning. On the one hand, there are methods that address the estimation of camera response or brightness transfer functions, mainly in the context of HDR imaging. Such approaches include the work of Grossberg and Nayar [16] who proposed to compute the brightness transfer function via histogram specification, as well as the papers of Debevec and Malik [9] and Grossberg and Nayar [17] on estimating the camera response function, the latter one using learned basis functions. On the other hand, there are approaches that represent appearance changes with basis functions for illumination changes. Such methods include the template tracking approach of Hager and Belhumeur [19] as well as the work on iconic changes by Black *et al.* [3]. Finally, there exist a few optical flow methods that make use of spatial or temporal basis functions to model the flow. This applies to the approaches by Nir *et al.* [31] on over-parametrized optical flow and Garg *et al.* on temporal tracking of non-rigid objects with subspace constraints [12].

Organization. In Section 2, we introduce our novel variational model based on brightness transfer basis functions and joint complementary coefficient regularization. Minimization issues are then discussed in Section 3. The estimation of the basis functions and the clustering step are explained in Section 4. Our results and a comparison to the literature are presented in Section 5. The paper ends with a summary in Section 6.

2 Variational Model

Let us consider a sequence of two images $f_i : \Omega \rightarrow \mathbb{R}$ ($i \in \{1,2\}$) defined on a rectangular domain $\Omega \subset \mathbb{R}^2$. Furthermore, let the optical flow field be denoted by $\boldsymbol{w} = (u,v)^\top \colon \Omega \rightarrow \mathbb{R}^2$ and let the illumination changes be parametrized by a coefficient field $\mathbf{c} : \Omega \rightarrow \mathbb{R}^n$. Then, inspired by the basic approach of Cornelius and Kanade [7], we propose to jointly compute the optical flow and the illumination changes as minimizer of an energy functional with the following structure:

$$E(\boldsymbol{w}, \mathbf{c}) = \int_\Omega \big(D(\boldsymbol{w}, \mathbf{c}) + R_{\text{flow}}(\boldsymbol{w}) + R_{\text{illum}}(\mathbf{c})\big)\, \mathrm{d}\boldsymbol{x}\,. \tag{1}$$

It consists of three terms: a data term D that relates two consecutive frames of the input image sequence via the optical flow and the parametrized illumination changes (in terms of coefficients), a flow regularization term R_{flow} which encourages a piecewise affine flow field, and a coefficient regularization term R_{illum} that assumes the coefficient fields to be piecewise smooth. Let us now discuss these terms in detail.

2.1 Data Term

Unlike traditional data terms for optical flow estimation that explain brightness changes in the image sequence exclusively by motion, our data term models changes in illumination as additional source for brightness variations. In order to estimate these changes jointly with the motion, we make use of a *parametrized* brightness transfer function (BTF) which was originally proposed by Grossberg and Nayar [17] in the context of photometric calibration for HDR imaging. This function maps intensities of the first frame to their intensities in the second frame. Given a set of n basis functions $\phi_j : \mathbb{R} \to \mathbb{R}$, the corresponding brightness transfer function reads

$$\Phi(\boldsymbol{c}, f) = \bar{\phi}(f) + \sum_{j=1}^{n} c_j \cdot \phi_j(f)\,, \tag{2}$$

where $\bar{\phi} : \mathbb{R} \to \mathbb{R}$ is the mean brightness transfer function and $\boldsymbol{c} = (c_1, \ldots, c_n)^\top$ are linear weights. Let us now discuss how to embed this general model for brightness changes into a data term. To this end, we propose the following combination of the *brightness* constancy assumption and the *gradient* constancy assumption which can be seen as an extension of [6]. Defining ν as positive weight and using $\boldsymbol{\nabla}\cdot$ as spatial gradient operator, our data term reads

$$D(\boldsymbol{w}, \boldsymbol{c}) = D_{\text{bright}}(\boldsymbol{w}, \boldsymbol{c}) + \nu D_{\text{grad}}(\boldsymbol{w}, \boldsymbol{c})\,, \tag{3}$$

with

$$D_{\text{bright}}(\boldsymbol{w}, \boldsymbol{c}) = \Psi_{\text{d}}\Big(\big(f_2\left(\boldsymbol{x}+\boldsymbol{w}\right) - \Phi\left(\boldsymbol{c}(\boldsymbol{x}), f_1(\boldsymbol{x})\right)\big)^2\Big)\,, \tag{4}$$

and

$$D_{\text{grad}}(\boldsymbol{w}, \boldsymbol{c}) = \Psi_{\text{d}}\Big(\left\|\boldsymbol{\nabla} f_2(\boldsymbol{x}+\boldsymbol{w}) - \boldsymbol{\nabla}\Phi(\boldsymbol{c}(\boldsymbol{x}), f_1(\boldsymbol{x}))\right\|_2^2\Big)\,, \tag{5}$$

where brightness changes are now modeled to be spatially variant, i.e. with non-constant coefficients $\boldsymbol{c}$. Thus, we allow different brightness transfer functions Φ at each position. For both assumptions, the same sub-quadratic penalizer $\Psi_{\text{d}}(s^2) = 2\lambda_{\text{d}}^2(1+s^2/\lambda_{\text{d}}^2)^{\frac{1}{2}}$ is used to render the approach more robust w.r.t. outliers [2].

Please note that flow variables and illumination coefficients have intentionally been distributed to different frames. This avoids products of unknowns when linearizing the assumptions later on and thus makes the minimization better tractable. Moreover, at first glance, it may seem counter-intuitive to combine our explicit estimation strategy with a gradient constancy assumption that is invariant under additive illumination changes. However, the additional gradient constancy term supports the estimation at those locations where the coefficients can not adapt or have not yet adapted perfectly to the illumination changes. This is for instance the case at the beginning of the estimation, when neither the flow nor the coefficients have converged to their final values yet.

2.2 Regularization Terms

Since the constancy assumptions in the data term may locally fail to provide any information, a spatial regularization of both the flow variables and the illumination coefficients is required. Moreover, it is not clear from the data term how to distribute observed brightness changes between motion and illumination. While the parametrization in terms of basis functions already provides a meaningful representation given by the coefficient fields, the concrete modeling of both regularization terms plays an important role in resolving this ambiguity. Let us now discuss how we model the two regularizers.

Flow Regularization. While first order regularization strategies have a long and successful tradition [22], recently, second-order smoothness terms received notable attention. In particular, such terms turned out to be highly useful for non-fronto-parallel motion, since they are tailored towards piecewise affine solutions [5,35,42,46]. Consequently, we make use of the following second-order regularizer that has already been used in the context of image denoising [26] and shape-from-shading [47]:

$$R_{\text{flow}}(\boldsymbol{w}) = \alpha \cdot \Psi_{\text{s}}\left(\|\boldsymbol{\mathcal{H}}u\|_F^2 + \|\boldsymbol{\mathcal{H}}v\|_F^2\right) . \tag{6}$$

Here, α is a positive weight, $\|\boldsymbol{\mathcal{H}}\cdot\|_F$ is the Frobenius norm of the Hessian, and $\Psi_{\text{s}}(s^2) = 2\lambda_{\text{s}}^2(1+s^2/\lambda_{\text{s}}^2)^{\frac{1}{2}}$ is a sub-quadratic penalizer that encourages piecewise affine solutions.

Coefficient Regularization. In contrast to the flow regularizer that models a piecewise affine flow field, we assume that neighboring pixels are subject to similar illumination changes, i.e. that the coefficients of the basis functions are piecewise constant. Additionally, discontinuities in the coefficient fields are assumed to be aligned with edges in the input images (e.g. shadow edges) [29]. Consequently, we follow the idea of Zimmer *et al.* [54] and employ the following anisotropic complementary regularization term

$$R_{\text{illum}}(\boldsymbol{c}) = \beta \cdot \sum_{i=1}^{2} \Psi_{\text{illum}}^{i}\Big(\sum_{j=1}^{n} \gamma_j \,(\boldsymbol{r}_i^\top \nabla c_j)^2\Big) , \tag{7}$$

where β is a positive weight and the two directions $\boldsymbol{r}_1$ and $\boldsymbol{r}_2 = \boldsymbol{r}_1^\perp$ allow to adapt the smoothing direction locally across and along image edges, respectively. As proposed in [54], these directions can be derived as the eigenvectors of the so-called regularization tensor. In our case, this tensor must be computed from the *photometric uncompensated* first frame f_1 to ensure that brightness information related to illumination changes is *not* discarded. Moreover, all coefficient fields are regularized jointly with a single penalizer function per direction, since spatial changes of the brightness transfer function typically result in discontinuities in all coefficient fields. In this context, the derivatives of the coefficients have to be balanced with weights γ_j to reflect the different magnitude ranges of the coefficient fields. How we can estimate these weights together with the basis functions is discussed in Section 4. Finally, we have to define the penalizer functions. As suggested in [54], we use the edge-enhancing Perona-Malik regularizer

$\Psi^1_{\text{illum}}(s^2) = \lambda_c^2 \log(1 + s^2/\lambda_c^2)$ as penalizer across edges (in $\boldsymbol{r}_1$-direction), while we apply the edge-preserving Charbonnier regularizer $\Psi^2_{\text{illum}}(s^2) = 2\lambda_c^2(1+s^2/\lambda_c^2)^{\frac{1}{2}}$ along them (in $\boldsymbol{r}_2$-direction).

3 Minimization

In order to handle large displacements, we follow the warping strategy of Brox *et al.* [6]. We split the unknowns, i.e. the flow field $\boldsymbol{w}$ and the coefficient fields $\boldsymbol{c}$, into a known part $\boldsymbol{w}^k$, $\boldsymbol{c}^k$ and an unknown increment $\boldsymbol{dw}^k$, $\boldsymbol{dc}^k$ and embed their overall estimation into a coarse-to-fine fixed point iteration. Moreover, within this (outer) fixed point iteration, we linearize the brightness and the gradient constancy assumptions in terms of the flow increments $\boldsymbol{dw}^k$ such that we finally approximate the original non-convex optimization problem by a series of convex optimization problems.

Actually, this strategy comes down to solving a differential formulation of the original energy (1) at each level k of the coarse-to-fine approach. If we denote the first frame by $f_1^k = f_1(x,y)$ and the motion compensated second frame by $f_2^k = f_2(x{+}u^k, y{+}v^k)$, the corresponding differential formulation of data and smoothness terms is given as follows. While the brightness and gradient constancy terms become

$$D^k_{\text{bright}} = \Psi_{\text{d}}\Big(\theta \cdot \Big(f^k_{2,x} du^k + f^k_{2,y} dv^k + f_2^k - \bar{\phi}(f_1^k) - \sum_{j=1}^{n} (c_j^k + dc_j^k) \cdot \phi_j(f_1^k)\Big)^2\Big) \tag{8}$$

and

$$\begin{aligned} D^k_{\text{grad}} = \Psi_{\text{d}}\Bigg(\Bigg\|\begin{pmatrix}\theta_x & 0\\ 0 & \theta_y\end{pmatrix}\Big(& \boldsymbol{\nabla} f^k_{2,x} du^k + \boldsymbol{\nabla} f^k_{2,y} dv^k + \boldsymbol{\nabla} f_2^k \\ & - \sum_{j=1}^{n} \phi_j(f_1^k) \cdot \boldsymbol{\nabla}(c_j^k + dc_j^k) \\ & - \Big(\bar{\phi}'(f_1^k) + \sum_{j=1}^{n} (c_j^k + dc_j^k) \cdot \phi_j'(f_1^k)\Big) \cdot \boldsymbol{\nabla} f_1^k\Big)\Bigg\|_2^2\Bigg), \end{aligned} \tag{9}$$

respectively, the flow regularizer is given by

$$R^k_{\text{flow}} = \alpha \cdot \Psi_{\text{s}}\left(\|\boldsymbol{\mathcal{H}}(u^k + du^k)\|_F^2 + \|\boldsymbol{\mathcal{H}}(v^k + dv^k)\|_F^2\right), \tag{10}$$

and the coefficient regularizer reads

$$R^k_{\text{illum}} = \beta \cdot \sum_{i=1}^{2} \Psi^i_{\text{illum}}\Big(\sum_{j=1}^{n} \gamma_j \,(\boldsymbol{r}_i^\top \boldsymbol{\nabla}(c_j^k + dc_j^k))^2\Big). \tag{11}$$

Additionally, constraint normalization has been applied to all constancy assumptions in terms of the weights θ, θ_x and θ_y as proposed in [44] for linearized constraints with more than two variables.

After discretizing the Euler-Lagrange equations of this differential energy with finite differences, we obtain a nonlinear system of equations due to the derivatives of the subquadratic penalizers Ψ_*. This nonlinear system is then solved by another (inner) fixed point iteration: All nonlinear expressions are repeatedly kept fixed, and the resulting linear systems are solved using the successive overrelaxation (SOR) method [52].

In order to speed up computations, the inner fixed point iteration is embedded in a cascadic multigrid scheme, i.e. finer levels are initialized with coarse-scale solutions [4]. This also explains why we use an incremental computation of the coefficient fields $\boldsymbol{c}^k$ although the corresponding expressions are linear in the original functional (1). As the cascadic multigrid approach always starts the computation from scratch, we need an increment ($\boldsymbol{dc}^k$) which can be initialized to zero without losing all previous information.

4 Basis Learning for Brightness Transfer Functions

In the previous sections, we have introduced our novel variational model and have sketched how to minimize the corresponding energy. The goal of this section is to explain how we estimate the mean BTF $\bar{\phi}(f)$, the basis functions ϕ_j as well as the associated weights γ_j for the joint regularizer of the coefficient fields. The basic strategy of this paper is inspired by the *Empirical Model of Response (EMoR)* of Grossberg and Nayar [17], where the camera response function of imaging systems is parametrized with a set of basis functions. However, our model acts on intensities instead of irradiances. As already mentioned in Section 2, input intensities f are mapped to output intensities via

$$\Phi(f) = \bar{\phi}(f) + \sum_{j=1}^{n} c_j \cdot \phi_j(f) . \tag{12}$$

Note that many kinds of polynomial and exponential illumination models can be represented using the appropriate basis functions. For instance, the affine model of Negahdaripour [30] fits into this framework by choosing

$$\bar{\phi}(f) = 0 , \qquad \phi_1(f) = 1 , \qquad \phi_2(f) = f . \tag{13}$$

The same holds also for the purely additive models in [7,28], i.e. if instead $\phi_2(f)=0$.

The recent KITTI Vision Benchmark Suite [14] offers a huge set of real-world image sequences together with ground truth optical flow fields. This gives us access to samples of input and output intensity levels of realistic scenarios. In particular, the availability of optical flow fields allows us to register consecutive frames and to analyze the behavior of the true BTF on a per-pixel basis.

Our general strategy to learn a basis from this massive amount of training data consists of three steps: In a first step, we segment and cluster the training images according to illumination changes along the ground truth flow. The segmentation is important, since we cannot expect that different image pairs provide fundamentally different *global* BTFs. Instead, we have to estimate multiple BTFs per image pair, since typical illumination changes such as drop shadows or specular reflections are *local* phenomena. In a second step, we use the segmented input images and compute for each region of each input image a separate BTF. In a third step, all these BTFs are used to perform a principal component analysis (PCA) in order to identify the most representative basis functions for the observed illumination changes. It is worth noting that these steps can be applied iteratively, i.e. the estimated basis functions can be used again to segment the input images and thus to obtain improved BTFs. Let us now detail on these steps.

Segmenting Illumination Changes. Let us assume that we are given the training image sequences with corresponding ground truth flows. In order to discriminate the image regions with distinct lighting situations, i.e. with different brightness transfer functions, for each image pair, we first have to determine the pointwise BTF for every pixel. However, although this pointwise BTF can be arbitrarily complex, the given images provide *only one* constraint per pixel: The unknown BTF must map the intensity of this pixel in the first frame to the intensity of the corresponding pixel in the second frame.

To relax this extremely under-determined problem, let us now assume we are already given an estimate of the basis functions. Then, the sought pointwise BTF can be approximated using the given basis, and our task comes down to computing the optimal coefficient vector $\mathbf{c}$ in each pixel. Consequently, this problem fits perfectly into our variational model from Section 2, with the difference that we *only* have to solve for the coefficients $\mathbf{c}$, since the optical flow is given and does not need to be estimated. However, as the ground truth might not be provided at every pixel (i.e. due to occlusions or due to sparse laser scans), we have to disable the data term at those positions where a flow vector is missing. Basically, this procedure leads to a variational inpainting method [49], because if the data term is disabled, only the coefficient regularization term contributes to the energy. Note that unlike in traditional inpainting scenarios, we are not interested in the coefficient values at positions with missing data. We only want to enforce global communication in order to avoid isolated estimates.

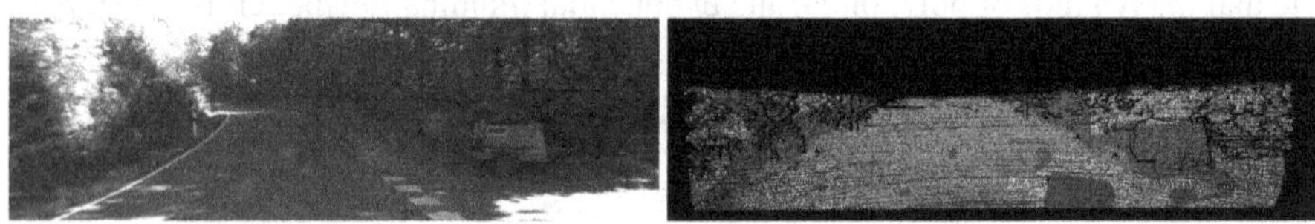

Fig. 1. Left: Frame 1 of KITTI training sequence #114. **Right:** Corresponding K-Means segmentation. Each color indicates a separate cluster, black pixels denote locations where ground truth is missing. The separation between the stronger brightening effect on the street and the weaker brightening effect in the environment becomes visible. Moreover, the inter-reflections at the windshield show off in terms of the three red spots on the street.

Once the coefficients are found, we perform a K-Means clustering (usually $K=5$) on the coefficients. This takes place exclusively in the n-dimensional coefficient space; spatial coordinates are intentionally ignored here in order to allow spatially disjoint regions belonging to the same segment. All pixels whose coefficients have been clustered together share a similar brightness transfer function and thus exhibit a similar lighting situation. Figure 1 shows an example where such a segmentation allows to distinguish regions in the image that undergo different brightening effects.

Estimating Brightness Transfer Functions. Given the previously computed segmentation, the next task is to estimate one brightness transfer function $g : \mathbb{R} \to \mathbb{R}$ per segment. To this end, we adopt the *global* idea of Grossberg and Nayar [16] *locally*: For each segment we construct the intensity histogram h_1 of the pixels in the first frame as well as the histogram h_2 of the corresponding intensities in the second frame. In this context, we only consider pixels with valid optical flow, i.e. a ground truth vector must be given and must not point out of the image domain. Once both histograms have been created, we compute the BTF that transforms h_1 into h_2 by means of a histogram specification. In this context, fully saturated segments or too small clusters may lead to wrong and unrealistic brightness transfer functions. To avoid this, we reject any segments in which more than 80% of all pixels have the same intensity, as well as segments in which more than one third of all possible intensities do not occur. Please note that the resulting function of the histogram specification is discrete and given by an arbitrary vector $\boldsymbol{g} \in \mathbb{R}^{256}$ that is not parametrized in terms of basis functions and coefficients. Along with the BTFs from other segments it serves as input for the following PCA.

Learning the Basis. After having performed the previous clustering and estimation steps on each of the p training image pairs we obtain $m \leq K \cdot p$ brightness transfer functions, so-called *observations*. In order to find one common set of basis functions for all of them, we perform a principal component analysis (PCA). After concatenating all observations $\boldsymbol{g}_i$ $(i=1,\ldots,m)$ into a so-called *observation matrix*

$$\boldsymbol{G} = (\boldsymbol{g}_1|\ldots|\boldsymbol{g}_m) \in \mathbb{R}^{256\times m}\,, \tag{14}$$

we compute the row-wise mean (i.e. the sample mean over all observations) $\bar{\boldsymbol{g}}$ of $\boldsymbol{G}$. Then we obtain the covariance matrix $\boldsymbol{C}$ as

$$\boldsymbol{C} = \boldsymbol{U}^\top \boldsymbol{\Sigma} \boldsymbol{U} = \frac{1}{m-1} \sum_{i=1}^{m} (\boldsymbol{g}_i - \bar{\boldsymbol{g}})(\boldsymbol{g}_i - \bar{\boldsymbol{g}})^\top . \tag{15}$$

From this principal component decompositon, the sought basis functions ϕ_j $(j=1,...,n)$ can be found as the eigenvectors of the covariance matrix (the columns of $\boldsymbol{U}$). Moreover, the row-wise mean $\bar{\boldsymbol{g}}$ coincides with the 0-th basis function which is the mean brightness transfer function $\bar{\phi}$. Furthermore, the diagonal matrix $\boldsymbol{\Sigma}$ contains the eigenvalues which represent the variance of the given data along the principal components. This is a well-suited estimate for the relative magnitude of the coefficients. Hence, we set the weights γ_j in the anisotropic coefficient regularization term (7) to be the inverse square roots of the eigenvalues.

Figure 2 shows the estimated bases for the KITTI Vision Benchmark Suite and compares it to an affine basis and the *EMoR* basis provided by [17]. We can see that compared to the EMoR basis our basis functions for the KITTI benchmark rather model illumination changes in the upper part of the dynamic range. Moreover, the mean brightness transfer function is rather linear, since we do not estimate a camera response function as in [17] but a mapping between intensities (where identity is expected as average).

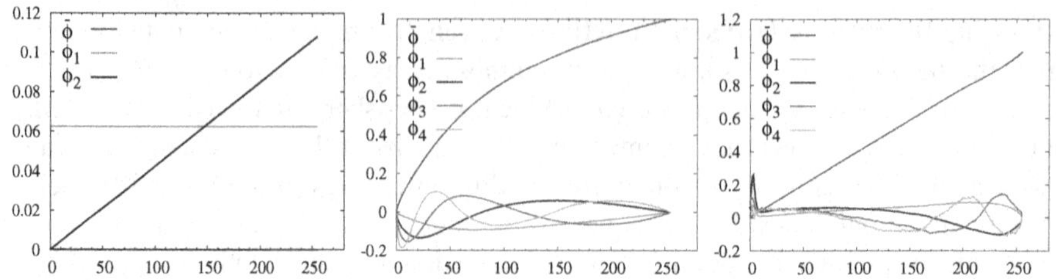

Fig. 2. Comparison of different basis functions. **From left to right:** (**a**) Normalized affine basis. (**b**) EMoR functions [16]. (**c**) Our basis functions learned from KITTI ground truth data.

Iterating the Estimation. The strategy we have described so far assumes a basis to be given for the clustering step. Initially, however, only the training images and ground truth flows are given. Thus, in our first iteration loop we omit the clustering step, treat the whole images as one segment, and estimate one global brightness transfer function per image pair. This leads to a first estimate for the basis which allows us then to perform the clustering as described. The impact of iterating the estimation of the basis functions on their shapes can be seen in Figure 3. While the mean BTF remains approximately the identity, the main support of the other basis functions is even further shifted towards the upper end of the dynamic range.

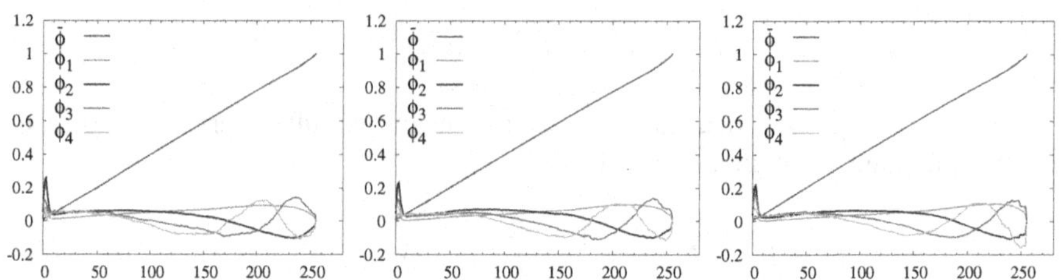

Fig. 3. Impact of iterating the estimation of the KITTI basis functions. **From left to right:** (**a**) Initial basis. (**b**) After one iteration. (**c**) After four iterations.

5 Evaluation

Our experiments are focused on the KITTI Vision Benchmark Suite [14] which offers a large amount of images depicting driving scenarios with challenging illumination changes. With our experiments we want to demonstrate that our method is very well suited for this kind of real-world imagery. The runtime of our single core implementation on an Intel XEON workstation with 3.2 GHz is about 80 seconds for each of the sequences (image size 1240×376). Results of our experiments are given in terms of the *bad pixel 3* (BP3) error measure that describes the percentage of estimated flow vectors that differ by more than 3 pixels from the respective ground truth.

Table 1. Comparison of different variants of our method on the full KITTI training set

Configuration	avg. BP3 error (occ)
Baseline (without illumination compensation)	11.17 %
Affine basis	11.07 %
EMoR basis	10.64 %
KITTI basis	10.71 %
KITTI basis (iterated)	10.19 %
KITTI basis (iterated, without gradient constancy)	10.65 %
KITTI basis (iterated, only gradient constancy)	10.95 %

Although our model contains a considerable number of parameters, effectively we set most of them fixed, and only adjusted the three main model parameters α, β, and ν. The contrast parameters for the sub-quadratic functions have been chosen fixed for all experiments as $(\lambda_{\mathrm{d}}, \lambda_{\mathrm{s}}, \lambda_{\mathrm{illum}}^{1,2}) = (0.01, 0.5, 0.01)$. Concerning the K-Means clustering step we kept $K = 5$ fixed as well. For the number n of basis functions we found $n = 4$ to be a good tradeoff between computational effort and accuracy.

Evaluation of Basis Functions. In our first experiment, we investigate the usefulness of illumination estimation in general and analyze the impact of choosing different sets of basis functions on the quality of the flow estimation. To this end, we have computed the average BP3 errors of our method – with different bases as well as without any illumination compensation – on the provided set of 194 training sequences. For each configuration, we have optimized the parameters of our model w.r.t. the average BP3 error for the whole training set using the ground truth including occluded pixels (*occ*).

The results of this experiment are presented in Table 1. On the one hand, they clearly show that the benefit of using the classical affine model of Gennert and Negahdaripour [15] is rather limited compared to the baseline method without any illumination compensation – on average the error does hardly decrease. On the other hand, we can observe a clear improvement when choosing or learning a more suitable (and less ad-hoc) set of basis functions. Moreover, our experiments show that refining the basis functions iteratively allows to further improve the results. In the end, our proposed illumination model has been able to impove results for 81% of all training sequences. Finally, we also analyze the impact of the gradient constancy assumption. To this end, we consider variants of our method where the gradient constancy term has either been disabled or is the only constancy assumption. The two last rows of Table 1 show that in both cases the results deteriorate. This underlines our considerations from Section 2: The gradient term provides an improved initialization of the flow in early iterations, where the coefficient fields have not yet converged. However, the gradient term alone cannot provide sufficient information for estimating the basis coefficients since it considers only local differences, but establishes a mapping between absolute grey values.

Analysis of Transfer Functions and Coefficient Fields. In our second experiment we shed light on the coefficients that are estimated jointly with the optical flow. To this end, we have picked one of the training sequences with moderate illumination changes, see

Figure 4, and another sequence with severe illumination changes, see Figure 5. The two figures show the first frame of the respective sequence together with the estimated flow as well as the four computed coefficient fields. Furthermore, we have highlighted interesting locations in the images using colored squares. The brightness transfer functions at those locations – that can be computed as linear combinations of the learned basis functions weighted by the estimated local coefficients – are jointly depicted in a graph using the corresponding colors.

For our first challenging example (Figure 4), the flow field appears reasonably accurate, which is confirmed by a BP3 error of only 9.41%. Since the lighting changes in that image sequence are rather global, the extracted brightness transfer functions are similar in shape. In fact, they only differ in the upper end of the dynamic range. As can be seen from the BTFs, the image becomes darker. This is mainly reflected by the strongly negative values in the coefficient field c_1 (that belongs to a positive basis function). Moreover, slight local variations of the BTFs can be observed in the coefficient plots, in particular in the plots of the coefficient fields c_2, c_3, c_4. An example, where our model has actually estimated significantly differing BTFs for different parts of the image is presented in Figure 5. Particularly challenging in this sequence are the inter-reflections in the windshield in front of the camera. However, the flow field is still of reasonable quality (BP3 of 5.33%). Apart of the spatially varying BTFs, one can also observe that the inter-reflections are reproduced by the corresponding coefficient fields.

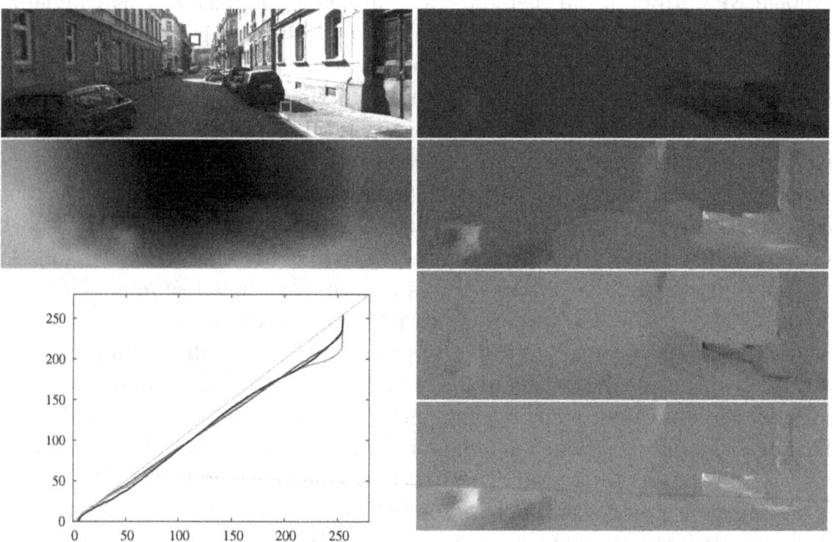

Fig. 4. Estimated coefficients and BTFs. **Left column, from top to bottom:** First frame of KITTI training sequence #15 with three highlighted positions, estimated optical flow field, plot of the three corresponding brightness transfer functions. Plot colors coincide with the marker colors. **Right column, from top to bottom:** Estimated coefficient fields c_1 to c_4. Coefficients have been shifted such that a grey value of 127 denotes a coefficient of 0. Brighter values denote positive coefficients, darker values negative coefficients.

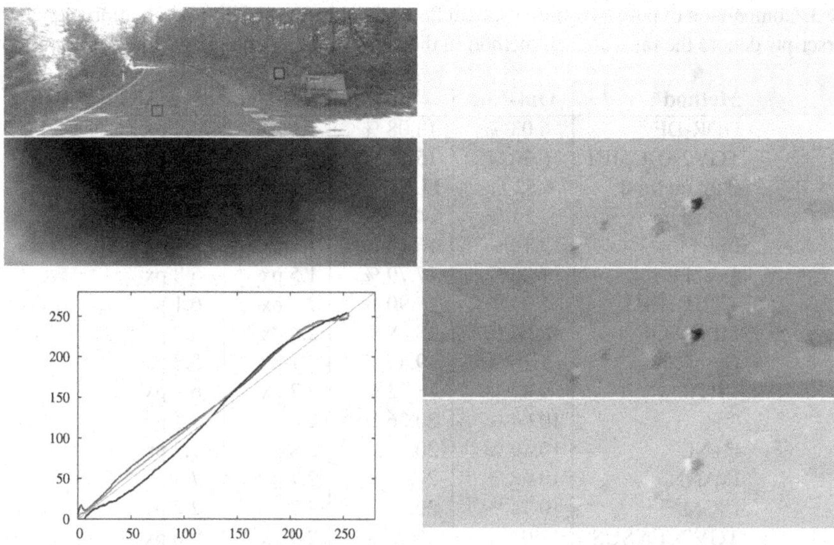

Fig. 5. Estimated coefficients and BTFs. **Left column, from top to bottom:** First frame of KITTI training sequence #114 with three highlighted positions, estimated optical flow field, plot of the three corresponding brightness transfer functions. Plot colors coincide with the marker colors. **Right column, from top to bottom:** Estimated coefficient fields c_1 to c_4. Coefficients have been shifted such that a grey value of 127 denotes a coefficient of 0. Brighter values denote positive coefficients, darker values negative coefficients.

Table 2. Error statistics of our method for the bad pixel measure with varying thresholds (BP2 - BP5), averaged over all sequences of the KITTI evaluation benchmark

Error	Out-Noc	Out-All	Avg-Noc	Avg-All
2 pixels	8.84 %	14.14 %	1.5 px	2.8 px
3 pixels	6.52 %	11.03 %	1.5 px	2.8 px
4 pixels	5.38 %	9.29 %	1.5 px	2.8 px
5 pixels	4.64 %	8.11 %	1.5 px	2.8 px

Comparison to the Literature. In our third experiment, we compare our method to other approaches from the literature. To this end, we evaluated our method on the KITTI test sequences using the optimized parameters (α, β, ν)=(5.2, 3, 6.25). The corresponding results are shown in Tables 2 and 3. While Table 2 gives detailed information on the performance of our algorithm in *non-occluded* and *all* regions for different thresholds of the bad pixel error measure (BP2 - BP5), Table 3 shows the performance of our algorithm compared to other *pure two-frame* optical flow methods *without stereo constraints* (such constraints are likely to fail in realistic scenarios with independently moving objects). As one can see, our method is among the leading optical flow approaches in this benchmark. In particular, when considering all pixels (i.e. also occluded regions), our method ranks first and is significantly more accurate than previous approaches. This clearly demonstrates that performing a joint estimation of illumination changes and motion can outperform methods discarding illumination information by using invariants.

Table 3. Comparison of pure two-frame optical flow methods for the KITTI evaluation sequences. Superscripts denote the rank of each method in the corresponding column at time of submission.

Method	Out-Noc	Out-All	Avg-Noc	Avg-All
DDR-DF	6.03 % [1]	13.08 % [2]	1.6 px [5]	4.2 px [3]
TGV2ADCSIFT	6.20 % [2]	15.15 % [4]	1.5 px [2]	4.5 px [4]
Our method	**6.52 %** [3]	**11.03 %** [1]	**1.5 px** [2]	**2.8 px** [1]
Data-Flow	7.11 % [4]	14.57 % [3]	1.9 px [6]	5.5 px [5]
EpicFlow	7.19 % [5]	16.15 % [5]	1.4 px [1]	3.7 px [2]
DeepFlow	7.22 % [6]	17.79 % [6]	1.5 px [2]	5.8 px [7]
TVL1-HOG	7.91 % [7]	18.90 % [10]	2.0 px [7]	6.1 px [8]
MLDP-OF	8.67 % [8]	18.78 % [9]	2.4 px [9]	6.7 px [11]
DescFlow	8.76 % [9]	19.45 % [11]	2.1 px [8]	5.7 px [6]
CRTflow	9.43 % [10]	18.72 % [8]	2.7 px [11]	6.5 px [9]
C++	10.04 % [11]	20.26 % [12]	2.6 px [10]	7.1 px [12]
C+NL	10.49 % [12]	20.64 % [13]	2.8 px [13]	7.2 px [13]
IVANN	10.68 % [13]	21.09 % [14]	2.7 px [11]	7.4 px [14]
fSGM	10.74 % [14]	22.66 % [15]	3.2 px [15]	12.2 px [15]
TGV2CENSUS	11.03 % [15]	18.37 % [7]	2.9 px [14]	6.6 px [10]

6 Conclusions and Outlook

In this work we have addressed the problem of estimating the optical flow under uncontrolled illumination. In contrast to recent state-of-the-art methods that simply discard illumination information, we have proposed a novel variational model for jointly estimating both illumination changes and optical flow. In this context, we have contributed in three different ways: (i) In order to find a meaningful representation of illumination changes we have learned brightness transfer basis functions from previously segmented training data. (ii) By imposing a complementary regularizer on the corresponding coefficient fields we have been able to achieve a sharp separation between areas of different illumination changes while maintaining smoothness of the resulting flow field itself. (iii) By embedding both the basis functions and the coefficient regularization into a recent variational framework, we achieve state-of-the-art accuracy on the KITTI benchmark, outperforming competing approaches based on illumination-invariant assumptions.

This shows that approaches that additionally estimate relevant information, such as illumination changes, are a worthwhile alternative to approaches that simply discard that information for the sake of robustness. Moreover, such approaches can be used to provide subsequent algorithms with this additional information improving the overall performance. Future work includes the online learning of basis functions as well as the development of efficient numerical schemes on the GPU to speed up the computation.

References

1. Barnes, C., Shechtman, E., Goldman, D.B., Finkelstein, A.: The generalized PatchMatch correspondence algorithm. In: Daniilidis, K., Maragos, P., Paragios, N. (eds.) ECCV 2010, Part II. LNCS, vol. 6312, pp. 29–43. Springer, Heidelberg (2010)

2. Black, M.J., Anandan, P.: Robust dynamic motion estimation over time. In: Proc. 1991 IEEE Computer Society Conference on Computer Vision and Pattern Recognition, pp. 292–302. IEEE Computer Society Press, Maui (1991)
3. Black, M.J., Fleet, D., Yacoob, Y.: Robustly estimating changes in image appearance. Computer Vision and Image Understanding 78(1), 8–31 (2000)
4. Bornemann, F., Deuflhard, P.: The cascadic multigrid method for elliptic problems. Numerische Mathematik 75, 135–152 (1996)
5. Braux-Zin, J., Dupont, R., Bartoli, A.: A general dense image matching framework combining direct and feature-based costs. In: Proc. IEEE International Conference on Computer Vision (ICCV), pp. 185–192. IEEE Press (2013)
6. Brox, T., Bruhn, A., Papenberg, N., Weickert, J.: High accuracy optical flow estimation based on a theory for warping. In: Pajdla, T., Matas, J(G.) (eds.) ECCV 2004. LNCS, vol. 3024, pp. 25–36. Springer, Heidelberg (2004)
7. Cornelius, N., Kanade, T.: Adapting optical-flow to measure object motion in reflectance and X-ray image sequences. Computer Graphics 18(1), 24–25 (1984)
8. Dalal, N., Triggs, B.: Histograms of oriented gradients for human detection. In: Schmid, C., Soatto, S., Tomasi, C. (eds.) Proc. IEEE Conference on Computer Vision and Pattern Recognition (CVPR), vol. 2, pp. 886–893 (2005)
9. Debevec, P.E., Malik, J.: Recovering high dynamic range radiance maps from photographs. In: Proc. SIGGRAPH 1997. Annual Conference Series, pp. 369–378. ACM Press (1997)
10. Dederscheck, D., Müller, T., Mester, R.: Illumination invariance for driving scene optical flow using comparagram preselection. In: Proc. IEEE Intelligent Vehicles Symposium (IV), pp. 742–747 (2012)
11. Demetz, O., Hafner, D., Weickert, J.: The complete rank transform: A tool for accurate and morphologically invariant matching of structures. In: Proceedings of the British Machine Vision Conference. BMVA Press (2013)
12. Garg, R., Roussos, A., Agapito, L.: A variational approach to video registration with subspace constraints. International Journal of Computer Vision 104(3), 286–314 (2013)
13. Garrido, P., Valgaerts, L., Wu, C., Theobalt, C.: Reconstructing detailed dynamic face geometry from monocular video. ACM Transactions on Graphics 32(6), 158:1–158:10 (2013)
14. Geiger, A., Lenz, P., Urtasun, R.: Are we ready for autonomous driving? The KITTI vision benchmark suite. In: Proc. IEEE Conference on Computer Vision and Pattern Recognition (CVPR), pp. 3354–3361. IEEE Computer Society (2012)
15. Gennert, M.A., Negahdaripour, S.: Relaxing the brightness constancy assumption in computing optical flow. Tech. Rep. 975, Artificial Intelligence Laboratory, Massachusetts Institute of Technology (June 1987)
16. Grossberg, M.D., Nayar, S.K.: What can be known about the radiometric response from images? In: Heyden, A., Sparr, G., Nielsen, M., Johansen, P. (eds.) ECCV 2002, Part I. LNCS, vol. 2350, pp. 189–205. Springer, Heidelberg (2002)
17. Grossberg, M.D., Nayar, S.K.: Modeling the space of camera response functions. IEEE Transactions on Pattern Analysis and Machine Intelligence 26(10), 1272–1282 (2004)
18. HaCohen, Y., Shechtman, E., Goldman, D.B., Lischinski, D.: Non-rigid dense correspondence with applications for image enhancement. ACM Transactions on Graphics 30(4), 70:1–70:9 (2011)
19. Hager, G.D., Belhumeur, P.N.: Real-time tracking of image regions with changes in geometry and illumination. In: Proc. IEEE Conference on Computer Vision and Pattern Recognition (CVPR), pp. 403–410 (1996)
20. Haussecker, H.W., Fleet, D.J.: Estimating optical flow with physical models of brightness variation. IEEE Transactions on Pattern Analysis and Machine Intelligence 23(6), 661–673 (2001)

21. Hermosillo, G., Chefd'Hotel, C., Faugeras, O.: Variational methods for multimodal image matching. International Journal of Computer Vision 50(3), 329–343 (2002)
22. Horn, B., Schunck, B.: Determining optical flow. Artificial Intelligence 17, 185–203 (1981)
23. Kim, T.H., Lee, H.S., Lee, K.M.: Optical flow via locally adaptive fusion of complementary data costs. In: Proc. IEEE International Conference on Computer Vision (ICCV), pp. 3344–3351. IEEE Press (2013)
24. Liu, C., Yuen, J., Torralba, A.: SIFT flow: Dense correspondence across scenes and its applications. IEEE Transactions on Pattern Analysis and Machine Intelligence 33(5), 978–994 (2011)
25. Lowe, D.L.: Distinctive image features from scale-invariant keypoints. International Journal of Computer Vision 60(2), 91–110 (2004)
26. Lysaker, M., Lundervold, A., Tai, X.C.: Noise removal using fourth-order partial differential equation with applications to medical magnetic resonance images in space and time. Transactions on Image Processing 12(12), 1579–1590 (2003)
27. Mileva, Y., Bruhn, A., Weickert, J.: Illumination-robust variational optical flow with photometric invariants. In: Hamprecht, F.A., Schnörr, C., Jähne, B. (eds.) DAGM 2007. LNCS, vol. 4713, pp. 152–162. Springer, Heidelberg (2007)
28. Mukawa, N.: Estimation of shape, reflection coefficients and illuminant direction from image sequences. In: Proc. IEEE International Conference on Computer Vision (ICCV), pp. 507–512 (1990)
29. Nagel, H.H., Enkelmann, W.: An investigation of smoothness constraints for the estimation of displacement vector fields from image sequences. IEEE Transactions on Pattern Analysis and Machine Intelligence 8, 565–593 (1986)
30. Negahdaripour, S., Yu, C.H.: A generalized brightness change model for computing optical flow. In: Proc. IEEE International Conference on Computer Vision (ICCV), pp. 2–11. IEEE Computer Society (1993)
31. Nir, T., Bruckstein, A.M., Kimmel, R.: Over-parameterized variational optical flow. International Journal of Computer Vision 76(2), 205–216 (2008)
32. Ochs, P., Malik, J., Brox, T.: Segmentation of moving objects by long term video analysis. IEEE Transactions on Pattern Analysis and Machine Intelligence (2013), early Access
33. Onkarappa, N., Sappa, A.: Speed and texture: an empirical study on optical-flow accuracy in ADAS scenarios. IEEE Transactions on Intelligent Transportation Systems 15(1), 136–147 (2014)
34. Papenberg, N., Bruhn, A., Brox, T., Didas, S., Weickert, J.: Highly accurate optic flow computation with theoretically justified warping. International Journal of Computer Vision 67(2), 141–158 (2006)
35. Ranftl, R., Gehrig, S., Pock, T., Bischof, H.: Pushing the limits of stereo using variational stereo estimation. In: IEEE Intelligent Vehicles Symposium, pp. 401–407 (2012)
36. Rashwan, H.A., Mohamed, M.A., García, M.A., Mertsching, B., Puig, D.: Illumination robust optical flow model based on histogram of oriented gradients. In: Weickert, J., Hein, M., Schiele, B. (eds.) GCPR 2013. LNCS, vol. 8142, pp. 354–363. Springer, Heidelberg (2013)
37. Sadek, R., Facciolo, G., Arias, P., Caselles, V.: A variational model for gradient-based video editing. International Journal of Computer Vision 103(1), 127–162 (2013)
38. Schnörr, C.: On functionals with greyvalue-controlled smoothness terms for determining optical flow. IEEE Transactions on Pattern Analysis and Machine Intelligence 15(10), 1074–1079 (1993)
39. Stein, F.J.: Efficient Computation of Optical Flow Using the Census Transform. In: Rasmussen, C.E., Bülthoff, H.H., Schölkopf, B., Giese, M.A. (eds.) DAGM 2004. LNCS, vol. 3175, pp. 79–86. Springer, Heidelberg (2004)

40. Steinbrücker, F., Pock, T., Cremers, D.: Advanced data terms for variational optic flow estimation. In: Magnor, M.A., Rosenhahn, B., Theisel, H. (eds.) Proceedings of the Vision, Modeling, and Visualization Workshop (VMV), pp. 155–164. DNB (2009)
41. Sun, D., Roth, S., Black, M.J.: A quantitative analysis of current practices in optical flow estimation and the principles behind them. International Journal of Computer Vision 106(2), 115–137 (2014)
42. Trobin, W., Pock, T., Cremers, D., Bischof, H.: An unbiased second-order prior for high-accuracy motion estimation. In: Rigoll, G. (ed.) DAGM 2008. LNCS, vol. 5096, pp. 396–405. Springer, Heidelberg (2008)
43. Uras, S., Girosi, F., Verri, A., Torre, V.: A computational approach to motion perception. Biological Cybernetics 60, 79–87 (1988)
44. Valgaerts, L., Bruhn, A., Zimmer, H., Weickert, J., Stoll, C., Theobalt, C.: Joint estimation of motion, structure and geometry from stereo sequences. In: Daniilidis, K., Maragos, P., Paragios, N. (eds.) ECCV 2010, Part IV. LNCS, vol. 6314, pp. 568–581. Springer, Heidelberg (2010)
45. van de Weijer, J., Gevers, T.: Robust optical flow from photometric invariants. In: Proc. IEEE International Conference on Image Processing (ICIP), pp. 1835–1838 (2004)
46. Vogel, C., Roth, S., Schindler, K.: An evaluation of data costs for optical flow. In: Weickert, J., Hein, M., Schiele, B. (eds.) GCPR 2013. LNCS, vol. 8142, pp. 343–353. Springer, Heidelberg (2013)
47. Vogel, O., Bruhn, A., Weickert, J., Didas, S.: Direct shape-from-shading with adaptive higher order regularisation. In: Sgallari, F., Murli, A., Paragios, N. (eds.) SSVM 2007. LNCS, vol. 4485, pp. 871–882. Springer, Heidelberg (2007)
48. Wedel, A., Pock, T., Zach, C., Bischof, H., Cremers, D.: An improved algorithm for TV-l^1 optical flow. In: Cremers, D., Rosenhahn, B., Yuille, A.L., Schmidt, F.R. (eds.) Statistical and Geometrical Approaches to Visual Motion Analysis. LNCS, vol. 5604, pp. 23–45. Springer, Heidelberg (2009)
49. Weickert, J., Welk, M.: Tensor field interpolation with PDEs. In: Weickert, J., Hagen, H. (eds.) Visualization and Processing of Tensor Fields, pp. 315–325. Springer (2006)
50. Werlberger, M., Pock, T., Bischof, H.: Motion estimation with non-local total variation regularization. In: Proc. IEEE Conference on Computer Vision and Pattern Recognition (CVPR), June 2010, pp. 2464–2471 (2010)
51. Xu, L., Jia, J., Matsushita, Y.: Motion detail preserving optical flow estimation. In: Proc. IEEE Conference on Computer Vision and Pattern Recognition (CVPR), pp. 1293–1300. IEEE Computer Society Press (2010)
52. Young, D.M.: Iterative Solution of Large Linear Systems. Academic Press, New York (1971)
53. Zabih, R., Woodfill, J.: Non-parametric local transforms for computing visual correspondence. In: Eklundh, J.-O. (ed.) ECCV 1994. LNCS, vol. 800, pp. 151–158. Springer, Heidelberg (1994)
54. Zimmer, H., Bruhn, A., Weickert, J.: Optic flow in harmony. International Journal of Computer Vision 93(3), 368–388 (2011)

Hipster Wars: Discovering Elements of Fashion Styles

M. Hadi Kiapour[1], Kota Yamaguchi[2], Alexander C. Berg[1], and Tamara L. Berg[1]

[1] University of North Carolina at Chapel Hill, NC, USA
{hadi,aberg,tlberg}@cs.unc.edu
[2] Tohoku University, Japan
kyamagu@vision.is.tohoku.ac.jp

Abstract. The clothing we wear and our identities are closely tied, revealing to the world clues about our wealth, occupation, and socio-identity. In this paper we examine questions related to what our clothing reveals about our personal style. We first design an online competitive Style Rating Game called *Hipster Wars* to crowd source reliable human judgments of style. We use this game to collect a new dataset of clothing outfits with associated style ratings for 5 style categories: hipster, bohemian, pinup, preppy, and goth. Next, we train models for between-class and within-class classification of styles. Finally, we explore methods to identify clothing elements that are generally discriminative for a style, and methods for identifying items in a particular outfit that may indicate a style.

1 Introduction

To me, clothing is a form of self-expression - there are hints about who you are in what you wear. – Marc Jacobs, fashion designer.

Clothing reveals information about its wearer's socio-identity, including hints about their wealth, occupation, religion, location, and social status. In this paper, we consider what clothing reveals about personal style, in particular focusing on recognizing styles of dress such as hipster, goth, or preppy. Personal style is closely tied to both how you perceive yourself, and how your identity is perceived by other people. At a broader level it even reflects and/or influences the people with whom you tend to interact and associate. We believe this makes it an important problem for consideration because it relates to improving our understanding and knowledge of human socio-identity. And, because clothing styles are generally composed of visual elements, computational vision techniques are the best avenue for automated exploration at a large scale.

Additionally, there are many potential research and commercial applications of style recognition. Imagine a billboard that could tailor which advertisements to show you as you walk by, based on what you're wearing. Another obvious application is personalized online shopping suggestions for clothing or other products. The annual revenue for online shopping alone totals over $200 Billion

D. Fleet et al. (Eds.): ECCV 2014, Part I, LNCS 8689, pp. 472–488, 2014.
© Springer International Publishing Switzerland 2014

dollars annually [33], making this a growing industry for automatic applications of computer vision. At a higher level, recognizing aspects of identity could be used in recommendation systems for compatible matches on dating and other social networks.

Toward efforts on style recognition, we first collect a new style dataset. The dataset consists of 1893 images depicting five different fashion styles – bohemian, goth, hipster, pinup, and preppy. For each image we want to identify not only which style is reflected, but also how strongly the style is displayed, e.g. is this person an uber hipster or only somewhat hipster. Since direct rating based measures (e.g. asking a person to rate the style from 1 to 10) often produce unstable scores (see Fig. 4), we designed *Hipster Wars* (www.hipsterwars.com), a new tournament based rating game to crowd source reliable style ratings across a large number of people. Hipster Wars presents a user with two images and asks, for example, which image is more hipster? A ranking algorithm is used to progressively determine style ratings based on user clicks, and to match up images with similar ratings to produce more accurate and fine-detailed scores efficiently. Our game was released to great success, attracting over 1700 users who provided over 30,000 votes at the time of submission. The number of users is growing every day.

Next, we perform a number of experiments on our new dataset related to style recognition. The first set of experiments explore multi-class classification between styles, e.g. which style does an image depict, hipster, goth, pinup, preppy, or bohemian (Sec 5.1). Next we look at within class classification (Sec 5.2). Here we want to identify the degree to which a style is exhibited, the main motivation for collecting the pairwise comparisons using Hipster Wars.

We also attempt to automatically identify which elements of clothing are associated with each style (Sec 6). This goal involves both exploring methods to identify clothing elements that are generally discriminative for a style, and methods for identifying items in a particular outfit that may indicate a style.

Though an exciting problem, style recognition has not been explored much to date in the computer vision community. Problems related to style in general have been explored in recent work on recognizing distinctive visual elements of cities [7] or cars [20]. More closely related to this paper, some work attempts recognizing urban tribes in group photos of people at different social events [25,17]. In that work, style recognition is treated as a multi-class classification problem where the goal is to predict which of k styles is depicted by a group of people. We take these efforts in a new direction by making use of state-of-the-art methods for clothing recognition to recognize style based only on the clothing that an individual person is wearing. Additionally, we examine two new problems: recognizing the strength of style depicted (e.g. how hipster is this person?), and recognizing which elements of clothing influence perception of style (e.g. which outfit items indicate that this person is a hipster?).

In summary, the main contributions of our paper are:

1. An online competitive *Rating Game* to collectively compute style ratings based on human judgments.

2. A new style dataset depicting different fashion styles with associated crowd sourced style ratings.
3. Between-Class classification of styles, i.e. differentiating between the different style categories.
4. Within-Class classification of styles, i.e. differentiating between high and low ranked images within a style category.
5. Experiments to identify the outfit elements that are most predictive for each style (what makes a hipster hip) or within an image (what makes this particular person so hipster).

2 Related Work

Clothing Recognition: Identifying clothing in images has drawn recent attention in the computer vision community due to the vast potential for commercial applications such as context-aware advertisements and visual online shopping. Recent papers have looked at the problem of parsing clothing (predicting pixel-wise labelings of garment items) [35,36] and clothing recognition for applications [22,23,11]. Parsing approaches take advantage of effective methods for human pose estimation [37]. Two different clothing parsing scenarios are examined, weakly supervised parsing where predictions are restricted to annotated garment item labels [35] and unrestricted parsing where the garment item labels are not provided [36]. The second scenario [36] is more appropriate for our task so we make use of this method here.

Attributes: Predicting useful mid-level semantic representations such as attributes have been well studied recently. Attribute methods have been applied to objects [16,26,14,18,9,32], scenes [21,34], and products [27,13,12]. Additionally attributes have been explored specifically in the context of clothing for describing attributes of upper body clothing [1] or for jointly estimating clothing attributes in a CRF based approach [4]. Work on attributes is related to our goal in that we also want to produce a mid-level representation. In our case we would like to predict the mid-level elements that are most indicative of a particular style of clothing. Currently we consider garments as our elements, but attributes would be a potential next step toward discovering distinctive predictors of a style.
Games for Image Annotation: Large-scale labeling of image data by people is becoming popular in the computer vision community, sometimes using domain experts for very specific labeling tasks [15], and alternatively addressing tasks requiring less specialized expertise or using a combination of human and computer feedback to allow non-experts to label imagery [13,2,3]. To more effectively leverage human labeling, some approaches make the labeling process into an entertaining game, as in the ESP Game [29] or [30]. More recently [6] uses a game setting to label important regions for fine-grained classification.

Recognizing Styles: Recently Doersch *et al* look at the problem of selecting discriminative patches that distinguish between the styles of different cities [7]. Lee *et al* use a related method to discover style elements connecting objects in space and time [20]. Most related to our work are methods to recognize social

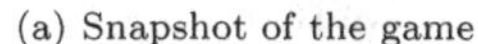

(a) Snapshot of the game

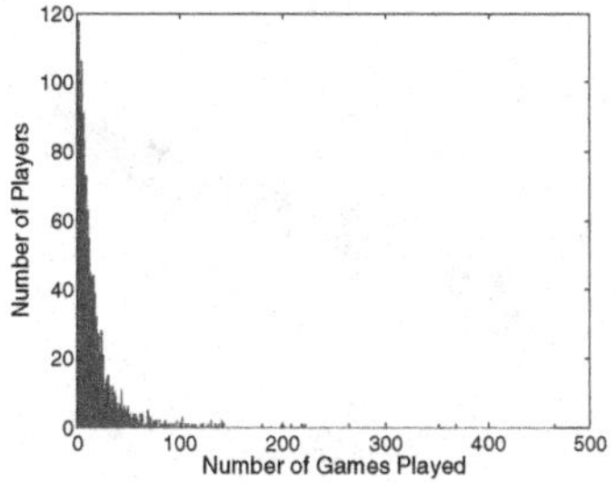

(b) Distribution of games played

Fig. 1. Left shows an example game for the hipster category on Hipster Wars. Users click on whichever image is more hipster or click "=" for a tie. Right shows the number of games played per player.

tribe of people in group photographs of events [25,17]. We address a somewhat different problem, considering photos of individuals instead of groups and not making use of any features from the image backgrounds. In addition we analyze and predict the degree to which a style is exhibited. We also consider a new problem of predicting which outfit items most indicate styles in general, and which outfit elements indicate a specific person's style.

3 Hipster Wars: Style Dataset and Rating Game

To study style prediction we first collect a new dataset depicting different fashion styles (Section 3.1). We then design a crowd-sourcing game called *Hipster Wars* to elicit style ratings for the images in our dataset (Section 3.2).

3.1 Data Collection

We collect a new dataset of images depicting five fashion styles, *Bohemian, Goth, Hipster, Pinup,* and *Preppy.* To construct our initial seed corpus, we query Google Image Search using each style name and download top ranked images. We then use Google's "Find Visually Similar Images" feature to retrieve thousands of additional visually similar images to our seed set and manually select images with good quality, full body outfit shots. We repeat this process with expanded search terms, e.g. "pinup clothing" or "pinup dress", to collect 1893 images in total. The images exhibit the styles to varying degrees.

3.2 Rating Game

We want to rate the images in each style category according to how strongly they depict the associated style. As we show in section 3.5, simply asking people to rate individual images directly can produce unstable results because each person may have a different internal scale for ratings. Therefore, we develop an online game to collectively crowd-source ratings for all images within each style category. A snapshot of the game is shown in Figure 1a.

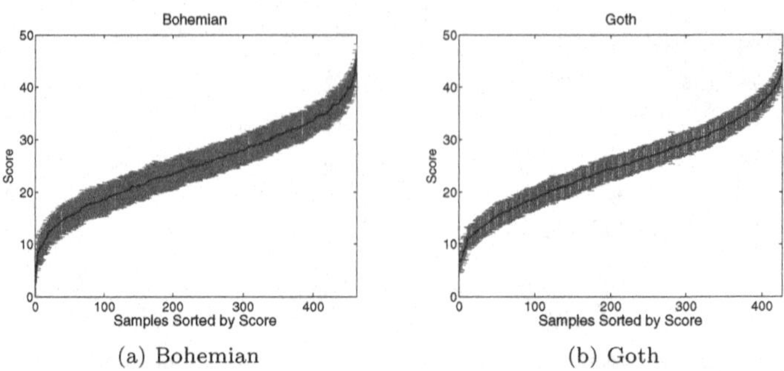

(a) Bohemian (b) Goth

Fig. 2. Style scores computed by our Style Rating Game, showing means and uncertainties for images sorted from smallest to largest mean

Our game is designed as a tournament where a user is presented with a pair of images from one of the style categories and asked to click on whichever image more strongly depicts the solicited style, or to select "Tie" if the images equally depict the style. For example, for images in the hipster category the user would be asked "Who's more hipster?" After each pair of images, the user is provided with feedback related to the winning and losing statistics of the pair from previous rounds of the tournament.

Because we cannot afford to gather comparisons for all pairs of images in our dataset, we make use of the TrueSkill algorithm [10]. This algorithm iteratively determines which pair of images to compare in each tournament, and based on user input successively updates the ratings of images in our dataset. TrueSkill is a popular ranking system, originally developed to pair users in XBox Live. Though it was originally developed to pair players and determine their gaming skill levels, it is a general model that can be applied in any competitive game. Here we apply it to images.

There are several reasons we choose the TrueSkill algorithm. For each tournament the algorithm pairs up images with similar estimated ratings. Therefore over time we are able to focus on finer-grained distinctions between images and minimize the number of comparisons we need to make to estimate the true image ratings. Additionally, the algorithm is online (as opposed to batch). Users can upload their own photos and merge them seamlessly into the tournaments even after the game has started. The algorithm is also efficient, allowing us to update rankings in real-time after each tournament even when many users are playing at once. It also explicitly allows for ties and models uncertainty in ratings. Finally, TrueSkill converges quickly, reducing the number of games necessary to compute ratings for images.

3.3 Game Details

Each image is associated with a *skill* variable, s, representing how strongly the image represents the associated style. Our goal is to determine this skill level for each image in the dataset. An image's skill is modeled by a Gaussian distribution with mean, μ, and variance, σ^2, where $s \sim \mathcal{N}(s; \mu, \sigma^2)$. As different users play the tournaments there may be variations in how the styles are perceived, this is modeled with another variable, p, a Gaussian distribution around skill level, $p \sim \mathcal{N}(p; s, \beta^2)$.

Updating after Win/Loss: After each tournament is played, if the tournament does not result in a tie, we update the skill estimates for the winning player as:

$$\mu_{\text{winner}} \leftarrow \mu_{\text{winner}} + \frac{\sigma^2_{\text{winner}}}{c}.\mathbb{V}\left(\frac{(\mu_{\text{winner}} - \mu_{\text{loser}})}{c}, \frac{\epsilon}{c}\right) \tag{1}$$

$$\sigma^2_{\text{winner}} \leftarrow \sigma^2_{\text{winner}}.\left(1 - \frac{\sigma^2_{\text{winner}}}{c^2}.\mathbb{W}\left(\frac{(\mu_{\text{winner}} - \mu_{\text{loser}})}{c}, \frac{\epsilon}{c}\right)\right) \tag{2}$$

$$\tag{3}$$

Where:

$$\mathbb{V}(a,b) = \frac{\mathcal{G}_{0,1}(a-b)}{\Phi_{0,1}(a-b)} \tag{4}$$

$$\mathbb{W}(a,b) = \mathbb{V}(a,b) \cdot (\mathbb{V}(a,b) + a - b) \tag{5}$$

$$c^2 = 2\beta^2 + \sigma^2_{\text{winner}} + \sigma^2_{\text{loser}} \tag{6}$$

Where $\mathcal{G}_{0,1}$ and $\Phi_{0,1}$ are the PDF and CDF of normal distributions with zero mean and unit variance. The intuition behind these updates is that if the win was expected, i.e. the difference between skills of the winner image and the losing image was large relative to the total uncertainty, c, then the update on image skill estimates will be small. However, if the outcome of the tournament was surprising, the updates will be larger. Similar update rules are applied for the loser of the tournament.

Updating after Tie: If a tournament is tied, $\mathbb{V}$ and $\mathbb{W}$ are computed as:

$$\mathbb{V}(a,b) = \frac{\mathcal{G}_{0,1}(-b-a) - \mathcal{G}_{0,1}(b-a)}{\Phi_{0,1}(b-a) - \Phi_{0,1}(-b-a)} \tag{7}$$

$$\mathbb{W}(a,b) = \mathbb{V}^2(a,b) + \frac{(b-a)\cdot\mathcal{G}_{0,1}(b-a) + (a+b)\cdot\mathcal{G}_{0,1}(a+b)}{\Phi_{0,1}(b-a) - \Phi_{0,1}(-b-a)} \tag{8}$$

Similar intuition applies here. If both images already had similar skill levels there are not significant updates on beliefs for either image. If the result was more surprising, updates are more significant.

Selecting Pairs: For each tournament we must select a pair of images to play against each other. We would like to optimize two things: every image should be played enough times to reliably determine its rating, and we would like to pair up images with similar ratings estimates in order to produce fine-grained estimates of their ratings. Therefore, to select pairs we first choose the least played image from the dataset and then we choose as its pair, the image with highest probability of creating a draw with that image (to maximize the informativeness of each tournament) which following [10] is computed as:

$$q_{\text{draw}}(\beta^2, \mu_i, \mu_j, \sigma_i, \sigma_j) \equiv \sqrt{\frac{2\beta^2}{2\beta^2 + \sigma_i^2 + \sigma_j^2}} \cdot \exp\left(-\frac{(\mu_i - \mu_j)^2}{2(2\beta^2 + \sigma_i^2 + \sigma_j^2}\right) \tag{9}$$

Fig. 3. Example results from our style rating game, *Hipster Wars*. Top and bottom rated for each style category.

Implementation Details: We design our game such that image scores fall into the range $[0, 50]$. Our ranking system initializes ratings for all images with $\mu = 25$ and uncertainty $\sigma = \frac{25}{3}$. Value for ϵ, the draw margin, is calculated based on a 10% chance of draw assumed in every game and default value for β is set to $\frac{25}{6}$. Finally the 'true skill' of each image is given by $\mu - 3\sigma$, a conservative estimate which ensures images with high skill means and least uncertainties will be placed on the top.

3.4 Game Results

Our style rating game was played by 1702 users for over 30,000 tournaments. On average users played about 18.5 tournaments, indicating reasonable engagement. Some users played hundreds of tournaments, with a max of 465. The distribution of number of games played per user is shown in Figure 1b. Scores sorted by their mean along with their uncertainty for two sample categories are shown in Figure 2.

This produces very reasonable ratings for each style category. Top and bottom rated images for each style are shown in Figure 3. Top rated images tend to depict very strong indications of the associated style while images rated toward the bottom of the set depict the style with much less strength.

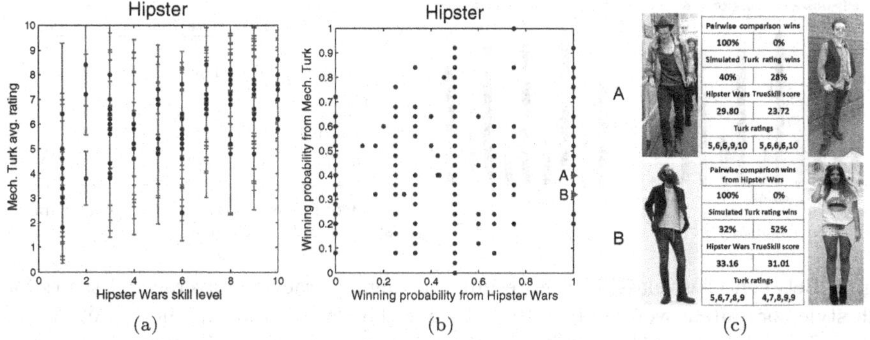

(a) (b) (c)

Fig. 4. Hipster Wars Pairwise ratings vs. individual ratings from Amazon Mech. Turk.

3.5 Pairwise vs. Individual Ratings

In order to evaluate the effectiveness of pairwise comparisons on Hipster Wars over a standard approach of rating style independently for each image, we used Amazon Mechanical Turk to conduct the following experiment. For each of the style categories, we divided the range of skills obtained from Hipster Wars into 10 equal size intervals which we call skill levels (1 :lowest, 10 :highest) and picked a subset of 100 images distributed uniformly over the intervals. For each of the images, we asked 5 individuals (on Mechanical Turk) to rate the degree of a particular style category. Example ratings from all skill levels were provided. Figure 4a shows a scatter plot of average ratings from Mechanical Turk vs the skill level estimated by Hipster Wars. Figure 4b shows the average ratings vs the actual win percentage of games on Hipster Wars. In general the ratings are much noisier than either the direct pairwise comparisons or the skill level estimated by Hipster Wars. Figure 4c shows example pairs where this discrepancy is very large. These results indicate that the pairwise comparison approach can provide more stable and useful ratings for subtle cues like style.

4 Style Representation

We represent the style of outfits using a number of visual descriptors found to be useful for clothing recognition tasks [36], including descriptors related to color, texture, and shape. In particular, we calculate a vector of the following features at each pixel within a patch centered around the pixel: a) RGB color value, b) Lab color value, c) MR8 texture response [28] (to encode local patterns) d) HOG descriptor [5] (to measure local object shape), e) Distance from image border, f) Probability of pixels belonging to skin and hair categories [36].

We form the Style Descriptor by accumulating these features following [36], but without dimensionality reduction to capture the details of clothing appearance. The exact procedure is the following: 1) We first estimate body pose [37]. 2) For each of the 24 estimated body part keypoints, we extract an image patch of size 32×32 pixels surrounding the keypoint. 3) We split each image patch into

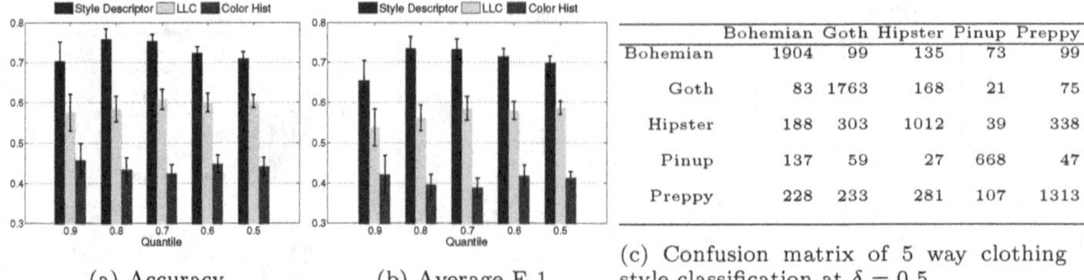

	Bohemian	Goth	Hipster	Pinup	Preppy
Bohemian	1904	99	135	73	99
Goth	83	1763	168	21	75
Hipster	188	303	1012	39	338
Pinup	137	59	27	668	47
Preppy	228	233	281	107	1313

(a) Accuracy (b) Average F-1 (c) Confusion matrix of 5 way clothing style classification at $\delta = 0.5$

Fig. 5. Between-Class classification results showing accuracy and average f-1 scores for each style computed over random 100 folds for the classification of the top δ% rated images. Error bars are 95% confidence intervals from statistical bootstrapping.

4×4 cells and mean-std pooling of the features described above are computed. 4) We concatenate all pooled features over all 24 patches, for a total of 39,168 dimensions.

We compared the classification performance of Style Descriptor against two other global visual descriptors computed on the detected bounding box by pose estimator: LLC encoding [31] of local SIFT [24] descriptors and color histogram. For LLC we extract SIFT features on a dense grid over the image and use LLC coding to transform each local descriptor into a sparse code and apply a multi-scale spatial pyramid (1×1, 2×2, 4×4) [19] max-pooling to obtain the final 43008-dimensional representation. Color histogram features were constructed by quantizing the R,G,B channels into 16 bins each, giving a final 4096-dimensional histogram for each image.

5 Predicting Clothing Styles

We consider two different style recognition tasks: Between-class classification - Classifying outfits into one of the five fashion styles (Sec 5.1). Within-class classification - differentiating between high and low rated images for each style (Sec 5.2). For each of these tasks, we compare Style Descriptor versus the other global descriptors which we considered as baseline. In all classification experiments we use a linear kernel SVM using the liblinear package [8].

5.1 Between-Class Classification

We consider classifying images as one of five styles. Results examine how performance varies for different splits of the data, defining a parameter δ which determines what percentage of the data is used in classification. We vary values of δ from 0.1 to 0.5 where $\delta = 0.1$ represents a classification task between the top rated 10% of images from each style (using the ratings computed in Sec 3.2). We use a $9:1$ train to test ratio, and repeat the train-test process 100 times. The results of our between-class classification are shown in Figure 5. Performance is good, varying slowly with δ, and the pattern of confusions is reasonable.

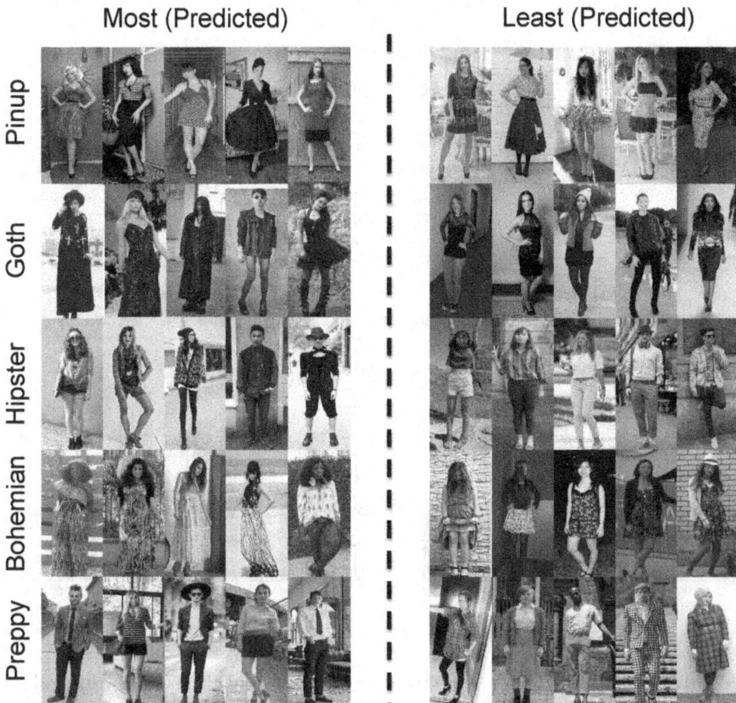

Fig. 6. Example results of within-classification task with $\delta = 0.5$. Top and bottom predictions for each style category are shown.

5.2 Within-Class Classification

Our next style recognition tasks considers classification between top rated and bottom rated examples for each style independently. Here we learn one linear SVM model for each style. The variable $\delta = 10\% \ldots 50\%$ determines the percentage of top and bottom ranked images considered. For example, $\delta = 0.1$ means the top rated 10% of images are used as positives and the bottom rated 10% of samples as negatives. We repeat the experiments for 100 random folds with a 9 : 1 train to test ratio. In each experiment, C, is determined using 5 fold cross-validation.

Results are reported in Figure 7. We observe that when δ is small we generally have better performance than for larger δ, probably because the classification task becomes more challenging as we add less extreme examples of each style. Additionally, we find best performance on the pinup category. Performance on the goth category comes in second. For the hipster category, we do quite well at differentiating between extremely strong or weak examples, but performance drops off quickly as δ increases. Example predictions for each style are shown in Figure 6.

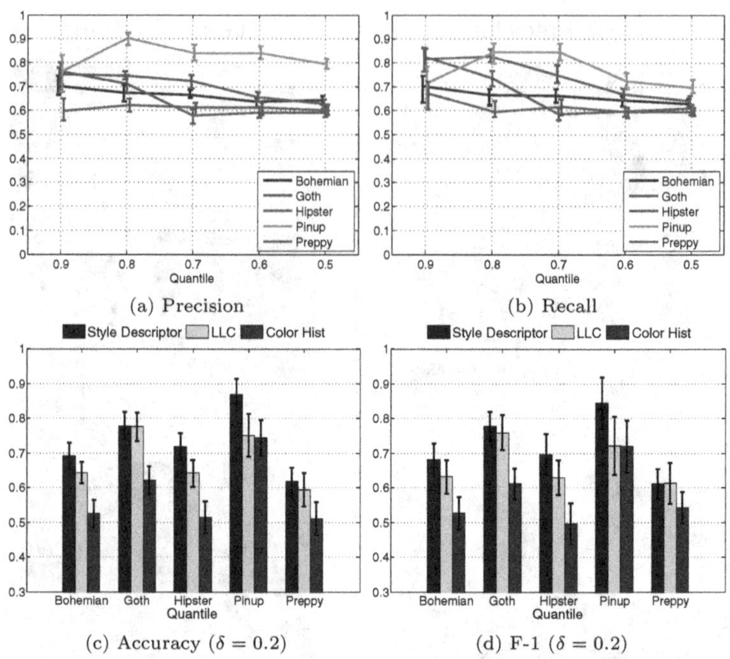

(a) Precision

(b) Recall

(c) Accuracy ($\delta = 0.2$)

(d) F-1 ($\delta = 0.2$)

Fig. 7. Within-Class classification results averaged for each style computed over random 100 folds balanced classification of the top and bottom δ% quartiles. Error bars are 95% confidence intervals from statistical bootstrapping.

6 Discovering the Elements of Styles

In this section, we are interested in two different questions: 1) what elements of style contribute to people in general being a hipster (or goth or preppy, etc), and 2) for a particular photo of a person, what elements of their outfit indicate that they are a hipster (or goth or preppy, etc)?

6.1 General Style Indicators

We would like to determine which garment items are most indicative of each style in general. For this, we compute clothing segmentation on all images of each style, and obtain the percentage of each predicted garment item present. Figure 8 shows the percentage of pixels occupied by each garment item across images of each style. Based on this automatic analysis, we can make some interesting observations using our clothing recognition predictions. For example, we find that pinups and bohemians tend to wear dresses whereas hipsters and preppies do not. Goths fall somewhere in between. Pinups also tend to display a lot of skin while this is less true for goths. Hipsters and preppies wear the most jeans and pants. Preppies tend to wear more blazers while goths and hipsters wear the most boots.

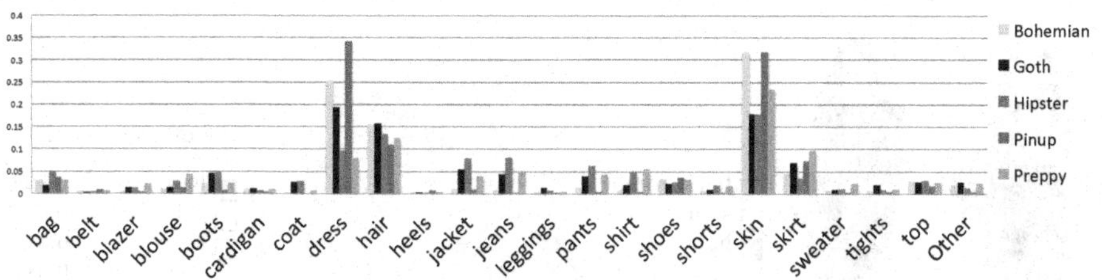

Fig. 8. Clothing items across styles

6.2 Style Indicators for Individuals

Our second approach is a bit more complex. In this model we make use of our models trained on Style Descriptors. We essentially transfer predictions from the Style Descriptor to the underlying parse while making use of computed priors on which garment items are most likely for each style.

Discriminative Part Discovery: Suppose we have a set of image features $\mathbf{x}_i$ from each part i that we locate from a pose estimator. Then our style prediction model can be described by a linear model:

$$y = \sum_{i \in \text{parts}} \mathbf{w}_i^{\mathrm{T}} \mathbf{x}_i + b, \tag{10}$$

where y is a decision value of the prediction, $\mathbf{w}_i$ is model parameters corresponding to part i, and b is a bias parameter.

In this paper, we specifically view the individual term $\mathbf{w}_i \mathbf{x}_i$ as a distance from the decision boundary for part i in the classification, and utilize the weights to *localize* where discriminative parts are located in the input image. This interpretation is possible when the input to the linear model is uniformly interpretable, i.e., same feature from different locations. Also to guarantee the equivalence of parts interpretation, we normalize the part features $\mathbf{x}_i$ to have zero-mean and uniform standard deviation in training data.

To calculate the score of the part i, we apply a sigmoid function on the decision value and get probabilities of a style given a single part:

$$p_i \equiv \frac{1}{1 + \exp\left(-\mathbf{w}_i^{\mathrm{T}} \mathbf{x}_i\right)}. \tag{11}$$

Learning is done in the same manner as within-class style classification, using L2-regularized logistic regression.

From Parts to Items: Part scores tell us which locations in the outfit are affecting style prediction. However, to convert these to an interpretable prediction, we map predicted garments back to garments predicted in the original parse. This produces a more semantic output, e.g. "She looks like a hipster because of her hat." To map parts to garments in the parse, we first compute a *saliency map* of parts; At each keypoint, we project the part score $p(\mathbf{x}_i)$ to all pixels in the patch

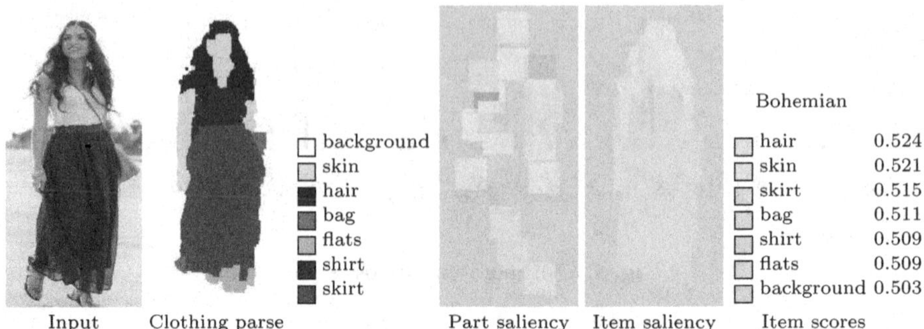

Fig. 9. From parts to items. We compute contributions of each part, and project them in image coordinates (Part saliency). Then, using clothing parse, we compute the scores of items. When the score is above 0.5, the associated item indicates a positive influence on the queried style. Note that the scores only show the relative strength of style-indication among items in the picture.

location. Articulated parts get the average score from all parts. Areas outside of any patch are set to 1/2 (i.e., decision boundary). Using the computed clothing segmentation [36], we compute the average score of each garment item from the *saliency map*. This produces, for each item k in the clothing parse of an image, a score p_k that we can use to predict items that strongly indicate a style. Figure 9 depicts this process.

Prior Filtering: The result of part-based factorization can still look noisy due to errors in pose estimation and clothing parsing. Therefore, we smooth our predictions with a prior on which garment items we expect to be associated with each style.

Our prior is constructed by building a linear classifier based on the area of each clothing item that we obtain from the clothing segmentation [36]. Denoting the log pixel-count of item k by x_k, we express the prior model by a linear function: $y = \sum_k w_k x_k + b$, where y is the decision value of style classification, and w_k and b are model parameters. Using the same idea from the previous subsections, we compute the score of each item by: $q_k \equiv \frac{1}{1+\exp(-w_k x_k)}$.

Once we compute the part-based score p_k and the prior score q_k, we merge them into the final indicator score r_k for garment-item k:

$$r_k \equiv \lambda_1 p_k + \lambda_2 \left[\frac{\sigma_p}{\sigma_q} \left(q_k - \frac{1}{2} \right) + \frac{1}{2} \right], \quad (12)$$

where λ_1 and λ_2, are weights given to each score, σ_p and σ_q are standard deviations of p_k and q_k at each image. The intuition here is that we assume both p_k and q_k follow a normal distribution with mean at 0.5. We adjust the shape of q_k distribution to that of p_k in the second term. Then, we use λ's to mix two scores and produce the final result. We set λ's to cross-validation accuracies of classification during training normalized to sum to a unit, so that the resulting score reflects the accuracy of style prediction.

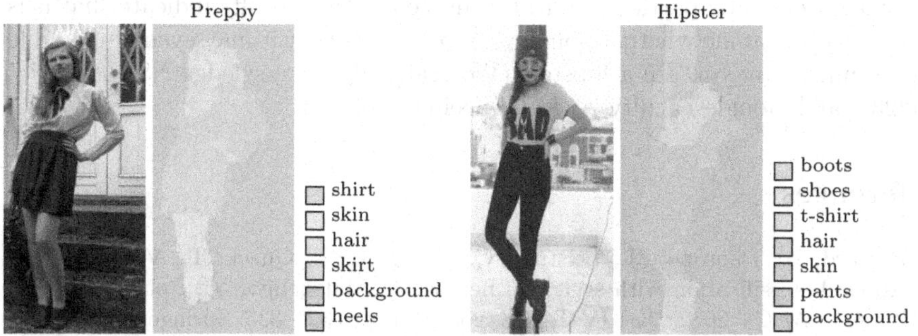

Fig. 10. Example predicted style indicators for individuals

Table 1. Ratio of images that include the top choice from crowds in the first 5 elements of our discovery method

Method	Bohemian	Goth	Hipster	Pinup	Preppy
Random	0.357	0.258	0.171	0.427	0.232
Our method	0.379	0.282	0.154	0.454	0.241

6.3 Analysis of Style Indicator for Individuals

Figure 10 shows examples of discovered style indicators for individuals. Predicted elements for each outfit are ordered by indicator scores. We find that our method captures the most important garment-items well such as shirt for preppy styles, graphic t-shirts for hipsters, or dresses for pinups.

We also attempted to quantitatively verify the results using crowdsourcing. We obtained the "ground truth" by asking workers to vote on which element they think is making a certain style. However, the naive application of this approach resulted in a number of problems; 1) workers tend to just vote on all visible items in the picture, 2) small items are ignored, 3) workers mark different items with a different name (e.g., shoes vs. flats) and 4) different workers are not consistent due to the great subjectivity in the question. We show in Table 1 the ratio of images from our discovery that included the worker's top choice. Our method achieved slightly better result than the random ordering. However, we note that the "ground truth" in this evaluation does not necessarily constitute a good measurement for benchmarking, leaving open the question of how to "ground truth" annotation for such subtle socially-defined signals.

7 Conclusions

We have designed a new game for gathering human judgments of style ratings and have used this game to collect a new dataset of rated style images. We have explored recognizing and estimating the degree of fashion styles. We have also begun efforts to recognize which elements of outfits indicate styles generally and which items in a particular outfit indicate a style. Results indicate that it is possible to determine whether you are a hipster and that it may even be possible to determine why you are a hipster! (We gratefully acknowledge NSF Award# 1444234, and Google Faculty Award, "Seeing Social".)

References

1. Bossard, L., Dantone, M., Leistner, C., Wengert, C., Quack, T., Van Gool, L.: Apparel classification with style. In: Lee, K.M., Matsushita, Y., Rehg, J.M., Hu, Z. (eds.) ACCV 2012, Part IV. LNCS, vol. 7727, pp. 321–335. Springer, Heidelberg (2013)
2. Bourdev, L., Malik, J.: Poselets: Body part detectors trained using 3D human pose annotations. In: 2009 IEEE 12th International Conference on Computer Vision, pp. 1365–1372. IEEE (2009)
3. Branson, S., Wah, C., Schroff, F., Babenko, B., Welinder, P., Perona, P., Belongie, S.: Visual recognition with humans in the loop. In: Daniilidis, K., Maragos, P., Paragios, N. (eds.) ECCV 2010, Part IV. LNCS, vol. 6314, pp. 438–451. Springer, Heidelberg (2010)
4. Chen, H., Gallagher, A., Girod, B.: Describing clothing by semantic attributes. In: Fitzgibbon, A., Lazebnik, S., Perona, P., Sato, Y., Schmid, C. (eds.) ECCV 2012, Part III. LNCS, vol. 7574, pp. 609–623. Springer, Heidelberg (2012)
5. Dalal, N., Triggs, B.: Histograms of oriented gradients for human detection. In: IEEE Computer Society Conference on Computer Vision and Pattern Recognition, CVPR 2005, vol. 1, pp. 886–893 (2005)
6. Deng, J., Krause, J., Fei-Fei, L.: Fine-grained crowdsourcing for fine-grained recognition. In: 2013 IEEE Conference on Computer Vision and Pattern Recognition (CVPR). IEEE (2013)
7. Doersch, C., Singh, S., Gupta, A., Sivic, J., Efros, A.A.: What makes paris look like paris? ACM Transactions on Graphics (SIGGRAPH) 31(4) (2012)
8. Fan, R.E., Chang, K.W., Hsieh, C.J., Wang, X.R., Lin, C.J.: Liblinear: A library for large linear classification. Journal of Machine Learning Research (2008)
9. Ferrari, V., Zisserman, A.: Learning visual attributes. In: NIPS (2007)
10. Herbrich, R., Minka, T., Graepel, T.: Trueskill(tm): A bayesian skill rating system. In: Advances in Neural Information Processing Systems, pp. 569–576 (2007)
11. Kalantidis, Y., Kennedy, L., Li, L.J.: Getting the look: clothing recognition and segmentation for automatic product suggestions in everyday photos. In: Proceedings of the 3rd ACM Conference on International Conference on Multimedia Retrieval, pp. 105–112. ACM (2013)
12. Kovashka, A., Grauman, K.: Attribute pivots for guiding relevance feedback in image search. In: ICCV (2013)
13. Kovashka, A., Parikh, D., Grauman, K.: Whittlesearch: Image search with relative attribute feedback. In: CVPR, pp. 2973–2980. IEEE (2012)
14. Kumar, N., Berg, A., Belhumeur, P., Nayar, S.: Attribute and simile classifiers for face verification. In: ICCV (2009)
15. Kumar, N., Belhumeur, P.N., Biswas, A., Jacobs, D.W., Kress, W.J., Lopez, I.C., Soares, J.V.B.: Leafsnap: A computer vision system for automatic plant species identification. In: Fitzgibbon, A., Lazebnik, S., Perona, P., Sato, Y., Schmid, C. (eds.) ECCV 2012, Part II. LNCS, vol. 7573, pp. 502–516. Springer, Heidelberg (2012)

16. Kumar, N., Berg, A.C., Belhumeur, P.N., Nayar, S.K.: Describable visual attributes for face verification and image search. IEEE Transactions on Pattern Analysis and Machine Intelligence, PAMI (October 2011)
17. Kwak, I.S., Murillo, A.C., Belhumeur, P., Belongie, S., Kriegman, D.: From bikers to surfers: Visual recognition of urban tribes. In: British Machine Vision Conference (BMVC), Bristol (September 2013)
18. Lampert, C., Nickisch, H., Harmeling, S.: Learning to detect unseen object classes by between-class attribute transfer. In: CVPR (2009)
19. Lazebnik, S., Schmid, C., Ponce, J.: Beyond bags of features: Spatial pyramid matching for recognizing natural scene categories. In: 2006 IEEE Conference on Computer Vision and Pattern Recognition (CVPR). IEEE (2006)
20. Lee, Y.J., Efros, A.A., Hebert, M.: Style-aware mid-level representation for discovering visual connections in space and time. In: ICCV (2013)
21. Li, L.-J., Su, H., Lim, Y., Fei-Fei, L.: Objects as attributes for scene classification. In: Kutulakos, K.N. (ed.) ECCV 2010 Workshops, Part I. LNCS, vol. 6553, pp. 57–69. Springer, Heidelberg (2010)
22. Liu, S., Feng, J., Song, Z., Zhang, T., Lu, H., Xu, C., Yan, S.: Hi, magic closet, tell me what to wear? In: ACM International Conference on Multimedia, pp. 619–628. ACM (2012)
23. Liu, S., Song, Z., Liu, G., Xu, C., Lu, H., Yan, S.: Street-to-shop: Cross-scenario clothing retrieval via parts alignment and auxiliary set. In: CVPR, pp. 3330–3337 (2012)
24. Lowe, D.: Object recognition from local scale-invariant features. In: ICCV, pp. 1150–1157 (1999)
25. Murillo, A.C., Kwak, I.S., Bourdev, L., Kriegman, D., Belongie, S.: Urban tribes: Analyzing group photos from a social perspective. In: CVPR Workshop on Socially Intelligent Surveillance and Monitoring (SISM), Providence, RI (June 2012)
26. Parikh, D., Grauman, K.: Interactively building a discriminative vocabulary of nameable attributes. In: CVPR (2011)
27. Parikh, D., Grauman, K.: Relative attributes. In: ICCV (2011)
28. Varma, M., Zisserman, A.: A statistical approach to texture classification from single images. Int. J. Comput. Vision 62(1-2), 61–81 (2005), `http://dx.doi.org/10.1007/s11263-005-4635-4`
29. Von Ahn, L., Dabbish, L.: Labeling images with a computer game. In: SIGCHI Conference on Human Factors in Computing Systems (CHI), pp. 319–326. ACM (2004)
30. Von Ahn, L., Liu, R., Blum, M.: Peekaboom: a game for locating objects in images. In: Conference on Human Factors in Computing Systems, CHI (2006)
31. Wang, J., Yang, J., Yu, K., Huang, T., Lv, F., Gong, Y.: Locality-constrained linear coding for image classification. In: 2010 IEEE Conference on Computer Vision and Pattern Recognition (CVPR). IEEE (2010)
32. Wang, Y., Mori, G.: A discriminative latent model of object classes and attributes. In: Daniilidis, K., Maragos, P., Paragios, N. (eds.) ECCV 2010, Part V. LNCS, vol. 6315, pp. 155–168. Springer, Heidelberg (2010)
33. Wu, S.: Online-retail spending at $200 billion annually and growing. Wall Street Journal Digits Blog (February 2012)

34. Xiao, J., Hays, J., Ehinger, K.A., Oliva, A., Torralba, A.: Sun database: Large-scale scene recognition from abbey to zoo. In: 2010 IEEE Conference on Computer Vision and Pattern Recognition (CVPR), pp. 3485–3492. IEEE (2010)
35. Yamaguchi, K., Kiapour, M.H., Berg, T.L.: Parsing clothing in fashion photographs. In: Proceedings of the 2012 IEEE Conference on Computer Vision and Pattern Recognition (CVPR 2012), pp. 3570–3577. IEEE Computer Society, Washington, DC (2012), http://dl.acm.org/citation.cfm?id=2354409.2355126
36. Yamaguchi, K., Kiapour, M.H., Berg, T.L.: Paper doll parsing: Retrieving similar styles to parse clothing items. In: 2013 IEEE International Conference on Computer Vision, ICCV (2013)
37. Yang, Y., Ramanan, D.: Articulated pose estimation with flexible mixtures-of-parts. In: CVPR, pp. 1385–1392 (2011)

From Low-Cost Depth Sensors to CAD: Cross-Domain 3D Shape Retrieval via Regression Tree Fields

Yan Wang[1], Jie Feng[2], Zhixiang Wu[2], Jun Wang[3], and Shih-Fu Chang[1,2]

[1] Dept. of Electrical Engineering, Columbia University, USA
{yanwang,sfchang}@ee.columbia.edu
[2] Dept. of Computer Science, Columbia University, USA
jiefeng@cs.columbia.edu, zw2229@columbia.edu
[3] IBM T. J. Watson Research Center, USA
wangjun@us.ibm.com

Abstract. The recent advances of low-cost and mobile depth sensors dramatically extend the potential of 3D shape retrieval and analysis. While the traditional research of 3D retrieval mainly focused on searching by a rough 2D sketch or with a high-quality CAD model, we tackle a novel and challenging problem of cross-domain 3D shape retrieval, in which users can use 3D scans from low-cost depth sensors like Kinect as queries to search CAD models in the database. To cope with the imperfection of user-captured models such as model noise and occlusion, we propose a cross-domain shape retrieval framework, which minimizes the potential function of a Conditional Random Field to efficiently generate the retrieval scores. In particular, the potential function consists of two critical components: one unary potential term provides robust cross-domain partial matching and the other pairwise potential term embeds spatial structures to alleviate the instability from model noise. Both potential components are efficiently estimated using random forests with 3D local features, forming a *Regression Tree Field* framework. We conduct extensive experiments on two recently released user-captured 3D shape datasets and compare with several state-of-the-art approaches on the cross-domain shape retrieval task. The experimental results demonstrate that our proposed method outperforms the competing methods with a significant performance gain.

1 Introduction

Shape-based retrieval and analysis of 3D models is an important research topic in computer vision, graphics, and computational geometry due to the wide applications in many domains such as archeology, architecture, medical imaging, and computer-aided design (CAD). In the past two decades, extensive efforts have been made to design effective 3D shape retrieval algorithms [1]. The existing work is mainly focused on two search scenarios, i.e., search by sketch [2][3] (Figure 1(a)) and search with CAD models as query input [1] (Figure 1(b)).Along

D. Fleet et al. (Eds.): ECCV 2014, Part I, LNCS 8689, pp. 489–504, 2014.
© Springer International Publishing Switzerland 2014

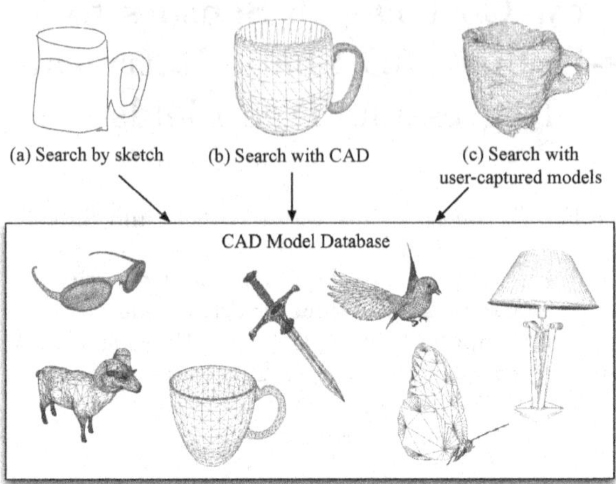

Fig. 1. Different 3D shape retrieval scenarios: (a) search by sketch; (b) search with CAD; and (c) cross-domain search with user-captured models from low-cost sensors

with the advances of low-cost depth sensors such as Microsoft Kinect, PrimeSense sensors, and the newly revealed mobile depth sensor from Google [4], there is tremendous growth of user-generated 3D data, which promotes the study of a new *cross-domain* retrieval problem, i.e., *search with user-captured models*, where the users capture potentially noisy depth data and images of the object to their interest, and then use reconstructed 3D models as queries to find similar 3D shapes from a large collection of high-quality CAD models as illustrated in Figure 1(c). Such a cross-domain scenario also promotes new applications for 3D shape retrieval, such as high-quality 3D scanning, manipulation and printing.

Note that the existing methods for search with CAD models are often specifically designed for high resolution models with a well-controlled level of quality, which differ from the 3D models captured with low-cost sensors in several aspects. First, the user-captured models often contain a significant level of noise generated in either the capturing or the reconstruction process. Second, the generated model in uncontrolled environment is often incomplete due to various reasons like occlusions or partial views. Hence, this new retrieval scenario with user-captured models brings significant challenges in various aspects of shape analysis and retrieval, including 3D shape descriptor extraction, model representation and matching.

More specifically, existing 3D shape retrieval approaches generally follow two popular frameworks, local feature matching with optional spatial verification [5][6][7][8][9] and the Bag-of-Feature scheme [10][11], both of which require effective 3D local features. Although great progress has been made in 3D feature design, such as spin-image based descriptor [6], MeshDOG/MeshHOG [7], Heat Kernel Signature (HKS) [8][11], and Intrinsic Shape Context (ISC) descriptor [9], these low-level shape features highly rely on the quality of the 3D models and

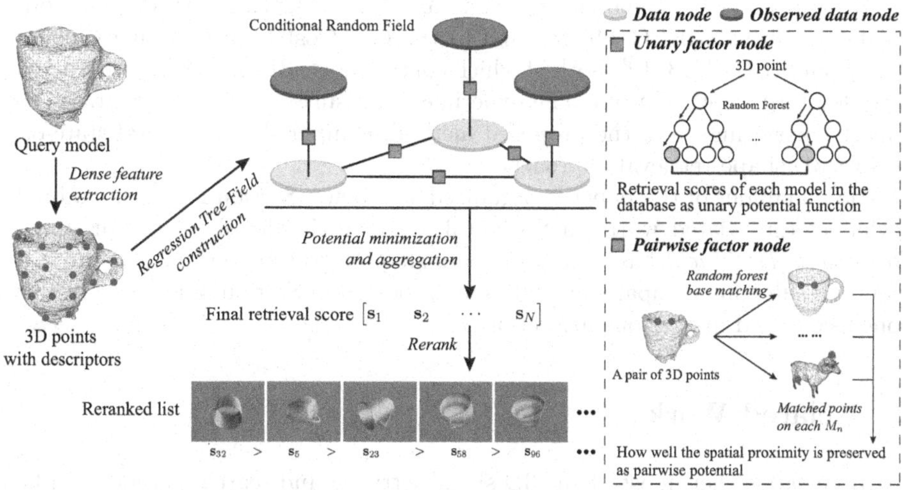

Fig. 2. Framework of our cross-domain 3D shape retrieval based on Regression Tree Fields. Best viewed in color.

tend to be sensitive to model noise that is often encountered with low-cost depth sensors. Furthermore, neither of these two frameworks explicitly address the challenge of partial models, resulting in degenerated performance in cross-domain 3D retrieval. For instance, previous study shows that the Scale-Invariant Heat Kernel Signature (SIHKS) achieves a high retrieval accuracy with CAD model queries [11], but significantly degrades for user-captured model queries [12]. To address these issues, spatial consistency checking has been used in both 2D [13] and 3D [10] cases. But the existing spatial consistency checking approaches such as pairwise feature quantization [10] and RANSAC [13] are still insufficient to handle the severe challenges associated with user-generated low-quality partial models, as observed in [12]. This is because the spatial consistency checking is often heuristic, and merely acts as a preprocessing or postprocessing, without principled optimization considering both feature similarity and spatial constraints.

To address the above two challenges, in this paper, we propose a robust and effective cross-domain shape retrieval approach by encoding local geometric structures in a Conditional Random Field (CRF), with a learned similarity measurement for robust feature matching. In particular, we build a CRF on the 3D points of the query model. Random forests are exploited to estimate rough similarity efficiently, thus to determine the unary potential. The geometric structures around each 3D point are embedded in the pairwise potential in a novel way, formulating the overall framework as a variant of *Regression Tree Field* [14], as show in Figure 2. Compared with the earlier approaches such as the Bag-of-Feature scheme and the existing partial matching algorithms, the proposed Regression Tree Field approach utilizes rich geometric information (instead of traditional pairwise spatial relationship checking) to compensate ill effects from model noise and incompletion. We evaluate our approach using two empirical study cases for cross-domain shape retrieval: a) the Querying with Partial Models dataset from SHREC '09 [15]; and b) the Low-Cost Depth Sensing Camera data from SHREC '13 [12], both of which contain noisy 3D models reconstructed from low-cost depth sensors. The experimental results clearly demonstrate the superior performance of the proposed method, compared with several state-of-the-art 3D shape retrieval approaches.

The remainder of the paper is organized as follows. Section 2 presents a brief review of the related work. In Section 3, we give the details of the proposed *Regression Tree Field* based cross-domain shape retrieval method. The experimental results and comparison studies are reported in Section 4, followed by our conclusions and discussions in Section 5.

2 Related Work

As discussed earlier, most of the 3D shape retrieval and search methods can be grouped into the following two major categories: a) search by sketch; b) search with CAD models. Below we briefly review the representative approaches in each category. Detailed survey papers of shape retrial methods can be found in [1][16].

Search by Sketch: As shown in Figure 1 (a), one first sketches a 2D projection of a 3D object and then uses the sketch as the query example to find similar 3D objects in a shape database, often containing CAD 3D models. Due to the simplicity, various techniques have been developed to retrieve 3D models whose 2D images match the query sketch. For instance, Funkhouser *et al.* used a variant of the 3D sphere harmonics to develop a shape search engine that accepts sketches as queries [2]. Yoon *et al.* employed suggestive contours and diffusion tensor fields to improve the robustness against shape and pose variance that often occurs in the user sketched images [17]. More recently, Shao *et al.* utilized a combination of contour-based representation and dense 2D matching to develop a robust approach that could perform partial matching between a query sketch and 3D models [18]. In summary, the sketch-based framework is still a popular choice for 3D shape retrieval and the influential SHape REtrieval Contest (SHREC) specifically has a sketch-based contest track. A comprehensive review on this topic is available in [16].

Search with CAD: The setting of search with CAD often requires the query sample to be a complete or partial CAD model. There have been two popular directions regarding to this task. One of them is to design powerful 3D shape signatures that can capture the intrinsic geometric information of the CAD models, with the motivation that the query and the database samples are essentially the same type of 3D models. To this end, various local features have been developed to describe the local geometry of 3D models, including MeshHoG as a 3D extension of the SIFT feature [7], Heat Kernel Signature [8][11], and Intrinsic Shape Context [9]. Realizing the sensitivity to model noise for those local descriptors [15], researchers also proposed to use high-level topological features [19][20], or aggregate low-level features to mid-level representations such as the extended

Bag-of-Words model [10][21] and graph correspondences [22]. Another direction is to map 3D models to a set of views, each of which can be represented using 2D descriptors [23][24]. Although such multi-view shape descriptors can benefit from the discriminative power of mature 2D features such as SIFT, they often overlook the important spatial information and suffer from expensive computational cost due to the matching of a large number of views.

Finally, the recent rapid growth of consumer 3D models promotes the study of a new shape search scheme, i.e, search with consumer models, which explores cross-domain shape retrieval using models generated from low-cost depth sensors to query CAD model database. Representative efforts include the "Querying with Partial Models" track in SHREC '09 [15] and "Low-Cost Depth Sensing Camera" track in SHREC '13 [12]. However, the evaluation of existing shape retrieval methods on these two test benchmarks shows unsatisfactory performance due to the challenging issues of model noise and incompletion. Therefore, it motivates us to design robust and accurate cross-domain shape retrieval techniques which can compensate the low quality of the consumer models.

3 Approach

To address the partial matching problem for 3D shape retrieval using noisy models captured by low-cost depth sensors, we here propose to use a potential minimization formulation on a Conditional Random Field (CRF) defined on the query model, where the potential functions are efficiently estimated through random forest prediction. This forms a variant of Regression Tree Field [14], with a difference that the potential is not learned fully jointly, resulting in more affordable training and testing time for larger-scale shape retrieval. Below, we will first introduce the notations, and then illustrate the potential function design, followed by our efficient method to determine the potential functions.

3.1 Background and Notations

Assume we are given a database consisting of N 3D mesh models $\{M_n\}_{n=1}^N$ with n as the index of models, and a possibly incomplete and noisy user-captured model M_q as the query. The goal of a cross-domain shape retrieval engine is to return a ranked list of the 3D models in the database, such that the models ranked higher are more similar to the query.

In our formulation, we first construct a conditional random field on M_q with an undirected graph representation $\mathcal{G} = (\mathcal{V}, \mathcal{E})$. Here we specifically use the 3D points in M_q as the vertices $\mathcal{V} = \{v_i\}_{i=1}^{|\mathcal{V}|}$ with $|\mathcal{V}|$ being the cardinality, and the edges $\mathcal{E}$ are the connections between nearby 3D points in an ϵ-ball manner. For a 3D point v_i in M_q, we compute the Scale-Invariant Spin Image (SISI) [25] to represent the local geometry of a *3D patch* centered at v_i. The calculated 128-dimensional SISI descriptor is used as the *observation* $\mathbf{x}_i$ of the CRF. Besides the observation $\mathbf{x}_i$, each vertex is also associated with a continuous vector $\mathbf{y}_i \in \mathbb{R}^N$ as the output variable conditioned on $\mathbf{x}$, where the n-th element $(\mathbf{y}_i)_n$

denotes the partial matching score between the i-th patch of the query model M_q and the n-th CAD model in the database. Compared to the standard CRF setting that often has a scalar as the output variable, in our CRF construction process, we have the output variable as a N-dimensional vector indicating the partial similarity between the 3D patch and each CAD model in the database. In the following, by designing the objective potential function to encode both the *shape similarity* and *geometric consistency*, we expect the inferred $\mathbf{y}$ to be a discriminant indicator for measuring the partial similarity between 3D patches and CAD models, while being robust to model noise and model incompletion in the cross-domain shape retrieval task.

3.2 Formulation

With the undirected graph model $(\mathcal{V}, \mathcal{E})$ and the associated random variables $\mathbf{x}, \mathbf{y}$, we can model the conditional distribution of the CRF. In particular, the optimal similarity scores $\mathbf{y}$ can be derived through minimizing the following potential function in a logarithmic form as

$$\mathbf{y}^* = \underset{\mathbf{y}}{\operatorname{argmin}} \log \Psi(\mathbf{y} \mid \mathbf{x}). \tag{1}$$

With the assumption that the conditional distribution obeys the Markov property with respect to the graph, the potential function $\Psi(\mathbf{y} \mid \mathbf{x})$ can be further decomposed as a *unary* term Ψ_u defined on each vertex and a *pairwise* term Ψ_p defined on each pair of connected vertices,

$$\log \Psi(\mathbf{y} \mid \mathbf{x}) = \lambda \sum_{v_i \in \mathcal{V}} \log \Psi_u(\mathbf{y}_i \mid \mathbf{x}_i) + (1 - \lambda) \sum_{(v_i, v_j) \in \mathcal{E}} \log \Psi_p(\mathbf{y}_i, \mathbf{y}_j \mid \mathbf{x}_i, \mathbf{x}_j), \tag{2}$$

where the coefficient λ is a parameter weighting contributions from these two terms. Note that the above two terms reflect important properties for shape retrieval. The unary term Ψ_u provides an robust estimation of similarity scores solely considering the local shape of the individual 3D patches, namely *shape similarity*. The pairwise term Ψ_p aims to further refine the scores by enforcing *geometric consistency* among neighbor patches. Through combining these two terms, our method can handle cross-domain partial matching with the unary term, while being less sensitive to model noise and incompletion due to the embedded geometric consistency in the pairwise term.

A natural concern of this formulation is the scalability, especially given that the optimization in Equation (1) may involve hundreds of variables with thousands of dimensions. But as we will show shortly, by exploring the sparsity of the problem and use discriminative random forests, inference on such CRFs can be very efficient and scalable to large-scale datasets.

Unary Potential. Following the standard practice of CRFs, the unary potential is used to penalize the variable $\mathbf{x}$ being far away from a rough estimation $\tilde{\mathbf{y}} = f(\mathbf{x})$. In particular, the unary potential is defined as a quadratic loss,

$$\log \Psi_u(\mathbf{y}_i \mid \mathbf{x}_i) = \frac{1}{2}(\mathbf{y}_i - f(\mathbf{x}_i))^T (\mathbf{y}_i - f(\mathbf{x}_i)). \tag{3}$$

Here the function $f : \mathbf{x} \in \mathbb{R}^{128} \rightarrow \mathbf{y} \in \mathbb{R}^N$ is a discriminative regressor which efficiently estimates similarity scores between a 3D patch in M_q and a database model $M_n, n = 1, \cdots, N$. We employ random forests as an ensemble learning method to build an efficient regression process, as discussed in Section 3.3.

Pairwise Potential. As a key difference from standard CRF formulation, the pairwise potential in our approach utilizes all the models in the database to help embed the local geometric structures. Intuitively, for a pair of neighbor vertices $(v_i, v_j) \in \mathcal{E}$ from the query model M_q, their corresponding vertices $v_i^{n\prime}, v_j^{n\prime}$ in a similar database model M_n should also be close by. Otherwise it indicates the spatial proximity of the neighbor vertices (v_i, v_j) is violated in the process of matching against the model M_n, and therefore M_n is not a spatially consistent candidate to the query. We define the pairwise term as

$$\log \Psi_p(\mathbf{y}_i, \mathbf{y}_j | \mathbf{x}_i, \mathbf{x}_j) = \sum_{n=1}^{N} \| \mathbf{v}_i^{n\prime}(\mathbf{x}_i) - \mathbf{v}_j^{n\prime}(\mathbf{x}_j) \|_2 \cdot (\mathbf{y}_i)_n (\mathbf{y}_j)_n. \tag{4}$$

Recall that $\mathbf{y}_i$ and $\mathbf{y}_j$ are the retrieval scores of the 3D patches $\mathbf{x}_i, \mathbf{x}_j$ in the query against all database models, with $(\mathbf{y}_i)_n$, $(\mathbf{y}_j)_n$ being the similarity scores against a database model M_n. Here, $\mathbf{v}_i^{n\prime}(\mathbf{x}_i)$ and $\mathbf{v}_j^{n\prime}(\mathbf{x}_j)$ are the 3D coordinates of the matched vertices in model M_n corresponding to 3D patches $\mathbf{x}_i$ and $\mathbf{x}_j$, respectively. Thus $\| \mathbf{v}_i^{n\prime}(\mathbf{x}_i) - \mathbf{v}_j^{n\prime}(\mathbf{x}_j) \|_2$ measures the Euclidean distance between two matched vertices in the model M_n. For well matched vertices $\mathbf{v}_i^{n\prime}(\mathbf{x}_i)$ and $\mathbf{v}_j^{n\prime}(\mathbf{x}_j)$, they are nearby with a small Euclidean distance, which indicates their similarity scores to the query patches will be less penalized recall we wish to minimize the potential function. On the contrary, if the matched vertices $\mathbf{v}_i^{n\prime}(\mathbf{x}_i)$ and $\mathbf{v}_j^{n\prime}(\mathbf{x}_j)$ are not spatially close to each other, indicating a large spatial distance, their similarity scores $(\mathbf{y}_i)_n, (\mathbf{y}_j)_n$ to the query patches will be suppressed since our objective is to minimize the above potential function. It is also worth noting that each model in the database is checked separately in the pairwise term computation, which does not require any pose estimation or calibration, thus being more reliable against sensor noise and incomplete models.

In practice, the straightforward local feature matching to find the corresponding vertices $\mathbf{v}_i^{n\prime}, \mathbf{v}_j^{n\prime}$ is unreliable under sensor noise. Therefore we further use random forests to robustly determine the vertex correspondences, as will be introduced in Section 3.3.

Inference. Let us define a matrix $\mathbf{V} \in \mathbb{R}^{N \times N}$ with its element V_{ij} calculated as $V_{ij} = \sum_{n=1}^{N} \left(\| \mathbf{v}_i^{n\prime} - \mathbf{v}_j^{n\prime} \|_2 \right)$. Then, the pairwise potential can be written in a compact matrix form as

$$\log \Psi_p(\mathbf{y}_i, \mathbf{y}_j) = \mathbf{y}_i^T V_{ij} \mathbf{y}_j. \tag{5}$$

Hence, the overall log pairwise potential is represented as

$$\sum_{(v_i, v_j) \in \mathcal{E}} \log \Psi_p(\mathbf{y}_i, \mathbf{y}_j) = \mathbf{y}^T V \mathbf{y}, \tag{6}$$

where $\mathbf{y} \in \mathbb{R}^{N|\mathcal{V}|}$ is the concatenation of all the column vectors $\mathbf{y}_i$, and V is a blockwise matrix with $|\mathcal{V}| \times |\mathcal{V}|$ blocks, each as V_{ij}. Substituting Ψ_u and Ψ_p

in Equation 2 by the above derivations, we can derive the objective potential function in a quadratic form as,

$$\mathbf{y}^* = \underset{\mathbf{y}}{\operatorname{argmin}} \log \Psi(\mathbf{y} \mid \mathbf{x}) = \underset{\mathbf{y}}{\operatorname{argmin}} \left(\frac{1}{2} \mathbf{y}^T H \mathbf{y} - \mathbf{c}^T \mathbf{y} \right), \tag{7}$$

where we have

$$H = \lambda I + (1 - \lambda) V$$
$$\mathbf{c} = \lambda \tilde{\mathbf{y}} = \lambda f(\mathbf{x}).$$

$\mathbf{y}$ and $\tilde{\mathbf{y}}$ are the column concatenation of $\mathbf{y}_i$ and $\tilde{\mathbf{y}}_i$ (c.f. Unary Potential above) respectively. However, the above quadratic problem is not necessary to be convex since H might not be positive semi-definite in practice. Therefore we use the stationary point that gives the solution to the linear system $H\mathbf{y} = \mathbf{c}$ as an approximate solution. Because H is high dimensional, it is computationally prohibitive to directly compute the analytical solution to the linear system. Following Regression Tree Fields [14], we use the conjugate gradient descent to obtain the solution efficiently in an iterative manner. In addition, since H is often sparse, the inference procedure is fairly efficient, which usually ends in 10 iterations within 0.1 seconds on a desktop i7 CPU.

After computing the locally optimal solution $\mathbf{y}^* = \{(\mathbf{y}_i^*)_n\}$ $(1 \leq i \leq |\mathcal{V}|, 1 \leq n \leq N)$, we can derive the final ranking score to a query model as $\mathbf{s}_n = \sum_{i=1}^{|\mathcal{V}|} (\mathbf{y}_i^*)_n$, which will be used for reranking.

However, in order to make this framework fast enough for real applications, two critical problems remain unresolved: a) to efficiently obtain the rough estimation of the similarity scores $\{\tilde{\mathbf{y}}_i = f(\mathbf{x}_i)\}$ for the unary term; and b) to perform efficient matching of (v_i, v_j) against every model in the database to determine the pairwise potential term. Below we present our choice by using random forests to accomplish these tasks in a sub-linear testing time.

3.3 Efficient Estimation of Potential Functions

To achieve fast estimation of the similarity score $\{\tilde{\mathbf{y}}_i = f(\mathbf{x}_i)\}_{i=1}^{|\mathcal{V}|}$ in the unary potential term, we propose to use the random forest method to carry out a regression process. The training data contains all the extracted features of 3D patches from the database models as inputs, and the indices of the associated model as discrete responses. For the random forest, each decision tree is trained recursively using the standard information gain algorithm with the linear classifiers for data splitting. Finally, each leaf node in a decision tree receives a score vector $\mathbf{p}_l = [p_{l1}, \cdots, p_{ln}, \cdots, p_{lN}]$ measuring the frequencies of the patches of a specific 3D model falling in that leaf with the element computed as

$$p_{ln} = \frac{\#\text{ of training examples from the model } n}{\#\text{ of training examples}}, n = 1, \cdots, N.$$

Here $l = 1, \cdots, L$ is the index of the decision tree with L being the number of decision trees in the random forest.

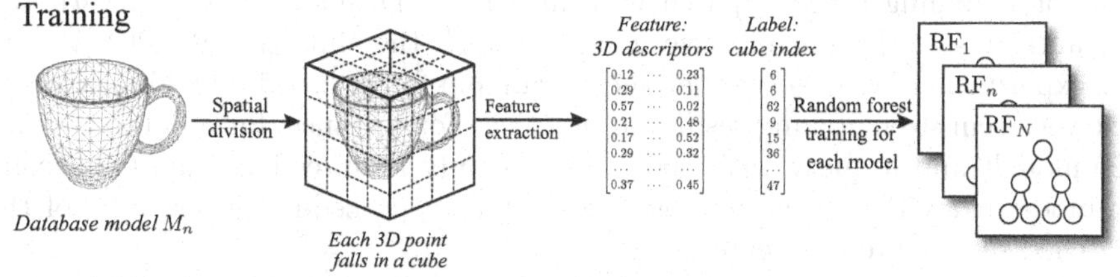

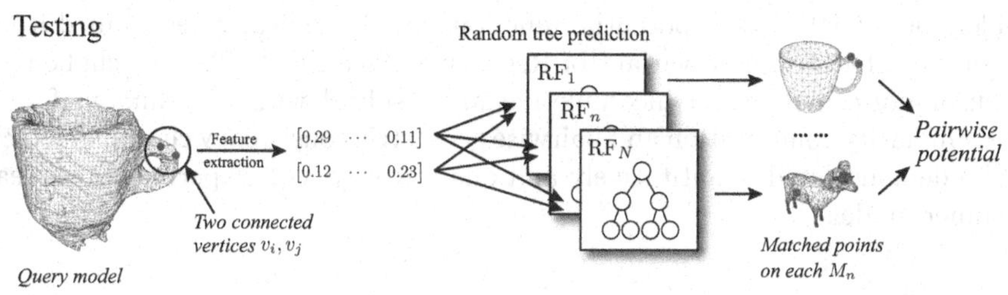

Fig. 3. Illustration of the efficient estimation of the pairwise potential term using random forests

Given a feature vector $\mathbf{x}_i$ from a 3D patch in the query model, we first conduct examination from the root node to leaf nodes through all the decision trees in the trained random forest. The rough estimation of the similarity scores between a patch in the query model $\mathbf{x}_i$ and the CAD models are computed via averaging the recomputed score $\mathbf{p}_l$ on the retrieved leaf nodes as $\tilde{\mathbf{y}}_i = \frac{1}{L}\sum_{l=1}^{L}\mathbf{p}_l$. Compared to the traditional way that computes the similarity score by performing exhaustive matching between features, the regression method utilizes a discriminative decision model that can capture the underlying distributions of the features, resulting more robust estimation against model noise. In addition, the random forests method also benefits from the computational efficiency with a sub-linear time complexity, that can be further sped up for handling large scale applications through easy parallel implementations.

To estimate the pairwise potential term, it is necessary to find the best matched patch in a CAD model M_n for a query patch $\mathbf{x}_i$ to derive the corresponding vertex $v_i^n{}'$. Here we propose to again employ random forests to perform fast matching in a classification manner, with the framework shown in Figure 3. In particular, we set 3D bounding boxes on each CAD model and partition the model into $d \times d \times d$ voxels, each of which contains a set of 3D vertices. Here d is often set as a small value, such as $d = 4$ in our experiments. Then we use those partitioned vertices as training data to build a random forest *for each model* with the leaf node generating the prediction of which voxel the query patch falls into. The random forests are trained in the same manner by using the information-gain based algorithm. Then for a given query patch $\mathbf{x}_i$, we can quickly retrieve a small voxel in M_n that could contain similar patch, and adopt the center of that voxel as the matched vertex $v_i^n{}'$. Providing random forests empirically provide testing time of $\mathcal{O}(\log C)$, in which C is the class number, the total time cost for matching a query patch with all the CAD models is $\mathcal{O}(N \log d)$, significantly faster than exhaustive matching with the time cost as $\mathcal{O}(N|\mathcal{V}|)$. In our experiments, we observe that such a random forest based matching achieves fast yet accurate matching results in practice. For instance, for a database with 720 models and a query with 500 points, it only requires less than 0.2 second on modern i7 CPUs to accomplish the matching procedure, where 80% of the matched results are the nearest vertices.

In summary, we formulate the cross-domain search as a potential minimization problem on a CRF, whose potential functions are dynamically determined from random forests, forming a variant of Regression Tree Field. The two challenges of sensor noise and model incompletion are resolved with the random forest based similarity computation and pairwise geometric consistency checking, which will be demonstrated quantitatively and qualitatively with experiments on real consumer models.

4 Experiments

To provide quantitative performance evaluation of the proposed cross-domain shape retrieval approach, we conduct experiments on two benchmarks from the well-known SHape REtrieval Contest (SHREC). The first dataset is from the Querying with the Partial Models track in the SHREC '09 [15], which consists of incomplete and noisy models captured from desktop 3D scanners. The second dataset contains query 3D models generated by Microsoft Kinect sensor that were used in the SHREC '13 [12]. Below we describe the details of the datasets, experimental settings, and evaluation results.

4.1 Datasets

The dataset from the Querying with Partial Models track of SHREC '09 is specifically designed to explore the frontier of 3D shape retrieval techniques in handling incomplete and possibly noisy query samples. It consists of a set of 720 high-quality CAD models as the database for querying. The CAD models are from 40 categories such as *bird, fish, mug* and *car* with 18 models for each category. In addition, it has two query sets, including a set of high-quality incomplete samples cropped from CAD models, and a set of user-captured models obtained with a desktop 3D scanner. Here we use the user-captured query set since it well represents the common challenges of cross-domain shape retrieval, such as surface noise and model incompletion due to self-occlusion. Examples of the physical objects used to capture the models are shown in Figure 4 (a), with the user-captured models shown in Figure 4 (b).

As another popular low-cost depth sensor, Microsoft Kinect is used to build 3D models using multiple range images [26]. Compared with single range image based 3D models like the SHREC '09 dataset, the Kinect-captured models tend to be more noisy due to non-smooth surfaces, and also with lower resolutions. In our experiments, we adopt the dataset from the Low-Cost Depth Sensing

(a)

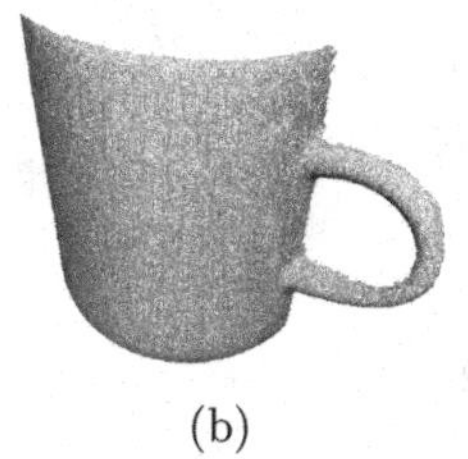
(b)

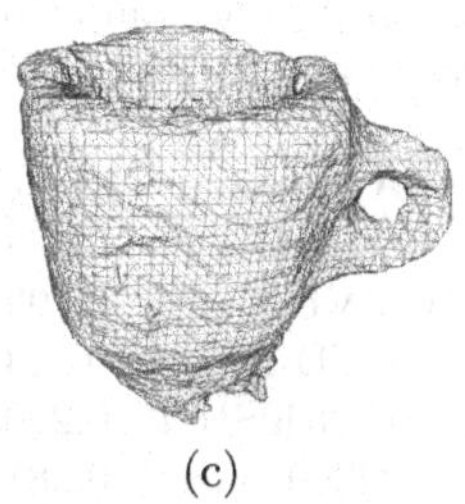
(c)

Fig. 4. Illustration of the physical objects and the user-captured 3D models from the benchmark dataset: a) Physical objects used to generate the 3D models for the SHREC '09 dataset (Figure cited from [15]); b) An incomplete query model of the SHREC '09 dataset captured by a 3D desktop scanner; c) A noisy and low-resolution query model of the SHREC '13 dataset captured by the Microsoft Kinect.

Camera track of the SHREC '13 [12], which contains a total of 192 Kinect models. Note that the original test in the SHREC '13 is designed for 3D retrieval with both queries and database containing Kinect models. To test the cross-domain performance, here we use the CAD models from the SHREC '09 dataset as the database and use the 192 Kinect models from the SHREC '13 as the query set. Figure 4 (c) demonstrates an example of the used Kinect models.

4.2 Experiment Settings

We conduct two types of empirical studies. On the SHREC '09 dataset, we provide quantitative performance evaluations and compared with several representative 3D shape retrieval methods. Since the query dataset from the SHREC '13 has no ground truth category information, we simply design qualitative evaluation by demonstrating the retrieval results.

For quantitative comparison, we compare with popular methods on CAD model retrieval and several approaches achieving state-of-the-art performance in the cross-domain contest track, including one 3D feature-based approach [10] and two 2D view-based approaches [15]. For our method, we also evaluate a variant that only uses the unary term without the pair-wise term of spatial consistency. Below we briefly describe the settings for each compared method.

- **Shape Google** [10]: We implement the Shape Google's approach [10], a shape retrieval approach for CAD models. For a fair comparison, we use the same Scale-Invariant Spin Image feature [25] as in our approach. A codebook with the size 10000 is built using the Approximate KMeans method [13].
- **CMVD-Depth** [15]: Achieving the best precision-recall in the SHREC '09 contest, the Compact Multi-View Descriptor (CMVD) extracts global 2D descriptors from the depth maps rendered from different views. The retrieval ranking is derived based on the minimum ℓ_1 distances between the signatures of the query and that of the database model.

Table 1. The computed MAP and NDCG on SHREC '09

Approach	MAP	NDCG
Shape Google	0.188	0.506
CMVD-Depth	0.193	0.521
CMVD-Binary	0.203	0.511
BF-GridSIFT	0.219	0.532
RTF-Unary	0.281	0.591
RTF	**0.315**	**0.611**

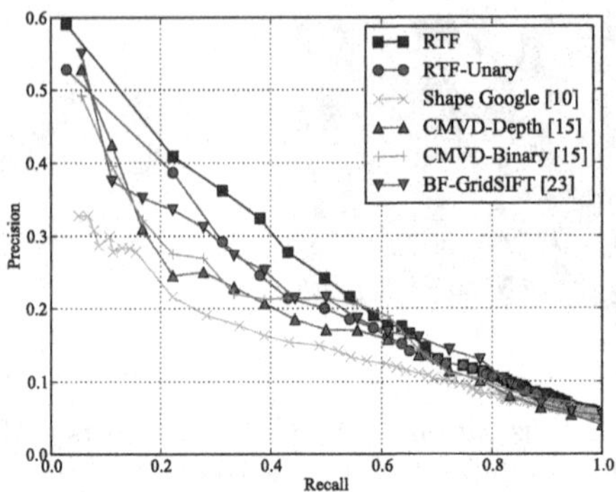

Fig. 5. Precision-recall curves of the evaluated approaches on the SHREC '09 dataset

- **CMVD-Binary** [15]: **CMVD-Binary** is another approach with strong perform on the consumer model retrieval task in the SHREC '09 [15]. Different with the **CMVD-Depth** method that renders depth images, **CMVD-Binary** renders binary masks of the model to achieve computational efficiency and robustness against model noise.
- **BF-GridSIFT** [27]: As a state-of-the-art approach for both generic and user-captured model 3D shape retrieval, **BF-GridSIFT** first performs pose normalization to the models, and then renders depth maps from uniformly distributed views. Then the Bag-of-Feature scheme is employed to aggregate the extracted 2D dense SIFT descriptors. In the retrieval stage, KL-Divergence is used to compute a non-symmetric distance between the query sample and a database model.
- **RTF-Unary**: It is a simplified version of the proposed Regression Tree Field (RTF) based approach, which only considers the unary term by setting $\lambda = 1$ in Equation 2 and 7. Note that the **RTF-Unary** approach is equivalent to only using the computed similarity score from partial matching with random forests to perform ranking.
- **RTF**: The proposed Regression Tree Fields (RTF) approach. In the implementation of both RTF based methods, i.e., the **RTF-Unary** and the **RTF**, we use 128 trees with the depth 12 in the unary term. For the pairwise term in the **RTF** method, we apply bounding boxes to partition each model into 64 voxels ($d = 4$) and build a random forest with four trees with the height as 6. The coefficients balancing the two potential terms is set as $\lambda = 0.9$ uniformly across all the experiments.

To measure the performance, we adopt the semantic category information to evaluate the retrieved results. In particular, we treat the models from the same category as *relevant* and the models from different categories as *irrelevant* to compute two quantitative measurements as the evaluation protocols. First, we compute the Mean Average Precision (MAP) that measures the average precision

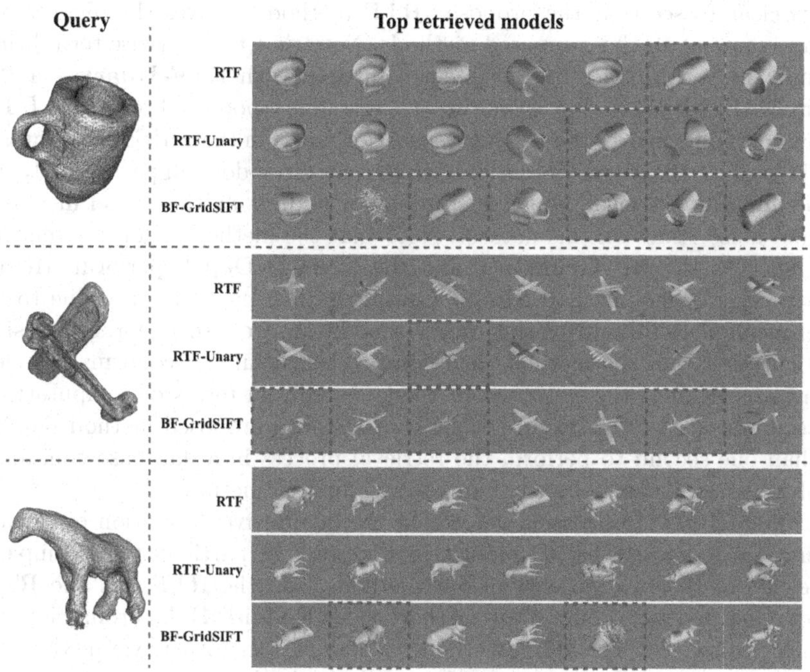

Fig. 6. Examples of the top results of the cross-domain shape retrieval, where the database contains CAD models from the SHREC '09 dataset and the query models are the user-captured models with the Microsoft Kinect. From the top to the bottom, the query models are *Mug*, *Airplane*, and *Quadruped*. And for each query, the three rows show the results from **RTF**, **RTF-Unary**, and **BF-GridSIFT** respectively. The results highlighted by red bounding boxes indicate the irrelevant 3D models.

scores across all queries [28]. Second, we employ the popular evaluation criteria, the Normalized Discounted Cumulative Gain (NDCG) that is defined as

$$\mathrm{NDCG} = \frac{\sum_{n=1}^{N} \frac{\mathrm{Relevant}_n}{\log_2(n+1)}}{\sum_{n=1}^{N} \frac{1}{\log_2(n+1)}},$$

where $\mathrm{Relevant}_n$ is 1 when the nth sample is relevant to the query, otherwise 0. By assigning larger weights to the results ranked higher, the NDCG favors high-ranked relevant instances because they are more important for user experience. Below we report the results for both quantitative and qualitative evaluations.

4.3 Results

For the results on the SHREC '09 dataset, we report the MAP and NDCG for all the compared methods in Table 1, with the performance of **CMVD-Depth**, **CMVD-Bianry** and **BF-GridSIFT** cited from [15].

It is clear to see that the proposed **RTF** method achieves the highest performance among all the compared methods. Note that the pairwise term brings a significant performance improvement compared with **RTF-Unary** – a 12% gain in MAP. Although only exploring a single unary potential term, the **RTF-Unary** method achieves the second best performance in the SHREC '09 dataset. This is because the unary potential term derives cross-domain partial matching based similarity retrieval, which is suitable for addressing the model incompletion and noise issues on this dataset. Note that the methods adopting multiple views such as the **BF-GridSIFT** and the **CMVD-Depth** perform stronger than the single-view method **Shape Google**, which might be also due to the model incompletion issue on this data. In addition, we also plot the precision-recall curves for all the methods in Figure 5, which further confirms the clear performance gain of the proposed methods. Finally in terms of computational cost, on a desktop PC with an i7 3.0GHz CPU, the proposed method requires less than one second to perform the retrieval process in a database containing 720 objects, significantly faster than other compared methods.

On the SHREC '13 dataset, we present the qualitative evaluation by demonstrating the top retrieved 3D models in Figure 6. In particular, we compared the results of the two variants of our methods, i.e., the **RTF** and the **RTF-Unary**, and a strong competitor method the **BF-GridSIFT**. From Figure 6, it is clear to see that the **RTF** method outperforms the other two methods by generating semantically consistent 3D models for both simple object like *mugs* and complicated object like *planes*.

5 Conclusions

This paper addresses an emerging cross-domain shape retrieval problem, where the query samples are captured by users using low-cost depth sensors and the database contains conventional high-quality CAD models. To tackle the challenging issues like noise and incompletion of the user-captured models, we present a novel retrieval method that explores the unique power of Regression Tree Fields. In particular, we formulate our objective as a minimization problem of the CRF potential function, which contains a unary term measuring the similarity of cross-domain partial matching and a pairwise term with embedded geometric consistency. Both of these two terms are determined using efficient random forest algorithms. We conduct extensive empirical studies on two benchmark datasets from the well-known SHape REtrieval Contest (SHREC). The results clearly corroborate the superior performance of the proposed method, compared with other representative shape retrieval algorithms. Our future directions include introducing online random forest training algorithms [29] to avoid the necessity of retraining when adding new models, and also extending the proposed method to explore cross-domain 3D shape recognition and classification.

References

1. Tangelder, J.W., Veltkamp, R.C.: A Survey of Content based 3D Shape Retrieval Methods. Multimedia Tools and Applications 39(3), 441–471 (2008)
2. Funkhouser, T., Min, P., Kazhdan, M., Chen, J., Halderman, A., Dobkin, D., Jacobs, D.: A Search Engine for 3D Models. ToG 22(1), 83–105 (2003)
3. Zeleznik, R.C., Herndon, K.P., Hughes, J.F.: SKETCH: An Interface for Sketching 3D Scenes. In: ACM SIGGRAPH 2007 Courses (2007)
4. Google Inc.: Project Tango, `http://www.google.com/atap/projecttango/`
5. Funkhouser, T., Kazhdan, M., Shilane, P., Min, P., Kiefer, W., Tal, A., Rusinkiewicz, S., Dobkin, D.: Modeling by Example. ToG 23(3), 652–663 (2004)
6. Johnson, A., Hebert, M.: Using Spin Images for Efficient Object Recognition in Cluttered 3D Scenes. IEEE Transactions on Pattern Analysis and Machine Intelligence 21(5), 433–449 (1999)
7. Zaharescu, A., Boyer, E., Varanasi, K., Horaud, R.: Surface Feature Detection and Description with Applications to Mesh Matching. In: Proc. of CVPR, pp. 373–380 (2009)
8. Sun, J., Ovsjanikov, M., Guibas, L.: A Concise and Provably Informative Multi-Scale Signature Based on Heat Diffusion. Computer Graphics Forum 28(5), 1383–1392 (2009)
9. Kokkinos, I., Bronstein, M.M., Litman, R., Bronstein, A.M.: Intrinsic Shape Context Descriptors for Deformable Shapes. In: Proc. of CVPR, pp. 159–166 (2012)
10. Bronstein, A.M., Bronstein, M.M., Guibas, L.J., Ovsjanikov, M.: Shape Google: Geometric Words and Expressions for Invariant Shape Retrieval. ToG 30(1) (February 2011)
11. Bronstein, M., Kokkinos, I.: Scale-Invariant Heat Kernel Signatures for Non-Rigid Shape Recognition. In: Proc. of CVPR, pp. 1704–1711 (2010)
12. Machado, J., Ferreira, A., Pascoal, P.B., Abdelrahman, M., Aono, M., El-Melegy, M.T., Farag, A.A., Johan, H., Li, B., Lu, Y., Tatsuma, A.: Shrec'13 track: Retrieval of objects captured with low-cost depth-sensing cameras. In: Proc. of EuroGraphics 3DOR, pp. 65–71 (2013)
13. Philbin, J., Chum, O., Isard, M., Sivic, J., Zisserman, A.: Object Retrieval with Large Vocabularies and Fast Spatial Matching. In: Proc. of CVPR (2007)
14. Jancsary, J., Nowozin, S., Sharp, T., Rother, C.: Regression Tree Fields - an Efficient, Non-Parametric Approach to Image Labeling Problems. In: Proc. of CVPR, 2376–2383 (2012)
15. Dutagaci, H., Godil, A., Axenopoulos, A., Daras, P., Furuya, T., Ohbuchi, R.: SHREC'09 Track: Querying with Partial Models. In: Proc. of Eurographics 3DOR, 69–76 (2009)
16. Li, B., Lu, Y., Godil, A., Schreck, T., Bustos, B., Ferreira, A., Furuya, T., Fonseca, M.J., Johan, H., Matsuda, T., Ohbuchi, R., Pascoal, P.B., Saavedra, J.M.: A Comparison of Methods for Sketch-Based 3D Shape Retrieval. CVIU 119, 57–80 (2014)
17. Yoon, S.M., Scherer, M., Schreck, T., Kuijper, A.: Sketch-based 3D Model Retrieval Using Diffusion Tensor Fields of Suggestive Contours. In: Proc. of ACM Multimedia, pp.193–200 (2010)
18. Shao, T., Xu, W., Yin, K., Wang, J., Zhou, K., Guo, B.: Discriminative Sketch-based 3D Model Retrieval via Robust Shape Matching. Computer Graphics Forum (PG), 2011–2020 (2011)

19. Tung, T., Matsuyama, T.: Topology dictionary for 3d video understanding. TPAMI 34, 1645–1657 (2012)
20. Huang, P., Hilton, A., Starck, J.: Shape similarity for 3D video sequences of people. IJCV 89(2-3), 362–381 (2010)
21. Pickup, D., Sun, X., Rosin, P.L., Martin, R.R., Cheng, Z., Lian, Z., Aono, M., Ben Hamza, A., Bronstein, A., Bronstein, M., Bu, S., Castellani, U., Cheng, S., Garro, V., Giachetti, A., Godil, A., Han, J., Johan, H., Lai, L., Li, B., Li, C., Li, H., Litman, R., Liu, X., Liu, Z., Lu, Y., Tatsuma, A., Ye, J.: SHREC'14 track: Shape retrieval of non-rigid 3D human models. In: EG 3DOR (2014)
22. Wang, C., Bronstein, M.M., Bronstein, A.M., Paragios, N.: Discrete minimum distortion correspondence problems for non-rigid shape matching. In: Bruckstein, A.M., ter Haar Romeny, B.M., Bronstein, A.M., Bronstein, M.M. (eds.) SSVM 2011. LNCS, vol. 6667, pp. 580–591. Springer, Heidelberg (2012)
23. Chen, D.Y., Tian, X.P., Shen, Y.T., Ouhyoung, M.: On Visual Similarity Based 3D Model Retrieval. Computer Graphics Forum (EuroGraphics) 22(3), 223–232 (2003)
24. Daras, P., Axenopoulos, A.: A 3D shape retrieval framework supporting multimodal queries. IJCV 89(2-3), 229–247 (2010)
25. Darom, T., Keller, Y.: Scale-Invariant Features for 3-D Mesh Models. TIP 21(5), 2758–2769 (2012)
26. Izadi, S., Kim, D., Hilliges, O., Molyneaux, D., Newcombe, R., Kohli, P., Shotton, J., Hodges, S., Freeman, D., Davison, A., Fitzgibbon, A.: KinectFusion: Real-time 3D Reconstruction and Interaction Using a Moving Depth Camera. In: Proc. of UIST, pp. 559–568 (2011)
27. Ohbuchi, R., Osada, K., Furuya, T., Banno, T.: Salient Local Visual Features for Shape-Based 3D Model Retrieval. In: Proc. of Shape Modeling and Applications, pp. 93–102 (June 2008)
28. Yilmaz, E., Aslam, J.A.: Estimating average precision with incomplete and imperfect judgments. In: Proc. of CIKM (2006)
29. Ben-Haim, Y., Tom-Tov, E.: A streaming parallel decision tree algorithm. JMLR 11, 849–872 (2010)

Fast and Accurate Texture Recognition with Multilayer Convolution and Multifractal Analysis

Hicham Badri, Hussein Yahia, and Khalid Daoudi

INRIA Bordeaux Sud-Ouest, 33405 Talence, France
{hicham.badri,hussein.yahia,khalid.daoudi}@inria.fr

Abstract. A fast and accurate texture recognition system is presented. The new approach consists in extracting locally and globally invariant representations. The locally invariant representation is built on a multi-resolution convolutional network with a local pooling operator to improve robustness to local orientation and scale changes. This representation is mapped into a globally invariant descriptor using multifractal analysis. We propose a new multifractal descriptor that captures rich texture information and is mathematically invariant to various complex transformations. In addition, two more techniques are presented to further improve the robustness of our system. The first technique consists in combining the generative PCA classifier with multiclass SVMs. The second technique consists of two simple strategies to boost classification results by synthetically augmenting the training set. Experiments show that the proposed solution outperforms existing methods on three challenging public benchmark datasets, while being computationally efficient.

1 Introduction

Texture classification is one of the most challenging computer vision and pattern recognition problems. A powerful texture descriptor should be invariant to scale, illumination, occlusions, perspective/affine transformations and even non-rigid surface deformations, while being computationally efficient. Modeling textures via statistics of spatial local textons is probably the most popular approach to build a texture classification system [1,2,3,4,5,6,7]. Based on this Bag-of-Words architecture, these methods try to design a robust local descriptor. Distributions over these textons are then compared using a proper distance and a nearest neighbor or kernel SVMs classifier [8]. Another alternative to regular histograms consists in using multifractal analysis [9,10,11,12,13]. The VG-fractal method [9] statistically represents the textures with the full PDF of the local fractal dimensions or lengths, while the methods in [10,11,12,13] make use of the box-counting method to estimate the multifractal spectrum. Multifractal-based descriptors are theoretically globally invariant to bi-Lipschitz transforms that include perspective transforms and texture deformations. A different approach recently presented in [14] consists in building a powerful local descriptor by cascading wavelet scattering transformations of image patches and using a generative PCA classifier [15]. Unfortunately, while these methods achieve high accuracy on some standard benchmark datasets, little attention is given to the computational efficiency, which is crucial in a real-world system.

D. Fleet et al. (Eds.): ECCV 2014, Part I, LNCS 8689, pp. 505–519, 2014.
© Springer International Publishing Switzerland 2014

We present in this paper a new texture classification system which is both accurate and computationally efficient. The motivation behind the proposed work comes from the success of multifractal analysis [10,9,11,12,13]. Given an input texture, the image is filtered with a small filter bank for various filter orientations. A pooling operator is then applied to improve robustness to local orientation change. This process is repeated for different resolutions for a richer representation. This first step generates various low-pass and high-pass responses that form a *locally* invariant representation. The mapping towards the final descriptor is done via multifractal analysis. It is well known that the *multifractal spectrum* encodes rich texture information. The methods in [10,11,12,13] use the box-counting method to estimate the multifractal spectrum. However, this method is unstable due the limited resolution of real-world images. We present a new multifractal descriptor that is more stable and improves invariance to bi-Lipschitz transformations. This improvement is validated by extensive experiments on public benchmark datasets. The second part of our work concerns training strategies to improve classification rates. We propose to combine the generative PCA classifier [14,15] with kernel SVMs [8] for classification. We also introduce two strategies called "synthetic training" to artificially add more training data based on illumination and scale change. Results outperforming the state-of-the-art are obtained over challenging public datasets, with high computational efficiency.

The paper is organized as follows : section 2 describes the proposed descriptor, section 3 presents the proposed training strategies, section 4 presents classification results conducted on 3 public datasets as well as a comparison with **9** state-of-the-art methods.

2 Robust Invariant Texture Representation

The main goal of a texture recognition system is to build an *invariant* representation, a mapping which reduces the large intra-class variability. This is a very challenging problem because the invariance must include various complex transformations such as translation, rotation, occlusion, illumination change, non-rigid deformations, perspective view, among others. As a result, two similar textures with different transformation parameters must have similar descriptors. An example is given in Figure 1. Not only the system should be accurate, but it should be also computationally efficient. Otherwise, its use in a real-world system would be limited due to the long processing time to extract the descriptor. Our goal in this paper is to build both an *accurate* and *fast* texture recognition system. Our Matlab non-optimized implementation takes around 0.7 second to extract the descriptor on a medium size image (480×640) using a modern laptop. The processing time can be further decreased by reducing the resolution of the image without sacrificing much the accuracy. This is due to the strong robustness of our descriptor to scale changes via accurate multifractal statistics that encode rich multi-scale texture information. We explain in this section how we build the proposed descriptor, the motivation behind the approach and the connection with previous work.

2.1 Overview of the Proposed Approach

The proposed descriptor is based on two main steps :

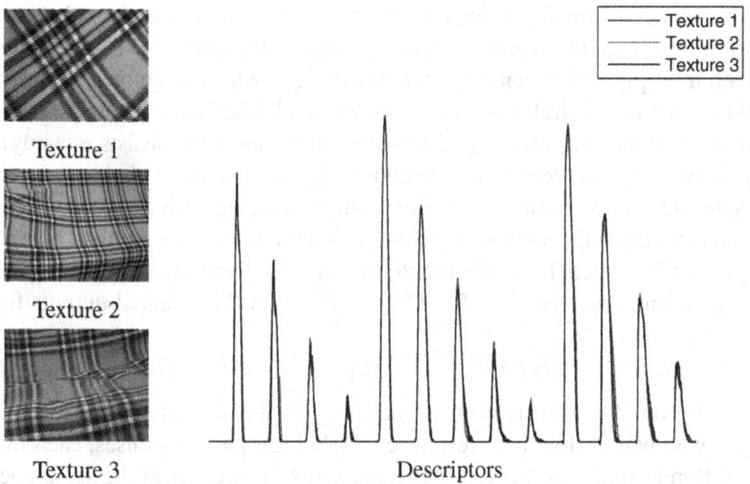

Fig. 1. Intra-class variability demonstration. The three textures 1, 2 and 3 exhibit strong changes in scale and orientation as well as non-rigid deformations. As can be seen, the proposed descriptor is nearly invariant to these transformations (see section 2).

1. Building a *locally* invariant representation : using multiple high-pass filters, we generate different sparse representations for different filter orientations. A pooling operator is applied on the orientation to increase the local invariance to orientation change. The process is repeated for multiple image resolutions for a richer representation.

2. Building a *globally* invariant representation : the first step generates various images that encode different texture information. We also include the multi-resolution versions of the input to provide low-pass information. We need a mapping that transforms this set of images into a stable, fixed-size descriptor. We use multifractal analysis to statistically describe each one of these images. We present a new method that extracts rich information directly from local singularity exponents. The local exponents encode rich multi-scale texture information. Their log-normalized distribution represents a stable mapping which is invariant to complex bi-Lipschitz transforms. As a result, the proposed multifractal descriptor is proven mathematically to be robust to strong environmental changes.

2.2 Locally Invariant Representation

A locally invariant representation aims at increasing the similarity of local statistics between textures of the same class. To build this representation, we construct a simple convolutional network where the input image is convolved with a filter bank for various orientations, and then pooled to reduce local orientation change. The multilayer extension consists in repeating the same process for various image resolutions on the low-pass output of the previous resolution, which offers a richer representation.

Given an input texture I, the image is first low-pass filtered with a filter ψ_l to reduce small image domain perturbations and produce an image $J_{1,0}$. This image is then filtered with multiple zero-mean high-pass filters $\psi_{k,\theta}$, where k denotes the filter number and θ its orientation. High-pass responses encode higher-order statistics that are not present in the low-pass response $J_{1,0}$. A more stable approach consists in applying the modulus on the high-pass responses, which imposes symmetric statistics and improves invariance of the local statistics. Applying multiple filtering with multiple different filters naturally increases the amount of texture information that are going to be extracted further via multifractal analysis. In order to increase the local invariance to orientation, we apply a pooling operator $\phi_\theta : \mathcal{R}^{i \times j \times n} \rightarrow \mathcal{R}^{i \times j}$ on the oriented outputs for each filter :

$$J_{1,k} = \phi_\theta(|J_{1,0} \star \psi_{k,\theta}| \, , \, \theta = \theta_1, ..., \theta_n) \quad , \quad k = 1, ..., K, \tag{1}$$

where n is the number of orientations and $i \times j$ is the size of the low-pass image. As a result, we obtain 1 low-pass response and K high-pass responses, each image is encoding different statistics. For a richer representation, we repeat the same operation for different resolutions $s = 2^{0,...,-L}$, where $s = 1$ is the finest resolution and $s = 2^{-L}$ is the coarsest resolution. The image generation process is then generalized as follows :

$$J_{s,k} = \begin{cases} I \star \psi_l & k = 0 \, , \, s = 1 \\ \downarrow (J_{2s,0} \star \psi_l) & k = 0 \, , \, s \neq 1 \\ \phi_\theta(|J_{s,0} \star \psi_{k,\theta}| \, , \, \theta = \theta_1, ..., \theta_n) & k = 1, ..., K, \end{cases} \tag{2}$$

where $\downarrow$ denotes the downsampling operator. We found that calculating statistics on multiple resolutions instead of a single one increases significantly the robustness of the descriptor. This can be expected because two textures may seem "more similar" at a lower resolution. As a result, the intra-class variability decreases as the resolution decreases, but keeping higher resolution images is important to ensure extra-class decorrelation.

Dimensionality Reduction with Pooling

Using multiple filters $\psi_{k,\theta}$ increases dramatically the size of the image set. Knowing that each image $J_{s,k}$ will be used to extract statistics using multifractal analysis, this will result in a very large descriptor. One resulting issue is the high dimensionality of the training set. Another one is the processing time as the statistics should be applied on each image. We propose to merge different high-pass responses $J_{s,k}$ together to reduce the number of images. A straightforward approach would be to gather various images $\{J_{s,k} \, , \, k = t, .., u\}$ and then apply a pooling operator ϕ_r that is going to merge each image subset into one single image $J_{s,k_{t,..,u}}$:

$$J_{s,k_{t,..,u}} = \phi_r(\, J_{s,k} \, , \, k = t, .., u). \tag{3}$$

As a result, the number of high-pass responses will be decreased ; this leads to a reduced size descriptor. The pooling operator ϕ_r can be either the mean or the min/max functions. We take ϕ_r as a maximum function in this paper. An example is given in Figure 2 for one resolution $s = 0$ using 6 high-pass filters and one low-pass filter. The

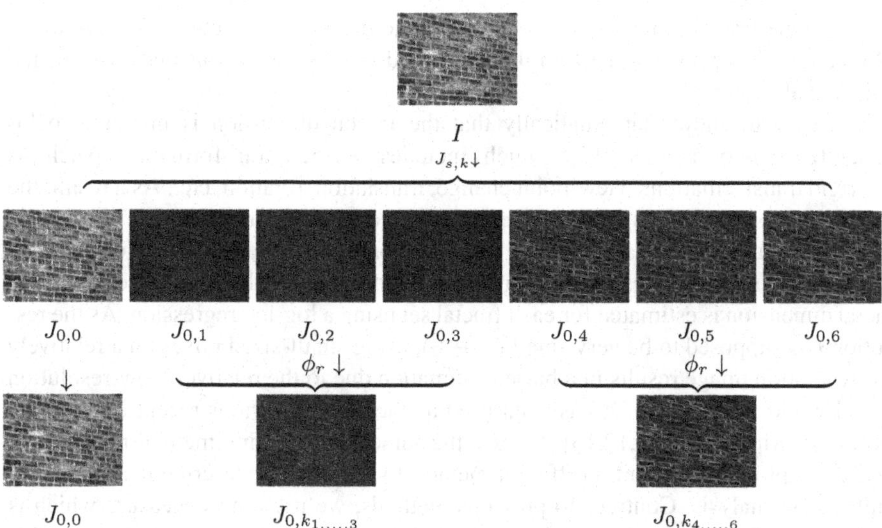

Fig. 2. Image generation example applied on the texture input I for one resolution using 6 high-pass filters. The images $J_{0,1\dots6}$ are a result of the orientation pooling (eq. 2). The 6 images are reduced to 2 images using a pooling operator ϕ_r on similar responses to reduce the dimensionality. The same process is repeated for multiple resolutions.

number of images is reduced from 7 to 3. For 5 resolutions ($s = 2^{0,\dots,-4}$), the total number of images goes from 35 to 15, which is an important reduction.

2.3 Globally Invariant Representation

Once the set of low-pass and high-pass images is generated, we need to extract global statistics, a mapping into a fixed-size descriptor, which is *globally* invariant to the complex physical transformations. We propose to use a new multifractal approach to statistically describe textures suffering from strong environmental changes. To understand the difference between the proposed method and the previous work, we first present the standard fractal and multifractal analysis framework used by the previous methods, we then introduce the proposed approach.

Multifractal Analysis. In a nutshell, a fractal object E is self-similar across scales. One characteristic of its irregularity is the so-called *box fractal dimension*. By measuring a fractal object on multiple scales r, the box fractal dimension is defined as a power-law relashionship between the scale r and the smallest number of sets of length r covering E [16]:

$$\dim(E) = \lim_{r\to 0} \frac{\log N(r,E)}{-\log r}, \quad (4)$$

Using squared boxes of size r, this dimension can be estimated numerically, known as the *box-counting* method. Multifractal analysis is an extension of this important notion. A multifractal object F is composed of many fractal components $F_{1,\dots,f}$. In this case, a single fractal dimension is not sufficient to describe this object. The *multifractal spectrum* is the collection of all the associated fractal dimensions that describe the multifractal object.

It is easy to show mathematically that the fractal dimension is invariant to bi-Lipschitz transformations [17], which includes various transformations such as non-rigid transformations, view-point change, translation, rotation, etc.. As a result, the multifractal spectrum is also invariant to these transformations. This makes the multifractal spectrum an attractive tool to globally describe textures. However, the box-counting method gives a rather crude estimation of the real fractal dimension. The fractal dimension is estimated for each fractal set using a log-log regression. As the resolution r is supposed to be very small ($r \to 0$), using small-sized boxes on a relatively low-resolution image results in a biased estimation due to the relatively low-resolution of real-world images [18]. It has been used as the core of various recent multifractal texture descriptors [10,11,12,13] that use the same box-counting method to build the final descriptor. We present a different method to statistically describe textures using multifractal analysis. Contrary to previous methods, we use a new measure which is based on the distribution of local singularity exponents. It can be shown in fact that this measure is related to the true multifractal spectrum, and its precision is proven by the high-accuracy of the proposed descriptor. Moreover, this approach is computationally efficient, which permits to achieve high accuracy at reduced processing time.

Proposed Multifractal Descriptor. The proposed method first estimates the local singularity exponents $h(x)$ on each pixel x, and then applies the empirical histogram followed by log operator to extract the global statistics $\varphi_h = \log(\rho_h + \epsilon)$. This operation is performed on all the resulting images of the first step, which results in multiple histograms φ_{h_i}. The concatenation of all these histograms forms the final descriptor.

Let J be an image, and $\mu_\psi(B(x,r)) = \int_{B(x,r)} (J \star \psi_r)(y)dy$ a positive measure, where ψ_r is an appropriate wavelet at scale r (Gaussian in our case) and $B(x,r)$ a closed disc of radius $r > 0$ centered at x. Multifractal analysis states that the wavelet projections scale as power laws in r [19,20,21]. We use a microcanonical evaluation [20] which consists in assessing an exponent $h(x)$ for each pixel x :

$$\mu_\psi(B(x,r)) \approx \alpha(x) r^{h(x)} \ , r \to 0. \tag{5}$$

The validity of equation (5) has been tested on a large dataset [21], which proves that natural images exhibit a strong multifractal behavior. Introducing the log, the formula is expressed as a linear fit :

$$\log(\mu_\psi(B(x,r))) \approx \log(\alpha(x)) + h(x)\log(r) \ , \ r \to 0. \tag{6}$$

Rewriting the equation in the matrix form permits to calculate all the exponents at once by solving the following linear system :

$$\underbrace{\begin{bmatrix} 1 \ \log(r_1) \\ \vdots \quad \vdots \\ 1 \ \log(r_l) \end{bmatrix}}_{A} \underbrace{\begin{bmatrix} \log(\alpha(x_1)) & \cdots & \log(\alpha(x_N)) \\ h(x_1) & \cdots & h(x_N) \end{bmatrix}}_{\eta} = \underbrace{\begin{bmatrix} \log(\mu_\psi(B(x_1,r_1))) & \ldots & \log(\mu_\psi(B(x_N,r_1))) \\ \vdots & \cdots & \vdots \\ \log(\mu_\psi(B(x_1,r_l))) & \ldots & \log(\mu_\psi(B(x_N,r_l))) \end{bmatrix}}_{b}, \tag{7}$$

$$\underset{\eta}{\operatorname{argmin}} \, ||A\eta - b||_2^2 \, , \, h(x_i) = \eta(2, i), \tag{8}$$

where N is the number of pixels of the image J, l is the number of scales used in the log-log regression. This matrix formulation is computationally efficient and plays an important role in the speed of the proposed method. Given the local exponents $h(x)$, which is an image of the same size of J that describes the local irregularities at each pixel, we need to extract now a fixed-size measure that globally describes the statistics of $h(x)$. Using the box-counting method, this would require extracting all the fractal fractal sets $F_h = \{x \,|\, h(x) \approx h\}$, and then calculating the box-counting dimension for each set F_h. As discussed before, this approach leads to a crude estimation of the true multifractal spectrum due to the actual low-resolution of real-world images. Moreover, a log-log regression should be performed on each fractal set. Instead, we propose to use the empirical histogram ρ_h followed by a log operator :

$$\varphi_h = \log(\rho_h + \epsilon), \tag{9}$$

where $\epsilon \geq 1$ is set to provide stability. The distribution of the local exponents is an invariant representation which encodes the multi-scale properties of the texture. The log acts as a normalization operator that nearly linearizes histogram scaling and makes the descriptor more robust to small perturbations. This way, we have access to reliable statistics [1]. This log-histogram is calculated on each image generated in the first step, which results in a set of histograms $\varphi_{h_{1,\ldots,M}}$, where M is the total number of generated images. The final descriptor φ is constructed by concatenating ($\biguplus$) all the generated histograms :

$$\varphi = \biguplus_{m}^{M} \varphi_{h_m}; \tag{10}$$

A descriptor example is given in Figure 3. This descriptor φ is the result of the concatenation of 14 log exponents histograms calculated on the images generated with the first step of the method presented in section 2.2 and further explained in Figure 2. Three images are generated for each scale s ; a low-pass response is presented in red, and two high-pass responses are presented in black and gray in the figure [2].

2.4 Analysis

The basic multifractal framework consists in generating multiple images and then extracting statistics using multifractal analysis. Multifractal descriptors are mathematically invariant to bi-Lipschitz transforms, which even includes non-rigid transformation and view-point change. The proposed method follows the same strategy, but is substantially different from the previous methods. The differences lie in both the image generation step and the statistical description. For instance, the WMFS method [13] generates

[1] A mathematical relationship between the log exponents histogram and the multifractal spectrum is presented in the supplementary material.

[2] A histogram was discarded for $s = 2^{-4}$ in the second high response (in gray) due to the large size of the filter which is larger than the actual size of the input image at resolution $s = 2^{-4}$.

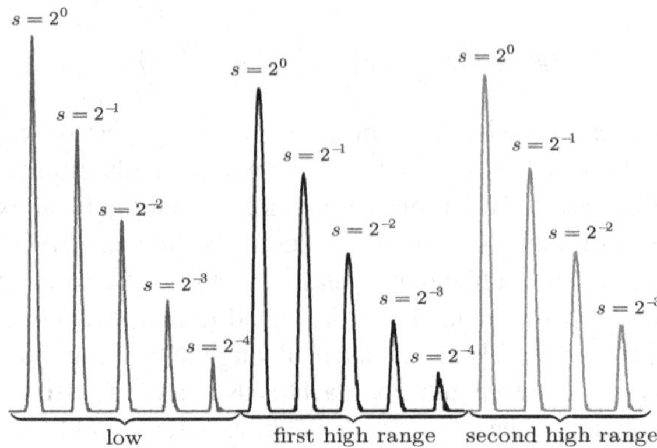

Fig. 3. A descriptor example using a low-pass response and two high-pass responses for 5 resolutions $s = 2^{0,\dots,-4}$. The exponents log-histogram is calculated for each response and for multiple image resolutions s.

multiple images for multiple orientations, each oriented image is then analyzed using Daubechies discrete wavelet transform as well as using the wavelet leaders [22]. The multifractal spectrum (*MFS*) is then estimated for each image, for a given orientation using the box-counting method. Each *MFS* is then concatenated for a given orientation and the final descriptor is defined as the mean of all the descriptors over the orientation. Contrary to this method, we use different high-pass filters instead of one single analyzing wavelet, which permits to extract different statistics. Generating multiple descriptors for multiple orientations is computationally expensive. In contrast, we generate only one descriptor. To ensure local robustness to orientation, we apply a pooling operator on the *filtered responses*. This approach is much more computationally efficient. Finally, the core of our method is the new multifractal descriptor which permits to extract accurate statistics, contrary to the popular box-counting method as explained in the previous section. The proposed method takes about 0.7 second to extract the whole descriptor on an image of size 480×640, compared to 37 seconds as reported in the state-of-the-art multifractal method [13]. Experiments show that the proposed descriptor permits also to achieve higher accuracy, especially in large-scale situations when the extra-class decorrelation is a challenging issue.

2.5 Pre and Post Processing

Pre-processing and post-processing can improve the robustness of a texture recognition system. For instance, the method in [12] performs a scale normalization step on each input texture using blob detection. This step first estimates the scale of the texture and then a normalization is applied, which aims at increasing the robustness to scale change. Other texture classification methods such as [9] use Weber's law normalization to improve robustness to illumination. We do not use any scale normalization step such as [12,13], we rather use sometimes histogram equalization to improve robustness to illumination change. We also use a post-processing on features vector φ using wavelet domain soft-thresholding [23]. This step aims at increasing the intra-class correlation by reducing small histogram perturbations (for more details, please refer to the supplementary material).

3 Classification and Training Strategies

The second part of our work concerns the training aspect of the texture recognition problem. The globally invariant representation offers a theoretically stable invariant representation via accurate multifractal statistics. However, there are other small transformations and perturbations that may occur in real-world images and this is where a good training strategy will help us to take advantage of the proposed descriptor in practice. We work on two ideas :

1. The choice of the classifier can improve recognition rates : we introduce a simple combination between the Generative PCA classifier [14] and SVMs [8].
2. The lack of data is an issue, how to get more data? : Given an input training texture image, we synthetically generate more images by changing its illumination and scale. We call this strategy "synthetic training".

Experiments on challenging public benchmark datasets, including a large-scale dataset with 250 classes, validates the robustness of the proposed solution.

3.1 Classification

Support Vector Machines. SVMs [8] are widely used in texture classification [10,12,12,13,7,6]. Commonly used kernels are mainly RBF Gaussian kernel, polynomials and χ^2 kernel. Extension to multiclass can be done via strategies such as one-vs-one and one-vs-all. In this paper, we use the one-vs-all strategy with an RBF-kernel. It consists in building a binary classifier for each class as follows : for each class, a positive label is assigned to the corresponding instances and a negative label is affected to all the remaining instances. The winning class c_{svm} can be chosen based on probability estimates [24] or a simple score maximization :

$$c_{svm} = \underset{1 \leq c \leq N_c}{\text{argmax}} \{f_{svm}(x, c)\} \quad , \quad f_{svm}(x, c) = \sum_{i=1}^{M_c} \alpha_i^c y_i^c \mathrm{K}(x_i^c, x) + b_c \ , \tag{11}$$

where α_i^c are the optimal Lagrange multipliers of the classifier representing the class c, x_i^c are the support vectors of the class c, y_i^c are the corresponding ± 1 labels, N_c is the number of classes and x is the instance to classify.

Generative PCA Classifier. The generative PCA (GPCA) classifier is a simple PCA-based classifier recently used in [15,14]. Given a test descriptor x, GPCA finds the closest class centroid $\mathbb{E}(\{x_c\})$ to x, after ignoring the first D principal variability directions. Let V_c be the linear space generated by the D eigenvectors of the covariance matrix of largest eigenvalues, and $V_c^{\perp}$ its orthogonal complement. The generative PCA classifier uses the projection distance associated to $P_{V_c^{\perp}}$:

$$c_{pca} = \underset{1 \leq c \leq N_c}{\text{argmin}} \; ||P_{V_c^{\perp}}(x - \mathbb{E}(\{x_c\}))||^2. \tag{12}$$

Classification consists in choosing the class c_{pca} with the minimum projection distance.

GPCA-SVM Classifier. We propose to combine GPCA and SVMs in one single classifier. The idea behind this combination comes from the observation that SVMs and GPCA often fail on different instances. As a result, a well-established combination of these classifiers should theoretically lead to improved performance. We propose a combination based on the distance between the score separation of each classifier output

$$c_{final} = \begin{cases} c_{svm} & \text{if } f_{svm}(x, c_{svm}) - f_{svm}(x, c_{pca}) \geq th_{svm} \\ c_{pca} & \text{otherwise,} \end{cases} \tag{13}$$

where th_{svm} is a threshold parameter. The score separation gives an idea of SVMs' accuracy to classify a given instance. Another similar approach would be using probability estimates [24] instead of the score. If the measure $f_{svm}(x, c_{svm}) - f_{svm}(x, c_{pca})$ is relatively important, this means that SVMs are quite "confident" about the result. Otherwise, the classifier selects the GPCA result. Determining the best threshold th_{svm} for each instance is an open problem. In this paper, we rather fix a threshold value for each experiment. We generally select a small threshold for small training sets and larger thresholds for larger sets. Even if this strategy is not optimal, experiments show that the combination improves the classification rates as expected.

3.2 Synthetic Training

One important problem in training is coping with the low amount of examples. We propose a simple strategy to artificially add more data to the training set by changing illumination and scale of each instance of the training set. While this idea seems simple, it can have a dramatic impact on the performance as we will see in the next section.

Multi-illumination Training. Given an input image I, multi-illumination training consists in generating other images of the same content of I but with different illumination. There are two illumination cases ; the first one consists in *uniform* changing by image scaling of the form aI, where a is a given scalar. The second case consists in *nonuniform* changing using histogram matching with a set of histograms. The histograms can come from external images, or even from the training set itself (for example by transforming or combining a set of histograms).

Multi-scale Training. Given an input image I, multi-scale training consists simply in generating other images of the same size as I by zooming-in and out. In this paper, we use around 4 generated images, 2 by zooming-in and 2 others by zooming-out.

4 Texture Classification Experiments

We present in this section texture classiffication results conducted on standard public datasets **UIUC** [25,1], **UMD** [26] and **ALOT** [27,28], as well as a comparison with **9** state-of-the-art methods.

Datasets Description. The **UIUC** dataset [25,1] is one of the most challenging texture datasets presented so far. It is composed of 25 classes, each class contains 40 grayscale images of size 480×640 with strong scale, rotation and viewpoint changes in uncontrolled illumination environment. Some images exhibit also strong non-rigid deformations. Some samples are presented in Figure 4. The **UMD** dataset [26] is similar to **UIUC** with higher resolution images (1280×960) but exhibits less non-rigid deformations and stronger illumination changes compared to **UIUC**. To evaluate the proposed method on a large-scale dataset, we choose the **ALOT** dataset [27,28]. It consists of **250** classes, 100 samples each. We use the same setup as the previous multifractal methods [13]: grayscale version with half resolution (768×512). The **ALOT** dataset is very challenging as it reprensents a significantly larger number of classes (250) compared to **UIUC** and **UMD** (25) and very strong illumination change (8 levels of illumination). The viewpoint change is however less dramatic compared to **UIUC** and **UMD**.

Fig. 4. Texture samples from the **UIUC** dataset [25,1]. Each row represents images from the same class with strong enviromental changes.

Implementation Details. In order to build a fast texture classification system, we use only two high-pass filtering responses, which results in 3 histograms per image resolution [3]. The number of the image scales is fixed to 5. The filter bank consists in high-pass wavelet filters (Daubechies, Symlets and Gabor). A more robust descriptor can be built by increasing the number of filters and orientations. Filtering can be parallelized for faster processing. While augmenting the number of filters slightly improves classification results, the minimalist setup presented above, coupled with the training strategies introduced in this paper, permits to outperform existing techniques while offering in addition computational efficiency.

Evaluation

We evaluate the proposed system and compare it with state-of-the-art methods for 50 random splits between training and testing. The evaluation consists in three steps :

[3] Except for **ALOT** dataset, we use 3 high-pass responses for a more robust representation.

1. log-histogram vs. box-counting : We evaluate the precision of our log-histogram method and compare it with the box-counting method used in previous methods.
2. Learning efficiency : We compare the proposed GPCA-SVM combination with single GPCA and SVM results and see how the proposed synthetic training strategy improves classification rates.
3. We compare our main results with **9** state-of-the-art results.

log-Histogram vs. Box-Counting. In this experiment, we replace the log-histogram step of our approach with the box-counting method widely used in the previous multifractal methods to see if the proposed log-histogram leads to a more accurate bi-Lipschitz invariance. The results are presented in Figure 5. As can be seen, the log-histogram approach leads to higher performance, especially when more data is available. This clearly shows that indeed, the log-histogram leads to a better bi-Lipschitz invariance, as theoretically discussed before. The log-histogram is a simple operation that permits our system to achieve high computational efficiency.

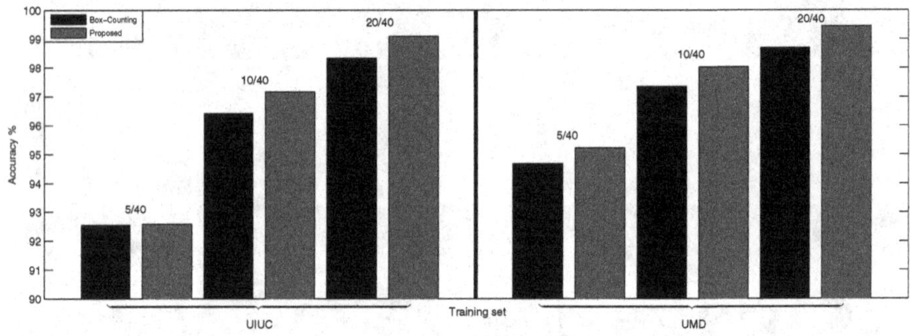

Fig. 5. Comparison between the box-counting method and the proposed log-histogram approach for various dataset training sizes (5, 10 and 20). The proposed approach leads to a more accurate descriptor

Learning Efficiency. In this experiment, we first compare the proposed GPCA-SVM combination with single GPCA and SVM classifiers using the proposed descriptor. Each dataset is presented in the form $D^x_{(y)}$ where x is the name of the dataset and y is the training size in number of images. The best results are in bold. As can be seen in Table 1, the GPCA-SVM does indeed improve classification rates. We expect to get even better results with a better strategy to set the threshold parameters th_{svm} as in the proposed experiments, the threshold is fixed for all the instances. Now we compare the results with and without the proposed synthetic training strategy. As can be seen, synthetic training leads to a dramatic improvement. This is a very interesting approach as it increases only the training time. The system can achieve higher recognition accuracy for almost the same computational effiency. For the **UMD** and **ALOT** datasets, we use uniform illumination change with the multiplicative parameter a in the range $[0.9, 0.95, 1.05, 1.1]$. For the **UIUC** dataset, we use the nonuniform illumination change with two histograms. For the multi-scale training, we use only four generated images (two by zooming-in and two other by zooming-out), which increases the training set 9 times in the **UMD** and **UIUC** datasets (no mutli-scale training is used for the **ALOT** dataset).

Table 1. Classification rates comparison using GPCA-SVM and synthetic training

		$D^{UIUC}_{(5)}$	$D^{UIUC}_{(10)}$	$D^{UIUC}_{(20)}$	$D^{UMD}_{(5)}$	$D^{UMD}_{(10)}$	$D^{UMD}_{(20)}$	$D^{ALOT}_{(10)}$	$D^{ALOT}_{(30)}$	$D^{ALOT}_{(50)}$
Proposed	GPCA	91.15%	97.12%	99.07%	95.07%	97.85%	99.40%	89.30%	98.03%	99.27%
	SVM	91.23%	96.30%	98.47%	94.43%	97.44%	99.25%	88.96%	98.16%	99.14%
	GPCA-SVM	**92.58%**	**97.17%**	**99.10%**	**95.23%**	**98.04%**	**99.44%**	**90.67%**	**98.45%**	**99.34%**
+ Synthetic Train	GPCA	95.84%	98.77%	99.67%	98.02%	99.13%	99.62%	91.54%	98.81%	99.59%
	SVM	95.40%	98.43%	99.46%	97.75%	99.06%	99.72%	92.23%	98.80%	99.51%
	GPCA-SVM	**96.13%**	**98.93%**	**99.78%**	**98.20%**	**99.24%**	**99.79%**	**92.82%**	**99.03%**	**99.64%**

Discussions. We compare the proposed method MCMA (Multilayer Convolution - Multifractal Analysis) with **9** state-of-the-art methods for 50 random splits between training and testing, for different training sizes. Results are presented in Table 2. The best results are in bold [4]. As can be seen, the proposed method outperforms the published results on the 3 datasets. Compared to the leading method [14], our system seems to better handle viewpoint change and non-rigid deformations. This is clearly shown in the results on the **UIUC** dataset that exhibits strong enviromental changes. This result can be expected as the scattering method builds invariants on translation, rotation and scale changes, which does not include viewpoint change and non-rigid deformations. Contrary to this, using accurate multifractal statistics, our solution produces descriptors that are invariant to these complex transformations. The proposed system maintains a high performance on the **UMD** dataset. It is worth noting that on this dataset, the images are of high resolution (1280 × 960), which gives an advantage over the **UIUC** dataset. However, we did not use the original resolution, we rather rescale the images to half-size for faster processing. The high accuracy shows that the proposed multifractal method is able to extract robust invariant statistics even on low-resolution images. On the large-scale dataset **ALOT**, the proposed method maintains high performance. Recall that this dataset contains **250** classes with 100 samples each. This is a very challenging dataset that evaluates the extra-class decorrelation of the produced descriptors. A robust descriptor should increase the intra-class correlation, but should also decrease the extra-class correlation and this has be evaluated on a large-scale data set which contains as many different classes as possible. The results on the **ALOT** dataset clearly show a significant performance drop of the leading multifractal method WMFS. The proposed solution in fact outperforms the WMFS method even without synthetic train as can be seen in Table 1. This proves that the proposed descriptor is able to extract a robust invariant representation.

[4] Detailed results with standard deviation can be found in the supplementary material.

Table 2. Classification rates on the **UIUC,UMD** and **ALOT** datasets

	$D^{UIUC}_{(5)}$	$D^{UIUC}_{(10)}$	$D^{UIUC}_{(20)}$	$D^{UMD}_{(5)}$	$D^{UMD}_{(10)}$	$D^{UMD}_{(20)}$	$D^{ALOT}_{(10)}$	$D^{ALOT}_{(30)}$	$D^{ALOT}_{(50)}$
MFS [10]	-	-	92.74%	-	-	93.93%	71.35%	82.57%	85.64%
OTF-MFS [11]	-	-	97.40%	-	-	98.49%	81.04%	93.45%	95.60%
WMFS [13]	93.40%	97.00%	97.62%	93.40%	97.00%	98.68%	82.95%	93.57%	96.94%
VG-Fractal [9]	85.35%	91.64%	95.40%	-	-	96.36%	-	-	-
Varma [29]	-	-	98.76%	-	-	-	-	-	-
Lazebnik [1]	91.12%	94.42%	97.02%	90.71%	94.54%	96.95%	-	-	-
BIF [5]	-	-	98.80%	-	-		-	-	-
SRP [7]	-	-	98.56%	-	-	99.30%	-	-	-
Scattering [14]	93.30%	97.80%	99.40%	96.60%	98.90%	99.70%	-	-	-
MCMA	**96.13%**	**98.93%**	**99.78%**	**98.20%**	**99.24%**	**99.79%**	**92.82%**	**99.03%**	**99.64%**

5 Conclusion

This paper presents a fast and accurate texture classification system. The proposed solution builds a locally invariant representation using a multilayer convolution architecture that performs convolutions with a filter bank, applies a pooling operator to increase the local invariance and repeats the process for various image resolutions. The resulting images are mapped into a stable descriptor via multifractal analysis. We present a new multifractal descriptor that extracts rich texture information from the local singularity exponents. The descriptor is mathematically validated to be invariant to bi-Lipschitz transformations, which includes complex environmental changes. The second part of paper tackles the training part of the recognition system. We propose the GPCA-SVM classifier that combines the generative PCA classifier with the popular kernel SVMs to achieve higher accuracy. In addition, a simple and efficient "synthetic training" strategy is proposed that consists in synthetically generating more training data by changing illumination and scale of the training instances. Results outperforming the state-of-the-art are obtained and compared with 9 recent methods on 3 challenging public benchmark datasets, while ensuring high computational efficiency.

Acknowledgements. Hicham Badri's PhD is funded by an INRIA (Direction of Research) CORDI-S grant. He is making a PhD in co-supervision with INRIA and Mohammed V-Agdal University - LRIT, Associated Unit to CNRST (URAC 29).

References

1. Lazebnik, S., Schmid, C., Ponce, J.: A sparse texture representation using local affine regions. PAMI 27, 1265–1278 (2005)
2. Zhang, J., Marszalek, M., Lazebnik, S., Schmid, C.: Local features and kernels for classification of texture and object categories: A comprehensive study. Int. J. Comput. Vision 73(2), 213–238 (2007)

3. Varma, M., Zisserman, A.: A statistical approach to material classification using image patch exemplars. PAMI 31(11), 2032–2047 (2009)
4. Ojala, T., Pietikäinen, M., Mäenpää, T.: Multiresolution gray-scale and rotation invariant texture classification with local binary patterns. PAMI 24(7), 971–987 (2002)
5. Crosier, M., Griffin, L.D.: Texture classification with a dictionary of basic image features. In: CVPR. IEEE Computer Society (2008)
6. Liu, L., Fieguth, P.W.: Texture classification from random features. PAMI 34(3), 574–586 (2012)
7. Liu, L., Fieguth, P.W., Kuang, G., Zha, H.: Sorted random projections for robust texture classification. In: ICCV, pp. 391–398 (2011)
8. Scholkopf, B., Smola, A.J.: Learning with Kernels: Support Vector Machines, Regularization, Optimization, and Beyond. MIT Press, Cambridge (2001)
9. Varma, M., Garg, R.: Locally invariant fractal features for statistical texture classification. In: CVPR, Rio de Janeiro, Brazil (October 2007)
10. Xu, Y., Ji, H., Fermuller, C.: A projective invariant for textures. In: 2006 CVPR, vol. 2, pp. 1932–1939 (2006)
11. Xu, Y., Huang, S.B., Ji, H., Fermüller, C.: Combining powerful local and global statistics for texture description. In: CVPR, pp. 573–580. IEEE (2009)
12. Xu, Y., Yang, X., Ling, H., Ji, H.: A new texture descriptor using multifractal analysis in multi-orientation wavelet pyramid. In: CVPR, pp. 161–168 (2010)
13. Ji, H., Yang, X., Ling, H., Xu, Y.: Wavelet domain multifractal analysis for static and dynamic texture classification. IEEE Transactions on Image Processing 22(1), 286–299 (2013)
14. Sifre, L., Mallat, S.: Rotation, scaling and deformation invariant scattering for texture discrimination. In: CVPR (2013)
15. Bruna, J., Mallat, S.: Invariant scattering convolution networks. PAMI 35(8), 1872–1886 (2013)
16. Falconer, K.: Techniques in Fractal Geometry. Wiley (1997)
17. Xu, Y., Ji, H., Fermüller, C.: Viewpoint invariant texture description using fractal analysis. Int. J. Comput. Vision 83(1), 85–100 (2009)
18. Arneodo, A., Bacry, E., Muzy, J.F.: The thermodynamics of fractals revisited with wavelets. Physica A: Statistical and Theoretical Physics 213(1-2), 232–275 (1995)
19. Turiel, A., del Pozo, A.: Reconstructing images from their most singular fractal manifold. IEEE Trans. Img. Proc. 11(4), 345–350 (2002)
20. Yahia, H., Turiel, A., Perez-Vicente, C.: Microcanonical multifractal formalism: a geometrical approach to multifractal systems. Part I: singularity analysis. Journal of Physics A: Math. Theor. (41) (2008)
21. Turiel, A., Parga, N.: The multifractal structure of contrast changes in natural images: From sharp edges to textures. Neural Computation 12(4), 763–793 (2000)
22. Wendt, H., Roux, S.G., Jaffard, S., Abry, P.: Wavelet leaders and bootstrap for multifractal analysis of images. Signal Process. 89(6), 1100–1114 (2009)
23. Donoho, D.L.: De-noising by soft-thresholding. IEEE Trans. Inf. Theor. 41(3), 613–627 (1995)
24. Chang, C.-C., Lin, C.-J.: LIBSVM: A library for support vector machines. ACM Transactions on Intelligent Systems and Technology 2, 27:1–27:27 (2011)
25. UIUC, http://www-cvr.ai.uiuc.edu/ponce_grp/data/
26. UMD, http://www.cfar.umd.edu/~fer/website-texture/texture.htm
27. Burghouts, G.J., Geusebroek, J.M.: Material-specific adaptation of color invariant features. Pattern Recognition Letters 30, 306–313 (2009)
28. ALOT, http://staff.science.uva.nl/~aloi/public_alot/
29. Varma, M.: Learning the discriminative powerinvariance trade-off. In: ICCV (2007)

Learning to Rank 3D Features*

Oncel Tuzel, Ming-Yu Liu, Yuichi Taguchi, and Arvind Raghunathan

Mitsubishi Electric Research Labs (MERL), Cambridge, MA, USA

Abstract. Representation of three dimensional objects using a set of oriented point pair features has been shown to be effective for object recognition and pose estimation. Combined with an efficient voting scheme on a generalized Hough space, existing approaches achieve good recognition accuracy and fast operation. However, the performance of these approaches degrades when the objects are (self-)similar or exhibit degeneracies, such as large planar surfaces which are very common in both man made and natural shapes, or due to heavy object and background clutter. We propose a max-margin learning framework to identify discriminative features on the surface of three dimensional objects. Our algorithm selects and ranks features according to their importance for the specified task, which leads to improved accuracy and reduced computational cost. In addition, we analyze various grouping and optimization strategies to learn the discriminative pair features. We present extensive synthetic and real experiments demonstrating the improved results.

Keywords: 3D pose estimation, feature selection, max-margin learning.

1 Introduction

Three dimensional object recognition and pose estimation tasks require identification and matching of scene measurements to the known object model. Various methods have been proposed. Many of them are based on selecting salient points in the 3D point cloud and using feature representations that can invariantly describe regions around the points [29,15,27,8,2,1,26]. These methods are known to produce successful results when the 3D object shape is rich and detailed, and the scene measurements are of high resolution and less noisy. However, under less ideal conditions their accuracy degrades rapidly. More importantly, partial measurements due to self occlusion and contaminating background clutter make a detailed region representation unavailable. Recently, using a set of simple pair features [33] has been shown to be useful for detection and pose estimation tasks. Drost *et al.* [7] used pairs of oriented points on the surface of the object in a voting framework. Even though the descriptor associated with the pair feature is not very discriminative, by accumulating evidence from a large number of pairs, it produces accurate results and becomes robust against moderate occlusion and background clutter. This

* Electronic supplementary material -Supplementary material is available in the online version of this chapter at `http://dx.doi.org/10.1007/978-3-319-10590-34`. Videos can also be accessed at `http://www.springerimages.com/videos/978-3-319-10589-5`

D. Fleet et al. (Eds.): ECCV 2014, Part I, LNCS 8689, pp. 520–535, 2014.
© Springer International Publishing Switzerland 2014

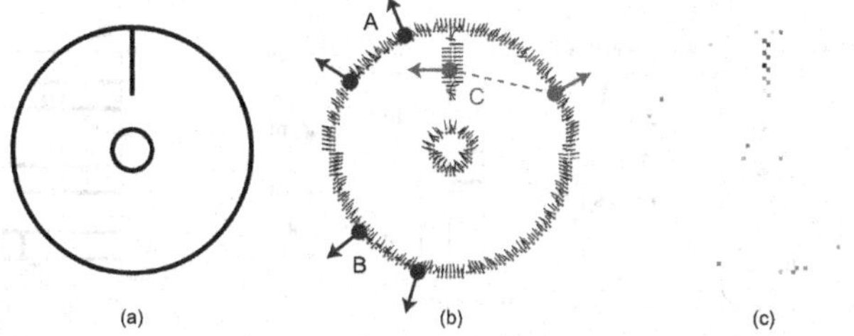

Fig. 1. Learning to rank features. (a) Input shape. Only the line at the center encodes orientation information. (b) Feature representation of the points using 2D location and orientation. Two points on the circle do not encode orientation information (the pairs A and B are indistinguishable). The orientation can be determined if one of the points is selected on the line as in the pair C. (c) Points selected by our learning algorithm are highlighted according to their weights. Primarily the points on the line are selected.

framework is also known to benefit from a carefully designed hashing and voting scheme, similar to geometric hashing [18], making the algorithm efficient.

Our observation is that not all the pairs of points have similar discriminative power or repeatability. In fact, certain features do not carry relevant information to the task in hand. For example, let us use the simple two dimensional shape shown in Figure 1(a), and define the task to be estimating the 2D pose (rotation and translation) of this shape in a scene. The feature is defined to be 2D point pair and their gradient orientations (Figure 1(b)). Under this setup, any point pair that is selected on the same circle (e.g., the pairs A and B) does not contain any information about the orientation of the shape, since they can simply match to many other pairs on the same circle. Hence a pair on the same circle is useless for the pose estimation task and should be identified and removed to improve both efficiency and robustness.

As mentioned above and more in [9,23,20], there are many methods to detect salient points on a scene or an object. Although these methods achieve major success for many tasks, it is unrealistic to expect a fixed recipe to be satisfactory for all the shapes and tasks. Instead, we propose a machine learning based approach to identify and rank important model features directly from the available data (image or a 3D model of an object) for the given task. A set of learned weights using our algorithm for the shape in Figure 1(a) is shown in Figure 1(c) with intensity values representing weights of the model features. As shown, our approach finds important points on the shape (the line segment that resolves rotation ambiguity) while removing unnecessary (on the circle) and unreliable points (points on the tip of the line has unreliable gradient orientations across synthesized rotations of the shape).

1.1 Contributions

The contributions of the paper are as follows:

- We present a max-margin learning framework for selecting and ranking discriminative features for voting-based 3D pose estimation and object recognition tasks.

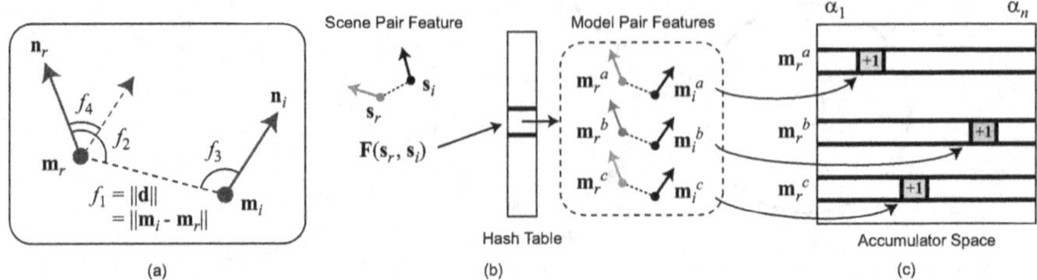

Fig. 2. Overview of the voting-based pose estimation algorithm [7,6]. (a) A point pair feature is defined using two oriented points. The 4D descriptor is defined by the distance between the points and angles between their orientations and the displacement vector. (b) Point pair features from the model are stored in a hash table using their descriptors as the keys. Each point pair feature from the scene is matched with multiple pair features from the model using the hash table. (c) Each matched model pair feature votes for an entry in a 2D accumulator space, corresponding to a particular pose.

- The learning task does not require manual labor for data collection and annotation, and uses data synthesized through rendering object models.
- The proposed approach enables various weighted voting strategies and can combine multiple different feature types.
- We present large scale real experiments on two challenging datasets and demonstrate improved results over the state-of-the-art.

2 Pose Estimation Using Point Pair Features

Figure 2 shows an overview of the voting-based pose estimation algorithm using point pair features [7,6]. A point pair feature consists of a pair of oriented points, denoted by their positions $\mathbf{m}_r$ and $\mathbf{m}_i$ and orientations $\mathbf{n}_r$ and $\mathbf{n}_i$ (e.g., normals or boundary directions). We refer to the first point $\mathbf{m}_r$ as the *reference* point. The descriptor of a point pair feature is given by

$$\mathbf{F}(\mathbf{m}_r, \mathbf{m}_i) = (f_1, f_2, f_3, f_4) = (\|\mathbf{d}\|_2, \angle(\mathbf{n}_r, \mathbf{d}), \angle(\mathbf{n}_i, \mathbf{d}), \angle(\mathbf{n}_r, \mathbf{n}_i)), \qquad (1)$$

where $\mathbf{d} = \mathbf{m}_i - \mathbf{m}_r$ and $\angle(.\ ,\ .)$ denotes the acute angle between two vectors, as shown in Figure 2(a). Note that this descriptor is pose invariant.

To recover the object pose, pair features from the scene are matched with those from the model. For efficiency, all the model pair features are stored in a hash table by using their quantized descriptors as the hash keys in an offline process. During pose estimation, a scene reference point is sampled and paired with another scene point to form a point pair feature. Its descriptor is then used to retrieve matched model pair features using the hash table, as shown in Figure 2(b). Each of the retrieved model pair feature in the hash bin votes for an entry in a 2D accumulator space, as shown in Figure 2(c). Each entry in the accumulator space corresponds to a specific object pose. After votes are accumulated for the sampled reference scene point by pairing it with multiple sampled scene points, poses supported by a certain number of votes are retrieved. The process is repeated for different reference scene points. Finally, clustering is performed to the retrieved poses to collect support from several reference points.

Drost *et al.* [7] used points on object surfaces and performed voting using surface-to-surface (S2S) pair features. Choi *et al.* [6] extended it using points on object boundaries and defined surface-to-boundary (S2B) and boundary-to-boundary (B2B) pair features. They showed that for planar objects, pair features including boundary points encode more information for pose estimation and provide better performance. However, (1) they were limited to the use of the individual pair features and (2) they did not provide how to select an optimal set of pair features given an object. Our framework allows us to combine different pair features by jointly learning optimal weights for all pair features.

3 Learning to Rank Features

The predicted pose of the object is given by the pose hypothesis that receives the maximum number of votes among all pose hypotheses. The goal of the learning is to select and weight the features to improve the chance that the correct hypothesis receives more votes than the others.

3.1 Weighted Voting

There are several different ways of weighting the features. The simplest form is based on weighting each model point pair with a different weight, and any scene point pair that maps to a given model point pair casts a vote equal to this weight. Although this weighting scheme is general, learning would be severely underdetermined due to high dimensional weight space.

Alternatively, we can group the features and constrain all the features within a group to have the same weight. One such strategy is *weighting hash table bins*: A weight is defined for each entry of the hash table and any scene pair feature that maps to the same hash table bin votes with the same weight. Since the point pairs are grouped into clusters that are mapping to the same hash table entry, the dimension of the weight space is reduced to the number of hash table bins. Another important advantage of this method is that it is possible to learn a weight vector that is sparse. Then the voting algorithm immediately removes any scene feature mapping to a bin with zero weight, improving the speed of the algorithm. A second grouping strategy is *weighting model points*: A weight is defined for each model point and any scene pair that maps to (either first or second point of the pair) this model point votes with this weight. This approach reduces the dimension of the weight space by an order, allowing efficient learning, and directly identifies important points on the model surface.

Given a 3D point cloud of a scene containing the target object, let S be the set of all scene pair features that are computed from this scene. Without loss of generality here we use the *weighting hash table bins* scheme. Let $\mathbf{y} \in SE(3)$ be a pose hypothesis. The corresponding data vector $\mathbf{x}_{\mathbf{y}} \in \mathbb{R}^M$ is given by the mapping $\mathbf{x} = \Phi(S, \mathbf{y})$[1] where M is the size of the hash table. Each dimension of the data vector, x^m, counts the number of times a scene pair feature, $s \in S$, maps to the hash table entry m and votes for the pose $\mathbf{y}$:

$$x^m = \Phi^m(S, \mathbf{y}) = \sum_{s \in S} \sum_{\mathbf{v} \in \mathbf{y}(s)} \mathbb{1}_{(h(s)=m \ \& \ \mathbf{y}=\mathbf{v})}, \tag{2}$$

where x^m is the mth dimension of the data vector $\mathbf{x}$, $\mathbb{1}_{(.)} \in \{0, 1\}$ is the indicator function, $h(s) \in \{1, \ldots, M\}$ is the hash function mapping the pair feature s to the corresponding hash table entry, and $\mathbf{y}(s)$ is the set of poses that the pair s votes. Note that a pair feature can cast votes for multiple poses, or even multiple votes for a single pose as explained in Section 2.

The weighted voting function can then be written using the linear map $\mathbf{w}^T\mathbf{x}$, where $\mathbf{w}$ is an M-dimensional weight vector. When $\mathbf{w} = \mathbf{1}_M$, this function is equivalent to the original (uniform) voting function.

3.2 Max-Margin Learning of Weights

Let I be a 3D scene and $\mathbf{y}^*$ be the true pose of the target object in the scene[2]. The learning to rank 3D features problem is the problem of finding a non-negative weight vector which satisfies the following constraints:

$$\mathbf{w}^T\mathbf{x}^* > \mathbf{w}^T\mathbf{x}, \ \forall \mathbf{y} \neq \mathbf{y}^*, \ \forall I. \tag{3}$$

This means that for all the 3D scenes I containing the target object, the true pose of the object $\mathbf{y}^*$ should have more *weighted* votes than any other poses.

Except for a few simple shapes, a closed form solution to this problem does not exist. Therefore, we proceed by optimizing the weights using a dataset of 3D scenes containing the target objects. Typically, collecting and labeling a dataset for each object is a labor intensive procedure. Since in our problem we have access to 3D models of the objects, we avoid this tedious task and generate dataset through simulation by rendering models according to the sampled poses. Let $\{(I_i, \mathbf{y}_i^*)\}_{i=1,\ldots,N}$ be the synthesized dataset consisting of N 3D scenes and ground truth poses of the target object. Still, the constraints given in (3) might not define a feasible set. Instead, we reformulate learning the weights as a regularized soft constraint optimization problem:

$$(\mathbf{w}^*, \xi^*) = \arg\min_{\mathbf{w},\xi} \sum_i \xi_i + \lambda R(\mathbf{w}) \tag{4}$$

$$s.t. \ \ \mathbf{w}^T(\mathbf{x}_i^* - \mathbf{x}) \geq \Delta(\mathbf{y}_i^*, \mathbf{y}) - \xi_i, \forall i, \ \forall \mathbf{y} \neq \mathbf{y}_i^* \tag{5}$$

$$w_u \geq \mathbf{w} \geq 0, \ \ \xi_i \geq 0, \tag{6}$$

which is similar to the margin re-scaling formulation of structured SVM learning [30,31] where $R(\mathbf{w})$ is a convex regularizer, λ controls the tradeoff between

[1] For ease of notation, we drop the subscript representing the dependency of the data vector $\mathbf{x}$ to the pose $\mathbf{y}$, and write $\mathbf{x}$ instead of $\mathbf{x}_\mathbf{y}$. For example $\mathbf{x}^*$ represents $\mathbf{x}_{\mathbf{y}^*}$.

[2] We assume that there is a single instance of the target object in the scene.

the margin and the training error, the loss function $\Delta(\mathbf{y}_i^*, \mathbf{y})$ penalizes larger pose deviation from the true pose more, and ξ_i are the slack variables corresponding to the constraint violations. In addition, we have an explicit upper bound w_u on the maximum weight (vote) a pair feature can have.

We use the loss function

$$\Delta(\mathbf{y}_i, \mathbf{y}) = 1 + \lambda_\theta \theta(\mathbf{y}_i, \mathbf{y}), \tag{7}$$

where $\theta(\mathbf{y}_i, \mathbf{y}) = \| \log(\mathbf{R}_{\mathbf{y}_i}^{-1} \mathbf{R}_{\mathbf{y}}) \|_F$ is the geodesic distance between the two rotation matrices encoded in 6-DOF poses $\mathbf{y}_i$ and $\mathbf{y}$. The constant 1 puts a fixed margin between two non-identical poses (Equation (5)) and λ_θ is a weighting factor between fixed margin and its scaled counterpart (the orientation difference)[3]. We ignore the translational component of the pose $\mathbf{y}$ since the observed pair features are largely insensitive to translation.

The form of the regularization function plays an important role on the accuracy and efficiency of the voting algorithm. Unless otherwise stated, in our experiments we used the quadratic regularization function $R(\mathbf{w}) = \mathbf{w}^T\mathbf{w}$. Using $L1$-norm regularizer $\|\mathbf{w}\|_1$ sparsifies the weight vector, leading to feature selection.

3.3 Optimization

Unlike standard structured learning problems that contain a combinatorial number of constraints due to a discrete label space, our labels, $\mathbf{y}$, are defined on a continuous pose space; therefore to optimally solve the problem an infinite number of constraints should be included to (5). However, we can still employ a cutting plane style optimization method [16] which has largely been used for discrete label space problems.

At each iteration k of the cutting plane algorithm, we use the previous set of weights $\mathbf{w}^{(k-1)}$ and solve the pose estimation problem for each scene I_i using the algorithm given in Section 2. In addition to the best pose, this algorithm provides a set of likely poses which are sorted according to the number of votes that they receive. For all the likely poses we evaluate the margin constraint (5):

$$(\mathbf{w}^{(k-1)})^T(\mathbf{x}_i^* - \mathbf{x}) \geq \Delta(\mathbf{y}_i^*, \mathbf{y}) \tag{8}$$

and add the most violated constraint to the selected constraint list. Let $\mathbf{y}^{(1:k)}$ and $\mathbf{x}^{(1:k)}$ be the set of all selected poses and constraints up to iteration k. Then the optimization problem at iteration k is given by

$$(\mathbf{w}^{(k)}, \xi^{(k)}) = \arg\min_{\mathbf{w},\xi} \sum_i \sum_j \xi_{i,j} + \lambda R(\mathbf{w}) \tag{9}$$

$$s.t. \;\; \mathbf{w}^T(\mathbf{x}_i^* - \mathbf{x}_{i,j}^{(1:k)}) \geq \Delta(\mathbf{y}_i^*, \mathbf{y}_{i,j}^{(1:k)}) - \xi_{i,j}, \; \forall i, \; j \tag{10}$$

$$w_u \geq \mathbf{w} \geq 0, \;\; \xi_{i,j} \geq 0 \tag{11}$$

[3] Two poses are considered identical if they have less than 12 degrees rotational distance.

Algorithm 1. Learning to Rank 3D Features

1. Input: Sampled 3D scenes and corresponding true poses: $\{(I_i, \mathbf{y}_i^*)\}_{i=1...N}$
2. Initialize $\mathbf{w}^0 = \mathbf{1}^M$, empty constraint set $\mathbf{x}_{i,j}^{(0)} = \{\}$, $k = 1$
3. **while** $k \leq max\ iteration$ **do**
4. For each scene I_i solve pose estimation (Section 2) using weights $\mathbf{w}^{(k-1)}$
5. For all the likely poses compute the most violated constraints using (8). Let $\mathbf{x}_{i,j}^{(k)}$ and $\mathbf{y}_{i,j}^{(k)}$ be the set of the most violated constraints and corresponding poses. If this list is empty **break**
6. Add most violated constraints to the constraint list $\mathbf{x}_{i,j}^{(1:k)} = \mathbf{x}_{i,j}^{(1:k-1)} \cup \mathbf{x}_{i,j}^{(k)}$
7. Solve optimization problem (9) using constraint set $\mathbf{x}_{i,j}^{(1:k)}$ to get new weights $\mathbf{w}^{(k)}$. $k = k + 1$
8. **end while**
9. Output: Learned weight vector $\mathbf{w}$

where $\mathbf{y}_{i,j}$ represents the jth violated pose in the ith scene. Optimization problem (9) is convex and has finite number of constraints which we solve optimally. Note that the dimensionality of the data vectors can be quite high $M >> 10^5$, and we can have as many as $N \simeq 10^5$ margin constraints, which require careful attention to memory and computation. Fortunately, data vectors are quite sparse and using sparse matrices and sparse linear algebra, optimization can be solved efficiently. We use an interior point solver [32] to solve (9).

In general, the algorithm requires fewer iterations when multiple violated constraints (8) are added to the supporting constraint set at a given time, leading to faster operation. We add the most violated 10% of all the violated constraints at a time and usually obtain the optimal solution in $k = 3 - 4$ iterations of the cutting plane method. We initialize the optimization with uniform weights, $\mathbf{w}^{(0)} = \mathbf{1}_M$, which provides a good initial constraint set and significantly speeds up the convergence of the algorithm. The parameters of the learning algorithm (λ, w_u) are tuned using a grid search on a synthesized validation set as explained in Section 4. The optimization algorithm is summarized in Algorithm 1.

4 Experiments

We conducted extensive experimental evaluation of the proposed algorithm using two challenging datasets: (1) Mian *et al.*'s dataset [22] which contains curvy objects, and (2) a large scale real dataset collected by us containing mostly piecewise planar industrial-style objects, and compared our results with the state-of-the-art.

4.1 Curvy Objects

In the first experiment, we tested our algorithm using the real dataset introduced by Mian *et al.* [22] which is the standard benchmark for evaluating 3D recognition and pose estimation algorithms. This dataset contains 50 scenes taken

Fig. 3. Examples of generated synthetic scenes used for training. Four target objects were rendered with random poses.

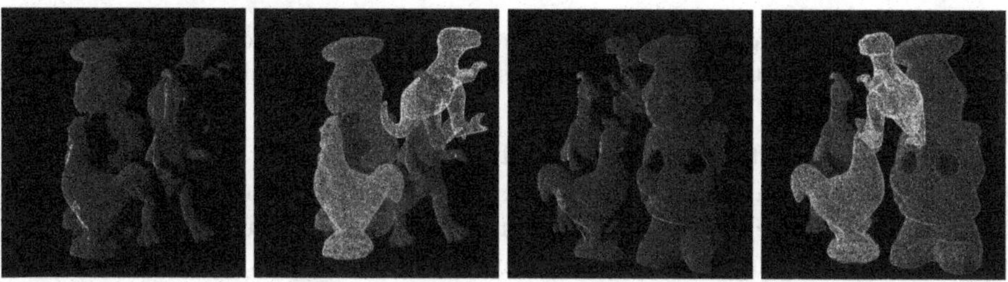

Fig. 4. Samples from Mian *et al.*'s dataset [22] and corresponding estimation results using learned weights (overlayed on the data)

using a Minolta range scanner where each scene contains four or five objects. These objects have smooth shapes with rich variations in surface normals. Since surface normals are more informative for these shapes, we used the S2S pair features in our algorithm. We used weighting hash table bins scheme to learn the weights. We generated two sets of synthetic datasets, one for training (used to learn the weights) and one for validation (used for tuning training parameters), each containing 500 3D scenes, by rendering 3D models of the objects according to randomly sampled rotation and translation parameters. In the simulation, maximum occlusion ratio was set to be 0.8. Example training images are shown in Figure 3.

We used the standard evaluation procedure defined in [7] which (1) excluded the rhino object and (2) labeled an estimation as correct if the retrieved translation and rotation are within the one-tenth of the object's diameter and 12° of the ground truth pose respectively. In Figure 5, we plot recognition rate vs. the occlusion ratio for our algorithm and four other leading algorithms: (1) Spin images [15], (2) Tensor matching [22], (3) Drost *et al.* [7] and (4) Support vector shape (SVS) [24]. In addition, we also included our implementation of the original Drost *et al.*'s algorithm which is equivalent to using uniform weights (labeled as "our implementation" in the figure).

As seen in Figure 5, the proposed algorithm produced equal or better results at all the occlusion rates than all the prior work. For all the objects with less

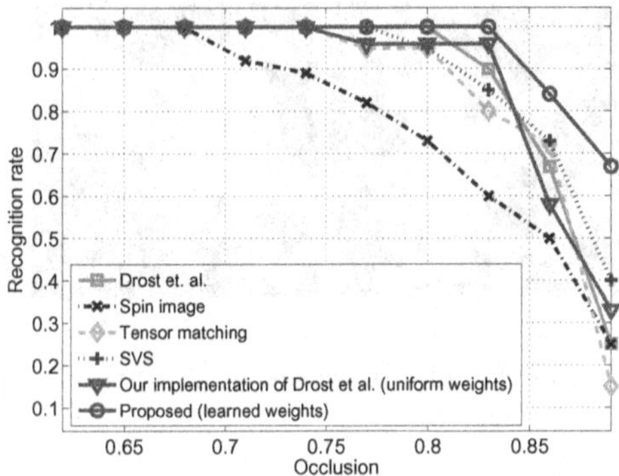

Fig. 5. Recognition rate vs. the occlusion rate on Mian *et al.*'s dataset. Our method improves the state-of-the-art significantly especially at larger occlusion rates.

than 0.84 occlusion, the reported recognition rates were 97% for Drost *et al.* and 96.7% for tensor matching, whereas our algorithm achieved 98.8% recognition rate. The improvement is even more prominent at larger occlusion rates. Our implementation using uniform weights is consistent with Drost *et al.* and achieved 95.8% recognition rate (only marginally lower) at less than 0.84 occlusion. By learning the weights, our algorithm significantly reduced the error by 71.4% for up to 0.84 occlusion and 55% for all the occlusion rates. This improvement was consistently observed for all of the four objects. Several examples of pose estimation using the proposed approach are shown in Figure 4. Note that Rodala *et al.* [26] have also reported competitive results on Mian *et al.*'s dataset. However, in that study the recognition rate was evaluated using the feature matching accuracy rather than the pose estimation error, therefore it is not possible to directly compare with our method.

4.2 Industrial Objects

In the second set of experiments, we conducted evaluation of the algorithm on both synthetic and real data using 5 industrial-style objects, namely circuit breaker (CB), clamp (CL), knob (KN), T-nut (TN), and L-shape (LS). These objects capture a wide spectrum of 3D object shape properties starting from simple planar shapes to more featured and semi-smooth surfaces to near and complete shape symmetries, generating various different challenges for recognition and pose estimation algorithms. Figure 6 shows renderings of 3D models of these objects on captured real scenes.

The real test scenes were captured using a structured light based 3D sensor under a challenging setup where all of these five shapes were placed in a bin in random poses to generate cluttered scenes with varying degrees of occlusion. We captured 450 such scenes and manually labeled ground truth poses of all 5 objects in each scene. A few example scenes and ground truth labels are shown in the top row of Figure 6, where labeled poses are overlayed on data. Since our

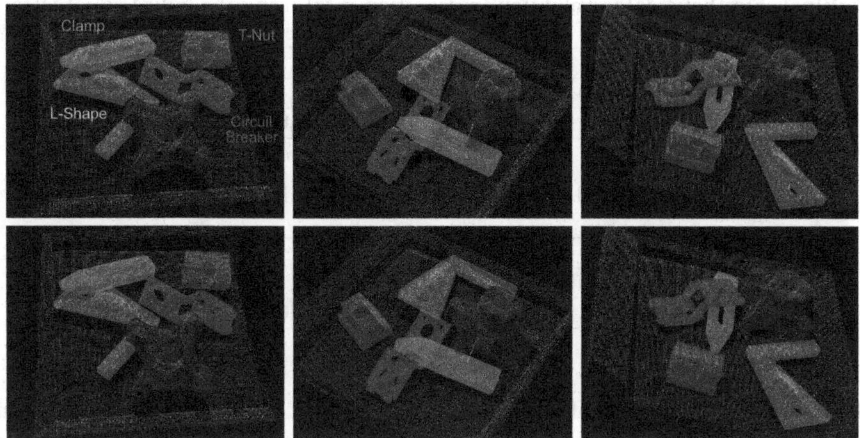

Fig. 6. Pose estimation examples for real industrial objects. (Top) Ground truth poses for each object. (Bottom) Estimated poses using weighted voting for each object.

results were saturated (only 1% failure case remained) using the Mian *et al.*'s dataset, this large scale and challenging test platform enabled us to better study the details of the proposed algorithm.

We replicated the real environment in simulation by rendering the 3D models of the objects under the same setup and generated training, validation and testing datasets, 500 each. In the simulation, maximum occlusion ratio was set to be 0.2 for training and validation and 0.6 for test scenes. Note that, similar to the previous experiment, training did not use any real data. In our evaluation, an estimated pose of the object was considered to be correct if the difference of the estimated pose and the ground truth pose was less than 5 millimeters in translation and 15 degrees in rotation, while the diameter of the largest object was 60 millimeters.

Many of these shapes contain large planar surfaces therefore edges encode valuable information. Unless otherwise stated, in all the experiments using this dataset we used the B2B pair feature, which was shown to provide a good compromise between speed and accuracy [6], and we used weighting hash table bins scheme to learn the weights.

Learning vs. Uniform Voting: We compared learning results with the baseline algorithm—uniform (equal) weights for each pair feature [7,6]. The results were computed for both synthetic and real data and are shown in Table 1 and Table 2, respectively. Synthetic and real experiments showed the same trend, and we achieved major performance boost (20% to 50% error reduction) with the learning framework except for the LS object. This shape is quite unique (distinct from other shapes and does not contain self symmetries), which was easy to identify using the B2B features; it was therefore reliably identified except for very large occlusions, leading to more modest improvement by learning. In

Table 1. Synthetic data evaluation (recognition rate) using the industrial objects

Objects	CB	CL	KN	TN	LS
Uniform	0.698	0.505	0.616	0.460	0.874
Learned	**0.834**	**0.708**	**0.852**	**0.528**	**0.876**

Table 2. Real data evaluation using the industrial objects

Objects	CB	CL	KN	TN	LS
Uniform	0.776	0.413	0.362	0.493	0.909
Learned	**0.871**	**0.720**	**0.522**	**0.684**	**0.922**

addition, synthetic and real data results were quite similar, showing that our synthesized scenes were good representations of the real scene leading to good generalization accuracy. Note that the performance difference for the KN object between synthetic and real data was due to small inaccuracy of the 3D model. In Figure 6, we superimpose the estimated poses on top of the captured data and observe that the estimations are very accurate.

Alternative Pair Features: We evaluated the learning algorithm for a different point pair feature, S2S, and also learned a fusion feature that is a combination of S2S and B2B features. In this experiment, we used the CB object and performed evaluation using real data. The S2S pair feature uses two points on the surface of the object. Since the CB object is mainly composed of two large planar surfaces, this feature is quite weak for the object. In addition, the scenes contained several large planes corresponding to the faces of the container bin, as seen in Figure 6. Due to these challenges, the S2S pair feature could only recover 19.6% of the poses in the scenes using uniform weights, and most of the time it confused the bin surfaces with the object (Table 3).

By learning the weights, the performance improved almost by an order to 36.4%. However, the performance was still far from the B2B feature due to the reasons explained above. Joint S2S and B2B feature retrieved 62.2% of the objects in the uniform case and this result improved to 83.7% using learning. Even though this result is not as high as just using B2B feature, we believe that an important factor contributing to the reduced performance was high dimensional feature space leading to overfitting and could be improved by generating more training data.

Weighting Strategies: We compared different weighting strategies that were discussed in Section 3: (1) weighting hash table bins and (2) weighting model points. The comparison is shown in Table 4. Both of the approaches led to significant improvement compared to the uniform weights. Weighting model points had only 1% less performance than weighting hash table bins strategy. For this experiment, using the CB object, learning the weights of hash table bins required optimization on a 39K dimensional space compared to 5.4K dimensions for weighting model points, one for each point.

Table 3. Comparison of different pair features for the CB object

Features	B2B	S2S	S2S+B2B
Uniform	0.776	0.196	0.622
Learned	**0.871**	**0.364**	**0.837**

Table 4. Comparison of weighting strategies for the CB object

Uniform	Weighting hash bins	Weighting model points
0.776	**0.871**	0.867

Figure 7 illustrates the output of the learning algorithm for the weighting model points strategy, where points with larger weights are drawn by bigger dots and more red in color. The learning algorithm identified non-robust boundary points, such as the ones on the small circles, which were not repeatable across different views, and deemphasized these points. This object has 180° near-symmetry, frequently causing confusion in pose estimation. This near-symmetry can only be resolved by the interior boundaries, which were highly weighted by the learning algorithm.

Effect of Regularization: We compared the different regularization schemes for the optimization problem. The results are given in Table 5. Although the performance difference is negligible, regularization based on $L1$-norm prefers a sparse set of weights, leading to a more strict feature selection. Compared to quadratic regularization which selects 24.5% of the hash table bins, $L1$-norm regularizer selects only 3.3%. This leads to an efficient implementation for the voting framework. However, rather than voting, the pose clustering process took the most computation in our implementation, hence no major speed improvement was observed. We note that, in other experiments, we observed that very sparse solutions can perform worse in challenging scenes such as large amount of noise and missing data.

Alternative Learning Strategies: We also tested other simple strategies for determining weights based on occupancy statistics: (1) Weights inversely proportional to the number of pairs that occupy the bin; (2) Weights inversely proportional to the square root of number of pairs within a bin. None of these simple strategies produced better results than uniform weighting. Even though some features may be repeated in the model many times or they frequently vote for incorrect poses, these features might still be necessary to resolve confusion among certain poses. Our max-margin framework optimizes for the voting function (difference of votes between correct and incorrect poses) jointly for all the features; thus it is optimal for the pose estimation task.

Cluttered Bin: We used the proposed algorithm to estimate the 3D poses of these objects in heavy clutter. Figure 8 shows three such scenes with our estimation results overlayed. As shown, the proposed algorithm was able to retrieve

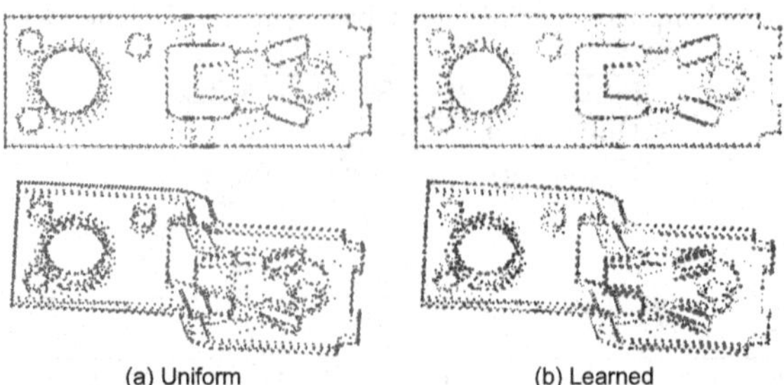

Fig. 7. Learning weights on model points. (a) Boundary points visualized with uniform weights used for B2B. (b) Boundary points visualized with weights (the larger the weights, the bigger and more red in color) learned by our algorithm.

Table 5. Comparison of regularization functions

Regularizer	Accuracy	# of selected hash bins	% of selected hash bins
Quadratic	0.871	9571	24.5%
$L1$-norm	**0.873**	**1275**	**3.3%**

several good pose candidates simultaneously. Please refer to the supplementary video for a robotic system using our algorithm in object grasping task.

Computational Requirement: Learning weights (offline) takes around 10 minutes per object model. Pose estimation time was less than 0.5s for industrial parts using 20% sampling of the B2B features ($\approx$ 1000 points). For the smooth object experiment, we sampled 5% of the dense S2S features ($\approx$ 4000 points). The pose estimation time in this experiment was 15s (vs. 85s in Drost *et al.* [7]).

5 Related Work and Discussion

Other than the local feature point based methods described in Section 1, there exists a large body of work that models 3D shapes globally such as using 2D/3D contours [3,4], shape templates [10,19], and feature histograms [33,12]. In general, these global methods require the target object in isolation and are more sensitive to occlusion. Also, the appearance change due to pose variations necessitates the use of a large number of shape templates, which has the drawback of increased memory footprint and matching time.

There exists many examples of learning interest point detectors and feature descriptors in computer vision, and here we discuss only a few closely related. Holzer *et al.* [11] presented a learning-based keypoint detector for range data. Unlike our approach, their learning model approximates an existing detector with a learned more efficient classifier, whereas our model identifies and weights features for a specific task and an object. Shotton *et al.* [28] combined simple

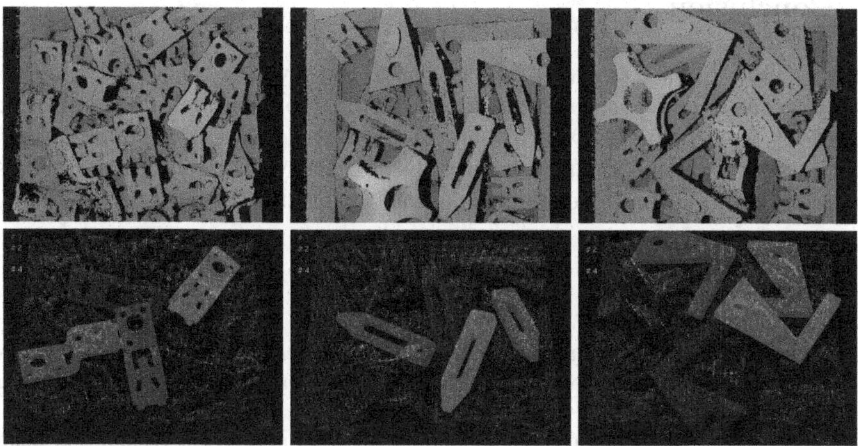

Fig. 8. Pose estimation for several different objects in cluttered bins

decision functions based on depth differences between pairs of points into a decision tree classifier for identification of human body parts. Moji and Malik [21] presented a 2D part based object detector where the contribution of each local part to a given object location is learned by optimizing a classification error cost. Similarly, Knopp *et al.* [17] proposed to weight the 3D features based on how often they vote for the correct shape center on a training set. In contrast, in our approach the 3D pose to vote is dynamically determined through matching features and the important features to match and their weights are learned by directly optimizing the voting function. In addition, our approach does not require a separate manually annotated training set and can learn the important features using only the 3D model of the object and simulation.

As explained in Section 3, to simplify the learning, we group sets of features and enforce them to have the same weight. The weighting scheme based on hash table bins has connection to well-known bag-of-words model, where hash keys can be considered the codewords mapping features to a histogram. However, even though the form of the function is the same, the setup of the learning problem is very different. In our problem, a hash table bin acts as a mid-level representation and votes for multiple different poses which are determined only during classification (based on matching between model and scene pairs features), rather than scoring a fixed set of classes which are predetermined as in bag-of-words model.

Similarly, learning the weights of a voting function has relations to learning ranking functions, which is extensively studied in machine learning community for information and image retrieval [14,5,13]. More notably, [25] learns mid-level object representations based on relative attributes. However, unlike these approaches, the relation of features to output is more indirect in our voting framework where a scene feature simultaneously votes for multiple poses and multiple different scene features vote for a given pose.

6 Conclusion

We presented a new framework to learn a weighted voting function for 3D object recognition and pose estimation tasks. Our approach identifies and ranks important features on a given 3D object by optimizing a discriminative cost function. We evaluated the algorithm on large scale synthetic and real datasets, and achieved major improvements compared to the state-of-the-art.

References

1. Bariya, P., Nishino, K.: Scale-hierarchical 3D object recognition in cluttered scenes. In: Proc. IEEE Conf. Computer Vision and Pattern Recognition (CVPR), pp. 1657–1664 (2010)
2. Belongie, S., Malik, J., Puzicha, J.: Shape matching and object recognition using shape contexts. IEEE Trans. Pattern Anal. Mach. Intell. 24(4), 509–522 (2002)
3. Bookstein, F.L.: Principal warps: Thin-plate splines and the decomposition of deformations. IEEE Trans. Pattern Anal. Mach. Intell. 11(6), 567–585 (1989)
4. Borgefors, G.: Hierarchical chamfer matching: A parametric edge matching algorithm. IEEE Trans. Pattern Anal. Mach. Intell. 10(6), 849–865 (1988)
5. Cao, Z., Qin, T., Liu, T.Y., Tsai, M.F., Li, H.: Learning to rank: From pairwise approach to listwise approach. In: Proc. Int'l Conf. Mach. Learning (ICML), pp. 129–136 (2007)
6. Choi, C., Taguchi, Y., Tuzel, O., Liu, M.Y., Ramalingam, S.: Voting-based pose estimation for robotic assembly using a 3D sensor. In: Proc. IEEE Int'l Conf. Robotics Automation (ICRA), pp. 1724–1731 (May 2012)
7. Drost, B., Ulrich, M., Navab, N., Ilic, S.: Model globally, match locally: Efficient and robust 3D object recognition. In: Proc. IEEE Conf. Computer Vision and Pattern Recognition (CVPR), pp. 998–1005 (June 2010)
8. Frome, A., Huber, D., Kolluri, R., Bülow, T., Malik, J.: Recognizing objects in range data using regional point descriptors. In: Pajdla, T., Matas, J. (eds.) ECCV 2004. LNCS, vol. 3023, pp. 224–237. Springer, Heidelberg (2004)
9. Harris, C., Stephens, M.: A combined corner and edge detector. In: Alvey Vision Conference, Manchester, UK, vol. 15, p. 50 (1988)
10. Hinterstoisser, S., Holzer, S., Cagniart, C., Ilic, S., Konolige, K., Navab, N., Lepetit, V.: Multimodal templates for real-time detection of texture-less objects in heavily cluttered scenes. In: Proc. IEEE Int'l Conf. Computer Vision (ICCV), pp. 858–865 (November 2011)
11. Holzer, S., Shotton, J., Kohli, P.: Learning to efficiently detect repeatable interest points in depth data. In: Fitzgibbon, A., Lazebnik, S., Perona, P., Sato, Y., Schmid, C. (eds.) ECCV 2012, Part I. LNCS, vol. 7572, pp. 200–213. Springer, Heidelberg (2012)
12. Horn, B.K.P.: Extended gaussian images. Proceedings of the IEEE 72(12), 1671–1686 (1984)
13. Jain, V., Varma, M.: Learning to re-rank: query-dependent image re-ranking using click data. In: Proc. Int'l Conf. World Wide Web, pp. 277–286 (2011)
14. Joachims, T.: Optimizing search engines using clickthrough data. In: Proceedings of the Eighth ACM SIGKDD International Conference on Knowledge discovery and Data Mining, pp. 133–142 (2002)

15. Johnson, A.E., Hebert, M.: Using spin images for efficient object recognition in cluttered 3D scenes. IEEE Trans. Pattern Anal. Mach. Intell. 21(5), 433–449 (1999)
16. Kelley Jr., J.E.: The cutting-plane method for solving convex programs. Journal of the Society for Industrial & Applied Mathematics 8(4), 703–712 (1960)
17. Knopp, J., Prasad, M., Willems, G., Timofte, R., Van Gool, L.: Hough transform and 3D SURF for robust three dimensional classification. In: Daniilidis, K., Maragos, P., Paragios, N. (eds.) ECCV 2010, Part VI. LNCS, vol. 6316, pp. 589–602. Springer, Heidelberg (2010)
18. Lamdan, Y., Wolfson, H.J.: Geometric hashing: A general and efficient model-based recognition scheme. In: Proc. IEEE Int'l Conf. Computer Vision (ICCV), vol. 88, pp. 238–249 (1988)
19. Liu, M.Y., Tuzel, O., Veeraraghavan, A., Chellappa, R.: Fast directional chamfer matching. In: Proc. IEEE Conf. Computer Vision and Pattern Recognition (CVPR), pp. 1696–1703 (June 2010)
20. Lowe, D.G.: Distinctive image features from scale-invariant keypoints. Int'l J. Computer Vision 60(2), 91–110 (2004)
21. Maji, S., Malik, J.: Object detection using a max-margin hough transform. In: Proc. IEEE Conf. Computer Vision and Pattern Recognition (CVPR), pp. 1038–1045 (2009)
22. Mian, A.S., Bennamoun, M., Owens, R.: Three-dimensional model-based object recognition and segmentation in cluttered scenes. IEEE Trans. Pattern Anal. Mach. Intell. 28, 1584–1601 (2006)
23. Mikolajczyk, K., Schmid, C.: Indexing based on scale invariant interest points. In: Proc. IEEE Int'l Conf. Computer Vision (ICCV), vol. 1, pp. 525–531 (2001)
24. Nguyen, H., Porikli, F.: Support vector shape: A classifier based shape representation. IEEE Trans. Pattern Anal. Mach. Intell. 35(4), 970–982 (2013)
25. Parikh, D., Grauman, K.: Relative attributes. In: Proc. IEEE Int'l Conf. Computer Vision (ICCV), pp. 503–510 (2011)
26. Rodolà, E., Albarelli, A., Bergamasco, F., Torsello, A.: A scale independent selection process for 3D object recognition in cluttered scenes. Int'l J. Computer Vision 102(1-3), 129–145 (2013)
27. Rusu, R.B., Blodow, N., Beetz, M.: Fast point feature histograms (FPFH) for 3D registration. In: Proc. IEEE Int'l Conf. Robotics Automation (ICRA), pp. 3212–3217 (May 2009)
28. Shotton, J., Fitzgibbon, A., Cook, M., Sharp, T., Finocchio, M., Moore, R., Kipman, A., Blake, A.: Real-time human pose recognition in parts from single depth images. In: Proc. IEEE Conf. Computer Vision and Pattern Recognition (CVPR), pp. 1297–1304 (June 2011)
29. Stein, F., Medioni, G.: Structural indexing: Efficient 3-D object recognition. IEEE Trans. Pattern Anal. Mach. Intell. 14(2), 125–145 (1992)
30. Taskar, B., Guestrin, C., Koller, D.: Max-margin markov networks. In: Proc. Neural Information Processing Systems (NIPS), vol. 16 (2003)
31. Tsochantaridis, I., Hofmann, T., Joachims, T., Altun, Y.: Support vector machine learning for interdependent and structured output spaces. In: Proc. Int'l Conf. Mach. Learning (ICML), p. 104 (2004)
32. Tutuncu, R., Toh, K., Todd, M.: Solving semidefinite-quadratic-linear programs using sdpt3. Mathematical Programming Ser. B 95, 198–217 (2003)
33. Wahl, E., Hillenbrand, U., Hirzinger, G.: Surflet-pair-relation histograms: A statistical 3D-shape representation for rapid classification. In: Proc. Int'l Conf. 3-D Digital Imaging and Modeling (3DIM), pp. 474–481 (October 2003)

Salient Color Names for Person Re-identification

Yang Yang[1], Jimei Yang[2], Junjie Yan[1],
Shengcai Liao[1], Dong Yi[1], and Stan Z. Li[1,⋆]

[1] Center for Biometrics and Security Research & National Laboratory of Pattern Recognition, Institute of Automation, Chinese Academy of Sciences
[2] University of California, Merced
{yang.yang,jjyan,scliao,dong.yi,szli}@nlpr.ia.ac.cn, jyang44@ucmerced.edu

Abstract. Color naming, which relates colors with color names, can help people with a semantic analysis of images in many computer vision applications. In this paper, we propose a novel salient color names based color descriptor (SCNCD) to describe colors. SCNCD utilizes salient color names to guarantee that a higher probability will be assigned to the color name which is nearer to the color. Based on SCNCD, color distributions over color names in different color spaces are then obtained and fused to generate a feature representation. Moreover, the effect of background information is employed and analyzed for person re-identification. With a simple metric learning method, the proposed approach outperforms the state-of-the-art performance (without user's feedback optimization) on two challenging datasets (VIPeR and PRID 450S). More importantly, the proposed feature can be obtained very fast if we compute SCNCD of each color in advance.

Keywords: Salient color names, color descriptor, feature representation, person re-identification.

1 Introduction

Person re-identification is an important topic in visual surveillance. Its goal is to recognize an individual over disjoint camera views. It is a very challenging task because the appearance of an individual can be of significant difference in different viewpoints, illumination, poses, etc. Partial occlusions, low resolution and background interference add to the intractability of person re-identification.

To address these challenges in person re-identification, many researchers have proposed different strategies which can be summarized as two stages: (1) **feature representation** (e.g. [1,4,18,15,13,31,12,7]), which is our main concern in this paper and (2) **person matching** (e.g. [30,19,28,6,11,5,32,14]).

Color and texture are the most commonly used appearance based features for person re-identification. Texture descriptors such as Maximally Stable Color Regions (MSCR) [1], Local Binary Patterns (LBP) [6,11,5] and 21 texture filters (8 Gablor filters and 13 Schmid fiters) [15] have been successfully applied to

⋆ Corresponding Author.

D. Fleet et al. (Eds.): ECCV 2014, Part I, LNCS 8689, pp. 536–551, 2014.
© Springer International Publishing Switzerland 2014

address the problem of person re-identification. But color information, in comparison with texture information, seems to be a more important cue due to the fact that in most cases, only low-resolution images can be obtained. Traditional color information such as color histogram, a simple yet effective feature representation, is most widely used in [1,4,18,15,13,31,12,19,6,11,5,32]. With the consideration of the influence of illumination variations, we calculate color histograms in different color spaces separately and fuse them to make the final feature more robust to illumination changes. However, the performance of feature representation by means of color histograms is sill not satisfactory. Since color names show good robustness to photometric variance [26], an alternative approach is to apply color names to describe colors [12,27,10,26].

In this paper, we propose a novel salient color names based color descriptor (SCNCD) for person re-identification. An example of SCNCD is illustrated in Fig. 1. Different from [27] which is based on Google images, we employ 16 colors[1] from 16-color palette in RGB color space as color names in SCNCD, including fuchsia, blue, aqua, lime, yellow, red, purple, navy, teal, green, olive, maroon, black, gray, silver and white. Inspired by the idea of saliency [8] which is also reflected in other classic coding strategies (e.g. locality-constrained linear coding (LLC) [24], salient coding (SC) [8], local manifold-constrained coding (LMC) [29] and localized soft-assignment coding (LSC) [16]) in image classification, we assign the color's salient color names with nonzero values. Salient color names indicate that one color only have a certain probability of being assigned to several nearest color names, and that the closer one owns a higher probability. For the purpose of making the SCNCD relatively less sensitive to small RGB value changes caused by variations of incident illumination, we employ index to make colors owning the same index have the same color descriptor. The role of index is similar to that of bins to color histogram or that of clusters to bag-of-words model.

To achieve the feature representation, we choose a part-based model [23] which divides each image into six horizontal stripes of equal size, shown in Fig. 2(a) and (c). On the basis of SCNCD, we can obtain the color distribution over the color names (named as color names distribution in this paper) in each part. Examples are shown in Fig. 2(b) and (d). Then, color names distributions of all parts are fused to form an image-level feature. In addition, due to the fact that the background can provide scene context for classification [21], the effect of background information is employed and analyzed for person re-identification. In the stage of person matching, we adopt a fast and effective approach - Keep It Simple and Straightforward MEtric (KISSME) [11,20]. Experimental results show that our proposed method greatly outperforms the state-of-the-art performance on two challenging datasets (VIPeR and PRID 450S).

Contributions. The main contributions of this paper can be summarized as follows. (1) A novel salient color names based color descriptor is proposed for person re-identification. Experimental results demonstrate that SCNCD has shown better

[1] Refer to: `http://www.wackerart.de/rgbfarben.html`

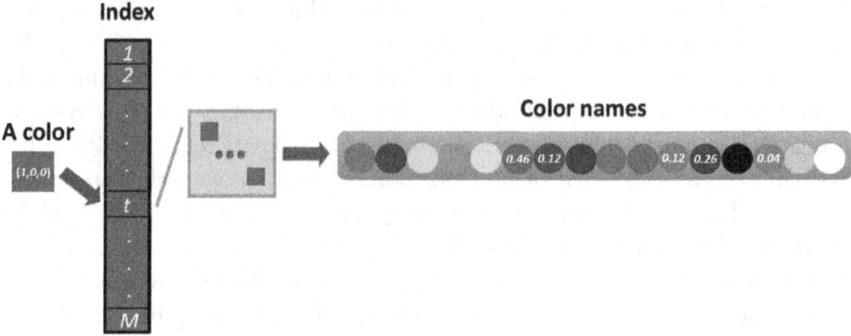

Fig. 1. An example of salient color names based color descriptor. The value corresponding to a color name denotes the probability of the set of colors, the indexes of which are the same, being assigned to this color name. It is noted that only several color names have nonzero values.

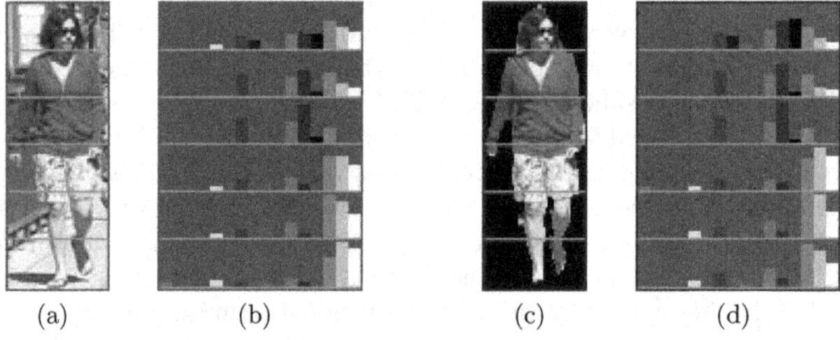

Fig. 2. An example of the color names distribution of a person image from VIPeR dataset. (a) Divide an image into six parts; (b) Color names distribution of each part of the image based on the SCNCD; (c) Divide the foreground (object of interest) into six parts; The mask used is automatically extracted by using the approach in [9]; (d) Color names distribution of each part of the foreground based on the SCNCD.

performance than the previous color descriptor. (2) Background information is exploited to enrich the feature representation for person re-identification. With it, we can obtain an image-foreground feature representation which is of good robustness against background interference and partial occlusion. (3) Since there is no single color model or descriptor which has the characteristic of robustness against all the types of illumination changes [2,22], features based on color names distributions and color histograms are fused to compensate each other which are computed in four different color spaces including original RGB, rgb, $l_1l_2l_3$ [2] and HSV.

2 Related Work

To tackle the problem of person re-identification, many researchers have proposed different approaches the focus of which can be roughly divided into **feature representation** and **person matching**.

Feature Representation. For the sake of describing a person's appearance, many of the existing approaches try to learn a stable as well as very distinctive feature representation. To address the problem of viewpoint changes, Gray *et al.* [4] propose an ensemble of localized features (ELF) to obtain a better representation. Farenzena *et al.* [1] extract three types of features to model the complementary aspects of human appearance, including weighted color histograms, maximally stable color regions (MSCR) and recurrent high-structured patches (RHSP). The algorithm reported in [1] achieves certain robustness against very low resolution, occlusions and pose, viewpoint and illumination changes. The drawback of this feature representation is that it is very time-consuming to extract these three types of features.

Features based on different color spaces and textures are all employed to represent the images, but what features are more important? In [15], Liu *et al.* present a novel unsupervised method to weigh the importance of different features. Experimental results show that the importance of features including different color spaces and textures is different under different circumstances and that instead of treating all features equally, endowing informative feature with a larger weight when different features are fused can lead to better results. The problem of person re-identification is revisited by means of color distribution in [13]. Kviatkovsky *et al.* [13] propose a novel illumination-invariant feature representation based on logchromaticity (log) color space and demonstrate that color as a single cue has a relatively good performance in identifying persons under greatly varying imaging conditions. In consideration of many existing approaches neglecting valuable salient information in matching persons, Zhao *et al.* [31] put forward an unsupervised framework to extract discriminative features for person re-identification and then patch matching is employed with adjacency constraint. The salience in [31] is specially designed to match persons and is robust to different pose, viewpoint variations and articulation. However, traditional color information may not be the optimal way of describing color. Thus, Kuo *et al.* [12] employ semantic color names, which are learned in [27] to describe color and achieve improvements over the state-of-art methods on VIPeR dataset.

Person Matching. Another line of research pays more attention to how to match persons efficiently. For instance, Zheng *et al.* [32] formulate person re-identification as a distance learning problem regardless of the choice of representation. A novel probabilistic relative distance comparison (PRDC) model is proposed which aims to maximise the probability of similar pairs having a smaller distance than that of dissimilar pairs. To solve the problem caused by different camera angles, Hirzer *et al.* [5] learn a Mahalanobis metric learning by employing similar pairs from different cameras. Then a linear projection is obtained that keeps similar pairs together whilst pushes impostors. In [6], a relaxed pairwise metric learning is presented to learn a discriminative Mahalanobis for matching persons from different cameras. It should be noted that a simple yet effective strategy named KISSME is introduced in [11] to learn a distance metric from equivalence constraints from a statistical inference perspective.

Recently, Zhao *et al.* [30] exploit salience matching, which is tightly integrated with patch matching in a unified structural RankSVM learning framework, to match persons over disjoint camera views. In [19], the local fisher discriminant analysis (LFDA) is applied to learn a distance metric for person re-identification problem. After dimensionality reduction, the obtained features can be classified by the nearest neighbor method. Different from the afore-mentioned matching approaches which refer to the target individual as a reference template, Xu *et al.* [28] represent an person image as a compositional part-based template, which introduces flexibility to the matching formulation of person re-identification.

3 Proposed Method

In this section, we first introduce salient color names to describe colors. Color names distribution of a person image is then obtained based on the SCNCD. In addition, background information is employed to form different feature representations that are then fused to obtain the final feature representation. At the end of this section, we will briefly review a simple metric learning method - KISSME.

3.1 Salient Color Names Based Color Descriptor

Color distribution [15,13,6,11,5,2,22] has been widely used to describe a person image in person re-identification. However, it is a challenging task to describe colors because many factors can lead to variations in RGB values, such as variations in illumination and viewpoints. To increase photometric invariance, different color models and descriptors have been presented and evaluated in [2,22]. But no single color model or descriptor has the characteristic of robustness against all the types of illumination changes. Worse still, photometric invariance is often increased at the cost of lowering discriminative ability. To make up the deficiency of RGB values, color names are employed as an alternative way of describing colors in [12,27,26,17]. Experimental results in [17] demonstrate that color description based on color names has a good robustness against photometric variance. Thus, the objective of this subsection is to present a novel approach of describing colors.

To describe colors based on color names, an appropriate mapping from RGB values of a image to color names is required. In this paper, we choose a probability distribution over the color names as a mapping method. Motivated by the idea of saliency, we put forward a novel concept of salient color names. To be specific, for each color to be named, salient color names indicate that this color only has a certain probability of being assigned to several nearest color names, and that the closer the color name is to the color, the higher probability the color has of being assigned to this color name. Fig. 1 gives an example of the salient color names representation of a color. Similar to color histogram or bag-of-words model which assigns a color (or a feature) to bins or 'words' respectively instead of all elements, we introduce index for our SCNCD. Through this way, we can assign multiple similar colors to the same index with the same color description. In the following, we explain in detail how to compute color description of these similar colors.

Throughout the paper, each channel in all color space is normalized to the range $[0, 1]$. The initial RGB color space is discretized into M indexes. In our case M is $32{\times}32 \times 32 = 32768$ of equally spaced grid points in the RGB cube. Therefore, there are $8 \times 8 \times 8 = 512$ colors for each index. We define $\boldsymbol{d} = \{\boldsymbol{w}_1, ..., \boldsymbol{w}_{512}\}$ as a set of colors the indexes of which are the same. The remaining question is how to calculate the salient color names representation of $\boldsymbol{d}$.

Assume $\boldsymbol{Z} = [\boldsymbol{z}_1, \boldsymbol{z}_2, ..., \boldsymbol{z}_{16}]$ denotes a set of 16 color names defined in the introduction, then the probability of assigning $\boldsymbol{d}$ to a color name $\boldsymbol{z}$ is

$$p(\boldsymbol{z}|\boldsymbol{d}) = \sum_{n=1}^{512} p(\boldsymbol{z}|\boldsymbol{w}_n) p(\boldsymbol{w}_n|\boldsymbol{d}), \tag{1}$$

with $p(\boldsymbol{z}|\boldsymbol{w}_n) =$

$$\begin{cases} \dfrac{\exp\left(-\|\boldsymbol{z}-\boldsymbol{w}_n\|^2 / \frac{1}{K-1}\sum_{\boldsymbol{z}_l \neq \boldsymbol{z}} \|\boldsymbol{z}_l-\boldsymbol{w}_n\|^2\right)}{\sum_{p=1}^{K} \exp\left(-\|\boldsymbol{z}_p-\boldsymbol{w}_n\|^2 / \frac{1}{K-1}\sum_{\boldsymbol{z}_s \neq \boldsymbol{z}_p} \|\boldsymbol{z}_s-\boldsymbol{w}_n\|^2\right)} , & if\ \boldsymbol{z} \in KNN(\boldsymbol{w}_n) \\ 0 , & otherwise \end{cases} \tag{2}$$

and

$$p(\boldsymbol{w}_n|\boldsymbol{d}) = \frac{\exp\left(-\alpha\|\boldsymbol{w}_n - \boldsymbol{\mu}\|^2\right)}{\sum_{l=1}^{512} \exp\left(-\alpha\|\boldsymbol{w}_l - \boldsymbol{\mu}\|^2\right)}. \tag{3}$$

where K means the number of nearest neighbors, $\boldsymbol{\mu}$ refers to the mean of $\boldsymbol{w}_n$ $(n = 1, ..., 512)$. In Eq. (2), $\boldsymbol{z}_p$, $\boldsymbol{z}_l$ and $\boldsymbol{z}_s$ $(p, l, s = 1, ..., K)$ belong to K nearest color names of $\boldsymbol{w}_n$. To reflect the saliency of the salient color names for $\boldsymbol{d}$, we first use the KNN algorithm to find K nearest color names of $\boldsymbol{w}_n$ in Euclidean space. Then, the difference between the one of K nearest color names to the other K - 1 color names is utilized to embody the saliency as in [8]. To calculate the saliency degree, we employ a better function $\Phi(t) = \exp(-t)$ instead of [8] which uses $\Phi(t) = 1-t$. After normalization, the probability distribution of $\boldsymbol{w}_n$ over 16 color names is defined as Eq. (2). To further obtain the final probability of $\boldsymbol{d}$ being assigned to color names, Eq. (3) is employed to weigh the contribution of w_n to the $\boldsymbol{d}$. It can be seen in Eq. (3) that the nearer of $\boldsymbol{w}_n$ to $\boldsymbol{\mu}$, the more it contributes to $\boldsymbol{d}$. With Eq. (1), we can describe each set of colors based on their salient color names. We refer to this type of color description as SCNCD in this paper. The biggest difference between salient coding and our SCNCD lies that SCNCD is a description of the probability distribution over its salient color names while salient coding has no relationship with probability distribution. Besides, based on SCNCD, multiple similar colors have the same color description, which increases its illumination invariance. In section 4, we will compare our SCNCD with salient coding which we take as a mapping method from RGB to color names in this paper.

Because all colors in the same set (or have the same index) possess the same salient color names, the salient color names representation of $\boldsymbol{d}$ is also that of the color belonging to the set $\boldsymbol{d}$. Moreover, it is easy to prove that the sum of the distribution of $\boldsymbol{d}$ over all color names $\boldsymbol{z}_m$, $m = 1, ..., 16$ is 1, i.e. $\sum_{m=1}^{16} p(\boldsymbol{z}_m|\boldsymbol{d}) = 1$.

SCNCD has the following advantages:

1. Each color in RGB color space is represented by the probability distribution over its salient color names. Furthermore, to get the salient color names representation, we not only compare the difference among salient color names, but also compare the probability of a color being assigned to each salient color name with that of a color being assigned to overall salient color names. In this way, a relatively reasonable probability distribution can be achieved.

2. It can achieve a certain amount of illumination invariance. Because small RGB value changes caused by illumination will have the same color description if only their indexes are the same.

3. It does not rely on complex optimization and is easy to implement. More importantly, it is very fast because all salient color names representation can be computed offline. Then, we just need to compute each color's index and assign it with its corresponding set's salient color names representation.

3.2 Feature Representation

Once we have achieved the distribution of each color over color names, we can employ them to describe all colors. To capture the color information of an image, we compute color names distribution of an image with the aid of SCNCD. In the following, we first explain in details how to calculate the color names distribution and then show different feature representations.

Color Names Distribution. Because the human body is not rigid, a part-based model [23] is selected instead of taking a person image as a whole. Similar to [15], we partition an image into six horizontal stripes of equal size, as is shown in Fig. 2(a) and (c).

We can find that six parts including the head, upper and lower torso, upper and lower legs and the feet are roughly captured. Let $\boldsymbol{H} = [\boldsymbol{h}_1, ..., \boldsymbol{h}_6]^T$ be the color names distribution of a person image, then the m-th, $m = 1, ..., 16$ element of the distribution of i-th part $\boldsymbol{h}_i = [h_{i1}, ..., h_{i16}]$ is defined as

$$h_{im} = \frac{\sum_{k=1}^{N} p(\boldsymbol{z}_m|\boldsymbol{x}_{ik})}{\sum_{m=1}^{16} \sum_{k=1}^{N} p(\boldsymbol{z}_m|\boldsymbol{x}_{ik})}, \tag{4}$$

where $\boldsymbol{x}_{ik}$, $k = 1, ..., N$, means the k-th color (or pixel) in part i, and N denotes the total number of colors in part i. An example of the color names distribution in each part of a person image is shown in Fig. 2(b) and (d). The bin of color name m denotes the probability of all colors in the corresponding part being assigned to color name m. Similar color names distribution can be obtained except the parts of head and feet between the image and foreground.

Foreground and Background Based Feature Representation. In image classification, it is demonstrated in [21] that background can provide scene context and improve classification accuracy. However, due to the fact that the background in person re-identification is not constant and may even include disturbing factors, background feature representation combined directly with the foreground feature representation will reduce the classification accuracy. To address this problem, we introduce image-foreground feature representation, which can be seen as that the foreground information is employed as the main information while the background information is treated as the secondary one. It alleviates the negative influence of noisy background.

We first introduce image-only and foreground feature representations. (1) **Image-only.** Inspired by the weighted color histograms [1], we endow each pixel $\boldsymbol{x}_{ik}$ with a different weight ω_{ik}:

$$\omega_{ik} = exp(-\frac{(y_{ik} - \mu)^2}{2\sigma^2}), \tag{5}$$

where $\mu = L/2$ and $\sigma = L/4$. In Eq. (5), y_{ik} denotes the column of $\boldsymbol{x}_{ik}$ in the image matrix whose column equals to the image width L. Then, h_{im} defined as Eq. 4 is transformed into

$$h_{im} = \frac{\sum_{k=1}^{N} \omega_{ik} p(\boldsymbol{z}_m|\boldsymbol{x}_{ik})}{\sum_{m=1}^{16}\sum_{k=1}^{N} \omega_{ik} p(\boldsymbol{z}_m|\boldsymbol{x}_{ik})}, \tag{6}$$

where ω_{ik} means the weight of the color $\boldsymbol{x}_{ik}$. (2) **Foreground.** To obtain the foreground representation, we need a mask to extract the object of interest. In this paper, we use the mask which is automatically obtained by the method [9] with the parameter settings used in [1]. It is a commonly used mask (or a revised mask) in person re-identification [1,18,23,20]. Color names distribution can be obtained according to Eq. (6) for foreground feature representation. Then, image-only and foreground feature representations are concatenated to form the **image-foreground** feature representation.

Fusion of Different Features. Since there is no single color model or descriptor which has the characteristic of robustness against all types of illumination changes [2,22], features based on four different color models including original RGB, normalized *rgb*, $l_1l_2l_3$ [2] and HSV are selected and fused to compensate each other. Because the range of pixel values of them in each channel are from 0 to 1, we can take them as a type of transformation of RGB values.

$$(\theta) = \mathcal{T}(\theta_o), \tag{7}$$

where θ_o (or θ) denotes the original RGB value (or the transformed RGB value) while $\mathcal{T}$ means a transformation approach. For example, the transformation for normalized *rgb* is

$$\mathcal{T}(a, b, c) = (a/(a + b + c), b/(a + b + c), c/(a + b + c)). \tag{8}$$

In addition, color histogram is also fused with color names distribution to improve the accuracy. Then, the final image-foreground feature representation is obtained by concatenating all image-foreground feature representations which are based on color names distribution and color histograms over the four different color models.

3.3 Person Matching

Mahalanobis distance learning has attracted considerable attention in computer vision. Given a pair of samples $\boldsymbol{x}_i$ and $\boldsymbol{x}_j$ ($\boldsymbol{x}_i, \boldsymbol{x}_j \in \mathcal{R}^d$), the Mahalanobis distance between them is

$$d_M^2(\boldsymbol{x}_i, \boldsymbol{x}_j) = (\boldsymbol{x}_i - \boldsymbol{x}_j)^T \boldsymbol{M} (\boldsymbol{x}_i - \boldsymbol{x}_j). \tag{9}$$

where $\boldsymbol{M} \geqslant 0$ is a positive semidefinite matrix. From a statistical inference point of view, KISSME defines the Mahalanobis distance matrix $\boldsymbol{M}$ by

$$\boldsymbol{M} = \Sigma_{\mathcal{S}}^{-1} - \Sigma_{\mathcal{D}}^{-1}. \tag{10}$$

where

$$\Sigma_{\mathcal{S}} = \frac{1}{|\mathcal{S}|} \sum_{\boldsymbol{x}_i, \boldsymbol{x}_j \in \mathcal{S}} (\boldsymbol{x}_i - \boldsymbol{x}_j)(\boldsymbol{x}_i - \boldsymbol{x}_j)^T, \tag{11}$$

$$\Sigma_{\mathcal{D}} = \frac{1}{|\mathcal{D}|} \sum_{\boldsymbol{x}_i, \boldsymbol{x}_j \in \mathcal{D}} (\boldsymbol{x}_i - \boldsymbol{x}_j)(\boldsymbol{x}_i - \boldsymbol{x}_j)^T. \tag{12}$$

denote the covariance matrices for similar pairs $\mathcal{S}$ and dissimilar pairs $\mathcal{D}$ respectively. Then, $\boldsymbol{M}$ can be learned easily from the training samples. More details can be found in KISSME [11,20].

4 Experiments

In this section, we evaluate our method on two publicly available datasets (VIPeR dataset [3] and PRID 450S dataset [20]). VIPeR dataset is commonly employed for single-shot re-identification while PRID 450S dataset is a recently published dataset and is more realistic than VIPeR dataset. Each person has one image pair in both datasets. Therefore, the single-shot evaluation strategy [1] (described specifically in the following experimental settings) can be used. All the results are shown in form of Cumulated Matching Characteristic (CMC) curve [25].

4.1 Settings

In our experiment, we randomly choose half image pairs for training and the remaining half image pairs are used for test. In the stage of test, images from one camera are treated as probe and those from the other camera as gallery.

Then, we switched the probe and gallery. The average of the results is regarded as one-trial CMC result. Similar to [19,11], we repeat 100 trials of evaluation and report the average result to achieve a more stable results in the following. When we calculate the SCNCD, the number of nearest neighbor of intermediate variable $\boldsymbol{w}_n$ in Eq. (2) is set to 5. α is set to 1 in Eq. (3). As in [11,20], the principal component analysis (PCA) is employed to reduce the computational efforts before KISSME is applied. When we compute the color histogram, the number of bins of each channel is set to 32 for all color models. In the following, we name **image**-only, **foreg**round and **image-f**oreground feature representations as *Img*, *Forg* and *ImgF* respectively.

(a)

(b)

Fig. 3. Some examples from the datasets: (a)VIPeR and (b) PRID 450S

4.2 VIPeR Dataset

This is a challenging dataset[2] for viewpoint invariant pedestrian recognition (VIPeR), suffering from arbitrary viewpoints, pose changes and illumination variations between two camera views. It contains 632 image pairs, which correspond to 632 persons and are captured by two cameras in outdoor academic environment. Images from Camera A are mostly captured from 0 degree to 90 degree and that from Camera B mostly from 90 degree to 180 degree. In experiments, we normalize all images to 128×48 pixels. Some examples from VIPeR are shown in Fig. 3(a).

Comparison with the State-of-the-art Methods. We compare our methods ($SCNCD_{all}$(*ImgF*) and Final(*ImgF*)) with the state-of-the-art methods on VIPeR dataset. $SCNCD_{all}$(*ImgF*) refers to *ImgF*s of SCNCD over four color models while Final(*ImgF*) means all the *ImgF*s of color names distributions and color histograms over four color spaces are concatenated. The compared methods are following the same evaluation protocol as ours. The dimensions of the features are reduced to 70 by PCA.

Table 1 shows that both $SCNCD_{all}$(*ImgF*) and Final(*ImgF*) outperform others. We can also find that when we fuse the $SCNCD_{all}$(*ImgF*) with different

[2] Available at: `http://vision.soe.ucsc.edu/?q=node/178`

Table 1. Comparison with the state-of-the-art methods on VIPeR dataset

Rank	1	5	10	15	20	25	30	50
PRDC[32]	15.7	38.4	53.9	-	70.1	-	-	-
Fusing+PRDC[15]	16.1	37.7	51.0	-	66.0	-	-	-
RPLM[6]	27	-	69	-	83	-	-	95
EIML[5]	22	-	63	-	78	-	-	93
KISSME[11]	19.6	-	62.2	-	-	80.7	-	91.8
KISSME*[20]	27.0	-	70.0	-	83.0	-	-	95
eSDC-ocsvm[31]	26.7	50.7	62.4	-	76.4	-	-	-
RankBoost[12]	23.9	45.6	56.2	-	68.7	-	-	-
LF[19]	24.2	-	67.1	-	-	85.1	-	94.1
Salience[30]	30.2	52.3	-	-	-	-	-	-
SCNCD$_{all}$(*ImgF*)	**33.7**	**62.7**	**74.8**	**81.3**	**85.0**	**87.7**	**89.6**	**93.8**
Final(*ImgF*)	**37.8**	**68.5**	**81.2**	**87.0**	**90.4**	**92.7**	**94.2**	**97.0**

color histograms, the obtained Final(*ImgF*) leads to a 4.1% improvement compared to $SCNCD_{all}$(*ImgF*) at rank 1. In addition, by comparing our approaches with approaches used in [11] and [20], our feature representation shows more effectiveness.

4.3 PRID 450S Dataset

PRID 450S dataset[3] is a new and more realistic dataset. It contains 450 single-shot image pairs captured over two spatially disjoint camera views. Fig 3(b) shows some examples from PRID 450S dataset. It is also a challenging person re-identification dataset due to different viewpoint changes, background interference, partial occlusion and viewpoint changes. In experiments, each image is normalized to 168×80 pixels.

Comparison with the State-of-the-art Methods. Because the PRID 450S is a new dataset, few methods have been tested on it. We only compare our approach with the best results reported in [20] which uses the existing methods. We use $SCNCD_{all}$(*ImgF*) and Final(*ImgF*). The dimensions of the features are reduced to 70 by PCA.

It is shown in Table 2 that our proposed methods outperform KISSME [11] and EIML [5] both of which employ the precise masks (generated manually). Specifically, the results of $SCNCD_{all}$(*ImgF*) and Final(*ImgF*) are at least 6.0% higher than the best result EIML[5] at rank 1. On the PRID 450S dataset, the improvement from $SCNCD_{all}$(*ImgF*) to Final(*ImgF*) is not as great as that in VIPeR dataset. This is because there are background noise and partial occlusion in PRID 450S dataset, which influences the performance of the color histograms.

[3] Available at: `https://lrs.icg.tugraz.at/download.php`

Table 2. Comparison with the state-of-the-art methods on PRID 450S dataset. KISSME* and EIML employ precise masks (generated manually). Our proposed methods employ the masks (generated automatically).

Rank	1	5	10	15	20	25	30	50
KISSME*[20]	33.0	-	71.0	-	79.0	-	-	90.0
EIML[5]	35	-	68	-	77	-	-	90
SCNCD$_{all}$(*ImgF*)	**41.5**	**66.6**	**75.9**	**81.1**	**84.4**	**86.7**	**88.4**	**92.4**
Final(*ImgF*)	**41.6**	**68.9**	**79.4**	**84.9**	**87.8**	**90.0**	**91.8**	**95.4**

4.4 Analysis of SCNCD

The performance of the proposed SCNCD is analyzed in the following:

Comparison with Other Color Descriptions. We compare our proposed SCNCD with several existing color descriptions on both VIPeR dataset and PRID 450S dataset, including color histogram, discriminative descriptor (DD) [10], the color names (CN) [27], semantic color names (SCN) [17] and salient coding representation (SCR) [8].

Table 3. Comparison with different color descriptions on VIPeR dataset. All six color descriptions are calculated in RGB color space. *Img* is employed for them.

Rank	1	5	10	15	20	25	30	50
Hist(RGB)	6.5	22.8	34.8	43.4	50.5	55.9	60.3	72.6
SCN[17]	11.9	32.3	45.9	55.0	61.8	67.1	71.4	83.7
SCR[8]	12.5	32.9	45.9	54.3	60.4	65.0	68.9	79.1
DD[10]	17.6	40.3	52.4	60.2	66.0	70.3	73.6	82.7
CN[27]	19.6	44.2	58.1	66.3	72.3	76.9	80.4	88.8
SCNCD(Ours)	**20.7**	**47.2**	**60.6**	**68.8**	**75.1**	**79.1**	**82.4**	**90.4**

For DD, we choose the best setting, namely 25 clusters. To obtain SCR, we employ salient coding [8] to map the color to color names and treat the mapping coefficients the color's description. To evaluate the performance of those six color descriptions fairly, we compute all of them based on *Img* in RGB color space while KISSME is employed as a matching method. The dimension is reduced to 34 (the same as in [11,20]) using PCA. It can be seen from Tables 3 and 4 that our proposed SCNCD outperforms all of other color descriptions on both datasets at all ranks.

***Img* v.s. *Forg* v.s. *ImgF*.** Three types of feature representations are shown in section 3.2, including *Img*, *Forg* and *ImgF*. We compare the performances of them on VIPeR and PRID 450S datasets. RGB color model is selected for

Table 4. Comparison with different color descriptions on PRID 450S dataset. All six color descriptions are calculated in RGB color space. *Img* is employed for them.

Rank	1	5	10	15	20	25	30	50
Hist(RGB)	4.9	17.6	28.7	36.7	43.6	49.2	54.0	68.0
SCN[17]	6.6	20.7	31.6	39.3	46.0	51.6	56.2	70.0
SCR[8]	9.6	26.2	37.0	44.4	49.8	54.8	59.1	70.4
DD[10]	17.6	40.3	52.4	60.2	66.0	70.3	73.6	82.7
CN[27]	20.4	42.6	53.3	60.3	65.3	68.9	71.8	79.3
SCNCD(Ours)	**26.9**	**52.9**	**64.2**	**70.4**	**74.9**	**78.0**	**80.4**	**87.3**

SCNCD. The dimension of *Img* (or *Forg*) is reduced to 34 by PCA while the dimension of *ImgF* 50.

In Fig. 4(a) and (b), *ImgF* shows better performance than traditional *Img* and *Forg* on the VIPeR and PRID 450S datasets. In addition, we can see from Fig. 4(a) that *Forg* yields similar results as *Img* on VIPeR dataset while Fig. 4(b) shows that *Forg* significantly outperforms *Img* on PRID 450S dataset. This phenomenon demonstrates that there is much more background noise in PRID 450S than in VIPeR. This is why the improvement in PRID 450S is not as great as in VIPeR when the background information is added in *ImF*.

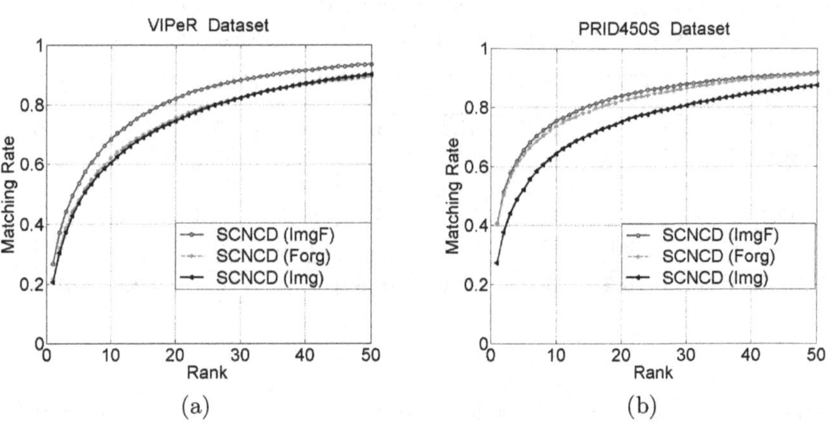

Fig. 4. Performances of different feature representations on: (a)VIPeR and (b) PRID 450S based on SCNCD in RGB color space.

SCNCD with Color Models. We employ four color models for SCNCD when we calculate the color names distribution of a person in section 3.2. Since these color modes are used to address the problems of illumination changes in [2,22], we choose VIPeR dataset to test our approach which suffers from illumination variations between two cameras. Features based on different color models including original RGB, normalized *rgb*, $l_1l_2l_3$ and HSV as well as feature obtained

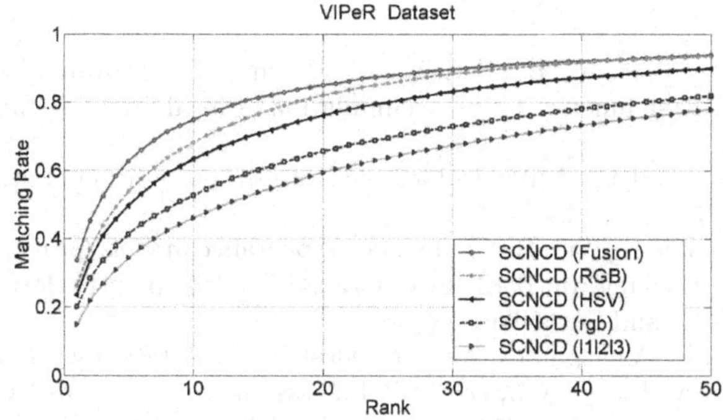

Fig. 5. Different color models are compared based on SCNCD

by fusing them are compared. *ImgF* is selected as the feature representation. The dimensions of features based on different color models are reduced to 50 by PCA while the dimension of the fusing feature 70. Fig. 5 shows the experimental results. It can be seen that among the four color models, SCNCD based on RGB achieves the best results. Thus, SCNCD shows a certain amount of illumination changes. Moreover, when we fuse these features computed under different color models, the recognition accuracy is improved significantly. It benefits from that these color models are invariant to different types of illumination [2].

5 Conclusion

In this paper, we propose a novel method to describe a color by its salient color names. It is very fast because each color can be represented by its corresponding index's color names representation which is precomputed. Then, color names distributions are computed over different color models and fused to address the illumination problem. Background information is added in the image-foreground feature representation. To improve the recognition accuracy, other color distribution methods based on different color histograms are also fused with color names distribution. Finally, we formulate the person re-identification problem as a color distribution matching problem. Experiments demonstrate that our proposed SCNCD possesses a certain robustness with background interference and partial occlusion and that the final image-foreground feature representation significantly improves the recognition accuracy of person re-identification.

Acknowledgments. This work was supported by the Chinese National Natural Science Foundation Projects #61105023, #61103156, #61105037, #61203267, #61375037, National Science and Technology Support Program Project #2013BAK02B01, Chinese Academy of Sciences Project No. KGZD-EW-102-2, and AuthenMetric R&D Funds.

References

1. Farenzena, M., Bazzani, L., Perina, A., Murino, V., Cristani, M.: Person re-identification by symmetry-driven accumulation of local features. In: Proc. CVPR (2010)
2. Gevers, T., Smeulders, A.W.: Color-based object recognition. Pattern Recognition 32(3), 453–464 (1999)
3. Gray, D., Brennan, S., Tao, H.: Evaluating appearance models for recognition, reacquisition, and tracking. In: IEEE International Workshop on Performance Evaluation for Tracking and Surveillance (2007)
4. Gray, D., Tao, H.: Viewpoint invariant pedestrian recognition with an ensemble of localized features. In: Forsyth, D., Torr, P., Zisserman, A. (eds.) ECCV 2008, Part I. LNCS, vol. 5302, pp. 262–275. Springer, Heidelberg (2008)
5. Hirzer, M., Roth, P.M., Bischof, H.: Person re-identification by efficient impostor-based metric learning. In: Proc. AVSS (2012)
6. Hirzer, M., Roth, P.M., Köstinger, M., Bischof, H.: Relaxed pairwise learned metric for person re-identification. In: Fitzgibbon, A., Lazebnik, S., Perona, P., Sato, Y., Schmid, C. (eds.) ECCV 2012, Part VI. LNCS, vol. 7577, pp. 780–793. Springer, Heidelberg (2012)
7. Hu, Y., Liao, S., Lei, Z., Li, S.Z.: Exploring structural information and fusing multiple features for person re-identification. In: Proc. CVPRW (2013)
8. Huang, Y., Huang, K., Yu, Y., Tan, T.: Salient coding for image classification. In: Proc. CVPR (2011)
9. Jojic, N., Perina, A., Cristani, M., Murino, V., Frey, B.: Stel component analysis: modeling spatial correlations in image class structure. In: Proc. CVPR (2009)
10. Khan, R., de Weijer, J.V., Khan, F.S., Muselet, D., Ducottet, C., Barat, C.: Discriminative color descriptors. In: Proc. CVPR (2013)
11. Kostinger, M., Hirzer, M., Wohlhart, P., Roth, P.M., Bischof, H.: Large scale metric learning from equivalence constraints. In: Proc. CVPR (2012)
12. Kuo, C.H., Khamis, S., Shet, V.: Person re-identification using semantic color names and rankboost. In: Proc. WACV (2013)
13. Kviatkovsky, I., Adam, A., Rivlin, E.: Color invariants for person reidentification. IEEE Trans. on PAMI 35(7), 1622–1634 (2013)
14. Li, Z., Chang, S., Liang, F., Huang, T.S., Cao, L., Smith, J.R.: Learning locally-adaptive decision functions for person verification. In: Proc. CVPR (2013)
15. Liu, C., Gong, S., Loy, C.C., Lin, X.: Person re-identification: What features are important? In: Fusiello, A., Murino, V., Cucchiara, R. (eds.) ECCV 2012 Ws/Demos, Part I. LNCS, vol. 7583, pp. 391–401. Springer, Heidelberg (2012)
16. Liu, L., Wang, L., Liu, X.: In defense of soft-assignment coding. In: Proc. ICCV (2011)
17. Liu, Y., Zhang, D., Lu, G., Ma, W.Y.: Region-based image retrieval with high-level semantic color names. In: Proceedings of the 11th International Multimedia Modelling Conference (2005)
18. Ma, B., Su, Y., Jurie, F.: Local descriptors encoded by fisher vectors for person re-identification. In: Fusiello, A., Murino, V., Cucchiara, R. (eds.) ECCV 2012 Ws/Demos, Part I. LNCS, vol. 7583, pp. 413–422. Springer, Heidelberg (2012)
19. Pedagadi, S., Orwell, J., Velastin, S., Boghossian, B.: Local fisher discriminant analysis for pedestrian re-identification. In: Proc. CVPR (2013)
20. Roth, P.M., Hirzer, M., Kostinger, M., Beleznai, C., Bischof, H.: Mahalanobis distance learning for person re-identification. Advances in Computer Vision and Pattern Recognition (2014)

21. Russakovsky, O., Lin, Y., Yu, K., Fei-Fei, L.: Object-centric spatial pooling for image classification. In: Fitzgibbon, A., Lazebnik, S., Perona, P., Sato, Y., Schmid, C. (eds.) ECCV 2012, Part II. LNCS, vol. 7573, pp. 1–15. Springer, Heidelberg (2012)
22. van de Sande, K.E., Gevers, T., Snoek, C.G.: Evaluating color descriptors for object and scene recognition. IEEE Trans. on PAMI 32(9), 1582–1596 (2010)
23. Satta, R.: Appearance descriptors for person re-identification: a comprehensive review. In: Proc. CoRR (2013)
24. Wang, J., Yang, J., Yu, K., Lv, F., Huang, T., Gong, Y.: Locality-constrained linear coding for image classification. In: Proc. CVPR (2010)
25. Wang, X., Doretto, G., Sebastian, T., Rittscher, J., Tu, P.: Shape and appearance context modeling. In: Proc. ICCV (2007)
26. van de Weijer, J., Schmid, C.: Applying color names to image description. In: Proc. ICIP (2007)
27. van de Weijer, J., Schmid, C., Verbeek, J., Larlus, D.: Learning color names for real-world applications. IEEE Trans. on Image Processing. 18(7), 1512–1523 (2009)
28. Xu, Y., Lin, L., Zheng, W.S., Liu, X.: Human re-identification by matching compositional template with cluster sampling. In: Proc. ICCV (2013)
29. Zhang, X., Yang, Y., Jiao, L., Dong, F.: Manifold-constrained coding and sparse representation for human action recognition. Pattern Recognition 46(7), 1819–1831 (2013)
30. Zhao, R., Ouyang, W., Wang, X.: Person re-identification by salience matching. In: Proc. ICCV (2013)
31. Zhao, R., Ouyang, W., Wang, X.: Unsupervised salience learning for person re-identification. In: Proc. CVPR (2013)
32. Zheng, W.S., Gong, S., Xiang, T.: Person re-identification by probabilistic relative distance comparison. In: Proc. CVPR (2011)

Learning Discriminative and Shareable Features for Scene Classification

Zhen Zuo[1], Gang Wang[1,2], Bing Shuai[1], Lifan Zhao[1],
Qingxiong Yang[3], and Xudong Jiang[1]

[1] Nanyang Technological University, Singapore
[2] Advanced Digital Sciences Center, Sinapore
[3] City University of Hong Kong

Abstract. In this paper, we propose to learn a discriminative and shareable feature transformation filter bank to transform local image patches (represented as raw pixel values) into features for scene image classification. The learned filters are expected to: (1) encode common visual patterns of a flexible number of categories; (2) encode discriminative and class-specific information. For each category, a subset of the filters are activated in a data-adaptive manner, meanwhile sharing of filters among different categories is also allowed. Discriminative power of the filter bank is further enhanced by enforcing the features from the same category to be close to each other in the feature space, while features from different categories to be far away from each other. The experimental results on three challenging scene image classification datasets indicate that our features can achieve very promising performance. Furthermore, our features also show great complementary effect to the state-of-the-art ConvNets feature.

Keywords: Feature learning, Discriminant analysis, Information sharing, Scene Classificsion.

1 Introduction

Generating robust, informative, and compact local features has been considered as one of the most critical factors for good performance in computer vision. In the last decade, numerous hand-crafted features, such as SIFT [1] and HOG [2], have ruled the local image representation area. Recently, a number of papers [3–9] have been published to learn feature representations from pixel values directly, aiming to extract data-adaptive features which are more suitable. However, most of these works operate in an unsupervised way without considering the class label information. We argue that extracting discriminative features is important for classification, as information on local patches is usually redundant, features which are discriminative for classification should be extracted.

In this paper, we develop a method to learn transformation filter bank to transform pixel values of local image patches into features, which is called Discriminative and Shareable Feature Learning (DSFL). As shown in Fig. 1, we

D. Fleet et al. (Eds.): ECCV 2014, Part I, LNCS 8689, pp. 552–568, 2014.
© Springer International Publishing Switzerland 2014

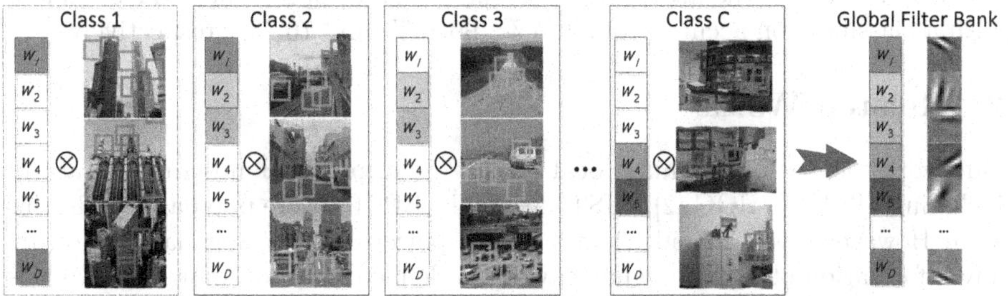

Fig. 1. Illustration of DSFL. $w_1, ..., w_D$ represent the filters in the global filter bank W. For each class, we force it to activate a small subset of filters to learn class-specific patterns, and different classes can share the same filters to learn shareable patterns. Finally, the feature of a image patch x_i can be represented as $f_i = \mathcal{F}(Wx_i)$. (Best viewed in color).

aim to learn an over-complete filter bank, which is able to cover the variances of images from different classes, meanwhile keeping the shareable correlation among different classes and discriminative power of each category. To build such a global filter bank, an intuitive way is to independently learn a filter bank for each class, and concatenate them together. However, if filters learned from different classes are not shared, the number of filters will increase linearly with the number of categories, which is not desirable for local feature representation. To learn a more compact global filter bank, we force each category to only activate a subset of the global filters during the learning procedure. Beyond reducing feature dimensions, sharing filters can also lead to more robust features. Images belonging to different classes do share some information in common (e.g. in scene classification, both 'computer room' and 'office' contain 'computer' and 'desk'). The amount of information shared depends on the similarity between different categories. Hence, we allow filters to be shared, meaning that the same filters can be activated by a number of categories. We introduce a binary selection variable vector to adaptively select what filters to share, and among what categories.

To improve the discrimination power, we introduce a discriminative term to force features from the same category to be close and features from different categories to be far away. (e.g. patches corresponding to bookshelf in 'office' can hardly be found in 'computer room'). However, not all the patches from the same categories are close, as they are very diverse. Hence, we introduce a method to select exemplars from each category, and a feature should be similar to a subgroup of the exemplars from the same category. Furthermore, not all the local patches from different classes should be forced to be separable, thus, we relax the discriminative term to allow sharing similar patches across different classes, and focus on separating the less similar patches from different classes.

We tested our method on three widely used scene image classification datasets: Scene 15, UIUC Sports, and MIT 67 Indoor. The experimental results show that our features can outperform most of the existing ones. By combining our feature with the ConvNets [3,10] features (supervised pretrained on ImageNet [11]), we can achieve state-of-the-art results on Scene 15, UIUC Sports and MIT 67 Indoor with a classification accuracy of 92.81% , 96.78%, and 76.23% respectively.

2 Related Works

Our work focuses on learning local feature descriptors. Hand-crafted features including SIFT [1], HOG [2], GIST [12], and LBP [13] were popular used in this area. However, even though they are very powerful, they can hardly capture any information other than what have been defined by prior knowledge. In this paper, we aim to learn a data adaptive local feature representation.

Recently, directly learning features from image pixel values [4–9,14–18] emerges as a hot research topic in computer vision because it is able to learn data adaptive features. And many of them have achieved superior performance on many important computer vision tasks such as digital image recognition [6], and action recognition [17]. However, most existing feature learning works adopt unsupervised learning methods to learn filters for feature extraction. Different from them, we argue that discriminative information can be critical for classification and discriminative patterns can be learned. We experimentally show that our discriminative feature learning works better than unsupervised feature learning on scene datasets by encoding the shareable and discriminative class correlation clues into feature representation. While in the supervised feature learning line, the ConvNets [3] is a very deep feature learning structure (5 convolutional layers, 2 fully connected layers, and 1 softmax layer), it focuses on progressively learning multi-levels of visual patterns. When pre-trained on ImageNet, it is the state-of-the-art feature extractor on many tasks [10,19,20]. In contrast, our DSFL focuses on encoding the shareable and discriminative correlation among different classes into each layer's feature transformation. In the Section 4, we will show that our DSFL learns significant complementary information to this powerful feature, and combines with which, we can update the current state-of-the-art on all of the three scene classification datasets.

There are also some related papers trying to extract discriminative representations from images. For example, [21–24] learn discriminative dictionaries to encode local image features. Another line of work [25–28] that represents scene images in terms of weakly-supervised mined discriminative parts gained increasingly popularity and success. The basic idea is to build a discriminative framework, and use it to mine a set of representative and distinct parts (multi-scale patches) for every class. Afterwards, images can be represented with the max pooled responses of such mid-level patterns. Different from these works, we focus on discriminatively learning filters to transform local image patches into features, and allowing sharing local feature transformation filters between different categories. To the best of our knowledge, this hasn't been done before. Furthermore, in [29, 30], object part filters at the middle level are shared to represent a large number of object categories for object detection. Compared to them, our training image patches don't have strong supervised labels except image-level class labels, so we develop an exemplar selection scheme and a nearest neighbour based maximum margin method to make it more robust to noise.

3 Discriminative and Shareable Feature Learning

In this section, we first describe the three components of our Discriminative and Shareable Feature Learning (DSFL) framework. Then we will provide an alternating optimization strategy to solve this problem.

3.1 DSFL Learning Components

We aim to learn features that can preserve the information of the original data, be shareable and be discriminative. To achieve these goals, we have three learning components in the DSFL learning framework. We write $x \in \mathbb{R}^{D_o}$ as a vector of raw pixel values of an image patch. Given a number of x from different categories, we aim to learn a feature transformation filter bank $W \in \mathbb{R}^{D \times D_0}$ (each row represents one filter, and there are D filters). By multiplying W with x, and applying an activation function $\mathcal{F}(\cdot)$, we expect to generate feature $f_i = \mathcal{F}(Wx_i)$, which is discriminative and as compact as possible. For this purpose, W should be learned to encode information which is discriminative among classes and only has a small number of rows (filters). In our learning framework, we force each class to activate a subset of filters in W to learn class-specific patterns. And we allow different classes to share filters to reduce the number of filters.

The Global Reconstruction Term. To ensure that the feature transformation matrix $W \in \mathbb{R}^{D \times D_0}$ can preserve the information hidden in the original data, we utilize a global reconstruction term, which aims to minimize the error between the reconstructed data and the original data. The cost function is shown as following:

$$
\begin{aligned}
L_u &= \sum_{i=1}^{N} \mathcal{L}_u(x_i, W) + \lambda_1 \sum_{i=1}^{N} \|f_i\|_1 \\
\text{where } & \mathcal{L}_u(x_i, W) = \left\|x_i - W^T W x_i\right\|_2^2 \\
\text{and } & f_i = \mathcal{F}(Wx_i),\ \mathcal{F}(\cdot) = \text{abs}(\cdot)
\end{aligned}
\tag{1}
$$

where N is the total number of training patches. $\mathcal{L}_u$ is the empirical loss function with respect to global filter bank W and unlabelled training patch x_i. $W^T W x_i$ denotes the reconstructed data of x_i. This auto-encoder [4,31] style reconstruction cost penalization term can not only prevent W from degeneration, but also allow W to be over-complete. The term $\|f_i\|_1$ is used to enforce the sparsity of the learned feature f_i. Following [5,17], we set $\mathcal{F}(\cdot) = \text{abs}(\cdot)$. Then the sparse term $\|f_i\|_1$ degenerates to summation of all the dimensions of f_i.

Shareable Constraint Term. Equation 1 can only learn a generative W without encoding any class-specific information. A method to overcome this limitation is to force a subset of filters to only respond to a specific class. Thus, we propose a constraint term to ensure that only a subset of the filters will be activated by one class, while the same filters can potentially be activated by multiple classes. For each class c, we write $\alpha^c \in \mathbb{R}^D$ as a binary vector to indicate the selection status of rows of W. If $\alpha_d^c = 1,\ d = 1, ..., D$, then the d-th row of W is activated. We use $A^c = \operatorname{diag}(\alpha^c)$ for representation convenience. The cost of our shareable constraint term of class c is formulated as following:

$$
\begin{aligned}
L_{\text{sha}}^c &= \sum_{j=1}^{N_c} \mathcal{L}_{\text{sha}}^c\left(x_j^c, A^c W\right) + \lambda_2 \|\alpha^c\|_0 \\
& s.t.\ \ \alpha_d^c \in \{0,1\}\,,\ d = 1, ..., D \\
\text{where } \mathcal{L}_{\text{sha}}^c\left(x_j^c, A^c W\right) &= \left\| x_j^c - \left(A^c W\right)^T \left(A^c W\right) x_j^c \right\|_2^2
\end{aligned}
\tag{2}
$$

where N_c is the number of training patches from class c, and C is the total number of classes. For the shareable term, similar to $\mathcal{L}_u$, $\mathcal{L}_{\text{sha}}^c$ is the reconstruction cost function with respect to the filter bank subset $\alpha^c W$ and training patch x_j^c from class c. We apply l_0 norm on α^c to force each class to activate a small number of rows. Consequently, for the d-th element in α^c, if it is only set to 1 for class c, then it means the d-th row of W will only be activated and learned with training patches from class c. If the d-th element is set to 1 for class c_1 and class c_2, then the d-th row of W is a shareable filter, which should be activated and learned with training data from class c_1 and c_2. When α^c is updated in each iteration, the corresponding training data for each filter will also be updated.

Discriminative Regularization Term. To enhance the discriminative power of feature descriptors, we further introduce a discriminative term based on the assumption that discriminative features should be close to the features from the same category, and be far away from the features from different categories in the feature space. In the image level scenario [32,33], labels are consistent with the targets. However, in patch level scenario, local features from the same class are inherently diverse, and directly forcing all of them to be similar to each other is not suitable. Similar to [34–36], we adopt the nearest neighbour based 'patch-to-class' distance metric to enforce discrimination. For a training patch x_j^c, its positive nearest neighbour patch set from the same category is denoted as $\Gamma\left(x_j^c\right)$; and its negative nearest neighbour patch set from the categories other than c is denoted as $\bar{\Gamma}\left(x_j^c\right)$. The k-th nearest neighbour in the two sets are represented as $\Gamma_k\left(x_j^c\right)$ and $\bar{\Gamma}_k\left(x_j^c\right)$ respectively.

In the class-specific feature space of class c (transformed by $A^c W$), the feature representation of the k-th positive and negative nearest neighbour patches sets are denoted as $\Gamma_k\left(f_j^c\right) = \mathcal{F}\left(A^c W \Gamma_k\left(x_j^c\right)\right)$ and $\bar{\Gamma}_k\left(f_j^c\right) = \mathcal{F}\left(A^c W \bar{\Gamma}_k\left(x_j^c\right)\right)$ correspondingly. We aim to minimize the distance between each feature to its positive nearest neighbours, while maximize the distance between each feature to its negative nearest neighbours. Furthermore, according to the maximum margin theory in learning, we should focus on the 'hard' training samples. Hence, we develop a 'hinge-loss' like objective function to learn $A^c W$:

$$L_{\text{dis}}^{c} = \sum_{j=1}^{N_c} \max\left(\delta + \text{Dis}\left(x_j^c, \Gamma\left(x_j^c\right)\right) - \text{Dis}\left(x_j^c, \bar{\Gamma}\left(x_j^c\right)\right), 0\right)$$

$$\text{where Dis}\left(x_j^c, \Gamma\left(x_j^c\right)\right) = \frac{1}{K}\sum_{k=1}^{K}\left\|f_j^c - \Gamma_k\left(f_j^c\right)\right\|_2^2 \tag{3}$$

$$\text{Dis}\left(x_j^c, \bar{\Gamma}\left(x_j^c\right)\right) = \frac{1}{K}\sum_{k=1}^{K}\left\|f_j^c - \bar{\Gamma}_k\left(f_j^c\right)\right\|_2^2$$

in which, δ is the margin, we set it to 1 in our experiments, and K is the number of nearest neighbours in the nearest neighbour patch sets, we fixed it as 5.

However, there are two limitations of the above nearest neighbour based learning method. Firstly, as mentioned in [36], the local patch level nearest neighbour search is likely to be dominated by noisy feature patches. Thus, some of the searched nearest neighbours in Equation 3 might not carry discriminative patterns, consequently the performance will be suppressed. Secondly, it is expensive to search nearest neighbours from the whole patch set. A straight forward solution is applying clustering and using the cluster centroids as the exemplars [36]. However, conventional clustering methods may consider non-informative dominant patterns as inliers of clusters, while treating informative class-specific patterns as outliers. Thus, we propose a method to select exemplars.

Inspired by the image-level exemplar selection method in [37], we propose an exemplar selection methods that is suitable for patch-level patterns. We firstly define the 'coverage set' of a patch x. Given X as the original global patch set, which is combined with patches densely extracted from all the training images. For each patch $x \in X$, we search its M nearest neighbours from X, and define these M patches as the 'coverage set' of x. Then for each class, we define their exemplar patches as the ones that cannot be easily covered by patches from many classes other than c. To reach this goal, we design a 'patch-to-database' (P2D) distance to measure the discriminative power of a patch x_i^c from class c:

$$\text{P2D}\left(x_j^c\right) = \frac{1}{C-1}\sum_{\bar{c}\neq c}\frac{1}{N_{\bar{c}}}\sum_{n=1}^{N_{\bar{c}}}\left\|x_j^c - x_n^{\bar{c}}\right\|_2 \tag{4}$$

where $x_n^{\bar{c}}$ is a patch from classes $\bar{c}, \bar{c} \neq c$, $N_{\bar{c}}$ is the number of patches from classes $\bar{c}$ whose coverage sets contain x_j^c, and C is the number of classes. If $\text{P2D}\left(x_j^c\right)$ is small, it means that x_j^c represents a common pattern among many classes, and should be removed, otherwise, it should be kept as a discriminative exemplar. For each class, we rank the patches based on their $\text{P2D}(\cdot)$ distances descendingly, and select the top 10% of them as discriminative exemplars. The selecting procedures are shown in Algorithm 1. The exemplars will replace the original patch set, and be used to search for the nearest neighbours in Equation 3. Specifically, for each training patch x_j^c, we search its nearest neighbours set $\Gamma\left(x_j^c\right)$ from the exemplars in class c, and search its negative nearest neighbours set $\bar{\Gamma}\left(x_j^c\right)$ from the exemplars belonging to classes other than c.

Algorithm 1. Discriminative Exemplar Selection

Input:
X: Global patch set
X_c: Patch set of class c
ε: Threshold for selecting discriminative exemplars
M: Number of patches in each coverage set
Output:
E_c: Exemplars of class c

1. Calculate the coverage set of each patch from X
for $c = 1$ to C **do**
  2. For each patch from X_c, calculate its P2D distance based on Equation 4
  3. Descendingly rank the patches from X_c based on their P2D distances.
  4. Select the top ε percent ranked patches as the exemplars E_c
end
return E_c

3.2 DSFL Objective Function and Optimization

Combining the global unsupervised reconstruction term L_u, the shareable constraint term L_{sha} and the discriminative regularization L_{dis}, we write the objective function of DSFL as:

$$\begin{aligned} &\min_{W,\alpha^c} L_u + \gamma \sum_{c=1}^{C} L_{\text{sha}}^c + \eta \sum_{c=1}^{C} L_{\text{dis}}^c \\ &\text{where } L_u = \sum_{i=1}^{N} \mathcal{L}_u\left(x_i, W\right) + \lambda_1 \sum_{i=1}^{N} \|f_i\|_1 \\ &L_{\text{sha}}^c = \sum_{j=1}^{N_c} \mathcal{L}_{\text{sha}}^c\left(x_j^c, A^c W\right) + \lambda_2 \|\alpha^c\|_0 \\ &L_{\text{dis}}^c = \sum_{j=1}^{N_c} \max\left(\delta + \text{Dis}\left(x_j^c, \Gamma\left(x_j^c\right)\right) - \text{Dis}\left(x_j^c, \bar{\Gamma}\left(x_j^c\right)\right), 0\right) \\ &\text{s.t. } \alpha_d^c \in \{0,1\}, d = 1, ..., D \end{aligned} \tag{5}$$

In Equation 5, when α^c is fixed, it is convex in W, and when W is fixed, a suboptimal α^c can also be obtained. However, the function cannot be jointly optimized. Thus, we adopt an alternating optimization strategy to iteratively update W and each α^c.

– ***Fix*** $\boldsymbol{\alpha^c}$ ***to update*** $\mathbf{W}$**:**

$$\min_{W} \sum_{i=1}^{N} \mathcal{L}_u\left(x_i, W\right) + \lambda_1 \sum_{i=1}^{N} \|f_i\|_1 + \gamma \sum_{c=1}^{C} \sum_{j=1}^{N_c} \mathcal{L}_{\text{sha}}^c\left(x_j^c, A^c W\right) + \eta \sum_{c=1}^{C} L_{\text{dis}}^c \tag{6}$$

Algorithm 2. DSFL: Discriminative and Shareable Feature Learning

Input:
x_i: Unlabelled training patch
x_j^c: Image-level labelled training patch from class c
D: Number of filters in the global filter bank
γ, η, λ_1, λ_2: Trade off parameters for controlling weight of shareable term, discriminative term, and sparsity
Output:
W: Global filter bank (feature transformation matrix)

1. Initialize $\alpha^c = \mathbf{0}^T$
2. Set W as a random number $D \times D_0$ matrix
3. Learn W with only unsupervised term L_u as the initialized W to the DSFL
4. Select exemplars for each class based on Equation 4
5. Search the positive and negative nearest neighbour exemplar sets for each x_j^c

while W and α^c not converge **do**
  for $c = 1$ to C **do**
    6. Fix W and solve Equation 7 by updating α^c
  end
  7. Fix $\alpha^c, c = 1, ..., C$ and solve Equation 6 by updating W
end
return W

As mentioned in Section 3.1, $\|f_i\|_1$ degenerates to summation of different dimensions in f_i, thus, Equation 6 can be easily optimized by unconstrained solvers, e.g. L-BFGS.

– ***Fix W to update $\boldsymbol{\alpha}^c$*:**

$$\min_{\alpha^c} \sum_{j=1}^{N_c} \mathcal{L}_{\text{sha}}^c \left(x_j^c, A^c W\right) + \lambda_2 \|\alpha^c\|_0 + \eta L_{\text{dis}}^c \tag{7}$$

For the optimization of α^c, we update one α^c each time for the c-th class, and fix $\alpha^{\bar{c}}$ ($\bar{c} \neq c$). To get such binary filter selection indicators, we apply a greedy optimization method. We first set all the elements in α^c as 0, then we search for the single best filter that can minimize Equation 7, and activate that filter by setting the corresponding element in α^c to 1. Afterwards, based on the previously activated filters, we search for next filter that can further minimize the cost function. After several rounds of searching, when the loss $\mathcal{L}_{\text{sha}}^c$ is smaller than a threshold, the optimization of α^c terminates, we stop updating α^c, and send the renewed α^c as the input to Equation 6 again to further optimize W.

The learning algorithm and initialization procedure are shown in Algorithm 2. The alternative optimization terminated until the values of both W and α^c converge (takes about 5 rounds).

3.3 Hierarchical Extension of DSFL

DSFL can be easily stacked to extract features at multiple levels. Features at lower level may represent edges and lines, while features at higher level may represent object parts, etc. In our implementation, we stack another layer on the top of the basic DSFL structure[1]. In the first layer DSFL network, 400 dimensional features are learned from 16x16 pixel raw images patches, which are densely extracted from the original/resized images with step size 4. In the second layer, another 400 dimensional feature is learned based on first layer features. To get the inputs for the second layer, we concatenate the first layer features densely extracted within 32x32 image areas. We further process PCA to reduce the dimension to 300 and send it to the second layer. Finally, we combine the features learned from both layers as our DSFL feature.

4 Experiments and Analysis

4.1 Datasets and Experiment Settings

We tested our DSFL method on three widely used scene image classification datasets: Scene 15 [38], UIUC Sports [39], and MIT 67 Indoor [40]. In order to make fair comparisons with other types of features, we only used gray scale information for all these datasets.

We tested on all the three datasets with the most standard settings: on Scene 15, we randomly selected 100 images per category for training, and the rest for testing; on UIUC sports, we randomly selected 70 images per class as training images, and 60 images per class as testing images; on MIT 67 Indoor, we followed the original splits in [40], which used around 80 training images and 20 testing images for each category. For UIUC sports and MIT 67 Indoor, since the resolution of the original images are too high for learning local features efficiently, we resized them to have maximum 300 pixels along the smaller axis. For Scene 15 and UIUC sports, we randomly split the training and testing dataset for 5 times. The average accuracy numbers over these 5 rounds are reported for comparison. For all the local features, we densely extracted features from six scales with rescaling factors $2^{-i/2}, i = 0, 1, ..., 5$. Specifically, RICA [4] and DSFL features were extracted with step size 3 for the first layer, and step size 6 for the second layer; SIFT features [1] were extracted from 16x16 patches with stride 3; HOG2x2 features [41] were extracted based on cells of size 8x8, and the stride is 1 cell; LBP features [13] were extracted from cells of size 8x8.

For each training image, we randomly picked 400 patches (200 for MIT Indoor), and used them as training data to learn W. In the objective function Equation 5, the value of margin δ was fixed as 1, and we sequentially learnt the weight parameters λ_1, λ_2, γ and η by cross validation. In Algorithm 1, the threshold of exemplar selection ε was set to 10%, and the coverage set size M

[1] Adding more layers can slightly improve the performance, but the computational cost is high, thus we apply two layer DSFL to reach a compromise.

Table 1. Comparison results between our feature and other features. (DeCAF is the feature learned by the deep ConvNets pre-trained on ImageNet).

Mehods	Scene 15	UIUC Sports	MIT 67 Indoor
GIST [12]	73.28%	-	22.00%
CENTRIST [42]	83.10%	78.50%	36.90%
SIFT [1]	82.06%	85.12%	45.86%
HOG2x2 [41]	81.58%	83.96%	43.76%
LBP [13]	82.95%	80.04%	39.25%
RICA [4]	79.85%	82.14%	47.89%
DSFL	84.19%	86.45%	52.24%
DeCAF [3, 10]	87.99%	93.96%	58.52%
SIFT [1] + DeCAF [3, 10]	89.90%	95.05%	70.51%
DSFL + DeCAF [3, 10]	92.81%	96.78%	76.23%

was set to 10. In Algorithm 2, the maximum number of iterations of updating W and α_c was set to 5.

We tested our local features based on the LLC framework [43], which used locality-constrained linear coding to encode local features, and performed max-pooling and linear-SVM afterwards. The size of the codebook was fixed as 2000, and each image was divided into 1x1, 2x2, and 4x4 spatial pooling regions [38]. We've also tested on other frameworks with different coding strategies (e.g. vector quantization) and pooling schemes (e.g. average pooling), our DSFL can consistently outperform traditional local features.

4.2 Comparison with Other Features

As shown in Table 1, we compared our DSFL with popular features which have shown good performance on scene images classification: SIFT [1], GIST [12], CENTRIST [42], and HoG [2, 44], LBP [13]. Our DSFL feature is able to outperform all of the hand crafted features. We also compared our DSFL with RICA [4], which is the baseline unsupervised feature learning method without encoding any discriminative or class-specific information. As shown in Table 1, our method consistently and significantly outperforms RICA. We've also tested the performance of only using the features learned by the first partially connected layer, and for the three datasets, the results were 82.61%, 83.92%, and 47.16%, which are less powerful than the two layer features.

In Table 1, the DeCAF feature [10] is an implementation of the 7 layer ConvNets [3]. Here we used the 6-th layer DeCAF feature. According to [10, 20], empirically the 6-th layer feature will lead to better results than the 7-th layer feature. On the three datasets, we also tested with the 7-th layer feature, and got 87.35%, 93.44%, and 58.27% respectively. Thus, the 6-th layer DeCAF features were used for evaluation. Although this pre-trained DeCAF feature is very powerful, yet directly comparing our feature with it is not fair. We do not utilize the huge amount of image data from ImageNet [11], we haven't used color

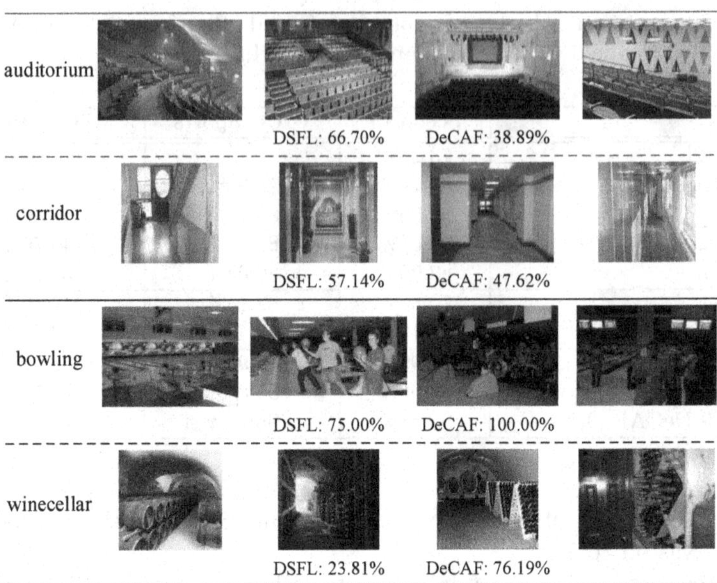

Fig. 2. Comparison results on MIT 67 Indoor. The first two rows show the two categories on which DSFL works better than DeCAF, the last two rows show the classes that are better represented by DeCAF. DSFL and DeCAF are complimentary. Combining them can result in better results for scene classification.

information, and we focus on local feature representation rather than global image representation. The ConvNets was trained on the ImageNet with a large amount of object images. We suppose the features learned from these two frameworks should be complementary. In Fig. 2, we tested on MIT 67 to show the complementary effect. In the first two rows, our DSFL worked better than DeCAF, and we show the testing images which were correctly classified by DSFL, but wrongly classified by DeCAF. In the last two rows, DeCAF outperformed DSFL, and we show the testing images which our DSFL failed to recognize but DeCAF could. To quantitatively analyze the complementation effect, we combined our DSFL with the DeCAF feature. As shown in the last row of Table 1, we are able to get much better performance than purely using the powerful ConvNets features and produce the state-of-the-art performance. We also tested the combination of SIFT and DeCAF. The accuracy numbers are not as good as those of the combination of DSFL and DeCAF, which indicates that our DSFL can learn more effective complementary information by considering data adaptive information. The traditional hand-crafted features such as SIFT usually extracted 'garbor-like' features, most of which can be learned by the lower levels in ConvNets. However, ConvNets adopts backpropagation for optimization based on huge training datasets, the bottom layers of the network were usually not well trained. In contrast, we explicitly used supervised information to train bottom layer features. Our method is more suitable for relatively small

Table 2. Comparison Results of our method and other popular methods on Scene 15, UIUC sports, and MIT 67 Indoor

Mehods	Scene 15	UIUC Sports	MIT 67 Indoor
ROI + GIST [40]	-	-	26.50%
DPM [45]	-	-	30.40%
Object Bank [46]	80.90%	76.30%	37.60%
Discriminative Patches [47]	-	-	38.10%
LDC [36]	80.30%	-	43.53%
macrofeatures [48]	84.30%	-	-
Visual Concepts + 3 combined features [25]	83.40%	84.80%	46.40%
MMDL + 5 combined features [49]	86.35%	**88.47%**	50.15%
Discriminative Part Detector [27]	86.00%	86.40%	51.40%
LScSPM [50]	**89.78%**	85.27%	-
IFV [28]	-	-	60.77%
MLrep + IFV [26]	-	-	**66.87%**
DSFL + DeCAF [3,10]	**92.81%**	**96.78%**	**76.23%**

datasets, as evidenced by the experimental results, while previous attempts on trying to train a CNN classifier on small datasets usually failed. So these two lines of works are expected to be complimentary.

We also compared our method (combining DSFL and DeCAF) with other methods applied on these three scene datasets. As shown in Table 2, our method achieved the highest accuracy on all of the three datasets. Note that Visual Elements [26] utilized numerous patches extracted at scales ranging from 80x80 to the full image size, and the patches were represented by standard HOG [2] plus a 8x8 color image in L*a*b space, and very high dimensional IFV [28] features. While MMDL [49] combined 5 types of features on 3 scales. Furthermore, most of the previous works were based on hand-crafted local feature descriptions, which means that our learned DSFL features can be combined with them to achieve better results. For example, LScSPM [50] focused on coding, which can be used to encode our DSFL features.

4.3 Analysis of the Effect of Different Components

In this section, we aim to compare our shareable and discriminative learning method to the baseline without encoding such information, which is equivalent to the RICA method in [4]. We first show the visualization of the filters learned from UIUC Sports in Fig. 3(a) and Fig. 3(b). We can see that our DSFL is able to capture more sharply localized patterns, corresponding to more class-specific visual information.

Effect of Learning Shareable Filter Bank. We tested the DSFL with or without the feature sharing terms, and got the intermediate results in Table 3. The first row of the table shows the baseline unsupervised RICA features

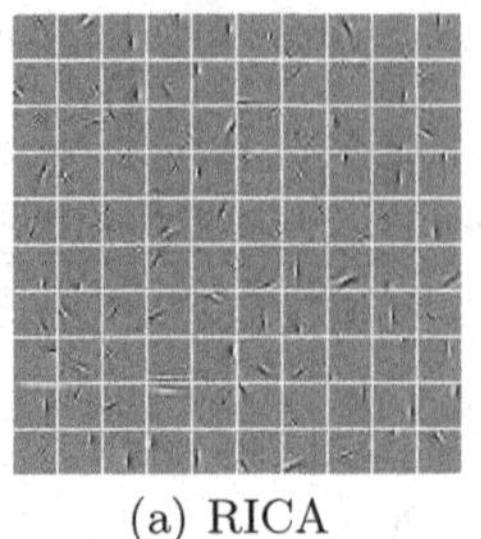

(a) RICA

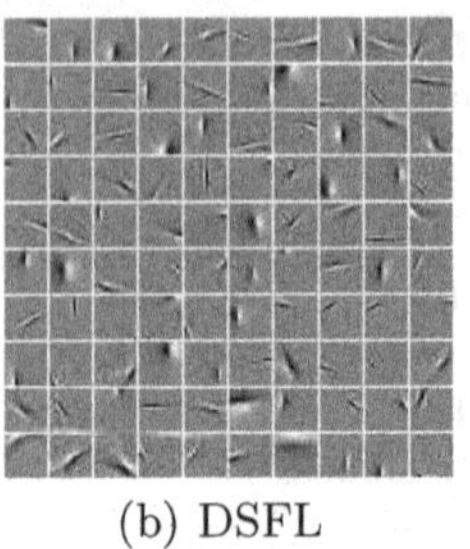

(b) DSFL

Fig. 3. Visualization of the filters learned by RICA and our DSFL on the UIUC Sports dataset

learned by solving Equation 1. In the second row, $L_u + L_{\text{sha}}$ corresponds to features learned with Equation 2. The improvement in accuracy shows that learning shareable features is effective for classification. However, if we removed the global reconstruction error term $\mathcal{L}_u$ and only kept the shareable terms, as shown in the third row, the performance dramatically dropped.

Effect of Discriminative Regularization and Exemplar Selection. According to the fourth row and the fifth row of Table 3, we can find that if we didn't select exemplars for learning, we could not achieve much improvement because noisy training examples might overwhelm the useful discriminative patterns. However, once we learned using selected exemplars, our method could achieve significant improvement in classification accuracy. This shows that discriminative exemplar selection is critical in our learning framework.

Furthermore, it's obvious that only using 10% of the whole patch set dramatically increased the efficiency of nearest neighbour search afterwards. Thus, our exemplar selection method is both effective and efficient.

Table 3. Analysis of the effect of each components

Mehods	Scene 15	UIUC Sports	MIT 67 Indoor
L_u (RICA [4])	79.85%	82.14%	47.89%
$L_u + L_{\text{sha}}$	82.01%	83.67%	49.70%
L_{sha}	72.69%	72.52%	24.12%
$L_u + L_{\text{sha}} + L_{\text{dis}}$ (without Exemplar)	82.50%	83.43%	51.28%
$L_u + L_{\text{sha}} + L_{\text{dis}}$ (Full DSFL)	84.19%	86.45%	52.24%

Effect of the Size of Filter Bank. To further analyze the influence caused by the size of filters, we test on Scene 15 dataset with 128, 256, 512, 1024, and 2048 filters for the DSFL. The results are shown in Fig. 4. At the beginning, when the size is small, the learned features are relatively weak. When the number of filters increases, and W becomes over-complete, the performance is substantially improved. Thus, learning over-complete filter bank does help to obtain better

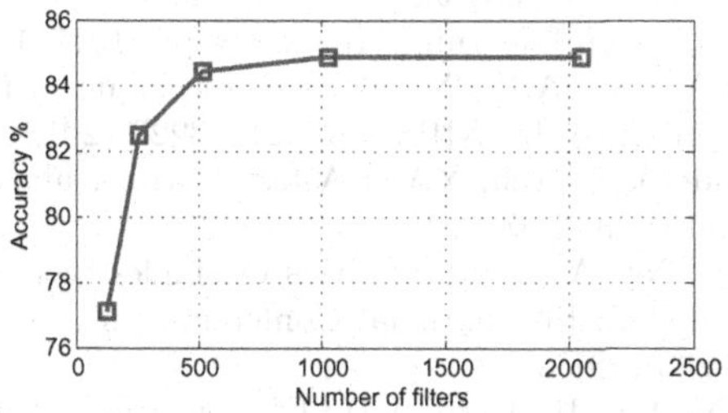

Fig. 4. Results of varying number of filters in Scene 15

feature representation because the resulting filter bank captures more information. However, when the number of filters further increases, the performance does not change much, while the learning process will be extremely slow. In our experiment, we use 400 as a compromise between efficiency and accuracy.

5 Conclusion

In this paper, we propose a weakly supervised feature learning method, called DSFL, to learn a discriminative and shareable filter bank to transform local image patches into features. In our DSFL method, we learn a flexible number of shared filters to represent common patterns shared across different categories. To enhance the discriminative power, we force the features from the same class to be locally similar, while features from different classes to be separable. We test our method on three widely used scene image classification benchmark datasets, and the results consistently show that our learned features can outperform most of the existing features. By combining our features with the ConvNets features pre-trained on ImageNet, we can greatly enhance the representation, and achieve state-of-the-art scene classification results. In the future, we will integrate our learning method with deeper learning structure to extract multi-level features for more effective classification.

Acknowledgement. The research is supported by MOE Tier 1 RG84/12, MOE Tier 2 ARC28/14 and SERC 1321202099.

References

1. Lowe, D.G.: Distinctive image features from scale-invariant keypoints. International Journal of Computer Vision 60(2), 91–110 (2004)
2. Dalal, N., Triggs, B.: Histograms of oriented gradients for human detection. In: CVPR, pp. 886–893 (2005)
3. Krizhevsky, A., Sutskever, I., Hinton, G.: Imagenet classification with deep convolutional neural networks. In: NIPS, pp. 1106–1114 (2012)

4. Le, Q.V., Karpenko, A., Ngiam, J., Ng, A.Y.: Ica with reconstruction cost for efficient overcomplete feature learning. In: NIPS, pp. 1017–1025 (2011)
5. Zou, W.Y., Zhu, S.Y., Ng, A.Y., Yu, K.: Deep learning of invariant features via simulated fixations in video. In: NIPS, pp. 3212–3220 (2012)
6. Hinton, G.E., Osindero, S., Teh, Y.W.: A fast learning algorithm for deep belief nets. Neural Computation (2006)
7. Coates, A., Lee, H., Ng, A.Y.: An analysis of single-layer networks in unsupervised feature learning. In: International Conference on Artificial Intelligence and Statistics, pp. 215–223 (2011)
8. Sohn, K., Jung, D.Y., Lee, H., Hero, A.O.: Efficient learning of sparse, distributed, convolutional feature representations for object recognition. In: ICCV, pp. 2643–2650 (2011)
9. Zuo, Z., Wang, G.: Learning discriminative hierarchical features for object recognition. Signal Processing Letters 21(9), 1159–1163 (2014)
10. Donahue, J., Jia, Y., Vinyals, O., Hoffman, J., Zhang, N., Tzeng, E., Darrell, T.: Decaf: A deep convolutional activation feature for generic visual recognition. In: ICML, pp. 647–655 (2014)
11. Deng, J., Berg, A.C., Li, K., Fei-Fei, L.: What does classifying more than 10,000 image categories tell us? In: Daniilidis, K., Maragos, P., Paragios, N. (eds.) ECCV 2010, Part V. LNCS, vol. 6315, pp. 71–84. Springer, Heidelberg (2010)
12. Oliva, A., Torralba, A.: Building the gist of a scene: The role of global image features in recognition. Progress in Brain Research 155, 23–36 (2006)
13. Ojala, T., Pietikainen, M., Maenpaa, T.: Multiresolution gray-scale and rotation invariant texture classification with local binary patterns. IEEE Transactions on Pattern Analysis and Machine Intelligence 24(7), 971–987 (2002)
14. Jarrett, K., Kavukcuoglu, K., Ranzato, M., LeCun, Y.: What is the best multi-stage architecture for object recognition? In: ICCV, pp. 2146–2153 (2009)
15. Taylor, G.W., Fergus, R., LeCun, Y., Bregler, C.: Convolutional learning of spatio-temporal features. In: Daniilidis, K., Maragos, P., Paragios, N. (eds.) ECCV 2010, Part VI. LNCS, vol. 6316, pp. 140–153. Springer, Heidelberg (2010)
16. Le, Q.V., Ranzato, M.A., Monga, R., Devin, M., Chen, K., Corrado, G.S., Dean, J., Ng, A.Y.: Building high-level features using large scale unsupervised learning. In: ICML (2012)
17. Le, Q.V., Zou, W.Y., Yeung, S.Y., Ng, A.Y.: Learning hierarchical invariant spatio-temporal features for action recognition with independent subspace analysis. In: CVPR, pp. 3361–3368 (2011)
18. Shen, X., Xu, L., Zhang, Q., Jia, J.: Multi-modal and multi-spectral registration for natural images. In: Fleet, D., Pajdla, T., Schiele, B., Tuytelaars, T. (eds.) ECCV 2014, Part IV. LNCS, vol. 8692, pp. 309–324. Springer, Heidelberg (2014)
19. Sermanet, P., Eigen, D., Zhang, X., Mathieu, M., Fergus, R., LeCun, Y.: Overfeat: Integrated recognition, localization and detection using convolutional networks. arXiv preprint arXiv:1312.6229 (2013)
20. Girshick, R., Donahue, J., Darrell, T., Malik, J.: Rich feature hierarchies for accurate object detection and semantic segmentation. arXiv preprint arXiv:1311.2524 (2013)
21. Jiang, Z., Lin, Z., Davis, L.S.: Learning a discriminative dictionary for sparse coding via label consistent k-svd. In: CVPR, pp. 1697–1704 (2011)
22. Mairal, J., Bach, F., Ponce, J., Sapiro, G., Zisserman, A.: Supervised dictionary learning. In: NIPS (2008)
23. Yang, M., Zhang, L., Feng, X., Zhang, D.: Fisher discrimination dictionary learning for sparse representation. In: ICCV, pp. 543–550 (2011)

24. Kong, S., Wang, D.: A dictionary learning approach for classification: Separating the particularity and the commonality. In: Fitzgibbon, A., Lazebnik, S., Perona, P., Sato, Y., Schmid, C. (eds.) ECCV 2012, Part I. LNCS, vol. 7572, pp. 186–199. Springer, Heidelberg (2012)
25. Li, Q., Wu, J., Tu, Z.: Harvesting mid-level visual concepts from large-scale internet images. In: CVPR (2013)
26. Doersch, C., Gupta, A., Efros, A.A.: Mid-level visual element discovery as discriminative mode seeking. In: NIPS, pp. 494–502 (2013)
27. Sun, J., Ponce, J., et al.: Learning discriminative part detectors for image classification and cosegmentation. In: ICCV (2013)
28. Juneja, M., Vedaldi, A., Jawahar, C., Zisserman, A.: Blocks that shout: Distinctive parts for scene classification. In: CVPR, pp. 923–930 (2013)
29. Song, H.O., Zickler, S., Althoff, T., Girshick, R., Fritz, M., Geyer, C., Felzenszwalb, P., Darrell, T.: Sparselet models for efficient multiclass object detection. In: Fitzgibbon, A., Lazebnik, S., Perona, P., Sato, Y., Schmid, C. (eds.) ECCV 2012, Part II. LNCS, vol. 7573, pp. 802–815. Springer, Heidelberg (2012)
30. Song, H.O., Darrell, T., Girshick, R.B.: Discriminatively activated sparselets. In: ICML, pp. 196–204 (2013)
31. Hinton, G.E., Salakhutdinov, R.R.: Reducing the dimensionality of data with neural networks. Science 313(5786), 504–507 (2006)
32. Wang, G., Forsyth, D., Hoiem, D.: Improved object categorization and detection using comparative object similarity. IEEE Transactions on Pattern Analysis and Machine Intelligence 35(10), 2442–2453 (2013)
33. Wang, Z., Gao, S., Chia, L.-T.: Learning class-to-image distance via large margin and L1-norm regularization. In: Fitzgibbon, A., Lazebnik, S., Perona, P., Sato, Y., Schmid, C. (eds.) ECCV 2012, Part II. LNCS, vol. 7573, pp. 230–244. Springer, Heidelberg (2012)
34. Boiman, O., Shechtman, E., Irani, M.: In defense of nearest-neighbor based image classification. In: CVPR, pp. 1–8 (2008)
35. McCann, S., Lowe, D.G.: Local naive bayes nearest neighbor for image classification. In: CVPR, pp. 3650–3656 (2012)
36. Wang, Z., Feng, J., Yan, S., Xi, H.: Linear distance coding for image classification. IEEE Transactions on Image Processing 22(2), 537–548 (2013)
37. Yao, B., Fei-Fei, L.: Action recognition with exemplar based 2.5D graph matching. In: Fitzgibbon, A., Lazebnik, S., Perona, P., Sato, Y., Schmid, C. (eds.) ECCV 2012, Part IV. LNCS, vol. 7575, pp. 173–186. Springer, Heidelberg (2012)
38. Lazebnik, S., Schmid, C., Ponce, J.: Beyond bags of features: Spatial pyramid matching for recognizing natural scene categories. In: CVPR, vol. 2, pp. 2169–2178 (2006)
39. Li, L.J., Fei-Fei, L.: What, where and who? classifying events by scene and object recognition. In: ICCV (2007)
40. Quattoni, A., Torralba, A.: Recognizing indoor scenes. In: CVPR (2009)
41. Xiao, J., Hays, J., Ehinger, K.A., Oliva, A., Torralba, A.: Sun database: Large-scale scene recognition from abbey to zoo. In: CVPR, pp. 3485–3492 (2010)
42. Wu, J., Rehg, J.M.: Centrist: A visual descriptor for scene categorization. IEEE Transactions on Pattern Analysis and Machine Intelligence 33(8), 1489–1501 (2011)
43. Wang, J., Yang, J., Yu, K., Lv, F., Huang, T., Gong, Y.: Locality-constrained linear coding for image classification. In: CVPR, pp. 3360–3367 (2010)
44. Felzenszwalb, P.F., Girshick, R.B., McAllester, D., Ramanan, D.: Object detection with discriminatively trained part-based models. IEEE Transactions on Pattern Analysis and Machine Intelligence 32(9), 1627–1645 (2010)

45. Pandey, M., Lazebnik, S.: Scene recognition and weakly supervised object localization with deformable part-based models. In: ICCV, pp. 1307–1314 (2011)
46. Li, L.J., Su, H., Fei-Fei, L., Xing, E.P.: Object bank: A high-level image representation for scene classification & semantic feature sparsification. In: NIPS (2010)
47. Singh, S., Gupta, A., Efros, A.A.: Unsupervised discovery of mid-level discriminative patches. In: Fitzgibbon, A., Lazebnik, S., Perona, P., Sato, Y., Schmid, C. (eds.) ECCV 2012, Part II. LNCS, vol. 7573, pp. 73–86. Springer, Heidelberg (2012)
48. Boureau, Y.L., Bach, F., Le Cun, Y., Ponce, J.: Learning mid-level features for recognition. In: CVPR (2010)
49. Wang, X., Wang, B., Bai, X., Liu, W., Tu, Z.: Max-margin multiple-instance dictionary learning. In: ICML (2013)
50. Gao, S., Tsang, I.H., Chia, L.T.: Laplacian sparse coding, hypergraph laplacian sparse coding, and applications. IEEE Transactions on Pattern Analysis and Machine Intelligence 35(1), 92–104 (2013)

Image Retrieval and Ranking via Consistently Reconstructing Multi-attribute Queries

Xiaochun Cao[1,2], Hua Zhang[1,⋆], Xiaojie Guo[2], Si Liu[3], and Xiaowu Chen[4]

[1] School of Computer Science and Technology, Tianjin University, Tianjin, China
[2] State Key Laboratory of Information Security, IIE, Chinese Academy of Sciences, China
[3] Department of Electrical & Computer Engineering, National University of Singapore
[4] State Key Laboratory of Virtual Reality Technology and Systems School of Computer Science and Engineering, Beihang University, Beijing, China

caoxiaochun@iie.ac.cn, huazhang@tju.edu.cn, xj.max.guo@gmail.com, dcslius@nus.edu.sg, chen@buaa.edu.cn

Abstract. Image retrieval and ranking based on the multi-attribute queries is beneficial to various real world applications. Traditional methods on this problem often utilize intermediate representations generated by attribute classifiers to describe the images, and then the images in the database are sorted according to their similarities to the query. However, such a scheme has two main challenges: 1) how to exploit the correlation between query attributes and non-query attributes, and 2) how to handle noisy representations since the pre-defined attribute classifiers are probably unreliable. To overcome these challenges, we discover the correlation among attributes via expanding the query representation, and imposing the group sparsity on representations to reduce the disturbance of noisy data. Specifically, given a multi-attribute query matrix with each row corresponding to a query attribute and each column the pre-defined attribute, we firstly expand the query based on the correlation of the attributes learned from the training data. Then, the expanded query matrix is reconstructed by the images in the dataset with the $\ell_{2,1}$ regularization. Furthermore, we introduce the ranking SVM into the objective function to guarantee the ranking consistency. Finally, we adopt a graph regularization to preserve the local visual similarity among images. Extensive experiments on LFW, CUB-200-2011, and Shoes datasets are conducted to demonstrate the effectiveness of our proposed method.

Keywords: Multi-Attribute Image, Image Retrieval & Ranking, Group Sparsity.

1 Introduction

The goal of image retrieval based on multi-attribute queries is to, from a database, recall images semantically similar to the query in a ranked order. It is beneficial yet challenging to many computer vision applications [8,17,15,14,23]. Different from single-attribute queries, a multi-attribute query can exploit the correlation among the query attributes and preferentially recommend the images similar to the whole attribute query. A traditional framework [16,9] first trains several attribute classifiers to describe the

⋆ Corresponding author.

D. Fleet et al. (Eds.): ECCV 2014, Part I, LNCS 8689, pp. 569–583, 2014.
© Springer International Publishing Switzerland 2014

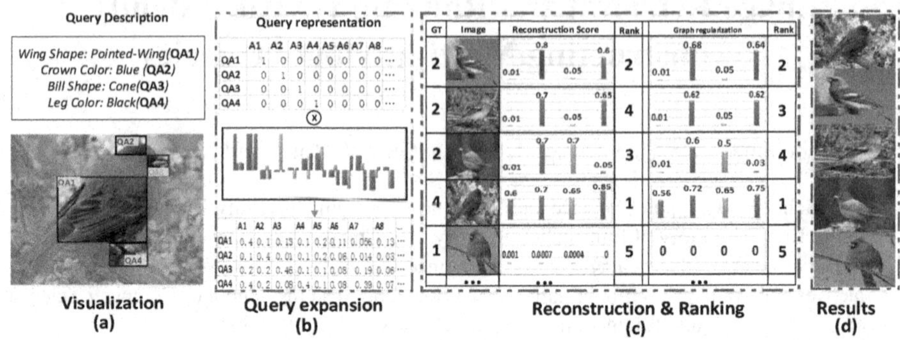

Fig. 1. An illustration of our proposed framework. Given a multi-attribute query (a), we first describe the query by a matrix. And then the query is expanded based on the correlation among attributes (Sec. 2.1). After that, we reconstruct the query by incorporating the ranking regularization into the objective function (Sec. 2.2 & 2.3). Furthermore, the graph regularization is introduced to enforce the local similarity (Sec. 2.4). Each column of the matrix (subgraph (b), top) indicates a visual attributes (A_j), while each row a query attribute (QA_i). In subgraph (c), GT is the number of query attributes in the corresponding images. The reconstruction score denotes the reconstruction values with ranking regularization. Graph regularization represents the reconstruction values with graph regularization. Finally, the retrieval results are shown in subgraph (d).

images, based on which, the candidate images are orderly feedback according to their similarities to the query. To improve the performance of retrieval, [17,23] introduce the non-query attributes as the context information to complement the query ones. More recently, [15] focuses on constructing more discriminative query classifiers by considering the distance among the query attributes. Impressive results have been achieved by previous work [17,15,14,23,16,9]. However, there are still three factors needed to be considered, which would significantly influence the retrieval and ranking performance. Firstly, due to the influence of various viewpoints, scales and occlusions, the trained classifier might not be sufficiently accurate. Secondly, considering the attributes in the query independently might lose the structure information. Thirdly, the correlation between the query and non-query attributes contains not only the co-occurrence but also the mutual inference correlation. In other words, a query attribute could be inferred by other attributes. For example, "Female" could be collated with "No Beard", "Wearing Lipstick", and "Wearing Necklace" *etc.*

In this paper, we propose a novel framework to handle imprecise and noisy image representations, consider the dependence among query attributes, and explicitly exploit the correlation between the query and non-query attributes. As shown in Fig. 1, our system has four main components: *Query expansion*, *Query reconstruction*, *Rank regularization*, and *Graph regularization*. The input is the multi-attribute query (QA_1,...,QA_4) as shown in Fig. 1 (a). In the first component, we first represent them as a matrix (top, Fig. 1(b)), each row of which is a query attribute (QA_i), and each column denotes a pre-defined attribute (A_j). Motivated by [22,11,4] on tag completion, we propose an attribute query expansion technique to expand the original query by using the correlation (middle, Fig. 1(b)). In the second component, we compute the similarity between the expanded query and the images in the database by using $\ell_{2,1}$ norm based reconstruction framework. This is inspired by the success of [19] in image annotation community. [19] shows that the semantic similarity between two images with overlapped labels can be well recovered in a reconstruction way. In the third component, since our goal is to retrieve and rank the similar images, beside the reconstruction error, the ranking error also needs to be considered in the objective function. We utilize the inequally contribution of different query reconstruction coefficients to boost the performance similar to [17,23]. In the fourth component, we introduce a graph regularization based on the low-level features of images into the objective function. It enforces the similar images to have similar reconstruction coefficients and rankings. The reason of introducing graph regularization is that two visually similar images might generate different intermediate representations because of various factors such as occlusions, scales. Extensive experiments are designed to validate the superior performance of our method, compared to state of the art alternatives, on LFW [10], CUB-200-2011 Bird [20], and Shoes [1] datasets.

The contributions of our work can be summarized as follows:

- We develop a reconstruction based framework to retrieve images by multi-attribute queries;
- A $\ell_{2,1}$ based constraint is introduced to retain the semantic structure of query;
- The query of our framework can be either the multi-attribute or the image.

1.1 Related Work

In this part, we briefly review the previous work that are closely related to ours. These work can be roughly divided into three groups:

1) *Attribute Classifier Based Image Retrieval.* In recent years, numerous algorithms in this category have been proposed, which can be further grouped into two categories. One focuses on modeling the multi-attribute query. Scheirer *et al.* [16] propose an attribute score calibration approach by considering the distribution of different detectors of the attribute. This method models the distribution of the query by taking advantage of the opposite side of the query attribute. However it is nontrivial to find the opposite of each attribute. [15] constructs the discriminative attribute detectors by analyzing the feature distance between attributes. As this method depends on the attribute distance, its performance is sensitive to the amount of training data. The other category is to explore the correlation among attributes: To model such interdependencies, Siddiquie *et al.* [17] design an image ranking and retrieval method by taking into account both query attributes and non-query attributes, which exploits the positive and negative correlations between the query and non-query attributes to improve the discriminative of image representation. Further, [23] introduces weak attributes to describe images by class names. This approach can handle large scale images and automatically select the correlation features. The approaches proposed in [17,23] focus on the presence of selected query attributes without the consideration of that the consistency of similar image would generate the similarity rank.

2) *Reconstruction Based Image Annotation and Retrieval.* Wang *et al.* [19] propose to annotate the query image by using sparse coding framework via the ℓ_1 norm. The

differences between our work are that first we want to retrieve the images based on the attribute query. Second, we use the group sparsity by $\ell_{2,1}$ norm instead of ℓ_1 norm. Zhang *et al.* [25] propose a group sparsity based method for the image annotation and retrieval task. In [25], features are divided into several groups to find the discriminative representation group by the constructed image pairs. In the testing phase, it automatically computes the similarity based on the feature weight between the test image and other images. Comparing with [25], our method uses not only the reconstruction error but also the ranking error and graph regularization into the objective function.

3) *Tag completion.* In [22], the authors propose to firstly complete the image tags based on the co-occurrence among tags, and then compute the similarity between the query and the images by using the tag relevance. The difference is that [22] uses the manual tags while our method utilizes the attribute. Moreover, [11] proposes to complete the image tags based on the image-tag association and tag-tag concurrence. And [4] gives an efficient approach by introducing a co-regularized framework. The difference between [11,4] and our method is that they focus on image annotation instead of image retrieval which would lead to the different framework.

2 Our Method

A multi-attribute query is represented by a matrix $\mathbf{Q} \in \{0, 1\}^{q \times m}$, where q is the number of query attributes and m denotes the feature dimension. The element $Q_{ij} = 1$ when the pre-defined attribute (A_j) is selected as the ith query attribute (QA_i). For example, in the Bird dataset, m is the number of pre-defined attributes, *i.e.* 312. If the query is "a bird with pointed-wing shape, blue crown, cone bill shape, and black leg" as shown in Fig. 1, we extract four attributes: "Wing shape: Pointed-Wing", "Crown Color: Blue", "Bill Shape: Cone", and "Leg color: Black", *i.e.* q is 4. Furthermore, Let $\mathbf{D} \in \mathbb{R}^{m \times N}$ represent a set of N training images, each of which is described by m-dimensional attribute scores.

2.1 Query Expansion

To characterize the correlation between query attributes and non-query attributes, we firstly collect the positive examples for the query from the training data $\mathbf{D}$, denoted as $\mathbf{D_q} \in \mathbb{R}^{m \times N_q}$, where N_q is the number of positive images. An image is positive when it contains all the query attributes. The goal is to compute the query dependent correlation matrix $\mathbf{B} \in \mathbb{R}^{m \times m}$. This problem is formalized as reconstructing $\mathbf{D_q} \in \mathbb{R}^{m \times N_q}$ from a "corrupted" $\widetilde{\mathbf{D}}_q \in \mathbb{R}^{m \times N_q}$. In order to mine the correlations among the attributes, we empty all the rows in $\mathbf{D}_q$ which represent the query attributes QA_i to obtain $\widetilde{\mathbf{D}}_q$ as:

$$\widetilde{\mathbf{D}}_q = (\mathbf{1}_{N_q \times m} - \mathbf{1}_{N_q \times q}\mathbf{Q})^T \odot \mathbf{D_q}, \tag{1}$$

where $\mathbf{1}_{r \times c}$ denotes a (r, c) matrix full of ones and $\odot$ is the Hadamard product. The correlation matrix $\mathbf{B}$ is expected to catch the correlation between non-query attributes in $\widetilde{\mathbf{D}}_q$ and query attributes in $\mathbf{D}$:

$$\mathbf{B} = \text{argmin} \, ||\mathbf{D}_q - \mathbf{B}\widetilde{\mathbf{D}}_q||^2 + \lambda||\mathbf{B}||_2, \tag{2}$$

where the second term is used to prevent overfitting and λ is the weighting parameter. This is an ordinary least squares regressor which has the closed form solution $\mathbf{B} = (\widetilde{\mathbf{D}}_q^T\widetilde{\mathbf{D}}_q + \lambda\mathbf{I})^{-1}\widetilde{\mathbf{D}}_q^T\mathbf{D}_\mathbf{q}$. Finally, we obtain the expanded query matrix $\mathbf{B}\mathbf{Q}^T$ as shown in Fig. 1 (b) bottom.

2.2 Query Reconstruction Based on Inducing Group Sparsity

Computing the similarity measure between the images and the expanded query by directly using the predicted attribute vectors might not handle the imprecise and noisy image representations caused by *e.g.* scale, occlusion. To overcome this limitation, we adopt a sparse reconstruction framework which has been proven to be effective in [19,21]. We use training data $\mathbf{D}$ as the base to sparsely reconstruct the expanded query attributes $\mathbf{B}\mathbf{Q}^T$ with $\ell_{2,1}$ norm constraint:

$$\mathbf{X} = \operatorname{argmin} ||\mathbf{B}\mathbf{Q}^\mathbf{T} - \mathbf{D}\mathbf{X}||_2^2 + \alpha||\mathbf{X}||_{2,1}, \tag{3}$$

where $\mathbf{X} \in \mathbb{R}^{N\times q}$ is the reconstruction coefficient, $||\cdot||_{2,1}$ is the $\ell_{2,1}$ norm, and α is the weighting parameter. The training images which have non-zero reconstruction coefficients are considered semantically related to the query. Specially, each row of $\mathbf{X}$ refers to the similarity scores of images with respect to corresponding query attributes.

In our work, we use $\ell_{2,1}$ norm instead of ℓ_1 for sparse recovery. The reasons of selecting $\ell_{2,1}$ norm regularization are twofold. Firstly, each image (column of $\mathbf{D}$) is restricted to be evenly similar to the expanded query attributes as imposed by the ℓ_2 norm. Secondly, the ℓ_1 norm is used to sum the similarities across images, and select only the reliable images by removing imprecise and noisy image representations. The group structure generated by $\ell_{2,1}$ norm ensures more robust and accurate results.

2.3 Ranking Regularization

Now, we have the reconstruction coefficient $\mathbf{X}$ whose non-zero rows indicate the images related to the query, moreover the value of each element denotes the degree of similarity. To rank the retrieved images based on their similarity to the query, an intuitive way is to sum the coefficient values and sort them. The assumption behind this way is that all the reconstruction coefficients contribute equally to the rank. We introduce a weighting scheme by ranking SVM [7] which embeds the ranking in its loss function. The training images are firstly collected from the training part of each dataset, which have the groundtruth labels. Then we define each query $\mathbf{Q}_t \subset Q$, where Q is the set of queries. The objective function of ranking SVM is:

$$\operatorname{argmin}\ \mathbf{W}^T\mathbf{W} + C\sum_t \xi_t,\ \forall t\ \ \mathbf{W}^T(\phi(\mathbf{Q}_t, \mathbf{y}_t^\star) - \phi(\mathbf{Q}_t, \mathbf{y}_t)) \geq \Delta(\mathbf{y}_t^\star, \mathbf{y}_t) - \xi_t, \tag{4}$$

where $\mathbf{W} \in \mathbb{R}^{q\times q}$ is the ranking weight, $\mathbf{y}^\star$ is the set of images which contains all the constituent attributes in query $\mathbf{Q}_t$. $\mathbf{y}$ represents the other set of images which do not include all the attributes in query $\mathbf{Q}_t$. $\Delta(\mathbf{y}_t^\star, \mathbf{y}_t)$ is the loss function as in [17,14]. C is a parameter which determines the trade-off between training accuracy and regularization.

ξ_t is a slack variable to handle the soft margin. $\phi(\cdot)$ is the feature map of images. Eq. 4 could be efficiently solved by cutting plane method [18].

Specifically, in our method we use the reconstruction coefficient $\mathbf{X}$ as the feature map. Then we can use the loss function to penalize outputs $\mathbf{y}_t$ that deviate from the correct output $\mathbf{y}_t^\star$ based on the performance metric we want to optimize for. We set the loss function as hamming loss:

$$\Delta(\mathbf{y}_t^\star, \mathbf{y}_t) = 1 - \frac{|\mathbf{y}_t \cap \mathbf{y}_t^\star| + |\bar{\mathbf{y}}_t \cap \bar{\mathbf{y}}_t^\star|}{N}. \tag{5}$$

The reason to choose hamming loss is that it computed efficiently which only needs $O(|y_t|)$ to solve Eq. 5 as discussed in [17,23], where $|y_t|$ is the number of training images. Eq. 3 only considers the reconstruction error while our aim is to rank the images. Motivated by [6] which merged the classification error to objective function to achieve a better classification results, we also embed the ranking error to the objective function which is denoted as $\Omega(\mathbf{W}, \mathbf{X})$. We define $\mathbf{y}_s$ as the prediction results of after computing the scores of training images $\mathbf{XW}$, and $\mathbf{y}_{gt}$ as the groundtruth ranking of training images under the current query $\mathbf{Q}_t$. The Normalized Discounted Cumulative Gains [3] is adopted as the ranking metric:

$$NDCG@k = \sum_{j=1}^{k} \frac{2^{rel(j)} - 1}{log(1 + j)}, \tag{6}$$

where $rel(j)$ is the relevance of the jth ranked image and Z is a normalization constant. And $NDCG@k$ represents the score of top k ranked images. The relevance is defined as the number of shared attributes between the query and the images. Then, $\Omega(\mathbf{W}, \mathbf{X}) = 1 - NDCG@k(\mathbf{y}_s, \mathbf{y}_{gt})$ where $k = 100$ in all our experiments.

To incorporate the ranking loss into the objective function, we could set $\Omega(\mathbf{W}, \mathbf{X})$ as a regularization term. Then the objective function Eq. 3 is rewritten as:

$$(\mathbf{W}, \mathbf{X}) = \text{argmin} \, ||\mathbf{BQ}^{\mathrm{T}} - \mathbf{DX}||_2^2 + \alpha||\mathbf{X}||_{2,1} + \gamma\Omega(\mathbf{W}, \mathbf{X}), \tag{7}$$

where γ is the weighting parameter.

2.4 Graph Regularization

Since we use the score of attribute classifiers as the intermediate representation (**D**) of the image, one limitation is that the visually similar images might generate different representations because of various factors such as occlusions and scales. Preserving the local visual similarity among images would boost the performance of our method. That is to say, when the images are visually similar, they should have similar scores to the query. Moreover, in the test phase, we utilize the such locality to make our method insensitive to the data variance. Graph regularization [26] is designed for such purpose in the reconstruction step. In our work, the goal of introducing the graph regularization into the objective function is to ensure the visually similar images to obtain the close rankings.

Mathematically, each image $\mathbf{f}_i = [h_1, h_2, ..., h_s]^T \in \mathbb{R}^{s\times 1}$ is represented by its low-level features, such as HOG, SIFT and Texton, where s denotes the dimension of the low level feature representation. We construct a graph $\mathbf{G}$ based on the nearest neighborhood method using the low-level feature distance, each vertex of which stands for an image. Let $\mathbf{S}$ be the weight matrix of graph $\mathbf{G}$, where $S_{i,j}$ is set to 1 when $\mathbf{f}_i$ is one of the k-nearest neighbors of $\mathbf{f}_j$ or equivalently $\mathbf{f}_j$ is one of the k-nearest neighbors of $\mathbf{f}_i$, otherwise $S_{i,j} = 0$. We define the degree of the image as $\mathbf{J} = diag\{j_1, j_2, ..., j_N\}$, where $j_n = \sum_{i=1}^{N} S_{ij}$. By considering the goal of this term, a reasonable method for choosing a graph regularizer is to minimize the following objective function:

$$\Psi(\mathbf{W}, \mathbf{X}) = \frac{1}{2}\sum_{i=1}^{N}\sum_{j=1}^{N}((\mathbf{x}_i - \mathbf{x}_j)^2 S_{ij} + (\mathbf{x}_i\mathbf{W} - \mathbf{x}_j\mathbf{W})^2 S_{ij}) = Tr((\mathbf{XW})^{\mathrm{T}}\mathbf{L}(\mathbf{XW}) + \mathbf{X}^{\mathrm{T}}\mathbf{LX}), \tag{8}$$

where $\mathbf{L} = \mathbf{S} - \mathbf{J}$ is the Laplacian matrix. $\mathbf{x}_i \in \mathbb{R}^{1\times q}$ denotes the reconstruction coefficient with respect to the ith image. This regularization enforces the similar images to obtain the close reconstruction coefficients and ranking scores. By incorporating the Laplacian regularizer Ψ into the objective (7), we have the final objective function:

$$(\mathbf{X}, \mathbf{W}) = \operatorname{argmin} \underbrace{\|\mathbf{BQ}^{\mathrm{T}} - \mathbf{DX}\|_2^2 + \alpha\|\mathbf{X}\|_{2,1}}_{sparse\ reconstruction} + \underbrace{\gamma\Omega(\mathbf{W}, \mathbf{X})}_{ranking\ regularization} + \underbrace{\beta\Psi(\mathbf{W}, \mathbf{X})}_{graph\ regularization}. \tag{9}$$

Recall that $\Omega(\mathbf{W}, \mathbf{X})$ denotes the ranking regularization term constructed based on the standard ranking SVM [7]. $\Psi(\mathbf{W}, \mathbf{X})$ is defined as the graph regularizer, which is used to keep the locality of the images. $\lambda, \alpha, \beta, \gamma$ are the weights associated with each regularization term.

2.5 Optimization

Since the local graph and global ranking consistency constraints in the objective function are quadratic, the objective function Eq. 9 is a convex problem, thus it could be solved by a gradient descent-based approach as shown in Algorithm 1.

Firstly, Eq. 2 could be considered as a rigid regression problem, which could be efficiently solved by gradient descent to get the correlation matrix $\mathbf{B}$. Then Eq. 9 is composed of two variables $(\mathbf{W}, \mathbf{X})$ to be optimized. We use an iterative strategy to solve it:

-Holding $\mathbf{W}$ fixed, learn the reconstruction coefficient $\mathbf{X}$ by solving a standard sparse coding problem. We use a similar algorithm described in [12] to solve this optimize problem.

-Holding $\mathbf{X}$ fixed, learn the ranking weight parameter $\mathbf{W}$ by employing a standard ranking SVM, which was proposed in [7].

The two steps are repeated until convergence. Furthermore, we observe that there needs to be about 2 ~ 4 iterations to convergence.

2.6 Test Phase

In the test phase, we firstly extract the attribute presentation $\mathbf{D}_t$ by using attribute classifiers. Then the similarity among testing images is computed based their low-level feature representation and therefore we have $\mathbf{S}_t$ and $\mathbf{L}_t$. Since we obtained the ranking weighting coefficients $\mathbf{W}$, query representation $\mathbf{BQ}^{\mathrm{T}}$ and the Laplacian matrix $\mathbf{L_t}$, we just need to solve a sparse reconstruction problem:

$$\mathbf{X}_t = \operatorname{argmin} ||\mathbf{BQ}^{\mathrm{T}} - \mathbf{D_t X_t}||_2^2 + \alpha ||\mathbf{X_t}||_{2,1} + \beta Tr((\mathbf{X_t W})^{\mathrm{T}} \mathbf{L_t} (\mathbf{X_t W}) + \mathbf{X_t^T L_t X_t}), \quad (10)$$

where $\mathbf{X}_t$ represents the reconstruction coefficients for the testing images. Finally, we use the reconstruction coefficients $\mathbf{X_t}$ and the ranking weight $\mathbf{W}$ to get the final image ranking list. α and β are determined on the validation dataset.

Algorithm 1. The main training steps of our method

1. **Input:** $\mathbf{B} \in \mathbb{R}^{m \times m}, \mathbf{Q} \in \mathbb{R}^{q \times m}, \mathbf{D} \in \mathbb{R}^{m \times n}, \lambda, \alpha, \beta, \gamma$
2. Initialize $\mathbf{W} = \mathbf{1}_{q \times q}, \mathbf{X} = \mathbf{0}$
3. **repeat**
4. Computing reconstruction coefficients $\mathbf{X}$ according to Eq. 9 with $\mathbf{W}$ fixed.
5. Computing image ranking weight $\mathbf{W}$ according to Eq. 4 with $\mathbf{X}$ fixed.
6. Update the solutions $\mathbf{W}$ and $\mathbf{X}$.
7. **until** convergence:$||\mathbf{BQ}^{\mathrm{T}} - \mathbf{DX}||_2 \leq \epsilon$ & $\Omega(\mathbf{W}, \mathbf{X}) \leq \rho$
8. **Output**:Reconstruction coefficients $\mathbf{X}$, Ranking weight $\mathbf{W}$;

3 Experiments

We have conducted extensive experiments to evaluate our image retrieval and ranking framework on three public datasets LFW [10], CUB-200-2011 [2], and Shoes dataset [1]. First, we show the effect of parameters to the performance. Second, compared with the state-of-the-art approaches, we validate the superior performance of our method. Third, we experiment on the shoes dataset to demonstrate our method can be applied on the case directly using images as queries.

3.1 Experimental Settings

Dataset. LFW[10] (Labeled Faces in the Wild) is originally constructed for face verification. In our experiments, a subset of images consisting of 9992 images is selected. In addition, each image is annotated with 73 attributes. We simply divide this subset into two parts: 50% of all the images are randomly chosen as the training data and the remaining are used for testing. **CUB-200-2011** [2] (Caltech-UCSD Birds-200-2011) is composed of 11,788 images from 200 bird categories, which are the uncropped images of birds with various statuses, such as flying, perched, swimming, truncated and occluded, in the wild. Furthermore, each bird has been described by 312 binary visual attributes. **Shoes dataset** [1]: contains 14,765 images of 10 classes of shoes. The images in this dataset are relatively clean without confounding visual challenges like clutters, occlusions *etc*.

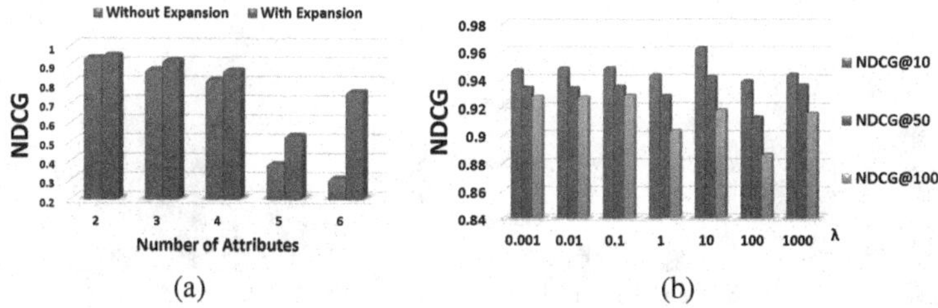

(a) (b)

Fig. 2. Evaluation of query expansion parameter: (a) The comparison results between with query expansion (Red histogram) and without query expansion (Blue histogram). The comparison is constructed on five types of queries. (b) NDCG Varies for Different Parameters: The weight of regularization λ and the number of top images.

Query. Since there are no pre-defined multi-attribute queries available for our task, we create the queries by ourselves based on the training part of each dataset. Two kinds of queries, *i.e.* semantic attribute queries (on LFW and CUB-200-2011) and image queries (on Shoes) are considered. For the semantic attribute ones, 5 different structures are involved, which contain various numbers, from 2 to 6, of attributes in the query. Specially, we randomly select the attributes from the training set to construct the query with the constraint that each query should contain at least 30 related images. For the image query, we randomly select the images from the training set used as queries.

Evaluation Metric: Instead of using a binary relevance, we design the relevance with multiple levels [13]. The more attributes an image shares with the query, the heavier the relevance is. As the common attributes become less, the relevance decreases. By considering that our goal is to rank the image, we select Normalized Discounted Cumulative Gains (NDCG) [3] as the evaluation criterion.

3.2 Component Evaluation

In this part, we use the validation dataset for tuning parameters and analyzing their corresponding influences to image retrieval and ranking performance. There are mainly four parameters of our proposed model including λ, α, β, and γ. λ controls the weight to avoid over-fitting when we expand query. α corresponds the sparsity of the representation, γ takes care of the contribution of ranking error in the objective function , while β determines the importance of the locality similarity among images. To evaluate the influence of each parameter, we randomly select 100 queries which are composed of two attributes from LFW. As for C in Eq. 4 and the number of nearest neighborhoods k in the graph regularization, we empirically set them to 0.1 and 5, respectively.

Query Expansion Evaluation. Firstly, we conduct experiments in this part to validate the advantage of the usage of the query expansion. In this validation, we test queries from 5 kinds of query structures, each of which consists of 100 queries. The experiment results are shown in Fig. 2(a). The advantage of the query expansion is not distinct when the number of attributes is small. However, as the number of query attributes grows, the query expansion shows its power. The reason is that when the query attributes are few,

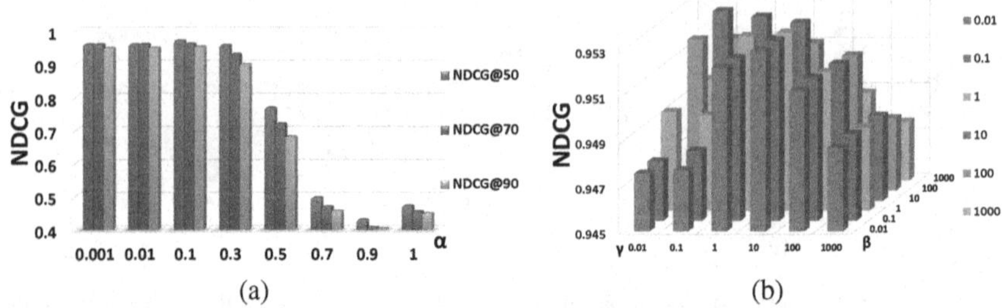

Fig. 3. Evaluation of weighting parameters in the objective function. (a) NDCG Varies for Different Sparsity: The higher value of α indicates more sparsity. (b) NDCG@100 results of different combinations of parameters β and γ.

for instance only two attributes, there are a lot of related images that limits the improvement. However, once the attributes becomes more, the number of the related images sharply drops, then the advantage of expansion gets outstanding. Besides, there is one more important parameter λ directly affecting the performance of the query expansion. The selected value of λ ranges from 10^{-3} to 10^{3} as shown in Fig. 2(b). The performance indicates that the query expansion is easily over-fitted when the value of λ is small.

Query Reconstruction Evaluation. We further investigate the influence of the group sparsity by varying α. Smaller value of α indicates that more images are involved in the ranking process, which would introduce more noises and increase the training time. While larger value of α would make a smaller subset of images response, which would give a desired ranking performance. As shown in Fig. 3(a), the optimal setting for α is around 0.1. Based on the results, the conclusion that the sparsity could help for preserving the related images and keeping the structure discriminative can be drawn. We also show how our algorithm performs given different β and γ values. The ranges for the two parameters are all set to be from 0.01 to 1000. From the results shown in Fig. 3(a), we observe that our algorithm achieves the best results when $\beta = 10$ and $\gamma = 0.1$. Please note that the bins in different colors in Fig. 3(a) represent different values of γ.

3.3 LFW Dataset

In this section, we test the performance of our method on LFW. The images in this dataset are evenly separated into two parts including the training set and the testing. We adopt the attributes defined in [10], say 73-dimensional scores of the attribute classifiers. We randomly generate $2,000$ queries to do the experiment. The number of queries from two to six attributes are 500, 400, 500, 300 and 300, respectively. The basic parameters of our model are set as $\lambda = 10$ the query expansion process, and $\alpha = 0.1, \beta = 10.5, \gamma = 0.5$ in the training. These parameters are fixed throughout this experiment.

Three related work on multi-attribute based image retrieval and ranking, *i.e. RMLL* [14], *MARR* [17] and *Weak Attributes* [23] are compared with our method. The parameters of the competitors are from the corresponding papers. To reveal the advantages of fusing the ranking regularization and graph regularization into the objective function,

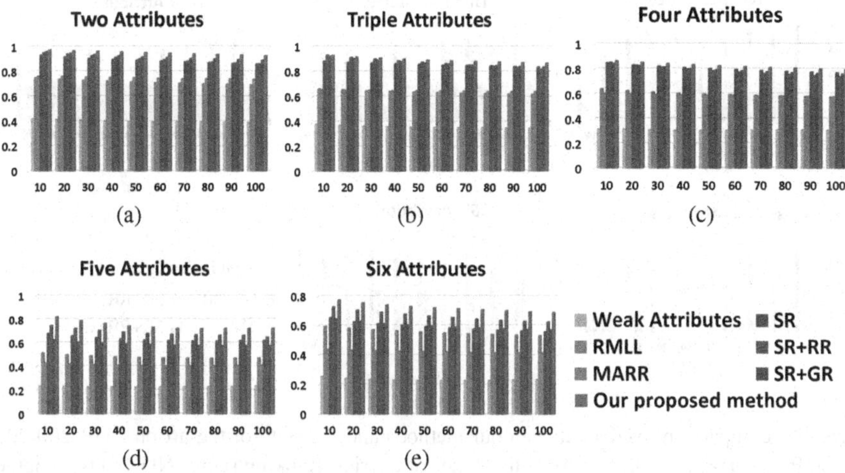

Fig. 4. The comparison results between our proposed methods and the state-of-the-art on LFW dataset. From (a)-(e) are the results of five types of queries. Ranking score (NDCG) is computed on 10 levels from top 10 to 100. The horizontal axis denotes the number of top retrieved images, and the vertical axis represents the score of NDCG.

we derivate three variations from our method to participate in the comparison. We use **SR** to represent the variation that only uses the sparse reconstruction. **SR+GR** denotes that we add the graph regularization into the objective function. **SR+RR** denotes that we add the ranking regularization into the objective function and our whole framework is represented by **SP+RR+GR**.

The comparison results are shown in Figure 4. We can observe that our method has achieved a significant improvement compared with the baselines [23,14,17] on all five types of queries. Four possible reasons may explain this situation: 1) The clean background of each image has little negative effect on training the attribute classifiers thus leads to the relative better intermediate representations. 2) The query expansion can generate the discriminative representation for the query. 3) The unified objective function can not only preserve the global ranking consistency by the ranking term but also hold the local similarity among images by the graph regularization (some examples corresponding to this point are shown in Fig. 6(a)). And 4) Few interruptions, such as viewpoint changes, occlusions and scales) in this dataset, which makes our results impressive.

3.4 CUB-200-2011 Dataset

To further test the effectiveness of our model, we experiment on a more challenging dataset CUB-200-2011 [20]. It contains 312 pre-defined binary attributes to describe a bird. The attributes can be summarized as 15 part categories: { *Beak, Belly, Throat, Crown, Tail, Back, Fore-head, Nape, Eye, Wing, Breast, Head, Leg, Body, Bird size*} and on average each part corresponds to two attributes on color or pattern. Instead of

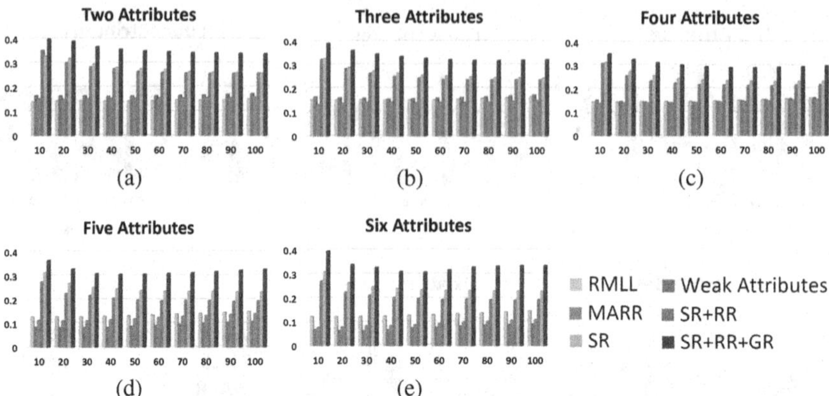

Fig. 5. The comparison results between our methods and the state-of-the-art on CUB-200-2011 dataset. From (a)-(e) are the results of five types of queries. Ranking score (NDCG) is computed on 10 levels from top 10 to 100. The horizontal axis denotes the number of top retrieved images, and the vertical axis represents the score of NDCG.

generating the queries from the binary attribute description, we develop the queries from the 15 category descriptions. We constrain that the query should contain different kinds of part categories and should include at least 30 related images. The number of queries on this dataset is 400. The parameters of this dataset is fixed as $\lambda = 10$ in the query expansion process, and $\alpha = 10, \beta = 100.5, \gamma = 0.5$ in the training.

Since there are not existing pre-trained attribute detectors, we employ a multi-label method [24] to train an multi-label attribute detector. Further, we use the image level description to describe each image: firstly we use the low level features which are provided by [5]. Three types of features including color(8), contour(128), and shape(54) are used to develop a descriptor with 216 dimensions. The comparison results of our method with the existing works are shown in Fig. 5. We observe that our proposed method achieves a significant better performance on this dataset than the other alternatives. This results further validate the robustness of our framework. While we also find that the average performance is degraded with the number of attributes growing. The main reasons are that the attribute detector has a lower recognition accuracy rate. When there are more attributes in the query, the errors accumulate. In addition, the decreasing number of positive images influences the performance of ranking SVM. Last but not least, the diverse bird appearances increase the difficulty of generating a robust classifier, even they are in the same class, which would reduce the positive effect of graph regularization. Some experiment results are shown in Fig. 6(b). We also show the qualitative retrieval example comparing with related methods as shown in Fig. 7.

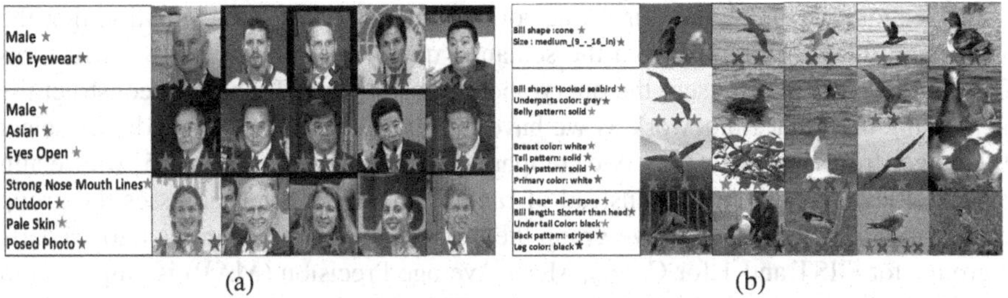

Fig. 6. (a) Top-5 retrieval results of our proposed approach based on different kinds of queries on LFW dataset. (b) Top-5 retrieval results of our proposed approach based on different kinds of queries of Bird dataset. The color of stars indicates the distinct attributes in the query and solid star represents the presence of corresponding attributes while the red cross states the image missing the corresponding query attribute.

Table 1. Image retrieval accuracy on shoes dataset. Comparing with [25], our proposed image retrieval framework significantly improves the accuracy.

Methods	10	30	50	70	90	Avg.
[25]	0.5811	0.4618	0.4076	0.3710	0.3417	0.4326
Our Method	0.6881	0.6033	0.5826	0.5718	0.5604	**0.6012**

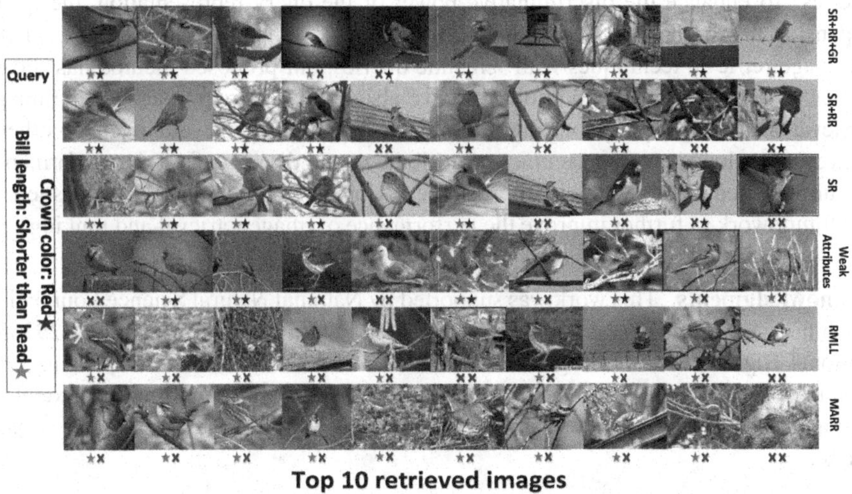

Fig. 7. Example of the retrieval results using the query "Bill length: Shorter than head" and "Crown color: Red" in the bird dataset. Top three rows show the results of our proposed methods, and the remaining rows display the results of the related work. The red cross states the image missing the corresponding query attribute. Better view in color.

3.5 Shoes Dataset

In this section, we show that our framework can be adopted to the situation that the query is an image. Different from the semantic query, we employ low level features (GIST and Color) to represent the query and corpus images. Then we reconstruct the query using the same framework as we have introduced. In total, we randomly select 100 images from the training set. We compare our ranking results with [25] whose aim was to retrieval similar images instead of ranking them. As [25] harnesses the group sparsity to retrieval images, so we group the proposed low level features into 10 parts (9 groups for GIST and 1 for Color). Mean Average Precision (**MAP**) is employed to measure the performance of different methods. The results are shown in Table 1, as can be seen, our method obtains 60.12% on average, compared with 43.26% of [25], thanks to that our method combines the ranking error into the objective function to gain a more better reconstruction results, and the graph regularization is capable to preserve the local similarity among images which helps to produce more robust results. Furthermore, comparing with [25] our proposed method add the graph and ranking regularization into the objective function which would decrease the distance between the query image and the similar reference images (Graph regularization) and increase the distance between the query image and the dissimilar reference images (Ranking regularizations).

4 Conclusion and Future Work

In this paper, we have proposed a framework for solving the multi-attribute query based image retrieval and ranking problem by minimizing both the reconstruction and the ranking errors. The proposed algorithm takes advantage of the structural sparsity of queries. To enhance the discriminative power of the query representation, the query expansion has been introduced into the framework. Compared with the state of the art image retrieval techniques with semantic queries, our proposed method has shown advanced performance. In addition, we have also applied our approach on the image retrieval with image query, our algorithm has achieved better results over the others. However, the low detection accuracy of attribute would directly affect the performance of our proposed method, how to improve the attribute prediction performance is left as our future work to further improve the performance of image retrieval and ranking.

Acknowledgments. This work was supported by National Natural Science Foundation of China (No.61332012), National Basic Research Program of China (2013CB329305), National High-tech R&D Program of China (2014BAK11B03), and 100 Talents Programme of The Chinese Academy of Sciences. X. Guo was supported by Excellent Young Talent of the Institute of Information Engineering, Chinese Academy of Sciences.

References

1. Berg, T.L., Berg, A.C., Shih, J.: Automatic attribute discovery and characterization from noisy web data. In: Daniilidis, K., Maragos, P., Paragios, N. (eds.) ECCV 2010, Part I. LNCS, vol. 6311, pp. 663–676. Springer, Heidelberg (2010)

2. Branson, S., Wah, C., Schroff, F., Babenko, B., Welinder, P., Perona, P., Belongie, S.: Visual recognition with humans in the loop. In: Daniilidis, K., Maragos, P., Paragios, N. (eds.) ECCV 2010, Part IV. LNCS, vol. 6314, pp. 438–451. Springer, Heidelberg (2010)
3. Chapelle, O., Le, Q., Smola, A.: Large margin optimization of ranking measures. In: NIPS Workshop on Learning to Rank (2007)
4. Chen, M., Zheng, A., Weinberger, K.: Fast image tagging. In: ICML (2013)
5. Duan, K., Parikh, D., Crandall, D., Grauman, K.: Discovering localized attributes for fine-grained recognition. In: CVPR (2012)
6. Jiang, Z., Lin, Z., Davis, L.: Label consistent k-svd: Learning a discriminative dictionary for recognition. TPAMI 35(11), 2651–2664 (2013)
7. Joachims, T.: Optimizing search engines using clickthrough data. In: KDD (2002)
8. Kovashka, A., Parikh, D., Grauman, K.: Whittlesearch: Image search with relative attribute feedback. In: CVPR (2012)
9. Kumar, N., Belhumeur, P., Nayar, S.: FaceTracer: A search engine for large collections of images with faces. In: Forsyth, D., Torr, P., Zisserman, A. (eds.) ECCV 2008, Part IV. LNCS, vol. 5305, pp. 340–353. Springer, Heidelberg (2008)
10. Kumar, N., Berg, A.C., Belhumeur, P.N., Nayar, S.K.: Attribute and simile classifiers for face verification. In: ICCV (2009)
11. Lin, Z., Ding, G., Hu, M., Wang, J., Ye, X.: Image tag completion via image-specific and tag-specific linear sparse reconstructions. In: CVPR (2013)
12. Liu, J., Ji, S., Ye, J.: Multi-task feature learning via efficient l2,1-norm minimization. In: UAI (2009)
13. Liu, S., Song, Z., Liu, G., Xu, C., Lu, H., Yan, S.: Street-to-shop: Cross-scenario clothing retrieval via parts alignment and auxiliary set. In: CVPR (2012)
14. Petterson, J., Caetano, T.: Reverse multi-label learning. In: NIPS (2010)
15. Rastegari, M., Diba, A., Parikh, D.: Multi-attribute queries: To merge or not to merge? In: CVPR (2013)
16. Scheirer, W., Kumar, N., Belhumeur, P.N., Boult, T.E.: Multi-attribute spaces: Calibration for attribute fusion and similarity search. In: CVPR (2012)
17. Siddiquie, B., Feris, R.S., Davis, L.S.: Image ranking and retrieval based on multi-attribute queries. In: CVPR (2011)
18. Tsochantaridis, I., Joachims, T., Hofmann, T., Altun, Y.: Large margin methods for structured and interdependent output variables. JMLR 6, 1453–1484 (2005)
19. Wang, C., Yan, S., Zhang, L., Zhang, H.J.: Multi-label sparse coding for automatic image annotation. In: CVPR (2009)
20. Welinder, P., Branson, S., Mita, T., Wah, C., Schroff, F., Belongie, S., Perona, P.: The caltech-ucsd birds-200-2011 dataset. California Institute of Technology, CNS-TR-2011-001 (2007)
21. Wright, J., Yang, A.Y., Ganesh, A., Sastry, S.S., Ma, Y.: Robust face recognition via sparse representation. TPAMI 31(2), 210–227 (2009)
22. Wu, L., Jin, R., Jain, A.K.: Tag completion for image retrieval. TPAMI 35(3), 716–727 (2013)
23. Yu, F., Ji, R., Tsai, M.H., Ye, G., Chang, S.F.: Weak attributes for large-scale image retrieval. In: CVPR (2012)
24. Zhang, M., Zhou, Z.: Ml-knn: A lazy learning approach to multi-label learning. PR 40(7), 2038–2048 (2007)
25. Zhang, S., Huang, J., Li, H., Metaxas, D.N.: Automatic image annotation and retrieval using group sparsity. TSMC, Part B, 838–849 (2012)
26. Zheng, M., Bu, J., Chen, C., Wang, C., Zhang, L., Qiu, G., Cai, D.: Graph regularized sparse coding for image representation. TIP 20(5), 1327–1336 (2011)

Neural Codes for Image Retrieval

Artem Babenko[1,3], Anton Slesarev[1],
Alexandr Chigorin[1], and Victor Lempitsky[2]

[1] Yandex, Russia
[2] Skolkovo Institute of Science and Technology (Skoltech), Russia
[3] Moscow Institute of Physics and Technology, Russia

Abstract. It has been shown that the activations invoked by an image within the top layers of a large convolutional neural network provide a high-level descriptor of the visual content of the image. In this paper, we investigate the use of such descriptors (neural codes) within the image retrieval application. In the experiments with several standard retrieval benchmarks, we establish that neural codes perform competitively even when the convolutional neural network has been trained for an unrelated classification task (e.g. Image-Net). We also evaluate the improvement in the retrieval performance of neural codes, when the network is retrained on a dataset of images that are similar to images encountered at test time.

We further evaluate the performance of the compressed neural codes and show that a simple PCA compression provides very good short codes that give state-of-the-art accuracy on a number of datasets. In general, neural codes turn out to be much more resilient to such compression in comparison other state-of-the-art descriptors. Finally, we show that discriminative dimensionality reduction trained on a dataset of pairs of matched photographs improves the performance of PCA-compressed neural codes even further. Overall, our quantitative experiments demonstrate the promise of neural codes as visual descriptors for image
retrieval.

Keywords: image retrieval, same-object image search, deep learning, convolutional neural networks, feature extraction.

1 Introduction

Deep convolutional neural networks [13] have recently advanced the state-of-the-art in image classification dramatically [10] and have consequently attracted a lot of interest within the computer vision community. A separate but related to the image classification problem is the problem of image retrieval, i.e. the task of finding images containing the same object or scene as in a query image. It has been suggested that the features emerging in the upper layers of the CNN learned to classify images can serve as good descriptors for image retrieval. In particular, Krizhevsky et al. [10] have shown some qualitative evidence for that.

D. Fleet et al. (Eds.): ECCV 2014, Part I, LNCS 8689, pp. 584–599, 2014.
© Springer International Publishing Switzerland 2014

Here we interesed in establishing the quantitative performance of such features (which we refer to as *neural codes*) and their variations.

We start by providing a quantitative evaluation of the image retrieval performance of the features that emerge within the convolutional neural network trained to recognize Image-Net [1] classes. We measure such performance on four standard benchmark datasets: INRIA Holidays [8], Oxford Buildings, Oxford Building 105K [19], and the University of Kentucky benchmark (UKB) [16]. Perhaps unsurprisingly, these deep features perform well, although not better than other state-of-the-art holistic features (e.g. Fisher vectors). Interestingly, the relative performance of different layers of the CNN varies in different retrieval setups, and the best performance on the standard retrieval datasets is achieved by the features in the middle of the fully-connected layers hierarchy.

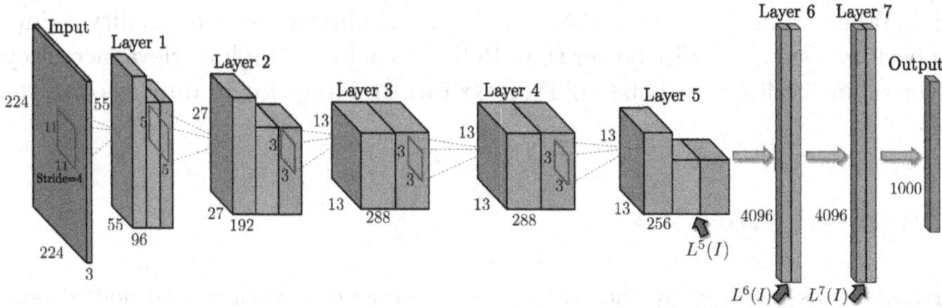

Fig. 1. The convolutional neural network architecture used on our experiments. Purple nodes correspond to input (an RGB image of size 224 × 224) and output (1000 class labels). Green units correspond to outputs of convolutions, red units correspond to the outputs of max pooling, and blue units correspond to the outputs of rectified linear (ReLU) transform. Layers 6, 7, and 8 (the output) are fully connected to the preceding layers. The units that correspond to the neural codes used in our experiments are shown with red arrows. Stride=4 are used in the first convolutional layer, and stride=1 in the rest.

The good performance of neural codes demonstrate their universality, since the task the network was trained for (i.e. classifying Image-Net classes) is quite different from the retrieval task we consider. Despite the evidence of such universality, there is an obvious possibility to improve the performance of deep features by adapting them to the task, and such adaptation is the subject of the second part of the paper. Towards this end, we assemble a large-scale image dataset, where the classes correspond to landmarks (similar to [14]), and retrain the CNN on this collection using the original image-net network parameters as initialization. After such training, we observe a considerable improvement of the retrieval performance on the datasets with similar image statistics, such as INRIA Holidays and Oxford Buildings, while the performance on the unrelated UKB dataset degrades. In the second experiment of this kind, we retrain the initial network on the Multi-view RGB-D dataset [12] of turntable views of different objects. As expected, we observe the improvement on the more related UKB dataset, while the performance on other datasets degrades or stays the same.

Finally, we focus our evaluation on the performance of the compact versions of the neural codes. We evaluate the performance of the PCA compression and observe that neural codes can be compressed very substantially, e.g. to 128 dimensions, with virtually no loss of the retrieval accuracy. Overall, the degradation from the PCA compression incurred by the neural codes is considerably smaller than the degradation incurred by other holistic descriptors. This makes the use of neural codes particularly attractive for large-scale retrieval applications, where the memory footprint of a descriptor often represents the major bottleneck.

Pushing the compression to the extreme, to e.g. 16 dimensions leads to considerable degradation, as long as PCA is used for the compression. We experiment with discriminative dimensionality reduction learned on an automatically collected large collection of pairs of photos depicting the same object (around 900K pairs). When trained on such a dataset, the discriminative dimensionality reduction performs substantially better than PCA and achieves high retrieval accuracy for very short codes (e.g. 0.368 mAP on Oxford Buildings for 16-dimensional features).

2 Related Work

Our paper was inspired by the strong performance of convolutional neural networks (CNN) in image classification tasks, and the qualitative evidence of their feasibility for image retrieval provided in [10]. A subsequent report [4] demonstrated that features emerging within the top layers of large deep CNNs can be reused for classification tasks dissimilar from the original classification task. Convolutional networks have also been used to produce descriptors suitable for retrieval within the *siamese architectures* [3].

In the domain of "shallow" architectures, there is a line of works on applying the responses of discriminatively trained multiclass classifiers as descriptors within retrieval applications. Thus, [24] uses the output of classifiers trained to predict membership of Flickr groups as image descriptors. Likewise, very compact descriptors based on the output of binary classifiers trained for a large number of classes (*classemes*) were proposed in [23]. Several works such as [11] used the outputs of discriminatively trained classifiers to describe human faces, obtaining high-performing face descriptors.

The current state-of-the-art holistic image descriptors are obtained by the aggregation of local gradient-based descriptors. Fisher Vectors [18] is the best known descriptor of this kind, however its performance has been recently superceded by the triangulation embedding suggested in [9] (another recent paper [22] have introduced descriptors that can also achieve very high performance, however the memory footprint of such descriptors is at least an order of magnitude larger than uncompressed Fisher vectors, which makes such descriptors unsuitable for most applications).

In [7], the dimensionality reduction of Fisher vectors is considered, and it is suggested to use Image-Net to discover discriminative low-dimensional subspace. The best performing variant of such dimensionality reduction in [7] is based on adding a hidden unit layer and a classifier output layer on top of Fisher vectors. After training on a subset of Image-Net, the low-dimensional activations of the hidden layer are used as descriptors for image retrieval. The architecture of [7] therefore is in many respects similar to those we investigate here, as it is deep (although not as multi-layered as in our case), and is trained on image-net classes. Still, the representations derived in [7] are based on hand-crafted features (SIFT and local color histograms) as opposed to neural codes derived from CNNs that are learned from the bottom up.

There is also a large body of work on dimensionality reduction and metric learning [26]. In the last part of the paper we used a variant of the discriminative dimensionality reduction similar to [21].

Independently and in parallel with our work, the use of neural codes for image retrieval (among other applications) has been investigated in [20]. Their findings are largely consistent with ours, however there is a substantial difference from this work in the way the neural codes are extracted from images. Specifically, [20] extract a large number of neural codes from each image by applying a CNN in a "jumping window" manner. In contrast to that, we focus on holistic descriptors where the whole image is mapped to a single vector, thus resulting in a substantially more compact and faster-to-compute descriptors, and we also investigate the performance of compressed holistic descriptors.

Furthermore, we investigate in details how retraining of a CNN on different datasets impact the retrieval performance of the corresponding neural codes. Another concurrent work [17] investigated how similar retraining can be used to adapt the Image-Net derived networks to smaller classification datasets.

3 Using Pretrained Neural Codes

Deep Convolutional Architecture. In this section, we evaluate the performance of neural codes obtained by passing images through a deep convolution network, trained to classify 1000 Image-Net classes [10]. In particular, we use our own reimplementation of the system from [10]. The model includes five convolutional layers, each including a convolution, a rectified linear (ReLU) transform ($f(x) = \max(x, 0)$), and a max pooling transform (layers 1, 2, and 2). At the top of the architecture are three fully connected layers ("layer 6", "layer 7", "layer 8"), which take as an input the output of the previous layer, multiply it by a matrix, and, in the case of layers 6, and 7 applies a rectified linear transform. The network is trained so that the layer 8 output corresponds to the one-hot encoding of the class label. The softmax loss is used during training. The results of the training on the ILSVRC dataset [1] closely matches the result of a single CNN reported in [10] (more precisely, the resulting accuracy is worse by 2%). Our network architecture is schematically illustrated on Figure 1.

The network is applicable to 224×224 images. Images of other dimensions are resized to 224×224 (without cropping). The CNN architecture is feed-forward, and given an image I, it produces a sequence of layer activations. We denote with $L^5(I)$, $L^6(I)$, and $L^7(I)$ the activations (output) of the corresponding layer *prior* to the ReLU transform. Naturally, each of these high-dimensional vectors represent a *deep* descriptor (a *neural code*) of the input image.

Benchmark Datasets. We evaluate the performance of neural codes on four standard datasets listed below. The results for top performing methods based on holistic descriptors (of dimensionality upto 32K) are given in Table 1.

Oxford Buildings Dataset [19] (Oxford). The dataset consists of 5062 photographs collected from Flickr and corresponding to major Oxford landmarks. Images corresponding to 11 landmarks (some having complex structure and comprising several buildings) are manually annotated. The 55 hold-out queries evenly distributed over those 11 landmarks are provided, and the performance of a retrieval method is reported as a mean average precision (mAP) [19] over the provided queries.

Oxford Buildings Dataset+100K [19] (Oxford 105K). The same dataset with the same associated protocol, but with additional 100K distractor images provided by the dataset authors.

INRIA Holidays Dataset [8] (Holidays). The dataset consists of 1491 vacation photographs corresponding to 500 groups based on same scene or object. One image from each group serves as a query. The performance is reported as mean average precision over 500 queries. Some images in the dataset are not in a natural orientation (rotated by ±90 degrees). As deep architectures that we consider are trained on the images in a normal orientation, we follow several previous works, and manually bring all images in the dataset to the normal orientation. In a sequel, all our results are for this modified dataset. We also experimented with an unrotated version and found the performance in most settings to be worse by about 0.03 mAP. Most of the performance drop can be regained back using data augmentation (rotating by ±90) on the dataset and on the query sides.

University of Kentucky Benchmark Dataset [16] (UKB). The dataset includes 10,200 indoor photographs of 2550 objects (4 photos per object). Each image is used to query the rest of the dataset. The performance is reported as the average number of same-object images within the top-4 results, and is a number between 0 and 4.

Results. The results for neural codes produced with a network trained on ILSVRC classes are given in the middle part of Table 1. All results were obtained using L2-distance on L2-normalized neural codes. We give the results corresponding to each of the layers 5, 6, 7. We have also tried the output of layer 8 (corresponding to the ILSVRC class probabilities and thus closely related to previous works that used class probabilities as descriptors), however it performed considerably worse (e.g. 0.02 mAP worse than layer 5 on Holidays).

Among all the layers, the 6th layer performs the best, however it is not uniformly better for all queries (see Figure 2 and Figure 3). Still, the results obtained using simple combination of the codes (e.g. sum or concatenation) were worse than $L^6(I)$-codes alone, and more complex non-linear combination rules we experimented with gave only marginal improvement.

Overall, the results obtained using $L^6(I)$-codes are in the same ballpark, but not superior compared to state-of-the-art. Their strong performance is however remarkable given the disparity between the ILSVRC classification task and the retrieval tasks considered here.

Fig. 2. A retrieval example on Holidays dataset where Layer 5 gives the best result among other layers, presumably because of its reliance on relatively low-level texture features rather than high level concepts. The left-most image in each row corresponds to the query, correct answers are outlined in green.

Fig. 3. A retrieval example on Holidays dataset where Layer 7 gives the best result among other layers, presumably because of its reliance on high level concepts. The left-most image in each row corresponds to the query, correct answers are outlined in green.

4 Retrained Neural Codes

A straightforward idea for the improvement of the performance of neural codes is to retrain the convolutional architecture on the dataset with image statistics and classes that are more relevant for datasets considered at test time.

The Landmarks Dataset. We first focus on collecting the dataset that is relevant to the landmark-type datasets (Holidays and Oxford Buildings). The collection of such dataset is an untrivial task, and we chose a (semi)-automated approach for that. We start by selecting 10,000 most viewed landmark Wikipedia pages (over the last month). For each page, we used the title of the page as a query to Yandex image search engine[1], and then downloaded 1000 top images returned in response to the query (or less, if the query returned less images).

At the second stage, we eyeballed the returned images by looking at the hundred of photographs from the top of the response and at an another hundred sampled uniformly from the remaining images (900 or less). We then manually classify the downloaded list into one of the following three classes: (1) "take all" (at least 80% in both hundreds are relevant, i.e. are actual photographs of the landmark), (2) "take top" (at least 80% in the first hundred are relevant, but the second hundred has more than 20% non-relevant images, including logos, maps, portraits, wrong scenes/objects), (3) "unsuitable" (more than 20% non-relevant images even within the first hundred). Overall, in this way we found 252 "take all" classes, and 420 "take top" images. Figure 4 shows two typical examples of classes in the collected dataset. We then assembled the dataset out of these classes, taking either top 1000 images (for "take all" classes) or top 100 images (for "take top" classes) for each query. Overall the resulting dataset has 672 classes and 213,678 images. During the collection, we excluded queries related to Oxford, and we also removed few near-duplicates with the Holidays dataset from the final dataset. We provide the list of the queries and the URLs at the project webpage[2].

Our approach for a landmark dataset collection is thus different from that of [14] that uses Flickr crawling to assemble a similar dataset in a fully automatic way. The statistics of images indexed by image search engines and of geotagged user photographs is different, so it would be interesting to try the adaptation using the Flickr-crawled dataset.

We then used the collected dataset to train the CNN with the same architecture as for the ILSVRC (except for the number of output nodes that we changed to 672). We initialized our model by the original ILSVRC CNN (again except for the last layer). Otherwise, the training was the same as for the original network.

Results for Retrained Neural Codes. The results for neural codes produced with a network retrained on the landmark classes are given in Table 1. As expected, the difference with respect to the original neural codes is related to the similarity between the landmark photographs and the particular retrieval

[1] `http://images.yandex.ru`

[2] `http://sites.skoltech.ru/compvision/projects/neuralcodes/`

Table 1. Full-size holistic descriptors: comparison with state-of-the-art (holistic descriptors with the dimensionality up to 32K). The neural codes are competitive with the state-of-the-art and benefit considerably from retraining on related datasets (Landmarks for Oxford Buildings and Holidays; turntable sequences for UKB). ⋆ indicate the results obtained for the rotated version of Holidays, where all images are set into their natural orientation.

Descriptor	Dims	Oxford	Oxford 105K	Holidays	UKB
Fisher+color[7]	4096	—	—	**0.774**	3.19
VLAD+adapt+innorm[2]	32768	0.555	—	0.646	—
Sparse-coded features[6]	11024	—	—	0.767	**3.76**
Triangulation embedding[9]	8064	**0.676**	**0.611**	0.771	3.53
Neural codes trained on ILSVRC					
Layer 5	9216	0.389	—	0.690*	3.09
Layer 6	4096	0.435	0.392	0.749*	3.43
Layer 7	4096	0.430	—	0.736*	3.39
After retraining on the Landmarks dataset					
Layer 5	9216	0.387	—	0.674*	2.99
Layer 6	4096	0.545	0.512	**0.793***	3.29
Layer 7	4096	0.538	—	0.764*	3.19
After retraining on turntable views (Multi-view RGB-D)					
Layer 5	9216	0.348	—	0.682*	3.13
Layer 6	4096	0.393	0.351	0.754*	3.56
Layer 7	4096	0.362	—	0.730*	3.53

dataset. Thus, there is a very big improvement for Oxford and Oxford 105K datasets, which are also based on landmark photographs. The improvement for the Holidays dataset is smaller but still very considerable. The performance of adapted $L^6(I)$ features on the Holidays dataset is better then for previously published systems based on holistic features (unless much higher dimensionality as in [22] is considered). Representative retrieval examples comparing the results obtained with the original and the retrained neural codes are presented in Figure 5. We also tried to train a CNN on the landmarks dataset with random initialization (i.e. trained from scratch) but observed poor performance due to a smaller number of training images and a higher ratio of irrelevant images compared to ILSVRC.

Interestingly, while we obtain an improvement by retraining the CNN on the Landmarks dataset, no improvement over the original neural codes was obtained by retraining the CNN on the SUN dataset [25]. Apparently, this is because each SUN class still correspond to *different* scenes with the same usage type, while each class in the Landmark dataset as well as in the Holidays and Oxford datasets corresponds to the same object (e.g. building).

Adaptation on the Turntable Sequences. After retraining on the Landmarks collection, the performance on the UKB dataset drops. This reflects the fact that the classes in the UKB dataset, which correspond to multiple indoor views of different small objects, are more similar to some classes within ILSVRC

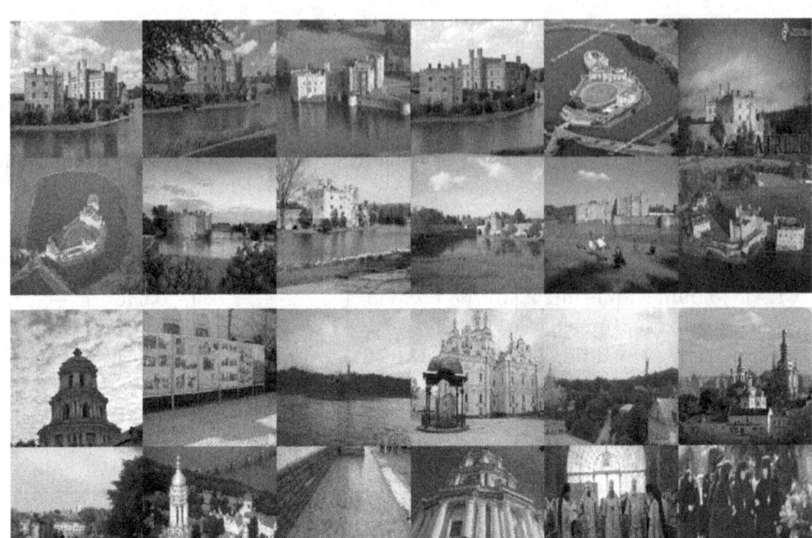

Fig. 4. Sample images from the "Leeds Castle" and "Kiev Pechersk Lavra" classes of the collected Landmarks dataset. The first class contains mostly "clean" outdoor images sharing the same building while the second class contains a lot of indoor photographs that do not share common geometry with the outdoor photos.

than to landmark photographs. To confirm this, we performed the second retraining experiment, where we used the Multi-view RGB-D dataset [12] which contains turntable views of 300 household objects. We treat each object as a separate class and sample 200 images per class. We retrain the network (again, initialized by the ILSVRC CNN) on this dataset of 60,000 images (the depth channel was discarded). Once again, we observed (Table 1) that this retraining provides an increase in the retrieval performance on the related dataset, as the accuracy on the UKB increased from 3.43 to 3.56. The performance on the unrelated datasets (Oxford, Oxford-105K) dropped.

5 Compressed Neural Codes

As the neural codes in our experiments are high-dimensional (e.g. 4096 for $L^6(I)$), albeit less high-dimensional than other state-of-the-art holistic descriptors, a question of their efficient compression arises. In this section, we evaluate two different strategies for such compression. First, we investigate how efficiency of neural codes degrades with the common PCA-based compression. An important finding is that this degradation is rather graceful. Second, we assess a more sophisticated procedure based on discriminative dimensionality reduction. We focus our evaluation on $L^6(I)$, since the performance of the neural codes

Fig. 5. Examples of Holidays queries with large differences between the results of the original and the retrained neural codes (retraining on Landmarks). In each row pair, the left-most images correspond to the query, the top row corresponds to the result with the original neural code, the bottom row corresponds to the retrained neural code. For most queries, the adaptation by retraining is helpful. The bottom row shows a rare exception.

Table 2. The performance of neural codes (original and retrained) for different PCA-compression rates. The performance of the descriptors is almost unaffected till the dimensionality of 256 and the degradation associated with more extreme compression is graceful.

Dimensions	16	32	64	128	256	512
Oxford						
Layer 6	0.328	0.390	0.421	0.433	0.435	0.435
Layer 6 + landmark retraining	0.418	0.515	0.548	0.557	0.557	0.557
Layer 6 + turntable retraining	0.289	0.349	0.377	0.391	0.392	0.393
Oxford 105K						
Layer 6	0.260	0.330	0.370	0.388	0.392	0.392
Layer 6 + landmark retraining	0.354	0.467	0.508	0.523	0.524	0.522
Layer 6 + turntable retraining	0.223	0.293	0.331	0.348	0.350	0.351
Holidays						
Layer 6	0.591	0.683	0.729	0.747	0.749	0.749
Layer 6 + landmark retraining	0.609	0.729	0.777	0.789	0.789	0.789
Layer 6 + turntable retraining	0.587	0.702	0.741	0.756	0.756	0.756
UKB						
Layer 6	2.630	3.130	3.381	3.416	3.423	3.426
Layer 6 + landmark retraining	2.410	2.980	3.256	3.297	3.298	3.300
Layer 6 + turntable retraining	2.829	3.302	3.526	3.552	3.556	3.557

associated with the sixth layer was consistently better than with the codes from other layers.

PCA Compression. We first evaluate the performance of different versions of neural codes after PCA compression to a different number of dimensions (Table 2). Here, PCA training was performed on 100,000 random images from the Landmark dataset.

The quality of neural codes $L^6(I)$ for different PCA compression rates is presented in Table 2. Overall, PCA works surprisingly well. Thus, the neural codes can be compressed to 256 or even to 128 dimensions almost without any quality loss. The advantage of the retrained codes persists through all compression rates. Table 3 further compares different holistic descriptors compressed to 128-dimensions, as this dimensionality has been chosen for comparison in several previous works. For Oxford and Holidays datasets, the landmark-retrained neural codes provide a new state-of-the-art among the low-dimensional global descriptors.

Discriminative Dimensionality Reduction. In this section, we further perform discriminative dimensionality reduction via the learning of a low-rank projection matrix W. The objective of the learning is to make distances between codes small in the cases when the corresponding images contain the same object and large otherwise, thus achieving additional tolerance for nuisance factors, such as viewpoint changes. For such learning, we collected a number of image pairs which contained the same object. Again, the challenge here was to collect a diverse set of pairs.

Table 3. The comparison of the PCA-compressed neural codes (128 dimensions) with the state-of-the-art holistic image descriptors of the same dimensionality. The PCA-compressed landmark-retrained neural codes establish new state-of-the-art on Holidays, Oxford, and Oxford 105K datasets.

Descriptor	Oxford	Oxford 105K	Holidays	UKB
Fisher+color[7]	—	—	0.723	3.08
VLAD+adapt+innorm[2]	0.448	0.374	0.625	—
Sparse-coded features[6]	—	—	0.727	**3.67**
Triangulation embedding[9]	0.433	0.353	0.617	3.40
Neural codes trained on ILSVRC				
Layer 6	0.433	0.386	0.747*	3.42
After retraining on the Landmarks dataset				
Layer 6	**0.557**	**0.523**	**0.789***	3.29
After retraining on turntable views (Multi-view RGB-D)				
Layer 6	0.391	0.348	0.756*	3.55

Fig. 6. Examples of queries with large differences between the results of the PCA-compressed and the discriminatively-compressed neural codes (for 32 dimensions). The correct answers are outlined in green.

To obtain such a dataset, we sample pairs of images within the same classes of the Landmark dataset. We built a matching graph using a standard image matching pipeline (SIFT+nearest neighbor matching with the second-best neighbor test [15] + RANSAC validation [5]). The pipeline is applied to all pairs of images belonging to the same landmark. Once the graph for the landmark is constructed, we took pairs of photographs that share at least one neighbor in

Table 4. The comparison of the performances of the PCA compression and a discriminative dimensionality reduction for the original neural codes on the Oxford dataset. Discriminative dimensionality reduction improves over the PCA reduction, in particular for the extreme dimensionality reduction.

D =	16	32	64	128
PCA-compression	0.328	0.390	0.421	0.433
Discriminative dimensionality reduction	0.368	0.401	0.430	0.439

the graph but are not neighbors themselves (to ensure that we do not focus the training process on near duplicates). Via such procedure we obtain 900K diverse image pairs (Figure 7). We further greedily select a subset of $100K$ pairs so that each photograph occurs at most once in such a subset, and use this subset of pairs for training.

Fig. 7. Examples of training pairs for discriminative dimensionality reduction. The pairs were obtained through time-consuming RANSAC matching of local features and simple analysis of the resulting match graph (see the text for more details).

Given a dataset of matching pairs we learn a linear projection matrix W via the method from [21]. In the experiments with large compression rates ($D = 16, 32$) we project original 4096-dimensional codes. For the dimensionality $D = 64$, 128, we observed significantn overfitting due to a large number of parameters within W. In this case we first performed PCA-compression to 1024 dimensions and then learned W for the preliminarily compressed 1024-dimensional codes.

The results of the two compression strategies (PCA and the discriminative reduction) are compared for non-retrained codes for the Oxford dataset in Table 4. As can be seen, the biggest gain from discriminative dimensionality reduction is achieved for the extremely compressed 16-dimensional codes. We have also evaluated the discriminative dimensionality reduction on the neural codes retrained on the Landmarks dataset. In this case, however, we did not observed any additional improvement from the discriminative reduction, presumably because the network retraining and the discriminative reduction were performed using overlapping training data.

6 Discussion

We have evaluated the performance of the deep neural codes within the image retrieval application. There are several conclusions and observations that one can draw from our experiments.

First of all, as was expected, neural codes perform well, even when one uses the CNN trained for the classification task and when the training dataset and the retrieval dataset are quite different from each other. Unsurprisingly, this performance can be further improved, when the CNN is retrained on photographs that are more related to the retrieval dataset.

We note that there is an obvious room for improvement in terms of the retrieval accuracy, in that all images are downsampled to low resolution (224×224) and therefore a lot of information about the texture, which can be quite discriminative, is lost. As an indication of potential improvement, our experiments with Fisher Vectors suggest that their drop in performance under similar circumstances is about 0.03 mAP on Holidays.

Interestingly, and perhaps unexpectedly, the best performance is observed not on the very top of the network, but rather at the layer that is two levels below the outputs. This effect persists even after the CNN is retrained on related images. We speculate, that this is because the very top layers are too much tuned for the classification task, while the bottom layers do not acquire enough invariance to nuisance factors.

We also investigate the performance of compressed neural codes, where plain PCA or a combination of PCA with discriminative dimensionality reduction result in very short codes with very good (state-of-the-art) performance. An important result is that PCA affects performance of neural codes much less than the one of VLADs, Fisher Vectors, or triangulation embedding. One possible explanation is that passing an image through the network discards much of the information that is irrelevant for classification (and for retrieval). Thus, CNN-based neural codes from deeper layers retain less (useless) information than unsupervised aggregation-based representations. Therefore PCA compression works better for neural codes.

One possible interesting direction for investigation, is whether good neural codes can be obtained directly by training the whole deep architecture using the pairs of matched images (rather than using the classification performance as the training objective), e.g. using siamese architecture of [3]. Automated collection of a suitable training collection having sufficient diversity would be an interesting task on its own. Finally, we note that the dimensionality reduction to a required dimensionality can be realized by choosing the size of a network layer used to produce the codes, rather than a post-hoc procedure.

References

1. Berg, A., Deng, J., Fei-Fei, L.: Large scale visual recognition challenge, ILSVRC (2010), http://www.image-net.org/challenges/LSVRC/2010/
2. Arandjelović, R., Zisserman, A.: All about VLAD. In: Computer Vision and Pattern Recognition (2013)
3. Chopra, S., Hadsell, R., LeCun, Y.: Learning a similarity metric discriminatively, with application to face verification. In: Computer Vision and Pattern Recognition (2005)
4. Donahue, J., Jia, Y., Vinyals, O., Hoffman, J., Zhang, N., Tzeng, E., Darrell, T.: Decaf: A deep convolutional activation feature for generic visual recognition. CoRR abs/1310.1531 (2013)
5. Fischler, M.A., Bolles, R.C.: Random sample consensus: A paradigm for model fitting with applications to image analysis and automated cartography. Commun. ACM (1981)
6. Ge, T., Ke, Q., Sun, J.: Sparse-coded features for image retrieval. In: British Machine Vision Conference (2013)
7. Gordo, A., Rodríguez-Serrano, J.A., Perronnin, F., Valveny, E.: Leveraging category-level labels for instance-level image retrieval. In: Computer Vision and Pattern Recognition (2012)
8. Jegou, H., Douze, M., Schmid, C.: Hamming embedding and weak geometric consistency for large scale image search. In: Forsyth, D., Torr, P., Zisserman, A. (eds.) ECCV 2008, Part I. LNCS, vol. 5302, pp. 304–317. Springer, Heidelberg (2008)
9. Jégou, H., Zisserman, A.: Triangulation embedding and democratic aggregation for image search. In: Computer Vision and Pattern Recognition (2014)
10. Krizhevsky, A., Sutskever, I., Hinton, G.E.: Imagenet classification with deep convolutional neural networks. In: Neural Information Processing Systems (2012)
11. Kumar, N., Berg, A.C., Belhumeur, P.N., Nayar, S.K.: Attribute and simile classifiers for face verification. In: International Conference on Computer Vision, pp. 365–372 (2009)
12. Lai, K., Bo, L., Ren, X., Fox, D.: A large-scale hierarchical multi-view rgb-d object dataset. In: Neural Information Processing Systems (2011)
13. LeCun, Y., Boser, B.E., Denker, J.S., Henderson, D., Howard, R.E., Hubbard, W.E., Jackel, L.D.: Handwritten digit recognition with a back-propagation network. In: Neural Information Processing Systems, pp. 396–404 (1989)
14. Li, Y., Crandall, D., Huttenlocher, D.: Landmark classification in large-scale image collections. In: International Conference on Computer Vision (2009)
15. Lowe, D.G.: Distinctive image features from scale-invariant keypoints. International Journal of Computer Vision (2004)
16. Nistér, D., Stewénius, H.: Scalable recognition with a vocabulary tree. In: Computer Vision and Pattern Recognition (2006)
17. Oquab, M., Bottou, L., Laptev, I., Sivic, J.: Learning and transferring mid-level image representations using convolutional neural networks. In: Computer Vision and Pattern Recognition (June 2014)
18. Perronnin, F., Sánchez, J., Mensink, T.: Improving the fisher kernel for large-scale image classification. In: Daniilidis, K., Maragos, P., Paragios, N. (eds.) ECCV 2010, Part IV. LNCS, vol. 6314, pp. 143–156. Springer, Heidelberg (2010)
19. Philbin, J., Chum, O., Isard, M., Sivic, J., Zisserman, A.: Object retrieval with large vocabularies and fast spatial matching. In: Computer Vision and Pattern Recognition (2007)

20. Razavian, A.S., Azizpour, H., Sullivan, J., Carlsson, S.: CNN features off-the-shelf: an astounding baseline for recognition. CoRR (2014)
21. Simonyan, K., Parkhi, O.M., Vedaldi, A., Zisserman, A.: Fisher Vector Faces in the Wild. In: British Machine Vision Conference (2013)
22. Tolias, G., Avrithis, Y., Jégou, H.: To aggregate or not to aggregate: selective match kernels for image search. In: International Conference on Computer Vision (2013)
23. Torresani, L., Szummer, M., Fitzgibbon, A.: Efficient object category recognition using classemes. In: Daniilidis, K., Maragos, P., Paragios, N. (eds.) ECCV 2010, Part I. LNCS, vol. 6311, pp. 776–789. Springer, Heidelberg (2010)
24. Wang, G., Hoiem, D., Forsyth, D.A.: Learning image similarity from flickr groups using stochastic intersection kernel machines. In: International Conference on Computer Vision (2009)
25. Xiao, J., Hays, J., Ehinger, K.A., Oliva, A., Torralba, A.: Sun database: Large-scale scene recognition from abbey to zoo. In: Computer Vision and Pattern Recognition (2010)
26. Yang, L., Jin, R.: Distance metric learning: A comprehensive survey, vol. 2. Michigan State Universiy (2006)

Architectural Style Classification Using Multinomial Latent Logistic Regression

Zhe Xu[1,2], Dacheng Tao[2], Ya Zhang[1], Junjie Wu[3], and Ah Chung Tsoi[4]

[1] Shanghai Key Laboratory of Multimedia Processing and Transmissions, Shanghai Jiao Tong University, Shanghai, China
[2] Centre for Quantum Computation & Intelligent Systems and Faculty of Engineering and Information Technology, University of Technology, Sydney, NSW, Australia
[3] School of Economics and Management, Beihang University, Beijing, China
[4] Faculty of Information Technology, Macau University of Science and Technology, Macau, China

Abstract. Architectural style classification differs from standard classification tasks due to the rich inter-class relationships between different styles, such as re-interpretation, revival, and territoriality. In this paper, we adopt Deformable Part-based Models (DPM) to capture the morphological characteristics of basic architectural components and propose Multinomial Latent Logistic Regression (MLLR) that introduces the probabilistic analysis and tackles the multi-class problem in latent variable models. Due to the lack of publicly available datasets, we release a new large-scale architectural style dataset containing twenty-five classes. Experimentation on this dataset shows that MLLR in combination with standard global image features, obtains the best classification results. We also present interpretable probabilistic explanations for the results, such as the styles of individual buildings and a style relationship network, to illustrate inter-class relationships.

Keywords: Latent Variable Models, Architectural Style Classification, Architectural Style Dataset.

1 Introduction

Buildings can be classified according to architectural styles, where each style possesses a set of unique and distinguishing features [5]. Some features, especially the façade and its decorations, enable automatic classification using computer vision methods. Architectural style classification has an important property that styles are not independently and identically distributed. The generation of architectural styles evolves as a gradual process over time, where characteristics such as territoriality and re-interpretation lead to complicated relationships between different architectural styles.

Most of existing architectural style classification algorithms focus on efficient extraction of discriminative local-based patches or patterns [1,3,4,8,14]. In a four-style classification problem, Chu *et al.* [3] extracted visual patterns by modeling

D. Fleet et al. (Eds.): ECCV 2014, Part I, LNCS 8689, pp. 600–615, 2014.
© Springer International Publishing Switzerland 2014

spatial configurations to address object scaling, rotation, and deformation. Goel *et al.* [8] achieved nearly perfect results on published datasets by mining word pairs and semantic patterns, and therefore tested this approach further on a more challenging five-class dataset collected from the internet. Zhang *et al.* [20] used "blocklets" to represent basic architectural components and adopted hierarchical sparse coding to model these blocklets. However, as argued in [17], some patches that look totally different can be very close in the feature space, which degrades the performance of local patches in understanding detail-rich architecture images. One recent study showed the possibility of cross-domain matching from sketches to building images [15], and this inspired us to employ sketch-like features to represent the building façades.

The Deformable Part-based Model (DPM) [6] is a popular scheme that employs sketch-like Histogram of Oriented Gradient (HOG) features. DPM models both global and local cues and enables flexible configuration of local parts by introducing so-called deformation costs. By adopting a latent SVM (LSVM) algorithm for training, the DPM-LSVM framework produces hard assignments to the labels as classification results. However, in order to enable rational explanation of the gradual transition and mixture of architectural styles, it would be preferable to provide soft assignments and introduce the concept of probability into the model.

In this paper, we propose an algorithm that introduces latent variables into logistic regression, which we term "*Multinomial Latent Logistic Regression*" (MLLR). MLLR is similar to latent SVM but provides efficient probabilistic analysis and straightforward multi-class extension using a multinomial model. MLLR overcomes some of the drawbacks of LSVM, such as dealing with imbalanced training data and the multi-class problem, while producing soft assignment results.

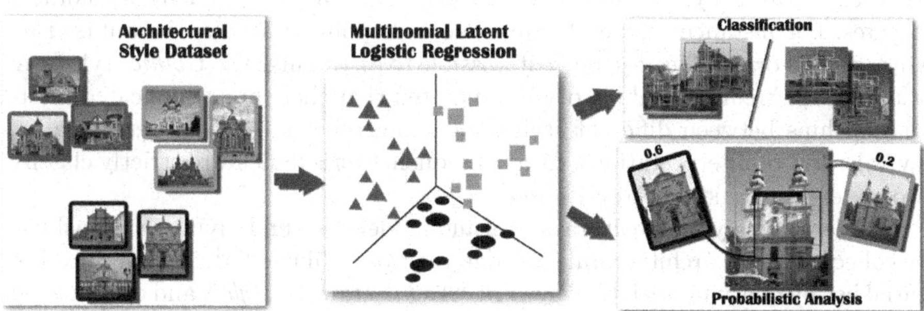

Fig. 1. Schematic illustration of architectural style classification using Multinomial Latent Logistic Regression (MLLR). Given a new large-scale architectural style dataset, we model the façade of buildings using deformable part-based models. In the middle figure, the smaller marks that surround the larger marks represent possible latent values for an object. The proposed latent variable algorithm simultaneously trains all the style models given a total objective function. The resulting classifiers can provide probabilistic analysis along with the standard classification results.

However, one reason why few previous studies focus on this problem is a lack of well-organized, large-scale datasets. Here, we collect a new and challenging dataset containing 25 architectural styles. The dataset possesses several preferred properties enclosing in architectural style classification, including multiple classes, inter-class relationships, hierarchical structure, change of views and scales. Our new dataset provides an improved platform for evaluating the performance of existing classification algorithms, and encourages the design of new ones. Fig. 1 summarizes the framework of the paper and illustrates the dataset, algorithm, and applications.

The contributions of this paper are:

- we create a multi-class and large-scale architectural style dataset and design several challenges based on this dataset. The rich set of inter-relationships between different architectural styles distinguish this dataset from standard scene classification datasets;
- we propose the MLLR algorithm, which introduces latent variables to logistic regression, analogous to latent SVM. The algorithm simultaneously trains classifiers for all classes. Thus, the detriment of the multi-class problem and unbalanced training data is minimized;
- by introducing the concept of "probability" to architectural style analysis, we analyze the inter-relationships of architectural styles probabilistically. Specifically, besides classification accuracies, the algorithm outputs a style relationship network and provides architectural style analysis for individual buildings.

2 Architectural Style Dataset

An architectural style is a specific construction, characterized by its notable features. For instance, unique features, such as pointed arches, rib vaults, rose windows and ornate façades, make it possible to distinguish the *Gothic* style from other styles. Architectural history has dictated that there are complicated inter-relationships between different styles, including rebellion, special territoriality, revivals, and re-interpretations. As a consequence, it is difficult to strictly classify two styles using a standard criterion.

In order to study architectural styles and model their underlying relationships, we collected a new architectural style dataset from Wikimedia[1]. We obtained the initial list by querying with the keyword *"Architecture_by_style"*, and downloaded images from subcategories following Wikimedia's hierarchy using the depth-first search strategy. The crawled images were manually filtered to exclude images of non-buildings, interior decorations, or part of a building. Therefore, the remaining images contained only the exterior façade of buildings. Styles with too few images were discarded, resulting in a total of 25 styles. The number of

[1] From Wikimedia commons.
`http://commons.wikimedia.org/wiki/Category:Architecture_by_style`.

images in each style varies from 60 to 300, and altogether the dataset contains approximately 5,000 images[2].

We propose several challenges to extensively exploit the data size and rich relationships between different architectural styles in this dataset. Fig. 2 illustrates the dataset.

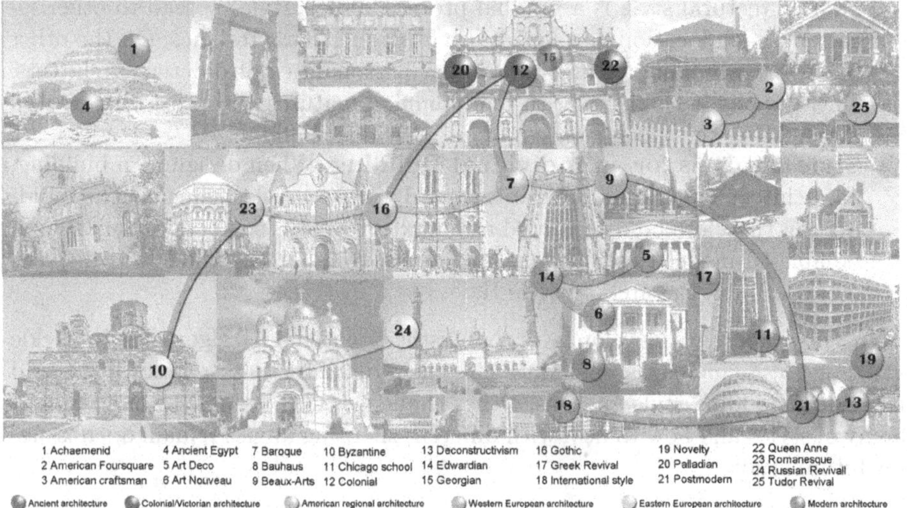

Fig. 2. Illustration of the architectural style dataset. Each of the 25 styles is represented by a circle with the respective number in the middle, where different colors indicate broad concepts, such as modern architecture and medieval architecture. The styles are arranged according to time order, where newer ones are placed in the right of ancient ones. Various inter-class relationships exist between the styles, e.g., lines between circles stand for following relationships; smaller circles around large ones indicate sub-categories. Typical images of the styles are shown in the background. Better viewed in color.

- **Multi-Class Classification**. To the best of our knowledge, this dataset is the largest publicly available dataset for architectural style classification. Other popular datasets related to buildings do exist, such as the Oxford Landmark dataset [14]. However, their main purpose is for the retrieval of individual landmark buildings rather than classification of architectural styles. A discussion of the difference between "style" and "content" can be found in [7]. There are some researches on different type of art styles, such as painting [18,21] and car designing [10], which may also provide cross-domain knowledge from other aspects of art styles.
- **Modeling Inter-Class Relationships between Styles.** Various relationships exist between the 25 architectural styles, e.g., following, revival, and against. Styles can be roughly classified into broad concepts, such as ancient

[2] `https://sites.google.com/site/zhexuutssjtu/projects/arch`

architecture, medieval architecture and modern architecture, and thus further be arranged in a hierarchical structure. For reference, we summarize the relationships between different styles verified by Wikipedia. It is of interest to explore whether computer vision algorithms can efficiently extract the underlying inter-class relationships.

- **Modeling Intra-Class Variance within a Style.** The establishment of an architectural style is a gradual process. When styles spread to other locations, each location develops its own unique characteristics. On the other hand, each building is unique due the personalities of different architects. Therefore, it is challenging to find common features within a style, as well highlighting the specific design of an individual building.
- **Style Analysis for an Individual Building.** When designing a building, an architect sometimes integrates several different style elements. The building can therefore be represented as a mixture of styles. An algorithm should be able to model this phenomenon, e.g., show that the window is inspired by style I and the arch by style II.

In this paper, we develop a probabilistic latent model algorithm to tackle some of these challenges, including classification, inter-class relationships, and individual building style analysis. Other challenges such as how to build a hierarchy of styles and how to deal with different shooting angles remain open issues for future study.

3 Model Description

A Deformable Part-based Model (DPM) [6] describes an image by a multi-scale HOG feature pyramid. The model consists of three parts: (i) a root filter that captures the outline of the object; (ii) a set of part filters that are applied to the image with twice the resolution of the root, conveying detailed information of the object; (iii) deformation costs that penalize deviations of the parts from their default locations with respect to the root.

In object detection tasks, a hypothesis x represents location of the root in the feature pyramid, and the part locations with respect to the root are treated as latent variables z. The filter response is given by the dot product of the HOG features and the model parameters, i.e., in the form of a score function:

$$s_\beta(x) = \max_{z \in Z(x)} \beta \cdot f(x, z), \tag{1}$$

where β is the vector of DPM parameters, $Z(x)$ stands for all possible relative positions between the root and parts. To introduce deformation costs, the model is parameterized by a concatenation of all the filters and deformation weights, and $f(x, z)$ is the concatenation of the HOG features and the part displacements.

To train the model parameters β, a latent SVM algorithm is adopted, whose objective function is defined analogically to classical SVMs as:

$$L(D) = \frac{1}{2}||\beta||^2 + C \sum_{i=1}^{N} \max(0, 1 - y_i s_\beta(x_i)), \tag{2}$$

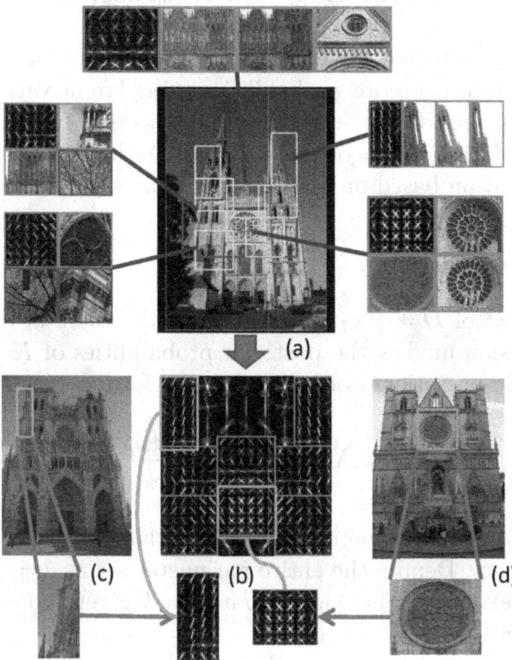

Fig. 3. Visualization of the use of DPM in architectural style classification. (a)(c)(d) show detection results for different testing images. The trained model for *Gothic* architectural style is shown in (b). The root model shows typical façade outline of *Gothic* style buildings, and the part filters captures discriminative architectural elements such as rose windows. Independently using each part filter cannot obtain convincing results, i.e., red boxes indicate incorrect detections with high scores given a part filter.

where $\max(0, 1 - y_i s_\beta(x_i))$ is the standard hinge loss and C is the soft margin parameter, which controls the weight of the regularization term. Due to the non-convex training objective function, latent SVM is solved using a coordinate descent framework.

Following [6], Pandey *et al.* [13] use DPM in a scene recognition and a weakly supervised object localization task. They point out that scene recognition can also be viewed as a "part-based" problem, where the root captures the entire image and the parts encompass moveable "regions of interest" (ROIs). In their experiments, they find that when the model is trained using the entire image as the root, the resulting performance is not as good as expected. They remark that the root filter should be allowed to move, and regarding the position of the root filter as another latent variable. We follow this setup, i.e., use a square root filter and restrict it to have at least 40% overlap with the image.

In our implementation, we exploit DPM as the detection model and introduce MLLR as the learning algorithm. A visualization of DPMs in architectural style classification is shown in Fig. 3.

4 Multinomial Latent Logistic Regression

In this section, we first review the concept and notation of logistic regression and then show the form of posterior probabilities using latent variables. By proving the semi-concavity property of the resulting objective function, we provide a gradient ascent solution analogous to latent SVM [6]. The training procedure has a clear explanation based on probabilistic analysis.

4.1 Logistic Regression

Given a training set of $D = \{(x_1, y_1), ..., (x_N, y_N)\}$, where $y_i \in \mathcal{Y} = [1, 2, ..., K]$, the logistic regression models the posterior probabilities of K classes via linear functions in x. The posterior probability has the form:

$$Pr(Y = k|X = x) = \frac{exp(\beta_k^T x)}{\sum_{l=1}^{K} exp(\beta_l^T x)}, \tag{3}$$

where β_k are the model parameters of the k-th class. We omit the bias term in the model for brevity. Denote the entire parameter set as $\theta = \{\beta_1^T, ..., \beta_K^T\}$. The probability of an example x belonging to a class k given model parameters θ is defined as $Pr(Y = k|X = x) = p_k(x; \theta)$.

Logistic regression models are typically fitted by maximizing the log-likelihood function, defined as:

$$l(\theta) = \sum_{i=1}^{N} \log p_{y_i}(x_i; \theta). \tag{4}$$

To maximize the log-likelihood function, gradient-based methods are generally used, such as the Newton-Raphson algorithm.

4.2 Latent Variables

In MLLR, each input example x is associated with a latent variable z. Let $f(x, z)$ be the feature vector of an example x with a latent variable z, where $z \in Z(x)$, and the $Z(x)$ define the possible latent value set for an example x.

Consider a score function of the form:

$$s(x; \beta_k) = \max_{z \in Z(x)} \beta_k \cdot f(x, z). \tag{5}$$

The score is obtained by finding the optimized latent value z that gives the highest score to example x given a model β_k. An example x is called a positive example with respect to model β_k if the respective training label $y = k$, and called a negative example with respect to model β_k if the label $y \neq k$.

The optimized latent value can then be denoted as:

$$z(\beta_k) = \arg\max_{z \in Z(x)} \beta_k \cdot f(x, z). \tag{6}$$

Analogous to standard logistic regression, we rewrite the posterior probability of the k-th class given an example x as:

$$p_k(x;\theta) = \frac{exp(s(x;\beta_k))}{\sum_{l=1}^{K} exp(s(x;\beta_l))}. \tag{7}$$

Given that the parameter space has a large volume, the training data might be easily overfit by MLLR; we therefore add a lasso regularizer to avoid overfitting. The log-likelihood function then becomes:

$$\begin{aligned} l(\theta) &= \sum_{i=1}^{N} \log p_{y_i}(x_i;\theta) - \lambda \sum_{l=1}^{K} |\beta_l| \\ &= \sum_{i=1}^{N} \log \frac{exp(s(x_i;\beta_{y_i}))}{\sum_{l=1}^{K} exp(s(x_i;\beta_l))} - \lambda \sum_{l=1}^{K} |\beta_l| \\ &= \sum_{i=1}^{N} s(x_i;\beta_{y_i}) - \sum_{i=1}^{N} \log \sum_{l=1}^{K} exp(s(x_i;\beta_l)) - \lambda \sum_{l=1}^{K} |\beta_l|, \end{aligned} \tag{8}$$

4.3 Semiconcavity

Maximizing the log-likelihood function of the standard logistic regression model in (4) leads to a concave optimization problem. However, after introducing latent variables to the log-likelihood function, the function is no longer concave with respect to the model β_k, due to the maximum operator in $s(x_i;\beta_{y_i})$. Similar to LSVM, MLLR has a semi-concavity property. Fixing the latent value for positive examples, the first term in (8) is reduced to a linear function of β_k, which is concave. We thus employ gradient ascent method based on the semi-concavity property to maximize the likelihood function.

Define $l(\theta, Z_p)$ as an auxiliary function that bounds the exact likelihood function by fixing the latent variable for each positive example, where $Z_p = \{z_i, i = 1, ..., N\}$ is a set of latent values specifying the positive configuration for all the N training examples. In particular, the auxiliary function is defined as:

$$l(\theta, Z_p) = \sum_{i=1}^{N} s'(x_i;\beta_{y_i}) - \sum_{i=1}^{N} \log \sum_{l=1}^{K} exp(s'(x_i;\beta_l)) - \lambda \sum_{l=1}^{K} |\beta_l|, \tag{9}$$

where

$$s'(x_i;\beta_l) = \begin{cases} \beta_l^T f(x_i, z_l), & y_i = l. \\ s(x_i;\beta_l), & y_i \neq l. \end{cases}$$

Considering that $l(\theta, Z_p)$ is a concave function, we maximize $l(\theta)$ using the coordinate ascent method, as follows.

1. *Optimize positive examples*: Optimize $l(\theta, Z_p)$ over Z_p. For each example x_i, find the optimized latent value for its respective model β_{y_i} using (5), $z_i^* = \arg\max_{z \in Z(x_i)} \beta_{y_i} \cdot f(x_i, z)$ and set $Z_p = \{z_i^*, i = 1, ..., N\}$.
2. *Optimize model parameters* θ. Optimize the concave function $l(\theta, Z_p)$ over θ and all possible latent values for negative examples.

4.4 Gradient Ascent

This process is to optimize model parameters θ and the latent value for negative examples. Although the lasso regularization term is non-differentiable, we can compute a subgradient of (8) with respect to β_k as:

$$\nabla l(\beta_k) = \sum_{i=1}^{N} f(x_i, z_i(\beta_k)) \cdot h(x_i, \beta_k) - \lambda \cdot sgn(\beta_k), \tag{10}$$

where

$$h(x_i, \beta_k) = \begin{cases} 1 - p_k(x_i; \theta) & ,x_i \text{ is positive for class } k. \\ -p_k(x_i; \theta) & ,x_i \text{ is negative for class } k. \end{cases}$$

The gradient ascent procedure iteratively updates model parameters and latent variables for negative examples, as follows:

1. In the $(t+1)$-th iteration, for all training examples x_i and all class models β_k, let $z_i(\beta_k^{(t)}) = \arg\max_{z \in Z(x_i)} \beta_k^{(t)} \cdot f(x_i, z)$, where $y_i \neq k$, and $z_i(\beta_k^{(t)}) = z_i^*$ if $y_i = k$, where $z_i^* \in Z_p$

2. For all class models, set $\beta_k^{(t+1)} = \beta_k^{(t)} + \alpha_t \cdot [\sum_{i=1}^{N} f(x_i, z_i(\beta_k^{(t)})) \cdot h(x_i, \beta_k^{(t)}) - \lambda \cdot sgn(\beta_k^{(t)})]$.

The form of $h(x_i, \beta_k)$ has a clear probabilistic explanation. Similar to the perceptron algorithm, the gradient ascent method repeatedly pushes the model β_k towards positive examples and away from negative examples. By adding a probabilistic multiplier, the algorithm assigns a larger penalization on "hard negative", where $p_k(x_i; \theta)$ is large. For positive examples, a "hard positive" indicates an example that has a smaller probability with respect to the current model, and plays a more important role in updating the model parameters.

The training procedure is outlined in Algorithm 1.

4.5 Comparison to the Latent SVM

MLLR and LSVM have many shared characteristics, such as the form of latent variables and the semi-convexity property. These similarities enable MLLR to incorporate existing latent variable models trained by LSVM, such as deformation part-based models. However, there are some notable differences between MLLR and LSVM, which make MLLR more suitable for the architectural style classification task.

First, it is argued that SVM tends to underperform when using imbalanced training data where negative examples far outnumber positive examples [19]. The vast "background" class in the object detection framework introduces a serious imbalance between positive and negative examples. Moreover, in LSVM, the training process needs to fix the latent value for positive examples, while keeping all possible latent values for negative examples. This process makes the imbalance problem even more severe.

Second, the dominant method for solving multi-class problems using SVM has been based on reducing a single multi-class problem to multiple binary problems. However, since each binary problem is trained independently, adopting this

Algorithm 1. Multinomial Latent Logistic Regression Training

```
Input: Training examples {(x_1, y_1), ..., (x_N, y_N)}
  Initial models θ = {β_1, ..., β_K}
Output: New models θ
  for posLoop:=1 to numPosLoop do
    {Relabel positive examples}
    for i:=1 to N do
      Optimize z_i^* = arg max_{z∈Z(x_i)} β_{y_i} · f(x_i, z).
    end for
    {Gradient Ascent}
    for t:=1 to numGradientAscentLoop do
      {Relabel negative examples}
      for i:=1 to N do
        for k:=1 to K and k ≠ y_i do
          Optimize z_i(β_k^(t)) = arg max_{z∈Z(x_i)} β_k^(t) · f(x_i, z).
        end for
      end for
      {Update model parameters}
      for k:=1 to K do
        Update β_k^(t+1) = β_k^(t) + α_t · [Σ_{i=1}^N f(x_i, z_i(β_k^(t))) · h(x_i, β_k^(t)) − λ · sgn(β_k^(t))].
      end for
    end for
  end for
```

strategy is problematic because it cannot capture correlations between different classes. As a result, the output decision values are not comparable, and this is known as the "calibration" problem. MLLR trains all classes simultaneously by introducing a unified objective function and in this way does not suffer from the hazard of different biases occurring with the multi-class problem and imbalanced training data.

Finally, SVM does not provide an effective probabilistic analysis with a soft boundary. Given an input example, the corresponding output of SVM is called the decision value, which is the distance from the example to the decision boundary. A previous work [12], in which a normalization process was proposed to convert the decision values of SVM to probabilistic outputs, does not provide a genuine probabilistic explanation. MLLR produces comparable classification results for multiple classes, and more reasonably turns them into probabilities.

5 Experiment

The experiment is presented in three steps. In the first step, we choose ten architectural styles that are relatively distinguishable by their façades and have lower intra-class variance. As a result, using sketch-like HOG features, DPM can clearly demonstrate the characteristics of these styles. Second, we evaluate the effect of a more extensive multi-class problem and larger intra-class variance using the full dataset. Given the probabilistic results, we formulate inter-class relationships using a style relationship map. The third part illustrates individual building style analysis of MLLR.

5.1 Classification Task

A ten-class sub-dataset is exploited for the first classification task, most of which have prominent façade or decoration features, such as pointed arches, the ribbed vaults and the flying buttresses characteristics of *Gothic* architecture. For each class, 30 images are randomly chosen as training images and the remaining images are used for testing, 1,716 in total. We run a ten-fold experiment. The proposed algorithm is denoted by DPM-MLLR. Table 1 compares the classification accuracy of DPM-MLLR with other algorithms, including GIST [16], Spatial Pyramid (SP) [9], Object Bank [11], and DPM-LSVM [13]. DPM-MLLR outperforms LSVM in terms of overall accuracy. It is noted that DPM and local patch-based algorithms, such as Spatial Pyramid, have complementary properties. We therefore combine their results using a naive softmax function and achieve the best result with nearly 70% accuracy.

Table 1. Results on the architectural style classification dataset. MLLR consistently outperforms LSVM. Multiple features are combined by adopting the softmax function on classifier outputs.

	GIST	SP	OB-Partless	OB-Part	DPM-LSVM	DPM-MLLR	MLLR+SP
10 classes	30.74	60.08	62.26	63.76	65.67	67.80	**69.17**
25 classes	17.39	44.52	42.50	45.41	37.69	42.55	**46.21**

Fig. 4 shows the trained models and typical detection results of MLLR. Close inspection of the results reveals that the models capture discriminative features of the styles. For instance, the model representing *American Queen Anne* architecture detects twin gables and allows them to move within limits (in the top of the root). Thus, the model is robust to slight view changes and intra-class variance.

5.2 Inter-Class Relationships between Styles

This part of the experiment is implemented on the full dataset. The 25-class dataset has stronger intra-class invariance and is harder to distinguish purely by the façades. The results show that algorithms that take the features of the entire image into consideration, i.e., Spatial Pyramid and Object Bank, achieve superior performance (Table 1). DPM-MLLR has slightly lower accuracy. However, compared to the result of the ten-class problem, MLLR outperforms LSVM by a larger margin due to the increased number of classes. Again, the combined MLLR-SP algorithm achieves the best result.

Despite classification accuracies, the proposed algorithm provides a probabilistic style distribution for each building image. By summing the probabilities,

Fig. 4. Testing results for the ten architectural styles. The first two columns visualize the result root and part filters for each model. From top to bottom: *Baroque, Chicago school, Gothic, Greek Revival, Queen Anne, Romanesque* and *Russian Revival* architecture. Detected root filters are displayed in red, and part filters are shown in yellow. Better viewed in color.

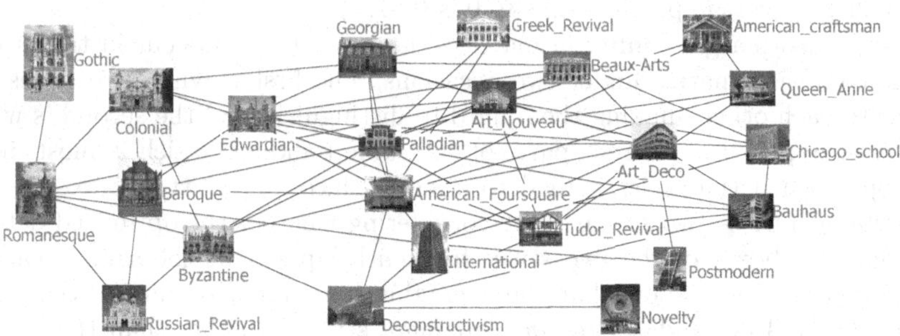

Fig. 5. An architectural style relationship map generated by the proposed algorithm. The confusion probability between style A and B is obtained by summing the probabilities with regard to B for all images labeled by A. Only links whose weight exceeds a given threshold are shown in the figure. Modern styles, such as *Postmodern* and *International* style, are connected, while the links between modern and medieval styles are weak. The figure is drawn using NetDraw [2].

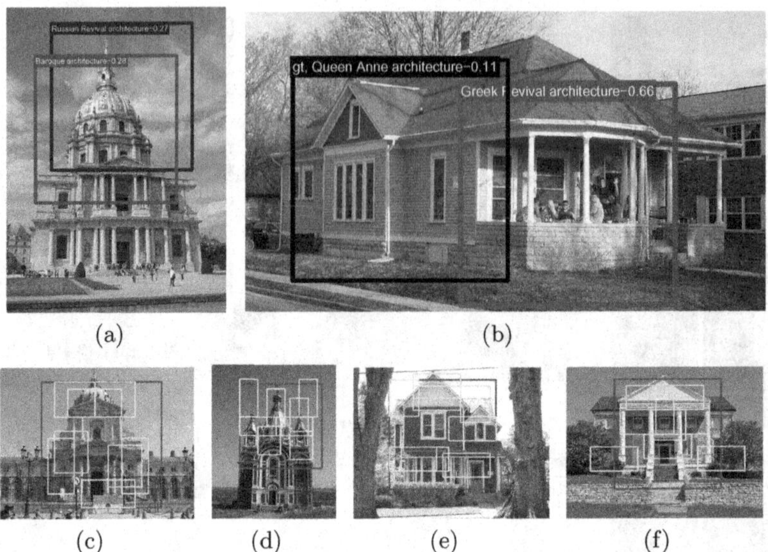

Fig. 6. MLLR detects the optimized latent position for each class and outputs a global list of probabilities for each class. (a) Parts shared by different styles. (b) A building that combines several styles. (c)-(f) Typical detection results for the four styles appearing in (a) and (b), i.e., from left to right, *Baroque, Russian Revival, Queen Anne* and *Greek Revival.*

we obtain a probabilistic confusion matrix, which is further decomposed into a style inter-relationship network by assigning an edge between two styles whose confusion probability exceeds a given threshold. Fig. 5 shows the resulting relationship map of the 25-class dataset. According to the set of relationships between styles collected from Wikipedia, the proposed algorithm gets a recall of 0.66, and the average precision $AP@10$ is 0.51.

Unlike hard-margin confusion matrices, large values can occur in the probabilistic confusion matrix under two occasions. The first is when two styles are similar to each other, making them hard to distinguish, and the second is when two styles appear on different parts of the same building, which is most likely to happen when the styles spread to a same place and start to mix. We try to distinguish these two scenarios by considering whether the optimized detecting bounding boxes of the two styles frequently appear at the same location. Experimental results show that the averaging bounding box intersection ratio of the *Queen Anne* and *American Craftsman* styles is higher than that of the *Baroque* and *Colonial* style (0.56 vs. 0.46), which means that the first two styles have a similar façade and should therefore be more dependent on local parts for classification. This phenomenon is in accordance with architectural history.

5.3 Individual Building Analysis

MLLR makes it possible to analyze the architectural style of a building probabilistically. Fig. 6 shows two typical situations in which the algorithm gives comparable scores for at least two styles, which correspond to the two scenarios discussed in the previous subsection. The first is when different architectural styles share similar features, such as pear-shaped domes in both *Baroque* and *Russian Revival* architecture. The second scenario appears when architects design new buildings that combine several different architectural styles. For instance, Fig. 6(b) shows a failed classification case in which the main body of the building follows the *Queen Anne* style, while the terrace shows a strong *Greek* sense. MLLR mistakenly classifies the building as *Greek Revival* style due to the unusual shooting angle, which places the main body in side view. However, MLLR discovers interesting patterns in the building that indicates a combination of different styles, and assigns probabilities for each style according to the training set.

6 Conclusions

We introduce Multinomial Latent Logistic Regression (MLLR), a latent variable algorithm that uses log-likelihood as the objective function and simultaneously trains multi-class models. Experimental results using a new, large-scale architectural style dataset show that the Deformable Part-based Model (DPM)-MLLR algorithm achieves the best performance when the styles have highly distinguishable façades. The algorithm is also competitive comparing with other state-of-the-art algorithms, even when using a more challenging experimental setup with large intra-class variance. The probabilistic analysis of MLLR makes it possible to interpret inter-class relationships between architectural styles and the combination of multiple styles in an individual building.

Acknowledgement. The work is partially supported by the High Technology Research and Development Program of China (2012AA011702,2014AA012303), National Natural Science Foundation of China (61003107,71322104, 71171007), the Australian Research Council Projects FT-130101457, ARC DP-120103730, and LP-140100569, Huawei Project 2014000353. We appreciate insightful discussions with Mr. Q. Xie at Huawei and valuable comments from anonymous reviewers.

References

1. Berg, A.C., Grabler, F., Malik, J.: Parsing images of architectural scenes. In: IEEE 11th International Conference on Computer Vision, ICCV 2007, pp. 1–8. IEEE (2007)
2. Borgatti, S.: Netdraw software for network visualization. Analytic Technologies (2002)
3. Chu, W.T., Tsai, M.H.: Visual pattern discovery for architecture image classification and product image search. In: Proceedings of the 2nd ACM International Conference on Multimedia Retrieval, p. 27. ACM (2012)
4. Doersch, C., Singh, S., Gupta, A., Sivic, J., Efros, A.A.: What makes paris look like paris? ACM Transactions on Graphics (TOG) 31(4), 101 (2012)
5. Dunlop, C.: Architectural Styles. Dearborn Real Estate (2003)
6. Felzenszwalb, P., Girshick, R., McAllester, D., Ramanan, D.: Object detection with discriminatively trained part-based models. IEEE Transactions on Pattern Analysis and Machine Intelligence 32(9), 1627–1645 (2010)
7. Freeman, W.T., Tenenbaum, J.B.: Learning bilinear models for two-factor problems in vision. In: Proceedings of the 1997 IEEE Computer Society Conference on Computer Vision and Pattern Recognition, pp. 554–560. IEEE (1997)
8. Goel, A., Juneja, M., Jawahar, C.: Are buildings only instances?: exploration in architectural style categories. In: Proceedings of the Eighth Indian Conference on Computer Vision, Graphics and Image Processing, p. 1. ACM (2012)
9. Lazebnik, S., Schmid, C., Ponce, J.: Beyond bags of features: Spatial pyramid matching for recognizing natural scene categories. In: 2006 IEEE Computer Society Conference on Computer Vision and Pattern Recognition, vol. 2, pp. 2169–2178 (2006)
10. Lee, Y.J., Efros, A.A., Hebert, M.: Style-aware mid-level representation for discovering visual connections in space and time. In: 2013 IEEE International Conference on Computer Vision (ICCV), pp. 1857–1864. IEEE (2013)
11. Li, L.J., Su, H., Fei-Fei, L., Xing, E.P.: Object bank: A high-level image representation for scene classification & semantic feature sparsification. In: Advances in Neural Information Processing Systems, pp. 1378–1386 (2010)
12. Lin, H.T., Lin, C.J., Weng, R.C.: A note on platts probabilistic outputs for support vector machines. Machine Learning 68(3), 267–276 (2007)
13. Pandey, M., Lazebnik, S.: Scene recognition and weakly supervised object localization with deformable part-based models. In: 2011 IEEE International Conference on Computer Vision (ICCV), pp. 1307–1314. IEEE (2011)
14. Philbin, J., Chum, O., Isard, M., Sivic, J., Zisserman, A.: Object retrieval with large vocabularies and fast spatial matching. In: IEEE Conference on Computer Vision and Pattern Recognition, CVPR 2007, pp. 1–8 (June 2007)
15. Shrivastava, A., Malisiewicz, T., Gupta, A., Efros, A.A.: Data-driven visual similarity for cross-domain image matching. ACM Transactions on Graphics (TOG) 30, 154 (2011)
16. Torralba, A., Murphy, K.P., Freeman, W.T., Rubin, M.A.: Context-based vision system for place and object recognition. In: Proceedings of the Ninth IEEE International Conference on Computer Vision, pp. 273–280. IEEE (2003)
17. Vondrick, C., Khosla, A., Malisiewicz, T., Torralba, A.: Hoggles: Visualizing object detection features. In: ICCV (2013)

18. Watanabe, S.: Discrimination of painting style and quality: pigeons use different strategies for different tasks. Animal Cognition 14(6), 797–808 (2011)
19. Wu, G., Chang, E.Y.: Class-boundary alignment for imbalanced dataset learning. In: ICML 2003 Workshop on Learning from Imbalanced Data Sets II, Washington, DC, pp. 49–56 (2003)
20. Zhang, L., Song, M., Liu, X., Sun, L., Chen, C., Bu, J.: Recognizing architecture styles by hierarchical sparse coding of blocklets. Information Sciences 254, 141–154 (2014)
21. Zujovic, J., Gandy, L., Friedman, S., Pardo, B., Pappas, T.N.: Classifying paintings by artistic genre: An analysis of features & classifiers. In: IEEE International Workshop on Multimedia Signal Processing, MMSP 2009, pp. 1–5. IEEE (2009)

Instance Segmentation of Indoor Scenes Using a Coverage Loss

Nathan Silberman, David Sontag, and Rob Fergus

Courant Institute of Mathematical Sciences, New York University

Abstract. A major limitation of existing models for semantic segmentation is the inability to identify individual instances of the same class: when labeling pixels with only semantic classes, a set of pixels with the same label could represent a single object or ten. In this work, we introduce a model to perform both semantic and instance segmentation simultaneously. We introduce a new higher-order loss function that directly minimizes the coverage metric and evaluate a variety of region features, including those from a convolutional network. We apply our model to the NYU Depth V2 dataset, obtaining state of the art results.

Keywords: Semantic Segmentation, Deep Learning.

1 Introduction

Semantic segmentation models have made great strides in the last few years. Following early efforts to densely label scenes [1], numerous approaches such as reasoning with multiple segmentations [2], higher-order label constraints [3] and fast inference mechanisms [4] have advanced the state of the art considerably. One limitation in all of these methods, however, is their inability to differentiate between different *instances* of the same class. This work introduces a novel algorithm for simultaneously producing both a semantic and instance segmentation of a scene. More specifically, given an image, we produce both a semantic label for every pixel and an instance label that differentiates between two instances of the same class, as illustrated in Fig. 1.

The ability to differentiate between instances of the same class is important for a variety of tasks. In image search, one needs to understanding instance information to properly understand count-based searches: "three cars waiting at a light" should retrieve different results from "a single car waiting at the light". Robots that interact with real world environments must understand instance information as well. For example, when lifting boxes a robot needs to distinguish between a single box and a stack of them. Finally, being able to correctly infer object instances drastically improves performance on high level scene reasoning tasks such as support inference [5] or inferring object extent [6] [7].

Unfortunately, searching over the space of all semantic and instance segmentations for a given image is computationally infeasible. Like many previous works in semantic segmentation [8] [4] [9], we use a heuristic to limit the search space by first performing a hierarchical segmentation of the image. This produces a set of nested segments that form a tree, referred to as a *segmentation tree.*

D. Fleet et al. (Eds.): ECCV 2014, Part I, LNCS 8689, pp. 616–631, 2014.
© Springer International Publishing Switzerland 2014

Our goal during inference is to (a) find the best non-overlapping subset of these segments such that each pixel is explained by a single region from the tree – referred to as *cutting the segmentation tree* – and (b) each selected region is labeled with a semantic label denoting the class and instance ID (e.g. chair #2). The inference procedure finds the cut through the segmentation tree that maximizes these two objectives. During learning, we will seek to maximize the Coverage Score [10], a measure of how similar two segmentations are, between our inferred semantic/instance segments and those produced by human annotators.

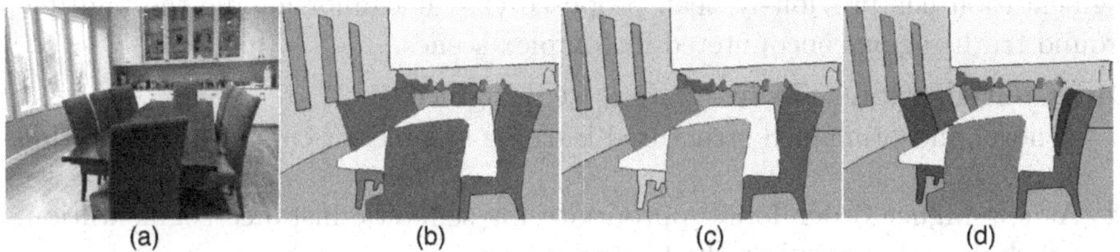

Fig. 1. An illustration of the limits of semantic segmentation: (a) the input image. (b) a perfect semantic segmentation; note all of the chair pixels are labeled blue. (c) a naive instance segmentation in which all connected components of the same class are considered separate instances of the chair class. (d) a correct instance segmentation, which correctly reasons about instances within contiguous segments and across occlusions.

While at a high level this approach is similar to many semantic segmentation methods, two main factors complicate the joint learning of semantic-instance segmentation models using segmentation trees:

The Ground Truth Mapping Problem: When using a reduced search space, such as one provided by a given hierarchical segmentation, it is extremely rare that the exact ground truth regions are among the set of bottom-up *proposed* regions, due to mistakes made at detecting object boundaries. Therefore, during training, we must be able to map the human-provided labels to a set of surrogate labels, defined on the set of proposed regions.

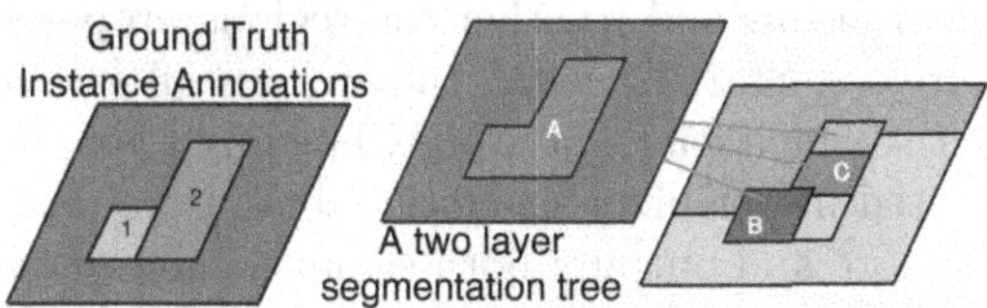

Fig. 2. Computing the best possible set of instances that overlap with the ground truth cannot be computed independently per ground truth region. For example, ground truth region 2 best overlaps with proposed region A and ground truth region 1 best overlaps with proposed region B. But both proposed regions A and B cannot be selected at the same time because they overlap.

Obtaining these surrogate labels is problematic for semantic-instance segmentation. The constraint that the regions must not non-overlap means the best possible subset of regions cannot be computed independently as the inclusion of one region may exclude the use of another (see Figure 2). Therefore, computing the 'best possible' instance segmentation with respect to a segmentation tree is an optimization problem in its own right.

Identifying a Good Loss Function: In semantic segmentation, it is easy to penalize mistakes: a region is either assigned the correct or incorrect label. In our setting, we require a more continuous measure, since an inferred region might not exactly match the 'best' region, but it might be extremely close (e.g. differing by a single pixel). While a continuous higher order loss function for binary segmentation has previously been proposed [11], it cannot handle the multiple ground truth regions encountered in complex scenes.

Our Contributions: To summarize, we introduce:

1. A novel and principled structured learning scheme for cutting segmentation trees.
2. A new higher order loss, appropriate for semantic-instance segmentation, which directly optimizes the Coverage score.
3. An efficient structured learning algorithm based on block-coordinate Frank Wolfe and a novel integer linear program for loss-augmented inference
4. A quantitative analysis of the use of features from state-of-the-art convolutional networks and their application to segmenting densely labeled RGB-D scenes.

2 Related Work

For certain classes of objects, such as cars or pedestrians, instance information can be recovered from detectors. While the state of the art in object localization [12] has improved dramatically, they perform best with large objects that occupy a significant portion of the image plane and struggle when the objects exhibit large amounts of occlusion. Furthermore, they do not in themselves produce a segmentation.

Motivated by the observation that a single segmentation of an image is unlikely to produce a perfect result, numerous approaches [13] [14] [15] [16] make use of multiple segmentations of an image. These approaches differ in how they use the various segmentations and whether the regions proposed are strictly hierarchical or structureless. Starting with [13], various efforts [3] [17] have used multiple independent segmentations in a pixel labeling task. While these works are ultimately interested in per-pixel semantic labels, ours reasons about which regions to select or ignore and outputs both semantic and instance labels.

Several works [18] [19] use a structureless bag of regions to perform segmentation in which inference comprises of a search for the best non-overlapping set of regions that respects object boundaries. However, neither work uses semantics for reasoning. Rather than use arbitrary or structureless regions as input, an increasing number of approaches [2] [8] [4] [9] have been introduced that utilize hierarchical segmentations to improve semantic segmentation. Like our approach, these models are trained to cut a segmentation tree. The major difference between these works and our own is that the product of these algorithms do not differentiate between instances of objects.

Higher order losses for segmentation have also been previously explored. Tarlow et al. [11] introduce the Pascal Loss which smoothly minimizes the overlap score [20] of a single foreground/background segmentation. The Pascal Loss is closely related to the Coverage loss. A crucial difference between the two is that in the case of Pascal Loss, the best overlapping region is specified a priori (there is only one region, the foreground), whereas in the Coverage Loss, the best overlapping region can only be computing by jointly reasoning over every proposed region.

3 Segmentation Trees

Because the space of all semantic-instance segmentations is so large, we must limit the solution space to make the problem tractable. Like previous work in semantic segmentation [2] [8] [4] [9], we make use of hierarchical segmentations, referred to as segmentation trees, to limit the search space to a more manageable size. A set of regions or segments $S = \{s_1, \ldots, s_R\}$ forms a valid segmentation tree $\mathcal{T} = \{S, P\}$ for an image $\mathcal{I}$ if it satisfies the following constraints:

Completeness: Every pixel $\mathcal{I}_i$ is contained in at least one region of S.
Tree Structure: Each region s_i has at most one parent: $P(s_i) \in \{\emptyset, s_j\}, j \neq i$
Strict Nesting: If $P(s_i) = s_j$, then the pixels in s_i form a strict subset of s_j

A cut $\mathcal{T}(A)$ of the tree selects a subset $S_A \subset S$ of segments that form a *planar segmentation*, a map $M : \mathcal{I}_i \mapsto \mathbb{Z}$ from each pixel $\mathcal{I}_i$ to exactly one region. The goal of this work is to take as input a segmentation tree and cut it such that the resulting planar segmentation is composed of a set of regions, each of which corresponds to a single object instance in the input image.

During training, we will make use of two types of segmentation trees: standard segmentation trees and *Biased Segmentation Trees.*

3.1 Standard Segmentation Trees

We use the term *standard segmentation tree* to refer to a hierarchical segmentation created by iteratively merging similar regions based on local boundary cues until a pre-specified stopping criteria is met. While various schemes [21] [10] have been introduced to perform this operation, we use the method of [22]. To summarize, given an image $\mathcal{I}$ of size $H \times W$, we begin by producing a grid $\mathcal{L}_{H,W}$ where each pixel corresponds to a node in the graph and edge weights between neighboring pixels indicate the probability that each neighboring pair of pixels are separated by a region boundary. As in [22], the edge weights are computed by first extracting gPb features [23] and calculating the Ultrametric Contour Map (UCM). To create a segmentation at a particular scale, edges with weights lower than some threshold are removed and the induced regions are the connected components of the resulting graph. This process is repeated with various thresholds to create finer or coarser regions. The unique superset of regions produced by the various thresholded region maps form a tree $\mathcal{T}$ such that each region is represented as a node and any pair of region r_i, r_j are the children of region r_k if r_i and r_j are both sub-regions of r_k.

3.2 Biased Segmentation Trees

Using only standard segmentations trees, one cannot properly evaluate whether the limitation of a particular tree cutting algorithm is the quality of the regions it has to select from or the capacity of the model itself. To separate these sources of error, we need a tree that contains, as a possible cut, a specified planar segmentation, which we refer to as a *biased segmentation tree.* In particular, we wish to take as input a ground truth planar segmentation provided by a human labeler and create a segmentation tree that contains the ground truth regions as a possible cut. With such trees, we are able to properly evaluate tree-cutting model errors independant of segmentation tree creation errors.

To create biased segmentation trees, we first threshold the UMC to obtain a base set of regions. Next, we split these regions further by taking the intersection of every ground truth region with the segmented regions. Edge weights for newly introduced boundaries are computed using the average gPb values for each pixel along each boundary. Any boundary aligned with a ground truth edge is given a weight of 0. Next, we use the same algorithm as in Section 3.1 to produce several fine segmentations culminating in the ground truth segmentation. Finally, a coarser set of regions is obtained by repeating this process starting from the ground truth regions. In this final step, any boundary inside a ground truth region is given a weight of 0 and any boundary aligned with a ground truth region is computed by averaging the gPb values along the boundary pixels.

4 Cutting Instance Segmentation Trees

Given an image and a segmentation tree, our goal is to find the best cut of the tree such that each of the resulting regions corresponds to a single *instance* of an object and is labeled with the appropriate semantic class.

Let a cut of the tree be represented by $\{\mathbf{A} : A_i \in \{0, 1\}, i = 1..R\}$, a vector indicating whether or not each of the R regions in the tree are selected. Let $\{\mathbf{C} : C_i \in \{1..K\}, i = 1..R\}$ be a vector indicating the semantic class (out of K classes) of each region. Finally let $y = \{\mathbf{A}, \mathbf{C}\}$ be the combined output of semantic labels and region instances.

4.1 Model

We perform structured prediction by optimizing over the space $\mathcal{Y}$ of region selections and semantic class assignments for a given segmentation tree. Formally, we predict using $y^* = \arg\max_{y \in \mathcal{Y}} w^T \phi(x, y)$, where x represents the input image, y encapsulates both the region selection vector A and class assignments C, and w represents a trained weight vector. ϕ is a feature function on the joint space of x and y such that $w^T \phi(x, y)$ can be interpreted as measuring the compatibility of x and y. $w^T \phi(x, y)$ can be decomposed as follows:

$$w_{\text{reg}}^T \phi_{\text{reg}}(x, y) + \sum_{k=1}^{K} w_{\text{sem:k}}^T \phi_{\text{sem:k}}(x, y) + w_{\text{pair}}^T \phi_{\text{pair}}(x, y) + \phi_{\text{tree}}(y)$$

The **generic region features** encode class-agnostic appearance features of selected regions: $\phi_{\text{reg}}(x, y) = \sum_{i=1}^{R} f_i^{\text{reg}}[A_i = 1]$, where f_i^{reg} are region features extracted from region i and $[\ldots]$ is the indicator function. The **semantic compatibility** features capture class-specific features of each region: $\phi_{\text{sem:k}}(x, y) = \sum_{i=1}^{R} f_i^{\text{sem}}[A_i = 1 \wedge C_i = k]$, where k is the semantic class and f_i^{sem} are semantic features extracted from region i.

The **pairwise** features $\phi_{\text{pair}}(x, y)$ are given by $\sum_{ij \in \mathcal{E}} f_{ij}^{\text{pair}}[A_i = 1 \wedge A_j = 1]$, where $\mathcal{E}$ is the set of all adjacent regions and f_{ij}^{pair} are pairwise features extracted along the boundary between regions i and j. Finally, the **tree-consistency function** $\phi_{\text{tree}}(y)$ ensures that exactly one region along every path from the leaf nodes to the root node of the tree is selected:

$$\phi_{\text{tree}}(y) = \sum_{\gamma \in \Gamma} -\infty \big[1 \neq \sum_{i \in \gamma} 1[y.A_i = 1]\big], \tag{1}$$

where Γ is the set of paths in the tree from the leaves to the root.

4.2 Learning

Let $D = \{(x^{(1)}, y^{(1)}), ...(x^{(N)}, y^{(N)})\}$ be a dataset of pairs of images and labels where $y^{(i)} = \{\mathbf{A}, \mathbf{C}\}$ comprises the best assignment (Section 6) of segments from the pool and semantic class labels for image i. We use a Structured SVM [24] formulation with margin re-scaling to learn weight vector w:

$$\min_{w,\, \xi \geq 0} \quad \frac{1}{2} w^T w + \frac{\lambda}{N} \sum_{i=1}^{N} \xi_i \tag{2}$$

$$\text{s.t.} \quad w \cdot [\phi(x^{(n)}, y^{(n)}) - \phi(x^{(n)}, y)] \geq \Delta(y, y^{(n)}) - \xi_n \quad \forall n,\ y \in \mathcal{Y}$$

where ξ_i are slack variables for each of the training samples $1..N$, and λ is a regularization parameter. The definition of the loss function $\Delta(y, y^{(n)})$ is discussed in more detail in Section 5.

4.3 Inference

We first show how the inference task, $\arg\max_{y \in \mathcal{Y}} w^T \phi(x, y)$, can be formulated as an integer linear program. To do so, we introduce binary variable matrices to encode the different states of $\mathbf{A}$ and $\mathbf{C}$ and auxiliary vector variables p to encode the pairwise states. Let $a \in \mathbb{B}^{R \times 2}$ encode the states of $\mathbf{A}$ such that $a_{i,0} = 0$ indicates that region i is inactive and $a_{i,1} = 1$ indicates that region i is active. Let $c_{i,k}$ encode the states of $\mathbf{C}$ such that $c_{i,k} = 1$ if $\mathbf{C}_i = k$ and 0 otherwise. Finally, let $p \in \mathbb{B}^{E \times 1}$ be a vector which encodes whether any neighboring pair of regions are both selected where E is the number of neighboring regions. Our integer linear program is then:

$$\arg\max_{a,c,p} \sum_{i=1}^{R} \theta_i^{\mathrm{r}} a_{i,1} + \sum_{i=1}^{R}\sum_{k=1}^{K} \theta_{i,k}^{\mathrm{s}} c_{i,k} + \sum_{ij\in\mathcal{E}} \theta_{ij}^{\mathrm{p}} p_{ij} \tag{3}$$

$$\text{s.t.} \quad a_{i,0} + a_{i,1} = 1 \tag{4}$$

$$\sum_{k=0}^{K} c_{i,k} = 1, \quad a_{i,0} = c_{i,0} \qquad \forall\, i \in R \tag{5}$$

$$\sum_{i\in\gamma} a_{i,1} = 1 \qquad \forall\, \gamma \in \Gamma \tag{6}$$

$$p_{ij} \le a_{i,1}, \quad p_{ij} \le a_{j,1}, \quad a_{i,1} + a_{j,1} - p_{ij} \le 1 \qquad \forall\, i,j \in \mathcal{E} \tag{7}$$

with generic region costs $\theta_i^r = w_{\text{reg}}^T f_i^{\text{reg}}$, semantic compatibility costs $\theta_{i,k}^s = w_{\text{sem:k}}^T f_i^{\text{reg}}$ and pairwise costs $\theta_{ij}^p = w_{\text{pair}}^T f_{ij}^{\text{pair}}$.

Equation 4 ensures that each region is either active or inactive. Equation 5 ensures that each region can take on at most a single semantic label (or no semantic label if the region is inactive). Equation 6 ensures that exactly one region in each of the paths of the tree (from each leaf to most coarse node) is active. Equation 7 ensures that the auxiliary pairwise variable p_{ij} is on if and only if both regions i and j are selected.

When there are no pairwise features we can give an efficient dynamic programming algorithm to exactly solve the maximization problem, having running time $O(RK)$. When pairwise features are included, this algorithm could be used together with dual decomposition to efficiently perform test-time inference [25]. However, the integer linear program formulation is particularly useful for loss-augmented inference during learning (see Section 5.1).

5 Coverage Loss

Let $G = \{r_1^G, ... r_{|G|}^G\}$ be a set of ground truth regions and $S = \{r_1^S, ... r_{|S|}^S\}$ be a set of proposed regions for a given image. For a given pair of regions r_j and r_k, the overlap between them is defined using the intersection over union score: $\text{Overlap}(r_j, r_k) = (r_j \cap r_k)/(r_j \cup r_k)$. The weighted coverage score [10] measures the similarity between two segmentations:

$$\text{Coverage}_{\text{weighted}}(G, S) = \frac{1}{|\mathcal{I}|} \sum_{j=1}^{|G|} |r_j^G| \max_{k=1..|S|} \text{Overlap}(r_j^G, r_k^S). \tag{8}$$

where $|\mathcal{I}|$ is the total number of pixels in the image and $|r_j^G|$ is the number of pixels in ground truth region r_j^G. We define the Coverage Loss function to be the amount of coverage score unattained by a particular segmentation:

$$\Delta_{\text{W}_1}(y, \bar{y}) = \frac{1}{|\mathcal{I}|} \sum_{j=1}^{|G|} |r_j^G| (1 - \max_{k:\bar{A}_k=1} \text{Overlap}(r_j^G, r_k^S)) \tag{9}$$

where $\bar{y}$ is a predicted cut of the segmentation tree and $\bar{A} \in \mathbb{B}^{|S|\times 1}$ the corresponding vector indicating which regions are selected.

5.1 Integer Program Formulation with Loss Augmentation

During training, most structured learning algorithms [26] [27] need to solve the *loss augmented inference* problem, in which we seek to obtain a high energy prediction that also has high loss:

$$y^* = \arg\max_{\bar{y} \in \mathcal{Y}} \Delta(y^{(i)}, \bar{y}) + w^T \phi(x, \bar{y}) \tag{10}$$

To solve the loss augmented inference problem, we introduce an additional auxiliary matrix $o \in \mathbb{B}^{G \times R}$ where G represents the number of ground truth regions and R represents the number of regions in the tree. The variable o_{gj} will be 1 if region r_j is the argmax in (9) for the ground truth region g (specified by $y^{(i)}$), and 0 otherwise. To ensure this, we add an additional set of constraints:

$$o_{gi} \leq a_{i,1} \qquad \forall\, g \in G,\ \forall i \in R \tag{11}$$

$$\sum_{i=1}^{R} o_{gi} = 1 \qquad \forall\, g \in G \tag{12}$$

$$o_{gi} + a_{j,1} \leq 1 \qquad \forall g \in G, i, j \in R \text{ s.t. } \text{Overlap}(s_g, s_j) > \text{Overlap}(s_g, s_i) \tag{13}$$

Equation (11) ensures that a prediction region i can only be considered the maximally overlapping region with ground truth region g if it is a selected region. Equation (12) ensures that every ground truth region is assigned exactly 1 overlap region. Finally, Equation (13) ensures that prediction region i can only be assigned the maximal region of g if and only if no other region j that has greater overlap with g is active.

The ILP objective is then altered to take into account the coverage loss:

$$\arg\max_{a,c,p,o} \quad \sum_{i=1}^{R} \theta_i^{\mathrm{r}} a_{i,1} + \sum_{i=1}^{R}\sum_{k=1}^{K} \theta_{i,k}^{\mathrm{s}} c_{i,k} + \sum_{ij \in \mathcal{E}} \theta_{ij}^{p} p_{ij} + \sum_{g=1}^{G}\sum_{i=1}^{R} \theta_{gi}^{\mathrm{o}} o_{gi} \tag{14}$$

where $\theta_{gi}^{o} = \text{Overlap}(r_g^G, r_s^S) - \text{Overlap}(r_g^G, r_i^S)$ encodes the loss incurred if region i is selected where r_s^S is the region specified by the surrogate labeling with the greatest overlap with ground truth region g.

6 Solving the Ground Truth Mapping Problem

Because the ground truth semantic and instance annotations are defined as a set of regions which are not among our segmentation tree-produced regions, we must map the ground truth annotations onto our segmented regions in order to learn. To do so, we build upon the ILP formulation described in the previous section.

Formally, given a ground truth set of instance regions $G = \{r_1^g, ... r_{R_G}^g\}$ and a proposed tree of regions $S = \{r_1, ... r_{R_P}\}$, the cut of the tree that maximizes the weighted coverage score is given by the following ILP:

$$\arg\min_{a,o} \quad \sum_{g=1}^{G}\sum_{i=1}^{R} \theta_{gi}^{\mathrm{o}} o_{gi}$$

subject to $a_{i,0} + a_{i,1} = 1 \; \forall i \in R$, $\sum_{i \in \gamma} a_{i,1} = 1 \; \forall \gamma \in \Gamma$, and Equations (11),(12), and (13).

6.1 Learning with Surrogate Labels

When the segmentation trees contain the ground truth regions as a possible cut, the minimal value of the Coverage Loss (Equation 9) is 0. However, in practice, segmentation trees provide a very small sample from the set of all possible regions and it is rare that the ground truth regions are among them. Consequently, we must learn to predict a set of surrogate labels $\{z^{(1)}, ..., z^{(N)}\}$ instead.

We modify the loss used in training to ensure that the magnitude of the surrogate loss of a prediction $\bar{y}_i$ is defined relative to the best possible cut $z^{(i)}$:

$$\Delta_{W_2}(z^{(i)}, \bar{y}) = \Delta_{W_1}(y^{(i)}, \bar{y}) - \Delta_{W_1}(y^{(i)}, z^{(i)}) \tag{15}$$

Note that the first term in the loss can be pre-computed and has the effect of scaling the loss such that the margin requested during learning is defined with respect to the best attainable cut in a given segment tree. It should be clear then when $y^{(i)} = z^{(i)}$, that $\Delta_{W_2} = \Delta_{W_1}$.

7 Convolutional Network Features for Dense Segmentation

While Convolutional Neural Networks (CNNs) have shown impressive performance in Classification [28] and Detection [12] tasks, it has not yet been demonstrated that CNN features improve dense segmentation performance. Recently [29] showed how to use a pretrained convolutional network to improve the ranking of foreground/background segmentations on the PASCAL VOC dataset. It is unclear, however, whether a similar scheme can be successfully applied to densely labeled scenes, where many of the images can only be identified via contextual cues. Furthermore, because CNNs are generally trained on RGB data (no RGBD data exists with enough labeled examples to properly train these deep models) it is unclear whether CNN features provide an additional performance boost when combined with depth features. To address these questions, we compare state of the art hand-crafted RGB+D features with features derived from the aforementioned CNN models, as well as combinations of the two feature sources. As in [29], we extract CNN-based region features as follows: for each arbitrarily shaped region, we first extract a sub-window that tightly bounds the region. Next, we feed the sub-window to the pre-trained network of [28]. We treat the activations from the first fully connected hidden layer of the model as the features for the region. While we experimented with using the final pooled convolutional layer and the second fully connected layer, we did not observe a major difference in performance when using these alternative feature sources.

Because a particular sub-window may contain multiple objects, there exists an inherent ambiguity with regard to which object in a sub-window is being classified by the CNN. To address this ambiguity, we experimented with three types of masking operations performed on each sub-window before the CNN features were computed. Firstly, we perform no masking (Normal Windows). Secondly, we blur the subwindow (Mask Blurred Windows) with a blur kernel whose radius increases with respect to the euclidean distance from the region mask. This produces a subwindow that appears *focused* on the object itself. Finally, we use the masking operation from [29] (Masked Windows) in which any pixels falling outside the mask are set to the image means so that the background regions have zero value after mean-subtraction.

We additionally experiment with a superset of region features from [30] and [5] as well as compare the convolutional network features to Sparse Coded SIFT features from [31]. Our pairwise region features are a superset of pairwise region and boundary features from [30] [5].

8 Experiments

To evaluate our instance-segmentation scheme, we use the NYU Depth V2 [5] dataset. While datasets like Pascal [20], Berkeley [32], Stanford Backgound [33] and MSRC [1] are frequently used to evaluate segmentation tasks, Stanford Background and MSRC do not provide instance labels and the Berkeley dataset provides neither semantic nor instance labels. Pascal only contains a few segmented objects per scene, mostly at the same scale. Conversely the NYU Depth dataset has densely labeled scenes with instance masks for objects of highly varying size and shape.

While the original NYU V2 dataset has over 800 semantic classes, we mapped these down to 20 classes: cabinet, bed, table, seating, curtain, picture, window, pillow, books, television person, sink, shelves, cloth, furniture, wall, ceiling, floor, prop and structure. We use the same classes for evaluating both the CNN features and the semantic instance segmentation.

8.1 Evaluating Segmentation Tree Proposal Methods

While numerous hierarchical segmentation strategies have been proposed, it has not been previously possible to estimate the upper bound coverage score of a particular segmentation tree. Our loss formulation addresses this by allowing us to directly measure the Coverage upper bound (CUB) scores achievable by a particular hierarchical segmentation. We evaluate several hierarchical segmentation proposal schemes in Table 1 by computing for each the surrogate labels that maximize the weighted coverage score. Unsurprisingly the depth signal raises the CUB score. [30] outperforms [5] both in terms of CUB score and requires far fewer regions. [21] and [10] both achieve the same weighted CUB scores but [21] is a bit more efficient requiring fewer regions. We use the method from [30] for all subsequent experiments.

8.2 Evaluating CNN Features

To evaluate the CNN features, we used the ground truth instance annotations from the NYU Depth V2 dataset. By evaluating on the ground truth regions,

Table 1. Segmentation results on the testing set

.

Input	Algorithm	Weighted CUB	Average Number of Regions
RGB	Hoiem et al [10]	50.7	117.7 ± 36.7
RGB	Zhile and Shakhnarovich [21]	50.7	102.4 ± 56.4
RGB+D	Silberman et al (RGBD) [5]	64.1	210.0 ± 106.0
RGB+D	Gupta et al [30]	70.6	62.5 ± 26.6

we can isolate errors inherent in evaluating poor regions from the abilities of the descriptor as well as avoid the ground truth mapping problem for assigning semantic labels. To prepare the inputs to the CNN we perform the following operations: For each instance mask in the dataset (a binary mask for a single object instance), we compute a tight bounding box around the object plus a small margin (10% of the height and width of the mask). If the bounding box is smaller than 140×140, we use a 140×140 bounding box and upsample to 244×244. Otherwise, we rescale the image to 244×244. During training, we use each original sub-window and its mirror image at several scales $(1.1, 1.3, 1.5, 1.7)$. Finally, we ignore regions whose original size is smaller than 20×20. We computed a random train/val/test split using the original 1449 images in the dataset of equal sizes. After performing each of the aforementioned masking operations and computing the CNN features from each subwindow, we normalize each output feature from the CNN by subtracting the mean and dividing by the variance, computed across the training set. We then train a L2-regularized logistic regressor to predict the correct semantic labels of each instance. The regularization parameters were chosen to maximize accuracy on the validation set and are found in the supplementary material.

As shown in Table 2, the CNN features perform surprisingly well, with Masked Windows computed on RGB only beating both RGBD Features and the combination of sparse coded SIFT and RGBD Features. Our Mask-Blurring operation does not do as well as Masking, with the combination of RGBD Features and CNN Features extracted from Masked regions performing the best.

Table 2. A comparison on region-feature descriptors on ground truth regions

Features	Accuracy	Conf Matrix Mean Diagonal
Normal Windows	48.8	23.5
Mask-Blurred Windows	56.6	36.8
Masked Windows [29]	60.8	42.3
RGBD Features [5]	59.9	32.1
Sparse Coded Sift + RGBD Features [31]	60.3	34.4
Unblurred Windows + RGBD Features	60.3	38.0
Mask-Blurred Windows + RGBD Features	63.1	46.1
Masked Windows + RGBD Features	64.9	46.9

8.3 Segmentation

To evaluate our semantic/instance segmentation results, we use the semantic and instance labels from [5]. We train and evaluate on the same train/test split as [5] and [34]. We computed the surrogate labels using the weighted coverage loss and report all of the results using the weighted coverage score. To train our model, we used the Block Coordinate Frank Wolf algorithm [27] for solving the structured SVM optizmiation problem, and the Gurobi[35] ILP solver for performing inference. Loss augmented inference takes several seconds per image whereas inference at test time takes half a second on average. The difference in speed is due to the addition of the overlap matrix (Section 5.1) used to implement loss augmented inference at training time.

Evaluating Semantic-Instance Segmentation Results
We evaluate several different types of Semantic-Instance Segmentation models. The model **SEG Trees, SIFT Features** uses the standard segmentation trees with Sparse Coded SIFT features, **SEG Trees, CNN Features** uses standard segmentation trees and CNN Features using the Masking strategy, **SEG + GT Trees, CNN Features** uses the CNN features as well but also trains with a set of height-1 trees created from the ground truth instance maps. Since these height-1 trees are by definition already segmented, during training we use the Coverage Loss for the SEG Trees and Hamming Loss on the semantic predictions for the GT Trees. The last model we evaluated, **GT-SEG Trees, CNN Features**, is a model trained on segmentation trees biased by the ground truth.

Table 3. Segmentation results on the NYU Depth V2 Dataset

Algorithm	Weighted Coverage
Silberman et al [5]	61.1
Jia et al [34]	61.7
Our Model - SEG Trees, SIFT Features	61.8
Our Model - SEG Trees, CNN Features without Pairwise terms	62.4
Our Model - SEG Trees, CNN Features	62.5
Our Model - SEG + GT Trees, CNN Features	62.8
Our Model - GT-SEG Trees, CNN Features	87.4

Table 4. Evaluating the use of the Coverage Loss

Loss Function	Weighted Coverage
Hamming Loss	61.4
Weighted Coverage Loss	62.5

As shown in Table 3 our model achieves state of the art performance in segmenting the dense scenes from the NYU Depth Dataset. While the use of SIFT features makes a negligible improvement with regard to previous work, using

Fig. 3. Random test images from the NYU Depth V2 dataset, overlaid with segmentations. 1st column: ground truth. 2nd column: segmentations from Jia et al [34]. 3rd colmun: our segmentations. 4th column: semantic labels, produced as a by-product of our segmentation procedure.

convolutional features provides almost a 1% improvement. **SEG + GT Trees, CNN Features**, which was trained to minimize coverage loss on the SEG trees and semantic loss on the ground truth performs slightly better. The addition of the GT trees to the training data acts as a regularizer for the semantic weights on the high dimensional CNN features by requiring that the weights are both useful for finding instances of imperfectly segmented objects and correctly labeling objects if a perfect region is made available. Qualitative results for this model are shown in Fig. 3 along with a comparison to [34]. As these figures illustrate, the model performs better on larger objects in the scene such as the couch in row 1, and the bed in row 4. Like [34] however, it struggles with smaller objects such as the clutter on the desk in row 5.

Finally **GT-SEG Trees, CNN Features** is a model trained on segmentation trees biased by the ground truth. This model achieves a coverage score of 87.4% which indicates that while our model shows improvement over previous methods at instance segmentation, it still does not achieve a perfect coverage score even when the ground truth is available as a possible cut.

Evaluating the Loss Function
To evaluate the effectiveness of using the Coverage Loss for instance segmentation, we use the same model but vary the loss function used to minimize the structural SVM. We compare against using the hamming loss. We use the use regularization parameter [1] for both experiments.

9 Conclusions

In this work, we introduce a scheme for jointly inferring dense semantic and instance labels for indoor scenes. We contribute a new loss function, the Coverage Loss, and demonstrate its utility in learning to infer semantic and instance labels. While we can now directly measure the maximum achievable coverage score given a set of regions, it is not yet clear whether this upper bound is actually attainable. While a particular cut of a segmentation tree may maximize the coverage score, it may be information theoretically impossible to find a generalizing model as different humans may disagree on the best surrogate labels, just as they may disagree on the best ground truth annotations. Furthermore, while our structured learning approach was applied to segmentation trees, it can be similarly applied to an unstructured "soup" of segments. In practice, we found that such an unstructured set of segments did not increase performance but instead slowed inference. This is due to the fact that the requirement that no two selected segments overlap can be efficiently represented by a small set of constraints when using segmentation trees where a "soup" of segments requires a very large number of non-overlap constraints. One limitation of our segmentation tree formulation is the inability of the model to merge instances which are non-neighbors in the image plane. We hope to tackle this problem in future work.

Acknowledgements: The authors would like to acknowledge support from ONR #N00014-13-1-0646, NSF #1116923 and Microsoft Research."

References

1. Shotton, J., Winn, J.M., Rother, C., Criminisi, A.: *TextonBoost*: Joint appearance, shape and context modeling for multi-class object recognition and segmentation. In: Leonardis, A., Bischof, H., Pinz, A. (eds.) ECCV 2006, Part I. LNCS, vol. 3951, pp. 1–15. Springer, Heidelberg (2006)

[1] $\lambda = .001$.

2. Ladicky, L., Russell, C., Kohli, P., Torr, P.H.: Associative hierarchical crfs for object class image segmentation. In: 2009 IEEE 12th International Conference on Computer Vision, pp. 739–746. IEEE (2009)
3. Kohli, P., Torr, P.H., et al.: Robust higher order potentials for enforcing label consistency. International Journal of Computer Vision 82(3), 302–324 (2009)
4. Lempitsky, V., Vedaldi, A., Zisserman, A.: A pylon model for semantic segmentation. In: NIPS (2011)
5. Silberman, N., Hoiem, D., Kohli, P., Fergus, R.: Indoor segmentation and support inference from RGBD images. In: Fitzgibbon, A., Lazebnik, S., Perona, P., Sato, Y., Schmid, C. (eds.) ECCV 2012, Part V. LNCS, vol. 7576, pp. 746–760. Springer, Heidelberg (2012)
6. Guo, R., Hoiem, D.: Beyond the line of sight: Labeling the underlying surfaces. In: Fitzgibbon, A., Lazebnik, S., Perona, P., Sato, Y., Schmid, C. (eds.) ECCV 2012, Part V. LNCS, vol. 7576, pp. 761–774. Springer, Heidelberg (2012)
7. Silberman, N., Shapira, L., Gal, R., Kohli, P.: A contour completion model for augmenting surface reconstructions. In: Fleet, D., Pajdla, T., Schiele, B., Tuytelaars, T. (eds.) ECCV 2014, Part III. LNCS, vol. 8691, pp. 488–503. Springer, Heidelberg (2014)
8. Munoz, D., Bagnell, J.A., Hebert, M.: Stacked hierarchical labeling. In: Daniilidis, K., Maragos, P., Paragios, N. (eds.) ECCV 2010, Part VI. LNCS, vol. 6316, pp. 57–70. Springer, Heidelberg (2010)
9. Farabet, C., Couprie, C., Najman, L., LeCun, Y.: Scene parsing with multiscale feature learning, purity trees, and optimal covers. arXiv preprint arXiv:1202.2160 (2012)
10. Hoiem, D., Efros, A.A., Hebert, M.: Recovering occlusion boundaries from an image. Int. J. Comput. Vision 91, 328–346 (2011)
11. Tarlow, D., Zemel, R.S.: Structured output learning with high order loss functions. In: International Conference on Artificial Intelligence and Statistics, pp. 1212–1220 (2012)
12. Sermanet, P., Eigen, D., Zhang, X., Mathieu, M., Fergus, R., LeCun, Y.: Overfeat: Integrated recognition, localization and detection using convolutional networks. CoRR abs/1312.6229 (2013)
13. Derek Hoiem, A.E., Hebert, M.: Geometric context from a single image. In: International Conference on Computer Vision (2005)
14. Malisiewicz, T., Efros, A.: Improving spatial support for objects via multiple segmentations. In: BVMC (2007)
15. Russell, B.C., Freeman, W.T., Efros, A.A., Sivic, J., Zisserman, A.: Using Multiple Segmentations to Discover Objects and their Extent in Image Collections. In: Computer Vision and Pattern Recognition (2006)
16. Pantofaru, C., Schmid, C., Hebert, M.: Object recognition by integrating multiple image segmentations. In: Forsyth, D., Torr, P., Zisserman, A. (eds.) ECCV 2008, Part III. LNCS, vol. 5304, pp. 481–494. Springer, Heidelberg (2008)
17. Kumar, M.P., Koller, D.: Efficiently selecting regions for scene understanding. In: 2010 IEEE Conference on Computer Vision and Pattern Recognition (CVPR), pp. 3217–3224. IEEE (2010)
18. Brendel, W., Todorovic, S.: Segmentation as maximum weight independent set. In: Neural Information Processing Systems, vol. 4 (2010)
19. Ion, A., Carreira, J., Sminchisescu, C.: Image segmentation by figure-ground composition into maximal cliques. In: 2011 IEEE International Conference on Computer Vision (ICCV), pp. 2110–2117. IEEE (2011)

20. Everingham, M., Van Gool, L., Williams, C.K., Winn, J., Zisserman, A.: The pascal visual object classes (voc) challenge. International Journal of Computer Vision 88(2), 303–338 (2010)
21. Ren, Z., Shakhnarovich, G.: Image segmentation by cascaded region agglomeration. In: 2013 IEEE Conference on Computer Vision and Pattern Recognition (CVPR), pp. 2011–2018. IEEE (2013)
22. Arbelaez, P.: Boundary extraction in natural images using ultrametric contour maps. In: Conference on Computer Vision and Pattern Recognition Workshop, CVPRW 2006, pp. 182. IEEE (2006)
23. Maire, M., Arbeláez, P., Fowlkes, C., Malik, J.: Using contours to detect and localize junctions in natural images. In: IEEE Conference on Computer Vision and Pattern Recognition, CVPR 2008, pp. 1–8. IEEE (2008)
24. Tsochantaridis, I., Joachims, T., Hofmann, T., Altun, Y.: Large Margin Methods for Structured and Interdependent Output Variables. J. Mach. Learn. Res. 6, 1453–1484 (2005)
25. Sontag, D., Globerson, A., Jaakkola, T.: Introduction to dual decomposition for inference. In: Sra, S., Nowozin, S., Wright, S.J. (eds.) Optimization for Machine Learning. MIT Press (2011)
26. Joachims, T., Finley, T., Yu, C.N.J.: Cutting-plane training of structural svms. Machine Learning 77(1), 27–59 (2009)
27. Lacoste-Julien, S., Jaggi, M., Schmidt, M., Pletscher, P.: Block-coordinate frank-wolfe optimization for structural svms. arXiv preprint arXiv:1207.4747 (2012)
28. Krizhevsky, A., Sutskever, I., Hinton, G.E.: Imagenet classification with deep convolutional neural networks. In: NIPS, vol. 1, p. 4 (2012)
29. Girshick, R., Donahue, J., Darrell, T., Malik, J.: Rich feature hierarchies for accurate object detection and semantic segmentation. arXiv preprint arXiv:1311.2524 (2013)
30. Gupta, S., Arbelaez, P., Malik, J.: Perceptual organization and recognition of indoor scenes from rgb-d images. In: 2013 IEEE Conference on Computer Vision and Pattern Recognition (CVPR), pp. 564–571. IEEE (2013)
31. Silberman, N., Fergus, R.: Indoor scene segmentation using a structured light sensor. In: Proceedings of the International Conference on Computer Vision - Workshop on 3D Representation and Recognition (2011)
32. Arbelaez, P., Maire, M., Fowlkes, C., Malik, J.: Contour detection and hierarchical image segmentation. IEEE Transactions on Pattern Analysis and Machine Intelligence 33(5), 898–916 (2011)
33. Gould, S., Fulton, R., Koller, D.: Decomposing a scene into geometric and semantically consistent regions. In: 2009 IEEE 12th International Conference on Computer Vision, pp. 1–8. IEEE (2009)
34. Jia, Z., Gallagher, A., Saxena, A., Chen, T.: 3D-based reasoning with blocks, support, and stability. In: 2013 IEEE Conference on Computer Vision and Pattern Recognition (CVPR), pp. 1–8. IEEE (2013)
35. Gurobi Optimization, Inc.: Gurobi optimizer reference manual (2014)

Superpixel Graph Label Transfer with Learned Distance Metric

Stephen Gould[1], Jiecheng Zhao[1], Xuming He[1,2], and Yuhang Zhang[1,3]

[1] Research School of Computer Science, ANU, Australia
[2] NICTA, Australia
[3] Chalmers University of Technology, Sweden

Abstract. We present a fast approximate nearest neighbor algorithm for semantic segmentation. Our algorithm builds a graph over superpixels from an annotated set of training images. Edges in the graph represent approximate nearest neighbors in feature space. At test time we match superpixels from a novel image to the training images by adding the novel image to the graph. A move-making search algorithm allows us to leverage the graph and image structure for finding matches. We then transfer labels from the training images to the image under test. To promote good matches between superpixels we propose to learn a distance metric that weights the edges in our graph. Our approach is evaluated on four standard semantic segmentation datasets and achieves results comparable with the state-of-the-art.

1 Introduction

Semantic segmentation, or multi-class pixel labeling, is a fundamental step in understanding images. In this task every pixel in the image is annotated with a category label, such as "sky", "tree", "water", "person", etc. Traditional methods learn a per-pixel classifier for each category of interest and combine these together with pairwise and higher-order constraints using a conditional Markov random field (CRF) [1, 2]. The difficulty with such methods is that they need re-training whenever new data becomes available or the set of categories of interest is changed. Furthermore, the per-pixel classifier evaluation is an expensive operation that must be performed for each test image.

The latter problem can be addressed by moving to a superpixel representation of the image. Here a bottom-up over-segmentation algorithm (e.g., [3, 4]) is used to divide the image into small contiguous regions of similar appearance. The number of superpixels is significantly smaller than the number of pixels but still capture important image characteristics (such as object boundaries). Thus inference time is dramatically reduced with negligible cost to accuracy.

Recently, nearest neighbor methods have been proposed to address the problem of growing datasets and changing categories [5–9]. These data driven approaches work by first matching regions in the image under test to regions from a large database of hand labelled images. Matches are found based on region and image-level appearance cues. Since the regions in the database are labelled,

D. Fleet et al. (Eds.): ECCV 2014, Part I, LNCS 8689, pp. 632–647, 2014.
© Springer International Publishing Switzerland 2014

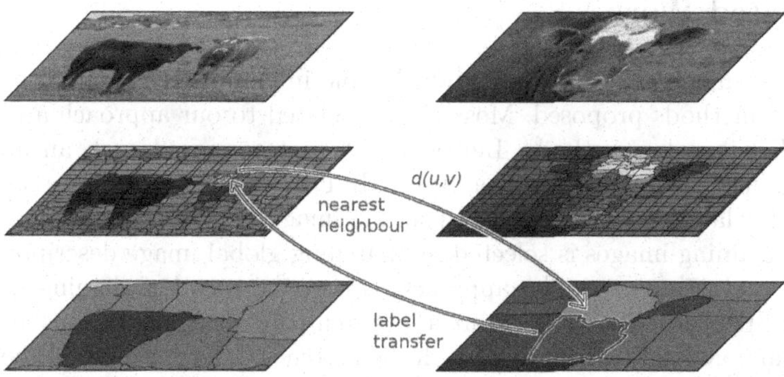

Fig. 1. Illustration of the idea of label transfer on a Superpixel Graph. The graph is built by finding good matches for each superpixel. These are represented by directed edges. Labels are then transferred backwards along the edges.

the target image can be annotated by transferring the labels of the matched regions. Clearly such methods can seamlessly integrate new data but they require a finely tuned distance function for finding matches—ideally one that correlates category labels (the thing we want) with appearance (the thing we observe).

In this paper we propose a nearest neighbor method for semantic segmentation that uses a learned distance function. Our method represents an image by a set of overlapping superpixels of different sizes. Associated with each superpixel is a feature vector that summarizes its appearance. By finding superpixels with similar features in a database of labelled images we can apply label transfer to annotate a new image. The idea is illustrated in Figure 1. Importantly, nearest neighbor matching is done per superpixel but annotation is done at the pixel level allowing pixel labels to be determined from overlapping superpixels.

We present an algorithm for rapidly finding good matches by adaptively constructing a graph where nodes represent superpixels and edges represent matches. Our algorithm can be viewed as an approximate nearest neighbor method, but one where we encourage spatial continuity during matching. This is in contrast to other methods that rely on matching at two different levels: global (image) and local (superpixel). To improve the accuracy of the annotation we learn a distance metric so that superpixels with the same label appear closer in feature space than those with different labels. Our key contribution is the integration of metric learning with graph construction. Specifically, we interleave graph construction and metric learning, and derive the metric learning problem based on the structure of the graph at hand.

We run extensive experiments on four standard datasets and compare our method with and without learning the distance metric. We also evaluate the effect of varying other algorithm parameters such as the number of superpixels and the database size. Our results show that metric learning helps to improve accuracy but as expected other factors, such as dataset size, are also important for achieving good performance.

2 Related Work

Semantic segmentation is a well studied topic in computer vision with a large number of methods proposed. Most closely related to our approach are the so-called label transfer methods. Liu et al. [9] first proposed such an approach with an innovative algorithm that uses SIFT descriptors to align scenes and then overlay labels from a subset of training images onto the target image. The subset of training images is selected by matching global image descriptors.

Zhang et al. [7] use a similar approach. However, instead of aligning scenes by matching SIFT descriptors they directly match pairs of image regions and use a Markov random field (MRF) to smooth the matches. Like our method they use a superpixel representation of the image to reduce complexity and provide spatial support for computing features. However, our method does not require matching (and hence label transfer from) an entire image. Moreover, we use multiple sets of different sized superpixels for representing a single image.

Many works attempt to explain an image by matching parts of it to regions in other images (e.g., [10, 11]). A label transfer approach along these lines, aimed at large scale labeling tasks, is the work of Tighe and Lazebnik [6]. This work also uses a superpixel representation of images but does not enforce spatial continuity during the matching process. Matches are used to construct pseudo-probability vectors for each superpixel in the test image and an MRF produces the final predictions. The approach uses a very large number of features and a pre-selection phase based on global image descriptors like the previous works to prune the images considered at test time. Nevertheless, they are able to label images in under 10s of total processing time.

An extension of this work [5] includes cues derived from per-exemplar object detectors, which have been shown to work well for the object detection task [12]. This improves performance on less abundant classes but comes at a substantial cost in features computed and processing time. Our approach, on the other hand, computes an order of magnitude fewer features and achieves similar results.

Conceptually similar to our work is the PatchMatchGraph method of Gould and Zhang [8] and the PatchWeb method of Barnes [13]. Like our approach, they build a graph over matched image regions. However, instead of using superpixels they use overlapping rectangular image patches. This makes the method expensive both in terms of memory and running time. Our superpixel representation provides a much more compact set of regions without compromising accuracy. To build the graph over image patches, Gould and Zhang [8] and Barnes [13] employ a search strategy motivated by the PatchMatch algorithm of Barnes et al. [14, 15]. We use a similar strategy adapted to superpixels, and also propose a new random projection move.

All of the above methods rely on hand tuned feature vectors for matching regions (patches or superpixels) across images. While this can give high quality results in terms of matching similar appearance there is no guarantee that the features chosen will match regions with similar semantics. Our approach differs by incorporating a learned distance metric. Specifically, we use a variant of the large margin nearest neighbor algorithm of Weinberger and Saul [16]. Eigen and

Fergus [17] also employ a nearest neighbor approach with learned metric but do so by scaling individual training set descriptors. Our metric is a generalized distance capable of arbitrary linear transforms in feature space.

3 Superpixel Graphs

In this section we describe our nearest neighbor algorithm for label transfer. We begin by describing our superpixel-based representation. Next, we introduce a superpixel graph for quickly finding similar superpixels in other images. Our approach is akin to the PATCHMATCHGRAPH [8] but rather than using rectangular patches we use superpixels. This gives us a much more compact image representation. Interleaved with our graph construction is the learning of the distance metric used to compare superpixels. At the end of the section we show how our graph can be used for label transfer.

3.1 Superpixel Embedding

We represent an image by a set of superpixels generated by an over-segmentation algorithm. However, a single over-segmentation of an image may fail to capture true object boundaries—too coarse a representation will miss small objects while too fine a representation results in many superpixels that are non-distinctive. Thus we produce many different over-segmentations resulting in an overlapping set of superpixels of different sizes. In our work, we use the superpixel algorithm of Zhang et al. [3] but our approach is not limited to this choice—any other over-segmentation algorithm can be used (e.g., [4]).

We embed our superpixels in a metric space by encoding the superpixels as feature vectors in $\mathbb{R}^n$. We denote the feature vector for superpixel u by $\boldsymbol{x}_u$. In this work we construct the feature vectors by averaging filter responses over the superpixel region. Our filters include the 17-dimensional "texton" filter [2], 13-dimensional dense HOG [18, 19], and 4-connected LBP histograms [20]. We also include the x- and y-location of the superpixel and its size to provide spatial context, and the entropy of each RGB color channel to provide a further measure of texture. To construct $\boldsymbol{x}_u$ we combine these features with the mean and standard deviation of the filter responses from neighboring regions at each of the four compass directions. This gives 510 features for each superpixel. Note that this is much smaller than the feature vectors used in other superpixel-based nearest neighbor methods (e.g., [6]).[1]

During metric learning and image annotation we require superpixel labels $y_u \in \{1, \ldots, C\}$. These are generated from ground truth pixel labels by computing the proportion of each class label within the superpixel. This gives an empirical probability estimate $\hat{P}_u(y)$. Most superpixels only contain pixels with the same label but some larger superpixels can have mixed labels. When a single hard label for superpixel u is required we take it as $y_u = \text{argmax}_y \hat{P}_u(y)$.

[1] We provide full source code for our method including superpixel generation, feature calculation, graph construction, metric learning, and label transfer as part of the DARWIN software package [21].

3.2 Building the Superpixel Graph

For finding nearest neighbor matches quickly we construct a graph over superpixels. Our graph is similar to the PatchMatchGraph proposed by Gould and Zhang [8], which uses ideas from Barnes et al. [15] for leveraging existing matches to find better ones. Formally, let $\mathcal{G} = \langle \mathcal{V}, \mathcal{E} \rangle$ be a graph with nodes $\mathcal{V}$ and edges $\mathcal{E}$. Each node $u \in \mathcal{V}$ represents a superpixel and each directed edge $(u, v) \in \mathcal{E}$ represents a match from superpixel u to superpixel v. Note that we do not require superpixel v to also match with u.

A weight associated with each edge (u, v) represents the cost of matching u to v. We define this cost to be the (generalized) distance between the feature vectors describing the two superpixels:

$$d_M(u, v) = (\boldsymbol{x}_u - \boldsymbol{x}_v)^T M (\boldsymbol{x}_u - \boldsymbol{x}_v) \tag{1}$$

where $\boldsymbol{x}_u$ and $\boldsymbol{x}_v$ are the feature vectors associated with superpixels u and v, respectively, and $M = LL^T \succeq 0$ is a positive semi-definite matrix that parameterizes the metric. When $M = I$ the metric is the Euclidean norm, and when $M = \hat{\Sigma}^{-1}$ the metric is the Mahalanobis distance, where $\hat{\Sigma}^{-1}$ is the inverse covariance matrix of the data.

The set of nodes adjacent to node u in the graph are $\mathcal{N}_u = \{v : (u, v) \in \mathcal{E}\}$. If the corresponding superpixels are those closest, in feature space, to u out of all $v \in \mathcal{V}$ then $\mathcal{N}_u$ is the set of exact nearest neighbors. Thus to find the set of k nearest neighbors for all superpixels u we need to solve the following optimization problem over the set of edges in the graph.

$$\begin{array}{ll} \text{minimize}_{\mathcal{E}} & \sum_{(u,v) \in \mathcal{E}} d_M(u, v) \\ \text{subject to} & \forall u \in \mathcal{V}\colon \deg(u) = k \\ & \forall (u, v) \in \mathcal{E}\colon \text{img}(u) \neq \text{img}(v) \\ & \forall (u, v), (u, w) \in \mathcal{E}\colon \text{img}(v) \neq \text{img}(w) \end{array} \tag{2}$$

where we constrain the out degree of each node to k and denote such a graph by $\mathcal{G}_k$. Furthermore, since we are interested in using our graph for label transfer there is no use in matching a superpixel to another one within the same image. Thus we add the constraint $\text{img}(u) \neq \text{img}(v)$, meaning superpixels u and v cannot come from the same image. Finally, as in Gould and Zhang [8] we would like to find a diverse set of matches and so restrict each superpixel to matching at most one superpixel from any single image. Consequently we are guaranteed that each superpixel matches to superpixels from k different images. This is encoded by the last constraint.

Equation 2 is a hard optimization problem since we are minimizing over the discrete set of edges in the graph. Therefore, we perform approximate optimization via a move-making algorithm that we describe below. Since finding nearest neighbors requires many distance computations we can accelerate the search by first transforming the features as $\boldsymbol{x}' = L^T \boldsymbol{x}$ so that $d_M(u, v) = \|\boldsymbol{x}'_u - \boldsymbol{x}'_v\|^2$.

Our overall algorithm for building a superpixel graph as described above is summarized in Algorithm 1.

Algorithm 1. Build Superpixel Graph.

input training images (and labels) and k
generate superpixels $\mathcal{V} = \{u\}$
compute superpixel features $\{\boldsymbol{x}_u\}$ and labels $\{y_u\}$
define feature transform matrix

$$L = \begin{cases} I & \text{euclidean} \\ \mathbf{diag}\,(1/\sigma_i) & \text{whitened} \\ \Sigma^{-1/2} & \text{mahalanobis} \\ \text{LMNN}_k(\{\boldsymbol{x}_u\}, \{y_u\}) & \text{learned (see §3.3)} \end{cases}$$

transform features $\forall u \in \mathcal{V}$, $\boldsymbol{x}'_u \leftarrow L^T \boldsymbol{x}_u$
initialize superpixel graph $\mathcal{G}_k = \langle \mathcal{V}, \mathcal{E} \rangle$ on features $\boldsymbol{x}'$
repeat
  attempt search moves for each $u \in \mathcal{V}$
until convergence
return graph $\mathcal{G}_k$ and feature transform matrix L^T

Move Making Optimization. Our search moves are motivated by the PATCHMATCH algorithm of Barnes et al. [15, 14]. We begin by initializing the graph with random edges that honor the constraints of Equation 2, i.e., each node has exactly k outgoing edges and no two edges emanating from a node terminate at nodes belonging to the same image. We then iterate over a sequence of search moves to incrementally improve the objective. We terminate after a fixed number of iterations or when the objective value (i.e., graph structure) does not change after attempting all moves.

Briefly, each move evaluates a set of candidate matches for one or more superpixels. These manifest as changes to the graph structure. Consider a candidate match v for superpixel u. To decide whether or not to add the edge (u, v) to the graph we examine the current outgoing edges from u. If one of these edges, say (u, w), points to a superpixel from the same image as v and if $d_M(u, v)$ is smaller than $d_M(u, w)$ we replace (u, w) with (u, v). Now, if none of the current outgoing edges from u point to a superpixel from the same image as v then we replace the highest cost outgoing edge with (u, v) if it has a smaller cost. This local update rule ensures that the objective of Equation 2 is non-increasing and the constraints are always satisfied.

An key aspect of our moves is that they are context enriched and encourage spatially coherent matches. That is, they are not simply based on local superpixel feature similarity. Nevertheless the moves can be computed in parallel for each superpixel u. This is important for scaling to larger image datasets as we progress towards solving the scene understanding challenge.

Exhaustive Search. The exhaustive search move is a naive move that finds the best k matches for a given superpixel u by comparing it to all superpixels in all other images. This is computationally expensive so we only apply it to a small number of superpixels per iteration. We randomly choose the superpixels from a distribution weighted by the cost of the current matches for each superpixels—that is, we are more likely to sample a superpixel that currently has bad matches than a superpixel that already has good ones. Our hope is that this will seed the graph with some very good edges that other search moves can exploit.

Random Projection. Motivated by locality-sensitive hashing (LSH) [22], the random projection move uses the fact that it is much easier to find nearest neighbors in a one-dimensional space than an n-dimensional space. Moreover, points close to each other in n dimensions will remain close to each other when projected onto a line. Of course, points that are distant may also end up close on the line. Nevertheless, the move is effective for finding some good matches especially during early move making iterations.

Concretely, we choose a random direction $\boldsymbol{z}$ in the n-dimensional feature space. We then project the feature vector for each superpixel onto this direction giving $\boldsymbol{z}^T \boldsymbol{x}_u \in \mathbb{R}$. Sorting by these values we can easily find nearby superpixels in direction $\boldsymbol{z}$ (not from the same image). We compute the distance between the superpixels in the full n-dimensional space with those within a fixed horizon h along direction $\boldsymbol{z}$ and perform the update rule described above.

Local Search and Propagate. Local search and propagate moves exploit image smoothness. For local search we consider candidate matches from the image neighborhood of the current match—that is, for edge $(u, v) \in \mathcal{E}$ we consider all superpixels adjacent to v in the image. For the propagation move we consider candidate matches where both superpixels are image-neighbors of a current match—that is, given an edge $(u, v) \in \mathcal{E}$ we consider the match (u', v') where u' and v' are superpixels adjacent to u and v in their respective images.

Enrichment. The last moves are the forward and inverse enrichment moves, which leverage properties of our graph $\mathcal{G}_k$. The forward enrichment move takes pairs of edges (u, v) and (v, w), and considers adding the candidate edge (u, w) to the graph. The inverse enrichment move takes an edge (u, v) and consider adding the reverse edge (v, u) to the graph. Both the forward and inverse enrichment moves tend to rapidly spread good matches across the graph.

3.3 Distance Metric Learning

As discussed above, it is important that our distance metric puts semantically similar superpixels closer than semantically different ones. However, the distance metric only has access to the observed superpixel features not their labels. There is no a priori guarantee that superpixel with similar features have the same category label since this is highly dependent on the features chosen and their relative scaling. Thus we need to learn a metric with the desired property that superpixels of the same label are clustered together. We do so using a variant of the large margin nearest neighbor (LMNN) algorithm of Weinberger and Saul [16].

Formally, let $\mathcal{N}_u^+ \subseteq \{v \in \mathcal{V} : y_v = y_u\}$ with $|\mathcal{N}_u^+| = k$ be the set of target superpixels within the neighborhood set of u, and let $\mathcal{N}_u^- = \{w \in \mathcal{V} : y_w \neq y_u\}$ be the set of so-called imposter superpixels with label differing from that of u. We wish to learn a metric so that all $v \in \mathcal{N}_u^+$ are closer to u than any $w \in \mathcal{N}_u^-$. The large margin nearest neighbor algorithm aims to find such a metric by solving the following convex optimization problem

$$\begin{array}{ll} \text{minimize}_M & \sum_{uv} d_M(u,v) + C \sum_{uvw} \xi_{uvw} \\ \text{subject to} & \forall uvw : d_M(u,w) - d_M(u,v) \geq 1 - \xi_{uvw} \\ & \xi_{uvw} \geq 0 \\ & M \succeq 0 \end{array} \tag{3}$$

where uv iterates over all $u \in \mathcal{V}$ and $v \in \mathcal{N}_u^+$, and uvw iterates over all $u \in \mathcal{V}$, $v \in \mathcal{N}_u^+$ and $w \in \mathcal{N}_u^-$. Here $C > 0$ trades off regularization of M with the margin constraint. The problem is a positive semi-definite program which we solve by the subgradient method on L (see Appendix A).

Our method differs from the implementation of Weinberger and Saul [16] in that the target and imposter nearest neighbors are chosen to satisfy the constraints of Equation 2. This is important because we wish to rule out adjacent superpixels in the same image as target nearest neighbors since these are unhelpful for label transfer. Given an annotated training set and initial distance metric M we run our graph construction algorithm using the following two label-augmented distance functions

$$d_M^+(u,v) = \begin{cases} d_M(u,v) & \text{if } y_u = y_v \\ \infty & \text{otherwise} \end{cases} \quad \text{and} \quad d_M^-(u,v) = \begin{cases} d_M(u,v) & \text{if } y_u \neq y_v \\ \infty & \text{otherwise} \end{cases} \tag{4}$$

to find $\mathcal{N}_u^+$ and $\mathcal{N}_u^-$, respectively. Specifically, the edges in the graph constructed using the first metric contain only target nearest neighbors and the edges in the graph constructed using the second metric contain only imposter nearest neighbors. We then iterate between learning the metric and refining the graph edges based on the newly learned metric, thus giving a principled way of learning the distance metric in our context-enriched nearest neighbor graph.

3.4 Label Transfer

The superpixel graph provides a simple mechanism for performing label transfer for semantic segmentation. First we build a superpixel graph on a set of training images. Then for each novel image, we introduce the image to the graph and run a small number of move-making iterations (50 in our experiments) with the existing edges fixed. We then transfer labels in the following way.

For each pixel p in the image we construct a distribution $P_p(y_p \mid \mathcal{G})$ over labels by considering all superpixels u that contain p. Formally, we have

$$P_p(y \mid \mathcal{G}) \propto \sum_{u \sim p} \sum_{v:(u,v) \in \mathcal{E}} \lambda_{uv} \hat{P}_v(y) \tag{5}$$

where $u \sim p$ indicates the that pixel p is in superpixel u, and $\hat{P}_v(y)$ is the empirical distribution over labels for superpixel v as described in Section 3.1. Here the term $\lambda_{uv} \geq 0$ controls the relative weight for each matching superpixel. In our work we set λ_{uv} to the inverse rank of v in the sorted list of nearest neighbors for u. Thus the closest match gets a weight of one, the next closest match a weight of one-half, etc. The inferred label for pixel p is then computed as $y_p^\star = \text{argmax}_y P_p(y \mid \mathcal{G})$.

4 Experimental Results

We conduct extensive experiments on four different scene understanding datasets:

- The Polo dataset [23] is a 6-class dataset comprising images related to the sport of polo. The dataset contains 317 unique images divided into a pre-defined training set of 80 images and test set of 237 images.[2]
- The MSRC dataset [24, 2] is a 21-class dataset consisting of a large variety of images.[3] The dataset contains 591 total images divided into a pre-defined training set of 276 images, validation set of 59 images, and evaluation (test) set of 256 images. We combine training and validation for our experiments.
- The Stanford Background Dataset [25] is an 8-class dataset consisting of 715 images of rural, urban and harbor scenes. Results in the literature report on a training set of size 572 images and test set of 143 images. However, a standard split is not provided.
- The SIFT Flow dataset [9] is a very large 33-class dataset. It consists of 2688 images divided into a pre-defined training set of 2488 images and test set of 200 images. While there are many classes only a few of them dominate.

In all experiments we report the average pixelwise accuracy on the set of test images. We also report the pixelwise accuracy averaged by class. Unless otherwise stated we set the parameters of our over-segmentation algorithm to generate five different sets of superpixels ranging in size from approximately 576 down to 16 superpixels per image.

Efficacy of Search Moves. We first examine the effectiveness of our search moves in constructing a superpixel graph. Figure 2 shows the objective value of Equation 2 as a function of number of iterations for different search strategies. Here we use the subset of training images from the MSRC dataset and do not consider labeling accuracy. The results lead to three interesting observations. First, the objective drops rapidly in the first few iterations with only small improvements in the objective occurring after about 5 or so iterations. Second, the exhaustive search move helps very little in terms of the global objective. This is not surprising given that this move only affects a small number of superpixels. Nevertheless, the move is cheap to compute (on a single superpixel) and does provide a small numerical improvement (barely noticeable in the plots).

The third observation is that propagate, local search, and enrichment moves when used on their own all converge very quickly to a local optimum. However,

[2] We remove the three images from the test set that originally appeared in both training and test sets in [23].

[3] The dataset actually contains 23 classes but standard practice is to remove the "horse" and "mountain" class due to their low occurrence.

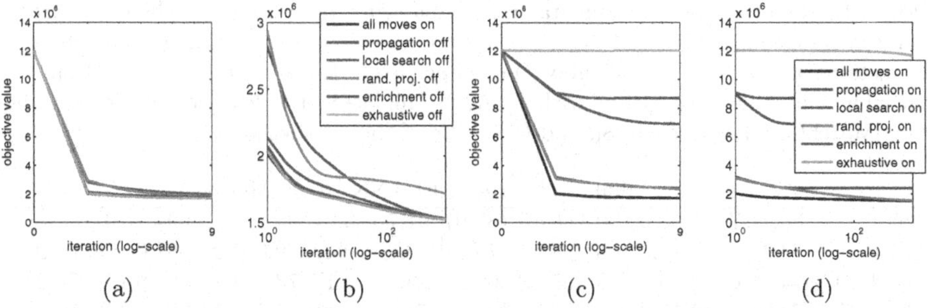

(a) (b) (c) (d)

Fig. 2. Objective value as a function of number of iterations for different search strategies: (a) all-but-one strategies from initialization for 10 iterations; (b) all-but-one strategies, initialization not shown, to 1000 iterations; (c) only-one strategy from initialization for 10 iterations; (d) only-one strategy, initialization not shown, to 1000 iterations. Note different vertical scale for (b).

with the other moves they are effective at accelerating the search. Random projection, propagate, and enrichment are all very powerful moves in reducing the objective value, and hence rapidly finding good superpixel matches. This is because these moves exploit the structure of the feature space (random projection), structure of images (propagate), and structure of the graph (enrichment).

Results on Standard Datasets. Our main interest is semantic segmentation accuracy. In this experiment we construct a superpixel graph $\mathcal{G}_k$ over the training set of images using Euclidean distance, diagonal Mahalanobis distance, and the distance metric learned by the large margin nearest neighbor algorithm (see Section 3.3). We then introduce the test images into the graph and evaluate label transfer on these images. Note that labels are only transferred from the training set images to the test set images. Figure 3 shows performance on each dataset as a function of the number of nearest neighbors k. Results for $k = 5$ are listed in Table 1. We conducted repeated runs of our method with different random seeds and found the results varied by less than 0.5%. We also include in the table results obtained by replacing our search method with FLANN [26] (for the learned distance metric), and a comparison to the conceptually similar PatchMatchGraph approach [8] as well as current state-of-the-art methods.

The results show some interesting trends. First, the learned distance metric outperforms the Euclidean norm and Mahalanobis distance, as expected. Moreover, the results are competitive with the state-of-the-art. For example, Ladicky et al. [27] report 87.0% (78.0%) on the MSRC dataset and Tighe and Lazebnik [5] achieve 78.6% (39.2%) on the SIFT Flow dataset compared to our 84.5% (73.8%) and 78.4% (25.7%), respectively. Our class-averaged pixelwise accuracy on the SIFT Flow dataset is low, which we attribute in part to our equal weighting of category labels. The state-of-the-art approach employ per-exemplar detectors to boost performance on less abundant classes, and it would be interesting to see if such an approach could improve our results too.

Table 1. Quantitative experimental results showing percentage pixelwise accuracy and percentage class-averaged accuracy in parentheses on test set images for different datasets at $k = 5$ nearest neighbors per superpixel. Table includes results from (i) replacing our search algorithm with FLANN [26] using the learned metric, (ii) the PatchMatchGraph approach [8], and (iii) state-of-the-art methods.

	Euclidean	Mahal.	Learned	FLANN [26]	PMG [8]	S-of-the-A
Polo	86.1 (71.0)	89.4 (80.1)	91.8 (85.9)	91.7 (85.8)	94.2 (91.7)	94.2 (91.7) [8]
MSRC	74.3 (61.4)	79.6 (68.2)	84.5 (73.8)	82.3 (70.4)	79.0 (72.8)	87.0 (78.0) [27]
Stanford	74.8 (64.4)	76.2 (66.0)	79.3 (69.4)	78.8 (69.1)	73.4 (62.0)	82.9 (74.5) [28]
SIFT Flow	74.5 (21.6)	75.9 (22.7)	78.4 (25.7)	77.5 (24.2)	65.2 (14.9)	78.6 (39.2) [5]

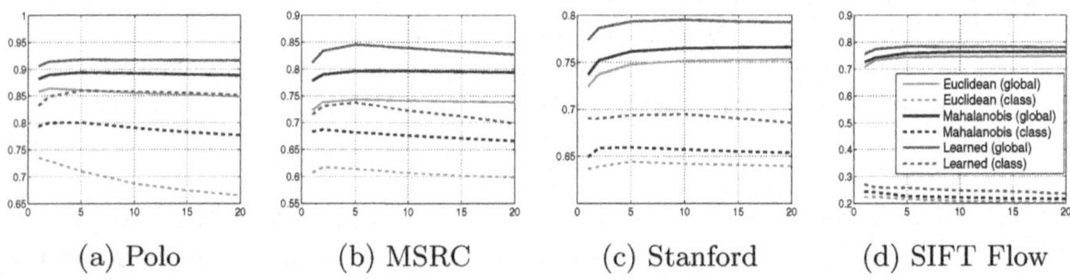

(a) Polo (b) MSRC (c) Stanford (d) SIFT Flow

Fig. 3. Pixelwise semantic segmentation accuracy as a function of the number of nearest neighbors. Shown are global averaged (solid lines) and class averaged (dashed lines) results for different distance metrics.

Second, it is clear from Figure 3 that accuracy saturates at about five nearest neighbors. Interestingly there is a drop in class-averaged accuracy (dashed line) for all metrics as we increase the number of nearest neighbors. This is most pronounced in the Polo dataset. We surmise that the drop is due to the class imbalance in the datasets—as k increases it is more likely that instances with abundant class labels appear in the nearest neighbor set adversely affecting the less abundant classes. The effect can also be seen to a lesser extent for the learned metric in the global-averaged results (solid line). We attribute this to the fact that satisfying the margin constraints is more difficult with larger k and that some classes only appear in a small number of images. For example, only 24 images in the MSRC dataset contain the class "cat".

A handful of qualitative results are shown in Figure 5. Observe that the annotations are quite blocky in parts. This is an artifact of using superpixels as our base representation. Note, however, we have not performed any post processing on the transferred labels. The application of a Markov random field (MRF) or bilateral filter to the results should remove many of these artifacts, but that is not the focus of our investigation here.

Despite the block artifacts, the annotations are generally very good. For example, the horses in the Polo dataset can be reliably detected at different scales, and in the SIFT Flow dataset we are able to correctly label quite difficult categories such as the sidewalk in the bottom right example. Note, however, that our method uses only local context and sometimes makes mistakes. The park

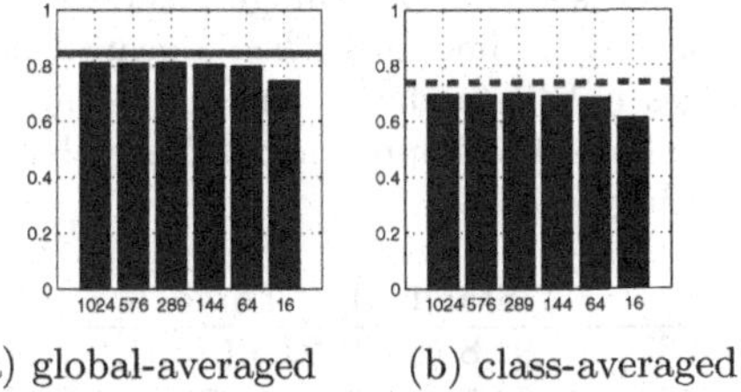

(a) global-averaged (b) class-averaged

Fig. 4. Results on the MSRC dataset showing global and class averaged accuracy for a single over-segmentation of the image as a function of (approximate) number of superpixels. Solid and dashed lines show performance from using all over-segmentations for global and class averaged accuracy, respectively.

bench in the bottom right MSRC example is partially mislabelled as building due to similarity in appearance. The bottom left SIFT Flow example also shows confusion in the transferred labels due to the unusual viewpoint of the scene. We believe that these types of mistakes can be corrected with larger datasets.

Effect of Superpixel Size. Next we evaluate the effect of superpixel size on the label transfer results. Here we generate six sets of over-segmentations where we choose the parameters to give between approximately 1024 superpixels to approximately 16 superpixels per image. We build a superpixel graph with learned distance metric on each set of over-segmentations and apply label transfer as described above. Figure 4 shows results on the MSRC dataset. Other datasets exhibit similar behavior.

The results clearly show that smaller superpixels (more per image) give better accuracy than larger ones (less per image). However, combining multiple over-segmentations leads to even better performance than any single over-segmentation. Moreover, beyond about 289 superpixels per image the accuracy tapers off. Note that in our experiments with combined over-segmentations we did not include the set of 1024 superpixels.

Effect of Dataset Size. An interesting question for all machine learning approaches is whether performance at the task is limited by the dataset size. The nature of our algorithm allows us to go some way in experimentally answering this question. Here we build a superpixel graph over all images in the dataset and perform label transfer, one at a time, to each image in the test set. This is akin to leave-one-out cross-validation, which is expensive to perform on methods with long training phases but easy to do with our approach. To keep our analysis compatible with the previous experiments we use the same distance metric learned on the training set of images with k set to 5 and report average accuracies only on the test set images. Results are shown in Table 2.

For the SIFT Flow dataset and the Stanford Background dataset the effect of increased dataset size is negligible. This can be explained by the already large dataset size in the case of SIFT Flow and the dominance of easy to label background classes in the Stanford Background dataset. More interesting are

Table 2. Quantitative results showing percentage pixelwise accuracy and percentage class-averaged accuracy on test set images for $k = 5$ nearest neighbors with matching against training set images only (standard) versus matching against entire dataset (large). The last column shows the improvement. Note that the distance metric is learned using the training images only.

	Standard	Large	Δ
Polo [23]	91.8 (85.9)	92.5 (87.4)	0.7 (1.5)
MSRC [24, 2]	84.5 (73.8)	86.3 (76.6)	1.8 (2.8)
Stanford [25]	79.3 (69.4)	79.6 (69.4)	0.3 (0.0)
SIFT Flow [9]	78.4 (25.7)	78.4 (25.4)	0.0 (-0.3)

the results for the other two datasets. The Polo dataset is a relatively easy dataset with only a small number of categories. However, the training set is small and accuracy is improved when additional images are available at test time. The MSRC dataset shows the greatest improvement in accuracy with the larger dataset, which can be explained by the diversity and difficulty of the classes in the MSRC dataset and the relatively small training set size. These results confirm the intuition that, at least for nearest neighbor techniques, larger datasets are required for recognizing a large and diverse set of classes.

Running Time. Finally, we evaluate the running time of the different steps in our algorithm. All running times were measured on a 3.4GHz Intel Xeon processor with eight cores. Most of the steps are very fast. It takes approximately 0.5s per image to compute the superpixels, 0.3s per image to compute the features, 1.5s per image to build the superpixel graph on the set of training images (for $k = 5$), and 0.4s per image to perform label transfer. Thus at test time it takes around 2.8s to label a novel image. The time depends on the number of superpixels in the test image but is robust to the size of the graph—only the cost of the random projection move scales with graph size but its overhead is small as long as we pre-compute the projections. Our graphs range in size from 320 thousand nodes for the Polo dataset to 2.6 million for the SIFT Flow dataset. Replacing our nearest neighbor search with FLANN reduced processing time per image to 1.2s but accuracy suffers (see Table 1). By far the most expensive step was the metric learning, taking over an hour. Fortunately, this step only needs to be done during training and is quick to apply on each test instance.

5 Discussion and Future Work

This paper has presented a novel approach to semantic segmentation by label transfer. The approach involves two key contribution. The first is the proposal of a method for rapidly building a graph over superpixels that can be thought of as an approximate nearest neighbor algorithm that is context enriched. The second is the inclusion of a learning step to provide a meaningful metric, which relates observed features to unobservable semantics. We performed extensive experiments on four standard datasets and showed that our approach is competitive

(a) Polo (b) MSRC

(c) Stanford (d) SIFT Flow

Fig. 5. Example annotation results on four standard semantic segmentation datasets using our superpixel graph label transfer method. Best viewed in color.

with state-of-the-art. Nevertheless, there is still room for improvement and we are excited about future opportunities suggested by our work.

For example, we would like to investigate learning a non-linear distance metric, which we believe would lead to even better results. This may be achieved, for example, via a kernelized metric learning approach or deep feature architecture (e.g., [29]). More interesting would be combining the metric learning with the superpixel graph construction, which may improve the efficiency of the metric learning algorithm and also facilitate adaptive metric learning on a long-lived and evolving superpixel graph. As dataset sizes grow we believe that nearest neighbor approaches using techniques such as those discussed in this paper will become more and more relevant for scene understanding.

A Derivation of Subgradient Update on L

Eliminating ξ_{uvw} we write Eqn. 3 as the minimization over $M = LL^T \succeq 0$ of

$$\sum_{uv} d_M(u,v) + C \sum_{uvw} \Big[1 - d_M(u,w) + d_M(u,v)\Big]_+ \tag{6}$$

where $[\cdot]_+ = \max\{\cdot, 0\}$. Now let $\mathcal{A} \subseteq \mathcal{V} \times \mathcal{V} \times \mathcal{V}$ be the set of uvw triplets with violated margin constraints, i.e., where $d_M(u,w) - d_M(u,v) < 1$ for $v \in \mathcal{N}_u^+$ and

$w \in \mathcal{N}_u^-$. Then

$$g = \sum_{uv} \nabla_L d_M(u,v) + C \sum_{uvw \in \mathcal{A}} \left(\nabla_L d_M(u,v) - \nabla_L d_M(u,w)\right)$$

is a subgradient of Equation 6, where $\nabla_L d_M(u,v) = 2L^T(\boldsymbol{x}_u - \boldsymbol{x}_v)(\boldsymbol{x}_u - \boldsymbol{x}_v)^T$.

References

1. He, X., Zemel, R.S., Carreira-Perpinan, M.: Multiscale conditional random fields for image labeling. In: CVPR (2004)
2. Shotton, J., Winn, J.M., Rother, C., Criminisi, A.: *TextonBoost*: Joint appearance, shape and context modeling for multi-class object recognition and segmentation. In: Leonardis, A., Bischof, H., Pinz, A. (eds.) ECCV 2006, Part I. LNCS, vol. 3951, pp. 1–15. Springer, Heidelberg (2006)
3. Zhang, Y., Hartley, R., Mashford, J., Burn, S.: Superpixels via pseudo-boolean optimization. In: ICCV (2011)
4. Achanta, R., Shaji, A., Smith, K., Lucchi, A., Fua, P., Susstrunk, S.: SLIC superpixels. Technical Report 149300, EPFL (2010)
5. Tighe, J., Lazebnik, S.: Finding things: Image parsing with regions and per-exemplar detectors. In: CVPR (2013)
6. Tighe, J., Lazebnik, S.: SuperParsing: Scalable nonparametric image parsing with superpixels. In: Daniilidis, K., Maragos, P., Paragios, N. (eds.) ECCV 2010, Part V. LNCS, vol. 6315, pp. 352–365. Springer, Heidelberg (2010)
7. Zhang, H., Xiao, J., Quan, L.: Supervised label transfer for semantic segmentation of street scenes. In: Daniilidis, K., Maragos, P., Paragios, N. (eds.) ECCV 2010, Part V. LNCS, vol. 6315, pp. 561–574. Springer, Heidelberg (2010)
8. Gould, S., Zhang, Y.: PatchMatchGraph: Building a graph of dense patch correspondences for label transfer. In: Fitzgibbon, A., Lazebnik, S., Perona, P., Sato, Y., Schmid, C. (eds.) ECCV 2012, Part V. LNCS, vol. 7576, pp. 439–452. Springer, Heidelberg (2012)
9. Liu, C., Yuen, J., Torralba, A.: Nonparametric scene parsing: Label transfer via dense scene alignment. In: CVPR (2009)
10. Faktor, A., Irani, M.: "Clustering by composition" – unsupervised discovery of image categories. In: Fitzgibbon, A., Lazebnik, S., Perona, P., Sato, Y., Schmid, C. (eds.) ECCV 2012, Part VII. LNCS, vol. 7578, pp. 474–487. Springer, Heidelberg (2012)
11. Malisiewicz, T., Efros, A.A.: Recognition by association via learning per-exemplar distances. In: CVPR (2008)
12. Malisiewicz, T., Gupta, A., Efros, A.A.: Ensemble of exemplar-svms for object detection and beyond. In: ICCV (2011)
13. Barnes, C.: PatchMatch: A Fast Randomized Matching Algorithm with Application to Image and Video. PhD thesis, Princeton University (2011)
14. Barnes, C., Shechtman, E., Finkelstein, A., Goldman, D.B.: PatchMatch: A randomized correspondence algorithm for structural image editing. In: SIGGRAPH (2009)
15. Barnes, C., Shechtman, E., Goldman, D.B., Finkelstein, A.: The generalized PatchMatch correspondence algorithm. In: Daniilidis, K., Maragos, P., Paragios, N. (eds.) ECCV 2010, Part III. LNCS, vol. 6313, pp. 29–43. Springer, Heidelberg (2010)

16. Weinberger, K., Saul, L.: Distance metric learning for large margin nearest neighbor classification. JMLR 10, 207–244 (2009)
17. Eigen, D., Fergus, R.: Nonparametric image parsing using adaptive neighbor sets. In: CVPR (2012)
18. Dalal, N., Triggs, B.: Histograms of oriented gradients for human detection. In: CVPR (2005)
19. Felzenszwalb, P., Girshick, R.B., McAllester, D., Ramanan, D.: Object detection with discriminatively trained part based models. PAMI (2010)
20. Ojala, T., Pietikainen, M., Maenpaa, T.: Multiresolution gray-scale and rotation invariant texture classification with local binary patterns. PAMI 24, 971–987 (2002)
21. Gould, S.: DARWIN: A framework for machine learning and computer vision research and development. JMLR 13, 3533–3537 (2012)
22. Indyk, P., Motwani, R.: Approximate nearest neighbor—towards removing the curse of dimensionality. In: 30th Symp. of Theory of Comp., pp. 604–613 (1998)
23. Zhang, H., Quan, L.: Partial similarity based nonparametric scene parsing in certain environment. In: CVPR (2011)
24. Criminisi, A.: Microsoft Research Cambridge (MSRC) object recognition pixel-wise labeled image database (version 2) (2004)
25. Gould, S., Fulton, R., Koller, D.: Decomposing a scene into geometric and semantically consistent regions. In: ICCV (2009)
26. Muja, M., Lowe, D.G.: Fast approximate nearest neighbors with automatic algorithm configuration. In: VISSAPP (2009)
27. Ladicky, L., Russell, C., Kohli, P., Torr, P.H.: Associative hierarchical random fields. PAMI (2013)
28. Ren, X., Bo, L., Fox, D.: RGB-(D) scene labeling: Features and algorithms. In: CVPR (2012)
29. Hu, J., Lu, J., Tan, Y.P.: Discriminative deep metric learning for face verification in the wild. In: CVPR (2014)

Precision-Recall-Classification Evaluation Framework: Application to Depth Estimation on Single Images

Guillem Palou Visa and Philippe Salembier

Technical University of Catalonia, Barcelona, Spain

Abstract. Many computer vision applications involve algorithms that can be decomposed in two main steps. In a first step, events or objects are detected and, in a second step, detections are assigned to classes. Examples of such "detection plus classification" problems can be found in human pose classification, object recognition or action classification among others. In this paper, we focus on a special case: depth ordering on single images. In this problem, the detection step consists of the image segmentation, and the classification step assigns a depth gradient to each contour or a depth order to each region. We discuss the limitations of the classical Precision-Recall evaluation framework for these kind of problems and define an extended framework called "Precision-Recall-Classfication" (PRC). Then, we apply this framework to depth ordering problems and design two specific PRC measures to evaluate both the local and the global depth consistencies. We use these measures to evaluate precisely state of the art depth ordering systems for monocular images. We also propose an extension to the method of [2] applying an optimal graph cut on a hierarchical segmentation structure. The resulting system is proven to provide better results than state of the art algorithms.

Keywords: Precision-Recall, Detection, Classification, Depth ordering.

1 Introduction

While humans are very effective at estimating the scene structure from monocular images or sequences, computers are still very limited for this task. Many systems have been proposed but, performances of current unsupervised systems cannot compete with human perception. The work [4] stated that low level depth cues could be used to retrieve a global depth order. Although humans use these cues, their reasoning is also based on high order statistics and a priori knowledge on the type of scene. Nevertheless, low level cues do offer a good starting point to determine depth order. Works such as [3,17] attempt to estimate the depth order through the explicit detection of occlusion cues and rely on two perceptual ideas: 1) convex regions appear to be occluding and 2) in case of T-junctions, the region forming the largest angle is the occluding region. [11] proposes an extension of the gPb algorithm [12] to provide a figure/ground order based on the convexity of detected contours. More recently, the work in [2] retrieves the depth order by computing the *probability of ownership* of a pixel to different components. The algorithm supposes that the image is generated by a dead leaves model [8]. The novelty of this approach is that it does not have to explicitly deal with cue detection but occlusion arises naturally from the image model.

D. Fleet et al. (Eds.): ECCV 2014, Part I, LNCS 8689, pp. 648–662, 2014.
© Springer International Publishing Switzerland 2014

Table 1. Performance measures of [17,9,18] using figure/ground classification accuracy. All measures are extracted from the respective papers. Segmentation information is unavailable.

Method	BPT+TJC [17]	UCM+TJC [17]	[9]	[18]
Accuracy (%)	71.3	69.3	69.1	68.9

Other approaches rely on higher level features such as surface orientation or semantics. In this research line, the work of [20] oversegments the image and infers depth maps using a random field. In [6], the surface layout detector [5] and other features are used to detect the orientation and type of surfaces present in the image to condition a posterior inference on their spatial position. These approaches heavily rely on a training step and suffer when the type of scene has not been observed during the training phase.

The problem is also related to figure/ground (f/g) assignment on contours. In this field, [18,10,6,9] assign a depth gradient to each detected contour. The difference between f/g and depth ordering is that in the former, closed contours and regions are not necessary. Depth ordering, on the other hand, produces an image partition and a global depth interpretation. Conversion from depth ordering to f/g is possible by computing the depth gradient of the produced partition (but the converse is in general not possible).

Assessing the performance of f/g systems is traditionally done by measuring the f/g accuracy on detected contours. Table 1 reports the performance of several methods: [17], [9] and [18]. The usual way to measure the performances is to decouple segmentation from depth classification by providing two independent measures. Thus, the final f/g score is the classification accuracy of the boundary recall. The main problem with this approach is that it completely ignores the quality of the segmentation, leading to biased results if only confident contours are detected. However, the f/g performance is generally strongly related to the segmentation quality. As stated in [13], the f/g assignment on confident contours is easier than the assignment on ambiguous ones. Therefore, if a system only provides the most confident contours, the f/g score will be biased towards high values. [18] or [10] show results on both human marked and automatically detected contours and, precisely, much better f/g scores can be obtained with perfect segmentations. In other words, there exists a compromise between the segmentation quality and the f/g labeling problem which, to this day, has not been fully addressed.

In [13], a first step is proposed by evaluating the f/g score versus the boundary recall for video frames, showing that, effectively, there exists a compromise between these two values. However, this approach loses the precision information and thus does not provide a complete evaluation. For instance, Fig. 1 shows an image with its ground-truth depth order along with four possible outcomes of four different depth ordering systems. Which one is the best? The answer is not simple, as the user may sacrifice some segmentation quality so as to obtain correct depth relations or vice versa. Therefore, the question that naturally arises is to know whether it is possible to evaluate at the same time precision, recall and classification accuracy. We show that using a precision-recall-classification (PRC) framework, it is possible to provide both contour detection and depth gradient classification in a single plot and provide a complete view of the algorithm performances.

Fig. 1. From left to right: original image, ground-truth depth order and four depth order results. A part from the second result, deciding which is the best result is a difficult task.

"Detection plus classification" problems arise in many fields. For example, structured prediction with latent variables [7] classifies objects into classes without knowing their localization. In these problems, latent variables (which correspond to the detection step) are not explicitly modeled but they are key to the performance of the system. In [7], the latent variable is a bounding box indicating the object localization. The system output is the classification of the detected objects into specific classes (human, animal...). Therefore, as for depth ordering, the problem involves the same two steps: 1) detection of object localization and 2) object classification. Most of the time, the better the object localization is, the better will the classifier perform. As detection and classification performance are not independent, it is interesting to have an evaluation framework capable of capturing all the information.

To this end, a Precision-Recall-Classification (PRC) framework is proposed in this paper and two particular instantiations for depth ordering are discussed. The main idea is to combine the detection problem (segmentation quality) and the classification (f/g accuracy) into a single evaluation framework, showing that it is a more accurate and appropriate way of assessing performances than relying on two different measures on segmentation and classification. Besides this contribution, we also propose a new depth ordering system extending the work of [2] to integrate high quality regions. Furthermore, we also publish new annotations of the BSDS500 Dataset [1] involving depth order ground-truth (available at *http://imatge.upc.edu*).

The paper is organized as follows. Sec. 2 discusses the detection plus classification evaluation problem and defines the PRC framework. Sec. 3 proposes two measures to evaluate depth ordered partitions and, in Sec. 4, an extension of the method of [2] is discussed. The new depth ordering annotations for the BSDS500 dataset along with the experimental results are discussed in Sec. 5. Finally, conclusions are reported in Sec. 6.

2 The PRC Evaluation Framework

2.1 Detection Performance Measures

In detection problems, systems are designed to decide whether a given event or feature is present or absent in a given space. Given a ground-truth annotation, the ideal system behavior is to detect all possible entities without giving any false alarms. Quantifying a system performance is normally done by combining True/False Positives/Negatives to

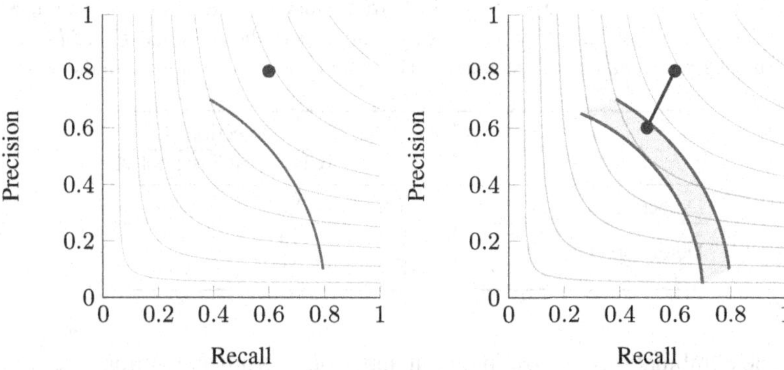

Fig. 2. Operating regions or points of two algorithms (red and blue) for the classic Precision-Recall (left) and the Precision-Recall-Classification (right) frameworks. Gray lines indicate points with the same F measure.

measure the *Precision* and *Recall*. Precision measures the rate of true positives among all detections, while Recall measures the percentage of detected ground truth annotations. They are defined by:

$$Precision = \frac{TP}{TP+FP}, \quad Recall = \frac{TP}{TP+FN} \tag{1}$$

The ideal system corresponds to precision and recall equal to one. In practice, a compromise between these two quantities exists: a system with a high recall is likely to have false positives, and a system with high precision is likely to miss some true annotations. Often, the two quantities are summarized into a single number, F, defined as the harmonic mean of precision and recall: $F = \frac{2PR}{P+R}$.

Generally, the system performance is plotted on a precision-recall plane. As most systems depend on a given set of parameters θ, the precision and recall values also depend on θ: $P(\theta)$ and $R(\theta)$. This generates a set of points on the precision recall plane which are generally represented as a curve, see Fig. 2.

2.2 Combining Detection and Classification

In classification problems, results are often represented with confusion matrices, where the miss-classification rate is observed among different classes. If ground-truth results are available, the classifier performance can easily be computed. However, if classified objects should be first detected by an algorithm, it is likely that the classification score will depend on the operating point of the detection system. For instance, if only confident detections are considered (low recall, high precision), a high classification score is likely to be obtained. On the contrary, if many detections are retrieved, (low precision, high recall), the classification performance is likely to be worse. To integrate the detection and classification problems, we introduce two concepts:

- Inconsistent Detection ID: a correct detection that has been erroneously classified.
- Consistent Detection CD: a correct detection that has been properly classified.

Table 2. Confusion matrix of the proposed PRC framework. $\emptyset$ indicates no detection, while 1 indicates a detection. A and not A are the possible outcomes of the classifier. TN, MD and FD stand for true negatives and missed detections. The other concepts are defined in the text.

		Detection: $\emptyset$	Detection: 1	
			Class: A	Class: not A
Detection: $\emptyset$		TN	MD	MD
Detection: 1	Class: A	FD	CD	ID
	Class: not A	FD	ID	CD

All possible combinations of system output and ground-truth annotations are shown in Table 2. Similarly to pure detection scores, these measures are combined to provide precision-recall measures. CD and ID should be interpreted with care. Note that IDs, although not desirable, are in some way "better" than miss-detections MD or false detections FD since a correct detection is present and a post-processing step may correct the classification. Let us consider two extreme cases of evaluation:

Pure Detection System. In this scenario, we ignore the classification and consider an outcome to be correct if the detection is correct. In this approach CD and ID are equivalent and $TP = CD + ID$, $FP = FD$ and $FN = MD$.

Pure Classification System. This scenario considers that an outcome is correct if and only if detection and classification are correct. Hence, one should consider that TP are only correctly detected events with the same classification as the ground-truth. In this context, $TP = CD$ while ID should be interpreted in two ways:

- Detecting an incorrect class is equivalent to detect an event/object that does not exist. Therefore $FP = FD + ID$.
- Detecting an incorrect class leaves a ground-truth result without correct detection. Therefore $FN = MD + ID$.

To consider a scenario in-between these two extremes, a parameter $0 \leq \beta \leq 1$ is introduced to define the compromise between segmentation and classification qualities. In this way, it is possible to redefine:

$$TP(\beta) = CD + \beta ID \tag{2}$$

$$FP(\beta) = FD + (1 - \beta)ID \tag{3}$$

$$FN(\beta) = MD + (1 - \beta)ID \tag{4}$$

Precision (P) can be redefined using (1), (2) and (3):

$$P(\beta) = \frac{CD + \beta ID}{CD + \beta ID + FD + (1 - \beta)ID} = \frac{CD + \beta ID}{CD + ID + FD} = C_p + \beta I_p \tag{5}$$

With $C_p = \frac{CD}{CD+ID+FD}$ and $I_p = \frac{ID}{CD+ID+FP}$ which are the consistent and inconsistent precision respectively. Similarly, the recall (R) can be redefined as:

$$R(\beta) = \frac{CD + \beta ID}{CD + ID + MD} = C_r + \beta I_r \tag{6}$$

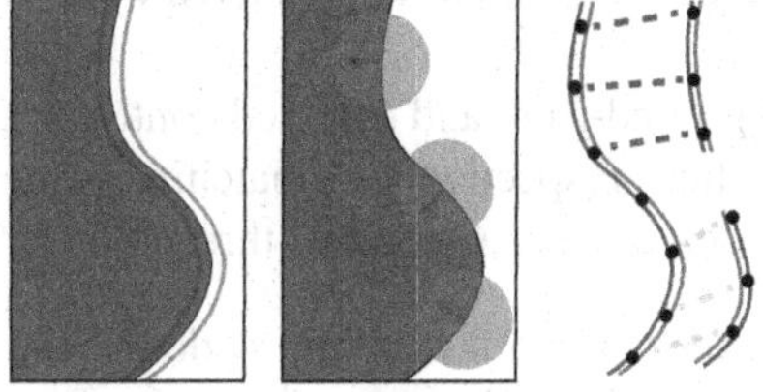

Fig. 3. Left: Depth partition with one contour. The green (red) overlay indicates the figure (ground) side. Center: Contour normals are estimated by averaging local orientations. Right: Bipartite matching of the ground-truth contour (right) and detected contours (left). Consistent (green) and inconsistent (yellow) matchings are shown.

C_r and I_r are the consistent and inconsistent recalls. Therefore, as shown in Fig. 2, each operating point establishes a line segment on the precision-recall (PR) plane depending on β. If the algorithm depends on a set of parameters θ, the evaluation produces a region in the PR plane. To differentiate these measures with respect to a classical detection approach, we will refer to them as Precision-Recall-Classification (PRC) framework.

The PRC plot of Fig. 2 gives insight about the system performance. Ideally, a system should reach $P(\beta) = R(\beta) = 1$ for all β values. Real systems however present a compromise between precision and recall. In the PRC framework, there is an additional compromise corresponding to the width of the operating region. A wide region indicates poor system performance in classification ($I_p, I_r \gg 0$), while a thin region ($I_p, I_r \approx 0$) indicates that the system is a good classifier. Moreover, as the operating point of the detection system detects only confident event/objects (low recall), the region width is expected to decrease, as classification is easier. Based on this framework, concrete PRC measures are proposed in the next section.

3 PRC Depth Measures

Equations (5), (6) defines the abstract PRC framework without specifying CD and ID for a specific problem. In this section, we show how the PRC framework suits a depth ordering evaluation task by proposing two measures.

3.1 Local Depth Consistency

We extend here the original bipartite matching for contour detection evaluation [14] to include the classification step: when a contour is correctly detected, it may be consistent (CD) with the ground-truth depth order (correct f/g assignment to both sides) or inconsistent (ID). Originally proposed in [18], the performance of a f/g classification algorithm is to simply measure $fg = \frac{CD}{CD+ID}$. The original matching scheme [14] is therefore modified to measure inconsistent matchings as follows (see Fig. 3):

1. From the depth partition, figure and ground sides are identified by examining the depth of each region.

2. The orientation of the depth gradient is estimated by averaging contour normals within a local window.
3. Bipartite matching of ground-truth and detected contours: CD and ID are marked with green and yellow lines respectively. A matching is inconsistent if the orientation of the depth gradient exceeds a specified threshold (15°).

Once CD and ID are defined, Equations 5 and 6 define the so-called Local Depth Consistency (LDC) as it measures local depth relations on contours.

F/G over Random Index. As previously mentioned, precision and recall curves are sometimes summarized by a single number, F. Here we define a similar number for the PRC framework. According to equations (5) and (6), precision and recall are divided into their consistent and inconsistent subparts. Consider a contour detection system S and two classification systems on the detections of S: S_i and S_r. Suppose that for S_i, depth gradients are assigned using some sort of reasoning; while, for S_r, the depth gradient is randomly assigned. Therefore, the classification performance of S_i is expected to be better than the one of S_r at every detection operating point.

Assume the operating point of S_i has a total of D detections with a given set of CD_i and ID_i with $D = CD_i + ID_i$. S_r uses the same detection system S so, detections are the same. If S_r assigns randomly the depth gradient on a contour, and as the depth gradient can have two directions, the chance of assigning a correct depth gradient is 50%. Therefore, $CD_r = ID_r = \frac{D}{2} = \frac{CD_i+ID_i}{2}$. It is possible to show with (5) and (6) that the precision, recall and F measure (P_r, R_r, F_r) of a random classification system are related to their counterparts of an "intelligent" classification system (P_i, R_i, F_i) with the same detection score by:

$$P_r = (1+\beta)P_i/2 \qquad P_r = (1+\beta)P_i/2 \qquad F_r = (1+\beta)F_i/2 \tag{7}$$

When $\beta = 1$, no misclassification is considered wrong, so all measures are essentially the same. On the contrary, when $\beta = 0$, only correct contours count for precision and recall. So in a random system, there is a 50% chance of getting a consistent detection. We have found that this is a reasonable assumption for partitions with no severe oversegmentation, as matched detected contours follow ground-truth boundary orientation. However, when a highly oversegmented partition is evaluated, contour orientation cannot be easily estimated and thus the accuracy ratio $fg = \frac{CD}{CD+ID}$ can be lower than 50%. See the results section for more details.

Therefore, assuming this baseline, precision, recall and F-measure are reduced to half with respect to an intelligent classification system. It is expected that a real system will behave better than pure random guesses, so this can represent a lower bound of the system performance. If the system depends on a set of parameters, the F measure is a function of two variables $F(\beta, \theta)$. Define $\theta_{max} = \arg\max F(1, \theta)$ and use it to find $F_{max} = F(1, \theta_{max})$ and $F_{min} = F(0, \theta_{max})$. It is then possible to define an over-random-index (ORI) as:

$$ORI = \max(0, \frac{F_{min} - F_{max}/2}{F_{max}/2}) \tag{8}$$

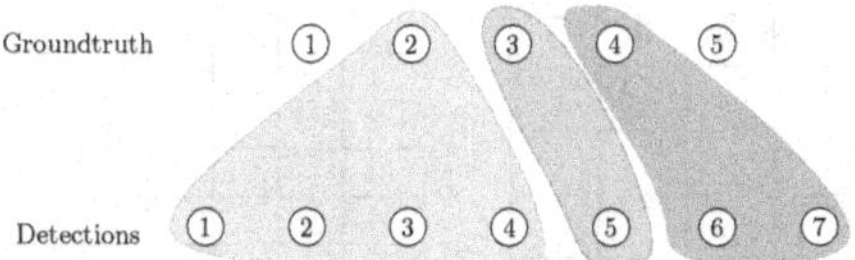

Fig. 4. Region matching example. Each detected region is matched to a ground-truth region. In case of subsegmentation, some ground-truth regions may not be matched. In case of oversegmentation, the same region may be matched multiple times.

When $ORI = 0$ the system behaves randomly, while when $ORI = 1$ the systems performs without misclassifications. Since ORI summarizes a whole region in the precision-recall plane into a single number, it only gives a rough indication of the system performance. The maximum operator is used to ensure positive ORI scores.

3.2 Global Depth Consistency

When estimating depth maps or figure/ground, it is important that the whole depth map is consistent with respect to a ground-truth. That is, the global depth image structure should be the same for the estimation and the ground-truth, even if the contours do not perfectly match. Therefore, a non local measure that quantifies the global depth consistency is desirable. To this end, similarly to the LDC, we have designed a region based precision-recall framework called Global Depth Consistency (GDC).

Assume the system output is a partition P_S formed by a set of regions $S = \{S_i\}$ and the ground-truth data is also a partition P_G with regions $G = \{G_i\}$. Unlike contours, regions by themselves do not incorporate the notion of relative order. However, if we consider pairs of regions, the notion of depth transition naturally arises. Since these pairs of regions do not necessarily need to be adjacent (unlike contours, which delimit two adjacent regions), evaluating all pairs of region order leads to a global depth interpretation of the estimated P_S with respect to P_G. Let Δ_i^S, Δ_i^G denote the depth of regions S_i, G_i. Prior to the evaluation, each region S_i is matched with a ground-truth region by finding its maximum Jaccard index (See Fig. 4):

$$m(S_i) = \widetilde{G}_i = \arg\max_{G_i} \frac{S_i \bigcap G_j}{S_i \bigcup G_j} \qquad \forall S_i, G_j \tag{9}$$

When matchings are available, FD (False Detection) is the number of detected pairs of regions matched to the same ground-truth region with different depth (See Fig. 5):

$$FD = \sum_{S_i, S_j \in S} \left(1 - \delta\left(\Delta_i^S, \Delta_j^S\right)\right) \delta\left(\widetilde{G}_i, \widetilde{G}_j\right) \tag{10}$$

where $\delta(a, b) = 1$ if $a = b$ and 0 otherwise. MD (Missed Detection) is the total number of missed transitions due to the region matching process (9). If the set of unmatched ground-truth regions is $\widetilde{G}$, the formal expression of MD is:

$$MD = |G|\left(|G| - 1\right)/2 - |\widetilde{G}|(|\widetilde{G}| - 1)/2 \tag{11}$$

	1	2	3	4	5
1					
2					
3					
4					
5					

	1	2	3	4	5	6	7
1							
2							
3							
4							
5							
6							
7							

Fig. 5. Tables showing all possible ground-truth pairs (left) and detected region pairs (right). Red squares count as MD, blue count as FD, green as CD and yellow as ID. See the text for an extended explanation.

where $|\cdot|$ denotes the set cardinality. CD and ID are found by examining each pair G_i, G_j and averaging the pairs of detected regions with the same and different depth order respectively. This is done to avoid counting the same ground-truth transition twice for two different pairs of S_i, S_j. Intuitively, CD and ID for a pair G_i, G_j measures how, in average, the detections are consistent with the ground-truth depth. Define α_{ij} and β_{ij} the number of consistent and inconsistent matches for a pair G_i, G_j respectively. $\gamma_{ij}^{G,S} = \mathrm{sgn}(\Delta_i^{G,S} - \Delta_j^{G,S})$ is an indicator of the order of the regions i, j in the sets G, S. Then, α_{ij}, β_{ij} are given by:

$$\alpha_{ij} = \sum \delta\left(\gamma_{kl}^{S}, \gamma_{ij}^{G}\right), \qquad \beta_{ij} = \sum 1 - \delta\left(\gamma_{kl}^{S}, \gamma_{ij}^{G}\right) \tag{12}$$

Both summations are performed over the regions S_k, S_l fulfilling $m(S_k) = \widetilde{G}_i$ and $m(S_l) = \widetilde{G}_j$. The final consistent and inconsistent measures are given by:

$$CD = \sum_{G_i, G_j} \frac{\alpha_{ij}}{\alpha_{ij} + \beta ij} \qquad ID = \sum_{G_i, G_j} \frac{\beta_{ij}}{\alpha_{ij} + \beta ij} \tag{13}$$

The GDC is more restrictive than LDC because it considers not only local relations but also non-adjacent depth transitions. Therefore it is expected that precision-recall values be lower than in the LDC measure as a global consistency is harder to attain than a local one. These two measures will be used in Sec. 5 to evaluate state of the art algorithms plus a new one that is presented in the following section and that is an extension of [2].

4 Depth through Probability of Ownership

The method of [2] estimates the relative depth by measuring the likelihood of a pixel to belong to different connected components, named Probability of Ownership (PO). The algorithm does not explicitly detect low level cues, but estimates the likelihood that a pixel $\boldsymbol{p}$ belongs to the connected components formed by a dead leaves model [8]. In this model, the image is assumed to be a superposition of objects of different sizes and depths. When objects are projected into the image plane, they are occluded by other objects of lower relative depth. If no occlusions were present, the projection of an object O_i would create a region X_i. When multiple objects occlude each other, the visible part of O_i becomes A_i ($A_i \subset X_i$) and the union of the visible parts A_i forms the image.

Although a pixel $\boldsymbol{p}$ belongs only to a visible component A_i, it may correspond to multiple (and occluded) X_i. The algorithm [2] exploits shape, distance and color features of A_i to determine a membership function, $Z(\boldsymbol{p})$, which estimates for each pixel $\boldsymbol{p}$ its probability to belong to several connected components of the image.

$$Z(\boldsymbol{p}) = \sum_{i=1}^{N} D(\boldsymbol{p}, A_i) \tag{14}$$

The density term $D(\boldsymbol{p}, A_i)$ estimates the likelihood that $\boldsymbol{p}$ belongs to X_i. It is defined using two principles: a pixel is more likely to belong to a set X_i if 1) the pixel is close to A_i and 2) the boundary is highly curved. The concrete expression of $D(\boldsymbol{p}, A_i)$ is rather complex and we refer the reader to [2] for more details. The function $Z(\boldsymbol{p})$ is an indicator of the number of X_i that a pixel belongs to. If $Z(\boldsymbol{p}) = 1$ the pixel belongs to a single component, while if $Z(\boldsymbol{p}) > 1$ the pixel belongs to more than one component. The only reason for a pixel to belong to more than one component is occlusion. Therefore, $Z(\boldsymbol{p})$ is a direct indicator of local depth without explicitly detecting occlusion cues. The higher $Z(\boldsymbol{p})$ is, the closer will be the pixel to the viewer. From now on, we will refer to $Z(\boldsymbol{p})$ values as the Probability of Ownership (PO).

4.1 Incorporating Regions

In practice, the sets A_i are formed by pixels with no semantic information. Therefore, the algorithm [2] is based on processing raw color pixel information. However, if higher level information, such as regions, needs to be extracted, the values $Z(\boldsymbol{p})$ can be used in conjunction with segmentation hierarchies to retrieve relevant objects. Here we propose to estimate the depth order map through an optimal graph cut applied on a hierarchical segmentation structure represented by a Binary Partition Tree (BPT) [19] which has been previously populated with PO values.

First, in order to construct the BPT, the ultrametric contour map (UCM) [1] of the image is computed. Then, the BPT is created by successively merging the pair of neighboring regions separated by the lowest salient contour as defined by the UCM. The leaves of the BPT correspond to the regions belonging to the finest UCM partition and the remaining BPT nodes represent regions obtained through the merging of pair of neighboring regions. The BPT root corresponds to the entire image support. Finally, the BPT edges describe the inclusion relationship between regions.

A partition can be naturally extracted from a BPT by selecting the regions represented by the tree leaves. If this is done on the original tree, the leaves correspond to the finest UCM partition and the process is trivial. However, if we prune the tree, that is if we cut branches at one location to reduce their length, a new tree, called a *pruned BPT* is created and the leaves of the pruned tree may define useful partitions. The pruning can be seen as a particular graph cut: Assume the tree root is connected to a *source* node and that all the tree leaves are connected to a *sink* node. A *pruning* is a graph cut that separates the tree into two connected components, one connected to the source and

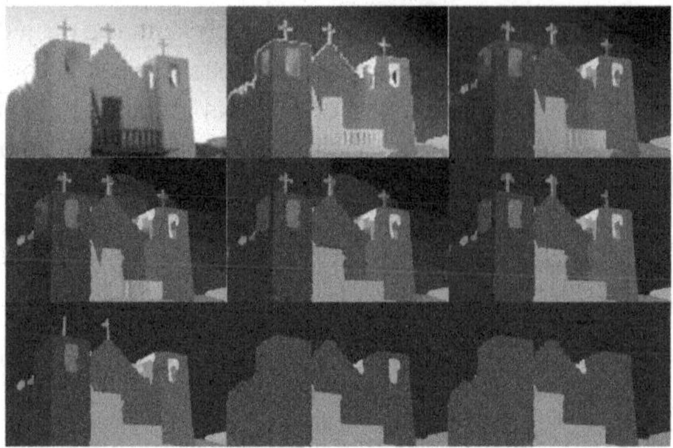

Fig. 6. Example of results using [2] and the proposed region-based approach. In raster order: original image, original depth map of [2] and depth maps found with increasing λ in Eq. (15). Note that the region-based system is able to resolve some error between the building and the sky.

the other to the sink, in such a way that any pair of siblings falls in the same connected component. The connected component that includes the root node is the pruned BPT and its leaves define a partition of the space.

To extract a depth order partition, the tree nodes, representing regions R_i, are populated by their mean PO value $\widehat{D}_i$ and their perimeter Γ_i. The pruning is defined by the graph cut minimizing a criterion inspired by the Mumford-Shah functional [15] over the hierarchy. If $\{R_i\}_{1 \leq i \leq N}$ denotes the set of regions corresponding to the leaves of the pruned BPT, the criterion to optimize is given by:

$$\sum_{i=1}^{N} \left(\sum_{p \in R_i} \left| \widehat{D}_i - D(\boldsymbol{p}) \right|^2 + \lambda |\Gamma|_i \right) \tag{15}$$

where $D(\boldsymbol{p})$ is the original estimated depth (PO) value for pixel $\boldsymbol{p}$ and λ a parameter controlling the partition granularity. The criterion defined by Eq. (15) can be very efficiently minimized by dynamic programming [19,21,16]. Small λ values create fine partitions with many regions, while for larger λ, coarser partitions are found. The final depth partition is formed by regions R_i with $\widehat{D}_i$ as depth value. Fig. 6 shows several partitions obtained with this optimum pruning.

5 Experiments and Results

In this section, we compare the classical depth ordering evaluation with the LDC and GDC measures. For the selection of the state of the art systems, the code of [18] and [9] are not public, so we could not run the algorithms for evaluation. Their performances as given in their respective papers are reported in Table 1. The LDC and GDC measures are reported for the BPT+TJC and UCM+TJC approaches of [17], the angular embedding (AE) of [11], the occlusion boundary detection (OB) of [6], the learning depth based (LD) approach of [20], the PO approach of [2] and the proposed algorithm using the region PO-based graph cut on BPT.

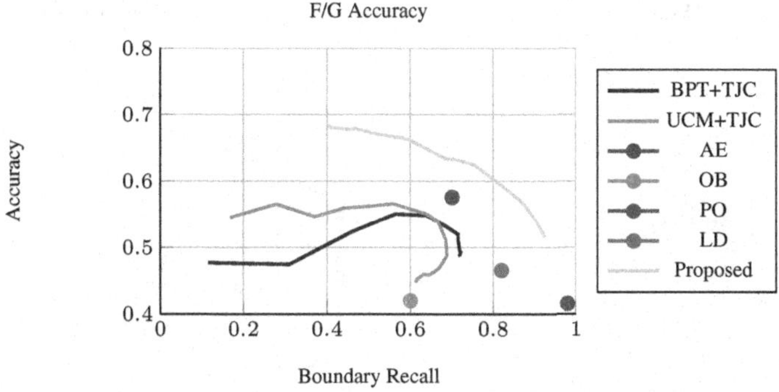

Fig. 7. Accuracy of the f/g classification as a function of the boundary recall

5.1 Dataset with Depth Annotation

We have found few public datasets incorporating relative depth ordering between objects present in images. One of the most popular datasets in image segmentation, the BSDS500 [1] incorporates figure/ground annotations for a subset of the images. Although it is the classical evaluation choice for figure/ground system, it does not involve closed contours and no global consistency is found in several cases. To solve this issue, we have chosen several segmentations for each of the 500 images and have annotated their regions with relative depth, creating a consistent depth map. Examples can be seen in the second column of Fig. 9. These annotations are publicly available at *http://imatge.upc.edu*.

5.2 LDC and GDC Results

Fig. 7 shows the figure/ground classification accuracy as a function of the boundary recall[1]. Although this plot is an interesting step for evaluating depth ordering systems, it is not found in the literature other than in [13] for f/g estimation in video frames.

It follows from Fig. 7 that the proposed system seems the one providing more consistent depth estimates. Nevertheless, the f/g accuracy does not provide the segmentation precision, a crucial segmentation measure. Moreover, if precision is not known, depending on the degree of recall that one may require, the proposed system can present lower accuracy than BPT+TJC, UCM+TJC and AE. Therefore, additional measures should be invloved to define the quality of each system.

To this purpose, these systems are evaluated with the LDC and GDC measures. Results are presented in Fig. 8. The first point to notice is that LDC gives higher scores than GDC: a global depth consistency is much harder to achieve than estimating local depth gradient on contour points. Second, the LDC measure does suffer for output

[1] The f/g matching process can lead to different results compared to the original papers, due to differences in contour distance and angle tolerance on the depth gradient. Following a strategy similar to [18], we only considered contours at a 3 pixels distance for matching. A depth gradient is considered correct if its orientation lies within $15°$ of the ground-truth orientation.

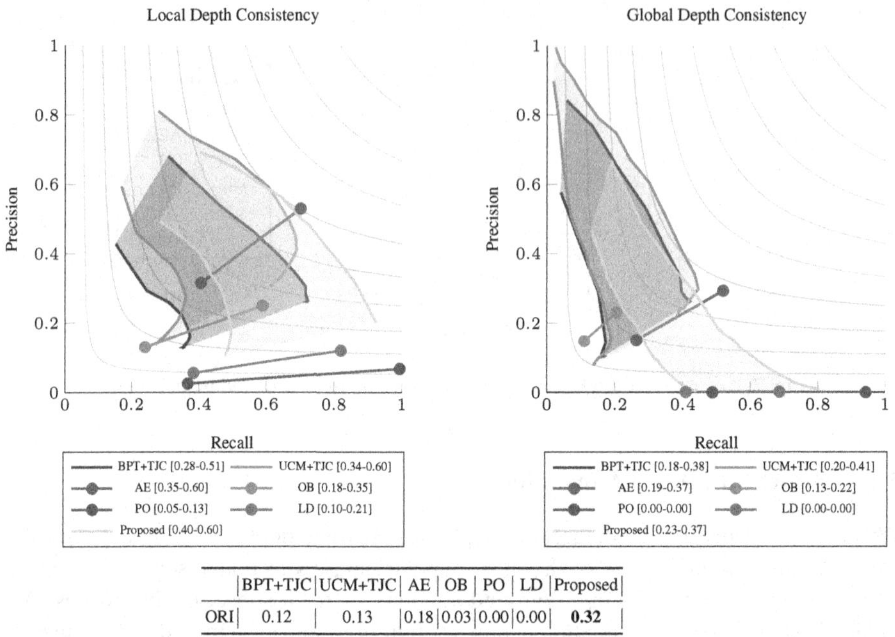

	BPT+TJC	UCM+TJC	AE	OB	PO	LD	Proposed
ORI	0.12	0.13	0.18	0.03	0.00	0.00	**0.32**

Fig. 8. LDC and GDC measures for state of the art system. F_{max} and F_{min} measures for each method are shown in brackets in both cases. The ORI is also shown in the table at the bottom.

with high recall values and low precision. The bipartite assignment for oversegmented solutions (such as the PO and LD systems) has problems to assign the depth gradient when many contours are potential matches. Since the assignment does not favor any particular orientation, the ORI index approaches 0 for high recall methods.

LDC: Overall, the system proposed in this paper is the best one in terms of segmentation quality and of depth ordering, as its ORI is more than 0.1 over the second best technique. Still, there is much room for improvement both in segmentation quality and depth ordering, since the maximum F measure is around 0.6, where the ground-truth assignments achieve an F measure of 0.78. The ORI index indicates that monocular depth ordering still can be improved, as the theoretical maximum ORI is 1 and the best kown technique has a much lower score (around 0.3).

GDC: Referring to a global depth interpretation, the precision values of the systems have much lower scores compared to LDC. Basically because small regions are missed unless very oversegmented solutions are considered. An important point to notice is that PO has the largest recall for classification, indicating that it is the technique detecting most depth transitions. Again, the small width of the proposed algorithm region indicates that it behaves quite well for global depth interpretation. However, techniques as UCM+TJC or BPT+TJC seem to provide higher quality regions. Overall, we can conclude that proposed system should be the choice if monocular depth ordering is needed due to its better scores in LDC, ORI and its competitive results in GDC.

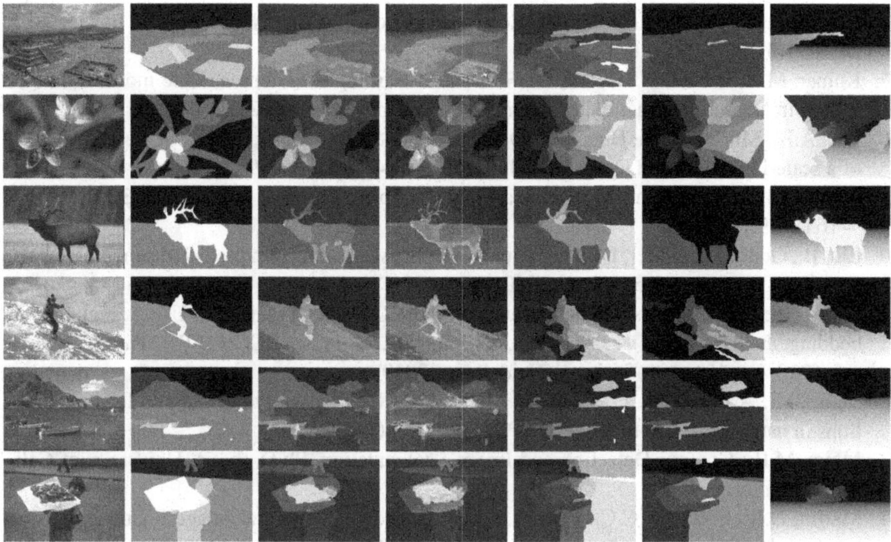

Fig. 9. From left to right. Original image, ground-truth relative depth order and results from the proposed system, PO, AE, the UCM+TJC and OB. The proposed methods is able to reduce noisy estimation of PO. More results can be found in the supplemental material.

6 Conclusions

We have proposed a new framework to evaluate problems encompassing detection and classification where the complete system performance can be seen in a single plot. Two particular applications of the PRC framework are shown for depth ordering, where local and global depth consistency measures are presented. Depth ordering annotations of the BSDS500 Dataset were also created for this particular problem and made public. State of the art methods and a new proposed algorithm are evaluated using both PRC measures. Results show that the proposed algorithmm is the one having the best results, although human depth perception is still unreachable for fully unsupervised systems.

References

1. Arbeláez, P., Maire, M., Fowlkes, C., Malik, J.: Contour detection and hierarchical image segmentation. IEEE TPAMI 33(5), 898–916 (2011)
2. Calderero, F., Caselles, V.: Recovering relative depth from low-level features without explicit T-junction detection and interpretation. IEEE IJCV (2013) (in Press)
3. Dimiccoli, M.: Monocular Depth Estimation for Image Segmentation and Filtering. Ph.D. thesis, Universitat Politecnica de Catalunya (2009)
4. Fowlkes, C.C., Martin, D.R., Malik, J.: Local figure-ground cues are valid for natural images. Journal of Vision 7(8), 2 (2007)
5. Hoiem, D., Efros, A.A., Hebert, M.: Recovering Surface Layout from an Image. IEEE IJCV 75(1), 151–172 (2007)

6. Hoiem, D., Efros, A.A., Hebert, M.: Recovering Occlusion Boundaries from an Image. IEEE IJCV 91(3), 328–346 (2011)
7. Kumar, M.P., Packer, B., Koller, D.: Self-paced learning for latent variable models. In: Advances in Neural Information Processing Systems, pp. 1189–1197 (2010)
8. Lee, A.B., Mumford, D., Huang, J.: Occlusion models for natural images: A statistical study of a scale-invariant dead leaves model. IEEE IJCV 41(1-2), 35–59 (2001)
9. Leichter, I., Lindenbaum, M.: Boundary ownership by lifting to 2.1D. In: IEEE ICCV, pp. 9–16 (2009)
10. Liu, B., Gould, S., Koller, D.: Single image depth estimation from predicted semantic labels. In: IEEE CVPR, pp. 1253–1260 (2010)
11. Maire, M.: Simultaneous Segmentation and Figure/Ground Organization Using Angular Embedding. In: Daniilidis, K., Maragos, P., Paragios, N. (eds.) ECCV 2010, Part II. LNCS, vol. 6312, pp. 450–464. Springer, Heidelberg (2010)
12. Maire, M., Arbelaez, P., Fowlkes, C., Malik, J.: Using contours to detect and localize junctions in natural images. In: IEEE CVPR, pp. 1–8 (2008)
13. Maire, M.R.: Contour Detection and Image Segmentation. Ph.D. thesis, University of California, Berkeley (2009)
14. Martin, D.R., Fowlkes, C.C., Malik, J.: Learning to detect natural image boundaries using local brightness, color, and texture cues. IEEE TPAMI 26(5), 530–549 (2004)
15. Mumford, D., Shah, J.: Optimal approximations by piecewise smooth functions and associated variational problems. Comm. on Pure and Applied Mathematics 42(5), 577–685 (1989)
16. Palou, G., Salembier, P.: Depth ordering on image sequences using motion occlusions. In: IEEE ICIP, Orlando, FL, USA (2012)
17. Palou, G., Salembier, P.: Monocular Depth Ordering Using T-junctions and Convexity Occlusion Cues. IEEE Trans. on Image Proc. (2013)
18. Ren, X., Fowlkes, C.C., Malik, J.: Figure/Ground Assignment in Natural Images. In: Leonardis, A., Bischof, H., Pinz, A. (eds.) ECCV 2006. LNCS, vol. 3952, pp. 614–627. Springer, Heidelberg (2006)
19. Salembier, P., Garrido, L.: Binary partition tree as an efficient representation for image processing, segmentation, and information retrieval. IEEE Trans. on Image Processing 9(4), 561–576 (2000)
20. Saxena, A., Ng, A., Chung, S.: Learning Depth from Single Monocular Images. In: IEEE NIPS, vol. 18 (2005)
21. Serra, J., Kiran, B.R., Cousty, J.: Hierarchies and Climbing Energies. In: Alvarez, L., Mejail, M., Gomez, L., Jacobo, J. (eds.) CIARP 2012. LNCS, vol. 7441, pp. 821–828. Springer, Heidelberg (2012)

A Multi-stage Approach to Curve Extraction

Yuliang Guo, Naman Kumar, Maruthi Narayanan, and Benjamin Kimia

Brown University, School of Engineering,
Providence, RI 02912, USA
{yuliang_guo,maruthi_narayanan,benjamin_kimia}@brown.edu,
namank@andrew.cmu.edu
http://vision.lems.brown.edu

Abstract. We propose a multi-stage approach to curve extraction where the curve fragment search space is iteratively reduced by removing unlikely candidates using geometric constrains, but without affecting recall, to a point where the application of an objective functional becomes appropriate. The motivation in using multiple stages is to avoid the drawback of using a global functional directly on edges, which can result in non-salient but high scoring curve fragments, which arise from non-uniformly distributed edge evidence. The process progresses in stages from local to global: (*i*) edges, (*ii*) curvelets, (*iii*) unambiguous curve fragments, (*iv*) resolving ambiguities to generate a full set of curve fragment candidates, (*v*) merging curve fragments based on a learned photometric and geometric cues as well a novel *lateral edge sparsity* cue, and (*vi*) the application of a learned objective functional to get a final selection of curve fragments. The resulting curve fragments are typically visually salient and have been evaluated in two ways. First, we measure the stability of curve fragments when images undergo visual transformations such as change in viewpoints, illumination, and noise, a critical factor for curve fragments to be useful to later visual processes but one often ignored in evaluation. Second, we use a more traditional comparison against human annotation, but using the CFGD dataset and CFGD evaluation strategy rather than the standard BSDS counterpart, which is shown to be not appropriate for evaluating curve fragments. Under both evaluation schemes our results are significantly better than those state of the art algorithms whose implementations are publicly available.

1 Introduction

Interest in *contour extraction*, an age-old fundamental problem in computer vision, which diminished beginning in the late 1990's with a paradigm shift towards the use of keypoint-based approaches, has recently seen a revival, especially in application to object recognition and multi-view applications. Contours, which along with regions have been a classic intermediate-level representation of images, are attractive since they are robust to illumination variation, view variation, and other visual transformations. An increasing number of approaches now rely on extracted contours for recognition [6,16,20,31,11], or for 3D object

D. Fleet et al. (Eds.): ECCV 2014, Part I, LNCS 8689, pp. 663–678, 2014.
© Springer International Publishing Switzerland 2014

recognition and pose estimation [21], and others, leading to a number of recent approaches to contour extraction [22,28]. Multiple terms such as boundary, contour, silhouette, curve, edges, *etc.*, have been used with some ambiguity to denote at least three distinct notions: (*i*) *edge maps*, line tokens, and other local and unorganized representations of a contour where a pixel/point is denoted as a contour point; (*ii*) *saliency maps* representing at each pixel the probability of a contour, or a subset of contours such as silhouette (boundaries), *e.g.*, Pb [18,2] and others; (*iii*) *curve fragments* which are essentially chains of long ordered edge points [27,13,14,15,5,22,11,17,4,24,9]. Relatively fewer papers address the latter, but it is a arguably the most useful. The focus of this paper is to extract contour fragments, Fig 1.

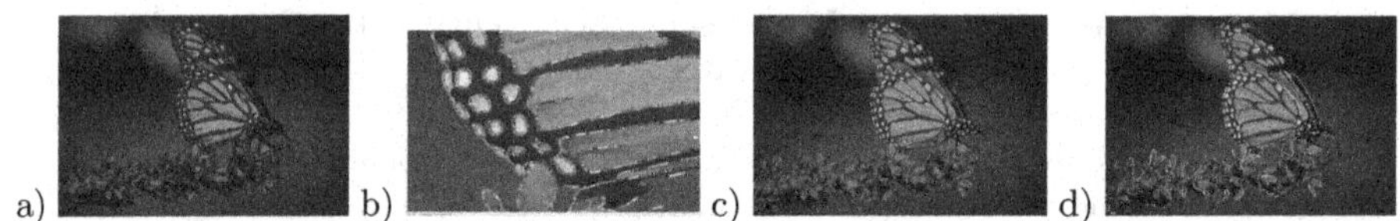

Fig. 1. A brief overview of some of the stages in our curve extraction approach: a) Initial Edge Map, b) Curvelet Map, zoomed in to show details, c) Contour fragments from [27], d) Contour Fragments resulting from this work. Readers are invited to zoom in to compare the two contour fragments shown in randomized color

The early work of Fischler *et al.* [8] is canonical of work which followed the next three decades in this area: a local road detector generates a spatial map which is then searched by the A^* algorithm for the minimum cost path between any two given points. We show in Section 2 that previous work essentially follows this pattern by searching the space of curves using a linear objective functional. The drawback of this type of a model is that for any given path depicting a low cost (high edge evidence), there is a *key underlying assumption that cost is uniformly distributed.* This assumption, however, is not always true and this caveat allows for paths passing through very high strength evidence but otherwise sparse, leading to either numerous false positives or missed detections.

Fig 2 shows examples of curve fragments achieving good response from the global optimization process which are not salient because they are in fact spatially sparse in edge evidence. The existence of such curves can overwhelm those arrangements of edges which have consistency but possibly low edge evidence. We posit that the jump from edges to curve fragments needs to be mediated by multiple stages of increasingly more global considerations, each maintaining recall while reducing the space of undesirable curves, thus safely limiting that the curve fragment search space. This is in analogy to the 20 question approach but done in stages.

Specifically, the curve extraction process proceeds in six stages: (*i*) edge maps are first computed at thresholds generating the highest recall, therefore also generating the highest level of false positives; (*ii*) the formation of curvelets from neighboring edges at each edge, identifies edges with geometrically consistent support and potential neighbors. This allows false positives to be reduced with

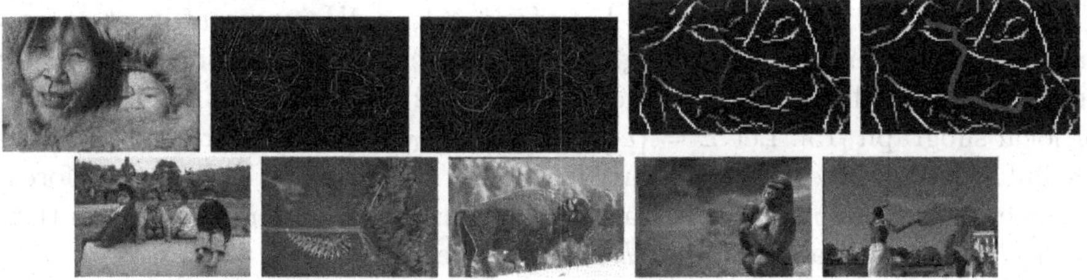

Fig. 2. An example demonstrating the drawback of directly going from edges to curve fragments: top row, left to right: original image and its edge map, some selected contours which score well based on a standard objective functional but which are not salient, the edge map zoomed in the area of the blue curve without and with the blue curve superimposed. Second row: additional examples.

a very insignificant drop in recall; (*iii*) edges whose local curvelet structure indicates an unambiguous groupings with their neighbors are grouped and all these edges are replaced with the resulting curve fragment; (*iv*) the ambiguity in grouping the remaining edges is explicitly represented in a hypothesis graph rooted at end-points of contour fragments formed in the previous stage. The ambiguity is then resolved by applying an objective functional operating locally which takes into account smoothness and minimizes gaps; (*v*) The resulting curve fragments are often over-fragmented, so geometric and photometric cues and a novel edge sparsity cue introduced here are learnt in combination to merge pairs of curves sharing an end-point; (*vi*) The resulting curve fragments are rated by a learned objective functional using cues almost identical with the above, to prune false positives. The end result of our process is a *contour fragment graph*, representing curve fragments and their relative arrangements at junctions.

The results are evaluated in two ways. First, the stability of curve fragments when images undergo visual transformations is examined. Second, results are compared against human annotations using the boundary evaluation framework introduced by [18] on the Berkeley Segmentation DataSet (BSDS) [18] as well as the curve evaluation framework introduced in [10] on the Curve Fragment Ground-Truth Dataset (CFGD). In all cases it is shown that our approach improves upon the state of the art.

2 Related Works

The need for non-linearity at the level of edge detection was identified by Iverson and Zucker [12] who proposed that instead of a linear sum over the support of an edge detector, a non-linear function in the form of a logical-linear operation be used. Our approach is similar to this idea at the level of curve fragments. A **Curve Fragment (CF)** is formally defined as a piecewise smooth parameterizable curve segment, $C(s) = (x(s), y(s)), s \in [0, 1]$. The literature on boundary detection is broad, diverse, and spans a few decades. Much of this work, however, focuses on edge or saliency map detection and relatively few focus on detecting curve fragments. We present a large portion of the existing literature in the following abstract framework. Let $V = \{v_i | i = 1, ..., N\}$ represent a set of possible samples along the curve fragments: These can be image pixels [5], image edges [30], or small grouping of edges (super-nodes) in the form of line tokens [14] or local subgraph [13]. Let $E = \{e_{ij} | d(v_i, v_j) < d_0, \forall v_i, \forall v_j\}$ represent all possible links among these candidate curve samples. The graph $G(V, E)$ is therefore a superset of all possible curve fragments. The curve extraction problem can then be cast as selecting a set of links $E^* \subset E$ where

$$E^* = \arg\min_{\bar{E} \subseteq E} [f_{fg}(\bar{E}) + f_{bg}(E \setminus \bar{E})], \tag{1}$$

and where f_{fg} and f_{bg} are objective functionals that capture characteristics of the foreground curve and the background clutter, respectively. For example, in the min-cover approach [5], v_i are image pixels and the algorithm seeks curves to minimizing an objective function in the form of Equation 1. The two approaches KGS [30,13] and FPG [14] follow a two-stage strategy: in KGS [30,13], normalized cut [26] divides the graph into clusters which then represent v_i as a super node. In FPG [14] short straight lines are first formed and represent v_i. Both methods then proceed to solve an optimization problem of the form described in Equation 1 using a linear objective function (see supplementary material for further detail). This two-stage optimization increases efficiency, but has serious drawbacks: The initial clustering in normalized cut can introduce spurious links in the k-way normalized cut [29], which includes non-convex optimization, random initialization results in random clusters which in turn lead to poor stability, *e.g.*, over a video sequence. Similarly, the initial stage in FPG [14] needs to be conservative due to the geometric limitations of the line model, leaving much of the work for the second stage.

In our approach, we have avoided both problems by employing a range of simple to complex models covering local to global information arranged in stages. Our approach bears a strong relationship with compositional systems such as [11,7], which begin with Gabor-like filters and progressively construct higher level constructs by composing simples structures. Our work, however has only bottom-up processing and may benefit from a full compositional structure. The work of Todorovic [22] is also hierarchical and generates a vast collection of contour fragment candidates which though extensive are selected to form a final output. The latter stage of this work can probably work with the results of this paper.

3 Managing Grouping Ambiguity

The goal of the multi-stage approach is to entertain all possible curve hypothesis and then progressively remove unlikely ones, *i.e.*, maintaining recall while increasing precision, all based on geometric constraints, as explained below.

Stage 1) Edge Detection: The set of candidate curves is significantly reduced by only initiating them through detected edges. The caveat is that curves with significant gaps would not have a representation in the gap area, so these curves would have to rely on representation in the non-gap areas to be initiated; see more below. The idea of initiating curve candidates from edges implies that the results of edge detection should not be pruned at this early stage. Rather, this step should maintain the highest possible recall at the expense of also maintaining numerous false positives, Fig 1. The edges are connected by a neighborhood graph:

Definition 1. The Edge Topology Graph *(ETG) is a graph whose nodes are image edges and where links exist between any two edges which are linked by some* curvelet, Fig 3 (d).

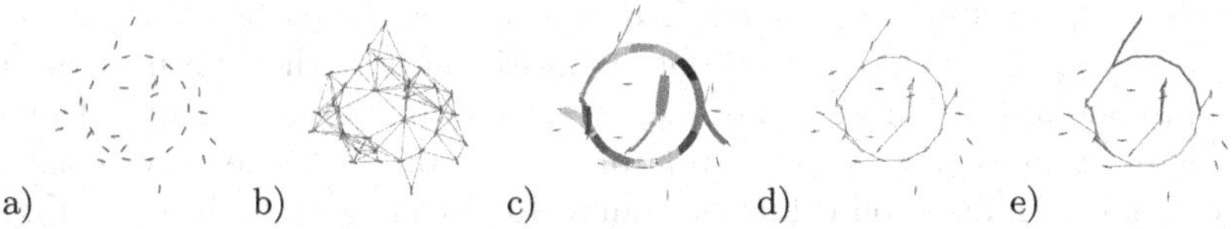

Fig. 3. (a) And edge map, (b) An Edge Neighborhood Graph connects each edge to every edge in a local neighborhood, (c) The set of discrete curvelets, (d) The Edge Topology Graph **(ETG)**, (e) The Curve Fragment Map **(CFG)** is formed by identifying unambiguous and geometrically viable 1-chains and replacing the image edges and connecting links by a single curve fragment

Stage 2) Curvelet Formation: The next stage in removing unlikely candidates is to require a curve segment to have more than one edge support. We follow the approach of [27] who considered all geometrically reasonable combinations of edges, referred to as *curvelets, in some neighborhood typically (7x7). The purpose of using* curvelets is twofold: (*i*) establish candidate pairing among edges from which candidate curve fragments can be constructed, and (*ii*) discarding all potential pairings which do not participate in a geometrically consistent relationship say in a set of say five edges. This stage removes only those curve fragments whose edge support is below five edges, which implies a very minimal reduction in recall, but a significant reduction in false positives. Note that this is quite different than a greedy approach where the most likely combination is considered. Rather, this approach retains almost all of the likely combinations, relegating the job of deciding which may be veridical to a later, global stage.

Stage 3) Forming unambiguous curve fragments: Since all pairings of edges which have passed the above stage are considered viable, ambiguities arise when an edge forms pairings with more than one edge, occurring often in junctions, corners, but also in other portions of a curve. However, in numerous other cases an edge forms pairing with only one other edge (each end of an edge is considered separately). In this case an unambiguous curve fragment forms, which need not be challenged [27]. The formation of these unambiguous curve fragments to replace all edges and their groupings which led to it helps resolves ambiguity in their neighborhood, as described next. Observe that thus far no objective function has been used, but rather the geometric configuration of edges with barely minimal contrast has been used to reduce the search space.

Definition 2. The Curve Fragment Graph *(CFG) is a transformation of the **ETG** where these nodes and links which form unambiguous and geometrically viable 1-chains are replaced by a single contour fragment, Fig 3 (e).*

Stage 4) Resolving Grouping Ambiguity: The approach to resolve the ambiguity in grouping the remaining edges is to first construct a graph of all possible groupings. The first observation is that grouping ambiguity occurs in clusters of edges, thanks to the formation of unambiguous curve fragments. The canonical curves can enumerated by considering possibilities starting from the end point of an existing unambiguous curve fragments: (i) The end point is truly an end point, with on continuities, *e.g.*, endpoint of A in Fig 4a. (ii) The curve continues to another curve with ambiguity in the specific paths among a cluster of options, *e.g.*, continuations of B onto C in Fig 4a. (iii) the continuations of a curve onto one or two curves or both, as in the continuations of C onto D and E as in Fig 4a, representing a Y-junction or T junction. (iv) The curve continues but does not terminate onto another curve fragment, *e.g.*, as in G in Fig 4a. Observe that in many cases clusters of possible curves agree on the underlying topology but disagree slightly about the geometry of connectivity. The set of possible continuations can be represented by a graph, Fig 4c:

Definition 3. The Contour Hypothesis Graph *(CHG) is a rooted graph with the root node representing a contour fragment end-point (the anchor contour end-point) with links representing the next edge selection and with with nodes representing image edges. The leaf nodes, each representing a unique path from the root, give the set of all contour fragments continuing the anchor contour at the root.*

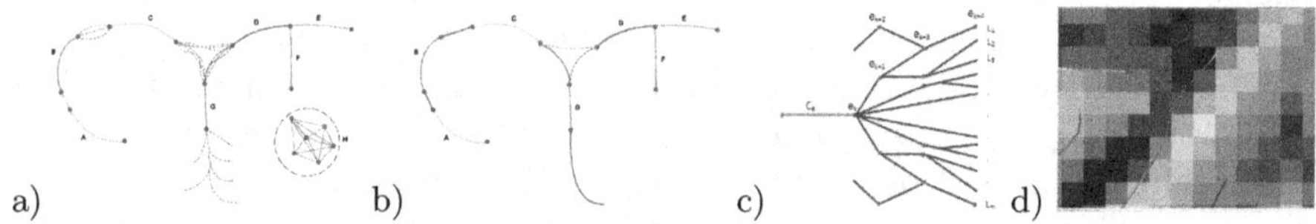

Fig. 4. a) Several distinct types of ambiguities with candidate paths from end-points. The region labeled "H" represents a noisy area not connected to any viable contour fragments. b) Newly formed **CFG** is shown after the resolution of the ambiguities using quality metric as described in the text. c) A Contour Hypotheses Graph **(CHG)** rooted at the end point e_K of contour fragment C_K. In this case, six contributions are possible which include e_{K+1}. d) A realistic example of how the CHG represents and manages ambiguity in grouping among three end-points.

The construction of CHG follows a best-first strategy guided by the quality of the path constructed thus far. Quality is represented by an energy functional **E** capturing the saliency of a contour is described below. Three limitations are imposed on the construction: *(i)* The total number of nodes cannot exceed $K = 1000$. This is experimentally never reached; *(ii)* The energy of a path can not exceed a Threshold E_0; and, *(iii)* the individual link energy cannot exceed a threshold E, a large threshold devised to prune away the very unlikely continuations. It should be noted that the contour hypothesis graph is typically very constrained since it represents local grouping ambiguity between contour fragment end-points, thus performance is not affected significantly by changes in the above system parameters.

Contour Saliency Measure: The contour hypothesis graph localizes ambiguities to clusters of topologically equivalent but geometrically different groupings. The latter can be resolved by employing a standard energy function, representing structural saliency [25]. Specifically, given an ordered sequence of edges, $C = (e_0, e_1, ...e_N)$, the energy $E(\mathcal{C})$ depends on two factors (i) maximizing smoothness by minimizing orientation difference $|\theta_{i+1} - \theta_i|$, where θ_i is the orientation of edge e_i, and (ii) minimizing the gap length or the Euclidean Distance between pairs of subsequent edges $|e_{i+1} - e_i|$. Finally, the energy is normalized by the number of edges to represent a measure that can fairly capture short and long sequences of edges:

$$E(\mathcal{C}) = \frac{1}{N+1} \sum_{i=0}^{N} (w * |e_{i+1} - e_i| + (1-w) * |\theta_{i+1} - \theta_i|), \quad 0 < w < 1 \tag{2}$$

where we set $w = 0.2$ which is optimized by grid search in $(0, 1)$ for highest F-measure.

It should be noted that the mutli-stage approach above does not attempt to bridge gaps beyond what is possible within a small local neighborhood. Rather, gaps beyond a couple of pixels need to be completed in a post processing stage such as those presented in [23,19].

4 Learning-Based Merging of Curve Fragments

The result of the previous set of stages is a set of curve fragments which are represented as a graph, where nodes represent curve fragment endpoints or junctions where two or more curve fragments come together Fig 5a. These curve fragments are typically small and cascaded, so that over-fragmentation of expected contour is perceptually evident. Thus, additional grouping is required. Consistent with the progression from local information (edges) to increasing more global information (curvelets, hypothesis graph) in previous stages, which chiefly involve geometric information, the next stage uses a slightly more global basis of reasoning. While the chief organizational principle has thus far been geometric continuity, the resulting curve fragments are typically sufficiently long to allow the use of photometric and geometric cues in deciding whether additional grouping is required and in disambiguating conflicts when such grouping is warranted. Specifically, the main question is whether two cascaded curve fragments, i.e., those that share an end point in exclusion of other curve fragments (no T or Y junctions) should be merged or not, essentially a classification problem, Fig 5b.

We consider the following set of photometric and geometric cues in relation to whether they contribute to the merge/not-merge decision and to what extent. First, the **photometric cues** are length-normalized integrals of those photometric cues traditionally used in edge detection: *(i) Brightness* gradient: $\int \nabla B(s)\, ds$; *(ii) Saturation* gradient: $\int \nabla S(s)\, ds$; *(iii)* Hue gradient: $\int \nabla H(s)\, ds$; These three cues are computed for each of the two curve fragments and then compared. *(iv)* Texture differences between the respective sides of the two connected curve fragments, i.e., differences between the texture attributes of regions 1 and 2

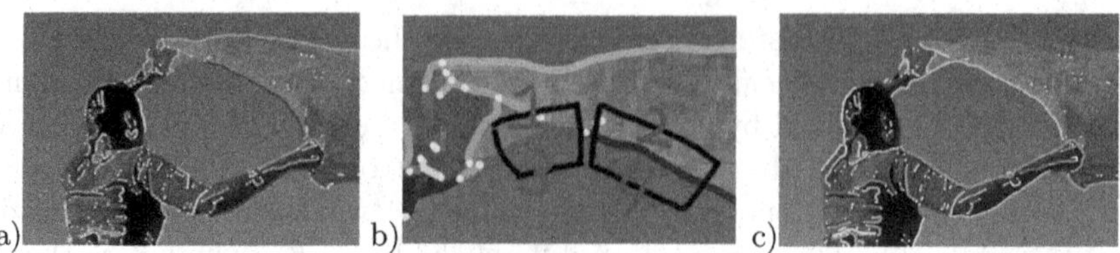

Fig. 5. (a) The curve fragment graph structure provides an opportunity to reduce the over-fragmentation by using various cues to label each node sharing two curve fragments as either "merge" or "do not merge." The decision uses only local portions of curve fragments as shown in b). (c) shows curve fragments after this stage.

in Fig 5(b), and regions 3 and 4, respectively. These differences are captured by the Chi-Square distance between the histograms of textons in each region, and then summed for the two pairs of regions.

Second, the **geometric cues** are also traditional measures: *(v)* Length-normalized integral of absolute curvature: $\int |\kappa(s)|\, ds$; *(vi) Wiggliness*: the number of inflection points along the curve fragment; These two cues are computed for each of the two curve fragments and then compared. Finally, *(vii) Geometric Continuity:* the angle between the tangents of the two curve fragments at their connecting node is a measure of how likely the two curve fragments are a single curve fragment.

Third, we introduce a **novel cue** which to the best of our knowledge has not been reported before, namely, *(viii) Lateral Edge Sparsity*: this is defined as the number of edges in a narrow neighborhood of the curve fragment, see the regions in Fig 5b. We observe that veridical contours lack edges in a small neighborhood and therefore conjecture that the cue is inversely correlated with the likelihood that a candidate curve is veridical (see next section). In addition to being a cue for veridicality, this cue can also be used as an attribute to the two potentially connecting curve fragments, expecting the number to be small for both curves.

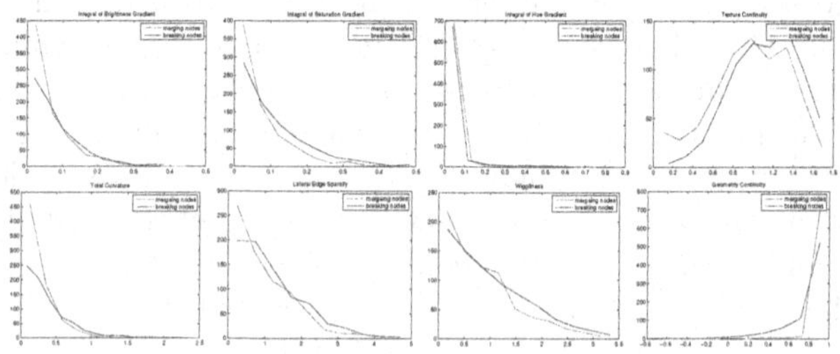

Fig. 6. The histogram of each of the eight cues, shown separately for "merge" in red and "do not merge" in blue. Observe that each cue in isolation offers a modest measure of distinction between the two cases, while the distinction is significantly compounded when all cues are used in conjunction with each other.

We explore the utility of these eight cues by using a logistic regression classifier on a training set where positive (merge) and negative (do not merge) examples are specified. Specifically, we train on the curve fragments annotated in the *Contour Fragment Ground-Truth Dataset* (CFGD) which is introduced in [10].

We use the first 20 images of the CFGD dataset for training and leave the remaining 30 for the testing stage . By matching the candidate pair of curve fragments to ground-truth curve fragments, the connection node is selected as "merge" or "do not merge" depending on whether the corresponding ground-truth curve is connected. The histograms of positive (merge) and negative (do not merge) samples for each cue reveal the discriminative power of each cue in isolation, Fig 6. The cues act in concert giving the probability of the "merge" vs "do not merge," which when exceeding a selected threshold (0.5 by default) leads to a concrete decision.

The above discussion has focused on augmenting the geometric continuity measures of previous stages with more global photometric and geometric measure with the goal of merging the typically over-fragmented curve fragments arising from local geometric grouping in previous stages. While this will be shown to be effective, the opposite problem must also be addressed: in certain instances, the geometric cues happen to be so powerful that they result in long curve fragments. In such cases, caution is required to verify that indeed the geometric factors are not inconsistent with photometric cues.[1] We therefore use the same machinery in reverse: we virtually break a long curve at the points along its length and consider whether the two pieces of the curve should be merged: the probability of (re)merging at each point of the curve is calculated, local minima are identified, and if the probability is below the merge threshold, breaks are introduced.

5 Learning-Based Sifting of Curve Fragments

The curve fragments obtained in our approach are the end result of a very cautious process: extremely low edge thresholds, maintaining all possible local groupings in the form of curvelets, stringing together unambiguous curvelets while sorting out ambiguous ones in a hypothesis graph, and resolving ambiguity by grouping cues all results in making sure that any contour hypotheses with the slightest degree of evidence is retained. As a result, it is unlikely that a veridical contour is missed in the process (very high recall), while at the same time it is highly likely that the process generates (hallucinates) false positives from scant data (low precision). Since the high degree of false positives can overwhelm processes relying on contour fragments, *e.g.*, for recognition, a final stage is needed to reduce the false positive while necessarily also reducing the recall.

This is done by learning a veridicality measure for curve fragments based on training data. Specifically, curve fragments are attributed with several image-based measures, essentially the same cues presented in the previous section, so that each curve fragment is represented as a point in a high-dimensional space. The ground-truth curve fragments of a training set from CFGD separate curve fragments into positive and negative exemplars: Veridical (or false positive) curve fragments are randomly sampled from those computed curve fragments which

[1] Since producing erroneously grouped curves can cause irreversible damage, *e.g.*, confusing object and background (as many camouflaged objects hope to achieve), it is wiser to er on the side of caution.

match (do not match) the ground truth curve fragments under the matching method of [10]. Finally, a query curve fragment interrogates this space to decide which class it belongs to. This approach is analogous to [18] who use training data in cue combination on edge data.

The cues used to indicate veridicality are very similar to those used to indicate whether two connected curve fragments should be merged. Specifically, these cues are the photometric cues of brightness, saturation, and hue gradients, and the geometric cues of total curvature, wiggliness, and finally lateral edge sparsity. We also use curve fragment length as a cue in addition[2]. Fig 7 shows the histograms of each cue on veridical and false positive contours, showing meaningful distinctions.

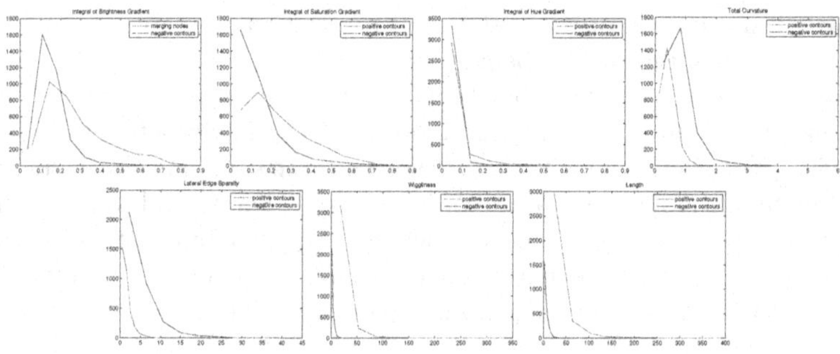

Fig. 7. The comparison of histograms of various cues for veridical (red) and false positive contours (blue), on the **CFGD** data depicting various degrees of separation

To combine the various cues we use a logistic regression classifier. The classifier is trained on the first 20 images of the CFGD and the rest are reserved for testing. Utilizing the resulting classifier output, each contour is assigned a probability of being veridical, and the curve fragment map is thresholded to yield a final set of curve fragments. This approach is quite flexible and the same framework can be applied to any other curve extraction system [13,14,15]. To quantitatively evaluate the extracted curve fragments the classifier probability is thresholded at varying levels to generate the PR curve, see Fig 13. The visual examples shown in Fig 1 and Fig 14 correspond to the highest F-measure of the PR curve.

6 Experiments

The algorithm is evaluated in two ways, one using stability analysis and one using human annotation. Both evaluations are compared to those curve extraction algorithms for which *(i)* code is available and *(ii)* an output is in the form of an independent set of ordered edges is available. Among a series of candidate algorithms we considered [13,14,15,5,22,23,11,28], only [13,14,15] satisfy these criteria.

[2] We have not included texture gradients due to technical difficulties arising just before the paper deadline.

6.1 Contour Stability/Self Consistency

A key requirement of extracted contour fragments is that they should remain stable as the viewing pose and viewing distance change, as illumination changes, as noise is introduced into the system, *etc.* Baker and Nayar [3] introduced global measures of coherence that reported self consistency of edge detectors, *e.g.* colinearity. We now expand on this idea to stability of extracted curves under general visual transformations as a form of evaluating contour fragments.

Illumination Stability Test: A requirement of contour fragment algorithms is stability with moderate illumination variations. Figure 8a) shows several frames of a sequence from the Robot Dataset [1] where the lighting is varied over a wide range. Despite the large range of variations, our method produces contour fragments, Figure 8b), that exhibit a high degree of invariance to illumination when compared to competing methods.

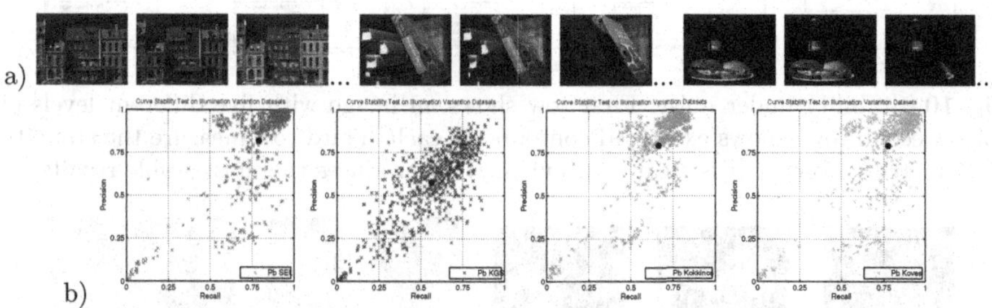

Fig. 8. Illumination Curve Stability Test: a) Several Images from the Robot Dataset [1] where images undergo illumination changes. b) Scatter plots where each dot represents an evaluation using [10] of curve fragments between two subsequent images.

Multi-View Stability Test: Fig 9 compares the stability of various curve extraction methods on multiple views of the same scene taking from slightly different poses.

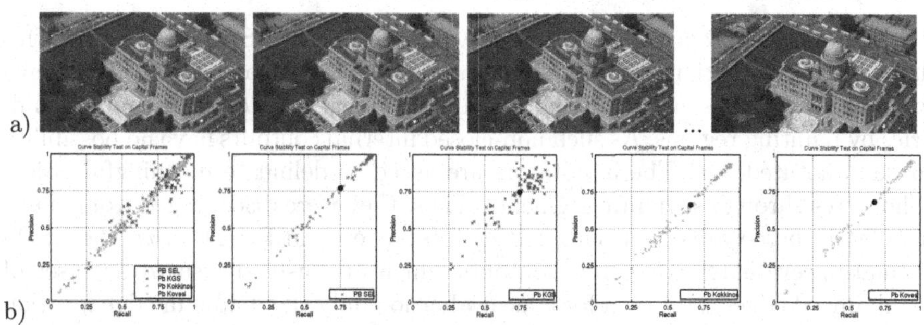

Fig. 9. Stability of curve fragments with slight changes in viewpoint is demonstrated on the Capitol Dataset images (a). Scatter plot where each dot represents an evaluation using [10] of curve fragments between two subsequent images is shown in (b).

Stability Test under Noise: A more sensitive evaluation is to test each contour extraction algorithm's stability under random noise. Fig 10 During this test, images are generated through adding five different level of Gaussian noise, and each algorithm's stability is measured by matching contour fragments generated from noise image to the curve fragments extracted from original image.

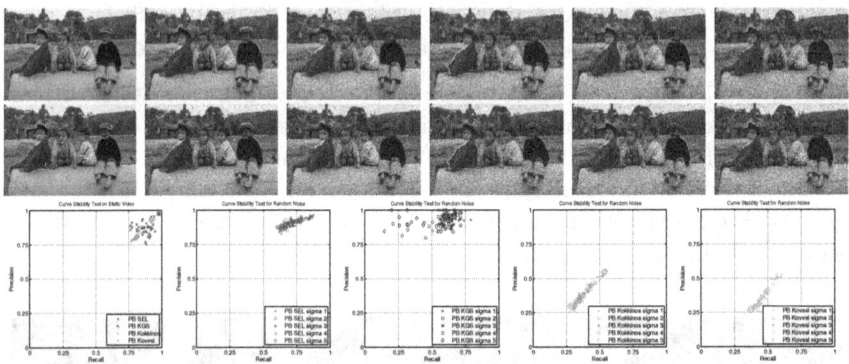

Fig. 10. Stability under noise: First row shows an image with five different levels of noise. Second rows shows extracted contours for each. Third row measure the stability of extracted contours. It is clear that our method produces the most stable results.

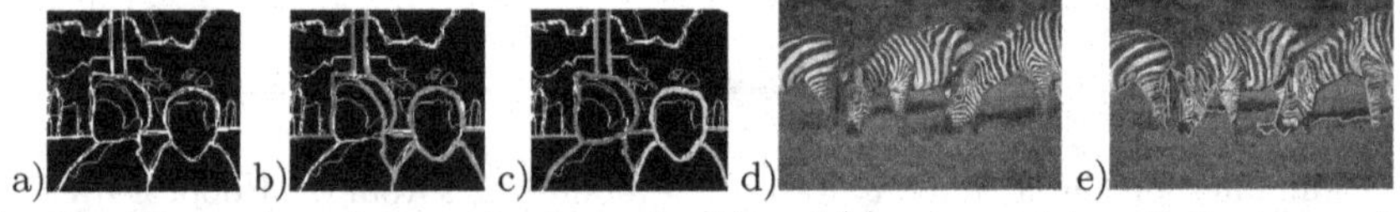

Fig. 11. The contour fragments shown in (b) and (c) represent two distinct groupings, yet at the edge map level (a), they are completely equivalent. BSDS evaluation takes into account edge position (not even edge orientation which by itself is very significant) but not which edges go together. This motivates a ground truth which explicitly represents ordering among edge points. BSDS only annotates silhouettes (d) as compared to CFGD [10] (e) which annotates all contours, including internal contours.

6.2 Evaluation Based on Human Annotation

The standard approach for boundary evaluation is the BSDS framework. This dataset and evaluation strategy is inappropriate for evaluating curve fragments for a number of reasons: *(i)* the human annotators are asked to delineate boundaries by painting regions. As such non-closed internal contours have no possibility to be annotated. *(ii)* The annotators are asked to delineate meaningful object silhouettes through semantic segments. Thus, they were discouraged from marking clearly perceivable contours, *e.g.,* zebra patterns in Fig 11. *(iii)* The BSDS evaluation evaluates edges not contours which are instead treated as a set of unorganized edges; *(iv)* even for edge evaluation only the match in edge location is checked but edge orientation, which is critical, is not included in the evaluation. Thus, random contours on a busy image have a good chance of matching ground truth. In fact, including edge orientation error in the evaluation changes the results and the rankings of algorithms.

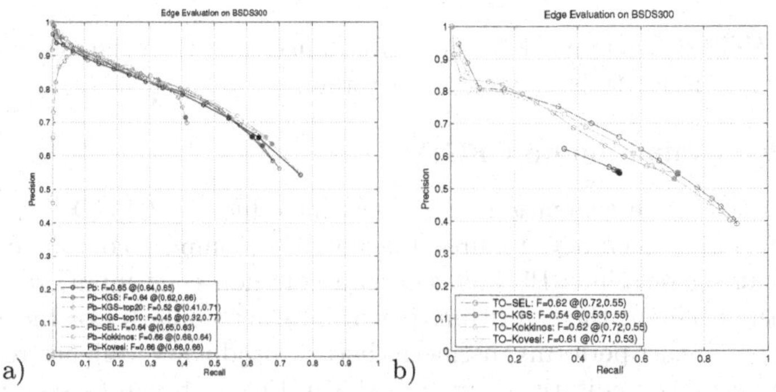

Fig. 12. Berkeley boundary evaluation on BSDS given the same edge input Pb [18] (a) and TO [27] (b), respectively, for a number of linkers. Applying our method on Pb does not improve the performance when compared to the raw Pb input. However, our full pipeline using TO with SEL results in higher recall compared to other methods. We note that KGS is limited on the total number of edges due to the limited range of the eigensolver system.

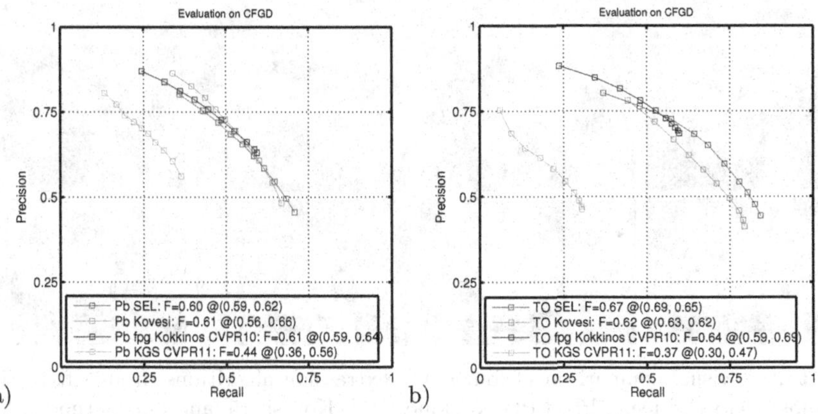

Fig. 13. Using the CFGD evaulation to compare the performance of several curve extraction algorithms using the Pb [18] (a) and TO [27] (b) edge input. Observe that SEL produces the highest recall for both edge maps.

6.3 Edge Evaluation on BSDS

Despite these shortcomings it is informative to evaluate the extracted contours based on the evaluation of edge detection. Using Pb [18] as the baseline and the input, we compare our algorithm's performance to KGS [13], FPG Kokkinos [14], Kovesi [15] in Fig 12a). The results show that the PR curves between Pb and Pb+Sel have nearly identical performance. This is due to the fact that the curve linking process maintains a high edge recall, throws out few edges. Identical performance between BSDS evaluation of edge detector output and edge linking output is consistent with other methods in Fig 12a), and can be seen from Fig 12 b) when comparing algorithms using the third order edge detector

(TO) [27]. KGS [13] gets much lower performance than the others because of its computational difficulty in solving eigensystem.

6.4 Curve Evaluation on CFGD

We rely on the curve evaluation framework introduce by CFGD [10] to evaluate edge grouping accuracy. Figures 13a and 13b compare contour extraction algorithms using retrained Pb and TO as a common edge input, respectively. While for the Pb input the algorithms perform rather similarly, for the TO input our algorithm (SEL) performs distinctly better, producing a higher recall rate. Visual comparisons qualitatively confirm this in Fig 14. It can be seen that SEL generates long smooth curve fragments covering most veridical boundaries while rarely groups boundaries from different objects or object parts together.

Fig. 14. A visual comparison of four curve extraction algorithms: from left to right columns: KGS [13] using Pb, FPG Kokkinos [14], Kovesi [15] and our method (SEL), all using TO. The selection of edge map type is based on which gives the best performance. Each is individually sifted by the veridicality probability threshold that gives the highest F-measure score. The color images are show in grey for better visualization.

7 Conclusion

There are three major contributions in this paper. First, a multi-stage approach is presented which relies on geometry in forming curve fragment pieces from edges and utilizes multiple curve-level cues in grouping over-segmented curve fragments as well as measuring the veridicality of curve fragments. Second, a hypothesis graph is proposed for the representation and management of grouping ambiguities in an approach based on "least early commitment" which demonstrably gives better contour fragments. Third, a learning-based approach and a novel and effective lateral edge sparsity cue is proposed that effectively reduces the false positive groupings and sifts out veridical curve fragments. The resulting system is shown to lead to improved contour fragments when validated against human-annotated data, and which is stable with noise, viewing and viewing angle variations, and to moderate illumination variation.

References

1. Aanæs, H., Dahl, A.L., Pedersen, K.S.: Interesting interest points - a comparative study of interest point performance on a unique data set. International Journal of Computer Vision 97(1), 18–35 (2012)
2. Arbelaez, P., Maire, M., Fowlkes, C., Malik, J.: Contour detection and hierarchical image segmentation. IEEE Trans. Pattern Anal. Mach. Intell. 33(5), 898–916 (2011)
3. Baker, S., Nayar, S.: Global measures of coherence for edge detector evaluation. In: CVPR, pp. II:373–II:379 (1999)
4. Coughlan, J.M., Yuille, A.L.: Bayesian a* tree search with expected o(n) node expansions: Applications to road tracking. Neural Computation 14(8), 1929–1958 (2002)
5. Felzenszwalb, P., McAllester, D.: A min-cover approach for finding salient curves. In: Conference on Computer Vision and Pattern Recognition Workshop, CVPRW 2006, p. 185 (June 2006)
6. Ferrari, V., Fevrier, L., Jurie, F., Schmid, C.: Groups of adjacent contour segments for object detection. IEEE Trans. Pattern Analysis and Machine Intelligence 30(1), 36–51 (2008)
7. Fidler, S., Berginc, G., Leonardis, A.: Hierarchical statistical learning of generic parts of object structure. In: Proceedings of the IEEE Computer Society Conference on Computer Vision and Pattern Recognition, pp. 182–189. IEEE Computer Society (2006)
8. Fischler, M., Tenenbaum, J., Wolf, H.: Detection of roads and linear structures in low-resolution aerial imagery using a multisource knowledge integration technique. Computer Graphics and Image Processing 15(3), 201–223
9. Geman, D., Jedynak, B.: An active testing model for tracking roads in satellite images. IEEE Trans. Pattern Anal. Mach. Intell. 18(1), 1–14 (1996)
10. Guo, Y., Kimia, B.B.: On evaluating methods for recovering image curve fragments. In: Proceedings of IEEE Workshop on Perceptual Organization in Computer Vision, POCV, pp. 9–16 (June 2012)
11. Hu, W., Wu, Y.N., Zhu, S.C.: Image representation by active curves. In: Proceedings of the IEEE International Conference on Computer Vision, pp. 1808–1815 (2011)
12. Iverson, L., Zucker, S.: Logical/linear operators for image curves. PAMI 17(10), 982–996 (1995)
13. Kennedy, R., Gallier, J., Shi, J.: Contour cut: Identifying salient contours in images by solving a hermitian eigenvalue problem. In: Proceedings of the 2011 IEEE Conference on Computer Vision and Pattern Recognition, CVPR 2011, pp. 2065–2072. IEEE Computer Society (2011)
14. Kokkinos, I.: Highly accurate boundary detection and grouping. In: Proceedings of the IEEE Computer Society Conference on Computer Vision and Pattern Recognition, pp. 2520–2527. IEEE Computer Society Press, San Francisco (2010)
15. Kovesi, P.D.: MATLAB and Octave functions for computer vision and image processing. School of Computer Science & Software Engineering, The University of Western Australia (2009), `http://www.csse.uwa.edu.au/~pk/research/matlabfns/`

16. Lin, L., Zeng, K., Liu, X., Zhu, S.C.: Layered graph matching by composite cluster sampling with collaborative and competitive interactions. In: Proceedings of the IEEE Computer Society Conference on Computer Vision and Pattern Recognition, pp. 1351–1358. IEEE Computer Society Press, Miami (2009)
17. Mahamud, S., Williams, L., Thornber, K., Xu, K.: Segmentation of multiple salient closed contours from real images. PAMI 25(4), 433–444 (2003)
18. Martin, D.R., Fowlkes, C.C., Malik, J.: Learning to detect natural image boundaries using local brightness, color, and texture cues. IEEE Transactions on Pattern Analysis and Machine Intelligence 26(5), 530–549 (2004)
19. Narayanan, M., Kimia, B.: To complete or not to complete: Gap completion in real images. In: Proceedings of IEEE Workshop on Perceptual Organization in Computer Vision, POCV, pp. 47–54 (June 2012)
20. Payet, N., Todorovic, S.: From a set of shapes to object discovery. In: Daniilidis, K., Maragos, P., Paragios, N. (eds.) ECCV 2010, Part V. LNCS, vol. 6315, pp. 57–70. Springer, Heidelberg (2010)
21. Payet, N., Todorovic, S.: From contours to 3D object detection and pose estimation. In: Proceedings of the IEEE International Conference on Computer Vision, pp. 983–990 (2011)
22. Payet, N., Todorovic, S.: Sledge: Sequential labeling of image edges for boundary detection. International Journal of Computer Vision 104(1), 15–37 (2013)
23. Ren, X., Fowlkes, C., Malik, J.: Learning probabilistic models for contour completion in natural images. International Journal of Computer Vision 77(1-3), 47–63 (2008)
24. Sharon, E., Brandt, A., Basri, R.: Segmentation and boundary detection using multiscale intensity measurements. In: Proceedings of the IEEE Computer Society Conference on Computer Vision and Pattern Recognition, December 9-14, pp. 469–476. IEEE Computer Society Press, Kauai (2001)
25. Shashua, A., Ullman, S.: Structural saliency: The detection of globally salient structures using a locally connected network. In: ICCV, pp. 321–327 (1988)
26. Shi, J., Malik, J.: Normalized cuts and image segmentation. In: Proceedings of the IEEE Computer Society Conference on Computer Vision and Pattern Recognition, pp. 731–737. IEEE Computer Society (1997)
27. Tamrakar, A., Kimia, B.B.: No grouping left behind: From edges to curve fragments. In: Proceedings of the IEEE International Conference on Computer Vision. IEEE Computer Society, Rio de Janeiro (2007)
28. Widynski, N., Mignotte, M.: A particle filter framework for contour detection. In: Fitzgibbon, A., Lazebnik, S., Perona, P., Sato, Y., Schmid, C. (eds.) ECCV 2012, Part I. LNCS, vol. 7572, pp. 780–793. Springer, Heidelberg (2012)
29. Yu, S.X., Shi, J.: Multiclass spectral clustering. In: Proceedings of the IEEE International Conference on Computer Vision, pp. 313–319. IEEE Computer Society, Nice (2003)
30. Zhu, Q., Song, G., Shi, J.: Untangling cycles for contour grouping. In: Proceedings of the IEEE International Conference on Computer Vision, pp. 1–8. IEEE Computer Society (2007)
31. Zhu, Q., Wang, L., Wu, Y., Shi, J.: Contour context selection for object detection: A set-to-set contour matching approach. In: Forsyth, D., Torr, P., Zisserman, A. (eds.) ECCV 2008, Part II. LNCS, vol. 5303, pp. 774–787. Springer, Heidelberg (2008)

Geometry Driven Semantic Labeling of Indoor Scenes

Salman Hameed Khan[1], Mohammed Bennamoun[1], Ferdous Sohel[1], and Roberto Togneri[2]

[1] School of CSSE, The University of Western Australia, 35 Stirling Highway, Crawley, WA 6009, Australia
[2] School of EECE, The University of Western Australia, 35 Stirling Highway, Crawley, WA 6009, Australia

Abstract. We present a discriminative graphical model which integrates geometrical information from RGBD images in its unary, pairwise and higher order components. We propose an improved geometry estimation scheme which is robust to erroneous sensor inputs. At the unary level, we combine appearance based beliefs defined on pixels and planes using a hybrid decision fusion scheme. Our proposed location potential gives an improved representation of the planar classes. At the pairwise level, we learn a balanced combination of various boundaries to consider the spatial discontinuity. Finally, we treat planar regions as higher order cliques and use graphcuts to make efficient inference. In our model based formulation, we use structured learning to fine tune the model parameters. We test our approach on two RGBD datasets and demonstrate significant improvements over the state-of-the-art scene labeling techniques.

1 Introduction

The task of indoor scene labeling is a relatively difficult problem compared to its outdoor counterpart. Indoor scenes have a large number of categories that are significantly different from each other (e.g., corridors, bookstores and kitchens). They also contain illumination variations, clutter, significant appearance variations and imbalanced representation of object categories [27]. Recently, inexpensive structured light sensors (e.g., Microsoft Kinect) are proving to be a rich source of information for indoor scenes. They provide co-registered color (RGB) and depth (D) images in real-time. Efficient use of this information for indoor scene labeling problems is a critical opportunity.

Several recent works focus on the use of RGBD images for scene labeling of indoor scenes. Koppula *et al.* [20] used Kinect fusion to create a 3D point cloud and then densely labeled it using a Markov Random Field (MRF) model. Silberman and Fergus [34] achieved a reasonable semantic labeling performance using a Conditional Random Field (CRF) with SIFT features and 3D location priors. Couprie *et al.* [3] used ConvNets to learn feature representations from RGBD data to label the images while Ren *et.al* [31] employed kernel descriptors to

D. Fleet et al. (Eds.): ECCV 2014, Part I, LNCS 8689, pp. 679–694, 2014.
© Springer International Publishing Switzerland 2014

capture the distinctive features. These works are focused on extracting discriminative features from RGBD data and have shown that the depth information can certainly improve the scene labeling performance. However, the question of how to adequately incorporate depth information to model local, pairwise and higher order interactions has not been fully addressed.

In this work, we propose a novel depth-based geometrical CRF model to more efficiently utilize the depth information along side the RGB data. *First*, we incorporate the geometrical information in the most important potential of our CRF model, namely the appearance potential. At the appearance level, we encode both the intensity and depth based characteristics in the feature space. These features are used to predict the unary potentials in a discriminative fashion. Likewise, planes, which are the fundamental geometric units of indoor scenes, are extracted using a new smoothness constraint based *region growing algorithm* (see Sec. 5). Compared to other plane detection methods (e.g.,[29, 35]), our method is robust to outer-boundary holes present in Kinect's depth maps. The geometric as well as the appearance based characteristics of these planar patches are learned and used to provide unary estimates. We propose a novel *hierarchical fusion scheme* to combine the pixel and planar based unary potentials. This hierarchical scheme first uses a number of contrasting opinion pools and finally combines them using a Bayesian framework (see Sec. 3.1).

Next, we turn our attention towards the *location potential*, which encodes the possible spatial locations of all classes. In contrast to the conventional 2D location prior (e.g., in [33, 34]), we propose to integrate the rough geometry of planar regions along with their location in each scene (see Sec. 3.1, 4.1). We also propose a novel *spatial discontinuity potential* (SDP) in the pairwise smoothness model. It combines a number of different boundaries (such as depth edges, contrast based edges and super-pixel edges) and learns a balanced combination of these using a quadratic cost function minimization procedure based on the manually segmented images of the training set (see Sec. 4.2). *Finally*, we add a higher order potential (HOP) in our CRF model which is defined on cliques that encompass planar patches. The proposed HOP increases the expressivity of the random field model by assimilating the geometric context. This encourages all pixels inside a planar patch to take the same class label (see Sec. 3.3).

In short, we have proposed a new random field formulation which elegantly combines the geometric information with the appearance information at various levels of the model hierarchy (Fig. 1).

2 Related Work

The use of depth sensors for scene analysis and understanding is increasing. Recent works employ depth information for various purposes e.g., object detection [8], semantic segmentation [11, 20], object grasping [30], door-opening [28] and object placement [14] tasks. For the case of semantic labeling, works such as [3, 31, 34, 35] demonstrate that depth information reasonably helps in achieving better performance. They however do not explore possible ways, other than the depth based features, to incorporate depth information. In this paper, we define

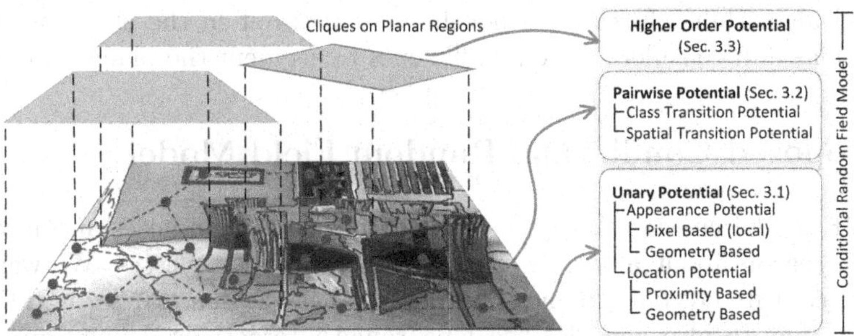

Fig. 1. Our approach combines geometrical information with low-level cues with in a CRF model. Only limited graph nodes are shown for the purpose of clear illustration.

various levels where depth information can be incorporated in a random field model and then explore how each level contributes to enhance the performance of semantic labeling. Our framework is particularly inspired by the works on semantic labeling of RGBD data [34, 35], considering long range interactions [19], parametric learning [36, 37] and geometric reconstruction [29].

The **scene parsing** problem has been studied extensively in recent years. Graphical models e.g., MRF and CRF have found success in modeling context and providing a consistent labeling [9, 12, 13, 23, 26]. Hierarchical MRFs are employed in [21] to make inference jointly on pixels and super-pixels. Huang *et al.* [13] trained the CRF on separate clusters of similar scenes and used them with standard CRF to label street images. Several research works (such as [3, 34, 41]) have shown that the depth based information enhances segmentation performance. They however remain limited to the use of depth based features and do not exploit the geometry of the regions and high level interactions.

An important challenge in scene labeling is to incorporate **long-range interactions** between graph nodes while making local decisions. Farabet *et al.* extracted dense features at a number of scales at each pixel location [5]. Other works incorporate wide context by generating a number of varying scale segmentations (often arranged as trees) to propose many possible labelings (e.g., [2, 21]). HOPs have been employed to model long range smoothness [19], shape based information [24], cardinality based potential [39] and label co-occurrences [22]. In contrast to previously proposed HOPs [18, 19], we propose to consider the geometrical structure of the scenes to model high level interactions.

Currently popular **parameter estimation** methods include partition function approximations [33], cross validation [33] or simply hand picked parameters [34]. We used a one-slack formulation [15] of the parameter learning technique of [36], which gives a more efficient optimization compared to [36, 37]. Further, we extend the parameter estimation problem to consider various different boundary potentials in the SDP and learn them using a tractable quadratic program.

Our **geometric reconstruction** scheme is close to those proposed in [29, 41]. Both these schemes use data from accurate laser scanners and can not handle the less accurate depth data acquired by a real time operating Kinect sensor. Our proposed algorithm relaxes the smoothness constraint in the erroneous depth map regions and considers more reliable cues to segment the planar patches.

3 Proposed Conditional Random Field Model

The CRF model considers the appearance, location, boundaries and layout of pixels to reason about a set of semantically meaningful classes. We want the model to capture not only the neighboring interactions in a standard grid graph structure, but to also consider the long range interactions defined on planar regions (Fig. 1). The CRF model is defined on a graph $\mathcal{G}(\mathcal{I}) = \langle \mathcal{V}, \mathcal{E}, \mathcal{C} \rangle$ composed of a set of vertices $\mathcal{V}$, edges $\mathcal{E}$ and cliques $\mathcal{C}$. The goal of multi-class image labeling is to segment an image $\mathcal{I}$ by labeling each pixel p_i with its correct class label $\ell_i \in \mathcal{L} = \{1..L\}$. The conditional distribution of output classes ($\mathbf{y}$) given an input image ($\mathbf{x}$) and parameters ($\mathbf{w}$) can be defined as a function of Gibbs energy: $\mathcal{P}(\mathbf{y}|\mathbf{x};\mathbf{w}) = \frac{1}{Z(\mathbf{w})}\exp(-\mathrm{E}(\mathbf{y},\mathbf{x};\mathbf{w}))$. This energy is defined in terms of negative log-likelihoods as:

$$\mathrm{E}(\mathbf{y},\mathbf{x};\mathbf{w}) = \sum_{i\in\mathcal{V}} \psi_i(y_i,\mathbf{x};\mathbf{w}_u) + \sum_{(i,j)\in\mathcal{E}} \psi_{ij}(y_{ij},\mathbf{x};\mathbf{w}_p) + \sum_{c\in\mathcal{C}} \psi_c(y_c,\mathbf{x};\mathbf{w}_c). \quad (1)$$

The three terms in Eq. 1 are the unary, pairwise and higher order energies respectively. The parameters introduced in Eq. 1 are learnt using a max-margin criterion, details of which are given in Sec. 4.2. At the inference stage, the most likely labeling is found by making a MAP estimate $\mathbf{y}^*$ upon a set of random variables $\mathbf{y} \in \mathcal{L}^N$: $\mathbf{y}^* = \underset{\mathbf{y}\in\mathcal{L}^N}{\mathrm{argmax}}\ \mathcal{P}(\mathbf{y}|\mathbf{x};\mathbf{w})$.

3.1 Unary Potentials

The unary potential in Eq. 1 is further divided into two components, appearance potential and location potential (Fig. 1):

$$\sum_{i\in\mathcal{V}} \psi_i(y_i,\mathbf{x};\mathbf{w}_u) = \sum_{i\in\mathcal{V}} \overbrace{\phi_i(y_i,\mathbf{x};\mathbf{w}_u^{app})}^{\text{appearance}} + \sum_{i\in\mathcal{V}} \overbrace{\phi_i(y_i,i;\mathbf{w}_u^{loc})}^{\text{location}} \quad (2)$$

We treat both terms separately in the following sections.

Appearance Potential: The proposed appearance potential in Eq. 2 is defined over both pixels and planar regions (Fig. 1). We used a hierarchical ensemble learning method to combine local appearance and geometric information (Fig. 2). We use the class predictions defined over planar regions to help in improving the posterior defined over pixels. In other words, planar features are used to aid in reinforcing beliefs on some dominant planar classes (e.g., walls, blinds, floor and ceiling). At the first level, m contrasting opinions ($\kappa_j : j \in [1,m]$) are used to combine the classifier outputs using linear opinion pooling (LOP) [4], $\mathcal{P}(y_i|\mathbf{x}_1,\ldots,\mathbf{x}_m) = \sum_{j=1}^{m} \kappa_j \mathcal{P}_j(y_i|\mathbf{x}_j)$, where $\mathbf{x}_j$'s denote the representation of an image in different feature spaces. Since we want to combine two classifiers: the pixel based classifier

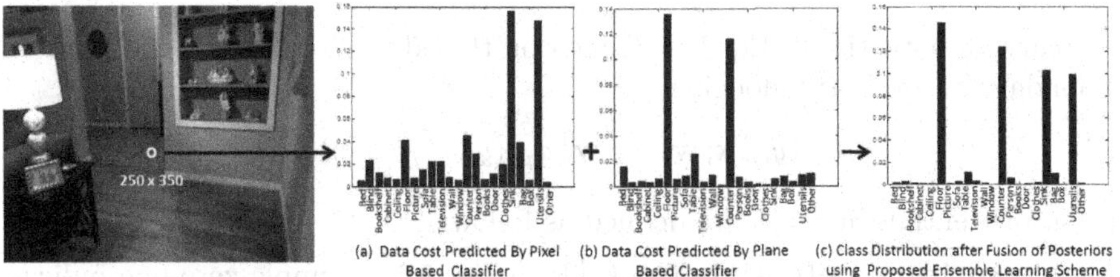

250 x 350
(a) Data Cost Predicted By Pixel Based Classifier
(b) Data Cost Predicted By Plane Based Classifier
(c) Class Distribution after Fusion of Posteriors using Proposed Ensemble Learning Scheme

Fig. 2. Effect of Ensemble Learning Scheme: At the pixel location shown in *left most* image, the pixel based appearance model favors class *Sink*. On the other hand, planar regions based appearance model takes care of geometrical properties of region and favors class *Floor*. The right most bar plot shows how our proposed ensemble learning scheme picks the correct class decision.

and the planar region based classifier, we therefore set $m = 2$. After unifying beliefs based on contrasting opinions, the Bayesian rule is used to combine them at the second stage. To try a number of weighting options (r configurations of weights κ) to generate contrasting opinions $\mathbf{o}$, we can represent our ensemble of probabilities as[1], $\mathcal{P}(y_i|\mathbf{o}_1,\ldots,\mathbf{o}_r) = \frac{\mathcal{P}(\mathbf{o}_1,\ldots,\mathbf{o}_r|y_i)\mathcal{P}(y_i)}{\mathcal{P}(\mathbf{o}_1,\ldots,\mathbf{o}_r)}$. Since $\mathbf{o}_1,\ldots,\mathbf{o}_r$ are independent measurements, we have, $\mathcal{P}(y_i|\mathbf{o}_1,\ldots,\mathbf{o}_r) = \frac{\mathcal{P}(\mathbf{o}_1|y_i)\ldots\mathcal{P}(\mathbf{o}_r|y_i)\mathcal{P}(y_i)}{\mathcal{P}(\mathbf{o}_1,\ldots,\mathbf{o}_r)}$. Again applying the Bayes rule and after simplification we get, $\mathcal{P}(y_i|\mathbf{o}_1,\ldots,\mathbf{o}_r) = \rho\frac{\mathcal{P}(y_i|\mathbf{o}_1)\ldots\mathcal{P}(y_i|\mathbf{o}_r)}{\mathcal{P}(y_i)^{r-1}}$. Here,
$\mathcal{P}(y_i)$ is the prior and ρ is a constant which depends on the data and is given by $\rho = \frac{\mathcal{P}(\mathbf{o}_1)\ldots\mathcal{P}(\mathbf{o}_r)}{\mathcal{P}(\mathbf{o}_1,\ldots,\mathbf{o}_r)}$ [4]. The appearance potential is therefore defined by:

$$\phi_i(y_i,\mathbf{x};\mathbf{w}_u^{app}) = \mathbf{w}_u^{app}\log\mathcal{P}(y_i|\mathbf{o}_1,\ldots,\mathbf{o}_r). \qquad (3)$$

The posterior probabilities $\mathcal{P}(y_i|\mathbf{x}_i)$ are estimated using the random forest (RF) classifier. It captures the discriminative features of an image which encode information about shape, texture, context and geometry. We trained the RF with 100 trees and 500 randomly sampled variables as candidates at each split.

Location Potential: The proposed location prior in Eq. 2 models the class distribution based on the orientation and spatial location:

$$\phi(y_i,i;\mathbf{w}_u^{loc}) = \mathbf{w}_u^{loc}\log\mathcal{F}_{loc}(y_i,i), \qquad (4)$$

where, $\mathcal{F}_{loc}(y_i,i)$ is defined in Sec. 4.1 and $\mathbf{w}_u^{loc}$ is the parameter. The function $\mathcal{F}_{loc}(y_i,i)$ is dependent on both the location and the orientation of a pixel (Fig. 1, see Sec. 4.1).

[1] In this work we set $r = 3$ and κ is set to $[0.25, 0.75]$, $[0.5, 0.5]$ and $[0.75, 0.25]$ respectively in each case. This choice is based on the validation set (see Sec. 6.2).

3.2 Pairwise Potentials

The pairwise potential in Eq. 1 is defined on the edges $\mathcal{E}$ and takes the form of a boundary aware Potts model:

$$\psi_{ij}(y_{ij}, \mathbf{x}; \mathbf{w}_p) = \mathbf{w}_p^{\mathrm{T}} \phi_{p_1}(y_i, y_j) \phi_{p_2}(\mathbf{x}). \tag{5}$$

The sub-potentials in Eq. 5 are defined as follows.

Class Transition Potential: The CTP in Eq. 5 is a simple zero-one indicator function which enforces a consistent labeling. It is defined as: $\phi_{p_1}(y_i, y_j) = a\mathbf{1}_{y_i \neq y_j}$. For this work we used $a = 10$ based on the validation set (Sec. 6.2).

Spatial Discontinuity Potential: The SDP in Eq. 5 encourages the label transition at the boundaries [32, 33]. It is defined as a combination of edges from the intensity image, depth image and the super-pixel edges extracted using Mean-shift [7] and Felzenswalb [6] segmentation: $\phi_{p_2}(\mathbf{x}) = \mathbf{w}_{p2}^{\mathrm{T}} \phi_{edges}(\mathbf{x})$. Weights assigned to each edge potential are learned using a quadratic program (see Sec. 4.2). In simple terms, edges which match with the manual annotations to a large extent contribute more in the SDP. The edge potential is given by:

$$\phi_{edges}(\mathbf{x}) = [\beta_x \exp(-\tfrac{\sigma_{ij}}{\langle\sigma_{ij}\rangle}), \beta_d \exp(-\tfrac{\sigma_{ij}^d}{\langle\sigma_{ij}^d\rangle}), \beta_{\text{sp-fw}} \mathcal{F}_{\text{sp-fw}}(\mathbf{x}), \beta_{\text{sp-ms}} \mathcal{F}_{\text{sp-ms}}(\mathbf{x}), \alpha]^{\mathrm{T}} \tag{6}$$

where, $\sigma_{ij} = \|x_i - x_j\|^2$, $\sigma_{ij}^d = \|x_i^d - x_j^d\|^2$ and $\langle . \rangle$ denotes the average contrast in an image. x_i and x_i^d shows the color and depth image pixels respectively. $\mathcal{F}_{\text{sp-ms}}$ and $\mathcal{F}_{\text{sp-fw}}$ are indicator functions which give all zeros except at the boundaries of the Mean-shift [7] or Felzenswalb [6] super-pixels respectively. For our case, we set $\alpha = 1$, $\beta_x = \beta_d = 150$ and $\beta_{\text{sp-ms}} = \beta_{\text{sp-fw}} = 5$ based on the validation set (see Sec. 6.2).

3.3 Higher Order Potentials

HOPs incorporate long range interactions and enhance the representational power of the CRF model (Eq. 1). We treat planar patches as n-order cliques and define HOPs on them to eliminate inconsistent variables by encouraging all variables in a clique to take the dominant label. The robust P^n model [19] poses this encouragement in a soft manner and some pixels in a clique may retain different labelings. Hence, it is a linear truncated function of the number of inconsistent variables in a clique. Our proposed HOP enforces consistency by applying a logarithmic penalty:

$$\psi_c(y_c, \mathbf{x}; \mathbf{w}_c) = \mathbf{w}_c \min_{\ell \in \mathcal{L}} \mathcal{F}_c(\tau_c), \tag{7}$$

where, $\mathcal{F}_c(.)$ is a function which takes the number of inconsistent pixels $\tau_c = \#c - n_\ell(\mathbf{y}_c)$ as its argument. $\mathcal{F}_c$ is a non-decreasing concave function of the form $\mathcal{F}_c(\tau_c) = \lambda_{max} - (\lambda_{max} - \lambda_\ell)\exp(-\eta\tau_c)$, where $\eta = \eta_0 / Q_\ell$ and $\eta_0 = 5$. Here η_0 is the slope parameter which decides the rate of increase of the penalty, with the increase in the number of pixels disagreeing with the dominant label. The parameters λ_{max} and λ_ℓ define the penalty range which is typically set to 1.5

and 0.15 respectively. Q_ℓ is the truncation parameter which provides the bound for the maximum number of disagreements in a clique. To apply the graph cuts algorithm, details regarding the disintegration of the HOP (Eq. 7) are given in the supplementary material.

4 Learning CRF Model

4.1 Learning Potentials

For a robust semantic labeling, all the characteristics of a class (including its texture, shape, context, geometry and spatial location) need to be taken into account. The procedure of learning this information is outlined as follows.

Features for Local Appearance Potential: The local appearance potential is modeled in a discriminative fashion using a trained classifier (RF in our case). We extract features densely at each point and then aggregate them at the super-pixel[2] level to reduce the computational load and to ensure that similar pixels get a unified representation in the feature space. A rich feature set is extracted which includes local binary patterns (LBP), texton features, SPIN images, scale invariant feature transform (SIFT), color SIFT, depth SIFT and histogram of gradients (HOG). Overall, these features form a high dimensional space (~640 dimensions) and it becomes computationally intensive to train the classifier with all these features. Moreover, some of these features are redundant while some others have a lower accuracy. We therefore employ a genetic search algorithm[3] to find the most useful set of features on the validation dataset (Sec. 6.2).

Features for Appearance Model on Planes: One of the most important features is the plane orientation which is characterized by the direction of its normal. We include the area and height (maximum z-axis value) of the planar region in the feature set to consider its extent and position. Since these measures may vary significantly and a relative measure is needed, we normalize each value with the largest instance in the scene. Moreover, color histograms in the HSV and CIE LAB color spaces are also included. The responses to various filters (in the same manner as *textons*) are calculated and aggregated at the planar level.

Learning Location Potential: Our formulation is based on the idea that the location of a class which has a characteristic geometric orientation can further be made specific, if any geometric information about the scene is available. For example, it is very unlikely to have a *bed* or *floor* at some location in an image, where we know a vertical plane exists. Therefore, we seek to minimize the location prior on the regions where the geometric properties of an object class do not match with the observation made from a scene. First, we average class occurrences over the ground truth for each class (y_i) at each ith location [33, 34]: $\mathcal{F}_{loc}(y_i, i) = \frac{N_{\{y_i,i\}}}{N_i}$. Next, we incorporate geometric information into the location prior. For this, we extract the planar patches (see Sec. 5) and divide them

[2] The super-pixels are obtained using a graph based segmentation method [6].

[3] We use the standard implementation of genetic search algorithm in Weka attribute selector tool [10] to choose the 256 best features.

into three distinct geometrical classes: *below-horizon horizontal regions*, *above-horizon horizontal regions* and *vertical* regions. Since the Kinect sensor gives the pitch and roll for each image, the RGBD images are rotated appropriately to remove any affine transformations. This makes the horizon (estimated using the accelerometer) to lie horizontally at the center of each image. We use this horizon to split the horizontal regions into *above-horizon* and *below-horizon* subclasses. For each planar object class, we retain the 2D location prior in the regions where the geometric properties of the class match with those of the planar region and reduce its value in regions where that class cannot be located. For example, the roof cannot lie on a horizontal plane in the below-horizon region or a vertical region. This effectively reduces the class location prior to only those regions which are consistent with the geometric context. It must be noted that this elimination procedure is only carried out for planar classes e,g., roof, floor, bed and blinds. Finally, the location prior is smoothed and the prior distribution is normalized to give $\sum_i \mathcal{F}_{loc}(y_i, i) = 1/L$ [34].

4.2 Learning Parameters

We used a structured large-margin learning method (S-SVM [36]) to efficiently adjust the probabilistic model parameters. Whilst Szummer *et al.* [36] used the n-slack formulation of cost function, we use a single slack formulation which results in a more efficient learning without any performance degradation[4] [15]. Algorithm 1 shows the learning procedure where the training set $\mathcal{T}$ consists of N training images, $\xi \in \mathbb{R}_+$ is a single slack variable, C is the regularization constant and $\Delta(\mathbf{y}, \mathbf{y}^n)$ is the hamming loss function [36]. It can be proved that the algorithm converges after $O(1/\epsilon)$ steps [15, 37]. The two major steps in this algorithm are the quadratic optimization step (line 8), which is solvable by off-the-shelf convex optimization problem solvers and the loss augmented prediction step (line 4), which can be solved by graph cuts. Although graph cuts move making algorithm gives an approximate solution, but it is efficient and well suited for the task [16, 36]. To further minimize any chance of getting sub-optimal solution, we initialize the parameters using validation set. With these good initial estimates, S-SVM training converged mostly with in 40 iterations.

We also learn the parameters of the boundary potentials to get a balanced representation of each edge in the SDP potential. In our approach, we define a weighted combination of various possible edge potentials (such as depth edges, contrast based edges, Felzenswalb and mean-shift super-pixels edges) to accommodate information from all these sources (see Sec. 3.2 and Eq. 6). We start with a heuristic based initialization (given by parameters such as β_x and α in Eq. 6) and iterate over the training samples to learn a more balanced representation. Note that here we use double parameterization to minimize the chances of getting into a local minimum. The weights for edges are restrained to be non-negative ($\mathbf{w}_{p2} > 0$) so that the energy remains sub-modular and the graph cuts

[4] Interested readers are referred to [15] for more details and efficiency comparisons between n-slack and 1-slack formulations.

Algorithm 1. S-SVM Training with Rescaled Margin Cutting Plane Algorithm

Input: Training set ($\mathcal{T}$), ϵ tolerance (or convergence threshold), initial parameters $\mathbf{w}_0$
Output: Learned parameters $\mathbf{w}^*$

$\mathbf{S} \leftarrow \emptyset$ (working set of low energy labelings that are used as active constraints)
while $U(y_n, x_n; \mathbf{w}) \geq \epsilon - \xi$ **do**
  for n = 1 ... N **do**
    $y^* = argmin_{y \in \mathcal{Y}} E(y, x^n; w) - \Delta(y, y^n)$
    $S = S \cup \{y^*\}$
  end for
  $(\mathbf{w}, \xi) \leftarrow \underset{\mathbf{w},\xi}{\text{argmin}} \ \frac{1}{2}\|\mathbf{w}\|^2 + C\xi$
s.t. $\frac{1}{N}\sum_{n=1}^{N}[E(\mathbf{y}, \mathbf{x}^n; \mathbf{w}) - E(\mathbf{y}^n, \mathbf{x}^n; \mathbf{w})] \geq \frac{1}{N}\sum_{n=1}^{N}\Delta(\mathbf{y}, \mathbf{y}^n) - \xi \quad ; \ C > 0, w_i \geq 0.$
end while
where, $U(y_n, x_n; \mathbf{w}) = \frac{1}{N}\sum_{n=1}^{N}[E(\mathbf{y}, \mathbf{x}^n; \mathbf{w}) - E(\mathbf{y}^n, \mathbf{x}^n; \mathbf{w})] - \frac{1}{N}\sum_{n=1}^{N}\Delta(\mathbf{y}, \mathbf{y}^n)$

inference can be applied. We use structured learning to learn SDP weights (Sec. 3.2) and the resulting quadratic program is given as follows:

$$\underset{\|\mathbf{w}_{p2}\|=1}{\text{argmax}} \ \gamma \qquad s.t. \ \ \{E_{\text{con}}, E_{\text{dep}}, E_{\text{fel-sp}}, E_{\text{ms-sp}}\} - E_{\text{grd}} \geq \gamma, \{\mathbf{w}_{p2}\} \geq 0, \qquad (8)$$

where, E_{grd} is the energy when the SDP is based on the manually identified edges from the training images. Energies for the case when the SDP is based on image contrast, image depth, Felzenswalb or mean-shift super-pixels are represented as $E_{\text{con}}, E_{\text{dep}}, E_{\text{fel-sp}}$ or $E_{\text{ms-sp}}$ respectively. The cost function given in Eq. 8 is optimized in a similar fashion as in Algorithm 1.

5 Plane Detection and Geometric Modeling Scheme

Indoor environments are predominantly composed of structures which can be decomposed into planar regions such as walls, ceilings, cupboards and blinds. We extract the dominant planes which best fit the sparse point clouds of indoor images (obtained from RGBD data) and use them in our model based representation (Fig. 1). It must be noted that depth map from Kinect contains many missing values e.g., along the outer boundaries of an image or when the scene contains a black or a specular surface. Traditional plane detection algorithms (e.g. [29, 35]) either make use of dense 3D point clouds or simply ignore the missing depth regions. In contrast, we propose an efficient plane detection algorithm which is robust to missing depth vlaues (often termed as *holes*) in the Kinect depth map. We expect that the inference made on the improved planar regions will help us achieve a better semantic labeling performance.

Our method[5] first aligns the 3D points with the principal directions of the room. Next, surface normals are computed at each point. Contiguous points in

[5] More details can be found in the supplementary material. Plane detection code is available at `http://www.csse.uwa.edu.au/~salman`

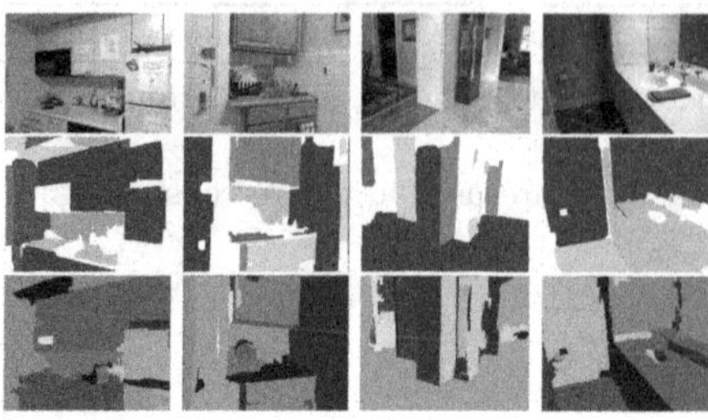

Fig. 3. Comparison of our algorithm (*last* row) with [35] (*middle* row) is shown. Note that the *white* color in middle row shows *non-planar* regions. The *last* row shows detected planes averaged over super-pixels.

Table 1. Comparison of plane detection results on the NYU-Depth v2 dataset. We report detection accuracies for 'exactly planar classes' (EPC) and 'exact and nearly planar classes' (E+NPC).

Performance Evaluation

Method	EPC Acc.	E+NPC Acc.
Silberman et al. [35]	0.69 ± 0.09	0.67 ± 0.10
Rabbani et al. [29]	0.60 ± 0.12	0.57 ± 0.14
This paper	$\mathbf{0.76 \pm 0.09}$	$\mathbf{0.81 \pm 0.07}$

Timing Comparison (averaged for NYU v2)
(for Matlab prog. running on single core, thread)

Silberman [35]	Rabbani [29]	This paper
41 sec	73 sec	3.1 sec

space are then clustered by a region growing algorithm which groups the 3D points in a way to maintain their continuity and smoothness. It is robust to erroneous normal orientations caused due to big holes mostly present along the borders of the depth image acquired via Kinect sensor (Fig. 3). The basic idea is to take help from appearance based cues when the depth information is not reliable. The algorithm begins with a seed point and at each step, a region is grown by including the points in the current region with normals pointing in the same direction. Iteratively, the region is extended and the newly included points are treated as seeds in the subsequent iteration. To deal with erroneous sensor measurements along the border and any other regions with missing depth measurements, we relax the smoothness constraint and use major line segments present in the image to decide about the region continuity.

The line segment detector (LSD) [38] is used to extract the major line segments. These line segments are grouped according to the vanishing points. Line segments in the direction of the major vanishing points contribute more in separating regions during the smoothness constraint based plane detection process. We, however, empirically found that the use of any simple edge detection method (e.g., canny edge detector) in our algorithm gives nearly similar performance with much better efficiency. We further increased the efficiency by replacing iterative region growing with k-means clustering for regions having valid depth values. The planar patches are grown from regions with valid depth values towards regions having missing depths. In this process, segmentation boundaries are predominantly defined by the appearance based edges in an image. Since the majority of the pixels have correct orientation, fitting a plane decreases the orientation errors and the approximate orientation of major surfaces is retained. An added benefit of our algorithm is that curved surfaces are not missed out during the region growing process, rather they are approximated by planes.

Once the regions are grown to the full extent, the small regions are dropped and only the regions with a significant number of pixels are retained. After that, planes are fitted onto the set of points belonging to each region using TLS (Total Least Square) fitting. The least square plane fitting is a non-linear problem, it however reduces to an eigenvalue problem in the case of planar patches. This makes the plane fitting process highly efficient. It is important to note that although the indoor surfaces are not strictly limited to planes, we assume that we are dealing with planar regions during the plane fitting process. It turns out that this assumption is not a hard constraint since the majority of the surfaces in an indoor environment are either strictly planar (e.g., walls, ceilings) or nearly planar (e.g., beds, doors). Finally, our algorithm is superior to other region growing algorithms (e.g., [29]) which are suitable for the segmentation of dense point clouds and fail to deal with the erroneous depth measurements from the Kinect sensor (Fig. 3 and Table 1).

6 Experiments and Analysis

6.1 Datasets

We evaluated our framework on the New York University (NYU) Depth dataset (v2) and a recent SUN3D dataset. The NYU dataset [34] consists of 1449 labeled images. SUN3D is a large scale indoor RGBD dataset [40], however it's still under development and only a small portion has been labeled. We extracted keyframes from SUN3D which amounted to 83 labeled images.

6.2 Results

In the NYU-Depth v2, around 900 different object classes are present in all indoor scenes. Since not all object classes have a sufficient representation, we follow the procedure in [34] to cluster the existing annotations into the 22 most frequently occurring classes. This clustering is performed using the Wordnet Natural Language Toolkit (NLTK). For the case of SUN3D dataset, 32 classes are present in the labeled images we acquired. We clustered them into 13 major classes using Wordnet. In both the datasets, a supplementary class labeled '*other*' is also included to model rarely occurring objects. In our evaluations, we exclude all unlabeled regions. For both the datasets, 60%/40% train/test split was used. A relatively small validation set consisting of 50 random images was extracted from NYU-Depth v2. This validation set was used with the genetic search algorithm for the selection of useful features and for the choice of the initial estimates of the parameters which gave the best performance (for SUN3D we used the same parameters). Afterwards, these parameters were optimized during the learning process as described in Sec. 4.2.

We used two popular evaluation metrics to assess our results, '*pixel accuracy*' and '*class accuracy*' (see Table 2). Pixel accuracy accounts for the average number of pixels which are correctly classified in the test set. Class accuracy measures the average of the correct class predictions which is essentially equal to the mean of the values occurring at the diagonal of the confusion matrix. We extensively evaluated our approach on both the NYU-Depth and SUN3D datasets. Our experimental results are shown in Table 2. The comparisons with state-of-the-art

Table 2. Semantic Labeling Performance: We report the results of our proposed framework when only variants of unary potentials were used (top 3 rows), a CRF with regular Potts model was used (second last row) and the improvements observed when more sophisticated priors and HOPs (last row) were added. Accuracies are reported for 22 and 13 class semantic labeling for NYU v2 and SUN3D datasets respectively.

Variants of Our Method	NYU-Depth v2		SUN3D	
	Pixel Accuracy	Class Acc.	Pixel Accuracy	Class Acc.
Feature Ensemble (FE)	$44.4 \pm 15.8\%$	39.2%	$41.9 \pm 11.1\%$	40.0%
FE + Planar Appearance Model (PAM)	$52.5 \pm 15.5\%$	42.4%	$48.3 \pm 11.5\%$	42.6%
FE + PAM + Planar Location Prior (PLP)	$55.3 \pm 15.8\%$	43.1%	$51.5 \pm 11.9\%$	43.3%
FE + PAM + PLP + CRF (Regular Potts Model)	$55.5 \pm 15.8\%$	43.2%	$51.8 \pm 12.0\%$	43.5%
FE + PAM + PLP + CRF (SDP + HOP)	$\mathbf{58.3 \pm 15.9\%}$	**45.1%**	$\mathbf{54.2 \pm 12.2\%}$	**44.7%**

Table 3. Comparison of results on the NYU-Depth v2 (4-class labeling task): Our method achieved best performance in terms of average pixel and class accuracies

Method	Semantic Classes				Pixel Accuracy	Class Accuracy
	Floor	Structure	Furniture	Props		
Supp. Inf. [35]	68	59	**70**	**42**	58.6	59.6
ConvNet [5]	68.1	87.8	51.1	29.9	63	59.2
ConvNet + D [3]	87.3	86.1	45.3	35.5	64.5	63.5
Im ∪ 3D [1]	**87.9**	79.7	63.8	27.1	67.0	64.3
This paper	87.1	**88.2**	54.7	32.6	**69.2**	**65.6**

techniques are shown in Tables 3, 4. Sample labelings for NYU-Depth v2 are presented in Fig. 4. Although the unlabeled portions in the annotated images are not considered during our evaluations, we observed that the labeling scheme mostly predicts accurate class labels (see Fig. 4).

We report our results in terms of average pixel and class accuracies in Table 2. Starting from a simple unary potential defined on pixels using an ensemble of features, we achieve pixel and class accuracies of 44.4% and 39.2% respectively on NYU-Depth v2. The corresponding accuracies for SUN3D are 41.9% and 40.0% respectively. Starting from these moderate accuracies we build up and get significant improvements. Upon the introduction of the planar appearance model, the pixel and class accuracies increased by 8.1% and 3.2% from their previous values for NYU-Depth v2. For the SUN3D database, we get an increase of 6.4% and 2.6% in pixel and class accuracies respectively. The addition of CRF and modified location potential along with the HOP enforced a better label consistency and the results were consequently improved by 5.8% and 2.7% for NYU-Depth v2, 5.9% and 2.4% for SUN3D datasets. By comparing last two rows in Table 2, it can be seen that the proposed SDP performs better much than the regular Potts model.

For the case of NYU-Depth v2, we compare our framework with a recent multi-scale ConvNet based technique [3, 5]. Whereas in [3, 5] evaluations were performed on just 13 classes, we use a broader range of 22 classes to report our results (see Table 4). To compare with the class *sofa*, we report the mean accuracies of the *sofa* and *chair* classes for a fair comparison[6]. We compare the *furniture* class in [3] with our *cabinet* class based on the details given in [3].

[6] If we sum up the class occurrences of the *chair* and *sofa* which are reported in [3], it supports such comparison.

Table 4. Class wise Accuracies on NYU-Depth v2: Our proposed framework achieves the highest accuracy on 19/22 classes. With nearly double number of classes used in [3, 5], we get $\sim$ 6% and $\sim$ 9% improvement in class and pixel accuracies respectively.

Method	Bed	Blind	Bookshelf	Cabinet	Ceiling	Floor	Picture	Sofa	Table	Television	Wall	Window	Counter	Person	Books	Door	Clothes	Sink	Bag	Box	Utensils	Other	Unlabeled	Mean Class Accuracy	Mean Pixel Accuracy	Classes
Class Freq.	4.7	2.0	4.2	10.7	1.4	10.8	2.2	6.2	2.6	0.5	22.8	2.3	2.7	1.7	0.9	2.3	1.7	0.3	1.7	0.8	0.2	0.1	17.4	-	-	-
ConvNet [5]	30.3	-	31.7	28.5	33.2	68.0	-	35.1	18.0	18.8	**89.4**	37.8	-	-	-	-	-	-	-	-	-	-	-	35.8	51.0	13
CNN+D [3]	**38.1**	-	13.7	42.4	62.6	**87.3**	-	29.8	10.2	6.0	86.1	15.9	-	-	-	-	-	-	-	-	-	-	-	36.2	52.4	13
This paper	32.3	**56.9**	**38.3**	**45.6**	**64.7**	75.8	**43.6**	**58.6**	**47.9**	**45.7**	77.5	**54.0**	**43.8**	**38.8**	**34.0**	**58.3**	**37.2**	**23.1**	**28.4**	**35.7**	**22.6**	**29.9**	-	**45.1**	**58.3**	22

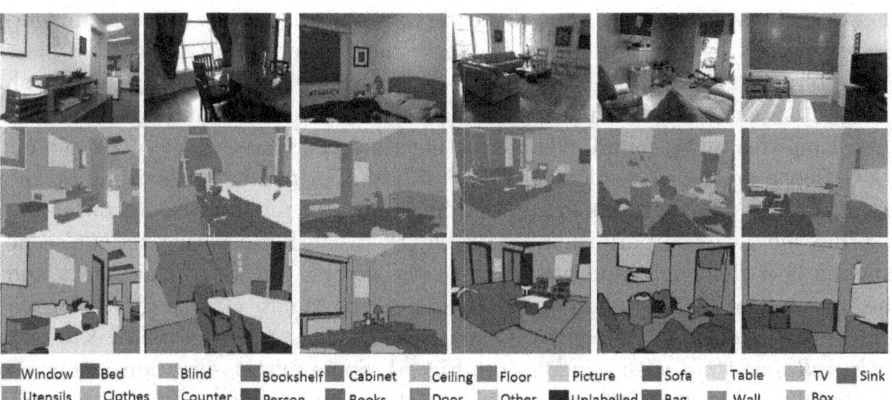

Fig. 4. Examples of semantic labeling results on the NYU-Depth v2 dataset. Figure shows intensity images (*top* row), ground truths (*bottom* row) and our results (*middle* row). Our framework performs well in many cases including some unlabeled regions.

Overall, we get superior performance compared to [3, 5] and also achieve best class accuracies in 19/22 classes.

On NYU-Depth v2, Silberman *et al.* defined just four semantic classes: *furniture*, *ground*, *structure* and *props* [35]. The main goal of [35] was to infer support relationships between objects, for which such a class selection was justified. For our application, such a small number of classes will be meaningless. However, for the sake of comparison we evaluated our method on the 4-class segmentation task as well. As shown in Table 3, we achieved the best performance over all. Particularly we performed well on planar classes such as *floor* and *structures*. In terms of pixel and class accuracies, we noted an improvement of 2.2% and 1.3% respectively. Very recently, Muller and Behnke [25] have reported state-of-the-art labeling performance on NYU-Depth v2. In comparison to [25], which reported results on just 4 classes, our method performs also well on a larger set of 22 classes which demonstrates its scalability.

One may wonder why the incorporation of geometrical context in the CRF model works and gives such high accuracies? In v2 of the NYU-Depth dataset, there are nearly ten out of 22 classes (bed, blind, cabinet, ceiling, floor, picture, table, wall, counter, door) which are planar and out of the remaining classes, 6 are loosely planar (tv, sofa, bookshelf, window, box, sink). The planar classes

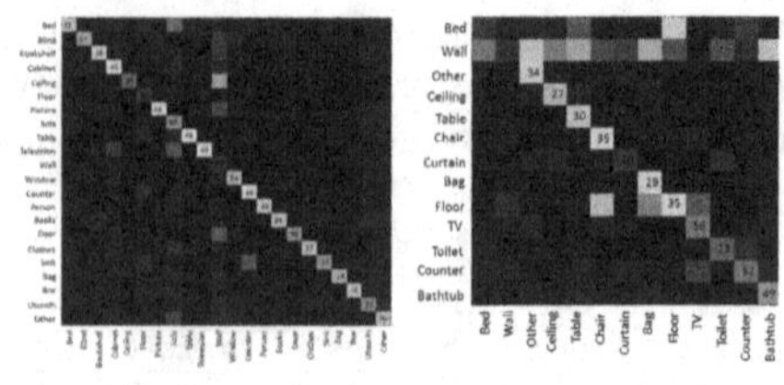

Fig. 5. Confusion Matrices for NYU-Depth v2 (*left*) and SUN3D *right* Databases. All the class accuracies shown on the diagonal are rounded to the closest integer for clarity.

correspond to 62.2% while the loosely planar classes correspond to 14.3% of the total labeled data. There is a similar trend on the SUN3D database. Note that classes such as *floor* or *wall* may have varying textures across different images. However, with depth information in place, we can determine the correct class of the object. Our approach is efficient at test time, since the proposed graph energies are sub-modular and approximate inference can be made using graph-cuts. Empirically, we found average testing time per image to be ~ 1.7 sec for NYU-Depth and ~ 1.4 sec for SUN3D database. For parameter learning on the training set, it took ~ 12 hrs for NYU-Depth and ~ 45 min for SUN3D database.

From the achieved performances (Table 2), it can be seen that indoor scene labeling is a challenging problem due to the diverse nature of the scenes and the presence of a large number of objects. Many times, class errors occurred due to the confusion between two similar classes e.g., *door* is usually confused with *wall* and *blind* with *window* (see Fig. 5). Some misclassifications occurred due to illumination variations, specular surfaces and shadows. In future work, we will explore the use of shadow removal methods like [17] to enhance the labeling accuracy. Lastly, the datasets are somewhat unbalanced and a sufficient representation of all classes is not present in the training set. The labeled portion of SUN3D database is really small (because the database has been released recently) and this is why the achieved accuarcies are on the lower side (see Table 2). The availability of more and higher quality training data for each class will certainly improve the quality of scene labelings.

7 Conclusion

With the availability of depth data for indoor scenes, a pressing issue is to leverage this information in a better way. We extract geometric information from indoor scenes using a novel region growing algorithm which uses dominant lines and surface normals to group the pixels. We use this information at a number of levels in the proposed CRF model. First, we accommodate a posterior defined on planar regions in the appearance based potential to reinforce our beliefs on the dominant planar classes. We also include geometry aware location priors and HOPs defined over n-order cliques to encourage the pixels lying on a planar region to adopt the same labeling. The pairwise potential in our model is defined as a combination of various edges learned using a quadratic program. We extensively evaluated our scheme on the NYU-Depth and the SUN3D databases and report comparisons and improvements over existing works.

Acknowledgments. This research was supported by the Australian Research Council (ARC) grants DP110102166 and DE120102960.

References

[1] Cadena, C., Košecká, J.: Semantic segmentation with heterogeneous sensor coverages (2014)

[2] Carreira, J., Sminchisescu, C.: Cpmc: Automatic object segmentation using constrained parametric min-cuts. TPAMI 34(7), 1312–1328 (2012)

[3] Couprie, C., Farabet, C., Najman, L., LeCun, Y.: Indoor semantic segmentation using depth information. In: ICLR (2013)

[4] Edwards, W., Miles Jr., R.F., Von Winterfeldt, D.: Advances in decision analysis: from foundations to applications. Cambridge University Press (2007)

[5] Farabet, C., Couprie, C., Najman, L., LeCun, Y.: Learning hierarchical features for scene labeling. TPAMI 35(8), 1915–1929 (2013)

[6] Felzenszwalb, P.F., Huttenlocher, D.P.: Efficient graph-based image segmentation. IJCV 59(2), 167–181 (2004)

[7] Fukunaga, K., Hostetler, L.: The estimation of the gradient of a density function, with applications in pattern recognition. TIT 21(1), 32–40 (1975)

[8] Gould, S., Baumstarck, et al.: Integrating visual and range data for robotic object detection. In: Workshop on M2SFA2 (2008)

[9] Gould, S., Fulton, R., Koller, D.: Decomposing a scene into geometric and semantically consistent regions. In: ICCV, pp. 1–8. IEEE (2009)

[10] Hall, M., Frank, E., Holmes, G., Pfahringer, B., Reutemann, P., Witten, I.H.: The weka data mining software: an update. ACM SIGKDD Explorations Newsletter 11(1), 10–18 (2009)

[11] Hayat, M., Bennamoun, M., An, S.: Learning non-linear reconstruction models for image set classification. In: 2014 IEEE Conference on Computer Vision and Pattern Recognition, CVPR (2014)

[12] He, X., Zemel, R.S., Carreira-Perpinán, M.A.: Multiscale conditional random fields for image labeling. In: CVPR, vol. 2, pp. II–695. IEEE (2004)

[13] Huang, Q., Han, M., Wu, B., Ioffe, S.: A hierarchical conditional random field model for labeling and segmenting images of street scenes. In: CVPR, pp. 1953–1960. IEEE (2011)

[14] Jiang, Y., Lim, M., et al.: Learning to place new objects in a scene. IJRR 31(9), 1021–1043 (2012)

[15] Joachims, T., Finley, T., Yu, C.N.J.: Cutting-plane training of structural svms. JML 77(1), 27–59 (2009)

[16] Kappes, J.H., Andres, B., Hamprecht, F.A., Schnorr, C., Nowozin, S., Batra, D., Kim, S., Kausler, B.X., Lellmann, J., Komodakis, N., et al.: A comparative study of modern inference techniques for discrete energy minimization problems. In: 2013 IEEE Conference on Computer Vision and Pattern Recognition (CVPR), pp. 1328–1335. IEEE (2013)

[17] Khan, S., Bennamoun, M., Sohel, F., Togneri, R.: Automatic feature learning for robust shadow detection. In: CVPR. IEEE (2014)

[18] Kohli, P., Kumar, M.P., Torr, P.H.: P3 & beyond: Solving energies with higher order cliques. In: CVPR, pp. 1–8. IEEE (2007)

[19] Kohli, P., Torr, P.H., et al.: Robust higher order potentials for enforcing label consistency. IJCV 82(3), 302–324 (2009)

[20] Koppula, H.S., Anand, A., et al.: Semantic labeling of 3D point clouds for indoor scenes. In: NIPS, pp. 244–252 (2011)

[21] Ladicky, L., Russell, C., Kohli, P., Torr, P.H.: Associative hierarchical crfs for object class image segmentation. In: ICCV, pp. 739–746. IEEE (2009)
[22] Ladický, L., Russell, C., et al.: Inference methods for crfs with co-occurrence statistics. IJCV, 1–13 (2013)
[23] Lempitsky, V., Vedaldi, A., Zisserman, A.: Pylon model for semantic segmentation. In: NIPS, pp. 1485–1493 (2011)
[24] Li, Y., Tarlow, D., Zemel, R.: Exploring compositional high order pattern potentials for structured output learning (June 2013)
[25] Muller, A., Behnke, S.: Learning depth-sensitive conditional random fields for semantic segmentation of rgb-d images. In: ICRA (2014)
[26] Munoz, D., Bagnell, J.A., Hebert, M.: Stacked hierarchical labeling. In: Daniilidis, K., Maragos, P., Paragios, N. (eds.) ECCV 2010, Part VI. LNCS, vol. 6316, pp. 57–70. Springer, Heidelberg (2010)
[27] Quattoni, A., Torralba, A.: Recognizing indoor scenes. In: CVPR, pp. 413–420 (2009)
[28] Quigley, M., Batra, S., et al.: High-accuracy 3D sensing for mobile manipulation: Improving object detection and door opening. In: ICRA, pp. 2816–2822. IEEE (2009)
[29] Rabbani, T., van Den Heuvel, F., Vosselmann, G.: Segmentation of point clouds using smoothness constraint. Intl. Archives of Photogrammetry, Remote Sensing and Spatial Information Sciences 36(5), 248–253 (2006)
[30] Rao, D., Le, Q.V., et al.: Grasping novel objects with depth segmentation. In: IROS, pp. 2578–2585. IEEE (2010)
[31] Ren, X., Bo, L., Fox, D.: Rgb-(d) scene labeling: Features and algorithms. In: CVPR, pp. 2759–2766. IEEE (2012)
[32] Rother, C., Kolmogorov, V., Blake, A.: Grabcut: Interactive foreground extraction using iterated graph cuts. TOG 23, 309–314 (2004)
[33] Shotton, J., Winn, J., Rother, C., Criminisi, A.: Textonboost for image understanding: Multi-class object recognition and segmentation by jointly modeling texture, layout, and context. IJCV 81(1), 2–23 (2009)
[34] Silberman, N., Fergus, R.: Indoor scene segmentation using a structured light sensor. In: ICCV Workshops, pp. 601–608. IEEE (2011)
[35] Silberman, N., Hoiem, D., Kohli, P., Fergus, R.: Indoor segmentation and support inference from RGBD images. In: Fitzgibbon, A., Lazebnik, S., Perona, P., Sato, Y., Schmid, C. (eds.) ECCV 2012, Part V. LNCS, vol. 7576, pp. 746–760. Springer, Heidelberg (2012)
[36] Szummer, M., Kohli, P., Hoiem, D.: Learning CRFs using graph cuts. In: Forsyth, D., Torr, P., Zisserman, A. (eds.) ECCV 2008, Part II. LNCS, vol. 5303, pp. 582–595. Springer, Heidelberg (2008)
[37] Tsochantaridis, I., Hofmann, T., Joachims, T., Altun, Y.: Support vector machine learning for interdependent and structured output spaces. In: ICML, p. 104. ACM (2004)
[38] Von Gioi, R.G., Jakubowicz, J., Morel, J.M., Randall, G.: Lsd: A fast line segment detector with a false detection control. TPAMI 32(4), 722–732 (2010)
[39] Woodford, O.J., Rother, C., Kolmogorov, V.: A global perspective on map inference for low-level vision. In: ICCV, pp. 2319–2326. IEEE (2009)
[40] Xiao, J., Owens, A., Torralba, A.: Sun3d: A database of big spaces reconstructed using sfm and object labels. In: ICCV. IEEE (2013)
[41] Xiong, X., Huber, D.: Using context to create semantic 3D models of indoor environments. In: BMVC, pp. 45–41 (2010)

A Novel Topic-Level Random Walk Framework for Scene Image Co-segmentation

Zehuan Yuan[1], Tong Lu[1,⋆], and Palaiahnakote Shivakumara[2]

[1] National Key Laboratory of Software Novel Technology, Nanjing University, China
[2] Faculty of Computer Science and Information Technology, University of Malaya

Abstract. Image co-segmentation is popular with its ability to detour supervisory data by exploiting the common information in multiple images. In this paper, we aim at a more challenging branch called scene image co-segmentation, which jointly segments multiple images captured from the same scene into regions corresponding to their respective classes. We first put forward a novel representation named *Visual Relation Network* (VRN) to organize multiple segments, and then search for meaningful segments for every image through voting on the network. Scalable topic-level random walk is then used to solve the voting problem. Experiments on the benchmark MSRC-v2, the more difficult LabelMe and SUN datasets show the superiority over the state-of-the-art methods.

Keywords: Image co-segmentation, voting, random walk, link analysis.

1 Introduction

As one of the recent developments in computer vision, image co-segmentation has attracted the interest of researchers [10][7][16][14][11][17][18][4][13][8] in the past years with its ability to remedy the loss of supervisory data by utilizing enhanced cues from co-occurring objects. However, although promising results have been achieved, most of them still face difficulties when dealing with scene images due to large intra-class variability and complex scene structures.

In this paper, we simultaneously analyze multiple images from the same scene and decompose each complex scene image into disjoint but meaningful segments with each corresponding to an instance of a scene element (e.g., tree and car). We propose a fully automatic co-segmentation method that exploits both the appearance consistency of the same class and the spatial scene context constraints of different classes. The core of our method is to derive a directed *flowing-graph* named *Visual Relation Network* (VRN) (Sec.3) to characterize "soup of segments" [19] and their relations. In VRN, each node corresponds to an image segment and its latent class label is indicated by the state variable of the node. The statement of the *flowing-graph* means that the weight of any edge varies over the state variables of its linked nodes, like a valve controlling the water volume flowing from the starting point to the end. VRN thus succeeds in modeling both the

⋆ Corresponding author.

D. Fleet et al. (Eds.): ECCV 2014, Part I, LNCS 8689, pp. 695–709, 2014.
© Springer International Publishing Switzerland 2014

appearance similarity and the spatial scene context relations between every two segments on class level by the form of adjustable weights. Note that compared to bad segments, meaningful segments are believed to have strong intra-class appearance consistencies and spatial inter-class context relations with other segments. Thus they are actually the hubs of the graph with more water flowing into them. Thereby, co-segmentation from multiple scene images can be formulated as voting on the large-scale network. By considering "classes" as "topics", we address it by a topic-level random walk algorithm (Sec.4) on the *flowing-graph* to search for the meaningful segments that have high ranking scores. Then for each image, we use a greedy strategy (Sec.5) to search for the optimized segment combination from the selected meaningful segments. The overview of the entire framework is shown in Fig. 1. Note that since scene spatial context is unknown in advance, we thereby adopt a recursive way to alternate co-segmentation and learning stable spatial scene context (Sec.6).

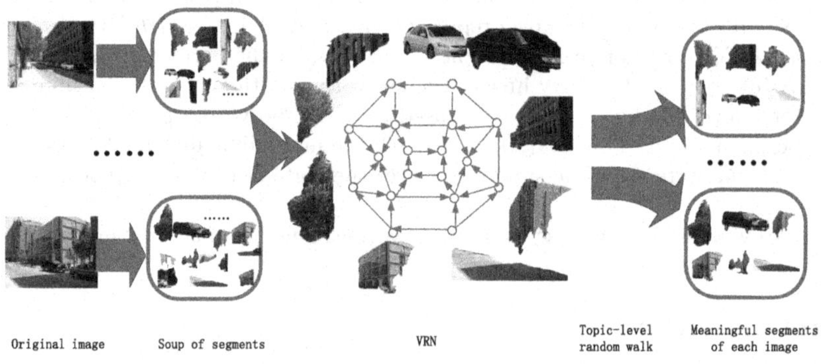

Fig. 1. The overview of the proposed method. The directed edges (blue arrow) in VRN model either the appearance similarity or the class-level spatial context relation between two segments (red circle).

Our main contributions include 1) the introduction of stable scene context into scene image co-segmentation, and 2) a new framework consisting of the VRN representation and the topic-level random walk on it to address the problem. Although topic-level random walk is familiar in mining social networks [26], it is novel for image co-segmentation to the best of our knowledge. According to the experiments on LabelMe [20] and SUN [1], we have averagely 10% improvement over the state-of-the-art methods. Moreover, the proposed VRN is sparse with few hubs [9] and thus is efficient for large scene datasets compared to popular pixel-label methods.

2 Related Work

There are two branches towards image co-segmentation: two-class co-segmentation and multi-class co-segmentation. Two-class image co-segmentation aims to divide every image into foreground or background regions with the former corresponding to common objects. However, multi-class image co-segmentation mainly focuses on the images consisting of many instances of different classes.

2.1 Two-Class Co-segmentation

The key step in these methods is to construct a proper appearance model to distinguish the two classes directly and robustly. Then it will be relatively easy to perform pixel-level labeling by using techniques like energy minimization. These methods are very different from each other in their selected features, such as color histogram [16], texture features [14], Garbos filters [6], stereo cues [11], objectness [24], and visual saliency [17].

To further propagate segmentation masks of common objects to different images, visually matching techniques across images have been introduced, typically consisting of region-level matching [18][4] and pixel-level correspondence [17]. [2] additionally models the shape of foreground objects explicitly by shape templates, thus getting better co-segmentation results by sharing shape templates among multiple foreground object instances. Recently, [25] further establishes consistent functional maps between two images in an reduced functional space to assist image co-segmentation. However, two-class co-segmentation algorithms can not be applied into the images that have many instances of different classes.

2.2 Multi-class Image Co-segmentation

As an extension to two-class co-segmentation, researchers have explored multi-class co-segmentation [10][7][13][8] recently. For example, [10] over-segments every image into multiple regions and labels each region under an combinatorial auction optimization framework. [7] converts the multi-class co-segmentation into the combination of spectral clustering and discriminative clustering, which well maintains the spatial structure of each image and the distinction of different classes. However, these methods only make use of the appearance consistency of the same class across images. Actually, there also exists stable scene class-level context that can be used for co-segmentation.

3 The Proposed VRN

We introduce the construction of VRN in this section. Essentially, VRN is a weighted directed graph (V, E, W) with V as its vertex set, E as its edge set, and W as the edge weight set. Node a_i represents the i-th segment in the "soup of segments" of image a. For any image, we adopt the same strategy as [19] to obtain its "soup of segments", namely, we perform multiple rounds of graph-cut segmentation with a different parameter setting in each round. In addition, we add category-independent object proposals [3] into the soup to ensure meaningful segments of objects can be included into the soup. Note that we assume there is at least one meaningful segment in the soup for every class in the image.

A segment 1) is described by the appearance A that is characterized by its pHOG, color distribution and texton distribution, and 2) has a class variable t belonging to $\{1, 2 \cdots, T\}$ and a distribution P that describes the probability of the segment belonging to one class in $\{1, 2 \cdots, T\}$. The unsupervised category discovery method [19] is used to initialize the distribution of every segment over different classes. The method clusters all segments by Latent Dirichlet allocation (LDA) and thus encourages the segments in the same cluster to manifest similar appearance. Finally, its class label is initialized by $t = arg\max_c P(c)$. Edges will then be created between segments either from different images or inside the same image. See the example VRN in Fig. 2(a).

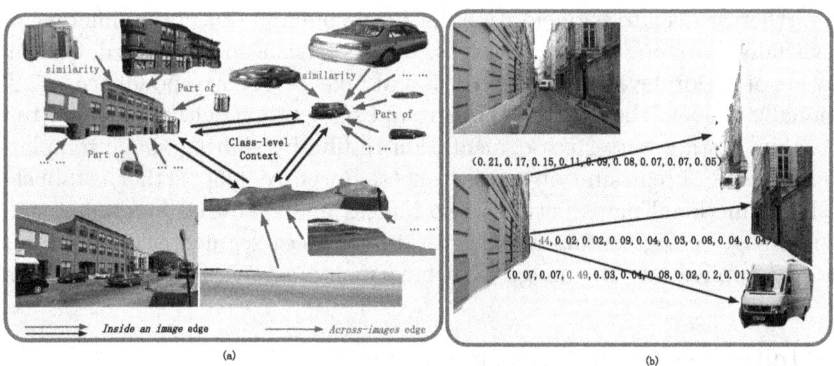

Fig. 2. An example VRN. (a) The VRN example, where three different object classes consisting of *building*, *sky* and *car* are denoted by class label 1, 2 and 3, respectively. (b) Class-level weight vectors, in which the 9 elements respectively correspond to class pairs (1,1), (1,2), (1,3), (2,1), (2,2), (2,3), (3,1), (3,2), (3,3). Note that for an edge between two pure segments, there is a significant peak in the weight vector compared to a flat distribution between mixed segments.

3.1 Edge Construction Across Images

It is observed that meaningful segments tend to have consistent matches and thus we encourage the segments of similar appearance to be linked. Specifically, for each VRN node a_i, we first search for its K-nearest neighbors from "soups of segments" of other scene images by defining the following similarity measure S between two segments a_i and b_j:

$$S(a_i, b_j) = \frac{1}{|\, c \,|} \sum_c K_{\chi^2}(A_c(a_i), A_c(b_j)) \tag{1}$$

where A_c denotes the cth type of appearance features consisting of pHOG, texton and color, and $K_{\chi^2}(\cdot, \cdot)$ is a χ^2 kernel function. Generally, two visually similar segments are more likely to belong to the same class, while the segments of different classes have dissimilar visual appearances. Note that no shape features are adopted to measure the similarity between two segments since the segment of an object may be a union of smaller ones due to over-segmentation or occlusion, and most importantly, many scene *stuffs* even have no explicit shapes.

Finally, let $\{b_j^k\}_{b \neq a}^{k=1,\cdots,K}$ denote the K-nearest neighbors of a_i, a *similarity* edge connecting a_i and b_j will be created, namely, the edge $a_i \to b_j$ as shown in Fig. 2(a) with its weight initialized as $S(a_i, b_j)$.

3.2 VRN Construction Inside an Image

We hypothesize that two segments in one image should be connected if there exists a class-level spatial *context* relation or a *part-of* relation.

Establishing *part-of* Edges. As known, it is difficult to distinguish a part and the entire object without any semantic information. For instance, the building in Fig. 2(a) may be over-segmented and it is easy to consider any small segment as an independent meaningful object. Based on Gestalt Principles, we are prone to reserve the larger segments. Thereby, we define there exists a *part-of* relation between two segments if one segment belongs to another one. For this case we add an edge to link them. That is, given two segments a_i and a_j with an overlapped scale $\frac{a_i \cap a_j}{\min(a_i, a_j)} > 0.95$, we add a directed edge (a_i, a_j) if the segment a_i is smaller, otherwise (a_j, a_i) is added. The weight of a *part-of* edge is fixed as $\tau = 0.52$.

Inter-Class Spatial Context. The inter-class spatial context represents that the instances of different classes in a scene have a roughly stable spatial layout. We take a street scene as an example and assume there exist instances of class 1, class 2 and class 3 which correspond to "pedestrian", "road" and "sky", respectively. The instances of class 1 always walk on the instances of class 2, and similarly the instances of class 3 will be above on all the instances of the rest two classes in this scene. However, due to perspective deformation, 3D spatial context of a scene manifests in a diverse way in 2D image space. In our method, we classify 2D inter-class spatial context into different clusters. In another word, the images that have similar spatial structures are grouped into the same cluster, and thus the inter-class spatial context for each cluster are consistent and stable. Each image has a cluster label that corresponds to the group it exists. Specifically, we first extract the global Gist feature [15] to represent its spatial structure for every image. Then the hierarchical agglomerative clustering is used since it chooses the number of clusters in an automatical way. Fig. 3 shows a tree view example of clusters, where the images that have visually similar elements and layout are categorized into the same cluster.

For each cluster c, we use image-dependent location probability maps [5] to model its inter-class spatial context. A map $M^c_{t_j|t_i}(\cdot, \cdot)$ models the preference of t_j at any relative location to pixel of t_i for the scene cluster c. For example, $M^c_{t_j|t_i}(x, y)$ encodes the probability of the pixel with (x, y) deviation to anyone pixel of t_i belonging to t_j.

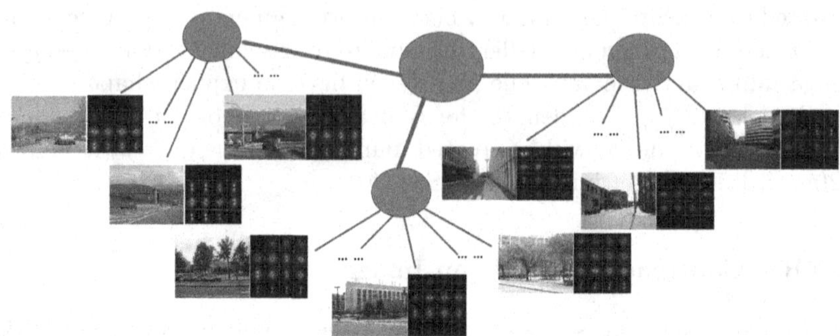

Fig. 3. A hierarchical tree view example after clustering. Example images and their corresponding Gist features are shown for each cluster.

Establishing Class-Level *context* Edges. Based on the learned inter-class spatial context model, *context* edges are added to include the inter-class spatial constraints between two segments in an image. Note that the strength of an edge is a function over the class variables of its linked segments. Specifically, given two segments a_i and a_j with the overlapped scale $\frac{a_i \cap a_j}{a_i \cup a_j} < 0.05$, we add two directed edges (a_i, a_j) and (a_j, a_i) into E. With each element corresponding to a class pair, the weight of (a_i, a_j) is a class-level vector $c(t_i, t_j)$ indicating the strength of spatial relation if a_i and a_j are equal to t_i and t_j, respectively:

$$c(t_i, t_j) = \frac{p(t_i|a_i)}{|\, a_i \,||\, a_j \,|} \sum_{\substack{(x,y) \in a_i \\ (x^*,y^*) \in a_j}} M^c_{t_j|t_i}(x^* - x, y^* - y) \tag{2}$$

where $|\, a_i \,|$ and $|\, a_j \,|$ are the number of pixels in a_i and a_j, respectively. $p(t_i|a_i)$ is the probability of a_i under class t_i, and $M^c_{t_j|t_i}(\cdot, \cdot)$ is the relative location map of t_j given t_i in the cluster c of a. Note that the weight of (a_j, a_i) may not be the same as that of (a_i, a_j) because of different relative location maps. Note that for an edge between two pure segments, there is a significant peak in the weight vector compared to a flat distribution between mixed segments (See Fig. 2(b)). This can be utilized by our topic-level random walk later to search for meaningful segments.

4 Topic-Level Random Walk on VRN

After initializing all the nodes and the edges in VRN, it is observed that meaningful segments perform the role of hubs to which many other nodes are directed. Thus we consider the weight of every directed edge as a vote from the starting segment to the ending one. Since the weight of a *context* edge is a function of class variables, we adopt a topic-level random walk method to improve the ranking quality by integrating class-level spatial context.

Specifically, given a node a_i, we introduce a ranking score vector $\{r[a_i,t]_{t=1,\cdots,T}\}$ to represent the importance of a_i under class t, rather than a simple important value used in Pagerank. Votes are then derived from either the linked segments in the same image a or those from other scene images b. The vote of a *similarity* edge is essentially intra-class. That is, for an edge (a_i,b_j), a_i only votes $r[a_i,t]$ to $r[b_j,t]$. However, for a *context* edge (a_i,a_j), the vote is inter-class. If a_i and a_j respectively have strong spatial relations under classes t_i and t_j, namely $c(t_i,t_j)$ is large, a_i votes $r[a_i,t_i]$ to $r[b_j,t_j]$. This encourages meaningful segments to have a higher ranking score under its correct class label. The vote of a *part-of* edge is not class-level because we prefer to the larger regions regardless of their classes. Mathematically, the topic-level ranking score of a_i under class t can be recursively defined by:

$$r(a_i,t)=\varepsilon\frac{p(t|a_i)}{|V|}+(1-\varepsilon)\Big(\kappa\sum_{(b_j,a_i)\in E}r(b_j,t)w_{b_ja_i}+ (1-\kappa)\sum_{(a_j,a_i)\in E}V(a_j,a_i,t)\Big)$$

$$V(a_j,a_i,t)=\begin{cases}\sum_{t_j}\tau r(a_j,t_j) & (a_j,a_i)\text{is } \textit{Part of}\\ \sum_{t_j}c_{a_ja_i}(t_j,t)r(a_j,t_j) & \text{Otherwise}\end{cases} \tag{3}$$

where ε is the damping factor and is set by its typical value 0.15. κ represents the balance factor between two types of edges. $w_{b_ja_i}$ is the normalized appearance similarity measure $S(a_i,b_j)$ and E represents all the edges in VRN. Intuitively, a VRN node with a relatively high ranking score is much likely to connect with the VRN nodes that also have high ranking scores.

The proposed topic-level random walk can be further reduced into a simple Pagerank representation. The details are included in the supplementary material. Accordingly, the iterative definition of topic-level random walk is promised to converge theoretically. The inference of $r[\cdot,t]$ of any node in VRN can thus be addressed by the Power method used for Pagerank.

5 Segments Selection and Class Inference

A meaningful segment in general has a relatively high ranking score. To search for meaningful segments for any scene image a, we adopt a greedy algorithm and the details are shown in Tab. 1. Since every segment has an importance vector, we calculate its overall importance. One segment with a high overall importance is considered more important. Note that we infer the class label for any selected segment a_i by $\bar{t}=\arg\max r(a_i,t)$.

Table 1. The greedy algorithm to choose meaningful segments

input: Image set D and all the candidate segments S
Output: The selected segments $segC$ for every image in D

For any image a in D
(**1**) Calculate the overall score $r_{overall}$ of a segment a_i and assign a class label $\bar{t}$ to it by $\bar{t} = \arg\max r(a_i, t), m_a = \frac{1}{|T|}\sum_t r(a_i, t), v_a = \frac{1}{|T|}\sum_t (r(a_i, t) - m_a)^2$, $r_{overall} = v_a * \max r(a_i, t)$;
(**2**) Sort all $\{a_i\}_{i=1,\cdots,S_a}$ by $r_{overall}$ and initialize the selected segments set $segC = []$;
(**3**) Select a_i in the descending order of $r_{overall}$;
(**4**) For $a_j \in segC$ calculate $Overlap = \frac{a_i \cap a_j}{a_i \cup a_j}$, if $Overlap > 0.1$ return (**3**);
(**5**) Add a_i into $segC$, if $\bigcup segC < 0.9 *$ imagesize of a, return (**3**).
End

6 Iterative Scene Image Co-segmentation Using VRN

After constructing VRN, we adopt an iterative strategy to perform co-segmentation and update scene spatial context. It will converge to an optimal solution when the scene spatial context are stable. The overall framework is as follows:

1. **Initialization-step:** Initialize the VRN representation as introduced in Sec. 3.
2. **Iteration-step:** Search for meaningful segments for every image iteratively:
   (a) Use topic-level random walk on the VRN to calculate ranking scores of all the nodes in it;
   (b) Select meaningful segments and infer their class variables for every scene image;
   (c) Calculate a new VRN representation by updating the inter-class spatial context for every cluster and the class distribution associated to each node.

In this stage, the *context* edges should be recalculated according to the new inter-class context model. Therefore, we first update inter-class spatial context for each scene cluster according to the selected segments and their class labels. That is, we need update a lot of relative location maps by recalculating $M^c_{t2|t1}$ between any two classes of $t2$ and $t1$ for each cluster c. Note that only the images with the cluster label c are used to update $M^c_{(\cdot,\cdot)}$. Specifically, given a pixel p_1 of the class $t1$, $M^c_{t2|t1}(u, v)$ counts the ratio of pixels p_2 at the offset (u, v) to any p_1 of the class $t1$ belonging to $t2$. The map $M^c_{t2|t1}(u, v)$ is maintained in normalized image coordinates $(u, v) \in [-1, 1] \times [-1, 1]$. We also have $\sum_{t2} M^c_{t2|t1}(u, v) = 1$ so that $M^c_{t2|t1}$ represents a proper conditional probability distribution over the class $t1$. See details in [5].

Next, for a segment a_i in V of VRN, we update its class distribution by

$$p(t_i|a_i) = \frac{r(a_i, t_i)}{\sum_t r(a_i, t)} \tag{4}$$

Accordingly, we have a new class distribution for every segment to construct a new VRN as in Sec. 3.

7 Experiments and Discussions

7.1 Experimental Settings

We employ the normalized cuts algorithm [21] to generate the "soup of segments" of every image in a scene. Specifically, we vary the segment number from 3 to 12 and accordingly run the algorithm 10 times. The top 10 object proposals are also added into the soup using [3]. Thus totally 85 segment candidates are obtained for every scene image in our dataset. We then use the algorithm [19] to initialize the class distribution for each candidate segment. The appearance characteristic A of each segment includes two types of Bag-of-features histograms: Texton Histograms (TH), Color Histograms (CH), and a pyramid of HOG (pHOG). We generate these histograms in the same way as [12]. κ is a weight to balance the importance of context and appearance in topic-level random walk, which is fixed as $\kappa = 0.65$ because we find κ and τ are unsensitive to specific scenes as long as the scenes have stable context. Thereby, we get their respective optimal values by a simple validation set.

7.2 Datasets

We evaluate our method on three datasets: MSRC-v2 [22], LabelMe [20] and SUN [1]. MSRC-v2 has altogether 21-classes (591 images). We pick up scenes that have more than 3 classes for testing and thus form a subset (380 images) consisting of 13 classes. The images from LabelMe and SUN are collected from realistic daily life scenes. We choose six scenes: office (180 images) (LabelMe), movie theater (32 images) (LabelMe), bathroom (350 images) (LabelMe) and bedroom (307 images) (LabelMe), static street scene (400 images) (SUN) and outdoor (137 images) (SUN), with each scene category consisting of more than five object classes. We normalize all the images from LabelMe and SUN into 256×256 to avoid scale variations. Note that all the images in our dataset have pixel-level ground-truth labels.

7.3 Evaluation

Firstly, we adopt the segmentation accuracy to quantitatively evaluate our results. For each class, we denote the ground-truth segments and the obtained segments with G and C , respectively. Then the segmentation accuracy can be defined as the ratio of the intersection of G and C to the union of them, namely $\frac{G \cap C}{G \cup C}$. Besides, *purity* score [23] is also adopted to measure the coherency of class labeling of our method over the entire dataset. For each selected segment, its ground-truth class label is the one that the majority of pixels in it belong to. Note that different class labels may be potentially assigned to the selected segments with the same ground-truth class label in different images.

7.4 Scene Co-segmentation Results

Segmentation Accuracy on MSRC-v2. For each image, we search for meaningful scene segments from its 85 segment candidates. Eight examples of four scenes in our subset of MSRC-v2 are illustrated in Fig. 4. It can be seen that most classes in these images are well segmented.

Fig. 4. Image co-segmentation examples of MSRC-V2. Two images are shown for each scene. The right images are the union of the selected meaningful segments of the same class from the original images.

The segmentation accuracies for MSRC-v2 are listed in Tab. 2. Firstly, we compare our complete version with the modified versions to test the effectiveness of the spatial context (see (b) in Tab. 2) and the *part-of* relation (see (c)) on MSRC-v2. Additionally, an appearance-only approach for image co-segmentation without constructing the *inside the same image* edges of VRN is also performed for comparisons (see (d)). It can be seen that the complete version of the proposed approach performs best. Thereby, the *part-of* relation helps avoid over-segmenting scene elements into smaller parts. Moreover, the spatial context and the *part-of* relations can supplement with each other to improve the performance.

We further compare our approach with the baseline algorithm [19], the recent unsupervised object discovery method [12] and another two state-of-the-art multi-class co-segmentation approaches Jour [7] and Kim [10]. Although the baseline [19] and [12] aim at category discovery, they also output segments of each category. Thus comparisons are available using their public codes. Note that we do not compare with [12] directly due to their priors of known scene elements. We adopt their version without object-graph. Similarly, we use public codes of [7] and [10], and then adjust parameters to get their best results. We can see our method performs best in 6/13 classes and obtains competing results over the others. The main reason is that most images consisting the rest 7 classes have few objects and large inter-class variability. Thus the methods based on only appearance is sufficient to discriminate them. Note that [10] performs relatively bad on MSRC-v2 due to their strong assumption for multi-class co-segmentation. Thereby, the results validate that the spatial context and *part-of* relation play a critical role in selecting meaningful segments.

Segmentation Accuracy on LabelMe and SUN. One example image and its segmentation results of every scene in LabelMe and SUN are shown in Fig. 5.

Table 2. Accuracy comparisons on MSRC-v2

Class	Propose	(b)Cont	(c)Part	(d)Appr	Russ[19]	Lee[12]	Jour[7]	Kim[10]
car	0.51	0.45	0.42	0.40	0.31	0.38	**0.57**	0.44
sky	**0.81**	0.75	0.79	0.73	0.67	0.75	0.80	0.52
Tree	0.57	0.51	0.54	0.47	0.57	0.48	**0.61**	0.49
Grass	0.56	0.56	0.55	0.51	0.49	0.53	**0.57**	0.50
Building	**0.63**	0.54	0.56	0.50	0.45	0.49	0.51	0.51
House	**0.67**	0.55	0.56	0.50	0.54	0.57	0.52	0.44
Road	**0.61**	0.59	0.58	0.57	0.41	0.44	0.60	0.51
Cow	0.53	0.46	0.51	0.51	0.40	**0.54**	**0.54**	0.49
Plane	**0.49**	0.47	0.42	0.40	0.38	0.44	0.45	0.31
Sheep	0.62	0.55	0.59	0.60	0.47	0.63	0.66	**0.68**
Bird	0.46	0.44	0.45	0.41	0.34	0.40	**0.47**	**0.47**
Dog	0.42	0.37	0.38	0.35	0.39	0.35	0.41	**0.47**
Boat	**0.38**	0.43	0.40	0.39	0.38	0.32	**0.38**	0.34

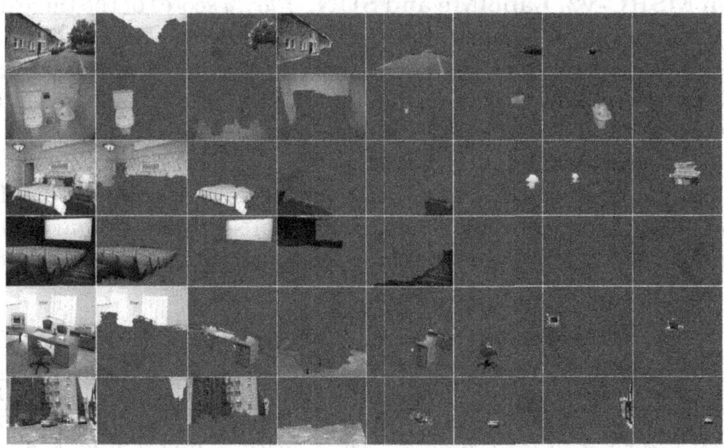

Fig. 5. Scene image co-segmentation examples on LabelMe and SUN. From top to bottom: Outdoor, Bathroom, Bedroom, Movie Theater, Static Office and Static Street. The first column represents an example image, while the rest columns are the results after co-segmentation. The selected segments are ranked in a decreasing order by their overall importance scores from left to right. The blue subgraphs at the tail of each row are only for alignment.

Although there are many object classes in these images, our method can well discriminate them and successfully select meaningful segments.

For the scene images from LabelMe and SUN, we average the segmentation accuracy of all the classes in each scene because of the large amounts of classes in them. The results are illustrated in Tab. 7.4. We find the average accuracy of MSRC-v2 is higher than those of LabelMe and SUN. This is due to the fact that most of the scenes in MSRC-v2 have fewer categories and large inter-class variability. From the comparison results, we can see our methods perform

Table 3. Accuracy comparisons on LabelMe and SUN

Scene	Propose	(b)Cont	(c)Part	(d)Appr	Russ[19]	Lee[12]	Jour[7]	Kim[10]
Office	**0.35**	0.29	0.22	0.20	0.25	0.30	0.29	0.24
Theater	**0.44**	0.40	0.34	0.29	0.31	0.34	0.35	0.31
Bathroom	**0.45**	0.39	0.38	0.39	0.35	0.32	0.33	0.39
Bedroom	**0.39**	0.32	0.30	0.25	0.30	0.29	0.30	0.38
Street	**0.52**	0.42	0.40	0.39	0.39	0.45	0.41	0.40
Indoor	**0.44**	0.35	0.32	0.30	0.36	0.30	0.37	0.33

overwhelmingly better that other methods. It follows our intuition that there exists stable scene context in each scene and they can help much to discriminate different classes. To conclude, our method succeeds in combining appearance, *part of* relation and the scene context to select meaningful segments.

Purity on MSRC-v2, LabelMe and SUN. *Purity* scores of the three datasets are illustrated in Tab. 4. We find that our method succeeds in assigning consistent class labels to each scene element. Averagely, the *purity* scores on LabelMe and SUN are lower than that on MSRC-v2 due to large intra-class variability. Since Jourlin [7]and Kim [10] perform pixel labeling, we calculate their *purity* scores at pixel-level. Overall, it is consistent with segmentation accuracy results and thus our method has advantages relatively over the three datasets. To conclude, our method can not only select meaningful segments for any image but also assign consistent class labels to these segments of the same category.

Table 4. Purity on MSRC-v2, LabelMe and SUN

Dataset	Propose	(b)Cont	(c)Part	(d)Appr	Russ[19]	Lee[12]	Jour[7]	Kim[10]
MSRC-v2	0.79	0.63	0.64	0.50	0.51	0.77	**0.80**	0.77
LabelMe	**0.52**	0.45	0.40	0.28	0.34	0.46	0.46	0.41
SUN	**0.58**	0.44	0.45	0.40	0.37	0.47	0.45	0.47

7.5 Impacts of Class Number

The class number T in our aforementioned experiments is fixed to achieve the best performance. In this section, we evaluate the influence of different T against *purity*. From the results on three datasets (the front two images in Fig. 6), we can see that the performance reaches the best when restricting the class number near 1.4× *Number of scene element categories.*

7.6 Impacts of the Sparsity Measurement of VRN

The sparsity of the VRN is controlled by K when constructing *across images* edges. Generally, a large K can cause the complexity of topic-level random

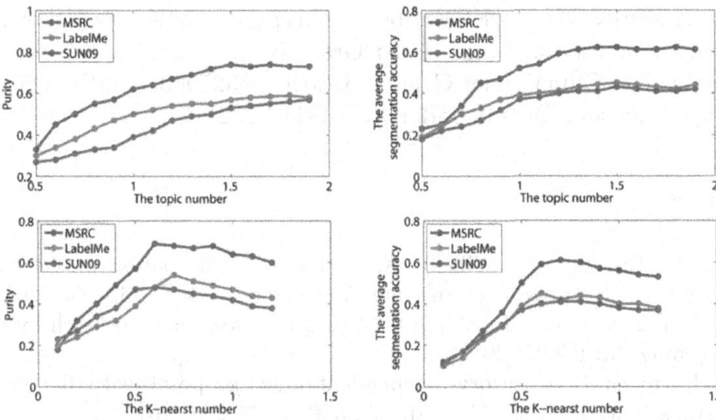

Fig. 6. The first two graphs show the performances as the class number varies, while the last two graphs correspond to the sparsity variations of VRN. In the temporary context, the class number and K-nearest number of the horizontal axis is a percentage to the total amount of scene element classes and scene image number, respectively.

walk, while a small K is insufficient to find enough matches during image co-segmentation. The last two images of Fig. 6 show that the range [0.6, 0.8] is the best choice. Moreover, too many matches can cause a negative impact. The main reason is that too many extra intra-class votes will mislead topic-level random walk to derive error importance scores.

7.7 Running Time

We implement our entire algorithm by Matlab and run on our machine with Intel i3-2130 CPU@ 3.40GHz. When "soups of segments" are available, the construction of VRN and the selection of meaningful segments are relatively quick. Without any optimization of codes, it takes about 10 mins to construct the overall VRN and 2 mins to select meaningful segments for each image. The overall co-segmentation requires 44 min till convergence for 400 images comprising totally 34000 segments. Compared to pixel-label methods, it is a valuable step that benefits from our introduction of topic level random walk.

8 Conclusion

In this paper, we present a novel *visual relation network* to model the relationship between scene segment candidates and perform topic-level random walk on the network to exploit scene co-segmentation. The experiments on different datasets show the effectiveness of our method. However, if unfortunately most of the candidate segments are "garbage" ones, the accuracy will be according decreased during image co-segmentation. Potentially it can be avoided by enriching "soup of segments". Our further work is to improve the accuracy of our unsupervised scene image co-segmentation by including more class-level context cues.

Acknowledgment. The work described in this paper was supported by the Natural Science Foundation of China under Grant No. 61272218 and No. 61321491, the 973 Program of China under Grant No. 2010CB327903, and the Program for New Century Excellent Talents under NCET-11-0232.

References

1. Choi, M.J., Torralba, A., Willsky, A.S.: A tree-based context model for object recognition. IEEE Trans. Pattern Anal. Mach. Intell. 34(2), 240–252 (2012)
2. Dai, J., Wu, Y.N., Zhou, J., Zhu, S.C.: Cosegmentation and cosketch by unsupervised learning. In: ICCV (2013)
3. Endres, I., Hoiem, D.: Category-independent object proposals with diverse ranking. IEEE Trans. Pattern Anal. Mach. Intell. 36(2), 222–234 (2014)
4. Faktor, A., Irani, M.: Co-segmentation by composition. In: ICCV (2013)
5. Gould, S., Rodgers, J., Cohen, D., Elidan, G., Koller, D.: Multi-class segmentation with relative location prior. International Journal of Computer Vision 80(3), 300–316 (2008)
6. Hochbaum, D.S., Singh, V.: An efficient algorithm for co-segmentation. In: ICCV, pp. 269–276 (2009)
7. Joulin, A., Bach, F., Ponce, J.: Multi-class cosegmentation. In: CVPR, pp. 542–549 (2012)
8. Joulin, A., Bach, F.R., Ponce, J.: Discriminative clustering for image co-segmentation. In: CVPR, pp. 1943–1950 (2010)
9. Kim, G., Faloutsos, C., Hebert, M.: Unsupervised modeling of object categories using link analysis techniques. In: CVPR (2008)
10. Kim, G., Xing, E.P.: On multiple foreground cosegmentation. In: CVPR, pp. 837–844 (2012)
11. Kowdle, A., Sinha, S.N., Szeliski, R.: Multiple view object cosegmentation using appearance and stereo cues. In: Fitzgibbon, A., Lazebnik, S., Perona, P., Sato, Y., Schmid, C. (eds.) ECCV 2012, Part V. LNCS, vol. 7576, pp. 789–803. Springer, Heidelberg (2012)
12. Lee, Y.J., Grauman, K.: Object-graphs for context-aware visual category discovery. IEEE Trans. Pattern Anal. Mach. Intell. 34(2), 346–358 (2012)
13. Ma, T., Latecki, L.J.: Graph transduction learning with connectivity constraints with application to multiple foreground cosegmentation. In: CVPR, pp. 1955–1962 (2013)
14. Mukherjee, L., Singh, V., Peng, J.: Scale invariant cosegmentation for image groups. In: CVPR, pp. 1881–1888 (2011)
15. Oliva, A., Torralba, A.: Modeling the shape of the scene: A holistic representation of the spatial envelope. International Journal of Computer Vision 42(3), 145–175 (2001)
16. Rother, C., Minka, T.P., Blake, A., Kolmogorov, V.: Cosegmentation of image pairs by histogram matching - incorporating a global constraint into mrfs. In: CVPR (1), pp. 993–1000 (2006)
17. Rubinstein, M., Joulin, A., Kopf, J., Liu, C.: Unsupervised joint object discovery and segmentation in internet images. In: CVPR, pp. 1939–1946 (2013)
18. Rubio, J.C., Serrat, J., López, A.M., Paragios, N.: Unsupervised co-segmentation through region matching. In: CVPR, pp. 749–756 (2012)

19. Russell, B.C., Freeman, W.T., Efros, A.A., Sivic, J., Zisserman, A.: Using multiple segmentations to discover objects and their extent in image collections. In: CVPR (2), pp. 1605–1614 (2006)
20. Russell, B.C., Torralba, A., Murphy, K.P., Freeman, W.T.: Labelme: A database and web-based tool for image annotation. International Journal of Computer Vision 77(1-3), 157–173 (2008)
21. Shi, J., Malik, J.: Normalized cuts and image segmentation. IEEE Trans. Pattern Anal. Mach. Intell. 22(8), 888–905 (2000)
22. Shotton, J., Winn, J.M., Rother, C., Criminisi, A.: *TextonBoost*: Joint appearance, shape and context modeling for multi-class object recognition and segmentation. In: Leonardis, A., Bischof, H., Pinz, A. (eds.) ECCV 2006, Part I. LNCS, vol. 3951, pp. 1–15. Springer, Heidelberg (2006)
23. Tan, P.N., Steinbach, M., Kumar, V.: Introduction to Data Mining. Addison-Wesley (2005)
24. Vicente, S., Rother, C., Kolmogorov, V.: Object cosegmentation. In: CVPR, pp. 2217–2224 (2011)
25. Wang, F., Huang, Q., Guibas, L.J.: Image co-segmentation via consistent functional maps. In: ICCV (2013)
26. Yang, Z., Tang, J., Zhang, J., Li, J., Gao, B.: Topic-level random walk through probabilistic model. In: Li, Q., Feng, L., Pei, J., Wang, S.X., Zhou, X., Zhu, Q.-M. (eds.) APWeb/WAIM 2009. LNCS, vol. 5446, pp. 162–173. Springer, Heidelberg (2009)

Surface Matching and Registration by Landmark Curve-Driven Canonical Quasiconformal Mapping

Wei Zeng[1] and Yi-Jun Yang[2]

[1] Florida International University, USA
[2] Shandong University, China

Abstract. This work presents a novel surface matching and registration method based on the landmark curve-driven canonical surface quasiconformal mapping, where an open genus zero surface decorated with landmark curves is mapped to a canonical domain with horizontal or vertical straight segments and the local shapes are preserved as much as possible. The key idea of the canonical mapping is to minimize the harmonic energy with the landmark curve straightening constraints and generate a quasi-holomorphic 1-form which is zero in one parameter along landmark and results in a quasiconformal mapping. The mapping exists and is unique and intrinsic to surface and landmark geometry. The novel shape representation provides a conformal invariant shape signature. We use it as Teichmüller coordinates to construct a subspace of the conventional Teichmüller space which considers geometry feature details and therefore increases the discriminative ability for matching. *Furthermore*, we present a novel and efficient registration method for surfaces with landmark curve constraints by computing an optimal mapping over the canonical domains with straight segments, where the curve constraints become linear forms. Due to the linearity of 1-form and harmonic map, the algorithms are easy to compute, efficient and practical. Experiments on human face and brain surfaces demonstrate the efficiency and efficacy and the potential for broader shape analysis applications.

1 Introduction

In computer vision, efficient shape representations for surfaces are highly desired to effectively deal with the shape analysis problems, such as shape indexing, matching, recognition, classification, and registration [6,8,9,16]. *Canonical* surface mappings such as conformal mappings provide shape representations with good properties, which are global and intrinsic and have the guarantee of existence and uniqueness.

In this work, we compute a special category of quasiconformal mappings for surfaces decorated landmark curves, whose angle distortion (quasiconformality) is implied by the landmark curve straightening constraints. Such mappings are *canonical* and *intrinsic*. They give a novel type of shape representation, which encodes the landmark curves' geometry and their relation to background surface context, and provides a global and intrinsic shape signature to classify surfaces in shape space. Specially, the shape signature is invariant if the surface encounters a conformal transformation (conformal invariant). Using this as the Teichmüller coordinates, we construct a landmark-driven Teichmüller space, which is a subspace of the conventional Teichmüller space, constrained by the

D. Fleet et al. (Eds.): ECCV 2014, Part I, LNCS 8689, pp. 710–724, 2014.
© Springer International Publishing Switzerland 2014

landmark curves. We then apply this canonical shape representation for matching and registration purposes for the case of *landmark curve decorated surfaces.*

1.1 Motivation

In practice, features on surface are preferred for surface matching and registration purposes. Such features usually include feature points, landmark curves, or regions of interest. For example, in medical applications, *anatomical* landmarks are used in computer-aided diagnosis and tumor or abnormality detection, such as sulci and gyri curves in brain mapping and facial symmetry curves in adolescent idiopathic scoliosis (AIS) and autism diagnosis. These landmarks may be manually labeled by doctors or automatically extracted. Conformal mapping is computed for *pure surfaces* without any interior constraints. Surfaces to be registered can be first mapped to 2D canonical domains conformally and then a mapping over them is built with feature constraints [7]. One strategy to handle landmark curve constraints is to slice surface open along them, and map them to boundaries of canonical domain by hyperbolic metric [18], but it is highly nonlinear.

In general, surface mapping will introduce angle and/or area distortions inevitably. If angle distortion is reduced to the limit (zero), then the mapping is *conformal* (C). If the angle distortion is bounded, then the mapping is *quasiconformal* (QC). Geometrically, conformal mapping maps infinitesimal circles to circles, while quasiconformal mapping maps infinitesimal ellipses to circles. The distortion from ellipse to circle is encoded into Beltrami coefficient, denoted as μ, which is complex-valued. A conformal mapping has zero μ everywhere. A quasiconformal mapping corresponds to a μ; and a μ determines a quasiconformal mapping uniquely up to a Möbius transformation.

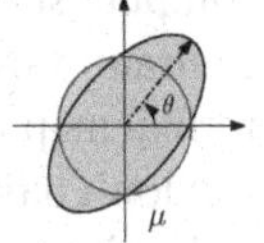

In practice, it is hard to prescribe μ for the desired mapping; however, it is easy to set target canonical shapes for landmark curves (straight lines or circular arcs/loops). Therefore, in this work, we use landmark straightening constraints to adapt surface conformal structure, such that the resulting quasiconformal mapping preserves the local shapes as much as possible (see Fig. 1). This mapping is intrinsic to surface and landmark geometry and reveals the characteristics of landmark curves.

This landmark-driven canonical form will pave a novel way for efficient and effective matching and registration of surfaces decorated with landmark curve cases. It provides a global shape signature by combining the conformal module of the background domain and the configuration of the canonically mapped landmark curves, and used to construct a Teichmüller space which considers more dimensional information (surface features) besides the surface itself. *For example*, conformal mapping cannot differentiate topological disk surfaces, because they share the same conformal structure. If we consider the landmark curve constraints, then the topological disks can be compared using the locations and sizes of the straightened landmark curves on the canonical domain. *Moreover*, the canonical quasiconformal mapping provides an approach to introducing the landmark curve constraints to registration process in a linear way, which is efficient. It deals with landmark curves with surface together, without changing topology, and is linear and easy to compute. It is fundamental and will foster a broad range of real applications with landmark curve constraints in both engineering and medicine.

(a) 3D surface

(b) conformal map

(c) canonical quasiconformal map

Fig. 1. Surface mapping for a human facial surface. The mouth landmark l_m is employed

1.2 Related Works

In the past decade, a lot of research [5,17] focuses on conformal mapping methods, including the least square conformal maps [11], differential forms [3], discrete curvature flows [2], and so on. According to surface uniformization theorem [4], any arbitrary surface can be conformally mapped to one of three canonical spaces, the unit sphere, the Euclidean plane or the hyperbolic disk, which has been carried out [7].

As a general mapping, quasiconformal mapping has been arousing more and more attention recently. The surface conformal mapping framework can be generalized to compute surface quasiconformal mappings by an auxiliary metric[22] or holomorphic Beltrami flow [12], with a given Beltrami coefficient μ. Recently, extremal quasiconformal map with a unique extremal μ becomes an active topic [19]. In our q.c. mapping, we don't have μ as input; μ is induced by the landmark constraints intrinsically.

Furthermore, feature landmarks, usually feature *points*, are applied to adapt the conformal mapping to be quasiconformal mapping such that the points are aligned to the prescribed targets and used for surface registration [22]. Sparse landmarks were also introduced in Kurtek et al.'s approach [10], which computes the registration and deformation process simultaneously for genus-0 surfaces. In this work, we focus on landmark *curves*, their mapping positions are not prescribed but computed automatically, thus the mapping is intrinsic to surface and landmark curve geometry. Recent work [18] treats landmark curves as surface boundaries based on nonlinear hyperbolic harmonic map.

Recently, Teichmüller space, which studies conformal equivalence class of surfaces, has been studied for shape indexing, dynamics analysis, and morphology analysis. Different Teichmüller coordinates were introduced. Classical geodesic length spectrum for high genus surfaces [8] and conformal module for genus zero surfaces with boundaries [23] describe surface conformal structure directly. Conformal welding signatures for 2D shapes by Sharon and Mumford [16,13] and for 3D shapes [24] describe correlation among non-intersecting *contour(s)* on surface through conformal structures of surface components surrounded by contours. All above are created on canonical conformal mappings. Instead, our proposed landmark-driven canonical quasiconformal mapping gives a novel Teichmüller coordinates, which describes correlation among *open curve(s)* and *non-trivial loop(s)* on surface through one single quasiconformal structure. Here, each landmark has no self-intersection; "horizontal" landmarks may only intersect "vertical" landmarks, and vice versa. Also, this signature is conformal invariant and intrinsic to surface and landmark geometry.

1.3 Approach Overview

In detail, for a genus zero surface with landmark curves, we map it to a canonical parameter domain $D(u,v)$ such that each landmark curve is mapped to a straight segment parallel to u-axis (horizontally) or v-axis (vertically), while the local shapes are preserved as much as possible. The computational strategy is to incorporate landmark straightening conditions into the computation of conformal mapping based on the holomorphic 1-form method. Mathematically, this problem is formulated as solving a sparse linear system with boundary conditions. According to Hodge decomposition theorem [4], any differential 1-form can be composed of a closed 1-form, an exact 1-form, and a harmonic 1-form. A conformal mapping can be generated by integrating a holomorphic 1-form of the surface. Correspondingly, a quasiconformal mapping can be induced by a harmonic 1-form, plus an exact 1-form which is also closed. We compute a special exact 1-form to constrain the final 1-form to be zero along landmark curves in u or v direction (vertically or horizontally), while minimizing the harmonic energy of the desired 1-form. The resulting 1-form is quasi-holomorphic and its integration generates a rectangular quasiconformal mapping. By an exponential map, the rectangular map can be mapped to a circle domain, where straight segments become concentric arcs. Figure 1 shows the mappings for a human facial surface (a small puncture at nose tip, which is mapped to the disk center), where the curved mouth landmark curve on conformal map is mapped to a circular (horizontal) arc on the canonical quasiconformal map. The variation from surface conformal structure is driven by landmark straightening constraints.

The result exists and is unique. Due to the linear nature of 1-form, the algorithm has linear time complexity, and is efficient and practical. The induced intrinsic shape signature, Teichüller coordinates, is then applied to construct a Teichmüller space surface matching. The L^2 norm between Teichmüller coordinates defines the similarity metric of two surfaces. Using the canonical mapping, the surfaces with landmark curve constraints can be registered over the canonical domains by linear harmonic map, where the landmark constraints between straight segments are converted to linear forms.

1.4 Contributions and Novelties

This work presents a *novel* method for surface matching and registration based on the *novel* canonical surface quasiconformal mapping for landmark curve decorated surfaces. To our best knowledge, this is the *first* work to conquer landmark curves on surface cases in the way of canonical quasiconformal map. The details are as follows:

1. To present a *novel* canonical surface quasiconformal mapping based on holomorphic 1-form, where the quasiconformality is driven by landmark curve straightening constraints intrinsically. Besides that, the mapping is coherent to surface uniformization theorem; surfaces are mapped to rectangle or circle domain and the local shapes are preserved as much as possible. We call this technique *Quasiconformal Straightening (QCS)*. The method is linear, stable and easy to compute.
2. To obtain a *novel* shape representation for landmark curve decorated surfaces, which generates an intrinsic, unique and global shape signature, called *QCS Signature*, as shape index for matching. We employ this conformal invariant as Teichmüller coordinates to construct a subspace of the conventional Teichmüller space,

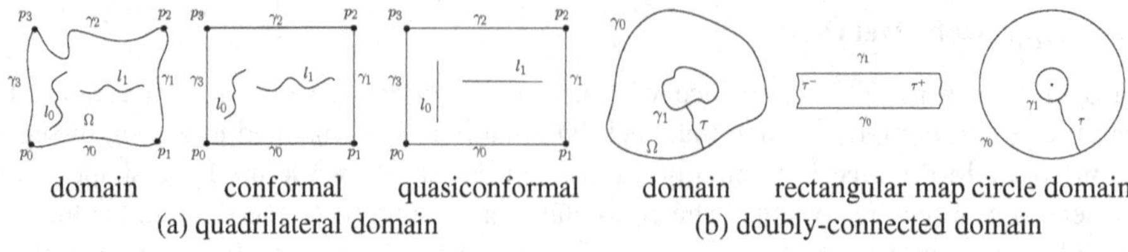

domain conformal quasiconformal domain rectangular map circle domain
(a) quadrilateral domain (b) doubly-connected domain

Fig. 2. Illustrations of canonical surface mappings

which is aware of geometry of landmark curves and increases the discriminative ability for real applications, such as to differentiate topological disks in Teichmüller space. The surface distance is given by the L^2 norm between the signatures.
3. To present a *novel* landmark curve constrained surface registration method using the proposed canonical quasiconformal mappings. The landmark curve decorated surfaces become straight segment decorated 2D domains; then an optimal mapping is built over them. By taking the linear advantage of straight segments, the curves can be easily aligned. Similarly, the method is linear, robust and efficient in practice.

Experiments on a diverse set of 3D human facial and brain surfaces were performed to demonstrate the efficiency and efficacy of the proposed framework for surface matching and registration. The proposed landmark-driven framework is fundamental and practical for general shape analysis purposes in various engineering and medical fields especially for those anatomical geometric data.

2 Theoretical Background

2.1 Quasiconformal Mapping

Consider a complex-valued function $\phi : \mathbb{C} \to \mathbb{C}$ mapping the z-plane to the w-plane, $z = x + iy$, $w = u + iv$. Suppose ϕ is differentiable. The *complex partial derivative* is defined as $\frac{\partial}{\partial z} := \frac{1}{2}(\frac{\partial}{\partial x} - i\frac{\partial}{\partial y})$, $\frac{\partial}{\partial \bar{z}} = \frac{1}{2}(\frac{\partial}{\partial x} + i\frac{\partial}{\partial y})$. The *Beltrami equation* for ϕ is given by

$$\frac{\partial \phi}{\partial \bar{z}} = \mu(z)\frac{\partial \phi}{\partial z}, \quad (1)$$

where μ is called the *Beltrami coefficient*, which is a complex-valued function. If $\mu = 0$, then ϕ satisfies the Cauchy-Riemann equations, $\frac{\partial u}{\partial x} = \frac{\partial v}{\partial y}$, $\frac{\partial u}{\partial y} = -\frac{\partial v}{\partial x}$, and is called a *holomorphic function*, which preserves angles. The resulting mapping is a *conformal mapping*. Otherwise, if $0 < \|\mu\|_\infty < 1$, where $\|\cdot\|_\infty$ denotes the L^∞ norm, then ϕ is a *quasiconformal mapping* with bounded angle distortion.

2.2 Holomorphic 1-form for Conformal Mapping

We use general genus zero surfaces with boundaries (embedded in $\mathbb{R}^2$ or $\mathbb{R}^3$) to illustrate the computational method of conformal mappings based on Hodge theory [4,7].

Quadrilateral Domain. For a *quadrilateral domain* Ω with four boundary segment components, $\partial\Omega = \gamma_0 + \gamma_1 + \gamma_2 + \gamma_3$, i.e., with four boundary corners, p_0, p_1, p_2, p_3, the holomorphic 1-form $\omega = (\tau_1, {}^*\tau_1)$ is computed by two exact harmonic 1-forms, $\tau_1 = df_1, \tau_2 = df_2$, such that

$$\begin{cases} \Delta f_1 = 0 \\ f_1|_{\gamma_3} = 0 \\ f_1|_{\gamma_1} = 1 \\ \frac{\partial f_1}{\partial \mathbf{n}}|_{\gamma_0 \cup \gamma_2} = 0 \end{cases} \text{ and } \begin{cases} \Delta f_2 = 0 \\ f_2|_{\gamma_0} = 0 \\ f_2|_{\gamma_2} = 1 \\ \frac{\partial f_2}{\partial \mathbf{n}}|_{\gamma_1 \cup \gamma_3} = 0 \end{cases}. \tag{2}$$

The conjugate ${}^*\tau_1 = c\tau_2$, where c is a scalar function. The integration of ω gives a rectangular conformal map, where γ_0, γ_2 are mapped to horizontal boundaries of the rectangle while γ_1, γ_3 are mapped to vertical ones (see Fig. 2(a)).

Doubly-Connected Domain. If a compact domain Ω has only two boundary components, $\partial\Omega = \gamma_0 - \gamma_1$, then it is called a *doubly-connected domain*. The whole domain is mapped to an annulus, where two boundaries are mapped to concentric circle boundaries. The holomorphic 1-form τ_1 or ${}^*\tau_1$ is orthogonal to both boundaries, $\tau_1 = \omega_1 + c^*\omega_1$, where ω_1 corresponds to γ_1, such that $\int_{\gamma_j} \omega_i = \delta_i^j$, where δ_i^j is the Kronecker symbol. The integration of such a holomorphic 1-form from base point p generates the rectangular map, where the domain is sliced open by a curve τ. Then by the exponential map, the circular map is generated (see Fig. 2(b)).

Simply-Connected Domain. Suppose Ω is a compact domain on the complex plane $\mathbb{C}$. If Ω has a single boundary component, then it is called a *simply-connected domain*. By a puncture at an interior point, the domain becomes a doubly-connected one and then the above computation can be applied. The whole domain is mapped to a unit disk. Such kind of mappings differ by Möbius transformations.

Multiply-Connected Domain. Suppose Ω has multiple boundary components, $\partial\Omega = \gamma_0 - \gamma_1 - \gamma_2 \cdots \gamma_n$, where γ_0 represents the exterior boundary component and $\gamma_i, i = 1..n$ represent the interior ones, then Ω is called a *multiply-connected domain*. It can be mapped to a unit disk with circular holes, called *circle domain*, where one boundary is mapped to the exterior unit circle, and others are mapped to inner circles. The computation is to iteratively perform the basic operation of mapping a doubly-connected domain to a canonical annulus based on Koebe's iteration method [7].

The existence and uniqueness of conformal and quasiconformal mappings for multiply-connected domains are guaranteed by the generalized Riemann mapping theorem [4] and the generalized measurable Riemann mapping theorem [1].

Theorem 1 (Generalized Measurable Riemann Mapping [1]). *Suppose $\Omega \subset \mathbb{C}$ is a multiply-connected domain. Suppose $\mu : \Omega \to \mathbb{C}$ is a measurable complex function, such that $\|\mu\|_\infty < 1$. There exists a quasiconformal mapping $\phi : \Omega \to D$ whose Beltrami coefficient is μ, where D is a circle domain. Such kind of quasiconformal mappings differ by Möbius transformations.*

2.3 Conformal Module

Let S be a topological surface and all the possible Riemannian metrics on S be $G = \{\mathbf{g}\}$. Two metrics $\mathbf{g}_1$, $\mathbf{g}_2$ are *conformally equivalent*, $\mathbf{g}_1 \sim \mathbf{g}_2$, if there exists a function $\lambda : S \to \mathbb{R}$, such that $\mathbf{g}_1 = e^{2\lambda}\mathbf{g}_2$.

All domains can be classified by conformal equivalence relation. Each class shares the same *conformal invariant*, called *conformal module*, which defines a unique and global shape signature. According to Reimann mapping theorem [4], every simply-connected domain is conformally equivalent to the open unit disk and such kind of mappings differ by Möbius transformations. Therefore,

Theorem 2. *All simply-connected domains are conformally equivalent.*

The conformal module for a rectangle domain is defined as the ratio of the height over the width. For a circle domain it is represented as the centers and radii of inner circles. By a Möbius normalization mapping one inner circle to be concentric, the topological annulus only requires 1 parameter in its conformal module. In general case, there are $n > 1$ inner circles, the conformal module requires $3n-3$ parameters. All conformal equivalence classes form a $3n-3$ Riemannian manifold, the so-called *Teichmüller space*. The conformal module can be treated as the *Teichmüller coordinates*.

3 Algorithm for Canonical Surface Quasiconformal Mapping

The main goal of our algorithm is to compute the canonical quasiconformal mapping with landmark straightening constraints for genus zero surfaces with boundaries. In practice, the surfaces are approximated by triangular meshes embedded in $\mathbb{R}^3$, denoted as $M = (V, E, F)$, where V, E, F are the sets of vertices, edges, and faces, respectively.

Assume the desire mapping is $f : (M, L) \to (D, \ell)$, surface mesh M is mapped to a planar parameter domain D, and D has the local coordinates (u, v). Here, we use the quadrilateral case for discussion. The computational pipeline is as follows:

Step 1: Prepare Landmark Curves. We use $L = \{l_k, k = 1..m\}$ to denote the set of m interior landmark curves on M. Assume $L = L^H \cup L^V$, where L^H, L^V are to be mapped to horizontal and vertical straight segments, respectively. Each landmark is represented as a chain of vertices, $l_k = [v_1, v_2, \ldots, v_{n_k}]$, where n_k is the number of the vertices on l_k.

Step 2: Compute Quasi-holomorphic 1-form. The quasi-holomorphic 1-form to be computed will be $\omega = \tau_1 + \sqrt{-1}{}^*\tau_1$, where $\tau_1 = df_1$, ${}^*\tau_1 = \lambda\tau_2$, and $\tau_2 = df_2$:
1. Compute the harmonic functions f_1, f_2: Combining the straightening constraint conditions into Eqn. (2), we have

$$\begin{cases} \Delta f_1 = 0 \\ f_1|_{\gamma_3} = 0 \\ f_1|_{\gamma_1} = 1 \\ \frac{\partial f_1}{\partial \mathbf{n}}|_{\gamma_0 \cup \gamma_2} = 0 \\ f_1|_{l_k^V} = s_k \end{cases} \text{and} \begin{cases} \Delta f_2 = 0 \\ f_2|_{\gamma_0} = 0 \\ f_2|_{\gamma_2} = 1 \\ \frac{\partial f_2}{\partial \mathbf{n}}|_{\gamma_1 \cup \gamma_3} = 0 \\ f_2|_{l_k^H} = t_k \end{cases}, \tag{3}$$

where $\mathbf{n}$ is the normal vector to the boundary, s_k, t_k are unknown variables, computed automatically for each landmark curve. Two types of straightening constraints are: 1)

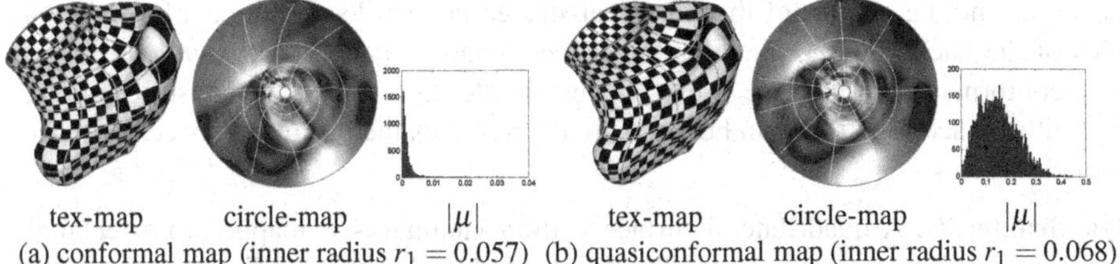

(a) conformal map (inner radius $r_1 = 0.057$) (b) quasiconformal map (inner radius $r_1 = 0.068$)

Fig. 3. Landmark-driven quasiconformal mapping for a doubly-connected domain. It contains four (4) horizontal landmarks (loops) and ten (10) vertical landmarks. Checker-board texture mappings and histograms of Beltrami coefficients (by $|\mu|$) demonstrate the quasiconformality.

Horizontal: for $l_k \in L^H$, $v(v_i) = s_k, i = 1 \dots n_k$; and 2) *Vertical*: $l_k \in L^V$, $u(v_i) = t_k, i = 1 \dots n_k$. The Laplace-Beltrami operator Δ is approximated by the cotangent weight w_{ij}, $\Delta f(v_i) = \sum_{[v_i,v_j] \in E} w_{ij}(f(v_j) - f(v_i))$. For edge $[v_i, v_j]$, suppose two adjacent faces are $[v_i, v_j, v_k]$ and $[v_j, v_i, v_l]$. Then its *weight* is defined as $w_{ij} = \cot\theta_k^{ij} + \cot\theta_l^{ij}$, $[v_i, v_j] \notin \partial M$; or $w_{ij} = \cot\theta_k^{ij}$, $[v_i, v_j] \in \partial M$, where θ_k^{ij} is the corner angle at v_k in $[v_i, v_j, v_k]$.
2. Compute harmonic 1-forms by gradient computation: $\tau_1 = \nabla f_1, \tau_2 = \nabla f_2$.
3. Compute conjugate 1-form of τ_1 *by Hodge star operator:* ${}^\star\tau_1 = \lambda \tau_2$ (λ is a scalar), by minimizing the energy $E(\lambda) = \sum_{[v_i,v_j,v_k] \in F} |\nabla f_2 - \lambda \mathbf{n} \times \nabla f_1|^2 A_{ijk}$, where A_{ijk} is the area of face $[v_i, v_j, v_k]$, and $\mathbf{n}$ is the normal vector to the face.
4. Compute $\omega = \tau_1 + \sqrt{-1}\,{}^\star\tau_1$.

The problem turns to minimizing the harmonic energy, $E(f) = \sum_{[v_i,v_j]} w_{ij}(f(v_j) - f(v_i))^2$, by considering the landmark constraints in Eqn. (3).

Step 3: Computing Quasiconformal Mapping. We generate the quasiconformal mapping by integrating the obtained quasi-holomorphic 1-form ω over M, $f(q) = \int_{\gamma(p,q) \in M} \omega$, $\forall q \in V$, where $\gamma(p,q)$ is an arbitrary path from the base vertex p to the current vertex q. On the planar domain, $f(p) = (0,0)$, $f(\gamma_i), f(l_k)$ are all straight lines.

The computational algorithms for other genus zero surface cases are similar. They share the same key component of minimizing harmonic energy with landmark straightening constraints. By the exponential map, the rectangular domain is converted to circle domain, where the straight lines are mapped to circular arcs. Figure 3 shows a doubly-connected case. The difference from the conformal map can be evaluated by the angle distortion of checker-board textures and the distributions of Beltrami coefficients (mean of $|\mu|$: 0.15 vs. 0.001). Figure 4 shows the examples for a human facial surface with multiple landmark curves. In theory, the solution exists and is unique [15]. The resulting mapping preserves local shapes as much as possible and is intrinsic to geometry of both surface and landmark curves. The algorithm solves sparse linear systems and have linear complexity. In practice, the conjugate gradient method is applied.

4 Algorithm for Surface Matching

The proposed quasiconformal mapping $\phi : (S, L) \to (D, \ell)$ offers an intrinsic canonical shape representation for surfaces decorated with landmark curves. We employ the positions and the lengths of the canonical-shaped landmarks and the conformal modules of the background domain as the shape signature, called *QCS signature*, which is a conformal invariant. We use it as Teichmüller coordinates to construct the Teichmüller space. The L^2 norm between signatures gives the distance between two decorated surfaces.

Quadrilaterals. A quadrilateral surface with m landmarks is mapped to a rectangle domain with horizontally or vertically straightened landmarks (see Fig. 4). Assume the bottom-left corner of the rectangle domain is set to be the origin $(0,0)$. Then the QCS signature is defined as

$$QCS(S) = \{\frac{x_j^H}{w}, \frac{y_j^H}{h}, \frac{d_j^H}{w}\} \bigcup \{\frac{x_k^V}{w}, \frac{y_k^V}{h}, \frac{d_k^V}{h}\} \bigcup \text{Mod}(D), \tag{4}$$

where h, w denote the height and the width of D, respectively, (x_j^H, y_j^H) represents the left endpoint of $\phi(l_j)$, $l_j \in L^H$, (x_k^V, y_k^V) represents the bottom endpoint of $\phi(l_k)$, $l_k \in L^V$, d_k denotes the length of the segment $\phi(l_k)$, $l_k \in L$, and Mod is the conformal module of D, h/w, as defined in Sect. 2. Then the Teichmüller space is $3m+1$ dimensional.

$(n+1)$**-Connected Domains.** General genus zero $(g=0)$ domains with $n+1$ boundaries and m landmarks are mapped to circle domains (normalized onto unit disk) with radial straight or concentric circular landmarks. Then the QCS signature is defined as

$$QCS(S) = \{r_j, \frac{\theta_j^1}{2\pi}, \frac{\theta_j^2}{2\pi}\} \bigcup \{r_k^1, r_k^2, \frac{\theta_k}{2\pi}\} \bigcup \text{Mod}(D), \tag{5}$$

where $(r_j, \theta_j^1, \theta_j^2)$ denotes the radius and argument angles of the concentric circular arc $\phi(l_j)$, $l_j \in L^H$; (r_k^1, r_k^2, θ_k) denotes the radii and the argument angle of the radial straight segment $\phi(l_k)$, $l_k \in L^V$, and Mod is the conformal module of circle domain D, including the center positions and radii of the inner circles, as defined in Sect. 2. Assume D is normalized by a Möbius transformation. We use $T_{0,n,m}$ to denote the Teichmüller space of open genus zero $(g=0)$ surfaces with n inner boundaries and m landmarks.

- For multiply-connected domains, $\dim T_{0,n>1,m>0} = 3m + (3n-3)$.
- For simply-connected domains, $\dim T_{0,n=0,m>0} = 3m-2$.
- For doubly-connected domains, $\dim T_{0,n=1,m>0} = (3m-1)+1 = 3m$.

For each open landmark curve with two endpoints on boundary in quadrilaterals or non-trivial landmark loop in connected domains, the total dimension decreases by 2.

5 Algorithm for Surface Registration

The main strategy is to map decorated surfaces to canonical planar domains with *canonically shaped* (*straight*) landmark curves using the proposed quasiconformal map and then convert surface registration problems to image registration problems, where the landmark curve constraints become *linear* constraints between images.

$$\begin{array}{ccc} (S_1,L_1) & \xrightarrow{f} & (S_2,L_2) \\ \phi_1 \downarrow & & \downarrow \phi_2 \\ (D_1,\ell_1) & \xrightarrow{h} & (D_2,\ell_2) \end{array}$$

Registration Framework. Suppose (S_k,L_k), $k=1,2$ are the *source* and *target* surfaces S_k decorated with landmark curves L_k, respectively. In order to compute the *registration* $f:(S_1,L_1)\rightarrow(S_2,L_2)$, we first map decorated surfaces to *decorated canonical domains*, $\phi_k:(S_k,L_k)\rightarrow(D_k,\ell_k)$, then construct the optimal mapping $h:(D_1,\ell_1)\rightarrow(D_2,\ell_2)$, such that straight line ℓ_1 is aligned with straight line ℓ_2 and the harmonic energy of the mapping is minimized. The registration is given by $f=\phi_2^{-1}\circ h\circ\phi_1$.

This novel quasiconformal map-based registration framework works for landmark *curve* constrained surfaces with general deformations, subsuming rigid motion, isometry, and conformal transformation. This framework can be generalized to more general surfaces and handle point-curve mixed constraints. In contrast, existing works using conformal map-based framework [22,21] mainly focus on registration of surfaces decorated with feature *point* constraints. They cannot introduce each landmark curve as a whole; accordingly, a heuristic alternative is to sample the curve to isolated points then apply the point-constrained registration method [14] .

Algorithm with Landmark Curve Constraints. The computation is based on the optimization of constrained harmonic energy to smooth out distortion as much as possible. We generate a harmonic map $h:(D_1,\ell_1)\rightarrow(D_2,\ell_2)$, $\nabla h=(h_1,h_2)$, to minimize the energy $E(h)=\int_{D_1}|\nabla\cdot\nabla h|^2dA$ with the Dirichlet and Neumann boundary conditions on both canonical domain boundaries and horizontal or vertical landmarks. Suppose D_k are rectangles, $\partial D_k=\gamma_0^k+\gamma_1^k+\gamma_2^k+\gamma_3^k$, where $(\gamma_i^1,\gamma_i^2), i=0..3$ denotes a pair of corresponding boundaries, and $L_k=L_k^H\bigcap L_k^V$. We use (l_1,l_2) and (p_1,p_2) to denote a pair of segments and endpoints to be aligned, respectively, and solve

$$\begin{cases} \Delta h_1=0 \\ h_1|_{\gamma_3^1}=\phi_2^u|_{\gamma_3^2}-\phi_1^u|_{\gamma_3^1} \\ h_1|_{\gamma_1^1}=\phi_2^u|_{\gamma_1^2}-\phi_1^u|_{\gamma_1^1} \\ \frac{\partial h_1}{\partial \mathbf{n}}|_{\gamma_0\cup\gamma_2}=0 \\ h_1|_{l_1^V}=\phi_2^u|_{l_2^V}-\phi_1^u|_{l_1^V} \\ h_1|_{p_1^H}=\phi_2^u|_{p_2^H}-\phi_1^u|_{p_1^H} \end{cases} \quad\text{and}\quad \begin{cases} \Delta h_2=0 \\ h_2|_{\gamma_0^1}=\phi_2^v|_{\gamma_0^2}-\phi_1^v|_{\gamma_0^1} \\ h_2|_{\gamma_2^1}=\phi_2^v|_{\gamma_2^2}-\phi_1^v|_{\gamma_2^1} \\ \frac{\partial h_2}{\partial \mathbf{n}}|_{\gamma_1\cup\gamma_3}=0 \\ h_2|_{l_1^H}=\phi_2^v|_{l_2^H}-\phi_1^v|_{l_1^H} \\ h_2|_{p_1^V}=\phi_2^v|_{p_2^V}-\phi_1^v|_{p_1^V} \end{cases}. \quad (6)$$

Then $h(p)=p+\nabla h(p), p\in D_1$. The desired mapping $f=\phi_2^{-1}\circ h\circ\phi_1$.

The registration accuracy can be evaluated by an energy form $E(f)=\int_{p\in S_1}(H(p)-H(f(p)))^2+(K(p)-K(f(p)))^2+(\lambda(p)-\lambda(f(p)))^2$, where H,K,λ denote the mean curvature, the Gauss curvature, and the conformal factor, respectively.

6 Experimental Results

The proposed landmark-driven canonical quasiconformal mapping provides a fundamental approach to surface matching and registration, and have broad applications in vision, graphics, and medical imaging. Here, we develop experiments on human facial and brain surfaces to demonstrate the efficiency and efficacy.

Experimental Settings. We consider a set of anatomical facial landmark curves: 1) the curve along eyebrows l_b; 2) the geodesic curve between inner eye corners l_e; 3)

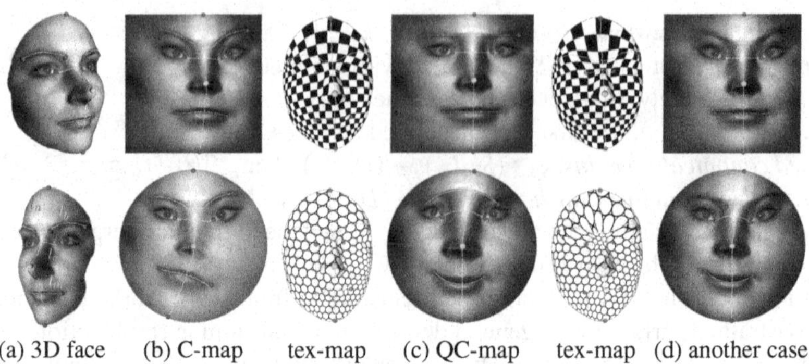

Fig. 4. Landmark-driven canonical quasiconformal mappings for a human facial surface

the geodesic curve between mouth corners l_m; and 4) the symmetry axis curve $l_n = l_{n_1} \cup l_{n_2}$, split into two parts by nose tip, as shown in Fig. 4(a). In canonical mapping, we set $L^H = \{l_b, l_e, l_m\}$ and $L^V = \{l_n\}$ or $\{l_{n_1}, l_{n_2}\}$. For brain surfaces, we consider the anatomical sulci and gyri curves. The algorithms are tested on a desktop with 3.7GHz CPU and 16GB RAM. The whole pipeline is automatic. For mapping a facial surface with 120k triangles and a brain surface with 20k triangles, the averaged running times are 10 seconds and 3 seconds, respectively. The registration process including two such q.c. maps and another mapping over 2D domains totally costs 3 times the mapping time.

6.1 Feature-Aware Shape Signature

Figure 4 shows the mapping results for a 3D facial surface decorated with multiple landmark curves. *Upper row*: Surface with prescribed four boundary corners, a quadrilateral, is mapped to a rectangle; *Bottom row*: Surface is mapped to a unit disk. *Column*: (a) 3D views of the landmark curve decorated surface; (b) conformal maps; (c) canonical quasiconformal maps with landmark straightening constraints; (d) quasiconformal maps with a constraint change on eyebrow landmark. The angle distortions are illustrated by the texture mapping results. Table 1 gives the numerical results for QCS signatures of the two cases in (c), computed by Eqn. (4).

6.2 Content-Based Surface Matching

As stated in Theorem 2, conformal mappings keep the same structure for the topological disk surfaces and cannot differentiate them in Teichmüller space. The QCS signature is aware of feature details and has the discriminative ability. In our experiments, we employ the QCS signature for shape matching on two categories of human facial scans which have been successfully tested: 1) 5 human facial expression sequences from the same subject (each has 400 frames) (see Fig. 5), and 2) human facial surfaces from different subjects (BU-3DFE database [20], 100 subjects with various expressions) (see Fig. 6). Table 1 gives the QCS signatures computed by Eqn. (5).

In Fig. 5, the expression change is mainly around mouth area, so we introduce one landmark l_m to study the dynamics to conquer the conformal equivalence of topological

Table 1. Shape signatures

Models	Signatures
Fig. 4(c) upper-bottom ($l_b;l_e;l_m;l_n;Mod$)	(0.260,0.849,0.638; 0.433,0.728,0.278; 0.371,0.285,0.398; 0.576; 0.954) (0.373,0.135,0.363; 0.238,0.141,0.346; 0.254,0.617,0.849; 0.475)
Fig. 5 left-right (l_m)	(0.508,0.214), (0.519,0.266), (0.492,0.294), (0.527,0.282)
Fig. 6 left-right ($l_m;l_e$)	(0.398,0.234;0.334,0.149,0.356), (0.415,0.223;0.344,0.145,0.36), (0.384,0.213;0.355,0.143,0.365), (0.426,0.183;0.307,0.147,0.376), (0.427,0.197;0.384,0.14,0.359), (0.463,0.236;0.366,0.156,0.343)

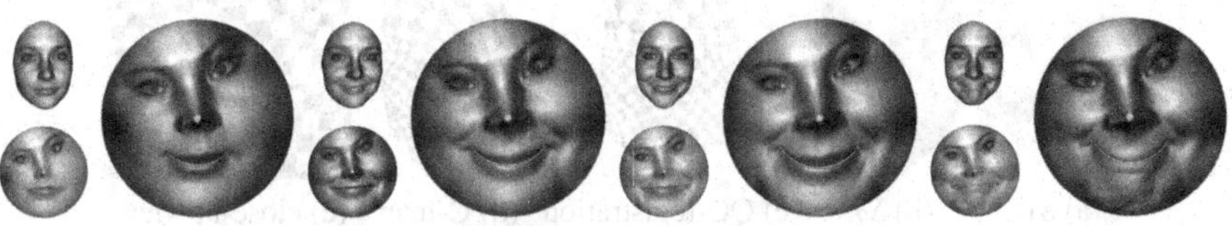

Fig. 5. Surface matching for a deforming facial expression sequence from the same subject. The mouth landmark l_m is employed. The bottom-left small disk shows the conformal mapping result.

disk faces. The L^2 norm geometric distances (similarity of expressions) to the leftmost expression $d(S_k,S_0) = 0, 0.053, 0.071, 0.082, k = 0..3$. In Fig. 6, we use QCS signatures to differentiate the faces from different subjects. The geometric distances (similarity of faces) to the leftmost $d(S_k,S_0) = 0, 0.023, 0.035, 0.067, 0.069, 0.074, k = 0..5$.

The experimental results show that the QCS signature is promising for large-scale content-based shape retrieval applications for 2D images and 3D objects, such as face recognition, brain surface classification, and general geometric search engine.

6.3 Landmark-Curve Constrained Surface Registration

Our registration algorithm has been successfully tested on two categories of 3D nonrigid surfaces: 1) human facial surfaces with different expressions from the same subject (see Fig. 7), and neutral faces from different subjects (see Fig. 8), and 2) human brain surfaces from control group and patient group (see Fig. 9). Each pair has big geometry variance and the deformation is quasiconformal. The geometric registration accuracy is evaluated by the energy form $E(f)$ in Sect. 5. $E(f) = 0.03$ for Fig. 7, $E(f) = 0.05$ for Fig.8, and $E(f) = 0.08$ for Fig. 9. The registration effects can also be visually checked by the consistent texture mapping results.

Our proposed method takes the curve constraints as linear constraints. For better understanding, we performed a comparison test, as shown in Fig. 8(b), where 9 point constraints are sampled to replace curve constraint. The result is not smooth, significantly different from our result (see the close-up view in (b)). The accuracy can be improved by dense sampling, but this will generate more cost. All the results demonstrate the advantages of our method in terms of the accuracy, efficiency and practicality.

6.4 Performance Discussion

Efficiency, Robustness and Generality: The 1-form method solves positive definite sparse linear systems, therefore has linear time complexity. The solution exists and is

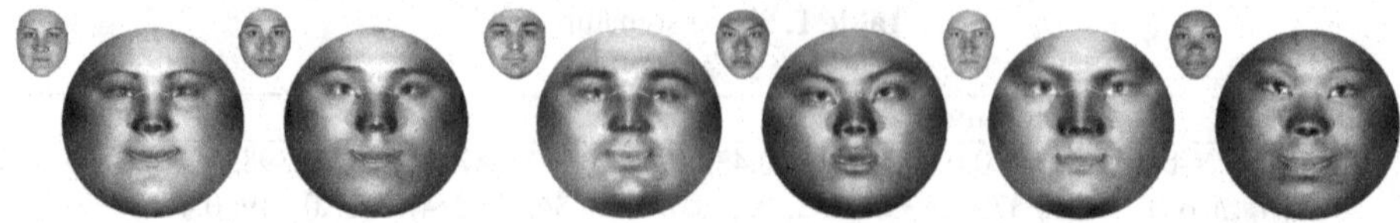

Fig. 6. Surface matching by landmark-driven quasiconformal mappings for neutral facial surfaces from different subjects. The inner eye corner and mouth landmarks l_e, l_m are employed.

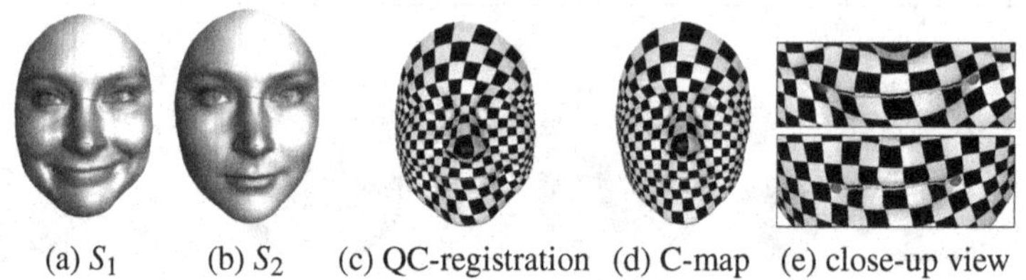

(a) S_1 (b) S_2 (c) QC-registration (d) C-map (e) close-up view

Fig. 7. Facial surface registration between different expressions from the same subject

unique in theory [15]. The 1-form method is stable and robust to handle small geometric and topological noises or variations under different modalities (resolution, quality, smoothness, boundary noise, small holes or handles) and multiple and complicated decorative landmark curves (open and closed); it is easy to implement and fast to compute. The proposed QCS technique can be incorporated into the 1-form computation for general topological surfaces [7]. *In addition*, due to the generality of quasiconformal map, the proposed registration method is general to handle any types and intensities of deformations, including small or significantly large rigid motions, isometries, conformal transformations, and quasiconformal deformations.

Novelty, Comparison and Practicability: To our best knowledge, this is the *first* work to compute landmark curve driven canonical quasiconformal map, and use the canonical shape representation for landmark curve-decorated surface matching and registration.

Compared with conformal maps of pure surfaces, the generated intrinsic canonical quasiconformal map studies the nature of curves in surface and the influence to conformal structure, and provides the feature-aware shape signature and global representation. The conformal welding signature [16,13] needs to divide the whole surface to multiple components by closed contours; it cannot deal with open curves. Different from other conformal invariant shape signatures of pure surfaces such as conformal modules [23,8], the QCS signature encodes landmark geometry, therefore is more capable to represent a shape both globally and locally; and especially it can be used to differentiate the topological disk surfaces.

Most existing conformal map based registration methods can only handle point constraints, or treat the landmark curves as isolated points in the mapping process [23,14]. The hyperbolic harmonic map method [18] slices the landmark curves open to be boundaries and uses the hyperbolic metric; the computation is highly nonlinear. Our proposed method has significant difference: it provides linear constraints between straightened curves and has practical advantage due to linearity of 1-forms. Our method deals with surface and landmark curves as a whole without changing topology. Kurtek

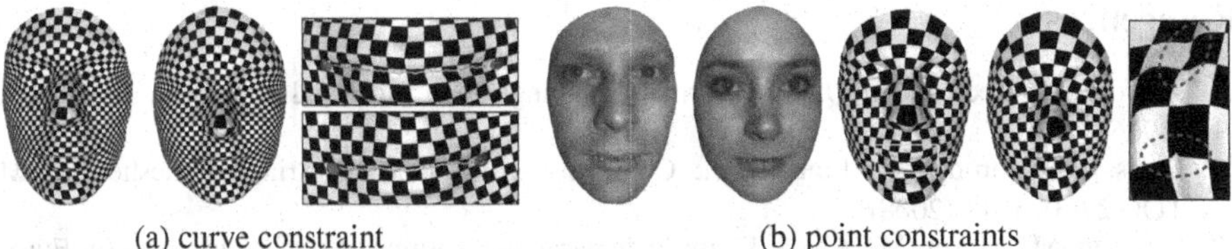

(a) curve constraint (b) point constraints

Fig. 8. Facial surface registration for two subjects. (a) lip landmark curve constraint is employed; (b) curve constraint is sampled as point constraints.

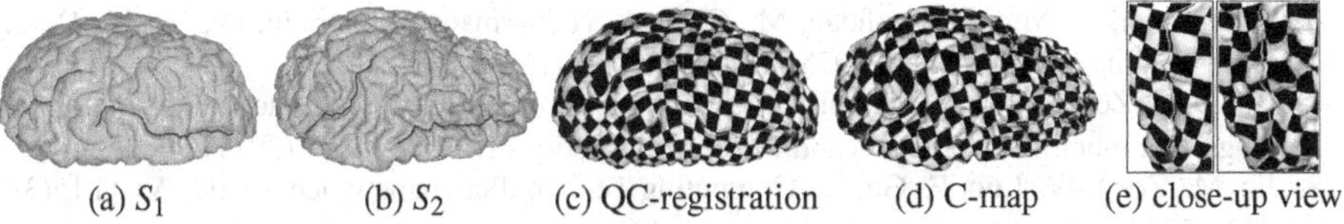

(a) S_1 (b) S_2 (c) QC-registration (d) C-map (e) close-up view

Fig. 9. Brain surface registration with convoluted landmark curves

et al.'s approach [10] handles sparse feature points; given two isometric surfaces with different embeddings, our shape metric gives 0, and theirs doesn't.

Flexibility and Potential Impacts: The user can freely select landmark curves and design their straightening styles according to the application needs. In order to arrange the landmarks properly and avoid large distortions, we can first observe their shapes on conformal mapping domain, for example in Fig. 4(b), where the styles can be automatically extracted by comparing the averaged slope of the curve with the u and v-axis. It has potential for artwork design and large-scale shape retrieval in industry.

7 Conclusion

We present the novel surface matching and registration method based on the intrinsic canonical surface quasiconformal mapping, which maps the landmark curves to be the horizontal or vertical straight lines on canonical 2D domain and preserves the local shapes as much as possible. The mapping is unique and intrinsic to surface and landmark curve geometry. It gives the novel conformal invariant shape signature to construct the feature-aware Teichmüller space for surface matching. It is easy to deal with surface registration with straightened landmark curve constraints. All the algorithms are based on 1-form and have linear time complexity and are efficient and practical. Experiments on matching and registering facial and brain scans demonstrate the efficiency and efficacy, which is promising for broader computer vision applications where landmark curves are naturally associated. In future, we will explore more under the proposed framework.

Acknowledgment. This work is partially supported by NSFC-61202146 and the Outstanding Young Scientist Research Award Fund of Shandong Province of China (BS2012DX014).

References

1. Ahlfors, L.: Lectures in Quasiconformal Mappings. Van Nostrand Reinhold, New York (1966)
2. Boris, S., Schröder, P., Pinkall, U.: Conformal equivalence of triangle meshes. ACM TOG 27(3), 1–11 (2008)
3. Desbrun, M., Meyer, M., Alliez, P.: Intrinsic parameterizations of surface meshes. In: Eurographics 2002, pp. 209–218 (2002)
4. Farkas, H.M., Kra, I.: Riemann Surfaces (Graduate Texts in Mathematics). Springer (1991)
5. Floater, M.S., Hormann, K.: Surface parameterization: a tutorial and survey, pp. 157–186. Springer
6. Funkhouser, T., Min, P., Kazhdan, M., Chen, J., Halderman, A., Dobkin, D., Jacobs, D.: A search engine for 3D models. ACM TOG 22(1), 83–105 (2003)
7. Gu, D.X., Zeng, W., Luo, F., Yau, S.T.: Numerical computation of surface conformal mappings. Computational Methods and Functional Theory 11(2), 747–787 (2011)
8. Jin, M., Zeng, W., Luo, F., Gu, X.: Computing Teichmüller shape space. IEEE TVCG 15(3), 504–517 (2009)
9. Kazhdan, M., Funkhouser, T., Rusinkiewicz, S.: Rotation invariant spherical harmonic representation of 3D shape descriptors. In: SGP 2003, pp. 156–164 (2003)
10. Kurtek, S., Srivastava, A., Klassen, E., Laga, H.: Landmark-guided elastic shape analysis of spherically-parameterized surfaces. Computer Graphics Forum (Proceedings of Eurographics 2013) 32(2), 429–438 (2013)
11. Levy, B., Petitjean, S., Ray, N., Maillot, J.: Least squares conformal maps for automatic texture atlas generation. In: SIGGRAPH 2002 (2002)
12. Lui, L.M., Wong, T.W., Zeng, W., Gu, X., Thompson, P.M., Chan, T.F., Yau, S.T.: Optimization of surface registrations using Beltrami holomorphic flow. J. of Scie. Comp. 50(3), 557–585 (2012)
13. Lui, L.M., Zeng, W., Yau, S.T., Gu, X.: Shape analysis of planar multiply-connected objects using conformal welding. IEEE TPAMI 36(7), 1384–1401 (2014)
14. Lui, L., Wang, Y., Chan, T., Thompson, P.: Automatic landmark tracking and its application to the optimization of brain conformal mapping, pp. II:1784–II:1792 (2006)
15. Schoen, R., Yau, S.T.: Lecture on Harmonic Maps, vol. 2. International Press Incorporated, Boston (1997)
16. Sharon, E., Mumford, D.: 2D-shape analysis using conformal mapping. IJCV 70, 55–75 (2006)
17. Sheffer, A., Praun, E., Rose, K.: Mesh parameterization methods and their applications, vol. 2 (2006)
18. Shi, R., Zeng, W., Su, Z., Damasio, H., Lu, Z., Wang, Y., Yau, S.T., Gu, X.: Hyperbolic harmonic mapping for constrained brain surface registration. In: IEEE CVPR 2013 (2013)
19. Weber, O., Myles, A., Zorin, D.: Computing extremal quasiconformal maps. Comp. Graph. Forum 31(5), 1679–1689 (2012)
20. Yin, L., Wei, X., Sun, Y., Wang, J., Rosato, M.J.: A 3D facial expression database for facial behavior research. In: IEEE FG 2006, pp. 211–216 (2006)
21. Zeng, W., Zeng, Y., Wang, Y., Yin, X., Gu, X., Samaras, D.: 3D non-rigid surface matching and registration based on holomorphic differentials. In: Forsyth, D., Torr, P., Zisserman, A. (eds.) ECCV 2008, Part III. LNCS, vol. 5304, pp. 1–14. Springer, Heidelberg (2008)
22. Zeng, W., Gu, X.: Registration for 3D surfaces with large deformations using quasi-conformal curvature flow. In: IEEE CVPR 2011 (2011)
23. Zeng, W., Samaras, D., Gu, X.D.: Ricci flow for 3D shape analysis. IEEE TPAMI 32(4), 662–677 (2010)
24. Zeng, W., Shi, R., Wang, Y., Yau, S.T., Gu, X.: Teichmüller shape descriptor and its application to Alzheimer's disease study. IJCV 105(2), 155–170 (2013)

Motion Words for Videos

Ekaterina H. Taralova, Fernando De la Torre, and Martial Hebert

Carnegie Mellon University, USA

Abstract. In the task of activity recognition in videos, computing the video representation often involves pooling feature vectors over spatially local neighborhoods. The pooling is done over the entire video, over coarse spatio-temporal pyramids, or over pre-determined rigid cuboids. Similarly to pooling image features over superpixels in images, it is natural to consider pooling spatio-temporal features over video segments, e.g., supervoxels. However, since the number of segments is variable, this produces a video representation of variable size. We propose Motion Words - a new, fixed size video representation, where we pool features over supervoxels. To segment the video into supervoxels, we explore two recent video segmentation algorithms. The proposed representation enables localization of common regions across videos in both space and time. Importantly, since the video segments are meaningful regions, we can interpret the proposed features and obtain a better understanding of *why* two videos are similar. Evaluation on classification and retrieval tasks on two datasets further shows that Motion Words achieves state-of-the-art performance.

Keywords: Video representations, action classification.

1 Introduction

Features for video classification and retrieval include low-level interest point features [33,34,8,4], mid-level patch-based features [15,1,35,38], and higher level, semantic features [22]. Even though low-level features are limited either in temporal scale [33,8], or in density [4], they robustly capture local information, and in fact obtain state-of-the-art classification performance on several datasets [23,17]. However, if we want to know why two videos are classified as similar, visualizing the low-level features does not allow us to interpret the results. On the other hand, mid-level video patches also perform well for activity classification [15,6,35], and we can visualize the cuboids learned as important for classification. These representations have been limited to cuboids of predetermined spatial and temporal sizes [15], or rectangles from object/foreground detectors [40]. High-level features provide semantic interpretation at the expense of additional annotations or training [22].

Ultimately, we seek a video representation that captures both low-level and region-based statistics. Furthermore, it is important that the representation enables interpretability. That is, when visualized, we want features that give us the power to understand which regions make two videos similar. We propose a video

D. Fleet et al. (Eds.): ECCV 2014, Part I, LNCS 8689, pp. 725–740, 2014.
© Springer International Publishing Switzerland 2014

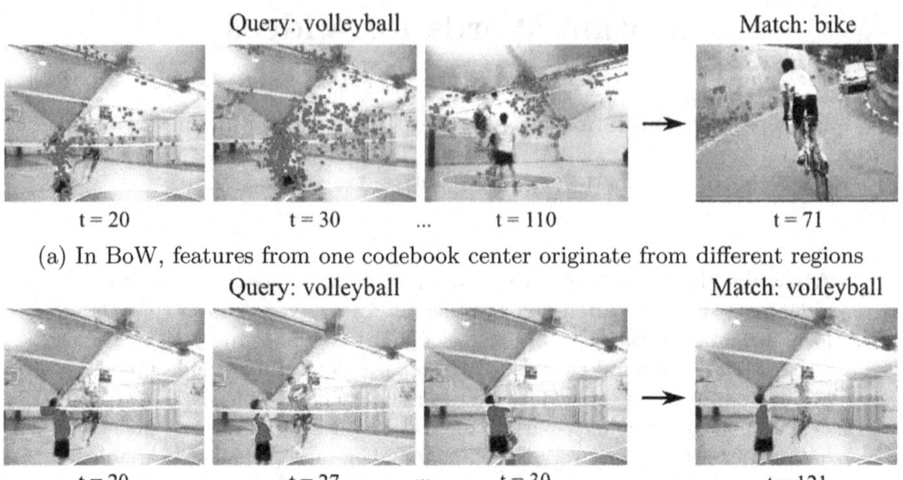

(a) In BoW, features from one codebook center originate from different regions

(b) In the proposed BMW, supervoxels from one Motion Words codebook center originate from similar regions, and are easy to interpret

Fig. 1. In standard BoW pooling (a), features match from regions of very different appearance and motion. In the proposed BMW representation (b), features pooled over supervoxels match similar regions and enable interpretability.

representation in which we pool low-level features over regions defined by a video segmentation. It is a natural idea to pool features over coherent spatio-temporal regions, e.g., supervoxels. In fact, work in image analysis shows that descriptors computed over segmentation regions (e.g., superpixels) provide more robust image representations [2]. Nevertheless, in video analysis, pooling is currently done either over the entire video [33,8], over coarse spatio-temporal pyramids [33], or over pre-determined rigid cuboids [19,9,27]. Each video is then represented by the concatenation of the regions.

However, pooling is not necessarily local in the feature vector space and widely dissimilar features may be pooled together [2]. We visualize such a scenario in Figure 1, where volleyball players and their interactions with the ball occur at various spatio-temporal locations in a video from the Youtube [23] action dataset. We take this video as a query and ask for the nearest neighbor from the dataset using the standard Bag of Words framework with state-of-the-art Dense Trajectory [33] features. The dataset contains a very similar video of the same players, in the same environment, performing a different golf swing trial. We are thus puzzled when the system retrieves an incorrect result, an outdoors "biking" video. If we pick a BoW codebook center and visualize the features that are encoded by this center in both the query and the match, we see that the features come from video regions with very different motion and appearance, e.g., players, wall, sidewalk, car (Figure 1a). While we can peek into BoW in this manner, this visualization does not provide any intuition as to what makes the videos similar.

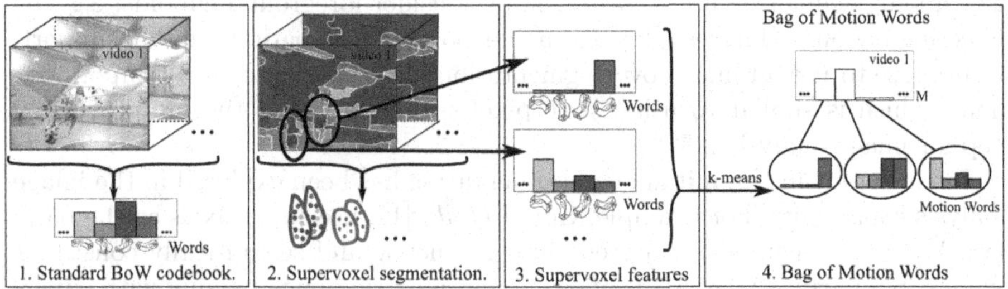

Fig. 2. In the proposed Bag of Motion Words framework we start with a standard BoW codebook (e.g., computed from Dense Trajectories [33]), compute a supervoxel segmentation, and pool the encoded low-level features over the supervoxels. We cluster the supervoxel-based feature vectors using k-means to learn a codebook of Motion Words.

On the other hand, video segments provide more flexible spatio-temporal support than cuboids of manually chosen spatial and temporal sizes. For example, in the above scenario, when we pool features over supervoxels, we obtain a much better match - the expected "volleyball" video (Figure 1b). However, each video can have a different number of segments, resulting in video representations of variable sizes. In this paper, we propose a simple way of constructing a fixed-size representation by using the popular Bag of Words (BoW) framework. Rather than constrain all videos to have the same number of regions, we treat each video segment as a feature vector and cluster the segments from training videos to learn Motion Words. Each video is then represented as a Bag of Motion Words (BMW), as shown in Figure 2. Furthermore, the proposed Motion Words representation enables localization and interpretation. Since segmentation algorithms produce meaningful spatio-temporal regions, we can visualize and interpret the "words" that are common to both videos (Figure 1, bottom).

We present the method overview and its components in Section 3. In Section 4 we discuss design choices and experimental setup. We evaluate the representation qualitatively in Section 5, and quantitatively in Section 6.

2 Related Work

2.1 Feature Pooling

Pooling is one of the key steps in computing video representations. For example, when applied to videos, the Bag of Words representation is computed either by pooling features in an unstructured way over the entire video [33,8,28], over a coarse spatio-temporal pyramid [33,28], or over predetermined cuboids chosen for convenience or computational reasons [19,9,27]. Pooling low-level features over cuboids is also a key step to many methods that learn mid-level representations [15,6,22,35]. Le *et.al.* [19] automatically learn features from video data over predetermined cuboids, which are also used at pooling time. Recent works use cuboids defined by users' gaze [25], or consider foreground cuboids, e.g., by detecting regions of interest [40]. To enable more robust spatio-temporal support, we propose to use an initial oversegmentation into coherent spatio-temporal regions, which is similar to using superpixel segmentation as the pre-processing step for image analysis [26].

The idea of using an initial over-segmentation has been explored in the image analysis community. For example, Gould *et.al.* [12] use superpixels as the basic data layer for decomposing a scene into geometric and semantically consistent regions. Similarly, Tighe [31] propose nonparametric image parsing with superpixels. Other works restrict pooling to inputs close in input space [16,39]. Image processing and de-noising works consider similar inputs to smooth noisy data over a homogeneous sample without throwing out the signal [5,7,24]. We hypothesize that in videos it is important to pool features locally in space and time, e.g., over supervoxels, which are regions coherent in motion and appearance.

In video analysis, works that first compute supervoxels followed by various task-specific processes include hierarchical grouping [13], long-range tracking [3,21], superpixel flow [32] and mid-level features [9]. On the other hand, Zhang *et.al.* [38] model combinations or co-occurances of low-level features, Essa *et.al.* [1] use n-grams and regular expressions to encode long-term motion information. Zhang *et.al.* [38] propose mid-level features that rely on the definition of a correspondence transform to compare videos with variable number of regions. Rather than develop new metrics to compare videos with a variable size representation, we simply perform a second clustering step to learn a codebook of the region-based features. This provides a fixed size representation for videos which can be used in standard classification methods.

2.2 Video Segmentation

In recent work on video segmentation, Brendel and Todorovic [3] segment videos into spatiotemporal tubes designed to represent moving objects. They propose a simple, blocky segmenter, which uses compression error to split and then merge image regions in a small temporal window, based on HSV color values and Lucas-Kanade optical flow. Others attempt to segment foreground objects while avoiding over-segmentation [20]. Grundmann [13] propose a hierarchical graph-based segmentation which extends the Felzenszwalb and Huttenlocher [10] method for segmenting images. They build a graph of color regions and connect them over time based on color and motion histogram distance. Xu *et.al.* [37] create a streaming version of this method that is computationally much more efficient and can be applied to videos with larger number of frames. The recent Uniform Entropy Slice [36] method provides a way to select supervoxels from different hierarchies of the segmentation based on a user-defined feature criterion, for example, "motionness." Selecting regions across the hierarchy alleviates the issue of under-segmentation at coarse levels and over-segmentation at fine levels.

To encode long-range motion cues, other algorithms build upon clusters of long trajectories [4]. Extending this work, Lezama *et.al.* [21] augment trajectories with local image information and seek a segmentation that respects

Fig. 3. Example supervoxels from the coarse and fine segmentation hierarchies of the streaming GBH algorithm [37]

object boundaries and associates these objects across frames. Raptis [29] also use clusters of long-term point trajectories, but require annotated bounding boxes and assume a fixed number of parts. Long-range trajectories are sparse and thus these methods ignore background motion, which is often very informative. Furthermore, finding a good track clustering function is essential, but not straightforward.

3 Motion Words

While pooling over rigid cuboids provides computational efficiency, it is natural to consider pooling features over more flexible spatio-temporal regions. Supervoxel segmentation algorithms provide excellent spatio-temporal support for feature pooling. Supervoxels are regions coherent in both appearance and motion over time, e.g., the streaming GBH segmentation [37] and the UES [36] methods (Figure 3). We propose a new video representation, Motion Words, where we pool low-level features over such coherent spatio-temporal regions. One way to represent a supervoxel would be to average the low-level descriptors within the supervoxel. However, averaging descriptors like HOG, HOF, MBH, STIPs, *etc.* with their neighbors results in the loss of a considerable amount of information [2]. Instead, we first encode the low-level descriptors to a standard Bag of Words codebook and average the codes within each supervoxel.

We construct the Motion Words representation in four steps (see Figure 2):

1. Compute a standard Bag of Words codebook from low-level descriptors;
2. Compute a supervoxel segmentation;
3. Pool the encoded low-level descriptors in each supervoxel to obtain supervoxel-based feature vectors.
4. Cluster the supervoxel-based vectors to learn a codebook of Motion Words.

3.1 Low-Level Features

Motion Words can be built from a variety of features and their combinations. For example, we can easily pool dense features (e.g., MBH [33], STIPs [18]) by simply counting those that fall within each supervoxel. On the other hand, features that span several frames, e.g., Dense Trajectories [33,34], with default length of 15 frames, can be pooled by defining a minimum temporal overlap threshold with a supervoxel to determine which trajectories should be counted. Similarly, we can pool cuboid-based features (e.g., automatically learned features via subspace analysis, ISA [19]) by defining a minimum volume overlap threshold with a supervoxel. While we can also use long trajectories (e.g., Brox and Malik [4]), or features extracted only at interest points, they are sparse and many supervoxels will be empty. Nevertheless, such sparse features can be used to complement dense features. In the experimental section we report performance using Dense Trajectories, Dense Descriptors and ISA features.

3.2 Video Segmentation

Video segmentation algorithms provide an unsupervised way to generate coherent spatio-temporal regions, which, while not necessarily corresponding to objects, are easy to interpret. We seek a segmentation into supervoxels of sizes determined by appearance and motion cues, and not necessarily regions that respect object boundaries. That is, rather than impose a fixed number of regions or fix their size, we allow the method to find the best segmentation for each video. Video segmentation algorithms that optimize jointly for appearance and motion at the pixel level, e.g., [13,37], are excellent first choices to consider for generating supervoxels for Motion Words. One property that we hypothesize is essential in the context of Motion Words is a stronger emphasis on respecting motion boundaries as opposed to respecting appearance boundaries. The Unified Entropy Slice (UES) [36] segmentation method provides a way to do so by selecting supervoxels across the segmentation hierarchy levels that optimize a user-specified property. In the case of Motion Words, the "motion-ness" property is most relevant, where the method optimizes for motion boundaries based on optical flow. In the experimental section we use the freely available streaming GBH method [37] and compare Motion Words obtained using the most coarse level of segmentation, the finest level, the union of three hierarchy levels, and the UES [36] segmentation.

3.3 Bag of Motion Words (BMW)

Each video is an unordered collection of a variable number of supervoxel-based feature vectors of the same dimension (k). There are several ways we can proceed to construct the video representation. For example, Zhang *et.al.* [38] develop an approach to handle a variable number of features per video by defining a correspondence transform for comparing videos. Instead, we propose to use the statistical power of the Bag of Words framework a second time (Figure 2). We cluster the supervoxel features of the training videos to learn a Motion Words codebook. The video representation is a Bag of Motion Words (BMW), that is, a normalized histogram of Motion Word counts.

Formally, let κ be a codebook of size k learned over a set of features in a standard BoW framework (e.g., Dense Trajectories [33], or features learned directly from video data [19]). Let $\Gamma^v = \{\gamma_1^v, \ldots, \gamma_n^v\}$ be a segmentation of video v into n spatio-temporal regions (e.g., obtained using the hierarchical method of Grundmann and Essa [13], or the streaming method of Xu *et.al.* [37]). We encode the low-level features to the codebook κ, and pool them within each region γ_i^v. That is, each supervoxel γ_i^v is represented as a histogram of size k (counts of the encoded low-level features within γ_i^v). We cluster the supervoxel histograms to learn a codebook of Motion Words of size M. Finally, the supervoxel histograms are encoded to the Motion Words codebook and each video v is represented as a histogram $\mathcal{M} = \{\mu_1, \ldots, \mu_M\}$ of Motion Word counts (see Figure 2).

4 Experimental Setup

There are several key design choices involved in building Motion Words. We discuss and evaluate the choice of low-level features, segmentation, quantization, and classifier methods.

4.1 Choice of Low-Level Features

For the underlying Bag of Words we consider three types of features that have been successfully used in activity classification: state-of-the-art Dense Trajectories (*DTs*) [33], automatically learned features through independent subspace analysis (*ISA*) [19], and dense HOG, HOF and MBH descriptors [33]. We extract features using code provided by the authors. Since we want to test pooling of different types of descriptors, we use the default settings without performing any parameter tuning.

4.2 Choice of Supervoxels

For the choice of spatio-temporal regions, we consider state-of-the-art video segmentation methods. The streaming graph-based algorithm of Xu *et.al.* [37] is well suited for Motion Words because it encodes properties such as spatio-temporal uniformity and coherence, and boundary detection. We find that the default parameters suggested by the authors are a good trade-off between size of supervoxels and motion boundary preservation. We extract three hierarchy levels and compare pooling over supervoxels from the coarsest level (GBH coarse), the finest level (GBH fine), and the union of all three levels (GBH combined).

Furthermore, we evaluate the Bag of Motion Words framework using the Uniform Entropy Slice segmentation algorithm [36], choosing to optimize for "motion-ness." Each video has 300 – 1000 supervoxels generated from the streaming GBH method at the finest level, 20 – 100 generated at the coarsest level, and 20 – 100 supervoxels generated by the UES method. We randomly sample 100,000 of the training supervoxels to learn a BMW codebook using k-means and Euclidean distance. We count trajectories as part of a supervoxel if at least half of the trajectory is contained in the supervoxel. In the case of ISA features, we count only those that overlap a supervoxel by at least 30%.

(a) Even when visualized, it is difficult to understand why DTs (shown in red) from the same codebook center originate from regions of different appearance and motion (e.g., static grass and mountains, and twisting torso). Best viewed in color.

(b) When visualized, Motion Words are easy to interpret - the SVs that quantize to the same codebook center as the manually chosen body region also correspond to the golfer's body. Best viewed in color.

Fig. 4. We manually select one point on the golfer's body and visualize all other descriptors that quantize to the same codebook center in two golf swing trials. Ideally, all descriptors will correspond to regions of the golfer's body.

Since extracting supervoxels is independent of the low-level descriptors, it can be done in parallel to the feature extraction. In our experiments, the time to segment videos took 1.3 times longer on average than extracting DTs.

4.3 Choice of Quantization Method

For computing the low-level feature codebook, we follow the setup of Wang *et.al.* [33] by randomly sampling 100,000 data points per feature channel, and clustering with k-means. To analyze the sensitivity of Motion Words we evaluate codebooks of sizes 5000, 1000, 500, and 200. Finally, for the Bag of Motion Words we consider k-means with 5000, 2500 and 1000 clusters using Euclidean distance.

Since the number of supervoxels per video can be very small, soft quantization is better suited in the encoding step. The smaller number of descriptors and their sparsity make the second quantization step much faster to compute than standard BoW. In our experiments, k-means for BMW took 0.3 the time to cluster DTs with the same number of codebook centers.

In our initial evaluation, we chose to pool the quantized supervoxel features over the entire video, not encoding temporal relationships across supervoxels. In

Fig. 5. Given a manually selected supervoxel on the golfer's body in the first video, we can visualize all other supervoxels that quantize to the same Motion Word center in other videos. Even though the environment and the golfers differ, the supervoxel descriptors capture the characteristic motion well, and indeed, the corresponding SVs in the second video also correspond to the golfer's body. Best viewed in color.

future work, these supervoxel features can be the input to methods which model temporal relationships, e.g., [3,11,30,35].

4.4 Datasets

We evaluate the framework on two datasets: the YouTube dataset [23], and the HMDB [17] dataset. The former dataset contains 11 action categories with a total of 1,168 sequences, with roughly 44 test videos per split. It is a challenging dataset due to large variations in camera motion and viewpoint, object appearance, pose, and scale. The HMDB dataset consists of 6849 clips divided into 51 action categories, with 1530 test videos per split. For both datasets, we use the train/test splits provided by the authors.

5 Interpretability

We seek video representations that enable interpretability. That is, when visualized, we want features that give us the power to understand which regions make two videos similar. For instance, given two videos, we can visualize DTs that quantize to the same codebook center. In Figure 4a we select one DT from the region of the golfer's body, find its corresponding codebook center, and then display all DTs that quantize to the same codebook center in two golf videos. Even

Fig. 6. For the action "juggle," we show some of the unique Motion Words (codebook centers) that are used (expressed) only in this class. They tend to correspond to the soccer ball and the player's legs. Best viewed in color.

Fig. 7. Supervoxels from one of the unique Motion Word centers for the action "horse riding" correspond to regions on the body of the horse when moving to the left. They are found in videos with both slow or fast translations, with or without camera motion. Best viewed in color.

though we can visualize low-level features in this manner, it is difficult to interpret why these DTs have been clustered together. In contrast, since supervoxels are interpretable, the proposed BMW representation enables interpretation of features common across videos. For the same two golf videos, we manually select a supervoxel on the golfer's body in one frame and in Figure 4b we visualize all regions that quantize to the same Motion Word center. We can now easily interpret the similar regions - they indeed correspond to the golfer's body, as expected. Furthermore, the supervoxel based descriptors are robust to environment changes. For a very different golf video, in Figure 5, we visualize supervoxels from from the same codebook center. We find that these regions also correspond to the golfer's body, as desired.

In addition, we can qualitatively evaluate how well the representation captures features specific to each action class. For example, Motion Words that appear only in videos from one action class are unique to that class. The total number of unique Words in the YouTube dataset using the BoW representation is only 83 out of $20,000$ Words, for STP it is 220, and for BMW it is 1280. In Figure 6 we visualize a few of these Motion Words for the action "juggle." The supervoxel

Fig. 8. The query "bike" video (left) is mistakenly classified as "juggle" (right) in a nearest neighbor retrieval task. We can visualize Motion Words that are common between the two videos. Yellow denotes the HOF channel, green the trajectory, and blue denotes multiple channels (including HOG and MBH).

regions roughly correspond to the soccer ball and the legs of the players. In Figure 7 we show a few of the unique Motion Words for the "horse riding" action class, which tend to correspond to the back and legs of the horse.

Furthermore, Motion Words give us the power to understand incorrect results. For example, in a retrieval task with a query "bike" video and a retrieved "juggle" video (Figure 8), we can easily visualize the regions that make the two videos similar in appearance (the soccer field) and the regions with similar motion (the children and cameras in each video move in the same manner).

6 Quantitative Evaluation

6.1 Classification

We learn a one-vs-all SVM [14] classifier with a χ^2 kernel and find the parameters via 5-fold cross validation on the training set. Similarly to Wang *et.al.* [33], we combine the feature channels and report average accuracy[1]. We evaluate the key components of BMW, namely, the supervoxel settings, the low-level features, and the size of the representation.

In Figure 9 we show classification accuracy on the Youtube dataset using Dense Trajectories and different codebook sizes. We compare standard Bag of Words (BoW), Spatio-Temporal Pyramids (STP) [33], three supervoxel methods obtained with the streaming GBH algorithm (GBH coarse, GBH fine, and GBH combined), and supervoxels obtained from the UES algorithm with the "motion-ness" objective. We find that very coarse supervoxels (GBH coarse) are not suitable for pooling dense trajectories. However, the other three supervoxel settings outperform both global pooling and STP. Motion Words based on

[1] We compute average classification accuracy by taking the label of the most confident classification among the one-vs-all SVM classifiers for each test video.

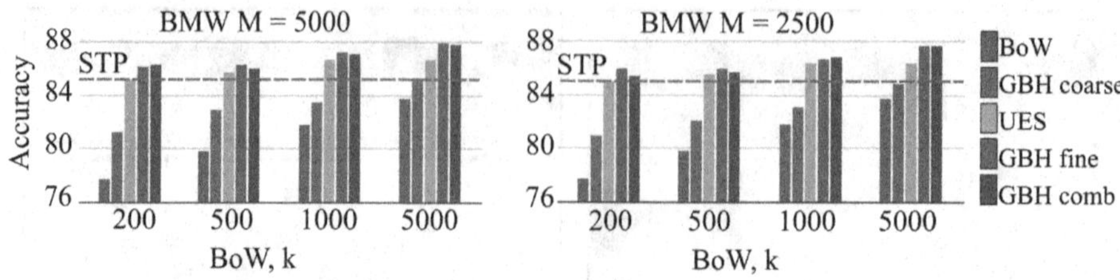

Fig. 9. Classification accuracy on the YouTube dataset using DTs and different codebook sizes. When pooling features over non-coarse supervoxels encoded to large codebooks, we obtain better classification performance compared to BoW and STP.

fine supervoxels improve performance by 3.5% (88.9) compared to coarse spatio-temporal pyramids (85.4 [34]), and similar performance to the recent Fisher vector (MBH and SIFT) representation pooled over STPs (89 [28]). Fine supervoxels better capture motion information compared to coarse supervoxels, which often group regions of different motion and appearance. We observe the same trend when learning Motion Word codebooks of sizes 5000 and 1000, showing that the performance of the proposed representation is not very sensitive to M.

Table 1. Pooling different types of low-level descriptors in BMW compared to standard pooling in the YouTube dataset (5000 codebook centers). DTs pooled over non-coarse supervoxels achieve highest classification accuracy.

	BoW	GBH coarse	GBH fine	GBH comb	UES
ISA [19]	75.8	75.9	76.4	77.2	76.1
Dense HOG,HOF,MBH [33]	81.4	82.8	85.7	85.8	83.6
Dense Trajectories [33]	**83.8**	**85.3**	**88.9**	**88.1**	**86.8**

Table 2. On the YouTube dataset, the proposed BMW achieves classification accuracy comparable to state-of-the-art methods, while enabling interpretation and clear visualization of the video representation

BoW	STP [33]	FV MBH+SIFT STP [28]	FV MBH STP [28]	BMW GBH fine
83.8	85.4	89	88.5	88.9

Next, using 5000 codebook centers, we evaluate performance of the underlying low-level features. In Table 1 we show classification accuracy on the YouTube dataset using the proposed Motion Words representation where we pool different types of low-level descriptors: DTs [33], which capture HOG, HOF, and MBH over 15 frames by tracking interest points; Dense Descriptors (HOG, HOF, MBH) [33] which do not track points; and automatically learned ISA features computed over cuboids. Compared to the standard BoW representation, pooling over supervoxels always performs better. The Dense Trajectories capture temporal information better than the Dense Descriptors and obtain higher performance. We find that the ISA features are not suitable for pooling over supervoxels since they are computed over cuboids of sizes much larger than the extracted supervoxels. Highest performance is achieved when pooling features that encode temporal information (DTs) over fine supervoxels (which robustly group pixels of similar motion and appearance).

Finally, we evaluate the BMW representation on the challenging HMDB dataset. In Table 3 we show classification performance compared to prior results reported by Wang *et.al.* [33,34] and Oneata *et.al.* [28]. Wang *et.al.* [33,34] use DTs with combined HOG, HOF and MBH channels, and pool over spatio-temporal pyramids. The latter work augments DTs to compensate for camera motion. Oneata *et.al.* [28] extract spatial Fisher vectors based on MBH and SIFT descriptors, pooling over spatio-temporal grids. We only evaluate non-coarse supervoxels using DTs and the combined HOG, HOF and MBH channels, learning codebooks of size 5000 centers. The proposed representation achieves state-of-the-art results, while enabling interpretability. We attribute the good performance of the fine supervoxels to the ability of the segmentation method to respect motion boundaries. BMW with fine supervoxels obtains 58.8% classification accuracy, which is 2.6% better than the 57.2% previously reported by Wang *et.al.* [34].

Table 3. Classification accuracy on the HMDB dataset using BMW with fine GBH and UES supervoxels and codebooks of size 5000 centers. Pooling over fine supervoxels obtains better performance compared to other pooling methods.

	Wang *et.al.* [33]	Oneata *et.al.* [28]	Wang *et.al.* [34]	GBH fine	UES
HMDB	48.3	54.8	57.2	**58.8**	57.9

Table 4. Nearest neighbor retrieval (average recall) on the YouTube dataset. When pooling DTs over non-coarse supervoxels, the Motion Words representation outperforms global and STP pooling methods for different codebook sizes.

	BoW	STP	GBH coarse	UES motion	GBH fine	GBH comb
$K = 500$	65.43	66.80	67.21	68.23	68.35	**68.69**
$K = 1000$	67.94	68.85	68.31	69.14	69.53	**69.59**
$K = 5000$	68.22	68.70	67.61	69.14	69.34	**69.52**

6.2 Retrieval

We analyze the usefulness of the proposed representation in the task of directly comparing videos using nearest neighbor. We simply concatenate the descriptors for each video, and treat the test set as query videos. In Table 4 we report average recall from a nearest neighbor retrieval task on the YouTube dataset using χ^2 distance, where we use the provided action labels to determined correct retrieval.

Similarly to the classification performance results, we find that coarse supervoxels do not provide good spatio-temporal support for pooling low-level features. However, we find that pooling over the other supervoxels settings outperforms BoW and STP representations in this very challenging task.

7 Conclusion

In this paper we propose Motion Words – a representation that builds upon BoW by pooling features over supervoxels and performing a second quantization step to obtain a robust and compact video representation. We show that this representation is well-suited for activity classification and retrieval, achieving state-of-the-art performance. The BMW representation achieves high performance when we encode non-coarse supervoxels to BoW codebooks of Dense Trajectories. Furthermore, Motion Words enable interpretability of the results, giving us the power to gain understanding of which features make videos similar.

References

1. Bettadapura, V., Schindler, G., Ploetz, T., Essa, I.: Augmenting bag-of-words: Data-driven discovery of temporal and structural information for activity recognition. In: CVPR (2013)
2. Boureau, Y.L., Le Roux, N., Bach, F., Ponce, J., LeCun, Y.: Ask the locals: Multi-way local pooling for image recognition. In: ICCV, pp. 2651–2658 (2011)
3. Brendel, W., Todorovic, S.: Video object segmentation by tracking regions. In: ICCV, pp. 833–840 (2009)
4. Brox, T., Malik, J.: Object segmentation by long term analysis of point trajectories. In: Daniilidis, K., Maragos, P., Paragios, N. (eds.) ECCV 2010, Part V. LNCS, vol. 6315, pp. 282–295. Springer, Heidelberg (2010)
5. Buades, A., Coll, B., Morel, J.M.: A non-local algorithm for image denoising. In: CVPR, pp. 60–65 (2005)
6. Carreira, J., Caseiro, R., Batista, J., Sminchisescu, C.: Semantic Segmentation with Second-Order Pooling. In: Fitzgibbon, A., Lazebnik, S., Perona, P., Sato, Y., Schmid, C. (eds.) ECCV 2012, Part VII. LNCS, vol. 7578, pp. 430–443. Springer, Heidelberg (2012)
7. Dabov, K., Foi, A., Katkovnik, V., Egiazarian, K.: Image denoising with block-matching and 3D filtering. In: Electronic Imaging (2006)
8. Dollar, P., Rabaud, V., Cottrell, G., Belongie, S.: Behavior recognition via sparse spatio-temporal features. In: International Workshop on Visual Surveillance and Performance Evaluation of Tracking and Surveillance (2005)
9. Everts, I., van Gemert, J.C., Gevers, T.: Evaluation of color STIPs for human action recognition. In: CVPR (2013)
10. Felzenszwalb, P.F., Huttenlocher, D.P.: Efficient graph-based image segmentation. IJCV (2), 167–181 (2004)
11. Gaidon, A., Harchaoui, Z., Schmid, C.: Actom Sequence Models for Efficient Action Detection. In: CVPR, pp. 3201–3208 (2011)
12. Gould, S., Fulton, R., Koller, D.: Decomposing a scene into geometric and semantically consistent regions. In: ICCV, pp. 1–8 (2009)

13. Grundmann, M., Kwatra, V., Han, M., Essa, I.: Efficient hierarchical graph-based video segmentation, In: CVPR (2010)
14. Hsu, C.W., Chang, C.C., Lin, C.J.: A practical guide to support vector classification. Tech. rep., National Taiwan University (2005)
15. Jain, A., Gupta, A., Rodriguez, M., Davis, L.S.: Representing Videos using Mid-level Discriminative Patches. In: CVPR (2013)
16. Jégou, H., Douze, M., Schmid, C., Pérez, P.: Aggregating local descriptors into a compact image representation. In: CVPR, pp. 3304–3311 (2010)
17. Kuehne, H., Jhuang, H., Garrote, E., Poggio, T., Serre, T.: HMDB: a large video database for human motion recognition. In: ICCV (2011)
18. Laptev, I., Lindeberg, T.: Local descriptors for spatio-temporal recognition. In: MacLean, W.J. (ed.) SCVMA 2004. LNCS, vol. 3667, pp. 91–103. Springer, Heidelberg (2006)
19. Le, Q.V., Zou, W.Y., Yeung, S.Y., Ng, A.Y.: Learning hierarchical invariant spatio-temporal features for action recognition with independent subspace analysis. In: CVPR (2011)
20. Lee, Y.J., Kim, J., Grauman, K.: Key-segments for video object segmentation. In: ICCV (2011)
21. Lezama, J., Alahari, K., Sivic, J., Laptev, I.: Track to the future: Spatio-temporal video segmentation with long-range motion cues. In: CVPR (2011)
22. Liu, J., Kuipers, B., Savarese, S.: Recognizing human actions by attributes. In: CVPR (2011)
23. Liu, J., Luo, J., Shah, M.: Recognizing realistic actions from videos "in the wild". In: CVPR (2009)
24. Mairal, J., Bach, F., Ponce, J., Sapiro, G., Zisserman, A.: Non-local sparse models for image restoration. In: ICCV, pp. 2272–2279 (2009)
25. Mathe, S., Sminchisescu, C.: Dynamic Eye Movement Datasets and Learnt Saliency Models for Visual Action Recognition. In: Fitzgibbon, A., Lazebnik, S., Perona, P., Sato, Y., Schmid, C. (eds.) ECCV 2012, Part II. LNCS, vol. 7573, pp. 842–856. Springer, Heidelberg (2012)
26. Moore, A., Prince, S., Warrell, J., Mohammed, U., Jones, G.: Superpixel lattices. In: CVPR (2008)
27. Nguyen, M.H., Torresani, L., De la Torre, F., Rother, C.: Weakly supervised discriminative localization and classification: a joint learning process. Tech. rep., Carnegie Mellon University (2009)
28. Oneata, D., Verbeek, J., Schmid, C.: Action and Event Recognition with Fisher Vectors on a Compact Feature Set. In: ICCV, pp. 1817–1824 (2013)
29. Raptis, M., Kokkinos, I., Soatto, S.: Discovering discriminative action parts from mid-level video representations. In: CVPR (2012)
30. Shapovalova, N., Vahdat, A., Cannons, K., Lan, T., Mori, G.: Similarity constrained latent support vector machine: An application to weakly supervised action classification. In: Fitzgibbon, A., Lazebnik, S., Perona, P., Sato, Y., Schmid, C. (eds.) ECCV 2012, Part VII. LNCS, vol. 7578, pp. 55–68. Springer, Heidelberg (2012)
31. Tighe, J., Lazebnik, S.: Superparsing: Scalable nonparametric image parsing with superpixels. In: Daniilidis, K., Maragos, P., Paragios, N. (eds.) ECCV 2010, Part V. LNCS, vol. 6315, pp. 352–365. Springer, Heidelberg (2010)
32. Vazquez-Reina, A., Avidan, S., Pfister, H., Miller, E.: Multiple hypothesis video segmentation from superpixel flows. In: Daniilidis, K., Maragos, P., Paragios, N. (eds.) ECCV 2010, Part V. LNCS, vol. 6315, pp. 268–281. Springer, Heidelberg (2010)

33. Wang, H., Kläser, A., Schmid, C., Cheng-Lin, L.: Action Recognition by Dense Trajectories. In: CVPR (2011)
34. Wang, H., Schmid, C.: Action Recognition with Improved Trajectories. In: ICCV (2013)
35. Wang, L., Qiao, Y., Tang, X.: Motionlets: Mid-level 3D parts for human motion recognition. In: CVPR (2013)
36. Xu, C., Whitt, S., Corso, J.: Flattening supervoxel hierarchies by the uniform entropy slice. In: ICCV (2013)
37. Xu, C., Xiong, C., Corso, J.J.: Streaming hierarchical video segmentation. In: Fitzgibbon, A., Lazebnik, S., Perona, P., Sato, Y., Schmid, C. (eds.) ECCV 2012, Part VI. LNCS, vol. 7577, pp. 626–639. Springer, Heidelberg (2012)
38. Zhang, Y., Liu, X., Chang, M.-C., Ge, W., Chen, T.: Spatio-temporal phrases for activity recognition. In: Fitzgibbon, A., Lazebnik, S., Perona, P., Sato, Y., Schmid, C. (eds.) ECCV 2012, Part III. LNCS, vol. 7574, pp. 707–721. Springer, Heidelberg (2012)
39. Zhou, X., Yu, K., Zhang, T., Huang, T.S.: Image classification using super-vector coding of local image descriptors. In: Daniilidis, K., Maragos, P., Paragios, N. (eds.) ECCV 2010, Part V. LNCS, vol. 6315, pp. 141–154. Springer, Heidelberg (2010)
40. Zhu, Y., Nayak, N.M., Roy-Chowdhury, A.K.: Context-aware modeling and recognition of activities in video. In: CVPR (2013)

Activity Group Localization by Modeling the Relations among Participants

Lei Sun[1], Haizhou Ai[1], and Shihong Lao[2]

[1] Computer Science & Technology Department, Tsinghua University, Beijing, China
[2] OMRON Social Solutions Co. Ltd., Kusatsu, Shiga, Japan
ahz@mail.tsinghua.edu.cn

Abstract. Beyond recognizing the actions of individuals, activity group localization aims to determine "who participates in each group" and "what activity the group performs". In this paper, we propose a latent graphical model to group participants while inferring each group's activity by exploring the relations among them, thus simultaneously addressing the problems of group localization and activity recognition. Our key insight is to exploit the relational graph among the participants. Specifically, each group is represented as a tree with an activity label while relations among groups are modeled as a fully connected graph. Inference of such a graph is reduced into an extended minimum spanning forest problem, which is casted into a max-margin framework. It therefore avoids the limitation of high-ordered hierarchical model and can be solved efficiently. Our model is able to provide strong and discriminative contextual cues for activity recognition and to better interpret scene information for localization. Experiments on three datasets demonstrate that our model achieves significant improvements in activity group. localization and state-of-the-arts performance on activity recognition.

Keywords: Action recognition, group localization, graphical model.

1 Introduction

Vision-based human action and activity analysis have attracted much attention in computer vision literature. There has been quite a lot of work focusing on single-person action recognition [2], interactive activity between a person and objects [14,11], or pair-activities between two persons [16]. Collective activities, i.e. multiple persons performing activities in groups, however, is more common in real scenarios, with typical examples like: shopper queuing in a shopping store to get checked, pedestrians crossing a road, and friends talking together with their kids playing around. The analysis of such collective activity is of great practical importance for many applications such as smart video surveillance and semantic video indexing.

In this paper, we go beyond recognizing collective activities of individuals and focus on activity group localization in videos, which involves two distinct but related tasks: activity recognition and group localization. We seek to jointly solve

D. Fleet et al. (Eds.): ECCV 2014, Part I, LNCS 8689, pp. 741–755, 2014.
© Springer International Publishing Switzerland 2014

these two tasks by grouping individuals and reasoning activities at the group level. Noticeably, this incorporation of group information is in sharp contrast to most recent research in collective activity recognition, in which no group information is considered (e.g. regarding persons nearby as context for single person activity recognition [17,18,6,7] or modeling interactions or activity co-occurrences among some closely related persons [17,5]), leaving the whole relations among persons unclear.

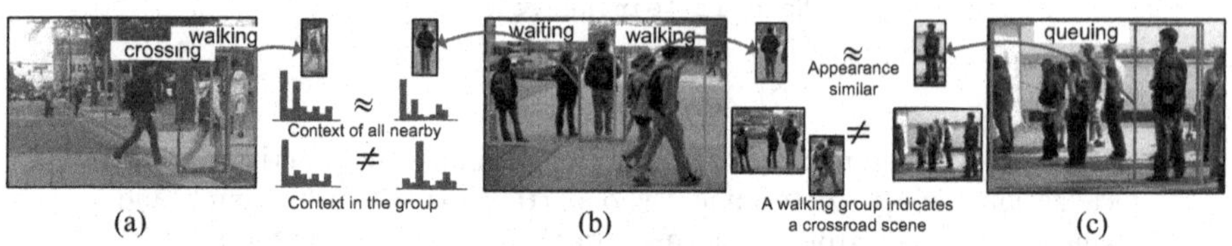

Fig. 1. Group helps action recognition. The green box denotes the activity group.

We argue that, instead of treating these two tasks separately, jointly addressing activity recognition and group localization enjoys many benefits. Firstly, it allows us to focus on recognizing activity on a group of persons and disregard those persons that are not discriminative or relevant. For example, in Fig. 1(a), the person in the red box is crossing. It will be confused to find his activities if we consider all his nearby persons as context. However, it will be much helpful if we only take the persons in his group and disregard the irrelevant persons in other groups. Secondly, it reduces the obscured relations of persons in the scene to person-person relations in each group and group-group relations among groups, thus enabling explicit modeling of such relations. In this way, by encapsulating individuals into groups, inter-group relations can better characterize the scene information. Take the queuing person boxed in red in Fig. 1(c) as an example, with similar appearance to the outlined person in Fig. 1(b), it still can be disambiguated since a co-existed "crossing" group implies a crossroad scenario. Last but not least, in perception, it is more sensible to discover activity groups than recognize individuals' actions. Group localization and activity recognition are mutually beneficial to each other. On one hand, group localization reveals the relations among participants in the scene, in which case more useful cues for activity recognition are obtained. On the other hand, activity recognition assists group localization in a more evident way, i.e., fusing activity information enables group localization at an activity level.

We propose a latent graphical model to jointly address two problems together, which we present in this work as a new problem called activity group localization. In particular, we employ a tree structure to represent each group and a fully connected graph to describe the relations among groups. Such graphical structure is quite sensible and is capable of capturing characteristics of group activities and co-occurrences among them. Then by dynamically inferring over this latent structure, the groups along with their activities can be consequently obtained.

Specifically, we treat it as an extended minimum spanning forest problem and utilize a max-margin framework to efficiently solve it.

The contributions of our work can be summarized in three-fold. Firstly, we advance prior work of individual activity recognition to activity group localization by jointly addressing group localization and activity recognition. Secondly, a relational graph is presented to model the relations among participants, which gives an interpretable description of the scene information and thus largely assists the activity recognition as well as group localization. Thirdly, we solve the graphical model as an extended spanning forest problem, and cast it into a max-margin framework which enables efficiently inference over the graph structure.

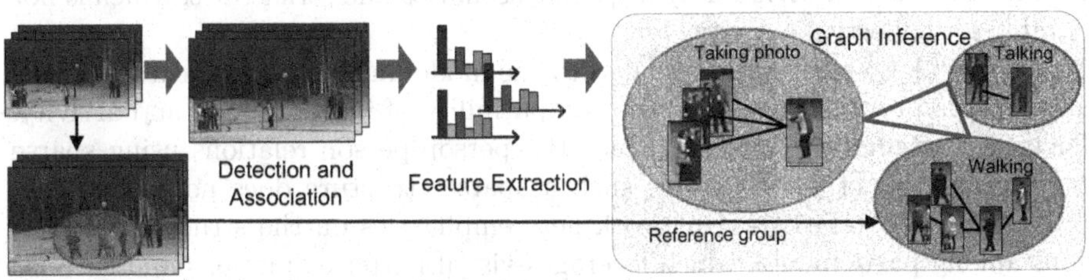

Fig. 2. System overview. First detect and associate the persons in the video, then a relational graph is constructed and inferred with respect to activities as well as groups.

2 Related Work

Many recent works on human action recognition model the context explicitly to assist recognition. For example, the contextual information is exploited by means of scenes[20], objects [14,11], or interactions between two or more objects[16]. The scene or role interactions are explored by many researchers using sophisticated models like dynamic Bayesian networks [23], CASE natural language representations [13], AND-OR graphs [12], and probabilistic first-order logic [21,3].

In group activity or collective activity recognition, context generally means what others are doing. Some methods attempt to provide contextual information for single person activity classification by concatenating the action scores of all the neighbor persons [17,18] or extracting spatiotemporal distributions of surroundings persons [6,7]. Some mid-level atomic interactions are captured to encode the relation between a pair of persons [5]. Unfortunately, such kind of interactions only provide useful information for interactive activities such as "talking" but rarely occur in other casual activities such as "crossing", and "waiting". Besides, involving the atomic interactions also complicates the problem. Rather than recognizing individual's activity in isolation, some approaches [17,18,5] attempt to jointly classify all people in a scene. In this case, a hierarchical model is often used to model the compatibility of the activities among person-person and person-group. To the best of our knowledge, none of previous approaches explicitly captures the overall relations among participants, which we believe is of critical importance for activity recognition. Another related issue in collective activity recognition is using the tracking information [19], e.g., to formulate multi-target tracking and action recognition into a constrained minimum cost flow problem [15], or to integrate tracking, atomic activities, interactions and collective activities together to form a hierarchical model, and infers them by combining belief propagation and branch and bound [5].

There is not much work about grouping activity groups. They typically focus on one aspect of this problem, e.g., to determine the group location by developing contextual spatial pyramid descriptor while neglecting individual activity [22], or to infer the individual activity by a chain model [1]. Some other approaches [4] attempt to cluster individual with specific scenarios and strict rules, which is not suitable for collective activity.

Our work is to some extent related to the model in [17,18], where a hierarchical model is proposed to model the compatibility of image, action and activity. They also attempt to implicitly infer the person-person relations using sparse loopy graph structure. However, such a sparse structure does not completely characterize the relations. Our work here emphasizes on the structure of relations among participants, which leverages visual patterns, motions and activity compatibility in terms of intra-group relations and inter-group relations.

3 System Overview

The proposed framework is illustrated in Fig. 2. Our main objective is to localize activity groups in a video. Haven the persons detected and associated, for each single image, we construct a relational graph, which is then inferred with respect to groups as well as their activity labels. Notice that there are some reference groups participated in the relational graph. Such groups, coming from previous frames of the video, are often those that have been identified as reliable activity groups. In this case, They play a role of authority for further verification. We each time select one reference group to participate in the graph inference and take the relational graph with the highest score as the final result.

Here we emphasize on how to model and solve the relational graph, which attempts to encode the relations among persons and groups. We assume that in each group every person closely coordinates with only one another, i.e. a tree structure. As for inter-group relations, we remain groups fully connected (Fig. 3(a)). Notice that, solving this relational graph is reduced to a clustering problem if no activity recognition is required, and such clustering can efficiently be modeled as a minimum spanning forest problem. Therefore, we seek to solve our activity localization problem tailoring an extended version of minimum spanning forest problem, of which the difference is that each tree is with an extra activity label and is connected to every other one. In the next, we start by explaining how to model such a graph in Section 4, then describe the learning of the model in Section 5 and model inference in Section 6.

4 Modeling Activity Group Localization

4.1 Model Formulation

Given a set of detected persons $\mathbf{x}$=$\{x_1, x_2, ..., x_m\}$ in the image and a reference group $(\mathbf{x}_r, g_r, a_r)$, the objective is to find the groups $\mathbf{g}$=$\{g_1, g_2, ..., g_n\}$ with activity labels $\mathbf{a}$=$\{a_1, a_2, ..., a_n\}$, where g_i=$(g_{i1}, g_{i2}, ..., g_{im})$ with $g_{ik} \in \{0, 1\}$ indicating whether the kth person belongs to the group g_i or not $(\sum_i g_i$=1_m,$\forall i, j, g_i g_j^T$=$0)$, and $a_i \in A$ with A being the set of all possible activity labels. Let h denote the relational graph structure, as shown in Fig. 3(a). It consists of n trees, h=$\{t_n\}$, each representing one activity group (g, a). We use $F_{\mathbf{w}}(\mathbf{x}, h, \mathbf{g}, \mathbf{a})$ to measure the compatibility among activity groups ($\mathbf{g}$, $\mathbf{a}$), graph structure h and persons $\mathbf{x}$. And by maximizing such a potential function, the optimum assignment of ($\mathbf{g}$, $\mathbf{a}$) for $\mathbf{x}$ can be obtained. Note that we include the reference group $(\mathbf{x}_r, g_r, a_r)$ into the current notation $(\mathbf{x}, \mathbf{g}, \mathbf{a})$ for simplicity, which will be discussed in detail in the following.

Two kinds of potentials are developed to measure the compatibility function. The first regards to intra-group potential, which we attempts to model the compatibility of a pair of individuals' belonging to one activity group, while the second, inter-group potential, characterizes the compatibility of a pair of activity groups belonging to the same scene. Therefore, the potential function $F_{\mathbf{w}}(\mathbf{x}, h, \mathbf{g}, \mathbf{a})$ is formulated as

$$F_{\mathbf{w}}(\mathbf{x}, h, \mathbf{g}, \mathbf{a}) = \mathbf{w}_p^T \psi_p(\mathbf{x}, h, \mathbf{g}, \mathbf{a}) + \mathbf{w}_g^T \psi_g(\mathbf{x}, h, \mathbf{g}, \mathbf{a}), \tag{1}$$

where $\mathbf{w}_p^T \psi_p(\mathbf{x}, h, \mathbf{g}, \mathbf{a})$ measures intra-group compatibility, $\mathbf{w}_g^T \psi_g(\mathbf{x}, h, \mathbf{g}, \mathbf{a})$ scores inter-group compatibility. The model parameters are the combination of $\mathbf{w}_p^T$ and $\mathbf{w}_g^T$, $\mathbf{w} = [\mathbf{w}_p^T \ \ \mathbf{w}_g^T]^T$. The details of Eq. 1 are described in the following.

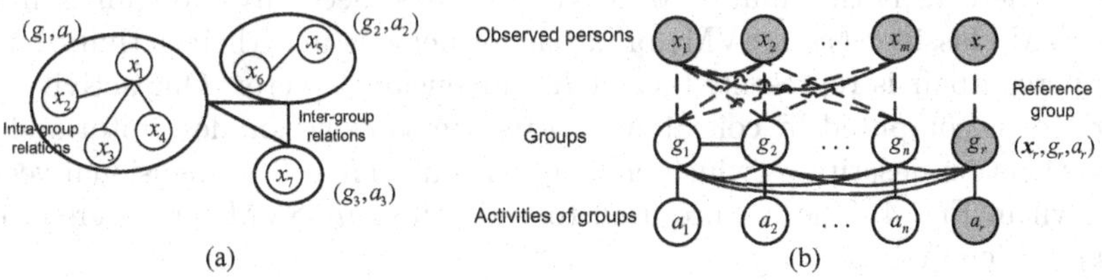

Fig. 3. (a) shows the relational graph. Grey node in (b) denote observable variants.

Intra-Group Potential $\mathbf{w}_p^T \psi_p(\mathbf{x}, h, \mathbf{g}, \mathbf{a})$: This function encodes the relation among a pair of persons and their belonged group. It is parameterized as:

$$\mathbf{w}_p^T \psi_p(\mathbf{x}, h, \mathbf{g}, \mathbf{a}) = \sum_{t \subseteq h} \sum_{(x_i, x_j) \in t} \sum_{b \in A} \mathbf{w}_{pb}^T \phi(x_i, x_j) \mathbf{1}(a_t = b), \tag{2}$$

where $\mathbf{1}(.)$ is the indicator function, and $\phi(x_i, x_j)$ denotes the person-person descriptor (Sec. 4.2). The parameter $\mathbf{w}_p$ is simply the concatenation of $\mathbf{w}_{pb}$ for all $b \in A$.

Inter-Group Potential $\mathbf{w}_g^T \psi_g(\mathbf{x}, h, \mathbf{g}, \mathbf{a})$: This function characterizes the relation between all pairs of groups. It is parameterized as:

$$\mathbf{w}_g^T \psi_g(\mathbf{x}, h, \mathbf{g}, \mathbf{a}) = \sum_{(t_i,t_j)\in h} \sum_{b,c\in A} \mathbf{w}_{gbc}^T \varphi(t_i, t_j) \mathbf{1}(a_{t_i} = b) \mathbf{1}(a_{t_j} = c), \quad (3)$$

where $\varphi(t_i, t_j)$ denotes the group-group descriptor (Sec. 4.2). By adding reference group in this term, additional group pairs are modeled with knowledge of reference group's activity label.

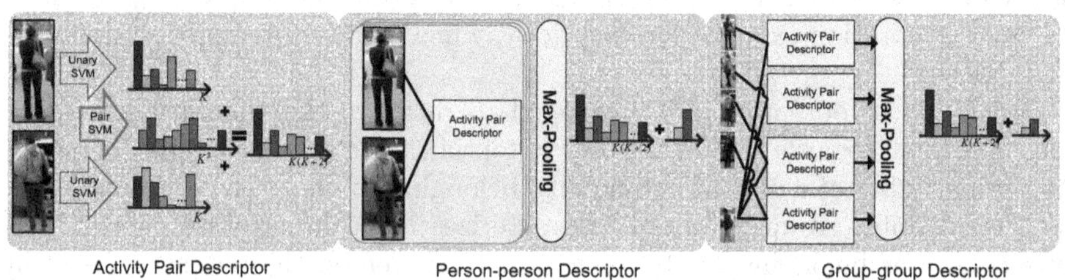

Fig. 4. Activity pair descriptor

4.2 Activity Pair Descriptor

We build this descriptor in two stages. Firstly, we train a multi-class SVM classifier (*unary* SVM) based on the person descriptors (e.g. HOG [8]) and their associated action labels, then each person can be represented as a K-dimensional vector, where K is the number of activity classes. Secondly, we train a multi-class SVM classifier (*pair* SVM) on a pair of persons and their activity labels. Each person pair is represented as an K_2-dimensional vector. Our activity pair descriptor is computed by concatenating two person's action descriptor and the pairwise action descriptor, which ends up with a $K(K+2)$-dimensional vector, as shown in Fig. 4. The feature used to train the *pair* SVM for a person pair (x_i, x_j) is denoted as

$$\mathbf{f}_{(x_i,x_j)}=[\mathbf{d}_{x_i}\ \mathbf{d}_{x_j}\ \mathbf{d}_{x_i}-\mathbf{d}_{x_j}\ \mathbf{d}_{x_i}\otimes\mathbf{d}_{x_j}\ \mathbf{c}], \quad (4)$$

where $\mathbf{d}_{x_i}$, $\mathbf{d}_{x_j}$ are the person descriptors of the person x_i and x_j, respectively. The operator $\otimes$ means element-wise multiplication. $\mathbf{c}$ is the bag-of-words representation of the scene's context.

Person-Person Descriptor $\phi(x_i, x_j)$: To compute the person-person descriptor for a person pair (x_i, x_j),we do not only consider the visual appearance in the current frame, but also take advantage of association which locates the persons in the neighbor frames. Let $N(x)$ be the set of tracked human across neighbor frames for person x, then we compute activity pair descriptors of all possible person pairs $P(x_i, x_j)$, of which the first is from $N(x_i)$ and the second is from $N(x_j)$. Note that, only reliable tracklets are used in our work, so if none of the tracklets coveres the person x, $N(x)$ will only have one element x. Finally we calculate the person-person descriptor as follows

$$\phi(x_i, x_j) = [\max_{p \in P(x_i, x_j)} S_{p,1}, ..., \max_{p \in P(x_i, x_j)} S_{p,K(K+2)}, \ l_x, \ l_y], \tag{5}$$

where $S_{p,k}$ denotes the kth value of the activity pair descriptor, l_x and l_y are the average relative deviations of all pairs at the x and y coordinates, respectively.

Group-Group Descriptor $\varphi(t_i.t_j)$: For all person pairs (x_m, x_n), where x_m comes from one group t_i and x_n comes from the other group t_j, we compute the person-person descriptors $\phi(x_m, x_n)$. The final group-group descriptor is obtained using the following equation

$$\varphi(t_i, t_j) = [\max_{x_m \in t_i, x_n \in t_j} \phi(x_m, x_n)_1, ..., \max_{x_m \in t_i, x_n \in t_j} \phi(x_m, x_n)_{K(K+2)}, \ l_x, \ l_y], \tag{6}$$

where $\phi(x_m, x_n)_k$ is the kth value in the person-person descriptor, l_x and l_y are the average relative deviations of all pairs at the x and y coordinates, respectively.

4.3 Reference Groups

Reference groups are those that have been identified as reliable activity groups in the previous frames. They, in a sense, serves as some explicit scene information. Given a *crossing* group in the scene, it is more likely to tell a group of standing persons to be a *waiting* group rather than a *talking* group. Specifically, the activity groups with confidence that exceeds a threshold (set empirically) are pushed into a reference group pool. And concerning the computation, we select a subset of reference groups with little overlap with the current groups' region (the total number of reference groups is discussed in Section 7.2). Such strategy is reasonable since our model favors seeing complete relational graph located in various regions.

5 Model Learning

Our scoring function can be converted into an inner product $\langle \mathbf{w}, \psi(\mathbf{x}, h, \mathbf{g}, \mathbf{a}) \rangle$, where $\mathbf{w} = [\mathbf{w}_p^T \ \mathbf{w}_g^T]^T$, $\psi(\mathbf{x}, h, \mathbf{g}, \mathbf{a}) = [\psi_p(\mathbf{x}, h, \mathbf{g}, \mathbf{a}) \ \ \psi_g(\mathbf{x}, h, \mathbf{g}, \mathbf{a})]$.

Given a set of N training examples $(\mathbf{x}^n, \mathbf{g}^n, \mathbf{a}^n)$ $(n = 1, 2, ..., N)$, we train the model parameter $\mathbf{w}$ to produce the correct groups $\mathbf{g}$ and activity labels $\mathbf{a}$. Note that the groups and activity labels can be observed on training data, but the graph structure h is unobserved. We adopt the latent SVM [10] formulation to train this model, which in our case can be written as follows

$$\begin{aligned}\mathbf{w}^* = \arg\min_{\mathbf{w}}\{\tfrac{1}{2}||\mathbf{w}||^2 - C\sum_{i=1}^{N}\mathbf{w}^T\psi(\mathbf{x}^i, h^i, \mathbf{g}^i, \mathbf{a}^i) \\ +C\sum_{i=1}^{N}\max_{(\hat{\mathbf{g}},\hat{h},\hat{\mathbf{a}})}[\mathbf{w}^T\psi(\mathbf{x}^i, \hat{h}^i, \hat{\mathbf{g}}^i, \hat{\mathbf{a}}^i) + \Delta(\mathbf{g}, \hat{\mathbf{g}}, \hat{h}, \mathbf{a}, \hat{\mathbf{a}})]\},\end{aligned} \tag{7}$$

where C controls the tradeoff betwen the errors in the training model and margin maximization and $\Delta(\mathbf{g}, \hat{\mathbf{g}}, \hat{h}, \mathbf{a}, \hat{\mathbf{a}})$ is the loss function. Naturally, this function need penalize both incorrect groups and incorrect activity labels. We define it as follows

$$\Delta(\mathbf{g}, \hat{\mathbf{g}}, \hat{h}, \mathbf{a}, \hat{\mathbf{a}}) = n(\mathbf{g}) - \sum_{(x_i,x_j)\in\hat{h}} l(\mathbf{g}, \mathbf{a}, \hat{\mathbf{a}}, (x_i, x_j)), \tag{8}$$

where $n(\mathbf{g})$ is the difference of the number of nodes and the number of groups. The function $l(\mathbf{g}, \mathbf{a}, \hat{\mathbf{a}}, (x_i, x_j))$ returns 1 if (x_i, x_j) belongs to the same group with the correct activity, returns 0 if (x_i, x_j) belongs to different groups but with the correct activity, and -1 otherwise. It is easy to show that such a loss function equals zero if and only if the individuals are clustered into correct groups and with correct activities.

6 Model Inference

Given the model parameter $\mathbf{w}$, the inference problem is to find the best group locations $\mathbf{g}$ along with the corresponding activity label $\mathbf{a}$ for each input $\mathbf{x}$. Using the latent SVM formulation, it can be written as:

$$F_{\mathbf{w}}(\mathbf{x}, \mathbf{g}, \mathbf{a}) = \max_{a}\max_{g,h} F_{\mathbf{w}}(\mathbf{x}, h, \mathbf{g}, \mathbf{a}). \tag{9}$$

Since groups $\mathbf{g}$, graph structure h and activities $\mathbf{a}$ are not independent with each other, the optimization of Eq. 10 is NP-hard. When the number of persons and activities are small and some spatial restrictions can be incorporated, we encourage a combinatorial search to generate exactly inference. In other cases, we approximately solve it by iterating the following three steps:

- Holding activities $\mathbf{a}$ and groups $\mathbf{g}$ fixed, optimize the graph structure h, using a standard spanning tree algorithm such as Kruskal's algorithm.
- Holding graph structure h and groups $\mathbf{g}$ fixed, optimize the activities $\mathbf{a}$ by enumerating all possible activities.
- Holding activities $\mathbf{a}$ fixed, generate new optimal groups $\mathbf{g}$ by merging two trees or splitting one tree with the same activity in the current structure h.

The three steps are iterated until converged. While this algorithm cannot guarantee a globally optimum solution, in our experiments it works well to find good solutions.

7 Experiments

Datasets. We evaluate our method on two collective activity datasets from [6,7] and a newly recorded dataset collected by ourselves. The first collective activity dataset is composed of 44 video clips with 5 activities, *crossing*, *walking*, *queuing*, *talking* and *waiting*. While the second is an extended dataset of the former. It includes two more classes of *dancing* and *jogging* and removes the ill-defined *walking* class, which results in 6 class of activities. We refer these two collective activity datasets as 5-class collective dataset and 6-class collective dataset, respectively. We use the activity annotations provided by [6] and further annotate the groups with bounding boxes. We also collect several 10-minute videos from a outdoor touring environment, and we segment them into 52 video clips, each having 800 to 1000 frames. Typical collective activities include *walking*, *bicycling*, *taking photos*, *standing*, and *talking*. This new dataset is referred as touring dataset. We annotate the activity label for each person and the groups in every tenth frame (4560 annotated frames including 5067 *walking*, 3126 *bicycling*, 3228 *taking photos*, 3850 *standing*,3027 *talking*).

Evaluation Metric. We stress that our objective is to localize activity groups, two aspects are evaluated: activity recognition and group localization. For localization, we compute a ratio of the intersection and union of detected and ground-truth bounding boxes of people participating in activities. The activity group is correct only if ratio > 0.5 and activity is correct.

Implementation Details. For the 5-class collective dataset and 6-class collective dataset, we apply the pedestrian detector in [9], and obtain some reliable tracklets by simply associating the detected bounding boxes in two neighboring frames using spatio-temporal locations and appearance similarity. For touring dataset, however, pedestrian detectors are not enough, we additionally apply background subtraction in [24] using Gaussian Mixture Model to obtain foreground objects. Instead of using raw features (e.g. HOG), we follow the setting in [17] to extract Action Context (AC) descriptor as the person descriptor. Also, the $\mathbf{c}$ in Eq. 4 is constructed by computing the histogram of visual-words within the persons appearing in neighbor frames. Specifically, we extract HOG feature of persons and apply k-means to generate 200 codewords.

7.1 Activity Recognition

In this part, we concentrate on activity recognition task. First we demonstrate the effective of our model by comparing to several baselines. Then we make comparisons with the state-of-the-art approaches with respect to three different validation schemes. We also analyze the behavior of our model in terms of learnt weights and total number of reference groups.

First we construct several baselines to demonstrate the capability of our model to interpret context in terms of a relational graph, activity pair descriptor and reference groups, which largely improves activity recognition. To evaluate the performance of our relational structure, three baselines with different graph structures are considered as shown in Fig. 5. The first (*unary person*) is a latent SVM model based on AC descriptor. It simply regards all nearby persons as context and attempts to infer their activities. It can be formulated as $F_{\mathbf{w}}(\mathbf{x}, \mathbf{g}, \mathbf{a}) = \sum_i \sum_b \mathbf{w}_b x_i \mathbf{1}(a_i = b)$, where $\mathbf{x}$ denotes all persons in a euclidean distance. The second (*sparse link*) adopts the structure in [18]. To our knowledge, [18] is the only work that has mentioned about the structure of participates, and in particular, they tend to find sparse but important links between persons by maximize the summation of all pairwise activity potential under a maximum limitation of each vertex's degree, which can be formulated as $F_{\mathbf{w}}(\mathbf{x}, \mathbf{g}, \mathbf{a}) = \sum_{(i,j)} \sum_{(b,c)} \mathbf{w}_{bc} \psi_p(x_i, x_j) \mathbf{1}(a_i = b) \mathbf{1}(a_j = c)$, *s.t.* $\forall i, d(x_i) \leqslant q$. $d(x_i)$ denotes the degree of the vertex while q is a threshold. The third baseline (*unary group*) ignores the pairwise group structure, which is equivalent to our model in Eq. 1 by removing inter-group potential term.

We also evaluate the performance of our activity pair descriptor by replacing it with a concatenated vector by two AC descriptors of a person pair in *full* model, which we called *2-AC*. And the performance of reference group (*non-reference*) is evaluated by removing them from our *full* model.

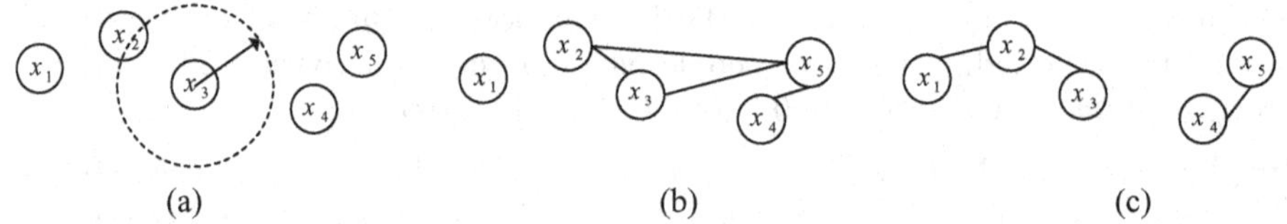

Fig. 5. (a)-(c) shows the graph structure of three baselines: *unary person model*, *sparse link model* and *unary group model*, respectively

Table 1. Mean average activity classification accuracy on three datasets

Dataset	unary person	sparse link	unary group	2-AC	non-reference	full
5-class collective dataset	54.8%	69.4%	62.3%	72.9%	71.6%	**74.8%**
6-class collective dataset	67.3%	80.2%	72.1%	83.2%	82.9%	**85.8%**
Touring dataset	49.2%	58.4%	53.6%	67.1%	66.2%	**68.3%**

Table 1 summarizes the results using leave-one-video-out validation strategy. We can see that our model significantly outperforms all baselines with respect to all the three datasets. Consider the structural baselines, the *unary person* model is almost unachievable, especially in a more complex scenario of touring dataset. This can be attributed to the unstructured context, drawing all persons nearby as context information introduces much noise as well as irrelevant persons. Compared to the *unary person* model, *unary group* model and *sparse link* model achieve a large improvement of performance, which further proves the effect of modeling the relations among participants. We can also see that *sparse link* has a better performance by about 6% than *unary group* model. It is quite reasonable, since *unary group* model imposes quite a few links on the relations while *sparse link* model might find multiple important pairwise relations. In comparisons to these three baselines, our *full* model has a significant boost in performance, showing the advantage of integrating groups into activity recognition and modeling pairwise group relations. We also observe a slight degradation in performance occurs when a combination of AC descriptor is used instead of activity pair descriptor, suggesting that our model is able to perform competitively well even with "poorer" descriptors. Moreover, we find that reference groups leads to better results by comparing *non-reference* model to *full* model. We attribute this to the complementary scene information from the video provided by reference groups.

Then we make quantitative comparisons with other state-of-the-art approaches on the 5-class and 6-class collective datasets, including RSTV approach in [7], a joint tracking and recognition flow model in [15], a complex hierarchical model in [5], a bayesian BORD method in [1] and a discriminative latent model in [17]. To be comparable to these reported results, we adopt their respective training/testing schemes and evaluation criteria.

We summarize the results using three validation schemes in Table 2. The first scheme is the leave-one-video-out (LOO) training/testing scheme and per-person activity classification is evaluated, which is used in [6,7,5,15]. Our model outperforms all approaches by achieving an overall accuracy of 74.8% on the 5-class collective dataset and 85.8% on the 6-class collective dataset. Notice that, the model from [5] yields competitive results as our model for the first dataset. However, it employs a complex hierarchical model, which requires additional pose orientations of each person, 3D trajectories and some interactive atomic actions. The second experiment is to train the model on three fourths of the dataset while testing on the remaining fourth, and to evaluate per-scene activity classification. We follow the same split of dataset suggested by [17], and achieve 81.2% on the 5-class collective dataset. It is superior than 79.1% and 80.4% reported in [17] and [5]. The last experiment adopts the scheme in [1], which merges 5-class collective dataset and 6-class collective dataset to form a 7-class collective dataset (*walking* activity is not removed). They use 2/3 and 1/3 of the videos from each class for training and testing. Our model reports 83.7% accuracy which is 2.2% higher than [1]. To demonstrate the effective of our model in a more complex scenario, we re-implement the adaptive structured latent SVM method in [18], and achieve 61.5% accuracy on touring dataset using leave-one-video-out validation scheme, which is 6.8% lower than our performance.

Table 2. Comparisons with the state of the art on two collective datasets

Validataion	Approaches	RSTV [7]	RSTV+MRF [7]	AC+Flow[15]	T.+A.+I.[5]	AC+LSVM[17]	BORDS[1]	full model
LOO	5-class	67.2%	70.9%	70.9%	74.4%	–	–	**74.8%**
LOO	6-class	71.7%	82.0%	83.7%	–	–	–	**85.8%**
one fourth	5-class	–	–	–	80.4%	79.1%	–	**81.2%**
one third	7-class	–	–	–	–	–	81.5%	**83.7%**

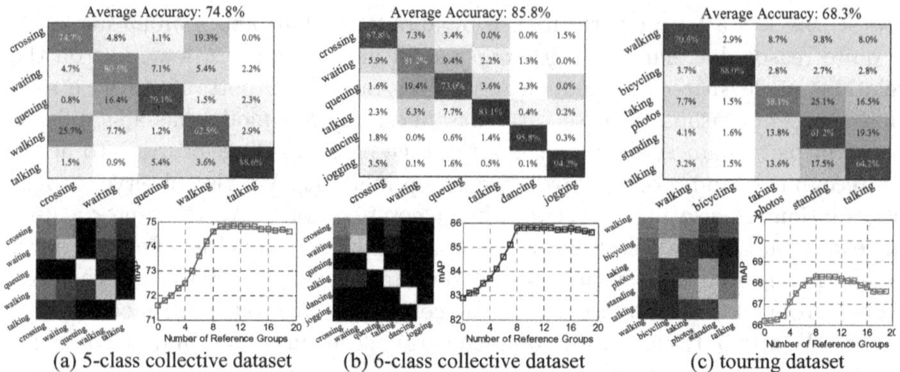

(a) 5-class collective dataset (b) 6-class collective dataset (c) touring dataset

Fig. 6. The confusion matrixes (upper row), the learnt weights across different activity groups and precision-reference groups curves (lower row)

At last, to give a clear insight into our model, we give the confusion matrixes and the learnt pairwise weights across different activity groups in Fig. 6. The learnt weights encode some scene information, which further demonstrates the benefits of including pairwise group relations. For example, *walking* groups are more likely to be co-existed with *crossing* groups, while *queuing* groups tend to be appear alone. *standing* groups have high co-occurrences with *taking photos* groups. Besides, the performance with different number of reference groups are illustrated in Fig. 6. It indicates that 8 to 15 is optimal, in which case larger causes computation issue while smaller leads to insufficient scene cues.

7.2 Activity Group Localization

In this part, we evaluate our model for the task of activity group localization. To our knowledge, there is only one work [22] about activity group localization, so we re-implement their method (*CSPM*), and compare our results with it. In order to investigate the capability of our model to localize activity groups, we construct two step-wise baselines: a) we estimate the activity label of each person (use the re-implemented version of [18]), followed by a mean-shift clustering algorithm (*activity-cluster*), and b) we remove the latent activity term in Eq. 1, to formulate a clustering method based on our activity pair descriptor (no reference groups), and then use a multi-class SVM to classify the activity of each group using the max-pooled AC descriptors within each group (*cluster-activity*).

As Fig. 7 shows, our model achieves a significant improvement with respect to all activity groups over [22] as well as two baselines. Such good performance resides in not only explicit activity inference but also the pairwise group relations modeling. The work in [22] proposes a contextual spatial pyramid descriptor and attempts to localize one particular group at one time. Though it might implicitly characterize the variations of activity, it lacks the ability to account for the correspondences between groups. The first baseline is a conventional step-wise

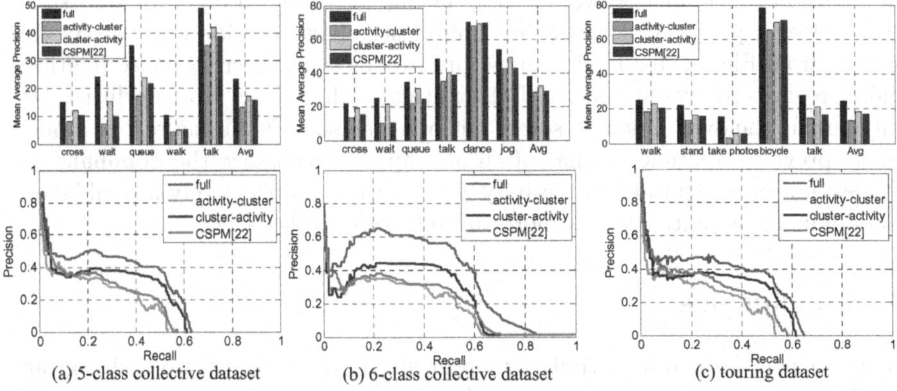

(a) 5-class collective dataset (b) 6-class collective dataset (c) touring dataset

Fig. 7. The mean average precisions and precision-recall curves of localization

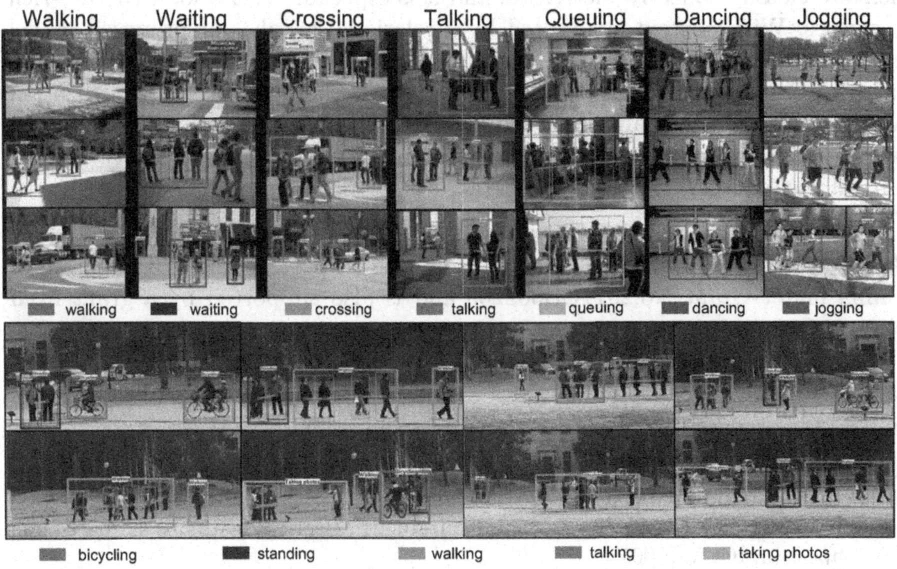

Fig. 8. Results on two collective datasets (upper row) and touring dataset (lower row). Bold rectangle denotes an activity group, with its color indicating its activity. Red line denotes an edge in the tree structure.

method to localize activity groups. It clearly suffers from the unreliable activity recognition. The second baseline, on the other hand, attempts to first cluster the groups and then to recognize their respective activities, of which the poor performance implies that clustering on visual cues is not sufficient.

We visualize the activity group localization results and the learned structure among participants in Fig. 8. Some interesting inner group tree structures are learnt, like a chain structure which connects all people for queuing activity, one or two connections between people facing each other for talking and short links between people nearby having similar standing pose for waiting. As can be seen from Fig. 8, this kind of structure reveals some discriminative relations and disregards irrelevant ones, and also mitigates the impact from occlusions by only linking the overlapped person to one other person. Furthermore, our model, unlike previous approaches that often attempts to recognize the dominant activities, favors seeing different activity groups, thus can effectively disambiguate non-dominant activities and is more suitable for complex scenes.

8 Conclusions

In this paper, we aim at activity group localization including two tasks: group localization and activity recognition. A relational graph is proposed to model the relations among participants, which is solved as an extended problem of minimum spanning forest. We demonstrated that the incorporation of group helps to classify collective activities, and it is especially useful for structure-rich activities. With context structured by a relational graph, our proposed model can achieve competitive results comparing with the state-of-the-art approaches using three different validation schemes. In return, the activity group localization accuracy is also significant improved by jointly inferring the activities. In future work, we plan to exploit this group structure to mine group activity in long surveillance videos.

Acknowledgements. This work is supported in part by the 973 Program of China under Grant No.2011CB302203 and is also supported by a grant from Omron Corporation.

References

1. Amer, M.R., Todorovic, S.: A chains model for localizing participants of group activities in videos. In: ICCV (2011)
2. Blank, M., Gorelick, L., Shechtman, E., Irani, M., Basri, R.: Actions as space-time shapes. In: ICCV (2005)
3. Brendel, W., Todorovic, S., Fern, A.: Probabilistic event logic for interval-based event recognition. In: CVPR (2011)
4. Chang, M.C., Krahnstoever, M., Lim, S., Yu, T.: Group level activity recognition in crowed environments across multiple cameras. In: Workshop on Activity Monitoring by Multi-camera Surveillance System (2010)
5. Choi, W., Savarese, S.: A unified framework for multi-target tracking and collective activity recognition. In: Fitzgibbon, A., Lazebnik, S., Perona, P., Sato, Y., Schmid, C. (eds.) ECCV 2012, Part IV. LNCS, vol. 7575, pp. 215–230. Springer, Heidelberg (2012)
6. Choi, W., Shahid, K., Savarese, S.: What are they doing?: Collective activity classification using spatio-temporal relationship among people. In: VSWS (2009)
7. Choi, W., Shahid, K., Savarese, S.: Learning context for collective activity recognition. In: CVPR (2011)

8. Dalal, N., Triggs, B.: Histogram of oriented gradients for human detection. In: CVPR (2005)
9. Duan, G., Huang, C., Ai, H., Lao, S.: Boosting associated pairing comparison features for pedestrian detection. In: Workshop of ICCV (2009)
10. Felzenszwalb, P., McAllester, D., Ramanan, D.: A discriminatively trained, multiscale, deformable part model. In: CVPR (2008)
11. Gupta, A., Davis, L.S.: Objects in action: An approach for combing action understanding and object perception. In: CVPR (2007)
12. Gupta, A., Srinivasan, P., Shi, J., Davis, L.S.: Understanding videos, constructing plots learning a visually grounded storyline model from annotated videos. In: CVPR (2009)
13. Hakeem, A., Shah, M.: Learning, detection and representation of multi-agent events in videos. Artificial Intelligence 171(8), 586–605 (2007)
14. Jain, A., Gupta, A., Davis, L.S.: Learning what and how of contextual models for scene labeling. In: Daniilidis, K., Maragos, P., Paragios, N. (eds.) ECCV 2010, Part IV. LNCS, vol. 6314, pp. 199–212. Springer, Heidelberg (2010)
15. Khamis, S., Morariu, V.I., Davis, L.S.: A flow model for joint action recognition and identity maintenance. In: CVPR (2012)
16. Lan, T., Wang, Y., Mori, G., Robinovitch, S.N.: Retrieving actions in group contexts. In: Kutulakos, K.N. (ed.) ECCV 2010 Workshops, Part I. LNCS, vol. 6553, pp. 181–194. Springer, Heidelberg (2012)
17. Lan, T., Wang, Y., Wang, W., Mori, G.: Beyond actions: Discriminative models for contextual group activities. In: NIPS (2010)
18. Lan, T., Wang, Y., Yang, W.L., Robinovitch, S.N., Mori, G.: Discriminative latent models for recognizeing contextual group activities. TPAMI 34(8), 1549–1562 (2012)
19. Liu, L., Ai, H.: Learning structure models with context information for visual tracking. Journal of Computer Science and Technology 28(5), 818–826 (2013)
20. Marszalek, M., Laptev, I., Shimid, C.: Actions in context. In: CVPR (2009)
21. Morariu, V.I., Davis, L.S.: Multi-agent event recognition in structured scenarios. In: CVPR (2011)
22. Odashima, S., Shimosaka, M., Kaneko, T., Fukui, R., Sato, T.: Collective activity localization with contextual spatial pyramid. In: Fusiello, A., Murino, V., Cucchiara, R. (eds.) ECCV 2012 Ws/Demos, Part III. LNCS, vol. 7585, pp. 243–252. Springer, Heidelberg (2012)
23. Xiang, T., Gong, S.: Beyond tracking: modeling activity and understanding behavior. IJCV 67(1), 21–51 (2006)
24. Xing, J., Liu, L., Ai, H.: Background subtraction through multiple life span modeling. In: ICIP (2011)

Finding Coherent Motions and Semantic Regions in Crowd Scenes: A Diffusion and Clustering Approach

Weiyue Wang[1], Weiyao Lin[1,*], Yuanzhe Chen[1], Jianxin Wu[2], Jingdong Wang[3], and Bin Sheng[4]

[1] Dept. Electronic Engr., Shanghai Jiao Tong Univ., China
[2] National Key Laboratory for Novel Software Technology, Nanjing Univ., China
[3] Microsoft Research, Beijing, China
[4] Dept. Computer Science & Engr., Shanghai Jiao Tong Univ., China

Abstract. This paper addresses the problem of detecting coherent motions in crowd scenes and subsequently constructing semantic regions for activity recognition. We first introduce a coarse-to-fine thermal-diffusion-based approach. It processes input motion fields (e.g., optical flow fields) and produces a coherent motion filed, named as thermal energy field. The thermal energy field is able to capture both motion correlation among particles and the motion trends of individual particles which are helpful to discover coherency among them. We further introduce a two-step clustering process to construct stable semantic regions from the extracted time-varying coherent motions. Finally, these semantic regions are used to recognize activities in crowded scenes. Experiments on various videos demonstrate the effectiveness of our approach.

1 Introduction

Coherent motions, which represent coherent movements of massive individual particles, are pervasive in natural and social scenarios. Examples include traffic flows and parades of people (cf. Fig. 1). Since coherent motions can effectively decompose scenes into meaningful semantic parts and facilitate the analysis of complex crowd scenes, they are of increasing importance in crowd-scene understanding and activity recognition.

In this paper, we focus on: (1) constructing an accurate coherent motion field to find coherent motions, and (2) finding stable semantic regions based on the detected coherent motions and recognizing activities in a crowd scene.

First, constructing an accurate coherent motion field is crucial to coherent motion detection. In Fig. 1, (c) is the input motion field and (d) is the coherent motion field which is constructed from (c) using the proposed approach. In (c), the motion vectors of particles at the beginning of the Marathon queue are far different from those at the end, and there are many inaccurate optical flow vectors. Due to such variations and input errors, it is difficult to achieve satisfying

* Corresponding author.

D. Fleet et al. (Eds.): ECCV 2014, Part I, LNCS 8689, pp. 756–771, 2014.
© Springer International Publishing Switzerland 2014

coherent detection results directly from (c). However, by transferring (c) into a coherent motion field where the coherent motions among particles are suitably highlighted (i.e., (d)), coherent motion detection is greatly facilitated. However, although many algorithms have been proposed for coherent motion detection [2,21,26,27,12], this problem is not yet effectively addressed. *We argue that a good coherent motion field should effectively be able to*: (1) *encode motion correlation among particles*, such that particles with high correlations can be grouped into the same coherent region; and, (2) *maintain motion information of individual particles*, such that activities in crowd scenes can be effectively parsed by the extracted coherent motion field. Based on these intuitions, we propose a thermal-diffusion-based approach, which can extract accurate coherent motion fields.

Second, constructing meaningful semantic regions for describing the activity patterns in a scene is another important issue. Coherent motions at different times may vary widely, e.g. in Fig 1(a), changing of traffic lights will lead to different coherent motions. Coherent motions alone may not effectively describe the overall semantic patterns in a scene. Therefore, semantic regions need to be extracted from these time-varying coherent motions to achieve stable and meaningful semantic patterns. However, most existing works only focus on the detection of coherent motions at some specific time, while the problem of handling time-varying coherent motions is less studied. We proposed a two-step custering process for this purpose.

Our contributions to crowd scene understand and activity recognition are:

(1) We propose a coarse-to-fine thermal diffusion process to transfer the input motion field into a thermal energy field (TEF), i.e., a more accurate coherent motion field. TEF effectively encodes both motion correlation among particles and motion trends of individual particles. To our knowledge, this is the first work that introduces thermal diffusion to detect coherent motions in crowd scenes. We also introduce a triangulation-based scheme to effectively identify coherent motion components from the TEF.

(2) We further propose a two-step clustering scheme to find semantic regions according to the correlations among coherent motions. The found semantic regions can effectively catch activity patterns in a scene. Thus crowd activity recognition based on these semantic regions can achieve good performance. Besides, the proposed clustering scheme can also effectively handle disconnectedness, which is caused by occlusion or low density regions in the crowd (cf. Fig. 1 (a), the yellow regions).

The remainder of this paper is organized as follows. Section 2 reviews related works. Section 3 describes the framework of the proposed approach. Sections 4-6 describe the details of our proposed thermal diffusion process, triangulation scheme, and two-step clustering scheme. Section 7 shows the experimental results and Section 8 concludes the paper.

2 Related Works

Although many works [2,21,26,27,12,17,25,9,5,10] have been proposed on coherent motion detection, due to the complex nature of crowd scenes, they are not

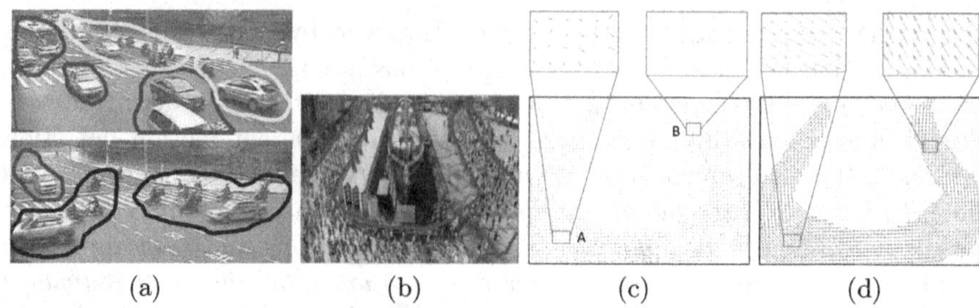

(a) (b) (c) (d)

Fig. 1. (a) Example time-varying coherent motions; (b) Example frame of a Marathon video sequence, the red curve is the ground truth coherent motion region; (c) Input motion vector field of (b); (d) Coherent motion field from (c) using the proposed approach (Best viewed in color)

yet mature for the accurate detection of coherent motion fields. Cremers and Soatto [9] and Brox et al. [5] model the intensity variation of optical flow by an objective functional minimization scheme. However, these methods are only suitable for motions with simple patterns and cannot effectively analyze complex crowd patterns such as the circular flow in Fig. 1 (b). Other works introduce external spatial-temporal correlation traits to model the motion coherency among particles [21,26,27]. Since these methods model particle correlations in more precise ways, they can achieve more satisfying results. However, most of these methods only consider short-distance particle motion correlation within a local region while neglecting long-distance correlation among distant particles, they will have limitations in handling low-density or disconnected coherent motions where the long-distance correlation is essential. Furthermore, without the information from distant particles, these methods are also less effective in identifying coherent motion regions in the case when local coherent motion patterns are close to their neighboring backgrounds. One example of this kind of scenario is showcased in the region B in Fig. 1 (c).

Besides the works on coherent motion detection, there are also other works related to motion modeling. One line of related works is advanced optical flow estimation. These methods try to improve the estimation accuracy of the input motion field by including global constraints over particles [23,14]. However, the focus of our approach is different from these methods. In our approach, we focus on enhancing the correlation among coherent particles to facilitate coherent motion detection. Thus, the motion vectors of coherent particles will be enhanced even if their actual motions are small, such as the region B in Fig. 1 (c) and (d). In contrast, advanced optical flow estimation methods focus on estimating the *actual* motion of particles. Thus, they are still less capable of creating precise results when applied on coherent motion detection.

Another thread of related works is the anisotropic-diffusion-based methods [18,22,20] used in image segmentation. However, our approach also differs from these methods. First, our approach not only embeds the motion correlation among particles, but also suitably maintains the original motion information from the input motion vector field. Comparatively, the anisotropic-diffusion-based methods are more focused on enhancing the correlation among particles while neglecting

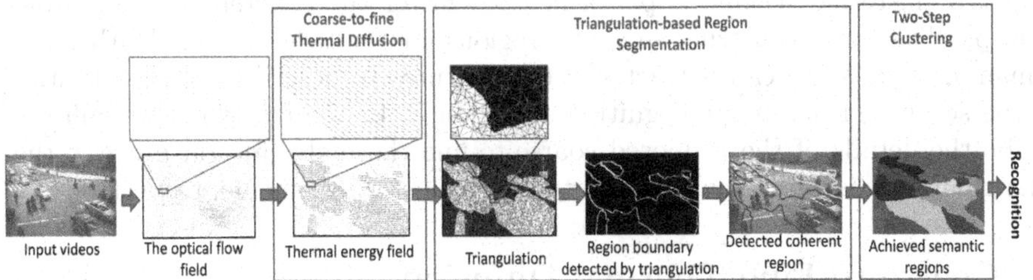

Fig. 2. The flowchart of the proposed approach (best viewed in color)

the particles original information. As aforementioned, maintaining particle motion information is important in parsing crowd scenes. More importantly, due to the complex nature of crowd scenes, many coherent region boundaries are vague, subtle and unrecognizable. Simply applying the anisotropic-diffusion methods [18,22,20] cannot identify the ideal boundaries. The proposed thermal diffusion process can achieve more satisfying results by modeling the motion direction, strength, and spatial correlation among particles.

Besides coherent motion detection, another important issue is the utilization of coherent motions to recognize crowd activities. However, most existing coherent motion works only focus on the extraction of coherent motions while the recognition of crowd activities is much less studied. In [2], Ali and Shah detected instability regions in a scene by comparing with its normal coherent motions. However, they assume coherent motions to be stable, while in practice, many coherent motions may vary widely over time, making it difficult to construct stable normal coherent motions. Furthermore, besides the works on coherent motion, there are also other works which directly extract global features from the entire scene to recognize crowd activities [19,24]. However, since they do not consider the semantic region correlations inside the scene, they have limitations in differentiating subtle differences among activities. Although there are some works [15,13] which recognize crowd activities by segmenting scenes into semantic regions, our approach differs from them in that: our approach finds the semantic regions by first extracting global coherent motion information, while these methods construct semantic regions from the particles' local features. As will be shown in this paper, information from the coherent motions can effectively enhance the correlation among particles, resulting in more meaningful semantic regions to facilitate activity recognition.

3 Overview of the Approach

Fig. 2 shows framework of the proposed approach. The input motion fields are first extracted from input videos. In this paper, optical flow fields [2,6] are extracted, and each pixel in the frame is viewed as a particle. Then, the coarse-to-fine thermal diffusion process is applied to transfer the input motion fields into coherent motion fields (i.e., thermal energy fields (TEFs)). After that, the triangulation-based scheme is applied to identify coherent motions. Finally, the two-step clustering scheme is performed to cluster the coherent motions from multiple TEFs and construct semantic regions for the target scene. With these semantic regions, we can extract effective features to describe crowd activities in the scene and perform recognition accordingly. In the following, we will describe the details of the proposed coarse-to-fine thermal diffusion process, the triangulation-based scheme, and the two-step clustering scheme, respectively.

4 Coarse-to-Fine Thermal Diffusion

In order to facilitate coherency detection, it is important to construct a coherent motion field to highlight the motion correlation among particles while still maintaining the original motion information. To achieve this requirement, we introduce a thermal diffusion process to model particle correlations. Given an input optical flow field, we view each particle as a "heat source" and it can diffuse energies to influence other particles. By suitably modeling this thermal diffusion process, precise correlation among particles can be achieved. Besides, we also argue that the following intuitions should be satisfied:

(1) Particles farther from heat source should achieve fewer thermal energies.

(2) Particles residing in the motion direction of the heat source particle should receive more thermal energies.

(3) Heat source particles with larger motions should carry more thermal energies.

4.1 Thermal Diffusion Process

Based on the above discussions, we borrow the idea from physical thermal propagation [7] and model the thermal diffusion process by Eqn. (1):

$$\frac{\partial \boldsymbol{E}_{\boldsymbol{P},l}}{\partial l} = k_p^2 \left(\frac{\partial^2 \boldsymbol{E}_{\boldsymbol{P},l}}{\partial x^2} + \frac{\partial^2 \boldsymbol{E}_{\boldsymbol{P},l}}{\partial y^2} \right) + \boldsymbol{F}_{\boldsymbol{P}} \tag{1}$$

where $\boldsymbol{E}_{\boldsymbol{P},l} = [E^x_{\boldsymbol{P},l}, E^y_{\boldsymbol{P},l}]$ is the thermal energy for the particle at location $\boldsymbol{P} = (p^x, p^y)$ after performing thermal diffusion for l seconds. $\boldsymbol{F}_{\boldsymbol{P}} = [f^x_{\boldsymbol{P}}, f^y_{\boldsymbol{P}}]$ is the input motion vector for particle $\boldsymbol{P}$, k_p is the propagation coefficient.

The first term in Eqn. (1) models the propagation of thermal energies over free space such that the spatial correlation among particles can be properly enhanced during thermal diffusion. The second term $\boldsymbol{F}_{\boldsymbol{P}}$ can be viewed as the external force added on the particle to affect its diffusion behavior, which preserves the original motion patterns. The inclusion of this term is one of the major differences between our approach and the anisotropic-diffusion methods [20]. Without the $\boldsymbol{F}_{\boldsymbol{P}}$ term, Eqn. (1) can be solved by:

$$\boldsymbol{E}_{\boldsymbol{P},l} = \frac{1}{wh} \sum_{\boldsymbol{Q} \in \boldsymbol{I}, \boldsymbol{Q} \neq \boldsymbol{P}} \boldsymbol{e}_{\boldsymbol{P},l}(\boldsymbol{Q}) \tag{2}$$

where $\boldsymbol{E}_{\boldsymbol{P},l}$ is the final diffused thermal energy for particle $\boldsymbol{P}$ after l seconds, $\boldsymbol{I}$ is the set of all particles in the frame, w and h are width height of the frame.

The individual thermal energy $\boldsymbol{e}_{\boldsymbol{P},l}(\boldsymbol{Q}) = [e^x_{\boldsymbol{P},l}(\boldsymbol{Q}), e^y_{\boldsymbol{P},l}(\boldsymbol{Q})]$ is diffused from the heat source particle $\boldsymbol{Q} = (q^x, q^y)$ to particle $\boldsymbol{P}$ after l seconds, as:

$$e^{\gamma}_{\boldsymbol{P},l}(\boldsymbol{Q}) = u^{\gamma}_{\boldsymbol{Q}} \cdot e^{\frac{-k_p}{l}||\boldsymbol{P}-\boldsymbol{Q}||^2} \tag{3}$$

where $\gamma \in \{x, y\}$, $\boldsymbol{U_Q} = (u^x_{\boldsymbol{Q}}, u^y_{\boldsymbol{Q}})$ is the current motion pattern for the heat source particle $\boldsymbol{Q}$ and it is initialized by $\boldsymbol{U_Q} = \boldsymbol{F_Q}$. $||\boldsymbol{P} - \boldsymbol{Q}||$ is the distance between particles $\boldsymbol{P}$ and $\boldsymbol{Q}$. In this paper, we fix l to be 1 to eliminate its effect.

However, when $\boldsymbol{F}$ in Eqn. (1) is non-zero, it is difficult to get the exact solution for Eqn. (1). So we introduce an additional term $e^{-k_f|\boldsymbol{F_Q}\cdot(\boldsymbol{P}-\boldsymbol{Q})|}$ to approximate the influence of $\boldsymbol{F_Q}$ where k_f is a force propagation factor. Moreover, in order to prevent unrelated particles from accepting too much heat from $\boldsymbol{Q}$, we restrict that only highly correlated particles will propagate energies to each other. The final individual thermal energy from $\boldsymbol{Q}$ to $\boldsymbol{P}$ is:

$$e^{\gamma}_{\boldsymbol{P},l}(\boldsymbol{Q}) = \begin{cases} u^{\gamma}_{\boldsymbol{Q}} \times e^{-k_p||\boldsymbol{P}-\boldsymbol{Q}||^2} \times e^{-k_f|\boldsymbol{F_Q}\cdot(\boldsymbol{P}-\boldsymbol{Q})|} & \text{if } \cos(\boldsymbol{F_P}, \boldsymbol{F_Q}) \geq \theta_c \\ 0 & \text{otherwise} \end{cases} \tag{4}$$

where $\boldsymbol{F_P}$ and $\boldsymbol{F_Q}$ are the input motion vectors of the current particle $\boldsymbol{P}$ and the heat source particle $\boldsymbol{Q}$, and $\cos(\boldsymbol{F_P}, \boldsymbol{F_Q})$ is the cosine similarity, θ_c is a threshold.

From Eqn. (2), we see that the diffused thermal energy $\boldsymbol{E_P}$ is the summation from all the other particles, which encodes the correlation among $\boldsymbol{P}$ and all other particles in the frame. Furthermore, in Eqn. (4), the first term preserves the motion pattern of the heat source. The second term considers the spatial correlation between source and target particles. And the third term guarantees that particles along the motion direction of the heat source receives more thermal energies. Furthermore, the cosine similarity measure $\cos(\boldsymbol{F_P}, \boldsymbol{F_Q})$ is introduced in Eqn. (4) such that particle $\boldsymbol{P}$ will not accept energy from $\boldsymbol{Q}$ if their input motion vectors are far different (or less-coherent) from each other. That is, Eqn. (4) successfully satisfies all the intuitions.

Fig. 3 shows one example of the thermal diffusion process, which reveals that: (1) Comparing Fig. 3 (b) and (a), the original motion information is indeed preseved in the TEF. Moreover, TEF further strengthens particle motion coherency by thermal diffusion, which integrates the influence among particles. Coherent motions become more recognizable, thus more accurate coherent motion extraction can be achieved.

(2) From Fig. 3 (c), we can see that the thermal energy for each heat source particle is propagated in a sector shape. Particles along the motion direction of the heat source (C and D) receive more energies than particles outside the motion direction (such as E). In Fig. 3 (d), since particles on the lower side of the heat source B have small (cosine) motion similarities with B, they do not accept thermal energies.

4.2 The Coarse-to-Fine Scheme

Although Eqn. (2) can effectively strengthen the coherency among particles, it is based on a single input motion field, and only short-term motion information is

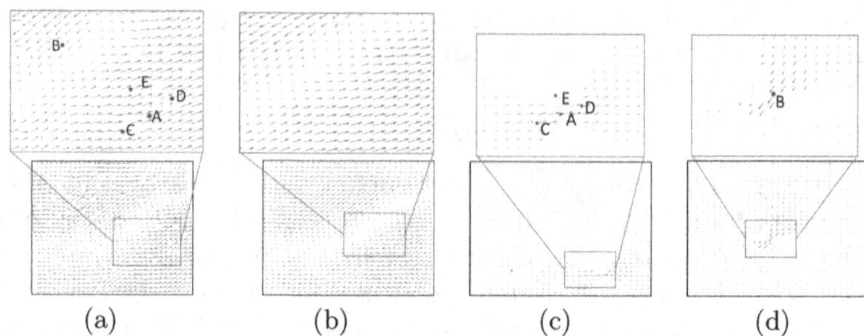

Fig. 3. (a),(b): One input optical flow field and its thermal energy field; (c), (d): Individual thermal diffusion result by diffusing from a single heat source particle A and B to the entire field

considered, which is volatile and noisy. Thus, we propose a coarse-to-fine scheme to include long-term motion information.

Algorithm 1: Coarse-to-Fine Thermal Diffusion Process

$T = T_{max}$.
calculate the input motion vector field $\boldsymbol{F_P}(T)$ with T-frame intervals.
$\boldsymbol{U_P} = \boldsymbol{F_P}(T)$.
for $n = 0$ to Num_{itr} // Num_{itr} is the total iteration time
  use Eqn. (2) to create the new thermal energy field $\boldsymbol{E_P^n}$ based on $\boldsymbol{F_P}(T)$ and $\boldsymbol{U_P}$.
  normalize the vector magnitudes in $\boldsymbol{E_P^n}$.
  $\boldsymbol{U_P} = \boldsymbol{E_P^n}$.
  $T = T - T_{step}$.
  if $T > 0$
    calculate $\boldsymbol{F_P}(T)$ with the new T.
  end if
end for
output $\boldsymbol{E_P^n}$

The entire coarse-to-fine thermal diffusion process is described in Algorithm 1. The long-term motion vector field with a large frame interval T_{max} is first calculated and used to create the thermal energy field. Then, the TEF is iteratively updated with shorter-term motion vector fields, i.e., $\boldsymbol{F_P}(T)$ with smaller T. Fig. 4 (c)-(d) show the TEF results after different iteration numbers. When more iterations are performed, more motion information with different intervals will be included in the thermal diffusion process. Thus, more precise results can be achieved in the TEF, as in Fig. 4 (d). Fig. 1 (d) shows another TEF result after the entire coarse-to-fine thermal diffusion scheme. We find that:

(1) TEF is an enhanced version of the input motion where particles' energy directions in the TEF are similar to their original motion directions. Besides, since TEF include both the motion correlation among particles and the short-/long-term motion information among frames, coherent motions are effectively strengthened and highlighted in TEF.

(2) As mentioned, input motion vectors may be disordered, e.g., region A in Fig. 1 (c). However, the thermal energies from other particles can help recognize these disordered motion vectors and make them coherent, e.g., Fig. 1 (d).

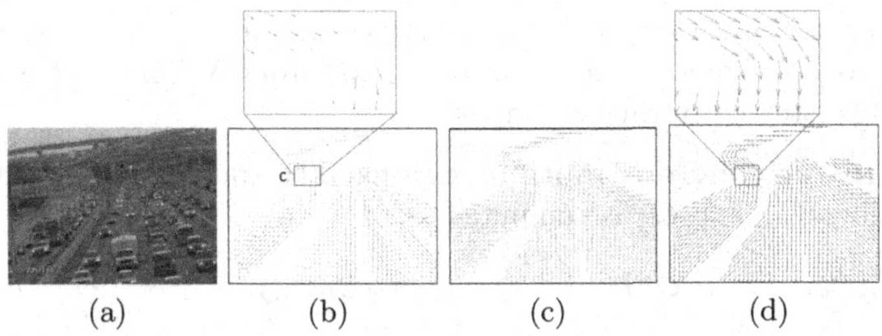

Fig. 4. (a),(b): An input video frame and its input motion vector field; (c),(d): TEF results of Algorithm 1 after 1 and 3 iterations, respectively (T_{max}=5 and T_{step}=1)

(3) Input motion vectors may be extremely small due to slow motion or occlusion by other objects (region B and C in Fig. 4 (b), respectively.) It is very difficult to include these particles into the coherent region by traditional methods [2,21,26,27] because they are close to the background motion vector. However, TEF can strengthen these small motion vectors by diffusing thermal energies from distant particles with larger motions.

5 Coherent Motion Extraction through Triangulation

Coherent motion regions can be achieved by performing segmentation on the TEF. We propose a triangulation-based scheme as follows:

Step 1: Triangulation. In this step, we randomly sample particles from the entire scene and apply the triangulation process [11] to link the sampled particles. The block labeled as "triangulation" in Fig. 2 shows one triangulation result, where red dots are the sampled particles and the lines are links created by the triangulation process [11].

Step 2: Boundary detection. We first obtain each triangulation link weight by:

$$\omega(\boldsymbol{P}, \boldsymbol{Q}) = \frac{||\boldsymbol{E_P} - \boldsymbol{E_Q}||}{||\boldsymbol{P} - \boldsymbol{Q}||} \tag{5}$$

where $\boldsymbol{P}$ and $\boldsymbol{Q}$ are two connected particles, $\boldsymbol{E_P}$ and $\boldsymbol{E_Q}$ are the thermal energy vectors of $\boldsymbol{P}$ and $\boldsymbol{Q}$ in the TEF. A large weight will be assigned if the connected particles are from different coherent motion regions (i.e., they have different thermal energy vectors). Thus, by thresholding on the link weights, we can find links crossing the boundaries. The block labeled as "detected region boundary" in Fig. 2 shows one boundary detection result after step 2.

Step 3: Coherent motion segmentation. Then, coherent motions can be easily segmented and we use the watershed algorithm [3]. The final coherent motions are shown in the block named "detected coherent motions" in Fig. 2.

6 Two-Step Clustering

Since coherent motions may vary over time, it is essential to construct semantic regions from time-varying coherent motions to catch the stable semantic patterns inside a scene, for which we propose a two-step clustering scheme. Assuming that in total M coherent motions ($\boldsymbol{C}_m$, $m = 1, ..., M$) from N TEFs extracted at N times, the two-step clustering scheme is:

Step 1: Cluster coherent motion regions. The similarity between two coherent motions $\boldsymbol{C}_m$ and $\boldsymbol{C}_k$ is computed as:

$$S(\boldsymbol{C}_m, \boldsymbol{C}_k) = \#\{(\boldsymbol{P}, \boldsymbol{Q}) | \boldsymbol{P} \in \boldsymbol{L}_m, \boldsymbol{Q} \in \boldsymbol{L}_k, \cos(\boldsymbol{E}_{\boldsymbol{P}}, \boldsymbol{E}_{\boldsymbol{Q}}) \cdot e^{-k_p ||\boldsymbol{P}-\boldsymbol{Q}||^2} > \theta_{bp}\} \tag{6}$$

where $\#\{\cdot\}$ is the number of elements in a set, and θ_{bp} is a threshold. Furthermore, $\boldsymbol{L}_m$ and $\boldsymbol{L}_k$ are the sets of "indicative particles" for $\boldsymbol{C}_m$ and $\boldsymbol{C}_k$:

$$\begin{cases} \boldsymbol{L}_m = \{\boldsymbol{P} | \cos(\boldsymbol{E}_{\boldsymbol{P}}, \boldsymbol{V}_{\boldsymbol{P}}) > \theta_c, \boldsymbol{P} \text{ is on the boundary of } \boldsymbol{C}_m\} \\ \boldsymbol{L}_k = \{\boldsymbol{Q} | \cos(\boldsymbol{E}_{\boldsymbol{Q}}, \boldsymbol{V}_{\boldsymbol{Q}}) > \theta_c, \boldsymbol{Q} \text{ is on the boundary of } \boldsymbol{C}_k\} \end{cases} \tag{7}$$

where $\boldsymbol{V}_{\boldsymbol{P}} = [v^x_{\boldsymbol{P}}, v^y_{\boldsymbol{P}}]$ is the outer normal vector at $\boldsymbol{P}$, i.e., perpendicular to the boundary and pointing outward the coherent motion region. θ_c is the same threshold as in Eqn. (4). That is, only particles which are on the boundaries of the coherent motion region and whose thermal energy vectors sharply point outward the region are selected as the indicative particles. Thus, we can avoid noisy particles and substantially reduce the required computations.

From Eqn. (6), we can see that we first extract the indicative particles, then only utilize those high-correlation pairs, and the total number of such pairs are the similarity value between two coherent motions. It should be noted that the similarity will be calculated between any coherent motion pairs even if they belong to different TEFs.

Then, we construct a similarity graph for the M coherent motions, and perform clustering [16] on this similarity graph with the optimal number of clusters being determined automatically, the cluster results are grouped coherent regions.

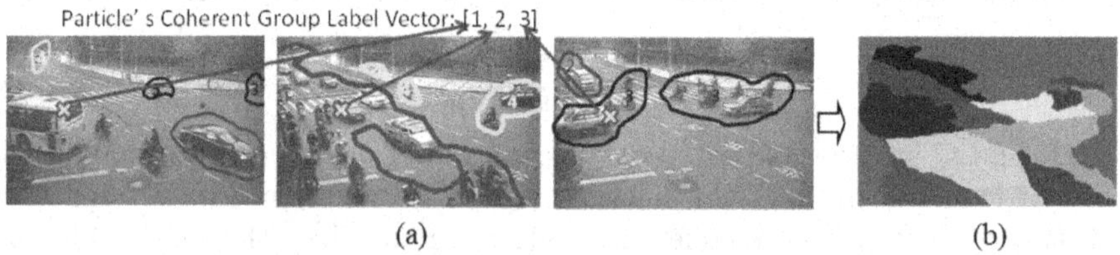

Fig. 5. (a) Step 1: Coherent regions in the three TEFs have been assigned different cluster labels by Step 1 and are displayed in different colors); (b) Find semantic regions by clustering the cluster label vectors of the particles (best viewed in color)

Step 2: Cluster to find semantic regions. Each coherent motion is assigned a cluster label in Step 1, as illustrated in Fig. 5 (a). However, due to the variation of coherent motions at different time, there exist many ambiguous particles. For example, in Fig. 5(a), the yellow cross particle belongs to different coherent motion clusters in different TEFs). This makes it difficult to directly use the clustered coherent motion results to construct reliable semantic regions. In order to address this problem, we further propose to encode particles in each

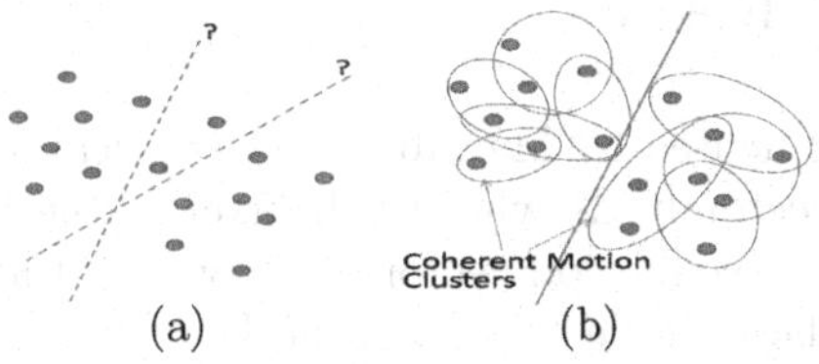

Fig. 6. (a) Directly segmenting semantic regions according to the particles' local features. (b) Segmenting semantic regions with the guidance of coherent motion clusters.

TEF by the cluster labels of the particles' affiliated coherent motions. And by concatenating the cluster labels over different TEFs, we can construct a "cluster label" vector for each particle, as in Fig. 5(a). And with these label vectors, the same spectral clustering process as Step 1 [16] can be performed on the particles to achieve the final semantic regions, as in Fig. 5 (b).

Comparing with previous semantic region segmentation methods [15,13] which perform clustering using local similarity among particles, our scheme utilizes the guidance from the global coherent motion clustering results to strengthen the correlations among particles. For example, in Fig. 6 (a), when directly segmenting the particles by their local features, its accuracy may be limited due to similar distances among particles. However, by utilizing cluster labels to encode the particles, similarities among particles can be suitably enhanced by the global coherent cluster information, as in Fig. 6 (b). Thus, more precise segmentation results can be achieved.

6.1 Activity Recognition

Based on the constructed semantic regions, we are able to recognize activities in the scene. In this paper, we simply average the TEF vectors in each semantic region and concatenate these averaged TEF vectors as the final feature vector for describing the activity patterns in a TEF. Then, a linear support vector machine (SVM) [8] is utilized to train and recognize activities. Experimental results show that with accurate TEF and precise semantic regions, we can achieve satisfying results using this simple method.

6.2 Merging Disconnected Coherent Motions

Since TEF also includes long-distance correlations between distant particles, by performing our clustering scheme, we also have the advantage of effectively merging disconnected coherent motions, which may be caused by the occlusion from other objects or low density of the crowd. For examples, the two disconnected blue regions in the right-most figure in Fig. 5 (a) are merged into the same cluster by our approach. Note that this issue is not well studied in the existing coherent motion research.

7 Experimental Results

Our algorithm is implemented by Matlab and the optical flow fields [6] are used as the input motion vector fields while each pixel in the frame is viewed as a particle. In order to achieve motion vector fields with T-frame intervals ($T = 10$ in our experiments), the particle advection method [2] is used which tracks the movement of each particle over T frames. Furthermore, the parameters k_p, k_f, θ_c, and θ_{bp} in Eqns (4) and (6) are set to be 0.2, 0.8, 0.7, and 0.7, respectively. These values are decided from the experimental statistics.

7.1 Results for Coherent Motion Detection

We perform experiments on a dataset including 30 different crowd videos collected from the UCF dataset [2], the UCSD dataset [1], the CUHK dataset [27], and our own collected set. This dataset covers various real-world crowd scene scenarios with both low- and high-density crowds and both rapid and slow motion flows. Some example frames of the dataset is shown in Fig. 7.

We compare our approach with four state-of-the-art coherent motion detection algorithms: The Lagrangian particle dynamics approach [2], the local-translation domain segmentation approach [21], the coherent-filtering approach [26], and the collectiveness measuring-based approach [27]. In order to further demonstrate the effectiveness of our approach, we also include the results of a general motion segmentation method [4] and an anisotropic-diffusion-based image segmentation method [22].

Qualitative Comparison on Coherent Motion Detection. Fig. 7 compares the coherent motion detection results for different methods. We include the manually labeled ground truth results in the first column. From Fig. 7, we can see that our approach can achieve better coherent motion extraction than the compared methods. For example, in sequence 1, our approach can effectively extract the circle-shape coherent motion. Comparatively, the method in [2] can only detect part of the circle while the methods in [26] and [27] fail to work since few reliable key points are extracted from this over-crowded scene. For sequences 2 and 4 where multiple complex motion flows exist, our approach can still precisely detect the small and less differentiable coherent motions, such as the pink region on the bottom and the blue region on the top in sequence 2 (a). The compared methods have low effectiveness in identifying these regions due to the interference from the neighboring motion regions. In sequences 3 and 6, since motions on the top of the frame are extremely small and close to the background, the compared methods fail to include these particles into the coherent motion region. However, in our approach, these small motions can be suitably strengthened and included through the thermal diffusion process. Furthermore, the methods in [4] and [22] do not show satisfying results, e.g., in sequences 5 and 6. This is because: (1) the crowd scenes are extremely complicated such that the extracted particle flows or trajectories become unreliable, thus making the general motion segmentation methods [4] difficult to create precise results;

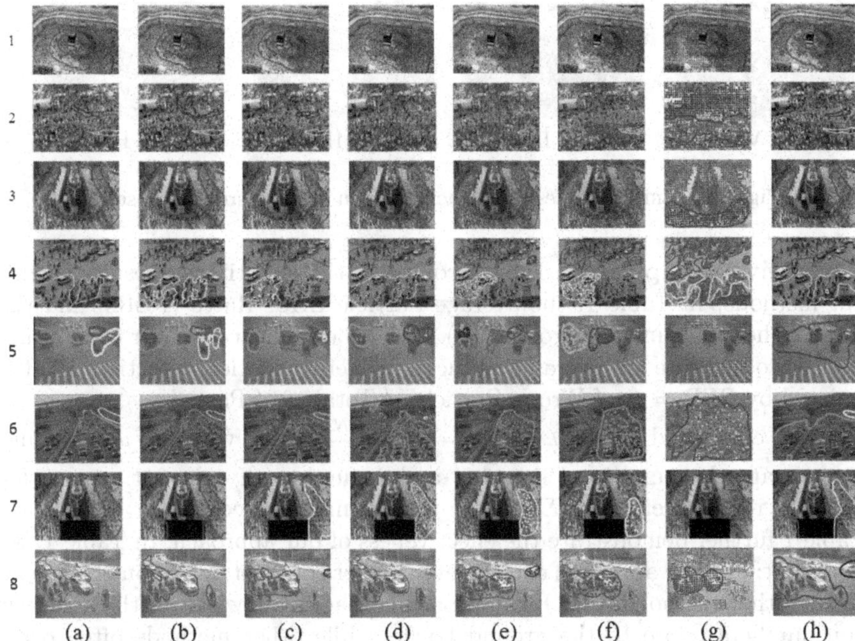

Fig. 7. Coherent motion extraction results. (a): Ground Truth, (b): Results of our approach, (c): Results of [2], (d): Results of [21], (e): Results of [26], (f): Results of [27], (g): Results of [4], (h): Results of [22]. (Best viewed in color).

(2) Since many coherent region boundaries in the crowd motion fields are rather vague and unrecognizable, good boundaries cannot be easily achieved without suitably utilizing the characteristics of the motion vector fields. Thus, simply applying the existing anisotropic-diffusion segmentation methods [22] cannot achieve satisfying results.

Table 1. Average PER and CNE for all sequences in the dataset

Methods	**Proposed**	[2]	[21]	[26]	[27]	[4]	[22]
Average PER (%)	**7.8**	32.5	19.5	25.6	24.1	66.4	21.4
Average CNE	**0.14**	1.24	0.93	1.05	0.96	1.78	0.84

Capability to Handle Disconnected Coherent Motions. Sequences 5-8 in Fig. 7 compare the algorithms' capability in handling disconnected coherent motions. In sequence 7, we manually block one part of the coherent motion region while in sequences 5, 6, and 8, the red or green coherent motion regions are disconnected due to occlusion by other objects or low density. Since the disconnected regions are separated far from each other, most compared methods wrongly segment them into different coherent motion regions. However, with our thermal diffusion process and two-step clustering scheme, these regions can be successfully merged into one coherent region.

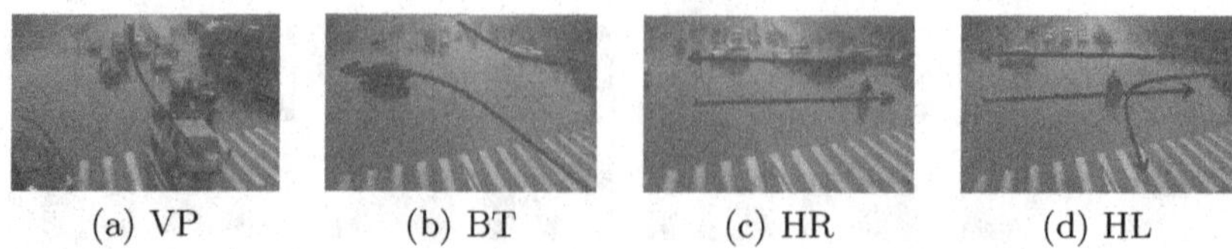

(a) VP (b) BT (c) HR (d) HL

Fig. 8. Example frames of the activities in the crossroad dataset

Quantitative Comparison. Table 1 compares the quantitative results for different methods. In Table 1, the average Particle Error Rates (PERs) and the average Coherent Number Error (CNE) for all the sequences in our dataset are compared to measure the overall accuracy of coherent motion detection. PER is calculated by PER = # of Wrong Particles / Total # of Particles.

CNE is calculated by $CNE = \frac{\sum_i |Num_d(i) - Num_{gt}(i)|}{\Sigma_i 1}$ where $Num_d(i)$ and $Num_{gt}(i)$ are the number of detected and ground-truth coherent regions for sequence i, respectively. And $\Sigma_i 1$ is the total number of sequences.

Table 1 further demonstrate the effectiveness of our approach. In Table 1, we can see that: (1) Our approach can achieve smaller coherent detection error rates than the other methods. (2) Our approach can accurately obtain the coherent region numbers (close to the ground truth) while other methods often over-segment or under-segment the coherent regions.

7.2 Results for Semantic Region Construction and Activity Recognition

We perform experiments on a dataset of a crowd crossroad scene. This dataset includes 400 video clips with each clip includes 20 frames. There are totally four crowd activities in the dataset: vertical pass (VP), both turn (BT), horizontal pass and right turn (HR), and horizontal pass and left turn (HL), as in Fig. 8. This is a challenging dataset in that: (1) the crowd density in the scene varies frequently including both high density as Fig. 8 (a) and low density clips as Fig. 8 (b); (2) The motion patterns are varying for different activities, making it difficult to construct meaningful and stable semantic regions; (3) There are large numbers of irregular motions that disturb the normal motion patterns (e.g., people running the red lights or bicycle following irregular paths); (4) The number of clips in the dataset is small, which increases the difficulty of constructing reliable semantic regions.

Accuracy on Semantic Region Construction. We randomly select 200 video clips to construct semantic regions. Fig. 9 compares the results of four methods: (1) Our approach ("Our"), (2) Directly cluster regions based on the particles' TEF vectors ("Direct", note that our approach differs from this method by clustering over the cluster label vectors), (3) Use [21] to achieve coherent motion regions and then apply our two-step clustering scheme to construct semantic regions ("[21]+Two-Step", we choose to show the results of [21] because from our experiments, [21] has the best semantic region construction results among the compared methods in Table 1), (4) The activity-based scene segmentation method in [15] ("[15]"). We also show original scene images and plot all major activity flows to ease the comparison ("original scene").

Fig. 9 shows that the methods utilizing "coherent motion cluster label" information ("our" and "[21]+two-step") create more meaningful semantic regions than the other methods (e.g., successfully identifying the horizontal motion regions in the middle of the scene). This shows that our cluster label features can effectively strengthen the correlation among particles to facilitate semantic region construction. Furthermore, comparing our approach with the "[21]+Two-Step" method, it is obvious that the semantic regions by our approach are more accurate (e.g., more precise semantic region boundaries and more meaningful segmentations in the scene). This further shows that more precise coherent motion detection results can result in more accurate semantic region results.

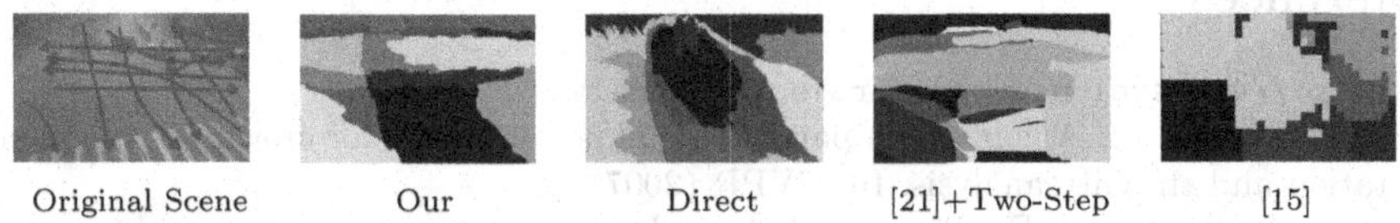

Fig. 9. Constructed semantic regions of different methods. (Best viewed in color).

Table 2. Recognition accuracy of different methods

Methods	Our	Our+OF	Direct	[21]+Two-Step	[15]	[19]
Accuracy	92.2%	87.75%	77.0%	89.5%	79.2%	67.0%

Performances on Activity Recognition. We randomly select 200 video clips and construct semantic regions by the methods in Fig. 9. After that, we derive features from the TEF and train SVM classifiers by the method in Section 6.1. Finally, we perform recognition on the other 200 video clips. Besides, we also include the results of two additional methods: (1) a state-of-the-art dense-trajectory-based recognition method [19] ("Dense-Traj"); (2) the method which uses our semantic regions but uses the input motion field (i.e., the optical flows) to derive the motion features in each semantic region ("Our+OF"). From the recognition accuracy shown in Table 2, we observe that:

(1) Methods using more meaningful semantic regions ("our", "our+OF", and "[21]+Two step") achieve better results than other methods. This shows that suitable semantic region construction can greatly facilitate activity recognition.

(2) Approaches using TEF ("Our") achieve better results than those using the input motion field ("Our+OF"). This demonstrates that compared with the input motion filed, our TEF can effectively improve the effectiveness in representing the semantic regions' motion patterns.

(3) The dense-trajectory method [19] which extracts global features does not achieve satisfying results. This is because the global features still have limitations in differentiating the subtle differences among activities. This further implies the usefulness of semantic region decomposition in analyzing crowd scenes.

8 Conclusion

In this paper, we study the problem of coherent motion detection and semantic region construction in crowd scenes, and introduce a thermal-diffusion-based algorithm together with a two-step clustering scheme, which can achieve more meaningful coherent motion and semantic region results. Experiments on various videos show that our approach achieves the state-of-the-art performance.

Acknowledgements. This work is supported in part by the following grants: National Science Foundation of China (No. 61001146, 61202154, 61025005, U1201255), Shanghai Pujiang Program (12PJ1404300), and Chinese National 973 Grants (2010CB731401).

References

1. http://www.svcl.ucsd.edu/projects/anomaly/
2. Ali, S., Shah, M.: A lagrangian particle dynamics approach for crowd flow segmentation and stability analysis. In: CVPR (2007)
3. Beucher, S., Meyer, F.: The morphological approach to segmentation: the watershed transformation. Optical Engineering (1992)
4. Brox, T., Malik, J.: Object segmentation by long term analysis of point trajectories. In: Daniilidis, K., Maragos, P., Paragios, N. (eds.) ECCV 2010, Part V. LNCS, vol. 6315, pp. 282–295. Springer, Heidelberg (2010)
5. Brox, T., Rousson, M., Deriche, R., Weickert, J.: Colour, texture, and motion in level set based segmentation and tracking. Image Vis. Comput. (2010)
6. Bruh, A., Weickert, J., Schnörr, C.: Lucas/Kanade meets Horn/Schunck: combining local and global optic flow methods. Int'l J. Computer Vision (2005)
7. Carslaw, H., Jaeger, J.: Conduction of Heat in Solids. IEEE Trans. Pattern Analysis and Machine Intelligence (1986)
8. Chang, C., Lin, C.: LIBSVM: A library for support vector machines. ACM Trans. Intell. Syst. Technol. 2, 1–27 (2011)
9. Cremers, D., Soatto, S.: Motion competition: A variational approach to piecewise parametric motion segmentation. Int. J. Comput. Vis. (2005)
10. Cui, X., Liu, Q., Gao, M., Metaxas, D.N.: Abnormal detection using interaction energy potentials. In: CVPR (2011)
11. Edelsbrunner, H., Shah, N.: Incremental topological flipping works for regular triangulations. Algorithmica (1996)
12. Hu, M., Ali, S., Shah, M.: Learning motion patterns in crowded scenes using motion flow field. In: ICPR (2008)
13. Li, J., Gong, S., Xiang, T.: Scene segmentation for behaviour correlation. In: Forsyth, D., Torr, P., Zisserman, A. (eds.) ECCV 2008, Part IV. LNCS, vol. 5305, pp. 383–395. Springer, Heidelberg (2008)
14. Lin, D., Grimson, E., Fisher, J.: Learning visual flows: a lie algebraic approach. In: CVPR (2009)
15. Loy, C.C., Xiang, T., Gong, S.: Multi-camera activity correlation analysis. In: CVPR (2009)
16. Lu, Z., Yang, X., Lin, W., Zha, H., Chen, X.: Inferring user image search goals under the implicit guidance of users. IEEE Trans. Circuits and Systems for Video Technology (2014)

17. Mehran, R., Oyama, A., Shah, M.: Abnormal crowd behavior detection using social force model. In: CVPR (2009)
18. Perona, P., Malik, J.: Scale-space and edge detection using anisotropic diffusion. IEEE Trans. Pattern Analysis and Machine Intelligence 12(7), 629–639 (1990)
19. Wang, H., Klaser, A., Schmid, C., Liu, C.: Action recognition by dense trajectories. In: CVPR (2011)
20. Weickert, J.: Anisotropic diffusion in image processing. Teubner, Stuttgart (1998)
21. Wu, S., Wong, H.: Crowd motion partitioning in a scattered motion field. IEEE Trans. Systems, Man, and Cybernetics (2012)
22. Wu, Y., Wang, Y., Jia, Y.: Adaptive diffusion flow active contours for image segmentation. Computer Vision and Image Understanding, 1421–1435 (2013)
23. Xu, L., Jia, J., Matsushita, Y.: Motion detail preserving optical flow estimation. IEEE Trans. Pattern Analysis and Machine Intelligence 34(9), 1744–1757 (2012)
24. Xu, T., Peng, P., Fang, X., Su, C., Wang, Y., Tian, Y., Zeng, W., Huang, T.: Single and multiple view detection, tracking and video analysis in crowded environments. In: AVSS (2012)
25. Zhan, B., Monekosso, D., Remagnino, P., Velastin, S., Xu, L.: Crowd analysis: a survey. Machine Vision and Applications (2008)
26. Zhou, B., Tang, X., Wang, X.: Coherent filtering: Detecting coherent motions from crowd clutters. In: Fitzgibbon, A., Lazebnik, S., Perona, P., Sato, Y., Schmid, C. (eds.) ECCV 2012, Part II. LNCS, vol. 7573, pp. 857–871. Springer, Heidelberg (2012)
27. Zhou, B., Tang, X., Wang, X.: Measuring crowd collectiveness. In: CVPR (2013)

Semantic Aware Video Transcription Using Random Forest Classifiers

Chen Sun and Ram Nevatia

University of Southern California, Institute for Robotics and Intelligent Systems, Los Angeles, CA 90089, USA

Abstract. This paper focuses on transcription generation in the form of subject, verb, object (SVO) triplets for videos in the wild, given off-the-shelf visual concept detectors. This problem is challenging due to the availability of sentence only annotations, the unreliability of concept detectors, and the lack of training samples for many words. Facing these challenges, we propose a Semantic Aware Transcription (SAT) framework based on Random Forest classifiers. It takes concept detection results as input, and outputs a distribution of English words. SAT uses video, sentence pairs for training. It hierarchically learns node splits by grouping semantically similar words, measured by a continuous skip-gram language model. This not only addresses the sparsity of training samples per word, but also yields semantically reasonable errors during transcription. SAT provides a systematic way to measure the relatedness of a concept detector to real words, which helps us understand the relationship between current visual detectors and words in a semantic space. Experiments on a large video dataset with 1,970 clips and 85,550 sentences are used to demonstrate our idea.

Keywords: Video transcription, random forest, skim-gram language model.

1 Introduction

Humans can easily describe a video in terms of actors, actions and objects. It would be desirable to make this process automatic, so that users can retrieve semantically related videos using text queries, and capture the gist of a video before watching it. The goal of this paper is generating video transcriptions, where each transcription consists of a subject, verb and object (SVO) triplet. We assume the videos to be unconstrained user captured videos possibly with overlaid captions and camera motion, but that they are pre-segmented to be short clips with a single activity, and a few objects of interest. One example is shown in Figure 1 left.

Video transcription with SVO is an extremely challenging problem for several reasons: first, as annotating actions and objects with spatio-temporal bounding boxes is time-consuming and boring, in most cases, only video-level sentence annotations are available for training (Figure 1 right). Second, although there

D. Fleet et al. (Eds.): ECCV 2014, Part I, LNCS 8689, pp. 772–786, 2014.
© Springer International Publishing Switzerland 2014

Human annotations:
Three men are biking in the woods
Two cyclist do tricks
Guys are riding motorcycles
People ride their bikes
...

Output of SAT:
Person rides bike

Fig. 1. *Left:* one example of the testing videos we used. *Right:* our algorithm utilizes sentence based annotations, and output subject, verb, object triplets.

are several action and object datasets with a large number of categories [7,26], a considerable amount of SVO terms are still not present in these categories. Finally, even for the detectors with corresponding SVO terms, many of them are still far from reliable when applied to videos in the wild [15].

Many papers on activity analysis have emerged recently. Usual goal is activity or event classification of pre-defined categories [32,27,18]. For video transcription problem where the combinatorial space of SVO triplets is much bigger and sparse, it is hard to apply these techniques directly and learn a classifier for every SVO triplet. Guadarrama *et al.* [14] proposed a video transcription method YouTube2Text: they learned an SVM classifier for each term in candidate subjects, verbs and objects, and used low-level and mid-level visual features [17] [30] for classification. All these approaches treat each class (either an *activity* or a *term*) independently, and ignore the semantic relationships between the classes.

We propose a semantic aware transcription framework (SAT) using Random Forest classifiers. Inputs for the Random Forest classifiers are detection responses from off-the-shelf action and object detectors. SAT's outputs are in the form of SVO triplets, which can then be used for sentence generation. To obtain the SVO terms for training, we parse human annotated sentences and retrieve the subject, verb and object terms. The labels of a training video contain the top k most commonly used subject, verb and object terms for that video. For example, the set of labels for video in Figure 1 may be (*person, motorcyclist, ride, do, bicycle, trick*).

The core innovation of SAT is to consider the semantic relationships of SVO labels during training. Semantic aware training is important when the labels are user provided without a pre-defined small vocabulary set. On one hand, humans may use different words to describe objects that are close visually or essentially the same (*bike* and *bicycle*). On the other hand, for problems with a large number of classes, semantically reasonable errors (*tomato* to *potato*) are more desirable than unreasonable ones (*tomato* to *guitar*). SAT provides a framework for semantic aware training: during node split selection of decision trees, it favors the clustering of semantically similar words. Similarity is measured by continuous word vectors, learned with the skip-gram model [21]. The skip-gram model optimizes context prediction power of words over a training corpus, and has been shown to produce word vector clusters with clear semantic similarities. Given the learned word vectors, SAT picks the best node split by computing differential entropy of word clusters. Each tree in the resulting forest divides training samples hierarchically into semantically consistent clusters.

The detector responses used in this paper can be seen as candidate action and object proposals. They are more suitable for the transcription task than low level features, as action and object locations are not provided in the annotations. Torresani *et al.* [29] showed that object detector responses provide competitive performance when used as features for image classification task. SAT goes one step further and provides a mechanism to measure the semantic map from a detector type to output labels. The map measures the influence of a detector's response on the output probabilities of labels. For example, *bicycle* detector may have high impact on both objects like *bike* or *motorcycle* as well as verbs like *ride*.

SAT has the following highlights:

Larger vocabulary support. A Random Forest classifier is naturally suited for multi-class classification. We can use a single Random Forest for arbitrary vocabulary size. For SVM-based frameworks, the number of one-vs-rest classifiers required grows linearly with vocabulary size.

Feature sharing for semantically similar words. By using a hierarchical structure, SAT allows sharing features for semantically similar words. For example, *horse* and *bicycle* may go through the same path in a decision tree until separated by a node with large tree depth. This is particularly useful for training as words with few occurrence can be trained together with similar words with more training samples.

Semantic reasonableness. SAT optimizes over semantic similarity instead of binary classification error. In our framework, *piano* is considered a *better* error for *guitar* than *pasta*. The resulting transcriptions are thus likely to be more semantically reasonable.

The contribution of this paper is two-fold: First, we propose a semantic aware learning algorithm for Random Forest classifiers, which has the potential of producing semantically reasonable results. Second, we provide a mechanism to compute semantic maps from detectors to words.

2 Related Work

Several recent papers have focused on generating descriptions for visual contents. Kulkarni *et al.* [16] proposed a method to detect candidate objects and their attributes from static images, and applied CRF for sentence generation. [1] used object detection and tracking results to describe videos with simple actions and fixed camera. In [15], the authors obtained the SVO triplets using object and action detectors and reranked the triplet proposals with language models. A related task to video description is event recounting, it asks a system to output supporting evidence for a video event. [6,19] used event labels as prior and built CRF or SVM models with concept detector responses. All these approaches assume that the detectors carry direct semantic meanings and require trained detectors for every action, object or attribute of interest. SAT is different from these as it learns a hierarchical mapping from detector response space to word space.

Alternatively, [25] proposed to classify semantic representations (SR) with low level features, and used a CRF to model the co-occurrences of SR. It formulated the conversion from SR to sentences as a statistical machine translation problem and tested the idea on an indoor kitchen dataset. However, global low level features may not be discriminative enough to identify actions and objects for videos in the wild.

The idea of utilizing semantic relationships of annotations have motivated several papers on image and video analysis. Topic model was used in [24] to convert text into topic distribution vectors and group mid-level actions. Deng *et al.* [8] observed the existence of a trade-off between accuracy and specificity for object categories and applied it to image classification. Specificity is measured by an object's depth in WordNet hierarchy. YouTube2Text system [14] extended this idea and used data-driven hierarchies to generate SVO video transcriptions. Both of them applied semantic hierarchy in the post-processing stage. Unlike these approaches, SAT uses word vectors in a continuous semantic space, and defines an adaptive similarity measurement for arbitrary word sets; semantic similarity is explicitly used to learn the word maps.

3 Proposed Method

This section describes the Semantic Aware Transcription framework. We first briefly introduce a vector based word representation in semantic space [21]. The structure of Random Forest classifiers and their inputs are then described. Next, we show how the semantic word vectors can be used to select the best node split in Random Forest classifier training, such that training samples after split become more similar in the semantic space. Finally, a mechanism is provided to compute the semantic map for a concept detector.

3.1 Continuous Word Representation

Many existing Natural Language Processing techniques can be used to measure semantic distances among different words. For example, WordNet [23] provides a database of hierarchical word trees, on which semantic distances can be defined. To learn data driven semantic structures, topic modeling techniques such as Latent Dirichlet Allocation have been found to be useful [3].

We adopt the continuous word representation learned by skip-gram model [22]. Given a sequence of training words $\{w_1, w_2, ..., w_T\}$, it searches for a vector representation for each word w_i, denoted by v_{w_i}, such that

$$\frac{1}{T}\sum_{t=1}^{T}\sum_{-c\leq j\leq c, j\neq 0}\log P(w_{t+j}|w_t) \quad (1)$$

is maximized. c controls the training context size, and the probability of w_{t+j} given w_t is defined by the softmax function

$$P(w_i|w_j) = \frac{\exp(v_{w_i}^T\ v_{w_j})}{\sum_w \exp(v_w^T\ v_{w_j})} \quad (2)$$

This objective function attempts to make the vector representation of semantically close words behave similarly in predicting their contexts. In practice, a hierarchical softmax function is used to make the training process computationally feasible. When trained on large text corpus, the Euclidean distances between vectors of semantically similar words are small.

Compared with rule-based WordNet and the topic modeling techniques, continuous word representation is both data-driven and flexible. Once word vectors are trained from an independent corpus, one can measure the semantic similarity for an arbitrary set of words.

3.2 Video and Annotation Preprocessing

We assume each training video has several one-sentence descriptions annotated via crowdsourcing. These sentences are parsed by a dependency parser [20], and only subject, verb and object components are kept. Denote D_s, D_v and D_o as the dictionary of subjects, verbs and objects, we store their word vectors as $V_s = \{v_{w_s}|w_s \in D_s\}$, $V_v = \{v_{w_v}|w_v \in D_v\}$, $V_o = \{v_{w_o}|w_o \in D_o\}$.

After annotation preprocessing, every training video has a set of SVO words. For subject and object words, although most of them correspond to concrete objects, we lack the bounding boxes to locate them. Meanwhile, an annotated verb may correspond to very different actions, like the verb *play* in *play guitar* and *play soccer*. It is hard to learn verb detectors based on these annotations directly.

We use off-the-shelf action and object detectors to represent a video [13,28]. Training data for these detectors are obtained from independent datasets. The types of trained detectors correspond to a very limited vocabulary and may not contain the words used in video transcriptions. To apply object detectors, we sample video frames and take the maximum response returned by a detector over all sampled frames; action detectors are applied with sliding windows, and are also combined by maximum pooling. The final video representation is a vector of action and object detector responses $S = [s_1\ s_2\ ...\ s_M]$. Each dimension corresponds to a type of action or object detector.

3.3 Random Forest Structure

As illustrated in Figure 2, we use a forest of randomly trained decision trees to map detector responses into posterior word probabilities.

Starting from the root, every non-leaf node k contains a simple classifier $\Phi_k(S)$ for vector S of detector responses based on a single type of detector response.

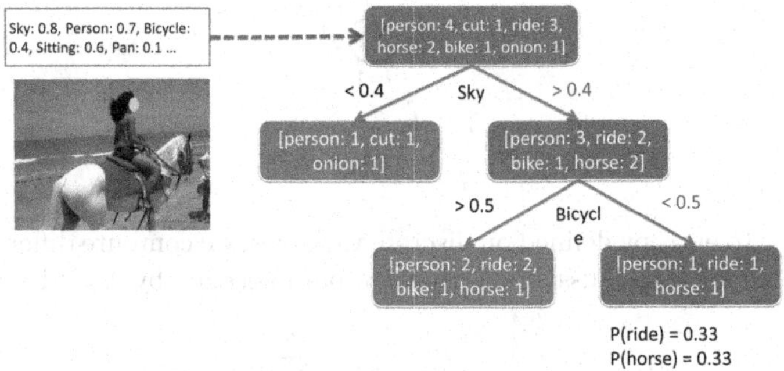

Fig. 2. Illustration of a single decision tree used in SAT. Detector responses for a video are used to traverse the tree nodes until reaching a leaf. Note that a horse detector may not be needed in the process.

We have

$$\Phi_k(S) = s_i - \tau \begin{cases} > 0 & \text{Go to left} \\ < 0 & \text{Go to right} \end{cases} \tag{3}$$

where s_i is the i-th concept in the vector, and τ is the threshold.

Leaf nodes store word count vectors; as in traditional decision trees, a word count vector is obtained by accumulating the SVO words from all training samples belonging to the leaf node. The final confidence score for word w_i is obtained by

$$f(w_i) = \frac{1}{T}\sum_{t=1}^{T} \frac{c_{t,w_i}}{\sum_w c_{t,w}} \tag{4}$$

where T is the forest size, $c_{t,w}$ is the count for word w at the leaf node of the t-th decision tree.

The subject, verb and object terms with the highest confidence scores respectively are selected to generate a sentence description for a video.

3.4 Learning Semantic Hierarchies

Ideally, we would like to learn a tree structure which encodes the semantic hierarchy of SVO words. Towards this goal, we use the continuous word vectors to measure the *semantic compactness* for a set of words.

Denote $W = \{w_1, w_2, ..., w_M\}$ as a group of words, and $V = \{v_{w_1}, v_{w_2}, ..., v_{w_M}\}$ the word vectors. Assume the underlying distribution of the word vectors is Gaussian, we have

$$g(v_w) = \frac{1}{\sqrt{(2\pi)^k|\Sigma|}} \exp\left(-\frac{1}{2}(v_w - \mu)^T \Sigma^{-1}(v_w - \mu)\right) \tag{5}$$

where k is the dimension of word vectors, $\mu = [\mu_1\ \mu_2\ ...\ \mu_k]$ is the mean vector, and $\Sigma = diag(\sigma_1, \sigma_2, ..., \sigma_k)$ is the diagonal covariance matrix. They can be estimated from V by

$$\mu_j = \frac{1}{M} \sum_{i=1}^{M} v_{w_i}^j \tag{6}$$

$$\sigma_j = \frac{1}{M} \sum_{i=1}^{M} (v_{w_i}^j - \mu_j)^2 \tag{7}$$

In analogy to entropy defined on discrete variables, we compute differential entropy $H(\mu, \Sigma)$ for the Gaussian distribution parametrized by Σ and μ following

$$H(\mu, \Sigma) = \frac{1}{2} \ln |(2\pi e)\Sigma| \sim \sum_{j=1}^{k} \ln \sigma_j + C \tag{8}$$

$H(\mu, \Sigma)$ measures the degree of uncertainty for the distribution: the lower the value, the more certain the distribution is. For word vectors, since semantically similar words lie close to each other, their estimated σ's should be small and the differential entropy low according to Equation 8. As a result, to achieve semantic compact node splits, we minimize the weighted differential entropy

$$\frac{|V_l|}{|V_l| + |V_r|} H(\mu_l, \Sigma_l) + \frac{|V_r|}{|V_l| + |V_r|} H(\mu_r, \Sigma_r) \tag{9}$$

where V_l and V_r are the two groups of word vectors after node split.

It has been shown that the generalization error of random forests is determined by the strength of individual trees and correlation of the trees [4]. To reduce correlation, we impose several types of randomness in training. First, only a subset of training videos is sampled to train each decision forest. Second, we randomly assign each node to consider only subject words, verb words or object words, and use the selected word to compute differential entropy as defined in Equation 8. Finally, we use the node split selection criteria similar to extremely randomized trees [12]: after a feature dimension is sampled, instead of finding the best threshold to minimize Equation 9, we only choose a small subset of candidate thresholds and pick the best one among them. The training algorithm is summarized in Algorithm 1.

3.5 Computing Semantic Maps

In Section 3.2, we showed how to obtain a video representation based on pre-trained action and object detectors. SAT does not require a detector to carry direct semantic meaning indicated by its name, but uses its response to traverse the semantic hierarchy defined by Random Forest classifiers.

Motivated by the variable importance estimation for Random Forest classifiers [4], we use a similar scheme to compute semantic maps from input detector types to output words. Let M be the number of action and object detectors, and F be the trained Random Forest classifier. Given a set S of detector response vectors, for each detector type m, we set its value for all vectors in S to the lowest possible and the highest possible, and fix the values of all the other dimensions.

Algorithm 1. SAT Training Algorithm

```
Input: A set S of training videos as concept response and word annotation pairs
Output: Random forest with T decision trees
for t = 1 to T do
    Sample a subset of S as S_t
    Call splitNode(S_t)
end for

splitNode(S):
if stop criteria not met then
    Randomly select a node type from SVO
    Randomly sample N_f feature dimension indices and N_t thresholds
    Apply each weak classifier to split set S
    Evaluate weak classifiers using words of selected type (Equation 9)
    Select the weak classifier which minimizes Equation 9
    Split S into S_l and S_r based on the selected weak classifier
    Call splitNode(S_l) and splitNode(S_r)
else
    Compute word counts and mark the node as leaf
end if
```

This produces two modified sets $\mathcal{S}'$ and $\mathcal{S}''$. We apply F on $\mathcal{S}'$ and $\mathcal{S}''$ to get the word probabilities. The correlation of the m-th detector and a word w is measure by

$$\varphi_m(w) = \sum_{i=1}^{N} |f'_w(i) - f''_w(i)| \tag{10}$$

Here $f'_w(i)$ is w's probability for the i-th sample in $\mathcal{S}'$, and $f''_w(i)$ is its probability for the i-th sample in $\mathcal{S}''$. Higher value of $\varphi_m(w)$ indicates a strong map between the detector type and the word.

3.6 Discussion

One major difference of SAT from traditional Random Forest classifiers is the node split criteria during training. SAT fits a group of semantic word vectors using a Gaussian distribution with diagonal covariance matrix, and computes differential entropy to measure the *semantic compactness*. The penalties of grouping semantic similar words are smaller. For example, the split of (*drive, ride*) and (*cut, slice*) should be better than (*drive, slice*) and (*cut, ride*). Traditional Random Forest classifiers cannot distinguish the two as their discrete entropies are the same. This difference makes SAT produce more semantically reasonable predictions.

Video transcription using SAT is fast (tens of comparisons for each decision tree, and hundreds of trees in total). For training, it only evaluates the randomly sampled thresholds instead of searching for the optimum, which can be done very efficiently. Since there is no interaction between different trees, both training and testing of SAT can be parallelized easily.

Our method to compute semantic map is related to, but different from, variable importance estimation: we measure only the change in output word probabilities; instead of filling in randomly selected values, we select only the maximum and minimum possible values for that dimension, so that all nodes using this dimension to make decision are toggled.

Computed semantic maps provide several indications: if the semantic meaning of a detector's name and its top mapped words are identical or very similar, it is quite likely that the detector outputs are reliable. Besides, if an object detector's top mapped words contain verbs or an action detector's top mapped words contain objects, the combination should appear frequently in training videos.

4 Experiments

In this section, we first describe our experiment setup and the dataset used for evaluations. Next, we compare the performance of SAT with several other video transcription frameworks. Semantic maps learned by SAT are shown at the end of this section.

4.1 Dataset

We used the YouTube dataset collected by Chen and Dolan [5]. There are 1,970 short video clips with 85,550 sentence-based video descriptions in English. Videos were annotated by Amazon Mechanical Turk workers.

Object detector training data were provided by PASCAL VOC challenge [9] and a subset of ImageNet [7]. There are 243 categories in total. For action detector training, we used UCF 101 dataset [26] with 101 categories.

4.2 Experimental Setup

We followed data partitioning used in [14], there are 1,300 training videos and 670 testing videos.

Stanford parser [20] was used to extract the subject, verb and object components from the sentence associated with the videos. Some of the extracted words are typos or occur only a few times, we filtered these words out; this results in a dictionary size of 517 words. As annotators tend to describe the same video with diverse words, each video was described by the one most common subject, the two most common verbs and the two most common objects. Unless otherwise specified, we used this set of words as the groundtruth to train the classifiers and measure the accuracy of video transcription.

We used the continuous word vectors pre-trained on Google News dataset. It was provided by the authors of [22]. The dimension of each word vector is 300.

Deformable part models (DPM) [11] were used to train object detectors. Part of the detector models were downloaded from [2]. The object detector works on static frames. We uniformly sampled frames every second, and used maximum pooling to merge the detector confidence scores for all sampled frames in the same video.

To learn action detectors, we first extracted motion compensated dense trajectory features with default parameters [31], and encoded the features with Fisher Vectors [28]. We set the number of clusters for Fisher Vectors as 512, and computed Fisher Vectors for the HOG, HOF and MBH components separately. A linear SVM [10] was then trained for each action category with a single type of features. We used average fusion to combine the classifier outputs.

Parameter set for Random Forest classifiers includes the number of decision trees T, the number of sampled feature dimensions N_f and thresholds N_t, as well as the max tree depth D. Parameters were selected by measuring out-of-bag errors (OOB) [4]. It was computed as the average of prediction errors for each decision tree, using the non-selected training data.

Table 1. Top correlated verb and object pairs in SAT

Verb	Top correlation
come	go
run	walk
spread	mix
fry	cook
put	pour

Object	Top correlation
scooter	bicycle
finger	hand
motorbike	car
vegetable	onion
computer	camera

4.3 Performance Evaluation

We first qualitatively show how SAT uses semantic similarity to group training samples. We computed correlation of two words based on their number of cooccurrences in SAT's leaf nodes. To avoid correlation introduced by multiple annotations for the same video, we used only a single SVO triplet for each video. Table 1 shows several subject or object words with their top correlated words. As we can see, most of the pairs are both semantically close and visually related.

For quantitative evaluation, we compare our proposed SAT framework with the following two baselines:

Random Forest with no semantic grouping (RF). Every word under this setting was treated as an independent class. Node split is selected by computing the discrete entropy.

Linear SVM (SVM). A linear SVM classifier was learned for every word, using the detector responses as input features.

We fixed $T = 150$ and $D = 40$ for SAT and RF. N_f and N_t were selected by OOB. For SVM system, we fixed the soft-margin penalty ratio between positive and negative samples as the inverse of their sample size ratio, and used cross validation to select the cost parameter.

Table 2. Accuracy comparison among our proposed SAT, a traditional RF and a linear SVM

Method	Subject accuracy	Verb accuracy	Object accuracy
SAT	**0.816**	**0.344**	**0.244**
RF	**0.816**	0.312	0.152
SVM	0.726	0.281	0.191

Table 2 shows the accuracy comparison for the three methods. It is easy to see that our proposed SAT provides better performance in both verb accuracy and object accuracy, compared with the other two systems which do not use semantic relationships during training. In Figure 3, we also show some of the transcription results. SAT provided the correct SVO triplets for the top two examples, and related triplets for the middle two examples. The bottom one is a case where SAT returned wrong result.

Table 3. Accuracy and WUP comparisons between our proposed method and YouTube2text [14]

Method	Subject accuracy	Verb accuracy	Object accuracy
SAT	0.792	**0.306**	**0.188**
YouTube2Text [14]	**0.809**	0.291	0.170
Method	Subject WUP	Verb WUP	Object WUP
SAT	**0.927**	**0.625**	**0.590**
YouTube2Text [14]	0.926	0.468	0.467

We also compare the performance of SAT with the YouTube2Text system proposed by [14]. It used semantic hierarchies to convert unconfident SVO proposals to terms with higher semantic hierarchy. Their evaluations included a binary accuracy measurement using only the most common SVO triplet per testing video, no semantic conversion was used for this evaluation. To make our results comparable, we used the groundtruth labels provided by the authors. WUP metric was also used for evaluation. It is computed by

$$s_{WUP}(w_1, w_2) = \frac{2 \cdot D_{lcs}}{D_{w_1} + D_{w_2}} \tag{11}$$

where lcs is the least common ancestor of w_1 and w_2 in the semantic tree defined by WordNet, and D_w is the depth of w in the semantic tree. It provides the semantic similarity of w_1 and w_2 defined by the rule-based WordNet. Since a word may have multiple entries in WordNet, we used the set of entries provided by [14].

In Table 3, the binary accuracy of SAT is comparable to YouTube2Text in subject terms, and better in verb and object terms. For the WUP measure where semantic relatedness is being considered, SAT outperforms the YouTube2Text system by a large margin.

GT: Person rides bicycle.
SAT: Person rides bicycle.
RF: Person tries ball.
SVM: Person rides bicycle.

GT: Person dances rain.
SAT: Person dances group.
RF: Person does hair.
SVM: Person kicks video.

GT: Person does exercise.
SAT: Person does exercise.
RF: Person does pistol.
SVM: Person gets pencil.

GT: Person runs ball.
SAT: Person plays ball.
RF: Person hits ball.
SVM: Person kicks garden.

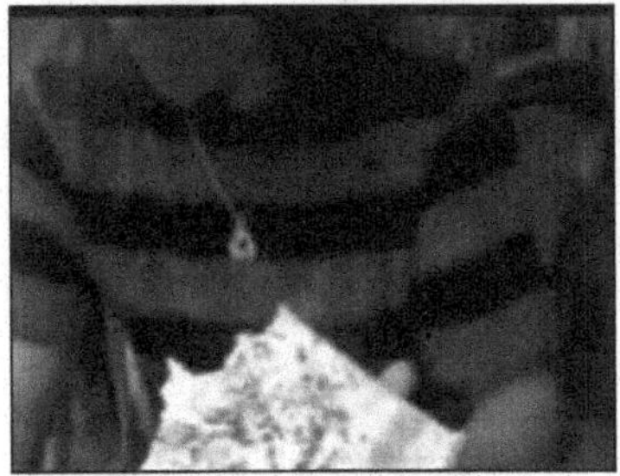

GT: Person eats pizza.
SAT: Person makes food.
RF: Person goes something.
SVM: Person makes box.

GT: Person drives car.
SAT: Person rides car.
RF: Person moves bicycle.
SVM: Person does pool.

Fig. 3. Testing videos with SVO triplets from groundtruth (GT), SAT, RF and SVM. Exact matches are marked in blue, semantic related verbs and objects are marked in red.

Fig. 4. Visualization of semantic maps for some action and object detectors

4.4 Visualization of Semantic Maps

Finally, we visualize some of the detector semantic maps in Figure 4. The maps were computed using testing videos. It can be seen that some of the detectors have semantically close mappings in the word space. Many action detectors we used involve objects, this is reflected by their top mapped words (*board* for *drawing on board* detector). It is also interesting to see that some detectors are connected with the top mapped words through motion patterns (the word *dance* and the *salsa spin* detector). This observation also holds for object detectors. The maps also illustrate how SAT handles the words outside the detectors' vocabulary.

5 Conclusion

We propose a Semantic Aware Video Transcription (SAT) system using Random Forest classifiers. SAT builds a hierarchical structure using the response of action and object detectors. It favors grouping of semantically similar words, and outputs the probabilities of subject, verb, object terms. SAT supports large vocabulary of output words, and is able to generate more semantic reasonable results. Experimental results on a web video dataset of 1970 videos and 85,550 sentences showed that SAT provides state-of-the-art transcription performance.

Acknowledgement. This work was supported by the Intelligence Advanced Research Projects Activity (IARPA) via the Department of Interior National Business Center (DoI/NBC), contract number D11PC0067. The U.S. Government is authorized to reproduce and distribute reprints for Governmental purposes notwithstanding any copyright annotation thereon. Disclaimer: The views and conclusions contained herein are those of the authors and should not be interpreted as necessarily representing the official policies or endorsements, either expressed or implied, of IARPA, DoI/NBC, or the U.S. Government.

References

1. Barbu, A., Bridge, A., Burchill, Z., Coroian, D., Dickinson, S.J., Fidler, S., Michaux, A., Mussman, S., Narayanaswamy, S., Salvi, D., Schmidt, L., Shangguan, J., Siskind, J.M., Waggoner, J.W., Wang, S., Wei, J., Yin, Y., Zhang, Z.: Video in sentences out. In: UAI (2012)
2. Batra, D., Agrawal, H., Banik, P., Chavali, N., Alfadda, A.: Cloudcv: Large-scale distributed computer vision as a cloud service (2013)
3. Blei, D.M., Ng, A.Y., Jordan, M.I.: Latent dirichlet allocation. JMLR (2003)
4. Breiman, L.: Random forests. Machine Learning (2001)
5. Chen, D., Dolan, W.B.: Collecting highly parallel data for paraphrase evaluation. In: ACL (2011)
6. Das, P., Xu, C., Doell, R.F., Corso, J.J.: A thousand frames in just a few words: Lingual description of videos through latent topics and sparse object stitching. In: CVPR (2013)
7. Deng, J., Dong, W., Socher, R., Li, L.-J., Li, K., Fei-Fei, L.: ImageNet: A Large-Scale Hierarchical Image Database. In: CVPR (2009)
8. Deng, J., Krause, J., Berg, A., Fei-Fei, L.: Hedging your bets: Optimizing accuracy-specificity trade-offs in large scale visual recognition. In: CVPR (2012)

9. Everingham, M., Van Gool, L., Williams, C.K.I., Winn, J., Zisserman, A.: The pascal visual object classes (voc) challenge. IJCV (2010)
10. Fan, R.E., Chang, K.W., Hsieh, C.J., Wang, X.R., Lin, C.J.: LIBLINEAR: A library for large linear classification. Journal of Machine Learning Research (2008)
11. Felzenszwalb, P.F., Girshick, R., McAllester, D., Ramanan, D.: Object detection with discriminatively trained part-based models. PAMI (2009)
12. Geurts, P., Ernst, D., Wehenkel, L.: Extremely randomized trees. Machine Learning (2006)
13. Girshick, R.B., Felzenszwalb, P.F., McAllester, D.: Discriminatively trained deformable part models, release 5
14. Guadarrama, S., Krishnamoorthy, N., Malkarnenkar, G., Mooney, R., Darrell, T., Saenko, K.: Youtube2text: Recognizing and describing arbitrary activities using semantic hierarchies and zero-shot recognition. In: ICCV (2013)
15. Krishnamoorthy, N., Malkarnenkar, G., Mooney, R.J., Saenko, K., Guadarrama, S.: Generating natural-language video descriptions using text-mined knowledge. In: AAAI (2013)
16. Kulkarni, G., Premraj, V., Dhar, S., Li, S., Choi, Y., Berg, A.C., Berg, T.L.: Baby talk: Understanding and generating image descriptions. In: CVPR (2011)
17. Li, L.J., Su, H., Xing, E.P., Li, F.F.: Object bank: A high-level image representation for scene classification & semantic feature sparsification. In: NIPS (2010)
18. Li, W., Yu, Q., Divakaran, A., Vasconcelos, N.: Dynamic pooling for complex event recognition. In: ICCV (2013)
19. Liu, J., Yu, Q., Javed, O., Ali, S., Tamrakar, A., Divakaran, A., Cheng, H., Sawhney, H.S.: Video event recognition using concept attributes. In: WACV (2013)
20. de Marneffe, M.C., MacCartney, B., Manning, C.D.: Generating typed dependency parses from phrase structure parses. In: LREC (2006)
21. Mikolov, T., Chen, K., Corrado, G., Dean, J.: Efficient estimation of word representations in vector space. CoRR (2013)
22. Mikolov, T., Sutskever, I., Chen, K., Corrado, G.S., Dean, J.: Distributed representations of words and phrases and their compositionality. In: NIPS (2013)
23. Miller, G.A.: Wordnet: A lexical database for English. CACM (1995)
24. Ramanathan, V., Liang, P., Fei-Fei, L.: Video event understanding using natural language descriptions. In: ICCV (2013)
25. Rohrbach, M., Qiu, W., Titov, I., Thater, S., Pinkal, M., Schiele, B.: Translating video content to natural language descriptions. In: ICCV (2013)
26. Soomro, K., Zamir, A.R., Shah, M.: Ucf101: A dataset of 101 human actions classes from videos in the wild. CRCV-TR-12-01
27. Sun, C., Nevatia, R.: Active: Activity concept transitions in video event classification. In: ICCV (2013)
28. Sun, C., Nevatia, R.: Large-scale web video event classification by use of fisher vectors. In: WACV (2013)
29. Torresani, L., Szummer, M., Fitzgibbon, A.: Efficient object category recognition using classemes. In: Daniilidis, K., Maragos, P., Paragios, N. (eds.) ECCV 2010, Part I. LNCS, vol. 6311, pp. 776–789. Springer, Heidelberg (2010)
30. Wang, H., Kläser, A., Schmid, C., Liu, C.L.: Action recognition by dense trajectories. In: CVPR (2011)
31. Wang, H., Schmid, C.: Action Recognition with Improved Trajectories. In: ICCV (2013)
32. Wang, L., Qiao, Y., Tang, X.: Mining motion atoms and phrases for complex action recognition. In: ICCV (2013)

Ranking Domain-Specific Highlights by Analyzing Edited Videos

Min Sun, Ali Farhadi, and Steve Seitz

University of Washington, Seattle, WA, USA

Abstract. We present a fully automatic system for ranking domain-specific highlights in unconstrained personal videos by analyzing online edited videos. A novel latent linear ranking model is proposed to handle noisy training data harvested online. Specifically, given a search query (domain) such as "surfing", our system mines the Youtube database to find pairs of raw and corresponding edited videos. Leveraging the assumption that edited video is more likely to contain highlights than the trimmed parts of the raw video, we obtain pair-wise ranking constraints to train our model. The learning task is challenging due to the amount of noise and variation in the mined data. Hence, a latent loss function is incorporated to robustly deal with the noise. We efficiently learn the latent model on a large number of videos (about 700 minutes in all) using a novel EM-like self-paced model selection procedure. Our latent ranking model outperforms its classification counterpart, a motion analysis baseline [15], and a fully-supervised ranking system that requires labels from Amazon Mechanical Turk. Finally, we show that impressive highlights can be retrieved without additional human supervision for domains like skating, surfing, skiing, gymnastics, parkour, and dog activity in unconstrained personal videos.

Keywords: Video highlight detection, latent ranking.

1 Introduction

We increasingly capture large amounts of video data, a trend that is likely to accelerate with new devices like Google Glass. On YouTube alone, 100 hours of video are uploaded every minute. Most video content, however, is not fun to watch; the best videos have usually been carefully and manually *edited* to feature the highlights and trim out the boring segments.

Wouldn't it be great if computers could do the editing for us? I.e., we'd provide raw video footage, and out would pop a high quality edited video. Indeed, both Google and Facebook recently released products that seek to achieve similar goals. Google's Auto-Awesome movie feature generates a video summary from all the footage of an event (complete with filters and background music!). However, Auto-Awesome works best when the event videos are short and contain only highlights. It is not clear how it can handle raw personal videos typically a few minutes long. Facebook's new *Look Back* feature provides similar functionality,

D. Fleet et al. (Eds.): ECCV 2014, Part I, LNCS 8689, pp. 787–802, 2014.
© Springer International Publishing Switzerland 2014

Fig. 1. Retrieving domain-specific highlights (e.g., for surfing) from unconstrained personal videos is an important step toward automatic video editing. Our system automatically learns how to rank the "highlightness" of every moment (a short 2 seconds clip) in a raw video by analyzing edited videos on Youtube. Here we show ranking results of our system on two raw videos (click to watch on Youtube link1, link2) captured by GoPro cameras, where each clip is represented by a frame sampled from the clip.

but focused on photos and your most popular posts instead of videos. These applications motivate the importance of research in automatic video editing.

As a step towards this goal, we address the problem of retrieving domain-specific *highlights* in raw videos (see Fig. 1). While prior research has explored the highlight selection problem in limited domains, e.g., [27,20,16,26,25,10,4,23], most methods require large amounts of human-crafted training data. Since the definition of a highlight is highly dependent on the domain of interest (e.g., blowing out the candles on a birthday cake, a ski jump, raising glasses in a toast), it's not clear that these techniques are scalable to handle video contents from all domains.

Instead, we ask a crucial question: can we learn to detect highlights by analyzing how users (with domain knowledge) edit videos? There is a wealth of edited video content on YouTube, along with the raw source material. This content captures highlights spanning a vast range of different activities and actions. Furthermore, we show that it's possible to identify the mapping of raw source material to edited highlights, leading to a wealth of training data. In this work, we introduce (1) a novel system to automatically harvest domain-specific information from Youtube, and (2) a novel latent ranking model which is trained with the harvested noisy data (see Fig. 2(a)). Leveraging the assumption that edited video is more likely to contain highlights than the trimmed parts of the raw video, we formulate the highlight selection problem as a pair-wise ranking problem between short video clips in the raw video. (see rank constraints in Fig. 2(b)). We introduce latent variables into the ranking model to accommodate variation of highlight selection across different users. For instance, user "A" might select a very long duration clip as a highlight, whereas user "B" prefers shorter clips (see Fig. 2(c)). We use a novel EM-like self-paced model selection procedure to learn the latent ranking model.

Our approach has several advantages. First, our latent ranking model consistently outperforms its classification counterpart (see Fig. 4). Second, it can be efficiently trained on a large number of videos by taking advantage of a newly developed solver [11] for linear ranking SVM. Third, our latent model nicely takes care of the noise in our automatically harvested training data (see Fig. 5). Finally, we demonstrate results using automatically harvested YouTube data that rival those obtained from a fully supervised ranking approach trained on specially constructed training sets commissioned on Amazon Mechanical Turk (see Fig. 6). Hence, we demonstrate state-of-the-art performance, while achieving much greater scalability (avoiding the need to manually construct new annotated datasets).

2 Related Work

Our work is highly related to video summarization. There is a large literature on video summarization (see review [1]), including techniques based on keyframes [13,3,17,15]. In the following, we focus on subjects most relevant to our work.

2.1 Content-Aware Video Summarization

Many methods have been recently proposed for summarizing a video with a known type of content. Given an ego-centric video, we know hands, objects, and faces are important cues. [14,12] propose to summarize a video according to discovered interesting objects and faces. Similarly, given a video uploaded to ecommerce websites for selling cars and trucks, [8] propose to use web-image priors (i.e., canonical viewpoints of cars and trucks online) to select frames to summarize the video. Our method is another step in this direction. However, our proposed system is not restricted to handling only ego-centric videos, where cues from hands and objects are easier to extract, nor does it rely on discovered canonical viewpoints which are shown to have generalization issues in other domains such as cooking [8]. Whereas, our method is feature independent and we directly harvest information about how users select domain-specific highlights to create their own edited videos.

2.2 Sports Video Analysis

Highlight detection in broadcast sport videos has attracted several researchers [27,20,16,26,25,10,4,23] due to the popularity of such videos. Compared to other video types, such as personal videos, broadcast sports videos have well defined structure and rules. A long sports game often can be divided into parts and only a few of these parts contain certain well defined highlights. For example, common highlights are the score event in soccer games, the hit event in baseball games, and the "bucket" event in basketball games. Due to the well defined structure, specifically designed mid-level and high-level audio-visual features, such as player trajectories, crowds, audience cheering, goal or score events, etc., are used in many methods. One exception is [23] which uses easy-to-extract low-level visual features. Most of the methods treat highlight detection as a binary classification task, where each part of a training video is labeled as true highlight or not. We argue that for unconstrained personal videos, it is ambiguous for humans to label highlights as binary labels. This also imposes extra burden for annotators. Hence, it is important for a method to scale-up by naturally harvesting crowd-sourced information online.

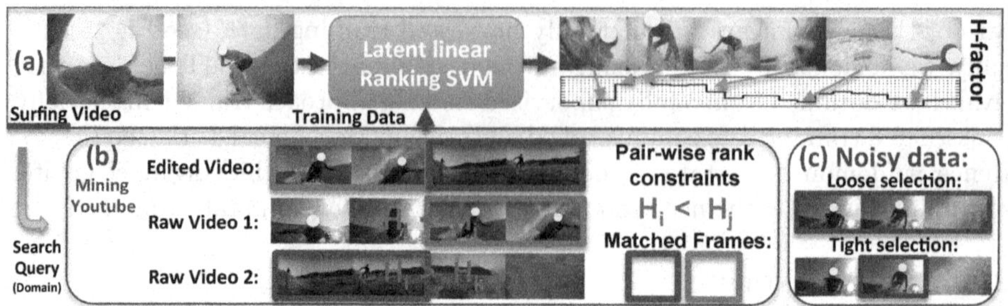

Fig. 2. System overview: Given "surfing" videos, we train a latent linear ranking SVM to predict the h-factors fully automatically (Panel (a)). Our system automatically harvests training data online by mining raw and edited videos in Youtube related to "surfing". The raw and edited pair of videos give us pair-wise rank constraints as shown in panel (b). Note that the harvested data is noisy due to the variation of highlights selected by the users on Youtube (Panel (c)).

2.3 Crowd-Sourced Highlight Discovery

Recently, many researchers have demonstrated the ability to discover highlights from crowd-sourced data such as Twitter. Olsen et al. show that user interaction data from an interactive TV application can be mined to detect events [18]. Hannon et al. use Twitter data in PASSEV [5], combining summaries of tweet frequency and user-specified search for terms in tweets to generate a highlight reel. The main difference between these approaches and others in computer vision is that crowd-sourced data (users' annotations but not the the video data) are always required as an input. Hence, these methods cannot work well on videos with no or very few associated crowd-sourced data. On the contrary, our method harvests both crowd-sourced and video data from Youtube for training our latent ranking model. After training, our model can be applied to rank highlights in any video.

2.4 Learning to Rank

Learning to rank is an important learning technique in recent years, because of its application to search engines and online advertisement. In computer vision, researchers have adopted the ranking approach mainly for the image retrieval task [6,21]. Recently, Parikh and Grauman have introduced the concept of relative attributes [19] which opens up new opportunities to learn human-nameable visual attributes using a ranking function. In this work, we propose one of the first ranking models for domain-specific video highlight retrieval. Our domains include popular actions such as skating, surfing, etc.

3 Video Highlights

A video highlight is a moment (a very short video clip) of major or special interest in a video. More formally, a highlightness measure h (later referred to as "h-factor") for every moment in a video can be defined such that moments with high h are typically selected as highlights. Hence, the goal of retrieving highlights is equivalent to learning a function $f(x)$ to predict the h-factor (i.e., $h = f(x)$) given features x extracted from a moment in the video (see Fig. 1).

One straight forward way to learn $f(x)$ is to treat it as a supervised regression problem. However, labeling the h-factor consistently across many videos is hard for humans. On the contrary, it is much easier for humans to rank pairs of moments based on their highlightness. Hence, we propose to formulate the video highlights problem as a pair-wise ranking problem described next.

3.1 Pair-Wise Ranking

To establish notation, we use i as a unique index for all moments in a set of videos. Each moment is associated to a tuple (y, q, x), where $y \in R$ is the relative h-factor, $q \in Q$ is the index of the video containing the moment, Q is a set of videos, and x is the features extracted from the moment. The set of ranking constraints corresponding to the qth video is defined as,

$$P_q \equiv \{(i,j)|q_i = q_j = q, y_i > y_j\} , \tag{1}$$

where $q_i = q_j = q$ ensures that only moments from the qth video are compared to each other according to the relative h-factor y. Note that y only needs to be a relative value to express the order within each video. The full set of pair-wise ranking constraints in the dataset is defined as,

$$P \equiv \cup_{q \in Q} P_q = \{(i,j)|q_i = q_j, y_i > y_j\} , \tag{2}$$

where $q_i = q_j$ ensures that only moments from the same video are enforced with the ranking constraints.

Our goal is to learn a function $f(x)$ such that

$$f(x_i) > f(x_j), \ \forall (i,j) \in P , \tag{3}$$

which means none of the pair-wise ranking constraints is violated. We adopt the L2 regularization and L2 loss linear ranking SVM formulation to learn $f(x; w) = w^T x$ as follows,

$$\min_w \tfrac{1}{2} w^T w + \lambda \textstyle\sum_{(i,j) \in P} \max(0, 1 - w^T(x_i - x_j))^2 , \tag{4}$$

where w is the linear model parameter and $\lambda > 0$ is a regularization parameter. Ideally, the optimal model parameters can be learned since the optimization problem is convex. However, the large number of pair-wise constraints ($|P|$) becomes the main difficulty in training the ranking SVM efficiently. We solve the problem efficiently by taking advantage of a newly proposed fast truncated newton solver which employs order-statistic trees to avoid evaluating all the pairs [11]. Note that other non-linear ranking methods can also be used. However, they are typically impractical to train on a large-scale dataset such as our videos dataset (about 700 minutes long in all).

3.2 Ranking from Edited Videos

Asking humans to order moments within each video is feasible but not scalable. Since the definition of a highlight is highly dependent on the domain of interest, human annotators without domain knowledge will find the task ambiguous and tedious. We argue that we can naturally harvest such information from edited videos. Assume we have raw videos which are used to create the edited videos, and users make a (somewhat) informed decision to select the moments in the raw video to include in the edited video. We now get the following ranking constraints,

$$y_i > y_j, \quad i \in E_q, j \in R_q \setminus E_q \ , \tag{5}$$

where q is the index of the raw video, E_q is the set of moments in the raw video which are included in the edited video, and R_q is the set of moments in the raw video. Eq. 5 states that the relative h-factors of moments included in the edited video (E_q) is higher than the rest of the moments in the raw video ($R_q \setminus E_q$) (see Fig. 2(b)).

Given many pairs of raw videos and their edited versions, the linear ranking SVM becomes

$$\min_w \tfrac{1}{2}\|w\|^2 + \lambda \textstyle\sum_{q \in Q} L(q; w) \ , \tag{6}$$

$$L(q; w) = \textstyle\sum_{i \in E_q} \sum_{j \in R_q \setminus E_q} \max(0, 1 - w^T(x_i - x_j))^2 \tag{7}$$

where Q is a set of raw videos, and $L(q; w)$ is the loss of violating ranking constraints in the qth raw video. As a result, we can even extract ranking constraints for training data where users edit their videos by simply trimming it. The main advantage of this approach is that a wealth of such data exists in the digital world. We describe in Sec. 3.5 how we can harvest such data online automatically.

3.3 Handling Noisy Data

Not all the users online are "experts". The start and end of a specific highlight can vary significantly depending on the users. For example, user "A" might select a loose highlight with a few minutes included in its edited version. In contrast, user "B" might select a tight highlight with a few seconds (see Fig 2(c)). Especially for the loose highlight, constraints expressed in Eq. 5 might not always be true. In order to address this problem, we propose a latent loss as follows,

$$L_{z_q}(q; w) = \textstyle\sum_{j \in R_q \setminus E_q} \max(0, 1 - w^T(x_{z_q} - x_j))^2 \ , \tag{8}$$

$$z_q = \arg\max_{i \in E_q} f(x_i; w) \ , \tag{9}$$

where z_q is the best highlighted moment in E_q. Note that the latent loss relaxes the constraints in Eq. 5 to

$$y_{z_q} > y_j, \quad j \in R_q \setminus E_q \ , \tag{10}$$

where only the the best highlighted moment z_q in E_q must have higher relative h-factor than the rest of the moment ($R_q \setminus E_q$) in the qth raw video.

Latent Linear Ranking SVM. A latent linear ranking SVM incorporating the latent loss is defined as,

$$\min_{w,Z} \frac{1}{2}\|w\|^2 + \lambda \left(\sum_{q \in Q_T} L(q; w) + \sum_{q \in Q_L} L_{z_q}(q; w) \right) , \tag{11}$$

where Q_T is a set of raw videos with tightly selected highlights, Q_L is a set of raw videos with loosely selected highlights, $\{Q_T, Q_L\}$ is a partition of Q (i.e., $Q_T \cap Q_L = \emptyset$, $Q_T \cup Q_L = Q$), and $Z = \{z_q\}_{q \in Q_L}$ is a set of latent best highlighted moments in Q_L.

EM-Like Approach. Given Q_T and Q_L, we solve the model parameters w and the set of latent best highlighted moments Z iteratively using a EM-like approach.

1. We set $Q = Q_T$ and obtain our initial w by solving Eq. 6.
2. Given the initial w, we estimate our initial Z by solving Eq. 9 (E-step).
3. Then, we obtain w by solving Eq. 11 while fixing Z (M-step).
4. Given w, we estimate Z by solving Eq. 9 (E-step).
5. Go to step 3 if the estimated latent variables Z have changed; otherwise, stop the procedure.

In our experiments, the EM-like approach stops typically within five iterations.

3.4 Self-Paced Model Selection

Identifying the loosely selected videos Q_L for our latent ranking SVM model is important. On the one hand, SVM is known to be sensitive to inconsistent labels, since they are very likely to become strong distractors (supporting vectors) which affect the learned model significantly. On the other hand, we essentially throw away most of the potentially good highlighted moments in E_q by moving a video q from Q_T to Q_L. Hence, it is important to automatically find a good trade-off between Q_T and Q_L.

We propose a self-paced model selection procedure to evaluate K partitions of Q guided by pair-wise accuracy of every video $A = \{a_q\}_q$ as follows.

1. We set $Q_T = Q$ and obtain w by solving Eq. 11.
2. Given the model w, we evaluate the pair-wise accuracy A on the training videos.
3. Given A, we order the videos from low to high pair-wise accuracy, and evenly split the videos into K mutually exclusive sets.
4. Starting from the set with the lowest accuracy, we remove one set at a time from Q_T to Q_L[1].
5. For each partition of Q_T and Q_L, we solve Eq. 11 to obtain a new model w and new pair-wise accuracy A on the training videos.
6. Finally, we select the model with the highest mean pair-wise accuracy $mean(A)$.

[1] Note that there are videos with highlights consisting of only one or two moments (a few seconds). We always keep these videos in Q_T.

The pair-wise accuracy a_q for the qth video is defined as,

$$a_q = \frac{\sum_{(i,j)\in P_q} \mathbf{1}(w^T x_i > w^T x_j)}{|P_q|} , \tag{12}$$

where $\mathbf{1}(\cdot)$ is a indicator function which is one if a pair-wise constraint is satisfied in our learned model ($w^T x$), P_q (defined in Eq. 1) is the set of pair-wise constraints for the qth video, and $|P_q|$ is the number of pairs. The pair-wise accuracy is a normalized value between 0 and 1. Hence, it is comparable for different pairs of Q_T and Q_L. Our results in Fig. 5 demonstrate that our novel latent linear ranking model can be effectively learned to achieve superior accuracy by our EM-like self-paced model selection procedure.

3.5 Harvesting Youtube Videos

Nowadays, many videos are shared online through websites such as Youtube. We propose to mine these videos online to harvest a large amount of data. In particular, we query the Youtube database with popular search queries to retrieve relevant videos. Given the retrieved videos, we can use [7] to efficiently identify duplicated frames between every pair of videos. Once a set of consecutively duplicated frames are matched for a pair of videos (q_1, q_2), we define these matched frames as the selected highlighted moments in E. Then, we identify either q_1 or q_2 as the raw video and treat the moments in the raw video as R. Note that [7] is robust, but it can miss matches when the video includes after effects. Hence, our dataset is built with high precision.

Theoretically, what we have proposed is feasible even for a large scale database such as Youtube. In particular, Google is already using a similar procedure to find videos with copyright violations. However, this is a daunting task for individual researchers like us, since we need to retrieve a large number of videos to find enough matched pairs of edited and raw videos. Fortunately, Youtube has an online editor called "Youtube video editor", which keeps track of the information of raw and edited pairs of videos. Hence, we use the Youtube API to query videos generated by "Youtube video editor" to retrieve a smaller set of raw and edited pairs of videos. Then, we use [7] to efficiently identify the duplicated frames as the highlighted moments. Inevitably, our current data is limited by the availability of videos generated by "Youtube video editor". Nevertheless, our current system works amazingly well for common action and animal related domains such as "skating", "dog", "parkour", etc. We describe in Sec. 4.3 about the selected domains and the data statistics. We also believe that a much larger dataset can be easily built by accessing Google's internal infrastructure.

3.6 Comparison to Binary Highlight Classification

Recall that previous highlight selection methods [27,20,16,26,25,10,4,23] formulate their problem as a binary highlight classification problem. Although we argue computing highlights is intrinsically a ranking problem, we show that our problem can also be considered as a binary classification problem by setting

$$\{y_i = +1; i \in E_q, q \in Q\} \ \ and \ \ \{y_j = -1; j \in R_q \setminus E_q, q \in Q\} , \tag{13}$$

where $y \in \{-1, +1\}$ becomes a binary label. Next we discuss the advantages and disadvantages of a binary classification problem.

The binary classification problem is highly related to a pair-wise ranking problem which ignores the video index and expresses the following constraints,

$$P \equiv \{(i, j); y_i > y_j\} \ . \tag{14}$$

In this case, moments are also compared to each other across videos. However, training a classification model is much more efficient than training a ranking model. This is because the huge number (i.e., quadratic to the number of moments) of pair-wise violation losses (Eq. 7) are replaced by losses with respect to a separation hyperplane as defined below,

$$L^C(q; w) = \textstyle\sum_{i; q_i = q} \max(0, 1 - y_i(w^T x_i)) \ . \tag{15}$$

The number of losses in Eq. 15 is linear to the number of moments. The advantages of a classification model is (1) it implicitly incorporates more pair-wise constraints in Eq. 14 than constraints in Eq. 2, and (2) it can be solved more efficiently using many existing methods. Nevertheless, the newly added pair-wise constraints which compare moments from two different videos (i.e., $\{(i, j); q_i \neq q_j, y_i > y_j\}$) could be harmful. For example, the highlight in video q_1 might be less interesting than many non-highlighted moments in video q_2.

We can also define a latent linear classification SVM to handle the noisy data by replacing $L(q; w)$ with $L^C(q; w)$ and $L_{z_q}(q; w)$ with $L^C_{z_q}(q; w)$ in Eq. 11, where $L^C_{z_q}(q; w)$ is defined as,

$$L^C_{z_q}(q; w) = \max(0, 1 - y_{z_q}(w^T x_{z_q}))^2 + \textstyle\sum_{j \in R_q \setminus E_q} max(0, 1 - y_j(w^T x_j))^2 \ ,$$
$$z_q = \arg\max_{i \in E_q} f(x_i; w) \ . \tag{16}$$

The latent linear binary classification SVM model can also be learned using our EM-like (Sec. 3.3) self-paced model selection (Sec. 3.4) procedure. In Fig. 4, we demonstrate that our proposed latent ranking model is consistently better than the latent classification model. This proves that the additional constraints in the latent classification model are indeed harmful.

4 Experiments

We conduct experiments on a newly created Youtube highlight dataset harvested by our system automatically. For analysis and evaluation purposes, we have labeled the dataset using Amazon Mechanical Turk. In the following sections, we first give details of our implementation such as feature representation, parameter setting, etc. Then, we report quantitative and qualitative results on our novel Youtube highlight dataset.

4.1 Implementation Details

We describe our representation and training parameters in detail.

Moment Definition. We first define each moment as a 100 frames clip evenly sampled across each raw video. The start and end frames of each moment is then aligned to nearby shot boundaries within 50 frames away.

Feature Representation. Given these moments, we extract the state-of-the-art dense trajectory motion feature [24] which is best for action classification (other scene, objects, and audio features can also be included in our framework). Then, the dimension of the dense trajectory features is reduced by half using PCA. The dense trajectory features within each moment are mapped to a learned Gaussian mixture codebook to generate a fisher vector with fix dimension (26000). The Gaussian mixture model with 200 mixture components is learned using the training raw videos for each domain.

Highlight Definition. During training, a moment is considered as a highlight (in E) if at least 70% of its frames are matched in the edited video. A moment is not considered as a highlight (in $R \setminus E$) if at most 30% of its frames are matched in the edited video. All the remaining moments are not included in training.

Model Training. All the regularization parameters λ in both the ranking and classification models are selected from 10 logarithmically spaced values from 0.001 to 10 to maximize the average pair-wise accuracy on the training data. We use the liblinear package [2] to train both models in their primal form with the same stopping criteria: maximum 10000 iterations, and $\epsilon = 0.0001$. For self-paced model selection, we set $K = 4$.

4.2 Evaluation Details

For evaluating our ranking results, ideally we would like to obtain a h-factor order of all moments in every video. However, it is time consuming and ambiguous to ask general people to order all the moments since often it is hard to compare the h-factors of two random moments. Hence, we found that it is more effective to ask multiple people to select a single highlight (i.e., a segment of consecutive moments) within each video. We use Amazon Mechanical Turk to collect these ground truth annotations. For each video, we collect a less than five seconds highlight from each turker, where there are five turkers assigned to each video. Since we are crowd-sourcing these annotations from a large number of turkers, our annotations will inevitably be noisy. Hence, we only keep the moments selected more than 2 times[2] as ground truth highlights for evaluation. As a result, our problem becomes a highlight detection task.

Highlight Detection. Within each video, the best method should first detect the ground truth highlighted moments rather than other moments. We calculate the average precision of highlight detection for each testing video and report the mean average precision (mAP) summarizing the performance of all videos. Note that unlike object detection which accumulates all the detections from images to

[2] For parkour and skiing, we found the turkers' annotation is noiser; hence, we only keep the moments selected more than 3 times.

Fig. 3. Statistics of our data harvested from Youtube

	skating	gymnastics	surfing	dog	parkour	skiing
# Training videos	37	46	81	49	43	98
# Testing videos	37	47	82	50	43	99
Total # videos	74	93	163	99	86	197
Total seconds	9003	8294	15348	9000	11698	32457
% relevant videos	64.86%	77.42%	55.83%	49.49%	65.12%	49.23%

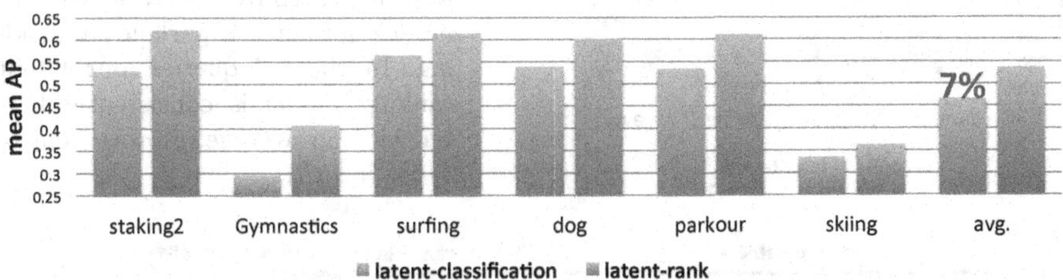

Fig. 4. Performance comparison between our latent ranking model and its classification counterpart. Latent ranking model is consistently better than latent classification model with an average improvement of ~ 7% in mAP.

calculate the average precision, highlight detection treats each video separately since a highlighted moment in one video is not necessary more interesting than a non-highlighted moment in another video.

4.3 Youtube Highlight Dataset

By harvesting freely available data from Youtube as described in Sec. 3.5, we have collected data for "skating", "gymnastics", "dog", "parkour", "surfing", and "skiing". These 6 domains are selected because about 20% of the retrieved raw videos in these domains are publicly downloadable. For each domain, there is about 100 videos with various length. The total accumulated time is 1430 minutes, which is at the similar scale as the state-of-the-art large scale action recognition dataset [9] (1600 minutes). Then, we split the data in half for training and testing. Our new dataset is very challenging since (1) it contains a variety of videos captured by portable devices, (2) the start and end of a specific highlight can vary significantly depending on the behavior of the users, and (3) there are irrelevant videos included in the dataset. For example, videos of interviews and slideshows of images are considered as irrelevant videos. Given all these challenges, our fully automatic system searches for the best latent configuration to limit the effects of the noise without human intervention. For testing, we evaluate on videos where turkers reach consensus on highlighted moments. The statistics of our collected data for each domain is shown in Fig. 3. The dataset and codes are available (see technical report [22] for details).

Our fully automatic system performs well on the novel Youtube highlight dataset with a mean average precision of 53.6% across six domains, which is significantly better than a motion analysis baseline (46%) [15]. We compare our system with other sophisticated methods below.

Latent Ranking v.s. Classification. In Fig. 4, we compare the mean average precision for every domain between our latent ranking model (Sec. 3.3)

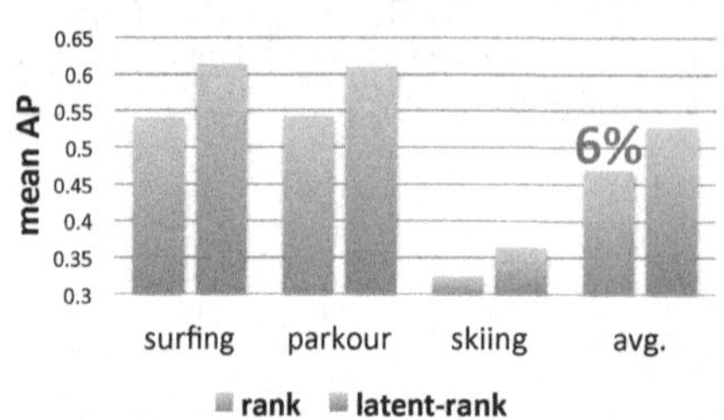

Fig. 5. Performance comparison between latent and non-latent ranking models. Our self-paced model selection procedure selects non-latent models for surfing, parkour, and skiing. In these 3 queries, our latent ranking model is consistently better with an average improvement of $\sim 6\%$ in mAP.

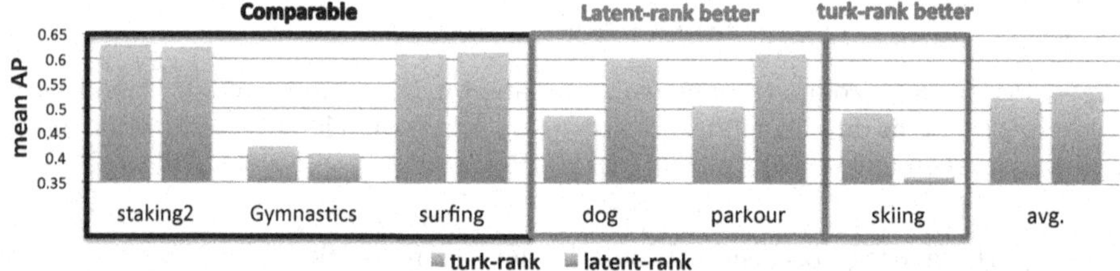

Fig. 6. Performance comparison between a fully supervised ranking model trained with turkers' annotations (referred to as "turk-ranking") and our latent ranking model trained with harvested data. Our model is very competitive compared to "turk-ranking", and suprisingly outperforms "turk-ranking" significantly on parkour and dog.

Fig. 7. Examples of moments ranking from high (left) to low (right) according to our predicted "h-factors" for skating, parkour, and skiing (see technical report [22] for more examples). We show one sampled frame from each moment to represent it.

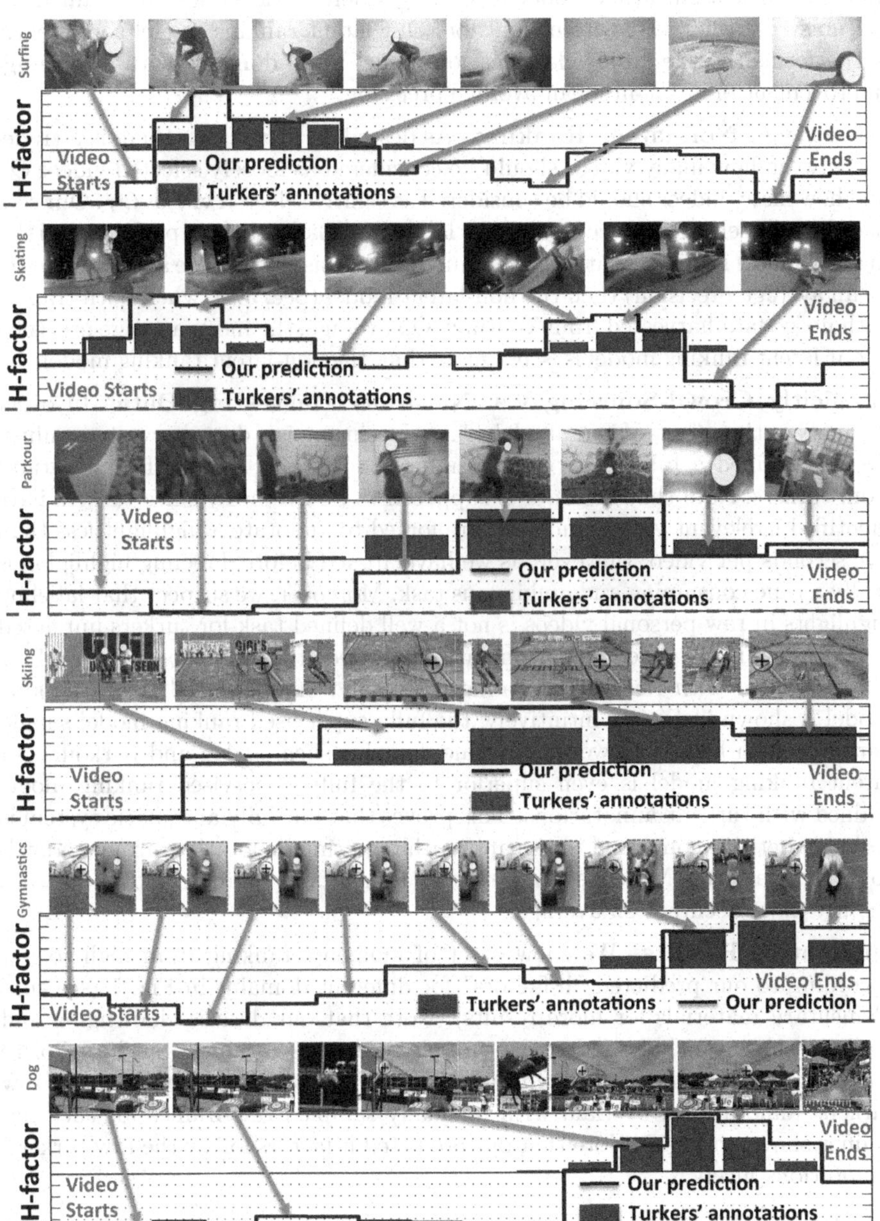

Fig. 8. Visualization of our predicted h-factors (black lines) and raw turkers' annotations (blue bars), overlaid with manually sampled raw frames. For gymnastics, dog, and skiing, the main characters in some frames are too small; hence, we show the manually cropped zoom-in version of the frames. Click to watch videos on Youtube: surfing link, skating link, parkour link, skiing link, Gymnastics link, dog link.

and a latent classification model (Sec. 3.6), where both models are trained using noisy data harvested from Youtube. Our latent ranking model consistently outperforms the the latent classification model in all domains with an average improvement of $\sim 7\%$ in mean average precision.

Latent v.s. Non-latent Ranking. As described in Sec. 3.4, there is a trade-off between how many videos should be considered as loosely selected videos Q_L and how many videos should be considered as tightly selected videos Q_T. Our self-paced model selection procedure selects latent models for surfing, parkour, and skiing[3]. We show in Fig. 5 that the latent model is consistently more accurate (larger mean average precision) then the non-latent model (Sec. 3.1), when both trained with noisy data harvested from Youtube. On average, the mean average precision of our latent ranking model is $\sim 6\%$ more than the non-latent ranking model.

Explicitly Crowd-Sourcing v.s. Naturally Harvesting Data. In order to analyze the effect of our model trained using noisy data harvested online, we also trained a fully supervised ranking model (Sec. 3.1) with annotations from turkers. Note that the data is supposed to be less noisy since turkers have identified irrelevant videos and they are forced to annotate a highlight less than five seconds per video. However, as we have argued before, labeling highlights is really a time consuming and ambiguous task. Moreover, we suspect that labeling highlights in raw personal videos is not a well defined task for turkers unrelated to the events in the videos. The comparison between the fully supervised ranking model trained with raw turkers' annotations and our proposed latent ranking model is shown in Fig. 6. Intuitively, the fully supervised ranking model should perform much better. However, in some domains such as dog and parkour, our latent ranking model is even superior to the fully supervised ranking model trained with turkers' annotations. This proves that our fully automatic system is very competitive compared to the approach requiring annotations from a crowd-sourcing platform. Moreover, our system is not only more scalable, but also slightly more accurate on average.

Qualitative Results. We show a set of moments ranking from high to low according to our predicted "h-factors" for different domains in Fig. 7 (see supplementary materials for more results). Note that our data is challenging and realistic, since it includes videos captured by widely used cameras such as GoPro and cellphone cameras. Detailed visualization of our predicted h-factors and raw turkers' annotations, overlaid with manually sampled raw frames for each domain is shown in Fig. 8. Note that our predicted h-factors follow the raw turkers' annotations nicely.

5 Conclusion

As a step towards automatic video editing, we introduce a fully automatic system for ranking video highlights in unconstrained personal videos by analyzing online

[3] For skating, gymnastics, and dog, our self-paced model selection procedure selects non-latent models (i.e., $Q_L = \emptyset$).

edited videos. Our system and the proposed novel latent ranking model are shown to be superior to its binary classification counterpart, a motion analysis baseline [15], a non-latent ranking model without handling noise in the harvested data, and a fully supervised ranking system requiring annotations from Amazon Mechanical Turk. We believe our system paves the way toward learning a large number of domain-specific highlights since more and more users' behavioral data can be harvested online. In the future, we would like to use a bank of domain-specific highlight rankers to describe every moment in a raw video. Given this high-level understanding of moments, we hope to automatically generate an edited video.

Acknowledgement. We thank Microsoft, Google, Intel, NSF IIS-1218683, ONR N00014-13-1-0720, and ONR MURI N00014-10-1-0934 for supporting this research.

References

1. Borgo, R., Chen, M., Daubney, B., Grundy, E., Heidemann, G., Hoferlin, B., Hoferlin, M., Janicke, H., Weiskopf, D., Xie, X.: A survey on video-based graphics and video visualization. In: EUROGRAPHICS (2011)
2. Fan, R.E., Chang, K.W., Hsieh, C.J., Wang, X.R., Lin, C.J.: LIBLINEAR: A library for large linear classification. Journal of Machine Learning Research 9, 1871–1874 (2008)
3. Gong, Y., Liu, X.: Video summarization using singular value decomposition. In: CVPR (2000)
4. Hanjalic, A.: Adaptive extraction of highlights from a sport video based on excitement modeling. IEEE Transactions on Multimedia (2005)
5. Hannon, J., McCarthy, K., Lynch, J., Smyth, B.: Personalized and automatic social summarization of events in video. In: IUI (2011)
6. Hu, Y., Li, M., Yu, N.: Multiple-instance ranking: Learning to rank images for image retrieval. In: CVPR (2008)
7. Jacobs, C.E., Finkelstein, A., Salesin, D.H.: Fast multiresolution image querying. In: SIGGRAPH (1995)
8. Khosla, A., Hamid, R., Lin, C.J., Sundaresan, N.: Large-scale video summarization using web-image priors. In: CVPR (2013)
9. Khurram Soomro, A.R.Z., Shah, M.: Ucf101: A dataset of 101 human action classes from videos in the wild. CRCV-TR (2013)
10. Kolekar, M., Sengupta, S.: Event-importance based customized and automatic cricket highlight generation. In: ICME (2006)
11. Lee, C.P., Lin, C.J.: Large-scale linear ranksvm. Neural Computation (2013)
12. Lee, Y.J., Ghosh, J., Grauman, K.: Discovering important people and objects for egocentric video summarization. In: CVPR (2012)
13. Liu, D., Hua, G., Chen, T.: A hierarchical visual model for video object summarization. TPAMI (2010)
14. Lu, Z., Grauman, K.: Story-driven summarization for egocentric video. In: CVPR (2013)
15. Mendi, E., Clemente, H.B., Bayrak, C.: Sports video summarization based on motion analysis. Computers and Electrical Engineering 39(3), 790–796 (2013)

16. Nepal, S., Srinivasan, U., Reynolds, G.: Automatic detection of goal segments in basketball videos. ACM Multimedia (2001)
17. Ngo, C., Ma, Y., Zhan, H.: Video summarization and scene detection by graph modeling. In: CSVT (2005)
18. Olsen, D.R., Moon, B.: Video summarization based on user interaction. In: EuroITV (2011)
19. Parikh, D., Grauman, K.: Relative attributes. In: ICCV (2011)
20. Rui, Y., Gupta, A., Acero, A.: Automatically extracting highlights for tv baseball programs. ACM Multimedia (2000)
21. Siddiquie, B., Feris, R., Davis, L.: Image ranking and retrieval based on multi-attribute queries. In: CVPR (2011)
22. Sun, M., Farhadi, A., Seitz, S.: Technical report of ranking domain-specific highlights, `http://homes.cs.washington.edu/~sunmin/projects/at-a-glace/`
23. Tang, H., Kwatra, V., Sargin, M., Gargi, U.: Detecting highlights in sports videos: Cricket as a test case. ICME (2011)
24. Wang, H., Kläser, A., Schmid, C., Liu, C.L.: Action Recognition by Dense Trajectories. In: CVPR (2011)
25. Xiong, Z., Radhakrishnan, R., Divakaran, A., Huang, T.: Highlights extraction from sports video based on an audio-visual marker detection framework. ICME (2005)
26. Wang, J., Xu, C., Chang, E., Tian, Q.: Sports highlight detection from keyword sequences using hmm. In: ICME (2004)
27. Yow, D., Yeo, B., Yeung, M., Liu, B.: Analysis and presentation of soccer highlights from digital video. In: ACCV (1995)

A Multi-transformational Model for Background Subtraction with Moving Cameras*

Daniya Zamalieva, Alper Yilmaz, and James W. Davis

The Ohio State University, Columbus OH, USA

Abstract. We introduce a new approach to perform background subtraction in moving camera scenarios. Unlike previous treatments of the problem, we do not restrict the camera motion or the scene geometry. The proposed approach relies on Bayesian selection of the transformation that best describes the geometric relation between consecutive frames. Based on the selected transformation, we propagate a set of learned background and foreground appearance models using a single or a series of homography transforms. The propagated models are subjected to MAP-MRF optimization framework that combines motion, appearance, spatial, and temporal cues; the optimization process provides the final background/foreground labels. Extensive experimental evaluation with challenging videos shows that the proposed method outperforms the baseline and state-of-the-art methods in most cases.

Keywords: Background subtraction, moving camera, moving object detection.

1 Introduction

Background subtraction is essential for many high level tasks in computer vision, including but not limited to object detection, object recognition, tracking, 3D scene recovery, and action recognition. Considering its precursory nature in the computer vision pipeline, the performance of background subtraction directly affects the quality of each task it precedes as well as the final results in the pipeline. For over two decades, a significant number of background subtraction methods have been published under the assumption that the camera capturing the scene is stationary. Needless to say, none of these algorithms are applicable in the case when the camera is moving. The ever increasing use of mobile phones and handheld cameras introduces a need for new background subtraction methods that alleviate a stationary camera requirement.

When the camera moves during acquisition, the pixels corresponding to background no longer maintain their positions in consecutive frames. This observation severely complicates the traditional background subtraction process and

* Electronic supplementary material -Supplementary material is available in the online version of this chapter at `http://dx.doi.org/10.1007/978-3-319-10590-52`. Videos can also be accessed at `http://www.springerimages.com/videos/978-3-319-10589-5`

D. Fleet et al. (Eds.): ECCV 2014, Part I, LNCS 8689, pp. 803–817, 2014.
© Springer International Publishing Switzerland 2014

requires compensation of the camera motion. The printed literature contains only a handful of studies on background subtraction for freely moving cameras [15,10,7,22,8,9,4,5]. A typical first step in all these methods is background motion estimation, which can be broadly classified into two categories: model-based estimation [10,8,9,7] and trajectory-based estimation [15,4,5]. The model-based methods assume that the majority of the visible scene is the background, and they estimate either the homography transform [10,7] or fundamental matrix [8,9] between frames. The homography transform, however, is valid only when the scene is planar or when the camera does not translate. On the other hand, the fundamental matrix is only valid for nonplanar scenes and can be computed when the camera translates creating parallax. Consequently, homography methods are prone to parallax, while fundamental matrix methods are susceptible to small camera motion. Since homography and fundamental matrices are complementary, neither can be used alone to model unknown camera motion. Alternatively to model-based methods, trajectory-based methods rely on dense long-term pixel trajectories to infer background motion [15,4,5]. These methods, however, are sensitive to tracking errors and short or incomplete trajectories especially when the camera motion is fast.

Methods in both categories remedy their drawbacks by employing appearance modeling and spatial smoothing. The appearance modeling is achieved by generating and transforming the background and foreground models for spectrally consistent results. Similarly, spatial smoothing ensures similar labeling results for proximal pixels. Both of these constraints work reasonably well in the case when the motion estimation prior to their application is acceptable; however, they are ineffectual when the motion estimation is incorrect.

In order to overcome the aforementioned problems related to implicit background motion estimation, we propose to use both the homography transform and the fundamental matrix (see Figure 1 for algorithmic flow). At each frame, we first estimate a dense motion field, then use it to compute the geometric transformations which are later used to propagate appearance models from the previous frame to the current frame. From among the two geometric transformations, the appropriate one is selected by adopting the Geometric Robust Information Criterion (GRIC) [18,6]. The application of the GRIC improves the motion estimation by choosing the appropriate geometric model for the short baseline case videos; hence, it makes the proposed background subtraction scheme immune to geometric degeneracies. In the case when the GRIC score favors the homography transform, the appearance propagation becomes a 1-1 mapping. On the other hand, if the fundamental matrix is chosen, we propagate the appearance models by estimating a series of homography transforms. The propagated appearance models provide the likelihood of each pixel used for background/foreground labeling. The appearance models we implement are similar to most background subtraction methods for stationary cameras, where the background appearances are modeled using a mixture of Gaussians per pixel [17]. Finally, we combine motion, appearance, spatial, and temporal cues in a MAP-MRF optimization framework to obtain the final background/foreground labels.

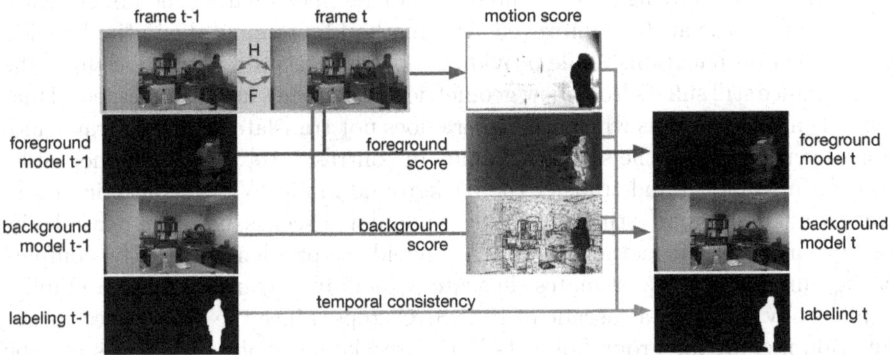

Fig. 1. Overview of the proposed method. First, the geometric transformation between frames $t-1$ and t is selected using the GRIC score, and the motion scores for each pixel are computed. Then, the appearance models from previous frame are propagated and compared with the current frame to obtain background/foreground scores. The motion and appearance scores are combined with the labeling of the previous frame to obtain the labeling for the current frame. Finally, the appearance models are updated accordingly.

The contributions of this paper can be summarized as follows. We provide novel methods in context of background subtraction for: 1) determining the best fitting geometric model that relates consecutive frames; 2) propagating learned background/foreground appearance via a multi-transformational model; 3) labeling pixels that is robust to occlusions and optical flow errors; 4) incorporating motion, appearance, spatial, and temporal cues for the final labeling.

2 Related Work

A common assumption for background subtraction methods is having a stationary camera for modeling the background appearance. The stationary camera assumption can be formulated as an identity transformation between the incoming frame and the background model. There are many papers in the literature that assume a stationary camera setup, and they have been discussed in comprehensive surveys [13,2]. There are also studies that perform background subtraction for stationary cameras but with dynamic backgrounds that exhibit non-stationary properties in time [12,16,11].

When the camera motion is not constrained, the background subtraction problem becomes complicated. Among the few papers published on this topic, a common treatment is to estimate the view geometric transformations such that the regions that do not fit the estimated transformations are labeled as foreground. Following this scheme, [9] uses the fundamental matrix for initial background/ foreground labeling, which is iteratively refined by imposing temporal and spatial smoothness. In their method, the image is divided into blocks and the temporal models of each block are propagated using optical flow. This method, however, is prone to small moving objects and degeneracies in estimating the fundamental matrix. In [8], the authors improved their method by refining the initial labeling using belief propagation. While providing a better postprocessing procedure, the performance still suffers from view geometric degeneracies in the fundamental matrix estimation, such as when the camera does not translate, frame-to-frame motion is very small, or the scene is planar. In contrast, [10] uses the homography transform to model and transfer the background model. View geometric degeneracies of homography estimation, such as nonplanar scenes, however, degrade the performance of their method. In order to avoid the problems caused by complex background scenes, [7] estimates separate homography transforms for a number of planes by applying a cascade of RANSAC steps. Since the points used for estimation include foreground objects, estimated homography transforms may be for non-existing planes which cause incorrect transformations. In addition, their method cannot tolerate when the first frame of the sequence contains moving objects or when the object enters the camera view together with a previously unseen part of the background. Alternative to implicit view geometry based methods, [22] performs full 3D recovery using a combination of structure from motion and bundle adjustment. Their approach requires a set of computationally expensive steps which is not suitable for background subtraction, which is usually considered an initial step in high-level computer vision tasks.

In contrast to the use of geometric transformations, some researchers analyze long-term trajectories to find moving objects in the sequence. In [15], the authors assume that the trajectories of background features form a 3D subspace, which can be estimated with factorization based shape-from-motion. In [4], a similar method is introduced, where the factorization is guided by group sparsity constraints defined for foreground. Both methods, however, strongly rely on long-term feature tracking which inhibits their real time application. A recent method [5] represents trajectories in a low-dimensional space and groups them by relearning the Gaussian Mixture Model at each frame. The decision of which trajectory groups belong to background or foreground is given by a set of heuristics such as compactness, surroundedness, and spatial closeness. These heuristics may fail for complex background scenes and non-rigid foreground objects.

In this paper, we model background motion by choosing appropriate geometric transformation for each frame instead of committing to a single model. Our method accommodates multiple transformational models for appearance model propagation, which are applied according to the selected geometric transformation.

3 Choosing Frame-to-Frame Transformations

Assuming the camera reference frame coincides with the world reference frame, the projection of a 3D point can be written as $\mathbf{x} = \mathtt{P}\mathbf{X} = \mathtt{K}[\mathtt{I}|\mathbf{0}]\mathbf{X}$, where $\mathtt{P}$ is a 3×4 projection matrix, $\mathtt{K}$ is the camera calibration matrix. When the camera rotates and translates, point $\mathbf{X}$ projects to the new image by $\mathbf{x}' = \mathtt{K}'[\mathtt{R}|\mathbf{t}]\mathbf{X}$. In this case, there is no one-to-one mapping between the image points $\mathbf{x}$ and $\mathbf{x}'$. These points, however, satisfy the fundamental matrix $\mathtt{F}$: $\mathbf{x}'^{\top}\mathtt{F}\mathbf{x} = 0$. The fundamental matrix is a geometrically valid transformation except for the following degenerate cases: 1) the camera does not translate and only rotates, 2) all matching points are coplanar. In addition, for small camera baseline the equation system for estimating fundamental matrix becomes ill-conditioned.

For the degenerate cases stated above the transformation becomes a 1-1 mapping. This can be shown by dropping the last column of the projection matrix $\mathtt{P}$, in the case when the camera does not translate: $\mathbf{x} = \mathtt{K}\mathbf{X}$ and $\mathbf{x}' = \mathtt{K}'\mathtt{R}\mathbf{X}$, such that 1-1 mapping between points becomes $\mathbf{x}' = (\mathtt{K}'\mathtt{R}\mathtt{K}^{-1})\mathbf{x} = \mathtt{H}_{\mathtt{R}}\mathbf{x}$, where $\mathtt{H}_{\mathtt{R}}$ is referred to as the rotational homography. For the second case in which all points are coplanar, without loss of generality, we can assume that the points lie on $Z = 0$ plane. In this case, the third column $\mathbf{p}_3$ of $\mathtt{P}$, which gets multiplied with the point's Z coordinate, is not relevant in projection and can be dropped. The resulting projections in case become $\mathbf{x} = [\mathbf{p}_1, \mathbf{p}_2, \mathbf{p}_4]\mathbf{X} = \mathtt{H}\mathbf{X}$, and $\mathbf{x}' = [\mathbf{p}'_1, \mathbf{p}'_2, \mathbf{p}'_4]\mathbf{X} = \mathtt{H}'\mathbf{X}'$, such that $\mathbf{x}' = (\mathtt{H}'\mathtt{H}^{-1})\mathbf{x} = (\mathtt{H}_\pi)\mathbf{x}$, where $\mathtt{H}_\pi$ is the homography transform with respect to plane π.

The homography transform and the fundamental matrix constitute all possible frame-to-frame geometric transformations for a static scene. In order words, when they are used interchangeably, they can model all camera motions and scene geometries. In order to realize this observation and allow a freely moving camera in arbitrary background, we use both geometric transformations instead of committing to only one of them (opposed to the published literature summarized in Section 2).

A straightforward selection of the appropriate geometric transformation for consecutive frames is to first estimate both transformations and compare the sum of fitting errors for each one individually. This approach, however, is not a well posed due to the fact that the homography transform is a bijective 2D map and results in a two-dimensional error; while the fundamental matrix is a many-to-one mapping and provides a one-dimensional error. In order to define a 1D geometric distance, we follow the convention described in [20,19], which computes the approximation of the squared geometric distance $e^2_{i,\mathtt{H}}$ and $e^2_{i,\mathtt{F}}$ from the 4D joint-space point $[\mathbf{x}_i; \mathbf{x}'_i]$ to the homography $\mathtt{H}$ and fundamental matrix $\mathtt{F}$ manifold, respectively.

Using these distance measures, [18] introduces the Geometric Robust Information Criterion (GRIC), which is a Bayesian model selection scheme for the two geometric transformations. In order to offset measurement errors in model estimation, a search region S is defined in which the distances are assumed acceptable. This model is later modified by [6] for a 3D scene recovery problem, where the authors suggest to add another search criteria R which defines the range of disparity along which the feature match is expected to occur. Since the original GRIC [18] is biased towards selection of homography transform as addressed in [6], we adopt the modified GRIC score for $m = \{\mathtt{H}, \mathtt{F}\}$ given as:

$$GRIC_m = \sum_i \rho_2 \left(\frac{e^2_{i,m}}{\sigma^2} \right) + n \left((D - d_m) \log 2\pi\sigma^2 + 2 \log \frac{c_m}{\gamma} \right) + k_m \log n, \quad (1)$$

where D is the dimensionality of an observation ($D = 4$ for a pair of 2D points), d_m is the dimensionality of the underlying model manifold ($d_H = 2$, $d_F = 3$), σ is

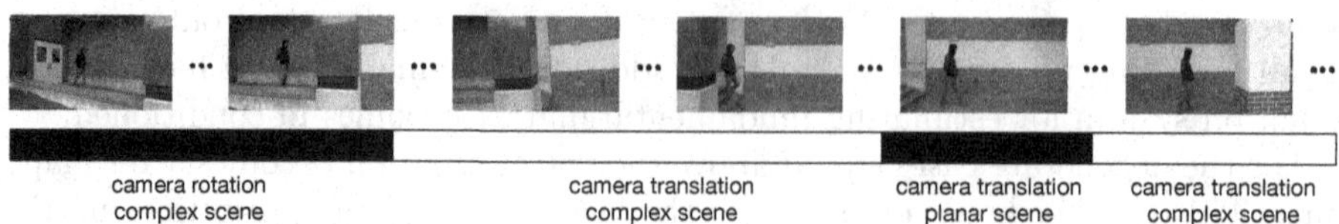

Fig. 2. GRIC score based selection for the *outdoor* sequence. The bar below exemplar frames indicates which geometric transformation is selected. Selection of H and F is respectively denoted by black and white regions.

the standard deviation of the measurement error, γ is the prior expectation that a correspondence is an inlier, k_m is the number of model parameters ($k_H = 8$, $k_F = 7$), n is the number of observations, and $\rho_2(x) = \min\{x, T_m\}$ with

$$T_m = 2\log\left(\frac{\gamma}{1-\gamma} \cdot \frac{\nu}{c_m}\right) - (D - d_m)\log 2\pi\sigma^2. \tag{2}$$

For an $L \times L$ image, while an arbitrary correspondence may occur in the volume $\nu = L \times L \times S \times S$, the GRIC score assumes an inlier correspondence is only distributed in the volume c_m, where $c_H = L \times L$ and $c_F = L \times L \times R$. In this framework, the lower GRIC score indicates the better geometric model.

In our implementation of the GRIC score, for each new frame I^t, we first compute point correspondences between I^t and I^{t-1} using optical flow. The matching features are then used to estimate both the fundamental matrix F and the homography transform H using RANSAC. Each geometric model is then subjected to Eqn. (1). The best fitting geometric model is selected based on the lowest GRIC score (see Figure 2). Once the model is chosen, the corresponding measurement error $e^2_{i,m}$ is used to assign each pixel $\mathbf{x}_i$ a motion based score $m(\mathbf{x}_i)$ which indicates the likelihood of $\mathbf{x}_i$ being a background pixel:

$$m(\mathbf{x}_i) = \exp\left(-\frac{e^2_{i,m}}{2\sigma^2_m}\right), \tag{3}$$

where σ_m controls the normalization of the motion score $m(\mathbf{x}_i)$.

4 Appearance Modeling

The motion score of a pixel $m(\mathbf{x})$ which is computed from the estimated motion model can be used to tentatively label a pixel as background or foreground. The resulting labeling based purely on motion is often noisy and prone to errors in optical flow; hence one can conjecture that the motion information alone is insufficient for the labeling. Besides motion, the appearance provides a strong clue indicating the presence or absence of a foreground object. To leverage the information provided by appearance changes, we maintain a background model $\mathcal{B}(\mathbf{x})$ and a foreground model $\mathcal{F}(\mathbf{x})$ for each pixel $\mathbf{x}$.

The challenge that makes background subtraction for a moving camera a hard problem is the requirement of registering the current frame with the background and foreground models. If such alignment is computed, any method proposed for a stationary camera can be applied to perform the background subtraction. In this paper, we adopt a commonly used Gaussian mixture model [17] to represent the background and foreground models.

The proposed method accommodates both the homography and a fundamental matrix based transformations by employing different mapping strategies. In the following text, we focus on how the selected geometric model can be used to compute an appearance based background and foreground scores from the generated appearance models.

4.1 Background Score for Homography Transform

When the GRIC metric results in selection of the homography transformation from the current frame, I^t, and the background model, $\mathcal{B}$, it can be directly used to map point $\mathbf{x}$ in I^t to background model $\mathcal{B}$:

$$\mathbf{x}' = \mathtt{H}_0\mathbf{x}. \tag{4}$$

The appearance based background score of $\mathbf{x}$ given the model $\mathcal{B}(\mathbf{x}')$ is then computed from:

$$s(\mathbf{x}|\mathcal{B}(\mathbf{x}')) = \sum_{j=1}^{g} w_j^b \exp\left(-\frac{1}{2}(I^t(\mathbf{x}) - \mu_j^b)^\top(\Sigma_j^b)^{-1}(I^t(\mathbf{x}) - \mu_j^b)\right) + w_0^b c, \tag{5}$$

where g is the number of mixture components at $\mathcal{B}(\mathbf{x}')$, $w_j^b, \mu_j^b, \Sigma_j^b$ are respectively the weight, mean, and covariance of jth component, c is a constant, and w_0 is the weight of a constant component which prevents from setting $w_1 = 1$ when the model is first initialized. Assuming independence of color channels, the covariance matrix is set to a diagonal matrix of the form $\Sigma = \sigma^2\mathbf{I}$.

4.2 Background Score for Fundamental Matrix

In the case when the GRIC metric chooses the fundamental matrix as the geometric transformation, the mapping between the image and the model becomes one-to-many, such that a point $\mathbf{x}$ in I^t maps to an epipolar line $\mathtt{F}\mathbf{x}$ in $\mathcal{B}$. This one-to-many mapping, however, does not register the image with the background model, and inhibits proper updating of the model. Geometrically, the choice of fundamental matrix suggests that the background scene contains more than a single physical plane, each of which can be transformed by a different homography transform that can be computed from a cascade of RANSAC steps.

In order to find such one-to-one mappings, correspondences with low motion score $m(\mathbf{x})$ given in Eqn. (3) are removed from the background pixel set due

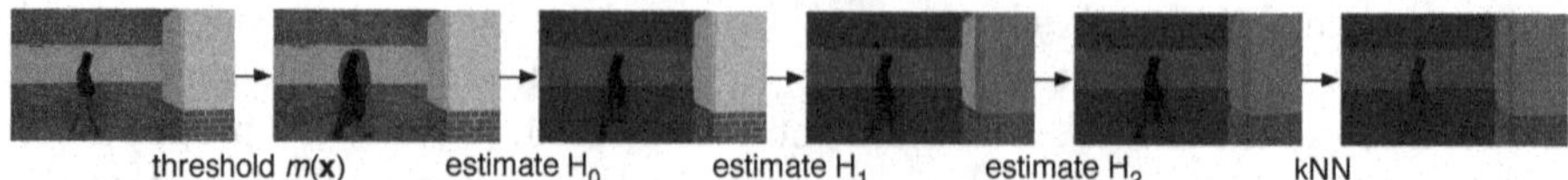

Fig. 3. The estimation of multiple homography transforms. First, the pixels with low motion scores are excluded (shaded with black in the second image). At each step, a homography transform $\mathtt{H}_i$ is estimated, and the inliers (shaded with navy, red, green) are excluded from subsequent homography estimations.

to the fact that they most likely correspond to foreground regions as discussed earlier. The remaining points are used to estimate the homography $\mathtt{H}_1$ using RANSAC. The inlier point set satisfying $\mathtt{H}_1$ are excluded from the set and the procedure is repeated for the remaining points to estimate $\mathtt{H}_2, \mathtt{H}_3, \ldots$ until the number of correspondences left is small (see Figure 3). In this scheme, each estimated homography transform $\mathtt{H}_i$ corresponds to a different plane π_i within the background scene and can be used to perform one-to-one mapping of pixels on respective planes to the background model by $\mathbf{x}'_i = \mathtt{H}_i\mathbf{x}$ for $i \geq 1$. While the inlier sets provide a list of pixels for each plane π_i, they by no means provide a complete set of pixels due to observation noise; hence, we transform each pixel in the image using all computed homography transforms and select the plane that satisfies:

$$\mathbf{x}' = \underset{\mathbf{x}'_i}{\operatorname{argmin}} ||I^t(\mathbf{x}) - I^{t-1}(\mathbf{x}'_i)||^2. \quad (6)$$

This process provides the transformation that best satisfy appearance similarity and the transformed pixel $\mathbf{x}'$ is used to compute the background score in Eqn. (5).

While this approach works well for visible background pixels, occluded background pixels that become visible after the foreground object moves require special treatment. This observations also holds for pixels with noisy optical flow. This is due to the fact the appearance constraint in Eqn. (6) is not satisfied. For such a pixel, we consider its k-nearest unoccluded pixels that are associated with one of the planes π_i and perform a majority voting to associate it to a plane. The corresponding homography is then used to compute the background score $s(\mathbf{x}|\mathcal{B}(\mathbf{x}'))$ using Eqn. (5).

Note that, if the homography transforms are estimated directly, one cannot avoid the estimation of a homography that maps the foreground objects between consecutive frames. If such a transformation is included, the foreground object will be incorporated into the background model after a number of frames. Moreover, moving objects present in the first frame would be directly included in the background model, and with the corresponding homography estimated, they cannot be distinguished from the background as the object moves. We avoid estimating the foreground homography by excluding the pixels with low scores $m(\mathbf{x})$ that indicate the presence of a moving object.

4.3 Foreground Score

Considering that the foreground objects can be non-rigid and nonplanar, we estimate the mapping of a pixel based on its optical flow:

$$\mathbf{x}' = \mathbf{x} + \boldsymbol{u}(\mathbf{x}), \tag{7}$$

where $\boldsymbol{u}(\mathbf{x})$ is optical flow of $\mathbf{x}$, and $\mathbf{x}'$ is the projected location we will use to estimate the foreground score. We should note that, for foreground objects, aside from having low background scores from Eqn. (5), the projections by optical flow and the estimated background homography transforms are different, which is encoded in the motion score $m(\mathbf{x})$. The foreground score $\mathcal{F}$ after the projection can be written similar to the background model of Eqn. (5):

$$s(\mathbf{x}|\mathcal{F}(\mathbf{x}')) = \sum_{j=1}^{g} w_j^f \exp\left(-\frac{1}{2}(I^t(\mathbf{x}) - \mu_j^f)^\top (\Sigma_j^f)^{-1} (I^t(\mathbf{x}) - \mu_j^f)\right) + w_0^f c, \tag{8}$$

where the subscript f indicates foreground.

5 Background/Foreground Labeling

Given the projection model, and the background and foreground scores for each pixel, our objective is to estimate a binary label $\mathcal{L}^t$ at time t, which denotes if the pixel belongs to background, $\mathcal{L}^t(\mathbf{x}) = 0$, or foreground, $\mathcal{L}^t(\mathbf{x}) = 1$. The cues introduced in the Section 3-4 provide necessary constraints for the labeling problem. In particular, the motion of pixel $\mathbf{x}$ and how well it satisfies the background motion based on Eqn. (3) can be used to reflect the cost of a background or foreground label:

$$\mathcal{M}(\mathbf{x}) = \begin{cases} 1 - m(\mathbf{x}) & \text{if } \mathcal{L}^t(\mathbf{x}) = 0 \\ m(\mathbf{x}) & \text{otherwise} \end{cases}. \tag{9}$$

In similar fashion, how well the appearance of the pixel fits to the background or the foreground model can be competed using Eqns. (5) and (8) by:

$$\mathcal{A}(\mathbf{x}) = \begin{cases} s(\mathbf{x}|\mathcal{F}(\mathbf{x} + \boldsymbol{u})) & \text{if } \mathcal{L}^t(\mathbf{x}) = 0 \\ s(\mathbf{x}|\mathcal{B}(\mathtt{H}_i\mathbf{x})) & \text{otherwise} \end{cases}, \tag{10}$$

where $i \geq 0$. Aside from the motion and appearance based terms, one can expect that the label of a pixel should be both temporally and spatially consistent. These constraints are typically introduced to the labeling cost function as smoothness terms that penalize the assignment of different labels to pixel's spatial or temporal neighborhood. Let a pixel $\mathbf{x}$ in frame t corresponds to pixel $\mathbf{x}'$ in the previous frame $t-1$. The temporal smoothness $T(\mathbf{x})$ is defined based on the neighborhood $G(\mathbf{x})$ of $\mathbf{x}$ and can be computed as:

$$T(\mathbf{x}) = (1 - \delta(\mathcal{L}^t(\mathbf{x}) - \mathcal{L}^{t-1}(\mathbf{x}'))) \exp\left(\frac{-\|I^t(\mathbf{x}) - I^{t-1}(\mathbf{x}')\|^2}{2\sigma_T^2}\right), \tag{11}$$

where $\delta(\cdot)$ is a Kronecker delta function.

The spatial smoothness $V(\mathbf{x}_i, \mathbf{x}_j)$ enforces the adjacent pixels $\mathbf{x}_i$ and $\mathbf{x}_j$ in frame I^t to have the same label and can be formulated as:

$$V(\mathbf{x}_i, \mathbf{x}_j) = (1 - \delta(\mathcal{L}^t(\mathbf{x}_i) - \mathcal{L}^t(\mathbf{x}_j))) \exp\left(\frac{-\|I^t(\mathbf{x}_i) - I^t(\mathbf{x}_j)\|^2}{2\beta}\right), \quad (12)$$

where the constant β is defined [9] as:

$$\beta = \frac{1}{n}\sum_{i=1}^{n} \sum_{\mathbf{x}_j \in G(\mathbf{x}_i)} \|I(\mathbf{x}_i) - I(\mathbf{x}_j)\|^2 \quad (13)$$

and $G(\mathbf{x}_i)$ is a set of neighboring pixels around $\mathbf{x}_i$. Given the motion, appearance, and smoothness constraints, the pixels can be labeled as foreground or background by minimizing the labeling cost function E is given by:

$$E(\mathcal{L}^t, \mathcal{X}) = \sum_{\mathbf{x}_i \in I^t} \mathcal{M}(\mathbf{x}_i) + \lambda_A \sum_{\mathbf{x}_i \in I^t} \mathcal{A}(\mathbf{x}_i) + \lambda_T \sum_{\mathbf{x}_i \in I^t} T(\mathbf{x}_i) + \lambda_S \sum_{\mathbf{x}_i, \mathbf{x}_j \in \mathcal{N}} V(\mathbf{x}_i, \mathbf{x}_j), \quad (14)$$

where the appearance, temporal, and spatial terms are weighted by λ_A, λ_T, λ_S, and $\mathcal{N}$ is the neighboring system on pixels. The solution of energy minimization can be efficiently computed using the graph-cut algorithm [3].

6 Appearance Model Update

Once the labels for all the pixels are assigned, the new background and foreground observations can be used to update the background and foreground models by mapping the pixels based on the associated transformations. Let $\mathbf{x}'$ be the model location of pixel $\mathbf{x}$ in frame I^t. For a pixel with background label $\mathbf{x}' = \mathtt{H}_i\mathbf{x}$ for $i \geq 0$, while for a pixel with foreground label $\mathbf{x}' = \mathbf{x} + \boldsymbol{u}$. In order to update the appropriate component of the Gaussian mixture in $\mathcal{B}(\mathbf{x})$ or $\mathcal{F}(\mathbf{x})$, the color at $I(\mathbf{x})$ is checked against each component until a match is found. The parameters of a distribution that matches the current pixel are updated as:

$$\mu_i^m(\mathbf{x}) \leftarrow (1 - \alpha)\mu_i^m(\mathbf{x}') + \alpha I^t(\mathbf{x}), \quad (15)$$

$$\sigma_i^m(\mathbf{x}) \leftarrow (1 - \alpha)\sigma_i^m(\mathbf{x}') + \alpha(I^t(\mathbf{x}) - \mu_i^m(\mathbf{x}'))^\top (I^t(\mathbf{x}) - \mu_i^m(\mathbf{x}')), \quad (16)$$

where i indicates the selected component of the mixture model, $m = \{f, b\}$, and α is the learning rate. In this process, the mean and standard deviation of the unmatched distributions remain unchanged. If the components are updated, the weight of the matching component in the new mixture distributions are computed as follows:

$$w_i \leftarrow (1 - \alpha)w_i + \alpha, \quad (17)$$

while the weight of the remaining mixture components are updated by:

$$w_j \leftarrow (1 - \alpha)w_j. \quad (18)$$

which are renormalized to satisfy $\sum_{i=0}^{g} w_i = 1$. If none of the g components of the mixture model match $I^t(\mathbf{x})$, the component with lowest weight is replaced by normal distribution $N(I^t(\mathbf{x}), \sigma_{init})$, where σ_{init} is set to a high value.

For the foreground model, the above procedure is applied to $\mathcal{F}^{t-1}(\mathbf{x}^f)$ to construct $\mathcal{F}^t(\mathbf{x})$ if $\mathcal{L}^t(\mathbf{x}) = 1$ or $m(\mathbf{x}) < 0.5$. Otherwise, we update only $w_0 = w_0 + \alpha$, while other parameters remain unchanged. This formulation prevents the foreground model from learning the background.

7 Experiments

In contrast to the stationary camera case, there is no benchmark dataset for evaluating performances of background subtraction methods for moving cameras. Due to this unavailability, some studies do not provide quantitative comparisons [22,10]. In this paper, we use a set of sequences from the Hopkins dataset [21] (*cars1-8, people1-2*) and from [14] (*cars, person*) which have been used by recent quantitative papers on the topic [9,8,15,5]. The sequences in Hopkins dataset, however, typically contain 20 to 50 frames and does not contain the challenges posed in realistic scenarios. Hence, we additionally include two very challenging sequences (*indoor, outdoor*) that reflect a real-world setting acquired with a smartphone camera. For quantitative evaluation, we generated the ground truth by manually extracting all moving objects in all frames.

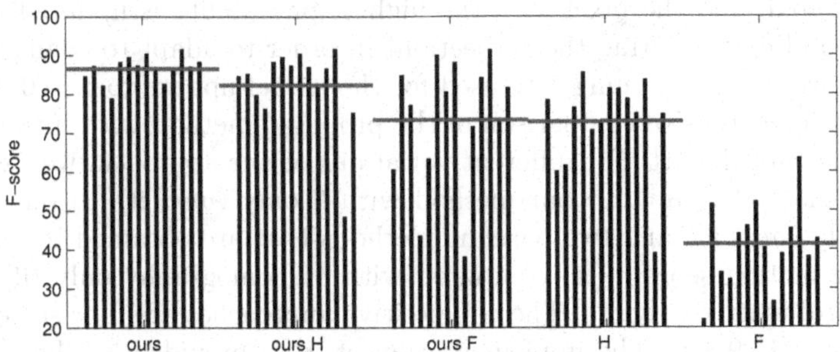

Fig. 4. The F-score computed from all sequences for our method and its variations. The bars in a group correspond to the sequences in the following order: *cars*, *person*, *cars1-8*, *people1-2*, *outdoor*, *indoor*. The red lines indicate the average F-score across the sequences for each approach.

Given a video sequence, our implementation generates dense point correspondences between consecutive frames from optical flow per pixel estimated using [1]. These correspondences are used to estimate both the fundamental matrix and the homograhy transform, which is followed by computing the respective GRIC score using Eqn. (1). The search region and the range of disparity in the GRIC are respectively set to $S = 30$, $R = 2$, $\sigma = 0.3$, and $\gamma = 0.6$. The geometric transformation providing the lowest GRIC score is selected to compute the

Table 1. Average precision (P), recall (R), and F-score (F) values for our and state-of-the-art methods. The best scores are denoted in bold.

	ours			Sheikh *et al.* [15]			Lim *et al.* [9]			Kwak *et al.* [8]		
	P	R	F	P	R	F	P	R	F	P	R	F
cars	**83.9**	**85.6**	**84.6**	65.1	84.6	72.7	79.4	64.4	71.0	59.5	62.6	60.7
person	82.3	93.6	**87.3**	69.6	**95.1**	80.0	**83.5**	83.1	82.7	53.9	62.8	56.8
cars1	72.9	**94.5**	**82.2**	68.5	74.3	67.9	63.0	87.2	72.6	**84.3**	73.8	78.5
cars2	69.8	**90.8**	78.9	54.7	81.7	63.6	**95.2**	77.2	**85.0**	67.9	74.1	70.5
cars3	**82.0**	95.6	**88.2**	62.8	**97.4**	76.1	70.6	87.7	77.9	80.4	80.2	80.2
cars4	**87.7**	**91.7**	**89.5**	68.5	88.3	76.2	80.8	73.1	75.1	57.5	67.9	62.1
cars5	**89.2**	**85.7**	**87.4**	62.7	79.7	66.2	69.4	82.5	75.3	62.3	68.0	64.5
cars6	**86.8**	94.2	**90.3**	68.8	**96.9**	79.8	64.4	73.1	68.4	62.4	89.0	73.1
cars7	80.2	**95.0**	86.9	81.3	94.4	**87.0**	**88.9**	84.2	86.2	66.2	72.9	69.1
cars8	73.7	**94.4**	**82.6**	**81.6**	85.4	82.2	73.7	76.2	74.9	77.5	76.6	76.7
people1	**92.5**	**81.6**	**86.6**	40.5	80.9	51.7	38.5	80.9	49.7	49.2	69.3	56.3
people2	**93.9**	89.5	**91.6**	72.6	88.0	78.2	71.6	**93.8**	80.5	85.0	77.4	80.8
outdoor	**91.3**	85.0	**87.0**	22.1	79.8	28.0	9.3	26.6	10.4	45.9	**86.4**	54.5
indoor	**91.6**	**87.4**	**88.3**	35.3	63.6	38.8	15.0	41.5	19.1	11.5	23.1	14.2

background model transformation (Section 4). The transformed model is used in the MAP-MRF framework with the following parameters $\lambda_A = 2$, $\lambda_T = 0.5$, $\lambda_S = 10$, and $\sigma_T = 10$. The final labels are then used to update the background and foreground models. During this step, a 3×3 window around projected pixel $\mathbf{x}'$ is evaluated, and the pixel with the highest probability is updated to avoid rounding and errors during the projection. In order to adapt to changes in appearance, we set the learning rate used for the model update to $\alpha = 0.05$.

We provide extensive comparison of the proposed method with its variations and the state-of-the-art. For different variations of our approach, we use 1) the complete method (*ours*), 2) our method with `H` only (*ours* `H`), 3) our method with `F` only (*ours* `F`), and two baseline methods that are obtained by theshold-ing of the motion score $m(\mathbf{x})$ computed with 4) homography only (`H`) and 5) fundamental matrix only (`F`). The competitive approaches are four state-of-the-art methods [15,9,8,7]. The implementation of [8] is provided by the authors[1], and we implemented the remaining methods. We selected the best parametric settings for all comparison after numerous experimental trials for quantitative evaluation. The overlap between the detected regions and the ground truth is analyzed by precision, recall, and their harmonic mean F-score.

In Figure 4, we plot the F-scores for different variations of our approach and two baseline methods. As expected, application of the appearance, spatial, and temporal constraints significantly improves the labeling compared to using only the motion scores (`H` and `F`). We observe that, for the Hopkins dataset and *cars*/*person* sequences, mostly the homography transform is chosen by GRIC. It can be attributed to the fact that the camera capturing these sequence moves very slowly, resulting in a very small baseline. As a result, for the aforementioned

[1] `http://cv.postech.ac.kr/research/gbs/`

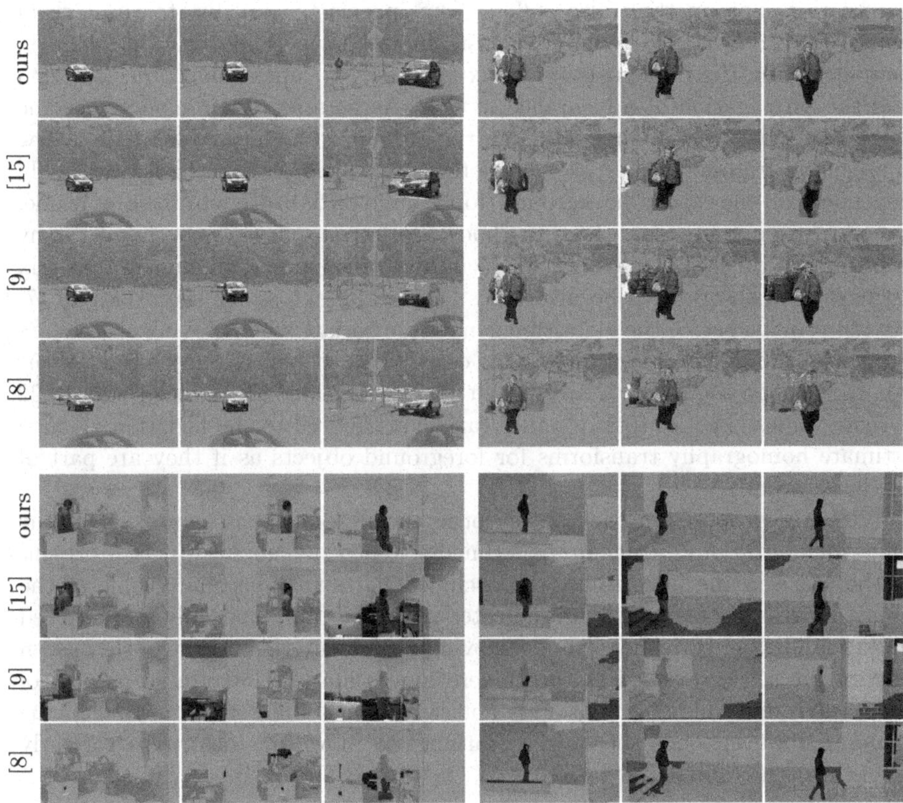

Fig. 5. Qualitative results for (row 1) the proposed method, (row 2) Sheikh *et al.* [15], (row 3) Lim *et al.* [9], and (row 4) Kwak *et al.* [8] for *cars4*, *people2*, *indoor* and *outdoor* sequences. Ten more sequences are included in supplemental material.

sequences, the performance of our method is comparable to the case where the homography transform alone is used (*ours* H). Note that, however, in many cases, our method results in a considerably higher performance compared to always choosing the fundamental matrix (*ours* F). The strength of our method can be realized in more complex sequences, that contain both camera rotation only and camera translation with complex scenes, such as the *indoor* and *outdoor* sequences. For these sequences, the alternated usage of H and F results in a higher performance than that of using H or F alone. Detailed results for this figure are tabulated in supplemental material.

In Table 1, we present quantitative comparisons of our method with the state-of-the-art methods. Note that our approach mostly outperforms the competitive methods, and it results in a significantly higher accuracy for long and realistic sequences (*indoor* and *outdoor*). As presented in qualitative results in Figure 5 (more results are included in supplemental material), we observe that [15] is susceptible to the noise in trajectories around the moving objects and image boundaries. This method also suffers from inconsistencies due to the lack of appearance models and temporal constraints. The methods introduced in [9] and [8] rely on the fundamental matrix for inferring camera and object motion and the propagation of appearance models. As a result, their models become corrupted when the fundamental matrix estimation is unsuccessful for a few consecutive frames. We also observed that, both of these methods are highly dependent on the correct background/foreground initialization in the first frame. Due to this requirement, these methods are initialized with the homography transform in the first frame in cases when the corresponding fundamental matrix estimation is observed to be incorrect. The results across the sequences for [7] are not provided since the algorithm is not appropriate when moving objects are present in the first frame, which is the case for all sequences except the *indoor*. For the *indoor* sequence, [7] results in 11.71 precision, 51.88 recall and 18.22 F-score values. The low performance can be attributed to the fact that [7] may estimate homography transforms for foreground objects as if they are part of the background.

While the proposed method outperforms the state-of-the-art, we observed the following limitations during our experiments. When the moving object is present in the scene in the first frame, the occluded parts that become visible as the object moves may be initially misdetected as foreground, especially for cluttered backgrounds. On the other hand, a moving object entering a previously unseen part of the scene revealed as the camera moves may be introduced as part of the background unless its motion is not significantly different from that of the camera. However, once the object continues to move, our algorithm correctly labels it as the foreground region.

8 Conclusions

We present a new method for background subtraction for moving cameras. Instead of committing to a single geometric transformation, we employ the Bayesian selection scheme to choose the model that best describes the transformation between the frames. As a result, the proposed method can adapt to various combinations of camera motions and scene structures. We maintain background and foreground models that are propagated using homography transform(s). The background/foreground labeling is obtained by combining the motion, appearance, spatial, and temporal cues in a MAP-MRF optimization framework. Extensive experimental results with challenging videos show that the proposed method outperforms the state-of-the-art in most cases.

References

1. Black, M.J., Anandan, P.: The robust estimation of multiple motions: parametric and piecewise-smooth flow fields. CVIU 63(1), 75–104 (1996)
2. Bouwmans, T.: Recent advanced statistical background modeling for foreground detection: A systematic survey. Recent Patents on Computer Science 4, 147–176 (2011)

3. Boykov, Y., Veksler, O., Zabih, R.: Fast approximate energy minimization via graph cuts. TPAMI 23(11), 1222–1239 (2001)
4. Cui, X., Huang, J., Zhang, S., Metaxas, D.N.: Background subtraction using low rank and group sparsity constraints. In: Fitzgibbon, A., Lazebnik, S., Perona, P., Sato, Y., Schmid, C. (eds.) ECCV 2012, Part I. LNCS, vol. 7572, pp. 612–625. Springer, Heidelberg (2012)
5. Elqursh, A., Elgammal, A.: Online moving camera background subtraction. In: Fitzgibbon, A., Lazebnik, S., Perona, P., Sato, Y., Schmid, C. (eds.) ECCV 2012, Part VI. LNCS, vol. 7577, pp. 228–241. Springer, Heidelberg (2012)
6. Gauglitz, S., Sweeney, C., Ventura, J., Turk, M., Höllerer, T.: Live tracking and mapping from both general and rotation-only camera motion. In: International Symposium on Mixed and Augmented Reality (2012)
7. Jin, Y., Tao, L., Di, H., Rao, N., Xu, G.: Background modeling from a free-moving camera by multi-layer homography algorithm. In: ICIP (2008)
8. Kwak, S., Lim, T., Nam, W., Han, B., Han, J.H.: Generalized background subtraction based on hybrid inference by belief propagation and Bayesian filtering. In: ICCV (2011)
9. Lim, T., Han, B., Han, J.H.: Modeling and segmentation of floating foreground and background in videos. PR 45(4), 1696–1706 (2012)
10. Liu, F., Gleicher, M.: Learning color and locality cues for moving object detection and segmentation. In: CVPR (2009)
11. Mahadevan, V., Vasconcelos, N.: Background subtraction in highly dynamic scenes. In: CVPR (2008)
12. Mittal, A., Paragios, N.: Motion-based background subtraction using adaptive kernel density estimation. In: CVPR, pp. 302–309 (2004)
13. Piccardi, M.: Background subtraction techniques: a review. In: Proc. IEEE International Conference on Systems, Man and Cybernetics, vol. 4, pp. 3099–3104 (2004)
14. Sand, P., Teller, S.: Particle video: long-range motion estimation using point trajectories. In: CVPR, pp. 2195–2202 (2006)
15. Sheikh, Y., Javed, O., Kanade, T.: Background subtraction for freely moving cameras. In: ICCV (2009)
16. Sheikh, Y., Shah, M.: Bayesian modeling of dynamic scenes for object detection. TPAMI 27(11), 1778–1792 (2005)
17. Stauffer, C., Eric, W., Grimson, L.: Learning patterns of activity using real-time tracking. TPAMI 22, 747–757 (2000)
18. Torr, P.H.S.: Bayesian model estimation and selection for epipolar geometry and generic manifold fitting. IJCV 50(1), 35–61 (2002)
19. Torr, P.H.S., Murray, D.W.: The development and comparison of robust methods for estimating the fundamental matrix. IJCV 24(3), 271–300 (1997)
20. Torr, P.H.S., Zisserman, A.: Mlesac: A new robust estimator with application to estimating image geometry. CVIU 78(1), 138–156 (2000)
21. Tron, R., Vidal, R.: A benchmark for the comparison of 3-D motion segmentation algorithms. In: CVPR (2007)
22. Zhang, G., Jia, J., Hua, W., Bao, H.: Robust bilayer segmentation and motion/depth estimation with a handheld camera. TPAMI 33, 603–617 (2011)

Visualizing and Understanding Convolutional Networks

Matthew D. Zeiler and Rob Fergus

Dept. of Computer Science,
New York University, USA
{zeiler,fergus}@cs.nyu.edu

Abstract. Large Convolutional Network models have recently demonstrated impressive classification performance on the ImageNet benchmark Krizhevsky *et al.* [18]. However there is no clear understanding of why they perform so well, or how they might be improved. In this paper we explore both issues. We introduce a novel visualization technique that gives insight into the function of intermediate feature layers and the operation of the classifier. Used in a diagnostic role, these visualizations allow us to find model architectures that outperform Krizhevsky *et al.* on the ImageNet classification benchmark. We also perform an ablation study to discover the performance contribution from different model layers. We show our ImageNet model generalizes well to other datasets: when the softmax classifier is retrained, it convincingly beats the current state-of-the-art results on Caltech-101 and Caltech-256 datasets.

1 Introduction

Since their introduction by LeCun *et al.* [20] in the early 1990's, Convolutional Networks (convnets) have demonstrated excellent performance at tasks such as hand-written digit classification and face detection. In the last 18 months, several papers have shown that they can also deliver outstanding performance on more challenging visual classification tasks. Ciresan *et al.* [4] demonstrate state-of-the-art performance on NORB and CIFAR-10 datasets. Most notably, Krizhevsky *et al.* [18] show record beating performance on the ImageNet 2012 classification benchmark, with their convnet model achieving an error rate of 16.4%, compared to the 2nd place result of 26.1%. Following on from this work, Girshick *et al.* [10] have shown leading detection performance on the PASCAL VOC dataset. Several factors are responsible for this dramatic improvement in performance: (i) the availability of much larger training sets, with millions of labeled examples; (ii) powerful GPU implementations, making the training of very large models practical and (iii) better model regularization strategies, such as Dropout [14].

Despite this encouraging progress, there is still little insight into the internal operation and behavior of these complex models, or how they achieve such good performance. From a scientific standpoint, this is deeply unsatisfactory. Without clear understanding of how and why they work, the development of better models is reduced to trial-and-error. In this paper we introduce a visualization

D. Fleet et al. (Eds.): ECCV 2014, Part I, LNCS 8689, pp. 818–833, 2014.
© Springer International Publishing Switzerland 2014

technique that reveals the input stimuli that excite individual feature maps at any layer in the model. It also allows us to observe the evolution of features during training and to diagnose potential problems with the model. The visualization technique we propose uses a multi-layered Deconvolutional Network (deconvnet), as proposed by Zeiler *et al.* [29], to project the feature activations back to the input pixel space. We also perform a sensitivity analysis of the classifier output by occluding portions of the input image, revealing which parts of the scene are important for classification.

Using these tools, we start with the architecture of Krizhevsky *et al.* [18] and explore different architectures, discovering ones that outperform their results on ImageNet. We then explore the generalization ability of the model to other datasets, just retraining the softmax classifier on top. As such, this is a form of supervised pre-training, which contrasts with the unsupervised pre-training methods popularized by Hinton *et al.* [13] and others [1,26].

1.1 Related Work

Visualization: Visualizing features to gain intuition about the network is common practice, but mostly limited to the 1st layer where projections to pixel space are possible. In higher layers alternate methods must be used. [8] find the optimal stimulus for each unit by performing gradient descent in image space to maximize the unit's activation. This requires a careful initialization and does not give any information about the unit's invariances. Motivated by the latter's short-coming, [19] (extending an idea by [2]) show how the Hessian of a given unit may be computed numerically around the optimal response, giving some insight into invariances. The problem is that for higher layers, the invariances are extremely complex so are poorly captured by a simple quadratic approximation. Our approach, by contrast, provides a non-parametric view of invariance, showing which patterns from the training set activate the feature map. Our approach is similar to contemporary work by Simonyan *et al.* [23] who demonstrate how saliency maps can be obtained from a convnet by projecting back from the fully connected layers of the network, instead of the convolutional features that we use. Girshick *et al.* [10] show visualizations that identify patches within a dataset that are responsible for strong activations at higher layers in the model. Our visualizations differ in that they are not just crops of input images, but rather top-down projections that reveal structures within each patch that stimulate a particular feature map.

Feature Generalization: Our demonstration of the generalization ability of convnet features is also explored in concurrent work by Donahue *et al.* [7] and Girshick *et al.* [10]. They use the convnet features to obtain state-of-the-art performance on Caltech-101 and the Sun scenes dataset in the former case, and for object detection on the PASCAL VOC dataset, in the latter.

2 Approach

We use standard fully supervised convnet models throughout the paper, as defined by LeCun *et al.* [20] and Krizhevsky *et al.* [18]. These models map a color

2D input image x_i, via a series of layers, to a probability vector $\hat{y_i}$ over the C different classes. Each layer consists of (i) convolution of the previous layer output (or, in the case of the 1st layer, the input image) with a set of learned filters; (ii) passing the responses through a rectified linear function ($relu(x) = \max(x, 0)$); (iii) [optionally] max pooling over local neighborhoods and (iv) [optionally] a local contrast operation that normalizes the responses across feature maps. For more details of these operations, see [18] and [16]. The top few layers of the network are conventional fully-connected networks and the final layer is a softmax classifier. Fig. 3 shows the model used in many of our experiments.

We train these models using a large set of N labeled images $\{x, y\}$, where label y_i is a discrete variable indicating the true class. A cross-entropy loss function, suitable for image classification, is used to compare $\hat{y_i}$ and y_i. The parameters of the network (filters in the convolutional layers, weight matrices in the fully-connected layers and biases) are trained by back-propagating the derivative of the loss with respect to the parameters throughout the network, and updating the parameters via stochastic gradient descent. Details of training are given in Section 3.

2.1 Visualization with a Deconvnet

Understanding the operation of a convnet requires interpreting the feature activity in intermediate layers. We present a novel way to *map these activities back to the input pixel space*, showing what input pattern originally caused a given activation in the feature maps. We perform this mapping with a Deconvolutional Network (deconvnet) Zeiler *et al.* [29]. A deconvnet can be thought of as a convnet model that uses the same components (filtering, pooling) but in reverse, so instead of mapping pixels to features does the opposite. In Zeiler *et al.* [29], deconvnets were proposed as a way of performing unsupervised learning. Here, they are not used in any learning capacity, just as a probe of an already trained convnet.

To examine a convnet, a deconvnet is attached to each of its layers, as illustrated in Fig. 1(top), providing a continuous path back to image pixels. To start, an input image is presented to the convnet and features computed throughout the layers. To examine a given convnet activation, we set all other activations in the layer to zero and pass the feature maps as input to the attached deconvnet layer. Then we successively (i) unpool, (ii) rectify and (iii) filter to reconstruct the activity in the layer beneath that gave rise to the chosen activation. This is then repeated until input pixel space is reached.

Unpooling: In the convnet, the max pooling operation is non-invertible, however we can obtain an approximate inverse by recording the locations of the maxima within each pooling region in a set of *switch* variables. In the deconvnet, the unpooling operation uses these switches to place the reconstructions from the layer above into appropriate locations, preserving the structure of the stimulus. See Fig. 1(bottom) for an illustration of the procedure.

Rectification: The convnet uses *relu* non-linearities, which rectify the feature maps thus ensuring the feature maps are always positive. To obtain valid feature reconstructions at each layer (which also should be positive), we pass the reconstructed signal through a *relu* non-linearity[1].

Filtering: The convnet uses learned filters to convolve the feature maps from the previous layer. To approximately invert this, the deconvnet uses transposed versions of the same filters (as other autoencoder models, such as RBMs), but applied to the rectified maps, not the output of the layer beneath. In practice this means flipping each filter vertically and horizontally.

Note that we do not use any contrast normalization operations when in this reconstruction path. Projecting down from higher layers uses the switch settings generated by the max pooling in the convnet on the way up. As these switch settings are peculiar to a given input image, the reconstruction obtained from a single activation thus resembles a small piece of the original input image, with structures weighted according to their contribution toward to the feature activation. Since the model is trained discriminatively, they implicitly show which parts of the input image are discriminative. Note that these projections are *not* samples from the model, since there is no generative process involved. The whole procedure is similar to backpropping a single strong activation (rather than the usual gradients), i.e. computing $\frac{\partial h}{\partial X_n}$, where h is the element of the feature map with the strong activation and X_n is the input image. However, it differs in that (i) the the *relu* is imposed independently and (ii) contrast normalization operations are not used. A general shortcoming of our approach is that it only visualizes a single activation, not the joint activity present in a layer. Nevertheless, as we show in Fig. 6, these visualizations are accurate representations of the input pattern that stimulates the given feature map in the model: when the parts of the original input image corresponding to the pattern are occluded, we see a distinct drop in activity within the feature map.

3 Training Details

We now describe the large convnet model that will be visualized in Section 4. The architecture, shown in Fig. 3, is similar to that used by Krizhevsky *et al.* [18] for ImageNet classification. One difference is that the sparse connections used in Krizhevsky's layers 3,4,5 (due to the model being split across 2 GPUs) are replaced with dense connections in our model. Other important differences relating to layers 1 and 2 were made following inspection of the visualizations in Fig. 5, as described in Section 4.1.

The model was trained on the ImageNet 2012 training set (1.3 million images, spread over 1000 different classes) [6]. Each RGB image was preprocessed by resizing the smallest dimension to 256, cropping the center 256x256 region, subtracting the per-pixel mean (across all images) and then using 10 different sub-crops of size 224x224 (corners + center with(out) horizontal flips). Stochastic gradient descent with a mini-batch size of 128 was used to update the parameters, starting with a learning rate of 10^{-2}, in conjunction with a momentum term of 0.9. We

[1] We also tried rectifying using the binary mask imposed by the feed-forward *relu* operation, but the resulting visualizations were significantly less clear.

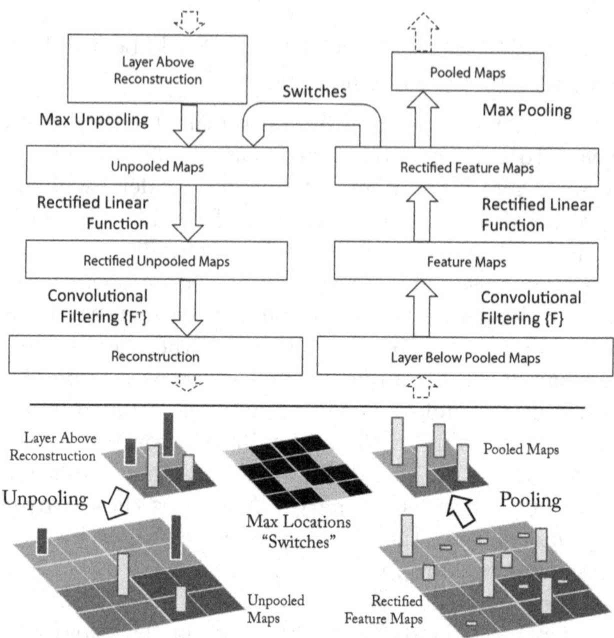

Fig. 1. Top: A deconvnet layer (left) attached to a convnet layer (right). The deconvnet will reconstruct an approximate version of the convnet features from the layer beneath. Bottom: An illustration of the unpooling operation in the deconvnet, using *switches* which record the location of the local max in each pooling region (colored zones) during pooling in the convnet. The black/white bars are negative/positive activations within the feature map.

anneal the learning rate throughout training manually when the validation error plateaus. Dropout [14] is used in the fully connected layers (6 and 7) with a rate of 0.5. All weights are initialized to 10^{-2} and biases are set to 0.

Visualization of the first layer filters during training reveals that a few of them dominate. To combat this, we renormalize each filter in the convolutional layers whose RMS value exceeds a fixed radius of 10^{-1} to this fixed radius. This is crucial, especially in the first layer of the model, where the input images are roughly in the [-128,128] range. As in Krizhevsky *et al.* [18], we produce multiple different crops and flips of each training example to boost training set size. We stopped training after 70 epochs, which took around 12 days on a single GTX580 GPU, using an implementation based on [18].

4 Convnet Visualization

Using the model described in Section 3, we now use the deconvnet to visualize the feature activations on the ImageNet validation set.

Feature Visualization: Fig. 2 shows feature visualizations from our model once training is complete. For a given feature map, we show the top 9 activations, each projected separately down to pixel space, revealing the different structures that excite that map and showing its invariance to input deformations. Alongside these visualizations we show the corresponding image patches. These have greater variation than visualizations which solely focus on the discriminant structure within each patch. For example, in layer 5, row 1, col 2, the patches appear to have little in common, but the visualizations reveal that this particular feature map focuses on the grass in the background, not the foreground objects.

The projections from each layer show the hierarchical nature of the features in the network. Layer 2 responds to corners and other edge/color conjunctions. Layer 3 has more complex invariances, capturing similar textures (e.g. mesh patterns (Row 1, Col 1); text (R2,C4)). Layer 4 shows significant variation, and is more class-specific: dog faces (R1,C1); bird's legs (R4,C2). Layer 5 shows entire objects with significant pose variation, e.g. keyboards (R1,C11) and dogs (R4).

Feature Evolution during Training: Fig. 4 visualizes the progression during training of the strongest activation (across all training examples) within a given feature map projected back to pixel space. Sudden jumps in appearance result from a change in the image from which the strongest activation originates. The lower layers of the model can be seen to converge within a few epochs. However, the upper layers only develop develop after a considerable number of epochs (40-50), demonstrating the need to let the models train until fully converged.

4.1 Architecture Selection

While visualization of a trained model gives insight into its operation, it can also assist with selecting good architectures in the first place. By visualizing the first and second layers of Krizhevsky *et al.* 's architecture (Fig. 5(a) & (c)), various problems are apparent. The first layer filters are a mix of extremely high and low frequency information, with little coverage of the mid frequencies. Additionally, the 2nd layer visualization shows aliasing artifacts caused by the large stride 4 used in the 1st layer convolutions. To remedy these problems, we (i) reduced the 1st layer filter size from 11x11 to 7x7 and (ii) made the stride of the convolution 2, rather than 4. This new architecture retains much more information in the 1st and 2nd layer features, as shown in Fig. 5(b) & (d). More importantly, it also improves the classification performance as shown in Section 5.1.

4.2 Occlusion Sensitivity

With image classification approaches, a natural question is if the model is truly identifying the location of the object in the image, or just using the surrounding context. Fig. 6 attempts to answer this question by systematically occluding different portions of the input image with a grey square, and monitoring the output of the classifier. The examples clearly show the model is localizing the objects within the scene, as the probability of the correct class drops significantly when the object is occluded. Fig. 6 also shows visualizations from the strongest feature map of the top convolution layer, in addition to activity in this map (summed over spatial locations) as a function of occluder position. When the

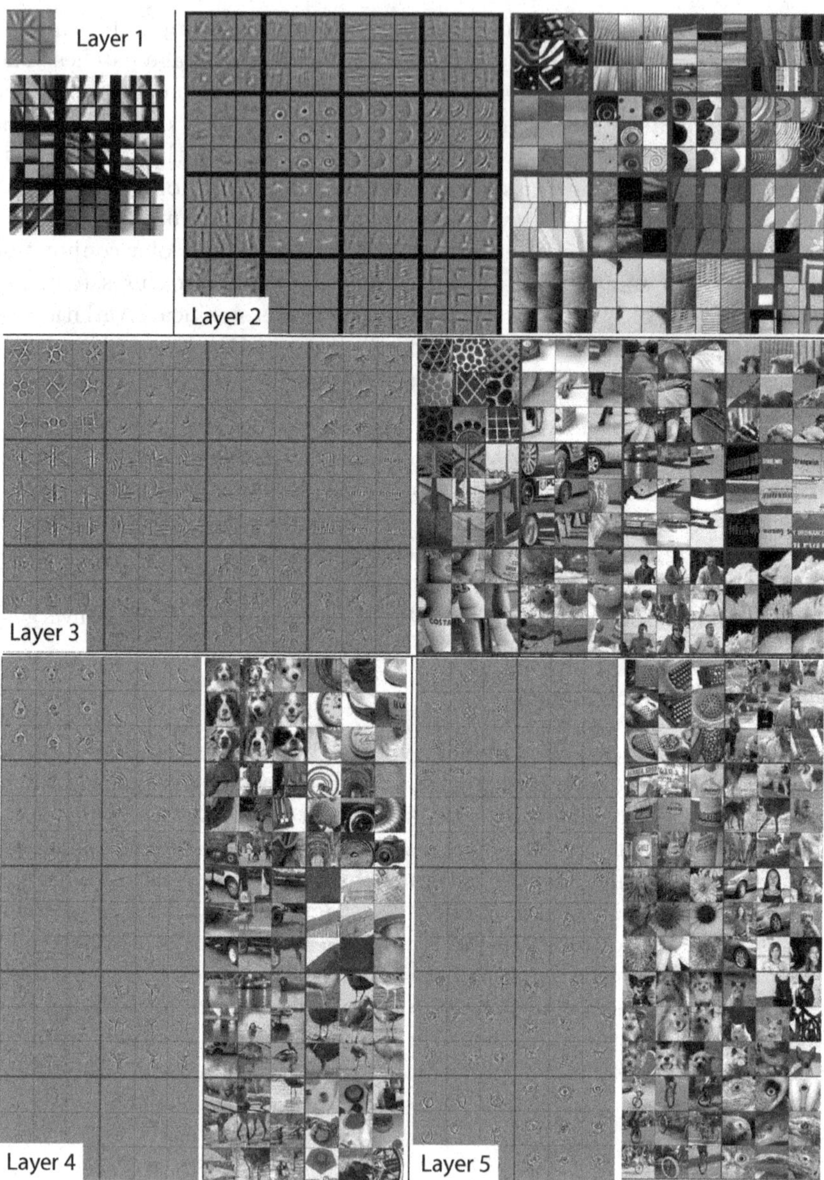

Fig. 2. Visualization of features in a fully trained model. For layers 2-5 we show the top 9 activations in a random subset of feature maps across the validation data, projected down to pixel space using our deconvolutional network approach. Our reconstructions are *not* samples from the model: they are reconstructed patterns from the validation set that cause high activations in a given feature map. For each feature map we also show the corresponding image patches. Note: (i) the the strong grouping within each feature map, (ii) greater invariance at higher layers and (iii) exaggeration of discriminative parts of the image, e.g. eyes and noses of dogs (layer 4, row 1, cols 1). Best viewed in electronic form. The compression artifacts are a consequence of the 30Mb submission limit, not the reconstruction algorithm itself.

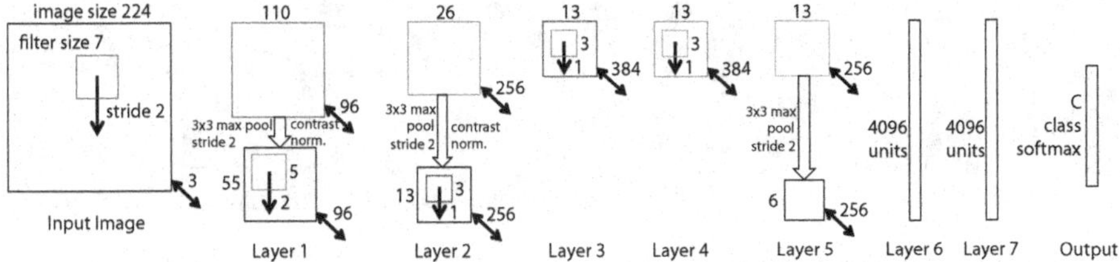

Fig. 3. Architecture of our 8 layer convnet model. A 224 by 224 crop of an image (with 3 color planes) is presented as the input. This is convolved with 96 different 1st layer filters (red), each of size 7 by 7, using a stride of 2 in both x and y. The resulting feature maps are then: (i) passed through a rectified linear function (not shown), (ii) pooled (max within 3x3 regions, using stride 2) and (iii) contrast normalized across feature maps to give 96 different 55 by 55 element feature maps. Similar operations are repeated in layers 2,3,4,5. The last two layers are fully connected, taking features from the top convolutional layer as input in vector form ($6 \cdot 6 \cdot 256 = 9216$ dimensions). The final layer is a C-way softmax function, C being the number of classes. All filters and feature maps are square in shape.

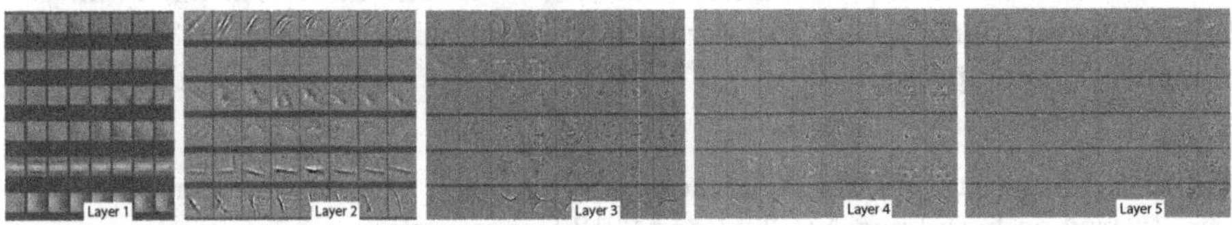

Fig. 4. Evolution of a randomly chosen subset of model features through training. Each layer's features are displayed in a different block. Within each block, we show a randomly chosen subset of features at epochs [1,2,5,10,20,30,40,64]. The visualization shows the strongest activation (across all training examples) for a given feature map, projected down to pixel space using our deconvnet approach. Color contrast is artificially enhanced and the figure is best viewed in electronic form.

occluder covers the image region that appears in the visualization, we see a strong drop in activity in the feature map. This shows that the visualization genuinely corresponds to the image structure that stimulates that feature map, hence validating the other visualizations shown in Fig. 4 and Fig. 2.

5 Experiments

5.1 ImageNet 2012

This dataset consists of 1.3M/50k/100k training/validation/test examples, spread over 1000 categories. Table 1 shows our results on this dataset.

Using the exact architecture specified in Krizhevsky *et al.* [18], we attempt to replicate their result on the validation set. We achieve an error rate within 0.1% of their reported value on the ImageNet 2012 validation set.

Next we analyze the performance of our model with the architectural changes outlined in Section 4.1 (7×7 filters in layer 1 and stride 2 convolutions in layers

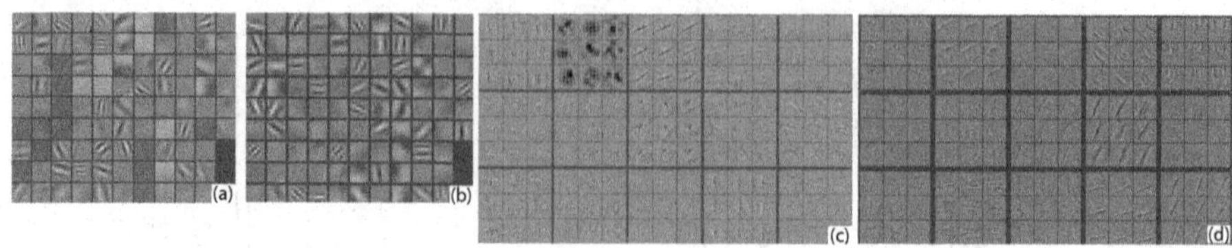

Fig. 5. (a): 1st layer features without feature scale clipping. Note that one feature dominates. (b): 1st layer features from Krizhevsky *et al.* [18]. (c): Our 1st layer features. The smaller stride (2 vs 4) and filter size (7x7 vs 11x11) results in more distinctive features and fewer "dead" features. (d): Visualizations of 2nd layer features from Krizhevsky *et al.* [18]. (e): Visualizations of our 2nd layer features. These are cleaner, with no aliasing artifacts that are visible in (d).

1 & 2). This model, shown in Fig. 3, significantly outperforms the architecture of Krizhevsky *et al.* [18], beating their single model result by 1.7% (test top-5). When we combine multiple models, we obtain a test error of 14.8%, an improvement of 1.6%. This result is close to that produced by the data-augmentation approaches of Howard [15], which could easily be combined with our architecture. However, our model is some way short of the winner of the 2013 Imagenet classification competition [28].

Table 1. ImageNet 2012/2013 classification error rates. The $*$ indicates models that were trained on both ImageNet 2011 and 2012 training sets.

Error %	Val Top-1	Val Top-5	Test Top-5
Gunji *et al.* [12]	-	-	26.2
DeCAF [7]	-	-	19.2
Krizhevsky *et al.* [18], 1 convnet	40.7	18.2	−−
Krizhevsky *et al.* [18], 5 convnets	38.1	16.4	16.4
Krizhevsky *et al.* *[18], 1 convnets	39.0	16.6	−−
Krizhevsky *et al.* *[18], 7 convnets	36.7	15.4	15.3
Our replication of Krizhevsky *et al.* , 1 convnet	40.5	18.1	−−
1 convnet as per Fig. 3	38.4	16.5	−−
5 convnets as per Fig. 3 – (a)	36.7	15.3	15.3
1 convnet as per Fig. 3 but with layers 3,4,5: 512,1024,512 maps – (b)	37.5	16.0	16.1
6 convnets, (a) & (b) combined	36.0	14.7	14.8
Howard [15]	-	-	13.5
Clarifai [28]	-	-	11.7

Varying ImageNet Model Sizes: In Table 2, we first explore the architecture of Krizhevsky *et al.* [18] by adjusting the size of layers, or removing them entirely. In each case, the model is trained from scratch with the revised architecture. Removing the fully connected layers (6,7) only gives a slight increase in error (in

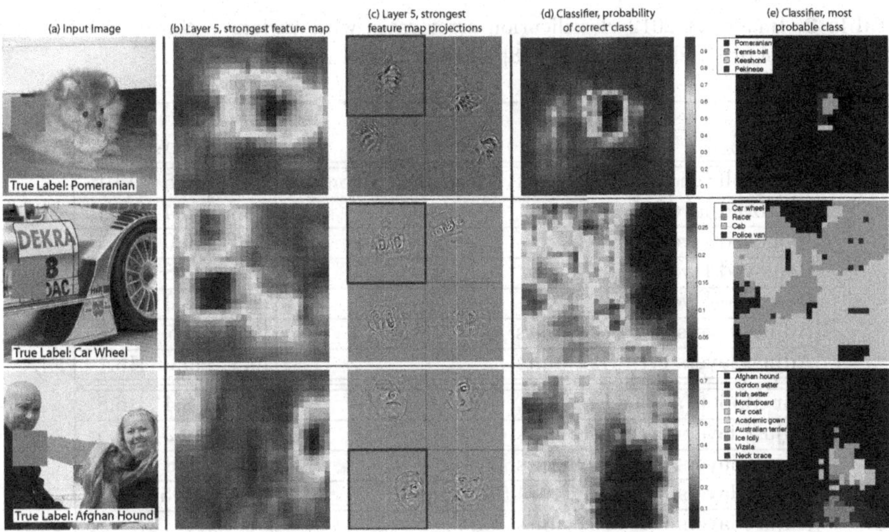

Fig. 6. Three test examples where we systematically cover up different portions of the scene with a gray square (1st column) and see how the top (layer 5) feature maps ((b) & (c)) and classifier output ((d) & (e)) changes. (b): for each position of the gray scale, we record the total activation in one layer 5 feature map (the one with the strongest response in the unoccluded image). (c): a visualization of this feature map projected down into the input image (black square), along with visualizations of this map from other images. The first row example shows the strongest feature to be the dog's face. When this is covered-up the activity in the feature map decreases (blue area in (b)). (d): a map of correct class probability, as a function of the position of the gray square. E.g. when the dog's face is obscured, the probability for "pomeranian" drops significantly. (e): the most probable label as a function of occluder position. E.g. in the 1st row, for most locations it is "pomeranian", but if the dog's face is obscured but not the ball, then it predicts "tennis ball". In the 2nd example, text on the car is the strongest feature in layer 5, but the classifier is most sensitive to the wheel. The 3rd example contains multiple objects. The strongest feature in layer 5 picks out the faces, but the classifier is sensitive to the dog (blue region in (d)), since it uses multiple feature maps.

the following, we refer to top-5 validation error). This is surprising, given that they contain the majority of model parameters. Removing two of the middle convolutional layers also makes a relatively small difference to the error rate. However, removing both the middle convolution layers and the fully connected layers yields a model with only 4 layers whose performance is dramatically worse. This would suggest that the overall depth of the model is important for obtaining good performance. We then modify our model, shown in Fig. 3. Changing the size of the fully connected layers makes little difference to performance (same for model of Krizhevsky *et al.* [18]). However, increasing the size of the middle convolution layers goes give a useful gain in performance. But increasing these, while also enlarging the fully connected layers results in over-fitting.

Table 2. ImageNet 2012 classification error rates with various architectural changes to the model of Krizhevsky *et al.* [18] and our model (see Fig. 3)

Error %	Train Top-1	Val Top-1	Val Top-5
Our replication of Krizhevsky *et al.* [18], 1 convnet	35.1	40.5	18.1
Removed layers 3,4	41.8	45.4	22.1
Removed layer 7	27.4	40.0	18.4
Removed layers 6,7	27.4	44.8	22.4
Removed layer 3,4,6,7	71.1	71.3	50.1
Adjust layers 6,7: 2048 units	40.3	41.7	18.8
Adjust layers 6,7: 8192 units	26.8	40.0	18.1
Our Model (as per Fig. 3)	33.1	38.4	16.5
Adjust layers 6,7: 2048 units	38.2	40.2	17.6
Adjust layers 6,7: 8192 units	22.0	38.8	17.0
Adjust layers 3,4,5: 512,1024,512 maps	18.8	**37.5**	**16.0**
Adjust layers 6,7: 8192 units and Layers 3,4,5: 512,1024,512 maps	**10.0**	38.3	16.9

5.2 Feature Generalization

The experiments above show the importance of the convolutional part of our ImageNet model in obtaining state-of-the-art performance. This is supported by the visualizations of Fig. 2 which show the complex invariances learned in the convolutional layers. We now explore the ability of these feature extraction layers to generalize to other datasets, namely Caltech-101 [9], Caltech-256 [11] and PASCAL VOC 2012. To do this, we keep layers 1-7 of our ImageNet-trained model fixed and train a new softmax classifier on top (for the appropriate number of classes) using the training images of the new dataset. Since the softmax contains relatively few parameters, it can be trained quickly from a relatively small number of examples, as is the case for certain datasets.

The experiments compare our feature representation, obtained from ImageNet, with the hand-crafted features used by other methods. In both our approach and existing ones the Caltech/PASCAL training data is only used to train the classifier. As they are of similar complexity (ours: softmax, others: linear SVM), the feature representation is crucial to performance. It is important to note that both representations were built using images beyond the Caltech and PASCAL training sets. For example, the hyper-parameters in HOG descriptors were determined through systematic experiments on a pedestrian dataset [5].

We also try a second strategy of training a model from scratch, i.e. resetting layers 1-7 to random values and train them, as well as the softmax, on the training images of the PASCAL/Caltech dataset.

One complication is that some of the Caltech datasets have some images that are also in the ImageNet training data. Using normalized correlation, we identified these few "overlap" images[2] and removed them from our Imagenet training set and then retrained our Imagenet models, so avoiding the possibility of train/test contamination.

Caltech-101: We follow the procedure of [9] and randomly select 15 or 30 images per class for training and test on up to 50 images per class reporting the average of the per-class accuracies in Table 3, using 5 train/test folds. Training took 17 minutes for 30 images/class. The pre-trained model beats the best reported result for 30 images/class from [3] by 2.2%. Our result agrees with the recently published result of Donahue *et al.* [7], who obtain 86.1% accuracy (30 imgs/class). The convnet model trained from scratch however does terribly, only achieving 46.5%, showing the impossibility of training a large convnet on such a small dataset.

Table 3. Caltech-101 classification accuracy for our convnet models, against two leading alternate approaches

# Train	Acc % 15/class	Acc % 30/class
Bo *et al.* [3]	–	81.4 ± 0.33
Yang *et al.* [17]	73.2	84.3
Non-pretrained convnet	22.8 ± 1.5	46.5 ± 1.7
ImageNet-pretrained convnet	$\mathbf{83.8 \pm 0.5}$	$\mathbf{86.5 \pm 0.5}$

Caltech-256: We follow the procedure of [11], selecting 15, 30, 45, or 60 training images per class, reporting the average of the per-class accuracies in Table 4. Our ImageNet-pretrained model beats the current state-of-the-art results obtained by Bo *et al.* [3] by a significant margin: 74.2% vs 55.2% for 60 training images/class. However, as with Caltech-101, the model trained from scratch does poorly. In Fig. 7, we explore the "one-shot learning" [9] regime. With our pre-trained model, just 6 Caltech-256 training images are needed to beat the leading method using 10 times as many images. This shows the power of the ImageNet feature extractor.

PASCAL 2012: We used the standard training and validation images to train a 20-way softmax on top of the ImageNet-pretrained convnet. This is not ideal, as PASCAL images can contain multiple objects and our model just provides a single exclusive prediction for each image. Table 5 shows the results on the test set, comparing to the leading methods: the top 2 entries in the competition and concurrent work from Oquab *et al.* [21] who use a convnet with a more appropriate classifier. The PASCAL and ImageNet images are quite different in nature, the former being full scenes unlike the latter. This may explain our mean

[2] For Caltech-101, we found 44 images in common (out of 9,144 total images), with a maximum overlap of 10 for any given class. For Caltech-256, we found 243 images in common (out of 30,607 total images), with a maximum overlap of 18 for any given class.

Table 4. Caltech 256 classification accuracies

# Train	Acc % 15/class	Acc % 30/class	Acc % 45/class	Acc % 60/class
Sohn *et al.* [24]	35.1	42.1	45.7	47.9
Bo *et al.* [3]	40.5 ± 0.4	48.0 ± 0.2	51.9 ± 0.2	55.2 ± 0.3
Non-pretr.	9.0 ± 1.4	22.5 ± 0.7	31.2 ± 0.5	38.8 ± 1.4
ImageNet-pretr.	**65.7 ± 0.2**	**70.6 ± 0.2**	**72.7 ± 0.4**	**74.2 ± 0.3**

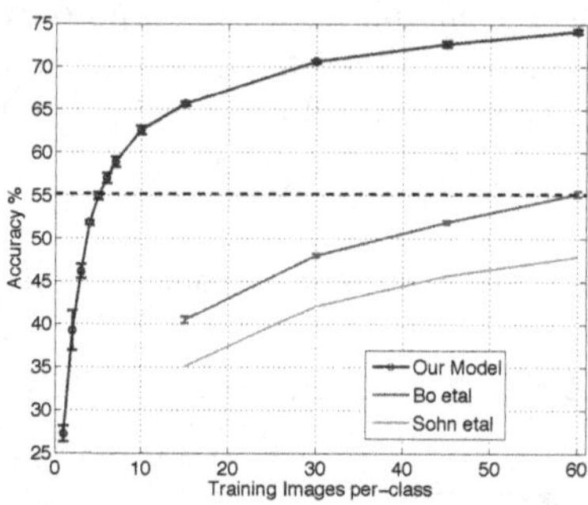

Fig. 7. Caltech-256 classification performance as the number of training images per class is varied. Using only 6 training examples per class with our pre-trained feature extractor, we surpass best reported result by Bo *et al.* [3].

Table 5. PASCAL 2012 classification results, comparing our Imagenet-pretrained convnet against the leading two methods and the recent approach of Oquab *et al.* [21]

Acc %	[22]	[27]	[21]	Ours	Acc %	[22]	[27]	[21]	Ours
Airplane	92.0	**97.3**	94.6	96.0	Dining table	63.2	**77.8**	69.0	67.7
Bicycle	74.2	**84.2**	82.9	77.1	Dog	68.9	83.0	**92.1**	87.8
Bird	73.0	80.8	88.2	**88.4**	Horse	78.2	87.5	**93.4**	86.0
Boat	77.5	85.3	60.3	**85.5**	Motorbike	81.0	**90.1**	88.6	85.1
Bottle	54.3	**60.8**	60.3	55.8	Person	91.6	95.0	**96.1**	90.9
Bus	85.2	**89.9**	89.0	85.8	Potted plant	55.9	57.8	**64.3**	52.2
Car	81.9	**86.8**	84.4	78.6	Sheep	69.4	79.2	**86.6**	83.6
Cat	76.4	89.3	90.7	**91.2**	Sofa	65.4	**73.4**	62.3	61.1
Chair	65.2	**75.4**	72.1	65.0	Train	86.7	**94.5**	91.1	91.8
Cow	63.2	77.8	**86.8**	74.4	Tv	77.4	**80.7**	79.8	76.1
Mean	74.3	82.2	**82.8**	79.0	# won	0	**11**	6	3

performance being 3.2% lower than the leading competition result [27], however we do beat them on 5 classes, sometimes by large margins.

5.3 Feature Analysis

We explore how discriminative the features in each layer of our Imagenet-pretrained model are. We do this by varying the number of layers retained from the ImageNet model and place either a linear SVM or softmax classifier on top. Table 6 shows results on Caltech-101 and Caltech-256. For both datasets, a steady improvement can be seen as we ascend the model, with best results being obtained by using all layers. This supports the premise that as the feature hierarchies become deeper, they learn increasingly powerful features.

Table 6. Analysis of the discriminative information contained in each layer of feature maps within our ImageNet-pretrained convnet. We train either a linear SVM or softmax on features from different layers (as indicated in brackets) from the convnet. Higher layers generally produce more discriminative features.

	Cal-101 (30/class)	Cal-256 (60/class)
SVM (1)	44.8 ± 0.7	24.6 ± 0.4
SVM (2)	66.2 ± 0.5	39.6 ± 0.3
SVM (3)	72.3 ± 0.4	46.0 ± 0.3
SVM (4)	76.6 ± 0.4	51.3 ± 0.1
SVM (5)	$\mathbf{86.2 \pm 0.8}$	65.6 ± 0.3
SVM (7)	$\mathbf{85.5 \pm 0.4}$	$\mathbf{71.7 \pm 0.2}$
Softmax (5)	82.9 ± 0.4	65.7 ± 0.5
Softmax (7)	$\mathbf{85.4 \pm 0.4}$	$\mathbf{72.6 \pm 0.1}$

6 Discussion

We explored large convolutional neural network models, trained for image classification, in a number ways. First, we presented a novel way to visualize the activity within the model. This reveals the features to be far from random, uninterpretable patterns. Rather, they show many intuitively desirable properties such as compositionality, increasing invariance and class discrimination as we ascend the layers. We also show how these visualization can be used to identify problems with the model and so obtain better results, for example improving on Krizhevsky *et al.* 's [18] impressive ImageNet 2012 result. We then demonstrated through a series of occlusion experiments that the model, while trained for classification, is highly sensitive to local structure in the image and is not just using broad scene context. An ablation study on the model revealed that having a minimum depth to the network, rather than any individual section, is vital to the model's performance.

Finally, we showed how the ImageNet trained model can generalize well to other datasets. For Caltech-101 and Caltech-256, the datasets are similar enough that we can beat the best reported results, in the latter case by a significant margin. Our convnet model generalized less well to the PASCAL data, perhaps suffering from dataset bias [25], although it was still within 3.2% of the best reported result, despite no tuning for the task. For example, our performance might improve if a different loss function was used that permitted multiple objects per image. This would naturally enable the networks to tackle the object detection as well.

Acknowledgments. The authors would like to thank Yann LeCun for helpful discussions and acknowledge support from NSERC, NSF grant #1116923 and Microsoft Research.

References

1. Bengio, Y., Lamblin, P., Popovici, D., Larochelle, H.: Greedy layer-wise training of deep networks. In: NIPS, pp. 153–160 (2007)
2. Berkes, P., Wiskott, L.: On the analysis and interpretation of inhomogeneous quadratic forms as receptive fields. Neural Computation (2006)
3. Bo, L., Ren, X., Fox, D.: Multipath sparse coding using hierarchical matching pursuit. In: CVPR (2013)
4. Ciresan, D.C., Meier, J., Schmidhuber, J.: Multi-column deep neural networks for image classification. In: CVPR (2012)
5. Dalal, N., Triggs, B.: Histograms of oriented gradients for pedestrian detection. In: CVPR (2005)
6. Deng, J., Dong, W., Socher, R., Li, L.J., Li, K., Fei-Fei, L.: ImageNet: A Large-Scale Hierarchical Image Database. In: CVPR 2009 (2009)
7. Donahue, J., Jia, Y., Vinyals, O., Hoffman, J., Zhang, N., Tzeng, E., Darrell, T.: DeCAF: A deep convolutional activation feature for generic visual recognition. arXiv:1310.1531 (2013)
8. Erhan, D., Bengio, Y., Courville, A., Vincent, P.: Visualizing higher-layer features of a deep network. Technical report, University of Montreal (2009)
9. Fei-fei, L., Fergus, R., Perona, P.: One-shot learning of object categories. IEEE Trans. PAMI (2006)
10. Girshick, R., Donahue, J., Darrell, T., Malik, J.: Rich feature hierarchies for accurate object detection and semantic segmentation. arXiv:1311.2524 (2014)
11. Griffin, G., Holub, A., Perona, P.: The caltech 256. Caltech Technical Report (2006)
12. Gunji, N., Higuchi, T., Yasumoto, K., Muraoka, H., Ushiku, Y., Harada, T., Kuniyoshi, Y.: Classification entry. Imagenet Competition (2012)
13. Hinton, G.E., Osindero, S., Teh, Y.: A fast learning algorithm for deep belief nets. Neural Computation 18, 1527–1554 (2006)
14. Hinton, G.E., Srivastave, N., Krizhevsky, A., Sutskever, I., Salakhutdinov, R.R.: Improving neural networks by preventing co-adaptation of feature detectors. In: arXiv:1207.0580 (2012)
15. Howard, A.G.: Some improvements on deep convolutional neural network based image classification. arXiv 1312.5402 (2013)
16. Jarrett, K., Kavukcuoglu, K., Ranzato, M., LeCun, Y.: What is the best multi-stage architecture for object recognition? In: ICCV (2009)
17. Jianchao, Y., Kai, Y., Yihong, G., Thomas, H.: Linear spatial pyramid matching using sparse coding for image classification. In: CVPR (2009)

18. Krizhevsky, A., Sutskever, I., Hinton, G.: Imagenet classification with deep convolutional neural networks. In: NIPS (2012)
19. Le, Q.V., Ngiam, J., Chen, Z., Chia, D., Koh, P., Ng, A.Y.: Tiled convolutional neural networks. In: NIPS (2010)
20. LeCun, Y., Boser, B., Denker, J.S., Henderson, D., Howard, R.E., Hubbard, W., Jackel, L.D.: Backpropagation applied to handwritten zip code recognition. Neural Comput. 1(4), 541–551 (1989)
21. Oquab, M., Bottou, L., Laptev, I., Sivic, J.: Learning and transferring mid-level image representations using convolutional neural networks. In: CVPR (2014)
22. Sande, K., Uijlings, J., Snoek, C., Smeulders, A.: Hybrid coding for selective search. In: PASCAL VOC Classification Challenge 2012 (2012)
23. Simonyan, K., Vedaldi, A., Zisserman, A.: Deep inside convolutional networks: Visualising image classification models and saliency maps. arXiv 1312.6034v1 (2013)
24. Sohn, K., Jung, D., Lee, H., Hero III, A.: Efficient learning of sparse, distributed, convolutional feature representations for object recognition. In: ICCV (2011)
25. Torralba, A., Efros, A.A.: Unbiased look at dataset bias. In: CVPR (2011)
26. Vincent, P., Larochelle, H., Bengio, Y., Manzagol, P.A.: Extracting and composing robust features with denoising autoencoders. In: ICML, pp. 1096–1103 (2008)
27. Yan, S., Dong, J., Chen, Q., Song, Z., Pan, Y., Xia, W., Huang, Z., Hua, Y., Shen, S.: Generalized hierarchical matching for sub-category aware object classification. In: PASCAL VOC Classification Challenge 2012 (2012)
28. Zeiler, M.: Clarifai (2013), `http://www.image-net.org/challenges/LSVRC/2013/results.php`
29. Zeiler, M., Taylor, G., Fergus, R.: Adaptive deconvolutional networks for mid and high level feature learning. In: ICCV (2011)

Part-Based R-CNNs for Fine-Grained Category Detection

Ning Zhang, Jeff Donahue, Ross Girshick, and Trevor Darrell

University of California, Berkeley, USA
{nzhang,jdonahue,rbg,trevor}@eecs.berkeley.edu

Abstract. Semantic part localization can facilitate fine-grained categorization by explicitly isolating subtle appearance differences associated with specific object parts. Methods for pose-normalized representations have been proposed, but generally presume bounding box annotations at test time due to the difficulty of object detection. We propose a model for fine-grained categorization that overcomes these limitations by leveraging deep convolutional features computed on bottom-up region proposals. Our method learns whole-object and part detectors, enforces learned geometric constraints between them, and predicts a fine-grained category from a pose-normalized representation. Experiments on the Caltech-UCSD bird dataset confirm that our method outperforms state-of-the-art fine-grained categorization methods in an end-to-end evaluation without requiring a bounding box at test time.

Keywords: Fine-grained recognition, object detection, convolutional models.

1 Introduction

The problem of visual fine-grained categorization can be extremely challenging due to the subtle differences in the appearance of certain parts across related categories. In contrast to basic-level recognition, fine-grained categorization aims to distinguish between different breeds or species or product models, and often requires distinctions that must be conditioned on the object pose for reliable identification. Facial recognition is the classic case of fine-grained recognition, and it is noteworthy that the best facial recognition methods jointly discover facial landmarks and extract features from those locations.

Localizing the parts in an object is therefore central to establishing correspondence between object instances and discounting object pose variations and camera view position. Previous work has investigated part-based approaches to this problem [7, 16, 29, 43, 46]. The bottleneck for many pose-normalized representations is indeed accurate part localization. The Poselet [8] and DPM [17] methods have previously been utilized to obtain part localizations with a modest degree of success; methods generally report adequate part localization only when given a known bounding box at test time [11, 20, 35, 36, 42]. By developing a novel deep part detection scheme, we propose an end-to-end fine grained categorization system which requires no knowledge of object bounding box at test time,

D. Fleet et al. (Eds.): ECCV 2014, Part I, LNCS 8689, pp. 834–849, 2014.
© Springer International Publishing Switzerland 2014

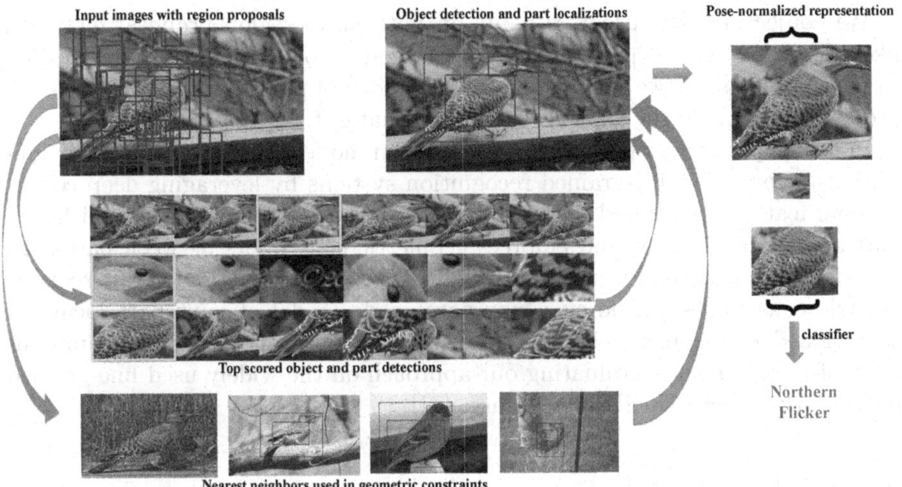

Fig. 1. Overview of our part localization Starting from bottom-up region proposals (top-left), we train both object and part detectors based on deep convolutional features. During test time, all the windows are scored by all detectors (middle), and we apply non-parametric geometric constraints (bottom) to rescore the windows and choose the best object and part detections (top-right). The final step is to extract features on the localized semantic parts for fine-grained recognition for a pose-normalized representation and then train a classifier for the final categorization. Best viewed in color.

and can achieve performance rivaling previously reported methods requiring the ground truth bounding box at test time to filter false positive detections.

The recent success of convolutional networks, like [26], on the ImageNet Challenge [22] has inspired further work on applying deep convolutional features to related image classification [14] and detection tasks [21]. In [21], Girshick et al. achieved breakthrough performance on object detection by applying the CNN of [26] to a set of bottom-up candidate region proposals [40], boosting PASCAL detection performance by over 30% compared to the previous best methods. Independently, OverFeat [37] proposed localization using a CNN to regress to object locations. However, the progress of leveraging deep convolutional features is not limited to basic-level object detection. In many applications such as fine-grained recognition, attribute recognition, pose estimation, and others, reasonable predictions demand accurate part localization.

Feature learning has been used for fine-grained recognition and attribute estimation, but was limited to engineered features for localization. DPD-DeCAF [47] used DeCAF [14] as a feature descriptor, but relied on HOG-based DPM [17] for part localization. PANDA [48] learned part-specific deep convolutional networks whose location was conditioned on HOG-based poselet models. These models lack the strength and detection robustness of R-CNN [21]. In this work we explore a unified method that uses the same deep convolutional representation for detection as well as part description.

We conjecture that progress made on bottom-up region proposal methods, like selective search [40], could benefit localization of smaller parts in addition to whole objects. As we show later, average recall of parts using selective search proposals is 95% on the Caltech-UCSD bird dataset.

In this paper, we propose a part localization model which overcomes the limitations of previous fine-grained recognition systems by leveraging deep convolutional features computed on bottom-up region proposals. Our method learns part appearance models and enforces geometric constraints between parts. An overview of our method is shown in Figure 1. We have investigated different geometric constraints, including a non-parametric model of joint part locations conditioned on nearest neighbors in semantic appearance space. We present state-of-the-art results evaluating our approach on the widely used fine-grained benchmark Caltech-UCSD bird dataset [41].

2 Related Work

2.1 Part-Based Models for Detection and Pose Localization

Previous work has proposed explicit modeling of object part appearances and locations for more accurate recognition and localization. Starting with pictorial structures [18, 19], and continuing through poselets [8] and related work, many methods have jointly localized a set of geometrically related parts. The deformable parts model (DPM) [17], until recently the state-of-the-art PASCAL object detection method, models parts with additional learned filters in positions anchored with respect to the whole object bounding box, allowing parts to be displaced from this anchor with learned deformation costs. The "strong" DPM [3] adapted this method for the strongly supervised setting in which part locations are annotated at training time. A limitation of these methods is their use of weak features (usually HOG [12]).

2.2 Fine-Grained Categorization

Recently, a large body of computer vision research has focused on the fine-grained classification problem in a number of domains, such as animal breeds or species [16, 25, 30, 32, 36, 45], plant species [1, 2, 5, 33, 34, 38], and man-made objects [31, 39].

Several approaches are based on detecting and extracting features from certain parts of objects. Farrell et al. [16] proposed a pose-normalized representation using poselets [8]. Deformable part models [17] were used in [36, 47] for part localization. Based on the work of localizing fiducial landmarks on faces [6], Liu et al. [30] proposed an exemplar-based geometric method to detect dog faces and extract highly localized image features from keypoints to differentiate dog breeds. Furthermore, Berg et al. [7] learned a set of highly discriminative intermediate features by learning a descriptor for each pair of keypoints. Moreover, in [29], the authors extend the non-parametric exemplar-based method of [6] by enforcing pose and subcategory consistency. Yao et al. [44] and Yang et al. [43] have investigated template matching methods to reduce the cost of sliding window approaches. All these part-based methods, however, require the ground truth bounding box at test time for part localization or keypoint prediction.

Human-in-the-loop methods [9, 13, 15] ask a human to name attributes of the object, click on certain parts or mark the most discriminative regions to improve classification accuracy. Segmentation-based approaches are also very effective for fine-grained recognition. Approaches such as [11, 20, 35, 36, 42] used region-level cues to infer the foreground segmentation mask and to discard the noisy visual information in the background. Chai et al. [10] showed that jointly learning part localization and foreground segmentation together can be beneficial for fine-grained categorization. Similar to most previous part-based approaches, these efforts require the ground truth bounding box to initialize the segmentation seed. In contrast, the aim of our work is to perform end-to-end fine-grained categorization with no knowledge at test time of the ground truth bounding box. Our part detectors use convolutional features on bottom-up region proposals, together with learned non-parametric geometric constraints to more accurately localize object parts, thus enabling strong fine-grained categorization.

2.3 Convolutional Networks

In recent years, convolutional neural networks (CNNs) have been incorporated into a number of visual recognition systems in a wide variety of domains. At least some of the strength of these models lies in their ability to *learn* discriminative features from raw data inputs (e.g., image pixels), in contrast to more traditional object recognition pipelines which compute hand-engineered features on images as an initial preprocessing step. CNNs were popularized by LeCun and colleagues who initially applied such models to digit recognition [27] and OCR [28] and later to generic object recognition tasks [23]. With the introduction of large labeled image databases [22] and GPU implementations used to efficiently perform the massive parallel computations required for learning and inference in large CNNs, these networks have become the most accurate method for generic object classification [26].

Most recently, generic object detection methods have begun to leverage deep CNNs and outperformed any competing approaches based on traditional features. OverFeat [37] uses a CNN to regress to object locations in a coarse sliding-window detection framework. Of particular inspiration to our work is the R-CNN method [21] which leverages features from a deep CNN in a region proposal framework to achieve unprecedented object detection results on the PASCAL VOC dataset. Our method generalizes R-CNN by applying it to model object parts in addition to whole objects, which our empirical results will demonstrate is essential for accurate fine-grained recognition.

3 Part-Based R-CNNs

While [21] demonstrated the effectiveness of the R-CNN method on a generic object detection task (PASCAL VOC), it did not explore the application of this method to simultaneous localization and fine-grained recognition. Because our work operates in this regime, we extend R-CNN to detect objects and localize their parts under a geometric prior. With hypotheses for the locations of individual semantic parts of the object of interest (e.g., the location of the head for an animal class), it becomes reasonable to model subtle appearance differences which tend to appear in locations that are roughly fixed with respect to these parts.

In the R-CNN method, for a particular object category, a candidate detection x with CNN feature descriptor $\phi(x)$ is assigned a score of $w_0^\intercal \phi(x)$, where w_0 is the learned vector of SVM weights for the object category. In our method, we assume a strongly supervised setting (e.g., [3]) in which at training time we have ground truth bounding box annotations not only for full objects, but for a fixed set of semantic parts $\{p_1, p_2, ..., p_n\}$ as well.

Given these part annotations, at training time all objects and each of their parts are initially treated as independent object categories: we train a one-versus-all linear SVM on feature descriptors extracted over region proposals, where regions with ≥ 0.7 overlap with a ground truth object or part bounding box are labeled as positives for that object or part, and regions with ≤ 0.3 overlap with any ground truth region are labeled as negatives. Hence for a single object category we learn whole-object ("root") SVM weights w_0 and part SVM weights $\{w_1, w_2, ..., w_n\}$ for parts $\{p_1, p_2, ..., p_n\}$ respectively. At test time, for each region proposal window we compute scores from all root and part SVMs. Of course, these scores do not incorporate any knowledge of how objects and their parts are constrained geometrically; for example, without any additional constraints the *bird head* detector may fire outside of a region where the *bird* detector fires. Hence our final joint object and part hypotheses are computed using the geometric scoring function detailed in the following section, which enforces the intuitively desirable property that pose predictions are consistent with the statistics of poses observed at training time.

3.1 Geometric Constraints

Let $X = \{x_0, x_1, \ldots, x_n\}$ denote the locations (bounding boxes) of object p_0 and n parts $\{p_i\}_{i=1}^n$, which are annotated in the training data, but unknown at test time. Our goal is to infer both the object location and part locations in a previously unseen test image. Given the R-CNN weights $\{w_0, w_1, \ldots, w_n\}$ for object and parts, we will have the corresponding detectors $\{d_0, d_1, \ldots, d_n\}$ where each detector score is $d_i(x) = \sigma(w_i^\intercal \phi(x))$, where $\sigma(\cdot)$ is the sigmoid function and $\phi(x)$ is the CNN feature descriptor extracted at location x. We infer the joint configuration of the object and parts by solving the following optimization problem:

$$X^* = \arg\max_X \Delta(X) \prod_{i=0}^{n} d_i(x_i) \tag{1}$$

where $\Delta(X)$ defines a scoring function over the joint configuration of the object and root bounding box. We consider and report quantitative results on several configuration scoring functions Δ, detailed in the following paragraphs.

Box constraints. One intuitive idea to localize both the object and parts is to consider each possible object window and all the windows inside the object and pick the windows with the highest part scores. In this case, we define the scoring function

$$\Delta_{\text{box}}(X) = \prod_{i=1}^{n} c_{x_0}(x_i) \tag{2}$$

where

$$c_x(y) = \begin{cases} 1 \text{ if region } y \text{ falls outside region } x \text{ by at most } \epsilon \text{ pixels} \\ 0 \text{ otherwise} \end{cases} \tag{3}$$

In our experiments, we let $\epsilon = 10$.

Geometric constraints. Because the individual part detectors are less than perfect, the window with highest individual part detector scores is not always correct, especially when there are occlusions. We therefore consider several scoring functions to enforce constraints over the layout of the parts relative to the object location to filter out incorrect detections. We define

$$\Delta_{\text{geometric}}(X) = \Delta_{\text{box}}(X) \left(\prod_{i=1}^{n} \delta_i(x_i) \right)^{\alpha} \tag{4}$$

where δ_i is a scoring function for the position of the part p_i given the training data. Following previous work on part localization from, e.g. [4, 17, 19], we experiment with three definitions of δ:

- $\delta_i^{MG}(x_i)$ fits a mixture of Gaussians model with N_g components to the training data for part p_i. In our experiments, we set $N_g = 4$.
- $\delta_i^{NP}(x_i)$ finds the K nearest neighbors in appearance space to $\tilde{x}_0$, where $\tilde{x}_0 = \arg\max d_0(x_0)$ is the top-scoring window from the root detector. We then fit a Gaussian model to these K neighbors. In our experiments, we set $K = 20$. Figure 2 illustrates some examples of nearest neighbors.

The DPM [17] models deformation costs with a per-component Gaussian prior. R-CNN [21] is a single-component model, motivating the δ^{MG} or δ^{NP} definitions. Our δ^{NP} definition is inspired by Belhumeur et al. [4], but differs in that we index nearest neighbors on appearance rather than geometry.

3.2 Fine-Grained Categorization

We extract semantic features from localized parts as well as the whole object. The final feature representation is $[\phi(x_0) \ldots \phi(x_n)]$ where x_0 and $x_{1 \ldots n}$ are whole-object and part location predictions inferred using one of the models from the previous section and $\phi(x_i)$ is the feature representation of part x_i.

Fig. 2. Illustration of geometric constant δ^{NP}. In each row, the first column is the test image with an R-CNN bounding box detection, and the rest are the top-five nearest neighbors in the training set, indexed using `pool5` features and cosine distance metric.

In one set of experiments, we extract deep convolutional features $\phi(x_i)$ from an ImageNet pre-trained CNN, similar to DeCAF [14]. In order to make the deep CNN-derived features more discriminative for the target task of fine-grained bird classification, we also fine-tune the ImageNet pre-trained CNN for the 200-way bird classification task from ground truth bounding box crops of the original CUB images. In particular, we replace the original 1000-way `fc8` classification layer with a new 200-way `fc8` layer with randomly initialized weights drawn from a Gaussian with $\mu = 0$ and $\sigma = 0.01$. We set fine-tuning learning rates as proposed by R-CNN [21], initializing the global rate to a tenth of the initial ImageNet learning rate and dropping it by a factor of 10 throughout training, but with a learning rate in the new `fc8` layer of 10 times the global learning rate. For the whole object bounding box and each of the part bounding boxes, we independently finetune the ImageNet pre-trained CNN for classification on ground truth crops of each region warped to the 227×227 network input size, always with 16 pixels on each edge of the input serving as context as in R-CNN [21]. At test time, we extract features for the predicted whole object or part region using the network fine-tuned for that particular whole object or part.

For training the classifier, we employ a one-versus-all linear SVM using the final feature representation. For a new test image, we apply the whole and part detectors with the geometric scoring function to get detected part locations and use the features for prediction. If a particular part i was not detected anywhere in the test image (due to all proposals falling below the part detector's threshold, set to achieve high recall), we set its features $\phi(x_i) = \mathbf{0}$ (zero vector).

4 Evaluation

In this section, we present a comparative performance evaluation of our proposed method. Specifically, we conduct experiments on the widely-used fine-grained benchmark Caltech-UCSD birds dataset [41] (CUB200-2011). The classification task is to discriminate among 200 species of birds, and is challenging for computer vision systems due to the high degree of similarity between categories. It contains 11,788 images of 200 bird species. Each image is annotated with its bounding box and the image coordinates of fifteen keypoints: the beak, back, breast, belly, forehead, crown, left eye, left leg, left wing, right eye, right leg, right wing, tail, nape and throat. We train and test on the splits included with the dataset, which contain around 30 training samples for each species. Following the protocol of [47], we use two semantic parts for the bird dataset: head and body.

We use the open-source package Caffe [24] to extract deep features and fine-tune our CNNs. For object and part detections, we use the Caffe reference model, which is almost identical to the model used by Krizhevsky et al. in [26]. We refer deep features from each layer as `conv`n, `pool`n, or `fc`n for the nth layer of the CNN, which is the output of a convolutional, pooling, or fully connected layer respectively. We use `fc6` to train R-CNN object and part detectors as well as image representation for classification. For δ^{NP}, nearest neighbors are computed using `pool5` and cosine distance metric.

4.1 Fine-Grained Categorization

We first present results on the standard fine-grained categorization task associated with the Caltech-UCSD birds dataset. The first set of results in Table 1 are achieved in the setting where the ground truth bounding box for the entire bird is known at test time, as most state-of-art methods assume, making the categorization task somewhat easier. In this setting, our part-based method with the local non-parametric geometric constraint δ^{NP} works the best without fine-tuning, achieving 68.1% classification accuracy without fine-tuning. Fine-tuning improves this result by a large margin, to over 76%. We compare our results against three state-of-the-art baseline approaches with results assuming the ground truth bounding box at test time. We use deep convolutional features as the authors of [14], but they use a HOG-based DPM as their part localization method. The increase in performance is likely due to better part localization (see Table 4). Oracle method uses the ground truth bounding box and part annotations for both training and test time.

The second set of results is in the less artificial setting where the bird bounding box is *unknown* at test time. Most of the literature on this dataset doesn't report performance in this more difficult, but more realistic setting. As Table 1 shows, in this setting our part-based method works much better than the baseline DPD model. We achieve 66.0% classification accuracy without finetuning , almost as good as the accuracy we can achieve when the ground truth bounding box is given. This means there is no need to annotate any box during test time to classify the bird species. With finetuned CNN models, our method achieves 73.89% classification accuracy. We are unaware of any other published results in this more difficult setting, but we note that our method outperforms previous state-of-the-art even without knowledge of the ground truth bounding box.

Table 1. Fine-grained categorization results on CUB200-2011 bird dataset. -ft means extracting deep features from finetuned CNN models using each semantic part. Oracle method uses the ground truth bounding box and part annotations for both training and test time.

Bounding Box Given	
DPD [47]	50.98%
DPD+DeCAF feature [14]	64.96%
POOF [7]	56.78%
Symbiotic Segmentation [10]	59.40%
Alignment [20]	62.70%
Oracle	72.83%
Oracle-ft	82.02%
Ours (Δ_{box})	67.55%
Ours ($\Delta_{\text{geometric}}$ with δ^{MG})	67.98%
Ours ($\Delta_{\text{geometric}}$ with δ^{NP})	68.07%
Ours-ft (Δ_{box})	75.34%
Ours-ft ($\Delta_{\text{geometric}}$ with δ^{MG})	**76.37%**
Ours-ft ($\Delta_{\text{geometric}}$ with δ^{NP})	76.34%
Bounding Box Unknown	
DPD+DeCAF [14] with no bounding box	44.94%
Ours (Δ_{null})	64.57%
Ours (Δ_{box})	65.22%
Ours ($\Delta_{\text{geometric}}$ with δ^{MG})	65.98%
Ours ($\Delta_{\text{geometric}}$ with δ^{NP})	65.96%
Ours-ft (Δ_{box})	72.73%
Ours-ft ($\Delta_{\text{geometric}}$ with δ^{MG})	72.95%
Ours-ft ($\Delta_{\text{geometric}}$ with δ^{NP})	**73.89%**

Another interesting experiment we did is to remove the part descriptors by only looking at the image descriptors inside the predicted bounding box. By having geometric constraints over part locations relative to object location, our method is able to help localize the object. As Table 2 shows, our method outperforms a single object detector using R-CNN, which means the geometric constraints helps our method better localize the object window. The detection of strong DPM is not as accurate as our method, which explains the performance drop. The "oracle" method uses the ground truth bounding box and achieves 57.94% accuracy, which is still much lower than the method in Table 1 of using both image descriptors inside object and parts.

4.2 Part Localization

We now present results evaluating in isolation the ability of our system to accurately localize parts. Our results in Table 4 are given in terms of the Percentage of Correctly Localized Parts (PCP) metric. For the first set of results, the whole object bounding box is given and the task is simply to correctly localize the parts inside of this bounding box, with parts having ≥ 0.5 overlap with ground truth counted as correct.

Table 2. Fine-grained categorization results on CUB200-2011 bird dataset with *no parts*. We trained a linear SVM using deep features on all the methods. Therefore only the bounding box prediction is the factor of difference. -ft is the result of extracting deep features from fine-tuned CNN model on bounding box patches.

Oracle (ground truth bounding box)	57.94%
Oracle-ft	68.29%
Strong DPM [3]	38.02%
R-CNN [21]	51.05%
Ours (Δ_{box})	50.17%
Ours ($\Delta_{\text{geometric}}$ with δ^{MG})	51.83%
Ours ($\Delta_{\text{geometric}}$ with δ^{NP})	52.38%
Ours-ft (Δ_{box})	62.13%
Ours-ft ($\Delta_{\text{geometric}}$ with δ^{MG})	62.06%
Ours-ft ($\Delta_{\text{geometric}}$ with δ^{NP})	**62.75%**

Table 3. Recall of region proposals produced by selective search methods on CUB200-2011 bird dataset. We use ground truth part annotations to compute the recall, as defined by the proportion of ground truth boxes for which there exists a region proposal with overlap at least 0.5, 0.6 and 0.7 respectively.

Overlap	0.50	0.60	0.70
Bounding box	96.70%	97.68%	89.50%
Head	93.34%	73.87%	37.57%
Body	96.70%	85.97%	54.68%

For the second set of results, the PCP metric is computed on top-ranked parts predictions using the objective function described in Sec. 3.2. Note that in this more realistic setting we do not assume knowledge of the ground truth bounding box at test time – despite this limitation, our system produces accurate part localizations.

As shown in Table 4, for both settings of given bounding box and unknown bounding box, our methods outperform the strong DPM [3] method. Adding a geometric constraint δ^{NP} improves our results (79.82% for body localization compared to 65.42%). In the fully automatic setting, the top ranked detection and part localization performance on head is 65% better than the baseline method. $\Delta_{\text{null}} = 1$ is the appearance-only case with no geometric constraints applied. Although the fine-grained classification results don't show a big gap between $\Delta_{\text{geometric}}$ and Δ_{box}, we can see the performance gap for part localization. The reason for the small performance gap might be that deep convolutional features are invariant to small translations and rotations, limiting the impact of small localization errors on our end-to-end accuracy.

We also evaluate the recall performance of selective search region proposals [40] for bounding box and semantic parts. The results of recall given different overlapping thresholds are shown in Table 3. Recall for the bird head and body parts is high when the overlap requirement is 0.5, which provides the foundation for localizing these parts given the region proposals. However, we also observe

Table 4. Part localization accuracy in terms of PCP (Percentage of Correctly Localized Parts) on the CUB200-2011 bird dataset. There are two different settings: with given bounding box and without bounding box.

Bounding Box Given		
	Head	Body
Strong DPM [3]	43.49%	75.15%
Ours (Δ_{box})	61.40%	65.42%
Ours ($\Delta_{\text{geometric}}$ with δ^{MG})	66.03%	76.62%
Ours ($\Delta_{\text{geometric}}$ with δ^{NP})	**68.19%**	**79.82%**
Bounding Box Unknown		
	Head	Body
Strong DPM [3]	37.44%	47.08%
Ours (Δ_{null})	60.50%	64.43%
Ours (Δ_{box})	60.56%	65.31%
Ours ($\Delta_{\text{geometric}}$ with δ^{MG})	**61.94%**	70.16%
Ours ($\Delta_{\text{geometric}}$ with δ^{NP})	61.42%	**70.68%**

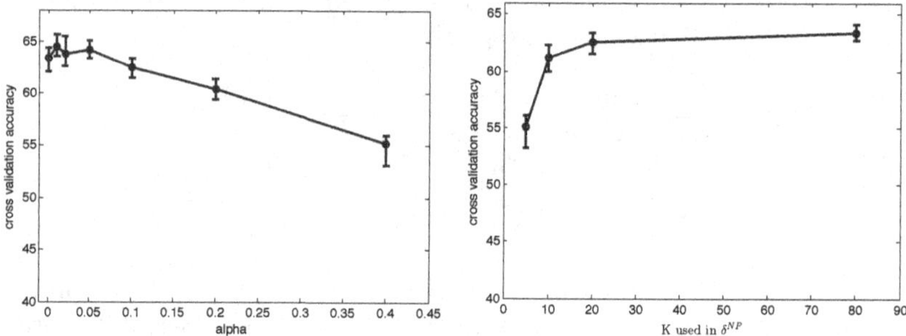

Fig. 3. Cross-validation results on fine-grained accuracy for different values of α (left) and K (right). We split the training data into 5 folds and use cross-validate each hyperparameter setting.

that the recall for head is below 40% when the overlap threshold is 0.7, indicating the bottom-up region proposals could be a bottleneck for precise part localization.

Other visualizations are shown in Figure 4. We show three detection and part localization for each image, the first column is the output from strong DPM, the second column is our methods with individual part predictions and the last column is our method with local prior. We used the model pretrained from [3] to get the results. We also show some failure cases of our method in Figure 5.

4.3 Component Analysis

To examine the effect of different values of α and K used in $\Delta_{\text{geometric}}$, we conduct cross-validation experiments. Results are shown in Figure 3. We fix $K = 20$ in

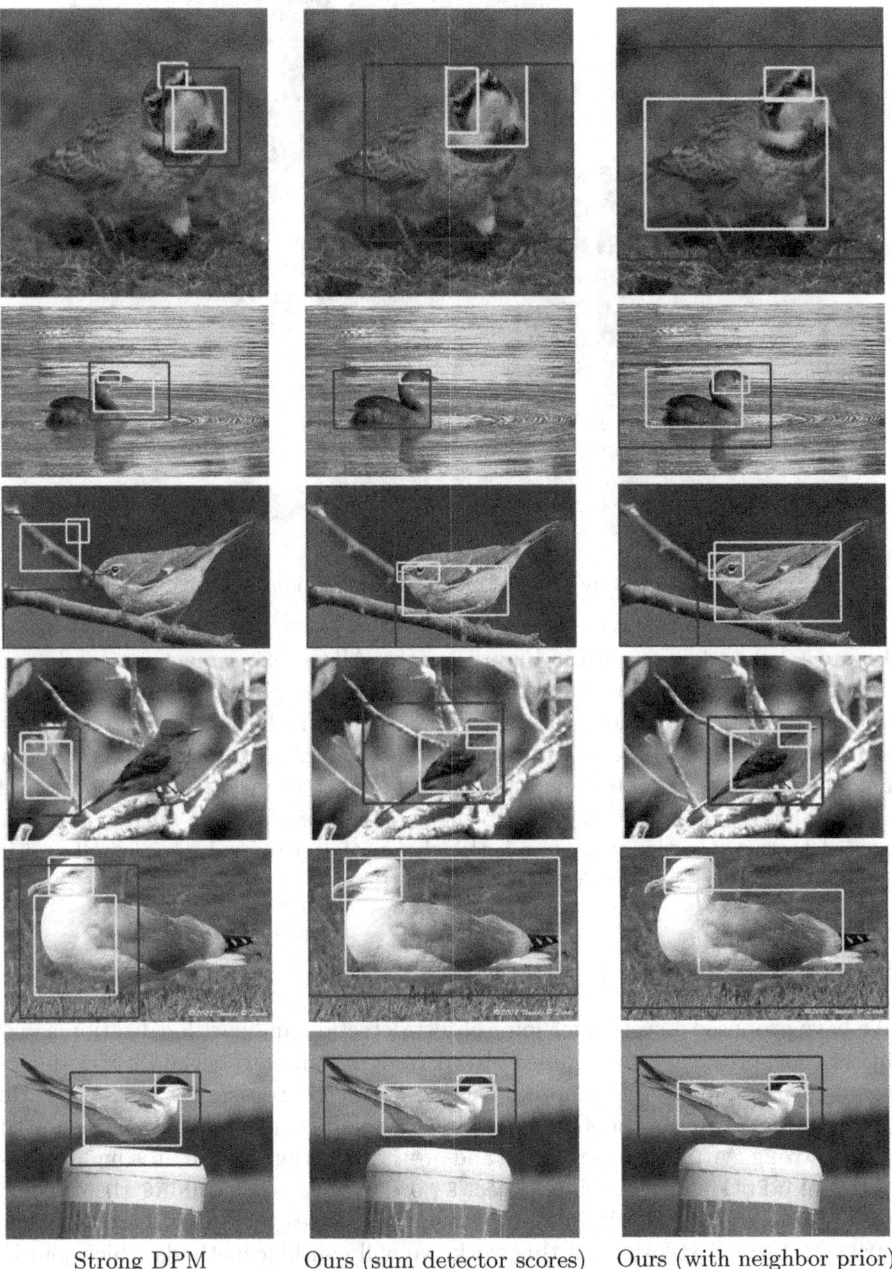

Strong DPM Ours (sum detector scores) Ours (with neighbor prior)

Fig. 4. Examples of bird detection and part localization from strong DPM [3] (left); our method using Δ_{box} part predictions (middle); and our method using δ^{NP}(right). All detection and localization results without any assumption of bounding box.

Fig. 5. Failure cases of our part localization using δ^{NP}

Figure 3, left and fix $\alpha = 0.1$ in Figure 3, right. All the experiments on conducted on training data in a cross-validation fashion and we split the training data into 5 folds. As the results show, the end-to-end fine-grained classification results are sensitive to the choice of α and $\alpha = 0$ is the case of Δ_{box} predictions without any geometric constraints. The reason why we have to pick a small α is the pdf of the Gaussian is large compared to the logistic score function output from our part detectors. On the other hand, the choice of K cannot be too small and it is not very sensitive when K is larger than 10.

5 Conclusion

We have proposed a system for joint object detection and part localization capable of state-of-the-art fine-grained object recognition. Our method learns detectors and part models and enforces learned geometric constraints between parts and with the object frame. Our experimental results demonstrate that even with a very strong feature representation and object detection system, it is highly beneficial to additionally model an object's pose by means of parts for the difficult task of fine-grained discrimination between categories with high semantic similarity. In future extensions of this work, we will consider methods which jointly model at training time the object category and each of its parts and deformation costs. We also plan to explore the weakly supervised setting in which we automatically discover and model parts as latent variables from only the object bounding box annotations. Finally, we will consider relaxing the use of selective search for smaller parts and employing dense window sampling.

References

1. Angelova, A., Zhu, S.: Efficient object detection and segmentation for fine-grained recognition. In: CVPR (2013)
2. Angelova, A., Zhu, S., Lin, Y.: Image segmentation for large-scale subcategory flower recognition. In: WACV (2013)
3. Azizpour, H., Laptev, I.: Object detection using strongly-supervised deformable part models. In: Fitzgibbon, A., Lazebnik, S., Perona, P., Sato, Y., Schmid, C. (eds.) ECCV 2012, Part I. LNCS, vol. 7572, pp. 836–849. Springer, Heidelberg (2012)
4. Belhumeur, P.N., Jacobs, D., Kriegman, D., Kumar, N.: Localizing parts of faces using a consensus of exemplars. In: CVPR (2011)
5. Belhumeur, P.N., et al.: Searching the world's herbaria: A system for visual identification of plant species. In: Forsyth, D., Torr, P., Zisserman, A. (eds.) ECCV 2008, Part IV. LNCS, vol. 5305, pp. 116–129. Springer, Heidelberg (2008)
6. Belhumeur, P.N., Jacobs, D.W., Kriegman, D.J., Kumar, N.: Localizing parts of faces using a consensus of exemplars. In: CVPR (2011)
7. Berg, T., Belhumeur, P.N.: POOF: Part-based one-vs.-one features for fine-grained categorization, face verification, and attribute estimation. In: CVPR (2013)
8. Bourdev, L., Malik, J.: Poselets: Body part detectors trained using 3D human pose annotations. In: ICCV (2009), `http://www.eecs.berkeley.edu/~lbourdev/poselets`
9. Branson, S., Wah, C., Schroff, F., Babenko, B., Welinder, P., Perona, P., Belongie, S.: Visual recognition with humans in the loop. In: Daniilidis, K., Maragos, P., Paragios, N. (eds.) ECCV 2010, Part IV. LNCS, vol. 6314, pp. 438–451. Springer, Heidelberg (2010)
10. Chai, Y., Lempitsky, V., Zisserman, A.: Symbiotic segmentation and part localization for fine-grained categorization. In: ICCV (2013)
11. Chai, Y., Rahtu, E., Lempitsky, V., Van Gool, L., Zisserman, A.: TriCoS: A tri-level class-discriminative co-segmentation method for image classification. In: Fitzgibbon, A., Lazebnik, S., Perona, P., Sato, Y., Schmid, C. (eds.) ECCV 2012, Part I. LNCS, vol. 7572, pp. 794–807. Springer, Heidelberg (2012)
12. Dalal, N., Triggs, B.: Histograms of oriented gradients for human detection. In: CVPR (2005)
13. Deng, J., Krause, J., Fei-Fei, L.: Fine-grained crowdsourcing for fine-grained recognition. In: CVPR (2013)
14. Donahue, J., Jia, Y., Vinyals, O., Hoffman, J., Zhang, N., Tzeng, E., Darrell, T.: DeCAF: A deep convolutional activation feature for generic visual recognition. In: ICML (2014)
15. Duan, K., Parkh, D., Crandall, D., Grauman, K.: Discovering localized attributes for fine-grained recognition. In: CVPR (2012)
16. Farrell, R., Oza, O., Zhang, N., Morariu, V.I., Darrell, T., Davis, L.S.: Birdlets: Subordinate categorization using volumetric primitives and pose-normalized appearance. In: ICCV (2011)
17. Felzenszwalb, P.F., Girshick, R.B., McAllester, D., Ramanan, D.: Object detection with discriminatively trained part based models. IEEE Transactions on Pattern Analysis and Machine Intelligence (2010)
18. Felzenszwalb, P.F., Huttenlocher, D.: Efficient matching of pictorial structure. In: CVPR (2000)

19. Fischler, M.A., Elschlager, R.A.: The representation and matching of pictorial structures. IEEE Transactions on Computers (January 1973), http://dx.doi.org/10.1109/T-C.1973.223602
20. Gavves, E., Fernando, B., Snoek, C., Smeulders, A., Tuytelaars, T.: Fine-grained categorization by alignments. In: ICCV (2013)
21. Girshick, R., Donahue, J., Darrell, T., Malik, J.: Rich feature hierarchies for accurate object detection and semantic segmentation. In: CVPR (2014)
22. ILSVRC: ImageNet Large-scale Visual Recognition Challenge (2010-2012), http://www.image-net.org/challenges/LSVRC/2011/
23. Jarrett, K., Kavukcuoglu, K., Ranzato, M., LeCun, Y.: What is the best multi-stage architecture for object recognition? In: ICCV (2009)
24. Jia, Y.: Caffe: An open source convolutional architecture for fast feature embedding (2013), http://caffe.berkeleyvision.org/
25. Khosla, A., Jayadevaprakash, N., Yao, B., Fei-Fei, L.: Novel dataset for fine-grained image categorization. In: FGVC Workshop, CVPR (2011)
26. Krizhevsky, A., Sutskever, I., Hinton, G.E.: Imagenet classification with deep convolutional neural networks. In: NIPS (2012)
27. LeCun, Y., Boser, B., Denker, J., Henderson, D., Howard, R.E., Hubbard, W., Jackel, L.D.: Backpropagation applied to hand-written zip code recognition. Neural Computation (1989)
28. Lecun, Y., Bottou, L., Bengio, Y., Haffner, P.: Gradient-based learning applied to document recognition. Proceedings of the IEEE, 2278–2324 (1998)
29. Liu, J., Belhumeur, P.N.: Bird part localization using exemplar-based models with enforced pose and subcategory consistency. In: ICCV (2013)
30. Liu, J., Kanazawa, A., Jacobs, D., Belhumeur, P.: Dog breed classification using part localization. In: Fitzgibbon, A., Lazebnik, S., Perona, P., Sato, Y., Schmid, C. (eds.) ECCV 2012, Part I. LNCS, vol. 7572, pp. 172–185. Springer, Heidelberg (2012)
31. Maji, S., Kannala, J., Rahtu, E., Blaschko, M., Vedaldi, A.: Fine-grained visual classification of aircraft. Tech. rep. (2013)
32. Martinez-Munoz, G., Larios, N., Mortensen, E., Zhang, W., Yamamuro, A., Paasch, R., Payet, N., Lytle, D., Shapiro, L., Todorovic, S., Moldenke, A., Dietterich, T.: Dictionary-free categorization of very similar objects via stacked evidence trees. In: CVPR (2009)
33. Nilsback, M.E., Zisserman, A.: A visual vocabulary for flower classification. In: CVPR (2006)
34. Nilsback, M.E., Zisserman, A.: Automated flower classification over a large number of classes. In: ICVGIP (2008)
35. Parkhi, O.M., Vedaldi, A., Jawahar, C.V., Zisserman, A.: The truth about cats and dogs. In: ICCV (2011)
36. Parkhi, O.M., Vedaldi, A., Zisserman, A., Jawahar, C.V.: Cats and dogs. In: CVPR (2012)
37. Sermanet, P., Eigen, D., Zhang, X., Mathieu, M., Fergus, R., LeCun, Y.: OverFeat: Integrated recognition, localization and detection using convolutional networks. CoRR abs/1312.6229 (2013)
38. Sfar, A.R., Boujemaa, N., Geman, D.: Vantage feature frames for fine-grained categorization. In: CVPR (2013)
39. Stark, M., Krause, J., Pepik, B., Meger, D., Little, J.J., Schiele, B., Koller, D.: Fine-grained categorization for 3D scene understanding. In: BMVC (2012)
40. Uijlings, J., van de Sande, K., Gevers, T., Smeulders, A.: Selective search for object recognition. IJCV (2013)

41. Welinder, P., Branson, S., Mita, T., Wah, C., Schroff, F., Belongie, S., Perona, P.: Caltech-UCSD Birds 200. Tech. Rep. CNS-TR-2010-001, California Institute of Technology (2010)
42. Xie, L., Tian, Q., Hong, R., Yan, S., Zhang, B.: Hierarchical part matching for fine-grained visual categorization. In: ICCV (2013)
43. Yang, S., Bo, L., Wang, J., Shapiro, L.: Unsupervised template learning for fine-grained object recognition. In: NIPS (2012)
44. Yao, B., Bradski, G., Fei-Fei, L.: A codebook-free and annotation-free approach for fine-grained image categorization. In: CVPR (2012)
45. Yao, B., Khosla, A., Fei-Fei, L.: Combining randomization and discrimination for fine-grained image categorization. In: CVPR (2011)
46. Zhang, N., Farrell, R., Darrell, T.: Pose pooling kernels for sub-category recognition. In: CVPR (2012)
47. Zhang, N., Farrell, R., Iandola, F., Darrell, T.: Deformable part descriptors for fine-grained recognition and attribute prediction. In: ICCV (2013)
48. Zhang, N., Paluri, M., Ranzato, M., Darrell, T., Bourdev, L.: PANDA: Pose aligned networks for deep attribute modeling. In: CVPR (2014)

Author Index

Printed in the United States
By Bookmasters